THE INTERLINEAR LITERAL TRANSLATION

OF THE

HEBREW OLD TESTAMENT

WITH

THE KING JAMES VERSION

AND

THE REVISED VERSION

CONVENIENTLY PLACED IN THE MARGINS FOR READY REFERENCE

AND WITH

EXPLANATORY TEXTUAL FOOTNOTES

SUPPLEMENTED BY TABLES OF THE HEBREW VERB, AND THE HEBREW ALPHABET

BY

GEORGE RICKER BERRY, PH.D.

OF THE UNIVERSITY OF CHICAGO AND COLGATE UNIVERSITY
DEPARTMENT OF SEMITIC LANGUAGES

GENESIS AND EXODUS

KREGEL PUBLICATIONS
GRAND RAPIDS, MICHIGAN 49501

Library of Congress Catalog Card No. 77-136092
ISBN 0-8254-2214-0

Reprinted complete and unabridged from
the 1897 Hinds & Noble edition.

First Kregel Publication Edition 1970
Second Printing 1972
Third Printing 1974
Fourth Printing 1975

Printed in the United States of America

INTRODUCTION

THIS volume is the beginning of a work designed to do in reference to the Old Testament that which has been done in the New by "The Interlinear New Testament." The general plan and scope of this volume are well set forth in the Introduction to that book. The circumstances of the case, however, make necessary many differences in the details of the method of treatment. Hebrew thought, constructions, and idioms are much farther removed from those of English than is the case with Greek. The chief object, therefore, of this Introduction is to explain such points as are necessary for a clear understanding of the methods employed.

This volume is intended to be of use to everyone who *studies the Bible.* Two classes, however, have been especially kept in mind in its preparation. One class consists of those who have more or less acquaintance with Hebrew, who will be able to grasp easily the exact force of each Hebrew word and expression by having it put side by side with its literal English equivalent. The other class includes those who study the Old Testament only in English, but who may obtain, from the new translation here given, added light upon the real meaning of this portion of God's Word.

It will be observed that the Authorized version is printed in the left-hand margin; the Revised version, in the right. The only changes made in these are that, as a matter of convenience, the verses of the Authorized version have been printed solid, with paragraphs instead of the paragraph sign, while in the Revised version the verse numbers have been transferred from the margin to the text. It has also been found impracticable to reproduce entirely the paragraphs of either version, although they have been followed as fully as it could be made convenient. In the rare cases in which the Hebrew chapter division varies from the ordinary English division, the Hebrew division has been followed in the body of the page, with the English division in the margins. In the interlinear translation it has been necessary, of course, for the English to read from right to left, following the order of the Hebrew.

It has been the aim to give, to the fullest possible extent, a literal rendering of the Hebrew. The opportunity given for easy comparison with the Authorized and Revised versions has made this practicable in many cases where otherwise there would have been danger of obscurity. A smooth translation has not been attempted, for that would often require the sacrifice of literalness. The aim has been to reproduce the force of the Hebrew just as closely as the English language will allow. The Hebrew idioms have been retained where they would be at all intelligible to an English reader. A slavish adherence to them, however, has been avoided. On the one hand, e.g. the expression דְּבַר יוֹם בְּיוֹמוֹ is rendered by transference of the idiom, *the matter of a day in its day;* on the other, a word like מַיִם, which is always in the plural, while the same idea is uniformly expressed in English by the singular, *water*, has been regularly rendered by the singular. These examples may serve as illustrations of the principles followed, although it has not always been easy to say which course should be adopted.

The Authorized version and, to a less degree, the Revised are deficient in appreciation of many of the characteristic constructions of the Hebrew. They apparently judged the Hebrew too much by English standards. Many of the peculiar uses of the tenses, the force of the circumstantial clause, and other idiomatic constructions have been often unrecognized. It is not claimed that this translation succeeds perfectly in supplying these deficiencies. In fact there is not entire agreement among Hebrew scholars upon some of these matters. But special attention has been paid to these points, and it is believed that in many passages an advance is made upon the ordinary versions. A *uniformity* of translation has been aimed at. So far as possible a Hebrew word, especially a technical word, has been rendered by the same English word. Yet this is possible only to a limited extent in the Old Testament, for as the Hebrew prose vocabulary is small, different meanings are often united in one word, e.g. תֵּבָה is used both of the vessel which Noah built and of that in which Moses was placed. To render both by one word, *ark*, as the English versions do, would give a wrong idea of their similarity. So also the use of different stems formed from the same root gives, especially to the verbs, many different shades of meaning which cannot be expressed by the same English word, e.g. נחם in the Pĭ'ēl stem means *to have compassion*, in the Nĭph'ăl, *to change one's mind.* Special attention has been paid to keeping distinct words which are similar in meaning and often confounded, e.g. עַד means *as far as*, used of attaining a given limit, אֶל, *towards* or *unto*, not implying such attainment. Obsolete English words have been generally avoided.

The square brackets [ ] have been used to inclose words *added* in the English which *are not* in the Hebrew, while the parentheses ( ) have been used for words which *are* in the Hebrew but of which the English usage requires the *omission*. Where it has been necessary to substitute some other English word for the literal rendering of the Hebrew, this has sometimes been done by inclosing the literal rendering in parentheses, while the rendering required in English precedes or follows this in square brackets. A word in Hebrew which has no equivalent in English has been left untranslated. This has rarely been done, however, except with the sign of the definite object אֵת. In the case of other words, which have an equivalent although not needed in English, it has usually been thought best to give the translation inclosed in parentheses.

The Hebrew order of words has always been followed in the English. Where a change of the Hebrew order is necessary in English it is indicated by numbering the words in the order in which they should be read. In some cases where the Hebrew order is regularly an inversion of the English, it has usually been allowed to stand, e.g. the subject following the predicate. Hebrew words connected by Măqqēph, corresponding to our hyphen, have been treated as one word, and translated in any order demanded by the context.

The division into paragraphs, both in our Hebrew text and English translations, has no original authority. Accordingly the paragraphs are based not upon either of these but upon what are thought to be the real divisions of thought. These will be found usually to correspond to those of the Revised version, but to depart from them in some cases.

The Hebrew text used is, for Genesis, that of Baer and Delitzsch. This is thought to be the best Masoretic text which has been published. For Exodus, the text of Baer and Delitzsch having not yet been published, that of Theile has been used, which is probably as correct as any. These texts have been followed with no changes except the omission of the Masoretic footnotes. Any corrected Hebrew text must be made from a comparison of the versions, and by the cautious employment of conjectural emendation. A thorough-going reconstruction like this is not practical, in accordance with the design of this book. Any changes less than this would only serve to unsettle the authority of the text, without introducing changes enough to be of substantial benefit. The translation has been regularly based upon this text, only departing from it in two or three cases which will be at once apparent.

The textual criticism of the Old Testament stands on a far different basis from that of the New, and presents much more difficulty in arriving at satisfactory results. Without entering into a general discussion of the subject, it will be sufficient to say that little help can be obtained for textual criticism from different *Hebrew* manuscripts, for the oldest of these comes from a date many centuries after Christ, and all present the same text with but slight variations. Many variations, however, are found in the Samaritan text, which is thus of interest, although its age and consequent value are not certain. The best attested text on the basis of the ordinary Hebrew manuscripts is all that our Hebrew Bibles aim to give us. The comparative lateness of these manuscripts would make it intrinsically probable that they contained many textual corruptions. The only substantial help for detecting these corruptions comes from the versions, which are centuries older than the oldest Hebrew manuscript, although still far removed from the original autographs. Of the versions, all those of importance have been collated, viz.: the Greek, commonly known as the Septuagint, the Syriac, called the Peshitto, the Latin, or Vulgate, and the Aramaic, or Targum of Onkelos, and the other Greek translations of Aquila, Symmachus and Theodotion, which are of much value, but are only preserved in a fragmentary form. Besides these are the Jerusalem Targum and the Arabic version, which are only rarely referred to. The Septuagint and Peshitto are of greatest value and their variations have been carefully collected and fully presented. Many characteristic changes of the Samaritan have been noted. The Vulgate is much more free on Genesis and Exodus than on many portions of the Old Testament, and hence of much less value. The Targum of Onkelos is never of high value, although on this portion it is remarkably literal. An *independent* variation of either Vulgate or Targum has seldom been thought worthy of being presented. Those who wish for fuller discussions of these versions than is possible here, may find them, among many other works, in Bleek's *Einleitung*, 6th ed., and Driver's *Notes on the Hebrew Text of the Books of Samuel.*

But little help in the textual notes has been obtained from any published commentary. The material has been obtained chiefly from a comparison of the texts themselves, the Septuagint in Swete's edition, the Peshitto in Lee's, the Vulgate in that of Heyse and Tischendorf, Aquila, Symmachus, and Theodotion in Field's edition of Origen's Hexapla, and the others in the London Polyglot. To present minute details, as e.g. the variant readings of different manuscripts of the Septuagint, has not often been attempted, since it was thought that it would be rather confusing than helpful. These notes do not claim to be absolutely complete, but to present everything of much value or interest. In their manner of presentation many questions have arisen. To give the readings in the original languages would have limited too much the number of those who could profit by them. The only courses open were to give them either in an English translation, or put as far as possible into the Hebrew original, or both. For the sake of making them accessible to those unacquainted with Hebrew, it has been thought best to place chief emphasis upon the English translation. This in many cases stands alone, in other cases followed by the Hebrew, when the employment of the Hebrew would add clearness to the reading. In rare cases the Hebrew alone has been given, when it expresses the meaning more clearly than an English translation would have done. The Hebrew has been left unpointed, except where the variation turns upon the pointing. It was impossible to have a uniform order of arrangement of the variations based upon the relative importance of the versions, for in many cases the nature of the variations themselves demanded a different order.

The letter indicating the textual note ordinarily stands at the end of the word affected, but at the beginning when an addition is made to the beginning of the word. When the letter stands with a single word, only that word is affected. Where several words are affected, the uniform method has been to put the *same* letter on the *first* and *last* words, thus including those between. Occasionally the same letter on two or more words indicates that the same note applies to each of them separately, but this will be plainly evident from the context.

The object of the textual notes, of course, is to give assistance in determining the true text. To obtain the most profit from them, what was said above of the different *value* of the testimony of the various versions must be kept in mind. It must also be remembered that the translations given are translations *of the versions,* not of the Hebrew text from which the versions were made. Hence they reproduce the peculiarities of the versions themselves. When, e.g. a version translates יהוה by its word for *Lord,* the English of the note gives the word *Lord.* So it is sometimes the case that the English is not an exact translation of the Hebrew by which it is followed, the English being the translation of one of the versions, and the Hebrew, the text from which it is *inferred* that the version was made. It must also not be forgotten that these versions, being translations, are subject to the defects of translations, and are liable to give paraphrastic, or abbreviated renderings. So a variation does not always argue a different Hebrew text. Such variations as these have in many cases not been given, but in those given it may be suspected that some are of this kind.

The words for money and measures in this part of the Old Testament are so few as to require no detailed treatment. Rarely the Hebrew word has been simply transliterated. Usually it has been possible to translate by terms in common use, which give a sufficiently correct idea of their meaning.

A list of the Hebrew letters with English equivalents is added, not for the purpose of teaching Hebrew, but for the sake of easy reference by those whose knowledge of the language may be a little rusty. The generally recognized English equivalents are given, which are sufficiently familiar to require no explanation.

The utmost care has been taken, both in the preparation of this work and in the proof-reading, to guard against mistakes. It would be too much to expect, however, that it is entirely free from them. It must be remembered that this is a kind of work in which they are especially liable to occur. It is hoped and believed, however, that such as may be found will be of such small magnitude, as not to give serious difficulty to anyone.

Besides lexicons and grammars, all the leading works on Genesis and Exodus have been consulted to a greater or less extent. The most help has been obtained from Wright on Genesis (in textual matters), Spurrell on Genesis, and the commentaries of Kalisch, Delitzsch, Strack, and Dillmann.

THE HEBREW VERB

These paradigms are given here for convenient reference by those to whom the Hebrew verb is not entirely familiar. They include the entire inflection of the strong verb, and the synopsis of the stems which differ materially from the strong verb in all the classes of weak verbs. The brief explanatory statements follow in general the order of the paradigms.

THE STRONG VERB

		Qăl (Stative) Middle O	Middle E	Hĭthpă'ēl	Hŏph'ăl	Hĭph'îl	Pŭ'ăl	Pĭ'ēl	Nĭph'ăl	Qăl		
Perfect	Sg. 3 m.	קָטֹל	קָטֵל	הִתְקַטֵּל	הָקְטַל	הִקְטִיל	קֻטַּל	קִטֵּל	נִקְטַל	קָטַל	Sg. 3 m.	Perfect
	3 f.	קָֽטְלָה	קָֽטְלָה	הִתְקַטְּלָה	הָקְטְלָה	הִקְטִילָה	קֻטְּלָה	קִטְּלָה	נִקְטְלָה	קָֽטְלָה	3 f.	
	2 m.	קָטֹלְתָּ	קָטַלְתָּ	הִתְקַטַּלְתָּ	הָקְטַלְתָּ	הִקְטַלְתָּ	קֻטַּלְתָּ	קִטַּלְתָּ	נִקְטַלְתָּ	קָטַלְתָּ	2 m.	
	2 f.	קָטֹלְתְּ	קָטַלְתְּ	הִתְקַטַּלְתְּ	הָקְטַלְתְּ	הִקְטַלְתְּ	קֻטַּלְתְּ	קִטַּלְתְּ	נִקְטַלְתְּ	קָטַלְתְּ	2 f.	
	1 c.	קָטֹלְתִּי	קָטַלְתִּי	הִתְקַטַּלְתִּי	הָקְטַלְתִּי	הִקְטַלְתִּי	קֻטַּלְתִּי	קִטַּלְתִּי	נִקְטַלְתִּי	קָטַלְתִּי	1 c.	
	Pl. 3 c.	קָֽטְלוּ	קָֽטְלוּ	הִתְקַטְּלוּ	הָקְטְלוּ	הִקְטִילוּ	קֻטְּלוּ	קִטְּלוּ	נִקְטְלוּ	קָֽטְלוּ	Pl. 3 c.	
	2 m.	קְטָלְתֶּם	קְטַלְתֶּם	הִתְקַטַּלְתֶּם	הָקְטַלְתֶּם	הִקְטַלְתֶּם	קֻטַּלְתֶּם	קִטַּלְתֶּם	נִקְטַלְתֶּם	קְטַלְתֶּם	2 m.	
	2 f.	קְטָלְתֶּן	קְטַלְתֶּן	הִתְקַטַּלְתֶּן	הָקְטַלְתֶּן	הִקְטַלְתֶּן	קֻטַּלְתֶּן	קִטַּלְתֶּן	נִקְטַלְתֶּן	קְטַלְתֶּן	2 f.	
	1 c.	קָטֹלְנוּ	קָטַלְנוּ	הִתְקַטַּלְנוּ	הָקְטַלְנוּ	הִקְטַלְנוּ	קֻטַּלְנוּ	קִטַּלְנוּ	נִקְטַלְנוּ	קָטַלְנוּ	1 c.	
Imperfect	Sg. 3 m.	יִקְטַל etc.	יִקְטַל	יִתְקַטֵּל	יָקְטַל	יַקְטִיל	יְקֻטַּל	יְקַטֵּל	יִקָּטֵל	יִקְטֹל	Sg. 3 m.	Imperfect
	3 f.		תִּקְטַל	תִּתְקַטֵּל	תָּקְטַל	תַּקְטִיל	תְּקֻטַּל	תְּקַטֵּל	תִּקָּטֵל	תִּקְטֹל	3 f.	
	2 m.		תִּקְטַל	תִּתְקַטֵּל	תָּקְטַל	תַּקְטִיל	תְּקֻטַּל	תְּקַטֵּל	תִּקָּטֵל	תִּקְטֹל	2 m.	
	2 f.		תִּקְטְלִי	תִּתְקַטְּלִי	תָּקְטְלִי	תַּקְטִילִי	תְּקֻטְּלִי	תְּקַטְּלִי	תִּקָּטְלִי	תִּקְטְלִי	2 f.	
	1 c.		אֶקְטַל	אֶתְקַטֵּל	אָקְטַל	אַקְטִיל	אֲקֻטַּל	אֲקַטֵּל	אֶקָּטֵל	אֶקְטֹל	1 c.	
	Pl. 3 m.		יִקְטְלוּ	יִתְקַטְּלוּ	יָקְטְלוּ	יַקְטִילוּ	יְקֻטְּלוּ	יְקַטְּלוּ	יִקָּטְלוּ	יִקְטְלוּ	Pl. 3 m.	
	3 f.		תִּקְטַלְנָה	תִּתְקַטֵּלְנָה	תָּקְטַלְנָה	תַּקְטֵלְנָה	תְּקֻטַּלְנָה	תְּקַטֵּלְנָה	תִּקָּטַלְנָה	תִּקְטֹלְנָה	3 f.	
	2 m.		תִּקְטְלוּ	תִּתְקַטְּלוּ	תָּקְטְלוּ	תַּקְטִילוּ	תְּקֻטְּלוּ	תְּקַטְּלוּ	תִּקָּטְלוּ	תִּקְטְלוּ	2 m.	
	2 f.		תִּקְטַלְנָה	תִּתְקַטֵּלְנָה	תָּקְטַלְנָה	תַּקְטֵלְנָה	תְּקֻטַּלְנָה	תְּקַטֵּלְנָה	תִּקָּטַלְנָה	תִּקְטֹלְנָה	2 f.	
	1 c.		נִקְטַל	נִתְקַטֵּל	נָקְטַל	נַקְטִיל	נְקֻטַּל	נְקַטֵּל	נִקָּטֵל	נִקְטֹל	1 c.	
Imperative	Sg. 2 m.		קְטַל	הִתְקַטֵּל		הַקְטֵל		קַטֵּל	הִקָּטֵל	קְטֹל	Sg. 2 m.	Imperative
	2 f.		קִטְלִי	הִתְקַטְּלִי		הַקְטִילִי		קַטְּלִי	הִקָּטְלִי	קִטְלִי	2 f.	
	Pl. 2 m.		קִטְלוּ	הִתְקַטְּלוּ		הַקְטִילוּ		קַטְּלוּ	הִקָּטְלוּ	קִטְלוּ	Pl. 2 m.	
	2 f.		קְטַלְנָה	הִתְקַטֵּלְנָה		הַקְטֵלְנָה		קַטֵּלְנָה	הִקָּטַלְנָה	קְטֹלְנָה	2 f.	
Infinitive	absolute		קָטוֹל	הִתְקַטֵּל	הָקְטֵל	הַקְטֵל	קֻטֹּל	קַטֹּל, קַטֵּל	הִקָּטֹל, נִקְטֹל	קָטוֹל	absolute	Infinitive
	construct		קְטַל, קְטֹל	הִתְקַטֵּל		הַקְטִיל		קַטֵּל	הִקָּטֵל	קְטֹל	construct	
Participle	active		קָטֵל	מִתְקַטֵּל		מַקְטִיל		מְקַטֵּל		קֹטֵל	active	Participle
	passive				מָקְטָל		מְקֻטָּל		נִקְטָל	קָטוּל	passive	

Abbreviations: Sg. = singular; Pl. = plural; m. = masculine; f. = feminine; c = common; 3 = third person; 2 = second person; 1 = first person.

THE HEBREW ALPHABET, WITH ENGLISH EQUIVALENTS

א	= '
בּ ב	= b, bh
גּ ג	= g, gh
דּ ד	= d, dh
ה	= h
ו	= w
ז	= z
ח	= ḥ
ט	= ṭ
י	= y
כּ כ ך	= k, kh
ל	= l
מ ם	= m
נ ן	= n
ס	= ṣ
ע	= '
פּ פ ף	= p, ph
צ ץ	= ç
ק	= q
ר	= r
שׂ שׁ	= s, sh
תּ ת	= t, th

THE HEBREW VOWEL SOUNDS, WITH ENGLISH EQUIVALENTS

A-Class		I-Class		U-Class	
ַ	ă	ִ	ĭ	ֻ	ŭ
ָ	â	ֶ	ĕ	ָ	ŏ
ָ	ā	ִי	î	וּ	û
ֶ	é	ֵי	ê	וֹ	ô
ְ	ᵉ	ֵ	ē	ֹ	ō
ֲ	ᵃ	ְ	ᵉ	ְ	ᵉ
		ֱ	ᵉ	ֳ	ᵒ

Synopsis of verb Pē (פ׳) Guttural

	Hŏph'ăl	Hĭph'îl	Nĭph'ăl	Qăl
Perf. 3 m. Sg.	הָעֳטַל	הֶעֱטִיל	נֶעֱטַל	עָטַל
Impf. 3 m. Sg.	יָעֳטַל	יַעֲטִיל	יֵעָטֵל	יַעֲטֹל, יֶעֱטַל
Impv. 2 m. Sg.		הַעֲטֵל	הֵעָטֵל	עֲטֹל, עֲטַל
Infinitive abs.	הָעֳטֵל	הַעֲטֵל	נַעֲטוֹל, הֵעָטֹל	עָטוֹל
Infinitive const.		הַעֲטִיל	הֵעָטֵל	עֲטֹל
Participle act.		מַעֲטִיל		עֹטֵל
Participle pass.	מָעֳטָל		נֶעֱטָל	עָטוּל

Synopsis of verb Lāmĕdh 'Ālĕph (ל״א)

	Hĭthpă'ēl	Hĭph'îl	Pĭ'ēl	Nĭph'ăl	Qăl
Perf. 3 m. Sg.	הִתְקַטֵּא	הִקְטִיא	קִטֵּא	נִקְטָא	קָטָא
Impf. 3 m. Sg.	יִתְקַטֵּא	יַקְטִיא	יְקַטֵּא	יִקָּטֵא	יִקְטָא
Impv. 2 m. Sg.	הִתְקַטֵּא	הַקְטֵא	קַטֵּא	הִקָּטֵא	קְטָא
Infinitive abs.		הַקְטֵא	קַטֹּא	נִקְטֹא	קָטוֹא
Infinitive const.	הִתְקַטֵּא	הַקְטִיא	קַטֵּא	הִקָּטֵא	קְטֹא
Participle act.	מִתְקַטֵּא	מַקְטִיא	מְקַטֵּא		קֹטֵא
Participle pass.				נִקְטָא	קָטוּא

Synopsis of verb Lāmĕdh Hē (ל״ה)

	Hĭthpă'ēl	Hŏph'ăl	Hĭph'îl	Pŭ'ăl	Pĭ'ēl	Nĭph'ăl	Qăl
Perf. 3 m. Sg.	הִתְקַטָּה	הָקְטָה	הִקְטָה	קֻטָּה	קִטָּה	נִקְטָה	קָטָה
Impf. 3 m. Sg.	יִתְקַטֶּה	יָקְטֶה	יַקְטֶה	יְקֻטֶּה	יְקַטֶּה	יִקָּטֶה	יִקְטֶה
Impv. 2 m. Sg.	הִתְקַטֵּה		הַקְטֵה		קַטֵּה	הִקָּטֵה	קְטֵה
Infinitive abs.		הָקְטֵה	הַקְטֵה		קַטֹּה, קַטֵּה	נִקְטֹה	קָטֹה
Infinitive const.	הִתְקַטּוֹת	הָקְטוֹת	הַקְטוֹת	קֻטּוֹת	קַטּוֹת	הִקָּטוֹת	קְטוֹת
Participle act.	מִתְקַטֶּה		מַקְטֶה		מְקַטֶּה		קֹטֶה
Participle pass.		מָקְטֶה		מְקֻטֶּה		נִקְטֶה	קָטוּי

Synopsis of verb 'Ăyĭn (ע׳) Guttural

	Hĭthpă'ēl	Pŭ'ăl	Pĭ'ēl	Nĭph'ăl	Qăl
Perf. 3 m. Sg.	הִתְקָאֵל	קֹאַל	קֵאֵל	נִקְאַל	קָאַל
Impf. 3 m. Sg.	יִתְקָאֵל	יְקֹאַל	יְקָאֵל	יִקָּאֵל	יִקְאַל
Impv. 2 m. Sg.	הִתְקָאֵל		קָאֵל	הִקָּאֵל	קְאַל
Infinitive abs.			קָאֵל	נִקְאוֹל	קָאוֹל
Infinitive const.	הִתְקָאֵל		קָאֵל	הִקָּאֵל	קְאֹל
Participle act.	מִתְקָאֵל		מְקָאֵל		קֹאֵל
Participle pass.		מְקֹאָל		נִקְאָל	קָאוּל

Synopsis of verb Lāmĕdh (ל׳) Guttural

	Hĭthpă'ēl	Hĭph'îl	Pĭ'ēl	Nĭph'ăl	Qăl
Perf. 3 m. Sg.	הִתְקַטַּח	הִקְטִיחַ	קִטַּח	נִקְטַח	קָטַח
Impf. 3 m. Sg.	יִתְקַטַּח	יַקְטִיחַ	יְקַטַּח	יִקָּטַח	יִקְטַח
Impv. 2 m. Sg.	הִתְקַטַּח	הַקְטַח	קַטַּח	הִקָּטַח	קְטַח
Infinitive abs.		הַקְטֵחַ	קַטֵּחַ	נִקְטוֹחַ	קָטוֹחַ
Infinitive const.	הִתְקַטַּח	הַקְטִיחַ	קַטַּח	הִקָּטַח	קְטֹחַ
Participle act.	מִתְקַטֵּחַ	מַקְטִיחַ	מְקַטֵּחַ		קֹטֵחַ
Participle pass.				נִקְטָח	קָטוּחַ

Synopsis of verb Pē Nûn (פ״ן)

	Hŏph'ăl	Hĭph'îl	Nĭph'ăl	Qăl
Perf. 3 m. Sg.	הֻטַּל	הִטִּיל	נִטַּל	נָטַל
Impf. 3 m. Sg.	יֻטַּל	יַטִּיל	יִנָּטֵל	יִטַּל, יִטֹּל
Impv. 2 m. Sg.		הַטֵּל	הִנָּטֵל	טַל, נְטֹל
Infinitive abs.	הֻטֵּל	הַטֵּל	הִנָּטֹל	נָטוֹל, נָטוֹל
Infinitive const.	הֻטַּל	הַטִּיל	הִנָּטֵל	טֶלֶת, נְטֹל
Participle act.		מַטִּיל		נֹטֵל
Participle pass.	מֻטָּל		נִטָּל	נָטוּל

Synopsis of verb Pē 'Ālĕph (פ״א)

	Qăl
Perf. 3 m. Sg.	אָטַל
Impf. 3 m. Sg.	יֹאטַל, יֹאטֵל
Impv. 2 m. Sg.	אֱטֹל
Infinitive abs.	אָטוֹל
Infinitive const.	אֱטֹל
Participle act.	אֹטֵל
Participle pass.	אָטוּל

Synopsis of verb 'Ăyĭn Yôdh (ע״י)

	Qăl
Perf. 3 m. Sg.	קָל
Impf. 3 m. Sg.	יָקִיל
Impv. 2 m. Sg.	קִיל
Infinitive abs.	קוֹל
Infinitive const.	קִיל
Participle act.	קָל
Participle pass.	קוּל, קִיל

Synopsis of verb 'Ăyĭn Doubled (ע״ע)

	Pô'āl	Pô'ēl	Hŏph'ăl	Hĭph'îl	Nĭph'ăl	Qăl
Perf. 3 m. Sg.	קוֹטַט	קוֹטֵט	הוּקַט	הֵקֵט	נָקַט	קַט
Impf. 3 m. Sg.	יְקוֹטַט	יְקוֹטֵט	יוּקַט, יֻקַּט	יָקֵט, יַקֵּט	יִקַּט	יָקֹט, יִקֹּט
Impv. 2 m. Sg.		קוֹטֵט		הָקֵט	הִקַּט	קֹט
Infinitive abs.	קוֹטַט	קוֹטֵט		הָקֵט	הִקּוֹט	קָטוֹט
Infinitive const.		קוֹטֵט		הָקֵט	הִקַּט	קֹט
Participle act.		מְקוֹטֵט		מֵקֵט		קֹטֵט
Participle pass.	מְקוֹטָט		מוּקָט		נָקָט	קָטוּט

Synopsis of verb Pē Wāw (פ״ו)

	Hŏph'ăl	Hĭph'îl	Nĭph'ăl	Qăl
Perf. 3 m. Sg.	הוּטַל	הוֹטִיל	נוֹטַל	יָטַל
Impf. 3 m. Sg.	יוּטַל	יוֹטִיל	יִוָּטֵל	יֵטֵל, יִיטַל
Impv. 2 m. Sg.		הוֹטֵל	הִוָּטֵל	טֵל, יְטַל
Infinitive abs.		הוֹטֵל		יָטוֹל, יָטוֹל
Infinitive const.	הוּטַל	הוֹטִיל	הִוָּטֵל	טֶלֶת, יְטֹל
Participle act.		מוֹטִיל	נוֹטָל	יֹטֵל
Participle pass.	מוּטָל			יָטוּל

Synopsis of verb 'Ăyĭn Wāw (ע״ו)

	Pôlăl	Pôlēl	Hŏph'ăl	Hĭph'îl	Nĭph'ăl	Qăl
Perf. 3 m. Sg.	קוֹלַל	קוֹלֵל	הוּקַל	הֵקִיל	נָקוֹל	קָל, קֵל
Impf. 3 m. Sg.	יְקוֹלַל	יְקוֹלֵל	יוּקַל	יָקִיל	יִקּוֹל	יָקוּל
Impv. 2 m. Sg.		קוֹלֵל		הָקֵל	הִקּוֹל	קוּל
Infinitive abs.				הָקֵל	הִקּוֹל	קוֹל
Infinitive const.		קוֹלֵל	הוּקַל	הָקִיל	הִקּוֹל	קוּל
Participle act.		מְקוֹלֵל		מֵקִיל		קָל
Participle pass.	מְקוֹלָל		מוּקָל		נָקוֹל	קוּל

Synopsis of verb Pē Yôdh (פ״י)

	Hĭph'îl	Qăl
Perf. 3 m. Sg.	הֵיטִיל	יָטַל
Impf. 3 m. Sg.	יֵיטִיל	יִיטַל
Impv. 2 m. Sg.	הֵיטֵל	יְטַל
Infinitive abs.	הֵיטֵל	יָטוֹל
Infinitive const.	הֵיטִיל	יְטֹל
Participle act.	מֵיטִיל	יֹטֵל
Participle pass.		יָטוּל

EXPLANATORY STATEMENTS

General Remarks. The root of a Hebrew verb has ordinarily three consonants called radicals. The verb has in common use a simple stem and six other stems which are modifications of the simple stem in form and meaning.

The Qăl is the simple stem.
The Nĭph'ăl has ordinarily the meaning of passive of the Qăl.
The Pĭ'ēl is intensive of the Qăl.
The Pŭ'ăl is the passive of the Pĭ'ēl.
The Hĭph'îl is causative of the Qăl.
The Hŏph'ăl is passive of the Hĭph'îl.
The Hĭthpă'ēl is reflexive of the Pĭ'ēl.

In some weak verbs occur stems known as Pô'ēl, Pôlēl and Pĭlpēl with the same meaning as the Pĭ'ēl; Pô'ăl and Pôlăl with the meaning of the Pŭ'ăl; and Hĭthpô'ēl, Hĭthpôlēl and Hĭthpălpēl with the meaning of the Hĭthpă'ēl. The forms of most of these will be seen from the Paradigms.

The Perfect tense corresponds most nearly to the past tense in English, and the Imperfect to the future, but with many differences. The Infinitive construct is used much like the Infinitive in English, only more widely, but the Infinitive absolute is chiefly used to intensify the meaning of a finite verb.

There is really only one conjugation of verbs in Hebrew. There are, however, certain variations in many verbs, caused by the nature of their consonants. The regular form of this conjugation is called the strong verb. Those which vary from the strong verb by reason of the peculiarities or weakness of certain consonants which they contain are called weak verbs. There are several classes of weak verbs. In the following statements are briefly enumerated the chief variations in the forms of these different classes of weak verbs from those of the strong verb. In the preceding Paradigms of weak verbs only the synopsis is given, the inflection being in most cases very similar to that of the strong verb. The stems omitted in any synopsis show no important variations from the strong verb.

Guttural Verbs. Pē ('פ) Guttural, 'Ăyĭn ('ע) Guttural, and Lāmĕdh ('ל) Guttural verbs are those respectively in which the first, second or third radical is a guttural, the gutturals being א, ה, ח, ע; ר is also often treated as a guttural. The chief variations of the guttural verbs are as follows:—

1. A guttural, including ר, rejects Dāghēš-forte (·), *i.e.*, it is never doubled This usually causes a short vowel which preceded the doubling to become long.

2. A guttural, usually not including ר, prefers the guttural or *a*-class vowel. Hence, in most forms the vowel immediately preceding the guttural is ă, and also in many forms the vowel immediately following the guttural.

3. A guttural, usually not including ר, prefers under it a compound Š^e^wâ (ֲ, ֱ, or ֳ, most frequently ֲ). Hence, a compound Š^e^wâ is regularly substituted for a simple Š^e^wâ (ְ) under the guttural, and usually for a silent Š^e^wâ (ְ), except in an accented syllable.

Lāmĕdh 'Ālĕph (ל״א) Verbs. Lāmĕdh 'Ālĕph (ל״א) verbs are those whose third radical is א.

1. א when final is silent, *i.e.*, loses its power as a consonant. Before it ă becomes ā.

2. א when medial is silent before consonantal additions. Before it a short vowel becomes long.

Lāmĕdh Hē (ל״ה) Verbs. Lāmĕdh Hē (ל״ה) verbs are those in which the third radical was originally ו, or more frequently י.

1. The י (or ו) when final is always lost, except in the Qăl passive Participle. A preceding short vowel becomes long, and ה is added as a vowel letter.

2. In inflection, before vowels the י is lost together with the preceding vowel.

3. Before consonants, contraction of י and the preceding vowel takes place, giving usually ֵי in the Perfects of the passive stems, ִי in the Perfects of the active stems, and ֶי in all Imperfects and Imperatives.

4. A final syllable ֶה or ֵה is frequently dropped.

Pē Nûn (פ״ן) Verbs. Pē Nûn (פ״ן) verbs are those in which the first radical is נ.

1. נ is regularly dropped together with the Š^e^wâ under it in the Qăl Impv. and Inf. const. of verbs which have ă as the stem vowel of the Impf.

2. נ is regularly assimilated, *i.e.*, disappears and is represented by Dāghēš-forte in the following consonant, whenever it stands at the close of a syllable.

Pē 'Ālĕph (פ״א) Verbs. The Pē 'Ālĕph (פ״א) verbs are six, אָבַד, אָבָה, אָחַז, אָכַל, אָמַר, אָפָה, in which א has become silent, *i.e.*, lost its power as a consonant. Their variations are only in the Qăl.

1. The preformative vowel is ô.

2. The stem vowel is ă or ē.

'Ăyĭn Yôdh (ע״י) Verbs. 'Ăyĭn Yôdh (ע״י) verbs are those in which the second radical is י. They do not differ materially from 'Ayĭn Wāw (ע״ו) verbs, except in the Qăl Impf., and in a few verbs in the Qăl Perfect.

'Ăyĭn Doubled (ע״ע) Verbs. 'Ăyĭn Doubled (ע״ע) verbs are those in which the second and third radicals are the same.

1. The second and third radicals are contracted into one, which has Dāghēš-forte before vowels, except in the Pĭ'ēl, Pŭ'ăl and Hĭthpă'ēl, and in the Inf. abs.

and Participles of the Qăl. The stem vowel then stands with the first radical instead of the second.

2. The preformative vowel is heightened, *i.e.*, a short vowel becomes long.

3. Before consonantal terminations a vowel is inserted, וֹ in Perfects, ֵי in Imperfects.

Pē Wāw (פ״ו) Verbs. The Pē Wāw (פ״ו) verbs are those in which the first radical was originally ו.

1. The original ו always becomes י when it is initial, elsewhere it usually remains ו.

2. In the Qăl some verbs have ē as the stem vowel of the Imperfect; these verbs drop the radical ו in the Impf., Impv., and Inf. construct. Other verbs have ă as the stem vowel of the Impf., and retain the first radical throughout.

3. ו is regularly contracted with an immediately preceding vowel, giving a naturally long vowel.

ʿĂyĭn Wāw (ע״ו) Verbs. ʿĂyĭn Wāw (ע״ו) verbs are those in which the second radical is ו.

1. ו never appears as a consonant; it is usually contracted with a preceding or following vowel, but is rejected with *a*.

2. The preformative vowel is usually heightened, *i.e.*, a short vowel becomes long.

3. Before consonantal terminations in Nĭphʿăl and Hĭphʿîl Perfects the vowel וֹ is inserted; in all Imperfects the vowel ֵי is inserted.

Pē Yôdh (פ״י) Verbs. The Pē Yôdh (פ״י) verbs are six, יָטַב, יָלַל, יָמַן, יָנַק, יָקַץ, יָשַׁר, whose first radical was originally י. They differ from Pē Wāw (פ״ו) verbs only in the Qăl and Hĭphʿîl.

LIST OF PRINCIPAL ABBREVIATIONS AND SIGNS USED

app.	= apparently.	*sing.*	= singular.
Aq.	= Aquila.	*Sm.*	= Samaritan.
Ar.	= Arabic.	*Sym.*	= Symmachus.
ess.	= essentially.	*T.*	= Targum of Onkelos.
fem.	= feminine.	*Theod.*	= Theodotion.
G.	= Septuagint.	*V.*	= Vulgate.
H.	= Hebrew text (unpointed).	[ ]	= an addition in the English which is not in the Hebrew.
masc.	= masculine.		
pl.	= plural.	( )	= an omission in the English of that which is in the Hebrew.
S.	= Peshitto.		

GENESIS בראשית

1

1 בְּרֵאשִׁית בָּרָא אֱלֹהִים אֵת הַשָּׁמַיִם וְאֵת הָאָרֶץ׃
,earth the and heavens the God created [when] beginning the In

2 וְהָאָרֶץ הָיְתָה תֹהוּ וָבֹהוּ וְחֹשֶׁךְ
[being] darkness and ,waste a and desolation a being earth the (and)

עַל־פְּנֵי תְהוֹם וְרוּחַ אֱלֹהִים מְרַחֶפֶת עַל־פְּנֵי
of face the upon hovering God of spirit the and ,abyss [the] of face the upon

3 הַמָּיִם׃ וַיֹּאמֶר אֱלֹהִים יְהִי־אוֹר וַיְהִי־אוֹר׃
.was light and be light Let :God said then ; waters the

4 וַיַּרְא אֱלֹהִים אֶת־הָאוֹר כִּי־טוֹב וַיַּבְדֵּל אֱלֹהִים
God divided and, good [was it] that light the God saw And

5 בֵּין הָאוֹר וּבֵין הַחֹשֶׁךְ׃ וַיִּקְרָא אֱלֹהִים ׀
God called And .darkness the (between) and light the between

לָאוֹר יוֹם וְלַחֹשֶׁךְ קָרָא לָיְלָה וַיְהִי־עֶרֶב
was evening and ; night called he darkness the to and ,day light the to

וַיְהִי־בֹקֶר יוֹם אֶחָד׃
.one[1] day[2] ,was morning and

6 וַיֹּאמֶר אֱלֹהִים יְהִי רָקִיעַ בְּתוֹךְ הַמָּיִם
,waters the of midst the in [2]expanse [1]an [3]be Let :God said And

7 וִיהִי מַבְדִּיל בֵּין מַיִם לָמָיִם׃[a] וַיַּעַשׂ אֱלֹהִים
God made And .waters to waters between dividing be it let and

אֶת־הָרָקִיעַ וַיַּבְדֵּל בֵּין הַמַּיִם אֲשֶׁר מִתַּחַת
under (from) [were] which waters the between divided he and ,expanse the

לָרָקִיעַ וּבֵין הַמַּיִם אֲשֶׁר מֵעַל
above (from) [were] which waters the (between) and expanse the (to)

8 לָרָקִיעַ וַיְהִי־כֵן׃[b] וַיִּקְרָא אֱלֹהִים לָרָקִיעַ
expanse the (to) God called And .so was it and ; expanse the (to)

שָׁמָיִם[c] וַיְהִי־עֶרֶב וַיְהִי־בֹקֶר יוֹם שֵׁנִי׃
.[1]second [2]day a ,was morning and was evening and ; heavens

IN the beginning God created the heaven and the earth. 2 And the earth was without form, and void; and darkness *was* upon the face of the deep. And the Spirit of God moved upon the face of the waters. 3 And God said, Let there be light: and there was light. 4 And God saw the light, that *it was* good: and God divided the light from the darkness. 5 And God called the light Day, and the darkness he called Night. And the evening and the morning were the first day. 6 And God said, Let there be a firmament in the midst of the waters, and let it divide the waters from the waters. 7 And God made the firmament, and divided the waters which *were* under the firmament from the waters which *were* above the firmament: and it was so. 8 And God called the firmament Heaven. And the evening and the morning were the second day.

IN the beginning God created the heaven and the earth. 2 And the earth was waste and void; and darkness was upon the face of the deep: and the spirit of God moved upon the face of the waters. 3 And God said, Let there be light: and there was light. 4 And God saw the light, that it was good: and God divided the light from the darkness. 5 And God called the light Day, and the darkness he called Night. And there was evening and there was morning, one day. 6 And God said, Let there be a firmament in the midst of the waters, and let it divide the waters from the waters. 7 And God made the firmament, and divided the waters which were under the firmament from the waters which were above the firmament: and it was so. 8 And God called the firmament Heaven. And there was evening and there was morning, a second day.

---

a G. adds *and it was so* ויהי־כן.
b G. omits *and it was so* ויהי־כן.
c G. adds, *and God saw that it was good* וירא אלהים כי טוב.

9 And God
said, Let the
waters under
the heaven be
gathered toge-
ther unto one
place, and let
the dry *land*
appear: and it
was so. 10 And
God called the
dry *land*
Earth; and the
gathering toge-
ther of the wa-
ters called he
Seas: and God
saw that *it was*
good. 11 And
God said, Let
the earth bring
forth grass,
the herb
yielding seed,
and the fruit
tree yielding
fruit after his
kind, whose seed
is in itself, upon
the earth: and
it was so. 12
And the earth
brought forth
grass, *and* herb
yielding seed
after his kind,
and the tree
yielding fruit,
whose seed *was*
in itself, after his
kind: and God
saw that *it was*
good. 13 And
the evening and
the morning
were the third
day.

14 And God
said, Let there
be lights in the
firmament of
the heaven to
divide the day
from the night;
and let them be
for signs, and
for seasons, and
for days, and
years: 15 And
let them be for
lights in the
firmament of
the heaven to
give light upon
the earth: and
it was so. 16

9 וַיֹּאמֶר אֱלֹהִים יִקָּווּ הַמַּיִם מִתַּחַת
under (from) waters the collected be Let :God said And

הַשָּׁמַיִם אֶל־מָקוֹם אֶחָד וְתֵרָאֶה הַיַּבָּשָׁה
; land dry the seen be let and ,[1]one [2]place unto heavens the

10 וַיְהִי־כֵן׃[a] וַיִּקְרָא אֱלֹהִים ׀ לַיַּבָּשָׁה אֶרֶץ
,earth land dry the to God called And .so was it and

וּלְמִקְוֵה הַמַּיִם קָרָא יַמִּים וַיַּרְא
saw and ;seas called he waters the of collection the to and

11 אֱלֹהִים כִּי־טוֹב׃ וַיֹּאמֶר אֱלֹהִים תַּדְשֵׁא
[6]forth [5]spring [4]to [3]cause Let :God said And .good [was it] that God

הָאָרֶץ דֶּשֶׁא עֵשֶׂב מַזְרִיעַ זֶרַע עֵץ[b] פְּרִי עֹשֶׂה פְּרִי
fruit making fruit of tree [and] ,seed seeding herb ,grass [2]earth [1]the

לְמִינוֹ אֲשֶׁר זַרְעוֹ־בוֹ עַל־הָאָרֶץ וַיְהִי־כֵן׃
.so was it and ; earth the upon ,(it in) seed its [is] which [in] ,kind its after

12 וַתּוֹצֵא הָאָרֶץ דֶּשֶׁא עֵשֶׂב מַזְרִיעַ זֶרַע
seed seeding herb ,grass [2]earth [1]the [6]forth [5]go [4]to [3]caused And

לְמִינֵהוּ וְעֵץ עֹשֶׂה־פְּרִי אֲשֶׁר זַרְעוֹ־בוֹ
(it in) seed its [is] which [in] fruit making tree and ,kind its after

13 לְמִינֵהוּ וַיַּרְא אֱלֹהִים כִּי־טוֹב׃ וַיְהִי־עֶרֶב
was evening And .good [was it] that God saw and ;kind its after

14 וַיְהִי־בֹקֶר יוֹם שְׁלִישִׁי׃ וַיֹּאמֶר אֱלֹהִים יְהִי מְאֹרֹת
[1]luminaries [2]be Let :God said And .[1]third [2]day a ,was morning and

בִּרְקִיעַ הַשָּׁמַיִם[c] לְהַבְדִּיל בֵּין הַיּוֹם וּבֵין
(between) and day the between divide to ,heavens the of expanse the in

הַלָּיְלָה וְהָיוּ לְאֹתֹת וּלְמוֹעֲדִים וּלְיָמִים
days for and ,seasons for and ,signs for be them let and ; night the

15 וְשָׁנִים׃ וְהָיוּ לִמְאוֹרֹת בִּרְקִיעַ הַשָּׁמַיִם
,heavens the of expanse the in luminaries for be them let and ; years and

16 לְהָאִיר עַל־הָאָרֶץ וַיְהִי־כֵן׃ וַיַּעַשׂ אֱלֹהִים אֶת־שְׁנֵי
two the God made And .so was it and ; earth the upon light give to

הַמְּאֹרֹת הַגְּדֹלִים אֶת־הַמָּאוֹר הַגָּדֹל לְמֶמְשֶׁלֶת
for ruling [1]greater [2]luminary the ;[1]great [2]luminaries

9 And God
said, Let the
waters under the
heaven be
gathered to-
gether unto one
place, and let
the dry land
appear: and it
was so. 10 And
God called the
dry land Earth;
and the gather-
ing together of
the waters called
he Seas: and
God saw that it
was good. 11
And God said,
Let the earth
put forth grass,
herb yielding
seed, *and* fruit
tree bearing
fruit after its
kind, wherein is
the seed thereof,
upon the earth:
and it was so.
12 And the
earth brought
forth grass, herb
yielding seed
after its kind,
and tree bearing
fruit, wherein is
the seed thereof,
after its kind:
and God saw
that it was good.
13 And there
was evening and
there was morn-
ing, a third
day.

14 And God
said, Let there
be lights in the
firmament of the
heaven to divide
the day from the
night; and let
them be for
signs, and for
seasons, and for
days and years:
15 and let them
be for lights in
the firmament of
the heaven to
give light upon
the earth: and it
was so. 16 And
God made the
two great

a G. adds, *and the water under the heaven was gathered unto their congregations, and the dry land was seen.*

b G., S. and V. read ועץ.

c G. adds *to give light upon the earth* להאיר על הארץ.

And God made
two great lights;
the greater light
to rule the day,
and the lesser
light to rule
the night: *he*
made the stars
also. 17 And
God set them in
the firmament of
the heaven to
give light upon
the earth, 18
And to rule over
the day and over
the night, and to
divide the light
from the dark-
ness: and God
saw that *it was*
good. 19 And
the evening and
the morning
were the fourth
day.
20 And God
said, Let the wa-
ters bring forth
abundantly the
moving crea-
ture that hath
life, and fowl
that may fly
above the earth
in the open fir-
mament of hea-
ven. 21 And
God created
great whales,
and every living
creature that
moveth, which
the waters
brought forth a-
bundantly, after
their kind, and
every winged
fowl after his
kind: and God
saw that *it was*
good. 22 And
God blessed
them, saying,
Be fruitful, and
multiply, and fill
the waters in the
seas, and let fowl
multiply in the
earth. 23 And
the evening and
the morning
were the fifth
day.
24 And God
said, Let the
earth bring
forth the living
creature after
his kind, cattle,
and creeping
thing, and beast

הַיּוֹם וְאֶת־הַמָּאוֹר הַקָּטֹן לְמֶמְשֶׁלֶת הַלַּיְלָה
;night the ruling for [1]smaller [2]luminary the and [1]day the

17 וְאֵת הַכֹּכָבִים׃ וַיִּתֵּן אֹתָם אֱלֹהִים
God them put And .stars the and

18 בִּרְקִיעַ הַשָּׁמָיִם לְהָאִיר עַל־הָאָרֶץ׃ וְלִמְשֹׁל
rule to and ,earth the upon light give to heaven the of expanse the in

בַּיּוֹם וּבַלַּיְלָה וּלֲהַבְדִּיל בֵּין הָאוֹר
light the between divide to and night the in and day the in

וּבֵין הַחֹשֶׁךְ וַיַּרְא אֱלֹהִים כִּי־טוֹב׃
.good [was it] that God saw and ;darkness the (between) and

19 וַיְהִי־עֶרֶב וַיְהִי -- בֹקֶר יוֹם רְבִיעִי׃
.[1]fourth [2]day a ,was morning and was evening And

20 וַיֹּאמֶר אֱלֹהִים יִשְׁרְצוּ הַמַּיִם שֶׁרֶץ נֶפֶשׁ חַיָּה
,life of soul ,swarms [with] [2]waters [1]the [3]swarm Let :God said And

וְעוֹף יְעוֹפֵף עַל־הָאָרֶץ עַל־פְּנֵי רְקִיעַ הַשָּׁמָיִם׃[a]
.heavens the of expanse the of face the upon ,earth the upon fly [1]let [2]fowl and

21 וַיִּבְרָא אֱלֹהִים אֶת־הַתַּנִּינִם הַגְּדֹלִים וְאֵת כָּל־נֶפֶשׁ
of souls the all and ,[1]great [2]sea-monsters the God created And

הַחַיָּה הָרֹמֶשֶׂת אֲשֶׁר שָׁרְצוּ הַמַּיִם לְמִינֵהֶם
,kinds their after ,waters the swarmed which [with] ,creep that life

וְאֵת כָּל־עוֹף כָּנָף לְמִינֵהוּ וַיַּרְא אֱלֹהִים
God saw and ; kind its after wing of fowl every and

22 כִּי־טוֹב׃ וַיְבָרֶךְ אֹתָם אֱלֹהִים לֵאמֹר
:saying ,God them blessed And .good [was it] that

פְּרוּ וּרְבוּ וּמִלְאוּ אֶת־הַמַּיִם בַּיַּמִּים
,seas the in waters the fill and ,multiply and ,fruitful Be

23 וְהָעוֹף יִרֶב בָּאָרֶץ׃ וַיְהִי־עֶרֶב וַיְהִי־בֹקֶר
,was morning and was evening And .earth the in multiply [1]let [3]fowl [2]the and

יוֹם חֲמִישִׁי׃
.[1]fifth [2]day a

24 וַיֹּאמֶר אֱלֹהִים תּוֹצֵא הָאָרֶץ נֶפֶשׁ חַיָּה
life of soul [2]earth [1]the [6]forth [5]go [4]to [3]cause let ,God said And

לְמִינָהּ בְּהֵמָה וָרֶמֶשׂ וְחַיְתוֹ־אֶרֶץ לְמִינָהּ
,kind its after earth [the] of beast and ,creeper and ,cattle ,kind its after

lights; the
greater light to
rule the day,
and the lesser
light to rule the
night: *he made*
the stars also.
17 And God
set them in the
firmament of the
heaven to give
light upon the
earth, 18 and to
rule over the day
and over the
night, and to
divide the light
from the dark-
ness: and God
saw that it was
good. 19 And
there was even-
ing, and there
was morning, a
fourth day.
20 And God
said, Let the wa-
ters bring forth
abundantly the
moving creature
that hath life,
and let fowl fly
above the earth
in the open fir-
mament of heav-
en. 21 And God
created the great
sea - monsters,
and every living
creature that
moveth, which
the waters
brought forth a-
bundantly, after
their kinds, and
every winged
fowl after its
kind: and God
saw that it was
good. 22 And
God blessed
them, saying, Be
fruitful, and
multiply, and
fill the waters in
the seas, and let
fowl multiply in
the earth. 23
And there was
evening and
there was mor-
ning, a fifth day.
24 And God
said, Let the
earth bring forth
the living crea-
ture after its
kind, cattle, and
creeping thing,
and beast of the
earth after its
kind; and it was

a G. adds, *and it was so* ויהי־כן.

of the earth after
his kind: and it
was so. 25 And
God made the
beast of the earth
after his kind,
and cattle after
their kind, and
every thing that
creepeth upon
the earth after
his kind: and
God saw that *it*
was good.
26 And God
said, Let us
make man in our
image, after our
likeness: and let
them have dominion over the
fish of the sea,
and over the
fowl of the air,
and over the
cattle, and over
all the earth, and
over every creeping thing that
creepeth upon
the earth. 27 So
God created
man in his *own*
image, in the
image of God
created he him;
male and female
created he them.
28 And God
blessed them,
and God said
unto them, Be
fruitful, and
multiply, and
replenish the
earth, and subdue it: and have
dominion over
the fish of the
sea, and over the
fowl of the air,
and over every
living thing that
moveth upon the
earth.
29 And God
said, Behold, I
have given you
every herb bearing seed, which
is upon the face
of all the earth,
and every tree, in
the which *is* the
fruit of a tree
yielding seed; to
you it shall be
for meat. 30 And
to every beast of
the earth, and
to every fowl of
the air, and to

25 וַיְהִי־כֵן׃ וַיַּעַשׂ אֱלֹהִים אֶת־חַיַּת הָאָרֶץ
earth the of beast the God made And .so was it and

לְמִינָהּ וְאֶת־הַבְּהֵמָה לְמִינָהּ וְאֵת כָּל־רֶמֶשׂ הָאֲדָמָה
ground the of creeper every and ,kind its after cattle the and ,kind its after

26 לְמִינֵהוּ וַיַּרְא אֱלֹהִים כִּי־טוֹב׃ וַיֹּאמֶר
said And .good [was it] that God saw and ;kind its after

אֱלֹהִים נַעֲשֶׂה אָדָם בְּצַלְמֵנוּ כִּדְמוּתֵנוּ[a]
; likeness our after ,image our in man make us Let :God

וְיִרְדּוּ בִדְגַת הַיָּם וּבְעוֹף
of fowl the over and ,sea the of fish the over dominion have them let and

הַשָּׁמַיִם וּבַבְּהֵמָה וּבְכָל־הָאָרֶץ וּבְכָל־הָרֶמֶשׂ
creeper every over and ,earth the all over and ,cattle the over and ,heavens the

27 הָרֹמֵשׂ עַל־הָאָרֶץ׃ וַיִּבְרָא אֱלֹהִים ׀ אֶת־הָאָדָם
man (the) God created And .earth the upon creeps that

בְּצַלְמוֹ[b] בְּצֶלֶם אֱלֹהִים בָּרָא אֹתוֹ זָכָר
male ,him created he God of image the in ,image his in

28 וּנְקֵבָה בָּרָא אֹתָם׃ וַיְבָרֶךְ אֹתָם
them blessed And .them created he female and

אֱלֹהִים וַיֹּאמֶר לָהֶם אֱלֹהִים[c] פְּרוּ וּרְבוּ
,multiply and ,fruitful Be :God them to said and ,God

וּמִלְאוּ אֶת־הָאָרֶץ וְכִבְשֻׁהָ וּרְדוּ בִּדְגַת
of fish the over dominion have and ; it subdue and ,earth the fill and

הַיָּם וּבְעוֹף הַשָּׁמַיִם[d] וּבְכָל־חַיָּה הָרֹמֶשֶׂת
creeps that beast every over and ,heavens the of fowl the over and ,sea the

29 עַל־הָאָרֶץ׃ וַיֹּאמֶר אֱלֹהִים הִנֵּה נָתַתִּי לָכֶם
you to given have I ,Behold :God said And .earth the upon

אֶת־כָּל־עֵשֶׂב ׀ זֹרֵעַ זֶרַע אֲשֶׁר עַל־פְּנֵי כָל־הָאָרֶץ וְאֶת
and ,earth the all of face the upon [is] which seed seeding herb every

כָּל־הָעֵץ אֲשֶׁר־בּוֹ פְרִי־עֵץ זֹרֵעַ זָרַע לָכֶם יִהְיֶה
be shall it you to ,seed seeding tree a of fruit the [is] which in tree every

30 לְאָכְלָה׃ וּלְכָל־חַיַּת הָאָרֶץ וּלְכָל־עוֹף הַשָּׁמַיִם
,heavens the of fowl the all to and ,earth the of beast every to and ; food for

וּלְכֹל ׀ רוֹמֵשׂ עַל־הָאָרֶץ אֲשֶׁר־בּוֹ נֶפֶשׁ
of soul a [is] which in ,earth the upon creeper every to and

so. 25 And God
made the beast
of the earth after
its kind, and the
cattle after their
kind, and every
thing that creepeth upon the
ground after its
kind: and God
saw that it was
good.
26 And God
said, Let us
make man in our
image, after our
likeness: and let
them have dominion over the
fish of the sea,
and over the
fowl of the air,
and over the
cattle, and over
all the earth, and
over every creeping thing that
creepeth upon
the earth. 27
And God created man in his
own image, in
the image of
God created he
him; male and
female created
he them. 28 And
God blessed
them: and God
said unto them,
Be fruitful, and
multiply, and replenish the earth
and subdue it,
and have dominion over the
fish of the sea,
and over the
fowl of the air,
and over every
living thing that
moveth upon the
earth.
29 And God
said, Behold, I
have given you
every herb yielding seed, which
is upon the face
of all the earth,
and every tree,
in the which is
the fruit of a tree
yielding seed;
to you it shall be
for meat: 30 and
to every beast of
the earth, and to
every fowl of
the air, and to
every thing that
creepeth upon

a and after our likeness, וכדמותנו is read by G. Aq., V.
b G. omits.
c to them God, להם-אלהים, is omitted by G. and V.
d S. adds, *and over the cattle*; G. adds, *and all the cattle and all the earth*.

every thing that
creepeth upon
the earth, where-
in *there is* life, *I*
have given every
green herb for
meat: and it was
so. 31 And God
saw every thing
that he had
made, and, be-
hold, *it was* very
good. And the
evening and the
morning were
the sixth day.

THUS the
heavens and the
earth were fin-
ished, and all
the host of them.
2 And on the
seventh day God
ended his work
which he had
made; and he
rested on the
seventh day
from all his
work which he
had made. 3
And God bless-
ed the seventh
day, and sanc-
tified it: because
that in it he
had rested from
all his work
which God cre-
ated and made.
4 These *are*
the genera-
tions of the
heavens and of
the earth when
they were cre-
ated, in the day
that the LORD
God made the
earth and the
heavens, 5 And
every plant of
the field before
it was in the
earth, and every
herb of the field
before it grew:
for the LORD
God had not
caused it to rain
upon the earth,
and *there was*
not a man to
till the ground.
6 But there went
up a mist from
the earth, and
watered the
whole face of the
ground. 7. And

חַיָּה אֶת־כָּל־יֶרֶק עֵשֶׂב לְאָכְלָה וַֽיְהִי־כֵן׃
.so was it and ;food for herb of greenness every [given have I], life

31 וַיַּרְא אֱלֹהִים אֶת־כָּל־אֲשֶׁר עָשָׂה וְהִנֵּה־טוֹב
[2]good [was it] ,behold and ,made had he which all God saw And

מְאֹד וַֽיְהִי־עֶרֶב וַֽיְהִי־בֹקֶר יוֹם הַשִּׁשִּׁי׃
.[1]sixth [2]day a ,was morning and was evening and ;[1]exceedingly

2

1 וַיְכֻלּוּ הַשָּׁמַיִם וְהָאָרֶץ וְכָל־צְבָאָם׃
.host their all and earth the and heavens the finished were And

2 וַיְכַל אֱלֹהִים בַּיּוֹם הַשְּׁבִיעִי[a] מְלַאכְתּוֹ אֲשֶׁר
which work his [1]seventh [2]day the in God finished And

עָשָׂה וַיִּשְׁבֹּת בַּיּוֹם הַשְּׁבִיעִי מִכָּל־מְלַאכְתּוֹ
work his all from [1]seventh [2]day the in rested he and ;made had he

3 אֲשֶׁר עָשָׂה׃ וַיְבָרֶךְ אֱלֹהִים אֶת־יוֹם הַשְּׁבִיעִי
[1]seventh [2]day the God blessed And .made had he which

וַיְקַדֵּשׁ אֹתוֹ כִּי בוֹ שָׁבַת מִכָּל־מְלַאכְתּוֹ
work his all from rested he it in because ;it sanctified and

4 אֲשֶׁר־בָּרָא אֱלֹהִים לַעֲשׂוֹת׃ אֵלֶּה
[are] These .make to God created had which

תוֹלְדוֹת הַשָּׁמַיִם וְהָאָרֶץ בְּהִבָּרְאָם
.created being their in earth the and heavens the of generations the

בְּיוֹם עֲשׂוֹת יְהוָה אֱלֹהִים אֶרֶץ וְשָׁמָיִם׃
;heavens and earth [2]God's [1]Jehovah [3]making of day the In

5 וְכֹל שִׂיחַ הַשָּׂדֶה טֶרֶם יִהְיֶה בָאָרֶץ
,earth the in being yet not field the of shrub any (and)

וְכָל־עֵשֶׂב הַשָּׂדֶה טֶרֶם יִצְמָח כִּי
for ;forth sprouted having yet not field the of herb any and

לֹא הִמְטִיר יְהוָה אֱלֹהִים עַל־הָאָרֶץ וְאָדָם
[there] man and ,earth the upon God Jehovah rain to caused had not

6 אַיִן לַעֲבֹד אֶת־הָאֲדָמָה׃ וְאֵד יַעֲלֶה
up go to accustomed being mist a and ;ground the till to not was

7 מִן־הָאָרֶץ וְהִשְׁקָה אֶת־כָּל־פְּנֵי־הָאֲדָמָה׃ וַיִּיצֶר
formed then ;ground the of face the all water to and earth the from

the earth,
wherein there is
life, *I have given*
every green herb
for meat: and it
was so. 31 And
God saw every
thing that he
had made, and,
behold, it was
very good. And
there was even-
ing and there
was morning,
the sixth day.

And the heav-
en and the earth
were finished,
and all the host
of them. 2 And
on the seventh
day God finished
his work which
he had made;
and he rested
on the seventh
day from all his
work which he
had made. 3
And God
blessed the sev-
enth day, and
hallowed it: be-
cause that in
it he rested from
all his work
which God had
created and
made.
4 These are
the generations
of the heaven
and of the earth
when they were
created, in the
day that the
LORD God made
earth and heav-
en. 5 And no
plant of the field
was yet in the
earth, and no
herb of the field
had yet sprung
up: for the
LORD God had
not caused it to
rain upon the
earth, and there
was not a man
to till the
ground; 6 but
there went up a
mist from the
earth, and wa-
tered the whole
face of the
ground. 7 And
the LORD God

a the sixth השׁשי, read by Sm., G. and S. An intentional change.

the LORD God
formed man *of*
the dust of the
ground, and
breathed into his
nostrils the
breath of life;
and man be-
came a living
soul. 8 ¶ And
the LORD God
planted a garden
eastward in
Eden; and there
he put the man
whom he had
formed. 9 And
out of the
ground made
the LORD God
to grow every
tree that is pleas-
ant to the sight,
and good for
food; the tree of
life also in the
midst of the gar-
den, and the
tree of knowl-
edge of good
and evil. 10
And a river
went out of
Eden to water
the garden; and
from thence it
was parted, and
became into four
heads. 11 The
name of the first
is Pison: that
is it which com-
passeth the
whole land of
Havilah, where
there is gold;
12 And the gold
of that land *is*
good: there *is*
bdellium and
the onyx stone.
13 And the name
of the second
river *is* Gihon:
the same *is* it
that compas-
seth the whole
land of Ethiopia.
14 And the
name of the
third river *is*
Hiddekel: that
is it which goeth
toward the east
of Assyria. And
the fourth river
is Euphrates. 15
And the LORD
God took the
man, and put
him into the
garden of Eden
to dress it and
to keep it. 16
And the LORD

יְהוָה אֱלֹהִים אֶת־הָאָדָם עָפָר מִן־הָאֲדָמָה
,ground the from dust [of out] man (the) God Jehovah

וַיִּפַּח בְּאַפָּיו נִשְׁמַת חַיִּים וַיְהִי הָאָדָם
[1]man (the) [2]became and ;life of breath nostrils his in breathed and

8 לְנֶפֶשׁ חַיָּה׃ וַיִּטַּע יְהוָה אֱלֹהִים גַּן בְּעֵדֶן
Eden in garden a God Jehovah planted And [1].living [2]soul a (for)

מִקֶּדֶם וַיָּשֶׂם שָׁם אֶת־הָאָדָם אֲשֶׁר יָצָר׃
.formed had he whom man the there placed and ,east [ward] (from)

9 וַיַּצְמַח יְהוָה אֱלֹהִים מִן־הָאֲדָמָה
ground the from God Jehovah sprout to caused And

כָּל־עֵץ נֶחְמָד לְמַרְאֶה וְטוֹב לְמַאֲכָל וְעֵץ
of tree the and ;food for good and appearance for pleasant tree every

הַחַיִּים בְּתוֹךְ הַגָּן וְעֵץ הַדַּעַת טוֹב
good knowing of tree the and ,garden the of midst the in life

10 וָרָע׃ וְנָהָר יֹצֵא מֵעֵדֶן לְהַשְׁקוֹת אֶת־הַגָּן
;garden the water to Eden from out going [was] river a And .evil and

וּמִשָּׁם יִפָּרֵד וְהָיָה לְאַרְבָּעָה רָאשִׁים׃
.heads four (for) became and divided was it thence from and

11 שֵׁם הָאֶחָד פִּישׁוֹן הוּא
[being] it ,Pishon [was] one the of name The

הַסֹּבֵב אֵת כָּל־אֶרֶץ הַחֲוִילָה אֲשֶׁר־שָׁם הַזָּהָב׃
.gold [is] where ,Havilah of land the all surrounding [one] the

12 וּזֲהַב הָאָרֶץ הַהִוא טוֹב שָׁם הַבְּדֹלַח
bdellium [being] there ;good [being] [1]that [2]land of gold the And

13 וְאֶבֶן הַשֹּׁהַם׃ וְשֵׁם־הַנָּהָר הַשֵּׁנִי
[was] [1]second [2]river the of name the And .onyx the of stone the (and)

גִּיחוֹן הוּא הַסּוֹבֵב אֵת כָּל־אֶרֶץ כּוּשׁ׃
.Cush of land the all surrounding [one] the [being] it ,Gihon

14 וְשֵׁם הַנָּהָר הַשְּׁלִישִׁי חִדֶּקֶל הוּא
[being] it ,Tigris [was] [1]third [2]river the of name the And

הַהֹלֵךְ קִדְמַת אַשּׁוּר וְהַנָּהָר הָרְבִיעִי הוּא פְרָת׃
.Euphrates is [1]fourth [2]river the and ;Assyria of eastward going[one]the

15 וַיִּקַּח יְהוָה אֱלֹהִים אֶת־הָאָדָם וַיַּנִּחֵהוּ בְגַן־עֵדֶן
Eden of garden the in him put and man the God Jehovah took And

16 לְעָבְדָהּ וּלְשָׁמְרָהּ׃ וַיְצַו יְהוָה אֱלֹהִים
God Jehovah commanded And .it guard to and it till to

formed man of
the dust of the
ground, and
breathed into his
nostrils the
breath of life;
and man became
a living soul. 8
And the LORD
God plant-
ed a garden east-
ward, in Eden;
and there he put
the man whom
he had formed.
9 And out of the
ground made
the LORD God
to grow every
tree that is pleas-
ant to the sight,
and good for
food; the tree
of life also in
the midst of the
garden, and the
tree of the
knowledge of
good and evil.
10 And a river
went out of
Eden to water
the garden; and
from thence it
was parted, and
became four
heads. 11 The
name of the first
is Pishon: that
is it which com-
passeth the
whole land
of Havilah,
where there is
gold; 12 and the
gold of that land
is good: there is
bdellium and
the onyx stone.
13 And the
name of the
second river is
Gihon: the same
is it that compas-
seth the whole
land of Cush.
14 And the name
of the third river
is Hiddekel:
that is it which
goeth in front of
Assyria. And
the fourth river
is Euphrates.
15 And the
LORD God took
the man, and
put him into the
garden of Eden
to dress it and
to keep it. 16
And the LORD
God command-
ed the man, say-
ing, Of every

God commanded the man, saying, Of every tree of the garden thou mayest freely eat: 17 But of the tree of the knowledge of good and evil, thou shalt not eat of it: for in the day that thou eatest thereof thou shalt surely die.

18 And the LORD God said, *It is* not good that the man should be alone; I will make him an help meet for him. 19 And out of the ground the LORD God formed every beast of the field, and every fowl of the air; and brought *them* unto Adam to see what he would call them: and whatsoever Adam called every living creature, that *was* the name thereof. 20 And Adam gave names to all cattle, and to the fowl of the air, and to every beast of the field; but for Adam there was not found an help meet for him. 21 And the LORD God caused a deep sleep to fall upon Adam, and he slept: and he took one of his ribs, and closed up the flesh instead thereof; 22 And the rib, which the LORD God had taken from man, made he a woman, and brought her unto the man. 23 And Adam said,

עַל־הָאָדָם לֵאמֹר מִכֹּל עֵץ־הַגָּן אָכֹל
eating garden the of tree every From :saying ,man the (upon)

17 תֹּאכֵל׃ וּמֵעֵץ הַדַּעַת טוֹב וָרָע לֹא
[3]not evil and good knowing of tree the from but ;eat mayest thou

תֹאכַל מִמֶּנּוּ כִּי בְּיוֹם אֲכָלְךָ מִמֶּנּוּ מוֹת
dying it from eating thy of day the in for ;it from eat [2]shalt [1]thou

תָּמוּת׃
.die shalt thou

18 וַיֹּאמֶר יְהוָה אֱלֹהִים לֹא־טוֹב הֱיוֹת
[2]being [[6]is] [8]good [7]Not :God Jehovah said And

הָאָדָם לְבַדּוֹ אֶעֱשֶׂה[a]־לּוֹ עֵזֶר
helper a him for make will I [5],separation [4]his [3]to [1]man's (the)

19 כְּנֶגְדּוֹ׃ וַיִּצֶר יְהוָה אֱלֹהִים מִן־הָאֲדָמָה
ground the from God Jehovah formed And .counterpart his as

כָּל־חַיַּת הַשָּׂדֶה וְאֵת כָּל־עוֹף הַשָּׁמַיִם וַיָּבֵא
brought and ,heavens the of fowl every and field the of beast every

אֶל־הָאָדָם לִרְאוֹת מַה־יִּקְרָא־לוֹ וְכֹל אֲשֶׁר
which all and ;it (to) call would he what see to man the unto

יִקְרָא־לוֹ הָאָדָם נֶפֶשׁ חַיָּה הוּא שְׁמוֹ׃
.name its was ,[1]living [2]soul a [to], ,man the it (to) call might

20 וַיִּקְרָא הָאָדָם שֵׁמוֹת לְכָל־הַבְּהֵמָה וּלְעוֹף
of fowl the to and cattle the all to names man the called And

הַשָּׁמַיִם וּלְכֹל חַיַּת הַשָּׂדֶה וּלְאָדָם
man a for and ;field the of beast every to and heavens the

21 לֹא־מָצָא עֵזֶר כְּנֶגְדּוֹ׃ וַיַּפֵּל יְהוָה
Jehovah fall to caused And .counterpart his as helper a find [2]did [1]he [3]not

אֱלֹהִים ׀ תַּרְדֵּמָה עַל־הָאָדָם וַיִּישָׁן וַיִּקַּח
took he and ;slept he and ,man the upon sleep heavy a God

22 אַחַת מִצַּלְעֹתָיו וַיִּסְגֹּר בָּשָׂר תַּחְתֶּנָּה׃ וַיִּבֶן
built And .it of instead flesh (the) closed and ,ribs his from one

יְהוָה אֱלֹהִים ׀ אֶת־הַצֵּלָע אֲשֶׁר־לָקַח מִן־הָאָדָם
man the from taken had he which rib the God Jehovah

23 לְאִשָּׁה וַיְבִאֶהָ אֶל־הָאָדָם׃ וַיֹּאמֶר הָאָדָם
,man the said And .man the unto her brought and ,woman a into

tree of the garden thou mayest freely eat: 17 but of the tree of the knowledge of good and evil, thou shalt not eat of it: for in the day that thou eatest thereof thou shalt surely die.

18 And the LORD God said, It is not good that the man should be alone; I will make him an help meet for him. 19 And out of the ground the LORD God formed every beast of the field, and every fowl of the air; and brought them unto the man to see what he would call them: and whatsoever the man called every living creature, that was the name thereof. 20 And the man gave names to all cattle, and to the fowl of the air, and to every beast of the field; but for man there was not found an help meet for him. 21 And the LORD God caused a deep sleep to fall upon the man, and he slept; and he took one of his ribs, and closed up the flesh instead thereof: 22 and the rib, which the LORD God had taken from the man, made he a woman, and brought her unto the man. 23 And the man

---

[a] *we will make*, נעשה, read by G. and V.

This *is* now bone of my bones, and flesh of my flesh: she shall be called Woman, because she was taken out of Man. 24 Therefore shall a man leave his father and his mother, and shall cleave unto his wife: and they shall be one flesh. 25 And they were both naked, the man and his wife, and were not ashamed.

זֹאת הַפַּעַם עֶצֶם מֵעֲצָמַי וּבָשָׂר מִבְּשָׂרִי
; flesh my from flesh and bones my from bone [is] ,last at now ,this

לְזֹאת יִקָּרֵא אִשָּׁה כִּי מֵאִישׁ[a] לֻקֳחָה־זֹּאת׃
.taken was this man from because ,woman called be shall it this to

24 עַל־כֵּן יַעֲזָב־אִישׁ אֶת־אָבִיו וְאֶת־אִמּוֹ
,mother his and father his leave shall man a Therefore

וְדָבַק בְּאִשְׁתּוֹ וְהָיוּ[b] לְבָשָׂר
[2]flesh (for) become shall they and ; wife his to cleave shall and

25 אֶחָד׃ וַיִּהְיוּ שְׁנֵיהֶם עֲרוּמִּים הָאָדָם וְאִשְׁתּוֹ וְלֹא
[3]not and ,wife his and man the ,naked two they were And .[1]one

יִתְבֹּשָׁשׁוּ׃
.other each before ashamed [2]were [1]they

said, This is now bone of my bones, and flesh of my flesh: she shall be called Woman, because she was taken out of Man. 24 Therefore shall a man leave his father and his mother, and shall cleave unto his wife: and they shall be one flesh. 25 And they were both naked, the man and his wife, and were not ashamed.

3

Now the serpent was more subtil than any beast of the field which the LORD God had made. And he said unto the woman, Yea, hath God said, Ye shall not eat of every tree of the garden? 2 And the woman said unto the serpent, We may eat of the fruit of the trees of the garden: 3 But of the fruit of the tree which *is* in the midst of the garden, God hath said, Ye shall not eat of it, neither shall ye touch it, lest ye die. 4 And the serpent said unto the woman, Ye shall not surely die: 5 For God doth know that in the day ye eat thereof, then your eyes shall be opened, and

1 וְהַנָּחָשׁ הָיָה עָרוּם מִכֹּל חַיַּת
of beast every (from) [above] crafty was serpent the And

הַשָּׂדֶה אֲשֶׁר עָשָׂה יְהוָה אֱלֹהִים וַיֹּאמֶר
said he and ; God Jehovah made had which field the

אֶל־הָאִשָּׁה אַף כִּי־אָמַר אֱלֹהִים לֹא תֹאכְלוּ
eat [2]shall [1]ye [3]Not :God said has that so [it Is] :woman the unto

2 מִכֹּל עֵץ הַגָּן׃ וַתֹּאמֶר הָאִשָּׁה אֶל־הַנָּחָשׁ
,serpent the unto woman the said And ?garden the of tree any from

מִפְּרִי עֵץ־הַגָּן נֹאכֵל׃
; eat may we garden the of trees the of fruit the From

3 וּמִפְּרִי הָעֵץ אֲשֶׁר בְּתוֹךְ־הַגָּן
,garden the of midst the in [is] which tree the of fruit the from but

אָמַר אֱלֹהִים לֹא תֹאכְלוּ מִמֶּנּוּ וְלֹא תִגְּעוּ
touch [2]shall [1]ye [3]not and ,it from eat [2]shall [1]ye [3]not ,God said has

4 בּוֹ פֶּן תְּמֻתוּן׃ וַיֹּאמֶר הַנָּחָשׁ אֶל־הָאִשָּׁה
,woman the unto serpent the said And .die ye lest ,it (in)

5 לֹא־מוֹת תְּמֻתוּן׃ כִּי יֹדֵעַ אֱלֹהִים כִּי בְּיוֹם
of day the in that God knowing [is] For .die [3]shall [2]ye [1]dying [4]not

אֲכָלְכֶם מִמֶּנּוּ וְנִפְקְחוּ עֵינֵיכֶם
,eyes your opened be shall then ,it from eating your

Now the serpent was more subtil than any beast of the field which the LORD God had made. And he said unto the woman, Yea, hath God said, Ye shall not eat of any tree of the garden? 2 And the woman said unto the serpent, Of the fruit of the trees of the garden we may eat: 3 but of the fruit of the tree which is in the midst of the garden, God hath said, Ye shall not eat of it, neither shall ye touch it, lest ye die. 4 And the serpent said unto the woman, Ye shall not surely die: 5 for God doth know that in the day ye eat thereof, then your eyes shall be

a from her husband מאישה, read by Sm., G. and T. *b they two*, שניהם, added by G., S. and V.

ye shall be as
gods, knowing
good and evil.
6 And when the
woman saw that
the tree *was*
good for food,
and that it *was*
pleasant to the
eyes, and a tree
to be desired to
make *one* wise,
she took of the
fruit thereof,
and did eat, and
gave also unto
her husband
with her, and he
did eat. 7 And
the eyes of them
both were open-
ed, and they
knew that they
were naked: and
they sewed fig
leaves together,
and made them-
selves aprons. 8
And they heard
the voice of the
LORD God
walking in the
garden in the
cool of the day:
and Adam and
his wife hid
themselves from
the presence of
the LORD God
amongst the
trees of the gar-
den. 9 And the
LORD God
called unto
Adam, and said
unto him,
Where *art*
thou? 10 And
he said, I heard
thy voice in the
garden, and I
was afraid, be-
cause I *was* na-
ked; and I hid
myself. 11 And
he said, Who
told thee that
thou *wast* na-
ked? Hast thou
eaten of the tree,
whereof I com-
manded thee
that thou
shouldest not
eat? 12 And
the man said,
The woman
whom thou gav-
est *to be* with
me, she gave me

6 וִהְיִיתֶם כֵּאלֹהִים יֹדְעֵי טוֹב וָרָע׃ וַתֵּרֶא
saw And .evil and good of knowers ,God like become shall ye and

הָאִשָּׁה כִּי טוֹב הָעֵץ לְמַאֲכָל וְכִי
that and ,food for ²tree ¹the ³[was] ⁴good that woman the

תַאֲוָה־הוּא לָעֵינַיִם וְנֶחְמָד הָעֵץ
tree the [was] desirable and ,eyes the to [²was] ¹it ⁴delight ³a

לְהַשְׂכִּיל וַתִּקַּח מִפִּרְיוֹ וַתֹּאכַל וַתִּתֵּן
gave she and ;ate and ,fruit its from took she and ,wise make to

7 גַּם־לְאִישָׁהּ עִמָּהּ וַיֹּאכַל[a]׃ וַתִּפָּקַחְנָה עֵינֵי
of eyes the opened were And .ate he and ,her with husband her to also

שְׁנֵיהֶם וַיֵּדְעוּ כִּי עֵירֻמִּם הֵם וַיִּתְפְּרוּ
sewed they and ;they [were] naked that knew they and ,two those

עֲלֵה תְאֵנָה וַיַּעֲשׂוּ לָהֶם חֲגֹרֹת׃
.girdles themselves for made and ,tree fig [the] of leaves

8 וַיִּשְׁמְעוּ אֶת־קוֹל יְהוָה אֱלֹהִים מִתְהַלֵּךְ בַּגָּן
garden the in about walking God Jehovah of sound the heard they And

לְרוּחַ הַיּוֹם וַיִּתְחַבֵּא הָאָדָם וְאִשְׁתּוֹ
wife his and man the themselves concealed and :day the of breeze the at

מִפְּנֵי יְהוָה אֱלֹהִים בְּתוֹךְ עֵץ
of trees the of midst the in God Jehovah of face the from

9 הַגָּן׃ וַיִּקְרָא יְהוָה אֱלֹהִים אֶל־הָאָדָם וַיֹּאמֶר
said and ,man the unto God Jehovah called And .garden the

10 לוֹ[b] אַיֶּכָּה׃ וַיֹּאמֶר אֶת־קֹלְךָ שָׁמַעְתִּי
heard I voice Thy ,said he And ?thou [art] Where :him to

בַּגָּן וָאִירָא כִּי־עֵירֹם אָנֹכִי
;I [am] naked because ,feared I and ,garden the in

11 וָאֵחָבֵא׃ וַיֹּאמֶר מִי הִגִּיד לְךָ
thee to known made Who :said he And .myself concealed I and

כִּי עֵירֹם אָתָּה הֲמִן־הָעֵץ אֲשֶׁר צִוִּיתִיךָ
thee commanded I which [from] tree the from ?thou [art] naked that

12 לְבִלְתִּי אֲכָל־מִמֶּנּוּ אָכָלְתָּ׃ וַיֹּאמֶר הָאָדָם
:man the said And ?eaten thou hast (it from) eat not to

הָאִשָּׁה אֲשֶׁר נָתַתָּה עִמָּדִי הִוא נָתְנָה־לִּי
me to gave she ,me with gavest thou whom woman The

opened, and ye
shall be as God,
knowing good
and evil. 6 And
when the wom-
an saw that
the tree was
good for food,
and that it was a
delight to the
eyes, and that
the tree was to
be desired to
make one wise,
she took of the
fruit thereof,
and did eat; and
she gave also
unto her hus-
band with her,
and he did eat.
7 And the eyes
of them both
were opened,
and they knew
that they were
naked; and they
sewed fig leaves
together, and
made them-
selves aprons. 8
And they heard
the voice of the
LORD God
walking in the
garden in the
cool of the day:
and the man and
his wife hid
themselves from
the presence of
the LORD GOD
amongst the
trees of the gar-
den. 9 And the
LORD God
called unto the
man, and said
unto him, Where
art thou? 10 And
he said, I heard
thy voice in the
garden, and I
was afraid, be-
cause I was na-
ked; and I hid
myself. 11 And
he said, Who
told thee that
thou wast na-
ked? Hast thou
eaten of the tree,
whereof I com-
manded thee
that thou
shouldest not
eat? 12 And the
man said, The
woman whom
thou gavest
to be with

a Sm. and G. have *and they ate*, ויאכלו.

b G. and S. add, *man*, אדם.

13 מִן־הָעֵץ וָאֹכֵל׃ וַיֹּאמֶר יְהוָה אֱלֹהִים לָאִשָּׁה
:woman the to God Jehovah said And .ate I and ,tree the from

מַה־זֹּאת עָשִׂית וַתֹּאמֶר הָאִשָּׁה הַנָּחָשׁ
serpent The :woman the said And ?done thou hast ,then ,What

14 הִשִּׁיאַנִי וָאֹכֵל׃ וַיֹּאמֶר יְהוָה אֱלֹהִים ׀
God Jehovah said And .ate I and me seduced

אֶל־הַנָּחָשׁ כִּי עָשִׂיתָ זֹּאת אָרוּר אַתָּה
thou [be] cursed ,this done hast thou Because :serpent the unto

מִכָּל־הַבְּהֵמָה וּמִכֹּל חַיַּת הַשָּׂדֶה עַל־גְּחֹנְךָ
belly thy upon ; field the of beasts all from and cattle the all from

15 תֵלֵךְ וְעָפָר תֹּאכַל כָּל־יְמֵי חַיֶּיךָ׃ וְאֵיבָה ׀
hostility And .life thy of days the all eat shalt thou dust and go shalt thou

אָשִׁית בֵּינְךָ וּבֵין הָאִשָּׁה וּבֵין זַרְעֲךָ
seed thy between and ,woman the (between) and thee between put will I

וּבֵין זַרְעָהּ הוּא יְשׁוּפְךָ רֹאשׁ וְאַתָּה
thou and head [the to as] thee bruise shall he ; seed her (between) and

16 תְּשׁוּפֶנּוּ עָקֵב׃ אֶל־[a]הָאִשָּׁה אָמַר
,said he woman the Unto .heel [the to as] him bruise shalt

הַרְבָּה אַרְבֶּה עִצְּבוֹנֵךְ וְהֵרֹנֵךְ בְּעֶצֶב
pain in ; conception thy and trouble thy multiply will I Multiplying

תֵּלְדִי בָנִים וְאֶל־אִישֵׁךְ
[be shall] husband thy unto and ; children forth bring shalt thou

17 תְּשׁוּקָתֵךְ וְהוּא יִמְשָׁל־בָּךְ׃ וּלְאָדָם אָמַר
,said he Adam to And .thee over rule shall he and longing thy

כִּי שָׁמַעְתָּ לְקוֹל אִשְׁתֶּךָ וַתֹּאכַל
eaten hast and ,wife thy of voice the to hearkened hast thou Because

מִן־הָעֵץ אֲשֶׁר צִוִּיתִיךָ לֵאמֹר לֹא
[3]Not :saying ,thee commanded I which [to as] tree the from

תֹאכַל מִמֶּנּוּ אֲרוּרָה הָאֲדָמָה בַּעֲבוּרֶךָ
; thee of account on ground the [be] cursed ; it from eat [2]shalt [1]thou

18 בְּעִצָּבוֹן תֹּאכְלֶנָּה כֹּל יְמֵי חַיֶּיךָ׃ וְקוֹץ
thorns and ; life thy of days the all it [of] eat shalt thou toil in

וְדַרְדַּר תַּצְמִיחַ לָךְ וְאָכַלְתָּ
eat shalt thou and ; thee for sprout to cause shall it thistles and

of the tree, and
I did eat. 13
And the LORD
God said unto
the woman,
What *is* this
that thou hast
done? And the
woman said,
The serpent
beguiled me,
and I did eat. 14
And the LORD
God said unto
the serpent, Because
thou hast
done this, thou
art cursed above
all cattle, and
above every
beast of the
field; upon thy
belly shalt thou
go, and dust
shalt thou eat
all the days of
thy life: 15 And
I will put enmity
between
thee and the woman,
and between
thy seed
and her seed; it
shall bruise thy
head, and thou
shalt bruise his
heel. 16 Unto
the woman he
said, I will greatly
multiply thy
sorrow and thy
conception; in
sorrow thou
shall bring forth
children; and
thy desire *shall*
be to thy husband,
and he
shall rule over
thee. 17 And
unto Adam he
said, Because
thou hast hearkened
unto the
voice of thy
wife, and hast
eaten of the tree,
of which I commanded
thee,
saying, Thou
shalt not eat of
it: cursed *is*
the ground for
thy sake; in
sorrow shalt
thou eat *of* it
all the days of
thy life; 18
Thorns also
and thistles shall
it bring forth to
thee; and thou

me, she gave
me of the tree,
and I did eat.
13 And the
LORD God said
unto the woman,
What is
this thou hast
done? And the
woman said,
The serpent beguiled
me, and I
did eat. 14 And
the LORD God
said unto the
serpent, Because
thou hast done
this, cursed art
thou above all
cattle, and above
every beast
of the field; upon
thy belly
shalt thou go,
and dust shalt
thou eat all the
days of thy life:
15 and I will put
enmity between
thee and the
woman, and between
thy seed
and her seed: it
shall bruise thy
head, and thou
shalt bruise his
heel. 16 Unto
the woman he
said, I will greatly
multiply thy
sorrow and thy
conception; in
sorrow thou
shalt bring forth
children; and
thy desire shall
be to thy husband,
and he
shall rule over
thee. 17 And unto
Adam he said,
Because thou
hast hearkened
unto the voice
of thy wife, and
hast eaten of
the tree, of
which I commanded
thee,
saying, Thou
shalt not eat of
it: cursed is the
ground for thy
sake; in toil shalt
thou eat of it
all the days of
thy life; 18
thorns also and
thistles shall it
bring forth to
thee; and thou
shalt eat the

a G., S. and V. have *and unto* ואל.

shalt eat the
herb of the field;
19 In the sweat
of thy face shalt
thou eat bread,
till thou return
unto the ground;
for out of it wast
thou taken: for
dust thou *art*,
and unto dust
shalt thou
return. 20 And
Adam called his
wife's name
Eve; because
she was the
mother of all
living. 21 Unto
Adam also and
to his wife did
the LORD God
make coats of
skins, and cloth-
ed them.

22 And the
LORD God
said, Behold,
the man is
become as one
of us, to know
good and evil:
and now, lest he
put forth his
hand, and take
also of the tree
of life, and eat,
and live for ever:
23 Therefore the
LORD God sent
him forth from
the garden of
Eden, to till the
ground from
whence he was
taken. 24 So he
drove out the
man; and he
placed at the
east of the gar-
den of Eden
Cherubims, and
a flaming sword
which turned
every way, to
keep the way of
the tree of life.

19 אֶת־עֵשֶׂב הַשָּׂדֶה׃ בְּזֵעַת אַפֶּיךָ תֹּאכַל לֶחֶם
,bread eat shalt thou nostrils thy of sweat the In .field the of herb the

עַד שׁוּבְךָ אֶל־הָאֲדָמָה כִּי מִמֶּנָּה לֻקָּחְתָּ כִּי־
for ; taken wast thou it from for ; ground the unto return thy until

20 עָפָר אַתָּה וְאֶל־עָפָר תָּשׁוּב׃ וַיִּקְרָא הָאָדָם
man the called And .return shalt thou dust unto and thou [art] dust

שֵׁם אִשְׁתּוֹ חַוָּה כִּי הִוא הָיְתָה אֵם כָּל־חָי׃
.[being]living every of mother became she for ; Eve wife his of name the

21 וַיַּעַשׂ יְהוָה אֱלֹהִים לְאָדָם וּלְאִשְׁתּוֹ
wife his for and Adam for God Jehovah made And

כָּתְנוֹת עוֹר וַיַּלְבִּשֵׁם׃
.them clothed and ,skin of tunics

22 וַיֹּאמֶר יְהוָה אֱלֹהִים הֵן הָאָדָם הָיָה
become has man the ,Behold :God Jehovah said And

כְּאַחַד מִמֶּנּוּ לָדַעַת טוֹב וָרָע וְעַתָּה
,now and ;evil and good know to ,us of one like

פֶּן־יִשְׁלַח יָדוֹ וְלָקַח גַּם מֵעֵץ הַחַיִּים וְאָכַל
,eat and ,life of tree the from also take and hand his forth put he lest

23 וָחַי לְעֹלָם׃ וַיְשַׁלְּחֵהוּ יְהוָה אֱלֹהִים מִגַּן־
of garden the from God Jehovah him sent [so] (and) — ever for live and

עֵדֶן לַעֲבֹד אֶת־הָאֲדָמָה אֲשֶׁר לֻקַּח מִשָּׁם׃
.(from there) taken was he whence [from] ground the till to Eden

24 וַיְגָרֶשׁ אֶת־הָאָדָם וַיַּשְׁכֵּן מִקֶּדֶם לְגַן־
of garden the (to)[of] East (from) stationed he and ,man the out drove he And

עֵדֶן אֶת־הַכְּרֻבִים וְאֵת לַהַט הַחֶרֶב הַמִּתְהַפֶּכֶת
about itself whirling sword the of flame the and Cherubim the Eden

לִשְׁמֹר אֶת־דֶּרֶךְ עֵץ הַחַיִּים׃
.life of tree the of way the guard to

herb of the field;
19 In the sweat
of thy face shalt
thou eat bread,
till thou return
unto the
ground; for out
of it wast thou
taken: for dust
thou art, and
unto dust shalt
thou return. 20
And the man
called his wife's
name Eve; be-
cause she was
the mother of
all living. 21
And the LORD
God made for
Adam and for
his wife coats of
skins, and
clothed them.

22 And the
LORD God said,
Behold, the man
is become as one
of us, to know
good and evil;
and now, lest he
put forth his
hand, and take
also of the tree
of life, and eat,
and live for ever:
23 therefore the
LORD God sent
him forth from
the garden of
Eden, to till the
ground from
whence he was
taken. 24 So he
drove out the
man; and he
placed at the
east of the gar-
den of Eden the
Cherubim, and
the flame of a
sword which
turned every
way, to keep the
way of the tree
of life.

4

AND Adam
knew Eve his
wife; and she
conceived, and
bare Cain, and
said, I have
gotten a man
from the LORD.

1 וְהָאָדָם יָדַע אֶת־חַוָּה אִשְׁתּוֹ וַתַּהַר וַתֵּלֶד
bore and ,conceived she and ; wife his Eve knew man the And

אֶת־קַיִן וַתֹּאמֶר קָנִיתִי אִישׁ אֶת־יְהוָה׃
,Jehovah [of help the] with man a acquired have I :said she and ; Cain

AND the
man knew Eve
his wife; and she
conceived, and
bare Cain, and
said, I have
gotten a man
with *the help* of

2 And she again
bare his brother
Abel. And Abel
was a keeper of
sheep, but Cain
was a tiller of
the ground. 3
And in process
of time it came
to pass, that
Cain brought of
the fruit of the
ground an offer-
ing unto the
LORD. 4 And
Abel, he also
brought of the
firstlings of his
flock and of the
fat thereof. And
the LORD had
respect unto
Abel and to his
offering: 5 But
unto Cain and
to his offering
he had not
respect. And
Cain was very
wroth, and his
countenance
fell. 6 And the
LORD said unto
Cain, Why art
thou wroth? and
why is thy
countenance
fallen? 7 If thou
doest well, shalt
thou not be ac-
cepted? and if
thou doest not
well, sin lieth
at the door. And
unto thee *shall*
be his desire, and
thou shalt rule
over him. 8 And
Cain talked with
Abel his brother:
and it came to
pass, when they
were in the field,
that Cain rose
up against Abel
his brother, and
slew him. 9 ¶
And the LORD
said unto Cain,
Where *is* Abel
thy brother?
And he said, I
know not: *Am*
I my brother's
keeper? 10 And
he said, What
hast thou done?
the voice of thy
brother's blood
crieth unto me
from the
ground. 11 And

2 וַתֹּסֶף לָלֶדֶת אֶת־אָחִיו אֶת־הָבֶל וַיְהִי־הֶבֶל
Abel became and ; Abel brother his bear to continued she And

רֹעֵה צֹאן וְקַיִן הָיָה עֹבֵד אֲדָמָה׃
.ground [the] of tiller a became Cain and ,flocks of shepherd a

3 וַיְהִי מִקֵּץ יָמִים וַיָּבֵא קַיִן
Cain brought that ,days of end the from pass to came it And

4 מִפְּרִי הָאֲדָמָה מִנְחָה לַיהוָה׃ וְהֶבֶל הֵבִיא
,brought Abel And .Jehovah to offering an ground the of fruit the from

גַם־הוּא מִבְּכֹרוֹת צֹאנוֹ וּמֵחֶלְבֵהֶן
.[pieces] fat their from even ,flocks his of firstlings the from ,he also

5 וַיִּשַׁע יְהוָה אֶל־הֶבֶל וְאֶל־מִנְחָתוֹ׃ וְאֶל־קַיִן
Cain unto And ; offering his unto and Abel unto Jehovah looked And

וְאֶל־מִנְחָתוֹ לֹא שָׁעָה וַיִּחַר לְקַיִן
Cain to burned [anger] and ,look [2]did[1]he [3]not offering his unto and

6 מְאֹד וַיִּפְּלוּ פָּנָיו׃ וַיֹּאמֶר יְהוָה אֶל־קָיִן
:Cain unto Jehovah said And .countenance his fell and exceedingly

לָמָּה חָרָה לָךְ וְלָמָּה נָפְלוּ פָנֶיךָ׃
?countenance thy fallen has why and thee to burned [anger] has Why

7 הֲלוֹא אִם־תֵּיטִיב שְׂאֵת וְאִם
if and ?[countenance of] up lifting a ,well doest thou if ,not [there] Is

לֹא תֵיטִיב לַפֶּתַח חַטָּאת רֹבֵץ וְאֵלֶיךָ
thee unto and ; crouching [is] sin door the at ,well [2]doest [1]thou [3]not

8 תְּשׁוּקָתוֹ וְאַתָּה תִּמְשָׁל־בּוֹ׃[a] וַיֹּאמֶר קַיִן
Cain said And .it over rule shalt thou and longing its [be shall]

אֶל־הֶבֶל אָחִיו[b] וַיְהִי בִּהְיוֹתָם בַּשָּׂדֶה
,field the in being their in ,pass to came it and ; brother his Abel unto

9 וַיָּקָם קַיִן אֶל־הֶבֶל אָחִיו וַיַּהַרְגֵהוּ׃ וַיֹּאמֶר
said And .him killed and brother his Abel unto Cain up rose that

יְהוָה אֶל־קַיִן אֵי הֶבֶל אָחִיךָ וַיֹּאמֶר לֹא
[3]Not ,said he And ?brother thy [is] Abel Where :Cain unto Jehovah

10 יָדַעְתִּי הֲשֹׁמֵר אָחִי אָנֹכִי׃ וַיֹּאמֶר[c] מֶה
What :said he And ?I [am] brother my of keeper the ;[2]know [1]I

עָשִׂיתָ קוֹל דְּמֵי אָחִיךָ צֹעֲקִים אֵלַי
me unto crying brother thy of blood the !voice A ?done thou hast

the LORD. 2
And again she
bare his brother
Abel. And Abel
was a keeper of
sheep, but Cain
was a tiller of
the ground. 3
And in process
of time it came
to pass, that
Cain brought of
the fruit of the
ground an offer-
ing unto the
LORD. 4 And
Abel, he also
brought of the
firstlings of his
flock and of the
fat thereof. And
the LORD had
respect unto
Abel and to his
offering: 5 But
unto Cain and
to his offering
he had not
respect. And
Cain was very
wroth, and his
countenance
fell. 6 And the
LORD said unto
Cain, Why art
thou wroth? and
why is thy
countenance
fallen? 7 If thou
doest well, shalt
thou not be ac-
cepted? and if
thou doest not
well, sin couch-
eth at the door:
and unto thee
shall be his de-
sire, and thou
shalt rule over
him. 8 And Cain
told Abel his
brother. And it
came to pass,
when they were
in the field, that
Cain rose up
against Abel his
brother, and
slew him. 9 And
the LORD said
unto Cain,
Where is Abel
thy brother?
And he said, I
know not: am I
my brother's
keeper? 10 And
he said, What
hast thou done?
the voice of thy
brother's blood
crieth unto me

a G., S. and T. vary much from H. in v. 7. The text is probably corrupt.

b Sm., G., S., V. add, *let us go into the field*, נלכה השדה.

c G. adds, *God;* V. adds, *to him;* S. adds, *to him Jehovah.*

now *art* thou
cursed from the
earth, which
hath opened her
mouth to receive
thy brother's
blood from thy
hand; 12 When
thou tillest the
ground, it shall
not henceforth
yield unto thee
her strength; a
fugitive and a
vagabond shalt
thou be in the
earth. 13 And
Cain said unto
the LORD, My
punishment *is*
greater than I
can bear. 14
Behold, thou
hast driven me
out this day from
the face of the
earth; and from
thy face shall I
be hid; and I
shall be a fug-
itive and a vag-
abond in the
earth; and it
shall come to
pass, *that* every
one that findeth
me shall slay
me. 15 And the
LORD said un-
to him, There-
fore whosoever
slayeth Cain,
vengence shall
be taken on
him sevenfold.
And the LORD
set a mark upon
Cain, lest any
finding him
should kill him.
16 And Cain
went out from
the presence of
the LORD, and
dwelt in the land
of Nod, on the
east of Eden. 17
And Cain knew
his wife; and she
conceived, and
bare Enoch: and
he builded a city,
and called the
name of the city,
after the name
of his son,
Enoch. 18 And
unto Enoch was
born Irad: and
Irad begat Me-
hujael: and Me-
hujael begat Me-
thusael: and

11 מִן־הָאֲדָמָה׃ וְעַתָּה אָרוּר אָתָּה מִן־הָאֲדָמָה אֲשֶׁר
which ,ground the from thou [be] cursed ,now And !ground the from

פָּצְתָה אֶת־פִּיהָ לָקַחַת אֶת־דְּמֵי אָחִיךָ מִיָּדֶךָ׃
.hand thy from brother thy of blood the receive to mouth its opened has

12 כִּי תַעֲבֹד אֶת־הָאֲדָמָה לֹא־תֹסֵף תֵּת־כֹּחָהּ
strength its give to continue not shall it ,ground the till shalt thou When

לָךְ נָע וָנָד תִּהְיֶה בָאָרֶץ׃
.earth the on become shalt thou wandering and unsettled ; thee to

13 וַיֹּאמֶר קַיִן אֶל־יְהוָה גָּדוֹל עֲוֺנִי מִנְּשֹׂא׃
.bearing (from) [beyond] iniquity my Great :Jehovah unto Cain said And

14 הֵן גֵּרַשְׁתָּ אֹתִי הַיּוֹם מֵעַל פְּנֵי
of face the (upon) from to-day [1]me [2]out driven hast thou ,Behold

הָאֲדָמָה וּמִפָּנֶיךָ אֶסָּתֵר וְהָיִיתִי
become shall I and ;hidden be shall I face thy from and ,ground the

נָע וָנָד בָּאָרֶץ וְהָיָה
pass to come will it [then] (and) ; earth the on wandering and unsettled

15 כָל־מֹצְאִי יַהַרְגֵנִי׃ וַיֹּאמֶר לוֹ יְהוָה לָכֵן[a]
Therefore :Jehovah him to said And .me kill will me finding anyone

כָּל־הֹרֵג קַיִן שִׁבְעָתַיִם יֻקָּם וַיָּשֶׂם
made And .avenged be shall [Cain] he sevenfold ,Cain killing one any

יְהוָה לְקַיִן אוֹת לְבִלְתִּי הַכּוֹת־אֹתוֹ כָּל־
one any him smite not to [order in] ,sign a Cain for Jehovah

16 מֹצְאוֹ׃ וַיֵּצֵא קַיִן מִלִּפְנֵי יְהוָה וַיֵּשֶׁב
settled and ,Jehovah before (to) from Cain out went And .him finding

17 בְּאֶרֶץ־נוֹד קִדְמַת־עֵדֶן׃ וַיֵּדַע קַיִן אֶת־אִשְׁתּוֹ
,wife his Cain knew And .Eden of eastward Nod of land the in

וַתַּהַר וַתֵּלֶד אֶת־חֲנוֹךְ וַיְהִי בֹּנֶה
building was he (and) [while] Enoch bore and ,conceived she and

עִיר וַיִּקְרָא שֵׁם הָעִיר כְּשֵׁם בְּנוֹ
,son his of name the after city the of name the called he and ,city a

18 חֲנוֹךְ׃ וַיִּוָּלֵד לַחֲנוֹךְ אֶת־עִירָד וְעִירָד יָלַד
begat Irad and ,Irad Enoch to born was And .Enoch

אֶת־מְחוּיָאֵל וּמְחִיָּיאֵל יָלַד אֶת־מְתוּשָׁאֵל וּמְתוּשָׁאֵל
Methushael and ,Methushael begat Mehujael and ,Mehujael

from the
ground. 11 And
now cursed art
thou from the
ground, which
hath opened her
mouth to receive
thy brother's
blood from thy
hand; 12 when
thou tillest the
ground, it shall
not henceforth
yield unto thee
her strength;
a fugitive and a
wanderer shalt
thou be in the
earth. 13 And
Cain said unto
the LORD, My
punishment is
greater than I
can bear. 14 Be-
hold, thou hast
driven me out
this day from
the face of the
ground; and
from thy face
shall I be hid;
and I shall be a
fugitive and a
wanderer in the
earth; and it
shall come to
pass, that who-
soever findeth
me shall slay me.
15 And the
LORD said unto
him, Therefore
whosoever slay-
eth Cain, ven-
gence shall be
taken on him
sevenfold. And
the LORD ap-
pointed a sign
for Cain, lest
any finding him
should smite
him.
16 And Cain
went out from
the presence of
the LORD, and
dwelt in the land
of Nod, on the
east of Eden. 17
And Cain knew
his wife; and she
conceived, and
bare Enoch:
and he builded a
city, and called
the name of the
city, after the
name of his son,
Enoch. 18 And
unto Enoch was
born Irad; and
Irad begat

a G., S. and V. *not so*, לא כן.

Methusael begat Lamech. 19 And Lamech took unto him two wives: the name of the one *was* Adah, and the name of the other Zillah. 20 And Adah bare Jabal: he was the father of such as dwell in tents, and *of such as have* cattle. 21 And his brother's name *was* Jubal: he was the father of all such as handle the harp and organ. 22 And Zillah, she also bare Tubal-cain, an instructor of every artificer in brass and iron: and the sister of Tubal-cain *was* Naamah. 23 And Lamech said unto his wives, Adah and Zillah, Hear my voice; ye wives of Lamech, hearken unto my speech: for I have slain a man to my wounding, and a young man to my hurt. 24 If Cain shall be avenged sevenfold, truly Lamech seventy and sevenfold. 25 And Adam knew his wife again; and she bare a son, aud called his name Seth: For God, *said she*, hath appointed me another seed instead of Abel, whom Cain slew. 26 And to Seth, to him also there was born a son; and he called his name Enos: then began men to call upon the name of the LORD.

19 יָלַד אֶת־לָמֶךְ׃ וַיִּקַּח־לוֹ לֶמֶךְ שְׁתֵּי נָשִׁים
,wives two Lamech himself for took And .Lamech begat

שֵׁם הָאַחַת עָדָה וְשֵׁם הַשֵּׁנִית
second the of name the and ,Adah [being] one the of name the

20 צִלָּה׃ וַתֵּלֶד עָדָה אֶת־יָבָל הוּא הָיָה אֲבִי
of father became he ;Jabal Adah bore And .Zillah [being]

21 יֹשֵׁב אֹהֶל וּמִקְנֶה׃ וְשֵׁם אָחִיו
brother his of name the And .cattle [with] and tents [in] dwellers

יוּבָל הוּא הָיָה אֲבִי כָּל־תֹּפֵשׂ כִּנּוֹר וְעוּגָב׃
.pipe and lyre on player every of father became he ;Jubal [was]

22 וְצִלָּה גַם־הִוא יָלְדָה אֶת־תּוּבַל קַיִן לֹטֵשׁ
of hammerer a ,Tubal-Cain bore ,she also ,Zillah And

כָּל־חֹרֵשׁ נְחֹשֶׁת וּבַרְזֶל וַאֲחוֹת
of sister the (and) ,iron and copper of tool sharp [of kind] every

23 תּוּבַל־קַיִן נַעֲמָה׃ וַיֹּאמֶר לֶמֶךְ לְנָשָׁיו עָדָה
Adah :wives his to Lamech said And .Naamah [being] Tubal-Cain

וְצִלָּה שְׁמַעַן קוֹלִי נְשֵׁי לֶמֶךְ הַאְזֵנָּה אִמְרָתִי
;speech my to hearken ,Lamech of wives ;voice my hear ,Zillah and

כִּי אִישׁ הָרַגְתִּי לְפִצְעִי וְיֶלֶד לְחַבֻּרָתִי׃
;scar my for men young and ,wound my for slay I men for

24 כִּי שִׁבְעָתַיִם יֻקַּם־קָיִן וְלֶמֶךְ שִׁבְעִים וְשִׁבְעָה
.seven [fold] and seventy Lamech and ,Cain avenged is sevenfold for

25 וַיֵּדַע אָדָם עוֹד אֶת־אִשְׁתּוֹ [a] וַתֵּלֶד [b] בֵּן וַתִּקְרָא
called she and ,son a bore she and ,wife his again Adam knew And

אֶת־שְׁמוֹ שֵׁת כִּי שָׁת־לִי אֱלֹהִים זֶרַע אַחֵר
[1]another [2]seed God me for appointed has for ;Seth name his

26 תַּחַת הֶבֶל כִּי הֲרָגוֹ קָיִן׃ וּלְשֵׁת גַּם־הוּא
,him [to] also ,Seth to And .Cain him slew for ,Abel of instead

יֻלַּד־בֵּן וַיִּקְרָא אֶת־שְׁמוֹ אֱנוֹשׁ אָז [c] הוּחַל [d]
begun was it then ;Enosh name his called he and ,son a born was

לִקְרֹא בְּשֵׁם יְהוָה׃
.Jehovah of name the on call to

Mehujael: and Mehujael begat Methushael: and Methushael begat Lamech. 19 And Lamech took unto him two wives; the name of the one was Adah, and the name of the other Zillah. 20 And Adah bare Jabal: he was the father of such as dwell in tents and *have* cattle. 21 And his brother's name was Jubal: he was the father of all such as handle the harp and pipe. 22 And Zillah, she also bare Tubal-cain, the forger of every cutting instrument of brass and iron: and the sister of Tubal-cain was Naamah. 23 And Lamech said unto his wives: Adah and Zillah, hear my voice: Ye wives of Lamech, hearken unto my speech: For I have slain a man, for wounding me, And a young men for bruising me. 24 If Cain shall be avenged seven fold, Truly Lamech seventy and seven fold. 25 And Adam knew his wife again; and she bare a son, and called his name Seth: For, *said she*, God hath appointed me another seed instead of Abel; for Cain slew him. 26 And to Seth, to him also there was born a son; and he called his name Enosh; then began men to call upon the name of the LORD.

---

a G. and S. *Eve his wife*, את חוה אשתו.
b G. and S. *and she conceived and bare*, ותהר ותלד.
c G. and V. omit.
d Sm., G., S. and V. *he began*, החל.

5

This is the
book of the gen-
erations of
Adam. In the
day that God
created man, in
the likeness of
God made he
him; 2 Male and
female created
he them; and
blessed them,
and called their
name Adam, in
the day when
they were cre-
ated.

3 And Adam
lived an hun-
dred and
thirty years, and
begat *a son* in
his own likeness,
after his image;
and called his
name Seth: 4
And the days of
Adam after he
had begotten
Seth were eight
hundred years:
and he begat
sons and daugh-
ters: 5 And all
the days that
Adam lived were
nine hundred
and thirty years:
and he died.

6 And Seth
lived an hun-
dred and five
years, and
begat Enos: 7
And Seth lived
after he begat
Enos eight hun-
dred and seven
years, and begat
sons and daugh-
ters: 8 And all
the days of Seth
were nine hun-
dred and twelve
years: and he
died.

9 And Enos
lived ninety
years, and begat
Cainan: 10 And
Enos lived after
he begat Cain-
an eight hun-
dred and fifteen
years, and begat
sons and daugh-

1 זֶה סֵפֶר תּוֹלְדֹת אָדָם בְּיוֹם
of day the in ;Adam of generations the of book the [is] This

בְּרֹא אֱלֹהִים אָדָם בִּדְמוּת אֱלֹהִים עָשָׂה אֹתוֹ׃
.him made he God of likeness the in ,Adam [1]God's [2]creating

2 זָכָר וּנְקֵבָה בְּרָאָם וַיְבָרֶךְ אֹתָם וַיִּקְרָא
called and ,them blessed he and ,them created he female and Male

3 אֶת־שְׁמָם אָדָם בְּיוֹם הִבָּרְאָם׃ וַיְחִי
lived And .created being their of day the in ,man name their

אָדָם שְׁלֹשִׁים וּמְאַת[a] שָׁנָה וַיּוֹלֶד בִּדְמוּתוֹ
,image his in [son a] begat and years hundred a and thirty Adam

4 כְּצַלְמוֹ וַיִּקְרָא אֶת־שְׁמוֹ שֵׁת׃ וַיִּהְיוּ יְמֵי
of days the were And .Seth name his called he and ;likeness his after

אָדָם אַחֲרֵי הוֹלִידוֹ אֶת־שֵׁת שְׁמֹנֶה מֵאֹת[b] שָׁנָה
,years hundred eight Seth begetting his after Adam

5 וַיּוֹלֶד בָּנִים וּבָנוֹת׃ וַיִּהְיוּ כָּל־יְמֵי אָדָם
Adam of days the all were And .daughters and sons begat he and

אֲשֶׁר־חַי תְּשַׁע מֵאוֹת שָׁנָה וּשְׁלֹשִׁים שָׁנָה וַיָּמֹת׃
.died he and ,years thirty and years hundred nine lived he which

6 וַיְחִי־שֵׁת חָמֵשׁ שָׁנִים וּמְאַת[c] שָׁנָה וַיּוֹלֶד
begat and ,years hundred a and years five Seth lived And

7 אֶת־אֱנוֹשׁ׃ וַיְחִי־שֵׁת אַחֲרֵי הוֹלִידוֹ אֶת־אֱנוֹשׁ שֶׁבַע
seven Enosh begetting his after Seth lived And .Enosh

שָׁנִים וּשְׁמֹנֶה מֵאוֹת[d] שָׁנָה וַיּוֹלֶד בָּנִים וּבָנוֹת׃
.daughters and sons begat he and ,years hundred eight and years

8 וַיִּהְיוּ כָּל־יְמֵי־שֵׁת שְׁתֵּים עֶשְׂרֵה שָׁנָה וּתְשַׁע
nine and years ten [and] two Seth of days the all were And

9 מֵאוֹת שָׁנָה וַיָּמֹת׃ וַיְחִי אֱנוֹשׁ תִּשְׁעִים[e] שָׁנָה
,years ninety Enosh lived And .died he and ,years hundred

10 וַיּוֹלֶד אֶת־קֵינָן׃ וַיְחִי אֱנוֹשׁ אַחֲרֵי הוֹלִידוֹ אֶת־קֵינָן
Kenan begetting his after Enosh lived And .Kenan begat and

חֲמֵשׁ עֶשְׂרֵה שָׁנָה וּשְׁמֹנֶה[f] מֵאוֹת שָׁנָה וַיּוֹלֶד
begat he and ,years hundred eight and years ten [and] five

This is the
book of the ge-
nerations of
Adam. In the
day that God
created man, in
the likeness of
God made he
him; 2 male and
female created
he them; and
blessed them,
and called their
name Adam, in
the day when
they were cre-
ated.

3 And Adam
lived an hun-
dred and
thirty years, and
begat *a son* in
his own likeness,
after his image;
and called his
name Seth: 4
and the days of
Adam after he
begat Seth were
eight hundred
years: and he
begat sons and
daughters. 5
And all the days
that Adam lived
were nine hun-
dred and thirty
years: and he
died.

6 And Seth
lived an hundred
and five years,
and begat
Enosh: 7 and
Seth lived after
he begat Enosh
eight hundred
and seven years,
and begat sons
and daughters:
8 and all the
days of Seth
were nine hun-
dred and twelve
years: and he
died.

9 And Enosh
lived ninety
years, and begat
Kenan: 10 and
Enosh lived aft-
er he begat Ken-
an eight hun-
dred and fif-
teen years, and
begat sons and

---

a G. reads, 230. *b* G. 700. *c* G. 205. *d* G. 707. *e* G. 190. *f* G. 715.

ters: 11 And all the days of Enos were nine hundred and five years: and he died.

12 And Cainan lived seventy years, and begat Mahalaleel: 13 And Cainan lived after he begat Mahalaleel eight hundred and forty years, and begat sons and daughters: 14 And all the days of Cainan were nine hundred and ten years: and he died.

15 And Mahalaleel lived sixty and five years, and begat Jared: 16 And Mahalaleel lived after he begat Jared eight hundred and thirty years, and begat sons and daughters: 17 And all the days of Mahalaleel were eight hundred ninety and five years: and he died.

18 And Jared lived an hundred sixty and two years, and he begat Enoch: 19 And Jared lived after he begat Enoch eight hundred years, and begat sons and daughters: 20 And all the days of Jared were nine hundred sixty and two years: and he died.

21 And Enoch lived sixty and five years, and begat Methuselah: 22 And Enoch walked with God after he begat Methuselah three hundred years, and

11 בָּנִים וּבָנוֹת׃ וַיִּהְיוּ כָּל־יְמֵי אֱנוֹשׁ חָמֵשׁ
five Enosh of days the all were And .daughters and sons

12 שָׁנִים וּתְשַׁע מֵאוֹת שָׁנָה וַיָּמֹת׃ וַיְחִי קֵינָן
Kenan lived And .died he and ,years hundred nine and years

13 שִׁבְעִים[a] שָׁנָה וַיּוֹלֶד אֶת־מַהֲלַלְאֵל׃ וַיְחִי קֵינָן אַחֲרֵי
after Kenan lived And .Mahalalel begat and ,years seventy

הוֹלִידוֹ אֶת־מַהֲלַלְאֵל אַרְבָּעִים שָׁנָה וּשְׁמֹנֶה מֵאוֹת[b]
hundred eight and years forty Mahalalel begetting his

14 שָׁנָה וַיּוֹלֶד בָּנִים וּבָנוֹת׃ וַיִּהְיוּ כָּל־יְמֵי
of days the all were And .daughters and sons begat he and ,years

קֵינָן עֶשֶׂר שָׁנִים וּתְשַׁע מֵאוֹת שָׁנָה וַיָּמֹת׃
.died he and ,years hundred nine and years ten Kenan

15 וַיְחִי מַהֲלַלְאֵל חָמֵשׁ שָׁנִים וְשִׁשִּׁים[c] שָׁנָה
,years sixty and years five Mahalalel lived And

16 וַיּוֹלֶד אֶת־יָרֶד׃ וַיְחִי מַהֲלַלְאֵל אַחֲרֵי הוֹלִידוֹ
begetting his after Mahalalel lived And .Jared begat and

אֶת־יֶרֶד שְׁלֹשִׁים שָׁנָה וּשְׁמֹנֶה מֵאוֹת[d] שָׁנָה וַיּוֹלֶד
begat he and ,years hundred eight and years thirty Jared

17 בָּנִים וּבָנוֹת׃ וַיִּהְיוּ כָּל־יְמֵי מַהֲלַלְאֵל חָמֵשׁ
five Mahalalel of days the all were And .daughters and sons

וְתִשְׁעִים שָׁנָה וּשְׁמֹנֶה מֵאוֹת שָׁנָה וַיָּמֹת׃
.died he and ,years hundred eight and years ninety and

18 וַיְחִי־יֶרֶד שְׁתַּיִם וְשִׁשִּׁים שָׁנָה וּמְאַת[e] שָׁנָה וַיּוֹלֶד
begat and ,years hundred a and years sixty and two Jared lived And

19 אֶת־חֲנוֹךְ׃ וַיְחִי־יֶרֶד אַחֲרֵי הוֹלִידוֹ אֶת־חֲנוֹךְ שְׁמֹנֶה
eight Enoch begetting his after Jared lived And .Enoch

20 מֵאוֹת[f] שָׁנָה וַיּוֹלֶד בָּנִים וּבָנוֹת׃ וַיִּהְיוּ
were And .daughters and sons begat he and ,years hundred

כָּל־יְמֵי־יֶרֶד שְׁתַּיִם וְשִׁשִּׁים שָׁנָה וּתְשַׁע מֵאוֹת[g] שָׁנָה
years hundred nine and years sixty and two Jared of days the all

21 וַיָּמֹת׃ וַיְחִי חֲנוֹךְ חָמֵשׁ וְשִׁשִּׁים[h] שָׁנָה וַיּוֹלֶד
begat and ,years sixty and five Enoch lived And .died he and

22 אֶת־מְתוּשָׁלַח׃ וַיִּתְהַלֵּךְ חֲנוֹךְ אֶת־הָאֱלֹהִים אַחֲרֵי
after God with Enoch walked And .Methushelah

daughters: 11 and all the days of Enosh were nine hundred and five years: and he died.

12 And Kenan lived seventy years, and begat Mahalalel: 13 and Kenan lived after he begat Mahalalel eight hundred and forty years, and begat sons and daughters: 14 and all the days of Kenan were nine hundred and ten years: and he died.

15 And Mahalalel lived sixty and five years, and begat Jared; 16 and Mahalalel lived after he begat Jared eight hundred and thirty years, and begat sons and daughters: 17 and all the days of Mahallalel were eight hundred ninety and five years: and he died.

18 And Jared lived an hundred sixty and two years, and begat Enoch: 19 and Jared lived after he begat Enoch eight hundred years, and begat sons and daughters: 20 and all the days of Jared were nine hundred sixty and two years: and he died.

21 And Enoch lived sixty and five years, and begat Methuselah: 22 and Enoch walked with God after he begat Methuselah three hundred years, and

a G. 170. *b* G. 740. *c* G. 165. *d* G. 730. *e* Sm. 62. *f* Sm. 785. *g* Sm. 847. *h* G. 165.

begat sons and
daughters: 23
And all the days
of Enoch were
three hundred
sixty and five
years: 24 And
Enoch walked
with God: and
he *was* not; for
God took him.

25 And Methu-
selah lived an
hundred eighty
and seven years,
and begat La-
mech. 26 And
Methuselah
lived after he
begat Lamech
seven hundred
eighty and two
years, and begat
sons and daugh-
ters: 27 And all
the days of Me-
thuselah were
nine hundred
sixty and nine
years: and he
died.

28 And La-
mech lived an
hundred eighty
and two years,
and begat a son:
29 And he called
his name Noah,
saying, This
same shall com-
fort us concern-
ing our work
and toil of our
hands, because
of the ground
which the LORD
hath cursed. 30
And Lamech
lived after he
begat Noah five
hundred ninety
and five years,
and begat sons
and daughters:
31 And all the
days of Lamech
were seven hun-
dred seventy and
seven years: and
he died.

32 And Noah
was five
hundred years
old: and Noah

הוֹלִידוֹ אֶת־מְתוּשֶׁלַח שְׁלֹשׁ מֵאוֹת[a] שָׁנָה וַיּוֹלֶד בָּנִים
sons begat he and ,years hundred three Methushelah begetting his

23 וּבָנוֹת׃ וַיְהִי כָּל־יְמֵי חֲנוֹךְ חָמֵשׁ וְשִׁשִּׁים
sixty and five Enoch of days the all were And .daughters and

24 שָׁנָה וּשְׁלֹשׁ מֵאוֹת שָׁנָה׃ וַיִּתְהַלֵּךְ חֲנוֹךְ אֶת־הָאֱלֹהִים
,God with Enoch walked And .years hundred three and years

25 וְאֵינֶנּוּ כִּי־לָקַח אֹתוֹ אֱלֹהִים׃ וַיְחִי מְתוּשֶׁלַח
Methushelah lived And .God him took for ,not was he and

שֶׁבַע וּשְׁמֹנִים שָׁנָה וּמְאַת[b] שָׁנָה וַיּוֹלֶד אֶת־לָמֶךְ׃
.Lamech begat and ,years hundred a and years eighty and seven

26 וַיְחִי מְתוּשֶׁלַח אַחֲרֵי הוֹלִידוֹ אֶת־לֶמֶךְ שְׁתַּיִם
two Lamech begetting his after Methushelah lived And

וּשְׁמוֹנִים שָׁנָה וּשְׁבַע מֵאוֹת[c] שָׁנָה וַיּוֹלֶד בָּנִים
sons begat he and ,years hundred seven and years eighty and

27 וּבָנוֹת׃ וַיִּהְיוּ כָּל־יְמֵי מְתוּשֶׁלַח תֵּשַׁע
nine Methushelah of days the all were And .daughters and

וְשִׁשִּׁים שָׁנָה וּתְשַׁע[d] מֵאוֹת שָׁנָה וַיָּמֹת׃
.died he and ,years hundred nine and years sixty and

28 וַיְחִי־לֶמֶךְ שְׁתַּיִם וּשְׁמֹנִים שָׁנָה וּמְאַת[e] שָׁנָה
,years hundred a and years eighty and two Lamech lived And

29 וַיּוֹלֶד בֵּן׃ וַיִּקְרָא אֶת־שְׁמוֹ נֹחַ לֵאמֹר זֶה[f]
This :saying ,Noah name his called he And .son a begat and

יְנַחֲמֵנוּ מִמַּעֲשֵׂנוּ וּמֵעִצְּבוֹן יָדֵינוּ
,hands our of toil the from and work our from us comfort shall

30 מִן־הָאֲדָמָה אֲשֶׁר אֵרְרָהּ יְהוָה׃ וַיְחִי־לֶמֶךְ
Lamech lived And .Jehovah (it) cursed which ground the from

אַחֲרֵי הוֹלִידוֹ אֶת־נֹחַ חָמֵשׁ וְתִשְׁעִים שָׁנָה וַחֲמֵשׁ
five and years ninety and five Noah begetting his after

31 מֵאֹת[g] שָׁנָה וַיּוֹלֶד בָּנִים וּבָנוֹת׃ וַיְהִי
were And .daughters and sons begat he and ,years hundred

כָּל־יְמֵי־לֶמֶךְ שֶׁבַע וְשִׁבְעִים שָׁנָה וּשְׁבַע
seven and years seventy and seven Lamech of days the all

32 מֵאוֹת[h] שָׁנָה וַיָּמֹת׃ וַיְהִי־נֹחַ בֶּן־חֲמֵשׁ מֵאוֹת
hundred five (of son a) Noah was And .died he and ,years hundred

begat sons and
daughters: 23
and all the days
of Enoch were
three hundred
sixty and five
years: 24 and
Enoch walked
with God: and
he was not; for
God took him.

25 And Methu-
selah lived an
hundred eighty
and seven years,
and begat La-
mech: 26 and
Methuselah
lived after he
begat Lamech
seven hundred
eighty and two
years, and be-
gat sons and
daughters; 27
and all the days
of Methuselah
were nine hun-
dred sixty and
nine years; and
he died.

28 And La-
mech lived an
hundred eighty
and two years,
and begat a son:
29 and he called
his name Noah,
saying, This
same shall com-
fort us for our
work and for the
toil of our
hands, because
of the ground
which the LORD
hath cursed. 30
And Lamech
lived after he
begat Noah five
hundred ninety
and five years,
and begat sons
and daughters:
31 and all the
days of Lamech
were seven hun-
dred seventy
and seven years:
and he died.

32 And Noah
was five hun-
dred years old;

---

a G. 200. *b* G. some mss. 167, some mss. 187, Sm. 67. *c* G. some mss. 802, some mss. 782. Sm. 653.
d Sm. 720 *e* G. 188. Sm. 53. *f* G., S. add, *and*, reading ומן. *g* G. has, 565; Sm. 600.
h G. has, 753; Sm. 653.

begat Shem,
Ham, and
Japheth.

שָׁנָה וַיּוֹלֶד נֹחַ אֶת־שֵׁם אֶת־חָם וְאֶת־יָפֶת׃

.Japheth and Ham Shem Noah begat and ,[old] years

and Noah be-
gat Shem, Ham,
and Japheth.

6

1 וַיְהִי כִּי־הֵחֵל הָאָדָם לָרֹב

many be to men began when pass to came it And

עַל־פְּנֵי הָאֲדָמָה וּבָנוֹת יֻלְּדוּ לָהֶם׃

;them to born were daughters and ,ground the of face the upon

2 וַיִּרְאוּ בְנֵי־הָאֱלֹהִים אֶת־בְּנוֹת הָאָדָם כִּי

that ,men of daughters the God of sons the saw [that] (and)

טֹבֹת הֵנָּה וַיִּקְחוּ לָהֶם נָשִׁים מִכֹּל

all (from) ,wives themselves for took they and ,they [were] comely

3 אֲשֶׁר בָּחָרוּ׃ וַיֹּאמֶר יְהוָה לֹא־יָדוֹן רוּחִי

spirit my rule shall Not : Jehovah said And .chose they which

בָאָדָם לְעֹלָם בְּשַׁגַּם הוּא בָשָׂר וְהָיוּ

be shall and ;flesh [is] he [since][1] ,erring their in ever for man in

4 יָמָיו מֵאָה וְעֶשְׂרִים שָׁנָה׃ הַנְּפִלִים הָיוּ

were Nephilim The .years twenty and hundred a days his

בָאָרֶץ בַּיָּמִים הָהֵם וְגַם אַחֲרֵי־כֵן אֲשֶׁר

when ,afterwards [especially] also and ;[1]those [2]days in earth the on

יָבֹאוּ בְּנֵי הָאֱלֹהִים אֶל־בְּנוֹת

of daughters the unto God of sons the in come to accustomed were

הָאָדָם וְיָלְדוּ לָהֶם הֵמָּה הַגִּבֹּרִים

heroes the [being] those ;them to bore they and ,men

אֲשֶׁר מֵעוֹלָם אַנְשֵׁי הַשֵּׁם׃

.name of men the ,time ancient from [were] which

5 וַיַּרְא יְהוָה כִּי רַבָּה רָעַת הָאָדָם

man of wickedness the [was] great that Jehovah saw And

בָּאָרֶץ וְכָל־יֵצֶר מַחְשְׁבֹת לִבּוֹ רַק

only [was] heart his of thoughts the of purpose every and earth the on

6 רַע כָּל־הַיּוֹם׃ וַיִּנָּחֶם יְהוָה כִּי־עָשָׂה

made had he that Jehovah regretted And .day whole the evil

7 אֶת־הָאָדָם בָּאָרֶץ וַיִּתְעַצֵּב אֶל־לִבּוֹ׃ וַיֹּאמֶר

said And .heart his unto grieved he and ,earth the on man

יְהוָה אֶמְחֶה אֶת־הָאָדָם אֲשֶׁר־בָּרָאתִי מֵעַל

upon from created have I whom man off wipe will I : Jehovah

AND it came
to pass, when
men began to
multiply on the
face of the
earth, and
daughters were
born unto
them, 2 That
the sons of God
saw the daugh-
ters of men that
they *were* fair;
and they took
them wives of
all which they
chose. 3 And
the LORD said,
My spirit shall
not always strive
with man, for
that he also *is*
flesh: yet his
days shall be an
hundred and
twenty years. 4
There were
giants in the
earth in those
days; and also
after that, when
the sons of God
came in unto
the daughters of
men, and they
bare *children* to
them, the same
became mighty
men which *were*
of old, men of
renown.
5 And GOD
saw that the
wickedness of
man *was*
great in the
earth, and *that*
every imagina-
tion of the
thoughts of his
heart *was* only
evil continually.
6 And it repent-
ed the LORD
that he had
made man on
the earth, and it
grieved him at
his heart. 7
And the LORD
said, I will
destroy man
whom I have
created from the
face of the
earth; both

AND it came
to pass, when
men began to
multiply on the
face of the
ground, and
daughters were
born unto them,
2 that the sons
of God saw the
daughters of
men that they
were fair; and
they took them
wives of all that
they chose. 3
And the LORD
said, My spirit
shall not strive
with man for-
ever, for that he
also is flesh: yet
shall his days be
an hundred and
twenty years. 4
The Nephilim
were in the
earth in those
days, and also
after that, when
the sons of God
came in unto
the daughters of
men, and they
bare children to
them: the same
were the mighty
men which were
of old, the men
of renown.
5 And the
LORD saw that
the wickedness
of man was great
in the earth, and
that every imag-
ination of the
thoughts of his
heart was only
evil continually.
6 And it repen-
ted the LORD
that he had
made man on
the earth, and it
grieved him at
his heart. 7 And
the LORD said,
I will destroy
man whom I
have created
from the face of
the ground;

man, and beast,
and the creeping
thing, and the
fowls of the air;
for it repenteth
me that I have
made them. 8
But Noah
found grace in
the eyes of the
LORD.

9 These *are*
the generations
of Noah: Noah
was a just man
and perfect in
his generations,
and Noah
walked with
God. 10 And
Noah begat
three sons,
Shem, Ham,
and Japheth 11
The earth also
was corrupt
before God; and
the earth was
filled with vio-
lence. 12 And
God looked
upon the earth,
and, behold, it
was corrupt; for
all flesh had cor-
rupted his way
upon the earth.
13 And God said
unto Noah, The
end of all flesh
is come before
me; for the
earth is filled
with violence
through them;
and, behold, I
will destroy
them with the
earth. 14 ¶ Make
thee an ark of
gopher wood;
rooms shalt
thou make in
the ark, and
shalt pitch it
within and with-
out with pitch.
15 And this *is*
the fashion
which thou
shalt make it
of: The length
of the ark *shall*
be three hun-
dred cubits, the
breadth of it
fifty cubits, and
the height of it
thirty cubits. 16
A window shalt
thou make to
the ark, and in
a cubit shalt
thou finish it
above; and the

פְּנֵי הָאֲדָמָה מֵאָדָם עַד־בְּהֵמָה עַד־רֶמֶשׂ
,creeper unto ,beast unto man from ,ground the of face the
וְעַד־עוֹף הַשָּׁמָיִם כִּי נִחַמְתִּי כִּי עֲשִׂיתִם׃
.them made have I that regret I for ;heavens the of fowl unto and
8 וְנֹחַ מָצָא חֵן בְּעֵינֵי יְהוָה׃
.Jehovah of eyes the in favor found Noah But

9 אֵלֶּה תּוֹלְדֹת נֹחַ נֹחַ אִישׁ צַדִּיק
,¹righteous ²man a ,Noah .Noah of generations the [are] These
תָּמִים הָיָה בְּדֹרֹתָיו אֶת־הָאֱלֹהִים הִתְהַלֶּךְ־נֹחַ׃
.Noah walked God with ;contemporaries his among ¹was ²blameless
10 וַיּוֹלֶד נֹחַ שְׁלֹשָׁה בָנִים אֶת־שֵׁם אֶת־חָם וְאֶת־יָפֶת׃
.Japheth and Ham Shem ,sons three Noah begat And
11 וַתִּשָּׁחֵת הָאָרֶץ לִפְנֵי הָאֱלֹהִים וַתִּמָּלֵא הָאָרֶץ
earth the filled was and ,God before earth the corrupted was And
12 חָמָס׃ וַיַּרְא אֱלֹהִים אֶת־הָאָרֶץ וְהִנֵּה
behold and ,earth the God saw And .violence [with]
נִשְׁחָתָה כִּי־הִשְׁחִית כָּל־בָּשָׂר אֶת־דַּרְכּוֹ
way his flesh all corrupted had for ,corrupted was it
13 עַל־הָאָרֶץ׃ וַיֹּאמֶר אֱלֹהִים לְנֹחַ קֵץ כָּל־בָּשָׂר בָּא
come has flesh all of end An :Noah to God said And .earth the upon
לְפָנַי כִּי־מָלְאָה הָאָרֶץ חָמָס מִפְּנֵיהֶם
; them before from violence [of] earth the full is for ,me before
14 וְהִנְנִי מַשְׁחִיתָם אֶת־הָאָרֶץ׃ עֲשֵׂה
Make .earth the with them destroy to about [am] I behold and
לְךָ תֵּבַת עֲצֵי־גֹפֶר קִנִּים תַּעֲשֶׂה
make shalt thou cells [in] ,cypress of timbers of ark an thee for
אֶת־הַתֵּבָה וְכָפַרְתָּ אֹתָהּ מִבַּיִת וּמִחוּץ
without (from) and within (from) it cover shalt thou and ;ark the
15 בַּכֹּפֶר׃ וְזֶה אֲשֶׁר תַּעֲשֶׂה אֹתָהּ שְׁלֹשׁ
three , ;it make shalt thou how [is] this And .asphalt with
מֵאוֹת אַמָּה אֹרֶךְ הַתֵּבָה חֲמִשִּׁים אַמָּה רָחְבָּהּ
,width its cubits fifty ,ark the of length the cubits hundred
16 וּשְׁלֹשִׁים אַמָּה קוֹמָתָהּ׃ צֹהַר תַּעֲשֶׂה לַתֵּבָה
ark the to make shalt thou Light .height its cubits thirty and
וְאֶל־אַמָּה תְּכַלֶּנָּה מִלְמַעְלָה
;above (to) from throughout it make shalt thou cubit a [of rate the] at and

both man, and
beast, and
creeping thing,
and fowl of the
air; for it re-
penteth me that
I have made
them. 8 But
Noah found
grace in the eyes
of the LORD.

9 These are
the generations
of Noah. Noah
was a righteous
man, *and* per-
fect in his gen-
erations: Noah
walked with
God. 10 And
Noah begat
three sons,
Shem, Ham,
and Japheth. 11
And the earth
was corrupt be-
fore God, and
the earth was
filled with viol-
ence. 12 And
God saw the
earth, and, be-
hold, it was cor-
rupt; for all
flesh had cor-
rupted his way
upon the earth.
13 And God
said unto Noah,
The end of all
flesh is come be-
fore me; for the
earth is filled
with violence
through them;
and, behold, I
will destroy
them with the
earth. 14 Make
thee an ark of
gopher wood;
rooms shalt thou
make in the ark,
and shalt pitch
it within and
without with
pitch. 15 And
this is how thou
shalt make it:
the length of
the ark three
hundred cubits,
the breadth of it
fifty cubits, and
the height of it
thirty cubits. 16
A light shalt
thou make to the
ark, and to a
cubit shalt thou
finish it upward;
and the door of
the ark shalt

door of the ark
shalt thou set in
the side thereof;
with lower, sec-
ond, and third
stories shalt
thou make it.
17 And, behold,
I, even I, do
bring a flood of
waters upon the
earth, to de-
stroy all flesh,
wherein *is* the
breath of life,
from under heav-
en; *and* every
thing that *is* in
the earth shall
die. 18 But with
thee will I es-
tablish my cove-
nant; and thou
shalt come into
the ark, thou,
and thy sons,
and thy wife,
and thy sons'
wives with thee.
19 And of every
living thing of
all flesh, two of
every *sort* shalt
thou bring into
the ark, to keep
them alive with
thee; they shall
be male and
female. 20 Of
fowls after their
kind, and of
cattle after their
kind, of every
creeping thing
of the earth
after his kind,
two of every
sort shall come
unto thee, to
keep *them* alive.
21 And take
thou unto thee
of all food that
is eaten, and
thou shalt gath-
er *it* to thee;
and it shall be
for food for
thee, and for
them. 22 Thus
did Noah; ac-
cording to all
that God com-
manded him, so
did he.

וּפֶתַח הַתֵּבָה בְּצִדָּהּ תָּשִׂים תַּחְתִּיִּם
[cells] lower in ; put shalt thou side its in ark the of door the and

17 שְׁנִיִּם וּשְׁלִשִׁים תַּעֲשֶׂהָ׃ וַאֲנִי הִנְנִי
I behold ,I And .it make shalt thou third and second

מֵבִיא אֶת־הַמַּבּוּל מַיִם עַל־הָאָרֶץ לְשַׁחֵת
destroy to ,earth the upon ,waters [even] ,flood the bring to about [am]

כָּל־בָּשָׂר אֲשֶׁר־בּוֹ רוּחַ חַיִּים מִתַּחַת
under from life of spirit the [is] which in flesh all

הַשָּׁמָיִם כֹּל אֲשֶׁר־בָּאָרֶץ יִגְוָע׃
.expire shall earth the in (is) which all ; heavens the

18 וַהֲקִמֹתִי אֶת־בְּרִיתִי אִתָּךְ וּבָאתָ
in go shalt thou and ,thee with covenant my establish will I And

אֶל־הַתֵּבָה אַתָּה וּבָנֶיךָ וְאִשְׁתְּךָ וּנְשֵׁי־בָנֶיךָ
sons thy of wives the and wife thy and ,sons thy and ,thou ,ark the unto

19 אִתָּךְ׃ וּמִכָּל־הָחַי מִכָּל־בָּשָׂר שְׁנַיִם מִכֹּל
[kind] every from two ,flesh all from thing living every from And .thee with

תָּבִיא אֶל־הַתֵּבָה לְהַחֲיֹת אִתָּךְ זָכָר
male ;thee with alive keep to ,ark the unto in bring shalt thou

20 וּנְקֵבָה יִהְיוּ׃ מֵהָעוֹף לְמִינֵהוּ וּמִן־
from and ,kind its after fowl the From .be shall they female and

הַבְּהֵמָה לְמִינָהּ מִכֹּל רֶמֶשׂ הָאֲדָמָה
ground the of creeper every from ,kind its after cattle the

לְמִינֵהוּ שְׁנַיִם מִכֹּל יָבֹאוּ אֵלֶיךָ
thee unto in come shall [kind] every from two ,kind its after

21 לְהַחֲיוֹת׃ וְאַתָּה קַח־לְךָ מִכָּל־מַאֲכָל אֲשֶׁר
which food all from thyself for take ,thou And .alive keep to

יֵאָכֵל וְאָסַפְתָּ אֵלֶיךָ וְהָיָה לְךָ
thee for be it let and ;thyself unto gather and ,eaten be may

22 וְלָהֶם לְאָכְלָה׃ וַיַּעַשׂ נֹחַ כְּכֹל אֲשֶׁר
which all to according ;[so] Noah did And .food for them for and

צִוָּה אֹתוֹ אֱלֹהִים כֵּן עָשָׂה׃
.did he so ,God him commanded

thou set in the
side thereof;
with lower, sec-
ond, and third
stories shalt
thou make it.
17 And I, be-
hold, I do bring
the flood of wa-
ters upon the
earth, to destroy
all flesh, where-
in is the breath
of life, from un-
der heaven;
every thing that
is in the earth
shalldie. 18 But
I will establish
my covenant
with thee; and
thou shalt
come into the
ark, thou, and
thy sons, and
thy wife and
thy sons' wives
with thee. 19
And of every
living thing of
all flesh, two of
every sort shalt
thou bring into
the ark, to keep
them alive with
thee; they shall
be male and fe-
male. 20 Of the
fowl after their
kind, and of the
cattle after their
kind, of every
creeping thing
of the ground
after its kind,
two of every sort
shall come unto
thee, to keep
them alive. 21
And take thou
unto thee of all
food that is
eaten, and gath-
er it to thee; and
it shall be for
food for thee,
and for them. 22
Thus did Noah;
according to all
that God com-
manded him, so
did he.

7

AND the
LORD said unto
Noah, Come
thou and all thy

1 וַיֹּאמֶר יְהוָה לְנֹחַ בֹּא־אַתָּה וְכָל־בֵּיתְךָ
house thy all and thou ,in Come ; Noah to Jehovah said And

AND the LORD
said unto Noah,
Come thou and
all thy house

house into the
ark; for thee
have I seen
righteous before
me in this gen-
eration. 2 Of
every clean
beast thou shalt
take to thee
by sevens, the
male and his
female; and of
beasts that *are*
not clean by two,
the male and his
female. 3 Of
fowls also of the
air by sevens,
the male and the
female; to keep
seed alive upon
the face of all
the earth. 4 For
yet seven days,
and I will cause
it to rain upon
the earth forty
days and forty
nights; and ev-
ery living sub-
stance that I
have made will I
destroy from off
the face of the
earth. 5 And
Noah did ac-
cording unto all
that the LORD
commanded
him. 6 And
Noah *was* six
hundred years
old when the
flood of waters
was upon the
earth.

אֶל־הַתֵּבָה כִּי־אֹתְךָ רָאִיתִי צַדִּיק לְפָנַי
me before righteous seen have I thee for ;ark the into

2 בַּדּוֹר הַזֶּה׃ מִכֹּל הַבְּהֵמָה הַטְּהוֹרָה תִּקַּח־
take shalt thou [1]clean [2]beast every From .[1]this [2]generation in

לְךָ שִׁבְעָה שִׁבְעָה אִישׁ וְאִשְׁתּוֹ וּמִן־הַבְּהֵמָה
beasts the from and ;female (his) and male ,seven [by] seven thyself for

3 אֲשֶׁר לֹא טְהֹרָה הִוא שְׁנַיִם[a] אִישׁ וְאִשְׁתּוֹ׃ גַּם
also ;female (his) and male ,two [1]are [3]clean [2]not which

מֵעוֹף הַשָּׁמַיִם[b] שִׁבְעָה שִׁבְעָה זָכָר וּנְקֵבָה
;female and male ,seven [by] seven ,heavens the of fowl the from

4 לְחַיּוֹת זֶרַע עַל־פְּנֵי כָל־הָאָרֶץ׃ כִּי לְיָמִים
[3]days after For .earth the all of face the upon seed alive keep to

עוֹד שִׁבְעָה אָנֹכִי מַמְטִיר עַל־הָאָרֶץ אַרְבָּעִים
forty ,earth the upon rain to cause to about [am] I [2]seven [1]yet

יוֹם וְאַרְבָּעִים לָיְלָה וּמָחִיתִי אֶת־כָּל־הַיְקוּם
thing existing every off wipe will I and ;nights forty and days

אֲשֶׁר עָשִׂיתִי מֵעַל פְּנֵי הָאֲדָמָה׃
.ground the of face the (upon) from made have I which

5 וַיַּעַשׂ נֹחַ כְּכֹל אֲשֶׁר־צִוָּהוּ יְהוָה׃
.Jehovah him commanded which all to according Noah did And

6 וְנֹחַ בֶּן־שֵׁשׁ מֵאוֹת שָׁנָה וְהַמַּבּוּל
flood the (and) ,[old] years hundred six (of son a) [being] Noah And

7 הָיָה מַיִם עַל־הָאָרֶץ׃ וַיָּבֹא נֹחַ
,Noah in went And .earth the upon ,waters [even] ,being into came

וּבָנָיו וְאִשְׁתּוֹ וּנְשֵׁי־בָנָיו אִתּוֹ
him with sons his of wives the and ,wife his and ,sons his and

8 אֶל־הַתֵּבָה מִפְּנֵי מֵי הַמַּבּוּל׃ מִן־הַבְּהֵמָה
[2]beasts the From .flood the of waters the before from ark the into

הַטְּהוֹרָה וּמִן־הַבְּהֵמָה אֲשֶׁר אֵינֶנָּה טְהֹרָה
,clean (they) not are which beasts the from and ,[1]clean

וּמִן־הָעוֹף וְכֹל אֲשֶׁר־רֹמֵשׂ עַל־הָאֲדָמָה׃
;ground the upon creeps which all and ,fowl the from and

9 שְׁנַיִם שְׁנַיִם בָּאוּ אֶל־נֹחַ אֶל־הַתֵּבָה זָכָר
male ,ark the into Noah unto in went they two [by] two

7 And
Noah went in,
and his sons, and
his wife, and
his sons' wives
with him, into
the ark, because
of the waters of
the flood. 8 Of
clean beasts, and
of beasts that
are not clean,
and of fowls,
and of every
thing that creep-
eth upon the
earth, 9 There
went in two and
two unto Noah
into the ark, the
male and the

into the ark;
for thee have I
seen righteous
before me in
this generation.
2 Of every clean
beast thou shalt
take to thee sev-
en and his fe-
male; and of
the beasts that
are not clean
two, the male
and his female;
3 of the fowl
also of the air,
seven and seven,
male and fe-
male; to keep
seed alive upon
the face of all
the earth. 4 For
yet seven days,
and I will cause
it to rain upon
the earth forty
days and forty
nights; and every
living thing that
I have made will
I destroy from
off the face of
the ground. 5
And Noah did
according unto
all that the
LORD com-
manded him. 6
And Noah was
six hundred
years old when
the flood of
waters was up-
on the earth.

7 And Noah
went in, and his
sons, and his
wife, and his
sons' wives with
him, into the
ark, because of
the waters of the
flood. 8 Of clean
beasts, and of
beasts that are
not clean, and
of fowls, and of
every thing that
creepeth upon
the ground, 9
there went in
two and two un-
to Noah into the
ark, male and

---

a For שנים *two*, Sm., G., S. and V. read *two by two*, שנים שנים.

b Sm., G., S. add, *the clean*, הטהור.

female, as God had commanded Noah. 10 And it came to pass after seven days, that the waters of the flood were upon the earth.

11 In the six hundredth year of Noah's life, in the second month, the seventeenth day of the month, the same day were all the fountains of the great deep broken up, and the windows of heaven were opened. 12 And the rain was upon the earth forty days and forty nights. 13 In the selfsame day entered Noah, and Shem, and Ham, and Japheth, the sons of Noah, and Noah's wife, and the three wives of his sons with them, into the ark; 14 They, and every beast after his kind, and all the cattle after their kind, and every creeping thing that creepeth upon the earth after his kind, and every fowl after his kind, every bird of every sort. 15 And they went in unto Noah into the ark, two and two of all flesh, wherein *is* the breath of life. 16 And they that went in, went in male and female of all flesh, as God had commanded him: and the LORD shut him in. 17 And the flood was forty days upon the earth; and the waters

וּנְקֵבָה כַּאֲשֶׁר צִוָּה אֱלֹהִים אֶת־נֹחַ׃
.Noah God commanded as according ,female and

10 וַיְהִי לְשִׁבְעַת הַיָּמִים וּמֵי
of waters the (and) ,days seven the after ,pass to came it And

11 הַמַּבּוּל הָיוּ עַל־הָאָרֶץ׃ בִּשְׁנַת
of year the In .earth the upon being into came flood the

שֵׁשׁ־מֵאוֹת שָׁנָה לְחַיֵּי־נֹחַ בַּחֹדֶשׁ הַשֵּׁנִי
,[1]second [2]month the in ,Noah of life the to years hundred six

בְּשִׁבְעָה־עָשָׂר יוֹם לַחֹדֶשׁ בַּיּוֹם הַזֶּה נִבְקְעוּ
cleft were [1]this [2]day on ,month the to day seventeenth the in

כָּל־מַעְיְנֹת תְּהוֹם רַבָּה וַאֲרֻבֹּת הַשָּׁמַיִם
heavens the of sluices the and ,[1]great [2]abyss the of fountains the all

12 נִפְתָּחוּ׃ וַיְהִי הַגֶּשֶׁם עַל־הָאָרֶץ אַרְבָּעִים
forty earth the upon rain gushing the was And .opened were

13 יוֹם וְאַרְבָּעִים לָיְלָה׃ בְּעֶצֶם הַיּוֹם הַזֶּה בָּא נֹחַ
Noah in went [1]this [3]day [2]very On .nights forty and days

וְשֵׁם־וְחָם וָיֶפֶת בְּנֵי־נֹחַ וְאֵשֶׁת
of wife the and ,Noah of sons the Japheth and Ham and Shem and

נֹחַ וּשְׁלֹשֶׁת נְשֵׁי־בָנָיו אִתָּם אֶל־הַתֵּבָה׃
;ark the unto them with sons his of wives three the and ,Noah

14 הֵמָּה וְכָל־הַחַיָּה לְמִינָהּ וְכָל־הַבְּהֵמָה לְמִינָהּ
,kind their after cattle all and ,kind its after beast every and they

וְכָל־הָרֶמֶשׂ הָרֹמֵשׂ עַל־הָאָרֶץ לְמִינֵהוּ
,kind its after earth the upon creeps that creeper every and

וְכָל־הָעוֹף לְמִינֵהוּ כֹּל צִפּוֹר כָּל־כָּנָף׃
.wing every of bird every ,kind its after fowl every and

15 וַיָּבֹאוּ אֶל־נֹחַ אֶל־הַתֵּבָה שְׁנַיִם שְׁנַיִם
two [by] two ,ark the unto Noah unto in went they And

16 מִכָּל־הַבָּשָׂר אֲשֶׁר־בּוֹ רוּחַ חַיִּים׃ וְהַבָּאִים
,in going those And .life of spirit the [was] which in flesh all from

זָכָר וּנְקֵבָה מִכָּל־בָּשָׂר בָּאוּ כַּאֲשֶׁר
as according ,in went they flesh all from female and male

צִוָּה אֹתוֹ אֱלֹהִים וַיִּסְגֹּר יְהֹוָה בַּעֲדוֹ׃
.him behind Jehovah shut and :God him commanded

17 וַיְהִי הַמַּבּוּל אַרְבָּעִים יוֹם עַל־הָאָרֶץ וַיִּרְבּוּ
increased and ,earth the upon days forty flood the was And

female, as God commanded Noah. 10 And it came to pass after the seven days, that the waters of the flood were upon the earth.

11 In the six hundredth year of Noah's life, in the second month, on the seventeenth day of the month, on the same day were all the fountains of the great deep broken up, and the windows of heaven were opened. 12 And the rain was upon the earth forty days and forty nights. 13 In the selfsame day entered Noah, and Shem, and Ham, and Japheth, the sons of Noah, and Noah's wife, and the three wives of his sons with them, into the ark; 14 they, and every beast after its kind, and all the cattle after their kind, and every creeping thing that creepeth upon the earth after its kind, and every fowl after its kind, every bird of every sort. 15 And they went in unto Noah into the ark, two and two of all flesh wherein is the breath of life. 16 And they that went in, went in male and female of all flesh, as God commanded him: and the LORD shut him in. 17 And the flood was forty days upon the earth; and the waters

increased, and
bare up the ark,
and it was lift
up above the
earth. 18 And
the waters pre-
vailed, and were
increased great-
ly upon the
earth; and the
ark went upon
the face of the
waters. 19 And
the waters pre-
vailed exceed-
ingly upon the
earth; and all the
high hills, that
were under the
whole heaven,
were covered. 20
Fifteen cubits
upward did the
waters prevail;
and the mount-
ains were cov-
ered. 21 And
all flesh died
that moved up-
on the earth,
both of fowl,
and of cattle,
and of beast,
and of every
creeping thing
that creepeth
upon the earth,
and every man:
22 All in whose
nostrils *was* the
breath of life,
of all that *was*
in the dry *land*,
died. 23 And
every living sub-
stance was
destroyed which
was upon the
face of the
ground, both
man, and cattle,
and the creep-
ing things, and
the fowl of the
heaven; and
they were de-
stroyed from the
earth: and Noah
only remained
alive, and they
that *were* with
him in the ark.

24 And the wa-
ters prevailed
upon the earth
an hundred and
fifty days.

הַמַּיִם וַיִּשְׂאוּ אֶת־הַתֵּבָה וַתָּרָם מֵעַל הָאָרֶץ׃

.earth the (upon) from rose it and ,ark the lifted and ,waters the

וַיִּגְבְּרוּ הַמַּיִם וַיִּרְבּוּ מְאֹד עַל־הָאָרֶץ 18

,earth the upon exceedingly increased and waters the mighty grew And

וַתֵּלֶךְ הַתֵּבָה עַל־פְּנֵי הַמָּיִם׃ וְהַמַּיִם 19

waters the And .waters the of face the upon ark the went and

גָּבְרוּ מְאֹד מְאֹד עַל־הָאָרֶץ וַיְכֻסּוּ

covered were and ;earth the upon exceedingly exceedingly mighty grew

כָּל־הֶהָרִים הַגְּבֹהִים אֲשֶׁר־תַּחַת כָּל־הַשָּׁמָיִם׃

;heavens the all under [were] which [1]high [2]mountains the all

חֲמֵשׁ עֶשְׂרֵה אַמָּה מִלְמַעְלָה גָּבְרוּ הַמָּיִם 20

,waters the mighty grew upwards (to from) cubits ten [and] five

וַיְכֻסּוּ הֶהָרִים׃ [a] וַיִּגְוַע כָּל־בָּשָׂר ׀ הָרֹמֵשׂ 21

creeps that flesh all expired And .mountains the covered were and

עַל־הָאָרֶץ בָּעוֹף וּבַבְּהֵמָה וּבַחַיָּה

,beasts (in) and cattle (in) and ,fowl (in) ,earth the upon

וּבְכָל־הַשֶּׁרֶץ הַשֹּׁרֵץ עַל־הָאָרֶץ וְכֹל

all and ,earth the upon swarms that swarmer every (in) and

הָאָדָם׃ כֹּל אֲשֶׁר נִשְׁמַת־רוּחַ חַיִּים 22

life of spirit the of breath the [was] [nostrils] whose [in] All .men

בְּאַפָּיו מִכֹּל אֲשֶׁר בֶּחָרָבָה מֵתוּ׃

.died ,land dry the on [was] which all from (nostrils his in)

וַיִּמַח אֶת־כָּל־הַיְקוּם ׀ אֲשֶׁר ׀ עַל־פְּנֵי 23

of face the upon [was] which thing existing every off wiped he And

הָאֲדָמָה מֵאָדָם עַד־בְּהֵמָה עַד־רֶמֶשׂ וְעַד־עוֹף

of fowl the unto and ,creeper unto ,cattle unto ,man from ,ground the

הַשָּׁמַיִם וַיִּמָּחוּ מִן־הָאָרֶץ וַיִּשָּׁאֶר

left was and ,earth the from off wiped were they and ;heavens the

אַךְ־נֹחַ וַאֲשֶׁר אִתּוֹ בַּתֵּבָה׃

.ark the in him with [were] who those and ,Noah only

וַיִּגְבְּרוּ הַמַּיִם עַל־הָאָרֶץ חֲמִשִּׁים וּמְאַת 24

hundred a and fifty earth the upon waters the mighty grew And

יוֹם׃

.days

increased, and
bare up the ark,
and it was lift
up above the
earth. 18 And
the waters pre-
vailed, and in-
creased greatly
upon the earth;
and the ark
went upon the
face of the wa-
ters. 19 And the
waters prevailed
exceedingly up-
on the earth;
and all the high
mountains that
were under the
whole heaven
were covered.
20 Fifteen cubits
upward did the
waters prevail;
and the moun-
tains were cov-
ered. 21 And
all flesh died
that moved
upon the earth,
both fowl, and
cattle, and beast,
and every creep-
ing thing that
creepeth upon
the earth, and
every man: 22
all in whose
nostrils was the
breath of the
spirit of life, of
all that was in
the dry land,
died. 23 And
every living
thing was de-
stroyed which
was upon the
face of the
ground, both
man, and cattle,
and creeping
thing, and fowl
of the heaven;
and they were
destroyed from
the earth: and
Noah only was
left, and they
that were with
him in the ark.

24 And the wa-
ters prevailed
upon the earth
an hundred and
fifty days.

---

a For ההרים, G. has, *all the high mountains;* S. *the high mountains.*

8

AND God re-
membered
Noah, and ev-
ery living thing,
and all the
cattle that *was*
with him in the
ark: and God
made a wind to
pass over the
earth, and the
waters assuaged;
2 The fountains
also of the deep
and the win-
dows of heaven
were stopped,
and the rain
from heaven
was restrained;
3 And the wa-
ters returned
from off the
earth continu-
ally: and after
the end of the
hundred and
fifty days the
waters were
abated. 4 And
the ark rested in
the seventh
month, on the
seventeenth day
of the month,
upon the mount-
ains of Ararat.
5 And the wa-
ters decreased
continually until
the tenth month:
in the tenth
month, on the
first *day* of the
month, were the
tops of the
mountains seen.

6 And it came
to pass at the
end of forty
days, that Noah
opened the win-
dow of the ark
which he had
made: 7 And
he sent forth a
raven, which
went forth to and
fro, until the
waters were
dried up from
off the earth.

1 וַיִּזְכֹּר אֱלֹהִים אֶת־נֹחַ וְאֵת כָּל־הַחַיָּה
beasts the all and Noah God remembered And

וְאֶת־כָּל־הַבְּהֵמָה אֲשֶׁר אִתּוֹ בַּתֵּבָה
;ark the in him with [were] which cattle the all and

וַיַּעֲבֵר אֱלֹהִים רוּחַ עַל־הָאָרֶץ וַיָּשֹׁכּוּ
sank and ,earth the upon wind a God over pass to caused and

2 הַמָּיִם׃ וַיִּסָּכְרוּ מַעְיְנֹת תְּהוֹם
abyss [the] of fountains the closed were And .waters the

וַאֲרֻבֹּת הַשָּׁמָיִם וַיִּכָּלֵא הַגֶּשֶׁם
rain gushing the checked was and ;heavens the of sluices the and

3 מִן־הַשָּׁמָיִם׃ וַיָּשֻׁבוּ הַמַּיִם מֵעַל הָאָרֶץ
,earth the upon from waters the retreated And .heavens the from

הָלוֹךְ וָשׁוֹב וַיַּחְסְרוּ הַמַּיִם מִקְצֵה
of end the from waters the diminished and ,retreating and going

4 חֲמִשִּׁים וּמְאַת יוֹם׃ וַתָּנַח הַתֵּבָה בַּחֹדֶשׁ
[2]month the in ark the rested And .days hundred a and fifty

הַשְּׁבִיעִי בְּשִׁבְעָה־עָשָׂר יוֹם לַחֹדֶשׁ עַל
upon ,month the to day seventeenth the in [1]seventh

5 הָרֵי אֲרָרָט׃ וְהַמַּיִם הָיוּ הָלוֹךְ וְחָסוֹר
diminishing and going were waters the And .Ararat of mountains the

עַד הַחֹדֶשׁ הָעֲשִׂירִי בָּעֲשִׂירִי בְּאֶחָד
[day] first the on [month] tenth the in ; [1]tenth [2]month the until

לַחֹדֶשׁ נִרְאוּ רָאשֵׁי הֶהָרִים׃
.mountains the of tops the visible became month the to

6 וַיְהִי מִקֵּץ אַרְבָּעִים יוֹם וַיִּפְתַּח
opened (and) ,days forty of end the from ,pass to came it And

נֹחַ אֶת־חַלּוֹן הַתֵּבָה אֲשֶׁר עָשָׂה׃
.made had he which ,ark the of window the Noah

7 וַיְשַׁלַּח אֶת־הָעֹרֵב וַיֵּצֵא יָצוֹא וָשׁוֹב[a]
,returning and out going ,out went it and ,raven a forth sent he And

עַד־יְבֹשֶׁת הַמַּיִם מֵעַל הָאָרֶץ׃
.earth the upon from waters the of up drying the until

AND God re-
membered
Noah, and ev-
ery living thing,
and all the cattle
that were with
him in the ark:
and God made a
wind to pass
over the earth,
and the wa-
ters assuaged;
2 the fount-
ains also of the
deep and the
windows of
heaven were
stopped, and
the rain from
heaven was re-
strained; 3 and
the waters re-
turned from off
the earth con-
tinually: and
after the end of
an hundred and
fifty days the
waters de-
creased. 4 And
the ark rested
in the seventh
month, on the
seventeenth day
of the month,
upon the mount-
ains of Ararat.
5 And the waters
decreased con-
tinually until the
tenth month: in
the tenth month,
on the first day
of the month,
were the tops of
the mountains
seen.

6 And it came
to pass at the
end of forty
days, that Noah
opened the win-
dow of the ark
which he had
made: 7 and he
sent forth a
raven, and it
went forth to
and fro, until
the waters were
dried up from
off the earth.

a For ושוב, Sm. has *and returned;* ושב; for יצוא ושוב, G., S. and V. have *and did not return.*

8 Also he sent
forth a dove
from him, to
see if the wa-
ters were abated
from off the
face of the
ground: 9 But
the dove found
no rest for the
sole of her foot,
and she returned
unto him into
the ark, for the
waters *were* on
the face of the
whole earth:
then he put
forth his hand,
and took her,
and pulled her
in unto him in-
to the ark. 10
And he stayed
yet other seven
days; and again
he sent forth the
dove out of the
ark: 11 And the
dove came in to
him in the even-
ing; and, lo, in
her mouth *was*
an olive leaf
pluckt off: so
Noah knew that
the waters were
abated from off
the earth. 12
And he stayed
yet other seven
days, and sent
forth the dove,
which returned
not again unto
him any more.

13 And it
came to pass, in
the six hun-
dredth and first
year, in the first
month, the first
day of the
month, the wa-
ters were dried
up from off the
earth: and Noah
removed the
covering of the
ark, and looked,
and, behold, the
face of the
ground was dry.
14 And in the
second month,
on the seven and
twentieth day of
the month, was
the earth dried.

8 וַיְשַׁלַּח אֶת־הַיּוֹנָה מֵאִתּוֹ לִרְאוֹת הֲקַלּוּ
decreased had whether see to ,him (with) from dove a forth sent he And

9 הַמַּיִם מֵעַל פְּנֵי הָאֲדָמָה׃ וְלֹא־מָצְאָה
[1]found [2]not and ;ground the of face the upon from waters the

הַיּוֹנָה מָנוֹחַ לְכַף־רַגְלָהּ וַתָּשָׁב
returned she and ; foot her of sole the for resting-place a dove the

אֵלָיו אֶל־הַתֵּבָה כִּי־מַיִם עַל־פְּנֵי
of face the upon [were] waters for ; ark the into him unto

כָל־הָאָרֶץ וַיִּשְׁלַח יָדוֹ וַיִּקָּחֶהָ וַיָּבֵא
brought and her took and hand his forth put he and ; earth the all

10 אֹתָהּ אֵלָיו אֶל־הַתֵּבָה׃ וַיָּחֶל עוֹד שִׁבְעַת יָמִים
[2]days seven still waited he And .ark the into him unto her

אֲחֵרִים וַיֹּסֶף שַׁלַּח אֶת־הַיּוֹנָה מִן־הַתֵּבָה׃
; ark the from dove the forth send to continued he and ;[1] other

11 וַתָּבֹא אֵלָיו הַיּוֹנָה לְעֵת עֶרֶב וְהִנֵּה
,behold and ,evening of time the at dove the him unto in came and

עֲלֵה־זַיִת טָרָף בְּפִיהָ וַיֵּדַע נֹחַ
Noah knew and ; mouth her in plucked freshly olive-tree an of leaf a

12 כִּי־קַלּוּ הַמַּיִם מֵעַל הָאָרֶץ׃ וַיִּיָּחֶל
waited he And .earth the upon from waters the decreased had that

עוֹד שִׁבְעַת יָמִים אֲחֵרִים וַיְשַׁלַּח אֶת־הַיּוֹנָה
,dove the forth sent he and [1]other [2]days seven still

13 וְלֹא־יָסְפָה שׁוּב־אֵלָיו עוֹד׃ וַיְהִי
pass to came it And .him unto return to continue not did she and

בְּאַחַת וְשֵׁשׁ־מֵאוֹת שָׁנָה בָּרִאשׁוֹן
[month] first the in year six-hundredth and one the in

בְּאֶחָד לַחֹדֶשׁ חָרְבוּ
up dried were ,month the to [day] first the on

הַמַּיִם מֵעַל הָאָרֶץ וַיָּסַר נֹחַ אֶת־מִכְסֵה
of covering the Noah removed and ; earth the upon from waters the

הַתֵּבָה וַיַּרְא וְהִנֵּה חָרְבוּ פְּנֵי הָאֲדָמָה׃
.ground the of face the dried was behold and ,saw and ,ark the

14 וּבַחֹדֶשׁ הַשֵּׁנִי בְּשִׁבְעָה וְעֶשְׂרִים יוֹם
day twentieth and seven the on [1]second [2]month the in And

לַחֹדֶשׁ יָבְשָׁה הָאָרֶץ׃
.earth the dry entirely was month the to

8 And he sent
forth a dove
from him, to see
if the waters
were abated
from off the face
of the ground;
9 but the dove
found no rest
for the sole of
her foot, and she
returned unto
him to the ark,
for the waters
were on the face
of the whole
earth: and he
put forth his
hand, and took
her, and brought
her in unto him
into the ark. 10
And he stayed
yet other seven
days; and again
he sent forth the
dove out of the
ark; 11 and the
dove came in to
him at eventide;
and, lo, in her
mouth an olive
leaf pluckt off:
so Noah knew
that the waters
were abated
from off the
earth. 12 And
he stayed yet
other seven
days; and sent
forth the dove;
and she returned
not again unto
him any more.

13 And it
came to pass in
the six hundred
and first year,
in the first
month, the first
day of the
month, the wa-
ters were dried
up from off the
earth: and Noah
removed the
covering of the
ark, and looked,
and, behold, the
face of the
ground was
dried. 14 And in
the second
month, on the
seven and twen-
tieth day of the
month, was the
earth dry.

15 And God
spake unto
Noah, saying,
16 Go forth of
the ark, thou,
and thy wife,
and thy sons,
and thy
sons' wives with
thee. 17 Bring
forth with thee
every living
thing that *is*
with thee, of all
flesh, *both* of
fowl, and of
cattle, and of
every creeping
thing that creep-
eth upon the
earth; that they
may breed a-
bundantly in the
earth, and be
fruitful, and
multiply upon
the earth. 18
And Noah went
forth, and his
sons, and his
wife, and his
sons' wives with
him: 19 Every
beast, every
creeping thing,
and every
fowl, *and* what-
soever creepeth
upon the earth,
after their
kinds, went
forth out of the
ark.

20 And Noah
builded an altar
unto the LORD;
and took of ev-
ery clean beast,
and of every
clean fowl, and
offered burnt
offerings on the
altar. 21 And the
LORD smelled a
sweet savour;
and the LORD
said in his
heart, I will not
again curse the
ground any
more for man's
sake; for the
imagination of
man's heart *is*
evil from his
youth; neither
will I again
smite any more
every thing liv-
ing, as I have
done. 22 While
the earth re-

15 16 וַיְדַבֵּר אֱלֹהִים אֶל־נֹחַ לֵאמֹר׃ צֵא מִן־הַתֵּבָה
,ark the from out Go ,saying ,Noah unto God spoke And

אַתָּה וְאִשְׁתְּךָ וּבָנֶיךָ וּנְשֵׁי־בָנֶיךָ אִתָּךְ׃
.thee with sons thy of wives the and ,sons thy and ,wife thy and thou

17 כָּל־הַחַיָּה אֲשֶׁר־אִתְּךָ מִכָּל־בָּשָׂר בָּעוֹף
,fowl (in) ,flesh all from thee with [is] which animal Every

וּבַבְּהֵמָה וּבְכָל־הָרֶמֶשׂ הָרֹמֵשׂ עַל־הָאָרֶץ
earth the upon creeps that creeper every (in) and cattle (in) and

הַוְצֵא אִתָּךְ וְשָׁרְצוּ בָאָרֶץ
,earth the in swarm them let and ,thee with out bring

וּפָרוּ וְרָבוּ עַל־הָאָרֶץ׃
.earth the upon multiply and fruitful be them let and

18 וַיֵּצֵא־נֹחַ וּבָנָיו וְאִשְׁתּוֹ וּנְשֵׁי־בָנָיו
sons his of wives the and ,wife his and ,sons his and ,Noah out went And

19 אִתּוֹ׃ [a]כָּל־הַחַיָּה [b]כָּל־הָרֶמֶשׂ וְכָל־הָעוֹף כֹּל
thing every ,fowl every and ,creeper every ,beast Every .him with

רוֹמֵשׂ עַל־הָאָרֶץ לְמִשְׁפְּחֹתֵיהֶם יָצְאוּ מִן־הַתֵּבָה׃
.ark the from out went ,families their after ,earth the upon creeping

20 וַיִּבֶן נֹחַ מִזְבֵּחַ לַיהוָה וַיִּקַּח מִכֹּל
all from took he and ;Jehovah to altar an Noah built And

הַבְּהֵמָה הַטְּהֹרָה וּמִכֹּל הָעוֹף הַטָּהֹר וַיַּעַל
up offered he and ,[1]clean [2]fowl all from and [1]clean [2]cattle

21 עֹלֹת בַּמִּזְבֵּחַ׃ וַיָּרַח יְהוָה אֶת־רֵיחַ
of odor the Jehovah smelled And .altar the on offerings burnt

הַנִּיחֹחַ וַיֹּאמֶר יְהוָה אֶל־לִבּוֹ לֹא
[3]Not ;heart his unto Jehovah said And .delight

אֹסִף לְקַלֵּל עוֹד אֶת־הָאֲדָמָה בַּעֲבוּר
of account on ground the still curse to [4]continue [2]will [1]I

הָאָדָם כִּי יֵצֶר לֵב הָאָדָם רַע
evil [is] man of heart the of purpose the because ,man

מִנְּעֻרָיו וְלֹא־אֹסִף עוֹד לְהַכּוֹת
smite to still coutinue not will I and ;youth his from

22 אֶת־כָּל־חַי כַּאֲשֶׁר עָשִׂיתִי׃ עֹד כָּל־יְמֵי
of days the all Still .done have I as according thing living every

15 And God
spake unto
Noah, saying,
16 Go forth of
the ark, thou,
and thy wife,
and thy sons,
and thy sons'
wives with thee.
17 Bring forth
with thee every
living thing that
is with thee of
all flesh, both
fowl, and cattle,
and every creep-
ing thing that
creepeth upon
the earth; that
they may breed
abundantly in
the earth, and
be fruitful, and
multiply upon
the earth. 18
And Noah went
forth, and his
sons, and his
wife, and his
sons' wives with
him: 19 every
beast, every
creeping thing,
and every fowl,
whatsoever
moveth upon
the earth, after
their families,
went forth out
of the ark.

20 And Noah
builded an altar
unto the LORD;
and took of
every clean
beast, and of
every clean
fowl, and
offered burnt
offerings on
the altar. 21
And the LORD
smelled the
sweet savour;
and the LORD
said in his heart,
I will not again
curse the ground
any more for
man's sake, for
that the imag-
ination of man's
heart is evil from
his youth; neith-
er will I again
smite any more
every thing liv-
ing, as I have
done. 22 While
the earth re-
maineth, seed-

a G., S., V. add, *and*, reading וכל. *b* G., S. add, *and*, reading וכל.

maineth, seed time and harvest, and cold and heat, and summer and winter, and day and night shall not cease.

הָאָרֶץ זֶרַע וְקָצִיר וְקֹר וָחֹם וְקַיִץ
summer and ,heat and cold and ,harvest and [time] seed ,earth the

וְחֹרֶף וְיוֹם וָלַיְלָה לֹא יִשְׁבֹּתוּ׃
.cease [1]shall [2]not night and day and ,winter and

time and harvest, and cold and heat, and summer and winter, and day and night shall not cease.

9

AND God blessed Noah and his sons, and said unto them, Be fruitful, and multiply, and replenish the earth. 2 And the fear of you and the dread of you shall be upon every beast of the earth, and upon every fowl of the air, upon all that moveth *upon* the earth, and upon all the fishes of the sea; into your hand are they delivered. 3 Every moving thing that liveth shall be meat for you; even as the green herb have I given you all things. 4 But flesh with the life thereof, *which is* the blood thereof, shall ye not eat. 5 And surely your blood of your lives will I require; at the hand of every beast will I require it, and at the hand of man; at the hand of every man's brother will I require the life of man. 6 Whoso sheddeth man's blood, by man shall his blood be shed: for in the image of God made he man. 7 And you, be ye fruitful, and multi-

1 וַיְבָרֶךְ אֱלֹהִים אֶת־נֹחַ וְאֶת־בָּנָיו וַיֹּאמֶר
said he and ,sons his and Noah God blessed And

לָהֶם פְּרוּ וּרְבוּ וּמִלְאוּ אֶת־הָאָרֶץ׃
.earth the fill and ,multiply and ,fruitful Be ;them to

2 וּמוֹרַאֲכֶם וְחִתְּכֶם יִהְיֶה עַל
upon be to come shall you of terror the and you of fear the And

כָּל־חַיַּת הָאָרֶץ וְעַל כָּל־עוֹף הַשָּׁמָיִם
,heavens the of fowl every upon and ,earth the of beast every

בְּכֹל[a] אֲשֶׁר תִּרְמֹשׂ הָאֲדָמָה וּבְכָל־דְּגֵי
of fish the all with and ,ground the creeps which [with] all with

3 הַיָּם בְּיֶדְכֶם נִתָּנוּ׃ כָּל־רֶמֶשׂ אֲשֶׁר־הוּא
is which creeper Every .given are they hand your into ; sea the

חַי לָכֶם יִהְיֶה לְאָכְלָה כְּיֶרֶק עֵשֶׂב
herb of greenness like ; food for be shall it you for ,alive

4 נָתַתִּי לָכֶם אֶת־כֹּל׃ אַךְ־בָּשָׂר בְּנַפְשׁוֹ דָמוֹ
,blood its [even] soul its with ,flesh But .all you to given have I

5 לֹא תֹאכֵלוּ׃ וְאַךְ אֶת־דִּמְכֶם לְנַפְשֹׁתֵיכֶם
souls your to [belonging] blood your yet And .eat [2]shall [1]ye [3]not

אֶדְרֹשׁ מִיַּד כָּל־חַיָּה אֶדְרְשֶׁנּוּ
,it demand will I beast every of hand the from ;demand will I

וּמִיַּד הָאָדָם מִיַּד אִישׁ
[5]one [4]each of hand the from ,man of hand the from and

6 אָחִיו[b] אֶדְרֹשׁ אֶת־נֶפֶשׁ הָאָדָם׃ שֹׁפֵךְ
of shedder The .man of soul the demand will I [3]of [2]brother [1][the] (his)

דַּם הָאָדָם בָּאָדָם[c] דָּמוֹ יִשָּׁפֵךְ כִּי
because ; shed be shall blood his man by ,man of blood the

7 בְּצֶלֶם אֱלֹהִים עָשָׂה אֶת־הָאָדָם׃ וְאַתֶּם פְּרוּ
fruitful be ,you And .man made he God of image the in

AND God blessed Noah and his sons, and said unto them, Be fruitful, and multiply, and replenish the earth. 2 And the fear of you and the dread of you shall be upon every beast of the earth, and upon every fowl of the air; with all wherewith the ground teemeth, and all the fishes of the sea, into your hand are they delivered. 3 Every moving thing that liveth shall be food for you; as the green herb have I given you all. 4 But flesh with the life thereof, *which is* the blood thereof, shall ye not eat. 5 And surely your blood, *the blood* of your lives, will I require; at the hand of every beast will I require it: and at the hand of man, even at the hand of every man's brother, will I require the life of man. 6 Whoso sheddeth man's blood, by man shall his blood be shed: for in the image of God made he man. 7 And you, be ye fruitful,

a G., S. add, *and*, reading, ובכל.
b Sm., S., V. add, *and*, reading ואחיו.
c V. omits; for באדם דמו, G. has, *in return for his blood.*

ply; bring forth abundantly in the earth, and multiply therein.

8 And God spake unto Noah, and to his sons with him saying, 9 And I, behold, I establish my covenant with you, and with your seed after you; 10 And with every living creature that *is* with you, of the fowl, of the cattle, and of every beast of the earth with you; from all that go out of the ark, to every beast of the earth. 11 And I will establish my covenant with you; neither shall all flesh be cut off any more by the waters of a flood; neither shall there any more be a flood to destroy the earth. 12 And God said, This *is* the token of the covenant which I make between me and you and every living creature that *is* with you, for perpetual generations: 13 I do set my bow in the cloud, and it shall be for a token of a covenant between me and the earth. 14 And it shall come to pass, when I bring a cloud over the earth, that the bow shall be seen in the cloud: 15 And I will remember my covenant, which *is* between me and you and every

8 וּרְבוּ שִׁרְצוּ בָאָרֶץ וּרְבוּ־בָהּ׃ וַיֹּאמֶר
said And .it in multiply and earth the in swarm ;multiply and

9 אֱלֹהִים אֶל־נֹחַ וְאֶל־בָּנָיו אִתּוֹ לֵאמֹר׃ וַאֲנִי
,I And ;saying ,him with sons his unto and Noah unto God

הִנְנִי מֵקִים אֶת־בְּרִיתִי אִתְּכֶם
you with covenant my establish to about [am] I behold

10 וְאֶת־זַרְעֲכֶם אַחֲרֵיכֶם׃ וְאֵת כָּל־נֶפֶשׁ הַחַיָּה אֲשֶׁר
which life of soul every with and ;you after seed your with and

אִתְּכֶם בָּעוֹף בַּבְּהֵמָה[a] וּבְכָל־חַיַּת
of beasts all (in) and cattle the (in) ,fowl the (in) ,you with [is]

הָאָרֶץ אִתְּכֶם מִכֹּל יֹצְאֵי הַתֵּבָה לְכֹל[b]
every to ,ark the from out going [are that] all from ,you with earth the

11 חַיַּת הָאָרֶץ׃[b] וַהֲקִמֹתִי אֶת־בְּרִיתִי אִתְּכֶם
,you with covenant my establish will I And .earth the of beast

וְלֹא־יִכָּרֵת כָּל־בָּשָׂר עוֹד מִמֵּי הַמַּבּוּל
,flood the of waters the from again flesh all off cut be not shall and

12 וְלֹא־יִהְיֶה עוֹד מַבּוּל לְשַׁחֵת הָאָרֶץ׃ וַיֹּאמֶר
said And .earth the destroy to flood a again be not shall and

אֱלֹהִים זֹאת אוֹת־הַבְּרִית אֲשֶׁר־אֲנִי
I which covenant the of sign the [is] This ;God

נֹתֵן בֵּינִי וּבֵינֵיכֶם וּבֵין
(between) and ,you (between) and me between make to about [am]

כָּל־נֶפֶשׁ חַיָּה אֲשֶׁר אִתְּכֶם לְדֹרֹת עוֹלָם׃
.eternity of generations for ,you with [is] which life of soul every

13 אֶת־קַשְׁתִּי נָתַתִּי בֶּעָנָן וְהָיְתָה לְאוֹת בְּרִית
covenant a of sign a for be shall it and ,clouds the in place I bow My

14 בֵּינִי וּבֵין הָאָרֶץ׃ וְהָיָה בְּעַנְנִי
gathering my in be shall it And .earth the (between) and me between

עָנָן עַל־הָאָרֶץ וְנִרְאֲתָה הַקֶּשֶׁת בֶּעָנָן׃
.clouds the in bow the seen be shall then ,earth the upon clouds

15 וְזָכַרְתִּי אֶת־בְּרִיתִי אֲשֶׁר בֵּינִי
me between [is] which covenant my remember will I And

וּבֵינֵיכֶם וּבֵין כָּל־נֶפֶשׁ חַיָּה בְּכָל־בָּשָׂר
,flesh all in life of soul every (between) and you (between) and

and multiply; bring forth abundantly in the earth, and multiply therein.

8 And God spake unto Noah, and to his sons with him, saying, 9 And I, behold, I establish my covenant with you, and with your seed after you; 10 and with every living creature that is with you, the fowl, the cattle, and every beast of the earth with you; of all that go out of the ark, even every beast of the earth. 11 And I will establish my covenant with you; neither shall all flesh be cut off any more by the waters of the flood; neither shall there any more be a flood to destroy the earth. 12 And God said, This is the token of the covenant which I make between me and you and every living creature that is with you, for perpetual generations: 13 I do set my bow in the cloud, and it shall be for a token of a covenant between me and the earth. 14 And it shall come to pass, when I bring a cloud over the earth, that the bow shall be seen in the cloud, 15 and I will remember my covenant, which is between me and you and every

a Sm., G., S. add, *and*, reading ובבהמה.

b G. omits.

living creature
of all flesh ; and
the waters shall
no more become
a flood to de-
stroy all flesh.
16 And the bow
shall be in the
cloud ; and I
will look upon
it, that I may
remember the
everlasting cov-
enant between
God and every
living creature
of all flesh that
is upon the
earth. 17 And
God said unto
Noah, This *is*
the token of the
covenant, which
I have estab-
lished between
me and all flesh
that *is* upon the
earth.

וְלֹא־יִהְיֶה עוֹד הַמַּיִם לְמַבּוּל לְשַׁחֵת
destroy to ,flood a (for) waters the again become not shall and

16 כָּל־בָּשָׂר׃ וְהָיְתָה הַקֶּשֶׁת בֶּעָנָן וּרְאִיתִיהָ
,it see shall I and clouds the in bow the be shall And .flesh all

לִזְכֹּר בְּרִית עוֹלָם בֵּין אֱלֹהִים וּבֵין
(between) and God between ,eternity of covenant a remember to

כָּל־נֶפֶשׁ חַיָּה בְּכָל־בָּשָׂר אֲשֶׁר עַל־הָאָרֶץ׃
.earth the upon [is] which flesh all in ,life of soul every

17 וַיֹּאמֶר אֱלֹהִים אֶל־נֹחַ זֹאת אוֹת־הַבְּרִית
covenant the of sign the [is] This ;Noah unto God said And

אֲשֶׁר הֲקִמֹתִי בֵּינִי וּבֵין כָּל־בָּשָׂר
flesh all (between) and me between established have I which

אֲשֶׁר עַל־הָאָרֶץ׃
.earth the upon [is] which

living creature
of all flesh ; and
the waters shall
no more become
a flood to de-
stroy all flesh.
16 And the bow
shall be in the
cloud ; and I
will look upon
it, that I may
remember the
everlasting cov-
enant between
God and every
living creature
of all flesh that
is upon the
earth. 17 And
God said unto
Noah, This is
the token of the
covenant which
I have estab-
lished between
me and all flesh
that is upon the
earth.

18 וַיִּהְיוּ בְנֵי־נֹחַ הַיֹּצְאִים מִן־הַתֵּבָה שֵׁם
Shem ,ark the from out going those ,Noah of sons the were And

18 And the
sons of Noah,
that went forth
of the ark, were
Shem, and
Ham, and Ja-
pheth: and Ham
is the father of
Canaan. 19
These *are* the
three sons of
Noah: and of
them was the
whole earth
overspread. 20
And Noah be-
gan *to be* a hus-
bandman, and
he planted a
vineyard : 21
And he drank of
the wine, and
was drunken ;
and he was un-
covered within
his tent. 22 And
Ham, the father
of Canaan, saw
the nakedness of
his father, and
told his two
brethren with-
out. 23 And
Shem and Ja-
pheth took a
garment, and
laid *it* upon both
their shoulders,
and went back-
ward, and cov-
ered the naked-
ness of their
father; and their

וְחָם וָיָפֶת וְחָם הוּא אֲבִי כְנָעַן׃
.Canaan of father the being Ham (and) ,Japheth and Ham and

19 שְׁלֹשָׁה אֵלֶּה בְּנֵי־נֹחַ וּמֵאֵלֶּה נָפְצָה
dispersed was these from and ;Noah of sons the [were] [1]these [2]Three

כָל־הָאָרֶץ׃
.earth the all

20 וַיָּחֶל נֹחַ אִישׁ הָאֲדָמָה וַיִּטַּע
planted and ,ground the of man a ,Noah began And

21 כָּרֶם׃ וַיֵּשְׁתְּ מִן־הַיַּיִן וַיִּשְׁכָּר
;drunken was and ,wine the from drank he and ;vineyard a

22 וַיִּתְגַּל בְּתוֹךְ אָהֳלֹה׃ וַיַּרְא חָם
Ham saw And .tent his of midst the in himself uncovered he and

אֲבִי כְנַעַן אֵת עֶרְוַת אָבִיו וַיַּגֵּד
known made and ,father his of nakedness the Canaan of father the

23 לִשְׁנֵי־אֶחָיו בַּחוּץ׃ וַיִּקַּח שֵׁם וָיֶפֶת
Japheth and Shem took And .outside brothers two his to

אֶת־הַשִּׂמְלָה וַיָּשִׂימוּ עַל־שְׁכֶם שְׁנֵיהֶם
,them of both of shoulders the upon [it] put and ,garment outer the

וַיֵּלְכוּ אֲחֹרַנִּית וַיְכַסּוּ אֵת עֶרְוַת אֲבִיהֶם
,father their of nakedness the covered and ,backwards went they and

18 And the
sons of Noah,
that went forth
of the ark, were
Shem, and
Ham, and Ja-
pheth: and Ham
is the father of
Canaan. 19
These three
were the sons
of Noah: and
of these was the
whole earth
overspread. 20
And Noah be-
gan to be an
husbandman,
and planted a
vineyard: 21
and he drank of
the wine, and
was drunken ;
and he was un-
covered within
his tent. 22 And
Ham, the father
of Canaan, saw
the nakedness of
his father, and
told his two
brethren with-
out. 23 And
Shem and Ja-
pheth took a
garment, and
laid it upon both
their shoulders,
and went back-
ward, and cover-
ed the naked-
ness of their

faces *were* backward, and they saw not their father's nakedness. 24 And Noah awoke from his wine, and knew what his younger son had done unto him. 25 And he said, Cursed *be* Canaan; a servant of servants shall he be unto his brethren. 26 And he said, Blessed *be* the LORD God of Shem; and Canaan shall be his servant. 27 God shall enlarge Japheth, and he shall dwell in the tents of Shem; and Canaan shall be his servant.

28 And Noah lived after the flood three hundred and fifty years. 29 And all the days of Noah were nine hundred and fifty years: and he died.

וּפְנֵיהֶם אֲחֹרַנִּית וְעֶרְוַת אֲבִיהֶם
father their of nakedness the and ,backward [being] faces their (and)

24 לֹא רָאוּ׃ וַיִּיקֶץ נֹחַ מִיֵּינוֹ וַיֵּדַע
knew he and ,wine his from Noah awoke And .²saw ¹they ³not

25 אֵת אֲשֶׁר־עָשָׂה לוֹ בְּנוֹ הַקָּטָן׃ וַיֹּאמֶר
;said he And .¹youngest ²son his him to done had which that

אָרוּר כְּנָעַן עֶבֶד עֲבָדִים יִהְיֶה לְאֶחָיו׃
.brethren his to be he may servants of servant a ;Canaan [be] Cursed

26 וַיֹּאמֶר בָּרוּךְ יְהוָה אֱלֹהֵי שֵׁם וִיהִי
be may and ,Shem of God the ,Jehovah [be] Blessed :said he And

27 כְנַעַן עֶבֶד לָמוֹ׃ יַפְתְּ אֱלֹהִים לְיֶפֶת
,Japheth to God enlargement give May .them to servant a Canaan

וְיִשְׁכֹּן בְּאָהֳלֵי־שֵׁם וִיהִי כְנַעַן עֶבֶד
servant a Canaan be may and ;Shem of tents the in dwell he may and

28 לָמוֹ׃ וַיְחִי־נֹחַ אַחַר הַמַּבּוּל שְׁלֹשׁ מֵאוֹת שָׁנָה
years hundred three flood the after Noah lived And .them to

29 וַחֲמִשִּׁים שָׁנָה׃ וַיְהִי כָּל־יְמֵי־נֹחַ תְּשַׁע מֵאוֹת
hundred nine Noah of days the all were And .years fifty and

שָׁנָה וַחֲמִשִּׁים שָׁנָה וַיָּמֹת׃
.died he and ,years fifty and years

father; and their faces were backward, and they saw not their father's nakedness. 24 And Noah awoke from his wine, and knew what his youngest son had done unto him. 25 And he said, Cursed be Canaan; A servant of servants shall he be unto his brethren. 26 And he said, Blessed be the LORD, the God of Shem; And let Canaan be his servant. 27 God enlarge Japheth, And let him dwell in the tents of Shem; And let Canaan be his servant.

28 And Noah lived after the flood three hundred and fifty years. 29 And all the days of Noah were nine hundred and fifty years: and he died.

10

Now these *are* the generations of the sons of Noah, Shem, Ham, and Japheth: and unto them were sons born after the flood. 2 The sons of Japheth; Gomer, and Magog, and Madai, and Javân, and Tubal, and Meshech, and Tiras. 3 And the sons of Gomer; Ashkenaz, and Riphath, and Togarmah. 4 And the sons of Javan; Elishah, and Tarshish, Kittim, and Dodanim. 5 By these were the isles of the Gentiles divided in their lands;

1 וְאֵלֶּה תּוֹלְדֹת בְּנֵי־נֹחַ שֵׁם חָם
Ham Shem ;Noah of sons the of generations the [are] these And

וָיָפֶת וַיִּוָּלְדוּ לָהֶם בָּנִים אַחַר הַמַּבּוּל׃
.flood the after sons them to born were And .Japheth and

2 בְּנֵי יֶפֶת גֹּמֶר וּמָגוֹג וּמָדַי וְיָוָן
,Javan ,Madai and ,Magog and ,Gomer ,Japheth of sons The

3 וְתֻבָל וּמֶשֶׁךְ וְתִירָס׃ וּבְנֵי גֹּמֶר אַשְׁכְּנַז
,Ashkenaz ;Gomer of sons the And .Tiras and ,Meshech and ,Tubal and

4 וְרִיפַת וְתֹגַרְמָה׃ וּבְנֵי יָוָן אֱלִישָׁה
,Elishah Javan of sons the And .Togarmah and ,Riphath and

5 וְתַרְשִׁישׁ כִּתִּים וְדֹדָנִים׃ מֵאֵלֶּה
these From .Dodanim the and Kittim the ,Tarshish and

נִפְרְדוּ אִיֵּי הַגּוֹיִם בְּאַרְצֹתָם
;lands their in ,nations the of lands coast the themselves separated

Now these are the generations of the sons of Noah, Shem, Ham and Japheth: and unto them were sons born after the flood. 2 The sons of Japheth; Gomer, and Magog, and Madai, and Javan, and Tubal, and Meshech, and Tiras. 3 And the sons of Gomer; Ashkenaz, and Riphath, and Togarmah. 4 And the sons of Javan; Elishah, and Tarshish, Kittim, and Dodanim. 5 Of these were the isles of the nations divided in their lands,

every one after
his tongue, after
their families, in
their nations.

6 And the
sons of Ham;
Cush, and Miz-
raim, and Phut,
and Canaan.
7 And the sons
of Cush; Seba,
and Havilah,
and Sabtah, and
Raamah, and
Sabtechah: and
the sons of Ra-
amah; Sheba,
and Dedan. 8
And Cush begat
Nimrod: he be-
gan to be a
mighty one
in the earth.
9 He was a
mighty hunter
before the
LORD: where-
fore it is said,
Even as Nim-
rod the mighty
hunter before
the LORD. 10
And the begin-
ning of his king-
dom was Babel,
and Erech, and
Accad, and Cal-
neh, in the land
of Shinar. 11
Out of that land
went forth As-
shur, and build-
ed Nineveh, and
the city Reho-
both, and Calah.
12 And Resen
between Nin-
eveh and Calah:
the same *is* a
great city. 13
And Mizraim be-
gat Ludim and
Anamim, and
Lehabim, and
Naphtuhim,
14 And Path-
rusim, and Cas-
luhim, (out of
whom came
Philistim,) and
Caphtorim.

15 And Ca-
naan begat
Sidon his first-
born, and Heth,
16 And the
Jebusite, and
the Amorite,
and the Girga-
site, 17 And the
Hivite, and the
Arkite, and the
Sinite, 18 And
the Arvadite,

אִישׁ לִלְשֹׁנוֹ לְמִשְׁפְּחֹתָם בְּגוֹיֵהֶם׃
.nations their in ,families their after ; tongue his after one each

6 וּבְנֵי חָם כּוּשׁ וּמִצְרַיִם וּפוּט וּכְנָעַן׃
.Canaan and ,Put and ,Mizraim and ,Cush ; Ham of sons the And

7 וּבְנֵי כּוּשׁ סְבָא וַחֲוִילָה וְסַבְתָּה
,Sabtah and ,Havilah and ,Seba ;Cush of sons the And

וְרַעְמָה וְסַבְתְּכָא וּבְנֵי רַעְמָה שְׁבָא וּדְדָן׃
.Dedan and Sheba ;Raamah of sons the And .Sabteca and ,Raamah and

8 וְכוּשׁ יָלַד אֶת־נִמְרֹד הוּא הֵחֵל לִהְיוֹת גִּבֹּר בָּאָרֶץ׃
.earth the in hero a be to began he ; Nimrod begat Cush And

9 הוּא־הָיָה גִבֹּר־צַיִד לִפְנֵי יְהוָה עַל־כֵּן יֵאָמַר
; said is it· therefore ;Jehovah before hunting of hero a was He

10 כְּנִמְרֹד גִּבּוֹר צַיִד לִפְנֵי יְהוָה׃ וַתְּהִי
was And .Jehovah before hunting of hero a Nimrod Like

רֵאשִׁית מַמְלַכְתּוֹ בָּבֶל וְאֶרֶךְ וְאַכַּד וְכַלְנֵה
Calneh and Accad and Erech and Babel kingdom his of beginning the

11 בְּאֶרֶץ שִׁנְעָר׃ מִן־הָאָרֶץ הַהִוא יָצָא אַשּׁוּר
,Assyria to out went he [1]that [2]land From .Shinar of land the in

12 וַיִּבֶן אֶת־נִינְוֵה וְאֶת־רְחֹבֹת עִיר וְאֶת־כָּלַח׃ וְאֶת־רֶסֶן
Resen and ,Calah and Ir ,Rehoboth and Nineveh built and

בֵּין נִינְוֵה וּבֵין כָּלַח הִוא הָעִיר
[2]city the [being] that ,Calah (between) and Nineveh between

13 הַגְּדֹלָה׃ וּמִצְרַיִם יָלַד אֶת־לוּדִים וְאֶת־עֲנָמִים
,Anamim the and ,Ludim the begat Mizraim And .[1]great

14 וְאֶת־לְהָבִים וְאֶת־נַפְתֻּחִים׃ וְאֶת־פַּתְרֻסִים
,Pathrusim the and ,Naphtuhim the and ,Lehabim the and

וְאֶת־כַּסְלֻחִים אֲשֶׁר יָצְאוּ מִשָּׁם פְּלִשְׁתִּים
,Philistines the (there from) out went whence ,Casluhim the and

וְאֶת־כַּפְתֹּרִים׃
.Caphtorim the and

15 וּכְנַעַן יָלַד אֶת־צִידֹן בְּכֹרוֹ וְאֶת־חֵת׃
,Heth and ,first-born his Zidon begat Canaan And

16 וְאֶת־הַיְבוּסִי וְאֶת־הָאֱמֹרִי וְאֵת הַגִּרְגָּשִׁי׃
,Girgashite the and ,Amorite the and ,Jebusite the and

17
18 וְאֶת־הַחִוִּי וְאֶת־הַעַרְקִי וְאֶת־הַסִּינִי׃ וְאֶת־הָאַרְוָדִי
,Arvadite the and ,Sinite the and ,Arkite the and ,Hivite the and

every one after
his tongue; after
their families,
in their nations.

6 And the sons
of Ham; Cush,
and Mizraim,
and Put, and
Canaan. 7 And
the sons of
Cush; Seba,
and Havilah,
and Sabtah, and
Raamah, and
Sabteca: and
the sons of Ra-
amah; Sheba,
and Dedan. 8
And Cush begat
Nimrod: he be-
gan to be a
mighty one in
the earth. 9 He
was a mighty
hunter before
the LORD:
wherefore it is
said, Like Nim-
rod a mighty
hunter before
the LORD. 10
And the begin-
ning of his king-
dom was Babel,
and Erech, and
Accad, and Cal-
neh, in the land
of Shinar. 11
Out of that land
he went forth
into Assyria,
and builded Nin-
eveh, and Re-
hoboth-Ir, and
Calah, 12 and
Resen between
Nineveh and
Calah (the same
is the great city).
13 And Mizraim
begat Ludim,
and Anamim,
and Lehabim,
and Naphtu-
him, 14 and
Pathrusim, and
Casluhim
(whence went
forth the Philis-
tines), and
Caphtorim.

15 And Ca-
naan begat Zi-
don his first-
born, and Heth;
16 And the Jeb-
usite, and the
Amorite, and
the Girgashite;
17 and the Hi-
vite, and the
Arkite, and the
Sinite; 18 and
the Arvadite,

and the Zem-
arite, and the
Hamathite: and
afterward were
the families of
the Canaanites
spread abroad.
19 And the bor-
der of the Ca-
naanites was
from Sidon, as
thou comest to
Gerar, unto
Gaza; as thou
goest, unto So-
dom, and Go-
morrah, and
Admah, and
Zeboim, even
unto Lasha. 20
These *are* the
sons of Ham,
after their fam-
ilies, after
their tongues, in
their countries,
and in their
nations.
21 Unto Shem
also, the father
of all the chil-
dren of Eber,
the brother of
Japheth the
elder, even to
him were *chil-
dren* born. 22
The children of
Shem; Elam
and Asshur, and
Arphaxad, and
Lud, and Aram.
23 And the chil-
dren of Aram;
Uz, and Hul,
and Gether, and
Mash. 24 And
Arphaxad begat
Salah; and Sa-
lah begat Eber.
25 And unto
Eber were born
two sons: the
name of one
was Peleg; for
in his days was
the earth divid-
ed; and his
brother's name
was Joktan. 26
And Joktan be-
gat Almodad,
and Sheleph,
and Hazarma-
veth, and Jerah,
27 And Hado-
ram, and Uzal,
and Diklah, 28
And Obal, and
Abimael, and
Sheba, 29 And
Ophir, and Hav-
ilah, and Jo-

וְאֶת־הַצְּמָרִי וְאֶת־הַחֲמָתִי וְאַחַר נָפֹצוּ
,Zemarite the and ;Hamathite the and afterwards and were spread abroad

מִשְׁפְּחוֹת הַכְּנַעֲנִי׃ וַיְהִי גְּבוּל הַכְּנַעֲנִי
of families the .Canaanite the was And of border the Canaanite the

19 מִצִּידֹן בֹּאֲכָה גְרָרָה עַד־עַזָּה
Zidon from going art thou [as] ,Gerar toward ;Gaza as far as

בֹּאֲכָה סְדֹמָה וַעֲמֹרָה וְאַדְמָה
going art thou [as] Sodom toward Gomorrah and Admah and

20 וּצְבֹיִם עַד־לָשַׁע׃ אֵלֶּה בְנֵי־חָם
,Zeboiim and .Lasha as far as These Ham of sons the [were]

לְמִשְׁפְּחֹתָם לִלְשֹׁנֹתָם בְּאַרְצֹתָם בְּגוֹיֵהֶם׃
,families their after ,tongues their after ,lands their in .nations their in

21 וּלְשֵׁם יֻלַּד גַּם־הוּא אֲבִי
Shem to And ,[offspring] born was ,him [to] also of father the

22 כָּל־בְּנֵי־עֵבֶר אֲחִי יֶפֶת הַגָּדוֹל׃ בְּנֵי
,Eber of sons the all the [2]brother [3]of [4]Japheth [1].elder of sons The

שֵׁם עֵילָם וְאַשּׁוּר וְאַרְפַּכְשַׁד וְלוּד וַאֲרָם׃[a]
:Shem Elam Asshur and Arpachshad and Lud and .Aram and

23 וּבְנֵי אֲרָם עוּץ וְחוּל וְגֶתֶר וָמַשׁ׃[b]
And the sons of :Aram Uz Hul and Gether and .Mash and

24 וְאַרְפַּכְשַׁד יָלַד[c] אֶת־שָׁלַח וְשֶׁלַח יָלַד אֶת־עֵבֶר׃
Arpachshad And begat Shelah Shelah and begat .Eber

25 וּלְעֵבֶר יֻלַּד שְׁנֵי בָנִים שֵׁם הָאֶחָד
Eber to And born were two ;sons of name the one the [being]

פֶּלֶג כִּי בְיָמָיו נִפְלְגָה הָאָרֶץ וְשֵׁם
,Peleg for days his in divided was earth the; of name the and

26 אָחִיו יָקְטָן׃ וְיָקְטָן יָלַד אֶת־אַלְמוֹדָד
brother his [being] .Joktan Joktan And begat ,Almodad

27 וְאֶת־שָׁלֶף וְאֶת־חֲצַרְמָוֶת וְאֶת־יָרַח׃ וְאֶת־הֲדוֹרָם
, Sheleph and ,Hazarmaveth and ,Jerah and ,Hadoram and

28 וְאֶת־אוּזָל וְאֶת־דִּקְלָה׃ וְאֶת־עוֹבָל וְאֶת־אֲבִימָאֵל
,Uzal and ,Diklah and ,Obal and ,Abimael and

29 וְאֶת־שְׁבָא׃ וְאֶת־אוֹפִר וְאֶת־חֲוִילָה וְאֶת־יוֹבָב כָּל־אֵלֶּה
,Sheba and ,Ophir and ,Havilah and ; Jobab and [were] these all

and the Zema-
rite, and the
Hamathite: and
afterward were
the families of
the Canaanite
spread abroad.
19 And the bor-
der of the Ca-
naanite was
from Zidon, as
thou goest to-
ward Gerar,
unto Gaza; as
thou goest to-
ward Sodom
and Gomorrah
and Admah and
Zeboiim, unto
Lasha. 20 These
are the sons of
Ham, after their
families, after
their tongues, in
their lands, in
their nations.
21 And unto
Shem, the fath-
er of all the
children of
Eber, the elder
brother of Ja-
pheth, to him
also were chil-
dren born. 22
The sons of
Shem; Elam,
and Asshur, and
Arpachshad,
and Lud, and
Aram. 23 And
the sons of
Aram; Uz, and
Hul, and Geth-
er, and Mash.
24 And Arpach-
shad begat
Shelah; and
Shelah begat
Eber. 25 And
unto Eber were
born two sons:
the name of the
one was Peleg;
for in his days
was the earth
divided; and his
brother's name
was Joktan. 26
And Joktan be-
gat Almodad,
and Sheleph,
and Hazarma-
veth, and Jerah;
27 and Hado-
ram, and Uzal,
and Diklah; 28
and Obal, and
Abimael, and
Sheba; 29 and
Ophir and Ha-
vilah, and Jo-

a G. adds, *and Cainan*.
b Sm. has ומשא: G. ומשך; cf. 1 Chron. 1: 17.
c G. adds, *Cainan, and Cainan begat;* cf. Luke 3: 36.

bab: all these *were* the sons of Joktan. 30 And their dwelling was from Mesha, as thou goest unto Sephar a mount of the east. 31 These *are* the sons of Shem, after their families, after their tongues, in their lands, after their nations. 32 These *are* the families of the sons of Noah, after their generations, in their nations: and by these were the nations divided in the earth after the flood.

30 בְּנֵי יָקְטָן׃ וַיְהִי מוֹשָׁבָם מִמֵּשָׁא
,Mesha from place dwelling their was And .Joktan of sons the

בֹּאֲכָה סְפָרָה הַר הַקֶּדֶם׃
.east the of mountain the [toward] ,Sephar toward going art thou [as]

31 אֵלֶּה בְנֵי־שֵׁם לְמִשְׁפְּחֹתָם לִלְשֹׁנֹתָם
,tongues their after ,families their after ,Shem of sons the [were] These

בְּאַרְצֹתָם לְגוֹיֵהֶם׃
.nations their after ,lands their in

32 אֵלֶּה מִשְׁפְּחֹת בְּנֵי־נֹחַ לְתוֹלְדֹתָם
,generations their after ,Noah of sons the of families the [were] These

בְּגוֹיֵהֶם וּמֵאֵלֶּה נִפְרְדוּ הַגּוֹיִם[a]
nations the themselves dispersed these from and ; nations their in

בָּאָרֶץ אַחַר הַמַּבּוּל׃
.flood the after earth the in

bab: all these were the sons of Joktan. 30 And their dwelling was from Mesha, as thou goest toward Sephar, the mountain of the east. 31 These are the sons of Shem, after their families, after their tongues, in their lands, after their nations. 32 These are the families of the sons of Noah, after their generations, in their nations: and of these were the nations divided in the earth after the flood.

11

AND the whole earth was of one language, and of one speech. 2 And it came to pass, as they journeyed from the east, that they found a plain in the land of Shinar; and they dwelt there. 3 And they said one to another, Go to, let us make brick, and burn them thoroughly. And they had brick for stone, and slime had they for mortar. 4 And they said, Go to, let us build us a city and a tower, whose top *may reach* unto heaven; and let us make us a name, lest we be scattered abroad upon the face of the whole earth.

1 וַיְהִי כָל־הָאָרֶץ שָׂפָה אֶחָת
[1]one [2]language [being] earth the all ,pass to came it And

2 וּדְבָרִים אֲחָדִים׃[b] וַיְהִי בְּנָסְעָם
migrating their in ,pass to came it (and) ; [2]same [1]the [3]words and

מִקֶּדֶם וַיִּמְצְאוּ בִקְעָה בְּאֶרֶץ
of land the in plain open an found they (and) eastward (from)

3 שִׁנְעָר וַיֵּשְׁבוּ שָׁם׃ וַיֹּאמְרוּ אִישׁ
one each ,said they And .there settled they and ,Shinar

אֶל־רֵעֵהוּ הָבָה נִלְבְּנָה לְבֵנִים וְנִשְׂרְפָה
burn us let and ,bricks make us let ,Come : neighbor his unto

לִשְׂרֵפָה וַתְּהִי לָהֶם הַלְּבֵנָה לְאָבֶן וְהַחֵמָר
bitumen the and stone for brick the them to was and ; burning to

4 הָיָה לָהֶם לַחֹמֶר׃ וַיֹּאמְרוּ הָבָה נִבְנֶה־לָּנוּ
us for build us let ,Come :said they And .mortar for them to was

עִיר וּמִגְדָּל וְרֹאשׁוֹ בַשָּׁמַיִם וְנַעֲשֶׂה־
make us let and ;heavens the in [being] top its (and) ,tower a and city a

לָּנוּ שֵׁם פֶּן־[c]נָפוּץ עַל־פְּנֵי כָל־הָאָרֶץ׃
.earth the all of face the upon scattered be we lest ,name a us for

And the whole earth was of one language and of one speech. 2 And it came to pass, as they journeyed east, that they found a plain in the land of Shinar; and they dwelt there. 3 And they said one to another, Go to, let us make brick, and burn them thoroughly. And they had brick for stone, and slime had they for mortar. 4 And they said, Go to, let us build us a city, and a tower, whose top *may reach* unto heaven, and let us make us a name; lest we be scattered abroad upon the face of the whole earth.

a Sm. G., have, *isles of the nations*, איי הגוים.
b G. adds, *to all.*
c G., V. have, *before.*

5 And the LORD
came down to
see the city and
the tower, which
the children of
men builded. 6
And the LORD
said, Behold,
the people *is*
one, and they
have all one
language; and
this they begin
to do: and now
nothing will be
restrained from
them, which
they have imag-
ined to do. 7
Go to, let us go
down, and there
confound their
language, that
they may not
understand one
another's
speech. 8 So the
LORD scattered
them abroad
from thence
upon the face
of all the earth:
and they left off
to build the city.
9 Therefore is
the name of it
called Babel;
because the
LORD did there
confound the
language of all
the earth: and
from thence did
the LORD scat-
ter them abroad
upon the face of
all the earth.

5 וַיֵּרֶד יְהוָה לִרְאֹת אֶת־הָעִיר וְאֶת־הַמִּגְדָּל
,tower the and city the see to Jehovah down came And

6 אֲשֶׁר בָּנוּ בְּנֵי הָאָדָם׃ וַיֹּאמֶר יְהוָה הֵן
,Behold ;Jehovah said And .men of sons the built had which

עַם אֶחָד וְשָׂפָה אַחַת לְכֻלָּם וְזֶה
[is] this and ;them of all to [1]one [2]language and ,[1]one [2]people

הַחִלָּם לַעֲשׂוֹת וְעַתָּה לֹא־יִבָּצֵר[a] מֵהֶם
them from off shut be not will now and ;do to beginning their

7 כֹּל אֲשֶׁר יָזְמוּ לַעֲשׂוֹת׃ הָבָה נֵרְדָה
down go us let ,Come .do to plan they which thing any

וְנָבְלָה שָׁם שְׂפָתָם אֲשֶׁר לֹא יִשְׁמְעוּ
hear [2]may [1]they [3]not that so ,language their there confuse and

8 אִישׁ שְׂפַת רֵעֵהוּ׃ וַיָּפֶץ יְהוָה
Jehovah scattered And .neighbor his of language the one each

אֹתָם מִשָּׁם עַל־פְּנֵי כָל־הָאָרֶץ וַיַּחְדְּלוּ
ceased they and ;earth the all of face the upon thence from them

9 לִבְנֹת הָעִיר׃[b] עַל־כֵּן קָרָא שְׁמָהּ בָּבֶל
,Babel name its called one Therefore .city the build to

כִּי־שָׁם בָּלַל יְהוָה שְׂפַת כָּל־הָאָרֶץ
,earth the all of language the Jehovah confused there because

וּמִשָּׁם הֱפִיצָם יְהוָה עַל־פְּנֵי
of face the upon Jehovah them scattered thence from and

כָּל־הָאָרֶץ׃
.earth the all

5 And the LORD
came down to
see the city and
the tower, which
the children of
men builded. 6
And the LORD
said, Behold,
they are one
people, and they
have all one lan-
guage; and this
is what they
begin to do:
and now noth-
ing will be
withholden from
them, which
they purpose to
do. 7 Go to, let
us go down, and
there confound
their language,
that they may
not understand
one another's
speech. 8 So the
LORD scattered
them abroad
from thence up-
on the face of
all the earth:
and they left off
to build the city.
9 Therefore was
the name of it
called Babel;
because the
LORD did there
confound the
language of all
the earth: and
from thence did
the LORD scat-
ter them abroad
upon the face of
all the earth.

10 These *are*
the generations
of Shem: Shem
was an hundred
years old, and
begat Arphaxad
two years after
the flood: 11 And
Shem lived after
he begat Ar-
phaxad five hun-
dred years, and
begat sons and
daughters. 12
And Arphaxad
lived five and
thirty years, and

10 אֵלֶּה תּוֹלְדֹת שֵׁם שֵׁם בֶּן־
(of son a) [being] Shem :Shem of generations the [are] These

מְאַת שָׁנָה וַיּוֹלֶד אֶת־אַרְפַּכְשָׁד שְׁנָתַיִם אַחַר
after years two ,Arpachshad begat (and) [old] years hundred a

11 הַמַּבּוּל׃ וַיְחִי־שֵׁם אַחֲרֵי הוֹלִידוֹ אֶת־אַרְפַּכְשָׁד
Arpachshad begetting his after Shem lived And .flood the

חֲמֵשׁ מֵאוֹת שָׁנָה וַיּוֹלֶד בָּנִים וּבָנוֹת׃[c]
.daughters and sons begat and ,years hundred five

12 וְאַרְפַּכְשַׁד חַי חָמֵשׁ וּשְׁלֹשִׁים[d] שָׁנָה וַיּוֹלֶד
begat and ,years thirty and five lived Arpachshad And

10 These are
the generations
of Shem. Shem
was an hundred
years old, and
begat Arpach-
shad two years
after the flood;
11 and Shem
lived after he
begat Arpach-
shad five hun-
dred years, and
begat sons and
daughters. 12
And Arpach-
shad lived five
and thirty years,
and begat She-

a S., V. have pl. act., *they will not desist.*
b Sm., G. add, *and the tower*, והמגדל.
c G. adds, *and he died*, וימת; Sm. adds, *and were all the days of Shem six hundred years and he died*, ויהי כל ימי שם שש מאות שנה וימת. Similar additions are made by G. and Sm. in vss. 13, 15, 17, 19, 21, 23, 25.
d Sm. and G. add, *and a hundred*, ומאת.

begat Salah: 13
And Arphaxad
lived after he
begat Salah four
hundred and
three years, and
begat sons and
daughters. 14
And Salah lived
thirty years, and
begat Eber: 15
And Salah lived
after he begat
Eber four hundred and three
years, and begat
sons and daughters. 16 And
Eber lived four
and thirty years,
and begat Peleg: 17 And
Eber lived after
he begat Peleg
four hundred
and thirty years,
and begat sons
and daughters.

13 אֶת־שָׁלַח׃ וַיְחִי אַרְפַּכְשַׁד אַחֲרֵי הוֹלִידוֹ
begetting his after Arpachshad lived And .Shelah

אֶת־שֶׁלַח[a] שָׁלֹשׁ[b] שָׁנִים וְאַרְבַּע[c] מֵאוֹת שָׁנָה וַיּוֹלֶד
begat and ,years hundred four and years three Shelah

14 בָּנִים וּבָנוֹת׃[d] וְשֶׁלַח חַי שְׁלֹשִׁים שָׁנָה[e] וַיּוֹלֶד
begat and ,years thirty lived Shelah And .daughters and sons

15 אֶת־עֵבֶר׃ וַיְחִי־שֶׁלַח אַחֲרֵי הוֹלִידוֹ אֶת־עֵבֶר
Eber begetting his after Shelah lived And .Eber

שָׁלֹשׁ[f] שָׁנִים וְאַרְבַּע[g] מֵאוֹת שָׁנָה וַיּוֹלֶד בָּנִים
sons begat and ,years hundred four and years three

16 וּבָנוֹת׃ וַיְחִי־עֵבֶר אַרְבַּע וּשְׁלֹשִׁים שָׁנָה[h]
,years thirty and four Eber lived And .daughters and

17 וַיּוֹלֶד אֶת־פָּלֶג׃ וַיְחִי־עֵבֶר אַחֲרֵי הוֹלִידוֹ
begetting his after Eber lived And .Peleg begat and

אֶת־פֶּלֶג שְׁלֹשִׁים שָׁנָה וְאַרְבַּע מֵאוֹת שָׁנָה[i] וַיּוֹלֶד
begat and ,years hundred four and years thirty Peleg

18 בָּנִים וּבָנוֹת׃ וַיְחִי־פֶלֶג שְׁלֹשִׁים שָׁנָה[j] וַיּוֹלֶד
begat and ,years thirty Peleg lived And .daughters and sons

19 אֶת־רְעוּ׃ וַיְחִי־פֶלֶג אַחֲרֵי הוֹלִידוֹ אֶת־רְעוּ תֵּשַׁע
nine Reu begetting his after Peleg lived And .Reu

שָׁנִים וּמָאתַיִם שָׁנָה[k] וַיּוֹלֶד בָּנִים וּבָנוֹת׃
.daughters and sons begat and ,years hundred two and years

20 וַיְחִי רְעוּ שְׁתַּיִם וּשְׁלֹשִׁים שָׁנָה[l] וַיּוֹלֶד אֶת־שְׂרוּג׃
.Serug begat and ,years thirty and two Reu lived And

21 וַיְחִי רְעוּ אַחֲרֵי הוֹלִידוֹ אֶת־שְׂרוּג שֶׁבַע שָׁנִים
years seven Serug begetting his after Reu lived And

22 וּמָאתַיִם שָׁנָה[m] וַיּוֹלֶד בָּנִים וּבָנוֹת׃ וַיְחִי
lived And .daughters and sons begat and ,years hundred two and

23 שְׂרוּג שְׁלֹשִׁים שָׁנָה[n] וַיּוֹלֶד אֶת־נָחוֹר׃ וַיְחִי שְׂרוּג
Serug lived And .Nahor begat and ,years thirty Serug

18 And Peleg
lived thirty
years, and begat
Reu: 19 And
Peleg lived after
he begat Reu
two hundred
and nine years,
and begat sons
and daughters.
20 And Reu
lived two and
thirty years, and
begat Serug:
21 And Reu
lived after he
begat Serug
two hundred
and seven years,
and begat sons
and daughters.
22 And Serug
lived thirty
years, and begat Nahor: 23
And Serug lived

lah: 13 and Ar-
pachshad lived
after he begat
Shelah four
hundred and
three years, and
begat sons and
daughters. 14
And Shelah
lived thirty
years, and begat Eber: 15 and
Shelah lived after he begat Eber four hundred
and three years,
and begat sons
and daughters.
16 And Eber
lived four and
thirty years, and
begat Peleg: 17
and Eber lived
after he begat
Peleg four hundred and thirty
years, and begat
sons and daughters.

18 And Peleg
lived thirty
years, and
begat Reu: 19
and Peleg lived
after he begat
Reu two hundred and nine
years, and begat sons and
daughters. 20
And Reu lived
two and thirty
years, and begat
Serug: 21 and
Reu lived after
he begat Serug
two hundred
and seven years,
and begat sons
and daughters.
22 And Serug
lived thirty
years, and begat
Nahor: 23 and
Serug lived after

a G. has, *Cainan*.

b G. has, *thirty*, שלשים.

c Sm., V. have, *three*, ושלש.

d G. adds, *and lived Cainan a hundred and thirty years and begat Sala. And lived Cainan after his begetting Sala three hundred and thirty years, and begat sons and daughters, and died.*

e Sm., G. add, *and a hundred* years, ומאת שנה.

f G. has, *thirty*, שלשים.

g Sm., G, have, *and three*, ושלש.

h Sm., G, add, *and a hundred.*

i Sm. has, *two hundred and seventy;* G. has, *three hundred and seventy.*

j Sm., G. *a hundred and thirty.*

k Sm. *a hundred and nine.*

l Sm., G. *a hundred and thirty two.*

m Sm. *a hundred and seven.*

n Sm., G. *a hundred and thirty.*

after he begat
Nahor two hun-
dred years, and
begat sons and
daughters. 24
And Nahor
lived nine and
twenty years,
and begat Te-
rah: 25 And
Nahor lived aft-
er he begat Te-
rah an hundred
and nineteen
years, and be-
gat sons and
daughters. 26
And Terah lived
seventy years,
and begat
Abram, Nahor,
and Haran.

אַחֲרֵי הוֹלִידוֹ אֶת־נָחוֹר מָאתַיִם שָׁנָה[a] וַיּוֹלֶד
begat and ,years hundred two Nahor begetting his after

24 בָּנִים וּבָנוֹת׃ וַיְחִי נָחוֹר תֵּשַׁע וְעֶשְׂרִים
twenty and nine Nahor lived And .daughters and sons

25 שָׁנָה[b] וַיּוֹלֶד אֶת־תָּרַח׃ וַיְחִי נָחוֹר אַחֲרֵי הוֹלִידוֹ
begetting his after Nahor lived And .Terah begat and ,years

אֶת־תֶּרַח תְּשַׁע־עֶשְׂרֵה שָׁנָה וּמְאַת שָׁנָה[c] וַיּוֹלֶד
begat and years hundred a and years nineteen Terah

בָּנִים וּבָנוֹת׃
.daughters and sons

26 וַיְחִי־תֶרַח שִׁבְעִים שָׁנָה וַיּוֹלֶד אֶת־אַבְרָם
,Abram begat and years seventy Terah lived And

27 אֶת־נָחוֹר וְאֶת־הָרָן׃ וְאֵלֶּה תּוֹלְדֹת
of generations the [are] these And .Haran and ,Nahor

תֶּרַח תֶּרַח הוֹלִיד אֶת־אַבְרָם אֶת־נָחוֹר וְאֶת־הָרָן
;Haran and ,Nahor ,Abram begat Terah .Terah

28 וְהָרָן הוֹלִיד אֶת־לוֹט׃ וַיָּמָת הָרָן עַל־פְּנֵי
of presence the in Haran died And .Lot begat Haran and

תֶּרַח אָבִיו בְּאֶרֶץ מוֹלַדְתּוֹ בְּאוּר[d] כַּשְׂדִּים׃
.Chaldees the of Ur in ,birth his of land the in father his Terah

29 וַיִּקַּח אַבְרָם וְנָחוֹר לָהֶם נָשִׁים שֵׁם
of name the ,wives themselves for Nahor and Abram took And

אֵשֶׁת־אַבְרָם שָׂרָי וְשֵׁם אֵשֶׁת־נָחוֹר
,Nahor of wife the of name the and ,Sarai [being] Abram of wife the

מִלְכָּה בַּת־הָרָן אֲבִי־מִלְכָּה וַאֲבִי
of father the and Milcha of father the ,Haran of daughter the ,Milcha

30 יִסְכָּה׃ וַתְּהִי שָׂרַי עֲקָרָה אֵין לָהּ וָלָד׃
.child a her to not was [there] ,barren Sarai was And .Iscah

31 וַיִּקַּח תֶּרַח אֶת־אַבְרָם בְּנוֹ וְאֶת־לוֹט בֶּן־הָרָן
Haran of son the Lot and ,son his Abram Terah took And

בֶּן־בְּנוֹ וְאֵת שָׂרַי כַּלָּתוֹ[e] אֵשֶׁת אַבְרָם
Abram of wife the daughter-in-law his Sarai and ,grandson his

27 Now these
are the genera-
tions of Terah:
Terah begat
Abram, Nahor,
and Haran; and
Haran begat
Lot. 28 And
Haran died be-
fore his father
Terah in the
land of his na-
tivity, in Ur of
the Chaldees. 29
And Abram and
Nahor took
them wives: the
name of A-
bram's wife *was*
Sarai; and the
name of Nahor's
wife, Milcha,
the daughter of
Haran, the fath-
er of Milcha,
and the father
of Iscah. 30 But
Sarai was bar-
ren; she *had* no
child. 31 And Te-
rah took Abram
his son, and
Lot the son of
Haran his son's
son, and Sarai
his daughter in
law, his son A-
bram's wife; and

he begat Nahor
two hundred
years, and begat
sons and daugh-
ters. 24 And
Nahor lived
nine and twenty
years, and begat
Terah: 25 and
Nahor lived aft-
er he begat Te-
rah an hundred
and nineteen
years, and be-
gat sons and
daughters. 26
And Terah lived
seventy years,
and begat A-
bram, Nahor,
and Haran.

27 Now these
are the genera-
tions of Terah.
Terah begat
Abram, Nahor,
and Haran; and
Haran begat
Lot. 28 And
Haran died in
the presence of
his father Terah
in the land of
his nativity, in
Ur of the Chal-
dees. 29 And
Abram and Na-
hor took them
wives: the name
of Abram's wife
was Sarai; and
the name of
Nahor's wife,
Milcha, the
daughter of Ha-
ran, the father
of Milcha, and
the father of
Iscah. 30 And
Sarai was bar-
ren; she had no
child. 31 And Te-
rah took Abram
his son, and
Lot the son of
Haran, his son's
son, and Sarai
his daughter in
law, his son
Abram's wife;

---

a Sm. *a hundred.*
b Sm., G. *seventy-nine.*
c Sm. *sixty-nine;* G. *a hundred and twenty-nine.*
d G. has, *in the land of*, בארץ.
e Sm. has, *and Milcah, his daughters-in-law,* ואת מלכה כלותיו.

they went forth
with them from
Ur of the Chal-
dees, to go into
the land of Ca-
naan; and they
came unto Ha-
ran, and dwelt
there. 32 And
the days of Te-
rah were two
hundred and
five years: and
Terah died in
Haran.

בְּנ֗וֹ[a] וַיֵּצְא֨וּ אִתָּ֜ם[b] מֵא֣וּר כַּשְׂדִּ֗ים
; son his | and they went out | with them | from Ur of | ,Chaldees the

לָלֶ֙כֶת֙ אַ֣רְצָה כְּנַ֔עַן וַיָּבֹ֥אוּ עַד־חָרָ֖ן
go to | of land the to | ;Canaan | came they and | Haran as far as

32 וַיֵּ֥שְׁבוּ שָֽׁם׃ וַיִּהְי֣וּ יְמֵי־תֶ֔רַח[c] חָמֵ֥שׁ שָׁנִ֖ים
settled and | .there | were And | Terah of days the | five | years

וּמָאתַ֣יִם שָׁנָ֑ה[d] וַיָּ֥מָת תֶּ֖רַח בְּחָרָֽן׃
hundred two and | ,years | died and | Terah | .Haran in

12

Now the
LORD had said
unto Abram, Get
thee out of thy
country, and
from thy
kindred, and
from thy father's
house, unto a
land that I will
shew thee: 2
And I will make
of thee a great
nation, and I
will bless thee,
and make thy
name great;
and thou shalt
be a blessing: 3
And I will bless
them that bless
thee, and curse
him that curseth
thee: and in thee
shall all families
of the earth be
blessed. 4 So
Abram depart-
ed, as the LORD
had spoken un-
to him; and Lot
went with him:
and Abram *was*
seventy and five
years old when
he departed out
of Haran. 5 And
Abram took
Sarai his wife,
and Lot his
brother's son,
and all their sub-
stance that they
had gathered,
and the souls

1 וַיֹּ֤אמֶר יְהוָה֙ אֶל־אַבְרָ֔ם לֶךְ־לְךָ֛ מֵאַרְצְךָ֥
said And | Jehovah | ; Abram unto | thyself for Go | land thy from

וּמִמּֽוֹלַדְתְּךָ֖ וּמִבֵּ֣ית אָבִ֑יךָ אֶל־הָאָ֖רֶץ
and from thy kindred | and from the house of | thy father | unto the land

2 אֲשֶׁ֥ר אַרְאֶֽךָּ׃ וְאֶֽעֶשְׂךָ֙ לְג֣וֹי גָּד֔וֹל
which | I shall show thee. | And I will make thee | (for) a nation[2] | great[1]

וַאֲבָרֶכְךָ֔ וַאֲגַדְּלָ֖ה שְׁמֶ֑ךָ וֶהְיֵ֖ה בְּרָכָֽה׃
and I will bless thee | and make great | thy name; | and be thou | a blessing.

3 וַאֲבָֽרְכָה֙ מְבָ֣רְכֶ֔יךָ וּמְקַלֶּלְךָ֖[e] אָאֹ֑ר
And I will bless | the blessers of thee, | and the despiser of thee | I will curse;

וְנִבְרְכ֣וּ בְךָ֔ כֹּ֖ל מִשְׁפְּחֹ֥ת הָאֲדָמָֽה׃[f]
and shall bless themselves | in thee | all | the families of | the ground.

4 וַיֵּ֣לֶךְ אַבְרָ֗ם כַּאֲשֶׁ֨ר דִּבֶּ֤ר אֵלָיו֙ יְהוָ֔ה וַיֵּ֥לֶךְ
And went | Abram | as | had spoken | unto him | Jehovah; | and went

אִתּ֖וֹ ל֑וֹט וְאַבְרָ֗ם בֶּן־חָמֵ֤שׁ שָׁנִים֙ וְשִׁבְעִ֣ים
with him | Lot, | (and) Abram | [being] (a son of) five | years | and seventy

5 שָׁנָ֔ה בְּצֵאת֖וֹ מֵחָרָֽן׃ וַיִּקַּ֣ח אַבְרָ֡ם
years | [old] in his going out | from Haran. | And took | Abram

אֶת־שָׂרַ֣י אִשְׁתּ֡וֹ וְאֶת־ל֣וֹט בֶּן־אָחִ֡יו וְאֶת־
Sarai | his wife, | and Lot | the son of his brother, | and

כָּל־רְכוּשָׁ֣ם אֲשֶׁ֣ר רָכָ֔שׁוּ וְאֶת־הַנֶּ֖פֶשׁ
all their movable property | which | they had acquired, | and the souls

Now the
LORD said unto
Abram, Get thee
out of thy coun-
try, and from
thy kindred, and
from thy father's
house, unto the
land that I will
shew thee: 2
and I will make
of thee a great
nation, and I
will bless thee,
and make thy
name great; and
be thou a bless-
ing: 3 and I will
bless them that
bless thee, and
him that curseth
thee will I curse:
and in thee shall
all the families
of the earth be
blessed. 4 So
Abram went, as
the LORD had
spoken unto
him; and Lot
went with him:
and Abram was
seventy and five
years old when
he departed out
of Haran. 5 And
Abram took
Sarai his wife,
and Lot his
brother's son,
and all their
substance that
they had gath-
ered, and the

---

a Sm. has, *and Nahor, his sons*, ונחור בניו.

b Sm., G., V. have, *and he brought them out*, וַיֹּצֵא אֹתָם; S. *and he went out with them*, וַיֵּצֵא אִתָּם.

c G. adds, *in Haran*.

d Sm. has, *a hundred and forty five*.

e Sm., G., S., V. have pl., מקלליך.

f G. adds, *and in thy seed*, ובזרעך.

that they had gotten in Haran; and they went forth to go into the land of Canaan; and into the land of Canaan they came.

אֲשֶׁר־עָשׂוּ בְחָרָן וַיֵּצְאוּ לָלֶכֶת
go to out went they and ; Haran in obtained had they whom

אַרְצָה כְּנַעַן וַיָּבֹאוּ אַרְצָה כְּנָעַן׃
.Canaan of land the to in came they and ,Canaan of land the to

souls that they had gotten in Haran; and they went forth to go into the land of Canaan; and into the land of Canaan they came.

6 And Abram passed through the land unto the place of Sichem, unto the plain of Moreh. And the Canaanite *was* then in the land. 7 And the LORD appeared unto Abram, and said, Unto thy seed will I give this land: and there builded he an altar unto the LORD, who appeared unto him. 8 And he removed from thence unto a mountain on the east of Beth-el, and pitched his tent, *having* Beth-el on the west, and Hai on the east: and there he builded an altar unto the LORD, and called upon the name of the LORD. 9 And Abram journeyed, going on still toward the south.

6 וַיַּעֲבֹר אַבְרָם בָּאָרֶץ[a] עַד מְקוֹם
of place the as far as land the in Abram through passed And

שְׁכֶם עַד אֵלוֹן מוֹרֶה[b] וְהַכְּנַעֲנִי
Canaanite the (and) ,Moreh of terebinth the as far as ,Shechem

7 אָז בָּאָרֶץ׃ וַיֵּרָא יְהוָֹה אֶל־אַבְרָם
,Abram unto Jehovah appeared And .land the in then [being]

וַיֹּאמֶר[c] לְזַרְעֲךָ אֶתֵּן אֶת־הָאָרֶץ הַזֹּאת וַיִּבֶן
built he and ; ¹this ²land give will I seed thy To :said and

8 שָׁם מִזְבֵּחַ לַיהוָֹה הַנִּרְאֶה אֵלָיו׃ וַיַּעְתֵּק
advanced he And .him unto appeared who Jehovah to altar an there

מִשָּׁם הָהָרָה מִקֶּדֶם לְבֵיתְאֵל וַיֵּט[d]
pitched and ; Bethel to east (from) mountain the to thence from

אָהֳלֹה בֵּיתְאֵל מִיָּם וְהָעַי מִקֶּדֶם
; east the on Ai and west the on [being] Bethel ,tent his

וַיִּבֶן־שָׁם מִזְבֵּחַ לַיהוָֹה וַיִּקְרָא בְּשֵׁם
of name the on called and ,Jehovah to altar an there built he and

9 יְהוָֹה׃ וַיִּסַּע אַבְרָם הָלוֹךְ וְנָסוֹעַ
journeying and going ,Abram journeyed And .Jehovah

הַנֶּגְבָּה׃
.land south the toward

6 And Abram passed through the land unto the place of Shechem, unto the oak of Moreh. And the Canaanite was then in the land. 7 And the LORD appeared unto Abram, and said, Unto thy seed will I give this land: and there builded he an altar unto the LORD, who appeared unto him. 8 And he removed from thence unto the mountain on the east of Beth-el, and pitched his tent, having Beth-el on the west, and Ai on the east: and there he builded an altar unto the LORD, and called upon the name of the LORD. 9 And Abram journeyed, going on still toward the South.

10 And there was a famine in the land: and Abram went down into Egypt to sojourn there; for the famine *was* grievous in the land. 11 And it came to pass, when he was come near to enter into Egypt, that he said unto Sarai his wife, Behold now, I know

10 וַיְהִי רָעָב בָּאָרֶץ וַיֵּרֶד אַבְרָם
Abram down went and ; land the in famine a was And

מִצְרַיְמָה לָגוּר שָׁם כִּי־כָבֵד הָרָעָב בָּאָרֶץ׃
.land the in famine the [was] severe for ,there sojourn to Egypt to

11 וַיְהִי כַּאֲשֶׁר הִקְרִיב לָבוֹא מִצְרָיְמָה
,Egypt to in come to near was he when pass to came it And

וַיֹּאמֶר אֶל־שָׂרַי אִשְׁתּוֹ הִנֵּה־נָא[e] יָדַעְתִּי כִּי
that know I ,now ,Behold :wife his Sarai unto said he (and)

10 And there was a famine in the land: and Abram went down into Egypt to sojourn there; for the famine was sore in the land. 11 And it came to pass, when he was come near to enter into Egypt, that he said unto Sarai his wife, Behold now, I know

---

a G. adds, *unto its length.*

b Sm. has, מורא; G. translates *lofty;* V. *illustrious;* S. has, *Mamre;* Sym. *Mambre.*

c Sm., G., S., V. add, *to him.*

d G., V. add, *there,* שם.

e G., V. omit, הנה נא.

that thou *art* a fair woman to look upon: 12 Therefore it shall come to pass, when the Egyptians shall see thee, that they shall say, This *is* his wife: and they will kill me, but they will save thee alive. 13 Say, I pray thee, thou *art* my sister: that it may be well with me for thy sake; and my soul shall live because of thee.

14 And it came to pass, that, when Abram was come into Egypt, the Egyptians beheld the woman that she *was* very fair. 15 The princes also of Pharaoh saw her, and commended her before Pharaoh: and the woman was taken into Pharaoh's house. 16 And he entreated Abram well for her sake: and he had sheep, and oxen, and he asses, and menservants, and maidservants, and she asses, and camels. 17 And the LORD plagued Pharaoh and his house with great plagues because of Sarai Abram's wife. 18 And Pharaoh called Abram, and said, What *is* this *that* thou hast done unto me? why didst thou not tell me that she *was* thy wife? 19 Why saidst thou, She *is* my sister? so I might have taken her to me

12 אִשָּׁה יְפַת־מַרְאֶה אָתְּ׃ וְהָיָה
,pass to come will it and ; thou [art] appearance of beautiful woman a

כִּי־יִרְאוּ אֹתָךְ הַמִּצְרִים וְאָמְרוּ אִשְׁתּוֹ זֹאת
; this [is] wife his ,say and ,Egyptians the thee see when

13 וְהָרְגוּ אֹתִי וְאֹתָךְ יְחַיּוּ׃ אִמְרִי־
,Say .alive leave will they thee and ,me kill will they (and)

נָא אֲחֹתִי אָתְּ לְמַעַן יִיטַב־לִי
me for prosperous be may it that order in ; thou [art] sister my ,now

בַעֲבוּרֵךְ וְחָיְתָה נַפְשִׁי בִּגְלָלֵךְ׃
.thee of because soul my live may and ,thee of account on

14 וַיְהִי כְּבוֹא אַבְרָם מִצְרָיְמָה וַיִּרְאוּ
saw that ,Egypt to Abram of coming the at ,pass to came it And

הַמִּצְרִים אֶת־הָאִשָּׁה כִּי־יָפָה הִוא מְאֹד׃
.exceedingly she [was] beautiful that woman the Egyptians the

15 וַיִּרְאוּ אֹתָהּ שָׂרֵי פַרְעֹה וַיְהַלְלוּ
commended they and ,Pharaoh of princes the her saw And

אֹתָהּ אֶל־פַּרְעֹה וַתֻּקַּח הָאִשָּׁה בֵּית
of house the to woman the taken was and ; Pharaoh unto her

16 פַּרְעֹה׃ וּלְאַבְרָם הֵיטִיב בַּעֲבוּרָהּ
; her of account on favor showed he Abram to And .Pharaoh

וַיְהִי־לוֹ צֹאן־וּבָקָר[a] וַחֲמֹרִים[b] וַעֲבָדִים
slaves male and ,asses and ,herds and flocks him to were and

17 וּשְׁפָחֹת וַאֲתֹנֹת וּגְמַלִּים׃ וַיְנַגַּע יְהוָה[c]
Jehovah struck And .camels and asses she and ,slaves female and

אֶת־פַּרְעֹה נְגָעִים גְּדֹלִים וְאֶת־בֵּיתוֹ עַל־דְּבַר
of account on ,house his and [1]great [2]strokes [with] Pharaoh

18 שָׂרַי אֵשֶׁת אַבְרָם׃ וַיִּקְרָא פַרְעֹה לְאַבְרָם
Abram to Pharaoh called And .Abram of wife the Sarai

וַיֹּאמֶר מַה־זֹּאת עָשִׂיתָ לִּי לָמָּה
why ? me to done hast thou this [is] What : said and

19 לֹא־הִגַּדְתָּ לִּי כִּי אִשְׁתְּךָ הִוא׃ לָמָה[d]
why ? she [was] wife thy that me to known made not thou hast

אָמַרְתְּ אֲחֹתִי הִוא וָאֶקַּח אֹתָהּ לִי
me to her took I so and ? she [is] sister my ,said thou hast

that thou art a fair woman to look upon: 12 and it shall come to pass, when the Egyptians shall see thee, that they shall say, This is his wife: and they will kill me, but they will save thee alive. 13 Say, I pray thee, thou art my sister: that it may be well with me for thy sake, and that my soul may live because of thee.

14 And it came to pass, that, when Abram was come into Egypt, the Egyptians beheld the woman that she was very fair. 15 And the princes of Pharaoh saw her, and praised her to Pharaoh: and the woman was taken into Pharaoh's house. 16 And he entreated Abram well for her sake: and he had sheep, and oxen, and he-asses, and menservants, and maidservants, and she-asses, and camels. 17 And the LORD plagued Pharaoh and his house with great plagues because of Sarai Abram's wife. 18 And Pharaoh called Abram, and said, What is this that thou hast done unto me? why didst thou not tell me that she was thy wife? 19 Why saidst thou, She is my sister? so that I took her to be

a Sm. adds, *an exceedingly valuable possession*, מקנה כבד מאד.

b Sm. puts after ושפחת.

c G. has, *God*, אלהים.

d Sm. and S. have, *and why*, ולמה.

to wife: now therefore behold thy wife, take *her*, and go thy way. 20 And Pharaoh commanded *his* men concerning him: and they sent him away, and his wife, and all that he had.

20 לְאִשָּׁה וְעַתָּה הִנֵּה אִשְׁתְּךָ קַח וָלֵךְ׃ וַיְצַו
commanded And .go and take ,wife thy behold now and wife a for

עָלָיו פַּרְעֹה אֲנָשִׁים וַיְשַׁלְּחוּ אֹתוֹ
him away sent they and ,men Pharaoh him concerning

וְאֶת־אִשְׁתּוֹ וְאֶת־כָּל־אֲשֶׁר־לוֹ[a]׃
.him to [was] which all and wife his and

my wife: now therefore behold thy wife, take her, and go thy way. 20 And Pharaoh gave men charge concerning him: and they brought him on the way, and his wife, and all that he had.

13

AND Abram went up out of Egypt, he, and his wife, and all that he had, and Lot with him, into the south. 2 And Abram *was* very rich in cattle, in silver, and in gold. 3 And he went on his journeys from the south even to Beth-el, unto the place where his tent had been at the beginning, between Beth-el and Hai; 4 Unto the place of the altar, which he had made there at the first: and there Abram called on the name of the LORD.

5 And Lot also, which went with Abram, had flocks, and herds, and tents. 6 And the land was not able to bear them, that they might dwell together: for their substance was great, so that they could not dwell together. 7 And there was a strife between the herdmen of Abram's cattle and the

1 וַיַּעַל אַבְרָם מִמִּצְרַיִם הוּא וְאִשְׁתּוֹ וְכָל־
all and wife his and he ,Egypt from Abram up went And

אֲשֶׁר־לוֹ וְלוֹט עִמּוֹ הַנֶּגְבָּה׃
; country south the to ,him with [being] Lot (and) ,him to [was] which

2 וְאַבְרָם כָּבֵד מְאֹד בַּמִּקְנֶה בַּכֶּסֶף וּבַזָּהָב׃
.gold in and silver in cattle in exceedingly rich [being] Abram (and)

3 וַיֵּלֶךְ לְמַסָּעָיו מִנֶּגֶב
country south the from stations his by went he And

וְעַד־בֵּית־אֵל עַד־הַמָּקוֹם אֲשֶׁר־הָיָה שָׁם
(there) been had where place the as far as ,Bethel as far as (and)

אָהֳלֹה בַּתְּחִלָּה בֵּין בֵּית־אֵל וּבֵין
(between) and Bethel between ,beginning the in tent his

4 הָעָי׃ אֶל־מְקוֹם הַמִּזְבֵּחַ אֲשֶׁר־עָשָׂה שָׁם
there made had he which altar the of place the unto ; Ai

בָּרִאשֹׁנָה וַיִּקְרָא שָׁם אַבְרָם בְּשֵׁם יְהוָֹה׃
.Jehovah of name the on Abram there called and ; first the at

5 וְגַם־לְלוֹט הַהֹלֵךְ אֶת־אַבְרָם הָיָה צֹאן
flocks were ,Abram with going one the ,Lot to also And

6 וּבָקָר וְאֹהָלִים׃ וְלֹא־נָשָׂא אֹתָם הָאָרֶץ
land the them bear not could And .tents and herds and

לָשֶׁבֶת יַחְדָּו כִּי־הָיָה רְכוּשָׁם רָב
,great property movable their become had for ; together dwell to

7 וְלֹא יָכְלוּ לָשֶׁבֶת יַחְדָּו׃ וַיְהִי־רִיב
strife be to came And .together dwell to able [2]were [1]they [3]not and

בֵּין רֹעֵי מִקְנֵה־אַבְרָם וּבֵין
(between) and Abram of cattle the of herdmen the between

AND Abram went up out of Egypt, he, and his wife, and all that he had, and Lot with him, into the South. 2 And Abram was very rich in cattle, in silver, and in gold. 3 And he went on his journeys from the South even to Beth-el, unto the place where his tent had been at the beginning, between Beth-el and Ai; 4 unto the place of the altar, which he had made there at the first: and there Abram called on the name of the LORD.

5 And Lot also, which went with Abram, had flocks, and herds, and tents. 6 And the land was not able to bear them, that they might dwell together: for their substance was great, so that they could not dwell together. 7 And there was a strife between the herdmen of Abram's cattle

---

a Sm. adds, *and Lot with him*, ולוט עמו.

herdmen of
Lot's cattle: and
the Canaanite
and the Perizzite
dwelled then in
the land. 8 And
Abram said unto
to Lot, Let
there be no
strife, I pray
thee, between
me and thee,
and between my
herdmen and
thy herdmen;
for we *be* breth-
ren. 9 *Is* not
the whole land
before thee?
separate thy-
self, I pray thee,
from me: if
thou wilt take
the left hand,
then I will go to
to the right; or
if *thou depart* to
the right hand,
then I will go to
the left. 10 And
Lot lifted up his
eyes, and beheld
all the plain of
Jordan, that it
was well water-
ed every where,
before the LORD
destroyed Sod-
om and Go-
morrah, *even* as
the garden of
the LORD, like
the land of
Egypt, as thou
comest unto
Zoar. 11 Then
Lot chose him
all the plain of
Jordan; and Lot
journeyed east:
and they separa-
ted themselves
the one from the
other. 12 Abram
dwelled in the
land of Canaan,
and Lot dwelled
in the cities of
the plain, and
pitched *his* tent
toward Sodom.
13 But the men
of Sodom *were*
wicked and sin-
ners before the
LORD exceed-
ingly.

14 And the
Lord said unto

רֹעֵי מִקְנֵה־לוֹט וְהַכְּנַעֲנִי
Canaanite the (and) ,Lot of cattle the of herdmen the

8 וְהַפְּרִזִּי אָז יֹשֵׁב בָּאָרֶץ׃ וַיֹּאמֶר אַבְרָם
Abram said And .land the in dwelling then Perizzite the and

אֶל־לוֹט אַל־נָא[a] תְהִי מְרִיבָה בֵּינִי
me between 4contention 5be 1let ,3pray ,2Not : Lot unto

וּבֵינֶךָ וּבֵין רֹעַי וּבֵין
(between) and herdmen my between and ,thee (between) and

9 רֹעֶיךָ כִּי־אֲנָשִׁים אַחִים אֲנָחְנוּ׃ הֲלֹא
not [Is] .we [are] brethren men for ; herdmen thy

כָל־הָאָרֶץ לְפָנֶיךָ הִפָּרֶד נָא[b] מֵעָלָי
; me (upon) from ,pray ,thyself separate ? thee before land the all

אִם־הַשְּׂמֹאל וְאֵימִנָה וְאִם־הַיָּמִין
,right the to if and ; right the to turn will I (and) ,left the to if

10 וְאַשְׂמְאִילָה׃ וַיִּשָּׂא־לוֹט אֶת־עֵינָיו וַיַּרְא
saw and eyes his Lot raised And .left the to turn will I (and)

אֶת־כָּל־כִּכַּר הַיַּרְדֵּן כִּי כֻלָּהּ מַשְׁקֶה
,place well-watered a [was] it of all that ,Jordan the of circuit the all

לִפְנֵי שַׁחֵת יְהוָה אֶת־סְדֹם וְאֶת־עֲמֹרָה
;Gomorrah and Sodom 1Jehovah's 2destroying before

כְּגַן־יְהוָה כְּאֶרֶץ מִצְרַיִם בֹּאֲכָה
going art thou [as] ,Egypt of land the like ,Jehovah of garden the like

11 צֹעַר׃ וַיִּבְחַר־לוֹ לוֹט אֵת כָּל־כִּכַּר הַיַּרְדֵּן
; Jordan the of circuit the all Lot himself for chose And .Zoar to

וַיִּסַּע לוֹט מִקֶּדֶם וַיִּפָּרְדוּ
,themselves separated they and ; eastward (from) Lot departed and

12 אִישׁ מֵעַל אָחִיו׃ אַבְרָם יָשַׁב בְּאֶרֶץ־
of land the in settled Abram .brother his (upon) from one each

כְּנָעַן וְלוֹט יָשַׁב בְּעָרֵי הַכִּכָּר
,circuit the of cities the in settled Lot and ; Canaan

13 וַיֶּאֱהַל עַד־סְדֹם׃ וְאַנְשֵׁי סְדֹם
Sodom of men the (and) ; Sodom as far as tents in journeyed and

14 רָעִים וְחַטָּאִים לַיהוָה מְאֹד׃ וַיהוָה[c]
Jehovah And .exceedingly Jehovah against sinners and wicked[being]

and the herdmen
of Lot's cattle:
and the Canaan-
ite and the Periz-
zite dwelled
then in the
land. 8 And Ab-
ram said unto
Lot, Let there be
no strife, I pray
thee, between
me and thee,
and between my
herdmen and
thy herdmen;
for we are breth-
ren. 9 Is not
the whole land
before thee?
separate thyself,
I pray thee,
from me: if
thou wilt take
the left hand,
then I will go to
the right; or if
thou take the
right hand, then
I will go to the
left. 10 And Lot
lifted up his
eyes, and beheld
all the Plain of
Jordan, that it
was well water-
ed every where,
before the LORD
destroyed Sod-
om and Go-
morrah, like the
garden of the
LORD, like the
land of Egypt,
as thou goest
unto Zoar. 11 So
Lot chose him
all the Plain of
Jordan; and Lot
journeyed east:
and they sepa-
rated themselves
the one from the
other. 12 A-
bram dwelled in
the land of Ca-
naan, and Lot
dwelled in the
cities of the
Plain, and
moved his tent
as far as Sodom.
13 Now the men
of Sodom were
wicked and sin-
ners against the
LORD exceed-
ingly.

14 And the
LORD said unto

a G., S. omit נא.
b G. omits.
c G. has, *and God*, ואלהים.

Abram, after
that Lot was
separated from
him, Lift up
now thine eyes,
and look from
the place where
thou art north-
ward, and south-
ward, and east-
ward, and west-
ward: 15 For all
the land which
thou seest, to
thee will I
give it, and to
thy seed for ever.
16 And I will
make thy seed
as the dust of the
earth: so that if
a man can num-
ber the dust of
the earth, *then*
shall thy seed
also be number-
ed. 17 Arise,
walk through
the land in the
length of it and
in the breadth
of it; for I will
give it unto thee.
18 Then Abram
removed *his*
tent, and came
and dwelt in the
plain of Mamre,
which *is* in He-
bron, and built
there an altar
unto the LORD.

אָמַר אֶל־אַבְרָם אַחֲרֵי הִפָּרֶד־לוֹט מֵעִמּוֹ
:him with from himself separating Lot's after Abram unto said

שָׂא נָא עֵינֶיךָ וּרְאֵה מִן־הַמָּקוֹם אֲשֶׁר־אַתָּה
[art] thou where place the from ,look and eyes thine ,now ,Raise

שָׁם צָפֹנָה וָנֶגְבָּה וָקֵדְמָה וָיָמָּה׃
.west the to and ,east the to and ,south the to and ,north the to ,(there)

15 כִּי אֶת־כָּל־הָאָרֶץ אֲשֶׁר־אַתָּה רֹאֶה לְךָ
thee to ,seeing [art] thou which land the all For

16 אֶתְּנֶנָּה וּלְזַרְעֲךָ עַד־עוֹלָם׃ וְשַׂמְתִּי
make will I And .ever for seed thy to and ,it give will I

אֶת־זַרְעֲךָ כַּעֲפַר הָאָרֶץ אֲשֶׁר אִם־יוּכַל אִישׁ
one any able is if that so ;earth the of dust the like seed thy

לִמְנוֹת אֶת־עֲפַר הָאָרֶץ גַּם זַרְעֲךָ יִמָּנֶה׃
.numbered be may seed thy also ,earth the of dust the number to

17 קוּם הִתְהַלֵּךְ בָּאָרֶץ לְאָרְכָּהּ וּלְרָחְבָּהּ
;breadth its to and length its to ,land the in about walk ,Rise

18 כִּי לְךָ אֶתְּנֶנָּה׃ וַיֶּאֱהַל[a] אַבְרָם וַיָּבֹא
,in came and ,Abram tent his moved And .it give will I thee to for

וַיֵּשֶׁב בְּאֵלֹנֵי מַמְרֵא[b] אֲשֶׁר בְּחֶבְרוֹן
;Hebron in [were] which Mamre of terebinths the by settled and

וַיִּבֶן־שָׁם מִזְבֵּחַ לַיהוָה׃
.Jehovah to altar an there built he and

Abram, after
that Lot was
separated from
him, Lift up
now thine eyes,
and look from
the place where
thou art, north-
ward and south-
ward and east-
ward and west-
ward: 15 for all
the land which
thou seest, to
thee will I give
it, and to thy
seed for ever. 16
And I will make
thy seed as the
dust of the earth:
so that if a man
can number the
dust of the earth,
then shall thy
seed also be
numbered. 17
Arise, walk
through the land
in the length of
it and in the
breadth of it;
for unto thee
will I give it. 18
And Abram
moved his tent,
and came and
dwelt by the
oaks of Mamre,
which are in
Hebron, and
built there an
altar unto the
LORD.

14

AND it came
to pass in the
days of Am-
raphel king of
Shinar, Arioch
king of Ellasar,
Chedorlaomer
king of Elam,
and Tidal king
of nations; 2
That these made
war with Bera
king of Sodom,
and with Birsha
king of Gomor-
rah, Shinab king

1 וַיְהִי בִּימֵי אַמְרָפֶל מֶלֶךְ־שִׁנְעָר
,Shinar of king Amraphel of days the in pass to came it And

אַרְיוֹךְ[c] מֶלֶךְ אֶלָּסָר כְּדָרְלָעֹמֶר[d] מֶלֶךְ עֵילָם
Elam of king Chedorlaomer ,Ellasar of king Arioch

2 וְתִדְעָל מֶלֶךְ גּוֹיִם׃ עָשׂוּ מִלְחָמָה אֶת־בֶּרַע
Bera with war made they ;Goiim of king Tidal and

מֶלֶךְ סְדֹם וְאֶת־בִּרְשַׁע מֶלֶךְ עֲמֹרָה שִׁנְאָב[e]
Shinab ,Gomorrah of king Birsha with and Sodom of king

AND it came
to pass in the
days of Am-
raphel king of
Shinar, Arioch
king of Ellasar,
Chedorlaomer,
king of Elam,
and Tidal king
of Goiim, 2 that
they made war
with Bera king
of Sodom, and
with Birsha
king of Gomor-
rah, Shinab

---

a Sm. *and he went*, וילך; so S.

b S. adds, *the Amorite.*

c Sm., S., V. have, *and Arioch*, ואריוך.

d G., S., V. have, *and Chedorlaomer*, וכדרלעמר.

e Sm., G., S., V. have, *and Shinab*, ושנאב.

of Admah, and
Shemeber king
of Zeboiim, and
the king of Bela,
which is Zoar. 3
All these were
joined together
in the vale of
Siddim, which is
the salt sea. 4
Twelve years
they served
Chedorlaomer,
and in the thir-
teenth year they
rebelled. 5 And
in the fourteenth
year came Che-
dorlaomer, and
the kings that
were with him,
and smote the
Rephaims in
Ashteroth Kar-
naim, and the
Zuzims in Ham,
and the Emims
in Shaveh Kiri-
athaim, 6 And
the Horites in
their mount
Seir, unto El-
paran, which *is*
by the wilder-
ness. 7 And they
returned, and
came to En-
mishpat, which
is Kadesh, and
smote all the
country of the
Amalekites, and
also the Amor-
ites, that dwelt
in Hazezon-
tamar.

8 And there
went out the
king of Sod-
om, and the
king of Gomor-
rah, and the
king of Admah,
and the king of
Zeboiim, and
the king of Bela,
(the same *is*
Zoar;) and they
joined battle
with them in the
vale of Siddim;
9 With Che-
dorlaomer the

מֶלֶךְ אַדְמָה וְשֶׁמְאֵבֶר מֶלֶךְ צְבֹיִים וּמֶלֶךְ
of king the and ,Zeboiim of king Shemeber and ,Admah of king

3 בֶּלַע הִיא־צֹעַר׃ כָּל־אֵלֶּה חָבְרוּ אֶל־עֵמֶק
of valley the unto allied came these All .Zoar [being] it ,Bela

4 הַשִּׂדִּים הוּא יָם הַמֶּלַח׃ שְׁתֵּים עֶשְׂרֵה
ten [and] Two .salt of sea the [being] it ,Siddim

שָׁנָה עָבְדוּ אֶת־כְּדָרְלָעֹמֶר וּשְׁלֹשׁ־עֶשְׂרֵה
thirteenth the [in] and ,Chedorlaomer served had they years

5 שָׁנָה מָרָדוּ׃ וּבְאַרְבַּע עֶשְׂרֵה שָׁנָה בָּא
in came year tenth [and] fourth the in And .rebelled they year

כְדָרְלָעֹמֶר וְהַמְּלָכִים אֲשֶׁר אִתּוֹ וַיַּכּוּ
smote they and ; him with [were] who kings the and ,Chedorlaomer

אֶת־רְפָאִים בְּעַשְׁתְּרֹת קַרְנַיִם וְאֶת־הַזּוּזִים[a] בְּהָם[b]
Ham in Zuzim the and Karnaim Ashteroth in Rephaim the

6 וְאֵת הָאֵימִים[c] בְּשָׁוֵה קִרְיָתָיִם[d]׃ וְאֶת־הַחֹרִי
Horites the and ; Kiriathaim of plain the in Emim the and

בְּהַרְרָם[e] שֵׂעִיר[e] עַד אֵיל פָּארָן אֲשֶׁר עַל־
by [is] which ,Paran El as far as ,Seir mountain their in

7 הַמִּדְבָּר׃ וַיָּשֻׁבוּ וַיָּבֹאוּ אֶל־עֵין מִשְׁפָּט
,Mishpat En unto came and turned they And .wilderness the

הִוא קָדֵשׁ[f] וַיַּכּוּ אֶת־כָּל־שְׂדֵה הָעֲמָלֵקִי
,Amalekites the of field the all smote and ,Kadesh [being] it

וְגַם אֶת־הָאֱמֹרִי הַיֹּשֵׁב בְּחַצְצֹן תָּמָר[g]׃
.Tamar Hazazon in dwelling those ,Amorites the also and

8 וַיֵּצֵא מֶלֶךְ־סְדֹם וּמֶלֶךְ עֲמֹרָה
,Gomorrah of king the and Sodom of king the out went And

וּמֶלֶךְ אַדְמָה וּמֶלֶךְ צְבֹיִים וּמֶלֶךְ
of king the and ,Zeboiim of king the and ,Admah of king the and

בֶּלַע הִוא־צֹעַר וַיַּעַרְכוּ אִתָּם
them against order in set they and ;Zoar [being] it ,Bela

9 מִלְחָמָה בְּעֵמֶק הַשִּׂדִּים׃ אֵת כְּדָרְלָעֹמֶר
Chedorlaomer with ; Siddim of valley the in battle

king of Admah,
and Shemeber
king of Zeboiim,
and the king of
Bela (the same
is Zoar). 3 All
these joined to-
gether in the
vale of Siddim
(the same is the
Salt Sea). 4
Twelve years
they served
Chedorlaomer,
and in the thir-
teenth year they
rebelled. 5 And
in the fourteenth
year came Che-
dorlaomer, and
the kings that
were with him,
and smote the
Rephaim in
Ashteroth-kar-
naim, and the
Zuzim in Ham,
and the Emim
in Shaveh-kiri-
athaim, 6 and
the Horites in
their mount
Seir, unto El-
paran, which is
by the wilder-
ness. 7 And they
returned, and
came to En-
mishpat (the
same *is* Ka-
desh), and smote
all the country
of the Amalek-
ites, and also
the Amorites,
that dwelt in
Hazazon-tamar.

8 And there
went out the
king of Sodom,
and the king of
Gomorrah, and
the king of Ad-
mah, and the
king of Zeboiim,
and the king of
Bela (the same
is Zoar); and
they set the
battle in array
against them in
the vale of Sid-
dim; 9 against
Chedorlaomer

---

a G. renders, *strong nations;* S., T. *the strong.*

b G., S., V. have, *with them,* בָּהֶם; T. *who were in Hemta.*

c G. has, *the Somaeans;* T. *the strong.*

d G. renders, *the city.*

e Sm., G., S., V. have, *in the mountains of Seir,* בהררי שעיר; T. *in the mountain of Seir.*

f S., T. have, *Rekam.*

g For *Hazazon Tamar*, S., T. have *Engedi.*

king of Elam, and with Tidal king of nations, and Amraphel king of Shinar, and Arioch king of Ellasar; four kings with five. 10 And the vale of Siddim *was full of* slimepits; and the kings of Sodom and Gomorrah fled, and fell there; and they that remained fled to the mountain. 11 And they took all the goods of Sodom and Gomorrah, and all their victuals, and went their way. 12 And they took Lot, Abram's brother's son, who dwelt in Sodom, and his goods, and departed.

מֶלֶךְ עֵילָם וְתִדְעָל מֶלֶךְ גּוֹיִם וְאַמְרָפֶל
Amraphel and ,Goiim of king Tidal and ,Elam of king

מֶלֶךְ שִׁנְעָר וְאַרְיוֹךְ מֶלֶךְ אֶלָּסָר אַרְבָּעָה
four ,Ellasar of king Arioch and Shinar of king

10 מְלָכִים אֶת־הַחֲמִשָּׁה׃ וְעֵמֶק הַשִּׂדִּים
[being] Siddim of valley the (And) .five against kings

בֶּאֱרֹת בֶּאֱרֹת חֵמָר וַיָּנֻסוּ מֶלֶךְ־סְדֹם
Sodom of king the fled (and) ,bitumen of springs ,springs

וַעֲמֹרָה[a] וַיִּפְּלוּ־שָׁמָּה וְהַנִּשְׁאָרִים
left ones the and ; there fell they and Gomorrah [of king the] and

11 הֶרָה נָּסוּ׃ וַיִּקְחוּ אֶת־כָּל־רְכֻשׁ[b]
of property movable the all took they And .fled mountain the to

סְדֹם וַעֲמֹרָה וְאֶת־כָּל־אָכְלָם וַיֵּלֵכוּ׃
.departed and ,provisions their all and Gomorrah and Sodom

12 וַיִּקְחוּ אֶת־לוֹט וְאֶת־רְכֻשׁוֹ בֶּן־אֲחִי
of brother the of son the, property movable his and Lot took they And

13 אַבְרָם וַיֵּלֵכוּ וְהוּא יֹשֵׁב בִּסְדֹם וַיָּבֹא
came And .Sodom in dwelling he (and) ,departed and ,Abram

13 And there came one that had escaped, and told Abram the Hebrew; for he dwelt in the plain of Mamre the Amorite, brother of Eshcol, and brother of Aner: and these *were* confederate with Abram. 14 And when Abram heard that his brother was taken captive, he armed his trained *servants*, born in his own house, three hundred and eighteen, and pursued *them* unto Dan. 15 And he divided himself against them, he and his servants, by night, and smote them,

הַפָּלִיט וַיַּגֵּד לְאַבְרָם הָעִבְרִי
; Hebrew the Abram to known made and fugitive the

וְהוּא שֹׁכֵן בְּאֵלֹנֵי מַמְרֵא
Mamre of terebinths the at dwelling [was] he [while] (and)

הָאֱמֹרִי אֲחִי אֶשְׁכֹּל וַאֲחִי עָנֵר
,Aner of brother and Eshcol of brother the ,Amorite the

14 וְהֵם בַּעֲלֵי בְרִית־אַבְרָם׃ וַיִּשְׁמַע
heard And .Abram of covenant the of possessors [being] they (and)

אַבְרָם כִּי נִשְׁבָּה אָחִיו[c] וַיָּרֶק
forth led he and ; brother his captured been had that Abram

אֶת־חֲנִיכָיו יְלִידֵי בֵיתוֹ שְׁמֹנָה עָשָׂר וּשְׁלֹשׁ
three and ten [and] eight ,house his of children ,men tried his

15 מֵאוֹת וַיִּרְדֹּף עַד־דָּן׃ וַיֵּחָלֵק
himself divided he And .Dan as far as pursued he and ,hundred

עֲלֵיהֶם לַיְלָה הוּא וַעֲבָדָיו וַיַּכֵּם
,them smote he and ; slaves his and he ,night at them against

king of Elam, and Tidal king of Goiim, and Amraphel king of Shinar, and Arioch king of Ellasar; four kings against the five. 10 Now the vale of Siddim was full of slime pits; and the kings of Sodom and Gomorrah fled, and they fell there, and they that remained fled to the mountain. 11 And they took all the goods of Sodom and Gomorrah, and all their victuals, and went their way. 12 And they took Lot, Abram's brother's son, who dwelt in Sodom, and his goods, and departed.

13 And there came one that had escaped, and told Abram the Hebrew: now he dwelt by the oaks of Mamre the Amorite, brother of Eshcol, and brother of Aner; and these were confederate with Abram. 14 And when Abram heard that his brother was taken captive, he led forth his trained men, born in his house, three hundred and eighteen, and pursued as far as Dan. 15 And he divided himself against them by night, he and his servants, and smote

a G., S., Sm. have, *and the king of Gomorrah,* ומלך עמרה.

b For רכש, G. has *horse,* סוס; so also in vss. 16 and 21.

c G., V. add, *Lot,* לוט; S. has, *son of his brother.*

and pursued
them unto
Hobah, which *is*
on the left hand
of Damascus. 16
And he brought
back all the
goods, and also
brought again
his brother Lot,
and his goods,
and the women
also, and the
people.

17 And the king
of Sodom went
out to meet him
after his return
from the slaugh-
ter of Chedorla-
omer, and of the
kings that *were*
with him, at the
valley of Sha-
veh, which *is*
the king's dale.
18 And Melchi-
zedek king of
Salem brought
forth bread and
wine: and he
was the priest of
the most high
God. 19 And he
blessed him, and
said, Blessed be
Abram of the
most high God,
possessor of
heaven and
earth: 20 And
blessed be the
most high God,
which hath de-
livered thine
enemies into thy
hand. And he
gave him tithes
of all. 21 And
the king of Sod-
om said unto
Abram, Give me
the persons, and
take the goods
to thyself. 22
And Abram said
to the king of
Sodom, I have
lift up mine
hand unto the
LORD, the most
high God, the
possessor of
heaven and
earth, 23 That
I will not *take*
from a thread
even to a shoe-
latchet, and that

וַיִּרְדְּפֵם עַד־חוֹבָה אֲשֶׁר מִשְּׂמֹאל
left the from is which ,Hobah as far as them pursued and

16 לְדַמָּשֶׂק׃ וַיָּשֶׁב אֵת כָּל־הָרְכֻשׁ[a] וְגַם
also and ; property movable the all back brought he And .Damascus to

אֶת־לוֹט אָחִיו[b] וּרְכֻשׁוֹ הֵשִׁיב
; back brought he property movable his and brother his Lot

17 וְגַם אֶת־הַנָּשִׁים וְאֶת־הָעָם׃ וַיֵּצֵא מֶלֶךְ־
of king the out went And .people the and women the also and

סְדֹם לִקְרָאתוֹ אַחֲרֵי שׁוּבוֹ מֵהַכּוֹת
smiting from about turning his after ,him meet to Sodom

אֶת־כְּדָרְלָעֹמֶר וְאֶת־הַמְּלָכִים אֲשֶׁר אִתּוֹ
,him with [were] which kings the and Chedorlaomer

אֶל־עֵמֶק שָׁוֵה הוּא עֵמֶק הַמֶּלֶךְ׃
.king the of valley the [being] it ,Shaveh of valley the unto

18 וּמַלְכִּי־צֶדֶק מֶלֶךְ שָׁלֵם הוֹצִיא לֶחֶם וָיָיִן
,wine and bread out brought Salem of king Melchizedek and

19 וְהוּא כֹהֵן לְאֵל עֶלְיוֹן׃ וַיְבָרְכֵהוּ[c]
him blessed he And .High Most God to priest a [being] he [and]

וַיֹּאמַר בָּרוּךְ אַבְרָם לְאֵל עֶלְיוֹן קֹנֵה
of possessor ,High Most God by Abram [be] Blessed : said and

20 שָׁמַיִם וָאָרֶץ׃ וּבָרוּךְ אֵל עֶלְיוֹן אֲשֶׁר־
who High Most God [be] blessed and ;earth and heavens

מִגֵּן צָרֶיךָ בְּיָדֶךָ וַיִּתֶּן־לוֹ
him to gave he and ; hand thy into oppressors thine over given has

21 מַעֲשֵׂר מִכֹּל׃ וַיֹּאמֶר מֶלֶךְ־סְדֹם אֶל־אַבְרָם
; Abram unto Sodom of king the said And .all from tithe a

תֶּן־לִי הַנֶּפֶשׁ וְהָרְכֻשׁ קַח־לָךְ׃
.thyself for take property movable the and ,souls the me to Give

22 וַיֹּאמֶר אַבְרָם אֶל־מֶלֶךְ סְדֹם הֲרִמֹתִי יָדִי
hand my up lift I ; Sodom of king the unto Abram said And

אֶל־יְהוָה[d] אֵל עֶלְיוֹן קֹנֵה שָׁמַיִם וָאָרֶץ׃
; earth and heavens of possessor ,High Most God ,Jehovah unto

23 אִם־מִחוּט וְעַד־שְׂרוֹךְ נַעַל וְאִם־
[not] (if and) ,sandal a of latchet a unto and thread a from [not] (if)

them, and pur-
sued them unto
Hobah, which is
on the left hand
of Damascus. 16
And he brought
back all the
goods, and also
brought again
his brother Lot,
and his goods,
and the women
also, and the
people.

17 And the
king of Sodom
went out to
meet him, after
his return from
the slaughter of
Chedorlaomer
and the kings
that were with
him, at the vale
of Shaveh (the
same is the
King's Vale).
18 And Melchiz-
edek king of
Salem brought
forth bread and
wine: and he
was priest of
God Most High.
19 And he bless-
ed him, and
said, Blessed be
Abram of God
Most High, pos-
sessor of heav-
en and earth: 20
and blessed be
God Most High,
which hath de-
livered thine
enemies into
thy hand. And
he gave him a
tenth of all. 21
And the king of
Sodom said un-
to Abram, Give
me the persons,
and take the
goods to thyself.
22 And Abram
said to the king
of Sodom, I
have lift up
mine hand unto
the LORD, God
Most High, pos-
sessor of heaven
and earth, 23
that I will not
take a thread
nor a shoelatchet
nor aught that

---

a G. adds, *of the Sodomites*, סדם.
b S., T. have, *son of his brother*.
c G. has, *and he blessed Abram*.
d For יהוה, Sm. has *God*, האלהים; G., S. omit.

I will not take any thing that *is* thine, lest thou shouldest say, I have made A-
bram rich: 24
Save only that which the young men have eaten, and the portion of the men which went with me, Aner, Eshcol, and Mamre; let them take their portion.

אֶקַּח מִכָּל־אֲשֶׁר־לָךְ וְלֹא תֹאמַר
; say ²mayest ¹thou ³not that ; thee to [is] which all from take I will

אֲנִי הֶעֱשַׁרְתִּי אֶת־אַבְרָם׃ בִּלְעָדַי רַק 24
only ,me for Nothing .Abram enriched have I

אֲשֶׁר אָכְלוּ הַנְּעָרִים וְחֵלֶק הָאֲנָשִׁים
men the of portion the and ,men young the eaten have what

אֲשֶׁר הָלְכוּ אִתִּי עָנֵר אֶשְׁכֹּל וּמַמְרֵא הֵם
they Mamre and Eshcol Aner ; me with went who

יִקְחוּ חֶלְקָם׃
.portion their take may

15

1 אַחַר הַדְּבָרִים הָאֵלֶּה הָיָה דְבַר־יְהֹוָה אֶל־
unto Jehovah of word the was ¹these ²things After

אַבְרָם בַּמַּחֲזֶה לֵאמֹר[a] אַל־תִּירָא אַבְרָם אָנֹכִי
I ; Abram ,fear not Do :saying vision in Abram

2 מָגֵן לָךְ שְׂכָרְךָ הַרְבֵּה מְאֹד׃ וַיֹּאמֶר
said And .exceedingly great is reward thy ,thee to shield a [am]

אַבְרָם אֲדֹנָי יֱהֹוִה מַה־תִּתֶּן־לִי וְאָנֹכִי
I [while] (and) ,me to give thou canst what ,Jehovah Lord O : Abram

הוֹלֵךְ עֲרִירִי וּבֶן־מֶשֶׁק בֵּיתִי
house my of possession of son the and ,childless departing [am]

3 הוּא דַּמֶּשֶׂק אֱלִיעֶזֶר׃ וַיֹּאמֶר אַבְרָם הֵן לִי
me to ,Behold : Abram said And .Eliezer ,Damascus is

לֹא נָתַתָּה זָרַע וְהִנֵּה בֶן־בֵּיתִי
house my of son the behold and ; seed given ²hast ¹thou ³not

4 יוֹרֵשׁ אֹתִי׃ וְהִנֵּה דְבַר־יְהֹוָה
Jehovah of word the ,behold And .me from inherit to about [is]

אֵלָיו לֵאמֹר לֹא יִירָשְׁךָ זֶה כִּי־אִם[b]
but ,one this thee from inherit shall Not ; saying him unto

אֲשֶׁר יֵצֵא מִמֵּעֶיךָ[c] הוּא יִירָשֶׁךָ׃
.thee from inherit shall he ,body thy from out go will who he

5 וַיּוֹצֵא אֹתוֹ הַחוּצָה וַיֹּאמֶר[d] הַבֶּט־נָא
,now, Look : said and ,outside him forth brought he And

AFTER these things the word of the LORD came unto A-
bram in a vision, saying, Fear not, Abram: I *am* thy shield, *and* thy exceeding great re-
ward. 2 And Abram said, Lord GOD, what wilt thou give me, seeing I go childless, and the steward of my house *is* this Eliezer of Damascus? 3
And Abram said, Behold, to me thou hast given no seed: and, lo, one born in my house is mine heir. 4 And, be-
hold, the word of the LORD *came* unto him, saying, This shall not be thine heir; but he that shall come forth out of thine own bowels shall be thine heir. 5
And he brought him forth a-
broad, and said, Look now to-

is thine, lest thou shouldest say, I have made Abram rich: 24
save only that which the young men have eaten, and the portion of the men which went with me; Aner, Eshcol, and Mamre, let them take their portion.

AFTER these things the word of the LORD came unto A-
bram in a vision, saying, Fear not, Abram: I am thy shield, *and* thy exceeding great re-
ward. 2 And A-
bram said, O Lord GOD, what wilt thou give me, seeing I go childless, and he that shall be possessor of my house is Dammesek E-
liezer? 3 And Abram said, Be-
hold, to me thou hast given no seed: and, lo, one born in my house is mine heir. 4 And, behold, the word of the LORD came unto him, saying, This man shall not be thine heir; but he that shall come forth out of thine own bowels shall be thine heir. 5
And he brought him forth a-
broad, and said, Look now to-

---

a S. adds, *to him.*
b S. adds, *thy son.*
c G. *from thee,* מִמְּךָ
d G., S., V. add, *to him.*

ward heaven, and tell the stars, if thou be able to number them: and he said unto him, So shall thy seed be. 6 And he believed in the LORD; and he counted it to him for righteousness. 7 And he said unto him, I *am* the LORD that brought thee out of Ur of the Chaldees, to give thee this land to inherit it. 8 And he said, Lord God, whereby shall I know that I shall inherit it? 9 And he said unto him, Take me an heifer of three years old, and a she goat of three years old, and a ram of three years old, and a turtledove, and a young pigeon.

10 And he took unto him all these, and divided them in the midst, and laid each piece one against another: but the birds divided he not. 11 And when the fowls came down upon the carcases, Abram drove them away. 12 And when the sun was going down, a deep sleep fell upon Abram; and, lo, an horror of great darkness fell upon him. 13 And he said unto Abram, Know of a surety that thy seed

הַשָּׁמַיְמָה וּסְפֹר הַכּוֹכָבִים אִם־תּוּכַל לִסְפֹּר
count to able art thou if ,stars the count and ,heavens the towards

אֹתָם וַיֹּאמֶר לוֹ[a] כֹּה יִהְיֶה זַרְעֶךָ׃
.seed thy become shall Thus :him to said he and ;them

6 וְהֶאֱמִן[b] בַּיהוָה וַיַּחְשְׁבֶהָ לּוֹ
him for it considered he and ,Jehovah in trusted he And

7 צְדָקָה׃ וַיֹּאמֶר אֵלָיו אֲנִי יְהוָה אֲשֶׁר
who ,Jehovah [am] I ;him unto said he And .righteousness

הוֹצֵאתִיךָ מֵאוּר כַּשְׂדִּים לָתֶת לְךָ
thee to give to ,Chaldees the of Ur from out thee brought

8 אֶת־הָאָרֶץ הַזֹּאת לְרִשְׁתָּהּ׃ וַיֹּאמַר
;said he And .it of possession take to [1]this [2]land

אֲדֹנָי יֱהוִה בַּמָּה אֵדַע כִּי אִירָשֶׁנָּה׃
? it of possession take shall I that know I may what by ,Jehovah Lord O

9 וַיֹּאמֶר אֵלָיו[c] קְחָה לִי עֶגְלָה מְשֻׁלֶּשֶׁת
,old years three heifer a me for Take :him unto said he And

וְעֵז מְשֻׁלֶּשֶׁת וְאַיִל מְשֻׁלָּשׁ
,old years three ram a and ,old years three goat she a and

10 וְתֹר וְגוֹזָל׃ וַיִּקַּח־לוֹ אֶת־
him for took he And .pigeon young a and ,dove turtle a and

כָּל־אֵלֶּה וַיְבַתֵּר אֹתָם בַּתָּוֶךְ וַיִּתֵּן אִישׁ־
,each put he and ;midst the in them cleft he and ,these all

בִּתְרוֹ לִקְרַאת רֵעֵהוּ וְאֶת־הַצִּפֹּר לֹא בָתָר׃
.cleave [2]did [1]he [3]not birds the but ;neighbor its meet to piece its

11 וַיֵּרֶד הָעַיִט עַל־הַפְּגָרִים[d] וַיַּשֵּׁב[e]
away scared and carcases the upon prey of birds the down came And

12 אֹתָם[e] אַבְרָם׃ וַיְהִי הַשֶּׁמֶשׁ לָבוֹא
,down go to about [being] sun the ,pass to came it And .Abram them

וְתַרְדֵּמָה נָפְלָה עַל־אַבְרָם וְהִנֵּה אֵימָה
,terror behold and ;Abram upon fell sleep deep (and)

13 חֲשֵׁכָה גְדֹלָה[f] נֹפֶלֶת עָלָיו׃ וַיֹּאמֶר לְאַבְרָם
;Abram to said he And .him upon falling [1],great [2]darkness

יָדֹעַ תֵּדַע כִּי־גֵר יִהְיֶה זַרְעֲךָ
seed thy become will sojourner a that know shalt thou Knowing

ward heaven, and tell the stars, if thou be able to tell them; and he said unto him, So shall thy seed be. 6 And he believed in the LORD: and he counted it to him for righteousness. 7 And he said unto him, I am the LORD that brought thee out of Ur of the Chaldees, to give thee this land to inherit it. 8 And he said, O Lord God, whereby shall I know that I shall inherit it? 9 And he said unto him, Take me an heifer of three years old, and a she goat of three years old, and a ram of three years old, and a turtledove, and a young pigeon.

10 And he took him all these, and divided them in the midst, and laid each half over against the other: but the birds divided he not. 11 And the birds of prey came down upon the carcases, and Abram drove them away. 12 And when the sun was going down, a deep sleep fell upon Abram; and, lo, an horror of great darkness fell upon him. 13 And he said unto Abram, Know of a surety that thy seed

a G. omits.

b G., S., V. add, *Abraham.*

c G. adds, *the Lord,* יהוה.

d G. adds, *the pieces of them.*

e G. *and sat with them,* וַיֵּשֶׁב אִתָּם.

f For אימה חשכה גדלה, S. has, *terror and great darkness;* V. *terror great and dark.*

shall be a stranger in a land *that is* not their's, and shall serve them; and they shall afflict them four hundred years;
14 And also that nation, whom they shall serve, will I judge: and afterward shall they come out with great substance.
15 And thou shalt go to thy fathers in peace; thou shalt be buried in a good old age.
16 But in the fourth generation they shall come hither again: for the iniquity of the Amorites *is* not yet full.
17 And it came to pass, that, when the sun went down, and it was dark, behold a smoking furnace, and a burning lamp that passed between those pieces.
18 In that same day the LORD made a covenant with Abram, saying, Unto thy seed have I given this land, from the river of Egypt unto the great river, the river Euphrates:
19 The Kenites, and the Kenizzites, and the Kadmonites,
20 And the Hittites, and the Perizzites, and the Rephaims,
21 And the Amorites, and the Canaanites, and the Girgashites, and the Jebusites.

בְּאֶרֶץ לֹא לָהֶם וַעֲבָדוּם [a] וְעִנּוּ
oppress shall they and ; them serve will they and ,them to not land a in

14 אֹתָם אַרְבַּע מֵאוֹת שָׁנָה׃ וְגַם אֶת־הַגּוֹי אֲשֶׁר
which nation the also And .years hundred four them

יַעֲבֹדוּ דָּן אָנֹכִי וְאַחֲרֵי־כֵן
afterward and ; I [am] judge to about ,serve will they

15 יֵצְאוּ בִּרְכֻשׁ גָּדוֹל׃ וְאַתָּה תָּבוֹא
go shalt thou And [1].great [3]property [2]movable with out go shall they

אֶל־אֲבֹתֶיךָ בְּשָׁלוֹם תִּקָּבֵר בְּשֵׂיבָה טוֹבָה׃
; [1]good [2]age a in buried be wilt thou ; peace in fathers thy unto

16 וְדוֹר רְבִיעִי יָשׁוּבוּ הֵנָּה כִּי
because ; hither return will they [1]fourth [2]generation a [as] and

לֹא שָׁלֵם עֲוֺן הָאֱמֹרִי עַד־הֵנָּה׃
.now until Amorites the of iniquity the [is] complete not

17 וַיְהִי הַשֶּׁמֶשׁ בָּאָה וַעֲלָטָה [b]
darkness dense and down gone having sun the ,pass to came it And

הָיָה וְהִנֵּה תַנּוּר עָשָׁן וְלַפִּיד
of torch a and smoke of oven an behold (and) ; be to come having

18 אֵשׁ אֲשֶׁר עָבַר בֵּין הַגְּזָרִים הָאֵלֶּה׃ בַּיּוֹם
[2]day In [1].these [2]pieces between by passed which ,fire

הַהוּא כָּרַת יְהוָה אֶת־אַבְרָם בְּרִית לֵאמֹר
: saying covenant a Abram with Jehovah cut [1]that

לְזַרְעֲךָ נָתַתִּי אֶת־הָאָרֶץ הַזֹּאת מִנְּהַר
of river the from ,[1]this [2]land give will I seed thy To

19 מִצְרַיִם עַד־הַנָּהָר הַגָּדֹל נְהַר־פְּרָת׃ אֶת־
; Euphrates of river the [1],great [2]river the as far as Egypt

20 הַקֵּינִי וְאֶת־הַקְּנִזִּי וְאֵת הַקַּדְמֹנִי׃ וְאֶת־הַחִתִּי
Hittite the and ,Kadmonite the and ,Kenizzite the and ,Kenite the

21 וְאֶת־הַפְּרִזִּי וְאֶת־הָרְפָאִים׃ וְאֶת־הָאֱמֹרִי וְאֶת־
and ,Amorite the and ,Rephaim the and ,Perizzite the and

הַכְּנַעֲנִי [c] וְאֶת־הַגִּרְגָּשִׁי וְאֶת־הַיְבוּסִי׃
.Jebusite the and ,Girgashite the and ,Canaanite the

shall be a stranger in a land that is not theirs, and shall serve them; and they shall afflict them four hundred years;
14 and also that nation, whom they shall serve, will I judge: and afterward shall they come out with great substance.
15 But thou shalt go to thy fathers in peace; thou shalt be buried in a good old age.
16 And in the fourth generation they shall come hither again: for the iniquity of the Amorite is not yet full.
17 And it came to pass, that, when the sun went down, and it was dark, behold a smoking furnace, and a flaming torch that passed between these pieces.
18 In that day the LORD made a covenant with Abram, saying, Unto thy seed have I given this land, from the river of Egypt unto the great river, the river Euphrates:
19 the Kenite, and the Kenizzite, and the Kadmonite,
20 and the Hittite, and the Perizzite, and the Rephaim,
21 and the Amorite, and the Canaanite, and the Girgashite, and the Jebusite.

---

a G., S., V., *and they will enslave them.*
b G. renders, *flame.*
c. G. adds, *and the Hivites.*

16

Now Sarai,
Abram's wife,
bare him no
children: and
she had an hand-
maid, an Egyp-
tian, whose
name *was* Ha-
gar. 2 And Sarai
said unto A-
bram, Behold
now, the LORD
hath restrained
me from bear-
ing: I pray thee,
go in unto my
maid; it may be
that I may ob-
tain children by
her. And Abram
hearkened to
the voice of
Sarai. 3 And
Sarai Abram's
wife took Ha-
gar her maid the
Egyptian, after
Abram had
dwelt ten years
in the land of
Canaan, and
gave her to her
husband Abram
to be his wife.

4 And he went
in unto Hagar,
and she con-
ceived: and
when she
saw that she had
conceived, her
mistress was
despised in her
eyes. 5 And
Sarai said unto
Abram, My
wrong *be* upon
thee: I have
given my maid
into thy bos-
om; and when
she saw that she
had conceived,
I was despised
in her eyes: the
LORD judge be-
tween me and
thee. 6 But A-
bram said unto
Sarai, Behold,
thy maid *is* in
thy hand; do to
her as it pleaseth
thee. And when

1 וְשָׂרַי אֵשֶׁת אַבְרָם לֹא יָלְדָה לוֹ
; him to — bear [1]did — [2]not — Abram — of wife — Sarai And

וְלָהּ שִׁפְחָה מִצְרִית וּשְׁמָהּ
[being] name her (and) — ,Egyptian an — ,slave female a — [was] her to and

2 הָגָר׃ וַתֹּאמֶר שָׂרַי אֶל־אַבְרָם הִנֵּה־נָא[a]
,now ,Behold — ;Abram unto — Sarai — said And — .Hagar

עֲצָרַנִי יְהוָה מִלֶּדֶת בֹּא־נָא אֶל־
unto — ,now ,in go — ,bearing from — Jehovah — me obstructed has

שִׁפְחָתִי אוּלַי[b] אִבָּנֶה מִמֶּנָּה[b] וַיִּשְׁמַע
hearkened and — ; her from — built be may I — perhaps — ,slave female my

3 אַבְרָם לְקוֹל שָׂרָי[c]׃ וַתִּקַּח שָׂרַי אֵשֶׁת
of wife the — Sarai — took And — .Sarai — of voice the to — Abram

אַבְרָם אֶת־הָגָר הַמִּצְרִית שִׁפְחָתָהּ מִקֵּץ
of end the from — ,slave female her — Egyptian the — Hagar — ,Abram

עֶשֶׂר שָׁנִים לְשֶׁבֶת אַבְרָם בְּאֶרֶץ כְּנָעַן
; Canaan — of land the in — [1]Abram's — [2]dwelling to — years — ten

וַתִּתֵּן אֹתָהּ לְאַבְרָם אִישָׁהּ לוֹ[d] לְאִשָּׁה׃
.wife a for — him to — ,husband her — Abram to — her — gave she and

4 וַיָּבֹא אֶל־הָגָר וַתַּהַר וַתֵּרֶא כִּי
that — saw she and — ; conceived she and — Hagar unto — in went he And

5 הָרָתָה וַתֵּקַל גְּבִרְתָּהּ בְּעֵינֶיהָ׃ וַתֹּאמֶר
said And — .eyes her in — mistress her — little was and — ,conceived had she

שָׂרַי אֶל־אַבְרָם חֲמָסִי[e] עָלֶיךָ[e] אָנֹכִי נָתַתִּי
gave — I — ; thee upon [is] — injury suffering My — :Abram unto — Sarai

שִׁפְחָתִי בְּחֵיקֶךָ וַתֵּרֶא כִּי הָרָתָה
;conceived had she — that — saw she and — ;bosom thy into — slave female my

וָאֵקַל בְּעֵינֶיהָ יִשְׁפֹּט יְהוָה[f] בֵּינִי
me between — Jehovah — judge let — ; eyes her in — little was I and

6 וּבֵינֶיךָ׃ וַיֹּאמֶר אַבְרָם אֶל־שָׂרַי[g] הִנֵּה
Behold — ; Sarai unto — Abram — said And — .thee (between) and

שִׁפְחָתֵךְ בְּיָדֵךְ[h] עֲשִׂי־לָהּ הַטּוֹב בְּעֵינָיִךְ
; eyes thine in — good the — her to do — ,hand thy in — [is] slave female thy

Now Sarai
Abram's wife
bare him no
children: and
she had an
handmaid, an
Egyptian,
whose name was
Hagar. 2 And
Sarai said unto
Abram, Behold
now, the LORD
hath restrained
me from bear-
ing; go in, I
pray thee, unto
my handmaid;
it may be that I
shall obtain
children by her.
And Abram
hearkened to
the voice of
Sarai. 3 And
Sarai Abram's
wife took Hagar
the Egyptian,
her handmaid,
after Abram had
dwelt ten years
in the land of
Canaan, and
gave her to A-
bram her hus-
band to be his
wife.

4 And he went
in unto Hagar,
and she con-
ceived: and
when she saw
that she had
conceived, her
mistress was
despised in her
eyes. 5 And
Sarai said unto
Abram, My
wrong be upon
thee: I gave my
handmaid into
thy bosom; and
when she saw
that she had
conceived, I was
despised in her
eyes: the LORD
judge between
me and thee. 6
But Abram said
unto Sarai, Be-
hold, thy maid
is in thy hand;
do to her that
which is good in
thine eyes. And

---

a G., S., V. omit נא.

b G., *in order that thou mayest beget children from her.*

c G., V. have, *her.*

d S., V. omit.

e For חמסי עליך, G. has, *I am wronged by thee;* V. *thou hast done wickedly towards me;* T. *a cause is to me against thee.*

f G. has, *God*, אלהים.

g S. adds, *his wife*, אשתו.

h For בידך, S. has, *is given over into thy hands.*

Sarai dealt hard-
ly with her, she
fled from her
face.
7 And the
angel of the
LORD found her
by a fountain of
water in the
wilderness, by
the fountain in
the way to Shur.
8 And he said,
Hagar, Sarai's
maid, whence
camest thou?
and whither
wilt thou go?
And she said,
I flee from the
face of my mis-
tress Sarai. 9
And the angel
of the LORD
said unto her,
Return to thy
mistress; and
submit thyself
under her
hands. 10 And
the angel of the
LORD said unto
her, I will mul-
tiply thy seed
exceedingly,
that it shall not
be numbered for
multitude. 11
And the angel
of the LORD said
unto her, Be-
hold, thou *art*
with child, and
shalt bear a son,
and shalt call
his name Ish-
mael; because
the LORD hath
heard thy afflic-
tion. 12 And he
will be a wild
man; his hand
will be against
every man, and
every man's
hand against
him; and he
shall dwell in
the presence of
all his brethren.
13 And she call-
ed the name of
the LORD that
spake unto her,
Thou God seest
me: for she said,
Have I also here

7 וַתְּעַנֶּהָ שָׂרַי[a] וַתִּבְרַח מִפָּנֶיהָ׃ וַיִּמְצָאָהּ
her found And .her before from fled she and ,Sarai her oppressed and

מַלְאַךְ יְהוָֹה[b] עַל־עֵין הַמַּיִם בַּמִּדְבָּר
;wilderness the in water of fountain the by Jehovah of angel the

8 עַל־הָעַיִן[c] בְּדֶרֶךְ שׁוּר׃ וַיֹּאמַר[d] הָגָר
Hagar :said he And .Shur of way the in fountain the by

שִׁפְחַת שָׂרַי אֵי־מִזֶּה בָאת וְאָנָה
whither and ,come thou hast (this from) whence ,Sarai of slave female

תֵלֵכִי וַתֹּאמֶר מִפְּנֵי שָׂרַי גְּבִרְתִּי
mistress my Sarai before From :said she And ?go thou dost

9 אָנֹכִי בֹּרַחַת׃ וַיֹּאמֶר לָהּ מַלְאַךְ יְהוָֹה
:Jehovah of angel the her to said And .fleeing am I

שׁוּבִי אֶל־גְּבִרְתֵּךְ וְהִתְעַנִּי תַּחַת יָדֶיהָ׃
.hands her under thyself humble and mistress thy unto Return

10 וַיֹּאמֶר לָהּ מַלְאַךְ יְהוָֹה הַרְבָּה אַרְבֶּה
multiply will I Multiplying :Jehovah of angel the her to said And

11 אֶת־זַרְעֵךְ וְלֹא יִסָּפֵר מֵרֹב׃ וַיֹּאמֶר
said And .multitude from numbered be [2]can [1]it [3]not and ,seed thy

לָהּ מַלְאַךְ יְהוָֹה הִנָּךְ הָרָה
,pregnant [art] thou Behold :Jehovah of angel the her to

וְיֹלַדְתְּ בֵּן וְקָרָאת שְׁמוֹ יִשְׁמָעֵאל
,Ishmael name his call shalt thou and ;son a bear wilt thou and

12 כִּי־שָׁמַע יְהוָֹה אֶל־עָנְיֵךְ׃ וְהוּא
he And .affliction thy unto Jehovah hearkened has because

יִהְיֶה פֶּרֶא אָדָם[e] יָדוֹ בַכֹּל
,one every against hand his ;man a of ass wild a become shall

וְיַד כֹּל בּוֹ וְעַל־פְּנֵי כָל־אֶחָיו
brethren his all before and ;him against one every of hand the and

13 יִשְׁכֹּן׃ וַתִּקְרָא שֵׁם־יְהוָֹה הַדֹּבֵר
speaking one the ,Jehovah of name the called she And .dwell shall he

אֵלֶיהָ[f] אַתָּה אֵל רֳאִי[g] כִּי אָמְרָה הֲגַם[h]
Even :said she for ;seeing of God a [art] Thou ;her unto

Sarai dealt hard-
ly with her, and
she fled from
her face.
7 And the
angel of the
LORD found her
by a fountain of
water in the
wilderness, by
the fountain in
the way to Shur.
8 And he said,
Hagar, Sarai's
handmaid,
whence camest
thou? and
whither goest
thou? and she
said, I flee from
the face of my
mistress Sarai. 9
And the angel
of the LORD said
unto her, Re-
turn to thy mis-
tress, and sub-
mit thyself un-
der her hands.
10 And the
angel of the
LORD said unto
her, I will great-
ly multiply thy
seed, that it
shall not be
numbered for
multitude. 11
And the angel
of the LORD
said unto her,
Behold, thou
art with child,
and shalt bear a
son; and thou
shalt call his
name Ishmael,
because the
LORD hath
heard thy afflic-
tion. 12 And he
shall be *as* a
wild-ass among
men; his hand
shall be against
every man, and
every man's
hand against
him; and he
shall dwell in
the presence of
all his breth-
ren. 13 And she
called the name
of the LORD
that spake unto
her, Thou art a

---

a G. adds, *her mistress.*

b G. adds, *the God*, האלהים.

c S., V. omit.

d S. adds, *to her;* G. *to her the angel of the Lord.*

e For פרא אדם, G. has, *a rough man*, so V.; Sym. *a man of the desert;* Theod, *separated from men.*

f S. adds, *and she said;* T. adds, *saying.*

g The versions have various interpretations, but their text is substantially that of H.; so with ראי below.

h G., S., V., T. apparently omit ה of הגם.

looked after
him that seeth
me? 14 Where-
fore the well was
called Beer-la-
hai-roi; behold,
it is between
Kadesh and
Bered.

15 And Hagar
bare Abram a
son: and Abram
called his son's
name, which
Hagar bare,
Ishmael. 16 And
Abram *was* four-
score and six
years old, when
Hagar bare Ish-
mael to Abram.

14 הֲלֹם רָאִיתִי אַחֲרֵי רֹאִי׃ עַל־כֵּן קָרָא[a]
called one Therefore ?me seeing one the after looked I have here

לַבְּאֵר בְּאֵר לַחַי רֹאִי הִנֵּה בֵין
between behold ;me seeing one living the of Well ,well the (to)

15 קָדֵשׁ וּבֵין בָּרֶד׃ וַתֵּלֶד הָגָר לְאַבְרָם בֵּן
,son a Abram to Hagar bore And .Bered (between) and Kadesh

וַיִּקְרָא אַבְרָם שֶׁם־בְּנוֹ[b] אֲשֶׁר־יָלְדָה הָגָר[c]
Hagar bore whom son his of name the Abram called and

16 יִשְׁמָעֵאל׃ וְאַבְרָם בֶּן־שְׁמֹנִים שָׁנָה וְשֵׁשׁ
six and years eighty (of son a) [being] Abram (and) ;Ishmael

שָׁנִים בְּלֶדֶת־הָגָר אֶת־יִשְׁמָעֵאל לְאַבְרָם׃
.Abram to Ishmael bearing Hagar's at [old] years

God that seeth:
for she said,
Have I even
here looked af-
ter him that
seeth me? 14
Wherefore the
well was called
Beer-lahai-roi;
behold, it is be-
tween Kadesh
and Bered.

15 And Hagar
bare Abram a
son: and Abram
called the name
of his son, which
Hagar bare, Ish-
mael. 16 And
Abram was four-
score and six
years old, when
Hagar bare Ish-
mael to Abram.

17

1 וַיְהִי אַבְרָם בֶּן־תִּשְׁעִים שָׁנָה
years ninety (of son a) [being] Abram ,pass to came it And

וְתֵשַׁע שָׁנִים וַיֵּרָא יְהוָה אֶל־אַבְרָם וַיֹּאמֶר
said and Abram unto Jehovah appeared that ,[old] years nine and

אֵלָיו אֲנִי־אֵל[d] שַׁדַּי[d] הִתְהַלֵּךְ לְפָנַי וֶהְיֵה
be and me before walk ,Almighty God [am] I ;him unto

2 תָמִים׃ וְאֶתְּנָה בְרִיתִי בֵּינִי וּבֵינֶךָ
,thee (between) and me between covenant my make will I and .spotless

3 וְאַרְבֶּה אוֹתְךָ בִּמְאֹד מְאֹד׃ וַיִּפֹּל
fell And .exceedingly exceedingly (in) thee increase will I and

אַבְרָם עַל־פָּנָיו וַיְדַבֵּר אִתּוֹ אֱלֹהִים לֵאמֹר׃
:saying God him with spoke and ,face his upon Abram

4 אֲנִי הִנֵּה[e] בְרִיתִי אִתָּךְ וְהָיִיתָ
become shalt thou and ;thee with [is] covenant my behold ,I

5 לְאַב הֲמוֹן גּוֹיִם׃ וְלֹא־יִקָּרֵא עוֹד
still called be not shall And .nations of multitude a of father (for)

אֶת־שִׁמְךָ אַבְרָם וְהָיָה שִׁמְךָ אַבְרָהָם כִּי
because ;Abraham name thy become shall and ,Abram name thy

AND when A-
bram was ninety
years old and
nine, the LORD
appeared to A-
bram, and said
unto him, I *am*
the Almighty
God; walk be-
fore me, and be
thou perfect. 2
And I will make
my covenant
between me and
thee, and will
multiply thee
exceedingly. 3
And Abram fell
on his face: and
God talked with
him, saying, 4
As for me, be-
hold, my cove-
nant *is* with
thee, and thou
shalt be a father
of many nations.
5 Neither shall
thy name any
more be called
Abram, but thy
name shall be
Abraham; for a

AND when A-
bram was ninety
years old and
nine, the LORD
appeared to A-
bram, and said
unto him, I am
God Almighty;
walk before me,
and be thou per-
fect. 2 And I
will make my
covenant be-
tween me and
thee, and will
multiply thee
exceedingly. 3
And Abram fell
on his face: and
God talked with
him, saying, 4
As for me, be-
hold, my cove-
nant is with
thee, and thou
shalt be the fath-
er of a multitude
of nations. 5
Neither shall
thy name any
more be called
Abram, but thy
name shall be
Abraham; for

a S. has, *she called*, קראה.
b S. adds, *who was born to him.*
c G., S. add, *to him.*
d For אל שדי, G. has, *thy God;* S. *El Shaddai God.*
e S., T. add, *I am establishing.*

father of many
nations have I
made thee. 6
And I will make
thee exceeding
fruitful, and I
will make na-
tions of thee,
and kings shall
come out of
thee. 7 And I
will establish
m y covenant
between me and
thee and thy
seed after thee
in their genera-
tions for an
everlasting co-
venant, to be a
God unto thee,
and to thy seed
after thee. 8
And I will give
unto thee, and
to thy seed after
thee, the land
wherein thou
art a stranger,
all the land of
Canaan, for an
everlasting pos-
session; and I
will be their
God.

9 And God
said unto Abra-
ham, Thou shalt
keep my cove-
nant therefore,
thou, and thy
seed after thee
in their genera-
tions. 10 This *is*
m y covenant,
which ye shall
keep, between
me and you and
thy seed after
thee; Every man
child among you
shall be circum-
cised. 11 And
ye shall circum-
cise the flesh of
your foreskin;
and it shall
be a token
of the covenant
betwixt me and
you. 12 And he
that is eight days
old shall be cir-
cumcised among
you, every man
child in your
generations, he

אַב־הֲמ֥וֹן גּוֹיִ֖ם נְתַתִּֽיךָ׃
.thee appointed have I   nations   of multitude a of father

6 וְהִפְרֵתִ֤י אֹֽתְךָ֙ בִּמְאֹ֣ד מְאֹ֔ד
; exceedingly   exceedingly (in)   thee   fruitful make will I And

וּנְתַתִּ֖יךָ לְגוֹיִ֑ם וּמְלָכִ֖ים מִמְּךָ֥[a] יֵצֵֽאוּ׃
.out go shall   thee from   kings and   ,nations (for)   thee make will I and

7 וַהֲקִמֹתִ֨י אֶת־בְּרִיתִ֜י בֵּינִ֣י וּבֵינֶ֗ךָ
,thee (between) and   ,me between   covenant my   establish will I And

וּבֵ֨ין זַרְעֲךָ֧ אַחֲרֶ֛יךָ לְדֹרֹתָ֖ם
,generations their to   ,thee after   seed thy   (between) and

לִבְרִ֣ית עוֹלָ֑ם לִהְי֤וֹת לְךָ֙ לֵֽאלֹהִ֔ים וּֽלְזַרְעֲךָ֖
seed thy to and   God a (for)   thee to   be to   ;eternity   of covenant a for

8 אַחֲרֶֽיךָ׃ וְנָתַתִּ֣י לְ֠ךָ וּלְזַרְעֲךָ֨ אַחֲרֶ֜יךָ אֵ֣ת
thee after   seed thy to and   thee to   give will I And   .thee after

אֶ֣רֶץ מְגֻרֶ֗יךָ אֵ֚ת כָּל־אֶ֣רֶץ כְּנַ֔עַן
,Canaan   of land the all   ,pilgrimage thy   of land the

לַאֲחֻזַּ֖ת עוֹלָ֑ם וְהָיִ֥יתִי לָהֶ֖ם לֵאלֹהִֽים׃
.God a (for)   them to   be will I and   ; eternity   of possession a for

9 וַיֹּ֤אמֶר אֱלֹהִים֙ אֶל־אַבְרָהָ֔ם וְאַתָּ֖ה אֶת־בְּרִיתִ֣י
covenant my   ,thou And   : Abraham unto   God   said And

תִשְׁמֹ֑ר אַתָּ֛ה וְזַרְעֲךָ֥ אַחֲרֶ֖יךָ לְדֹרֹתָֽם׃
; generations their to   thee after   seed thy and   thou   ,keep shalt thou

10 זֹ֣את[b] בְּרִיתִ֞י אֲשֶׁ֣ר תִּשְׁמְר֗וּ בֵּינִי֙
,me between   keep shall you   which   covenant my   [is] this

וּבֵ֣ינֵיכֶ֔ם וּבֵ֥ין זַרְעֲךָ֖ אַחֲרֶ֑יךָ הִמּ֥וֹל
[7]circumcised [6]be [5]to,   thee after   seed thy   (between) and   ,you (between) and

11 לָכֶ֖ם כָּל־זָכָֽר׃ וּנְמַלְתֶּ֕ם אֵ֖ת בְּשַׂ֣ר
of flesh the [to as]   circumcised be shall ye And   .[2]male [1]every   [4]you [3]to

עָרְלַתְכֶ֑ם וְהָיָה֙ לְא֣וֹת בְּרִ֔ית
covenant a   of sign a (for)   become shall it and   ; foreskin your

12 בֵּינִ֖י וּבֵינֵיכֶֽם׃ וּבֶן־שְׁמֹנַ֣ת יָמִ֗ים
[old] days   eight (of son a) And   .you (between) and   me between

יִמּ֥וֹל לָכֶ֛ם כָּל־זָכָ֖ר לְדֹרֹתֵיכֶ֑ם
; generations your to   male every   you for   circumcised be shall

the father of a
multitude of
nations have I
made thee. 6
And I will make
thee exceeding
fruitful, and I
will make na-
tions of thee,
and kings shall
come out of
thee. 7 And I
will establish my
covenant be-
tween me and
thee and thy
seed after thee
throughout their
generations for
an everlasting
covenant, to be
a God unto thee
and to thy seed
after thee. 8
And I will give
unto thee, and
to thy seed af-
ter thee, the
land of thy so-
journings, all
the land of Ca-
naan, for an
everlasting pos-
session; and I
will be their
God.

9 And God
said unto Abra-
ham, And as for
thee, thou shalt
keep my cove-
nant, thou, and
thy seed after
thee throughout
their genera-
tions. 10 This is
my covenant,
which ye shall
keep, between
me and you and
thy seed after
thee; every male
among you shall
be circumcised.
11 And ye shall
be circumcised
in the flesh of
your foreskin;
and it shall be a
token of a cov-
enant betwixt
me and you. 12
And he that is
eight days old
shall be circum-
cised among
you, every male
throughout your
generations, he

a S. has, *from thy body*, ממעיך; cf. 15: 4.

b G., *and this*, וזאת.

that is born in
the house, or
bought with
money of any
stranger, which
is not of thy
seed. 13 He that
is born in thy
house, and he
that is bought
with thy money,
must needs be
circumcised:
and my covenant shall be in
your flesh for an
everlasting covenant. 14 And
the uncircumcised man child
whose flesh of
his foreskin is
not circumcised,
that soul shall
be cut off from
his people; he
hath broken my
covenant.

15 And God
said unto Abraham, As for
Sarai thy wife,
thou shalt not
call her name
Sarai, but Sarah
shall her name
be. 16 And I
will bless her,
and give thee a
son also of her:
yea, I will bless
her, and she
shall be *a mother* of nations;
kings of people
shall be of her.
17 Then Abraham fell upon
his face, and
laughed, and
said in his heart,
Shall *a child* be
born unto him
that is an hundred years old?
and shall Sarah,
that is ninety
years old, bear?
18 And Abraham said unto
God, O that
Ishmael might
live before
thee! 19

יְלִיד בָּיִת וּמִקְנַת־כֶּסֶף מִכֹּל[a] [a]בֶּן־נֵכָר
strangeness of son any from money of purchase a and house the of son a

13 אֲשֶׁר לֹא מִזַּרְעֲךָ הוּא׃ הִמּוֹל[b] יִמּוֹל
circumcised be shall Surely .he [is] seed thy from not which

יְלִיד בֵּיתְךָ וּמִקְנַת [b]כַּסְפֶּךָ
;money thy of purchase the and ,house thy of child the

וְהָיְתָה בְרִיתִי בִּבְשַׂרְכֶם לִבְרִית
of covenant a (for) flesh your in covenant my become shall and

14 עוֹלָם׃ וְעָרֵל זָכָר אֲשֶׁר לֹא־יִמּוֹל
circumcised not is who male a ,one uncircumcised an And .eternity

אֶת־בְּשַׂר [c]עָרְלָתוֹ וְנִכְרְתָה הַנֶּפֶשׁ
[2]soul off cut be shall (and) ,foreskin his of flesh the [to as]

הַהִוא [d]מֵעַמֶּיהָ אֶת־בְּרִיתִי הֵפַר׃
.broken has he covenant my ;countrymen fellow his from [1]that

15 וַיֹּאמֶר אֱלֹהִים אֶל־אַבְרָהָם שָׂרַי אִשְׁתְּךָ
—wife thy Sarai ;Abraham unto God said And

[e]לֹא־תִקְרָא אֶת־שְׁמָהּ שָׂרָי כִּי שָׂרָה שְׁמָהּ׃
.name her [be shall] Sarah for ;Sarai name her call not shalt thou

16 וּבֵרַכְתִּי אֹתָהּ וְגַם נָתַתִּי מִמֶּנָּה לְךָ בֵּן
;son a thee to her from give will I also and ,her bless will I And

וּבֵרַכְתִּיהָ[f] וְהָיְתָה לְגוֹיִם [g]מַלְכֵי
of kings ,nations (for) become shall she and ,her bless will I and

17 עַמִּים מִמֶּנָּה יִהְיוּ׃ וַיִּפֹּל אַבְרָהָם עַל־פָּנָיו
face his upon Abraham fell And .be to come shall her from peoples

וַיִּצְחָק וַיֹּאמֶר [h]בְּלִבּוֹ הַלְּבֶן
[one] (of son a) To :heart his in said he and ;laughed and

מֵאָה־שָׁנָה [i]יִוָּלֵד וְאִם־שָׂרָה
—Sarah or (and) born be [child a] shall [old] years hundred a

18 הֲבַת־תִּשְׁעִים שָׁנָה תֵּלֵד׃ וַיֹּאמֶר
said And ?bear [1]shall [5][old] [4]years [3]ninety [2][one] (of daughter a)

אַבְרָהָם אֶל־הָאֱלֹהִים [j]לוּ [j]יִשְׁמָעֵאל יִחְיֶה לְפָנֶיךָ׃
.thee before live might Ishmael that Would :God unto Abraham

that is born in
the house, or
bought with
money of any
stranger, which
is not of thy
seed. 13 He
that is born in
thy house, and
he that is
bought with thy
money, must
needs be circumcised: and my
covenant shall
be in your flesh
for an everlasting covenant. 14
And the uncircumcised male
who is not circumcised in the
flesh of his foreskin, that soul
shall be cut off
from his people;
he hath broken
my covenant.

15 And God
said unto Abraham, As for
Sarai thy wife,
thou shalt not
call her name
Sarai, but Sarah
shall her name
be. 16 And I
will bless her,
and moreover I
will give thee a
son of her: yea,
I will bless her,
and she shall be
a mother of nations; kings of
peoples shall be
of her. 17 Then
Abraham fell
upon his face,
and laughed,
and said in his
heart, Shall a
child be born
unto him that is
an hundred
years old? and
shall Sarah,
that is ninety
years old, bear?
18 And Abraham said unto
God, Oh that
Ishmael might
live before thee!

---

a V. omits, מכל בן נכר, and adds, *shall be circumcised.*
b V. omits, המול---כספך.
c Sm., G. add, *on the eighth day.*
d G., V. add, *because* כי.
e G. has, *shall not be called,* לֹא תִקָּרֵא.
f G., S., V. have, *and I will bless him,* וברכתיו; also masc. in והיתה and ממנה.
g G., Sm., S., V. *and kings,* ומלכי.
h G. adds, *saying,* לאמר.
i G., S., V. *shall a son be born;* T. *shall there be a son.*
j For לו ישמעאל, G. has, *this Ishmael.*

And God said, Sarah thy wife shall bear thee a son indeed; and thou shalt call his name Isaac: and I will establish my covenant with him for an everlasting covenant, *and* with his seed after him. 20 And as for Ishmael, I have heard thee; Behold, I have blessed him, and will make him fruitful, and will multiply him exceedingly; twelve princes shall he beget, and I will make him a great nation. 21 But my covenant will I establish with Isaac, which Sarah shall bear unto thee at this set time in the next year. 22 And he left off talking with him, and God went up from Abraham.

23 And Abraham took Ishmael his son, and all that were born in his house, and all that were bought with his money, every male among the men of Abraham's house; and circumcised the flesh of their foreskin in the selfsame day, as God had said unto him. 24 And Abraham *was* ninety years old and nine,

19 וַיֹּאמֶר אֱלֹהִים[a] אֲבָל[b] שָׂרָה אִשְׁתְּךָ יֹלֶדֶת
bear to about [is] wife thy Sarah ,Indeed : God said And

לְךָ בֵּן וְקָרָאתָ אֶת־שְׁמוֹ יִצְחָק
; Isaac name his call shalt thou and ,son a thee to

וַהֲקִמֹתִי אֶת־בְּרִיתִי אִתּוֹ לִבְרִית
of covenant a for him with covenant my establish will I and

20 עוֹלָם לְזַרְעוֹ[c] אַחֲרָיו׃ וּלְיִשְׁמָעֵאל[d] שְׁמַעְתִּיךָ
;thee heard have I ,Ishmael for as And .him after seed his for ,eternity

הִנֵּה[e] בֵּרַכְתִּי אֹתוֹ וְהִפְרֵיתִי אֹתוֹ
,him fruitful make will and ,him bless will I behold

וְהִרְבֵּיתִי אֹתוֹ בִּמְאֹד מְאֹד שְׁנֵים־עָשָׂר
twelve ; exceedingly exceedingly (in) him multiply will and

21 נְשִׂיאִם[f] יוֹלִיד וּנְתַתִּיו לְגוֹי גָּדוֹל׃
.¹great ²nation a for him appoint will I and beget shall he princes

וְאֶת־בְּרִיתִי אָקִים אֶת־יִצְחָק אֲשֶׁר תֵּלֵד
bear shall whom ,Isaac with establish will I covenant my And

לְךָ שָׂרָה לַמּוֹעֵד הַזֶּה בַּשָּׁנָה הָאַחֶרֶת׃
.¹next ²year the in ¹this ²season at Sarah thee to

22 וַיְכַל לְדַבֵּר אִתּוֹ וַיַּעַל אֱלֹהִים
God ascended (and) him with speak to ended had he [when] And

23 מֵעַל אַבְרָהָם׃ וַיִּקַּח אַבְרָהָם אֶת־יִשְׁמָעֵאל בְּנוֹ
,son his Ishmael Abraham took And .Abraham with from

וְאֵת כָּל־יְלִידֵי בֵיתוֹ וְאֵת כָּל־מִקְנַת כַּסְפּוֹ
,money his of purchase the all and house his of children the all and

כָּל־זָכָר בְּאַנְשֵׁי בֵּית אַבְרָהָם
; Abraham of house the of men the among male every

וַיָּמָל אֶת־בְּשַׂר[g] עָרְלָתָם בְּעֶצֶם
(of bone the) in foreskin their of flesh the circumcised he and

הַיּוֹם הַזֶּה כַּאֲשֶׁר דִּבֶּר אִתּוֹ אֱלֹהִים׃
; God him with spoken had as according ¹this ²day

24 וְאַבְרָהָם בֶּן־תִּשְׁעִים וָתֵשַׁע שָׁנָה
[old] years nine and ninety (of son a) being Abraham (and)

19 And God said, Nay, but Sarah thy wife shall bear thee a son; and thou shalt call his name Isaac: and I will establish my covenant with him for an everlasting covenant for his seed after him. 20 And as for Ishmael, I have heard thee: behold, I have blessed him, and will make him fruitful, and will multiply him exceedingly; twelve princes shall he beget, and I will make him a great nation. 21 But my covenant will I establish with Isaac, which Sarah shall bear unto thee at this set time in the next year. 22 And he left off talking with him, and God went up from Abraham.

23 And Abraham took Ishmael his son, and all that were born in his house, and all that were bought with his money, every male among the men of Abraham's house, and circumcised the flesh of their foreskin in the selfsame day, as God had said unto him. 24 And Abraham was ninety years old and

a G., S., V. add, *unto Abraham.*
b Sm., G. add, *behold,* הנה.
c Sm., G., V. have, *and for his seed,* ולזרעו.
d G. adds, *behold,* הנה.
e G. has, *and.*
f G. has, *nations.*
g. G. omits.

when he was circumcised in the
flesh of his foreskin. 25 And
Ishmael his son *was* thirteen
years old, when he was circumcised in the flesh
of his foreskin.
26 In the selfsame day was
Abraham circumcised, and
Ishmael his son.
27 And all the men of his
house, born in the house, and
bought with money of the
stranger, were circumcised
with him.

25 בְּהִמֹּלוֹ בְּשַׂר עָרְלָתוֹ׃ וְיִשְׁמָעֵאל
Ishmael and ; [5]foreskin his[4] [3]of [2]flesh [1]the [7]circumcised [6]being at

בְּנוֹ בֶּן־שְׁלֹשׁ עֶשְׂרֵה שָׁנָה בְּהִמֹּלוֹ
circumcised being at [old] years ten [and] three (of son a) [being] son his

26 אֵת בְּשַׂר עָרְלָתוֹ׃ בְּעֶצֶם הַיּוֹם הַזֶּה נִמּוֹל
circumcised was [1]this [2]day (of bone the) in ; foreskin his of flesh the

27 אַבְרָהָם וְיִשְׁמָעֵאל בְּנוֹ׃ וְכָל־אַנְשֵׁי בֵיתוֹ
,house his of men the all And .son his Ishmael and ,Abraham

יְלִיד[a] בָּיִת וּמִקְנַת־כֶּסֶף מֵאֵת בֶּן־
of son a (with) from money of purchase a and house the of child a

נֵכָר נִמֹּלוּ אִתּוֹ[b]׃
.him with circumcised were ,strangeness

nine, when he was circumcised
in the flesh of his foreskin.
25 And Ishmael his son was thirteen years old, when he was
circumcised in the flesh of his
foreskin. 26 In the selfsame day
was Abraham circumcised,
and Ishmael his son. 27 And
all the men of his house, those
born in the house, and those
bought with money of the
stranger, were circumcised with
him.

18

AND the LORD appeared unto
him in the plains of Mamre: and
he sat in the tent door in the
heat of the day;
2 And he lift up his eyes and
looked, and, lo, three men stood
by him: and when he saw
them, he ran to meet them
from the tent door, and bowed
himself toward the ground. 3
And said, My Lord, if now I
have found favour in thy
sight, pass not away, I pray
thee, *from* thy servant: 4 Let
a little water, I pray you, be
fetched, and wash your feet,
and rest yourselves under the
tree: 5 And I will fetch a
morsel of bread, and comfort ye

1 וַיֵּרָא אֵלָיו יְהוָה[c] בְּאֵלֹנֵי מַמְרֵא
,Mamre of terebinths the by Jehovah him unto appeared And

וְהוּא יֹשֵׁב פֶּתַח־הָאֹהֶל כְּחֹם
of heat the at tent the of door the at sitting [was] he [while] (and)

2 הַיּוֹם׃ וַיִּשָּׂא עֵינָיו וַיַּרְא וְהִנֵּה שְׁלֹשָׁה
three behold and saw and ,eyes his raised he And .day the

אֲנָשִׁים נִצָּבִים עָלָיו וַיַּרְא וַיָּרָץ לִקְרָאתָם
them meet to ran and ,saw he and ;him by standing men

מִפֶּתַח הָאֹהֶל וַיִּשְׁתַּחוּ אָרְצָה׃
,earth the to himself prostrated he and ; tent the of door the from

3 וַיֹּאמַר אֲדֹנָי אִם־נָא מָצָאתִי חֵן בְּעֵינֶיךָ
,eyes thine in favor found have I ,now ,if ,Lord O : said and

אַל־נָא תַעֲבֹר מֵעַל עַבְדֶּךָ׃
.servant thy (upon) from away pass thou ,pray ,not do

4 יֻקַּח־נָא[d] מְעַט־מַיִם[e] וְרַחֲצוּ[f] רַגְלֵיכֶם וְהִשָּׁעֲנוּ
recline and ,feet your wash and ,water little a ,now ,taken be Let

5 תַּחַת הָעֵץ׃ וְאֶקְחָה פַת־לֶחֶם[g] וְסַעֲדוּ
ye strengthen and ,bread of crumb a take me let And .tree the under

And the LORD appeared unto
him by the oaks of Mamre,
as he sat in the tent door in the
heat of the day;
2 and he lift up his eyes and
looked, and, lo, three men stood
over against him: and when
he saw them, he ran to meet
them from the tent door, and
bowed himself to the earth, 3
and said, My Lord, if now I
have found favor in thy sight,
pass not away, I pray thee, from
thy servant: 4 let now a little
water be fetched, and
wash your feet, and rest yourselves under the tree: 5 and I
will fetch a morsel of bread,
and comfort ye

---

a G., V. add, *and*, ויליד.

b For נמלו אתו, G. has, *he circumcised them;* S. *he circumcised with him.*

c G. has, *God*, אלהים.

d For יקח, G. has, *I will take;* T. *let them bring;* V. *I will bring.*

e G. omits, *little*, מעט.

f G. *and let one wash;* S. *and I will wash.*

g G. omits, *crumb*, פת.

your hearts; af-
ter that ye shall
pass on: for
therefore are
ye come to
your servant.
And they said,
So do, as thou
hast said. 6
And Abraham
hastened into
the tent unto
Sarah, and said,
Make ready
quickly three
measures of fine
meal, knead *it*,
and make cakes
upon the hearth.
7 And Abraham
ran unto the
herd, and
fetcht a calf
tender and
good, and gave
it unto a young
man; and he
hasted to dress
it. 8 And he
took butter, and
milk, and the calf
which he had
dressed, and set
it before them;
and he stood by
them under the
tree, and they
did eat.
9 And they
said unto him,
Where *is* Sarah
thy wife? And
he said, Behold,
in the tent. 10
And he said, I
will certainly re-
turn unto thee
according to
the time of life;
and, lo, Sarah
thy wife shall
have a son.
And Sarah
heard *it* in the
tent door, which
was behind him.
11 Now Abra-
ham and Sarah
were old *and*
well stricken in
age; *and* it
ceased to be
with Sarah af-
ter the manner
of women. 12
Therefore Sarah
laughed within

לִבְּכֶם אַחַר[a] תַּעֲבֹרוּ כִּֽי־עַל־כֵּן עֲבַרְתֶּם
come have ye that because ,on pass may ye afterwards ;heart your

עַל־עַבְדְּכֶם וַיֹּאמְרוּ כֵּן תַּעֲשֶׂה כַּאֲשֶׁר
as according ,do thou do So :said they And .servant your unto

6 דִּבַּרְתָּ׃ וַיְמַהֵר אַבְרָהָם הָאֹהֱלָה אֶל־שָׂרָה
,Sarah unto tent the into Abraham hastened And .spoken hast thou

וַיֹּאמֶר מַהֲרִי שְׁלֹשׁ סְאִים קֶמַח סֹלֶת לוּשִׁי
,knead ;meal fine ,meal of seahs three quickly Bring :said and

7 וַעֲשִׂי עֻגוֹת׃ וְאֶל־הַבָּקָר רָץ אַבְרָהָם וַיִּקַּח
took and ,Abraham ran herd the unto And .cakes make and

בֶּן־בָּקָר רַךְ וָטוֹב וַיִּתֵּן אֶל־הַנַּעַר
;youth a unto gave and ,good and tender herd the of son a

8 וַיְמַהֵר לַעֲשׂוֹת אֹתוֹ׃ וַיִּקַּח חֶמְאָה וְחָלָב
,milk and curds took he And .it prepare to hastened he and

וּבֶן־הַבָּקָר אֲשֶׁר עָשָׂה וַיִּתֵּן
placed he and ;prepared had he which herd the of son the and

לִפְנֵיהֶם וְהוּא עֹמֵד עֲלֵיהֶם תַּחַת
under them by standing [was] he [while] (and) ,them before

9 הָעֵץ וַיֹּאכֵלוּ[b]׃ וַיֹּאמְרוּ[c] אֵלָיו אַיֵּה
[is] Where :him unto said they And .ate they and ;tree the

10 שָׂרָה אִשְׁתֶּךָ וַיֹּאמֶר הִנֵּה בָאֹהֶל׃ וַיֹּאמֶר
:said he And .tent the in ,Behold :said he and ;wife thy Sarah

שׁוֹב אָשׁוּב אֵלֶיךָ כָּעֵת חַיָּה[d]
,[1]reviving [2]time the at thee unto return will I Returning

וְהִנֵּה־בֵן לְשָׂרָה אִשְׁתֶּךָ וְשָׂרָה שֹׁמַעַת
hearing [was] Sarah and ;wife thy Sarah to son a behold and

11 פֶּתַח הָאֹהֶל וְהוּא[e] אַחֲרָיו׃ וְאַבְרָהָם
Abraham (And) .him behind [being] it (and) ,tent the of door the at

וְשָׂרָה זְקֵנִים בָּאִים בַּיָּמִים חָדַל לִהְיוֹת
to be ceased had there ,days in advanced ,old being Sarah and

12 לְשָׂרָה אֹרַח כַּנָּשִׁים׃ וַתִּצְחַק שָׂרָה
Sarah laughed And .women like custom [the] Sarah to

your heart; af-
ter that ye shall
pass on: foras-
much as ye are
come to your
servant. And
they said, So do,
as thou hast
said. 6 And A-
braham hast-
ened into the
tent unto Sarah,
and said, Make
ready quickly
three measures
of fine meal,
knead it, and
make cakes. 7
And Abraham
ran unto the
herd, and
fetched a calf
tender and
good, and gave
it unto the serv-
ant; and he
hasted to dress
it. 8 And he
took butter, and
milk, and the
calf which he
had dressed, and
set it before
them; and he
stood by them
under the tree,
and they did
eat.
9 And they
said unto him,
Where is Sarah
thy wife? And
he said, Behold,
in the tent. 10
And he said, I
will certainly re-
turn unto thee
when the season
cometh round;
and, lo, Sarah
thy wife shall
have a son. And
Sarah heard in
the tent door,
which was be-
hind him. 11
Now Abraham
and Sarah were
old, *and* well
stricken in age;
it had ceased to
be with Sarah
after the manner
of women. 12
And Sarah
laughed within

---

a Sm., G., S. add, *and*, ואחר.

b G. puts after לפניהם; V. omits.

c G. sing., *and he said*, ויאמר.

d For כעת חיה, G. has, *according to this season, at the time.*

e G. has, *she*, היא; Sm. *and she*, והיא; V. for the clause, has, *Sarah laughed behind the door of the tent.*

herself, saying,
After I am wax-
ed old shall I
have pleasure,
my lord being
old also? 13
And the LORD
said unto Abra-
ham, Where-
fore did Sarah
laugh, saying,
Shall I of a
surety bear a
child, which am
old? 14 Is any
thing too hard
for the LORD?
At the time ap-
pointed I will
return unto
thee, according
to the time of
life, and Sarah
shall have a son.
15 Then Sarah
denied, saying,
I laughed not;
for she was a-
fraid. And he
said, Nay; but
thou didst
laugh.
16 And the
men rose up
from thence,
and looked to-
ward Sodom:
and Abraham
went with them
to bring them
on the way. 17
And the LORD
said, Shall I
hide from Abra-
ham that thing
which I do; 18
Seeing that A-
braham shall
surely become a
great and
mighty nation,
and all the na-
tions of the
earth shall be
blessed in him?
19 For I know
him, that he
will command
his children and
his household
after him, and
they shall keep
the way of the
LORD, to do
justice and judg-
ment; that the
LORD may bring

בְּקִרְבָּהּ לֵאמֹר אַחֲרֵי בְלֹתִי הָיְתָה־לִּי [a]
[4]me [3]to [2]be should out worn being my After :saying herself within

עֶדְנָה וַאדֹנִי זָקֵן׃ וַיֹּאמֶר יְהוָה אֶל־ 13
unto Jehovah said And ? old [being] lord my (and) ,[1]pleasure

אַבְרָהָם לָמָּה זֶּה צָחֲקָה שָׂרָה [b] לֵאמֹר הַאַף
Indeed : saying ,Sarah laughed then Why : Abraham

אֻמְנָם אֵלֵד וַאֲנִי זָקַנְתִּי׃ הֲיִפָּלֵא מֵיְהוָה 14
Jehovah for unattainable Is ? old am I when ,bear I shall certainly

דָּבָר לַמּוֹעֵד אָשׁוּב אֵלֶיךָ כָּעֵת
[2]time the at ,thee unto return will I season the At ? thing [any]

חַיָּה [c] וּלְשָׂרָה בֵן׃ וַתְּכַחֵשׁ שָׂרָה לֵאמֹר לֹא 15
[3]Not : saying ,Sarah denied And .son a Sarah to and ;[1]reviving

צָחַקְתִּי כִּי יָרֵאָה וַיֹּאמֶר [d] לֹא [e] כִּי צָחָקְתְּ׃
.laughedst thou but ,No : said he and ; afraid was she for ,[2]laughed [1]I

וַיָּקֻמוּ מִשָּׁם הָאֲנָשִׁים וַיַּשְׁקִפוּ עַל־פְּנֵי סְדֹם [f] 16
,Sodom towards looked and ,men the thence from up rose And

וְאַבְרָהָם הֹלֵךְ עִמָּם לְשַׁלְּחָם.
.them accompany to ,them with going was Abraham [while] (and)

וַיהוָה אָמָר הַמְכַסֶּה אֲנִי מֵאַבְרָהָם [g] אֲשֶׁר 17
which that Abraham from [1]I [2]hide Do : said Jehovah And

אֲנִי עֹשֶׂה׃ וְאַבְרָהָם הָיוֹ יִהְיֶה 18
become will surely Abraham [while] (and) ;do to about [am] I

לְגוֹי גָּדוֹל וְעָצוּם וְנִבְרְכוּ־בוֹ
him in themselves bless will and ,strong and great nation a (for)

כֹּל גּוֹיֵי הָאָרֶץ׃ כִּי יְדַעְתִּיו לְמַעַן 19
order in ,him known have I For ? earth the of nations the all

אֲשֶׁר יְצַוֶּה אֶת־בָּנָיו וְאֶת־בֵּיתוֹ אַחֲרָיו
; him after house his and sons his command may he that

וְשָׁמְרוּ דֶּרֶךְ יְהוָה לַעֲשׂוֹת צְדָקָה
righteousness do to ,Jehovah of way the observe may they and

וּמִשְׁפָּט לְמַעַן הָבִיא יְהוָה עַל־אַבְרָהָם
Abraham upon Jehovah bring [may] that order in : judgment and

herself, saying,
After I am
waxed old shall
I have pleasure,
my lord being
old also? 13
And the LORD
said unto Abra-
ham, Wherefore
did Sarah laugh,
saying, Shall I
of a surety bear
a child, which
am old? 14 Is
any thing too
hard for the
LORD? At the
set time I will
return unto thee,
when the season
cometh round,
and Sarah shall
have a son. 15
Then Sarah de-
nied, saying, I
laughed not; for
she was afraid.
And he said,
Nay; but thou
didst laugh.
16 And the
men rose up
from thence,
and looked to-
ward Sodom:
and Abraham
went with them
to bring them
on the way. 17
And the LORD
said, Shall I
hide from Abra-
ham that which
I do; 18 seeing
that Abraham
shall surely be-
come a great
and mighty
nation, and all
the nations of
the earth shall
be blessed in
him? 19 For I
have known
him, to the end
that he may
command his
children and his
household after
him, that they
may keep the
way of the
LORD, to do
justice and judg-
ment; to the
end that the
LORD may bring

---

a For אחרי בלתי היתה לי עדנה, G. has, *not yet has it happened to me until now*, prob. reading, בִּלְתִּי הָיְתָה־לִּי עֲדֶנָה.

b G. adds, *within herself*, בלבה.

c G. omits.

d G. adds, *to her*.

e Sm. has, *to her*.

f G. adds, *and Gomorrah*.

g G. *from Abraham my servant;* S. *from my servant Abraham*.

upon Abraham that which he hath spoken of him. 20 And the LORD said, Because the cry of Sodom and Gomorrah is great, and because their sin is very grievous, 21 I will go down now, and see whether they have done altogether according to the cry of it, which is come unto me; and if not, I will know. 22 And the men turned their faces from thence, and went toward Sodom: but Abraham stood yet before the LORD.

23 And Abraham drew near, and said, Wilt thou also destroy the righteous with the wicked? 24 Peradventure there be fifty righteous within the city: wilt thou also destroy and not spare the place for the fifty righteous that *are* therein? 25 That be far from thee to do after this manner, to slay the righteous with the wicked: and that the righteous should be as the wicked, that be far from thee: Shall not the Judge of all the earth do right? 26 And the LORD said, If I find in Sodom fifty righteous within the city, then I will spare all the

20 אֵת אֲשֶׁר־דִּבֶּר[a] עָלָיו׃ וַיֹּאמֶר יְהוָה
: Jehovah said And .him concerning spoken has he which that

זַעֲקַת סְדֹם וַעֲמֹרָה כִּי־רָבָּה[b]
; great is it indeed ,Gomorrah and Sodom [over] (of) cry The

21 וְחַטָּאתָם כִּי[c] כָבְדָה מְאֹד׃ אֵרְדָה־נָּא
,now ,down go will I .exceedingly heavy is it indeed ,sin their and

וְאֶרְאֶה הַכְּצַעֲקָתָהּ הַבָּאָה
comes that it of cry the to according whether see will I and

22 אֵלַי עָשׂוּ כָּלָה וְאִם־לֹא אֵדָעָה[d]׃ וַיִּפְנוּ
turned And .know will I ,not if and ; all at done have they me unto

מִשָּׁם הָאֲנָשִׁים וַיֵּלְכוּ סְדֹמָה וְאַבְרָהָם
Abraham [while] (and) ,Sodom toward went and ,men the thence from

23 עוֹדֶנּוּ עֹמֵד לִפְנֵי יְהוָה׃ וַיִּגַּשׁ אַבְרָהָם
Abraham near drew And .Jehovah before standing [was] (he) still

וַיֹּאמַר הַאַף[e] תִּסְפֶּה צַדִּיק עִם־רָשָׁע[f]׃
? wicked with righteous away sweep thou wilt Even : said and

24 אוּלַי יֵשׁ חֲמִשִּׁים צַדִּיקִם בְּתוֹךְ הָעִיר
; city the of midst the in righteous fifty are [there] Perhaps

הַאַף[e] תִּסְפֶּה וְלֹא־תִשָּׂא[g] לַמָּקוֹם לְמַעַן
of because place the (to) forgive not and away sweep thou wilt even

25 חֲמִשִּׁים הַצַּדִּיקִם אֲשֶׁר[h] בְּקִרְבָּהּ׃ חָלִלָה
it be Far ?it of midst the in [are] who ,righteous the ,fifty

לְּךָ מֵעֲשֹׂת כַּדָּבָר הַזֶּה לְהָמִית צַדִּיק עִם־
with righteous kill to ,[1]this [2]word like doing from thee to

רָשָׁע וְהָיָה כַצַּדִּיק כָּרָשָׁע חָלִלָה
it be far ;wicked the like righteous the like be would it and ;wicked

לָּךְ הֲשֹׁפֵט כָּל־הָאָרֶץ לֹא[i] יַעֲשֶׂה
execute [1]shall [2]he [3]not ,earth the all of judge the ,thee to

26 מִשְׁפָּט[c]׃ וַיֹּאמֶר יְהוָה אִם־אֶמְצָא בִסְדֹם חֲמִשִּׁים
fifty Sodom in find I If : Jehovah said And ? judgment

צַדִּיקִם בְּתוֹךְ הָעִיר וְנָשָׂאתִי
forgive will I [then] (and) ,city the of midst the in righteous

upon Abraham that which he hath spoken of him. 20 And the LORD said, Because the cry of Sodom and Gomorrah is great, and because their sin is very grievous; 21 I will go down now, and see whether they have done altogether according to the cry of it, which is come unto me; and if not, I will know. 22 And the men turned from thence, and went toward Sodom: but Abraham stood yet before the LORD.

23 And Abraham drew near, and said, Wilt thou consume the righteous with the wicked? 24 Peradventure there be fifty righteous within the city: wilt thou consume and not spare the place for the fifty righteous that are therein? 25 That be far from thee to do after this manner, to slay the righteous with the wicked, that so the righteous should be as the wicked; that be far from thee: shall not the Judge of all the earth do right? 26 And the LORD said, If I find in Sodom fifty righteous within the city, then I will spare

---

a For אשר, G., V. have, *all which*, כל אשר.

b G., V. omit כי.

c G., S., V. omit.

d G., V. *that I may know*, כי ארעה.

e S. *in one anger;* T. *in anger.*

f G. adds, *and the righteous shall be as the wicked.*

g G. omits ו; G., S., V. connect with the following.

h G., V. have, *if they are.*

i For לא יעשה משפט, S. has, *this judgment shall not be done;* V. *thou wilt by no means do this judgment;* Sym, for השפט---משפט has, *the one asking every man to do right, thou shouldst not do this unjustly.*

place for their
sakes. 27 And
Abraham an-
swered and said,
Behold now, I
have taken up-
on me to speak
unto the Lord,
which *am but*
dust and ashes:
28 Peradventure
there shall lack
five of the fifty
righteous: wilt
thou destroy all
the city for *lack*
of five? And he
said, If I find
there forty and
five, I will not
destroy *it*. 29
And he spake
unto him yet a-
gain, and said,
Peradventure
there shall be
forty found
there. And he
said, I will not
do *it* for forty's
sake. 30 And
he said *unto*
him, Oh let not
the Lord be
angry, and I
will speak: Per-
adventure there
shall thirty be
found there.
And he said, I
will not do *it*,
if I find thirty
there. 31 And
he said, Behold
now, I have
taken upon me
to speak unto
the Lord: Per-
adventure there
shall be twenty
found there.
And he said, I
will not destroy
it for twenty's
sake. 32 And he
said, Oh let not
the Lord be
angry, and I
will speak yet
but this once:
Peradventure
ten shall be
found there.
And he said,
I will not
destroy *it* for
ten's sake. 33

27 לְכָל־הַמָּקוֹם בַּעֲבוּרָם׃ וַיַּעַן אַבְרָהָם
Abraham answered And .them of sake the for place the all (to)

וַיֹּאמַר הִנֵּה־נָא הוֹאַלְתִּי לְדַבֵּר אֶל־אֲדֹנָי
,Lord the unto speak to undertaken have I ,now ,Behold : said and

28 וְאָנֹכִי עָפָר וָאֵפֶר׃ אוּלַי יַחְסְרוּן
from lacking be will perhaps ;ashes and dust [being] I (and)

חֲמִשִּׁים הַצַּדִּיקִם חֲמִשָּׁה הֲתַשְׁחִית בַּחֲמִשָּׁה
,five for ,destroy thou wilt ;five righteous fifty the

אֶת־כָּל־הָעִיר וַיֹּאמֶר לֹא אַשְׁחִית אִם־אֶמְצָא
find I if ,destroy [2]will [1]I [3]Not : said he And ?city the all

29 שָׁם אַרְבָּעִים וַחֲמִשָּׁה׃ וַיֹּסֶף עוֹד לְדַבֵּר
speak to still continued he And .five and forty there

אֵלָיו וַיֹּאמַר אוּלַי יִמָּצְאוּן שָׁם אַרְבָּעִים [a]
: forty there found be will Perhaps : said and ,him unto

וַיֹּאמֶר לֹא אֶעֱשֶׂה [b] בַּעֲבוּר הָאַרְבָּעִים׃
.forty the of sake the for ,do [2]will [1]I [3]Not : said he and

30 וַיֹּאמֶר אַל־נָא יִחַר [c] לַאדֹנָי וַאֲדַבֵּרָה
; speak may I that ,Lord the to be anger [1]let ,[3]now ,[2]Not :said he And

אוּלַי יִמָּצְאוּן שָׁם שְׁלֹשִׁים וַיֹּאמֶר לֹא אֶעֱשֶׂה [d]
,do [2]will [1]I [3]Not : said he and ; thirty there found be will perhaps

31 אִם־אֶמְצָא שָׁם שְׁלֹשִׁים׃ וַיֹּאמֶר הִנֵּה־נָא
,now ,Behold : said he And .thirty there find I if

הוֹאַלְתִּי לְדַבֵּר אֶל־אֲדֹנָי אוּלַי יִמָּצְאוּן
found be will perhaps ; Lord the unto speak to undertaken have I

שָׁם עֶשְׂרִים וַיֹּאמֶר לֹא אַשְׁחִית בַּעֲבוּר
of sake the for ,destroy [2]will [1]I [3]Not : said he and ; twenty there

32 הָעֶשְׂרִים׃ וַיֹּאמֶר אַל־נָא יִחַר לַאדֹנָי
,Lord the to be anger [1]let ,[3]now ,[2]Not : said he And .twenty the

וַאֲדַבְּרָה אַךְ־הַפַּעַם אוּלַי יִמָּצְאוּן שָׁם עֲשָׂרָה
; ten there found be will perhaps ; time this only speak may I that

וַיֹּאמֶר לֹא אַשְׁחִית בַּעֲבוּר הָעֲשָׂרָה׃
.ten the of sake the for destroy [2]will [1]I [3]Not : said he and

all the place for
their sake. 27
And Abraham
answered and
said, Behold
now, I have
taken upon me
to speak unto
the Lord,
which am but
dust and ashes:
28 peradventure
there shall lack
five of the fifty
righteous: wilt
thou destroy all
the city for lack
of five? And he
said, I will not
destroy it, if I
find there forty
and five. 29
And he spake
unto him yet
again, and said,
Peradventure
there shall be
forty found
there. And he
said, I will not
do it for the
forty's sake. 30
And he said, Oh
let not the Lord
be angry, and I
will speak: per-
adventure there
shall thirty be
found there.
And he said, I
will not do
it, if I find thirty
there. 31 And
he said, Behold
now, I have
taken upon me
to speak unto
the Lord: per-
adventure there
shall be twenty
found there.
And he said, I
will not de-
stroy it for the
twenty's sake.
32 And he said,
Oh let not the
Lord be angry,
and I will speak
yet but this once:
peradventure
ten shall be
found there.
And he said, I
will not destroy
it for the ten's

---

a V. adds, *what wilt thou do?*

b G., Sm., S., V. have, *I will destroy*, אשחית; T. *I will make an end.*

c G. omits, so in vs. 32.

d As in vs. 29, except that here V. is like H.

And the LORD went his way, as soon as he had left communing with Abraham : and Abraham returned unto his place.

33 וַיֵּלֶךְ יְהוָה כַּאֲשֶׁר כִּלָּה לְדַבֵּר אֶל־
unto speak to finished had he when Jehovah away went And

אַבְרָהָם וְאַבְרָהָם שָׁב לִמְקֹמוֹ׃
.place his to returned Abraham [while] (and) ,Abraham

sake. 33 And the LORD went his way, as soon as he had left communing with Abraham : and Abraham returned unto his place.

19

AND there came two angels to Sodom at even ; and Lot sat in the gate of Sodom : and Lot seeing *them* rose up to meet them ; and he bowed himself with his face toward the ground ; 2 And he said, Behold now, my lords, turn in, I pray you, into your servant's house, and tarry all night, and wash your feet, and ye shall rise up early, and go on your ways. And they said, Nay; but we will abide in the street all night. 3 And he pressed upon them greatly; and they turned in unto him, and entered into his house; and he made them a feast, and did bake unleavened bread, and they did eat. 4 But before they lay down, the men of the city, *even* the men of Sodom, compassed the house round, both old and young, all the people from every quarter : 5 And they called unto Lot, and said unto him, Where *are* the men which came in to thee this night? bring them out unto us, that we may

1 וַיָּבֹאוּ שְׁנֵי הַמַּלְאָכִים סְדֹמָה בָּעֶרֶב
,evening at Sodom to angels two the in came And

וְלוֹט יֹשֵׁב בְּשַׁעַר־סְדֹם וַיַּרְא־לוֹט
saw Lot and ,Sodom of gate the in sitting [was] Lot [while] (and)

וַיָּקָם לִקְרָאתָם וַיִּשְׁתַּחוּ אַפַּיִם
face his [with] ,himself prostrated and ,them meet to up rose and

2 אָרְצָה׃ וַיֹּאמֶר הִנֶּה[a] נָּא־אֲדֹנַי סוּרוּ
,aside turn ,lords my ,now ,Behold : said he And .earth the towards

נָא אֶל־בֵּית עַבְדְּכֶם וְלִינוּ וְרַחֲצוּ
wash and ,night the spend and ,servant your of house the unto ,pray

רַגְלֵיכֶם וְהִשְׁכַּמְתֶּם וַהֲלַכְתֶּם לְדַרְכְּכֶם וַיֹּאמְרוּ
: said they and ; way your (to) go and early rise and ; feet your

3 לֹּא כִּי בָרְחוֹב נָלִין׃ וַיִּפְצַר־בָּם[b]
them urged he And .night the spend will we way broad the in for ;No

מְאֹד[c] וַיָּסֻרוּ אֵלָיו וַיָּבֹאוּ
in came and ,him unto aside turned they and ,exceedingly

אֶל־בֵּיתוֹ וַיַּעַשׂ לָהֶם מִשְׁתֶּה וּמַצּוֹת
cakes unleavened and ,feast a them for made he and ;house his unto

4 אָפָה[d] וַיֹּאכֵלוּ׃ טֶרֶם יִשְׁכָּבוּ[e] וְאַנְשֵׁי
of men the and ,down lain [2]had [1]they [4]yet [3]Not .ate they and ,baked he

הָעִיר אַנְשֵׁי סְדֹם נָסַבּוּ עַל־הַבַּיִת
; house the (upon) surrounded ,Sodom of men the ,city the

מִנַּעַר וְעַד־זָקֵן [f]כָּל־הָעָם מִקָּצֶה׃
.end the from people the all ,aged unto (and) youth from

5 וַיִּקְרְאוּ אֶל־לוֹט וַיֹּאמְרוּ לוֹ אַיֵּה הָאֲנָשִׁים
men the [are] Where :him to said and Lot unto called they And

אֲשֶׁר־בָּאוּ אֵלֶיךָ הַלָּיְלָה הוֹצִיאֵם אֵלֵינוּ
,us unto out them Bring ?to night thee unto in came who

And the two angels came to Sodom at even; and Lot sat in the gate of Sodom: and Lot saw them, and rose up to meet them; and he bowed himself with his face to the earth; 2 and he said, Behold now, my lords, turn aside, I pray you, into your servant's house, and tarry all night, and wash your feet, and ye shall rise up early, and go on your way. And they said, Nay ; but we will abide in the street all night. 3 And he urged them greatly; and they turned in unto him, and entered into his house; and he made them a feast, and did bake unleavened bread, and they did eat. 4 But before they lay down, the men of the city, *even* the men of Sodom, compassed the house round, both young and old, all the people from every quarter; 5 and they called unto Lot, and said unto him, Where are the men which came in to thee this night? bring them out unto us, that we may

a S., V., T. omit.
b S. adds, *Lot*, לוט.
c G. omits.
d G., S., T. add, *for them*, להם.
e G. connects, טרם ישכבו with vs. 3.
f S. adds, *and*, וכל-העם.

know them. 6 And Lot went out at the door unto them, and shut the door after him, 7 And said, I pray you, brethren, do not so wickedly. 8 Behold now, I have two daughters which have not known man; let me, I pray you, bring them out unto you, and do ye to them as *is* good in your eyes: only unto these men do nothing; for therefore came they under the shadow of my roof. 9 And they said, Stand back. And they said *again*, This one *fellow* came in to sojourn, and he will needs be a judge: now will we deal worse with thee, than with them. And they pressed sore upon the man, *even* Lot, and came near to break the door. 10 But the men put forth their hand, and pulled Lot into the house to them, and shut to the door. 11 And they smote the men that *were* at the door of the house with blindness, both small and great: so that they wearied themselves to find the door.

6 וְנֵדְעָה אֹתָם׃ וַיֵּצֵא אֲלֵהֶם לוֹט
Lot them unto out went And .them know may we that

7 הַפֶּתְחָה[a] וְהַדֶּלֶת סָגַר אַחֲרָיו׃ וַיֹּאמַר[b]
: said he and ; him behind closed he door the and ,entrance the to

8 אַל־נָא אַחַי תָּרֵעוּ׃ הִנֵּה־נָא[c] לִי
[are] me to ,now ,Behold .wickedly act ¹do ,⁵brethren ⁴my ,³pray ²,Not

שְׁתֵּי בָנוֹת אֲשֶׁר לֹא־יָדְעוּ[d] אִישׁ אוֹצִיאָה־נָּא
,pray ,out bring me let ;man known not have who ,daughters two

אֶתְהֶן אֲלֵיכֶם וַעֲשׂוּ לָהֶן כַּטּוֹב
good the to according them to do and ,you unto them

בְּעֵינֵיכֶם רַק לָאֲנָשִׁים הָאֵל אַל־תַּעֲשׂוּ דָבָר[e]
; thing a do not do ¹these ²men to only ; eyes your in

כִּי־עַל־כֵּן[f] בָּאוּ בְּצֵל קֹרָתִי׃
.roof my of shadow the into come have they therefore for

9 וַיֹּאמְרוּ גֶּשׁ־הָלְאָה וַיֹּאמְרוּ הָאֶחָד[g] בָּא־[g]
,in came one This : said they and ; away Move : said they And

לָגוּר וַיִּשְׁפֹּט שָׁפוֹט עַתָּה נָרַע
evil do will we now ; continually judge as acts he and sojourn to

לְךָ מֵהֶם וַיִּפְצְרוּ בָאִישׁ
,man the upon pressed they and ; them [to] than [more] thee to

בְּלוֹט[h] מְאֹד וַיִּגְּשׁוּ לִשְׁבֹּר הַדָּלֶת׃
.door the break to near drew and ,exceedingly ,Lot upon

10 וַיִּשְׁלְחוּ הָאֲנָשִׁים אֶת־יָדָם וַיָּבִיאוּ אֶת־לוֹט אֲלֵיהֶם
them unto Lot brought and ,hands their men the out put And

11 הַבָּיְתָה[i] וְאֶת־הַדֶּלֶת[j] סָגָרוּ׃ וְאֶת־הָאֲנָשִׁים
men the And .shut they door the and ,house the into

אֲשֶׁר־פֶּתַח הַבַּיִת הִכּוּ בַּסַּנְוֵרִים
,blindness with smote they house the of door the [at] [were] who

מִקָּטֹן וְעַד־גָּדוֹל וַיִּלְאוּ
themselves wearied they and ; great the unto and small the from

12 לִמְצֹא הַפָּתַח׃ וַיֹּאמְרוּ הָאֲנָשִׁים[k] אֶל־לוֹט עֹד[a]
Still : Lot unto men the said And .entrance the find to

know them. 6 And Lot went out unto them to the door, and shut the door after him. 7 And he said, I pray you, my brethren, do not so wickedly. 8 Behold now, I have two daughters which have not known man; let me, I pray you, bring them out unto you, and do ye to them as is good in your eyes: only unto these men do nothing; forasmuch as they are come under the shadow of my roof. 9 And they said, Stand back. And they said, This one fellow came in to sojourn, and he will needs be a judge; now will we deal worse with thee, than with them. And they pressed sore upon the man, even Lot, and drew near to break the door. 10 But the men put forth their hand, and brought Lot into the house to them, and shut to the door. 11 And they smote the men that were at the door of the house with blindness, both small and great: so that they wearied themselves to find the door.

12 And the men said unto Lot, Hast thou

12 And the men said unto Lot, Hast thou

---

a G., V. omit.
b G., S. add, *unto them.*
c G. has, *but;* V. omits.
d S., T. have sing. ידע, *whom a man has not known.*
e G. adds, *wicked;* so V.
f S., V. omit, *therefore,* על כן.
g G. has, *thou camest in.*
h S. has, *and Lot strove with the men.*
i V. omits.
j G. *the door of the house,* דלת הבית.
k Sm. *the angels,* המלאכים.

here any besides? son in
law, and thy
sons, and thy
daughters, and
whatsoever
thou hast in the
city, bring *them*
out of this
place: 13 For
we will destroy
this place, because the cry of
them is waxen
great before the
face of the Lord;
and the LORD
hath sent us to
destroy it. 14
And Lot went
out, and spake
unto his sons in
law, which married his daughters, and said,
Up, get you out
of this place; for
the LORD will
destroy this city.
But he seemed
as one that
mocked unto
his sons in law.
15 And when
the morning
arose, then the
angels hastened
Lot, saying,
Arise, take thy
wife, and thy
two daughters,
which are here;
lest thou be consumed in the
iniquity of the
city. 16 And
while he lingered, the men
laid hold upon
his hand, and
upon the
hand of his
wife, and upon
the hand of his
two daughters;
the LORD being
merciful unto
him: and they
brought him
forth, and set
him without the
city.
17 And it
came to pass,
when they had
brought them
forth abroad,

מִי־לְךָ פֹה[a] חָתָן וּבָנֶיךָ וּבְנֹתֶיךָ
,daughters thy and ,sons thy and ,Son-in-law ?here thee to [is] who

וְכֹל אֲשֶׁר־לְךָ בָּעִיר[b] הוֹצֵא מִן־הַמָּקוֹם׃[c]
.place the from forth bring ;city the in thee to [are] who all and

13 כִּי־מַשְׁחִתִים אֲנַחְנוּ אֶת־הַמָּקוֹם הַזֶּה כִּי־
because ;[1]this [2]place [2][are] [1]we [5]destroy [4]to [3]about For

גָדְלָה[d] צַעֲקָתָם אֶת־פְּנֵי יְהוָה
,Jehovah before them [over] (of) cry the great become has

14 וַיְשַׁלְּחֵנוּ יְהוָה לְשַׁחֲתָהּ׃ וַיֵּצֵא לוֹט וַיְדַבֵּר
spoke and Lot out went And .it destroy to Jehovah us sent has and

אֶל־חֲתָנָיו לֹקְחֵי בְנֹתָיו וַיֹּאמֶר קוּמוּ
,ye Rise :said he and ,daughters his of takers the ,sons-in-law his unto

צְאוּ מִן־הַמָּקוֹם הַזֶּה כִּי־מַשְׁחִית יְהוָה
[2][is] [1]Jehovah [5]destroy [4]to [3]about for [1]this [2]place from out go

אֶת־הָעִיר[e] וַיְהִי כִמְצַחֵק בְּעֵינֵי
of eyes the in mocking one like was he and ;city the

15 חֲתָנָיו׃ וּכְמוֹ הַשַּׁחַר עָלָה וַיָּאִיצוּ הַמַּלְאָכִים
angels the urged then ,arose dawn the when And .sons-in-law his

בְּלוֹט לֵאמֹר[f] קוּם קַח אֶת־אִשְׁתְּךָ וְאֶת־שְׁתֵּי בְנֹתֶיךָ
daughters [1]thy [2]two and wife thy take ,Rise :saying Lot (on)

הַנִּמְצָאֹת[g] פֶּן־תִּסָּפֶה בַּעֲוֺן הָעִיר׃
.city the of punishment the in away swept be thou lest ;found [are] who

16 וַיִּתְמַהְמָהּ[h] וַיַּחֲזִיקוּ הָאֲנָשִׁים[i] בְּיָדוֹ וּבְיַד־
of hand the (on) and hand his (on) men the seized and ;loitered he But

אִשְׁתּוֹ וּבְיַד שְׁתֵּי בְנֹתָיו בְּחֶמְלַת
[2]sparing in daughters [1]his [2]two of hand the (on) and wife his

יְהוָה עָלָיו וַיֹּצִאֻהוּ[j] וַיַּנִּחֻהוּ
him of go let and ,forth him brought they and ;him (upon) [1]Jehovah's

17 מִחוּץ לָעִיר׃[j] וַיְהִי[k] כְהוֹצִיאָם
forth bringing their at pass to came it And .city the to outside from

אֹתָם הַחוּצָה[k] וַיֹּאמֶר[l] הִמָּלֵט עַל־נַפְשֶׁךָ אַל־תַּבִּיט
look not do ,life thy for Escape :said he that ,outside them

here any besides? son in
law, and thy
sons, and thy
daughters, and
whomsoever
thou hast in the
city; bring them
out of the place:
13 for we will
destroy this
place, because
the cry of them
is waxen great
before the
LORD; and the
LORD hath sent
us to destroy it.
14 And Lot
went out, and
spake unto his
sons in law,
which married
his daughters,
and said, Up,
get you out of
this place; for
the LORD will
destroy the city.
But he seemed
unto his sons in
law as one that
mocked.
15 And when
the morning arose, then the
angels hastened
Lot, saying,
Arise, take thy
wife, and thy two
daughters which
are here; lest
thou be consumed in the
iniquity of the
city. 16 But he
lingered; and
the men laid
hold upon his
hand, and upon
the hand of his
wife, and upon
the hand of his
two daughters;
the LORD being
merciful unto
him: and they
brought him
forth, and set
him without the
city.
17 And it
came to pass,
when they had
brought them
forth abroad,

---

a S. has, *what art thou doing here?*

b V. omits.

c G., S. have, *from this place*, מן המקום הזה; V. *from the city.*

d For גדלה, G. has, *has gone up*, עלתה.

e V. *this city;* S. *it.*

f S. adds, *to him.*

g G. adds, *and go forth.*

h S. adds, *Lot*, לוט.

i G., S., *the angels*, המלאכים; V. omits.

j G. omits ויצאהו--לעיר.

k V. omits ויהו--החוצה.

l G., S., V. pl. *and they said*, ויאמרו; S. adds, *to him.*

that he said,
Escape for thy
life; look not
behind thee,
neither stay
thou in all the
plain; escape to
the mountain,
lest thou be
consumed. 18
And Lot said
unto them, Oh,
not so, my Lord:
19 Behold now,
thy servant hath
found grace in
thy sight, and
thou hast mag-
nified thy mercy,
which thou hast
shewed unto me
in saving my
life; and I can-
not escape to
the mountain,
less some evil
take me, and I
die: 20 Behold
now, this city *is*
near to flee un-
to, and it *is* a
little one: O,
let me escape
thither, (*is* it not
a little one?)
and my soul
shall live. 21
And he said un-
to him, See I
have accepted
thee concerning
this thing also,
that I will not
overthrow this
city, for the
which thou hast
spoken. 22
Haste thee, es-
cape thither;
for I cannot do
any thing till
thou be come
thither. There-
fore the name of
the city was call-
ed Zoar.
23 The sun
was risen upon
the earth when
Lot entered in-
to Zoar. 24 Then
the LORD rained
upon Sodom
and Gomorrah
brimstone and
fire from the
LORD out of
heaven; 25 And

אַחֲרֶיךָ וְאַל־תַּעֲמֹד בְּכָל־הַכִּכָּר הָהָרָה
mountain the to ;circuit the all in remain not do and ,thee behind

18 הִמָּלֵט פֶּן־תִּסָּפֶה׃ וַיֹּאמֶר[a] לוֹט אֲלֵהֶם
:them unto Lot said And .away swept be thou lest ,escape

19 אַל־נָא[b] אֲדֹנָי׃ הִנֵּה־נָא[c] מָצָא עַבְדְּךָ חֵן
favor servant thy found has ,now ,Behold .Lord O ,pray ,No

בְּעֵינֶיךָ וַתַּגְדֵּל חַסְדְּךָ אֲשֶׁר
which kindness thy great made hast thou and ,eyes thine in

עָשִׂיתָ עִמָּדִי לְהַחֲיוֹת אֶת־נַפְשִׁי וְאָנֹכִי לֹא
not I and ;soul my alive preserve to ,me with done hast thou

אוּכַל לְהִמָּלֵט הָהָרָה פֶּן־תִּדְבָּקַנִי הָרָעָה
evil the me to cling lest ,mountain the to escape to able am

20 וָמַתִּי׃ הִנֵּה־נָא הָעִיר הַזֹּאת קְרֹבָה לָנוּס שָׁמָּה
,thither flee to near [is] [1]this [2]city ,now ,Behold .die I and

וְהִוא מִצְעָר אִמָּלְטָה נָּא שָׁמָּה הֲלֹא
[2]not [is] ,thither ,pray ,escape me let ;thing small a [being] it (and)

21 מִצְעָר הִוא וּתְחִי נַפְשִׁי[d]׃ וַיֹּאמֶר אֵלָיו
,him unto said he And .soul my live may that ?[1]it [5]thing [4]small [3]a

הִנֵּה נָשָׂאתִי פָנֶיךָ גַּם לַדָּבָר הַזֶּה לְבִלְתִּי
[2]not to ,[1]this [2]thing for also face thy up lifted have I Behold

22[e] הָפְכִּי אֶת־הָעִיר אֲשֶׁר דִּבַּרְתָּ׃ מַהֵר
Hasten .about spoken hast thou which city the destroying [1]my

הִמָּלֵט שָׁמָּה כִּי לֹא אוּכַל לַעֲשׂוֹת דָּבָר עַד־
until ,thing a do to able [2]am [1]I [3]not for ,thither escape to

בֹּאֲךָ שָׁמָּה עַל־כֵּן קָרָא שֵׁם־הָעִיר
city the of name the called [one] therefore ;thither coming thy

23 צוֹעַר׃ הַשֶּׁמֶשׁ יָצָא עַל־הָאָרֶץ וְלוֹט בָּא
in came Lot (and) ,earth the upon risen having sun The .Zoar

24 צֹעֲרָה׃ וַיהוָה הִמְטִיר עַל־סְדֹם וְעַל־עֲמֹרָה
Gomorrah upon and Sodom upon rained Jehovah And .Zoar to

גָּפְרִית וָאֵשׁ מֵאֵת יְהוָה מִן־הַשָּׁמָיִם׃
.heavens the from Jehovah (with) from ,fire and brimstone

that he said,
Escape for thy
life; look not
behind thee,
neither stay thou
in all the Plain;
escape to the
mountain, lest
thou be con-
sumed. 18 And
Lot said unto
them, Oh, not
so, my lord: 19
behold now,
thy servant hath
found grace in
thy sight, and
thou hast mag-
nified thy mer-
cy, which thou
hast shewed un-
to me in saving
my life; and I
cannot escape
to the mountain,
lest evil overtake
me, and I die:
20 behold now,
this city is near
to flee unto,
and it is a little
one: Oh, let me
escape thither,
(is it not a little
one?) and my
soul shall live.
21 And he said
unto him, See, I
have accepted
thee concerning
this thing also,
that I will not
overthrow the
city of which
thou hast
spoken. 22
Haste thee, es-
cape thither;
for I cannot do
any thing till
thou be come
thither. There-
fore the name
of the city was
called Zoar.

23 The sun
was risen upon
the earth when
Lot came unto
Zoar. 24 Then
the LORD rained
upon Sodom
and upon Go-
morrah brim-
stone and fire
from the LORD
out of heaven,

---

a S. adds, *to them.*
b G., S., T., V. omit אל.
c G., V. have, *since.*
d G. adds. *on account of thee.*
e G. adds, *therefore.*

he over-
threw those
cities, and all
the plain, and
all the inhab-
itants of the
cities, and that
which grew up-
on the ground.
26 But his
wife looked
back from be-
hind him, and
she became a
pillar of salt.
27 And Abra-
ham gat up
early in the
morning to the
place where he
stood before the
the LORD: 28
And he looked
toward Sodom
and Gomorrah,
and toward all
the land of the
plain, and be-
held, and, lo,
the smoke of the
country went up
as the smoke of
a furnace.
29 And it
came to pass,
when God de-
stroyed the cit-
ies of the plain,
that God re-
membered A-
braham, and
sent Lot out of
the midst of the
overthrow,
when he over-
threw the cities
in the which
Lot dwelt.
30 And Lot
went up out of
Zoar, and dwelt
in the mountain,
and his two
daughters with
him; for he
feared to dwell
in Zoar: and he
dwelt in a cave,
he and his two
daughters. 31
And the first-
born said unto
the younger,
Our father *is*

25 וַיַּהֲפֹךְ אֶת־הֶעָרִים הָאֵל[a] וְאֵת כָּל־הַכִּכָּר וְאֵת
and ,circuit the all and ,[1]these [2]cities overthrew he And

כָּל־יֹשְׁבֵי הֶעָרִים[b] וְצֶמַח[c] הָאֲדָמָה׃
.ground the of growth the and ,cities the of inhabitants the all

26 וַתַּבֵּט אִשְׁתּוֹ מֵאַחֲרָיו וַתְּהִי
became she and ,him behind from wife his away looked And

27 נְצִיב מֶלַח׃ וַיַּשְׁכֵּם אַבְרָהָם בַּבֹּקֶר
morning the in Abraham early rose And .salt of pillar a

אֶל־הַמָּקוֹם אֲשֶׁר־עָמַד שָׁם אֶת־פְּנֵי יְהוָה׃
.Jehovah before (there) stood had he where place the unto

28 וַיַּשְׁקֵף עַל־פְּנֵי סְדֹם וַעֲמֹרָה וְעַל
upon and ,Gomorrah and Sodom of face the upon out looked he And

כָּל־פְּנֵי[d] אֶרֶץ הַכִּכָּר וַיַּרְא וְהִנֵּה
,behold and ,saw he and ;circuit the of land the of face the all

עָלָה קִיטֹר הָאָרֶץ כְּקִיטֹר הַכִּבְשָׁן׃
.smelting-oven a of vapor the like land the of vapor the up gone had

29 וַיְהִי בְּשַׁחֵת אֱלֹהִים[e] אֶת־עָרֵי הַכִּכָּר
,circuit the of cities the [1]God's [2]destroying in ,pass to came it And

וַיִּזְכֹּר אֱלֹהִים אֶת־אַבְרָהָם וַיְשַׁלַּח אֶת־לוֹט
Lot sent and ,Abraham God remembered that

מִתּוֹךְ הַהֲפֵכָה בַּהֲפֹךְ[f] אֶת־הֶעָרִים
cities the overthrowing in ,overthrow the of midst the from

30 אֲשֶׁר־יָשַׁב בָּהֵן לוֹט׃ וַיַּעַל לוֹט מִצּוֹעַר
Zoar from Lot up went And .Lot (them in) dwelt which [in]

וַיֵּשֶׁב בָּהָר וּשְׁתֵּי בְנֹתָיו עִמּוֹ
;him with [being] daughters [1]his [2]two (and) ,mountain the in dwelt and

כִּי יָרֵא לָשֶׁבֶת בְּצוֹעַר וַיֵּשֶׁב בַּמְּעָרָה הוּא
he ,cave the in dwelt he and ;Zoar in dwell to feared he for

31 וּשְׁתֵּי בְנֹתָיו[g]׃ וַתֹּאמֶר הַבְּכִירָה אֶל־הַצְּעִירָה
:younger the unto firstborn the said And .daughters [1]his [2]two and

אָבִינוּ זָקֵן וְאִישׁ אֵין בָּאָרֶץ לָבוֹא
in come to ,land the in not is man a and ,old is father Our

25 and he over-
threw those cit-
ies, and all the
Plain, and all
the inhabitants
of the cities, and
that which grew
upon the
ground.
26 But his
wife looked back
from behind
him, and she be-
came a pillar of
salt.
27 And Abra-
ham gat up early
in the morning
to the place
where he had
stood before
the LORD: 28
and he looked
toward Sodom
and Gomorrah,
and toward all
the land of the
Plain, and be-
held, and, lo,
the smoke of the
land went up as
the smoke of a
furnace.
29 And it
came to pass,
when God de-
stroyed the cit-
ies of the Plain,
that God re-
membered A-
braham, and
sent Lot out of
the midst of the
overthrow,
when he over-
threw the cities
in the which
Lot dwelt.
30 And Lot
went up out of
Zoar, and dwelt
in the mountain,
and his two
daughters with
him; for he
feared to dwell
in Zoar: and he
dwelt in a cave,
he and his two
daughters. 31
And the first-
born said unto
the younger,
Our father is
old, and there
is not a man in

---

a G. adds, *in which Lot dwelt*.
b S. has, *the land*, הארץ.
c G., V. add, *all*, וכל צמח.
d G. omits כל.
e G. has, *Lord*, יהוה.
f G. adds, *Lord*, יהוה.
g Sm., G., V. add, *with him*, עמו.

old, and *there is* not a man in the earth to come in unto us after the manner of all the earth: 32 Come, let us make our father drink wine, and we will lie with him, that we may preserve seed of our father. 33 And they made their father drink wine that night: and the firstborn went in, and lay with her father; and he perceived not when she lay down, nor when she arose. 34 And it came to pass on the morrow, that the firstborn said unto the younger, Behold, I lay yesternight with my father; let us make him drink wine this night also; and go thou in, *and* lie with him, that we may preserve seed of our father. 35 And they made their father drink wine that night also; and the younger arose, and lay with him; and he perceived not when she lay down, nor when she arose. 36 Thus were both the daughters of Lot with child by their father. 37 And the firstborn bare a son, and called his name Moab: the same *is* the father of the Moabites unto this day. 38 And the younger, she bare a son also, and called his name Ben-ammi: the same *is* the father of the children of Ammon unto this day.

עָלֵינוּ כְּדֶרֶךְ כָּל־הָאָרֶץ׃ לְכָה נַשְׁקֶה 32
drink to cause us let ,Come .earth the all of way the after us unto

אֶת־אָבִינוּ יַיִן וְנִשְׁכְּבָה עִמּוֹ וּנְחַיֶּה
alive preserve may we that ;him with lie us let and ,wine father our

33 מֵאָבִינוּ זָרַע׃ וַתַּשְׁקֶיןָ אֶת־אֲבִיהֶן יַיִן
wine father their drink to caused they And .seed father our from

בַּלַּיְלָה הוּא וַתָּבֹא הַבְּכִירָה וַתִּשְׁכַּב אֶת־אָבִיהָ [a]
;father her with lay and firstborn the in came and ;[1]that [2]night in

וְלֹא־יָדַע בְּשִׁכְבָהּ וּבְקוּמָהּ׃
.up rising her in and down lying her in know not did he and

34 וַיְהִי מִמָּחֳרָת וַתֹּאמֶר הַבְּכִירָה אֶל־
unto firstborn the said that morrow the from pass to came it And

הַצְּעִירָה הֵן־שָׁכַבְתִּי אֶמֶשׁ אֶת־אָבִי [b]
;father my with night [last] lay I Behold :younger the

נַשְׁקֶנּוּ יַיִן גַּם־הַלַּיְלָה וּבֹאִי
,in thou go and ;tonight also wine drink to him cause us let

שִׁכְבִי עִמּוֹ וּנְחַיֶּה מֵאָבִינוּ
father our from alive preserve may we that ;him with lie

35 זָרַע׃ וַתַּשְׁקֶיןָ גַּם בַּלַּיְלָה הַהוּא
[1]that [2]night in also drink to caused they And .seed

אֶת־אֲבִיהֶן יָיִן וַתָּקָם [c] הַצְּעִירָה וַתִּשְׁכַּב עִמּוֹ [d]
;him with lay and younger the up rose and :wine father their

וְלֹא־יָדַע בְּשִׁכְבָהּ וּבְקֻמָהּ׃
.up rising her in and down lying her in know not did he and

36 37 וַתַּהֲרֶיןָ שְׁתֵּי בְנוֹת־לוֹט מֵאֲבִיהֶן׃ וַתֵּלֶד
bore And .father their from Lot of daughters two the conceived And

הַבְּכִירָה בֵּן וַתִּקְרָא שְׁמוֹ מוֹאָב [e] הוּא
he ;Moab name his called she and ,son a firstborn the

38 אֲבִי־מוֹאָב עַד־הַיּוֹם׃ וְהַצְּעִירָה גַם־הִוא
,she also ,younger the And .day this unto Moab of father the [being]

יָלְדָה בֵּן וַתִּקְרָא שְׁמוֹ בֶּן־עַמִּי [f] הוּא
[being] he ;Ben-ammi name his called she and ,son a bore

אֲבִי בְנֵי־עַמּוֹן עַד־הַיּוֹם׃
.day this unto Ammon of sons the of father the

the earth to come in unto us after the manner of all the earth: 32 come, let us make our father drink wine, and we will lie with him, that we may preserve seed of our father. 33 And they made their father drink wine that night: and the firstborn went in, and lay with her father; and he knew not when she lay down, nor when she arose. 34 And it came to pass on the morrow, that the firstborn said unto the younger, Behold, I lay yesternight with my father: let us make him drink wine this night also; and go thou in, and lie with him, that we may preserve seed of our father. 35 And they made their father drink wine that night also: and the younger arose, and lay with him; and he knew not when she lay down, nor when she arose. 36 Thus were both the daughters of Lot with child by their father. 37 And the firstborn bare a son, and called his name Moab: the same is the father of the Moabites unto this day. 38 And the younger, she also bare a son, and called his name Ben-ammi: the same is the father of the children of Ammon unto this day.

---

a G. adds, *that night*.
b G. *our father*, אבינו.
c G., V. have, *and she came in*, ותבא.
d G. *with her father*.
e G. adds, *saying, from my father*.
f G. has, *Amman, the son of my people*; similar V. *Ammon, that is, son of my people*.

20

AND Abraham
journeyed from
thence toward
the south coun-
try, and dwelled
between Ka-
desh and Shur,
and sojourned
in Gerar. 2
And Abraham
said of Sarah
his wife, She *is*
my sister: and
Abimelech king
of Gerar sent,
and took Sarah.
3 But God came
to Abimelech
in a dream by
night, and
said to him,
Behold, thou
art but a dead
man, for the
woman which
thou hast taken;
for she *is* a
man's wife. 4
But Abimelech
had not come
near her: and
he said, Lord,
wilt thou slay al-
so a righteous
nation? 5 Said
he not unto me,
She *is* my sister?
and she, even
she herself said,
He *is* my broth-
er: in the integ-
rity of my heart
and innocency
of my hands
have I done
this. 6 And
God said unto
him in a dream,
Yea, I know
that thou didst
this in the integ-
rity of thy heart;
for I also with-
held thee from
sinning against
me: therefore
suffered I thee
not to touch her.

1 וַיִּסַּע מִשָּׁם אַבְרָהָם אַרְצָה
of land the to Abraham thence from departed And

הַנֶּגֶב וַיֵּשֶׁב בֵּין־קָדֵשׁ וּבֵין שׁוּר
; Shur (between) and Kadesh between dwelt and ,country south the

2 וַיָּגָר בִּגְרָר׃ וַיֹּאמֶר אַבְרָהָם אֶל־שָׂרָה
Sarah concerning Abraham said And .Gerar in sojourned he and

אִשְׁתּוֹ אֲחֹתִי הִוא[a] וַיִּשְׁלַח אֲבִימֶלֶךְ מֶלֶךְ גְּרָר
Gerar of king Abimelech sent and ; she [is] sister My :wife his

3 וַיִּקַּח אֶת־שָׂרָה׃ וַיָּבֹא אֱלֹהִים אֶל־אֲבִימֶלֶךְ בַּחֲלוֹם
dream a in Abimelech unto God came And .Sarah took and

הַלָּיְלָה וַיֹּאמֶר לוֹ הִנְּךָ מֵת
die to about [art] thou Behold : him to said and ,night by

עַל־הָאִשָּׁה אֲשֶׁר־לָקַחְתָּ וְהִוא
[being] she (and) ,taken hast thou whom woman the of account on

4 בְּעֻלַת בָּעַל׃ וַאֲבִימֶלֶךְ לֹא קָרַב אֵלֶיהָ
; her unto approached [1]had [2]not Abimelech And .husband a to married

וַיֹּאמַר אֲדֹנָי הֲגוֹי גַּם־צַדִּיק[b] תַּהֲרֹג׃
? slay thou wilt righteous even nation a ,Lord O : said he and

5 הֲלֹא הוּא אָמַר־לִי[c] אֲחֹתִי הִוא וְהִיא־גַם־הִוא
,she even ,she And ? she [is] sister My : me to say [1]did [3]he [2]Not

אָמְרָה[d] אָחִי הוּא בְּתָם־לְבָבִי
heart my of integrity the In ? he [is] brother My : said

6 וּבְנִקְיֹן כַּפַּי עָשִׂיתִי זֹאת׃ וַיֹּאמֶר אֵלָיו
him unto said And .this did I hands my of cleanness the in and

הָאֱלֹהִים בַּחֲלֹם גַּם אָנֹכִי יָדַעְתִּי כִּי בְתָם־
of integrity the in that know I Also : dream a in God

לְבָבְךָ עָשִׂיתָ זֹּאת וָאֶחְשֹׂךְ גַּם־אָנֹכִי אוֹתְךָ
thee ,I even ,restrained I and ; this didst thou heart thy

מֵחֲטוֹ־לִי עַל־כֵּן לֹא־נְתַתִּיךָ לִנְגֹּעַ
touch to thee allowed not have I therefore ; me against sinning from

And Abra-
ham journeyed
from thence to-
ward the land
of the South,
and dwelt be-
tween Kadesh
and Shur; and
he sojourned
in Gerar. 2 And
Abraham said of
Sarah his wife,
She is my sister:
and Abimelech
king of Gerar
sent, and took
Sarah. 3 But
God came to
Abimelech in a
dream of the
night, and said
to him, Behold,
thou art but a
dead man, be-
cause of the
woman which
thou hast taken;
for she is a man's
wife. 4 Now
Abimelech had
not come near
her: and he
said, Lord,
wilt thou slay
even a righteous
nation? 5 Said
he not himself
unto me, She is
my sister? and
she, even she
herself said, He
is my brother:
in the integrity
of my heart and
the innocency
of my hands
have I done
this. 6 And
God said unto
him in the
dream, Yea, I
know that in the
integrity of thy
heart thou hast
done this, and I
also withheld
thee from sin-
ning against me:
therefore suffer-
ed I thee not to

---

a G. adds, *for he feared to say, She is my wife, lest the men of the city might slay him on account of her.*

b G., V. have, *ignorant and righteous.*

c S. omits לִי.

d G. adds, *to me,* לִי.

7 Now there-
fore restore the
man *his* wife;
for he *is* a pro-
phet, and he
shall pray for
thee, and thou
shalt live: and
if thou restore
her not, know
thou that thou
shalt surely die,
thou, and all
that *are* thine. 8
Therefore A-
bimelech rose
early in the
morning, and
called all his
servants, and
told all these
things in their
ears: and the
men were sore
afraid. 9 Then
Abimelech call-
ed Abraham,
and said unto
him, What hast
thou done unto
us? and what
have I offended
thee, that thou
hast brought on
me and on my
kingdom a great
sin? thou hast
done deeds unto
me that ought
not to be done.
10 And Abi-
melech said un-
to Abraham,
What sawest
thou, that thou
hast done this
thing? 11 And
Abraham said,
Because I
thought, surely
the fear of God
is not in this
place; and they
will slay me for
my wife's sake.
12 And yet in-
deed *she is* my
sister; she *is* the
daughter of my
father, but not
the daughter of
my mother;
and she be-
came my wife.
13 And it came
to pass, when
God caused me
tc wander from

7 אֵלֶיהָ׃ וְעַתָּה הָשֵׁב אֵשֶׁת־הָאִישׁ [a] כִּי־נָבִיא
prophet a for ,man the of wife the return now And .her (unto)

הוּא וְיִתְפַּלֵּל בַּעַדְךָ וֶחְיֵה וְאִם־אֵינְךָ
not art thou if and ;thou live and ,thee for pray him let and ,he [is]

מֵשִׁיב דַּע כִּי־מוֹת תָּמוּת אַתָּה וְכָל־אֲשֶׁר־
which all and thou ,die shalt thou dying that know ,returning

8 לָךְ׃ וַיַּשְׁכֵּם אֲבִימֶלֶךְ בַּבֹּקֶר וַיִּקְרָא
called and ,morning the in Abimelech early rose And .thee to [is]

לְכָל־עֲבָדָיו וַיְדַבֵּר אֶת־כָּל־הַדְּבָרִים הָאֵלֶּה בְּאָזְנֵיהֶם
;ears their in [1]these [2]words all spoke and ,servants his all (to)

9 וַיִּירְאוּ הָאֲנָשִׁים [b] מְאֹד׃ וַיִּקְרָא אֲבִימֶלֶךְ לְאַבְרָהָם
Abraham (to) Abimelech called And .exceedingly men the feared and

וַיֹּאמֶר לוֹ מֶה־עָשִׂיתָ [c] לָּנוּ [c] וּמֶה־חָטָאתִי [d]
sinned I have what [in] And ?us to done thou hast What :him to said and

לָךְ כִּי־הֵבֵאתָ עָלַי וְעַל־מַמְלַכְתִּי
kingdom my upon and me upon in brought hast thou that ,thee against

חֲטָאָה גְדֹלָה מַעֲשִׂים אֲשֶׁר לֹא־יֵעָשׂוּ עָשִׂיתָ
done hast thou done be not should which deeds ?[1]great [2]sin

10 עִמָּדִי׃ וַיֹּאמֶר אֲבִימֶלֶךְ אֶל־אַבְרָהָם מָה רָאִיתָ
seen thou hast What :Abraham unto Abimelech said And .me with

11 כִּי עָשִׂיתָ אֶת־הַדָּבָר הַזֶּה׃ וַיֹּאמֶר אַבְרָהָם [e] כִּי
Because :Abraham said And ?[1]this [2]thing done hast thou that

אָמַרְתִּי רַק אֵין־יִרְאַת אֱלֹהִים בַּמָּקוֹם הַזֶּה
;[1]this [2]place in God of fear the not is [there] Surely :said I

12 וַהֲרָגוּנִי עַל־דְּבַר אִשְׁתִּי׃ וְגַם־אָמְנָה אֲחֹתִי
sister my truly also And .wife my of account on me kill will they and

בַת־אָבִי [f] הִוא אַךְ לֹא בַת־אִמִּי [g]
;mother my of daughter the not only ,she [is] father my of daughter the

13 וַתְּהִי־לִי לְאִשָּׁה׃ וַיְהִי כַּאֲשֶׁר
when pass to came it And .wife a (for) me to became she and

הִתְעוּ אֹתִי אֱלֹהִים מִבֵּית אָבִי
;father my of house the from [1]God [3]me [5]wander [4]to [2]caused

touch her. 7
Now therefore
restore the
man's wife; for
he is a prophet,
and he shall
pray for thee,
and thou shalt
live: and if thou
restore her not,
know thou that
thou shalt surely
die, thou, and
all that are
thine. 8 And
Abimelech rose
early in the
morning, and
called all his
servants, and
told all these
things in their
ears: and the
men were sore
afraid. 9
Then Abimel-
ech called A-
braham, and
said unto him,
What hast thou
done unto us?
and wherein
have I sinned
against thee,
that thou hast
brought on me
and on my king-
dom a great
sin? thou hast
done deeds un-
to me that ought
not to be done.
10 And Abi-
melech said un-
to Abraham,
What sawest
thou, that thou
hast done this
thing? 11 And
Abraham said,
Because I
thought, Surely
the fear of God
is not in this
place; and they
will slay me for
my wife's sake.
12 And more-
over she is in-
deed my sister,
the daughter of
my father, but
not the daughter
of my mother;
and she became
my wife: 13 and
it came to pass,
when God

---

a G. *the woman to the man;* V. *the wife to her husband.*

b Sm., G., V. have, *all the men,* כל האנשים.

c G. *what is this thou hast done to us?* S. *what have I done to thee?*

d G., V. *have we sinned,* חטאנו.

e Sm. adds, *because I feared,* כי יראתי.

f G. *from father.*

g G. *from mother.*

my father's house, that I said unto her, This *is* thy kindness which thou shalt shew unto me; at every place whither we shall come, say of me, He *is* my brother.
14 And Abimelech took sheep, and oxen, and menservants, and womenservants, and gave *them* unto Abraham, and restored him Sarah his wife.
15 And Abimelech said, Behold my land is before thee: dwell where it pleaseth thee.
16 And unto Sarah he said, Behold, I have given thy brother a thousand *pieces* of silver: behold, he *is* to thee a covering of the eyes, unto all that *are* with thee, and with all *other*: thus she was reproved.
17 So Abraham prayed unto God: and God healed Abimelech, and his wife, and his maidservants; and they bare *children*.
18 For the LORD had fast closed up all the wombs of the house of Abimelech, because of Sarah, Abraham's wife.

וָאֹמַר לָהּ זֶה[a] חַסְדֵּךְ [a]אֲשֶׁר תַּעֲשִׂי
do shalt thou which kindness thy [is] This : her to said I that

עִמָּדִי אֶל כָּל־הַמָּקוֹם אֲשֶׁר נָבוֹא שָׁמָּה
,(there) in come we whither place every at ;me with

14 אִמְרִי־לִי אָחִי הוּא׃ וַיִּקַּח אֲבִימֶלֶךְ[b] צֹאן וּבָקָר
herds and flocks Abimelech took And .he [is] brother My : me of say

וַעֲבָדִים וּשְׁפָחֹת וַיִּתֵּן לְאַבְרָהָם
; Abraham to gave and ,slaves female and slaves male and

15 וַיָּשֶׁב לוֹ אֵת שָׂרָה אִשְׁתּוֹ׃ וַיֹּאמֶר אֲבִימֶלֶךְ[c]
: Abimelech said And .wife his Sarah him to returned he and

הִנֵּה אַרְצִי לְפָנֶיךָ בַּטּוֹב בְּעֵינֶיךָ שֵׁב׃
.dwell eyes thine in good the in ; thee before [is] land my Behold

16 וּלְשָׂרָה אָמַר הִנֵּה נָתַתִּי אֶלֶף
[of shekels] thousand a give I Behold : said he Sarah to And

כֶּסֶף לְאָחִיךְ הִנֵּה הוּא־לָךְ כְּסוּת
of covering a [is] ,thee for ,it behold ; brother thy to silver

עֵינַיִם לְכֹל[d] אֲשֶׁר אִתָּךְ וְאֵת־כֹּל וְנֹכָחַת[e]׃
.justified art thou (and) all with and ; thee with [are] who all for eyes

17 וַיִּתְפַּלֵּל אַבְרָהָם אֶל־הָאֱלֹהִים וַיִּרְפָּא אֱלֹהִים
God healed and ,God unto Abraham prayed And

אֶת־אֲבִימֶלֶךְ וְאֶת־אִשְׁתּוֹ וְאַמְהֹתָיו וַיֵּלֵדוּ׃
.bore they and concubines his and wife his and Abimelech

18 כִּי־עָצֹר עָצַר יְהוָה בְּעַד כָּל־רֶחֶם
womb every of entrance the Jehovah closed had closing For

לְבֵית אֲבִימֶלֶךְ עַל־דְּבַר שָׂרָה אֵשֶׁת
of wife the Sarah of account on ,Abimelech of house the to

אַבְרָהָם׃
.Abraham

caused me to wander from my father's house, that I said unto her, This is thy kindness which thou shalt shew unto me; at every place whither we shall come, say of me, He is my brother.
14 And Abimelech took sheep and oxen, and menservants and womenservants, and gave them unto Abraham, and restored him Sarah his wife.
15 And Abimelech said, Behold, my land is before thee. dwell where it pleaseth thee.
16 And unto Sarah he said, Behold, I have given thy brother a thousand pieces of silver: behold, it is for thee a covering of the eyes to all that are with thee; and in respect of all thou art righted.
17 And Abraham prayed unto God: and God healed Abimelech, and his wife, and his maidservants; and they bare children.
18 For the LORD had fast closed up all the wombs of the house of Abimelech, because of Sarah Abraham's wife.

21

AND the LORD visited Sarah as he had said, and the LORD did unto Sarah as he had spoken. 2

1 וַיהוָה פָּקַד[f] אֶת־שָׂרָה כַּאֲשֶׁר אָמָר
,said had he as according ,Sarah visited Jehovah And

וַיַּעַשׂ יְהוָה לְשָׂרָה כַּאֲשֶׁר דִּבֵּר׃
.spoken had he as according Sarah to Jehovah did and

AND the LORD visited Sarah as he had said, and the LORD did unto Sarah as he had spoken. 2 And

a For זה הסרך אשר, G., S.; V. have, *this kindness.*
b Sm. adds, *a thousand* [*shekels*] *of silver*, אלף כסף; so G.
c G., S. add, *to Abraham.*
d Sm., G., T. have, *and for all*, ולכל.
e G., S. omit ו.
f S., T. *remembered.*

For Sarah con-
ceived, and bare
Abraham a son
in his old age,
at the set time
of which God
had spoken to
him. 3 And A-
braham called
the name of his
son that was
born unto him,
whom Sarah
bare to him,
Isaac. 4 And A-
braham circum-
cised his son
Isaac, being
eight days old,
as God had
commanded
him. 5 And A-
braham was an
hundred years
old, when his
son Isaac was
born unto him.
6 And Sarah
said, God hath
made me to
laugh, *so that*
all that hear
will laugh with
me. 7 And she
said, Who
would have said
unto Abraham,
that Sarah
should have giv-
en children
suck? for I have
born *him* a son
in his old age. 8
And the child
grew, and was
weaned: and
Abraham made
a great feast the
same day that
Isaac was
weaned.
9 And Sarah
saw the son of
Hagar the E-
gyptian, which
she had born
unto Abraham,
mocking. 10
Wherefore she
said unto Abra-
ham, Cast out
this bondwoman
and her son: for
the son of this
bondwoman
shall not be
heir with my
son, *even* with

וַתַּהַר וַתֵּלֶד שָׂרָה לְאַבְרָהָם בֵּן לִזְקֻנָיו[a]
;age old his to son a Abraham to Sarah bore and conceived And

3 לַמּוֹעֵד אֲשֶׁר־דִּבֶּר אֹתוֹ אֱלֹהִים׃ וַיִּקְרָא
called And .God him with spoken had which of season the at

אַבְרָהָם אֶת־שֶׁם־בְּנוֹ הַנּוֹלַד־לוֹ אֲשֶׁר־
whom ,him to born one the ,son his of name the Abraham

4 יָלְדָה־לּוֹ שָׂרָה יִצְחָק׃ וַיָּמָל אַבְרָהָם אֶת־יִצְחָק
Isaac Abraham circumcised And .Isaac ,Sarah him to bore

בְּנוֹ[b] בֶּן־שְׁמֹנַת יָמִים כַּאֲשֶׁר צִוָּה
commanded had as according ,[old] days eight (of son) ,son his

5 אֹתוֹ אֱלֹהִים׃ וְאַבְרָהָם בֶּן־מְאַת שָׁנָה
[old] years hundred a (of son) [was] Abraham And .God him

6 בְּהִוָּלֶד לוֹ אֵת יִצְחָק בְּנוֹ׃ וַתֹּאמֶר שָׂרָה
:Sarah said And .son his Isaac him to born being the in

צְחֹק עָשָׂה לִי אֱלֹהִים[c] כָּל־הַשֹּׁמֵעַ
hearing one every ;God me for made has Laughter

7 יִצְחַק־לִי׃ וַתֹּאמֶר מִי מִלֵּל לְאַבְרָהָם
,Abraham to said have could Who :said she And .me at laugh will

הֵינִיקָה בָנִים[d] שָׂרָה כִּי־יָלַדְתִּי[e] בֵן לִזְקֻנָיו[f]׃
.age old his to son a borne have I for ,Sarah children suckle Will

8 וַיִּגְדַּל הַיֶּלֶד וַיִּגָּמַל וַיַּעַשׂ אַבְרָהָם
Abraham made and ;weaned was and child the grew And

מִשְׁתֶּה גָדוֹל בְּיוֹם הִגָּמֵל אֶת־יִצְחָק[g]׃
.1Isaac's 3weaned 2being of day the on ,1great 2feast a

9 וַתֵּרֶא שָׂרָה אֶת־בֶּן־הָגָר הַמִּצְרִית אֲשֶׁר־
whom ,Egyptian the Hagar of son the Sarah saw And

10 יָלְדָה לְאַבְרָהָם מְצַחֵק[h]׃ וַתֹּאמֶר לְאַבְרָהָם
:Abraham to said she And .playing ,Abraham to borne had she

גָּרֵשׁ הָאָמָה הַזֹּאת וְאֶת־בְּנָהּ כִּי לֹא יִירַשׁ
inherit 1shall 2not for ;son her and 1this 2maidservant away Drive

בֶּן־הָאָמָה הַזֹּאת[i] עִם־בְּנִי עִם־יִצְחָק׃
.Isaac with ,son my with 1this 2maidservant of son the

Sarah con-
ceived, and bare
Abraham a son
in his old age,
at the set time of
which God had
spoken to him. 3
And Abraham
called the name
of his son that
was born unto
him, whom Sa-
rah bare to him,
Isaac. 4 And A-
braham circum-
cised his son
Isaac when he
was eight days
old, as God had
commanded
him. 5 And A-
braham was an
hundred years
old, when his
son Isaac was
born unto him.
6 And Sarah
said, God hath
made me to
laugh; every
one that heareth
will laugh with
me. 7 And she
said, Who
would have said
unto Abraham,
that Sarah
should give chil-
dren suck? for I
have borne him
a son in his old
age. 8 And the
child grew, and
was weaned:
and Abraham
made a great
feast on the day
that Isaac was
weaned.
9 And Sarah
saw the son of
Hagar the E-
gyptian, which
she had borne
unto Abraham,
mocking. 10
Wherefore she
said unto Abra-
ham, Cast out
this bondwoman
and her son: for
the son of this
bondwoman
shall not be heir
with my son,
even with Isaac.

---

a G. omits suffix; V. has, *her*.
b G. omits.
c S. adds, *today*.
d G. sing. *child*.
e S., V. *she has borne*.
f G. *in my old age*, לזקני.
g Sm., G. add, *his son*, בנו.
h G., V. add, *with Isaac her son*.
i G., V. omit.

Isaac. 11 And the thing was very grievous in Abraham's sight because of his son.

12 And God said unto Abraham, Let it not be grievous in thy sight because of the lad, and because of thy bondwoman; in all that Sarah hath said unto thee, hearken unto her voice; for in Isaac shall thy seed be called. 13 And also of the son of the bondwoman will I make a nation, because he *is* thy seed. 14 And Abraham rose up early in the morning, and took bread, and a bottle of water, and gave *it* unto Hagar, putting *it* on her shoulder, and the child, and sent her away: and she departed, and wandered in the wilderness of Beer-Sheba. 15 And the water was spent in the bottle, and she cast the child under one of the shrubs. 16 And she went, and sat her down over against *him* a good way off, as it were a bowshot: for she said, Let me not see the death of the child. And she sat over against *him*, and lift up her voice, and wept. 17 And God heard the voice of the lad; and the

11 וַיֵּרַע הַדָּבָר מְאֹד בְּעֵינֵי אַבְרָהָם עַל
on Abraham of eyes the in exceedingly thing the evil was And

12 אוֹדֹת בְּנוֹ׃ [a] וַיֹּאמֶר אֱלֹהִים אֶל־אַבְרָהָם אַל־
not it Let :Abraham unto God said And .son his of account

יֵרַע [b] בְּעֵינֶיךָ עַל־הַנַּעַר וְעַל־אֲמָתֶךָ
;maidservant thy of because and youth the of because eyes thine in evil be

כֹּל אֲשֶׁר תֹּאמַר אֵלֶיךָ שָׂרָה שְׁמַע בְּקֹלָהּ כִּי
for ;voice her to hearken ,Sarah thee unto says which all

13 בְיִצְחָק יִקָּרֵא לְךָ זָרַע׃ וְגַם אֶת־בֶּן־
son the also And .seed a thee for called be shall Isaac in

הָאָמָה [c] לְגוֹי [d] אֲשִׂימֶנּוּ כִּי זַרְעֲךָ
[is] seed thy for ;him make will I nation a (for) ,maidservant the of

14 הוּא׃ וַיַּשְׁכֵּם אַבְרָהָם׀ בַּבֹּקֶר וַיִּקַּח־לֶחֶם
,bread took and morning the in Abraham early rose And .he

וְחֵמַת מַיִם וַיִּתֵּן אֶל־הָגָר שָׂם [e] עַל־
upon putting ,Hagar unto gave and ,water of skin a and

שִׁכְמָהּ וְאֶת־הַיֶּלֶד וַיְשַׁלְּחֶהָ וַתֵּלֶךְ
went she and ;away her sent and ,child the and ,shoulder her

15 וַתֵּתַע בְּמִדְבַּר בְּאֵר שָׁבַע׃ וַיִּכְלוּ
consumed was And .Sheba Beer of wilderness the in wandered and

הַמַּיִם מִן־הַחֵמֶת וַתַּשְׁלֵךְ אֶת־הַיֶּלֶד תַּחַת אַחַד
of one under child the cast she and ,skin the from water the

16 הַשִּׂיחִם׃ וַתֵּלֶךְ וַתֵּשֶׁב לָהּ מִנֶּגֶד
,against over herself for sat and went she And .shrubs the

הַרְחֵק כִּמְטַחֲוֵי קֶשֶׁת כִּי אָמְרָה אַל־אֶרְאֶה
look not me Let ;said she for ,bow a of shot a about distant

בְּמוֹת הַיָּלֶד וַתֵּשֶׁב מִנֶּגֶד [f] וַתִּשָּׂא [g]
raised and ,against over sat she and ;child the of death the upon

17 אֶת־קֹלָהּ וַתֵּבְךְּ׃ [g] וַיִּשְׁמַע אֱלֹהִים אֶת־קוֹל הַנַּעַר [h]
;youth the of voice the God heard And .wept and voice her

וַיִּקְרָא מַלְאַךְ אֱלֹהִים׀ אֶל־הָגָר מִן־הַשָּׁמַיִם
,heavens the from Hagar unto God of angel the called and

11 And the thing was very grievous in Abraham's sight on account of his son.

12 And God said unto Abraham, Let it not be grievous in thy sight because of the lad, and because of thy bondwoman; in all that Sarah saith unto thee, hearken unto her voice; for in Isaac shall thy seed be called. 13 And also of the son of the bondwoman will I make a nation, because he is thy seed. 14 And Abraham rose up early in the morning, and took bread and a bottle of water, and gave it unto Hagar, putting it on her shoulder, and the child, and sent her away: and she departed, and wandered in the wilderness of Beer-sheba. 15 And the water in the bottle was spent, and she cast the child under one of the shrubs. 16 And she went, and sat her down over against him a good way off, as it were a bowshot: for she said, Let me not look upon the death of the child. And she sat over against him, and lift up her voice, and wept. 17 And God heard the voice of the lad; and the angel of God called to

---

a G. adds, *Ishmael.*
b G. adds, *the word,* הדבר.
c Sm., G. add, *this,* הזאת.
d G., Sm., S., V. add, *great,* גדל.
e G., S. וישם.
f G. adds, *at a distance,* הרחק.
g G. prob., *and she wailed for the crying child.*
h G. adds, *from the place where he was.*

וַיֹּאמֶר לָהּ מַה־לָּךְ הָגָר אַל־תִּירְאִי כִּי־
for ,fear not Do ? Hagar ,thee to What : her to said he and

שָׁמַע אֱלֹהִים אֶל־קוֹל הַנַּעַר בַּאֲשֶׁר הוּא־
he where (in) ,youth the of voice the (unto) God heard has

18 שָׁם׃ קוּמִי שְׂאִי אֶת־הַנַּעַר וְהַחֲזִיקִי
fast make and ,youth the up take ,Rise .(there) [is]

אֶת־יָדֵךְ בּוֹ כִּי־לְגוֹי גָּדוֹל אֲשִׂימֶנּוּ׃
.him make will I [1]great [2]nation a (to) for ; him upon hand thy

19 וַיִּפְקַח אֱלֹהִים אֶת־עֵינֶיהָ וַתֵּרֶא בְּאֵר מָיִם [a]
;water of spring a saw she and ,eyes her God opened And

וַתֵּלֶךְ וַתְּמַלֵּא אֶת־הַחֵמֶת מַיִם וַתַּשְׁקְ
to drink gave and ,water [with] skin the filled and went she and

20 אֶת־הַנָּעַר׃ וַיְהִי אֱלֹהִים אֶת־הַנַּעַר וַיִּגְדָּל
,up grew he and ,youth the with God was And .youth the

וַיֵּשֶׁב בַּמִּדְבָּר [b] וַיְהִי רֹבֶה קַשָּׁת׃
.bow the [with] archer an became and ,wilderness the in dwelt he and

21 וַיֵּשֶׁב [c] בְּמִדְבַּר פָּארָן וַתִּקַּח־לוֹ אִמּוֹ
mother his him for took and ,Paran of wilderness the in dwelt he And

אִשָּׁה מֵאֶרֶץ מִצְרָיִם׃
.Egypt of land the from wife a

22 וַיְהִי בָּעֵת הַהִוא וַיֹּאמֶר אֲבִימֶלֶךְ [d]
Abimelech said that ,[1]that [2]time at pass to came it And

וּפִיכֹל שַׂר־צְבָאוֹ אֶל־אַבְרָהָם לֵאמֹר
:saying Abraham unto host his of commander the Phicol and

אֱלֹהִים עִמְּךָ בְּכֹל אֲשֶׁר־אַתָּה עֹשֶׂה׃
.doing [art] thou which all in thee with [is] God

23 וְעַתָּה הִשָּׁבְעָה לִּי בֵאלֹהִים הֵנָּה [e] אִם־תִּשְׁקֹר
lie not wilt thou that ,here God by me to swear now And

לִי וּלְנִינִי וּלְנֶכְדִּי
;posterity my to and offspring my to and ,me to

כַּחֶסֶד אֲשֶׁר־עָשִׂיתִי עִמְּךָ
,thee with showed have I which kindness the to according

תַּעֲשֶׂה עִמָּדִי וְעִם־הָאָרֶץ אֲשֶׁר־גַּרְתָּה
sojourned hast thou which [in] land the with and ,me with show wilt thou

angel of God
called to Hagar
out of heaven,
and said unto
her, What aileth
thee, Hagar?
fear not; for
God hath heard
the voice of the
lad where he *is*.
18 Arise, lift up
the lad, and
hold him in
thine hand; for
I will make him
a great nation.
19 And God
opened her
eyes, and she
saw a well of
water; and she
went, and filled
the bottle with
water, and gave
the lad drink.
20 And God was
with the lad;
and he grew,
and dwelt in the
wilderness, and
became an ar-
cher. 21 And he
dwelt in the
wilderness of
Paran: and his
mother took him
a wife out of
the land of E-
gypt.

22 And it
came to pass at
that time, that
Abimelech and
Phichol the
chief captain of
his host spake
unto Abraham,
saying, God *is*
with thee in all
that thou doest:
23 Now there-
fore swear unto
me here by God
that thou wilt
not deal falsely
with me, nor
with my son,
nor with my
son's son: *but*
according to the
kindness that I
have done unto
thee, thou shalt
do unto me, and

Hagar out of
heaven, and said
unto her, What
aileth thee, Ha-
gar? fear not;
for God hath
heard the voice
of the lad where
he is. 18 Arise,
lift up the lad,
and hold him
in thine hand;
for I will make
him a great na-
tion. 19 And
God opened her
eyes, and she
saw a well of
water; and she
went, and filled
the bottle with
water, and gave
the lad drink. 20
And God was
with the lad,
and he grew;
and he dwelt in
the wilderness,
and became an
archer. 21 And
he dwelt in the
wilderness of
Paran: and his
mother took him
a wife out of the
land of Egypt.

22 And it
came to pass at
that time, that
Abimelech and
Phicol the cap-
tain of his host
spake unto A-
braham, saying,
God is with
thee in all that
thou doest: 23
now therefore,
swear unto me
here by God
that thou wilt
not deal falsely
with me, nor
with my son,
nor with my
son's son: but
according to the
kindness that I
have done unto
thee, thou shalt
do unto me, and

---

a G. adds, *living*.
b S. adds, *of Paran*.
c S. omits.
d G. adds, ואחזת מרעהו, so also in vs. 32; cf. 26: 26.
e G. V. omit.

to the land wherein thou hast sojourned. 24 And Abraham said, I will swear. 25 And Abraham reproved Abimelech because of a well of water, which Abimelech's servants had violently taken away. 26 And Abimelech said, I wot not who hath done this thing: neither didst thou tell me, neither yet heard I *of it*, but to-day. 27 And Abraham took sheep and oxen, and gave them unto Abimelech; and both of them made a covenant. 28 And Abraham set seven ewe lambs of the flock by themselves. 29 And Abimelech said unto Abraham, What *mean* these seven ewe lambs which thou hast set by themselves? 30 And he said, For *these* seven ewe lambs shalt thou take of my hand, that they may be a witness unto me, that I have digged this well. 31 Wherefore he called that place Beer-sheba; because there they sware both of them. 32 Thus they made a covenant at Beer-sheba: then Abimelech rose up, and Phichol the chief captain of his host, and they returned into the land of the Philistines.
33 And *Abraham* planted a

24 25 כָּה׃ וַיֹּאמֶר אַבְרָהָם אָנֹכִי אִשָּׁבֵעַ׃ וְהוֹכִחַ
reproved And .swear I :Abraham said And .(it in)
אַבְרָהָם אֶת־אֲבִימֶלֶךְ עַל־אֹדוֹת בְּאֵר[a] הַמַּיִם[b]
water of well the of account on Abimelech Abraham
26 אֲשֶׁר גָּזְלוּ עַבְדֵי אֲבִימֶלֶךְ׃ וַיֹּאמֶר[c]
said And .Abimelech of slaves the seized had which
אֲבִימֶלֶךְ לֹא יָדַעְתִּי מִי עָשָׂה אֶת־הַדָּבָר הַזֶּה
,[1]this [2]thing did who know [2]do [1]I [3]Not :Abimelech
וְגַם־אַתָּה לֹא־הִגַּדְתָּ לִּי וְגַם אָנֹכִי לֹא
[2]not I also and ,me to known made not hast thou also and
27 שָׁמַעְתִּי בִּלְתִּי הַיּוֹם׃ וַיִּקַּח אַבְרָהָם צֹאן וּבָקָר
herds and flocks Abraham took And .to day except ,heard [1]have
וַיִּתֵּן לַאֲבִימֶלֶךְ וַיִּכְרְתוּ שְׁנֵיהֶם בְּרִית׃
.covenant a two they cut and ; Abimelech to gave and
28 וַיַּצֵּב אַבְרָהָם אֶת־שֶׁבַע כִּבְשֹׂת הַצֹּאן
flock the of lambs ewe seven Abraham placed And
29 לְבַדְּהֶן׃ וַיֹּאמֶר אֲבִימֶלֶךְ אֶל־אַבְרָהָם מָה הֵנָּה
are What : Abraham unto Abimelech said And .apart
שֶׁבַע כְּבָשֹׂת הָאֵלֶּה אֲשֶׁר הִצַּבְתָּ לְבַדָּנָה׃
? apart placed hast thou which [1]these [4]lambs [3]ewe [2]seven
30 וַיֹּאמֶר[d] כִּי אֶת־שֶׁבַע כְּבָשֹׂת[e] תִּקַּח
take shalt thou lambs ewe seven the (That) :said he And
מִיָּדִי בַּעֲבוּר תִּהְיֶה־לִּי[f] לְעֵדָה
,witness a (for) me for become may it that order in ,hand my from
31 כִּי חָפַרְתִּי אֶת־הַבְּאֵר הַזֹּאת׃ עַל־כֵּן
Therefore .[1]this [2]well digged I that
קָרָא לַמָּקוֹם הַהוּא בְּאֵר שָׁבַע כִּי שָׁם
there because ,Sheba Beer [1]that [2]place to called [one]
32 נִשְׁבְּעוּ שְׁנֵיהֶם׃ וַיִּכְרְתוּ בְרִית בִּבְאֵר שָׁבַע
; Sheba Beer in covenant a cut they And .two they swore
וַיָּקָם אֲבִימֶלֶךְ וּפִיכֹל שַׂר־צְבָאוֹ
,host his of commander the Phicol and ,Abimelech up rose and
33 וַיָּשֻׁבוּ אֶל־אֶרֶץ פְּלִשְׁתִּים׃ וַיִּטַּע[g]
planted he And .Philistines the of land the unto returned and

to the land wherein thou hast sojourned. 24 And Abraham said, I will swear. 25 And Abraham reproved Abimelech because of the well of water, which Abimelech's servants had violently taken away. 26 And Abimelech said, I know not who hath done this thing: neither didst thou tell me, neither yet heard I of it, but to-day. 27 And Abraham took sheep and oxen, and gave them unto Abimelech; and they two made a covenant. 28 And Abraham set seven ewe lambs of the flock by themselves. 29 And Abimelech said unto Abraham, What mean these seven ewe lambs which thou hast set by themselves? 30 And he said, These seven ewe lambs shalt thou take of my hand, that it may be a witness unto me, that I have digged this well. 31 Wherefore he called that place Beer-sheba; because there they sware both of them. 32 So they made a covenant at Beer-sheba: and Abimelech rose up, and Phicol the captain of his host, and they returned into the land of the Philistines.

33 And *Abraham* planted a

---

a G. pl.
b S. adds, *which the slaves of Abraham had dug.*
c G. adds, *to him.*
d Sm., G. add, *Abraham.*
e G. adds, *these.*
f G. omits, לִי.
g G., S. add, *Abraham.*

grove in Beer-sheba, and called there on the name of the LORD, the everlasting God. 34 And Abraham sojourned in the Philistines' land many days.

אֶשֶׁל בִּבְאֵר שָׁבַע וַיִּקְרָא־שָׁם בְּשֵׁם
of name the on there called and Sheba Beer in tamarisk a

34 יְהוָה אֵל עוֹלָם׃ וַיָּגָר אַבְרָהָם
Abraham sojourned And .eternity of God the ,Jehovah

בְּאֶרֶץ פְּלִשְׁתִּים יָמִים רַבִּים׃
.[1]many [2]days Philistines the of land the in

tamarisk tree in Beer-sheba, and called there on the name of the LORD, the Everlasting God. 34 And Abraham sojourned in the land of the Philistines many days.

22

AND it came to pass after these things, that God did tempt Abraham, and said unto him, Abraham: and he said, Behold, *here* I *am*. 2 And he said, Take now thy son, thine only *son* Isaac, whom thou lovest, and get thee into the land of Moriah; and offer him there for a burnt offering upon one of the mountains which I will tell thee of.

3 And Abraham rose up early in the morning, and saddled his ass, and took two of his young men with him, and Isaac his son, and clave the wood for the burnt offering, and rose up, and went unto the place of which God had told him. 4 Then on the third day Abraham lifted up his eyes, and saw the place afar off. 5 And Abraham said unto his young men, Abide ye here with the ass; and I and the lad will go

1 וַיְהִי אַחַר הַדְּבָרִים הָאֵלֶּה וְהָאֱלֹהִים[a]
God (and) ,[1]these [2]things after pass to came it And

נִסָּה אֶת־אַבְרָהָם וַיֹּאמֶר אֵלָיו אַבְרָהָם[b]
; Abraham :him unto said he that ,Abraham testing

2 וַיֹּאמֶר הִנֵּנִי׃ וַיֹּאמֶר[c] קַח־נָא אֶת־בִּנְךָ
,son thy ,now ,Take :said he And .me Behold :said he and

אֶת־יְחִידְךָ אֲשֶׁר־אָהַבְתָּ אֶת־יִצְחָק וְלֶךְ־לְךָ
thyself for go and ; Isaac ,lovest thou whom ,one only thine

אֶל־אֶרֶץ הַמֹּרִיָּה וְהַעֲלֵהוּ שָׁם לְעֹלָה
burnt-offering a for there him offer and ,Moriah of land the unto

עַל אַחַד הֶהָרִים אֲשֶׁר אֹמַר אֵלֶיךָ׃
.thee unto say will I which ,mountains the of one upon

3 וַיַּשְׁכֵּם אַבְרָהָם בַּבֹּקֶר וַיַּחֲבֹשׁ אֶת־חֲמֹרוֹ
ass his saddled and ,morning the in Abraham early rose And

וַיִּקַּח אֶת־שְׁנֵי נְעָרָיו אִתּוֹ וְאֵת יִצְחָק בְּנוֹ
;son his Isaac and ,him with youths [1]his [2]two took and

וַיְבַקַּע עֲצֵי עֹלָה וַיָּקָם וַיֵּלֶךְ[d]
went and up rose and ,burnt-offering a of wood split he and

4 אֶל־הַמָּקוֹם אֲשֶׁר־אָמַר־לוֹ הָאֱלֹהִים׃ בַּיּוֹם
[2]day the On .God him to said had which place the unto

הַשְּׁלִישִׁי וַיִּשָּׂא אַבְרָהָם אֶת־עֵינָיו וַיַּרְא
saw and ,eyes his Abraham up lifted (and) [1]third

5 אֶת־הַמָּקוֹם מֵרָחֹק׃ וַיֹּאמֶר אַבְרָהָם[e] אֶל־נְעָרָיו
: youths his unto Abraham said And .distance a from place the

שְׁבוּ־לָכֶם פֹּה עִם־הַחֲמוֹר וַאֲנִי וְהַנַּעַר
youth the and I and ; ass the with here yourselves for Stay

AND it came to pass after these things, that God did prove Abraham, and said unto him, Abraham; and he said, Here am I. 2 And he said, Take now thy son, thine only son, whom thou lovest, even Isaac, and get thee into the land of Moriah; and offer him there for a burnt offering upon one of the mountains which I will tell thee of.

3 And Abraham rose early in the morning, and saddled his ass, and took two of his young men with him, and Isaac his son; and he clave the wood for the burnt offering, and rose up, and went unto the place of which God had told him. 4 On the third day Abraham lifted up his eyes, and saw the place afar off. 5 And Abraham said unto his young men, Abide ye here with the ass, and I and the lad will go

---

a G. omits ו.
b G., V. repeat.
c S., V. add, *to him*.
d G. adds, *and he came*, ויבא.
e S., V. omit.

yonder and worship, and come again to you. 6 And Abraham took the wood of the burnt offering, and laid *it* upon Isaac his son; and he took the fire in his hand, and a knife; and they went both of them together. 7 And Isaac spake unto Abraham his father, and said, My father: and he said, Here *am* I, my son. And he said, Behold the fire and the wood: but where *is* the lamb for a burnt offering? 8 And Abraham said, My son, God will provide himself a lamb for a burnt offering: so they went both of them together.

9 And they came to the place which God had told him of; and Abraham built an altar there, and laid the wood in order, and bound Isaac his son, and laid him on the altar upon the wood. 10 And Abraham stretched forth his hand, and took the knife to slay his son. 11 And the angel of the LORD called unto him out of heaven, and said, Abraham, Abraham: and he said, Here *am* I. 12 And he said, Lay not thine hand upon the lad,

נֵלְכָה עַד־כֹּה וְנִשְׁתַּחֲוֶה וְנָשׁוּבָה
return may and ,worship may we that ;yonder go will

6 אֲלֵיכֶם׃ וַיִּקַּח אַבְרָהָם אֶת־עֲצֵי הָעֹלָה
,burnt-offering the of wood the Abraham took And .you unto

וַיָּשֶׂם עַל־יִצְחָק בְּנוֹ וַיִּקַּח בְּיָדוֹ אֶת־
the hand his in took he and ;son his Isaac upon put and

הָאֵשׁ וְאֶת־הַמַּאֲכֶלֶת וַיֵּלְכוּ שְׁנֵיהֶם יַחְדָּו׃
.together two they went and ;knife the and fire

7 וַיֹּאמֶר יִצְחָק אֶל־אַבְרָהָם אָבִיו וַיֹּאמֶר אָבִי
;father My :said he and ,father his Abraham unto Isaac said And

וַיֹּאמֶר הִנֶּנִּי[a] בְנִי וַיֹּאמֶר הִנֵּה הָאֵשׁ
fire the Behold :said he And .son my ,me Behold :said he and

8 וְהָעֵצִים וְאַיֵּה הַשֶּׂה לְעֹלָה׃ וַיֹּאמֶר
said And ?burnt-offering a for lamb the where and ,wood the and

אַבְרָהָם אֱלֹהִים יִרְאֶה־לּוֹ הַשֶּׂה לְעֹלָה
,burnt-offering a for lamb the himself for see will God :Abraham

9 בְּנִי וַיֵּלְכוּ שְׁנֵיהֶם יַחְדָּו׃ וַיָּבֹאוּ אֶל־
unto in came they And .together two they went and ;son my

הַמָּקוֹם אֲשֶׁר אָמַר־לוֹ הָאֱלֹהִים וַיִּבֶן שָׁם
there built and ,God him to said had which place the

אַבְרָהָם אֶת־הַמִּזְבֵּחַ וַיַּעֲרֹךְ אֶת־הָעֵצִים
;wood the arranged and ,altar the Abraham

וַיַּעֲקֹד אֶת־יִצְחָק בְּנוֹ וַיָּשֶׂם אֹתוֹ עַל־הַמִּזְבֵּחַ
,altar the upon ,him put and son his Isaac bound he and

10 מִמַּעַל לָעֵצִים׃ וַיִּשְׁלַח אַבְרָהָם
Abraham out stretched And .wood the (to) above (from)

אֶת־יָדוֹ וַיִּקַּח[b] אֶת־הַמַּאֲכֶלֶת לִשְׁחֹט אֶת־בְּנוֹ׃
.son his slay to knife the took and ,hand his

11 וַיִּקְרָא אֵלָיו מַלְאַךְ יְהוָה[c] מִן־הַשָּׁמַיִם
,heavens the from Jehovah of angel the him unto called And

וַיֹּאמֶר[d] אַבְרָהָם ׀ אַבְרָהָם וַיֹּאמֶר הִנֵּנִי׃
.me Behold :said he and ,Abraham ,Abraham :said and

12 וַיֹּאמֶר[e] אַל־תִּשְׁלַח יָדְךָ אֶל־הַנַּעַר
,youth the unto hand thine out stretch not Do :said he And

yonder; and we will worship, and come again to you. 6 And Abraham took the wood of the burnt offering, and laid it upon Isaac his son; and he took in his hand the fire and the knife; and they went both of them together. 7 And Isaac spake unto Abraham his father, and said, My father: and he said, Here am I, my son. And he said, Behold the fire and the wood: but where is the lamb for a burnt offering? 8 And Abraham said, God will provide himself the lamb for a burnt offering, my son: so they went both of them together.

9 And they came to the place which God had told him of; and Abraham built the altar there, and laid the wood in order, and bound Isaac his son, and laid him on the altar, upon the wood. 10 And Abraham stretched forth his hand, and took the knife to slay his son. 11 And the angel of the LORD called unto him out of heaven, and said, Abraham, Abraham: and he said, Here am I. 12 And he said, Lay not thine hand upon the lad, neither

---

a G. *what is it?* V. *what do you wish?*
b G. *to take*, לקחת.
c S. has, *God*, אלהים.
d G. adds, *to him.*
e S., V. add, *to him.*

neither do thou any thing unto him: for now I know that thou fearest God, seeing thou hast not withheld thy son, thine only *son* from me.
13 And Abraham lifted up his eyes, and looked, and behold, behind *him* a ram caught in a thicket by his horns: and Abraham went and took the ram, and offered him up for a burnt offering in the stead of his son. 14 And Abraham called the name of that place Jehovah-jireh: as it is said *to* this day, In the mount of the LORD it shall be seen.

15 And the angel of the LORD called unto Abraham out of heaven the second time, 16 And said, By myself have I sworn, saith the LORD, for because thou hast done this thing, and hast not withheld thy son thine only *son*: 17 That in blessing I will bless thee, and in multiplying I will multiply thy seed as the stars of the heaven, and as the sand which *is* upon the sea shore; and thy seed shall possess the gate of his enemies; 18 And in thy seed

וְאַל־תַּעַשׂ לוֹ מְאוּמָה כִּי עַתָּה יָדַעְתִּי כִּי־
that know I now for ;thing any him to do not do and

יְרֵא אֱלֹהִים אַתָּה וְלֹא חָשַׂכְתָּ
withheld [2]hast [1]thou [3]not and ,thou [art] God of fearer a

13 אֶת־בִּנְךָ אֶת־יְחִידְךָ מִמֶּנִּי׃ וַיִּשָּׂא אַבְרָהָם
Abraham up lifted And .me from ,one only thine ,son thy

אֶת־עֵינָיו וַיַּרְא וְהִנֵּה־אַיִל אַחַר[a]
[which] ,behind ram a behold and ,saw and eyes his

נֶאֱחַז בַּסְּבַךְ בְּקַרְנָיו וַיֵּלֶךְ אַבְרָהָם
Abraham went and ; horns its by thicket a in entangled was

וַיִּקַּח אֶת־הָאַיִל וַיַּעֲלֵהוּ לְעֹלָה תַּחַת[b]
of instead burnt-offering a for him offered and ram the took and

14 בְּנוֹ׃ וַיִּקְרָא אַבְרָהָם שֵׁם־הַמָּקוֹם הַהוּא
,[1]that [2]place of name the Abraham called And .son his

יְהֹוָה יִרְאֶה אֲשֶׁר יֵאָמֵר הַיּוֹם בְּהַר[c]
,mount [the] In :today said is it that so ;Jireh Jehovah

15 יְהֹוָה יֵרָאֶה׃[d] וַיִּקְרָא מַלְאַךְ יְהֹוָה אֶל־
unto Jehovah of angel the called And .seen is Jehovah

16 אַבְרָהָם שֵׁנִית מִן־הַשָּׁמָיִם׃ וַיֹּאמֶר בִּי
myself By ;said and ,heavens the from time second a Abraham

נִשְׁבַּעְתִּי נְאֻם־יְהֹוָה כִּי יַעַן אֲשֶׁר עָשִׂיתָ
done hast thou (that) because that ,Jehovah of saying a ,swear I

אֶת־הַדָּבָר הַזֶּה וְלֹא חָשַׂכְתָּ אֶת־בִּנְךָ
,son thy withheld [1]hast [2]not and ,[1]this [2]thing

17 אֶת־יְחִידֶךָ׃[e] כִּי־בָרֵךְ[f] אֲבָרֶכְךָ וְהַרְבָּה
increasing and ,thee bless will I blessing that ; one only thine

אַרְבֶּה אֶת־זַרְעֲךָ כְּכוֹכְבֵי הַשָּׁמַיִם
,heavens the of stars the like seed thy increase will I

וְכַחוֹל אֲשֶׁר עַל־שְׂפַת הַיָּם וְיִרַשׁ
possess shall and ; sea the of shore the upon [is] which sand the like and

18 זַרְעֲךָ אֵת שַׁעַר[g] אֹיְבָיו׃ וְהִתְבָּרְכוּ
themselves bless shall and ; enemies his of gate the seed thy

do thou any thing unto him: for now I know that thou fearest God, seeing thou hast not withheld thy son, thine only son, from me. 13 And Abraham lifted up his eyes, and looked, and behold, behind *him* a ram caught in the thicket by his horns: and Abraham went and took the ram, and offered him up for a burnt offering in the stead of his son. 14 And Abraham called the name of that place Jehovah-jireh: as it is said to this day, In the mount of the LORD it shall be provided.

15 And the angel of the LORD called unto Abraham a second time out of heaven, 16 and said, By myself have I sworn, saith the LORD, because thou hast done this thing, and hast not withheld thy son, thine only son: 17 that in blessing I will bless thee, and in multiplying I will multiply thy seed as the stars of the heaven, and as the sand which is upon the sea shore; and thy seed shall possess the gate of his enemies; 18 and in thy seed shall

a G., S., T. *one*, אחד.
b G. adds, *Isaac.*
c S. adds, *this.*
d S., V. *will see*, יִרְאֶה.
e Sm., G., S., V. add, *from me*, ממני.
f G., S. omit כי.
g G., T. have, *cities*, ערי; S. *lands*, ארעת; V. *gates*, שערי.

shall all the na-
tions of the
earth be blessed;
because thou
hast obeyed my
voice. 19 So A-
braham return-
ed unto his
young men, and
they rose up and
went together to
Beer-sheba; and
Abraham dwelt
at Beer-sheba.

20 And it
came to pass
after these
things, that it
was told Abra-
ham, saying,
Behold, Milcah,
she hath also
borne children
unto thy brother
Nahor; 21 Huz
his firstborn,
and Buz his
brother, and
Kemuel the fa-
ther of Aram,
22 And Chesed,
and Hazo, and
Pildash, and
Jidlaph, and
Bethuel. 23 And
Bethuel begat
Rebekah: these
eight Milcah did
bear to Nahor,
Abraham's
brother. 24 And
his concubine,
whose name
was Reumah,
she bare also
Tebah, and
Gaham, and
Thahash, and
Maachah.

בְזַרְעֲךָ כֹּל גּוֹיֵי הָאָרֶץ[a] עֵקֶב אֲשֶׁר
(that) because ;earth the of nations the all seed thy in

19 שָׁמַעְתָּ בְּקֹלִי׃ וַיָּשָׁב אַבְרָהָם אֶל־
unto Abraham returned And .voice my to hearkened hast thou

נְעָרָיו וַיָּקֻמוּ וַיֵּלְכוּ יַחְדָּו[b] אֶל־בְּאֵר שָׁבַע
;Sheba Beer unto together went and up rose they and ,youths his

וַיֵּשֶׁב אַבְרָהָם בִּבְאֵר שָׁבַע׃
.Sheba Beer at Abraham dwelt and

20 וַיְהִי אַחֲרֵי הַדְּבָרִים הָאֵלֶּה וַיֻּגַּד
told was it that ,[1]these [2]things after pass to came it And

לְאַבְרָהָם לֵאמֹר הִנֵּה יָלְדָה מִלְכָּה גַם־הִוא בָּנִים
sons ,she also ,Milcah borne has Behold : saying Abraham to

21 לְנָחוֹר אָחִיךָ׃ אֶת־עוּץ בְּכֹרוֹ וְאֶת־בּוּז אָחִיו
,brother his Buz and ,firstborn his Uz ;brother thy Nahor to

22 וְאֶת־קְמוּאֵל אֲבִי אֲרָם׃ וְאֶת־כֶּשֶׂד וְאֶת־חֲזוֹ
Hazo and Kesed and ;Aram of father the Kemuel and

23 וְאֶת־פִּלְדָּשׁ וְאֶת־יִדְלָף וְאֵת בְּתוּאֵל׃ וּבְתוּאֵל
Bethuel And .Bethuel and Jidlaph and Pildash and

יָלַד אֶת־רִבְקָה שְׁמֹנָה אֵלֶּה יָלְדָה מִלְכָּה לְנָחוֹר
,Nahor to Milcah bore these eight ;Rebekah begat

24 אֲחִי אַבְרָהָם׃ וּפִילַגְשׁוֹ וּשְׁמָהּ רְאוּמָה
,Reumah [being] name her (and) ,concubine his And .Abraham of brother

וַתֵּלֶד גַּם־הִוא אֶת־טֶבַח וְאֶת־גַּחַם וְאֶת־תַּחַשׁ
Tahash and Gaham and Tebah also she bore (and)

וְאֶת־מַעֲכָה׃
.Maacah and

all the nations
of the earth be
blessed; be-
cause thou hast
obeyed my
voice. 19 So A-
braham return-
ed unto his
young men, and
they rose up
and went to-
gether to Beer-
sheba; and A-
braham dwelt at
Beer-sheba.

20 And it
came to pass
after these
things, that it
was told Abra-
ham, saying,
Behold, Milcah,
she also hath
borne children
unto thy broth-
er Nahor; 21 Uz
his firstborn,
and Buz his
brother, and
Kemuel the fa-
ther of Aram;
22 and Chesed,
and Hazo, and
Pildash, and
Jidlaph, and
Bethuel. 23 And
Bethuel begat
Rebekah: these
eight did Milcah
bear to Nahor,
Abraham's
brother. 24 And
his concubine,
whose name was
Reumah, she
also bare Tebah,
and Gaham, and
Tahash, and
Maacah.

23

AND Sarah
was an hundred
and seven and
twenty years
old: *these were*
the years of the
life of Sarah. 2
And Sarah died
in Kirjath-arba;
the same *is*
Hebron in the
land of Canaan:
and Abraham
came to mourn

1 וַיִּהְיוּ חַיֵּי שָׂרָה מֵאָה שָׁנָה וְעֶשְׂרִים
twenty and years hundred a Sarah of life the was And

שָׁנָה וְשֶׁבַע שָׁנִים שְׁנֵי[c] חַיֵּי שָׂרָה[c]׃
.Sarah of life the of years the ,years seven and years

2 וַתָּמָת שָׂרָה בְּקִרְיַת אַרְבַּע[d] הִוא חֶבְרוֹן בְּאֶרֶץ
of land the in ,Hebron [being] it ,Arba Kiriath in Sarah died And

AND the life
of Sarah was
an hundred
and seven and
twenty years:
these were the
years of the life
of Sarah. 2
And Sarah died
in Kiriath-arba
(the same is
Hebron), in the
land of Canaan:
and Abraham

---

a G. omits.
b G. omits.
c G., V. omit שני חיי שרה.
d Sm. adds, *in a valley*, אל עמק.

for Sarah, and
to weep for her.
3 And Abra-
ham stood up
from before his
dead, and spake
unto the sons of
Heth, saying, 4
I *am* a stranger
and a sojourner
with you: give
me a possession
of a burying-
place with you,
that I may bury
my dead out of
my sight. 5 And
the children of
Heth answered
Abraham, say-
ing unto him, 6
Hear us, my
lord: thou *art* a
mighty prince
among us: in
the choice of
our sepulchres
bury thy dead;
none of us shall
withhold from
thee his sepul-
chre, but that
thou mayest
bury thy dead.
7 And Abraham
stood up, and
bowed himself
to the people of
the land, *even* to
the children of
Heth. 8 And he
communed with
them, saying, If
it be your mind
that I should
bury my dead
out of my sight;
hear me, and
intreat for me
to Ephron the
son of Zohar, 9
That he may
give me the
cave of Mach-
pelah, which he
hath, which *is*
in the end of his
field; for as
much money as
it is worth he
shall give it me
for a possession
of a burying-
place amongst
you. 10 And
Ephron dwelt
among the
children of
Heth: and Eph-
ron the Hittite
answered Abra-

כְּנָעַן וַיָּבֹא אַבְרָהָם לִסְפֹּד לְשָׂרָה
Sarah for mourn to Abraham went and ; Canaan

3 וְלִבְכֹּתָהּ׃ וַיָּקָם אַבְרָהָם מֵעַל פְּנֵי
of face the (upon) from Abraham up rose And .her for weep to and

4 מֵתוֹ וַיְדַבֵּר[a] אֶל־בְּנֵי־חֵת לֵאמֹר׃ גֵּר־
stranger A :saying Heth of sons the unto spoke and dead his

וְתוֹשָׁב אָנֹכִי עִמָּכֶם תְּנוּ לִי אֲחֻזַּת־קֶבֶר
possession burial a me to ye give ; you with I [am] sojourner and

5 עִמָּכֶם וְאֶקְבְּרָה מֵתִי מִלְּפָנָי[b]׃ וַיַּעֲנוּ
answered And .me before from dead my bury may I that ,you with

6 בְנֵי־חֵת אֶת־אַבְרָהָם לֵאמֹר לוֹ[c]׃ [d]שְׁמָעֵנוּ
,us Hear :him to saying ,Abraham Heth of sons the

אֲדֹנִי נְשִׂיא אֱלֹהִים אַתָּה בְּתוֹכֵנוּ
; us of midst the in thou [art] God of prince a ; lord my

בְּמִבְחַר קְבָרֵינוּ קְבֹר אֶת־מֵתֶךָ[e] אִישׁ
each ,dead thy bury sepulchres our of choicest the in

מִמֶּנּוּ אֶת־קִבְרוֹ לֹא־יִכְלֶה מִמְּךָ מִקְּבֹר
burying from ,thee from refuse not will sepulchre his us of

7 מֵתֶךָ[f]׃ וַיָּקָם אַבְרָהָם וַיִּשְׁתַּחוּ לְעַם־
people the to himself prostrated and Abraham up rose And .dead thy

8 הָאָרֶץ לִבְנֵי־חֵת׃ וַיְדַבֵּר[g] אִתָּם לֵאמֹר
:saying them with spoke he And .Heth of sons the to ,land the of

אִם־יֵשׁ אֶת־נַפְשְׁכֶם לִקְבֹּר אֶת־מֵתִי מִלְּפָנַי
; me before from dead my bury to soul your with is it If

שְׁמָעוּנִי וּפִגְעוּ־לִי בְּעֶפְרוֹן בֶּן־צֹחַר[h]׃
; Zohar of son the Ephron (in) me for beseech and ,me hear

9 וְיִתֶּן־לִי אֶת־מְעָרַת הַמַּכְפֵּלָה אֲשֶׁר־
[is] which ,Makpelah of cave the me to give may he that

לוֹ אֲשֶׁר בִּקְצֵה שָׂדֵהוּ בְּכֶסֶף מָלֵא
[1]full [2]money for :field his of end the in [is] which ,him to

יִתְּנֶנָּה לִּי בְּתוֹכְכֶם לַאֲחֻזַּת־קָבֶר׃
.possession burial a for ,you of midst the in me to it give him let

10 וְעֶפְרוֹן יֹשֵׁב בְּתוֹךְ בְּנֵי־חֵת
,Heth of sons the of midst the in sitting [was] Ephron And

came to mourn
for Sarah, and
to weep for her.
3 And Abra-
ham rose up
from before his
dead, and spake
unto the chil-
dren of Heth,
saying, 4 I am a
stranger and a
sojourner with
you: give me a
possession of a
buryingplace
with you, that I
may bury my
dead out of my
sight. 5 And the
children of Heth
answered Abra-
ham, saying un-
to him, 6 Hear
us, my lord:
thou art a might-
y prince among
us: in the choice
of our sepul-
chres bury thy
dead; none of
us shall with-
hold from thee
his sepulchre,
but that
thou mayest
bury thy dead. 7
And Abraham
rose up, and
bowed himself
to the people of
the land, even
to the children
of Heth. 8 And
he communed
with them, say-
ing, If it be your
mind that I
should bury my
dead out of my
sight, hear me,
and intreat for
me to Ephron
the son of Zo-
har, 9 that he
may give me
the cave of
Machpelah,
which he hath,
which is in the
end of his field;
for the full price
let him give it to
me in the midst
of you for a
possession of a
buryingplace. 10
Now Ephron
was sitting in

a G. adds, *Abraham.*
b G. has, *there;* V. omits.
c G., V. omit.
d G. adds, before שמענו, *Nay, but.*
e G. adds, *for,* כי.
f G. adds, *there.*
g G. adds, *Abraham.*
h Sm. adds, *the Hittite.*

ham in the audience of the children of Heth, *even* of all that went in at the gate of his city, saying, 11 Nay, my lord, hear me: the field give I thee, and the cave that *is* therein, I give it thee; in the presence of the sons of my people give I it thee: bury thy dead. 12 And Abraham bowed down himself before the people of the land. 13 And he spake unto Ephron in the audience of the people of the land, saying, But if thou *wilt give it*, I pray thee, hear me: I will give thee money for the field; take *it* of me, and I will bury my dead there. 14 And Ephron answered Abraham, saying unto him, 15 My lord, hearken unto me: the land *is worth* four hundred shekels of silver; what *is* that betwixt me and thee? bury therefore thy dead. 16 And Abraham hearkened unto Ephron; and Abraham weighed to Ephron the silver, which he had named in the audience of the sons of Heth, four hundred shekels of silver, current *money* with the merchant.

וַיַּעַן עֶפְרוֹן הַחִתִּי אֶת־אַבְרָהָם [a] בְּאָזְנֵי

of ears the in Abraham Hittite the Ephron answered and

בְנֵי־חֵת [b] לְכֹל בָּאֵי [c] שַׁעַר־עִירוֹ לֵאמֹר׃

: saying ,city his of gate the entering all to ,Heth of sons the

11 לֹא־אֲדֹנִי [d] שְׁמָעֵנִי [e] הַשָּׂדֶה נָתַתִּי לָךְ וְהַמְּעָרָה

cave the and ,thee to give I field the ;me hear ,lord my ,No

אֲשֶׁר־בּוֹ לְךָ [f] נְתַתִּיהָ לְעֵינֵי בְנֵי־

of sons the of eyes the before ;it give I thee to ,it in [is] which

12 עַמִּי נְתַתִּיהָ לָּךְ קְבֹר מֵתֶךָ׃ וַיִּשְׁתַּחוּ

himself prostrated And .dead thy bury ,thee to it give I people my

13 אַבְרָהָם לִפְנֵי עַם־הָאָרֶץ׃ וַיְדַבֵּר אֶל־עֶפְרוֹן

Ephron unto spoke he And .land the of people the before Abraham

בְּאָזְנֵי עַם־הָאָרֶץ [g] לֵאמֹר אַךְ אִם־אַתָּה

—thou if Only : saying land the of people the of ears the in

לוּ [h] שְׁמָעֵנִי נָתַתִּי כֶּסֶף הַשָּׂדֶה [i] קַח מִמֶּנִּי

; me from take ,field the of money the give I ; me hear pray

14 וְאֶקְבְּרָה [j] אֶת־מֵתִי שָׁמָּה׃ וַיַּעַן עֶפְרוֹן [k]

Ephron answered And .there dead my bury may I that

15 אֶת־אַבְרָהָם לֵאמֹר לוֹ׃ [l] אֲדֹנִי [m] שְׁמָעֵנִי [m] אֶרֶץ [n]

of land ; me hear ,lord My : him to saying Abraham

אַרְבַּע מֵאֹת שֶׁקֶל־כֶּסֶף בֵּינִי וּבֵינְךָ

thee (between) and me between ,silver of shekels hundred four

16 מַה־הִוא וְאֶת־מֵתְךָ קְבֹר׃ וַיִּשְׁמַע אַבְרָהָם

Abraham hearkened And .bury dead thy and ?it [is] what

אֶל־עֶפְרוֹן וַיִּשְׁקֹל אַבְרָהָם לְעֶפְרֹן אֶת־הַכֶּסֶף אֲשֶׁר

which money the Ephron to Abraham weighed and ; Ephron unto

דִּבֶּר בְּאָזְנֵי בְנֵי־חֵת אַרְבַּע מֵאוֹת

hundred four ,Heth of sons the of ears the in spoken had he

שֶׁקֶל כֶּסֶף עֹבֵר לַסֹּחֵר׃

.merchant the with passes [which] ,silver of shekels

the midst of the children of Heth: and Ephron the Hittite answered Abraham in the audience of the children of Heth, even of all that went in at the gate of his city, saying, 11 Nay, my lord, hear me: the field give I thee, and the cave that is therein, I give it thee; in the presence of the sons of my people give I it thee: bury thy dead. 12 And Abraham bowed himself down before the people of the land. 13 And he spake unto Ephron in the audience of the people of the land, saying, But if thou wilt, I pray thee, hear me: I will give the price of the field; take it of me, and I will bury my dead there. 14 And Ephron answered Abraham, saying unto him, 15 My lord, hearken unto me: a piece of land worth four hundred shekels of silver, what is that betwixt me and thee? bury therefore thy dead. 16 And Abraham hearkened unto Ephron; and Abraham weighed to Ephron the silver, which he had named in the audience of the children of Heth, four hundred shekels of silver, current *money* with the merchant.

---

a G. adds, *and said*, ויאמר; S. adds the same, before את אברהם.

b G., S. *and all*, וכל; V. omits בני חת ל.

c G. *the city*.

d For לא, G. app. has, *to me*, לי.

e G. adds ו.

f G. omits לך נתתיה.

g G. *all the people of the land*.

h Sm., G. *to me*, לי.

i G. omits; S. adds, *to thee*.

j G. *and bury*, וקבר.

k S. adds, *and said*.

l G. omits; V. omits את אברהם לאמר לו.

m G. has, *Nay, Lord, for I have heard*.

n G. omits.

17 And the
field of Ephron,
which *was* in
Machpelah,
which *was* be-
fore Mamre, the
field, and the
cave which *was*
therein, and all
the trees that
were in the field,
that *were* in all
the borders
round about,
were made sure
18 Unto Abra-
ham for a pos-
session in the
presence of the
children of
Heth, before all
that went in at
the gate of his
city. 19 And aft-
er this, Abra-
ham buried Sa-
rah his wife in
the cave of the
field of Mach-
pelah before
Mamre: the
same *is* Hebron
in the land of
Canaan. 20 And
the field, and
the cave that *is*
therein, were
made sure unto
Abraham for a
possession of a
buryingplace by
the sons of
Heth.

17 וַיָּקָם ׀ שְׂדֵה[a] עֶפְרוֹן אֲשֶׁר בַּמַּכְפֵּלָה
,Makpelah in [was] which Ephron of field the confirmed was And

אֲשֶׁר לִפְנֵי מַמְרֵא הַשָּׂדֶה וְהַמְּעָרָה אֲשֶׁר־
which cave the and field the ; Mamre before [was] which

בּוֹ וְכָל־הָעֵץ אֲשֶׁר בַּשָּׂדֶה אֲשֶׁר
[were] which ,field the in [were] which trees the all and ,it in [was]

18 בְּכָל־גְּבֻלוֹ[b] סָבִיב׃ לְאַבְרָהָם לְמִקְנָה
possession purchased a for Abraham to ; about round border its all in

לְעֵינֵי בְנֵי־חֵת בְּכֹל[c] בָּאֵי שַׁעַר־
of gate the entering all with ,Heth of sons the of eyes the before

19 עִירוֹ׃[d] וְאַחֲרֵי־כֵן[e] קָבַר אַבְרָהָם אֶת־שָׂרָה אִשְׁתּוֹ
,wife his Sarah Abraham buried afterward And .city his

אֶל־מְעָרַת שְׂדֵה הַמַּכְפֵּלָה עַל־פְּנֵי[f] מַמְרֵא הִוא
[being] it ,Mamre before Makpelah of field the of cave the at

20 חֶבְרוֹן בְּאֶרֶץ כְּנָעַן׃ וַיָּקָם הַשָּׂדֶה
,field the confirmed was And .Canaan of land the in ,Hebron

וְהַמְּעָרָה אֲשֶׁר־בּוֹ לְאַבְרָהָם לַאֲחֻזַּת־קָבֶר
possession burial a for Abraham to ,it in [was] which cave the and

מֵאֵת בְּנֵי־חֵת׃
.Heth of sons the (with) from

17 So the field
of Ephron,
which was in
Machpelah,
which was be-
fore Mamre, the
field, and the
cave which was
therein, and all
the trees that
were in the
field, that were
in all the border
thereof round
about, were
made sure 18
unto Abraham
for a possession
in the presence
of the children
of Heth, be-
fore all that
went in at the
gate of his city.
19 And after
this, Abraham
buried Sarah his
wife in the cave
of the field of
Machpelah be-
fore Mamre (the
same is He-
bron), in the land
of Canaan. 20
And the field,
and the cave
that is therein,
were made sure
unto Abraham
for a possession
of a burying-
place by the chil-
dren of Heth.

24

AND Abra-
ham was old,
and well strick-
en in age: and
the LORD had
blessed Abra-
ham in all
things. 2 And
Abraham said
unto his eldest
servant of his
house, that
ruled over all
that he had,
Put, I pray thee,
thy hand under
my thigh: 3 And
I will make thee
swear by the
LORD, the God

1 וְאַבְרָהָם זָקֵן בָּא בַּיָּמִים וַיהוָה
Jehovah and ,days in advanced ,old [was] Abraham And

2 בֵּרַךְ אֶת־אַבְרָהָם בַּכֹּל׃ וַיֹּאמֶר[g] אַבְרָהָם אֶל־עַבְדּוֹ
,slave his unto Abraham said And .all in Abraham blessed had

זְקַן בֵּיתוֹ הַמֹּשֵׁל בְּכָל־אֲשֶׁר־לוֹ
:him to [was] which all in ruling one the ,house his of oldest the

3 שִׂים־נָא יָדְךָ תַּחַת יְרֵכִי׃ וְאַשְׁבִּיעֲךָ
swear to thee cause will I and ;thigh my under hand thy ,pray ,Put

בַּיהוָה אֱלֹהֵי הַשָּׁמַיִם וֵאלֹהֵי[h] הָאָרֶץ אֲשֶׁר
that ,earth the of God and heavens the of God Jehovah by

And Abra-
ham was old,
and well strick-
en in age: and
the LORD had
blessed Abra-
ham in all
things. 2 And
Abraham said
unto his servant,
the elder of his
house, that ruled
over all that he
had, Put, I pray
thee, thy hand
under my thigh:
3 and I will make
thee swear by
the LORD, the
God of heaven

---

a S. *the field of the cave;* so in vs. 20.
b G., S. omit כל.
c G., S., V. *and all,* וכל.
d G. *the city.*
e G., S. omit ו.
f G., S., T., V. *which is before*, adding אשר.
g S. *and called,* ויקרא.
h G., V. omit אלהי.

of heaven, and
the God of the
earth, that thou
shalt not take a
wife unto my
son of the
daughters of the
Canaanites, a-
mong whom I
dwell: 4 But
thou shalt go
unto my coun-
try, and to my
kindred, and
take a wife unto
my son Isaac. 5
And the servant
said unto him,
Peradventure
the woman will
not be willing to
follow me unto
this land: must
I needs bring
thy son again
unto the land
from whence
thou camest? 6
And Abraham
said unto him,
Beware thou
that thou bring
not my son
thither again.

7 The LORD
God of heav-
en, which took
me from my
father's house,
and from the
land of my
kindred, and
which spake un-
to me, and that
sware unto me,
saying, Unto
thy seed will I
give this land;
he shall send
his angel be-
fore thee, and
thou shalt take
a wife unto my
son from thence.
8 And if the
woman will not
be willing to
follow thee, then
thou shalt be
clear from this
my oath: only
bring not my
son thither a-
gain. 9 And the
servant put his
hand under the

לֹֽא־תִקַּח אִשָּׁה לִבְנִי [a] מִבְּנוֹת
of daughters the from — son my for — wife a — take not wilt thou

הַכְּנַעֲנִי אֲשֶׁר אָנֹכִי יוֹשֵׁב בְּקִרְבּוֹ׃
.[3]midst [2]whose [1]in — [6]dwelling [5][am] — [4]I — (which) — ,Canaanite the

4 כִּי אֶל־אַרְצִי [b] וְאֶל־מוֹלַדְתִּי תֵּלֵךְ
,go shalt thou — kindred my unto and — land my unto — But

5 וְלָקַחְתָּ אִשָּׁה לִבְנִי לְיִצְחָק [c]׃ וַיֹּאמֶר אֵלָיו
him unto — said And — .Isaac for — son my for — wife a — take shalt and

הָעֶבֶד אוּלַי לֹא־תֹאבֶה הָאִשָּׁה לָלֶכֶת
go to — woman the — willing be not will — Perhaps — :slave the

אַחֲרַי אֶל־הָאָרֶץ הַזֹּאת הֶהָשֵׁב אָשִׁיב אֶת־בִּנְךָ
son thy — return I shall — returning —[1]this — [2]land unto — me after

6 אֶל־הָאָרֶץ אֲשֶׁר־יָצָאתָ מִשָּׁם׃ וַיֹּאמֶר
said And — ? [2]whence [1]from — [5]out [4]wentest [3]thou (which) — land the unto

אֵלָיו אַבְרָהָם הִשָּׁמֶר לְךָ פֶּן־תָּשִׁיב
return thou lest — thyself for — care Take — :Abraham — him unto

7 אֶת־בְּנִי שָׁמָּה׃ יְהוָה אֱלֹהֵי הַשָּׁמַיִם [d] אֲשֶׁר לְקָחַנִי
me took — who — heavens the — of God — Jehovah — .thither — son my

מִבֵּית אָבִי וּמֵאֶרֶץ מוֹלַדְתִּי
,birth my — of land the from and — father my — of house the from

וַאֲשֶׁר [e] דִּבֶּר־לִי וַאֲשֶׁר נִשְׁבַּע־לִי לֵאמֹר [f]
:saying — me to swore — who and — me to spoke — who and

לְזַרְעֲךָ [g] אֶתֵּן אֶת־הָאָרֶץ הַזֹּאת הוּא יִשְׁלַח
send [1]may — [2]He — ;[1]this — [2]land — give will I — seed thy To

מַלְאָכוֹ לְפָנֶיךָ וְלָקַחְתָּ אִשָּׁה לִבְנִי [h]
son my for — wife a — take thou mayest and — ,thee before — angel his

8 מִשָּׁם׃ וְאִם־לֹא תֹאבֶה הָאִשָּׁה לָלֶכֶת אַחֲרֶיךָ [i]
,thee after — go to — woman the — willing [1]is — [2]not if And — .thence from

וְנִקִּיתָ מִשְּׁבֻעָתִי זֹאת רַק אֶת־בְּנִי לֹא
[3]not — son my — only — ;[1]this — [3]oath [2]my from — released art thou then

9 תָשֵׁב שָׁמָּה׃ וַיָּשֶׂם הָעֶבֶד אֶת־יָדוֹ תַּחַת
under — hand his — slave the — put And — .thither — return [2]shalt [1]thou

and the God of
the earth, that
thou shalt not
take a wife for
my son of the
daughters of the
Canaanites, a-
mong whom I
dwell: 4 but
thou shalt go
unto my coun-
try, and to my
kindred, and
take a wife for
my son Isaac. 5
And the servant
said unto him,
Peradventure
the woman will
not be willing to
follow me unto
this land: must
I needs bring thy
son again unto
the land from
whence thou
camest? 6 And
Abraham said
unto him, Be-
ware thou that
thou bring not
my son thither
again.

7 The LORD,
the God of heav-
en, that took me
from my father's
house, and from
the land of my
nativity, and
that spake unto
me, and that
sware unto me,
saying, Unto
thy seed will I
give this land;
he shall send
his angel before
thee, and thou
shalt take a wife
for my son from
thence. 8 And if
the woman be
not willing to
follow thee, then
thou shalt be
clear from this
my oath; only
thou shalt not
bring my son
thither again. 9
And the servant
put his hand
under the thigh

a G. adds, *Isaac.*
b G. adds, *where I was born.*
c G. adds, *thence*, משם; so V.
d G. adds, *and God of the earth*, ואלהי הארץ.
e G. omits ו.
f S. omits.
g G. has, *to thee and to thy seed*, לך ולזרעך.
h G. adds, *Isaac.*
i G. adds, *unto this land.*

thigh of Abra-
ham his master,
and sware to
him concerning
that matter.

10 And the
servant took ten
camels of the
camels of his
master, and de-
parted: for all
the goods of his
master *were* in
his hand; and he
arose, and went
to Mesopota-
mia, unto the
city of Nahor.
11 And he made
his camels to
kneel down
without the city
by a well of wa-
ter at the time of
the evening, *e-
ven* the time
that women go
out to draw *wa-
ter*. 12 And he
said, O LORD
God of my mas-
ter Abraham, I
pray thee, send
me good speed
this day, and
shew kindness
unto my master
Abraham. 13
Behold, I stand
here by the well
of water; and
the daughters of
the men of the
city come out to
draw water: 14
And let it come
to pass, that the
damsel to whom
I shall say, Let
down thy pitch-
er, I pray thee,
that I may drink;
and she shall
say, Drink, and
I will give thy
camels drink al-
so: *let the same
be* she *that* thou
hast appointed
for thy servant
Isaac; and
thereby shall I
know that thou
hast shewed

יֶרֶךְ אַבְרָהָם אֲדֹנָיו וַיִּשָּׁבַע לוֹ עַל־
concerning | him to | swore and | ,master his | Abraham | of thigh the

10 הַדָּבָר הַזֶּה׃ וַיִּקַּח הָעֶבֶד עֲשָׂרָה גְמַלִּים
camels | ten | slave the | took And | .[1]this | [2]thing

מִגְּמַלֵּי אֲדֹנָיו וַיֵּלֶךְ[a] וְכָל־[b]
[of kinds] all (and) | ,went and | master his | of camels the from

טוּב אֲדֹנָיו בְּיָדוֹ וַיָּקָם
up rose he and | ; hand his in | [being] master his | of things precious

וַיֵּלֶךְ אֶל־אֲרַם נַהֲרַיִם אֶל־עִיר נָחוֹר׃
.Nahor | of city the unto | ,rivers two the | of Aram unto | went and

11 וַיַּבְרֵךְ הַגְּמַלִּים מִחוּץ לָעִיר
city the (to) | without from | camels the | kneel to caused he And

אֶל־בְּאֵר הַמָּיִם לְעֵת עֶרֶב לְעֵת
of time the at | ,evening | of time the at | water | of well the at

12 צֵאת הַשֹּׁאֲבֹת׃ וַיֹּאמַר[c]
: said he And | .[waters of] drawers women the | of out going the

יְהוָה אֱלֹהֵי אֲדֹנִי אַבְרָהָם הַקְרֵה־נָא
,meet to [it] cause | ,Abraham | master my | of God | Jehovah

לְפָנַי הַיּוֹם וַעֲשֵׂה־חֶסֶד עִם אֲדֹנִי
master my | with | kindness do and | ,to day | me (before) ,pray I

13 אַבְרָהָם׃ הִנֵּה אָנֹכִי נִצָּב עַל־עֵין
of fountain the by | standing [am] | I | Behold | .Abraham

הַמָּיִם וּבְנוֹת אַנְשֵׁי הָעִיר יֹצְאֹת
out going [are] | city the | of men the | of daughters the and | ,water

14 לִשְׁאֹב מָיִם׃ וְהָיָה[d] הַנַּעֲרָ אֲשֶׁר
whom [unto] | maiden the | [that] be it may And | .water | draw to

אֹמַר אֵלֶיהָ הַטִּי־נָא כַדֵּךְ וְאֶשְׁתֶּה
; drink may I that | ,pitcher thy | ,pray ,down Let | : (her unto) | say shall I

וְאָמְרָה[e] שְׁתֵה וְגַם־גְּמַלֶּיךָ אַשְׁקֶה[f] אֹתָהּ
her—drink give will I | camels thy also and | Drink | : say will she and

הֹכַחְתָּ לְעַבְדְּךָ לְיִצְחָק וּבָהּ אֵדַע
know shall I | it by and | ; Isaac for | ,servant thy for | designed hast thou

of Abraham his
master, and
sware to him
concerning this
matter.

10 And the
servant took ten
camels, of the
camels of his
master, and de-
parted; having
all goodly things
of his master's
in his hand: and
he arose, and
went to Meso-
potamia, unto
the city of Na-
hor. 11 And he
made the camels
to kneel down
without the city
by the well of
water at the
time of even-
ing, the time
that women go
out to draw
water. 12 And
he said, O
LORD, the God
of my master A-
braham, send
me, I pray
thee, good speed
this day, and
shew kindness
unto my master
Abraham. 13
Behold, I stand
by the fountain
of water; and
the daughters of
the men of the
city come out to
draw water: 14
and let it come
to pass, that the
damsel to whom
I shall say, Let
down thy pitch-
er, I pray thee,
that I may drink;
and she shall
say, Drink, and
I will give thy
camels drink al-
so: Let the same
be she that thou
hast appointed
for thy servant
Isaac; and there-
by shall I know
that thou hast

---

a G. omits.
b For וכל, G., S. have, *and from all;* V. *from.*
c S. *and he prayed and said.*
d S. omits היה.
e G., S. add, *to me.*
f G. adds, *until they cease to drink.*

kindness unto
my master.

15 And it
came to pass,
before he had
done speaking,
that, behold,
Rebekah came
out, who was
born to Bethuel,
son of Milcah,
the wife of Na-
hor, Abraham's
brother, with
her pitcher up-
on her shoulder.
16 And the dam-
sel *was* very fair
to look upon, a
virgin, neither
had any man
known her: and
she went down
to the well, and
filled her pitch-
er, and came
up. 17 And the
servant ran to
meet her, and
said, Let me, I
pray thee, drink
a little water of
thy pitcher. 18
And she said,
Drink, my lord:
and she hasted,
and let down her
pitcher upon her
hand, and gave
him drink. 19
And when she
had done giving
him drink, she
said, I will draw
water for thy
camels also, un-
til they have
done drinking.
20 And she hast-
ed, and emptied
her pitcher into
the trough, and
ran again unto
the well to draw
water, and drew
for all his cam-
els. 21 And the
man wondering
at her held his
peace, to wit
whether the
LORD had made

15 כִּי־עָשִׂיתָ חֶסֶד[a] עִם־אֲדֹנִי[b]: וַיְהִי־הוּא[c]
he ,pass to came it And .master my with kindness done hast thou that

טֶרֶם כִּלָּה לְדַבֵּר[d] וְהִנֵּה רִבְקָה
Rebekah behold [that] (and) ,speak to finished having yet not

יֹצֵאת אֲשֶׁר יֻלְּדָה לִבְתוּאֵל בֶּן־מִלְכָּה
Milcah of son the ,Bethuel to born was who ,out going [was]

אֵשֶׁת נָחוֹר אֲחִי[e] אַבְרָהָם וְכַדָּהּ
pitcher her (and) ,Abraham of brother the Nahor of wife the

16 עַל־שִׁכְמָהּ: וְהַנַּעֲרָ טֹבַת מַרְאֶה
appearance of fair [was] maiden the And .shoulder her upon [being]

מְאֹד בְּתוּלָה וְאִישׁ לֹא יְדָעָהּ
; her known having not man a (and) ,virgin a ,exceedingly

וַתֵּרֶד הָעַיְנָה וַתְּמַלֵּא כַדָּהּ
,pitcher her filled and ,fountain the to down went she and

17 וַתָּעַל: וַיָּרָץ הָעֶבֶד לִקְרָאתָהּ וַיֹּאמֶר
: said and ,her meet to slave the ran And .up came and

18 הַגְמִיאִינִי נָא מְעַט־מַיִם מִכַּדֵּךְ: וַתֹּאמֶר[f]
: said she And .pitcher thy from water little a ,pray I ,sip me Let

שְׁתֵה אֲדֹנִי וַתְּמַהֵר וַתֹּרֶד כַּדָּהּ עַל־
upon pitcher her down let and hastened she and ; lord my ,Drink

19 יָדָהּ וַתַּשְׁקֵהוּ: וַתְּכַל[g] לְהַשְׁקֹתוֹ[g]
,drink him give to finished she And .drink him gave and ,hand her

וַתֹּאמֶר גַּם לִגְמַלֶּיךָ אֶשְׁאָב עַד[h] אִם־
(if) until ,draw will I camels thy for Also : said she and

20 כִּלּוּ לִשְׁתֹּת[h]: וַתְּמַהֵר וַתְּעַר
emptied and hastened she And .drink to finished have shall they

כַּדָּהּ אֶל־הַשֹּׁקֶת וַתָּרָץ עוֹד אֶל־הַבְּאֵר
well the unto again ran and ,trough the into pitcher her

21 לִשְׁאֹב[i] וַתִּשְׁאַב לְכָל־גְּמַלָּיו: וְהָאִישׁ מִשְׁתָּאֵה[j]
observing [was] man the And .camels his all for drew and ,draw to

לָהּ מַחֲרִישׁ לָדַעַת הַהִצְלִיחַ יְהוָה
Jehovah prospered had whether know to ,silent keeping ,her (to)

shewed kindness
unto my master.

15 And it came
to pass, before
he had done
speaking, that,
behold, Rebek-
ah came out,
who was born to
Bethuel the son
of Milcah, the
wife of Nahor,
Abraham's
brother, with
her pitcher up-
on her shoulder.
16 And the dam-
sel was very fair
to look upon, a
virgin, neither
had any man
known her; and
she went down
to the fountain,
and filled her
pitcher, and
came up. 17
And the servant
ran to meet her,
and said, Give
me to drink, I
pray thee, a
little water of
thy pitcher. 18
And she said,
Drink, my lord:
and she hasted,
and let down
her pitcher up-
on her hand,
and gave him
drink. 19 And
when she had
done giving him
drink, she said,
I will draw for
thy camels also,
until they have
done drinking.
20 And she hast-
ed, and emptied
her pitcher into
the trough, and
ran again unto
the well to
draw, and drew
for all his cam-
els. 21 And the
man looked
steadfastly on
her; holding his
peace, to know
whether the
LORD had made

---

a S. adds, *and justice*.

b Sm., G. add, *Abraham*.

c S. omits יהי.

d Sm. adds, *in his heart*, בלבו; so G., V.

e G. ואחי.

f S. adds, *to him*.

g G. connects with vs. 18 and has, *until he ceased drinking*.

h For עד אם כלו לשתת, G., V. have, *until all drink*.

i G. adds, *water*.

j S. *giving to drink and watching*, apparently double translation, one reading מַשְׁקָה.

his journey pros-
perous or not. 22 And it came
to pass, as the
camels had done
drinking, that
the man took a
golden earring
of half a shekel
weight, and two
bracelets for her
hands of ten
shekels weight of
gold; 23 And
said, Whose
daughter *art*
thou? tell me,
I pray thee: is
there room *in*
thy father's
house for us to
lodge in? 24
And she said
unto him, I *am*
the daughter of
Bethuel, the son
of Milcah, which
she bare unto
Nahor. 25
She said more-
over unto him,
We have both
straw and prov-
ender enough,
and room to
lodge in. 26
And the man
bowed down his
head, and wor-
shipped the
LORD. 27 And
he said, Blessed
be the LORD
God of my mas-
ter Abraham,
who hath not
left destitute my
master of his
mercy and his
truth: I *being* in
the way, the
LORD led me
to the house of
my master's
brethren. 28
And the dam-
sel ran, and
told *them of* her
mother's house
these things.

22 דַּרְכּוֹ אִם־לֹא׃ וַיְהִי[a] כַּאֲשֶׁר כִּלּוּ[b]
finished had when ,pass to came it And .not or ,way his

הַגְּמַלִּים לִשְׁתּוֹת וַיִּקַּח הָאִישׁ[c] נֶזֶם זָהָב
,gold of nose-ring a man the took that ,drink to camels the

בֶּקַע מִשְׁקָלוֹ[d] וּשְׁנֵי צְמִידִים עַל־יָדֶיהָ
,hands her upon bracelets two and ,weight its [being] half-shekel a

23 עֲשָׂרָה זָהָב מִשְׁקָלָם׃ וַיֹּאמֶר[e] בַּת־
of daughter The :said he And .weight their [being] gold [of shekels] ten

מִי אַתְּ הַגִּידִי נָא לִי הֲיֵשׁ
[there] Is .me to ,pray ,known make ?thou [art] whom

24 בֵּית־אָבִיךְ מָקוֹם לָנוּ לָלִין׃ וַתֹּאמֶר
said she And ?night the pass to us for place father thy of house the at

אֵלָיו בַּת־בְּתוּאֵל אָנֹכִי בֶּן־מִלְכָּה
,Milcah of son the ,I [am] Bethuel of daughter The :him unto

25 אֲשֶׁר יָלְדָה לְנָחוֹר׃ וַתֹּאמֶר אֵלָיו גַּם־תֶּבֶן
straw Both :him unto said she And .Nahor to bore she whom

גַּם־מִסְפּוֹא רַב עִמָּנוּ גַּם־מָקוֹם[f] לָלוּן׃
.night the pass to place a and ,us with plenty [are] fodder and

26 27 וַיִּקֹּד הָאִישׁ[g] וַיִּשְׁתַּחוּ לַיהוָה׃ וַיֹּאמֶר
:said he And .Jehovah to himself prostrated and ,man the bowed And

בָּרוּךְ יְהוָה אֱלֹהֵי אֲדֹנִי אַבְרָהָם אֲשֶׁר
who ,Abraham master my of God Jehovah [be] Blessed

לֹא־עָזַב חַסְדּוֹ וַאֲמִתּוֹ מֵעִם אֲדֹנִי
;master my with (from) truth his and kindness his discontinued not has

אָנֹכִי בַּדֶּרֶךְ נָחַנִי יְהוָה בֵּית
of house the to Jehovah me guided way the in ,me [for as]

28 אֲחֵי אֲדֹנִי[h]׃ וַתָּרָץ הַנַּעֲרָ וַתַּגֵּד
known made and ,maiden the ran And .master my of brothers the

לְבֵית אִמָּהּ כַּדְּבָרִים[i] הָאֵלֶּה׃
.¹these ²things to according mother her of house the to

his journey
prosperous or
not. 22 And it
came to pass, as
the camels had
done drinking,
that the man
took a golden
ring of half a
shekel weight,
and two brace-
lets for her
hands of ten
shekels weight
of gold; 23 and
said, Whose
daughter art
thou? tell me,
I pray thee. Is
there room in
thy father's
house for us to
lodge in? 24
And she said un-
to him, I am the
daughter of Be-
thuel the son of
Milcah, which
she bare unto
Nahor. 25 She
said moreover
unto him, We
have both straw
and provender
enough, and
room to lodge
in. 26 And the
man bowed his
head, and wor-
shipped the
LORD. 27 And
he said, Blessed
be the LORD,
the God of my
master Abra-
ham, who hath
not foresaken
his mercy and
his truth to-
ward my master:
as for me, the
LORD hath led
me in the way
to the house of
my master's
brethren. 28
And the damsel
ran, and told
her mother's
house according
to these words.

29 And Re-
bekah had a
brother, and his

29 וּלְרִבְקָה אָח וּשְׁמוֹ לָבָן
,Laban [being] name his (and) ,brother a [was] Rebekah to And

29 And Re-
bekah had a
brother, and his

---

a S. omits יהי.
b G. adds, *all*, prob. a double rendering.
c S. *the slave*, העבד.
d Sm. adds, *and he put upon* [*her*] *nose*, וישם על אפה.
e G. *and he answered her and said;* S. adds, *to her*.
f For גם, Sm., S. have וגם.
g S. adds, *upon the earth*, על הארץ.
h S. adds, *to take the daughter of the brother of my lord for his son*.
i S. omits כ.

name *was* La-
ban: and Laban
ran out unto
the man, unto
the well. 30 And
it came to pass,
when he saw the
earring and
bracelets upon
his sister's
hands, and
when he heard
the words of
Rebekah his
sister, saying,
Thus spake the
man unto me;
that he came
unto the man;
and, behold, he
stood by the
camels at the
well. 31 And he
said, Come in,
thou blessed of
the LORD;
wherefore
standest thou
without? for I
have prepared
the house, and
room for the
camels.
32 And the
man came into
the house: and
he ungirded his
camels, and
gave straw and
provender for
the camels, and
water to wash
his feet, and the
men's feet that
were with him.
33 And there
was set *meat*
before him to
eat: but he said,
I will not eat,
until I have told
mine errand.
And he said,
Speak on. 34
And he said, I
am Abraham's
servant. 35 And
the LORD hath
blessed my mas-
ter greatly; and
he is become
great: and he
hath given him
flocks, and
herds, and sil-
ver, and gold,
and menserv-

וַיָּרָץ לָבָן אֶל־הָאִישׁ הַחוּצָה אֶל־הָעָיִן׃
.fountain the unto ,outside man the unto Laban ran and

30 וַיְהִי כִּרְאֹת אֶת־הַנֶּזֶם וְאֶת־
and ,nose-ring the seeing [his] at pass to came it And

הַצְּמִדִים עַל־יְדֵי אֲחֹתוֹ וּכְשָׁמְעוֹ
hearing his at and ,sister his of hands the upon bracelets the

אֶת־דִּבְרֵי רִבְקָה אֲחֹתוֹ לֵאמֹר כֹּה־דִבֶּר אֵלַי
me unto spoke Thus :saying sister his Rebekah of words the

הָאִישׁ וַיָּבֹא אֶל־הָאִישׁ וְהִנֵּה[a] עֹמֵד
standing [was he] behold and ,man the unto came he then ;man the

31 עַל־הַגְּמַלִּים עַל־הָעָיִן׃ וַיֹּאמֶר[b] בּוֹא
,in thou Come :said he And .fountain the at camels the by

בְּרוּךְ יְהוָה לָמָּה תַעֲמֹד בַּחוּץ
,street the in stand thou dost why ,Jehovah of blessed

וְאָנֹכִי פִּנִּיתִי הַבַּיִת וּמָקוֹם לַגְּמַלִּים׃
?camels the for place a and house the prepared have I [seeing] (and)

32 וַיָּבֹא[c] הָאִישׁ הַבַּיְתָה וַיְפַתַּח הַגְּמַלִּים
,camels the unloaded he and ,house the to man the in came And

וַיִּתֵּן תֶּבֶן וּמִסְפּוֹא לַגְּמַלִּים וּמַיִם לִרְחֹץ[d]
wash to water and ,camels the to fodder and straw gave and

רַגְלָיו וְרַגְלֵי הָאֲנָשִׁים אֲשֶׁר אִתּוֹ׃
.him with [were] who men the of feet the and ,feet his

33 וַיּוּשַׂם לְפָנָיו[e] לֶאֱכֹל וַיֹּאמֶר לֹא אֹכַל
eat [2]will [1]I [3]Not :said he and ; eat to him before put was [food] and

34 עַד אִם־דִּבַּרְתִּי דְּבָרָי וַיֹּאמֶר[f] דַּבֵּר׃ וַיֹּאמַר
:said he And .Speak :said he and ; words my spoken have I (if) until

35 עֶבֶד אַבְרָהָם אָנֹכִי׃ וַיהוָה בֵּרַךְ
blessed has Jehovah And .I [am] Abraham of slave The

אֶת־אֲדֹנִי מְאֹד וַיִּגְדָּל וַיִּתֶּן־
given has he and ;great become has he and ,exceedingly master my

לוֹ[g] צֹאן וּבָקָר וְכֶסֶף וְזָהָב וַעֲבָדִם[h]
slaves male and ,gold and silver and ,herds and flocks him to

name was La-
ban: and La-
ban ran out unto
the man, unto
the fountain. 30
And it came to
pass, when he
saw the ring,
and the brace-
lets upon his sis-
ter's hands, and
when he heard
the words of
Rebekah his sis-
ter, saying,
Thus spake the
man unto me;
that he came
unto the man;
and, behold, he
stood by the
camels at the
fountain. 31
And he said,
Come in, thou
blessed of the
LORD; where-
fore standest
thou without?
for I have pre-
prepared the
house, and room
for the camels.
32 And the man
came into the
house, and he
ungirded the
camels; and he
gave straw and
provender for
the camels, and
water to wash
his feet and the
men's feet that
were with him.
33 And there
was set meat
before him to
eat: but he said,
I will not eat,
until I have told
mine errand.
And he said,
Speak on. 34
And he said, I
am Abraham's
servant. 35 And
the LORD hath
blessed my mas-
ter greatly; and
he is become
great: and he
hath given him
flocks and herds,
and silver and
gold, and men-
servants and

---

a S. *and he;* G. *he.*
b G., S. add, *to him.*
c V. has, *and he brought in,* וַיָּבֵא.
d G. omits רחץ.
e G. adds, *bread.*
f V. adds, *to him;* S. has, *they said to him.*
g S. *and there are to him.*
h G., V. omit ו.

ants, and maidservants, and camels, and asses. 36 And Sarah my master's wife bare a son to my master when she was old: and unto him hath he given all that he hath. 37 And my master made me swear, saying, Thou shalt not take a wife to my son of the daughters of the Canaanites, in whose land I dwell: 38 But thou shalt go unto my father's house, and to my kindred, and take a wife unto my son. 39 And I said unto my master, Peradventure the woman will not follow me. 40 And he said unto me, The LORD, before whom I walk, will send his angel with thee, and prosper thy way; and thou shalt take a wife for my son of my kindred, and of my father's house: 41 Then shalt thou be clear from *this* my oath, when thou comest to my kindred; and if they give not thee *one*, thou shalt be clear from my oath. 42 And I came this day unto the well, and said, O LORD God of my master Abraham, if now thou do prosper

36 וּשְׁפָחֹת[a] וּגְמַלִּים[b] וַחֲמֹרִים׃ וַתֵּלֶד שָׂרָה
Sarah bore And .asses and camels and ,slaves female and

אֵשֶׁת אֲדֹנִי בֵן[c] לַאדֹנִי אַחֲרֵי זִקְנָתָהּ
;old becoming her after ,master my to son a master my of wife the

37 וַיִּתֶּן־לוֹ אֶת־כָּל־אֲשֶׁר־לוֹ׃ וַיַּשְׁבִּעֵנִי
swear to me caused And .him to [was] which all him to given has he and

אֲדֹנִי לֵאמֹר[d] לֹא־תִקַּח אִשָּׁה לִבְנִי
son my for wife a take not shalt Thou :saying master my

מִבְּנוֹת הַכְּנַעֲנִי אֲשֶׁר אָנֹכִי יֹשֵׁב
[6]dwelling [5][am] [4]I (which) ,Canaanite the of daughters the from

38 בְּאַרְצוֹ׃ אִם־לֹא אֶל־בֵּית־אָבִי תֵּלֵךְ
,go shalt thou father my of house the unto But .[3]land [2]whose [1]in

וְאֶל־מִשְׁפַּחְתִּי וְלָקַחְתָּ אִשָּׁה לִבְנִי׃[e]
.son my for wife a take shalt thou and ;family my unto and

39 וָאֹמַר אֶל־אֲדֹנִי אֻלַי לֹא־תֵלֵךְ הָאִשָּׁה
woman the go not will Perhaps :master my unto said I And

40 אַחֲרָי׃ וַיֹּאמֶר אֵלָי[f] יְהוָה אֲשֶׁר הִתְהַלַּכְתִּי
[4]walk [3]I (whom) ,Jehovah : me unto said he And .me after

לְפָנָיו יִשְׁלַח מַלְאָכוֹ אִתָּךְ וְהִצְלִיחַ
prosper he may and ,thee with angel his send he may [2].whom [1]before

דַּרְכֶּךָ וְלָקַחְתָּ אִשָּׁה לִבְנִי מִמִּשְׁפַּחְתִּי
family my from son my for wife a take thou do and ; way thy

41 וּמִבֵּית אָבִי׃ אָז[g] תִּנָּקֶה
released art thou Then .father my of house the from and

מֵאָלָתִי כִּי תָבוֹא אֶל־מִשְׁפַּחְתִּי וְאִם־לֹא
[3]not if and ; family my unto comest thou when ,oath my from

יִתְּנוּ לָךְ וְהָיִיתָ[h] נָקִי מֵאָלָתִי׃[h]
.oath my from released art thou then ,thee to [2]give [1]they

42 וָאָבֹא הַיּוֹם אֶל־הָעָיִן וָאֹמַר יְהוָה אֱלֹהֵי
of God Jehovah : said I and ,fountain the unto today came I And

אֲדֹנִי אַבְרָהָם אִם־יֶשְׁךָ־נָּא מַצְלִיחַ דַּרְכִּי
,way my prosper to about ,pray I ,art thou if ,Abraham master my

maidservants, and camels and asses. 36 And Sarah my master's wife bare a son to my master when she was old: and unto him hath he given all that he hath. 37 And my master made me swear, saying, Thou shalt not take a wife for my son of the daughters of the Canaanites, in whose land I dwell: 38 But thou shalt go unto my father's house, and to my kindred, and take a wife for my son. 39 And I said unto my master, Peradventure the woman will not follow me. 40 And he said unto me, The LORD, before whom I walk, will send his angel with thee and prosper thy way; and thou shalt take a wife for my son of my kindred, and of my father's house: 41 then shalt thou be clear from my oath, when thou comest to my kindred; and if they give her not to thee, thou shalt be clear from my oath. 42 And I came this day unto the fountain, and said, O LORD, the God of my master Abraham, if now thou do prosper

---

a S. adds, *and she-asses*, ואתנת.
b G., V. omit ו.
c G. has, *one son.*
d S adds, *to me.*
e G., S. add, *thence*, משם.
f S. adds, *my lord*, ארני.
g S. ואז.
h V. omits והיית נקי מאלתי.

my way which I
go: 43 Behold,
I stand by the
well of water;
and it shall
come to pass,
that when the
virgin cometh
forth to draw
water, and I say
to her, Give me,
I pray thee, a
little water of thy
pitcher to drink;
44 And she
say to me, Both
drink thou, and
I will also draw
for thy camels:
let the same *be*
the woman
whom the LORD
hath appointed
out for my mas-
ter's son. 45 And
before I had
done speaking
in mine heart,
behold, Rebek-
ah came forth
with her pitcher
on her shoulder;
and she went
down unto the
well, and drew
water: and I said
unto her, Let
me drink, I pray
thee. 46 And she
made haste, and
let down her
pitcher from her
shoulder, and
said, Drink, and
I will give thy
camels drink al-
so: so I drank,
and she made
the camels drink
also. 47 And I
asked her, and
said, Whose
daughter *art*
thou? And she
said, The
daughter of Be-
thuel, Nahor's
son, whom Mil-
cah bare unto
him: and I put
the earring up-
on her face, and
the bracelets up-

43 אֲשֶׁר אָנֹכִי הֹלֵךְ עָלֶיהָ׃ הִנֵּה אָנֹכִי
I Behold .(it upon) go to about [am] I which [upon]

נִצָּב עַל־עֵין הַמָּיִם[a] וְהָיָה[b]
,pass to come it let and ; water of fountain the at standing [am]

הָעַלְמָה הַיֹּצֵאת לִשְׁאֹב[c] וְאָמַרְתִּי אֵלֶיהָ
: her unto say I and ,draw to out going maiden the [that]

44 הַשְׁקִינִי־נָא מְעַט־מַיִם מִכַּדֵּךְ׃ וְאָמְרָה
says she and ; pitcher thy from water little a ,pray I ,drink me Let

אֵלַי גַּם־אַתָּה שְׁתֵה וְגַם לִגְמַלֶּיךָ אֶשְׁאָב
—draw will I camels thy for also and ,drink ,thou Also : me unto

הִוא הָאִשָּׁה אֲשֶׁר־הֹכִיחַ יְהוָה לְבֶן־
of son the for Jehovah designed has whom woman the [be] she [may]

45 אֲדֹנִי[d]׃ אֲנִי[e] טֶרֶם אֲכַלֶּה לְדַבֵּר אֶל־לִבִּי
,heart my unto speak to finished had yet not I .master my

וְהִנֵּה רִבְקָה יֹצֵאת וְכַדָּהּ עַל־
upon [being] pitcher her (and) ,out going Rebekah behold and

שִׁכְמָהּ וַתֵּרֶד הָעַיְנָה וַתִּשְׁאָב
; drew and fountain the to down went she and ; shoulder her

46 וָאֹמַר אֵלֶיהָ הַשְׁקִינִי נָא׃[f] וַתְּמַהֵר
hastened she And .pray I ,drink me Let : her unto said I and

וַתּוֹרֶד כַּדָּהּ מֵעָלֶיהָ וַתֹּאמֶר[g] שְׁתֵה
,Drink : said and ,her upon from pitcher her down let and

וְגַם־גְּמַלֶּיךָ אַשְׁקֶה וָאֵשְׁתְּ וְגַם
also and ,drank I and ; drink give will I camels thy also and

47 הַגְּמַלִּים הִשְׁקָתָה[h]׃ וָאֶשְׁאַל אֹתָהּ וָאֹמַר
; said I and ,her asked I And .drink gave she camels the

בַּת־מִי אַתְּ[i] וַתֹּאמֶר בַּת־
of daughter The : said she And ? thou [art] whom of daughter The

בְּתוּאֵל בֶּן־נָחוֹר אֲשֶׁר יָלְדָה־לּוֹ מִלְכָּה
; Milcah him to bore whom ,Nahor of son the Bethuel

וָאָשִׂם הַנֶּזֶם עַל־אַפָּהּ וְהַצְּמִידִים עַל־
upon bracelets the and nose her upon ring the put I and

my way which I
go: 43 behold, I
stand by the
fountain of wa-
ter; and let it
come to pass,
that the maiden
which cometh
forth to draw,
to whom I shall
say, Give me, I
pray thee, a
little water of
thy pitcher to
drink; 44 and
she shall say to
me, Both drink
thou, and I will
also draw for
thy camels: let
the same be the
woman whom
the LORD hath
appointed for
my master's son.
45 And before I
had done speak-
ing in mine
heart, behold,
Rebekah came
forth with her
pitcher on her
shoulder; and
she went down
unto the fount-
ain, and drew:
and I said unto
her, Let me
drink, I pray
thee. 46 And she
made haste, and
let down her
pitcher from her
shoulder, and
said, Drink, and
I will give thy
camels drink al-
so: so I drank,
and she made
the camels drink
also. 47 And I
asked her, and
said, Whose
daughter art
thou? And she
said, The
daughter of Be-
thuel, Nahor's
son, whom Mil-
cah bare unto
him: and I put
the ring upon
her nose, and
the bracelets up-

---

a S. adds, *and the daughters of the men of the city will go out to draw water*, cf. vs. 13.

b S., V. omit היה.

c S. adds, *water*.

d G. has, *for his servant Isaac*, cf. vs. 14; G. adds, *and in this I shall know that thou hast done kindness to my lord Abraham*, cf. vs. 14.

e G. adds, before ויהי ,אני.

f Sm., S. add, *a little water from thy pitcher*; V. adds, *a little*.

g S. adds, *to me*.

h S. *I gave drink*, השקיתי.

i G. adds, *tell me*.

on her hands. 48
And I bowed
down my head,
and worshipped
the LORD, and
blessed the
LORD God of
my master A-
braham, which
had led me in
the right way to
take my master's
brother's daugh-
ter unto his son.
49 And now, if
ye will deal
kindly and truly
with my master,
tell me: and if
not, tell me;
that I may turn
to the right
hand, or to the
left. 50 Then
Laban and Be-
thuel answered
and said, The
thing proceedeth
from the LORD:
we cannot speak
unto thee bad or
good. 51 Be-
hold, Rebekah
is before thee;
take *her*, and
go, and let her
be thy master's
son's wife, as the
LORD hath
spoken. 52 And
it came to pass,
that, when A-
braham's serv-
ant heard their
words, he wor-
shipped the
LORD, *bowing*
himself to the
earth. 53 And
the servant
brought forth
jewels of silver,
and jewels of
gold, and rai-
ment, and gave
them to Rebek-
ah: he gave
also to her broth-
er and to her
mother precious
things. 54 And
they did eat and
drink, he and
the men that
were with him,
and tarried all
night; and they
rose up in the
morning, and he

יָדֶיהָ׃ וָאֶקֹּד וָאֶשְׁתַּחֲוֶה לַיהוָה 48
; Jehovah to myself prostrated and bowed I And .hands her

וָאֲבָרֵךְ אֶת־יְהוָה אֱלֹהֵי אֲדֹנִי אַבְרָהָם אֲשֶׁר
who ,Abraham lord my of God Jehovah blessed I and

הִנְחַנִי בְּדֶרֶךְ אֱמֶת[a] לָקַחַת אֶת־בַּת־
of daughter the take to ,truth of way a in me guided had

אֲחִי אֲדֹנִי לִבְנוֹ׃ וְעַתָּה אִם־יֶשְׁכֶם 49
are you if ,now And .son his for master my of brother the

עֹשִׂים חֶסֶד וֶאֱמֶת אֶת־אֲדֹנִי הַגִּידוּ
known make ,master my with truth and kindness do to about

לִי וְאִם־לֹא[b] הַגִּידוּ לִי וְאֶפְנֶה עַל־
unto turn may I that ; me to known make ,not if and ; me to

יָמִין אוֹ עַל־שְׂמֹאל׃ וַיַּעַן לָבָן וּבְתוּאֵל 50
Bethuel and Laban answered And .left the unto or right the

וַיֹּאמְרוּ מֵיְהוָה יָצָא הַדָּבָר לֹא נוּכַל
able ²are ¹we ³not ; thing the goes Jehovah From : said and

דַּבֵּר אֵלֶיךָ רַע אוֹ־טוֹב[c]׃ הִנֵּה־רִבְקָה לְפָנֶיךָ 51
,thee before Rebekah Behold .good or evil thee unto speak to

קַח וָלֵךְ וּתְהִי אִשָּׁה לְבֶן־אֲדֹנֶיךָ
,master thy of son the for wife a become her let and ,go and take

כַּאֲשֶׁר דִּבֶּר יְהוָה׃ וַיְהִי[d] כַּאֲשֶׁר 52
when ,pass to came it And .Jehovah spoken has as according

שָׁמַע עֶבֶד אַבְרָהָם אֶת־דִּבְרֵיהֶם וַיִּשְׁתַּחוּ
himself prostrated he that words their Abraham of slave the heard

אַרְצָה לַיהוָה׃ וַיּוֹצֵא הָעֶבֶד כְּלֵי־ 53
of vessels slave the out brought And .Jehovah unto earth the to

כֶסֶף וּכְלֵי זָהָב וּבְגָדִים וַיִּתֵּן לְרִבְקָה
; Rebekah to gave and ,garments and ,gold of vessels and ,silver

וּמִגְדָּנֹת נָתַן לְאָחִיהָ[e] וּלְאִמָּהּ׃ וַיֹּאכְלוּ 54
ate they And .mother her to and ,brother her to gave he jewels and

וַיִּשְׁתּוּ הוּא וְהָאֲנָשִׁים אֲשֶׁר־עִמּוֹ
,him with [were] who men the and he ,drank and

וַיָּלִינוּ וַיָּקוּמוּ בַבֹּקֶר
,morning the in up rose they and ; night the passed they and

on her hands.
48 And I bowed
my head, and
worshipped the
LORD, and
blessed the
LORD, the God
of my master A-
braham, which
had led me in
the right way to
take my master's
brother's daugh-
ter for his son.
49 And now if
ye will deal
kindly and truly
with my master,
tell me: and if
not, tell me;
that I may turn
to the right
hand, or to the
left. 50 Then
Laban and Be-
thuel answered
and said, The
thing proceed-
eth from the
LORD: we can-
not speak unto
thee bad or
good. 51 Be-
hold, Rebekah
is before thee,
take her, and
go, and let her
be thy master's
son's wife, as
the LORD hath
spoken. 52 And
it came to pass,
that, when A-
braham's serv-
ant heard their
words, he bowed
himself down to
the earth unto
the LORD. 53
And the servant
brought forth
jewels of silver,
and jewels of
gold, and rai-
ment, and gave
them to Rebek-
ah: he gave al-
so to her broth-
er and to her
mother precious
things. 54 And
they did eat and
drink, he and
the men that
were with him,
and tarried all
night; and they
rose up in the
morning, and he

---

a S. adds, *to the house of the brother of my lord*, cf. vs. 27.

b G. omits ואם לא הגידו לי.

c G. *for good*, לטוב; V. *beyond his will.*

d S. omits יהי.

e S., V. pl. לְאַחֶיהָ.

said, Send me
away unto my
master. 55 And
her brother and
her mother said,
Let the damsel
abide with us *a*
few days, at the
least ten; after
that she shall
go. 56 And he
said unto them,
Hinder me not,
seeing the LORD
hath prospered
my way; send
me away that I
may go to my
master. 57 And
they said, We
will call the
damsel, and en-
quire at her
mouth. 58 And
they called Re-
bekah, and said
unto her, Wilt
thou go with
this man? and
she said, I will
go. 59 And they
sent away Re-
bekah their sis-
ter, and her
nurse, and A-
braham's serv-
ant, and his
men. 60 And
they blessed
Rebekah, and
said unto her,
Thou *art* our
sister, be thou
the mother of
thousands of
millions, and let
thy seed possess
the gate of those
which hate
them.
61 And Rebek-
ah arose, and
her damsels,
and they rode
upon the cam-
els, and follow-
ed the man: and
the servant took
Rebekah, and
went his way. 62
And Isaac came
from the way of
the well Lahai-
roi; for he dwelt
in the south
country. 63 And
Isaac went out

55 ויאמר[a] שלחני[b] לאדני: ויאמר[c] אחיה[d]
brother her said And .master my to me Send ; said he and

ואמה תשב הנער אתנו ימים[e] או
or days us with maiden the stay Let : mother her and

56 עשור[e] אחר[f] תלך: ויאמר אלהם אל-
not Do : them unto said he And .go her let afterwards ,ten

תאחרו אתי ויהוה הצליח דרכי
; way my prospered has Jehovah [seeing] (and) ,me detain

57 שלחוני ואלכה לאדני: ויאמרו נקרא
call us Let ; said they And .master my to go may I that ,me send

58 לנער ונשאלה את-פיה: ויקראו
called they And .mouth her ask us let and ,maiden the (to)

לרבקה ויאמרו אליה התלכי עם-האיש
²man with go thou Wilt ; her unto said and ,Rebekah (to)

59 הזה ותאמר אלך: וישלחו את-רבקה
Rebekah sent they And .go will I : said she and ? ¹this

אחתם ואת-מנקתה ואת-עבד אברהם
,Abraham of slave the and ,nurse her and ,sister their

60 ואת-אנשיו: ויברכו את-רבקה[g] ויאמרו לה
: her to said and Rebekah blessed they And .men his and

אחתנו את היי לאלפי[h] רבבה[h] ויירש
possess may and ,myriads of thousands (for) ¹become ²thou ,sister Our

61 זרעך את שער[i] שנאיו: ותקם רבקה
,Rebekah arose And .them hating those of gate the seed thy

ונערתיה ותרכבנה על-הגמלים ותלכנה
went they and camels the upon rode they and ,maidens her and

אחרי האיש ויקח העבד את-רבקה וילך:
.went and Rebekah slave the took and ; man the after

62 ויצחק בא מבוא[j] באר לחי[k] ראי
,Roi Lahai Beer [towards] going from come had Isaac And

63 והוא יושב בארץ הנגב: ויצא
out gone had and — south the of land the in dwelling [was] he [for] (and)

said, Send me a-
way unto my
master. 55 And
her brother and
her mother said,
Let the damsel
abide with us *a*
few days, at the
least ten; after
that she shall
go. 56 And he
said unto them,
Hinder me not,
seeing the LORD
hath prospered
my way; send
me away that I
may go to my
master. 57 And
they said, We
will call the
damsel, and in-
quire at her
mouth. 58 And
they called Re-
bekah, and said
unto her, Wilt
thou go with
this man? And
she said, I will
go. 59 And they
sent away Re-
bekah their sis-
ter, and her
nurse, and A-
braham's serv-
ant, and his
men. 60 And
they blessed Re-
bekah and said
unto her, Our
sister, be thou
the mother of
thousands of ten
thousands, and
let thy seed pos-
sess the gate of
those which hate
them.

61 And Re-
bekah arose,
and her damsels,
and they rode
upon the cam-
els, and follow-
ed the man: and
the servant took
Rebekah, and
went his way.
62 And Isaac
came from the
way of Beer-la-
hai-roi; for he
dwelt in the land
of the South. 63
And Isaac went

a S. adds, *to them.*

b G., S., V. add, *that I may depart.*

c. S. adds, *to him.*

d G., S., V. pl. *her brothers,* אֶחֶיהָ.

e Sm. *days or a month,* ימים או חדש; G. *days about ten;* S. *a month of days;* T. *a little time or ten months;* V. *at least ten days.*

f G., Sm., V. have, *and afterwards,* ואחר; S. *and then.*

g G., S. add, *their sister;* so V. omitting רבקה.

h S., T. have, *for thousands and myriads.*

i G., T. *cities;* S. *lands;* V. *gates.*

j Sm. has, *in the wilderness,* במדבר; so G.

k G. omits.

to meditate in the field at the eventide: and he lifted up his eyes, and saw, and, behold, the camels *were* coming. 64 And Rebekah lifted up her eyes, and when she saw Isaac, she lighted off the camel. 65 For she *had* said unto the servant, What man *is* this that walketh in the field to meet us? And the servant *had* said, It *is* my master: therefore she took a vail, and covered herself. 66 And the servant told Isaac all things that he had done. 67 And Isaac brought her into his mother Sarah's tent, and took Rebekah, and she became his wife; and he loved her: and Isaac was comforted after his mother's *death*.

יִצְחָק לָשׂוּחַ בַּשָּׂדֶה לִפְנוֹת עָרֶב
—evening of approach the at field the in meditate to Isaac

וַיִּשָּׂא עֵינָיו וַיַּרְא וְהִנֵּה[a] גְמַלִּים בָּאִים׃
.coming camels behold and ,saw and eyes his raised he and

64 וַתִּשָּׂא רִבְקָה אֶת־עֵינֶיהָ וַתֵּרֶא אֶת־יִצְחָק
; Isaac saw she and ,eyes her Rebekah raised And

65 וַתִּפֹּל מֵעַל הַגָּמָל׃ וַתֹּאמֶר אֶל־
unto said she And .camel the upon from down sprung she and

הָעֶבֶד מִי־הָאִישׁ הַלָּזֶה הַהֹלֵךְ בַּשָּׂדֶה
field the in going one the ,[1]yonder [2]man [is] Who : slave the

לִקְרָאתֵנוּ וַיֹּאמֶר הָעֶבֶד הוּא אֲדֹנִי
.master my [is] He : slave the said And ? us meet to

66 וַתִּקַּח הַצָּעִיף וַתִּתְכָּס׃ וַיְסַפֵּר
related And .herself covered and mantle the took she And

הָעֶבֶד לְיִצְחָק אֵת כָּל־הַדְּבָרִים אֲשֶׁר עָשָׂה׃
.done had he which things the all Isaac to slave the

67 וַיְבִאֶהָ[b] יִצְחָק הָאֹהֱלָה שָׂרָה[c] אִמּוֹ
,mother his Sarah to ,tent the to Isaac in her brought And

וַיִּקַּח אֶת־רִבְקָה וַתְּהִי־לוֹ לְאִשָּׁה
,wife a (for) him to became she and ,Rebekah took he and

וַיֶּאֱהָבֶהָ וַיִּנָּחֵם יִצְחָק אַחֲרֵי[d] אִמּוֹ׃
.mother his after Isaac comforted was and ; her loved he and

out to meditate in the field at the eventide: and he lifted up his eyes, and saw, and, behold, there were camels coming. 64 And Rebekah lifted up her eyes, and when she saw Isaac, she lighted off the camel. 65 And she said unto the servant, What man is this that walketh in the field to meet us? And the servant said, It is my master: and she took her veil, and covered herself. 66 And the servant told Isaac all the things that he had done. 67 And Isaac brought her into his mother Sarah's tent, and took Rebekah, and she became his wife; and he loved her: and Isaac was comforted after his mother's death.

25

THEN again Abraham took a wife, and her name *was* Keturah. 2 And she bare him Zimran, and Jokshan, and Medan, and Midian, and Ishbak, and Shuah. 3 And Jokshan begat Sheba, and Dedan. And the sons of De-

1 וַיֹּסֶף אַבְרָהָם וַיִּקַּח אִשָּׁה וּשְׁמָהּ
[being] name her (and) ,wife a took and Abraham continued And

2 קְטוּרָה׃ וַתֵּלֶד לוֹ אֶת־זִמְרָן וְאֶת־יָקְשָׁן
Jokshan and Zimran him to bore she And .Keturah

וְאֶת־מְדָן וְאֶת־מִדְיָן וְאֶת־יִשְׁבָּק וְאֶת־שׁוּחַ׃
.Shuah and Jishbak and Midian and Medan and

3 וְיָקְשָׁן יָלַד אֶת־שְׁבָא[e] וְאֶת־דְּדָן וּבְנֵי
of sons the And .Dedan and Sheba begat Jokshan And

And Abraham took another wife, and her name was Keturah. 2 And she bare him Zimran, and Jokshan, and Medan, and Midian, and Ishbak, and Shuah. 3 And Jokshan begat Sheba, and Dedan. And the sons of De-

---

a G. omits.
b G. *and came in*, וַיָּבֹא.
c G. omits.
d G. adds, *Sarah*.
e G. adds, *and Taiman*.

dan were As-
shurim, and
Letushim, and
Leummim. 4
And the sons of
Midian; Ephah,
and Epher, and
Hanoch, and
Abidah, and
Eldaah. All
these *were* the
children of Ke-
turah.

5 And Abra-
ham gave all
that he had un-
to Isaac. 6 But
unto the sons of
the concubines,
which Abraham
had, Abraham
gave gifts, and
sent them away
from Isaac his
son, while he
yet lived, east-
ward, unto the
east country. 7
And these *are*
the days of the
years of Abra-
ham's life which
he lived, an hun-
dred threescore
and fifteen
years. 8 Then A-
braham gave up
the ghost, and
died in a good
old age, an old
man, and full
of years; and
was gathered to
his people. 9
And his sons
Isaac and
Ishmael buried
him in the cave
of Machpelah,
in the field of
Ephron the son
of Zohar the
Hittite, which *is*
before Mamre;
10 The field
which Abraham
purchased of the
sons of Heth:
there was Abra-
ham buried, and
Sarah his wife.

11 And it
came to pass af-
ter the death of

דְּדָ֑ן הָי֛וּ[a] אַשּׁוּרִ֥ם וּלְטוּשִׁ֖ם וּלְאֻמִּֽים׃
.Leummites and Letushites and Asshurites were Dedan

4 וּבְנֵ֣י מִדְיָ֗ן עֵיפָ֤ה וָעֵ֙פֶר֙ וַחֲנֹ֔ךְ
Hanoch and Epher and Ephah ,Midian of sons the And

וַאֲבִידָ֖ע וְאֶלְדָּעָ֑ה כָּל־אֵ֖לֶּה בְּנֵ֥י קְטוּרָֽה׃
.Keturah of sons the these all ; Eldaah and Abida and

5 וַיִּתֵּ֧ן אַבְרָהָ֛ם אֶת־כָּל־אֲשֶׁר־ל֖וֹ לְיִצְחָֽק׃[b]
.Isaac to him to [was] which all Abraham gave And

6 וְלִבְנֵ֤י הַפִּֽילַגְשִׁים֙ אֲשֶׁ֣ר[c] לְאַבְרָהָ֔ם[c]
,Abraham to [were] which ,concubines the of sons the to And

נָתַ֥ן אַבְרָהָ֖ם מַתָּנֹ֑ת וַֽיְשַׁלְּחֵ֞ם מֵעַ֨ל
(upon) from away them sent he and ; gifts Abraham gave

יִצְחָ֤ק בְּנוֹ֙ בְּעוֹדֶ֣נּוּ חַ֔י קֵ֖דְמָה אֶל־אֶ֥רֶץ
of land a unto eastward ,alive [being] still his in ,son his Isaac

7 קֶֽדֶם׃ וְאֵ֗לֶּה יְמֵ֛י שְׁנֵֽי־חַיֵּ֥י אַבְרָהָ֖ם
,Abraham of life the of years the of days the [were] these And .east the

אֲשֶׁר־חָ֑י מְאַ֥ת שָׁנָ֛ה וְשִׁבְעִ֥ים שָׁנָ֖ה וְחָמֵ֥שׁ
five and years seventy and years hundred a ,lived he which

8 שָׁנִֽים׃ וַיִּגְוַ֨ע וַיָּ֧מָת אַבְרָהָ֛ם בְּשֵׂיבָ֥ה טוֹבָ֖ה זָקֵ֣ן
old ,[1]good [2]age a in Abraham died and expired And .years

9 וְשָׂבֵ֑עַ[d] וַיֵּאָ֖סֶף אֶל־עַמָּֽיו׃ וַֽיִּקְבְּר֨וּ
buried And .people his unto gathered was he and ; satisfied and

אֹת֜וֹ יִצְחָ֤ק וְיִשְׁמָעֵאל֙ בָּנָ֔יו[e] אֶל־מְעָרַ֖ת הַמַּכְפֵּלָ֑ה
,Makpelah of cave the at ,sons his Ishmael and Isaac him

אֶל־שְׂדֵ֞ה עֶפְרֹ֣ן בֶּן־צֹ֗חַר הַֽחִתִּ֔י אֲשֶׁ֖ר
[is] which ,Hittite the Zohar of son the Ephron of field the at

10 עַל־פְּנֵ֥י מַמְרֵֽא׃ הַשָּׂדֶ֛ה[f] אֲשֶׁר־קָנָ֥ה אַבְרָהָ֖ם
Abraham purchased had which field the ; Mamre before

מֵאֵ֣ת בְּנֵי־חֵ֑ת[g] שָׁ֛מָּה קֻבַּ֥ר אַבְרָהָ֖ם
,Abraham buried was there ; Heth of sons the (with) from

11 וְשָׂרָ֥ה אִשְׁתּֽוֹ׃ וַיְהִ֗י אַחֲרֵי֙ מ֣וֹת
of death the after pass to came it And .wife his Sarah and

dan were As-
shurim, and Le-
tushim, and Le-
ummim. 4 And
the sons of Mid-
ian; Ephah,
and Epher, and
Hanoch, and
Abida, and El-
daah. All these
were the chil-
dren of Keturah.

5 And Abra-
ham gave all
that he had un-
to Isaac. 6 But
unto the sons of
the concubines,
which Abraham
had, Abraham
gave gifts; and
he sent them a-
way from Isaac
his son, while
he yet lived,
eastward, unto
the east country.
7 And these are
the days of the
years of Abra-
ham's life which
he lived, an hun-
dred threescore
and fifteen
years. 8 And A-
braham gave up
the ghost, and
died in a good
old age, an old
man, and full *of*
years; and was
gathered to his
people. 9 And
Isaac and Ish-
mael his sons
buried him in
the cave of
Machpelah, in
the field of E-
phron the son of
Zohar the Hit-
tite, which is be-
fore Mamre; 10
the field which
Abraham pur-
chased of the
children of
Heth: there
was Abraham
buried, and Sa-
rah his wife.

11 And it came
to pass after
the death of A-

---

a G. adds, *Raguel and Nabdeel and.*
b G., S. add, *his son.*
c For אשר לאברהם G. has, *his;* S. *of Abraham;* V. omits.
d Sm. adds, *days,* ימים; so G., S., V.
e G. *his two sons.*
f G. adds, *and the cave.*
g S. adds, *for a burial possession.*

Abraham, that
God blessed his
son Isaac; and
Isaac dwelt by
the well Lahai-
roi.

12 Now these
are the genera-
tions of Ish-
mael, Abra-
ham's son,
whom Hagar
the Egyp-
tian, Sarah's
handmaid, bare
unto Abraham:
13 And these
are the names
of the sons of
Ishmael, by
their names, ac-
cording to their
generations: the
firstborn of Ish-
mael, Nebajoth;
and Kedar, and
Adbeel, and
Mibsam, 14 And
Mishma, and
Dumah, and
Massa, 15 Ha-
dar, and Tema,
Jetur, Naphish,
and Kedemah:
16 These *are* the
sons of Ishmael,
and these *are*
their names,
by their towns,
and by their
castles; twelve
princes accord-
ing to their na-
tions. 17 And
these *are* the
years of the life
of Ishmael, an
hundred and
thirty and seven
years: and he
gave up the
ghost and died;
and was gather-
ed unto his peo-
ple. 18 And they
dwelt from Ha-
vilah unto Shur,
that *is* before
Egypt, as thou
goest toward
Assyria: *and* he
died in the pres-
ence of all his
brethren.

19 And these
are the genera-
tions of Isaac,
Abraham's son:

אַבְרָהָם וַיְבָרֶךְ אֱלֹהִים אֶת־יִצְחָק בְּנוֹ וַיֵּשֶׁב
dwelt and ,son his Isaac God blessed that Abraham

יִצְחָק עִם־בְּאֵר [a]לַחַי רֹאִי׃
.Roi Lahai Beer at Isaac

12 וְאֵלֶּה תֹּלְדֹת יִשְׁמָעֵאל בֶּן־אַבְרָהָם
,Abraham of son the ,Ishmael of generations the [are] these And

אֲשֶׁר יָלְדָה הָגָר הַמִּצְרִית[b] שִׁפְחַת שָׂרָה
Sarah of maidservant the Egyptian the Hagar bore whom

13 לְאַבְרָהָם׃ וְאֵלֶּה שְׁמוֹת בְּנֵי יִשְׁמָעֵאל
,Ishmael of sons the of names the [were] these And .Abraham to

בִּשְׁמֹתָם לְתוֹלְדֹתָם בְּכֹר יִשְׁמָעֵאל
,Ishmael of first-born the :generations their to ,names their by

14 נְבָיֹת וְקֵדָר וְאַדְבְּאֵל וּמִבְשָׂם׃ וּמִשְׁמָע
,Mishma and ,Mibsam and ,Adbeel and ,Kedar and ;Nebayoth

15 וְדוּמָה וּמַשָּׂא׃ [c]חֲדַד וְתֵימָא [d]יְטוּר [d]נָפִישׁ
,Naphish ,Jetur ,Tema and ,Hadad ,Massa and ,Dumah and

16 וָקֵדְמָה׃ אֵלֶּה הֵם בְּנֵי יִשְׁמָעֵאל וְאֵלֶּה
these and ,Ishmael of sons the were these ;Kedemah and

שְׁמֹתָם בְּחַצְרֵיהֶם וּבְטִירֹתָם
;encampments their in and settlements their in names their [were]

17 שְׁנֵים־עָשָׂר נְשִׂיאִם לְאֻמֹּתָם׃ וְאֵלֶּה
[were] these And .tribes their to according princes twelve

שְׁנֵי חַיֵּי יִשְׁמָעֵאל מְאַת שָׁנָה וּשְׁלֹשִׁים
thirty and years hundred a ,Ishmael of life the of years the

שָׁנָה וְשֶׁבַע שָׁנִים וַיִּגְוַע וַיָּמָת וַיֵּאָסֶף
gathered was and ,died and expired he and ;years seven and years

18 אֶל־עַמָּיו׃ וַיִּשְׁכְּנוּ[e] מֵחֲוִילָה עַד־שׁוּר אֲשֶׁר
is which ,Shur as far as Havilah from dwelt they And .people his unto

עַל־פְּנֵי מִצְרַיִם בֹּאֲכָה אַשּׁוּרָה עַל־פְּנֵי
before ;Assyria toward coming art thou [as] ,Egypt before

כָל־אֶחָיו נָפָל׃
.settled he brethren his all

19 וְאֵלֶּה תּוֹלְדֹת יִצְחָק בֶּן־אַבְרָהָם
;Abraham of son the Isaac of generations the [are] these And

braham, that
God blessed
Isaac his son;
and Isaac dwelt
by Beer-lahai-
roi.

12 Now these
are the genera-
tions of Ish-
mael, Abra-
ham's son,
whom Hagar
the Egyptian,
Sarah's hand-
maid, bare unto
Abraham: 13
and these are the
names of the
sons of Ishmael,
by their names,
according to
their genera-
tions: the first-
born of Ishmael,
Nebaioth; and
Kedar, and Ad-
beel, and Mib-
sam, 14 and
Mishma, and
Dumah, and
Massa; 15 Ha-
dad, and Tema,
Jetur, Naphish,
and Kedemah:
16 these are the
sons of Ishmael,
and these are
their names, by
their villages,
and by their en-
campments;
twelve princes
according to
their nations. 17
And these are
the years of the
life of Ishmael,
an hundred and
thirty and seven
years: and he
gave up the
ghost and died;
and was gather-
ed unto his peo-
ple. 18 And they
dwelt from Ha-
vilah unto Shur
that is before
Egypt, as thou
goest toward
Assyria: he a-
bode in the
presence of all
his brethren.

19 And these
are the genera-
tions of Isaac,
Abraham's son:

---

a G. omits.
b G. omits.
c G., S. add ו.
d G., S., V. add ו.
e G., V. sing. *and he dwelt*, וישכן.

Abraham begat
Isaac: 20 And
Isaac was forty
years old when
he took Rebek-
ah to wife,
the daugh-
ter of Bethuel
the Syrian of
Padan-aram,
the sister to La-
ban the Syrian.
21 And Isaac
intreated the
LORD for his
wife, because
she *was* barren;
and the LORD
was intreated of
him, and Rebek-
ah his wife con-
ceived. 22 And
the children
struggled to-
gether within
her; and she
said, If *it be* so,
why *am* I thus?
And she went
to enquire of the
LORD. 23 And
the LORD said
unto her, Two
nations *are* in
thy womb, and
two manner of
people shall be
separated from
thy bowels; and
the one people
shall be stronger
than *the other*
people; and the
elder shall serve
the younger.

24 And when
her days to be
delivered
were fulfilled,
behold, *there*
were twins in
her womb. 25
And the first
came out red,
all over like an
hairy garment;
and they called
his name Esau.
26 And after
that came his
brother out, and
his hand took
hold on Esau's
heel; and his
name was called
Jacob: and
Isaac *was* three-
score years old
when she bare
them. 27 And

20 אַבְרָהָם הוֹלִיד אֶת־יִצְחָק׃ וַיְהִי יִצְחָק בֶּן־אַרְבָּעִים
forty (of son a) Isaac was And .Isaac begat Abraham
שָׁנָה בְּקַחְתּוֹ אֶת־רִבְקָה בַּת־בְּתוּאֵל
Bethuel of daughter the Rebekah taking his in ,[old] years
הָאֲרַמִּי מִפַּדַּן אֲרָם אֲחוֹת לָבָן הָאֲרַמִּי
Aramean the Laban of sister the ,Aram Paddan from ,Aramean the
21 לוֹ לְאִשָּׁה׃ וַיֶּעְתַּר יִצְחָק לַיהוָה לְנֹכַח
of behalf on Jehovah (to) Isaac entreated And .wife a for him to
אִשְׁתּוֹ כִּי עֲקָרָה הִוא וַיֵּעָתֶר לוֹ
him by entreated was and ; she [was] barren for ,wife his
22 יְהוָה וַתַּהַר רִבְקָה אִשְׁתּוֹ׃ וַיִּתְרֹצֲצוּ
other each thrust And .wife his Rebekah conceived and ,Jehovah
הַבָּנִים בְּקִרְבָּהּ וַתֹּאמֶר אִם־כֵּן [a] לָמָּה זֶּה
then what for ,so If : said she and ,midst her in sons the
23 אָנֹכִי [b] וַתֵּלֶךְ לִדְרֹשׁ אֶת־יְהוָה׃ וַיֹּאמֶר
said And .Jehovah seek to went she And ?I [am]
יְהוָה לָהּ שְׁנֵי גֹיִים בְּבִטְנֵךְ וּשְׁנֵי
two and ,womb thy in nations Two : her to Jehovah
לְאֻמִּים מִמֵּעַיִךְ יִפָּרֵדוּ וּלְאֹם
people a and ; separated be shall bowels thy from peoples
מִלְאֹם יֶאֱמָץ וְרַב יַעֲבֹד
serve shall elder the and ,[3]stronger [2]be [1]shall [6]people [5]a [4]than
24 צָעִיר׃ וַיִּמְלְאוּ יָמֶיהָ לָלֶדֶת וְהִנֵּה
behold and ,forth bring to days her full were And .younger the
25 תוֹמִם בְּבִטְנָהּ׃ וַיֵּצֵא הָרִאשׁוֹן אַדְמוֹנִי
,reddish-brown first the out went And .womb her in twins
כֻּלּוֹ כְּאַדֶּרֶת שֵׂעָר וַיִּקְרְאוּ שְׁמוֹ עֵשָׂו׃
.Esau name his called they and ; hair of mantle a like him of all
26 וְאַחֲרֵי־כֵן יָצָא אָחִיו וְיָדוֹ אֹחֶזֶת
holding hand his [with] (and) ,brother his out went afterward And
בַּעֲקֵב עֵשָׂו וַיִּקְרָא שְׁמוֹ יַעֲקֹב וְיִצְחָק
Isaac (and) ; Jacob name his called [one] and ,Esau of heel the to
בֶּן־שִׁשִּׁים שָׁנָה בְּלֶדֶת אֹתָם׃ [c]
.them bearing [her] at [old] years sixty (of son a) [being]

Abraham begat
Isaac: 20 and
Isaac was forty
years old when
he took Rebek-
ah, the daugh-
ter of Bethuel
the Syrian of
Paddan-aram,
the sister of La-
ban the Syrian,
to be his wife.
21 And Isaac in-
treated the
LORD for his
wife, because
she was barren;
and the LORD
was intreated of
him, and Rebek-
ah his wife con-
ceived. 22 And
the children
struggled to-
gether within
her; and she
said, If it be so,
wherefore do I
live? And she
went to inquire
of the LORD. 23
And the LORD
said unto her,
Two nations are
in thy womb,
And two peo-
ples shall be
separated even
from thy bowels:
And the one
people shall be
stronger than
the other peo-
ple; And the
elder shall serve
the younger.

24 And when
her days to be
delivered were
fulfilled, behold,
there were twins
in her womb. 25
And the first
came forth red,
all over like an
hairy garment;
and they call-
ed his name E-
sau. 26 And af-
ter that came
forth his broth-
er, and his hand
had hold on E-
sau's heel; and
his name was
called Jacob;
and Isaac was
threescore years
old when she
bare them. 27

a G., V. have, *if so it is about to be to me.*
b S. adds, *living.*
c G. adds, *Rebekah.*

the boys grew:
and Esau was a
cunning hunter,
a man of the
field; and Jacob
was a plain man,
dwelling in
tents. 28 And
Isaac loved E-
sau, because he
did eat of *his*
venison: but
Rebekah loved
Jacob.

29 And Jacob
sod pottage: and
Esau came from
the field, and he
was faint: 30
And Esau said
to Jacob, Feed
me, I pray thee,
with that same
red *pottage*; for
I *am* faint:
therefore was
his name called
Edom. 31 And
Jacob said, Sell
me this day thy
birthright. 32
And Esau said,
Behold, I *am* at
the point to die:
and what profit
shall this birth-
right do to me?
33 And Jacob
said, Swear to
me this day; and
he sware unto
him; and he sold
his birthright
unto Jacob. 34
Then Jacob
gave Esau bread
and pottage of
lentiles; and
he did eat and
drink, and rose
up, and went
his way. Thus
Esau despised
his birthright.

27 וַיִּגְדְּלוּ הַנְּעָרִים וַיְהִי עֵשָׂו אִישׁ יֹדֵעַ
with acquainted man a Esau became and ;boys the up grew And

צַיִד אִישׁ שָׂדֶה וְיַעֲקֹב אִישׁ תָּם
[1],amiable [2]man an ,Jacob and ; field the of man a ,hunting

28 יֹשֵׁב[a] אֹהָלִים׃ וַיֶּאֱהַב יִצְחָק אֶת־עֵשָׂו כִּי־
because ,Esau Isaac loved And .tents in dwelling

צַיִד[b] בְּפִיו וְרִבְקָה אֹהֶבֶת אֶת־יַעֲקֹב׃
.Jacob loving [was] Rebekah and ; mouth his in [was] venison

29 וַיָּזֶד יַעֲקֹב נָזִיד וַיָּבֹא עֵשָׂו מִן־הַשָּׂדֶה
,field the from Esau in came and ,pottage Jacob boiled And

30 וְהוּא עָיֵף׃ וַיֹּאמֶר עֵשָׂו אֶל־יַעֲקֹב הַלְעִיטֵנִי
,devour me Let : Jacob unto Esau said And .faint [being] he (and)

נָא מִן־הָאָדֹם[c] הָאָדֹם הַזֶּה כִּי עָיֵף אָנֹכִי
; I [am] faint for ,[1]this [2]red ,[stuff] red the of ,pray I

31 עַל־כֵּן קָרָא־שְׁמוֹ אֱדוֹם׃ וַיֹּאמֶר יַעֲקֹב[d]
: Jacob said And .Edom name his called [one] therefore

32 מִכְרָה כַיּוֹם אֶת־בְּכֹרָתְךָ לִי׃ וַיֹּאמֶר עֵשָׂו[e]
: Esau said And .me to birth-right thy today Sell

הִנֵּה אָנֹכִי הוֹלֵךְ לָמוּת וְלָמָּה־זֶּה לִי
me to ,then ,what for and ; die to going [am] I Behold

33 בְּכֹרָה[f]׃ וַיֹּאמֶר[g] יַעֲקֹב הִשָּׁבְעָה לִּי כַּיּוֹם
; today me to Swear : Jacob said And ? birth-right a

וַיִּשָּׁבַע לוֹ וַיִּמְכֹּר[h] אֶת־בְּכֹרָתוֹ לְיַעֲקֹב׃
.Jacob to birth-right his sold and ,him to swore he and

34 וְיַעֲקֹב נָתַן לְעֵשָׂו לֶחֶם וּנְזִיד עֲדָשִׁים
; lentils of pottage and bread Esau to gave Jacob And

וַיֹּאכַל וַיֵּשְׁתְּ וַיָּקָם וַיֵּלַךְ וַיִּבֶז
lightly valued and ; departed and up rose and ,drank and ,ate he And

עֵשָׂו אֶת־הַבְּכֹרָה׃
.birth-right the Esau

And the boys
grew: and Esau
was a cunning
hunter, a man of
the field; and
Jacob was a
plain man,
dwelling in
tents. 28 Now
Isaac loved E-
sau, because he
did eat of his
venison: and
Rebekah loved
Jacob.

29 And Jacob
sod pottage;
and Esau came
in from the field,
and he was
faint: 30 and
Esau said to Ja-
cob, Feed me, I
pray thee, with
that same red
pottage; for I
am faint: there-
fore was his
name called E-
dom. 31 And
Jacob said, Sell
me this day thy
birthright. 32
And Esau said,
Behold, I am at
the point to die:
and what profit
shall the birth-
right do to me?
33 And Jacob
said, Swear to
me this day;
and he sware
unto him: and
he sold his birth-
right unto Ja-
cob. 34 And
Jacob gave
Esau bread and
pottage of len-
tils; and he did
eat and drink,
and rose up, and
went his way: so
Esau despised
his birthright.

26

AND there was
a famine in the
land, besides the

1 וַיְהִי רָעָב בָּאָרֶץ מִלְּבַד הָרָעָב
[2]famine the besides ,land the in famine a was [there] And

And there was
a famine in the
land, beside the

a S. *and dwelling*, וישב.
b Sm., G., S., T., V. have, *his venison*, צידו.
c G., V. have, *pottage*, נזיד.
d G. adds, *to Esau;* S. *to him;* V. *to whom.*
e S, *in his heart*, בלבו.
f G. *these birth-rights.*
g G., S. add, *to him.*
h G. adds, *Esau.*

first famine that
was in the days
of Abraham.
And Isaac went
unto Abimelech
king of the Phi-
listines unto
Gerar. 2 And
the LORD ap-
peared unto
him, and said,
Go not down
into Egypt;
dwell in the land
which I shall
tell thee of. 3
Sojourn in this
land, and I will
be with thee,
and will bless
thee; for unto
thee, and unto
thy seed, I will
give all these
countries, and
I will perform
the oath which
I sware unto A-
braham thy
father; 4 And I
will make thy
seed to multiply
as the stars of
heaven, and will
give unto thy
seed all these
countries; and
in thy seed shall
all the nations
of the earth be
blessed; 5 Be-
cause that A-
braham obeyed
my voice, and
kept my charge,
my command-
ments, my sta-
tutes, and my
laws.

6 And Isaac
dwelt in Gerar:
7 And the men
of the place ask-
ed *him* of his
wife; and he
said, She *is* my
sister: for he
feared to say,
She is my wife;
lest, *said he*, the
men of the place
should kill me
for Rebekah;
because she *was*
fair to look up-
on. 8 And it
came to pass,
when he had
been there a
long time, that

הָרִאשׁוֹן אֲשֶׁר הָיָה בִּימֵי אַבְרָהָם וַיֵּלֶךְ
went and ;Abraham of days the in was which [1]former

יִצְחָק אֶל־אֲבִימֶלֶךְ מֶלֶךְ־פְּלִשְׁתִּים גְּרָרָה׃
.Gerar to ,Philistines the of king Abimelech unto Isaac

2 וַיֵּרָא אֵלָיו יְהוָה וַיֹּאמֶר אַל־תֵּרֵד
down go not Do :said and Jehovah him unto appeared And

מִצְרָיְמָה שְׁכֹן[a] בָּאָרֶץ אֲשֶׁר אֹמַר אֵלֶיךָ׃
.thee unto say shall I which land the in remain ,Egypt to

3 גּוּר[b] בָּאָרֶץ הַזֹּאת וְאֶהְיֶה עִמְּךָ וַאֲבָרְכֶךָּ
;thee bless and thee with be will I and ,[1]this [2]land in Sojourn

כִּי־לְךָ וּלְזַרְעֲךָ אֶתֵּן אֶת־כָּל־הָאֲרָצֹת[c]
[2]lands all give will I seed thy to and thee to for

הָאֵל[c] וַהֲקִמֹתִי אֶת־הַשְּׁבֻעָה אֲשֶׁר נִשְׁבַּעְתִּי
swore I which oath my establish will I and ;[1]these

4 לְאַבְרָהָם אָבִיךָ׃ וְהִרְבֵּיתִי אֶת־זַרְעֲךָ
seed thy increase will I And .father thy Abraham to

כְּכוֹכְבֵי הַשָּׁמַיִם וְנָתַתִּי לְזַרְעֲךָ אֵת כָּל־
all seed thy to give will I and ,heavens the of stars the like

הָאֲרָצֹת הָאֵל וְהִתְבָּרְכוּ בְזַרְעֲךָ כֹּל
all seed thy in themselves bless shall and ;[1]these [2]lands

5 גּוֹיֵי הָאָרֶץ׃ עֵקֶב אֲשֶׁר־שָׁמַע אַבְרָהָם[d]
Abraham hearkened (that) because ;earth the of nations the

בְּקֹלִי וַיִּשְׁמֹר מִשְׁמַרְתִּי מִצְוֹתַי[e] חֻקּוֹתַי[e]
,statutes my ,commandments my ,charge my observed and voice my to

6 7 וְתוֹרֹתָי׃ וַיֵּשֶׁב יִצְחָק בִּגְרָר׃ וַיִּשְׁאֲלוּ אַנְשֵׁי
of men the asked and ;Gerar in Isaac dwelt And .laws my and

הַמָּקוֹם לְאִשְׁתּוֹ[f] וַיֹּאמֶר אֲחֹתִי הִוא כִּי
because ;she [is] sister My :said he and ,wife his about place the

יָרֵא לֵאמֹר אִשְׁתִּי פֶּן־יַהַרְגֻנִי[g] אַנְשֵׁי הַמָּקוֹם
place the of men the me kill lest ;wife My :say to feared he

עַל־רִבְקָה כִּי־טוֹבַת מַרְאֶה הִוא׃
.she [is] appearance of fair for ,Rebekah of account on

8 וַיְהִי כִּי־אָרְכוּ־לוֹ שָׁם הַיָּמִים
;days the there him to long become had when pass to came it And

first famine that
was in the days
of Abraham.
And Isaac went
unto Abimelech
king of the Phi-
listines unto
Gerar. 2 And
the LORD ap-
peared unto
him, and said,
Go not down in-
to Egypt; dwell
in the land
which I shall
tell thee of: 3
sojourn in this
land, and I will
be with thee,
and will bless
thee; for unto
thee, and unto
thy seed, I will
give all these
lands, and I
will establish
the oath which I
sware unto A-
braham thy fa-
ther; 4 and I
will multiply
thy seed as the
stars of heaven,
and will give
unto thy seed all
these lands; and
in thy seed shall
all the nations
of the earth be
blessed; 5 be-
cause that Abra-
ham obeyed my
voice, and kept
my charge, my
commandments,
my statutes, and
my laws.

6 And Isaac
dwelt in Gerar:
7 and the men of
the place asked
him of his wife;
and he said, She
is my sister: for
he feared to say,
My wife; lest,
said he, the
men of the place
should kill me
for Rebekah: be-
cause she was
fair to look up-
on. 8 And it
came to pass,
when he had
been there a
long time, that

a G. *and dwell*, וישכן.
b G., V. have, *and sojourn*, וגור.
c G. sing. *this land;* so in vs. 4.
d Sm., G. add, *thy father*.
e G., S., V. add, *and* ו.
f G. has, *about Rebekah his wife*.
g G., S., V. have suffix, ***him***.

Abimelech, king
of the Philis-
tines looked out
at a window,
and saw, and,
behold, Isaac
was sporting
with Rebekah
his wife. 9 And
Abimelech call-
ed Isaac,
and said, Be-
hold, of a sure-
ty she *is* thy
wife: and how
saidst thou, She
is my sister?
And Isaac said
unto him, Be-
cause I said,
Lest I die for
her. 10 And A-
bimelech said,
What *is* this
thou hast done
unto us? one of
the people
might lightly
have lien with
thy wife, and
thou shouldest
have brought
guiltiness upon
us. 11 And A-
bimelech charg-
ed all *his* peo-
ple, saying, He
that toucheth
this man or his
wife shall surely
be put to death.
12 Then Isaac
sowed in that
land, and re-
ceived in the
same year an
hundred fold:
and the LORD
blessed him. 13
And the man
waxed great,
and went for-
ward, and grew
until he became
very great: 14
For he had pos-
session of flocks,
and possession
of herds, and
great store of
servants: and
the Philistines
envied him. 15
For all the wells
which his fath-
er's servants had
digged in the
days of Abra-
ham his father,
the Philistines
had stopped

וַיַּשְׁקֵף אֲבִימֶלֶךְ מֶלֶךְ פְּלִשְׁתִּים[a] בְּעַד הַחַלּוֹן
,window the through Philistines the of king Abimelek looked that

וַיַּרְא וְהִנֵּה[b] יִצְחָק מְצַחֵק אֵת רִבְקָה אִשְׁתּוֹ׃
.wife his Rebekah caressing Isaac behold and ,saw and

9 וַיִּקְרָא אֲבִימֶלֶךְ לְיִצְחָק וַיֹּאמֶר[c] אַךְ הִנֵּה
behold Certainly :said and Isaac [to] Abimelek called And

אִשְׁתְּךָ הִוא וְאֵיךְ אָמַרְתָּ אֲחֹתִי הִוא
?she [is] sister My :said thou hast how and ,she [is] wife thy

וַיֹּאמֶר אֵלָיו יִצְחָק כִּי אָמַרְתִּי פֶּן־אָמוּת
die I Lest :said I Because :Isaac him unto said And

10 עָלֶיהָ׃ וַיֹּאמֶר[d] אֲבִימֶלֶךְ מַה־זֹּאת עָשִׂיתָ
done hast thou this is What :Abimelek said And .her of account on

לָּנוּ כִּמְעַט שָׁכַב אַחַד הָעָם[e] אֶת־אִשְׁתֶּךָ
,wife thy with people the of one lain had Almost ?us to

11 וְהֵבֵאתָ עָלֵינוּ אָשָׁם׃ וַיְצַו
commanded And .guilt us upon brought have wouldst thou and

אֲבִימֶלֶךְ אֶת־כָּל־הָעָם[f] לֵאמֹר הַנֹּגֵעַ בָּאִישׁ
[2]man [on] touching one The :saying people the all Abimelek

12 הַזֶּה וּבְאִשְׁתּוֹ מוֹת יוּמָת׃ וַיִּזְרַע יִצְחָק
Isaac sowed And .killed be shall dying ,wife his (on) and [1]this

בָּאָרֶץ הַהִוא וַיִּמְצָא בַּשָּׁנָה הַהִוא[g] מֵאָה שְׁעָרִים[h]
; measures hundred a [1]that [2]year in found and ,[1]that [2]land in

13 וַיְבָרְכֵהוּ יְהוָה׃ וַיִּגְדַּל הָאִישׁ וַיֵּלֶךְ
,went he and ;man the great became And .Jehovah him blessed and

הָלוֹךְ וְגָדֵל עַד כִּי־גָדַל מְאֹד׃
.exceedingly great became he (that) until ,great becoming and going

14 וַיְהִי־לוֹ מִקְנֵה־צֹאן וּמִקְנֵה
of possessions and flocks of possessions him to were [there] And

בָקָר וַעֲבֻדָּה רַבָּה וַיְקַנְאוּ אֹתוֹ
him envied and ;[1]many [3]slaves [2]household and ,herds

15 פְּלִשְׁתִּים׃ וְכָל־הַבְּאֵרֹת אֲשֶׁר חָפְרוּ עַבְדֵי
of slaves the dug had which wells the all And .Philistines the

אָבִיו בִּימֵי אַבְרָהָם[i] אָבִיו סִתְּמוּם
them obstructed ,father his Abraham of days the in ,father his

Abimelech king
of the Philis-
tines looked out
at a window, and
saw, and, be-
hold, Isaac was
sporting with
Rebekah his
wife. 9 And A-
bimelech called
Isaac, and said,
Behold, of a
surety she is
thy wife: and
how saidst thou,
She is my sister?
And Isaac said
unto him, Be-
cause I said,
Lest I die for
her. 10 And A-
bimelech said,
What is this
thou hast done
unto us? one of
the people
might lightly
have lien with
thy wife, and
thou shouldest
have brought
guiltiness upon
us. 11 And A-
bimelech charg-
ed all the peo-
ple, saying, He
that toucheth
this man or his
wife shall surely
be put to death.
12 And Isaac
sowed in that
land, and found
in the same year
an hundred fold:
and the LORD
blessed him. 13
And the man
waxed great,
and grew more
and more until
he became very
great: 14 and he
had possessions
of flocks, and
possessions of
herds, and a
great household:
and the Philis-
tines envied
him. 15 Now all
the wells which
his father's ser-
vants had dig-
ged in the days
of Abraham his
father, the Phi-
listines had stop-
ped them, and
filled them with

a G. has, *Gerar*.
b G., S., V. omit.
c G., S. add, *to him*.
d G., S. add, *to him*.
e G. has, *my people*.
f For העם, G., S. have, *his people*.
g S. omits.
h G., S. have, *barley*.
i G. omits.

them, and filled them with earth. 16 And Abimelech said unto Isaac, Go from us; for thou art much mightier than we.

17 And Isaac departed thence, and pitched his tent in the valley of Gerar, and dwelt there. 18 And Isaac digged again the wells of water, which they had digged in the days of Abraham his father; for the Philistines had stopped them after the death of Abraham: and he called their names after the names by which his father had called them. 19 And Isaac's servants digged in the valley, and found there a well of springing water. 20 And the herdmen of Gerar did strive with Isaac's herdmen, saying, The water *is* ours; and he called the name of the well Esek; because they strove with him. 21 And they digged another well, and strove for that also: and he called the name of it Sitnah. 22 And he removed from thence, and digged another well; and for that they strove not: and he called the name of it Rehoboth; and he said, For now the LORD hath made room for us, and we shall be fruitful in the land. 23 And he went up

16 פְלִשְׁתִּים וַיְמַלְאוּם עָפָר׃ וַיֹּאמֶר אֲבִימֶלֶךְ
Abimelek said And .dirt [with] them filled and ,Philistines the

אֶל־יִצְחָק לֵךְ מֵעִמָּנוּ כִּי־עָצַמְתָּ מִמֶּנּוּ
⁴we ³than ²stronger art thou for ,us (with) from Go ; Isaac unto

17 מְאֹד׃ וַיֵּלֶךְ מִשָּׁם יִצְחָק וַיִּחַן
encamped he and ; Isaac thence from went And .¹much

18 בְּנַחַל־גְּרָר וַיֵּשֶׁב שָׁם׃ וַיָּשָׁב יִצְחָק
Isaac returned And .there dwelt and ,Gerar of valley the in

וַיַּחְפֹּר אֶת־בְּאֵרֹת הַמַּיִם אֲשֶׁר חָפְרוּ[a] [b]בִּימֵי
of days the in dug had they which water of wells the dug and

אַבְרָהָם אָבִיו וַיְסַתְּמוּם פְּלִשְׁתִּים אַחֲרֵי
after Philistines the them obstructed had and ; father his Abraham

מוֹת אַבְרָהָם[c] וַיִּקְרָא לָהֶן שֵׁמוֹת כַּשֵּׁמֹת
names the like ,names them to called he and ; Abraham of death the

19 אֲשֶׁר־קָרָא לָהֶן[d] אָבִיו׃ וַיַּחְפְּרוּ עַבְדֵי־יִצְחָק
Isaac of slaves the dug And .father his them to called had which

[e]בַּנָּחַל וַיִּמְצְאוּ־שָׁם בְּאֵר מַיִם חַיִּים׃
.living water of well a there found they and ,valley the in

20 וַיָּרִיבוּ רֹעֵי גְרָר עִם־רֹעֵי יִצְחָק
Isaac of shepherds the with Gerar of shepherds the contended And

לֵאמֹר לָנוּ הַמָּיִם וַיִּקְרָא שֵׁם־הַבְּאֵר
well the of name the called he and ; water the [is] us To :saying

21 עֵשֶׂק כִּי הִתְעַשְּׂקוּ עִמּוֹ׃ [f]וַיַּחְפְּרוּ בְּאֵר
²well dug they And .him with quarreled they because ,Esek

אַחֶרֶת וַיָּרִיבוּ גַּם־עָלֶיהָ וַיִּקְרָא
called he and ; it about also contended they and ,¹another

22 שְׁמָהּ שִׂטְנָה׃ וַיַּעְתֵּק מִשָּׁם וַיַּחְפֹּר[g]
dug and ,thence from departed he And .Sitnah name its

בְּאֵר אַחֶרֶת וְלֹא רָבוּ עָלֶיהָ וַיִּקְרָא
called he and ; it about ²contended ¹they ³not and ,¹another ²well

שְׁמָהּ רְחֹבוֹת וַיֹּאמֶר כִּי־עַתָּה[h] הִרְחִיב
broad [it] made has now Truly : said he and ; Rehoboth name its

23 יְהוָה לָנוּ וּפָרִינוּ בָאָרֶץ׃ וַיַּעַל
up went he And .land the in fruitful be may we and ,us for Jehovah

earth. 16 And Abimelech said unto Isaac, Go from us; for thou art much mightier than we.

17 And Isaac departed thence, and encamped in the valley of Gerar, and dwelt there. 18 And Isaac digged again the wells of water, which they had digged in the days of Abraham his father; for the Philistines had stopped them after the death of Abraham: and he called their names after the names by which his father had called them. 19 And Isaac's servants digged in the valley, and found there a well of springing water. 20 And the herdmen of Gerar strove with Isaac's herdmen, saying, The water is ours: and he called the name of the well Esek; because they contended with him. 21 And they digged another well, and they strove for that also: and he called the name of it Sitnah. 22 And he removed from thence, and digged another well; and for that they strove not: and he called the name of it Rehoboth; and he said, For now the LORD hath made room for us, and we shall be fruitful in the land. 23 And he went up from thence to

a S. adds, *the servants of his father.*
b For בימי, Sm., G., V. have, *the slaves of*, עבדי.
c G. adds, *his father.*
d G., V. omit; G. adds, *Abraham.*
e G. adds, *of Gerar.*
f G. adds, at beginning of verse, *and Isaac departed thence*, cf. vs. 22.
g Sm., G. have pl.. ויחפרו.
h S., V. omit כי.

from thence to
Beer-sheba. 24
And the LORD
appeared unto
him the same
night, and said,
I *am* the God
of Abraham thy
father: fear not,
for I *am* with
thee, and will
bless thee, and
multiply thy
seed for my
servant Abra-
ham's sake. 25
And he builded
an altar there,
and called upon
the name of the
LORD, and
pitched his tent
there: and there
Isaac's servants
digged a well.

26 Then A-
bimelech went
to him from
Gerar, and A-
huzzath one of
his friends, and
Phichol the
chief captain of
his army. 27
And Isaac said
unto them,
Wherefore
come ye to me,
seeing ye hate
me, and have
sent me away
from you? 28
And they said,
We saw certain-
ly that the LORD
was with thee:
and we said, Let
there be now an
oath betwixt us,
even betwixt us
and thee, and
let us make a
covenant with
thee; 29 That
thou wilt do us
no hurt, as we
have not touch-
ed thee, and as
we have done
unto thee noth-
ing but good,
and have sent
thee away in
peace: thou *art*
now the blessed
of the LORD. 30
And he made
them a feast,
and they did
eat and drink.

24 מִשָּׁם בְּאֵר שָׁבַע׃ וַיֵּרָא אֵלָיו יְהוָה
Jehovah him unto appeared And .Sheba Beer [to] thence from

בַּלַּיְלָה הַהוּא וַיֹּאמֶר[a] אָנֹכִי אֱלֹהֵי אַבְרָהָם
Abraham of God the [am] I :said and ,[1]that [2]night in

אָבִיךָ אַל־תִּירָא כִּי־אִתְּךָ אָנֹכִי וּבֵרַכְתִּיךָ
,thee bless will I and ;I [am] thee with for ,fear not do ;father thy

וְהִרְבֵּיתִי אֶת־זַרְעֲךָ בַּעֲבוּר אַבְרָהָם עַבְדִּי[b]׃
.servant my Abraham of account on ,seed thy increase and

25 וַיִּבֶן שָׁם מִזְבֵּחַ וַיִּקְרָא בְּשֵׁם יְהוָה
,Jehovah of name the on called and altar an there built he And

וַיֶּט־שָׁם אָהֳלוֹ וַיִּכְרוּ־שָׁם עַבְדֵי־יִצְחָק
Isaac of slaves the there dug and ;tent his there pitched he and

26 בְּאֵר׃ וַאֲבִימֶלֶךְ הָלַךְ אֵלָיו מִגְּרָר וַאֲחֻזַּת
Ahuzzath and ,Gerar from him unto went Abimelek And .well a

27 מֵרֵעֵהוּ וּפִיכֹל שַׂר־צְבָאוֹ׃ וַיֹּאמֶר
said And .host his of commander the Phicol and ,friend his

אֲלֵהֶם יִצְחָק מַדּוּעַ בָּאתֶם אֵלָי וְאַתֶּם[c]
you and ,me unto come you do Why :Isaac them unto

28 שְׂנֵאתֶם אֹתִי וַתְּשַׁלְּחוּנִי מֵאִתְּכֶם׃ וַיֹּאמְרוּ[d]
,said they And ?you [with] from away me sent and ,me hated

רָאוֹ רָאִינוּ כִּי־הָיָה יְהוָה עִמָּךְ
,thee with Jehovah was that seen have we Seeing

וַנֹּאמֶר תְּהִי נָא אָלָה בֵּינוֹתֵינוּ[e]
,us between oath an ,now ,be [there] Let ;said have we and

בֵּינֵינוּ וּבֵינֶךָ וְנִכְרְתָה בְרִית עִמָּךְ׃
;thee with covenant a cut us let and ,thee (between) and us between

29 אִם־תַּעֲשֵׂה עִמָּנוּ רָעָה כַּאֲשֶׁר לֹא
[3]not as ,evil us with do [not] wilt thou [that] (if)

נְגַעֲנוּךָ וְכַאֲשֶׁר עָשִׂינוּ עִמְּךָ רַק־טוֹב[f]
,good only thee with did we as and ,thee touch [2]did [1]we

וַנְּשַׁלֵּחֲךָ בְּשָׁלוֹם אַתָּה עַתָּה בְּרוּךְ
of blessed now [being] thou ;peace in away thee sent we and

30 יְהוָה׃ וַיַּעַשׂ לָהֶם מִשְׁתֶּה וַיֹּאכְלוּ וַיִּשְׁתּוּ׃
.drank and ate they and ,feast a them for made he And .Jehovah

Beer-sheba. 24
And the LORD
appeared unto
him the same
night, and said,
I am the God of
Abraham thy fa-
ther: fear not,
for I am with
thee, and will
bless thee, and
multiply thy
seed for my serv-
ant Abraham's
sake. 25 And he
builded an altar
there, and called
upon the name
of the LORD,
and pitched his
tent there: and
there Isaac's
servants digged
a well.

26 Then A-
bimelech went
to him from
Gerar, and A-
huzzath his
friend, and Phi-
col the captain
of his host. 27
And Isaac said
unto them,
Wherefore are
ye come unto
me, seeing ye
hate me, and
have sent me a-
way from you?
28 And they
said, We saw
plainly that the
LORD was with
thee: and we
said, Let there
now be an oath
betwixt us, even
betwixt us and
thee, and let us
make a cove-
nant with thee;
29 that thou wilt
do us no hurt,
as we have not
touched thee,
and as we have
done unto thee
nothing but
good, and have
sent thee away
in peace: thou
art now the
blessed of the
LORD. 30 And
he made them a
feast, and they
did eat and
drink. 31 And

a S. adds *to him*.
b G. has, *thy father*.
c S. omits ו.
d S. adds, *to him*.
e G., S., V. omit; T. has, *which was between our fathers*.
f G., S. omit רק.

31 And they rose up betimes in the morning, and sware one to another: and Isaac sent them away, and they departed from him in peace. 32 And it came to pass the same day, that Isaac's servants came, and told him concerning the well which they had digged, and said unto him, We have found water. 33 And he called it Shebah: therefore the name of the city *is* Beer-sheba unto this day.

34 And Esau was forty years old when he took to wife Judith the daughter of Beeri the Hittite, and Bashemath the daughter of Elon the Hittite: 35 Which were a grief of mind unto Isaac and to Rebekah.

31 וַיַּשְׁכִּימוּ בַבֹּקֶר וַיִּשָּׁבְעוּ אִישׁ לְאָחִיו
; brother his to each ,swore and morning the in early rose they And

וַיְשַׁלְּחֵם יִצְחָק וַיֵּלְכוּ מֵאִתּוֹ בְּשָׁלוֹם׃
.peace in him (with) from went they and ,Isaac away them sent and

32 וַיְהִי ׀ בַּיּוֹם הַהוּא וַיָּבֹאוּ עַבְדֵי
of slaves the in came that ,[1]that [2]day on pass to came it And

יִצְחָק וַיַּגִּדוּ לוֹ[a] עַל־אֹדוֹת הַבְּאֵר אֲשֶׁר
which well the to regard with him to told and Isaac

חָפָרוּ וַיֹּאמְרוּ לוֹ מָצָאנוּ מָיִם׃
.water found have We ; him to said and ,digging been had they

33 וַיִּקְרָא אֹתָהּ שִׁבְעָה[b] עַל־כֵּן[c] שֵׁם־הָעִיר
[is] city the of name the therefore ; Shibah it called he And

בְּאֵר[d] שֶׁבַע[d] עַד הַיּוֹם הַזֶּה׃
.[1]this [2]day until Sheba Beer

34 וַיְהִי עֵשָׂו בֶּן־אַרְבָּעִים שָׁנָה וַיִּקַּח
took he and ; [old] years forty (of son a) Esau was And

אִשָּׁה אֶת־יְהוּדִית בַּת־בְּאֵרִי הַחִתִּי וְאֶת־
and ,Hittite the Beeri of daughter the ,Judith wife a

35 בָּשְׂמַת בַּת־אֵילֹן הַחִתִּי[e]׃ וַתִּהְיֶיןָ
became they and ; Hittite the Elon of daughter the Basemath

מֹרַת רוּחַ לְיִצְחָק וּלְרִבְקָה׃
.Rebekah to and Isaac to spirit of bitterness a

they rose up betimes in the morning, and sware one to another: and Isaac sent them away, and they departed from him in peace. 32 And it came to pass the same day, that Isaac's servants came, and told him concerning the well which they had digged, and said unto him, We have found water. 33 And he called it Shibah: therefore the name of the city is Beer-sheba unto this day.

34 And when Esau was forty years old he took to wife Judith the daughter of Beeri the Hittite, and Basemath the daughter of Elon the Hittite: 35 and they were a grief of mind unto Isaac and to Rebekah.

27

AND it came to pass, that when Isaac was old, and his eyes were dim, so that he could not see, he called Esau his eldest son, and said unto him, My son: and he said unto him, Behold, *here am* I. 2 And he said, Behold now, I am old, I know not the day of my death: 3

1 וַיְהִי כִּי־זָקֵן יִצְחָק וַתִּכְהֶיןָ
weak become had and ,Isaac old was when ,pass to came it And

עֵינָיו מֵרְאֹת וַיִּקְרָא אֶת־עֵשָׂו ׀ בְּנוֹ הַגָּדֹל
,[1]elder [2]son his Esau called he that ; seeing from eyes his

וַיֹּאמֶר אֵלָיו בְּנִי וַיֹּאמֶר אֵלָיו[f] הִנֵּנִי׃
.me Behold : him unto said he and ; son My : him unto said and

2 וַיֹּאמֶר[g] הִנֵּה־נָא זָקַנְתִּי לֹא יָדַעְתִּי
[2]know [1]I [3]not ,old am I ,now ,Behold : said he And

And it came to pass, that when Isaac was old, and his eyes were dim, so that he could not see, he called Esau his elder son, and said unto him, My son: and he said unto him, Here am I. 2 And he said, Behold now, I am old, I know not the day of my death.

a G. *not*, לא; V. omits.
b S., V., Aq., Sym., *satisfaction*, שָׂבָע.
c G. adds, *he called.*
d S., Aq., Sym., *well of satisfaction.*
e Sm., G., S. have, *the Hivite*, החוי.
f S., T. omit.
g S. adds, *to him Isaac:* V. *the father*.

Now therefore
take, I pray
thee, thy weap-
ons, thy quiver
and thy bow,
and go out to the
field, and take
me *some* ven-
ison;4And make
me savoury
meat, such as I
love, and bring
it to me, that I
may eat; that
my soul may
bless thee be-
fore I die. 5
And Rebekah
heard when
Isaac spake to
Esau his son.
And Esau went
to the field to
hunt *for* ven-
ison, *and* to
bring *it*.

6 And Re-
bekah spake un-
to Jacob her
son, saying, Be-
hold, I heard
thy father speak
unto Esau thy
brother, saying,
7 Bring me ven-
ison, and make
me savoury
meat, that I
may eat, and
bless thee before
the LORD
before my
death. 8 Now
therefore, my
son, obey my
voice according
to that which I
command thee.
9 Go now to the
flock, and fetch
me from thence
two good kids of
the goats; and I
will make them
savoury meat
for thy father,
such as he lov-
eth: 10 And
thou shalt bring
it to thy father,
that he may eat,
and that he may
bless thee before

3 יוֹם מוֹתִי׃ וְעַתָּה שָׂא־נָא כֵלֶיךָ
,weapons thy ,pray I ,up take now And .death my of day the

תֶּלְיְךָ[a] וְקַשְׁתֶּךָ וְצֵא הַשָּׂדֶה וְצוּדָה לִּי[b]
me for hunt and field the to out go and ; bow thy and quiver thy

4 צֵידָה׃ וַעֲשֵׂה־לִי מַטְעַמִּים כַּאֲשֶׁר אָהַבְתִּי
,love I as delicacies me for make and ; game

וְהָבִיאָה לִּי[c] וְאֹכֵלָה בַּעֲבוּר תְּבָרֶכְךָ
thee bless may that order in ; eat may I that me to in bring and

5 נַפְשִׁי בְּטֶרֶם אָמוּת׃ וְרִבְקָה שֹׁמַעַת בְּדַבֵּר
[2]speaking in hearing [was] Rebekah And .die I before ,soul my

יִצְחָק אֶל־עֵשָׂו בְּנוֹ וַיֵּלֶךְ עֵשָׂו הַשָּׂדֶה
field the to Esau went and ; son his Esau unto [1]Isaac's

6 לָצוּד צַיִד לְהָבִיא[d]׃ וְרִבְקָה אָמְרָה אֶל־יַעֲקֹב
Jacob unto said Rebekah And .in bring to game hunt to

בְּנָהּ לֵאמֹר[e] הִנֵּה שָׁמַעְתִּי אֶת־אָבִיךָ מְדַבֵּר
speaking father thy heard I Behold :saying ,son her

7 אֶל־עֵשָׂו אָחִיךָ לֵאמֹר[f]׃ הָבִיאָה לִּי צַיִד
game me to in Bring : saying ,brother thy Esau unto

וַעֲשֵׂה־לִי מַטְעַמִּים וְאֹכֵלָה וַאֲבָרֶכְכָה
thee bless may and ,eat may I that delicacies me for make and

8 לִפְנֵי יְהוָה לִפְנֵי מוֹתִי׃ וְעַתָּה[g] בְנִי שְׁמַע
hearken ,son my ,now And .dying my before Jehovah before

בְּקֹלִי לַאֲשֶׁר אֲנִי מְצַוָּה
commanding [am] I which that to reference in ,voice my to

9 אֹתָךְ׃ לֶךְ־נָא[h] אֶל־הַצֹּאן וְקַח־לִי מִשָּׁם שְׁנֵי
two thence from me for take and ,flock the unto ,now ,Go .thee

גְּדָיֵי עִזִּים טֹבִים[i] וְאֶעֱשֶׂה אֹתָם
them make will I and ; [1]good [5]goats [4]the [3]of [2]kids

10 מַטְעַמִּים לְאָבִיךָ כַּאֲשֶׁר אָהֵב׃ וְהֵבֵאתָ
in bring thou do and ; loves he as father thy for delicacies [into]

לְאָבִיךָ וְאָכָל בַּעֲבֻר אֲשֶׁר יְבָרֶכְךָ[j]
thee bless may he that order in ; eat him let and father thy to

3 Now therefore
take, I pray
thee, thy weap-
ons, thy quiver
and thy bow,
and go out to
the field, and
take me venison;
4 and make me
savoury meat,
such as I love,
and bring it to
me, that I may
eat; that my
soul may bless
thee before I
die. 5 And Re-
bekah heard
when Isaac
spake to Esau
his son. And E-
sau went to the
field to hunt for
venison, and to
bring it.

6 And Re-
bekah spake un-
to Jacob her
son, saying, Be-
hold, I heard thy
father speak un-
to Esau thy
brother, saying,
7 Bring me ven-
ison, and make
me savoury
meat, that I may
eat, and bless
thee before the
LORD before my
death. 8 Now
therefore, my
son, obey my
voice ac-
cording to that
which I com-
mand thee. 9
Go now to the
flock, and fetch
me from thence
two good kids of
the goats; and I
will make them
savoury meat for
thy father, such
as he loveth: 10
and thou shalt
bring it to thy
father, that he
may eat, so that
he may bless
thee before his

---

a S., T. have, *thy sword.*

b S., V. omit.

c S. omits.

d G. *for his father,* לאביו.

e G. has, *the younger,* הקטן; V., S. omit.

f S. omits.

g S. omits ו.

h G. adds *and,* ו.

i G. has, *tender and good.*

j G. adds, *thy father;* S. adds, *before Jehovah.*

his death. 11
And Jacob said
to Rebekah his
mother, Behold,
Esau my brother
is a hairy man,
and I *am* a
smooth man: 12
My father per-
adventure will
feel me, and I
shall seem to
him as a deceiv-
er; and I shall
bring a curse
upon me, and
not a blessing.
13 And his
mother said un-
to him, Upon
me *be* thy curse,
my son: only
obey my voice,
and go fetch me
them. 14 And he
went and fetch-
ed, and brought
them to his
mother: and his
mother made
savoury meat,
such as his fath-
er loved. 15 And
Rebekah took
goodly rai-
ment of her eld-
est son Esau,
which *were* with
her in the house,
and put them
upon Jacob her
younger son: 16
And she put the
skins of the kids
of the goats up-
on his hands,
and upon the
smooth of his
neck: 17 And
she gave the
savoury meat
and the bread,
which she had
prepared, into
the hand of her
son Jacob.

18 And he
came unto his
father, and said,
My father: and
he said, Here *am*
I, who *art* thou,
my son? 19 And
Jacob said unto
his father, I *am*
Esau thy first-
born; I have
done according

11 לִפְנֵי מוֹתוֹ׃ וַיֹּאמֶר יַעֲקֹב אֶל־רִבְקָה אִמּוֹ
: mother his Rebekah unto Jacob said And .dying his before

הֵן עֵשָׂו אָחִי אִישׁ שָׂעִר וְאָנֹכִי
I and ,[1]hairy [2]man a [is] brother my Esau Behold

12 אִישׁ חָלָק׃ אוּלַי יְמֻשֵּׁנִי אָבִי
,father my me feel will perhaps ; [1]smooth [2]man a [am]

וְהָיִיתִי בְעֵינָיו כִּמְתַעְתֵּעַ וְהֵבֵאתִי
bring shall I and ; mocking one like eyes his in be shall I and

13 עָלַי קְלָלָה וְלֹא בְרָכָה׃ וַתֹּאמֶר לוֹ
him to said And .blessing a not and curse a myself upon

אִמּוֹ עָלַי קִלְלָתְךָ בְּנִי אַךְ שְׁמַע
hearken only ; son my ,curse thy [be let] me Upon : mother his

14 בְּקֹלִי וְלֵךְ קַח־לִי׃ וַיֵּלֶךְ וַיִּקַּח
,took and ,went he And .me for take go and ,voice my to

וַיָּבֵא לְאִמּוֹ וַתַּעַשׂ אִמּוֹ מַטְעַמִּים
,delicacies mother his made and ; mother his to brought and

15 כַּאֲשֶׁר אָהֵב אָבִיו׃ וַתִּקַּח רִבְקָה אֶת־בִּגְדֵי
of garments the Rebekah took And .father his loved as

עֵשָׂו בְּנָהּ הַגָּדֹל הַחֲמֻדֹת אֲשֶׁר אִתָּהּ
her with [were] which ,ones costly the ,[1]elder [2]son her Esau

בַּבָּיִת וַתַּלְבֵּשׁ אֶת־יַעֲקֹב בְּנָהּ הַקָּטָן׃
; [1]younger [2]son her Jacob clothed she and ; house the in

16 וְאֵת עֹרֹת גְּדָיֵי הָעִזִּים הִלְבִּישָׁה עַל־יָדָיו
,hands his upon put she goats the of kids the of skins the and

17 וְעַל חֶלְקַת צַוָּארָיו׃ וַתִּתֵּן אֶת־הַמַּטְעַמִּים
,delicacies the gave she and ; neck his of smoothness the upon and

וְאֶת־הַלֶּחֶם אֲשֶׁר עָשָׂתָה בְּיַד יַעֲקֹב
Jacob of hand the into ,made had she which bread the and

18 בְּנָהּ׃ וַיָּבֹא[a] אֶל־אָבִיו וַיֹּאמֶר אָבִי
; father My : said and ,father his unto in came he And .son her

19 וַיֹּאמֶר הִנֶּנִּי[b] מִי אַתָּה בְּנִי׃ וַיֹּאמֶר
said And ? son my ,thou [art] who ; me Behold : said he and

יַעֲקֹב[c] אֶל־אָבִיו אָנֹכִי עֵשָׂו בְּכֹרֶךָ עָשִׂיתִי
done have I ,firstborn thy Esau [am] I : father his unto Jacob

death. 11 And
Jacob said to
Rebekah his
mother, Behold,
Esau my brother
is a hairy man,
and I am a
smooth man. 12
My father per-
adventure will
feel me, and I
shall seem to
him as a deceiv-
er; and I shall
bring a curse up-
on me, and not
a blessing. 13
And his mother
said unto him,
Upon me be thy
curse, my son:
only obey my
voice, and go
fetch me them.
14 And he went,
and fetched, and
brought them to
his mother: and
his mother made
savoury meat,
such as his fath-
er loved. 15 And
Rebekah took
the goodly rai-
ment of Esau
her elder son,
which were with
her in the house,
and put them
upon Jacob her
younger son: 16
and she put the
skins of the kids
of the goats up-
on his hands,
and upon the
smooth of his
neck: 17 and she
gave the savoury
meat and the
bread, which she
had prepared,
into the hand of
her son Jacob.

18 And he
came unto his
father, and said,
My father: and
he said, Here
am I; who art
thou, my son?
19 And Jacob
said unto his
father, I am E-
sau thy first-
born; I have
done according

---

a G., S. have, *and he brought in*, וַיָּבֵא.

b S. adds, *and he said.*

c G. adds, *his son*, בנו.

as thou badest
me; arise, I pray
thee, sit and eat
of my venison,
that thy soul
may bless me.
20 And Isaac
said unto his
son, How *is it*
that thou hast
found *it* so
quickly, my son?
And he said,
Because the
LORD thy God
brought *it* to
me. 21 And I-
saac said unto
Jacob, Come
near, I pray
thee, that I may
feel thee, my
son, whether
thou *be* my very
son Esau or not.
22 And Jacob
went near unto
Isaac his father;
and he felt him,
and said, The
voice *is* Jacob's
voice, but the
hands *are* the
hands of Esau.
23 And he dis-
cerned him not,
because his
hands were
hairy, as his
brother Esau's
hands: so he
blessed him.

24 And he said,
Art thou my
very son Esau?
And he said, I
am. 25 And he
said, Bring *it*
near to me, and
I will eat of my
son's venison,
that my soul
may bless thee.
And he brought
it near to him,
and he did eat:
and he brought
him wine, and
he drank. 26
And his father
Isaac said unto
him, Come near
now, and kiss
me, my son. 27

כַּאֲשֶׁר דִּבַּרְתָּ אֵלָי קוּם־נָא שְׁבָה וְאָכְלָה
eat and ,sit ,pray ,rise ; me unto speak didst thou as

20 מִצֵּידִי בַּעֲבוּר תְּבָרְכַנִּי נַפְשֶׁךָ׃ וַיֹּאמֶר
said And .soul thy me bless may that order in ; venison my from

יִצְחָק אֶל־בְּנוֹ מַה־זֶּה מִהַרְתָּ לִמְצֹא
,find to hastened thou hast ,then ,How : son his unto Isaac

בְּנִי וַיֹּאמֶר כִּי[a] הִקְרָה יְהוָה
Jehovah meet to [it] caused Because :said he And ?son my

21 אֱלֹהֶיךָ לְפָנָי׃ וַיֹּאמֶר יִצְחָק אֶל־יַעֲקֹב[b] גְּשָׁה־
,near Come : Jacob unto Isaac said And .me (before) God thy

נָּא[c] וַאֲמֻשְׁךָ בְּנִי הַאַתָּה זֶה בְּנִי
son my then [art] thou whether ;son my ,thee feel may I that ,pray

22 עֵשָׂו אִם־לֹא׃ וַיִּגַּשׁ יַעֲקֹב אֶל־יִצְחָק אָבִיו
,father his Isaac unto Jacob near came And .not or ,Esau

וַיְמֻשֵּׁהוּ וַיֹּאמֶר הַקֹּל[d] קוֹל יַעֲקֹב
,Jacob of voice the [is] voice The : said he and ; him felt he and

23 וְהַיָּדַיִם[e] יְדֵי עֵשָׂו׃[e] וְלֹא הִכִּירוֹ
,him recognize ²did ¹he ³not And .Esau of hands the hands the and

כִּי־הָיוּ יָדָיו כִּידֵי עֵשָׂו אָחִיו
,brother his Esau of hands the like hands his were because

24 שְׂעִרֹת וַיְבָרְכֵהוּ׃ וַיֹּאמֶר אַתָּה זֶה
,then ,thou [Art] :said he And .him blessed he and ; hairy

25 בְּנִי עֵשָׂו וַיֹּאמֶר אָנִי׃ וַיֹּאמֶר[f] הַגִּשָׁה
near Bring : said he And .[am] I : said he And ? Esau son my

לִּי וְאֹכְלָה מִצֵּיד[g] בְּנִי לְמַעַן
that ; son my of venison the from eat me let and ,me to

תְּבָרֶכְךָ נַפְשִׁי וַיַּגֶּשׁ־לוֹ וַיֹּאכַל
; ate he and ,him to near brought he And .soul my thee bless may

26 וַיָּבֵא לוֹ יַיִן וַיֵּשְׁתְּ׃ וַיֹּאמֶר אֵלָיו
him unto said And .drank he and wine him to brought he and

יִצְחָק אָבִיו גְּשָׁה־נָּא וּשְׁקָה־לִּי בְּנִי׃
.son my ,me (to) kiss and ,pray ,near Come : father his Isaac

as thou badest
me; arise, I pray
thee, sit and
eat of my ven-
ison, that thy
soul may bless
me. 20 And I-
saac said unto
his son, How
is it that thou
hast found it so
quickly, my son?
And he said, Be-
cause the LORD
thy God sent
me good speed.
21 And Isaac
said unto Jacob,
Come near, I
pray thee, that
I may feel thee,
my son, whether
thou be my very
son Esau or not.
22 And Jacob
went near unto
Isaac his father;
and he felt him,
and said, The
voice is Jacob's
voice, but the
hands are the
hands of Esau.
23 And he dis-
cerned him not,
because his
hands were
hairy, as his
brother Esau's
hands: so he
blessed him.

24 And he said,
Art thou my
very son Esau?
And he said, I
am. 25 And he
said, Bring it
near to me, and
I will eat of my
son's venison,
that my soul
may bless thee.
And he brought
it near to him,
and he did eat:
and he brought
him wine, and
he drank. 26
And his father
Isaac said unto
him, Come near
now, and kiss
me, my son. 27

---

a G., S. have *what*, אשר.
b S. adds, *his son*.
c For נא, G. has *to me*.
d S. omits.
e For והידים ידי עשו, S. has, *and the feeling of the hands* [*is*] *Esau's*.
f S. adds, *to him*.
g G. V. have, *from thy venison*, מצידך.

And he came near, and kissed him: and he smelled the smell of his raiment, and blessed him, and said, See, the smell of my son *is* as the smell of a field which the LORD hath blessed: 28 Therefore God give thee of the dew of heaven, and the fatness of the earth, and plenty of corn and wine: 29 Let people serve thee, and nations bow down to thee: be lord over thy brethren, and let thy mother's sons bow down to thee: cursed *be* every one that curseth thee, and blessed *be* he that blesseth thee.

30 And it came to pass, as soon as Isaac had made an end of blessing Jacob, and Jacob was yet scarce gone out from the presence of Isaac his father, that Esau his brother came in from his hunting. 31 And he also had made savoury meat, and brought it unto his father, and said unto his father, Let my father arise, and eat of his son's venison, that thy soul may bless me. 32 And Isaac his father said unto him, Who *art* thou? And he said, I

27 וַיִּגַּשׁ וַיִּשַּׁק־לוֹ וַיָּרַח אֶת־רֵיחַ
of smell the smelled he and ; him (to) kissed and near came he And

בְּגָדָיו וַיְבָרְכֵהוּ וַיֹּאמֶר רְאֵה רֵיחַ בְּנִי
son my of smell the ,See :said and ,him blessed and ,garments his

כְּרֵיחַ שָׂדֶה[a] אֲשֶׁר בֵּרֲכוֹ יְהוָה׃
.Jehovah (it) blessed has which ,field a of smell the like [is]

28 וְיִתֶּן־לְךָ[b] הָאֱלֹהִים מִטַּל הַשָּׁמַיִם[c]
,heavens the of dew the from God thee to give may And

וּמִשְׁמַנֵּי הָאָרֶץ וְרֹב דָּגָן וְתִירֹשׁ׃
.wine and corn of abundance and ; earth the of fatness the from and

29 יַעַבְדוּךָ[d] עַמִּים וְיִשְׁתַּחֲוּ לְךָ לְאֻמִּים[e]
; peoples thee to themselves prostrate and ,nations thee serve May

הֱוֵה[f] גְבִיר לְאַחֶיךָ[g] וְיִשְׁתַּחֲווּ לְךָ
thee to themselves prostrate may and ,brethren thy to ruler a be

בְּנֵי אִמֶּךָ[h] אֹרְרֶיךָ[i] אָרוּר[j]
,cursed [be] thee cursing those [May] .mother thy of sons the

30 וּמְבָרֲכֶיךָ[i] בָּרוּךְ[j]׃ וַיְהִי[k] כַּאֲשֶׁר
when ,pass to came it And .blessed [be] thee blessing those and

כִּלָּה יִצְחָק לְבָרֵךְ אֶת־יַעֲקֹב[l] וַיְהִי[k] אַךְ[m]
hardly ,pass to came it and ; Jacob bless to Isaac finished had

יָצֹא יָצָא יַעֲקֹב מֵאֵת פְּנֵי יִצְחָק
Isaac before (with) from Jacob out gone having

אָבִיו וְעֵשָׂו אָחִיו בָּא מִצֵּידוֹ׃
.hunting his from in came brother his Esau (and) ; father his

31 וַיַּעַשׂ גַּם־הוּא מַטְעַמִּים וַיָּבֵא לְאָבִיו
; father his to in brought and ,delicacies also he made And

וַיֹּאמֶר לְאָבִיו יָקֻם אָבִי וְיֹאכַל
eat and ,father my rise Let : father his to said he and

מִצֵּיד בְּנוֹ בַּעֲבֻר תְּבָרֲכַנִּי נַפְשֶׁךָ׃
.soul thy me bless may that order in ; son his of venison the from

32 וַיֹּאמֶר לוֹ יִצְחָק אָבִיו מִי־אָתָּה וַיֹּאמֶר
: said he And ? thou [art] Who : father his Isaac him to said And

And he came near, and kissed him: and he smelled the smell of his raiment, and blessed him, and said, See, the smell of my son Is as the smell of a field which the LORD hath blessed: 28 And God give thee of the dew of heaven, And of the fatness of the earth, And plenty of corn and wine: 29 Let peoples serve thee, And nations bow down to thee: Be lord over thy brethren, And let thy mother's sons bow down to thee: Cursed be every one that curseth thee, And blessed be every one that blesseth thee.

30 And it came to pass, as soon as Isaac had made an end of blessing Jacob, and Jacob was yet scarce gone out from the presence of Isaac his father, that Esau his brother came in from his hunting. 31 And he also made savoury meat, and brought it unto his father; and he said unto his father, Let my father arise, and eat of his son's venison, that thy soul may bless me. 32 And Isaac his father said unto him, Who art thou? And he said, I am thy

a Sm. adds *plentiful*, מלא; so G. V.
b S., V. omit ו.
c G. adds, *above*, מעל.
d G., V. add, *and*, ויעבדוך.
e G. has, *rulers*.
f G. adds, *and* והוה.
g G. has sing. לְאָחִיךָ.
h G. has, *thy father*, אביך.
i G., T., V. have sing.
j S., T. have pl.
k S., V. omit יהי.
l G. adds, *his son*.
m S., V. omit.

am thy son,
thy firstborn, E-
sau. 33 And I-
saac trembled
very exceed-
ingly, and said,
Who? where *is*
he that hath tak-
en venison, and
brought *it* me,
and I have eaten
of all before
thou camest,
and have blessed
him? yea, *and*
he shall be bless-
ed. 34 And when
Esau heard the
words of his
father, he cried
with a great and
exceeding bitter
cry, and said un-
to his father,
Bless me, *even*
me also, O my
father. 35 And
he said, Thy
brother came
with subtlety,
and hath taken
away thy bless-
ing. 36 And he
said, Is not he
rightly named
Jacob? for he
hath supplanted
me these two
times: he took
away my birth-
right; and, be-
hold, now he
hath taken away
my blessing.
And he said,
Hast thou not
reserved a bless-
ind for me?

37 And Isaac
answered and
said unto Esau,
Behold, I have
made him thy
lord, and all his
brethren have I
given to him for
servants; and
with corn and
wine have I sus-
tained him: and
what shall I do
now unto thee,
my son? 38 And
Esau said unto

33 אֲנִ֖י בִּנְךָ֥ בְּכֹרְךָ֖ עֵשָֽׂו׃ וַיֶּחֱרַ֨ד יִצְחָ֜ק
Isaac terrified was And .Esau ,firstborn thy ,son thy [am] I

חֲרָדָה֙ גְּדֹלָ֣ה עַד־מְאֹ֔ד וַיֹּ֡אמֶר מִֽי־
,Who : said he and ,exceedingly (unto) [1]great [2]terror [with]

אֵפ֡וֹא ה֣וּא הַצָּֽד־צַיִד֩ [a] וַיָּ֨בֵא לִ֜י
;me to in brought and ,game hunted who one the was ,then

וָאֹכַ֥ל מִכֹּ֛ל בְּטֶ֥רֶם תָּב֖וֹא וָאֲבָרְכֵ֑הוּ
? him blessed I and ,in camest thou before all from ate I and

34 גַּם־בָּר֖וּךְ יִהְיֶֽה׃ [b] כִּשְׁמֹ֤עַ עֵשָׂו֙ אֶת־דִּבְרֵ֣י [c]
of words the [1]Esau's [2]hearing At ! be shall he blessed also

אָבִ֔יו [d] וַיִּצְעַ֣ק צְעָקָ֔ה גְּדֹלָ֥ה וּמָרָ֖ה
bitter and great cry a [with] out cried he (and) ,father his

עַד־מְאֹ֑ד וַיֹּ֣אמֶר לְאָבִ֔יו [e] בָּרְכֵ֥נִי גַם־אָ֖נִי
,me also ,me Bless : father his to said he and ; exceedingly (unto)

35 אָבִֽי׃ וַיֹּ֕אמֶר [f] בָּ֥א אָחִ֖יךָ בְּמִרְמָ֑ה
,deceit with brother thy in Came : said he And .father my

36 וַיִּקַּ֖ח בִּרְכָתֶֽךָ׃ וַיֹּ֡אמֶר [g] הֲכִי֩ [h] קָרָ֨א
called has one that [it Is] : said he And .blessing thy took and

שְׁמ֜וֹ יַעֲקֹ֗ב וַֽיַּעְקְבֵ֙נִי֙ זֶ֣ה פַעֲמַ֔יִם
? twice now me overreached has he and ,Jacob name his

אֶת־בְּכֹרָתִ֣י לָקָ֔ח וְהִנֵּ֥ה [i] עַתָּ֖ה לָקַ֣ח
taken has he now behold and ,took he birth-right My

בִּרְכָתִ֑י וַיֹּאמַ֕ר [j] הֲלֹא־אָצַ֥לְתָּ לִּ֖י בְּרָכָֽה׃ [k]
? blessing a me for preserved not thou Hast : said he And .blessing my

37 וַיַּ֨עַן יִצְחָ֜ק וַיֹּ֣אמֶר לְעֵשָׂ֗ו הֵ֣ן [l] גְּבִ֞יר
ruler a ,Behold :Esau to said and Isaac answered And

שַׂמְתִּ֥יו לָךְ֙ וְאֶת־כָּל־אֶחָ֗יו נָתַ֤תִּי
given have I brethren his all and ,thee for him made have I

ל֔וֹ לַעֲבָדִ֔ים וְדָגָ֥ן וְתִירֹ֖שׁ סְמַכְתִּ֑יו
; him sustained have I wine and corn [with] and ; slaves for him to

38 וּלְכָ֣ה אֵפ֔וֹא מָ֥ה אֶעֱשֶׂ֖ה בְּנִֽי׃ וַיֹּ֥אמֶר
said And ? son my ,do I can what ,then ,thee for and

son, thy first-
born, Esau. 33
And Isaac trem-
bled very ex-
ceedingly, and
said, Who then
is he that hath
taken venison,
and brought it
me, and I have
eaten of all be-
fore thou cam-
est, and have
blessed him?
yea, *and* he
shall be blessed.
34 When Esau
heard the words
of his father, he
cried with an
exceeding great
and bitter cry,
and said unto
his father, Bless
me, even me al-
so, O my father.
35 And he said,
Thy brother
came with guile,
and hath taken
away thy bless-
ing. 36 And he
said, Is not he
rightly named
Jacob? for he
hath supplanted
me these two
times; he took
away my birth-
right; and, be-
hold, now he
hath taken away
my blessing.
And he said,
Hast thou not
reserved a bless-
ing for me?

37 And Isaac
answered and
said unto E-
sau, Behold,
I have made
him thy lord,
and all his
brethren have I
given to him for
servants; and
with corn and
wine have I sus-
tained him: and
what then shall
I do for thee,
my son? 38 And
Esau said unto

---

a G. adds, *for me.*

b Sm., G. add, *and it came to pass,* ויהי; S. adds, *and,* ו.

c G. adds, *Isaac.*

d G., S. omit ו; G. adds, *Esau.*

e G., V. omit.

f G. adds, *to him*; S. adds, *to him his father.*

g S. adds, *Esau.*

h G., S., T., V. have, *justly.*

i G., V. omit הנה.

j G., S. add, *Esau to his father;* V. adds, *to the father.*

k G. adds, *father.*

l G. has, *if.*

his father, Hast
thou but one
blessing, my fa-
ther ? bless me,
even me also, O
my father. And
Esau lifted up
his voice, and
wept. 39 And I-
saac his father
answered and
said unto him,
Behold, thy
dwelling shall be
the fatness of the
earth, and of the
dew of heaven
from above ; 40
And by thy
sword shalt thou
live, and shalt
serve thy broth-
er ; and it shall
come to pass
when thou shalt
have the domin-
ion, that thou
shalt break his
yoke from off
thy neck.

41 And Esau
hated Jacob be-
cause of the
blessing where-
with his father
blessed him: and
Esau said in his
heart, The days
of mourning for
my father are at
hand ; then will
I slay my broth-
er Jacob. 42
And these words
of Esau her eld-
er son were told
to Rebekah :
and she sent and
called Jacob her
younger son,
and said unto
him, Behold,
thy brother E-
sau, as touching
thee, doth com-
fort himself,
purposing to kill
thee. 43 Now
therefore, my
son, obey my
voice; and arise,
flee thou to La-
ban my brother,
to Haran; 44
And tarry with
him a few days,
until thy broth-
er's fury turn a-
way ; 45 Until

עשו אל־אביו[a] הברכה אחת הוא־לך אבי
? father my ,thee to [1]is [2]one [3]Blessing : father his unto Esau

ברכני גם־אני אבי וישא[b] עשו קלו
voice his Esau up lifted and ; father my ,me also ,me bless

39 ויבך[b]׃ ויען יצחק אביו ויאמר אליו
: him unto said and ,father his Isaac answered And .wept and

הנה משמני הארץ יהיה מושבך
,dwelling thy be shall earth the of fatness the from ,Behold

40 ומטל השמים מעל׃ ועל־חרבך
sword thy by And .above from heavens the of dew the from and

תחיה ואת־אחיך תעבד והיה[c]
,pass to come shall it and ;serve shalt thou brother thy and ,live shalt thou

כאשר תריד[c] ופרקת עלו מעל
upon from yoke his off break shalt thou (and) ,strivest thou when

41 צוארך׃ וישטם עשו את־יעקב על־
of account on ,Jacob [against] Esau enmity cherished And .neck thy

הברכה אשר ברכו אביו ויאמר
said and ; father his him blessed had which [with] blessing the

עשו בלבו יקרבו ימי אבל אבי
,father my [for] mourning of days the near Are : heart his in Esau

42 ואהרגה את־יעקב אחי׃ ויגד לרבקה
Rebekah to told were And .brother my Jacob kill will I and

את־דברי עשו בנה הגדל ותשלח ותקרא
called and sent she and ; [1]elder [2]son her Esau of words the

ליעקב בנה הקטן ותאמר אליו הנה
,Behold : him unto said she and ,[1]younger [2]son her Jacob (to)

עשו אחיך מתנחם לך להרגך׃
.thee kill to ,thee on himself comfort to about [is] brother thy Esau

43 ועתה בני שמע בקלי וקום ברח־לך[d]
thyself for flee ,rise and ; voice my to hearken ,son my ,now And

44 אל־לבן אחי חרנה׃ וישבת עמו ימים
[2]days him with dwell And .Haran to brother my Laban unto

45 אחדים עד[e] אשר־תשוב חמת אחיך׃ עד־
until ; brother thy of fury the turns that until ,[1]some

his father, Hast
thou but one
blessing, my fa-
ther ? bless me,
even me also, O
my father. And
Esau lifted up
his voice, and
wept. 39 And
Isaac his father
answered and
said unto him,
Behold, of the
fatness of the
earth shall be
thy dwelling,
And of the dew
of heaven from
above ; 40 And
by thy sword
shalt thou live,
and thou shalt
serve thy broth-
er ; And it shall
come to pass
when thou shalt
break loose,
That thou shalt
shake his yoke
from off thy
neck.

41 And Esau
hated Jacob be-
cause of the
blessing where-
with his father
blessed him: and
Esau said in his
heart, The days
of mourning for
my father are at
hand ; then will
I slay my broth-
er Jacob. 42 And
the words of E-
sau her elder son
were told to
Rebekah ; and
she sent and
called Jacob her
younger son,
and said unto
him, Behold,
thy brother E-
sau, as touching
thee, doth com-
fort himself,
purposing to
kill thee. 43
Now therefore,
my son, obey
my voice ; and
arise, flee thou to
Laban my broth-
er to Haran ; 44
and tarry with
him a few days,
until thy broth-
er's fury turn a-
way; 45 until thy

a G. *unto Isaac his father.*
b G. omits וישא----ויבך.
c For והיה----תריד, S. has, *and if thou repentest;* T. *and when his sons transgress the words of the law;* V. *and the time shall come when thou shalt shake off.*
d G. adds, *to Mesopotamia.*

שׁוּב[a] אַף־אָחִיךָ מִמְּךָ[a] וְשָׁכַח אֵת
forgets he and ,thee from brother thy of anger the of turning the

אֲשֶׁר־עָשִׂיתָ לּוֹ וְשָׁלַחְתִּי וּלְקַחְתִּיךָ
thee take and send will I and ;him to done hast thou what

מִשָּׁם לָמָה[b] אֶשְׁכַּל גַּם־שְׁנֵיכֶם יוֹם
2day [in] two you of also bereaved be I should why ;thence from

אֶחָד׃
?1one

46 וַתֹּאמֶר רִבְקָה אֶל־יִצְחָק קַצְתִּי בְחַיַּי
,life my of tired am I :Isaac unto Rebekah said And

מִפְּנֵי בְּנוֹת חֵת אִם־לֹקֵחַ יַעֲקֹב אִשָּׁה
wife a Jacob takes if ;Heth of daughters the before from

מִבְּנוֹת־חֵת[c] כָּאֵלֶּה[dc] מִבְּנוֹת הָאָרֶץ[d]
,land the of daughters the from these like ,Heth of daughters the from

לָמָּה לִּי חַיִּים׃
?life [is] me to what for

28

1 וַיִּקְרָא יִצְחָק אֶל־יַעֲקֹב וַיְבָרֶךְ אֹתוֹ
;him blessed and Jacob (unto) Isaac called And

וַיְצַוֵּהוּ וַיֹּאמֶר[e] לוֹ[e] לֹא־תִקַּח אִשָּׁה
wife a take not shalt Thou ;him to said and him commanded he and

2 מִבְּנוֹת כְּנָעַן׃ קוּם לֵךְ[f] פַּדֶּנָה אֲרָם
,Aram Paddan to go ,Rise .Canaan of daughters the from

בֵּיתָה בְתוּאֵל אֲבִי אִמֶּךָ וְקַח־לְךָ
thyself for take and ;mother thy of father the Bethuel of house the to

מִשָּׁם אִשָּׁה מִבְּנוֹת לָבָן אֲחִי
of brother the Laban of daughters the from ,wife a thence from

3 אִמֶּךָ׃ וְאֵל[g] שַׁדַּי[g] יְבָרֵךְ אֹתְךָ
,thee bless 1may 3Almighty 2God And .mother thy

וְיַפְרְךָ וְיַרְבֶּךָ וְהָיִיתָ
become thou mayest and ,thee multiply and ,fruitful thee make and

4 לִקְהַל עַמִּים׃ וְיִתֶּן־לְךָ אֶת־בִּרְכַּת
of blessing the thee to give he may and ;nations of company a (for)

thy brother's
anger turn away
from thee, and
he forget *that*
which thou hast
done to him:
then I will send,
and fetch thee
from thence.
Why should I be
deprived also of
you both in one
day?

46 And Re-
bekah said to
Isaac, I am
weary of my
life because of
the daughters of
Heth: if Jacob
take a wife of
the daughters of
Heth, such as
these *which are*
of the daughters
of the land,
what good shall
my life do me?

AND Isaac
called Jacob,
and blessed him,
and charged
him, and said
unto him, Thou
shalt not take a
wife of the
daughters of
Canaan. 2 Arise,
go to Padan-
aram, to the
house of Bethu-
el thy mother's
father; and
take thee a wife
from thence of
the daughters of
Laban thy
mother's broth-
er. 3 And God
Almighty bless
thee, and make
thee fruitful,
and multiply
thee, that thou
mayest be a
multitude of
people; 4 And
give thee the
blessing of A-

brother's anger
turn away from
thee, and he for-
get that which
thou hast done
to him: then I
will send, and
fetch thee from
thence: why
should I be
bereaved of you
both in one
day?

46 And Re-
bekah said to
Isaac, I am
weary of my life
because of the
daughters of
Heth: if Jacob
take a wife of
the daughters of
Heth, such as
these, of the
daughters of the
land, what good
shall my life do
me?

And Isaac
called Jacob and
blessed him, and
charged him,
and said unto
him, Thou shalt
not take a wife
of the daughters
of Canaan. 2
Arise, go to
Paddan - aram,
to the house of
Bethuel thy
mother's father;
and take thee a
wife from thence
of the daugh-
ters of Laban
thy mother's
brother. 3 And
God Almighty
bless thee, and
make thee fruit-
ful, and multi-
ply thee, that
thou mayest be
a company of
peoples; 4 and
give thee the
blessing of A-

a For עד אשר תשוב---ממך, G. has, *until the anger and wrath of thy brother turn from thee.*

b G. has, *lest.*

c G., V. omit.

d For כאלה מבנות הארץ, S. has, *like these daughters of the land.*

e G. has, *saying,* לאמר.

f S. adds, *for thyself,* לְךָ.

g For אל שדי, G. has, *my God.*

braham, to thee,
and to thy seed
with thee; that
thou mayest in-
herit the land
wherein thou art
a stranger,
which God gave
unto Abraham.
5 And Isaac sent
away Jacob:
and he went to
Padan-aram, un-
to Laban, son of
Bethuel the
Syrian, the
brother of Re-
bekah, Jacob's
and Esau's
mother.

6 When Esau
saw that Isaac
had blessed Ja-
cob, and sent
him away to
Padan-aram, to
take him a wife
from thence;
and that as he
blessed him he
gave him a
charge, saying,
Thou shalt not
take a wife of
the daughters of
Canaan; 7 And
that Jacob obey-
ed his father
and his mother,
and was gone to
Padan-aram; 8
And Esau see-
ing that the
daughters of
Canaan pleased
not Isaac his
father; 9 Then
went Esau unto
Ishmael, and
took unto the
wives which he
had, Mahalath
the daughter of
Ishmael, Abra-
ham's son, the
sister of Neba-
joth, to be his
wife.

10 And Jacob
went out from
Beer-sheba, and
went toward
Haran. 11 And
he lighted upon
a certain place,
and tarried
there all
night, because

אַבְרָהָם[a] לְךָ וּלְזַרְעֲךָ אִתָּךְ לְרִשְׁתְּךָ
possessing thy for ;thee with seed thy to and thee to ,Abraham

אֶת־אֶרֶץ מְגֻרֶיךָ אֲשֶׁר־נָתַן אֱלֹהִים לְאַבְרָהָם׃
.Abraham to God gave which ,sojournings thy of land the

5 וַיִּשְׁלַח יִצְחָק אֶת־יַעֲקֹב וַיֵּלֶךְ פַּדֶּנָה אֲרָם
;Aram Paddan to went he and ,Jacob Isaac away sent And

אֶל־לָבָן בֶּן־בְּתוּאֵל הָאֲרַמִּי אֲחִי[b]
of brother the ,Aramean the Bethuel of son the Laban unto

6 רִבְקָה אֵם יַעֲקֹב וְעֵשָׂו׃ וַיַּרְא עֵשָׂו
Esau saw And .Esau and Jacob of mother the ,Rebekah

כִּי־בֵרַךְ יִצְחָק אֶת־יַעֲקֹב[c] וְשִׁלַּח אֹתוֹ פַּדֶּנָה
Paddan to him away sent and ,Jacob Isaac blessed had that

אֲרָם לָקַחַת־לוֹ מִשָּׁם[d] אִשָּׁה בְּבָרֲכוֹ
blessing his in [and] ;wife a thence from himself for take to ,Aram

אֹתוֹ וַיְצַו עָלָיו לֵאמֹר
:saying him (upon) commanded had he (and) him

לֹא־תִקַּח אִשָּׁה מִבְּנוֹת כְּנָעַן׃
;Canaan of daughters the from wife a take not shalt Thou

7 וַיִּשְׁמַע יַעֲקֹב אֶל־אָבִיו וְאֶל־אִמּוֹ
,mother his unto and father his unto Jacob hearkened had and

8 וַיֵּלֶךְ פַּדֶּנָה אֲרָם׃ וַיַּרְא עֵשָׂו כִּי רָעוֹת
evil [were] that Esau saw and ;Aram Paddan to gone had and

9 בְּנוֹת כְּנָעַן בְּעֵינֵי יִצְחָק אָבִיו׃ וַיֵּלֶךְ
went and ;father his Isaac of eyes the in Canaan of daughters the

עֵשָׂו אֶל־יִשְׁמָעֵאל וַיִּקַּח אֶת־מָחֲלַת בַּת־יִשְׁמָעֵאל
Ishmael of daughter the Mahalath took and ,Ishmael unto Esau

בֶּן־אַבְרָהָם אֲחוֹת נְבָיוֹת עַל־נָשָׁיו לוֹ
him to ,wives his to addition in ,Nebaioth of sister the ,Abraham of son the

לְאִשָּׁה׃
.wife a for

10 וַיֵּצֵא יַעֲקֹב מִבְּאֵר שָׁבַע וַיֵּלֶךְ[e] חָרָנָה׃
.Haran to went and Sheba Beer from Jacob out went And

11 וַיִּפְגַּע בַּמָּקוֹם וַיָּלֶן שָׁם
,there night the passed and ,place a upon happened he And

braham, to thee,
and to thy
seed with thee;
that thou mayest
inherit the land
of thy sojourn-
ings, which God
gave unto Abra-
ham. 5 And I-
saac sent away
Jacob: and he
went to Paddan-
aram unto La-
ban, son of
Bethuel the
Syrian, the
brother of Re-
bekah, Jacob's
and Esau's
mother.

6 Now Esau saw
that Isaac had
blessed Jacob
and sent him a-
way to Paddan-
aram, to take
him a wife from
thence; and that
as he blessed
him he gave
him a charge,
saying, Thou
shalt not take a
wife of the
daughters of
Canaan; 7 and
that Jacob obey-
ed his father and
mother, and was
gone to Paddan-
aram: 8 and E-
sau saw that the
daughters of
Canaan pleased
not Isaac his
father; 9 and E-
sau went unto
Ishmael, and
took unto the
wives which he
had Mahalath
the daughter of
Ishmael Abra-
ham's son, the
sister of Ne-
baioth, to be his
wife.

10 And Jacob
went out from
Beer-sheba, and
went toward
Haran. 11 And
he lighted upon
a certain place,
and tarried there
all night, be-

a Sm., G. add, *thy father*.
b G. adds, *and*, ואחי.
c S. adds, *his brother*.
d G. omits.
e Sm., S. have, *to go*, ללכת.

the sun was set; and he took of the stones of that place, and put *them for* his pillows, and lay down in that place to sleep. 12 And he dreamed, and behold a ladder set up on the earth, and the top of it reached to heaven: and behold the angels of God ascending and descending on it. 13 And, behold, the LORD stood above it, and said, I *am* the LORD God of Abraham thy father, and the God of Isaac: the land whereon thou liest, to thee will I give it, and to thy seed; 14 And thy seed shall be as the dust of the earth, and thou shalt spread abroad to the west, and to the east, and to the north, and to the south: and in thee and in thy seed shall all the families of the earth be blessed. 15 And, behold, I *am* with thee, and will keep thee in all *places* whither thou goest, and will bring thee again into this land; for I will not leave thee, until I have done *that* which I have spoken to thee of.

16 And Jacob awaked out of his sleep, and he said, Surely the LORD is in

כִּי־בָא הַשֶּׁמֶשׁ וַיִּקַּח מֵאַבְנֵי הַמָּקוֹם
,place the of stones the from [some] took he and ; sun the set had for

וַיָּשֶׂם מְרַאֲשֹׁתָיו וַיִּשְׁכַּב בַּמָּקוֹם הַהוּא׃
.[1]that [2]place in down lay he and ; head his at put and

12 וַיַּחֲלֹם וְהִנֵּה סֻלָּם מֻצָּב אַרְצָה
,earth the on placed ladder a behold and ,dreamed he And

וְרֹאשׁוֹ מַגִּיעַ הַשָּׁמָיְמָה וְהִנֵּה[a] מַלְאֲכֵי
of angels the behold and ; heavens the to reaching top its (and)

13 אֱלֹהִים עֹלִים וְיֹרְדִים בּוֹ׃ וְהִנֵּה[b] יְהוָה
Jehovah behold And .it on descending and ascending God

נִצָּב עָלָיו וַיֹּאמַר אֲנִי יְהוָה[c] אֱלֹהֵי
of God the ,Jehovah [am] I : said he and ,him by standing

אַבְרָהָם אָבִיךָ וֵאלֹהֵי יִצְחָק[d] הָאָרֶץ
land the ; Isaac of God the and ,father thy Abraham

אֲשֶׁר אַתָּה שֹׁכֵב עָלֶיהָ לְךָ אֶתְּנֶנָּה
it give will I thee to ,(it upon) lying [art] thou which [upon]

14 וּלְזַרְעֶךָ׃ וְהָיָה זַרְעֲךָ כַּעֲפַר[e] הָאָרֶץ[e]
,earth the of dust the like seed thy become shall And .seed thy to and

וּפָרַצְתָּ יָמָּה וָקֵדְמָה וְצָפֹנָה
north the to and east the to and west the to spread shalt thou and

וָנֶגְבָּה וְנִבְרְכוּ בְךָ כָּל־מִשְׁפְּחֹת
of families the all thee in themselves bless shall and ; south the to and

15 הָאֲדָמָה וּבְזַרְעֶךָ׃ וְהִנֵּה אָנֹכִי עִמָּךְ
,thee with [be will] I ,behold And .seed thy in and ,ground the

וּשְׁמַרְתִּיךָ בְּכֹל אֲשֶׁר־תֵּלֵךְ
,go mayest thou which [in] [place] every in thee guard will and

וַהֲשִׁבֹתִיךָ אֶל־הָאֲדָמָה הַזֹּאת כִּי לֹא
[3]not for ;[1] this [2]land unto thee return will and

אֶעֱזָבְךָ עַד אֲשֶׁר אִם־עָשִׂיתִי אֵת[f] אֲשֶׁר־
which that done have shall I (if) that until ,thee forsake [2]will [1]I

16 דִּבַּרְתִּי לָךְ׃ וַיִּיקַץ יַעֲקֹב מִשְּׁנָתוֹ וַיֹּאמֶר
: said and ,sleep his from Jacob awoke And .thee to spoke I

אָכֵן[g] יֵשׁ יְהוָה בַּמָּקוֹם הַזֶּה וְאָנֹכִי לֹא
[2]not I [while] (and) ,[1]this [2]place in Jehovah is Surely

cause the sun was set; and he took one of the stones of the place, and put it under his head, and lay down in that place to sleep. 12 And he dreamed, and behold a ladder set up on the earth, and the top of it reached to heaven: and behold the angels of God ascending and descending on it. 13 And, behold, the LORD stood above it, and said, I am the LORD, the God of Abraham thy father, and the God of Isaac: the land whereon thou liest, to thee will I give it, and to thy seed; 14 and thy seed shall be as the dust of the earth, and thou shalt spread abroad to the west, and to the east, and to the north, and to the south: and in thee and in thy seed shall all the families of the earth be blessed. 15 And, behold, I am with thee, and will keep thee whithersoever thou goest, and will bring thee again into this land; for I will not leave thee, until I have done that which I have spoken to thee of.

16 And Jacob awaked out of his sleep, and he said, Surely the LORD is in this

---

a G. omits *behold*, הנה.
b G., V. omit, *behold*, הנה.
c G. omits.
d G. adds, *do not fear*.
e G. *like the sand of the sea*.
f G., V. add, *all*, כל.
g G. has, *for*, כי.

this place; and I
knew *it* not. 17
And he was a-
fraid, and said,
How dreadful
is this place!
this *is* none
other but the
house of God,
and this *is* the
gate of heaven.
18 And Jacob
rose up early in
the morning,
and took the
stone that he
had put *for* his
pillows, and set
it up *for* a pillar,
and poured oil
upon the top of
it. 19 And he
called the name
of that place
Beth-el: but the
name of that
city *was called*
Luz at the first.

20 And Jacob
vowed a vow,
saying, If God
will be with me,
and will keep
me in this way
that I go, and
will give me
bread to eat, and
raiment to put
on, 21 So that I
come again to
my father's
house in peace;
then shall the
LORD be my
God: 22 And
this stone which
I have set *for* a
pillar, shall be
God's house:
and of all that
thou shalt give
me I will surely
give the tenth
unto thee.

17 יָדָֽעְתִּי׃ וַיִּירָא[a] וַיֹּאמַר מַה־נּוֹרָא הַמָּקוֹם
[2]place terrible How : said and feared he And .know [1]did

הַזֶּה[b] אֵין זֶה כִּי אִם־בֵּית אֱלֹהִים וְזֶה
this and ,God of house the (if) except [1]this [3]not [2]is ![1]this

18 שַׁעַר הַשָּׁמָיִם׃ וַיַּשְׁכֵּם יַעֲקֹב בַּבֹּקֶר
,morning the in Jacob early rose And .heavens the of gate the

וַיִּקַּח אֶת־הָאֶבֶן אֲשֶׁר־שָׂם[c] מְרַאֲשֹׁתָיו וַיָּשֶׂם
put and ,head his at put had he which stone the took and

אֹתָהּ מַצֵּבָה וַיִּצֹק שֶׁמֶן עַל־רֹאשָׁהּ׃
.top its upon oil poured he and ;pillar memorial a [as] it

19 וַיִּקְרָא[d] אֶת־שֵׁם־הַמָּקוֹם הַהוּא בֵּית־אֵל וְאוּלָם
contrary the on (and) ,Bethel [1]that [2]place of name the called he And

20 לוּז שֵׁם־הָעִיר[e] לָרִאשֹׁנָה׃ וַיִּדַּר יַעֲקֹב
Jacob vowed And .first at city the of name the [being] Luz

נֶדֶר לֵאמֹר אִם־יִהְיֶה[f] אֱלֹהִים עִמָּדִי וּשְׁמָרַנִי
me guard and ,me with God be If ;saying vow a

בַּדֶּרֶךְ הַזֶּה אֲשֶׁר אָנֹכִי הוֹלֵךְ וְנָתַן־לִי
me to give and ,going [am] I which [in] [1]this [2]way in

21 לֶחֶם לֶאֱכֹל וּבֶגֶד לִלְבֹּשׁ׃ וְשַׁבְתִּי[g] בְשָׁלוֹם
peace in return I and ; wear to clothing and eat to bread

אֶל־בֵּית אָבִי וְהָיָה יְהוָה לִי
me to Jehovah become shall then ,father my of house the unto

22 לֵאלֹהִים׃ וְהָאֶבֶן הַזֹּאת אֲשֶׁר־שַׂמְתִּי מַצֵּבָה
pillar memorial a [as] put have I which [1]this [2]stone and ,God a (for)

יִהְיֶה[h] בֵּית אֱלֹהִים וְכֹל אֲשֶׁר תִּתֶּן־לִי
,me to give shalt thou which all and ; God of house a become shall

עַשֵּׂר אֲעַשְּׂרֶנּוּ לָךְ׃
.thee for tithe will I tithing

place; and I
knew it not. 17
And he was a-
fraid, and said,
How dreadful is
this place! this
is none other
but the house of
God, and this is
the gate of heav-
en. 18 And Ja-
cob rose up early
in the morning,
and took the
stone that he
had put under
his head, and
set it up for a
pillar, and pour-
ed oil upon the
top of it. 19
And he called
the name of that
place Beth-el:
but the name of
the city was Luz
at the first.

20 And Jacob
vowed a vow,
saying, If God
will be with me,
and will keep me
in this way that
I go, and will
give me bread to
eat, and raiment
to put on, 21 so
that I come a-
gain to my fath-
er's house in
peace, then shall
the LORD be my
God, 22 and this
stone, which I
have set up for
a pillar, shall be
God's house:
and of all that
thou shalt give
me I will surely
give the tenth
unto thee.

29

THEN Jacob
went on his
journey, and
came into the
land of the peo-

1 וַיִּשָּׂא יַעֲקֹב רַגְלָיו וַיֵּלֶךְ אַרְצָה
of land the to went and ,feet his Jacob up lifted And

Then Jacob
went on his
journey, and
came to the
land of the chil-

---

a S. adds, *Jacob with a great fear.*

b S. adds, *to-day.*

c G. has, *which he had put there,* a double translation for שם.

d G., S. add, *Jacob.*

e For העיר, S. has *that place.*

f G. adds, *Lord,* יהוה.

g G. *and he causes me to return.*

h G. adds, *for me.*

ple of the east.
2 And he looked,
and behold a
well in the field,
and, lo, there
were three flocks
of sheep lying
by it; for out of
that well they
watered the
flocks; and a
great stone *was*
upon the well's
mouth. 3 And
thither were all
the flocks gath-
ered: and they
rolled the stone
from the well's
mouth, and wa-
tered the sheep,
and put the
stone again up-
on the well's
mouth in his
place.
4 And Jacob
said unto them,
My breth-
ren, whence *be*
ye? And they
said, Of Haran
are we. 5 And
he said unto
them, Know ye
Laban the son
of Nahor? And
they said, We
know *him*. 6 And
he said unto
them, *Is* he well?
And they said,
He is well: and,
behold, Rachel
his daughter
cometh with the
sheep. 7 And he
said, Lo, *it is*
yet high day,
neither *is it* time
that the cattle
should be gath-
ered together:
water ye the
sheep, and go
and feed *them*.
8 And they said,

2 בְּנֵי־קֶדֶם׃[a] וַיַּרְא וְהִנֵּה בְאֵר בַּשָּׂדֶה
; field the in well a behold and ,saw he And .east the of sons the
וְהִנֵּה־שָׁם[b] שְׁלֹשָׁה עֶדְרֵי־צֹאן רֹבְצִים עָלֶיהָ
; it by lying [were] sheep of flocks three there behold and
כִּי מִן־הַבְּאֵר הַהִוא יַשְׁקוּ[c]
water to accustomed were they [1]that [2]well from for
הָעֲדָרִים וְהָאֶבֶן גְּדֹלָה עַל־פִּי
of mouth the upon great [being] stone the (and) ,flocks the
3 הַבְּאֵר׃ וְנֶאֶסְפוּ־שָׁמָּה כָל־
all thither gathered be to accustomed were And .well the
הָעֲדָרִים וְגָלֲלוּ אֶת־הָאֶבֶן
stone the roll to accustomed were they and ,flocks the
מֵעַל פִּי הַבְּאֵר וְהִשְׁקוּ אֶת־הַצֹּאן
,sheep the water to and ,well the of mouth the upon from
וְהֵשִׁיבוּ אֶת־הָאֶבֶן עַל־פִּי הַבְּאֵר
well the of mouth the upon stone the return to and
4 לִמְקֹמָהּ׃ וַיֹּאמֶר לָהֶם יַעֲקֹב אַחַי
,brethren My : Jacob them to said And .place its to
מֵאַיִן אַתֶּם וַיֹּאמְרוּ מֵחָרָן אֲנָחְנוּ׃
.we [are] Haran From ; said they And ? ye [are] whence from
5 וַיֹּאמֶר לָהֶם הַיְדַעְתֶּם אֶת־לָבָן בֶּן־
of son the Laban know ye Do ; them to said he And
6 נָחוֹר וַיֹּאמְרוּ יָדָעְנוּ׃ וַיֹּאמֶר לָהֶם
: them to said he And .know We : said they And ? Nahor
הֲשָׁלוֹם לוֹ וַיֹּאמְרוּ שָׁלוֹם[d] וְהִנֵּה רָחֵל
Rachel behold and ; Peace ; said they And ? him to peace [Is]
7 בִּתּוֹ בָּאָה עִם־הַצֹּאן׃[e] וַיֹּאמֶר[f] הֵן[g] עוֹד
still ,Behold : said he And .sheep the with coming is daughter his
הַיּוֹם גָּדוֹל לֹא־עֵת הֵאָסֵף
[4]gathered [3]being of time the not [is it] great [is] day the
8 הַמִּקְנֶה הַשְׁקוּ הַצֹּאן וּלְכוּ רְעוּ׃ וַיֹּאמְרוּ
:said they And .[them] feed ,go and , sheep the ye water ;[2]cattle's [1]the

dren of the east.
2 And he looked,
and behold a
well in the field,
and, lo, three
flocks of sheep
lying there by it;
for out of that
well they water-
ed the flocks:
and the stone
upon the well's
mouth was
great. 3 And
thither were all
the flocks gath-
ered: and they
rolled the stone
from the well's
mouth, and wa-
tered the sheep,
and put the
stone again up-
on the well's
mouth in its
place.
4 And Jacob
said unto
them, My breth-
ren, whence be
ye? And they
said, Of Haran
are we. 5 And
he said unto
them, Know ye
Laban the son
of Nahor?
And they said,
We know him. 6
And he said un-
to them, Is it
well with him?
And they said,
It is well; and
behold, Rachel
his daughter
cometh with the
sheep. 7 And he
said, Lo, it is
yet high day,
neither is it
time that the
cattle should be
gathered to-
gether: water ye
the sheep, and
go and feed
them. 8 And
they said, We

a G. omits בני; G. adds, *to Laban the son of Bethuel the Syrian, and brother of Rebekah, the mother of Jacob and Esau*, cf. 28: 5.

b G., S. omit הנה.

c S. *drink* יִשְׁקוּ.

d G. adds *he was still speaking*.

e G. adds *her father*.

f G., V. add *Jacob;* S. adds, *Jacob to them;* Sm. adds, *to them*.

g G. omits.

We cannot, until all the flocks be gathered together, and *till* they roll the stone from the well's mouth; then we water the sheep.
9 And while he yet spake with them, Rachel came with her father's sheep: for she kept them. 10 And it came to pass, when Jacob saw Rachel the daughter of Laban his mother's brother, and the sheep of Laban his mother's brother, that Jacob went near, and rolled the stone from the well's mouth, and watered the flock of Laban his mother's brother. 11 And Jacob kissed Rachel, and lifted up his voice and wept. 12 And Jacob told Rachel that he *was* her father's brother, and that he *was* Rebekah's son: and she ran and told her father. 13 And it came to pass, when Laban heard the tidings of Jacob his sister's son, that he ran to meet him, and embraced him, and kissed him, and brought him to his house. And he told Laban all these things. 14 And

לֹא נוּכַל עַד אֲשֶׁר יֵאָסְפוּ כָל־הָעֲדָרִים
,flocks the all gathered are that until ,able [2]are [1]we [3]Not

וְגָלְלוּ אֶת־הָאֶבֶן מֵעַל פִּי הַבְּאֵר
,well the of mouth the upon from stone the roll they and

9 עִמָּם מְדַבֵּר עוֹדֶנּוּ הַצֹּאן׃ וְהִשְׁקִינוּ
,them with speaking [was] still he [As] .sheep the water we and

וְרָחֵל ׀ [a] בָּאָה עִם־הַצֹּאן אֲשֶׁר לְאָבִיהָ
,father her to [were] which sheep the with came Rachel (and)

10 כִּי רֹעָה הִוא׃ [b] וַיְהִי כַּאֲשֶׁר רָאָה
saw when pass to came it And .she [was] shepherdess a for

יַעֲקֹב אֶת־רָחֵל בַּת־לָבָן אֲחִי אִמּוֹ
,mother his of brother the Laban of daughter the Rachel Jacob

וְאֶת־צֹאן [c] לָבָן אֲחִי אִמּוֹ [c] וַיִּגַּשׁ יַעֲקֹב
Jacob near came that ;mother his of brother the Laban of sheep the and

וַיָּגֶל אֶת־הָאֶבֶן מֵעַל פִּי הַבְּאֵר
,well the of mouth the upon from stone the rolled and

וַיַּשְׁקְ אֶת־צֹאן לָבָן אֲחִי אִמּוֹ׃
.mother his of brother the Laban of sheep the watered and

11 וַיִּשַּׁק יַעֲקֹב לְרָחֵל וַיִּשָּׂא אֶת־קֹלוֹ וַיֵּבְךְּ׃
.wept and ,voice his up lifted and ,Rachel (to) Jacob kissed And

12 וַיַּגֵּד יַעֲקֹב [d] לְרָחֵל כִּי אֲחִי אָבִיהָ
[was] father her of brother the that Rachel to Jacob told And

הוּא וְכִי בֶן־רִבְקָה הוּא וַתָּרָץ וַתַּגֵּד
told and ran she and ;he [was] Rebekah of son the that and he

13 לְאָבִיהָ׃ [e] וַיְהִי כִשְׁמֹעַ לָבָן אֶת־
[1]Laban's [2]hearing at pass to came it And .father her to

שֵׁמַע ׀ [f] יַעֲקֹב בֶּן־אֲחֹתוֹ וַיָּרָץ [g] לִקְרָאתוֹ
,him meet to ran he that ,sister his of son the Jacob of report the

וַיְחַבֶּק־לוֹ וַיְנַשֶּׁק־לוֹ וַיְבִיאֵהוּ
in him brought and ,him (to) kissed and ,him (to) embraced and

אֶל־בֵּיתוֹ וַיְסַפֵּר לְלָבָן אֵת כָּל־הַדְּבָרִים הָאֵלֶּה׃
.[1]these [2]things all Laban to related he and ;house his unto

cannot, until all the flocks be gathered together, and they roll the stone from the well's mouth; then we water the sheep.
9 While he yet spake with them, Rachel came with her father's sheep; for she kept them. 10 And it came to pass, when Jacob saw Rachel the daughter of Laban his mother's brother, and the sheep of Laban his mother's brother, that Jacob went near, and rolled the stone from the well's mouth, and watered the flock of Laban his mother's brother. 11 And Jacob kissed Rachel, and lifted up his voice, and wept. 12 And Jacob told Rachel that he was her father's brother, and that he was Rebekah's son: and she ran and told her father. 13 And it came to pass, when Laban heard the tidings of Jacob his sister's son, that he ran to meet him, and embraced him, and kissed him, and brought him to his house. And he told Laban all these things. 14 And

---

a G. adds, *the daughter of Laban.*

b G. adds, *the sheep of her father;* V. adds, *the flock.*

c G. omits, ואת-צאן---אמו.

d G. omits.

e G. adds, *according to these words.*

f G. has, for שמע, *name,* שֵׁם

g G., S., V. omit ו.

Laban said to
him, Surely thou
art my bone and
my flesh. And
he abode with
him the space of
a month.
15 And Laban
said unto Jacob,
Because thou
art my brother,
shouldest thou
therefore serve
me for nought?
tell me, what
shall thy wages
be? 16 And
Laban had
two daugh-
ters: the name
of the elder *was*
Leah, and the
name of the
younger *was*
Rachel. 17 Leah
was tender eyed;
but Rachel was
beautiful and
well favoured. 18
And Jacob loved
Rachel; and said
I will serve thee
seven years for
Rachel thy
younger daugh-
ter. 19 And La-
ban said, *It is*
better that I
give her to thee,
than that I
should give her
to another man:
abide with me.
20 And Jacob
served seven
years for Ra-
chel; and they
seemed unto
him *but* a few
days, for the
love he had to
her.
21 And Jacob
said unto La-
ban, Give *me*
my wife, for my
days are fulfill-
ed, that I may
go in unto her.
22 And Laban
gathered togeth-
er all the men
of the place,
and made a
feast. 23 And it
came to pass in
the evening,
that he took
Leah his daugh-
ter, and brought
her to him; and

14 וַיֹּאמֶר לוֹ לָבָן אַךְ[a] עַצְמִי וּבְשָׂרִי
[art] flesh my and bone my Surely :Laban him to said And

15 אָתָּה וַיֵּשֶׁב עִמּוֹ חֹדֶשׁ יָמִים׃ וַיֹּאמֶר
said And .days of month a him with dwelt he and ;thou

לָבָן לְיַעֲקֹב הֲכִי־אָחִי אַתָּה וַעֲבַדְתַּנִי
me serve shouldest and ,[art] thou brother my that [it Is] :Jacob to Laban

16 חִנָּם הַגִּידָה לִּי מַה־מַּשְׂכֻּרְתֶּךָ׃ וּלְלָבָן
[were] Laban to And ?wages thy what ,me to Tell ?nothing for

שְׁתֵּי בָנוֹת שֵׁם הַגְּדֹלָה לֵאָה וְשֵׁם
of name the and ,Leah [being] elder the of name the ,daughters two

17 הַקְּטַנָּה רָחֵל׃ וְעֵינֵי לֵאָה רַכּוֹת
,weak [were] Leah of eyes the And .Rachel younger the

וְרָחֵל הָיְתָה יְפַת־תֹּאַר וִיפַת מַרְאֶה׃
.appearance of beautiful and form of beautiful was Rachel and

18 וַיֶּאֱהַב יַעֲקֹב אֶת־רָחֵל וַיֹּאמֶר אֶעֱבָדְךָ
thee serve will I :said he and ,Rachel Jacob loved And

19 שֶׁבַע שָׁנִים בְּרָחֵל בִּתְּךָ הַקְּטַנָּה׃ וַיֹּאמֶר[b]
said And .[1]younger [2]daughter thy Rachel for years seven

לָבָן טוֹב תִּתִּי אֹתָהּ לָךְ מִתִּתִּי
giving my [than rather] (from) thee to her giving my [is] Good :Laban

20 אֹתָהּ לְאִישׁ אַחֵר שְׁבָה עִמָּדִי׃ וַיַּעֲבֹד יַעֲקֹב
Jacob served And .me with dwell ;[1]another [2]man to her

בְּרָחֵל שֶׁבַע שָׁנִים וַיִּהְיוּ[c] בְעֵינָיו כְּיָמִים
[2]days like eyes his in were they and ;years seven Rachel for

21 אֲחָדִים בְּאַהֲבָתוֹ אֹתָהּ׃[c] וַיֹּאמֶר יַעֲקֹב אֶל־לָבָן
:Laban unto Jacob said And .her loving his in ,[1]some

הָבָה[d] אֶת־אִשְׁתִּי כִּי מָלְאוּ יָמָי וְאָבוֹאָה
in go me let and ,days my full are because ,wife my Give

22 אֵלֶיהָ׃ וַיֶּאֱסֹף לָבָן אֶת־כָּל־אַנְשֵׁי הַמָּקוֹם
,place the of men the all Laban gathered And .her unto

23 וַיַּעַשׂ מִשְׁתֶּה׃ וַיְהִי[e] בָעֶרֶב[e] וַיִּקַּח[f]
took he that ,evening the in pass to came it And .feast a made and

אֶת־לֵאָה בִתּוֹ וַיָּבֵא אֹתָהּ אֵלָיו[g]
;him unto her brought and ,daughter his Leah

Laban said unto
him, Surely thou
art my bone and
my flesh. And
he abode with
him the space of
a month.
15 And Laban
said unto Jacob,
Because thou
art my brother,
shouldest thou
therefore serve
me for nought?
tell me, what
shall thy wages
be? 16 And La-
ban had two
daughters: the
name of the
elder was Leah,
and the name of
the younger was
Rachel. 17 And
Leah's eyes
were tender;
but Rachel was
beautiful and
well favoured. 18
And Jacob loved
Rachel; and he
said, I will serve
thee seven years
for Rachel thy
younger daugh-
ter. 19 And La-
ban said, It is
better that I
give her to thee,
than that I
should give her
to another man:
abide with me.
20 And Jacob
served seven
years for Ra-
chel; and they
seemed unto
him but a few
days, for the
love he had to
her.
21 And Jacob
said unto La-
ban, Give me
my wife, for my
days are fulfill-
ed, that I may
go in unto her.
22 And Laban
gathered to-
gether all the
men of the place,
and made a
feast. 23 And it
came to pass in
the evening,
that he took
Leah his daugh-
ter, and brought
her to him; and

a G., V. omit.
b G. adds, *to him;* S., V. omit ו.
c G. omits ויהיו---אתה.
d G., S. add, *to me.*
e G. omits ב; so S. rendering, *and when it was evening.*
f G. adds, *Laban.*
g G. *unto Jacob.*

he went in unto her. 24 And Laban gave unto his daughter Leah, Zilpah his maid *for* an handmaid. 25 And it came to pass, that in the morning, behold, it *was* Leah: and he said to Laban, What *is* this thou hast done unto me? did not I serve with thee for Rachel? wherefore then hast thou beguiled me? 26 And Laban said, It must not be so done in our country, to give the younger before the firstborn. 27 Fulfil her week, and we will give thee this also, for the service which thou shalt serve with me yet seven other years. 28 And Jacob did so, and fulfilled her week: and he gave him Rachel his daughter to wife also. 29 And Laban gave to Rachel his daughter, Bilhah his handmaid, to be her maid. 30 And he went in also unto Rachel, and he loved also Rachel more than Leah, and served with him yet seven other years.

31 And when the LORD saw that Leah *was* hated, he opened her womb:

24 וַיָּבֹא אֵלֶיהָ[a]: וַיִּתֵּן לָבָן לָהּ אֶת־זִלְפָּה
Zilpah her to Laban gave And .her unto in came he and

שִׁפְחָתוֹ לְלֵאָה בִתּוֹ שִׁפְחָה׃
.slave female a [as] daughter his Leah to ,slave female his

25 וַיְהִי[b] בַבֹּקֶר[b] וְהִנֵּה־הִוא[c] לֵאָה
; Leah [was] she behold and ,morning the in pass to came it And

וַיֹּאמֶר[d] אֶל־לָבָן מַה־זֹּאת עָשִׂיתָ לִּי
? me to done hast thou this [is] What : Laban unto said he and

הֲלֹא[e] בְרָחֵל עָבַדְתִּי עִמָּךְ וְלָמָּה[f]
why and ? thee with serve I Rachel for not [Did]

26 רִמִּיתָנִי׃ וַיֹּאמֶר לָבָן[g] לֹא־יֵעָשֶׂה כֵן
so done not is It :Laban said And ? me deceived thou hast

27 בִּמְקוֹמֵנוּ לָתֵת הַצְּעִירָה לִפְנֵי הַבְּכִירָה׃ מַלֵּא
Fill .first-born the before younger the give to ,place our in

שְׁבֻעַ זֹאת וְנִתְּנָה[h] לְךָ גַּם־אֶת־זֹאת
,one [other] this also thee to given be let and ,one this of week the

בַּעֲבֹדָה אֲשֶׁר תַּעֲבֹד עִמָּדִי עוֹד שֶׁבַע־
seven still me with serve shalt thou which service a for

28 שָׁנִים אֲחֵרוֹת׃ וַיַּעַשׂ יַעֲקֹב כֵּן וַיְמַלֵּא שְׁבֻעַ
of week the filled he and ,so Jacob did And .[1]other [2]years

זֹאת וַיִּתֶּן־לוֹ[i] אֶת־רָחֵל בִּתּוֹ לוֹ
him to daughter his Rachel him to gave he and ;one this

29 לְאִשָּׁה׃ וַיִּתֵּן לָבָן לְרָחֵל בִּתּוֹ אֶת־בִּלְהָה
Bilhah daughter his Rachel to Laban gave And .wife a for

30 שִׁפְחָתוֹ לָהּ לְשִׁפְחָה׃ וַיָּבֹא גַּם[j]
also in came he And .slave female a for her for ,slave female his

אֶל־רָחֵל וַיֶּאֱהַב[j] גַּם־אֶת־רָחֵל מִלֵּאָה
;Leah (from) [than more] Rachel also loved he and ,Rachel unto

וַיַּעֲבֹד עִמּוֹ עוֹד[j] שֶׁבַע־שָׁנִים אֲחֵרוֹת׃
.[1]other [2]years seven still him with served he and

31 וַיַּרְא יְהוָה[k] כִּי־שְׂנוּאָה לֵאָה וַיִּפְתַּח
opened he and ,Leah hated [was] that Jehovah saw And

he went in unto her. 24 And Laban gave Zilpah his handmaid unto his daughter Leah for an handmaid. 25 And it came to pass in the morning that, behold, it was Leah: and he said to Laban, What is this thou hast done unto me? did not I serve with thee for Rachel? wherefore then hast thou beguiled me? 26 And Laban said, It is not so done in our place, to give the younger before the firstborn. 27 Fulfil the week of this one, and we will give thee the other also for the service which thou shalt serve with me yet seven other years. 28 And Jacob did so, and fulfilled her week: and he gave him Rachel his daughter to wife. 29 And Laban gave to Rachel his daughter Bilhah his handmaid to be her handmaid. 30 And he went in also unto Rachel, and he loved also Rachel more than Leah, and served with him yet seven other years.

31 And the LORD saw that Leah was hated, and he opened

a Sm., G. add *Jacob.*

b G. omits ב; so S. rendering, *and when it was morning.*

c For הנה, S. has, *he saw* חזה.

d G. adds, *Jacob.*

e S. has *behold,* הנה.

f S., V. omit, *and,* ו.

g S. adds, *to Jacob.*

h Sm., G., S., V. have, *and I will give,* ואתנה.

i G. omits לו, and adds, *Laban.*

j G. omits.

k G. adds, *God.*

but Rachel *was*
barren. 32 And
Leah conceived,
and bare a son,
and she called
his name Reu-
ben: for she
said, Surely the
LORD hath
looked upon
my affliction;
now therefore
my husband
will love me. 33
And she con-
ceived again,
and bare a son;
and said, Be-
cause the LORD
hath heard that
I *was* hated, he
hath therefore
given me this
son also: and
she called his
name Simeon.
34 And she con-
ceived again,
and bare a son;
and said, Now
this time will
my husband be
joined unto me,
because I have
born him three
sons: therefore
was his name
called Levi. 35
And she con-
ceived again,
and bare a son:
and she said,
Now will I
praise the LORD:
therefore she
called his name
Judah; and
left bearing.

אֶת־רַחְמָהּ וְרָחֵל עֲקָרָה׃ וַתַּהַר לֵאָה 32
Leah conceived And .barren [being] Rachel (and) ,womb her

וַתֵּלֶד בֵּן[a] וַתִּקְרָא שְׁמוֹ רְאוּבֵן כִּי[b] אָמְרָה[b]
:said she for ;Reuben name his called she and ,son a bore and

כִּי־רָאָה יְהוָה[c] בְּעָנְיִי כִּי[d] עַתָּה יֶאֱהָבַנִי
me love will now for ,affliction my upon Jehovah looked has Surely

אִישִׁי׃ וַתַּהַר עוֹד[e] וַתֵּלֶד בֵּן[f] וַתֹּאמֶר 33
:said and ,son a bore and again conceived she And .husband my

כִּי־שָׁמַע יְהוָה כִּי־שְׂנוּאָה אָנֹכִי וַיִּתֶּן
given has and ,I [am] hated that Jehovah heard has Surely

לִי גַּם־אֶת־זֶה וַתִּקְרָא שְׁמוֹ שִׁמְעוֹן׃
.Simeon name his called she and ;one this also me to

וַתַּהַר עוֹד וַתֵּלֶד בֵּן וַתֹּאמֶר עַתָּה 34
Now :said she and ;son a bore and again conceived she And

הַפַּעַם יִלָּוֶה אִישִׁי אֵלַי כִּי־
because ,me unto husband my attached be will time [this] (the)

יָלַדְתִּי לוֹ שְׁלֹשָׁה בָנִים עַל־כֵּן קָרָא[g]־שְׁמוֹ
name his called one therefore ;sons three him to borne have I

לֵוִי׃ וַתַּהַר עוֹד וַתֵּלֶד בֵּן וַתֹּאמֶר 35
:said she and ;son a bore and again conceived she And .Levi

הַפַּעַם אוֹדֶה אֶת־יְהוָה עַל־כֵּן קָרְאָה
called she therefore ;Jehovah praise I time [this] (The)

שְׁמוֹ יְהוּדָה וַתַּעֲמֹד מִלֶּדֶת׃
.bearing from ceased she and ;Judah name his

her womb: but
Rachel was
barren. 32 And
Leah conceived,
and bare a son,
and she called
his name Reu-
ben: for she
said, Because
the LORD hath
looked upon
my affliction;
for now my hus-
band will love
me. 33 And she
conceived a-
gain, and bare
a son; and said,
Because the
LORD hath
heard that I
am hated, he
hath therefore
given me this
son also: and
she called his
name Simeon.
34 And she con-
ceived again,
and bare a son;
and said, Now
this time will
my husband be
joined unto me,
because I have
borne him three
sons: therefore
was his name
called Levi. 35
And she con-
ceived again,
and bare a son:
and she said,
This time will I
praise the
LORD: therefore
she called his
name Judah;
and she left
bearing.

30

AND when
Rachel saw that
she bare Jacob
no children,
Rachel envied
her sister; and
said unto Jacob,
Give me chil-
dren, or else I
die. 2 And Ja-
cob's anger was

וַתֵּרֶא רָחֵל כִּי לֹא יָלְדָה לְיַעֲקֹב 1
,Jacob to bear [1]did [2]she [3]not that Rachel saw And

וַתְּקַנֵּא רָחֵל בַּאֲחֹתָהּ וַתֹּאמֶר אֶל־יַעֲקֹב
: Jacob unto said she and ;sister her of Rachel jealous was and

הָבָה־לִּי בָנִים וְאִם־אַיִן מֵתָה אָנֹכִי׃ וַיִּחַר 2
glowed And .I [am] die to about ,not if and ,sons me to Give

And when
Rachel saw that
she bare Jacob
no children,
Rachel envied
her sister; and
she said unto
Jacob, Give me
children, or else
I die. 2 And
Jacob's anger

---

a G. adds, *to Jacob.*
b G., V. have *saying*, לֵאמֹר.
c S. has, *God.*
d G., S., V omit.
e G. adds, *Leah.*
f G. has, *a second son to Jacob.*
g Sm., S. have, *she called*, קָרְאָה.

kindled against Rachel: and he said, *Am* I in God's stead, who hath withheld from thee the fruit of the womb? 3 And she said, Behold my maid Bilhah, go in unto her; and she shall bear upon my knees, that I may also have children by her. 4 And she gave him Bilhah her handmaid to wife: and Jacob went in unto her. 5 And Bilhah conceived, and bare Jacob a son. 6 And Rachel said, God hath judged me, and hath also heard my voice, and hath given me a son: therefore called she his name Dan. 7 And Bilhah Rachel's maid conceived again, and bare Jacob a second son.

8 And Rachel said, With great wrestlings have I wrestled with my sister, and I have prevailed: and she called his name Naphtali. 9 When Leah saw that she had left bearing, she took Zilpah her maid, and gave her Jacob to wife. 10 And Zilpah Leah's maid bare Jacob a son. 11 And Leah said, A troop cometh: and she called his name Gad.

אַף יַעֲקֹב בְּרָחֵל וַיֹּאמֶר[a] הֲתַחַת
of place In :said he and ; Rachel against Jacob of anger the

אֱלֹהִים אָנֹכִי אֲשֶׁר־מָנַע מִמֵּךְ פְּרִי־בָטֶן׃
?womb the of fruit the thee from back kept has who ,I [am] God

3 וַתֹּאמֶר[b] הִנֵּה אֲמָתִי בִלְהָה בֹּא אֵלֶיהָ
;her unto in go ,Bilhah maidservant my Behold :said she And

וְתֵלֵד עַל־בִּרְכַּי וְאִבָּנֶה גַם־אָנֹכִי
,I also ,built be me let and ,knees my upon bear her let and

4 מִמֶּנָּה׃ וַתִּתֶּן־לוֹ אֶת־בִּלְהָה שִׁפְחָתָהּ[c]
,slave female her Bilhah him to gave she And .her from

5 לְאִשָּׁה וַיָּבֹא אֵלֶיהָ יַעֲקֹב[d]׃ וַתַּהַר בִּלְהָה[e]
,Bilhah conceived And .Jacob her unto in came and ;wife a for

6 וַתֵּלֶד לְיַעֲקֹב בֵּן׃ וַתֹּאמֶר רָחֵל דָּנַנִּי
me judged Has : Rachel said And .son a Jacob to bore And

אֱלֹהִים וְגַם[f] שָׁמַע בְּקֹלִי וַיִּתֶּן־לִי
me to given has and ,voice my to hearkened has also and God

7 בֵּן עַל־כֵּן קָרְאָה שְׁמוֹ דָּן׃ וַתַּהַר עוֹד
again conceived And .Dan name his called she therefore ;son a

וַתֵּלֶד בִּלְהָה שִׁפְחַת רָחֵל בֵּן שֵׁנִי לְיַעֲקֹב׃
.Jacob to [1]second [2]son a Rachel of slave female the Bilhah bore and

8 וַתֹּאמֶר רָחֵל נַפְתּוּלֵי אֱלֹהִים נִפְתַּלְתִּי עִם־
with struggled have I God of Struggles : Rachel said And

אֲחֹתִי גַּם־יָכֹלְתִּי[g] וַתִּקְרָא שְׁמוֹ נַפְתָּלִי׃
.Naphtali name his called she and ;prevailed have I also ,sister my

9 וַתֵּרֶא לֵאָה כִּי עָמְדָה מִלֶּדֶת וַתִּקַּח
took she and ,bearing from ceased had she that Leah saw And

אֶת־זִלְפָּה שִׁפְחָתָהּ וַתִּתֵּן אֹתָהּ לְיַעֲקֹב לְאִשָּׁה׃
.wife a for Jacob to her gave and ,slave female her Zilpah

10 וַתֵּלֶד[h] זִלְפָּה שִׁפְחַת לֵאָה לְיַעֲקֹב בֵּן׃
.son a Jacob to Leah of slave female the Zilpah bore and

11 וַתֹּאמֶר לֵאָה בָּגָד[i] וַתִּקְרָא אֶת־שְׁמוֹ גָּד׃
.Gad name his called she and ;fortune With : Leah said And

was kindled against Rachel: and he said, Am I in God's stead, who hath withheld from thee the fruit of the womb? 3 And she said, Behold my maid Bilhah, go in unto her; that she may bear upon my knees, and I also may obtain children by her. 4 And she gave him Bilhah her handmaid to wife; and Jacob went in unto her. 5 And Bilhah conceived, and bare Jacob a son. 6 And Rachel said, God hath judged me, and hath also heard my voice, and hath given me a son: therefore called she his name Dan. 7 And Bilhah Rachel's handmaid conceived again, and bare Jacob a second son.

8 And Rachel said, With mighty wrestlings have I wrestled with my sister, and have prevailed; and she called his name Naphtali. 9 When Leah saw that she had left bearing, she took Zilpah her handmaid, and gave her to Jacob to wife. 10 And Zilpah Leah's handmaid bare Jacob a son. 11 And Leah said, Fortunate! and she called his name Gad. 12

---

a G., S., V. add, *to her.*

b S. adds, *to him;* G. adds, *Rachel to Jacob.*

c G. adds, *to him.*

d S. omits.

e G. adds, *the maidservant of Rachel.*

f G., V. omit גם.

g Sm., S. add, *and,* וגם.

h G. adds, *and Jacob came in unto her and she conceived.*

i S. *my fortune comes;* T., Aq. *fortune comes;* Sym. *Gad has come;* all prob. read בא גד.

12 And Zilpah
Leah's maid
bare Jacob a
second son. 13
And Leah said,
Happy am I,
for the daugh-
ters will call me
blessed: and
she called his
name Asher.
14 And Reu-
ben went in
the days of
wheat harvest,
and found man-
drakes in the
field, and
brought them
unto his mother
Leah. Then Ra-
chel said to
Leah, Give me,
I pray thee, of
thy son's man-
drakes. 15 And
she said unto
her, *Is it* a
small matter
that thou hast
taken my hus-
band? and
wouldest thou
take away my
son's man-
drakes also?
And Rachel
said, Therefore
he shall lie with
thee to night for
thy son's man-
drakes. 16 And
Jacob came out
of the field in
the evening,
and Leah went
out to meet him,
and said, Thou
must come in un-
to me; for sure-
ly I have hired
thee with my
son's man-
drakes. And he
lay with her that
night. 17 And
God hearkened
unto Leah, and
she conceived,
and bare Jacob
the fifth son. 18
And Leah said,
God hath given
me my hire, be-
cause I have giv-
en my maiden to
my husband; and

12 [a]וַתֵּלֶד זִלְפָּה שִׁפְחַת לֵאָה בֵּן שֵׁנִי לְיַעֲקֹב׃
.Jacob to [1]second [2]son a Leah of slave female the Zilpah bore And

13 וַתֹּאמֶר לֵאָה בְּאָשְׁרִי כִּי אִשְּׁרוּנִי
happy me call to sure are for ; happiness my In : Leah said And

14 בָּנוֹת [b] וַתִּקְרָא אֶת־שְׁמוֹ אָשֵׁר׃ וַיֵּלֶךְ רְאוּבֵן
Reuben went And .Asher name his called she and ; daughters

בִּימֵי קְצִיר־חִטִּים וַיִּמְצָא דוּדָאִים בַּשָּׂדֶה
,field the in love-apples found and ,wheat of harvest the of days the in

וַיָּבֵא אֹתָם אֶל־לֵאָה אִמּוֹ וַתֹּאמֶר רָחֵל
Rachel said and ; mother his Leah unto them brought he and

אֶל־לֵאָה תְּנִי־נָא לִי מִדּוּדָאֵי בְּנֵךְ׃
.son thy of love-apples the from me to ,pray ,Give : Leah unto

15 וַתֹּאמֶר לָהּ [c] הַמְעַט קַחְתֵּךְ אֶת־אִישִׁי
,[4]husband [3]my [2]taking [1]thy [5]little Is : her to said she and

וְלָקַחַת גַּם אֶת־דּוּדָאֵי בְּנִי וַתֹּאמֶר
said And ? son my of love-apples the also taking for [thou art] and

רָחֵל לָכֵן [d] יִשְׁכַּב עִמָּךְ הַלַּיְלָה תַּחַת
for return in tonight thee with lie shall he Therefore : Rachel

16 דּוּדָאֵי בְנֵךְ׃ וַיָּבֹא יַעֲקֹב מִן־הַשָּׂדֶה
field the from Jacob in came And .son thy of love-apples the

בָּעֶרֶב וַתֵּצֵא לֵאָה לִקְרָאתוֹ וַתֹּאמֶר אֵלַי
me Unto : said she and ,him meet to Leah out went and ,evening at

תָּבוֹא [e] כִּי שָׂכֹר שְׂכַרְתִּיךָ
thee hired have I hiring because ,in come shouldest thou

בְּדוּדָאֵי בְּנִי וַיִּשְׁכַּב עִמָּהּ בַּלַּיְלָה
[2]night in her with lay he and ; son my of love-apples the with

17 הוּא׃ וַיִּשְׁמַע אֱלֹהִים אֶל־לֵאָה [f] וַתַּהַר
conceived she and ,Leah unto God hearkened And .[1]that

18 וַתֵּלֶד לְיַעֲקֹב בֵּן חֲמִישִׁי׃ וַתֹּאמֶר לֵאָה נָתַן
given Has : Leah said And .[1]fifth [2]son a Jacob to bore and

אֱלֹהִים שְׂכָרִי אֲשֶׁר־נָתַתִּי שִׁפְחָתִי לְאִישִׁי
; husband my to slave female my gave I because ,hire my God

And Zilpah
Leah's hand-
maid bare Jacob
a second son. 13
And Leah said,
Happy am I!
for the daugh-
ters will call me
happy: and she
called his name
Asher.
14 And Reu-
ben went in the
days of wheat
harvest, and
found man-
drakes in the
field, and
brought them
unto his mother
Leah. Then
Rachel said to
Leah, Give me,
I pray thee, of
thy son's man-
drakes. 15 And
she said unto
her, Is it a small
matter that thou
hast taken a-
way my hus-
band? and
wouldest thou
take away my
son's man-
drakes also?
And Rachel
said, Therefore
he shall lie with
thee to-night for
thy son's man-
drakes. 16 And
Jacob came
from the field
in the evening,
and Leah went
out to meet
him, and said,
Thou must
come in unto
me; for I have
surely hired thee
with my son's
mandrakes.
And he lay with
her that night.
17 And God
hearkened unto
Leah, and she
conceived, and
bare Jacob a
fifth son. 18
And Leah said,
God hath given
me my hire, be-
cause I gave my
handmaid to my

---

a G. adds, *and she conceived again.*

b G. has, *all the women.*

c G. has, *Leah,* לאה; S. adds, *Leah.*

d G. has, *not so,* לֹא כֵן.

e Sm. adds, *tonight,* הלילה; G. perh. the same, rendering, *today.*

f G. has, *her.*

she called his
name Issachar.
19 And Leah
conceived again,
and bare Jacob
the sixth son. 20
And Leah said,
God hath en-
dued me *with*
a good dowry;
now will my
husband dwell
with me, be-
cause I have
borne him six
sons: and she
called his name
Zebulun. 21 And
afterwards she
bare a daughter,
and called her
name Dinah.

22 And God
remembered
Rachel, and
God hearkened
to her, and o-
pened her
womb. 23 And
she conceived,
and bare a son;
and said, God
hath taken a-
way my re-
proach: 24 And
she called his
name Joseph;
and said, The
LORD shall add
to me another
son.

25 And it
came to pass,
when Rachel
had born Jo-
seph, that Jacob
said unto La-
ban, Send me
away, that I
may go unto
mine own place,
and to my coun-
try. 26 Give *me*
my wives and
my children,
for whom I
have served
thee, and let me
go: for thou
knowest my
service which I
have done thee.
27 And Laban
said unto him, I
pray thee, if I
have found
favour in thine
eyes, *tarry: for*
I have learned
by experience

19 וַתִּקְרָא שְׁמוֹ יִשָּׂשכָר[a]׃ וַתַּהַר עוֹד לֵאָה
Leah again conceived And .Issachar name his called she and

20 וַתֵּלֶד בֵּן־שִׁשִּׁי לְיַעֲקֹב׃ וַתֹּאמֶר לֵאָה זְבָדַנִי
me [to] presented Has :Leah said And .Jacob to son sixth a bore and

אֱלֹהִים ׀ אֹתִי זֵבֶד טוֹב הַפַּעַם יִזְבְּלֵנִי
me exalt will time [this] (the) ;[1]good [2]present a (me) God

אִישִׁי כִּי־יָלַדְתִּי לוֹ שִׁשָּׁה בָנִים
;sons six him to borne have I because ,husband my

21 וַתִּקְרָא אֶת־שְׁמוֹ זְבֻלוּן[b]׃ וְאַחַר יָלְדָה
bore she afterwards And .Zebulun name his called she and

22 בַּת וַתִּקְרָא אֶת־שְׁמָהּ דִּינָה׃ וַיִּזְכֹּר
remembered And .Dinah name her called and ,daughter a

אֱלֹהִים אֶת־רָחֵל וַיִּשְׁמַע אֵלֶיהָ אֱלֹהִים וַיִּפְתַּח
opened and ,God her unto hearkened and ,Rachel God

23 אֶת־רַחְמָהּ׃ וַתַּהַר וַתֵּלֶד בֵּן[c] וַתֹּאמֶר[d]
:said she and ,son a bore and conceived she And .womb her

24 אָסַף אֱלֹהִים אֶת־חֶרְפָּתִי׃ וַתִּקְרָא אֶת־שְׁמוֹ
name his called she And .reproach my God removed Has

יוֹסֵף לֵאמֹר יֹסֵף יְהוָה[e] לִי בֵּן אַחֵר׃
.[1]another [2]son me to Jehovah add May :saying ,Joseph

25 וַיְהִי כַּאֲשֶׁר יָלְדָה רָחֵל אֶת־יוֹסֵף
,Joseph Rachel borne had when ,pass to came it And

וַיֹּאמֶר יַעֲקֹב אֶל־לָבָן שַׁלְּחֵנִי וְאֵלְכָה
go me let and away me Send :Laban unto Jacob said that

26 אֶל־מְקוֹמִי וּלְאַרְצִי׃ תְּנָה[f] אֶת־נָשַׁי וְאֶת־יְלָדַי
,children my and wives my Give .land my to and place my unto

אֲשֶׁר עָבַדְתִּי אֹתְךָ בָּהֵן וְאֵלֵכָה
;go me let and ,(them for) thee served have I whom [for]

כִּי אַתָּה יָדַעְתָּ אֶת־עֲבֹדָתִי אֲשֶׁר עֲבַדְתִּיךָ׃
.thee served have I which [with] service my knowest thou for

27 וַיֹּאמֶר אֵלָיו[g] לָבָן אִם־נָא מָצָאתִי חֵן
favor found have I ,pray I ,If :Laban him unto said And

בְּעֵינֶיךָ נִחַשְׁתִּי וַיְבָרְכֵנִי
me blessed has and omens the observed have I — eyes thine in

husband: and
she called his
name Issachar.
19 And Leah
conceived a-
gain, and bare a
sixth son to
Jacob. 20 And
Leah said, God
hath endowed
me with a good
dowry; now will
my husband
dwell with me,
because I have
borne him six
sons: and she
called his name
Zebulun. 21
And afterwards
she bare a
daughter, and
called her name
Dinah.

22 And God
remembered
Rachel, and
God hearkened
to her, and open-
ed her womb. 23
And she con-
ceived, and
bare a son: and
said, God hath
taken away my
reproach: 24
and she called
his name Jo-
seph, saying,
The LORD add
to me another
son.

25 And it
came to pass,
when Rachel
had borne Jo-
seph, that Ja-
cob said unto
Laban, Send
me away, that I
may go unto
mine own place,
and to my coun-
try. 26 Give me
my wives and
my children for
whom I have
served thee,
and let me go:
for thou know-
est my service
wherewith I
have served
thee. 27 And
Laban said unto
him, If now I
have found fa-
vor in thine
eyes, *tarry:*
for I have
divined that the

a G. adds, *which is hire.*
b G. adds, *and she ceased to bear.*
c G. adds, *to Jacob.*
d G. adds, *Rachel.*
e G., S. have, *God.*
f S., V. add, *to me.*
g S. has, *to Jacob.*

that the LORD
hath blessed me
for thy sake. 28
And he said, Ap-
point me thy
wages, and I will
give *it*. 29 And
he said unto him,
Thou knowest
how I have
served thee, and
how thy cattle
was with me. 30
For *it was* little
which thou
hadst before I
came, and it is
now increased
unto a multi-
tude; and the
LORD hath
blessed thee
since my com-
ing: and now
when shall I
provide for mine
own house also?
31 And he said,
What shall I
give thee? And
Jacob said,
Thou shalt not
give me any
thing: if thou
wilt do this thing
for me, I will
again feed *and*
keep thy flock.
32 I will pass
through all thy
flock to day, re-
moving from
thence all the
speckled and
spotted cattle,
and all the
brown cattle a-
mong the sheep,
and the spotted
and speckled a-
mong the goats:
and *of such*
shall be my hire.
33 So shall my
righteousness
answer for me
in time to come,
when it shall
come for my

28 יְהוָה [a] בִּגְלָלֶךָ׃ וַיֹּאמַר [b] נָקְבָה שְׂכָרְךָ
wages thy Designate : said he And .thee of account on Jehovah

29 עָלַי וְאֶתֵּנָה׃ וַיֹּאמֶר אֵלָיו [c] אַתָּה יָדַעְתָּ
knowest Thou :him unto said he And .give me let and ,me upon

אֵת אֲשֶׁר עֲבַדְתִּיךָ וְאֵת אֲשֶׁר־הָיָה
⁴become ³have what and ,thee served have I [how] (what)

30 מִקְנְךָ אִתִּי׃ כִּי מְעַט אֲשֶׁר־הָיָה לְךָ [d] לְפָנַי
,me before thee to was which ,little a For .me with ²cattle ¹thy

וַיִּפְרֹץ לָרֹב וַיְבָרֶךְ יְהוָה אֹתְךָ
thee Jehovah blessed has and ,multitude a into spread has (and)

לְרַגְלִי וְעַתָּה מָתַי [e] אֶעֱשֶׂה גַם־אָנֹכִי לְבֵיתִי׃ [f]
? house my for ,I also ,work I shall when now and ; foot my at

31 וַיֹּאמֶר [g] מָה אֶתֶּן־לָךְ וַיֹּאמֶר [h] יַעֲקֹב
: Jacob said And ? thee to give I shall What : said he And

לֹא־תִתֶּן־לִי מְאוּמָה אִם־תַּעֲשֶׂה־לִּי הַדָּבָר
²thing me for do wilt thou if ; thing a me to give not shalt Thou

הַזֶּה [i] אָשׁוּבָה אֶרְעֶה צֹאנְךָ [j] אֶשְׁמֹר׃
.[it] keep will [and] ,flock thy tend will I ,return will I ,¹this

32 אֶעֱבֹר [k] בְּכָל־צֹאנְךָ [l] הַיּוֹם הָסֵר [m] מִשָּׁם
thence from removing ,today flock thy all in over pass will I

כָּל־שֶׂה [n] נָקֹד וְטָלוּא וְכָל־שֶׂה־חוּם
black sheep every and ;spotted and speckled sheep every

בַּכְּשָׂבִים [o] וְטָלוּא [p] וְנָקֹד בָּעִזִּים
goats the among speckled and spotted and ,lambs the among

33 וְהָיָה [q] שְׂכָרִי׃ וְעָנְתָה־בִּי צִדְקָתִי
rectitude my me for testify shall And .wages my be shall (and)

בְּיוֹם מָחָר כִּי־תָבוֹא [r] עַל־שְׂכָרִי [r]
wages my about in come mayest thou when tomorrow of day the in

LORD hath
blessed me for
thy sake. 28
And he said,
Appoint me thy
wages, and I
will give it. 29
And he said un-
to him, Thou
knowest how I
have served
thee, and how
thy cattle hath
fared with me.
30 For it was
little which thou
hadst before I
came, and it
hath increased
unto a multi-
tude; and the
LORD hath
blessed thee
whithersoever
I turned: and
now when shall
I provide for
mine own house
also? 31 And he
said, What shall
I give thee?
And Jacob said,
Thou shalt not
give me aught:
if thou wilt do
this thing for
me, I will a-
gain feed thy
flock and keep
it. 32 I will pass
through all thy
flock to-day, re-
moving from
thence every
speckled and
spotted one,
and every black
one among the
sheep, and the
spotted and
speckled among
the goats: and
of such shall be
my hire. 33 So
shall my right-
eousness answer
for me hereaft-
er, when thou
shalt come con-

---

a G., S., V. have, *God*.
b G., V. omit.
c G., S. add, *Jacob*.
d G. omits.
e S. has, *what*, מה.
f G. has, *for myself a house*, לי בית.
g G., S. add, *to him Laban*.
h G., S. add, *to him*.
i For הזה, S. has, *which I say to thee*.
j G., S. add, *and*, ואשמר.
k G. has, *let one pass over*; V. *pass over*.
l G. omits כל.
m V. *and separate*; S, *and I will separate for myself*.
n G. omits, נקד וטלוא וכל שה.
o S. has, *among the white ones*; so in vss. 33, 35.
p G. adds. *all*, וכל טלוא.
q G. omits *and*, ו.
r G. omits על and renders, *when my hire shall be*.

hire before thy face: every one that *is* not speckled and spotted among the goats, and brown among the sheep, that shall be counted stolen with me.
34 And Laban said, Behold, I would it might be according to thy word.
35 And he removed that day the he goats that were ringstraked and spotted, and all the she goats that were speckled and spotted, *and* every one that had *some* white in it, and all the brown among the sheep, and gave *them* into the hand of his sons.
36 And he set three days' journey betwixt himself and Jacob: and Jacob fed the rest of Laban's flocks.
37 And Jacob took him rods of green poplar, and of the hazel and chesnut tree; and pilled white strakes in them, and made the white appear which *was* in the rods.
38 And he set the rods which he had pilled before the flocks in the gutters in the watering troughs when the flocks came to drink, that they should conceive when they came to drink.
39 And the flocks conceived before the rods, and brought forth cattle ringstraked,

[a]לְפָנֶיךָ כֹּל אֲשֶׁר־אֵינֶנּוּ נָקֹד וְטָלוּא
spotted and speckled (it) not is that one every ; thee before (to)

בָּעִזִּים וְחוּם בַּכְּשָׂבִים גָּנוּב הוּא אִתִּי׃
.me with it [is] stolen ,lambs the among black and goats the among

34 [a]וַיֹּאמֶר לָבָן הֵן[b] לוּ[b] יְהִי כִדְבָרֶךָ׃
.word thy to according be it let ,verily ,Yea : Laban said And

35 וַיָּסַר בַּיּוֹם הַהוּא אֶת־הַתְּיָשִׁים הָעֲקֻדִּים
[1]striped [4]rams the [1]that [2]day in removed he And

וְהַטְּלֻאִים וְאֵת כָּל־הָעִזִּים הַנְּקֻדּוֹת וְהַטְּלֻאֹת
,[3]spotted [2]and [1]speckled [4]goats the all and ,[3]spottted [2]and

[c]כֹּל אֲשֶׁר־לָבָן בּוֹ וְכָל־חוּם
one black every and ,(it in) white [was] which [in] one every

36 בַּכְּשָׂבִים וַיִּתֵּן בְּיַד־בָּנָיו׃ וַיָּשֶׂם
put he And .sons his of hand the into gave he and ; lambs the among

דֶּרֶךְ שְׁלֹשֶׁת יָמִים בֵּינוֹ[d] וּבֵין יַעֲקֹב[e]
,Jacob (between) and him between days three of journey a

וְיַעֲקֹב רֹעֶה אֶת־צֹאן לָבָן הַנּוֹתָרֹת׃[f]
.remained that Laban of flocks the feeding [was] Jacob [while] (and)

37 וַיִּקַּח־לוֹ יַעֲקֹב מַקַּל לִבְנֶה לַח
,[1]fresh [5]storax [4]the [3]of [2]rods Jacob himself for took And

וְלוּז וְעַרְמוֹן וַיְפַצֵּל בָּהֵן פְּצָלוֹת
[2]stripes them in peeled he and ; tree plane the and almond the and

לְבָנוֹת[g] מַחְשֹׂף הַלָּבָן אֲשֶׁר עַל־הַמַּקְלוֹת׃
.rods the on [was] which white the bare laying [1]white

38 וַיַּצֵּג אֶת־הַמַּקְלוֹת אֲשֶׁר פִּצֵּל בָּרֳהָטִים
,troughs the by peeled had he which rods the placed he And

בְּשִׁקֲתוֹת הַמָּיִם אֲשֶׁר תָּבֹאןָ הַצֹּאן לִשְׁתּוֹת
,drink to flocks the in came whither ,water of troughs the by

לְנֹכַח הַצֹּאן[h] וַיֵּחַמְנָה[h] בְּבֹאָן לִשְׁתּוֹת׃
.drink to coming their in paired they and ; flocks the against over

39 וַיֶּחֱמוּ הַצֹּאן אֶל־הַמַּקְלוֹת וַתֵּלַדְןָ הַצֹּאן עֲקֻדִּים
,striped flocks the bore and ,rods the by flocks the paired And

cerning my hire that is before thee: every one that is not speckled and spotted among the goats, and black among the sheep, that *if found* with me shall be counted stolen.
34 And Laban said, Behold, I would it might be according to thy word.
35 And he removed that day the he-goats that were ringstraked and spotted, and all the she-goats that were speckled and spotted, every one that had white in it, and all the black ones among the sheep, and gave them into the hand of his sons;
36 and he set three days' journey betwixt himself and Jacob: and Jacob fed the rest of Laban's flocks.
37 And Jacob took him rods of fresh poplar, and of the almond and of the plane tree: and peeled white strakes in them, and made the white appear which was in the rods.
38 And he set the rods which he had peeled over against the flocks in the gutters in the watering troughs where the flocks came to drink; and they conceived when they came to drink.
39 And the flocks conceived before the rods, and the

---

a G., S. add, *to him.*
b G. omits; Sm., *and behold not*, והן לא.
c G., S. add, *and*, וכל.
d Sm., G. *between them.*
e S. has, *Laban.*
f Sm. here adds, with slight modifications and additions, ch. 31: 11—13.
g G. adds, *stripping off the green.*
h G. omits, and adds, *the rods.*

speckled, and
spotted. 40 And
Jacob did sep-
arate the lambs,
and set the faces
of the flocks to-
ward the ring-
straked, and
all the brown in
the flock of La-
ban; and he put
his own flocks
by themselves,
and put them
not unto La-
ban's cattle. 41
And it came to
pass, whenso-
ever the stronger
cattle did con-
ceive, that Ja-
cob laid the rods
before the eyes
of the cattle in
the gutters, that
they might con-
ceive among the
rods. 42 But
when the cattle
were feeble, he
put *them* not in:
so the feebler
were Laban's,
and the strong-
er Jacob's. 43
And the man in-
creased exceed-
ingly, and had
much cattle, and
maidservants,
and menserv-
ants, and cam-
els, and asses.

40 נְקֻדִּים וּטְלֻאִים׃ וְהַכְּשָׂבִים הִפְרִיד יַעֲקֹב וַיִּתֵּן
set and ,Jacob separated lambs the And .spotted and ,speckled

פְּנֵי הַצֹּאן אֶל־עָקֹד[a] וְכָל־חוּם
one black every and striped the towards flock the of faces the

בְּצֹאן לָבָן[b] וַיָּשֶׁת לוֹ עֲדָרִים לְבַדּוֹ
,apart droves himself for put he and ;Laban of flocks the in

41 וְלֹא שָׁתָם עַל־צֹאן לָבָן׃ וְהָיָה
,be to used it And .Laban of flock the with them put [2]did [1]he [3]not and

בְּכָל־יַחֵם הַצֹּאן הַמְקֻשָּׁרוֹת וְשָׂם
place to accustomed was (and) ,[1]strong [2]flocks the paired whenever

יַעֲקֹב אֶת־הַמַּקְלוֹת לְעֵינֵי הַצֹּאן בָּרְהָטִים
;troughs the by flocks the of eyes the before rods the Jacob

42 לְיַחְמֵנָּה בַּמַּקְלוֹת׃ וּבְהַעֲטִיף הַצֹּאן
[2]flocks' [1]the [4]weak [3]being in And .rods the by pair might they that

לֹא יָשִׂים וְהָיָה הָעֲטֻפִים
weak the become to used and ;place to accustomed [2]was [1]he [3]not

43 לְלָבָן וְהַקְּשֻׁרִים לְיַעֲקֹב׃ וַיִּפְרֹץ הָאִישׁ
man the increased And .Jacob for strong the and ,Laban for

מְאֹד מְאֹד וַיְהִי־לוֹ צֹאן רַבּוֹת[c]
,[1]many [2]flocks him to were and ;exceedingly ,exceedingly

וּשְׁפָחוֹת[d] וַעֲבָדִים[ed] וּגְמַלִּים וַחֲמֹרִים׃
.asses and camels and ,slaves male and ,slaves female and

flocks brought
forth ring-
straked, speck-
led, and spotted.
40 And Jacob
separated the
lambs, and set
the faces of the
flocks toward
the ringstraked
and all the black
in the flock of
Laban; and he
put his own
droves apart,
and put them
not unto La-
ban's flock. 41
And it came to
pass, whenso-
ever the strong-
er of the flock
did conceive,
that Jacob laid
the rods before
the eyes of the
flock in the
gutters, that
they might con-
ceive among
the rods; 42 but
when the flock
were feeble, he
put them not in:
so the feebler
were Laban's,
and the stronger
Jacob's. 43 And
the man in-
creased exceed-
ingly, and had
large flocks, and
maidservants
and menserv-
ants, and cam-
els and asses.

31

AND he heard
the words of La-
ban's sons, say-
ing, Jacob hath
taken away all
that *was* our
father's; and of
that which *was*
our father's
hath he gotten
all this
glory. 2 And
Jacob beheld
the countenance
of Laban, and,
behold, it *was*

1 וַיִּשְׁמַע[f] אֶת־דִּבְרֵי בְנֵי־לָבָן לֵאמֹר
:saying ,Laban of sons the of words the heard he And

לָקַח יַעֲקֹב אֵת כָּל־אֲשֶׁר לְאָבִינוּ
;father our to [was] which all Jacob taken Has

וּמֵאֲשֶׁר לְאָבִינוּ עָשָׂה אֵת כָּל־הַכָּבֹד
[2]wealth all made has he father our to [was] what from and

2 הַזֶּה׃ וַיַּרְא יַעֲקֹב אֶת־פְּנֵי לָבָן וְהִנֵּה
behold and ,Laban of face the Jacob saw And .[1]this

And he heard
the words of
Laban's sons,
saying, Jacob
hath taken a-
way all that was
our fathers;
and of that
which was our
father's hath he
gotten all this
glory. 2 And Ja-
cob beheld the
countenance of
Laban, and,
behold, it was

a For אל, Sm., G. have, *ram*, איל: T. *all*, כל; S. *sheep*.
b. G, omits.
c G. adds, *and cattle*.
d G., S. transpose, reading ועבדים ושפחות.
e S. adds, *and she-asses*, ואתנת.
f G., S. add, *Jacob*.

not toward him
as before. 3 And
the LORD said
unto Jacob, Re-
turn unto the
land of thy fa-
thers, and to
thy kindred;
and I will be
with thee. 4 And
Jacob sent and
called Rachel
and Leah to the
field unto his
flock, 5 And
said unto them,
I see your fath-
er's counte-
nance, that it *is*
not toward me
as before; but
the God of my
father hath been
with me. 6 And
ye know that
with all my
power I have
served your
father.
7 And your
father hath de-
ceived me, and
changed my
wages ten times;
but God suffer-
ed him not to
hurt me. 8 If he
said thus, The
speckled shall
be thy wages;
then all the
cattle bare
speckled: and if
he said thus,
The ringstrak-
ed shall be thy
hire; then bare
all the cattle
ringstraked. 9
Thus God hath
taken away the
cattle of your fa-
ther, and given
them to me. 10
And it came to
pass at the time
that the cattle
conceived, that I
lifted up mine
eyes, and saw in
a dream, and,
behold, the
rams which
leaped upon the

3 אֵינֶנּוּ עִמּוֹ כִּתְמוֹל שִׁלְשׁוֹם׃ וַיֹּאמֶר
said And .day third the [and] yesterday like ,him with not was it

יְהוָה אֶל־יַעֲקֹב שׁוּב אֶל־אֶרֶץ אֲבוֹתֶיךָ
,fathers thy of land the unto Return : Jacob unto Jehovah

4 וּלְמוֹלַדְתֶּךָ וְאֶהְיֶה עִמָּךְ׃ וַיִּשְׁלַח יַעֲקֹב
Jacob sent And .thee with be will I and ,kindred thy to and

וַיִּקְרָא לְרָחֵל וּלְלֵאָה הַשָּׂדֶה אֶל־צֹאנוֹ׃
.flock his unto field the [into] Leah (to) and Rachel (to) called and

5 וַיֹּאמֶר לָהֶן רֹאֶה אָנֹכִי אֶת־פְּנֵי אֲבִיכֶן
,father your of face the [1]I [3]seeing [[2]Am] : them to said he And

כִּי־אֵינֶנּוּ אֵלַי כִּתְמֹל שִׁלְשֹׁם וֵאלֹהֵי
of God the and ;day third the [and] yesterday like me unto not is it that

6 אָבִי הָיָה עִמָּדִי׃ וְאַתֵּנָה יְדַעְתֶּן כִּי בְּכָל־כֹּחִי
strength my all with that know ye And .me with been has father my

7 עָבַדְתִּי אֶת־אֲבִיכֶן׃ וַאֲבִיכֶן הֵתֶל בִּי
,me (in) cheated has father your And .father your served have I

וְהֶחֱלִף אֶת־מַשְׂכֻּרְתִּי עֲשֶׂרֶת מֹנִים וְלֹא־
not has and ;times ten wages my changed has and

8 נְתָנוֹ אֱלֹהִים[a] לְהָרַע עִמָּדִי׃ אִם־כֹּה יֹאמַר
: say to were he thus If .me with evil do to God him allowed

נְקֻדִּים יִהְיֶה שְׂכָרֶךָ וְיָלְדוּ כָל־הַצֹּאן
flocks the all bear to used then ,wages thy be shall ones Speckled

נְקֻדִּים וְאִם־כֹּה יֹאמַר עֲקֻדִּים יִהְיֶה
be shall ones Striped : say to were he thus if and ;speckled

שְׂכָרֶךָ וְיָלְדוּ כָל־הַצֹּאן עֲקֻדִּים׃
.striped flocks the all bear to used then ,wages thy

9 וַיַּצֵּל אֱלֹהִים אֶת־מִקְנֵה[b] אֲבִיכֶם
father your of cattle the God away taken has And

10 וַיִּתֶּן־לִי׃ וַיְהִי בְּעֵת
[when] time the at ,pass to came it And .me to given has and

יַחֵם הַצֹּאן וָאֶשָּׂא[c] עֵינַי וָאֵרֶא[c]
saw I and eyes my raised I that ,flocks the pair to accustomed were

בַּחֲלוֹם וְהִנֵּה הָעַתֻּדִים[d] הָעֹלִים עַל־
upon up going were that he-goats the behold and ,dream a in

not toward him
as beforetime.
3 And the LORD
said unto Jacob,
Return unto the
land of thy fa-
thers, and to thy
kindred; and I
will be with
thee. 4 And Ja-
cob sent and
called Rachel
and Leah to the
field unto his
flock, 5 and said
unto them, I
see your father's
countenance,
that it is not to-
ward me as be-
foretime; but
the God of my
father hath been
with me. 6 And
ye know that
with all my pow-
er I have serv-
ed your father.
7 And your fa-
ther hath de-
ceived me, and
changed my
wages ten times;
but God suffer-
ed him not to
hurt me. 8 If he
said thus, The
speckled shall be
thy wages; then
all the flock
bare speckled:
and if he said
thus, The ring-
straked shall be
thy wages; then
bare all the flock
ringstraked. 9
Thus God hath
taken away the
cattle of your
father, and giv-
en them to me.
10 And it came
to pass at the
time that the
flock conceived,
that I lifted up
mine eyes, and
saw in a dream,
and, behold, the
he-goats which
leaped upon the

---

a Sm. has, *Jehovah*, יהוה; so in vss. 9, 16a.
b G. has, *all the cattle;* S., T. *from the cattle.*
c For ואשא עיני וארא, G. has, *and I saw with the eyes.*
d G. has, *the rams and he-goats;* so in vs. 12.

cattle *were* ring-
straked, speck-
led, and griz-
zled. 11 And the
angel of God
spake unto me
in a dream, *say-
ing*, Jacob : and
I said, Here *am*
I. 12 And he
said, Lift up now
thine eyes, and
see, all the rams
which leap up-
on the cattle
are ringstraked,
speckled, and
grizzled : for I
have seen all
that Laban
doeth unto thee.

13 I *am* the
God of Beth-el,
where thou an-
ointedst the
pillar, *and*
where thou
vowedst a vow
unto me : now
arise, get thee
out from this
land, and re-
turn unto the
land of thy
kindred. 14 And
Rachel and Le-
ah answered and
said unto him,
Is there yet any
portion or in-
heritance for us
in our father's
house ? 15 Are
we not counted
of him stran-
gers? for he hath
sold us, and
hath quite de-
voured also our
money. 16 For
all the riches
which God hath
taken from our
father, that *is*
our's, and our
children's : now
then, whatso-
ever God hath
said unto thee,
do.

11 [a]הַצֹּאן עֲקֻדִּים נְקֻדִּים וּבְרֻדִּים׃ [b]וַיֹּאמֶר
said And .dappled and ,speckled ,striped [were] flock the

אֵלַי מַלְאַךְ הָאֱלֹהִים בַּחֲלוֹם יַעֲקֹב[c] וָאֹמַר
: said I and ; Jacob ,dream a in God of angel the me unto

12 הִנֵּנִי׃ וַיֹּאמֶר שָׂא־נָא עֵינֶיךָ וּרְאֵה
;see and eyes thine ,now ,Raise : said he And .me Behold

כָּל־הָעַתֻּדִים הָעֹלִים עַל־הַצֹּאן עֲקֻדִּים
,striped [are] flock the upon up going are that he-goats the all

נְקֻדִּים וּבְרֻדִּים כִּי רָאִיתִי אֵת כָּל־אֲשֶׁר לָבָן
Laban which all seen have I for ; dappled and ,speckled

13 עֹשֶׂה לָּךְ׃ אָנֹכִי הָאֵל[d] בֵּית־אֵל[d] אֲשֶׁר
where Bethel of God the [am] I .thee to doing [is]

מָשַׁחְתָּ[e] שָּׁם מַצֵּבָה [f]אֲשֶׁר נָדַרְתָּ לִּי
me to vowedst thou where ,pillar memorial a (there) anointedst thou

שָׁם נֶדֶר [g]עַתָּה קוּם צֵא מִן־הָאָרֶץ הַזֹּאת
,[1]this [2]land from out go ,rise now ; vow a (there)

14 וְשׁוּב אֶל־אֶרֶץ מוֹלַדְתֶּךָ׃[h] וַתַּעַן רָחֵל
Rachel answered And .nativity thy of land the unto return and

וְלֵאָה וַתֹּאמַרְנָה לוֹ הַעוֹד לָנוּ חֵלֶק
portion a us to still [there Is] : him to said and ,Leah and

15 וְנַחֲלָה בְּבֵית אָבִינוּ׃ הֲלוֹא
[3]Not ? father our of house the in inheritance an and

[i]נָכְרִיּוֹת נֶחְשַׁבְנוּ לוֹ כִּי מְכָרָנוּ
; us sold has he for ? him by [4]considered [2]we [1]are [5]strangers

16 וַיֹּאכַל [j]גַּם־אָכוֹל אֶת־כַּסְפֵּנוּ׃ כִּי[k] כָל־הָעֹשֶׁר[l]
riches the all For .price our entirely also devoured has he and

אֲשֶׁר הִצִּיל אֱלֹהִים מֵאָבִינוּ לָנוּ הוּא
,it [is] us to ,father our from God away taken has which

וּלְבָנֵינוּ וְעַתָּה כֹּל אֲשֶׁר אָמַר אֱלֹהִים אֵלֶיךָ
,thee unto God said has which all now and ; sons our to and

flock were ring-
straked, speck-
led, and grisled.
11 And the an-
gel of God said
unto me in the
dream, Jacob :
and I said, Here
am I. 12 And he
said, Lift up
now thine eyes,
and see, all the
he-goats which
leap upon the
flock are ring-
straked, speck-
led, and grisled:
for I have seen
all that Laban
doeth unto thee.

13 I am the
God of Beth-el,
where thou an-
ointedst a pil-
lar, where thou
vowedst a vow
unto me : now
arise, get thee
out from this
land, and re-
turn unto the
land of thy na-
tivity. 14 And
Rachel and
Leah answered
and said unto
him, Is there yet
any portion or
inheritance for
us in our fath-
er's house ? 15
Are we not
counted of
him strangers?
for he hath sold
us, and hath
also quite de-
voured our mon-
ey. 16 For all
the riches which
God hath taken
away from our
father, that is
ours and our
children's : now
then, whatso-
ever God hath
said unto thee,
do.

---

a For הצאן, G. has, *the sheep and the goats ;* so in vs. 12.

b G. *ash-colored, sprinkled.*

c G. repeats.

d T. has, *the God who appeared to thee at Bethel ;* G. has, *the God who appeared to thee in the place.*

e G., S. add, *to me.*

f Sm., G., T. add, *and,* ואשר.

g Sm. adds, *and,* ועתה; so G., V.

h G. adds, *and I will be with thee.*

i G., S., V. add, *like,* כנכריות.

j G., V. omit גם.

k G. omits.

l G. adds, *and the glory.*

17 Then Ja-
cob rose up, and
set his sons and
his wives upon
camels; 18 And
he carried away
all his cattle,
and all his
goods which he
had gotten, the
cattle of his get-
ting, which he
had gotten in
Padan-aram, for
to go to Isaac
his father in the
land of Canaan.
19 And Laban
went to shear
his sheep: and
Rachel had
stolen the imag-
es that *were* her
father's. 20 And
Jacob stole a-
way unawares to
Laban the Sy-
rian, in that he
told him not
that he fled. 21
So he fled with
all that he had;
and he rose up,
and passed over
the river, and
set his face *to-
ward* the mount
Gilead.

22 And it
was told La-
ban on the third
day that Jacob
was fled. 23 And
he took his
brethren with
him, and pur-
sued after him
seven days'
journey; and
they overtook
him in the
mount Gilead.
24 And God
came to Laban
the Syrian in a
dream by night,
and said unto
him, Take heed
that thou speak
not to Jacob
either good or
bad.

25 Then La-
ban overtook
Jacob. Now Ja-

17 עשה: ויקם יעקב וישא את־בניו[a] ואת־נשיו[a]
wives his and sons his put and ,Jacob arose And .do

18 על־הגמלים: וינהג את־כל־מקנהו ואת־
all and cattle his all away carried he And .camels upon

כל־רכשו אשר רכש מקנה[b] קנינו
,property his of cattle the ,acquired had he which property movable his

אשר רכש[b] בפדן ארם לבוא אל־יצחק
Isaac unto come to ;Aram Paddan in acquired had he which

19 אביו ארצה כנען: ולבן הלך לגזז
shear to gone had Laban And .Canaan of land the to ,father his

את־צאנו ותגנב רחל את־התרפים אשר
[were] which teraphim the Rachel stole and ,sheep his

20 לאביה: ויגנב יעקב את־לב לבן הארמי
,Aramean the Laban of heart the Jacob stole And .father her to

על־בלי הגיד לו כי ברח הוא:
.he [was] flee to about that him to tell [2]did [1]he [3]not because

21 ויברח הוא וכל־אשר־לו ויקם[c]
arose he and ; him to [was] which all and he ,fled he And

ויעבר את־הנהר וישם את־פניו
face his set and ,[Euphrates] river the over passed and

22 הר הגלעד: ויגד ללבן[d] ביום
[2]day the in Laban to told was it And .Gilead of mountain the toward

23 השלישי כי ברח יעקב: ויקח את־אחיו[e]
brethren his took he And .Jacob fled had that ,[1]third

עמו וירדף אחריו דרך שבעת ימים
;days seven of journey a ,him after pursued and ,him with

24 וידבק אתו בהר הגלעד: ויבא
came And .Gilead of mountain the in him overtook he and

אלהים אל־לבן הארמי בחלם הלילה
,night the of dream a in Aramean the Laban unto God

ויאמר לו השמר לך פן־תדבר עם־יעקב
,Jacob with speak thou lest thyself for careful Be :him to said and

25 מטוב[f] עד־רע[f]: וישג לבן את־יעקב
,Jacob [1]Laban [4]with [3]up [2]caught And .bad unto good from

17 Then Ja-
cob rose up, and
set his sons and
his wives upon
the camels; 18
and he carried
away all his cat-
tle, and all his
substance which
he had gather-
ed, the cattle of
his getting,
which he had
gathered in Pad-
dan-aram, for to
go to Isaac his
father unto the
land of Canaan.
19 Now Laban
was gone to
shear his sheep:
and Rachel stole
the teraphim
that were her
father's. 20 And
Jacob stole a-
way unawares to
Laban the Sy-
rian, in that he
told him not
that he fled. 21
So he fled with
all that he had;
and he rose up,
and passed over
the River, and
set his face to-
ward the mount-
ain of Gilead.

22 And it was
told Laban on
the third day
that Jacob was
fled. 23 And he
took his breth-
ren with him,
and pursued aft-
er him seven
days' journey;
and he overtook
him in the
mountain of
Gilead. 24 And
God came to
Laban the Sy-
rian in a dream
of the night,
and said unto
him, Take heed
to thyself that
thou speak not
to Jacob either
good or bad.

25 And Laban
came up with
Jacob. Now Ja-

a Sm., G. transpose, *his wives and his sons*, את נשיו ואת בניו.

b G., S. omit מקנה---רכש.

c G., V. omit.

d G. adds, *the Syrian*.

e G. adds, *all*, את כל אחיו.

f G., V. omit מטוב עד.

cob had pitched
his tent in the
mount; and La-
ban with his
brethren pitched
in the mount of
Gilead. 26 And
Laban said to
Jacob, What
hast thou done,
that thou hast
stolen away un-
awares to me,
and carried a-
way my daugh-
ters, as captives
taken with the
sword? 27
Wherefore didst
thou flee away
secretly, and
steal away from
me; and didst
not tell me, that
I might have
sent thee away
with mirth, and
with songs, with
tabret, and with
harp? 28 And
hast not suffered
me to kiss my
sons and my
daughters? thou
hast now done
foolishly in *so*
doing. 29 It is in
the power of my
hand to do you
hurt: but the
God of your
father spake un-
to me yester-
night, saying,
Take thou heed
that thou speak
not to Jacob
either good or
bad. 30 And
now, *though*
thou wouldest
needs be gone,
because thou
sore longedst
after thy fa-
ther's house, *yet*
wherefore hast
thou stolen my
gods? 31 And
Jacob answer-
ed and said to
Laban, Because
I was afraid: for
I said, Perad-
venture thou
wouldest take
by force thy
daughters from
me. 32 With

וְיַעֲקֹב תָּקַע אֶת־אָהֳלוֹ בָּהָר וְלָבָן
Laban and ,mountain the in tent his pitched having Jacob (and)

תָּקַע אֶת־אֶחָיו בְּהַר הַגִּלְעָד׃
; Gilead of mountain the in brethren his with pitched having

26 וַיֹּאמֶר לָבָן לְיַעֲקֹב מֶה עָשִׂיתָ וַתִּגְנֹב[a]
stolen hast thou that done thou hast What : Jacob to Laban said and

אֶת־לְבָבִי[a] וַתְּנַהֵג אֶת־בְּנֹתַי כִּשְׁבֻיוֹת
of captives like daughters my away carried and ,heart my

27 חָרֶב׃ לָמָּה[b] נַחְבֵּאתָ לִבְרֹחַ וַתִּגְנֹב
stolen hast and ,flee to secretly acted thou hast Why ? sword the

אֹתִי[b] וְלֹא־הִגַּדְתָּ לִּי וָאֲשַׁלֵּחֲךָ
away thee sent have would I and ; me to told not hast and ,me

28 בְּשִׂמְחָה וּבְשִׁרִים בְּתֹף[c] וּבְכִנּוֹר׃ וְלֹא
3not and ; harp with and tabret with ,songs with and rejoicing with

נְטַשְׁתַּנִי לְנַשֵּׁק לְבָנַי וְלִבְנֹתָי עַתָּה
now ?daughters my (to) and sons my (to) kiss to me allowed 2hast 1thou

29 הִסְכַּלְתָּ עֲשׂוֹ׃[d] יֶשׁ־לְאֵל יָדִי לַעֲשׂוֹת
do to hand my of power the in is It .do to foolish been hast thou

עִמָּכֶם[e] רָע וֵאלֹהֵי אֲבִיכֶם[f] אֶמֶשׁ אָמַר
spoke night [last] father your of God the but ; evil you with

אֵלַי לֵאמֹר[g] הִשָּׁמֶר לְךָ מִדַּבֵּר עִם־יַעֲקֹב
,Jacob with speaking from thyself for careful Be : saying me unto

30 מִטּוֹב עַד־רָע׃ וְעַתָּה הָלֹךְ[h] הָלַכְתָּ[h] כִּי־
because ,go didst thou going now And .evil unto good from

נִכְסֹף נִכְסַפְתָּה לְבֵית אָבִיךָ לָמָּה[i]
why — father thy of house the for longest thou longing

31 גָּנַבְתָּ אֶת־אֱלֹהָי׃ וַיַּעַן יַעֲקֹב וַיֹּאמֶר
said and Jacob answered And ?gods my stolen thou hast

לְלָבָן כִּי יָרֵאתִי כִּי אָמַרְתִּי פֶּן־
Lest :said I for ; feared I Because : Laban to

32 תִּגְזֹל אֶת־בְּנוֹתֶיךָ מֵעִמִּי׃[j] עִם[k]
With .me (with) from daughters thy forcibly take shouldest thou

cob had pitched
his tent in the
mountain: and
Laban with his
brethren pitched
in the mountain
of Gilead. 26
And Laban said
to Jacob, What
hast thou done,
that thou hast
stolen away un-
awares to me,
and carried a-
way my daugh-
ters as captives
of the sword?
27 Wherefore
didst thou flee
secretly, and
steal away from
me; and didst
not tell me, that
I might have
sent thee away
with mirth and
with songs, with
tabret and with
harp; 28 and
hast not suffer-
ed me to kiss
my sons and my
daughters? now
hast thou done
foolishly. 29 It
is in the power
of my hand to
do you hurt: but
the God of your
father spake un-
to me yester-
night, saying,
Take heed to
thyself that thou
speak not to
Jacob either
good or bad. 30
And now,
though thou
wouldest needs
be gone, be-
cause thou sore
longedst after
thy father's
house, *yet*
wherefore hast
thou stolen my
gods? 31 And
Jacob answered
and said to La-
ban, Because I
was afraid: for
I said, Lest
thou shouldest
take thy daugh-
ters from me by
force. 32 With

---

a G. has, *why hast thou fled secretly and hast robbed me?* cf. vs. 27.
b G. omits למה---אתי.
c S., V. add, *and*, ובתף.
d S. has, *in what thou hast done.*
e Sm. G., V. have sing. suff. עמך.
f Sm., G. have sing. suff. אביך.
g S. omits.
h G. *go*, הֵלֵךְ.
i G. adds, *and*, ולמה.
j G. adds, *and all my things*, וכל אשר לי.
k G. adds, *and Jacob said to him.*

whomsoever
thou findest thy
gods, let him
not live: before
our brethren
discern thou
what *is* thine
with me, and
take *it* to thee.
For Jacob knew
not that Rachel
had stolen them.
33 And Laban
went into Jacob's
tent, and into
Leah's tent, and
into the two
maidservants'
tents; but he
found *them* not.
Then went he
out of Leah's
tent, and enter-
ed into Rachel's
tent. 34 Now
Rachel had
taken the imag-
es, and put them
in the camels
furniture, and
sat upon them.
And Laban
searched all the
tent, but found
them not. 35
And she said to
her father, Let
it not displease
my lord that I
cannot rise up
before thee; for
the custom of
women *is* upon
me. And he
searched, but
found not the
images.

36 And Jacob
was wroth, and
chode with La-
ban: and Jacob
answered and
said to Laban,
What *is* my
trespass? what
is my sin, that
thou hast so
hotly pursued
after me? 37
Whereas thou
hast searched all

אֲשֶׁר תִּמְצָא[a] אֶת־אֱלֹהֶיךָ לֹא יִחְיֶה נֶגֶד
before ; live [2]shall [1]he [3]not ,gods thy findest thou whomsoever

אַחֵינוּ הַכֶּר־לְךָ[b] מָה[b] עִמָּדִי וְקַח־לָךְ[c]
;thyself for take and ,me with [is] what thyself for observe brethren our

33 וְלֹא־יָדַע יַעֲקֹב כִּי רָחֵל[d] גְּנָבָתַם׃ וַיָּבֹא
in came And .them stolen had Rachel that Jacob know not did and

לָבָן[e] בְּאֹהֶל־יַעֲקֹב וּבְאֹהֶל לֵאָה
,Leah of tent the into and ,Jacob of tent the into Laban

וּבְאֹהֶל שְׁתֵּי הָאֲמָהֹת וְלֹא מָצָא
;find [2]did [1]he [3]not and ,maidservants two the of tent the into and

וַיֵּצֵא מֵאֹהֶל לֵאָה[f] וַיָּבֹא בְּאֹהֶל
of tent the into came and Leah of tent the from out went he and

34 רָחֵל׃ וְרָחֵל לָקְחָה אֶת־הַתְּרָפִים וַתְּשִׂמֵם
them put and teraphim the taken had Rachel And .Rachel

בְּכַר הַגָּמָל וַתֵּשֶׁב עֲלֵיהֶם
;them upon sitting was she and ,camel the of saddle the into

וַיְמַשֵּׁשׁ[g] לָבָן אֶת־כָּל־הָאֹהֶל וְלֹא מָצָא[g]׃
.find [2]did [1]he [3]not and ,tent the all Laban felt and

35 וַתֹּאמֶר[h] אֶל־אָבִיהָ אַל־יִחַר בְּעֵינֵי
of eyes the in anger be not [there] Let ; father her unto said she And

אֲדֹנִי כִּי לוֹא אוּכַל לָקוּם מִפָּנֶיךָ כִּי־
for ,thee before from rise to able [2]am [1]I [3]not that ,lord my

דֶרֶךְ נָשִׁים לִי וַיְחַפֵּשׂ[i] וְלֹא
[2]not and ,carefully searched he and ; me to [is] women of way the

36 מָצָא אֶת־הַתְּרָפִים׃ וַיִּחַר לְיַעֲקֹב
,Jacob to anger was [there] And .teraphim the find [1]did

וַיָּרֶב בְּלָבָן וַיַּעַן יַעֲקֹב וַיֹּאמֶר
said and Jacob answered and ; Laban with contended he and

לְלָבָן מַה־פִּשְׁעִי מַה[j] חַטָּאתִי כִּי
that ,sin my [is] what ,transgression my [is] What : Laban to

37 דָלַקְתָּ אַחֲרָי׃ [k]כִּי־מִשַּׁשְׁתָּ אֶת־כָּל־
all felt hast thou For ? me after fiercely pursued hast thou

whomsoever
thou findest thy
gods, he shall
not live: before
our brethren
discern thou
what is thine
with me, and
take it to thee.
For Jacob knew
not that Rachel
had stolen them.
33 And Laban
went into Ja-
cob's tent, and
into Leah's tent,
and into the tent
of the two maid-
servants; but he
found them not.
And he went
out of Leah's
tent, and enter-
ed into Rachel's
tent. 34 Now
Rachel had
taken the tera-
phim, and put
them in the
camel's furni-
ture, and sat up-
on them. And
Laban felt a-
bout all the tent,
but found them
not. 35 And she
said to her fa-
ther, Let not
my lord be angry
that I cannot
rise up before
thee; for the
manner of wom-
en is upon me.
And he search-
ed, but found
not the tera-
phim.

36 And Jacob
was wroth, and
chode with La-
ban: and Jacob
answered and
said to Laban,
What is my
trespass? what
is my sin, that
thou hast hotly
pursued after
me? 37 Whereas
thou hast felt

a S. has pl. pass., *are found*, יִמָּצְאוּ.
b G., V. transpose, reading, מָה לְךָ.
c G. adds. *and he did not know by himself anything*.
d G. adds, *his wife*.
e Sm., G. add, *and searched*, ויחפש.
f G. transfers here באהל יעקב and באהל---האמהת, and adds, at beginning, *he searched*, and at end *and he did not find*.
g G. omits, וימשש---מצא.
h S. adds, *Rachel*.
i G. adds, *Laban in all the tent*.
j Sm., G., S., V. add, *and*, ומה.
k Sm., G. add, *and*, וכי; S. has, *behold*.

my stuff, what
hast thou found
of all thy house-
hold stuff? set
it here before
my brethren and
thy brethren,
that they may
judge betwixt
us both. 38
This twenty
years *have* I *been*
with thee; thy
ewes and thy
she goats have
not cast their
young, and the
rams of thy flock
have I not eaten.
39 That which
was torn *of*
beasts I brought
not unto thee;
I bare the loss
of it; of my
hand didst thou
require it,
whether stolen
by day, or stolen
by night. 40
Thus I was;
in the day
the drought
consumed me,
and the frost by
night; and my
sleep departed
from mine eyes.
41 Thus have I
been twenty
years in thy
house; I served
thee fourteen
years for thy
two daughters,
and six years for
thy cattle: and
thou hast chang-
ed my wages
ten times. 42
Except the God
of my father, the
God of A-
braham, and the
fear of Isaac,
had been with
me, surely thou
hadst sent me
away now emp-
ty. God hath
seen mine afflic-
tion and the
labour of my
hands, and re-
buked *thee*
yesternight.
43 And Laban
answered and

כֵּלַי[a] מַה־מָּצָאתָ מִכֹּל כְּלֵי־בֵיתֶךָ
?house thy of utensils the all from found thou hast what ,utensils my

שִׂים כֹּה נֶגֶד אַחַי וְאַחֶיךָ וְיוֹכִיחוּ
decide them let and ,brethren thy and brethren my before here Put

38 בֵּין שְׁנֵינוּ׃ זֶה[b] עֶשְׂרִים שָׁנָה אָנֹכִי עִמָּךְ
;thee with [been have] I years twenty ,Now .two us between

רְחֵלֶיךָ וְעִזֶּיךָ לֹא שִׁכֵּלוּ וְאֵילֵי[c]
of rams the and ,bear to failed [1]have [2]not she-goats thy and ewes thy

39 צֹאנְךָ לֹא אָכָלְתִּי׃ טְרֵפָה לֹא־הֵבֵאתִי
in bring not did I mangled The .eaten [2]have [1]I [3]not flock thy

אֵלֶיךָ אָנֹכִי[d] אֲחַטֶּנָּה[d] מִיָּדִי תְּבַקְשֶׁנָּה[e]
,it exact to used thou hand my from ;it replace to used I ,thee unto

40 גְּנֻבְתִי[f] יוֹם וּגְנֻבְתִי[g] לָיְלָה׃ הָיִיתִי
—was I .night [by] (of) stolen the and ,day [by] (of) stolen the

בַיּוֹם אֲכָלַנִי[h] חֹרֶב וְקֶרַח בַּלָּיְלָה וַתִּדַּד
departed and ;night by cold and ,heat me consumed day by

41 שְׁנָתִי מֵעֵינָי׃ זֶה־לִּי עֶשְׂרִים שָׁנָה בְּבֵיתֶךָ
;house thy in years twenty me to ,Now .eyes mine from sleep my

עֲבַדְתִּיךָ אַרְבַּע־עֶשְׂרֵה שָׁנָה בִּשְׁתֵּי בְנֹתֶיךָ
,daughters [1]thy [2]two for years fourteen thee served I

וְשֵׁשׁ שָׁנִים בְּצֹאנֶךָ וַתַּחֲלֵף אֶת־מַשְׂכֻּרְתִּי
wages my changedst thou and ;flocks thy for years six and

42 עֲשֶׂרֶת מֹנִים׃ לוּלֵי אֱלֹהֵי אָבִי אֱלֹהֵי[i] אַבְרָהָם
Abraham of God the ,father my of God the Unless .times ten

וּפַחַד יִצְחָק הָיָה לִי כִּי[j] עַתָּה רֵיקָם
empty now indeed ,me for been had ,Isaac of fear the and

שִׁלַּחְתָּנִי אֶת־עָנְיִי וְאֶת־יְגִיעַ
of toil the and affliction my ;away me sent have wouldst thou

כַּפַּי רָאָה אֱלֹהִים וַיּוֹכַח[k] אָמֶשׁ׃
.night [last] decided he and ;God seen has hands my

43 וַיַּעַן לָבָן וַיֹּאמֶר אֶל־יַעֲקֹב הַבָּנוֹת
daughters The :Jacob unto said and Laban answered And

about all my
stuff, what hast
thou found of
all thy house-
hold stuff? Set
it here before
my brethren and
thy brethren,
that they may
judge betwixt
us two. 38 This
twenty years
have I been
with thee; thy
ewes and thy
she-goats have
not cast their
young, and the
rams of thy
flocks have I not
eaten. 39 That
which was torn
of beasts I
brought not un-
to thee; I bare
the loss of it; of
my hand didst
thou require it,
whether stolen
by day or stolen
by night. 40
Thus I was; in
the day the
drought con-
sumed me, and
the frost by
night; and my
sleep fled from
mine eyes. 41
These twenty
years have I
been in thy
house; I served
thee fourteen
years for thy
two daughters,
and six years for
thy flock: and
thou hast chang-
ed my wages
ten times. 42
Except the God
of my father,
the God of A-
braham, and the
Fear of Isaac,
had been with
me, surely now
hadst thou sent
me away empty.
God hath seen
mine affliction
and the labour
of my hands,
and rebuked
thee yester-
night.
43 And Laban

---

a For כלי, G. has, *the things of my house.*
b G. adds, *to me;* S. has, *behold.*
c G. omits ו.
d T. has, *what was lacking.*
e Sm., G. omit.
f T. has, *I watched.*
g T. has, *and I watched.*
h G. has *consumed,* אָכוּל; so V.
i G., V. omit.
j G., S. omit.
k G., S., V. add, *thee,* ויוכחך.

said unto Jacob,
These daughters
are my daugh-
ters, and *these*
children *are* my
children, and
these cattle *are*
my cattle, and
all that thou
seest *is* mine:
and what can I
do this day unto
these my daugh-
ters, or unto
their children
which they have
born? 44 Now
therefore come
thou, let us
make a cove-
nant, I and
thou; and let it
be for a witness
between me and
thee. 45 And
Jacob took a
stone, and set
it up *for* a pil-
lar. 46 And Ja-
cob said unto
his brethren,
Gather stones;
and they took
stones, and
made an heap:
and they did eat
there upon the
heap. 47 And
Laban called it
Jegar-sahadu-
tha: but Jacob
called it Galeed.
48 And Laban
said, This heap
is a witness be-
tween me and
thee this day.
Therefore was
the name of it
called Galeed;
49 And Mizpah;
for he said, The
LORD watch be-
tween me and
thee, when we
are absent one
from another.
50 If thou shalt
afflict my daugh-
ters, or if thou
shalt take
other wives
beside my
daughters, no
man *is* with us;
see, God *is* wit-

בְּנֹתַי וְהַבָּנִים בָּנַי וְהַצֹּאן
flocks the and ; sons my [are] sons the and daughters my [are]

צֹאנִי וְכֹל אֲשֶׁר־אַתָּה רֹאֶה לִי הוּא
; [is] it me to ,seeing [art] thou which all and ,flocks my [are]

וְלִבְנֹתַי מָה־אֶעֱשֶׂה לָאֵלֶּה הַיּוֹם אוֹ לִבְנֵיהֶן
sons their to or ,today these to do I can what—daughters my to and

44 אֲשֶׁר יָלָדוּ׃ וְעַתָּה לְכָה נִכְרְתָה בְרִית
,covenant a cut us let ,come now And ? borne have they whom

אֲנִי וָאָתָּה וְהָיָה לְעֵד בֵּינִי
me between witness a for be it let and ; thou and I

45 וּבֵינֶךָ[a]׃ וַיִּקַּח יַעֲקֹב אָבֶן וַיְרִימֶהָ
up it set and ,stone a Jacob took And .thee between and

46 מַצֵּבָה׃ וַיֹּאמֶר יַעֲקֹב לְאֶחָיו לִקְטוּ
Gather : brethren his to Jacob said And .pillar memorial a [as]

אֲבָנִים וַיִּקְחוּ אֲבָנִים וַיַּעֲשׂוּ־גָל וַיֹּאכְלוּ[b] שָׁם
there ate they and ; heap a made and stones took they and ; stones

47 עַל־הַגָּל[c]׃ וַיִּקְרָא־לוֹ לָבָן יְגַר שָׂהֲדוּתָא
; sahadutha Jegar Laban it to called And .heap the upon

48 וְיַעֲקֹב קָרָא לוֹ גַּלְעֵד׃ וַיֹּאמֶר[d] לָבָן הַגַּל
[2]Heap : Laban said And .Galeed it to called Jacob and

הַזֶּה עֵד בֵּינִי וּבֵינְךָ הַיּוֹם[d]
; today thee (between) and me between witnesss a [is] [1]this

49 עַל־כֵּן קָרָא־שְׁמוֹ גַּלְעֵד[e]׃ וְהַמִּצְפָּה[f] אֲשֶׁר
because ,Mizpah and ; Galeed name its called he therefore

אָמַר יִצֶף יְהוָה בֵּינִי וּבֵינֶךָ כִּי
when ,thee (between) and me between Jehovah watch May : said he

50 נִסָּתֵר אִישׁ מֵרֵעֵהוּ׃ אִם־תְּעַנֶּה
afflict [not] wilt thou (If) .neighbor his from each concealed are we

אֶת־בְּנֹתַי וְאִם־תִּקַּח[g] נָשִׁים עַל־
to addition in wives take [not] wilt thou (if) and ,daughters my

בְּנֹתַי[h] אֵין אִישׁ עִמָּנוּ רְאֵה[i] אֱלֹהִים
God ,see ,us with man a not is [there] ; daughters my

answered and
said unto Jacob,
The daughters
are my daugh-
ters, and the
children are my
children, and
the flocks are my
flocks, and all
that thou seest
is mine: and
what can I do
this day unto
these my daugh-
ters, or unto
their children
which they have
borne? 44 And
now come, let
us make a cove-
nant, I and
thou; and let it
be for a witness
between me and
thee. 45 And Ja-
cob took a stone,
and set it up for
a pillar. 46 And
Jacob said unto
his brethren,
Gather stones;
and they took
stones, and
made an heap:
and they did eat
there by the
heap. 47 And
Laban called it
Jegar-sahadu-
tha: but Jacob
called it Galeed.
48 And Laban
said, This heap
is witness be-
tween me and
thee this day.
Therefore was
the name of it
called Galeed:
49 and Mizpah,
for he said, The
LORD watch be-
tween me and
thee, when we
are absent one
from another. 50
If thou shalt
afflict my
daughters, and
if thou shalt
take wives be-
side my daugh-
ters, no man is
with us; see,
God is witness

---

a G. adds, *and Jacob said to him: Behold no one is with us; behold God is witness between me and thee.*

b G. adds, *and drank.*

c G adds, *and Laban said to him: This heap shall witness between me and thee today;* cf. vs. 48.

d G. omits 48 a, to היום, cf. vs. 46, and transfers to this place vss. 51 and 52 a, to המצבה.

e V. adds, *that is, heap of witness.*

f Sm. has, *and the memorial pillar,* והמצבה.

g G. omits ו.

h G. adds, *see,* רְאֵה.

i G. omits ראה---ובינך.

ness betwixt me
and thee. 51
And Laban said
to Jacob, Behold
this heap, and
behold *this* pil-
lar, which I have
cast betwixt me
and thee; 52
This heap *be*
witness, and *this*
pillar *be* witness,
that I will not
pass over this
heap to thee,
and that thou
shalt not pass
over this heap
and this pillar
unto me, for
harm. 53 The
God of Abra-
ham, and the
God of Nahor,
the God of their
father, judge
betwixt us. And
Jacob sware by
the fear of his
father Isaac.

54 Then Jacob
offered sacri-
fice upon the
mount, and call-
ed his brethren
to eat bread:
and they did eat
bread, and tar-
ried all night in
the mount. 55
And early in the
morning Laban
rose up, and
kissed his sons
and his daugh-
ters, and blessed
them: and La-
ban departed,
and returned
unto his place.

AND Jacob
went on his way,
and the angels

51 עֵד בֵּינִי וּבֵינֶךָ׃ וַיֹּאמֶר לָבָן
Laban said And .thee (between) and me between witness [is]

לְיַעֲקֹב הִנֵּה הַגַּל הַזֶּה וְהִנֵּה הַמַּצֵּבָה
,pillar memorial the behold and ,[1]this [2]heap Behold :Jacob to

52 אֲשֶׁר יָרִיתִי בֵּינִי וּבֵינֶךָ׃ עֵד
[5]witness [4]A .thee (between) and me between put have I which

הַגַּל הַזֶּה וְעֵדָה הַמַּצֵּבָה אִם־אָנִי
,I (if) ;pillar memorial the [is] witness a and [[3]is] [1]this [2]heap

לֹא־אֶעֱבֹר אֵלֶיךָ אֶת־הַגַּל הַזֶּה וְאִם־אַתָּה
,thou (if) and ;[1]this [2]heap thee unto over pass I will neither

לֹא־תַעֲבֹר אֵלַי אֶת־הַגַּל הַזֶּה וְאֶת־
and [1]this [2]heap me unto over pass thou wilt nor

53 הַמַּצֵּבָה הַזֹּאת לְרָעָה׃ אֱלֹהֵי אַבְרָהָם
,Abraham of God The .evil for ,[1]this [3]pillar [2]memorial

וֵאלֹהֵי נָחוֹר יִשְׁפְּטוּ[a] בֵינֵינוּ אֱלֹהֵי[b] אֲבִיהֶם[b]
;father their of gods the ,us between judge let ,Nahor of God the and

54 וַיִּשָּׁבַע יַעֲקֹב בְּפַחַד אָבִיו יִצְחָק׃ וַיִּזְבַּח
sacrificed And .Isaac father his of fear the by Jacob swore and

יַעֲקֹב זֶבַח בָּהָר וַיִּקְרָא לְאֶחָיו
brethren his (to) called and ,mountain the in sacrifice a Jacob

לֶאֱכָל־לָחֶם[c] וַיֹּאכְלוּ[d] לֶחֶם[c] וַיָּלִינוּ
night the passed and ,bread ate they and ;bread eat to

בָּהָר׃
.mountain the in

32

1 וַיַּשְׁכֵּם לָבָן בַּבֹּקֶר וַיְנַשֵּׁק לְבָנָיו
sons his (to) kissed and ,morning the in Laban early rose And

וְלִבְנוֹתָיו וַיְבָרֶךְ אֶתְהֶם וַיֵּלֶךְ[e] וַיָּשָׁב[e]
returned and went and ;them blessed and ,daughters his (to) and

2 לָבָן לִמְקֹמוֹ׃ וְיַעֲקֹב הָלַךְ לְדַרְכּוֹ[f] וַיִּפְגְּעוּ־בוֹ
him (in) met and ,way his to went Jacob And .place his to Laban

betwixt me and
thee. 51 And
Laban said to
Jacob, Behold
this heap, and
behold the pil-
lar, which I
have set be-
twixt me and
thee. 52 This
heap be witness,
and the pillar be
witness, that I
will not pass
over this heap to
thee, and that
thou shalt not
pass over this
heap and this
pillar unto me,
for harm. 53 The
God of Abra-
ham, and the
God of Nahor,
the God of their
father, judge be-
twixt us. And
Jacob sware by
the Fear of his
father Isaac.

54 And Jacob
offered a sacri-
fice in the
mountain, and
called his breth-
ren to eat bread:
and they did
eat bread, and
tarried all night
in the mount-
ain. 55 And
early in the
morning Laban
rose up, and
kissed his sons
and his daugh-
ters, and blessed
them: and La-
ban departed,
and returned
unto his place.

And Jacob
went on his way,
and the angels

---

a Sm., G., S., V. have sing., ישפט.

b S. has, *the God of our fathers;* Sm., *the God of Abraham*; G. omits.

c G. omits.

d G. adds, *and they drank.*

e G., S. transpose; V. omits וילך.

f G. adds, *and lifting up his eyes he saw the camp of God drawn up in battle order.*

of God met him. 2 And when Jacob saw them, he said, This *is* God's host: and he called the name of that place Mahanaim. 3 And Jacob sent messengers before him to Esau his brother unto the land of Seir, the country of Edom. 4 And he commanded them, saying, Thus shall ye speak unto my lord Esau; Thy servant Jacob saith thus, I have sojourned with Laban, and stayed there until now: 5 And I have oxen, and asses, flocks, and menservants, and womenservants: and I have sent to tell my lord, that I may find grace in thy sight.

6 And the messengers returned to Jacob, saying, We came to thy brother Esau, and also he cometh to meet thee, and four hundred men with him. 7 Then Jacob was greatly afraid and distressed: and he divided the people that *was* with him, and the flocks, and herds, and the camels, into two bands; 8 And

3 מַלְאֲכֵי אֱלֹהִים׃ וַיֹּאמֶר יַעֲקֹב כַּאֲשֶׁר רָאָם
: them saw he when Jacob said And .God of angels the

מַחֲנֵה אֱלֹהִים זֶה וַיִּקְרָא שֵׁם־הַמָּקוֹם
[2]place of name the called he and ;this [is] God of camp The

הַהוּא מַחֲנָיִם׃
.Mahanaim [1]that

4 וַיִּשְׁלַח יַעֲקֹב מַלְאָכִים לְפָנָיו[a] אֶל־עֵשָׂו
Esau unto him before messengers Jacob sent And

אָחִיו אַרְצָה שֵׂעִיר שְׂדֵה אֱדוֹם׃
.Edom of field the ,Seir of land the to ,brother his

5 וַיְצַו אֹתָם לֵאמֹר[b] כֹּה תֹאמְרוּן לַאדֹנִי
,lord my to say shall you Thus ;saying them commanded he And

לְעֵשָׂו כֹּה אָמַר עַבְדְּךָ יַעֲקֹב עִם־לָבָן
Laban With :Jacob servant thy says Thus ;Esau to

6 גַּרְתִּי וָאֵחַר עַד־עָתָּה׃ וַיְהִי־לִי
me to be to come have And .now until tarried and ,sojourned have I

שׁוֹר וַחֲמוֹר[c] צֹאן וְעֶבֶד וְשִׁפְחָה וָאֶשְׁלְחָה
sent have I and ;slaves female and slaves and ,flocks ,asses and oxen

7 לְהַגִּיד לַאדֹנִי[d] לִמְצֹא־חֵן[e] בְּעֵינֶיךָ׃ וַיָּשֻׁבוּ
returned And .eyes thine in favor find to ,lord my to tell to

הַמַּלְאָכִים אֶל־יַעֲקֹב לֵאמֹר[f] בָּאנוּ אֶל־אָחִיךָ
,brother thy unto came We :saying Jacob unto messengers the

אֶל־עֵשָׂו וְגַם[g] הֹלֵךְ לִקְרָאתְךָ וְאַרְבַּע־
four (and) ,thee meet to coming [is he] also and ,Esau unto

8 מֵאוֹת אִישׁ עִמּוֹ׃ וַיִּירָא יַעֲקֹב מְאֹד[h]
exceedingly Jacob feared And .him with [being] men hundred

וַיֵּצֶר לוֹ[h] וַיַּחַץ אֶת־הָעָם
people the divided he and ; him to distress was [there] and

אֲשֶׁר־אִתּוֹ וְאֶת־הַצֹּאן וְאֶת־הַבָּקָר
,herds the and ,flocks the and ,him with [were] who

9 וְהַגְּמַלִּים[i] לִשְׁנֵי מַחֲנוֹת׃ וַיֹּאמֶר[j] אִם־יָבוֹא
comes If :said he And .camps two into ,camels the and

of God met him. 2 And Jacob said when he saw them, This is God's host: and he called the name of that place Mahanaim. 3 And Jacob sent messengers before him to Esau his brother unto the land of Seir, the field of Edom. 4 And he commanded them, saying, Thus shall ye say unto my lord Esau; Thus saith thy servant Jacob, I have sojourned with Laban, and stayed until now: 5 and I have oxen, and asses *and* flocks, and menservants and maidservants: and I have sent to tell my lord, that I may find grace in thy sight.

6 And the messengers returned to Jacob, saying, We came to thy brother Esau, and moreover he cometh to meet thee, and four hundred men with him. 7 Then Jacob was greatly afraid and was distressed: and he divided the people that was with him, and the flocks, and the herds, and the camels, into two companies; 8 and he said, If

a G. omits.
b S. adds, *to them.*
c Sm., G., S., V. add, *and*, reading וצאן.
d G. adds, *Esau.*
e G. adds, *thy servant.*
f S. adds, *to him.*
g G. omits ו; S. has, *and behold also.*
h S. puts מאד after לו.
i G. omits.
j G., S. add, *Jacob.*

said, If Esau
come to the one
company, and
smite it, then
the other com-
pany which is
left shall escape.
9 And Jacob
said, O God of
my father Abra-
ham, and God
of my father
Isaac, the LORD
which saidst un-
to me, Return
unto thy coun-
try, and to thy
kindred, and I
will deal well
with thee: 10 I
am not worthy
of the least of all
the mercies and
of all the truth,
which thou hast
shewed unto
thy servant; for
with my staff
I passed over
this Jordan;
and now I am
become two
bands. 11 De-
liver me, I pray
thee, from the
hand of my
brother, from
the hand of E-
sau: for I fear
him, lest he will
come and smite
me, *and* the
mother with the
children. 12 And
thou saidst, I
will surely do
thee good, and
make thy seed
as the sand of
the sea, which
cannot be num-
bered for multi-
tude.
13 And he
lodged there
that same night;
and took of that
which came to
his hand a pres-
ent for Esau his
brother; 14 Two
hundred she
goats and twen-
ty he goats, two
hundred ewes,
and twenty
rams, 15 Thirty

עֵשָׂו[a] אֶל־הַמַּחֲנֶה הָאַחַת וְהִכָּהוּ וְהָיָה
be shall (and) ,it smites and ¹one ²camp unto Esau

10 הַמַּחֲנֶה הַנִּשְׁאָר[b] לִפְלֵיטָה׃ וַיֹּאמֶר[c] יַעֲקֹב[c] אֱלֹהֵי
of God : Jacob said And .escape for left is that camp the

אָבִי אַבְרָהָם וֵאלֹהֵי[d] אָבִי יִצְחָק יְהוָה
,Jehovah ; Isaac father my of God and Abraham father my

הָאֹמֵר אֵלַי שׁוּב לְאַרְצְךָ[fe] וּלְמוֹלַדְתְּךָ[e]
,kindred thy to and land thy to Return : me unto saying wast who

11 וְאֵיטִיבָה עִמָּךְ׃ קָטֹנְתִּי מִכֹּל
all [for] (from) small [too] am I .thee with well deal will I and

הַחֲסָדִים וּמִכָּל־הָאֱמֶת אֲשֶׁר עָשִׂיתָ אֶת־
with done hast thou which truth the all and mercies the

עַבְדֶּךָ כִּי בְמַקְלִי[g] עָבַרְתִּי אֶת־הַיַּרְדֵּן הַזֶּה
,¹this ²Jordan over crossed I staff my with for ; servant thy

12 וְעַתָּה הָיִיתִי לִשְׁנֵי מַחֲנוֹת׃ הַצִּילֵנִי נָא
,pray I ,me Deliver .camps two (for) become have I now and

מִיַּד אָחִי מִיַּד[h] עֵשָׂו כִּי־
for ; Esau of hand the from ,brother my of hand the from

יָרֵא אָנֹכִי אֹתוֹ פֶּן־יָבוֹא וְהִכַּנִי אֵם[i]
mother—me smite and come he lest ,him ¹I ³fearing ²[am]

13 עַל־בָּנִים׃ וְאַתָּה אָמַרְתָּ הֵיטֵב אֵיטִיב
well deal will I well Dealing : saidst thou And .children upon

עִמָּךְ וְשַׂמְתִּי אֶת־זַרְעֲךָ כְּחוֹל הַיָּם
,sea the of sand the like seed thy make will I and ,thee with

14 אֲשֶׁר לֹא־יִסָּפֵר מֵרֹב׃ וַיָּלֶן שָׁם
there lodged he And .multitude from numbered be not can which

בַּלַּיְלָה הַהוּא וַיִּקַּח מִן־הַבָּא בְיָדוֹ
,hand his into come had what from took he and ; ¹that ²night in

15 מִנְחָה[j] לְעֵשָׂו אָחִיו׃ עִזִּים מָאתַיִם וּתְיָשִׁים[k]
he-goats and ,hundred two She-goats .brother his Esau for present a

16 עֶשְׂרִים רְחֵלִים מָאתַיִם וְאֵילִים[k] עֶשְׂרִים׃ גְּמַלִּים
camels ; twenty rams and ,hundred two ewes ; twenty

Esau come to
the one com-
pany, and smite
it, then the
company which
is left shall es-
cape.
9 And Ja-
cob said, O God
of my father A-
braham, and
God of my fa-
ther Isaac, O
LORD, which
saidst unto me,
Return unto
thy country, and
to thy kindred,
and I will do
thee good: 10 I
am not worthy
of the least of
all the mercies,
and of all the
truth, which
thou hast shew-
ed unto thy
servant; for
with my staff I
passed over this
Jordan; and
now I am be-
come two com-
panies. 11 De-
liver me, I pray
thee, from the
hand of my
brother, from
the hand of E-
sau: for I fear
him, lest he
come and smite
me, the mother
with the chil-
dren. 12 And
thou saidst, I
will surely do
thee good, and
make thy seed
as the sand of
the sea, which
cannot be num-
bered for multi-
tude.
13 And he
lodged there
that night; and
took of that
which he had
with him a
present for E-
sau his brother;
14 two hundred
she-goats and
twenty he-goats,
two hundred
ewes and twenty
rams, 15 thirty

---

a S. adds, *my brother*.
b G. has, *the second*, השני.
c S. has, *and Jacob prayed and said*.
d S. omits, *and*, ו.
e G. has, *to the land of thy nativity*.
f S. has, *to the land of thy fathers*.
g T. has, *alone*.
h G., S., V. omit.
i G., S. add, *and*, reading ואם.
j G. adds, *and sent*.
k G. omits, *and*, ו.

milch camels
with their colts,
forty kine, and
ten bulls, twen-
ty she asses, and
ten foals. 16
And he deliver-
ed *them* into the
hand of his
servants, every
drove by them-
selves; and said
unto his serv-
ants, Pass over
before me, and
put a space be-
twixt drove and
drove. 17 And
he commanded
the foremost,
saying, When
Esau my brother
meeteth thee,
and asketh thee,
saying, Whose
art thou? and
whither goest
thou? and
whose *are* these
before thee? 18
Then thou shalt
say, *They be*
thy servant Ja-
cob's; it *is* a
present sent un-
to my lord E-
sau: and, be-
hold, also he *is*
behind us.

19 And so com-
manded he the
second, and the
third, and all
that followed
the droves, say-
ing, On this
manner shall
ye speak unto
Esau, when ye
find him. 20
And say ye
moreover, Be-
hold, thy serv-
ant Jacob *is*
behind us. For
he said, I will
appease him
with the present
that goeth be-
fore me, and
afterward I will
see his face;
peradventure he

מֵינִיקוֹת וּבְנֵיהֶם שְׁלֹשִׁים פָּרוֹת אַרְבָּעִים וּפָרִים
bulls and ,forty cows ;thirty colts their and suck giving

17 עֲשָׂרָה אֲתֹנֹת עֶשְׂרִים וַעְיָרִם עֲשָׂרָה׃ וַיִּתֵּן
gave he and ;ten asses young and ,twenty she-asses ;ten

בְּיַד־עֲבָדָיו עֵדֶר עֵדֶר לְבַדּוֹ וַיֹּאמֶר
said he and ;separately ,drove ,drove ,slaves his of hand the into

אֶל־עֲבָדָיו עִבְרוּ לְפָנַי וְרֶוַח תָּשִׂימוּ
put shall you space wide a and me before over Pass :slaves his unto

18 בֵּין עֵדֶר וּבֵין עֵדֶר׃ וַיְצַו
commanded he And .drove (between) and drove between

אֶת־הָרִאשׁוֹן לֵאמֹר[a] כִּי יִפְגָשְׁךָ עֵשָׂו אָחִי
brother my Esau thee meets When ;saying first the

וּשְׁאֵלְךָ לֵאמֹר[b] לְמִי־אַתָּה וְאָנָה תֵלֵךְ
?thou goest whither and ,thou [art] whom To :saying ,thee asks and

19 וּלְמִי אֵלֶּה לְפָנֶיךָ׃ וְאָמַרְתָּ
:say shalt thou And ?thee before these [are] whom to and

לְעַבְדְּךָ לְיַעֲקֹב מִנְחָה הִוא שְׁלוּחָה[c] לַאדֹנִי
,lord my to sent ,[is] it gift a ,Jacob to ,servant thy To

20 לְעֵשָׂו וְהִנֵּה [d]גַם־הוּא אַחֲרֵינוּ׃ וַיְצַו[e]
commanded he And .us behind [is] he also behold and ;Esau to

גַּם אֶת־הַשֵּׁנִי גַּם אֶת־הַשְּׁלִישִׁי גַּם
and ,third the and ,second the both

אֶת־כָּל־הַהֹלְכִים אַחֲרֵי הָעֲדָרִים לֵאמֹר כַּדָּבָר
[2]word Like :saying ,droves the after going those all

הַזֶּה תְּדַבְּרוּן אֶל־עֵשָׂו בְּמֹצַאֲכֶם אֹתוֹ׃
.him finding your in Esau unto speak shall ye [1]this

21 וַאֲמַרְתֶּם[f] גַּם[g] הִנֵּה עַבְדְּךָ יַעֲקֹב[h] אַחֲרֵינוּ
.us behind [is] Jacob servant thy ,behold ,Also :say shall ye And

כִּי־אָמַר אֲכַפְּרָה פָנָיו בַּמִּנְחָה הַהֹלֶכֶת
going one the present the by face his cover will I :said he For

לְפָנָי[i] וְאַחֲרֵי־כֵן אֶרְאֶה פָנָיו אוּלַי
perhaps ,face his see will I afterwards and ;me before

milch camels
and their colts,
forty kine and
ten bulls,
twenty she-asses
and ten foals. 16
And he deliver-
ed them into the
hand of his serv-
ants, every
drove by itself;
and said unto
his servants,
Pass over before
me, and put a
space betwixt
drove and drove.
17 And he com-
manded the
foremost, say-
ing, When E-
sau my brother
meeteth thee,
and asketh thee,
saying, Whose
art thou? and
whither goest
thou? and
whose are these
before thee? 18
then thou shalt
say, *They be* thy
servant Jacob's;
it is a present
sent unto my
lord Esau: and,
behold, he also
is behind us.

19 And he com-
manded also the
second, and the
third, and all
that followed
the droves, say-
ing, On this
manner shall ye
speak unto E-
sau, when ye
find him; 20
and ye shall say,
Moreover, be-
hold, thy serv-
ant Jacob is be-
hind us. For he
said, I will ap-
pease him with
the present that
goeth before
me, and after-
ward I will see
his face; perad-
venture he will

---

a S. adds, *to him*.
b S. adds, *to thee*.
c G., S., V. have, *he has sent*.
d G. omits גם.
e G. adds, *the first*.
f S. adds, *to him*.
g G. omits.
h Sm., G., T., V. add, *comes*, בא
i G. has, *before him*, לפניו.

will accept of
me. 21 So went
the present over
before him: and
himself lodged
that night in the
company. 22
And he rose up
that night, and
took his two
wives, and his
two womenserv-
ants, and his
eleven sons, and
passed over the
ford Jabbok. 23
And he took
them, and sent
them over the
brook, and sent
over that he
had.

24 And Jacob
was left alone;
and there wres-
tled a man with
him until the
breaking of the
day. 25 And
when he saw
that he prevail-
ed not against
him, he touched
the hollow of
his thigh; and
the hollow of
Jacob's thigh
was out of joint,
as he wrestled
with him. 26
And he said,
Let me go, for
the day break-
eth. And he
said, I will not
let thee go, ex-
cept thou bless
me. 27 And he
said unto him,
What *is* thy
name? And he
said, Jacob. 28
And he said,
Thy name shall
be called no
more Jacob, but
Israel; for as a
prince hast thou
power with
God and with
men, and hast
prevailed. 29

22 יִשָּׂא פָנָי׃ וַתַּעֲבֹר הַמִּנְחָה עַל־פָּנָיו
; him before present the over passed And .face my up lift will he

23 וְהוּא לָן בַּלַּיְלָה־הַהוּא בַּמַּחֲנֶה׃ וַיָּקָם ׀
arose he And .camp the in night that in lodged he and

בַּלַּיְלָה הוּא וַיִּקַּח אֶת־שְׁתֵּי נָשָׁיו וְאֶת־שְׁתֵּי
[2]two and ,wives [1]his [2]two took and [1]that [2]night in

שִׁפְחֹתָיו וְאֶת־אַחַד עָשָׂר יְלָדָיו
,children [1]his [4]ten [3][and] [2]one and ,slaves female [1]his

24 וַיַּעֲבֹר[a] אֵת מַעֲבַר[b] יַבֹּק׃ וַיִּקָּחֵם
,them took he And .Jabbok the of crossing the over crossed and

וַיַּעֲבִרֵם[c] אֶת־הַנָּחַל וַיַּעֲבֵר
cross to caused he and ; brook the cross to them caused and

25 אֶת־אֲשֶׁר[d]־לוֹ׃ וַיִּוָּתֵר יַעֲקֹב לְבַדּוֹ וַיֵּאָבֵק
wrestled and ,alone Jacob left was And .him to [was] what

26 אִישׁ עִמּוֹ עַד עֲלוֹת הַשָּׁחַר׃ וַיַּרְא
saw he And .dawn the of up going the until him with man a

כִּי לֹא יָכֹל לוֹ וַיִּגַּע
struck he and ; him against prevailed [2]had [1]he [3]not that

בְּכַף־יְרֵכוֹ וַתֵּקַע כַּף־יֶרֶךְ
of hip the of socket the dislocated was and ,hip his of socket the (on)

27 יַעֲקֹב בְּהֵאָבְקוֹ עִמּוֹ׃ וַיֹּאמֶר[e] שַׁלְּחֵנִי
,away me Send : said he And .him with wrestling his in Jacob

כִּי עָלָה הַשָּׁחַר וַיֹּאמֶר לֹא אֲשַׁלֵּחֲךָ
away thee send [2]will [1]I [3]Not : said he And .dawn the up gone has for

28 כִּי אִם־בֵּרַכְתָּנִי׃ וַיֹּאמֶר אֵלָיו מַה־
[is] What : him unto said he And .me bless thou (if) unless

29 שְּׁמֶךָ וַיֹּאמֶר יַעֲקֹב׃ וַיֹּאמֶר[f] לֹא יַעֲקֹב
Jacob Not : said he And .Jacob : said he And ? name thy

יֵאָמֵר עוֹד שִׁמְךָ כִּי אִם־יִשְׂרָאֵל[g] כִּי־
because ; Israel (if) but ,name thy still called be shall

שָׂרִיתָ עִם־אֱלֹהִים[h] וְעִם־אֲנָשִׁים[i] וַתּוּכָל[j]׃
.prevailed hast and men with and God with fought hast thou

accept me. 21
So the present
passed over be-
fore him: and
he himself lodg-
ed that night in
the company. 22
And he rose up
that night, and
took his two
wives, and his
two handmaids,
and his eleven
children, and
passed over the
ford of Jabbok.
23 And he took
them, and sent
them over the
stream, and sent
over that he
had.

24 And Jacob
was left alone;
and there wres-
tled a man with
him until the
breaking of the
day. 25 And
when he saw
that he pre-
vailed not a-
gainst him, he
touched the hol-
low of his thigh;
and the hollow
of Jacob's thigh
was strained, as
he wrestled with
him. 26 And he
said, Let me go,
for the day
breaketh. And
he said, I will
not let thee go,
except thou
bless me. 27
And he said un-
to him, What is
thy name? And
he said, Jacob.
28 And he said,
Thy name shall
be called no
more Jacob, but
Israel: for thou
hast striven with
God and with
men, and hast
prevailed. 29

---

a S. has, *and caused them to cross over*, ויעבירם.
b S. has, *wilderness*, מדבר.
c G. has, *and he crossed*, וַיַּעֲבֹר.
d G., S., V. have, *all which*, כל אשר.
e G., S. add, *to him*.
f G., S. add, *to him*.
g G. adds, *shall be thy name*.
h S. has, *the angel*.
i S. has sing., *man*.
j G. omits, *and*, ו.

And Jacob asked *him*, and said, Tell *me*, I pray thee, thy name. And he said, Wherefore *is* it *that* thou dost ask after my name? And he blessed him there. 30 And Jacob called the name of the place Peniel: for I have seen God face to face, and my life is preserved. 31 And as he passed over Penuel the sun rose upon him, and he halted upon his thigh. 32 Therefore the children of Israel eat not *of* the sinew which shrank, which *is* upon the hollow of the thigh, unto this day: because he touched tbe hollow of Jacob's thigh in the sinew that shrank.

30 וַיִּשְׁאַל[a] יַעֲקֹב וַיֹּאמֶר הַגִּידָה־נָּא[b] שְׁמֶךָ

.name thy ,pray I ,Tell : said and Jacob asked And

וַיֹּאמֶר[c] לָמָּה זֶּה תִּשְׁאַל לִשְׁמִי

? name my about ask thou dost ,then ,Why :said he And

31 וַיְבָרֶךְ אֹתוֹ שָׁם׃ וַיִּקְרָא יַעֲקֹב שֵׁם

of name the Jacob called And .there him blessed he And

הַמָּקוֹם פְּנִיאֵל כִּי־רָאִיתִי אֱלֹהִים[d] פָּנִים אֶל־פָּנִים

,face unto face God saw I because ,Peniel place the

32 וַתִּנָּצֵל נַפְשִׁי׃ וַיִּזְרַח־לוֹ הַשֶּׁמֶשׁ כַּאֲשֶׁר

as sun the him for rose And .soul my preserved was yet and

עָבַר אֶת־פְּנוּאֵל וְהוּא צֹלֵעַ

limping [was] he [while] (and) ; Penuel over passed he

33 עַל־יְרֵכוֹ׃ [e]עַל־כֵּן לֹא־יֹאכְלוּ בְנֵי־

of children the eat to accustomed not are Therefore .hip his upon

יִשְׂרָאֵל אֶת־גִּיד הַנָּשֶׁה[f] אֲשֶׁר עַל־כַּף

of socket the upon [is] which ,hip the of sinew the Israel

הַיָּרֵךְ[g] עַד הַיּוֹם הַזֶּה כִּי נָגַע בְּכַף־

of socket the (on) struck he because ,[1]this [2]day until ,hip the

יֶרֶךְ יַעֲקֹב בְּגִיד הַנָּשֶׁה׃[f]

.hip the of sinew the (on) ,Jacob of hip the

And Jacob asked him, and said, Tell me, I pray thee, thy name. And he said, Wherefore is it that thou dost ask after my name? And he blessed him there. 30 And Jacob called the name of the place Peniel: for, *said he*, I have seen God face to face, and my life is preserved. 31 And the sun rose upon him as he passed over Penuel, and he halted upon his thigh. 32 Therefore the children of Israel eat not the sinew of the hip which is upon the hollow of the thigh, unto this day: because he touched the hollow of Jacob's thigh in the sinew of the hip.

33

AND Jacob lifted up his eyes, and looked, and, behold, Esau came, and with him four hundred men. And he divided the children unto Leah, and unto Rachel, and unto the two handmaids. 2 And he put the handmaids and their children foremost, and Leah and her children after, and Rachel and

1 וַיִּשָּׂא יַעֲקֹב עֵינָיו וַיַּרְא וְהִנֵּה עֵשָׂו[h]

Esau behold and ,saw and eyes his Jacob raised And

בָּא וְעִמּוֹ אַרְבַּע מֵאוֹת אִישׁ וַיַּחַץ[i]

divided he and ; men hundred four him with and ,coming

אֶת־הַיְלָדִים עַל־לֵאָה וְעַל־רָחֵל וְעַל שְׁתֵּי

two the unto and ,Rachel unto and ,Leah unto children the

2 הַשְּׁפָחוֹת׃ וַיָּשֶׂם[j] אֶת־הַשְּׁפָחוֹת[k] וְאֶת־יַלְדֵיהֶן

children their and slaves female the put he And .slaves female

רִאשֹׁנָה וְאֶת־לֵאָה וִילָדֶיהָ אַחֲרֹנִים וְאֶת־רָחֵל

Rachel and ; behind children her and Leah and ; first

And Jacob lifted up his eyes, and looked, and, behold, Esau came, and with him four hundred men. And he divided the children unto Leah, and unto Rachel, and unto the two handmaids. 2 And he put the handmaids and their children foremost, and Leah and her children after, and Rachel

---

a S. adds, *him*.
b G., S., V. add, *to me*.
c S. adds, *to him*.
d S. has, *the angel;* T. *the angel of God*.
e G. adds, *because*.
f S. has, *of woman*.
g G., V. add, *of Jacob*.
h G. adds, *his brother*.
i G. adds, *Jacob*.
j S. has, *and he caused to cross over*, וַיַּעֲבֵר.
k G., V. add, *two*.

Joseph hinder-
most. 3 And he
passed over be-
fore them, and
bowed himself
to the ground
seven times, un-
til he came
near to his
brother. 4 And
Esau ran to
meet him, and
embraced him,
and fell on his
neck, and kissed
him: and they
wept. 5 And he
lifted up his
eyes, and saw
the women and
the children;
and said, Who
are those with
thee? And he
said, The chil-
dren which God
hath graciously
given thy serv-
ant.
6 Then the
handmaidens
came near, they
and their chil-
dren, and they
bowed them-
selves. 7 And
Leah also with
her children
came near, and
bowed them-
selves: and after
came Joseph
near and Ra-
chel, and they
bowed them-
selves. 8 And he
said, What
meanest thou by
all this drove
which I met?
And he said,
These are to find
grace in the
sight of my
lord. 9 And E-
sau said, I have
enough, my
brother; keep
that thou hast
unto thyself. 10
And Jacob said,
Nay, I pray
thee, if now I
have found
grace in thy
sight, then re-
ceive my present

3 וְאֶת־יוֹסֵף אַחֲרֹנִים׃ וְהוּא עָבַר לִפְנֵיהֶם
; them before over passed he And .behind Joseph and

וַיִּשְׁתַּחוּ אַרְצָה שֶׁבַע פְּעָמִים עַד־
until ,times seven earth the to himself prostrated he and

4 גִּשְׁתּוֹ[a] עַד־אָחִיו׃[a] וַיָּרָץ עֵשָׂו לִקְרָאתוֹ
,him meet to Esau ran And .brother his unto even approaching his

וַיְחַבְּקֵהוּ וַיִּפֹּל עַל־צַוָּארָו וַיִּשָּׁקֵהוּ[b]
; him kissed and ,neck his upon fell and ,him embraced and

5 וַיִּבְכּוּ׃[c] וַיִּשָּׂא[d] אֶת־עֵינָיו וַיַּרְא אֶת־הַנָּשִׁים
women the saw and eyes his raised he And .wept they and

וְאֶת־הַיְלָדִים וַיֹּאמֶר מִי־אֵלֶּה לָּךְ׃
? thee for these [are] Who ; said he and children the and

וַיֹּאמַר הַיְלָדִים אֲשֶׁר־חָנַן אֱלֹהִים
God favored has whom [with] children The : said he And

6 אֶת־עַבְדֶּךָ׃ וַתִּגַּשְׁןָ הַשְּׁפָחוֹת הֵנָּה[e]
they ,slaves female the approached And .servant thy

7 וְיַלְדֵיהֶן וַתִּשְׁתַּחֲוֶיןָ׃ וַתִּגַּשׁ
approached And .themselves prostrated they and ,children their and

גַּם־לֵאָה[f] וִילָדֶיהָ וַיִּשְׁתַּחֲווּ וְאַחַר
afterwards and ,themselves prostrated and children her and Leah also

8 נִגַּשׁ יוֹסֵף[g] וְרָחֵל[g] וַיִּשְׁתַּחֲווּ׃ וַיֹּאמֶר[h]
: said he And .themselves prostrated and Rachel and Joseph approached

מִי[i] לְךָ כָּל־הַמַּחֲנֶה הַזֶּה אֲשֶׁר פָּגָשְׁתִּי
? met I which ,[1]this [2]camp all [is] ,thee for ,Who

9 וַיֹּאמֶר[j] לִמְצֹא־חֵן[k] בְּעֵינֵי אֲדֹנִי׃ וַיֹּאמֶר
said And .lord my of eyes the in favor find To : said he And

עֵשָׂו יֶשׁ־לִי רָב אָחִי יְהִי לְךָ
thee to be [that] let ; brother my ,much me to is [There] : Esau

10 אֲשֶׁר־לָךְ׃ וַיֹּאמֶר יַעֲקֹב אַל־נָא[l] אִם־נָא
,now ,if ;pray I ,Nay : Jacob said And .thee to [is] which

מָצָאתִי חֵן בְּעֵינֶיךָ וְלָקַחְתָּ מִנְחָתִי
present my take (and) ,eyes thine in favor found have I

and Joseph hin-
dermost. 3 And
he himself pass-
ed over before
them, and bow-
ed himself to the
ground seven
times, until he
came near to his
brother. 4 And
Esau ran to
meet him, and
embraced him,
and fell on his
neck, and kissed
him: and they
wept. 5 And he
lifted up his
eyes, and saw
the women and
the children;
and said, Who
are these with
thee? And he
said, The chil-
dren which God
hath graciously
given thy serv-
ant.
6 Then the
handmaids came
near, they and
their children,
and they bowed
themselves. 7
And Leah also
and her chil-
dren came near,
and bowed
themselves: and
after came Jo-
seph near and
Rachel, and
they bowed
themselves. 8
And he said,
What meanest
thou by all this
company which
I met? And he
said, To find
grace in the
sight of my lord.
9 And Esau
said, I have e-
nough; my
brother, let that
thou hast be
thine. 10 And
Jacob said, Nay,
I pray thee, if
now I have
found grace in
thy sight, then
receive my pre-
sent at my hand:

---

a G., V. have, *until his brother's approaching.*
b G. puts after ויחבקהו.
c G. adds, *both,* שניהם.
d S. adds, *Esau.*
e G. omits.
f G. omits גם.
g G., S. transpose, reading רחל ויוסף.
h S. adds, *Esau to Jacob.*
i G. adds, *these.*
j S. adds, *to him Jacob.*
k G. adds, *thy servant;* S. *I.*
l G. omits; S. has, *to him.*

at my hand: for
therefore I have
seen thy face, as
though I had
seen the face of
God, and thou
wast pleased
with me. 11
Take, I pray
thee, my bless-
ing that is
brought to thee;
because God
hath dealt gra-
ciously with me,
and because I
have enough.
And he urged
him, and he
took *it*. 12 And
he said, Let us
take our jour-
ney, and let us
go, and I will
go before thee.
13 And he said
unto him, My
lord knoweth
that the chil-
dren *are* tender,
and the flocks
and herds with
young *are* with
me: and if men
should overdrive
them one day,
all the flock will
die. 14 Let my
lord, I pray thee,
pass over before
his servant: and
I will lead on
softly, accord-
ing as the cattle
that goeth be-
fore me and the
children be able
to endure, until
I come unto my
lord unto Seir.
15 And Esau
said, Let me
now leave with
thee *some* of the
folk that *are*
with me. And
he said, What
needeth it? let
me find grace in
the sight of my
lord.

16 So Esau
returned that
day on his way

מִיָּדִי כִּי־עַל־כֵּן רָאִיתִי פָנֶיךָ כִּרְאֹת
seeing like ,face thy seen have I that because ; hand my from

פְּנֵי אֱלֹהִים[a] וַתִּרְצֵנִי׃ קַח־נָא 11
,pray I ,Take .me to favorable been hast thou and ,God of face the

אֶת־בִּרְכָתִי אֲשֶׁר הֻבָאת[b] לָךְ כִּי־חַנַּנִי
me favored has because ,thee to brought been has which blessing my

אֱלֹהִים וְכִי יֶשׁ־לִי־כֹל וַיִּפְצַר־בּוֹ
,him (on) urged he and ; all me to is [there] because and ,God

וַיִּקָּח׃ וַיֹּאמֶר[c] נִסְעָה וְנֵלֵכָה וְאֵלְכָה[d] 12
go will I and ,go and depart us Let : said he And .took he and

לְנֶגְדֶּךָ[e]׃ וַיֹּאמֶר אֵלָיו אֲדֹנִי יֹדֵעַ 13
knowing [is] lord My : him unto said he And .presence thy in

כִּי־הַיְלָדִים רַכִּים וְהַצֹּאן וְהַבָּקָר
herds the and flocks the and ,tender [are] children the that

עָלוֹת עָלָי וּדְפָקוּם[f]
them overdrive they [if] and ; me upon [are which] suck giving [are]

יוֹם אֶחָד וָמֵתוּ כָּל־הַצֹּאן׃ יַעֲבָר־נָא 14
,pray I ,over pass Let .flocks the all die will (and) ,[1]one [2]day

אֲדֹנִי לִפְנֵי עַבְדּוֹ וַאֲנִי אֶתְנָהֲלָה
slowly on move will I and ,servant his before lord my

לְאִטִּי לְרֶגֶל הַמְּלָאכָה אֲשֶׁר־
[is] which property the of pace the to according ; ease my at

לְפָנַי וּלְרֶגֶל הַיְלָדִים עַד אֲשֶׁר־
(that) until ; children the of pace the to according and ,me before

אָבֹא אֶל־אֲדֹנִי שֵׂעִירָה׃ וַיֹּאמֶר עֵשָׂו אַצִּיגָה־ 15
,place me Let : Esau said And .Seir to ,lord my unto in come I

נָּא עִמְּךָ מִן־הָעָם אֲשֶׁר אִתִּי
.me with [are] who people the of [some] thee with ,pray I

וַיֹּאמֶר[g] לָמָּה זֶּה אֶמְצָא־חֵן בְּעֵינֵי
of eyes the in favor find me let ? then ,Why :said he And

אֲדֹנִי׃ וַיָּשָׁב בַּיּוֹם הַהוּא עֵשָׂו לְדַרְכּוֹ 16
,way his to Esau [1]that [2]day in returned And .lord my

forasmuch as I
have seen thy
face, as one
seeth the face of
God, and thou
wast pleased
with me. 11
Take, I pray
thee, my gift
that is brought
to thee; because
God hath dealt
graciously with
me, and because
I have enough.
And he urged
him, and he
took it. 12 And
he said, Let us
take our jour-
ney, and let us
go, and I will
go before thee.
13 And he said
unto him, My
lord knoweth
that the chil-
dren are tender,
and that the
flocks and herds
with me give
suck: and if they
overdrive them
one day, all the
flocks will die.
14 Let my lord,
I pray thee, pass
over before his
servant: and I
will lead on
softly, accord-
ing to the pace
of the cattle
that is before
me and accord-
ing to the pace
of the children,
until I come un-
to my lord unto
Seir. 15 And E-
sau said, Let me
now leave with
thee some of
the folk that are
with me. And he
said, What
needeth it? let
me find grace in
the sight of my
lord.

16 So Esau
returned that
day on his way

---

a S. has, *an angel;* T. *princes.*

b Sm., G., S., V. have, *I have brought*, הבאתי.

c S. adds, *to him Esau.*

d G. omits.

e G. has, *at once.*

f Sm., G., S., V. have first person, ודפקתים.

g S. adds, *Jacob.*

unto Seir. 17
And Jacob journeyed to Succoth, and built him an house, and made booths for his cattle: therefore the name of the place is called Succoth.

18 And Jacob came to Shalem, a city of Shechem, which *is* in the land of Canaan, when he came from Padan-aram; and pitched his tent before the city. 19 And he
bought a parcel of a field, where he had spread his tent, at the hand of the children of Hamor, Shechem's father, for an hundred pieces of money. 20 And
he erected there an altar, and called it El-elohe-Israel.

17 שֵׂעִירָה׃ וְיַעֲקֹב נָסַע סֻכֹּתָה וַיִּבֶן
built he and ,Succoth to journeyed Jacob And .Seir toward

לוֹ[a] בָּיִת וּלְמִקְנֵהוּ עָשָׂה סֻכֹּת עַל־כֵּן
therefore ; booths made he cattle his for and house a himself for

קָרָא שֵׁם־הַמָּקוֹם סֻכּוֹת׃
.Succoth place the of name the called he

18 וַיָּבֹא יַעֲקֹב שָׁלֵם עִיר שְׁכֶם אֲשֶׁר
[is] which ,Shechem of city the to safety in Jacob came And

בְּאֶרֶץ כְּנַעַן בְּבֹאוֹ מִפַּדַּן אֲרָם
; Aram Paddan from coming his in ,Canaan of land the in

19 וַיִּחַן אֶת־פְּנֵי הָעִיר׃ וַיִּקֶן אֶת־
bought he And .city the before encamped he and

חֶלְקַת הַשָּׂדֶה אֲשֶׁר נָטָה־שָׁם אָהֳלוֹ
,tent his (there) pitched had he where field the of portion the

מִיַּד בְּנֵי־חֲמוֹר[b] אֲבִי שְׁכֶם
,Shechem of father the Hamor of sons the of hand the from

20 בְּמֵאָה קְשִׂיטָה׃ וַיַּצֶּב־שָׁם[c] מִזְבֵּחַ
,altar an there established he And .Kesitah hundred a for

וַיִּקְרָא־לוֹ[d] אֵל[d] אֱלֹהֵי יִשְׂרָאֵל׃
.Israel of God the El ,it to called he and

unto Seir. 17
And Jacob journeyed to Succoth, and built him an house, and made booths for his cattle: therefore the name of the place is called Succoth.

18 And Jacob came in peace to the city of Shechem, which is in the land of Canaan, when he came from Paddan-aram: and encamped before the city.
19 And he bought the parcel of ground, where he had spread his tent, at the hand of the children of Hamor, Shechem's father, for an hundred pieces of money.
20 And he erected there an altar, and called it El-elohe-Israel.

34

AND Dinah the daughter of Leah, which she bare unto Jacob, went out to see the daughters of the land.
2 And when Shechem the son of Hamor the Hivite, prince of the country, saw her, he took her, and lay with her, and defiled her. 3 And his
soul clave unto Dinah the daughter of Jacob, and he loved

1 וַתֵּצֵא דִינָה בַּת־לֵאָה אֲשֶׁר יָלְדָה
bore she whom ,Leah of daughter the Dinah out went And

2 לְיַעֲקֹב לִרְאוֹת בִּבְנוֹת הָאָרֶץ׃ וַיַּרְא
saw And .land the of daughters the upon look to Jacob to

אֹתָהּ שְׁכֶם בֶּן־חֲמוֹר הַחִוִּי[e] נְשִׂיא
of prince the Hivite the Hamor of son the ,Shechem her

הָאָרֶץ וַיִּקַּח אֹתָהּ[f] וַיִּשְׁכַּב אֹתָהּ וַיְעַנֶּהָ׃
.her humiliated and ,her with lay and her took he and ,land the

3 וַתִּדְבַּק[g] נַפְשׁוֹ בְּדִינָה[g] בַּת־יַעֲקֹב וַיֶּאֱהַב
loved he and ; Jacob of daughter the Dinah to soul his clung And

And Dinah the daughter of Leah, which she bare unto Jacob, went out to see the daughters of the land. 2 And Shechem the son of Hamor the Hivite, the prince of the land, saw her; and he took her, and lay with her, and humbled her. 3 And his soul clave unto Dinah the daughter of Jacob, and he loved the dam-

a G. adds, *there.*
b G. omits בני.
c S. adds, *and he pitched there his tent.*
d G. omits לו אל.
e G. has, *the Horite,* החרי.
f S. has, *Dinah.*
g G. has, *and he devoted himself to the soul of Din: h.*

ed the damsel, and spake kindly unto the damsel. 4 And Shechem spake unto his father Hamor, saying, Get me this damsel to wife. 5 And Jacob heard that he had defiled Dinah his daughter: now his sons were with his cattle in the field: and Jacob held his peace until they were come.

6 And Hamor the father of Shechem went out unto Jacob to commune with him. 7 And the sons of Jacob came out of the field when they heard *it*: and the men were grieved, and they were very wroth, because he had wrought folly in Israel in lying with Jacob's daughter; which thing ought not to be done. 8 And Hamor communed with them, saying, The soul of my son Shechem longeth for your daughter: I pray you give her him to wife. 9 And make ye marriages with us, *and* give your daughters unto us, and take our daughters unto you. 10 And ye shall dwell with us: and the land shall be before you; dwell and trade ye therein, and get you pos-

4 אֶת־הַנַּעֲרָ וַיְדַבֵּר עַל־לֵב הַנַּעֲרָ[a]: וַיֹּאמֶר
said And .maid the of heart the unto spoke and maid the

שְׁכֶם אֶל־חֲמוֹר אָבִיו לֵאמֹר[b] קַח־לִי
me for Take : saying ,father his Hamor unto Shechem

5 אֶת־הַיַּלְדָּה הַזֹּאת לְאִשָּׁה: וְיַעֲקֹב שָׁמַע כִּי
that heard had Jacob And .wife a for [1]this [2]girl

טִמֵּא[c] אֶת־דִּינָה בִתּוֹ וּבָנָיו הָיוּ
were sons his [while] (and) ,daughter his Dinah defiled had he

אֶת־מִקְנֵהוּ בַּשָּׂדֶה וְהֶחֱרִשׁ יַעֲקֹב עַד־
until Jacob silent was and ; field the in cattle his with

6 בֹּאָם: וַיֵּצֵא חֲמוֹר אֲבִי־שְׁכֶם
Shechem of father the Hamor went And .coming their

7 אֶל־יַעֲקֹב לְדַבֵּר אִתּוֹ: וּבְנֵי יַעֲקֹב
Jacob of sons the And .him with speak to ,Jacob unto

בָּאוּ מִן־הַשָּׂדֶה כְּשָׁמְעָם[d] וַיִּתְעַצְּבוּ[e]
furious were and ,hearing their at field the from in came

הָאֲנָשִׁים וַיִּחַר לָהֶם מְאֹד כִּי נְבָלָה
folly because ; exceedingly them to was anger and ,men the

עָשָׂה[f] בְיִשְׂרָאֵל לִשְׁכַּב אֶת־בַּת־יַעֲקֹב
,Jacob of daughter the with lie to Israel in done had he

8 וְכֵן לֹא יֵעָשֶׂה: וַיְדַבֵּר חֲמוֹר אִתָּם
them with Hamor spoke And .done be [2]should [1]it [3]not so and

לֵאמֹר[g] שְׁכֶם בְּנִי חָשְׁקָה נַפְשׁוֹ בְּבִתְּכֶם
; daughter your to soul his bound is ,son my Shechem : saying

9 תְּנוּ נָא אֹתָהּ לוֹ לְאִשָּׁה: וְהִתְחַתְּנוּ
with ye intermarry and ; wife a for him to her ,pray I ,ye give

אֹתָנוּ בְּנֹתֵיכֶם תִּתְּנוּ־לָנוּ וְאֶת־בְּנֹתֵינוּ
daughters our and ,us to give daughters your ,us

10 תִּקְחוּ לָכֶם[h]: וְאִתָּנוּ תֵּשֵׁבוּ וְהָאָרֶץ[i]
land the (and) ; dwell us with And .yourselves for take

תִּהְיֶה[j] לִפְנֵיכֶם שְׁבוּ וּסְחָרוּהָ וְהֵאָחֲזוּ
fast yourselves hold and ,it in traffic and dwell ,you before being

sel, and spake kindly unto the damsel. 4 And Shechem spake unto his father Hamor, saying, Get me this damsel to wife. 5 Now Jacob heard that he had defiled Dinah his daughter; and his sons were with his cattle in the field: and Jacob held his peace until they came.

6 And Hamor the father of Shechem went out unto Jacob to commune with him. 7 And the sons of Jacob came in from the field when they heard it: and the men were grieved, and they were very wroth, because he had wrought folly in Israel in lying with Jacob's daughter; which thing ought not to be done. 8 And Hamor communed with them, saying, The soul of my son Shechem longeth for your daughter: I pray you give her unto him to wife. 9 And make ye marriages with us; give your daughters unto us, and take our daughters unto you. 10 And ye shall dwell with us: and the land shall be before you; dwell and trade ye therein, and get you posses-

---

a G. adds, *to her.*

b S. omits.

c G. adds, *the son of Hamor.*

d S., V. add, *and,* ו.

e S., V. omit ו.

f G. adds, *Shechem.*

g S. adds, *to them.*

h G. has, *for your sons;* V. omits.

i G., S. have, *and behold the land.*

j G. has, *broad.*

sessions therein. 11 And Shechem said unto her father and unto her brethren, Let me find grace in your eyes, and what ye shall say unto me I will give. 12 Ask me never so much dowry and gift, and I will give according as ye shall say unto me: but give me the damsel to wife. 13 And the sons of Jacob answered Shechem and Hamor his father deceitfully, and said, because he had defiled Dinah their sister: 14 And they said unto them, We cannot do this thing, to give our sister to one that is uncircumcised; for that *were* a reproach unto us: 15 But in this will we consent unto you: If ye will be as we *be*, that every male of you be circumcised; 16 Then will we give our daughters unto you, and we will take your daughters to us, and we will dwell with you, and we will become one people. 17 But if ye will not hearken unto us, to be circumcised; then will we take our daughter, and we will be gone.

בָּהּ׃ וַיֹּאמֶר שְׁכֶם אֶל־אָבִיהָ וְאֶל־אַחֶיהָ 11
:brothers her unto and ,father her unto Shechem said And .it in

אֶמְצָא־חֵן בְּעֵינֵיכֶם וַאֲשֶׁר תֹּאמְרוּ אֵלַי[a]
me unto say you what and ,eyes your in favor find me Let

אֶתֵּן[a]׃ הַרְבּוּ עָלַי[b] מְאֹד מֹהַר וּמַתָּן[c] 12
,dowry and price exceedingly me upon Increase .give will I

וְאֶתְּנָה כַּאֲשֶׁר תֹּאמְרוּ אֵלָי [d]וּתְנוּ־לִי
me to give and — me unto say you as give will I and

אֶת־הַנַּעֲרָ לְאִשָּׁה׃ וַיַּעֲנוּ בְנֵי־יַעֲקֹב 13
Jacob of sons the answered And .wife a for maid the

אֶת־שְׁכֶם וְאֶת־חֲמוֹר אָבִיו בְּמִרְמָה[e] וַיְדַבֵּרוּ[f]
; spoke and ,deceit with father his Hamor and Shechem

אֲשֶׁר טִמֵּא[g] אֵת דִּינָה אֲחֹתָם׃ וַיֹּאמְרוּ 14
said they And .sister their Dinah defiled had he because

אֲלֵיהֶם[h] לֹא נוּכַל לַעֲשׂוֹת הַדָּבָר הַזֶּה לָתֵת
give to ,¹this ²thing do to able ²are ¹we ³Not ; them unto

אֶת־אֲחֹתֵנוּ לְאִישׁ אֲשֶׁר־לוֹ עָרְלָה כִּי־
for ; uncircumcision [is] whom to man a to sister our

חֶרְפָּה הִוא לָנוּ׃ אַךְ־בְּזֹאת[i] נֵאוֹת[j] 15
consent will we [condition] this on Only .us to [is] it reproach a

לָכֶם[j] אִם תִּהְיוּ כָמֹנוּ לְהִמֹּל לָכֶם
you to circumcised be to ,us like become will you if ; you to

כָּל־זָכָר[k]׃ וְנָתַנּוּ אֶת־בְּנֹתֵינוּ לָכֶם 16
,you to daughters our give will we [then] (and) ; male every

וְאֶת־בְּנֹתֵיכֶם נִקַּח־לָנוּ[l] וְיָשַׁבְנוּ אִתְּכֶם
,you with dwell will we And .us for take will we daughters your and

וְהָיִינוּ לְעַם אֶחָד׃ וְאִם־לֹא תִשְׁמְעוּ 17
hearken ²do ¹you ³not if And .¹one ²people (for) become will we and

אֵלֵינוּ לְהִמּוֹל וְלָקַחְנוּ אֶת־בִּתֵּנוּ
daughter our take will we (and) ; circumcised be to us unto

sions therein. 11 And Shechem said unto her father and unto her brethren, Let me find grace in your eyes, and what ye shall say unto me I will give. 12 Ask me never so much dowry and gift, and I will give according as ye shall say unto me: but give me the damsel to wife. 13 And the sons of Jacob answered Shechem and Hamor his father with guile, and spake, because he had defiled Dinah their sister, 14 and said unto them, We cannot do this thing, to give our sister to one that is uncircumcised; for that were a reproach unto us: 15 only on this condition will we consent unto you: if ye will be as we be, that every male of you be circumcised; 16 then will we give our daughters unto you, and we will take your daughters to us, and we will dwell with you, and we will become one people. 17 But if ye will not hearken unto us, to be circumcised; then will we take our daughter, and we will be gone.

18 And their words pleased Hamor, and She-

וְהָלָכְנוּ׃ וַיִּיטְבוּ דִבְרֵיהֶם בְּעֵינֵי חֲמוֹר 18
Hamor of eyes the in words their good seemed And .go will we and

18 And their words pleased Hamor, and

a G. has, *unto us we will give.*
b G., V. omit.
c G. omits.
d S. omits, *and,* וְ.
e S. puts after וידברו.
f G., S. add, *to them.*
g Sm., G., S. have pl.
h S., V. omit; G adds, *Simeon and Levi the brothers of Dinah and sons of Leah;* cf. vs. 25.
i G. omits אַךְ.
j G. has, *we will become like you and will dwell among you.*
k S. adds, *as we are circumcised.*
l G. adds, *wives.*

chem Hamor's son. 19 And the young man deferred not to do the thing, because he had delight in Jacob's daughter: and he *was* more honourable than all the house of his father.

20 And Hamor and Shechem his son came unto the gate of their city, and communed with the men of their city, saying, 21 These men *are* peaceable with us; therefore let them dwell in the land, and trade therein; for the land, behold, *it is* large enough for them; let us take their daughters to us for wives, and let us give them our daughters. 22 Only herein will the men consent unto us for to dwell with us, to be one people, if every male among us be circumcised, as they *are* circumcised. 23 *Shall* not their cattle and their substance and every beast of theirs *be* our's? only let us consent unto them, and they will dwell with us. 24 And unto Hamor and unto Shechem his son hearkened all that went out of the gate of his city; and ev-

19 וּבְעֵינֵי שְׁכֶם בֶּן־חֲמוֹר[a]: וְלֹא־אֵחַר
delay not did And .Hamor of son the Shechem of eyes the in and

הַנַּעַר לַעֲשׂוֹת הַדָּבָר כִּי חָפֵץ בְּבַת־
of daughter the in delighted he because ,thing the do to youth the

יַעֲקֹב וְהוּא נִכְבָּד מִכֹּל בֵּית
of house the all than more ,honored [being] he (and) ;Jacob

20 אָבִיו: וַיָּבֹא חֲמוֹר וּשְׁכֶם בְּנוֹ אֶל־
unto son his Shechem and Hamor in came And .father his

שַׁעַר עִירָם וַיְדַבְּרוּ אֶל־אַנְשֵׁי עִירָם
city their of men the unto spoke they and ;city their of gate the

21 לֵאמֹר[b]: הָאֲנָשִׁים הָאֵלֶּה שְׁלֵמִים הֵם אִתָּנוּ
: us with they [are] peaceable ,[1]these [2]Men ; saying

וְיֵשְׁבוּ[c] בָאָרֶץ וְיִסְחֲרוּ אֹתָהּ וְהָאָרֶץ
,land the (and) ,it in traffic and land the in dwell them let and

הִנֵּה רַחֲבַת־יָדַיִם לִפְנֵיהֶם אֶת־בְּנֹתָם
daughters their ; them before hands both [on] wide [being] ,behold

נִקַּח־לָנוּ לְנָשִׁים וְאֶת־בְּנֹתֵינוּ נִתֵּן
give us let daughters our and ,wives for ourselves for take us let

22 לָהֶם: אַךְ־בְּזֹאת יֵאֹתוּ לָנוּ הָאֲנָשִׁים
men the us to consent will [condition] this on Only .them to

לָשֶׁבֶת אִתָּנוּ לִהְיוֹת לְעָם אֶחָד
; [1]one [2]people (for) become to ,us with dwell to

בְּהִמּוֹל לָנוּ כָּל־זָכָר כַּאֲשֶׁר הֵם נִמֹּלִים:
.circumcised [are] they as ,male every us to circumcised being in

23 מִקְנֵהֶם[d] וְקִנְיָנָם וְכָל־בְּהֶמְתָּם
,burden of beasts their all and ,property their and ,cattle Their

הֲלוֹא[e] לָנוּ הֵם אַךְ[f] נֵאוֹתָה לָהֶם
,them to consent us let Only ? [2]they [[4]be [1]will] [6]us [5]to [3]not

24 וְיֵשְׁבוּ אִתָּנוּ: וַיִּשְׁמְעוּ אֶל־חֲמוֹר[g] וְאֶל־
unto and ,Hamor unto hearkened And .us with dwell them let and

שְׁכֶם בְּנוֹ[g] כָּל־יֹצְאֵי שַׁעַר עִירוֹ
;city his of gate the [from] (of) out going those all ,son his Shechem

Shechem Hamor's son. 19 And the young man deferred not to do the thing, because he had delight in Jacob's daughter: and he was honoured above all the house of his father.

20 And Hamor and Shechem his son came unto the gate of their city, and communed with the men of their city, saying, 21 These men are peaceable with us; therefore let them dwell in the land, and trade therein; for, behold, the land is large enough for them; let us take their daughters to us for wives, and let us give them our daughters. 22 Only on this condition will the men consent unto us to dwell with us, to become one people, if every male among us be circumcised, as they are circumcised. 23 Shall not their cattle and their substance and all their beasts be ours? only let us consent unto them, and they will dwell with us. 24 And unto Hamor and unto Shechem his son hearkened all that went out of the gate of his city; and

a S., V. have, *his son*, בנו.
b S. adds, *to them.*
c G., Sm., S. omit *and*, ו.
d G. adds, *and*, ו.
e V. omits; S. omits, and adds, *they*.
f G., V. add, *in this.*
g S. has, *unto Shechem and Hamor his father;* V. omits.

ery male was
circumcised, all
that went out of
the gate of his
city.

25 And it
came to pass on
the third day,
when they were
sore, that two of
the sons of Ja-
cob, Simeon and
Levi, Dinah's
brethren, took
each man his
sword, and
came upon the
city boldly, and
slew all the
males. 26 And
they slew Ha-
mor and She-
chem his son
with the edge
of the sword,
and took Dinah
out of She-
chem's house,
and went out.
27 The sons of
Jacob came up-
on the slain,
and spoiled the
city, because
they had defiled
their sister. 28
They took their
sheep, and their
oxen, and their
asses, and that
which *was* in
the city, and
that which *was*
in the field, 29
And all their
wealth, and all
their little ones,
and their wives
took they cap-
tive, and spoiled
even all that
was in the
house. 30 And
Jacob said to
Simeon and
Levi, Ye have
troubled me to
make me to
stink among the
inhabitants of
the land, among
the Canaanites

וַיִּמֹּלוּ[a] כָּל־זָכָר[a] כָּל־יֹצְאֵי[b]
(of) out going those all ,male every ,circumcised were they and

25 שַׁעַר עִירוֹ׃[b] וַיְהִי בַיּוֹם
[2]day the on pass to came it And .city his of gate the [from]

הַשְּׁלִישִׁי בִּהְיוֹתָם כֹּאֲבִים וַיִּקְחוּ שְׁנֵי־בְנֵי־יַעֲקֹב
,Jacob of sons two the took (and) ;sick being their in ,[1]third

שִׁמְעוֹן וְלֵוִי אֲחֵי דִינָה[c] אִישׁ חַרְבּוֹ
;sword his each ,Dinah of brothers ,Levi and Simeon

וַיָּבֹאוּ עַל־הָעִיר בֶּטַח וַיַּהַרְגוּ כָּל־זָכָר׃
.male every killed and ,security in city the upon came they and

26 וְאֶת־חֲמוֹר וְאֶת־שְׁכֶם בְּנוֹ הָרְגוּ
killed they son his Shechem and Hamor And

לְפִי־חָרֶב וַיִּקְחוּ אֶת־דִּינָה מִבֵּית
of house the from Dinah took they and ;sword the of mouth the at

27 שְׁכֶם וַיֵּצֵאוּ׃ [d]בְּנֵי יַעֲקֹב בָּאוּ עַל־הַחֲלָלִים
,slain the upon came Jacob of sons The .out went and Shechem

וַיָּבֹזּוּ הָעִיר אֲשֶׁר טִמְּאוּ[e] אֲחוֹתָם׃
.sister their defiled had they because ;city the plundered and

28 [f]אֶת־צֹאנָם וְאֶת־בְּקָרָם וְאֶת־חֲמֹרֵיהֶם וְאֵת
and ,asses their and herds their and flocks Their

אֲשֶׁר־בָּעִיר וְאֶת־אֲשֶׁר בַּשָּׂדֶה לָקָחוּ׃
.took they ,field the in [was] what and ,city the in [was] what

29 וְאֶת־כָּל־חֵילָם וְאֶת־כָּל־טַפָּם[g] וְאֶת־
and ,ones little their all and ,wealth their all And

נְשֵׁיהֶם שָׁבוּ וַיָּבֹזּוּ וְאֵת[h] כָּל־אֲשֶׁר
which all (and) ,plundered and captive carried they ,wives their

30 בַּבָּיִת[h]׃ וַיֹּאמֶר יַעֲקֹב אֶל־שִׁמְעוֹן וְאֶל־
unto and Simeon unto Jacob said And .house the in [was]

לֵוִי עֲכַרְתֶּם אֹתִי לְהַבְאִישֵׁנִי
stink me make to ,me disturbed have You :Levi

בְּיֹשֵׁב הָאָרֶץ בַּכְּנַעֲנִי
Canaanites the among ,land the of inhabitants the among

every male was
circumcised, all
that went out
of the gate of
his city.

25 And it
came to pass on
the third day,
when they were
sore, that two of
the sons of Ja-
cob, Simeon
and Levi, Di-
nah's brethren,
took each man
his sword, and
came upon the
city unawares,
and slew all the
males. 26 And
they slew Ha-
mor and She-
chem his son
with the edge of
the sword, and
took Dinah out
of Shechem's
house, and went
forth. 27 The
sons of Jacob
came up-
on the slain,
and spoiled the
city, because
they had defiled
their sister. 28
They took their
flocks and their
herds and their
asses, and that
which was in
the city, and
that which was
in the field; 29
and all their
wealth, and all
their little ones
and their wives,
took they cap-
tive and spoiled,
even all that
was in the
house. 30 And
Jacob said to
Simeon and
Levi, Ye have
troubled me, to
make me to
stink among the
inhabitants of
the land, a-
mong the Ca-

---

a G. has, *and they circumcised the flesh of their fore-skin, every male.*

b G., V. omit.

c S., V. add, *their sister.*

d Sm., G., S. add, *and,* ו.

e G., S. add, *Dinah.*

f Sm., G., S. add, *and,* ו.

g Sm., V. omit, *and all,* ואת-כל.

h G. has, *all which was in the city and all which was in the houses.*

-and the Periz-
zites: and I
being few in
number, they
shall gather
themselves to-
gether against
me, and slay
me; and I shall
be destroyed, I
and my house.
31 And they
said, Should he
deal with our
sister as with an
harlot?

וּבַפְּרִזִּי וַאֲנִי מְתֵי מִסְפָּר
; number of men [being] I (and) ; Perizzites the among and

וְנֶאֶסְפוּ עָלַי וְהִכּוּנִי
,me smite will they (and) ,me against gathered are they [if] and

31 וְנִשְׁמַדְתִּי אֲנִי וּבֵיתִי׃ וַיֹּאמְרוּ
:said they And .house my and I ,destroyed be shall I and

הַכְזוֹנָה יַעֲשֶׂה אֶת־אֲחוֹתֵנוּ׃
? sister our treat one should harlot a Like

naanites and
the Perizzites:
and, I being
few in number,
they will gather
themselves to-
gether against
me and smite
me; and I shall
be destroyed, I
and my house.
31 And they
said, Should he
deal with our
sister as with an
harlot?

35

AND God said
unto Jacob, A-
rise, go up to
Beth-el, and
dwell there: and
make there an
altar unto God,
that appeared
unto thee when
thou fleddest
from the face of
Esau thy broth-
er. 2 Then Ja-
cob said unto
his household,
and to all that
were with him,
Put away the
strange gods
that *are* among
you, and be
clean, and
change your
garments: 3 And
let us arise, and
go up to Beth-
el; and I will
make there an
altar unto God,
who answered
me in the day of
my distress,
and was with me
in the way
which I went. 4
And they gave
unto Jacob all
the strange gods
which *were* in
their hand, and
all their ear-
rings which
were in their
ears; and Jacob

1 וַיֹּאמֶר אֱלֹהִים אֶל־יַעֲקֹב קוּם עֲלֵה בֵית־אֵל
,Bethel to up go ,Arise :Jacob unto God said And

וְשֶׁב־שָׁם וַעֲשֵׂה־שָׁם מִזְבֵּחַ לָאֵל הַנִּרְאֶה
appeared who God to altar an there make and ; there dwell and

2 אֵלֶיךָ בְּבָרְחֲךָ מִפְּנֵי עֵשָׂו אָחִיךָ׃ וַיֹּאמֶר
said And .brother thy Esau before from fleeing thy in thee unto

יַעֲקֹב אֶל־בֵּיתוֹ וְאֶל כָּל־אֲשֶׁר עִמּוֹ
: him with [were] who all unto and ,house his unto Jacob

הָסִרוּ אֶת־אֱלֹהֵי הַנֵּכָר אֲשֶׁר[a] בְּתֹכְכֶם[a]
,midst your in [are] which strangeness of gods the Remove

3 וְהִטַּהֲרוּ וְהַחֲלִיפוּ שִׂמְלֹתֵיכֶם׃ וְנָקוּמָה
arise us let And .clothing your change and ,yourselves purify and

וְנַעֲלֶה בֵּית־אֵל [b]וְאֶעֱשֶׂה־שָּׁם מִזְבֵּחַ לָאֵל
God to altar an there make will I and ; Bethel to up go and

הָעֹנֶה אֹתִי בְּיוֹם צָרָתִי וַיְהִי עִמָּדִי[c]
me with was he and ; misery my of day the in me answered who

4 בַּדֶּרֶךְ אֲשֶׁר הָלָכְתִּי׃ וַיִּתְּנוּ אֶל־יַעֲקֹב
Jacob unto gave they And .went I which [in] way the in

אֵת [d]כָּל־אֱלֹהֵי הַנֵּכָר אֲשֶׁר בְּיָדָם וְאֶת־
and ,hand their in [were] which strangeness of gods the all

הַנְּזָמִים אֲשֶׁר בְּאָזְנֵיהֶם וַיִּטְמֹן אֹתָם יַעֲקֹב
Jacob them hid and ; ears their in [were] which rings the

And God said
unto Jacob, A-
rise, go up to
Beth-el, and
dwell there:
and make there
an altar unto
God, who ap-
peared unto thee
when thou fled-
dest from the
face of Esau thy
brother. 2 Then
Jacob said unto
his household,
and to all that
were with him,
Put away the
strange gods
that are among
you, and purify
yourselves, and
change your
garments: 3 and
let us arise, and
go up to Beth-
el; and I will
make there an
altar unto God,
who answered
me in the day of
my distress, and
was with me in
the way which I
went. 4 And
they gave unto
Jacob all the
strange gods
which were in
their hand,
and the rings
which were in
their ears; and
Jacob hid them

a G., S. have, *from your midst*, מתככם.
b For ואעשה, G., V. have, *and we will make.*
c G. adds, *and kept me.*
d G. omits, *all*, כל.

hid them under the oak which *was* by Shechem. 5 And they journeyed: and the terror of God was upon the cities that *were* round about them, and they did not pursue after the sons of Jacob.

6 So Jacob came to Luz, which *is* in the land of Canaan, that *is*, Beth-el, he and all the people that *were* with him. 7 And he built there an altar, and called the place El-beth-el: because there God appeared unto him, when he fled from the face of his brother. 8 But Deborah Rebekah's nurse died, and she was buried beneath Beth-el under an oak: and the name of it was called Allon-bachuth.

9 And God appeared unto Jacob again, when he came out of Padan-aram, and blessed him. 10 And God said unto him, Thy name *is* Jacob: thy name shall not be called any more Jacob, but Israel shall be thy name: and he called his name Israel. 11 And God said unto him, I *am* God Almighty:

5 תַּחַת הָאֵלָה אֲשֶׁר עִם־שְׁכֶם[a]׃ וַיִּסָּעוּ[b]
,journeyed they And .Shechem near [was] which terebinth the under
וַיְהִי חִתַּת אֱלֹהִים עַל־הֶעָרִים אֲשֶׁר
[were] which cities the upon God of terror the was and
סְבִיבוֹתֵיהֶם וְלֹא רָדְפוּ אַחֲרֵי בְּנֵי[c]
of sons the after pursue ²did ¹they ³not and ; them about round
6 יַעֲקֹב[c]׃ וַיָּבֹא יַעֲקֹב לוּזָה אֲשֶׁר בְּאֶרֶץ
of land the in [is] which ,Luz to Jacob came And .Jacob
כְּנַעַן הִוא בֵּית־אֵל הוּא וְכָל־הָעָם אֲשֶׁר־
[were] who people the all and he ; Bethel [being] it ,Canaan
7 עִמּוֹ׃ וַיִּבֶן שָׁם מִזְבֵּחַ וַיִּקְרָא לַמָּקוֹם
place the (to) called and ,altar an there built he And .him with
אֵל[d] בֵּית־אֵל· כִּי שָׁם נִגְלוּ אֵלָיו
him unto himself revealed there because ;Bethel El
8 הָאֱלֹהִים בְּבָרְחוֹ מִפְּנֵי[e] אָחִיו׃ וַתָּמָת
died And .brother his before from fleeing his in ,God
דְּבֹרָה מֵינֶקֶת רִבְקָה וַתִּקָּבֵר[f] מִתַּחַת
below (from) buried was and ,Rebekah of nurse the Deborah
לְבֵית־אֵל תַּחַת הָאַלּוֹן וַיִּקְרָא[g] שְׁמוֹ אַלּוֹן
Allon name its called he and ; terebinth the under Bethel (to)
בָּכוּת׃
.Bakuth
9 וַיֵּרָא אֱלֹהִים אֶל־יַעֲקֹב עוֹד[h] בְּבֹאוֹ
coming his in ,again Jacob unto God appeared And
10 מִפַּדַּן אֲרָם וַיְבָרֶךְ אֹתוֹ[i]׃ וַיֹּאמֶר־לוֹ
him to said And .him blessed he and ;Aram Paddan from
אֱלֹהִים שִׁמְךָ[j] יַעֲקֹב[j] לֹא יִקָּרֵא שִׁמְךָ
name thy called be shall not :Jacob [is] name Thy :God
עוֹד יַעֲקֹב כִּי אִם־יִשְׂרָאֵל יִהְיֶה שְׁמֶךָ וַיִּקְרָא[k]
called he and ;name thy be shall Israel (if) but ,Jacob still
11 אֶת־שְׁמוֹ יִשְׂרָאֵל[k]׃ וַיֹּאמֶר לוֹ אֱלֹהִים אֲנִי אֵל[l]
God [am] I :God him to said And .Israel name his

under the oak which was by Shechem. 5 And they journeyed: and a great terror was upon the cities that were round about them, and they did not pursue after the sons of Jacob.

6 So Jacob came to Luz, which is in the land of Canaan (the same is Beth-el), he and all the people that were with him. 7 And he built there an altar, and called the place El-beth-el: because there God was revealed unto him, when he fled from the face of his brother. 8 And Deborah Rebekah's nurse died, and she was buried below Beth-el under the oak: and the name of it was called Allon-bacuth.

9 And God appeared unto Jacob again, when he came from Paddan-aram, and blessed him. 10 And God said unto him, Thy name is Jacob: thy name shall not be called any more Jacob, but Israel shall be thy name: and he called his name Israel. 11 And God said unto him, I am God Almighty:

---

a G. adds, *and he destroyed them until this day.*

b G. adds, *Israel from Shechem.*

c G. has, *sons of Israel;* S. *Jacob and his sons;* V. *those departing.*

d G., S., V. omit.

e G., S. add, *Esau.*

f G. omits.

g G. adds, *Jacob.*

h G. adds, *in Luz.*

i Sm., G. add, *God.*

j G., S., V. omit.

k G. omits.

l For אל שדי G. has, *thy God.*

be fruitful and multiply: a nation and a company of nations shall be of thee, and kings shall come out of thy loins; 12 And the land which I gave Abraham and Isaac, to thee I will give it, and to thy seed after thee will I give the land. 13 And God went up from him in the place where he talked with him. 14 And Jacob set up a pillar in the place where he talked with him, *even* a pillar of stone: and he poured a drink offering thereon, and he poured oil thereon. 15 And Jacob called the name of the place where God spake with him, Beth-el.

16 And they journeyed from Beth-el; and there was but a little way to come to Ephrath: and Rachel travailed, and she had hard labour. 17 And it came to pass, when she was in hard labour, that the midwife said unto her, Fear not; thou shalt have this son also. 18 And it came to pass, as her soul was in departing, (for she died) that she called his name Ben-oni: but his father called

שַׁדַּי פְּרֵה וּרְבֵה גּוֹי[a] וּקְהַל
of company a and nation a ; multiply and fruitful be ,Almighty

גּוֹיִם יִהְיֶה מִמֶּךָּ וּמְלָכִים מֵחֲלָצֶיךָ יֵצֵאוּ׃
; forth go let loins thy from kings and ,thee from be let nations

12 וְאֶת־הָאָרֶץ אֲשֶׁר נָתַתִּי[b] לְאַבְרָהָם וּלְיִצְחָק לְךָ
thee to ,Isaac to and Abraham to gave I which land the and

אֶתְּנֶנָּה וּלְזַרְעֲךָ אַחֲרֶיךָ אֶתֵּן אֶת־הָאָרֶץ׃
.land the give will I thee after seed thy to and ; it give will I

13 וַיַּעַל מֵעָלָיו אֱלֹהִים בַּמָּקוֹם אֲשֶׁר־
where place the in ,God him (upon) from up went And

14 דִּבֶּר אִתּוֹ׃ וַיַּצֵּב יַעֲקֹב מַצֵּבָה
pillar memorial a Jacob established And .him with spoken had he

בַּמָּקוֹם אֲשֶׁר־דִּבֶּר אִתּוֹ מַצֶּבֶת
of pillar memorial a ,him with spoken had he where place the in

אָבֶן וַיַּסֵּךְ עָלֶיהָ נֶסֶךְ וַיִּצֹק
poured he and ; libation a it upon out poured he and ; stone

15 עָלֶיהָ שָׁמֶן׃ וַיִּקְרָא יַעֲקֹב אֶת־שֵׁם הַמָּקוֹם
place the of name the Jacob called And .oil it upon

אֲשֶׁר דִּבֶּר אִתּוֹ שָׁם אֱלֹהִים בֵּיתְאֵל׃
.Bethel God (there) him with spoken had where

16 וַיִּסְעוּ[c] מִבֵּיתְאֵל[d] וַיְהִי־עוֹד כִּבְרַת־
kibrah a still was [there] and ,Bethel from journeyed they And

הָאָרֶץ לָבוֹא אֶפְרָתָה וַתֵּלֶד רָחֵל
,Rachel forth brought and ; Ephrath to come to land of

17 וַתְּקַשׁ בְּלִדְתָּהּ׃ וַיְהִי
,pass to came it And .forth bringing her in difficulty found she and

בְהַקְשֹׁתָהּ בְלִדְתָּהּ[e] וַתֹּאמֶר לָהּ
her to said that ,forth bringing her in difficulty finding her in

הַמְיַלֶּדֶת אַל־תִּירְאִי כִּי־גַם־זֶה לָךְ[f] בֵּן׃
.son a thee to now also for ,fear not Do : midwife the

18 וַיְהִי בְּצֵאת נַפְשָׁהּ כִּי מֵתָה
,died she for ,[2]soul's [1]her [4]forth [3]going in pass to came it And

וַתִּקְרָא שְׁמוֹ בֶּן־אוֹנִי וְאָבִיו קָרָא־לוֹ
him (to) called father his but ;Benoni name his called she that

be fruitful and multiply; a nation and a company of nations shall be of thee, and kings shall come out of thy loins; 12 and the land which I gave unto Abraham and Isaac, to thee I will give it, and to thy seed after thee will I give the land. 13 And God went up from him in the place where he spake with him. 14 And Jacob set up a pillar in the place where he spake with him, a pillar of stone: and he poured out a drink offering thereon, and poured oil thereon. 15 And Jacob called the name of the place where God spake with him, Beth-el.

16 And they journeyed from Beth-el; and there was still some way to come to Ephrath: and Rachel travailed, and she had hard labour. 17 And it came to pass, when she was in hard labour, that the midwife said unto her, Fear not; for now thou shalt have another son. 18 And it came to pass, as her soul was in departing (for she died), that she called his name Ben-oni: but his father called

a V. has, *nations;* G. *and nations.*

b S. has, *I swore,* נשבעתי.

c G., S., V. have sing.; G. adds, *Jacob.*

d G. adds, *and pitched his tent beyond the tower of Gader;* which is transferred from 21 b.

e S. omits.

f G. omits.

him Benjamin.
19 And Rachel
died, and was
buried in the
way to Eph-
rath, which *is*
Beth-lehem. 20
And Jacob set a
pillar upon her
grave: that *is*
the pillar of Ra-
chel's grave un-
to this day.

21 And Israel
journeyed, and
spread his tent
beyond the tow-
er of Edar. 22
And it came to
pass, when Is-
rael dwelt in
that land, that
Reuben went
and lay with
Bilhah his fath-
er's concubine:
and Israel heard
it. Now the
sons of Jacob
were twelve: 23
The sons of
Leah; Reuben,
Jacob's first-
born, and Sim-
eon, and Levi,
and Judah, and
Issachar, and
Zebulun: 24 The
sons of Rachel;
Joseph, and
Benjamin: 25
And the sons of
Bilhah, Rachel's
handmaid; Dan,
and Naphtali:
26 And the sons
of Zilpah,
Leah's hand-
maid; Gad, and
Asher: these
are the sons of
Jacob, which
were born to
him in Padan-
aram.

27 And Jacob
came unto Isaac
his father unto
Mamre, unto the
city of Arbah,

19 בִּנְיָמִין׃ וַתָּמָת רָחֵל וַתִּקָּבֵר בְּדֶרֶךְ
of way the in buried was and Rachel died And .Benjamin

20 אֶפְרָתָה הִוא בֵּית לָחֶם׃ וַיַּצֵּב יַעֲקֹב
Jacob established And .Lehem Beth [being] it ,Ephrath

מַצֵּבָה עַל־קְבֻרָתָהּ[a] הִוא מַצֶּבֶת
of pillar memorial the [being] it ,grave her upon pillar memorial a

21 [b]קְבֻרַת־רָחֵל עַד־הַיּוֹם׃ [c]וַיִּסַּע יִשְׂרָאֵל
Israel departed And ;today until Rachel of grave the

וַיֵּט אָהֳלֹה מֵהָלְאָה לְמִגְדַּל־עֵדֶר׃
.flocks the of tower the to side other the from tent his pitched and

22 וַיְהִי בִּשְׁכֹּן יִשְׂרָאֵל בָּאָרֶץ הַהִוא
;[1]that [2]land in Israel of abiding the in pass to came it And

וַיֵּלֶךְ רְאוּבֵן וַיִּשְׁכַּב אֶת־בִּלְהָה פִּילֶגֶשׁ
of concubine the Bilhah with lay and Reuben went that

אָבִיו וַיִּשְׁמַע יִשְׂרָאֵל[d]
.Israel heard and ,father his

23 וַיִּהְיוּ בְנֵי־יַעֲקֹב שְׁנֵים עָשָׂר׃ בְּנֵי
of sons The .ten [and] two Jacob of sons the were And

לֵאָה בְּכוֹר יַעֲקֹב רְאוּבֵן [e]וְשִׁמְעוֹן [e]וְלֵוִי
,Levi and ,Simeon and ;Reuben Jacob of firstborn the ;Leah

24 [e]וִיהוּדָה [e]וְיִשָּׂשכָר [e]וּזְבוּלֻן׃ [f]בְּנֵי רָחֵל יוֹסֵף
,Joseph ,Rachel of sons the ;Zebulun and ,Issachar and ,Judah and

25 וּבִנְיָמִן׃ וּבְנֵי בִלְהָה שִׁפְחַת רָחֵל
,Rachel of slave female the Bilhah of sons the and ;Benjamin and

26 דָּן וְנַפְתָּלִי׃ וּבְנֵי זִלְפָּה שִׁפְחַת
of slave female the Zilpah of sons the and ;Naphtali and ,Dan

לֵאָה גָּד וְאָשֵׁר אֵלֶּה בְּנֵי יַעֲקֹב אֲשֶׁר
who ,Jacob of sons the [were] these ;Asher and ,Gad ,Leah

27 יֻלַּד־לוֹ בְּפַדַּן אֲרָם׃ וַיָּבֹא יַעֲקֹב
Jacob in came And .Aram Paddan in him to born were

אֶל־יִצְחָק אָבִיו מַמְרֵא קִרְיַת הָאַרְבַּע הִוא
[being] it ,Arba Kiriath to ,Mamre to father his Isaac unto

him Benjamin.
19 And Rachel
died, and was
buried in the
way to Ephrath
(the same is
Beth-lehem). 20
And Jacob set
up a pillar upon
her grave: the
same is the Pil-
lar of Rachel's
grave unto this
day.

21 And Israel
journeyed, and
spread his tent
beyond the tow-
er of Eder. 22
And it came to
pass, while Isra-
el dwelt in that
land, that Reu-
ben went and
lay with Bilhah
his father's con-
cubine: and Is-
rael heard of it.
Now the sons of
Jacob were
twelve: 23 the
sons of Leah;
Reuben, Jacob's
firstborn, and
Simeon, and
Levi, and Ju-
dah, and Issa-
char, and Zeb-
ulun: 24 the
sons of Ra-
chel; Joseph
and Benjamin.
25 and the sons
of Bilhah, Ra-
chel's hand-
maid; Dan and
Naphtali: 26
and the sons of
Zilpah, Leah's
handmaid; Gad
and Asher:
these are the
sons of Jacob,
which were born
to him in Pad-
dan-aram.

27 And Jacob
came unto Isaac
his father to
Mamre, to Kir-
iath-arba (the

---

a S. has, *tomb of Rachel*.

b G. omits, *grave*, קברת.

c G. omits vs. 21.

d G. adds, *and it appeared evil before him*, probably וירע בעיניו.

e G. omits, *and*, ו.

f Sm., G., S. add, *and*, ו.

which *is* Hebron, where Abraham and Isaac sojourned. 28 And the days of Isaac were an hundred and fourscore years. 29 And Isaac gave up the ghost, and died, and was gathered unto his people, *being* old and full of days: and his sons Esau and Jacob buried him.

חֶבְרוֹן [a] אֲשֶׁר־גָּר־שָׁם אַבְרָהָם וְיִצְחָק׃ וַיִּהְיוּ 28
were And .Isaac and Abraham sojourned where ; Hebron

יְמֵי יִצְחָק [b] מְאַת שָׁנָה וּשְׁמֹנִים שָׁנָה׃ וַיִּגְוַע 29
expired And .years eighty and years hundred a Isaac of days the

יִצְחָק וַיָּמָת וַיֵּאָסֶף אֶל־עַמָּיו זָקֵן
old ,people his unto gathered was and died and Isaac

וּשְׂבַע יָמִים וַיִּקְבְּרוּ אֹתוֹ עֵשָׂו וְיַעֲקֹב
Jacob and Esau him buried and ; days [with] (of) satisfied and

בָּנָיו׃ [c]
.sons his

same is Hebron), where Abraham and Isaac sojourned. 28 And the days of Isaac were an hundred and fourscore years. 29 And Isaac gave up the ghost, and died, and was gathered unto his people, old and full of days: and Esau and Jacob his sons buried him.

36

Now these *are* the generations of Esau, who is Edom. 2 Esau took his wives of the daughters of Canaan; Adah the daughter of Elon the Hittite, and Aholibamah the daughter of Anah the daughter of Zibeon the Hivite; 3 And Bashemath Ishmael's daughter, sister of Nebajoth. 4 And Adah bare to Esau Eliphaz; and Bashemath bare Reuel; 5 And Aholibamah bare Jeush, and Jaalam, and Korah: these *are* the sons of Esau, which were born unto him in the land of Canaan. 6 And Esau took his wives, and his sons, and his daughters, and all the persons of his house, and his cattle,

וְאֵלֶּה תֹּלְדוֹת עֵשָׂו [d] הוּא אֱדוֹם׃ 1
.Edom [being] he ,Esau of generations the are these And

[e] עֵשָׂו לָקַח [f] אֶת־נָשָׁיו מִבְּנוֹת כְּנָעַן 2
; Canaan of daughters the from wives his took Esau

אֶת־עָדָה בַּת־אֵילוֹן הַחִתִּי וְאֶת־אָהֳלִיבָמָה
Oholibamah and ,Hittite the Elon of daughter the Adah

בַּת־עֲנָה [g] בַּת־צִבְעוֹן הַחִוִּי׃ וְאֶת־ 3
and ,Hivite the Zibeon of daughter the Anah of daughter the

בָּשְׂמַת בַּת־יִשְׁמָעֵאל אֲחוֹת נְבָיוֹת׃ וַתֵּלֶד 4
bore And .Nebaioth of sister the ,Ishmael of daughter the Basemath

עָדָה לְעֵשָׂו אֶת־אֱלִיפָז וּבָשְׂמַת יָלְדָה אֶת־רְעוּאֵל 5
; Reuel bore Basemath and ; Eliphaz Esau to Adah

וְאָהֳלִיבָמָה יָלְדָה אֶת־יְעִישׁ וְאֶת־יַעְלָם וְאֶת־קֹרַח
; Korah and ,Jalam and ,Jeush bore Oholibamah and

אֵלֶּה בְּנֵי עֵשָׂו אֲשֶׁר יֻלְּדוּ־לוֹ בְּאֶרֶץ
of land the in him to born were who ,Esau of sons the [were] these

כְּנָעַן׃ וַיִּקַּח עֵשָׂו אֶת־נָשָׁיו וְאֶת־בָּנָיו 6
,sons his and ,wives his Esau took And .Canaan

וְאֶת־בְּנֹתָיו וְאֶת־כָּל־נַפְשׁוֹת בֵּיתוֹ וְאֶת־
and ; house his of souls the all and ,daughters his and

Now these are the generations of Esau (the same is Edom). 2 Esau took his wives of the daughters of Canaan; Adah the daughter of Elon the Hittite, and Oholibamah the daughter of Anah, the daughter of Zibeon the Hivite; 3 and Basemath Ishmael's daughter, sister of Nebaioth. 4 And Adah bare to Esau Eliphaz; and Basemath bare Reuel; 5 and Oholibamah bare Jeush, and Jalam, and Korah: these are the sons of Esau, which were born unto him in the land of Canaan. 6 And Esau took his wives, and his sons, and his daughters, and all the souls of his house, and

a G., S. add, *in the land of Canaan*, בארץ כנען.

b G. adds, *which he lived*, אשר חי.

c S. adds, *in the grave which Abraham his father had bought*.

d S. adds, *Esau*, a second time.

e G. adds, *and*, ו.

f G. adds, *for himself*.

g Instead of בת Sm., G., S. have, *son*, בן.

and all his
beasts, and all
his substance,
which he had got
in the land of
Canaan; and
went into the
country from the
face of his
brother Jacob. 7
For their riches
were more than
that they might
dwell together;
and the land
wherein they
were strangers
could not bear
them because of
their cattle. 8
Thus dwelt Esau
in mount Seir:
Esau *is* Edom.
9 And these
are the genera-
tions of Esau
the father of the
Edomites in
mount Seir: 10
These *are* the
names of Esau's
sons; Eliphaz
the son of Adah
the wife of E-
sau, Reuel the
son of Bashe-
math the wife of
Esau. 11 And
the sons of Eli-
phaz were Te-
man, Omar,
Zepho, and Ga-
tam, and Ke-
naz. 12 And
Timna was con-
cubine to Eli-
phaz Esau's son;
and she bare to
Eliphaz Ama-
lek: these *were*
the sons of Adah,
Esau's wife. 13
And these *are*
the sons of Re-
uel; Nahath,
and Zerah,
Shammah, and
Mizzah: these
were the sons of
Bashemath, E-
sau's wife.
14 And these
were the sons of
Aholibamah,
the daughter of
Anah the
daughter of Zib-

מִקְנֵהוּ[a] וְאֶת־כָּל־בְּהֶמְתּוֹ וְאֵת כָּל־קִנְיָנוֹ
property his all and ; burden of beasts his all and ,cattle his

אֲשֶׁר רָכַשׁ בְּאֶרֶץ כְּנָעַן וַיֵּלֶךְ
went he and ; Canaan of land the in acquired had he which

7 אֶל־אֶרֶץ[b] מִפְּנֵי יַעֲקֹב אָחִיו׃ כִּי־הָיָה
become had Because .brother his Jacob before from ,land a unto

רְכוּשָׁם רָב מִשֶּׁבֶת יַחְדָּו וְלֹא יָכְלָה
able was not and ; together dwelling from great possessions their

אֶרֶץ מְגוּרֵיהֶם לָשֵׂאת אֹתָם מִפְּנֵי[c] מִקְנֵיהֶם׃
.cattle their before from them bear to sojournings their of land the

8 וַיֵּשֶׁב עֵשָׂו בְּהַר שֵׂעִיר עֵשָׂו הוּא אֱדוֹם
.Edom being Esau ,Seir of mountain the in Esau dwelt And

9 וְאֵלֶּה תֹּלְדוֹת עֵשָׂו אֲבִי אֱדוֹם
,Edom of father the Esau of generations the [are] these And

10 בְּהַר שֵׂעִיר׃ [d]אֵלֶּה שְׁמוֹת בְּנֵי־עֵשָׂו
; Esau of sons the of names the [are] these ; Seir of mountain the in

אֱלִיפַז בֶּן־עָדָה אֵשֶׁת עֵשָׂו [e]רְעוּאֵל בֶּן־
of son the Reuel ; Esau of wife the Adah of son the Eliphaz

11 בָּשְׂמַת אֵשֶׁת עֵשָׂו׃ וַיִּהְיוּ בְּנֵי אֱלִיפָז
Eliphaz of sons the were And .Esau of wife the Basemath

12 תֵּימָן אוֹמָר צְפוֹ וְגַעְתָּם[f] וּקְנַז׃ וְתִמְנַע
Timna And .Kenaz and ,Gatam and Zepho ,Omar ,Teman

הָיְתָה פִילֶגֶשׁ לֶאֱלִיפַז בֶּן־עֵשָׂו וַתֵּלֶד
bore she.(and) ,Esau of son the Eliphaz to concubine a being

לֶאֱלִיפַז אֶת־עֲמָלֵק אֵלֶּה בְּנֵי עָדָה אֵשֶׁת
of wife the Adah of sons the [were] these ; Amalek Eliphaz to

13 עֵשָׂו׃ וְאֵלֶּה בְּנֵי רְעוּאֵל נַחַת וָזֶרַח[g]
,Zerah and ,Nahath ;Reuel of sons the [were] these And .Esau

שַׁמָּה וּמִזָּה אֵלֶּה הָיוּ בְּנֵי בָשְׂמַת
Basemath of sons the were these ; Mizzah and ,Shammah

14 אֵשֶׁת עֵשָׂו׃ וְאֵלֶּה הָיוּ בְּנֵי אָהֳלִיבָמָה
Oholibamah of sons the were these And .Esau of wife the

his cattle, and
all his beasts,
and all his pos-
sessions, which
he had gather-
ed in the land of
Canaan; and
went into a land
away from his
brother Jacob. 7
For their sub-
stance was too
great for them
to dwell togeth-
er; and the land
of their sojourn-
ings could not
bear them be-
cause of their
cattle. 8 And E-
sau dwelt in
mount Seir: E-
sau is Edom.
9 And these
are the genera-
tions of Esau
the father of
the Edomites in
mount Seir:
10 these are
the names of
Esau's sons;
Eliphaz the son
of Adah the
wife of Esau,
Reuel the son of
Basemath the
wife of Esau. 11
And the sons of
Eliphaz were
Teman, Omar,
Zepho, and Ga-
tam, and Ke-
naz. 12 And
Timna was con-
cubine to Eli-
phaz Esau's son;
and she bare to
Eliphaz Ama-
lek: these are
the sons of A-
dah Esau's
wife. 13 And
these are the
sons of Reuel;
Nahath, and
Zerah, Sham-
mah, and Miz-
zah: these were
the sons of Base-
math Esau's
wife.
14 And these
were the sons of
Oholibamah the
daughter of A-
nah, the daugh-

---

a S. omits; G. has, *and all his cattle.*

b S. adds, *Seir;* T., V. add, *another;* Sm., G. have, *from the land of Canaan.*

c G., V. have, *from the multitude of.*

d Sm., G., S., V. add, *and,* ו.

e G., S., V. add, *and,* ו.

f G. omits, *and,* ו.

g G. omits, *and,* ו.

eon, Esau's
wife: and she
bare to Esau
Jeush, and Ja-
alam, and Ko-
rah.

15 These *were*
dukes of the
sons of Esau:
the sons of Eli-
phaz the first-
born *son* of E-
sau; duke Te-
man, duke O-
mar, duke Ze-
pho, duke Ke-
naz, 16 Duke
Korah, duke
Gatam, *and*
duke Amalek:
these *are* the
dukes *that came*
of Eliphaz in the
land of Edom;
these *were* the
sons of Adah.

17 And these
are the sons of
Reuel Esau's
son; duke Na-
hath, duke Ze-
rah, duke Sham-
mah, duke Miz-
zah: these *are*
the dukes *that*
came of Reuel
in the land of
Edom; these
are the sons of
Bashemath, E-
sau's wife.

18 And these
are the sons of
Aholibamah, E-
sau's wife; duke
Jeush, duke Ja-
alam, duke Ko-
rah: these *were*
the dukes *that*
came of Aholi-
bamah, the
daughter of A-
nah, Esau's
wife. 19 These
are the sons of
Esau, who *is*
Edom, and
these *are* their
dukes.

20 These *are*
the sons of Seir
the Horite, who
inhabited the
land; Lotan,
and Shobal, and
Zibeon, and A-
nah, 21 And
Dishon, and E-

בַּת־עֲנָה [a]בַּת־צִבְעוֹן אֵשֶׁת עֵשָׂו
; Esau of wife the Zibeon of daughter the Anah of daughter the

וַתֵּלֶד לְעֵשָׂו אֶת־יְעִישׁ וְאֶת־יַעְלָם וְאֶת־קֹרַח׃
.Korah and ,Jalam and ,Jeush Esau to bore she and

15 אֵלֶּה אַלּוּפֵי בְנֵי־עֵשָׂו בְּנֵי אֱלִיפַז
Eliphaz of sons the ; Esau of sons the of princes the [were] These

בְּכוֹר עֵשָׂו אַלּוּף תֵּימָן אַלּוּף אוֹמָר אַלּוּף
prince ,Omar prince ,Teman prince : Esau of firstborn the

16 צְפוֹ אַלּוּף קְנַז׃ אַלּוּף־קֹרַח[b] אַלּוּף גַּעְתָּם אַלּוּף
prince ,Gatham prince ,Korah prince ,Kenaz prince ,Zepho

עֲמָלֵק אֵלֶּה אַלּוּפֵי אֱלִיפַז בְּאֶרֶץ
of land the in Eliphaz of princes the [were] these ; Amalek

17 אֱדוֹם אֵלֶּה בְּנֵי עָדָה׃ וְאֵלֶּה
these And .Adah of sons the [were] these ; Edom

בְּנֵי רְעוּאֵל בֶּן־עֵשָׂו אַלּוּף נַחַת
,Nahath prince ; Esau of son the Reuel of sons the [were]

אַלּוּף זֶרַח אַלּוּף שַׁמָּה אַלּוּף מִזָּה אֵלֶּה
[were] these ; Mizzah prince ,Shammah prince ,Zerah prince

אַלּוּפֵי רְעוּאֵל בְּאֶרֶץ אֱדוֹם אֵלֶּה
these ;Edom of land the in Reuel of princes the

18 בְּנֵי בָשְׂמַת אֵשֶׁת עֵשָׂו׃ וְאֵלֶּה
these And .Esau of wife the Basemath of sons the [were]

בְּנֵי אָהֳלִיבָמָה אֵשֶׁת עֵשָׂו אַלּוּף יְעוּשׁ
,Jeush prince ; Esau of wife the Oholibamah of sons the [were]

אַלּוּף יַעְלָם אַלּוּף קֹרַח אֵלֶּה אַלּוּפֵי
of princes the [were] these ; Korah prince ,Jalam prince

19 אָהֳלִיבָמָה בַּת־עֲנָה אֵשֶׁת עֵשָׂו׃ אֵלֶּה
[were] These .Esau of wife the Anah of daughter the Oholibamah

בְנֵי־עֵשָׂו וְאֵלֶּה אַלּוּפֵיהֶם[c] הוּא אֱדוֹם׃
.Edom [being] he ,princes their [were] these and Esau of sons the

20 [d]אֵלֶּה בְנֵי־שֵׂעִיר הַחֹרִי יֹשְׁבֵי הָאָרֶץ
; land the in dwelling ,Horite the Seir of sons the [were] These

21 לוֹטָן וְשׁוֹבָל וְצִבְעוֹן וַעֲנָה׃ וְדִשׁוֹן וְאֵצֶר
,Ezer and ,Dishon and ,Anah and ,Zibeon and ,Shobal and ,Lotan

ter of Zibeon,
Esau's wife:
and she bare to
Esau Jeush, and
Jalam, and Ko-
rah.

15 These are
the dukes of
the sons of E-
sau: the sons of
Eliphaz the first-
born of Esau;
duke Teman,
duke Omar,
duke Zepho,
duke Kenaz, 16
duke Korah,
duke Gatam,
duke Amalek:
these are the
dukes that came
of Eliphaz in the
land of Edom;
these are the
sons of Adah.

17 And these
are the sons of
Reuel Esau's
son; duke Na-
hath, duke Ze-
rah, duke Sham-
mah, duke Miz-
zah: these are
the dukes that
came of Reuel
in the land of
Edom; these are
the sons of Base-
math Esau's
wife.

18 And these
are the sons of
Oholibamah E-
sau's wife; duke
Jeush, duke
Jalam, duke
Korah: these
are the dukes
that came of
Oholibamah the
daughter of A-
nah, Esau's
wife. 19 These
are the sons of
Esau, and these
are their dukes:
the same is E-
dom.

20 These are
the sons of Seir
the Horite, the
inhabitants of
the land; Lotan
and Shobal and
Zibeon and A-
nah, 21 and Di-
shon and Ezer

---

a Instead of בת G. has, *son*, בן.

b S. puts after געתם; Sm. omits; cf. v. 18.

c Sm., S. add, *Esau;* G. has, *these are their princes, sons of Edom.*

d Sm., G., S. add, *and*, ו.

zer, and Dishan: these *are* the dukes of the Horites, the children of Seir in the land of Edom. 22 And the children of Lotan were Hori and Hemam; and Lotan's sister *was* Timna. 23 And the children of Shobal *were* these; Alvan, and Manahath, and Ebal, Shepho, and Onam. 24 And these *are* the children of Zibeon; both Ajah, and Anah: this *was that* Anah that found the mules in the wilderness, as he fed the asses of Zibeon his father. 25 And the children of Anah *were* these; Dishon, and Aholibamah the daughter of Anah. 26 And these *are* the children of Dishon; Hemdan, and Eshban, and Ithran, and Cheran. 27 The children of Ezer *are* these; Bilhan, and Zaavan, and Akan. 28 The children of Dishan *are* these; Uz, and Aran. 29 These *are* the dukes *that came* of the Horites; duke Lotan, duke Shobal, duke Zibeon, duke Anah, 30 Duke Dishon, duke Ezer, duke Dishan: these *are* the dukes *that came* of Hori, among their dukes in the land of Seir.

וְדִישָׁן אֵֽלֶּה אַלּוּפֵי הַחֹרִי בְּנֵי
of sons the ,Horites the of princes the [were] these ; Dishan and

22 שֵׂעִיר בְּאֶרֶץ אֱדוֹם׃ וַיִּהְיוּ בְנֵי־לוֹטָן חֹרִי
Hori ,Lotan of sons the were And .Edom of land the in ,Seir

23 וְהֵימָם וַאֲחוֹת לוֹטָן תִּמְנָע׃ וְאֵלֶּה
[were] these And .Timna [was] Lotan of sister the and ;Hemam and

בְּנֵי שׁוֹבָל עַלְוָן וּמָנַחַת וְעֵיבָל [a]שְׁפוֹ
,Shepho ,Ebal and ,Manahath and ,Alvan ;Shobal of sons the

24 וְאוֹנָם׃ וְאֵלֶּה בְנֵי־צִבְעוֹן [b]וְאַיָּה
,Aiah (and) ,Zibeon of sons the [were] these And .Onam and

וַעֲנָה הוּא עֲנָה אֲשֶׁר מָצָא [c]אֶת־הַיֵּמִם
springs hot the found who Anah [being] he ,Anah and

בַּמִּדְבָּר בִּרְעֹתוֹ אֶת־הַחֲמֹרִים לְצִבְעוֹן
Zibeon for asses the tending his in wilderness the in

25 אָבִיו׃ וְאֵלֶּה בְנֵי־עֲנָה דִּשֹׁן
,Dishon ; Anah of sons the [were] these And .father his

26 וְאָהֳלִיבָמָה בַּת־עֲנָה[d]׃ וְאֵלֶּה בְּנֵי
of sons the [were] these And .Anah of daughter the Oholibamah and

דִישָׁן חֶמְדָּן וְאֶשְׁבָּן וְיִתְרָן וּכְרָן׃
.Cheran and Ithran and Eshban and ,Hemdan ; Dishan

27 [e]אֵלֶּה בְּנֵי־אֵצֶר בִּלְהָן וְזַעֲוָן וַעֲקָן׃
.Akan and Zaavan and ,Bilhan ; Ezer of sons the [were] These

28 [f]אֵלֶּה בְנֵי־דִישָׁן עוּץ וַאֲרָן׃ אֵלֶּה
29 [were] These .Aran and Uz ,Dishan of sons the [were] These

אַלּוּפֵי הַחֹרִי אַלּוּף לוֹטָן אַלּוּף שׁוֹבָל אַלּוּף
prince ,Shobal prince ,Lotan prince ; Horites the of princes the

30 צִבְעוֹן אַלּוּף עֲנָה׃ אַלּוּף דִּשֹׁן אַלּוּף אֵצֶר אַלּוּף
prince ,Ezer prince ,Dishon prince ,Anah prince ,Zibeon

דִּישָׁן אֵלֶּה אַלּוּפֵי הַחֹרִי [g]לְאַלֻּפֵיהֶם
princes their to according ,Horites the of princes the [were] these ;Dishan

בְּאֶרֶץ שֵׂעִיר׃
.Seir of land the in

and Dishan: these are the dukes that came of the Horites, the children of Seir in the land of Edom. 22 And the children of Lotan were Hori and Hemam; and Lotan's sister was Timna. 23 And these are the children of Shobal: Alvan and Manahath and Ebal, Shepho and Onam. 24 And these are the children of Zibeon; Aiah and Anah: this is Anah who found the hot springs in the wilderness, as he fed the asses of Zibeon his father. 25 And these are the children of Anah; Dishon and Oholibamah the daughter of Anah. 26 And these are the children of Dishon; Hemdan and Eshban and Ithran and Cheran. 27 These are the children of Ezer; Bilhan and Zaavan and Akan. 28 These are the children of Dishan; Uz and Aran. 29 These are the dukes that came of the Horites; duke Lotan, duke Shobal, duke Zibeon, duke Anah, 30 duke Dishon, duke Ezer, duke Dishan: these are the dukes that came of the Horites, according to their dukes in the land of Seir.

---

a Sm., S., V. add, *and*, ו.

b Sm., G., S., V. omit, *and*, ו; cf. 1 Chr. 1: 40.

c G., Aq., Sym., Theod. transliterate; Sm., T. have, *the Emim*, האימים; S. *the water*, המים; V. *hot springs;* Ar. *mules*.

d S. omits.

e Sm., G., S., V., T. add, *and*, ו.

f Sm., G., S., V. add, *and*, ו.

g G. has, *by their divisions*, perhaps לְאַלְפֵיהֶם.

31 And these *are* the kings that reigned in the land of E-dom, before there reigned any king over the children of Israel. 32 And Bela the son of Beor reigned in Edom: and the name of his city *was* Din-habah. 33 And Bela died, and Jobab the son of Zerah of Boz-rah reigned in his stead. 34 And Jobab died, and Husham of the land of Te-mani reigned in his stead. 35 And Husham died, and Ha-dad the son of Bedad, who smote Midian in the field of Moab, reigned in his stead: and the name of his city *was* A-vith. 36 And Hadad died, and Samlah of Masrekah reign-ed in his stead. 37 And Samlah died, and Saul of Rehoboth *by* the river reign-ed in his stead. 38 And Saul died, and Baal-hanan the son of Achbor reign-ed in his stead. 39 And Baal-hanan the son of Achbor d i e d, a n d H a d a r reigned i n h i s stead: and the name of his city *was* Pau; and his wife's name *was* Mehetabel, the daughter of Matred, t h e daughter of Me-zahab. 40 And these *are* the names of the dukes *that came* of Esau, accord-	**31** וְאֵ֣לֶּה הַמְּלָכִים אֲשֶׁ֤ר מָלְכוּ֙ בְּאֶ֣רֶץ of land the in　reigned　who　kings the　[were] these And אֱד֔וֹם לִפְנֵ֥י מְלָךְ־מֶ֖לֶךְ לִבְנֵ֥י יִשְׂרָאֵֽל׃ .Israel　of children the to　king a of reigning the　before　,Edom **32** וַיִּמְלֹ֤ךְ בֶּאֱדוֹם֙ בֶּ֔לַע בֶּן־בְּע֑וֹר וְשֵׁ֥ם of name the (and)　,Beor of son the　Bela　Edom in　reigned And **33** עִיר֖וֹ דִּנְהָֽבָה׃ וַיָּ֖מָת בָּ֑לַע וַיִּמְלֹ֣ךְ reigned and　,Bela　died And　.Dinhabah　[being] city his **34** תַּחְתָּ֗יו יוֹבָ֛ב בֶּן־זֶ֖רַח מִבָּצְרָֽה׃ וַיָּ֖מָת died And　.Bozrah from　Zerah of son the　Jobab　him of instead יוֹבָ֑ב וַיִּמְלֹ֣ךְ תַּחְתָּ֗יו חֻשָׁם֙ מֵאֶ֣רֶץ of land the from　Husham　him of instead　reigned and　,Jobab **35** הַתֵּימָנִֽי׃ וַיָּ֖מָת חֻשָׁ֑ם וַיִּמְלֹ֣ךְ תַּחְתָּ֗יו him of instead　reigned and　,Husham　died And　.Temanites the הֲדַ֣ד בֶּן־בְּדַ֗ד הַמַּכֶּ֤ה אֶת־מִדְיָן֙ בִּשְׂדֵ֣ה of field the in　Midian [of]　smiter the　,Bedad of son the　Hadad **36** מוֹאָ֔ב וְשֵׁ֥ם עִיר֖וֹ עֲוִֽית׃ וַיָּ֖מָת died And　.Avith　[being] city his　of name the (and)　; Moab הֲדָ֑ד וַיִּמְלֹ֣ךְ תַּחְתָּ֗יו שַׂמְלָ֖ה מִמַּשְׂרֵקָֽה׃ .Masrekah from　Samlah　him of instead　reigned and　,Hadad **37** וַיָּ֖מָת שַׂמְלָ֑ה וַיִּמְלֹ֣ךְ תַּחְתָּ֗יו שָׁא֖וּל Shaul　him of instead　reigned and　,Samlah　died And **38** מֵרְחֹב֥וֹת הַנָּהָֽר׃ וַיָּ֖מָת שָׁא֑וּל וַיִּמְלֹ֣ךְ reigned and　,Shaul　died And　.river the　of Rehoboth from **39** תַּחְתָּ֗יו בַּ֤עַל חָנָן֙ בֶּן־עַכְבּֽוֹר׃ וַיָּ֖מָת died And　.Akbor of son the　Hanan　Baal　him of instead בַּֽעַל־חָנָ֣ן בֶּן־עַכְבּוֹר֙ａ וַיִּמְלֹ֣ךְ תַּחְתָּ֗יו הֲדַ֔ר ,Hadar　him of instead　reigned and　,Akbor of son the　Baal-Hanan וְשֵׁ֥ם עִיר֖וֹ פָּ֑עוּ וְשֵׁ֣ם אִשְׁתּ֗וֹ wife his　of name the and　,Pau　[being] city his　of name the (and) מְהֵֽיטַבְאֵ֙ל בַּת־מַטְרֵ֔ד בַּ֖תｂ מֵ֥י Me　of daughter the　Matred of daughter the　Mehetabel [being] **40** זָהָֽב׃ וְאֵ֣לֶּה שְׁמ֞וֹת אַלּוּפֵ֥י עֵשָׂ֖ו ,Esau　of princes the　of names the [were]　these And　.Zahab	**31** And these are the kings that reigned in the land of E-dom, before there reigned any king over the children of Israel. 32 And Bela the son of Beor reigned in Edom ; and the name of his city was Dinhabah. 33 And Bela died, and Jobab the son of Zerah of Bozrah reign-ed in his stead. 34 And Jobab died, and Hush-am of the land of the Teman-ites reigned in his stead. 35 And Husham died, and Hadad the son of Bedad, who smote Midian in the field of Moab, reigned in his stead: and the name of his city was Avith. 36 A n d Hadad died, and Sam-lah of Masrekah reigned in his stead. 37 And Samlah died, and Shaul of Rehoboth b y the River reign-ed in his stead. 38 And Shaul died, and Baal-hanan the son of Achbor reigned in his stead. 39 And Baal-hanan the son of Ach-bor died, a n d Hadar reigned in his stead: and the name of his city was Pau; and his wife's name was Me-hetabel, t h e daughter o f Matred, t h e daughter of Me-zahab. 40 And these are the names of the dukes that came of Esau, accord-

---

a Sm., V. omit; cf .1 Chr. 1: 50.　　　　　*b* G., S. have, *son*, בֶּן.

ing to their fam-
ilies, after their
places, by their
names; duke
Timnah, duke
Alvah, duke Je-
theth, 41 Duke
Aholibamah,
duke Elah, duke
Pinon, 42 Duke
Kenaz, duke Te-
man, duke
Mibzar, 43 Duke
Magdiel, duke
Iram: these *be*
the dukes of E-
dom, according
to their habita-
tions in the land
of their possess-
ion: he *is* Esau
the father of the
Edomites.

לְמִשְׁפְּחֹתָם לִמְקֹמֹתָם [a] בִּשְׁמֹתָם [b] אַלּוּף תִּמְנָע
,Timna prince ; names their by ,places their to ,families their to

41 אַלּוּף עַלְוָה אַלּוּף יְתֵת׃ אַלּוּף אָהֳלִיבָמָה אַלּוּף
prince ,Oholibamah prince ,Jetheth prince ,Alvah prince

42 אַלּוּף אֵלָה אַלּוּף פִּינֹן׃ אַלּוּף קְנַז אַלּוּף תֵּימָן אַלּוּף
prince ,Teman prince ,Kenaz prince ,Pinon prince ,Elah

43 מִבְצָר׃ אַלּוּף מַגְדִּיאֵל אַלּוּף עִירָם אֵלֶּה
[were] these ; Iram prince ,Magdiel prince ,Mibzar

אַלּוּפֵי אֱדוֹם לְמֹשְׁבֹתָם [c] בְּאֶרֶץ
of land the in ,dwellings their to ,Edom of princes the

אֲחֻזָּתָם הוּא עֵשָׂו אֲבִי אֱדוֹם׃
.Edom of father the ,Esau [being] he ,possession their

ing to their fam-
ilies, after their
places, by their
names; duke
Timnah, duke
Alvah, duke
Jetheth; 41 duke
Oholibamah,
duke Elah, duke
Pinon; 42 duke
Kenaz, duke
Teman, duke
Mibzar; 43 duke
Magdiel, duke
Iram: these be
the dukes of
Edom, accord-
ing to their ha-
bitatations in
the land of their
possession. This
is Esau the fath-
er of the E-
domites.

37

AND Jacob
dwelt in the land
wherein his fa-
ther was a
stranger, in the
land of Canaan.
2 These *are* the
generations of
Jacob. Joseph
being seventeen
years old, was
feeding the flock
with his breth-
ren; and the lad
was with the
sons of Bilhah,
and with the
sons of Zilpah,
his father's
wives: and Jo-
seph brought
unto his father
their evil report.
3 Now Israel lov-
ed Joseph more
than all his chil-
dren, because he
was the son of
his old age; and
he made him a
coat of *many*
colours. 4 And
when his breth-
ren saw that

1 וַיֵּשֶׁב יַעֲקֹב בְּאֶרֶץ מְגוּרֵי אָבִיו
,father his of sojournings the of land the in Jacob dwelt And

2 בְּאֶרֶץ כְּנָעַן׃ אֵלֶּה [d] תֹּלְדוֹת יַעֲקֹב
.Jacob of generations the [are] These .Canaan of land the in

יוֹסֵף בֶּן־שְׁבַע־עֶשְׂרֵה שָׁנָה הָיָה רֹעֶה
tending was ,[old] years seventeen (of son a) [being] Joseph

אֶת־אֶחָיו בַּצֹּאן וְהוּא נַעַר [e] אֶת־
with ; youth a [being] he (and) ,flock the (in) ,brethren his with

בְּנֵי בִלְהָה וְאֶת־בְּנֵי זִלְפָּה נְשֵׁי
of wives the Zilpah of sons the with and Bilhah of sons the

אָבִיו וַיָּבֵא יוֹסֵף אֶת־דִּבָּתָם רָעָה
,one evil an ,report their Joseph brought and ; father his

3 אֶל־אֲבִיהֶם׃ וְיִשְׂרָאֵל [f] אָהַב אֶת־יוֹסֵף מִכָּל־
all than more Joseph loved Israel And .father their unto

בָּנָיו כִּי־בֶן־זְקֻנִים הוּא לוֹ וְעָשָׂה
made he and ,him to [was] he age old of son a because ,sons his

4 לוֹ כְּתֹנֶת פַּסִּים׃ וַיִּרְאוּ אֶחָיו
brethren his saw And .feet the to reaching tunic a him for

And Jacob
dwelt in the
land of his fath-
er's sojournings,
in the land of
Canaan. 2 These
are the genera-
tions of Jacob.
Joseph, being
seventeen years
old, was feeding
the flock with his
brethren; and
he was a lad
with the sons of
Bilhah, and
with the sons of
Zilpah, his fath-
er's wives: and
Joseph brought
the evil report
of them unto
their father. 3
Now Israel lov-
ed Joseph more
than all his chil-
dren, because he
was the son of
his old age: and
he made him a
coat of many
colours. 4 And
his brethren saw

---

a S. has, *to their generations.*

b G. has, *in their countries and in their nations;* cf. 10: 20, 31.

c Sm. has, *to their families,* למשפחותם.

d G., S., V. add, *and,* ו.

e S., T. have, *was brought up.*

f G. has, *and Jacob.*

their father loved him more than all his brethren, they hated him, and could not speak peaceably unto him.

5 And Joseph dreamed a dream, and he told *it* his brethren: and they hated him yet the more. 6 And he said unto them, Hear, I pray you, this dream which I have dreamed: 7 For, behold, we *were* binding sheaves in the field, and, lo, my sheaf arose, and also stood upright; and, behold, your sheaves stood round about, and made obeisance to my sheaf. 8 And his brethren said to him, Shalt thou indeed reign over us? or shalt thou indeed have dominion over us? And they hated him yet the more for his dreams, and for his words.

9 And he dreamed yet another dream, and told it his brethren, and said, Behold, I have dreamed a dream more; and, behold, the sun and the moon and the eleven stars made obeisance to me. 10 And he told *it* to his father, and to his brethren: and his father rebuked him, and said unto him, What *is* this dream that

כִּי־אֹתוֹ אָהַב אֲבִיהֶם מִכָּל־אֶחָיו[a]
him that loved father their ,brethren his all than more

וַיִּשְׂנְאוּ אֹתוֹ וְלֹא יָכְלוּ דַּבְּרוֹ
hated they and ; him [3]not and [1]they [2]were able to address him,

5 לְשָׁלֹם׃ וַיַּחֲלֹם יוֹסֵף חֲלוֹם וַיַּגֵּד לְאֶחָיו
.peace for dreamed And Joseph ,dream a told and ,brethren his to

6 וַיּוֹסִפוּ[b] עוֹד שְׂנֹא אֹתוֹ[b]׃ וַיֹּאמֶר אֲלֵיהֶם
continued they and still hate to .him said he And : them unto

שִׁמְעוּ־נָא הַחֲלוֹם הַזֶּה אֲשֶׁר חָלָמְתִּי׃
Hear, now [2]dream [1]this which .dreamed have I

7 וְהִנֵּה אֲנַחְנוּ מְאַלְּמִים אֲלֻמִּים בְּתוֹךְ
(And) behold [were] we binding sheaves in the midst of

הַשָּׂדֶה וְהִנֵּה קָמָה אֲלֻמָּתִי וְגַם־נִצָּבָה
,field the behold and arose ,sheaf my and also stood;

וְהִנֵּה תְסֻבֶּינָה אֲלֻמֹּתֵיכֶם וַתִּשְׁתַּחֲוֶיןָ
behold and around moving were ,sheaves your and prostrated themselves

8 לַאֲלֻמָּתִי׃ וַיֹּאמְרוּ לוֹ אֶחָיו הֲמָלֹךְ
.sheaf my to said And him to ; brethren his Reigning

תִּמְלֹךְ עָלֵינוּ אִם־מָשׁוֹל תִּמְשֹׁל בָּנוּ
shalt thou reign ,us over or ruling shalt thou rule (on) us?

וַיּוֹסִפוּ עוֹד שְׂנֹא אֹתוֹ עַל־חֲלֹמֹתָיו
And they continued still to hate ,him on account of his dreams,

9 וְעַל־דְּבָרָיו׃ וַיַּחֲלֹם עוֹד חֲלוֹם
and on account of his words. And he dreamed again [2]dream

אַחֵר וַיְסַפֵּר אֹתוֹ לְאֶחָיו[c] וַיֹּאמֶר[d] הִנֵּה
[1]another, and related it ,brethren his to : said and Behold

חָלַמְתִּי חֲלוֹם עוֹד וְהִנֵּה הַשֶּׁמֶשׁ וְהַיָּרֵחַ
I have dreamed a dream ,again and behold the sun and the moon

וְאַחַד עָשָׂר כּוֹכָבִים מִשְׁתַּחֲוִים לִי׃
and one ten [and] stars [were] prostrating themselves to .me

10 וַיְסַפֵּר[e] אֶל־אָבִיו וְאֶל־אֶחָיו[e] וַיִּגְעַר
And he related unto his father and unto his brethren; and rebuked

בּוֹ אָבִיו וַיֹּאמֶר לוֹ מָה הַחֲלוֹם הַזֶּה
him (in) ,father his and said : him to What [2]dream [is] [1]this

that their father loved him more than all his brethren; and they hated him, and could not speak peaceably unto him.

5 And Joseph dreamed a dream, and he told it to his brethren: and they hated him yet the more. 6 And he said unto them, Hear, I pray you, this dream which I have dreamed: 7 for, behold, we were binding sheaves in the field, and, lo, my sheaf arose, and also stood upright; and, behold, your sheaves came round about, and made obeisance to my sheaf. 8 And his brethren said to him, Shalt thou indeed reign over us? or shalt thou indeed have dominion over us? And they hated him yet the more for his dreams, and for his words.

9 And he dreamed yet another dream, and told it to his brethren, and said, Behold, I have dreamed yet a dream; and, behold, the sun and the moon and eleven stars, made obeisance to me. 10 And he told it to his father, and to his brethren; and his father rebuked him, and said unto him, What is this dream that

a Instead of אחיו Sm., G., V. have, *his sons;* S. has, ולאחיו *them.*

b G. omits.

c G. has, *to his father and to his brethren,* לאביו

d S. adds, *to them.*

e G. omits.

thou hast
dreamed? Shall
I and thy moth-
er and thy breth-
ren indeed come
to bow down
ourselves to thee
to the earth? 11
And his breth-
ren envied him;
but his father
observed the
saying.
12 And his
brethren went to
feed their fath-
er's flock in She-
chem. 13 And
Israel said unto
Joseph, Do not
thy brethren
feed *the flock* in
Shechem? come,
and I will send
thee unto them.
And he said to
him, Here *am I.*
14 And he said
to him, Go, I
pray thee, see
whether it be
well with thy
brethren, and
well with the
flocks; and
bring me word
again. So he
sent him out of
the vale of He-
bron, and he
came to She-
chem.
15 And a cer-
tain man found
him, and, be-
hold, *he was*
wandering in
the field: and
the man asked
him, saying,
What seekest
thou? 16 And he
said, I seek my
brethren: tell
me, I pray thee,
where they feed
their flocks. 17
And the man
said, They are
departed hence;
for I heard them
say, Let us go
to Dothan. And
Joseph went af-
ter his brethren,
and found them
in Dothan. 18
And when they

אֲשֶׁר חָלָמְתָּ הֲבוֹא נָבוֹא אֲנִי
I ,come we shall Coming ?dreamed hast thou which

וְאִמְּךָ וְאַחֶיךָ לְהִשְׁתַּחֲוֺת לְךָ
thee to ourselves prostrate to ,brethren thy and mother thy and

11 אָרְצָה׃ וַיְקַנְאוּ־בוֹ אֶחָיו וְאָבִיו
father his but ;brethren his him of jealous were And ?earth the to

12 שָׁמַר אֶת־הַדָּבָר׃ וַיֵּלְכוּ אֶחָיו[a] לִרְעוֹת אֶת־צֹאן
of flock the tend to brethren his went And .word the kept

13 אֲבִיהֶם בִּשְׁכֶם׃ וַיֹּאמֶר יִשְׂרָאֵל אֶל־יוֹסֵף
:Joseph unto Israel said And .Shechem in father their

הֲלוֹא אַחֶיךָ רֹעִים בִּשְׁכֶם לְכָה
,come ?Shechem in tending brethren thy not [Are]

וְאֶשְׁלָחֲךָ אֲלֵיהֶם וַיֹּאמֶר לוֹ הִנֵּנִי׃
.me Behold ,him to said he And .them unto thee send will I and

14 וַיֹּאמֶר לוֹ[b] לֶךְ־נָא רְאֵה אֶת־שְׁלוֹם אַחֶיךָ
brethren thy of welfare the see ,now ,Go :him to said he And

וְאֶת־שְׁלוֹם[c] הַצֹּאן וַהֲשִׁבֵנִי דָּבָר
;word me [to] back bring and ,flock the of welfare the and

וַיִּשְׁלָחֵהוּ[d] מֵעֵמֶק חֶבְרוֹן וַיָּבֹא שְׁכֶמָה׃
.Shechem to came he and ,Hebron of valley the from him sent he and

15 וַיִּמְצָאֵהוּ אִישׁ וְהִנֵּה[e] תֹעֶה בַּשָּׂדֶה
;field the in wandering [was he] behold and , man a him found And

16 וַיִּשְׁאָלֵהוּ הָאִישׁ לֵאמֹר[f] מַה־תְּבַקֵּשׁ׃ וַיֹּאמֶר
:said he And ?seek thou dost What :saying ,man the him asked and

אֶת־אַחַי אָנֹכִי מְבַקֵּשׁ הַגִּידָה־נָּא לִי אֵיפֹה הֵם
they where ,me to ,pray I ,tell ;seeking [am] I brethren My

17 רֹעִים׃ וַיֹּאמֶר[g] הָאִישׁ נָסְעוּ מִזֶּה
,here from departed have They :man the said And .tending [are]

כִּי שָׁמַעְתִּי אֹמְרִים נֵלְכָה דֹּתָיְנָה וַיֵּלֶךְ
went and ;Dothan towards go us Let :saying [them] heard I for

18 יוֹסֵף אַחַר אֶחָיו וַיִּמְצָאֵם בְּדֹתָן׃ וַיִּרְאוּ
saw they And .Dothan in them found and ,brethren his after Joseph

thou hast
dreamed? Shall
I and thy moth-
er and thy breth-
ren indeed come
to bow down
ourselves to thee
to the earth? 11
And his breth-
ren envied him;
but his father
kept the saying
in mind.
12 And his
brethren went to
feed their fath-
er's flock in
Shechem. 13
And Israel said
unto Joseph,
Do not thy
brethren feed
the flock in She-
chem? come,
and I will send
thee unto them.
And he said to
him, Here am I.
14 And he said
to him, Go now,
see whether it be
well with thy
brethren, and
well with the
flock; and bring
me word again.
So he sent him
out of the vale
of Hebron, and
he came to She-
chem.
15 And a cer-
tain man found
him, and, be-
hold, he was
wandering in
the field: and
the man asked
him, saying,
What seekest
thou? 16 And he
said, I seek my
brethren: tell
me, I pray thee,
where they are
feeding *the
flock.* 17 And
the man said,
They are de-
parted hence:
for I heard them
say, Let us go to
Dothan. And
Joseph went af-
ter his brethren,
and found them
in Dothan. 18
And they saw

---

a S. has, *the brothers of Joseph.*
b G. adds, *Israel;* S. adds, *his father.*
c G. omits, *welfare,* שָׁלוֹם.
d S. adds, *Jacob.*
e G., V. omit.
f S. adds, *to him.*
g G., S., V. add, *to him.*

saw him afar off,
even before he
came near unto
them, they con-
spired against
him to slay him.
19 And they said
one to another,
Behold, this
dreamer com-
eth. 20 Come
now therefore,
and let us slay
him, and cast
him into some
pit, and we will
say, Some evil
beast hath de-
voured him:
and we shall see
what will be-
come of his
dreams. 21 And
Reuben heard
it, and he de-
livered him out
of their hands;
and said, Let us
not kill him. 22
And Reuben
said unto them,
Shed no blood,
but cast him into
this pit that *is*
in the wilder-
ness, and lay no
hand upon him;
that he might
rid him out of
their hands, to
deliver him to
his father again.

23 And it
came to pass,
when Joseph
was come unto
his brethren,
that they stript
Joseph out
of his coat, *his*
coat of *many*
colours that *was*
on him; 24 And
they took him,
and cast him in-
to a pit: and the
pit *was* empty,
there was no
water in it. 25
And they sat
down to eat
bread: and they
lifted up their
eyes and looked,
and, behold, a
company of Ish-
maelites came
from Gilead
with their cam-
els bearing

אֹתוֹ מֵרָחֹק וּבְטֶרֶם יִקְרַב אֲלֵיהֶם
them unto near came he before and ;afar from him

19 וַיִּתְנַכְּלוּ אֹתוֹ לַהֲמִיתוֹ׃ וַיֹּאמְרוּ אִישׁ
each ,said they And .him kill to him against plotted they (and)

אֶל־אָחִיו הִנֵּה בַּעַל הַחֲלֹמוֹת הַלָּזֶה בָּא׃
!coming [1]this [4]dreams [3]of [2]master ,Behold :brother his unto

20 וְעַתָּה ׀[a] לְכוּ וְנַהַרְגֵהוּ וְנַשְׁלִכֵהוּ בְּאַחַד הַבֹּרוֹת
,pits the of one into him cast and ,him kill us let and ,come now And

וְאָמַרְנוּ חַיָּה רָעָה אֲכָלָתְהוּ וְנִרְאֶה
see us let and ;him eaten has [1]evil [2]beast A :say us let and

21 מַה־יִּהְיוּ חֲלֹמֹתָיו׃ וַיִּשְׁמַע רְאוּבֵן וַיַּצִּלֵהוּ
him delivered and Reuben heard And .[2]dreams [1]his [4]become [3]will what

מִיָּדָם וַיֹּאמֶר[b] לֹא נַכֶּנּוּ נָפֶשׁ׃
.life [to as] him smite [2]us [1]let [3]Not :said and ,hand their from

22 וַיֹּאמֶר אֲלֵהֶם ׀ רְאוּבֵן אַל־תִּשְׁפְּכוּ־דָם [c]הַשְׁלִיכוּ
cast ;blood shed not Do :Reuben them unto said And

אֹתוֹ אֶל־הַבּוֹר הַזֶּה אֲשֶׁר בַּמִּדְבָּר וְיָד
hand a and ,wilderness the in [is] which ,[1]this [2]pit into him

אַל־תִּשְׁלְחוּ־בוֹ לְמַעַן הַצִּיל אֹתוֹ מִיָּדָם
,hand their from him deliver to order in ;him on forth put not do

23 [d]לַהֲשִׁיבוֹ אֶל־אָבִיו׃ וַיְהִי כַּאֲשֶׁר־בָּא יוֹסֵף
Joseph came when pass to came it And .father his unto him return to

אֶל־אֶחָיו וַיַּפְשִׁיטוּ אֶת־יוֹסֵף אֶת־כֻּתָּנְתּוֹ[e]
,tunic his Joseph [from] stripped they that ,brethren his unto

אֶת־כְּתֹנֶת הַפַּסִּים אֲשֶׁר עָלָיו׃
.him upon [was] which ,feet the to reaching tunic the

24 וַיִּקָּחֻהוּ וַיַּשְׁלִכוּ אֹתוֹ הַבֹּרָה וְהַבּוֹר
pit the (and) ,pit the into him cast and ,him took they And

25 רֵק[f] אֵין בּוֹ מָיִם׃ וַיֵּשְׁבוּ לֶאֱכָל־לֶחֶם
;bread eat to down sat they And .water it in being not ,empty [being]

וַיִּשְׂאוּ עֵינֵיהֶם וַיִּרְאוּ וְהִנֵּה אֹרְחַת
of caravan a behold and ,saw and ,eyes their up lifted they and

יִשְׁמְעֵאלִים[g] בָּאָה מִגִּלְעָד וּגְמַלֵּיהֶם נֹשְׂאִים
bearing camels their (and) ;Gilead from coming Ishmaelites

him afar off,
and before he
came near unto
them, they con-
spired against
him to slay him.
19 And they
said one to an-
other, Behold,
this dreamer
cometh. 20
Come now
therefore, and
let us slay him,
and cast him in-
to one of the
pits, and we
will say, An evil
beast hath de-
voured him: and
we shall see
what will be-
come of his
dreams. 21 And
Reuben heard
it, and delivered
him out of their
hand; and said,
Let us not take
his life. 22 And
Reuben said un-
to them, Shed
no blood; cast
him into this
pit that is in the
wilderness, but
lay no hand up-
on him: that he
might deliver
him out of their
hand, to restore
him to his fath-
er.
23 And it
came to pass,
when Joseph
was come unto
his brethren,
that they stript
Joseph of his
coat, the coat of
many colours
that was on him;
24 and they took
him, and cast
him into the
pit: and the pit
was empty,
there was no
water in it. 25
And they sat
down to eat
bread: and
they lifted up
their eyes and
looked, and,
behold, a travel-
ling company of
Ishmaelites
came from Gil-
ead, with their

a S., V. omit.
b S. adds, *to them.*
c G., V. add, *and*, ו.
d G., S., V. add, *and*, ו.
e G., S., V. omit.
f G. omits.
g S., T. have, *Arabs.*

spicery and
balm and
myrrh, going to
carry *it* down
to Egypt. 26
And Judah said
unto his breth-
ren, What profit
is it if we slay
our brother, and
conceal his
blood? 27 Come,
and let us sell
him to the Ish-
meelites, and let
not our hand
be upon him;
for he *is* our
brother *and* our
flesh. And his
brethren were
content. 28
Then there pass-
ed by Midian-
ites, merchant-
men; and they
drew and lifted
up Joseph out
of the pit, and
sold Joseph to
the Ishmeelites
for twenty
pieces of silver:
and they
brought Joseph
into Egypt.

29 And Reu-
ben returned
unto the pit;
and, behold,
Joseph *was* not
in the pit; and
he rent his
clothes. 30 And
he returned un-
to his brethren,
and said, The
child *is* not; and
I, whither shall
I go? 31 And
they took Jo-
seph's coat, and
killed a kid of
the goats, and
dipped the coat
in the blood; 32
And they sent
the coat of
many colours,
and they
brought *it* to
their father;
and said, This
have we found:
know now
whether it *be*

נְכֹאת וּצְרִי וָלֹט [a]הוֹלְכִים לְהוֹרִיד
down carry to going ,ladanum and balsam and tragacanth

26 מִצְרָיְמָה׃ וַיֹּאמֶר יְהוּדָה אֶל־אֶחָיו מַה־בֶּצַע כִּי
that ,gain What : brethren his unto Judah said And .Egypt to

27 נַהֲרֹג אֶת־אָחִינוּ וְכִסִּינוּ אֶת־דָּמוֹ׃ לְכוּ
,Come ?blood his conceal and ,brother our kill we

וְנִמְכְּרֶנּוּ לַיִּשְׁמְעֵאלִים[b] וְיָדֵנוּ אַל־תְּהִי־
be not let hand our and ,Ishmaelites the to him sell us let and

בוֹ כִּי־אָחִינוּ בְשָׂרֵנוּ הוּא וַיִּשְׁמְעוּ[c]
heard and ; he [is] flesh our ,brother our for ; him on

28 אֶחָיו׃ וַיַּעַבְרוּ אֲנָשִׁים מִדְיָנִים סֹחֲרִים
; traders ,Midianites men by passed And .brethren his

וַיִּמְשְׁכוּ וַיַּעֲלוּ אֶת־יוֹסֵף[d] מִן־הַבּוֹר
; pit the from Joseph up brought and drew they and

וַיִּמְכְּרוּ אֶת־יוֹסֵף לַיִּשְׁמְעֵאלִים[e] בְּעֶשְׂרִים
[of shekels] twenty for Ishmaelites the to Joseph sold they and

29 כָּסֶף וַיָּבִיאוּ אֶת־יוֹסֵף מִצְרָיְמָה׃ וַיָּשָׁב
returned And .Egypt to Joseph brought they and ; silver

רְאוּבֵן אֶל־הַבּוֹר וְהִנֵּה[f] אֵין־יוֹסֵף[f] בַּבּוֹר[g]
; pit the in not was Joseph behold and ; pit the unto Reuben

30 וַיִּקְרַע אֶת־בְּגָדָיו׃ וַיָּשָׁב אֶל־אֶחָיו
brethren his unto returned he And .garments his rent he and

וַיֹּאמַר[h] הַיֶּלֶד אֵינֶנּוּ[i] וַאֲנִי אָנָה אֲנִי־בָא׃
? go I shall whither ,I and ; not is he ,child The : said and

31 וַיִּקְחוּ אֶת־כְּתֹנֶת יוֹסֵף וַיִּשְׁחֲטוּ שְׂעִיר
of he-goat a slaughtered and ,Joseph of tunic the took they And

32 עִזִּים וַיִּטְבְּלוּ אֶת־הַכֻּתֹּנֶת בַּדָּם׃ וַיְשַׁלְּחוּ
sent they And .blood the in tunic the dipped and ,goats the

אֶת־כְּתֹנֶת הַפַּסִּים וַיָּבִיאוּ אֶל־אֲבִיהֶם
,father their unto brought they and ,feet the to reaching tunic the

וַיֹּאמְרוּ זֹאת מָצָאנוּ הַכֶּר־נָא הַכְּתֹנֶת
,tunic the ,now ,observe : found have we This : said and

camels bearing
spicery and balm
and myrrh,
going to carry
it down to E-
gypt. 26 And
Judah said unto
his brethren,
What profit is
it if we slay our
brother and con-
ceal his blood?
27 Come, and
let us sell him
to the Ish-
maelites, and let
not our hand be
upon him; for
he is our broth-
er, our flesh.
And his breth-
ren hearkened
unto him. 28
And there pass-
ed by Midi-
anites, mer-
chantmen; and
they drew and
lifted up Joseph
out of the pit,
and sold Joseph
to the Ish-
maelites for
twenty pieces of
silver. And they
brought Joseph
into Egypt.

29 And Reu-
ben returned
unto the pit;
and, behold,
Joseph was not
in the pit; and
he rent his
clothes. 30 And
he returned un-
to his brethren,
and said, The
child is not; and
I, whither shall
I go? 31 And
they took Jo-
seph's coat, and
killed a he-goat,
and dipped the
coat in the
blood; 32 and
they sent the
coat of many
colours, and
they brought it
to their father;
and said, This
have we found;
know now
whether it be

---

a G., S. add, *and*, ו.
b S., T. have, *to the Arabs*.
c S., T. add, *from him*; V. adds, *his words*.
d S., V. have, *him*.
e S., T. have, *to the Arabs*.
f For הנה אין G. has, *he does not see*; V. has, *he did not find*.
g S. has, *in it*; V. omits.
h S. adds, *to them*.
i S. has, *where is he?*

thy son's coat or
no. 33 And he
knew it, and
said, *It is* my
son's coat; an
evil beast hath
devoured him;
Joseph is with-
out doubt rent
in pieces. 34
And Jacob rent
his clothes, and
put sackcloth
upon his loins,
and mourned
for his son many
days. 35 And all
his sons and all
his daughters
rose up to com-
fort him; but he
refused to be
comforted; and
he said, For I
will go down
into the grave
unto my son
mourning. Thus
his father wept
for him. 36 And
the Midianites
sold him into E-
gypt unto Poti-
phar, an officer
of Pharaoh's,
and captain of
the guard.

33 בִּנְךָ הִוא אִם־לֹא׃ וַיַּכִּירָהּ וַיֹּאמֶר
:said and it observed he And ?not or ,it [is] son thy [of]

כְּתֹנֶת[a] בְּנִי[a] חַיָּה רָעָה אֲכָלָתְהוּ טָרֹף[b]
surely ; him eaten has [1]evil [2]beast A !son my of tunic The

34 טֹרַף[b] יוֹסֵף׃[c] וַיִּקְרַע יַעֲקֹב שִׂמְלֹתָיו וַיָּשֶׂם
put and ,clothes his Jacob rent And .Joseph pieces in torn is

שַׂק בְּמָתְנָיו וַיִּתְאַבֵּל עַל־בְּנוֹ יָמִים
[2]days son his for mourned he and ; loins his on sackcloth

35 רַבִּים׃ וַיָּקֻמוּ[d] כָל־בָּנָיו וְכָל־בְּנֹתָיו[e]
daughters his all and sons his all arose And .[1]many

לְנַחֲמוֹ וַיְמָאֵן לְהִתְנַחֵם וַיֹּאמֶר
: said and ,comforted be to refused he and ; him comfort to

כִּי־אֵרֵד אֶל־בְּנִי אָבֵל שְׁאֹלָה וַיֵּבְךְּ
for wept and ; Sheol to ,mourning son my unto down go will I (That)

36 אֹתוֹ אָבִיו׃ וְהַמְּדָנִים מָכְרוּ אֹתוֹ[f] אֶל־
into him sold Midianites the And .father his him

מִצְרָיִם לְפוֹטִיפַר סְרִיס פַּרְעֹה[g] שַׂר
of chief the ,Pharaoh of officer an ,Potiphar to ,Egypt

הַטַּבָּחִים׃
.executioners the

thy son's coat or
not. 33 And he
knew it, and
said, It is my
son's coat; an
evil beast hath
devoured him;
Joseph is with-
out doubt torn
in pieces. 34
And Jacob rent
his garments,
and put sack-
cloth upon his
loins, and
mourned for his
son many days.
35 And all his
sons and all his
daughters rose
up to comfort
him; but he re-
fused to be com-
forted; and he
said, For I will
go down to the
grave to my son
mourning. And
his father wept
for him. 36 And
the Midianites
sold him into
Egypt unto Po-
tiphar, an of-
ficer of Pha-
raoh's, the cap-
tain of the
guard.

38

AND it came
to pass at that
time, that Judah
went down from
his brethren,
and turned in to
a certain Adul-
lamite, whose
name *was* Hi-
rah. 2 And Ju-
dah saw there a
daughter of a
certain Canaan-
ite, whose
name *was* Shu-
ah; and he took
her, and went in
unto her. 3 And
she conceived,
and bare a son;

1 וַיְהִי בָּעֵת הַהִוא וַיֵּרֶד יְהוּדָה
Judah down went that [1],that [2]time at pass to came it And

מֵאֵת אֶחָיו וַיֵּט עַד־אִישׁ עֲדֻלָּמִי
,Adullamite an man a unto aside turned he and ; brethren his with from

2 וּשְׁמוֹ חִירָה׃ וַיַּרְא־שָׁם יְהוּדָה
Judah there saw And .Hirah [being] name his (and)

בַּת־אִישׁ כְּנַעֲנִי וּשְׁמוֹ־שׁוּעַ[h]
;Shua [being] name his (and) ,Canaanite a man a of daughter a

3 וַיִּקָּחֶהָ וַיָּבֹא אֵלֶיהָ׃ וַתַּהַר וַתֵּלֶד[i]
bore and conceived she And .her unto in came and her took he and

And it came
to pass at that
time, that Ju-
dah went down
from his breth-
ren, and turned
in to a certain
Adullamite,
whose name
was Hirah. 2
And Judah saw
there a daugh-
ter of a certain
Canaanite
whose name was
Shua; and he
took her, and
went in unto
her. 3 And she
conceived, and
bare a son; and

---

a Sm. omits.
b G., V. have, *a beast has torn.*
c S. adds, *my son.*
d G., V. have *and were collected,* וַיִּקָּווּ.
e G. adds, *and came,* ויבאו.
f Sm., G. have, *Joseph.*
g S. puts after, הטבחים.
h For ושמו G., S. have, *and her name* ושמה.
i S. adds, *to him.*

and he called his name Er. 4 And she conceived again, and bare a son; and she called his name Onan. 5 And she yet again conceived, and bare a son; and called his name Shelah: and he was at Chezib, when she bare him. 6 And Judah took a wife for Er his first-born, whose name *was* Tamar. 7 And Er, Judah's first-born, was wicked in the sight of the LORD; and the LORD slew him. 8 And Judah said unto Onan, Go in unto thy brother's wife, and marry her, and raise up seed to thy brother. 9 And Onan knew that the seed should not be his; and it came to pass, when he went in unto his brother's wife, that he spilled *it* on the ground, lest that he should give seed to his brother. 10 And the thing which he did displeased the LORD: wherefore he slew him also. 11 Then said Judah to Tamar his daughter in law, Remain a widow at thy father's house, till Shelah my son be grown: for he said, Lest peradventure he die also, as his brethren *did*. And Tamar went and dwelt in her father's house.

4 בֵּן וַיִּקְרָא[a] אֶת־שְׁמוֹ עֵר׃ וַתַּהַר עוֹד
again conceived she And .Er name his called he and ;son a

5 וַתֵּלֶד בֵּן וַתִּקְרָא[b] אֶת־שְׁמוֹ אוֹנָן׃ וַתֹּסֶף
continued she And .Onan name his called she and ;son a bore and

עוֹד וַתֵּלֶד בֵּן וַתִּקְרָא אֶת־שְׁמוֹ שֵׁלָה
;Shelah name his called she and ;son a bore and ,still

6 וְהָיָה בִכְזִיב[c] בְּלִדְתָּהּ אֹתוֹ[d]׃ וַיִּקַּח יְהוּדָה אִשָּׁה
wife a Judah took And .him bearing her in Chezib at was he and

7 לְעֵר בְּכוֹרוֹ וּשְׁמָהּ תָּמָר׃ וַיְהִי עֵר
Er was And .Tamar [being] name her (and) ,first-born his Er for

בְּכוֹר יְהוּדָה רַע בְּעֵינֵי יְהוָה[e] וַיְמִתֵהוּ
him slew and ,Jehovah of eyes the in evil Judah of first-born the

8 יְהוָה׃ וַיֹּאמֶר יְהוּדָה לְאוֹנָן[f] בֹּא אֶל־אֵשֶׁת
of wife the unto in Go :Onan to Judah said And .Jehovah

אָחִיךָ וְיַבֵּם אֹתָהּ וְהָקֵם זֶרַע
seed up raise and ;her with marriage brother-in-law's a make and ,brother thy

9 לְאָחִיךָ׃ וַיֵּדַע אוֹנָן כִּי לֹּא־לוֹ יִהְיֶה הַזָּרַע
;seed the be would him to not that Onan knew And .brother thy to

וְהָיָה אִם־בָּא אֶל־אֵשֶׁת אָחִיו
,brother his of wife the unto in went he whenever ,pass to came it and

וְשִׁחֵת אַרְצָה לְבִלְתִּי נְתָן־זֶרַע לְאָחִיו׃
.brother his to seed give not to ;ground the to [it] destroyed he (and)

10 וַיֵּרַע[g] בְּעֵינֵי יְהוָה אֲשֶׁר עָשָׂה וַיָּמֶת
slew he and ,did he what Jehovah of eyes the in evil was And

11 גַּם־אֹתוֹ׃ וַיֹּאמֶר יְהוּדָה לְתָמָר כַּלָּתוֹ
:daughter-in-law his Tamar to Judah said And .him also

שְׁבִי אַלְמָנָה בֵית־אָבִיךְ עַד־יִגְדַּל
up grown is until ,father thy of house the in widow a Dwell

שֵׁלָה בְנִי כִּי אָמַר פֶּן־יָמוּת גַּם־הוּא כְּאֶחָיו
;brothers his like he also die Lest :said he for ;son my Shelah

וַתֵּלֶךְ תָּמָר וַתֵּשֶׁב בֵּית אָבִיהָ׃
.father her of house the in dwelt and ,Tamar went and

he called his name Er. 4 And she conceived again, and bare a son; and she called his name Onan. 5 And she yet again bare a son, and called his name Shelah: and he was at Chezib, when she bare him. 6 And Judah took a wife for Er his first-born, and her name was Tamar. 7 And Er, Judah's first-born, was wicked in the sight of the LORD; and the LORD slew him. 8 And Judah said unto Onan, Go in unto thy brother's wife, and perform the duty of an husband's brother unto her, and raise up seed to thy brother. 9 And Onan knew that the seed should not be his; and it came to pass, when he went in unto his brother's wife, that he spilled it on the ground, lest he should give seed to his brother. 10 And the thing which he did was evil in the sight of the LORD: and he slew him also. 11 Then said Judah to Tamar his daughter in law, Remain a widow in thy father's house, till Shelah my son be grown up: for he said, Lest he also die, like his brethren. And Tamar went and dwelt

---

a Sm., G. have, *and she called*, as in vs. 4, 5.
b S. has, *and he called.*
c S., V. have, *ceasing.*
d G. has pl., *them.*
e G. has, *God.*
f S., V. add, *his son.*
g G., S. add *the thing.*

12 And in
process of time
the daughter of
Shuah Judah's
wife died; and
Judah was com-
forted, and went
up unto his
sheepshearers to
Timnath, he
and his friend
Hirah the Adul-
lamite. 13 And
it was told Ta-
mar, saying,
Behold thy
father in law
goeth up to
Timnath to
shear his sheep.

14 And she
put her widow's
garments off
from her, and
covered her
with a vail, and
wrapped her-
self, and sat in
an open place,
which *is* by the
way to Tim-
nath; for she
saw that She-
lah was grown,
and she was not
given unto him
to wife. 15
When Judah
saw her, he
thought her *to
be* an harlot; be-
cause she had
covered her
face. 16 And he
turned unto her
by the way, and
said, Go to, I
pray thee, let
me come in un-
to thee; (for he
knew not that
she *was* his
daughter in
law.) And she
said, What wilt
thou give me,
that thou may-
est come in un-
to me? 17 And
he said, I will
send *thee* a kid
from the flock.
And she said,

12 וַיִּרְבּוּ הַיָּמִים וַתָּמָת בַּת־שׁוּעַ[a]
Shua of daughter the died and ,days the many were And
אֵשֶׁת־יְהוּדָה וַיִּנָּחֶם יְהוּדָה וַיַּעַל
up went and ,Judah comforted was and ; Judah of wife the
עַל־גֹּזְזֵי צֹאנוֹ הוּא וְחִירָה רֵעֵהוּ
friend his Hirah and he ,flocks his of shearers the unto
13 הָעֲדֻלָּמִי תִּמְנָתָה׃ וַיֻּגַּד לְתָמָר[b] לֵאמֹר
: saying Tamar to told was it And .Timnah to ,Adullamite the
הִנֵּה חָמִיךְ עֹלֶה תִמְנָתָה לָגֹז
shear to Timnah to up going [is] father-in-law thy Behold
14 צֹאנוֹ׃ וַתָּסַר בִּגְדֵי אַלְמְנוּתָהּ
widowhood her of garments the removed she And .flocks his
מֵעָלֶיהָ וַתְּכַס בַּצָּעִיף וַתִּתְעַלָּף
; herself disguised and ,veil a with herself covered and ,her upon from
וַתֵּשֶׁב בְּפֶתַח[c] עֵינַיִם[c] אֲשֶׁר עַל־דֶּרֶךְ
way the upon [is] which ,Enaim of entrance the at sat she and
תִּמְנָתָה כִּי רָאֲתָה כִּי־גָדַל שֵׁלָה[d] וְהִוא[e]
she (and) ,Shelah up grown was that saw she for ; Timnah to
15 לֹא־נִתְּנָה[e] לוֹ לְאִשָּׁה[f]׃ וַיִּרְאֶהָ יְהוּדָה
,Judah her saw And .wife a for him to given been having not
וַיַּחְשְׁבֶהָ לְזוֹנָה כִּי כִסְּתָה פָּנֶיהָ[g]׃
.face her covered had she because ;harlot a (for) her considered he and
16 וַיֵּט אֵלֶיהָ אֶל־הַדֶּרֶךְ וַיֹּאמֶר[h] הָבָה
,Come : said and ,way the unto her unto aside turned he And
נָּא אָבוֹא אֵלַיִךְ כִּי לֹא יָדַע כִּי
that know [2]did [1]he [3]not for ; thee unto in come me let ,now
כַּלָּתוֹ הִוא וַתֹּאמֶר[i] מַה־תִּתֶּן־
give thou wilt What : said she And .she [was] daughter-in-law his
17 לִּי[j] כִּי תָבוֹא אֵלָי׃ וַיֹּאמֶר אָנֹכִי
I : said he And ? me unto in come mayest thou that ,me to
אֲשַׁלַּח[k] גְּדִי־עִזִּים מִן־הַצֹּאן וַתֹּאמֶר אִם־
If : said she and ;flock the from goats the of kid a send will

in her father's
house.
12 And in
process of time
Shua's daugh-
ter, the wife of
Judah, died;
and Judah was
comforted, and
went up unto
his sheepshear-
ers to Timnah,
he and his
friend Hirah
the Adullamite.
13 And it was
told Tamar,
saying, Behold,
thy father in
law goeth up
to Timnah to
shear his sheep.
14 And she put
off from her the
garments of her
widowhood,
and covered
herself with her
veil, and wrap-
ped herself, and
sat in the gate
of Enaim,
which is by the
way to Timnah;
for she saw that
Shelah was
grown up, and
she was not
given unto him
to wife. 15
When Judah
saw her, he
thought her to
be an harlot;
for she had cov-
ered her face. 16
And he turned
unto her by the
way, and said,
Go to, I pray
thee, let me
come in unto
thee: for he
knew not that
she was his
daughter in law.
And she said,
What wilt
thou give me,
that thou may-
est come in unto
me? 17 And he
said, I will send
thee a kid of
the goats from
the flock. And
she said, Wilt

---

a G. omits.
b Sm., G. add, *his daughter-in-law*.
c S., V., T. have, *at the parting of the ways*.
d G. adds, *his son*.
e G. has, *and he had not given her*, וְהוּא לֹא נְתָנָהּ.
f S. omits.
g G. adds, *and he did not know her*; V. adds, *that she might not be known*.
h G., S. add, *to her*.
i S. adds, *to him*.
j S. omits לִי.
k G., V. add, *to thee*.

Wilt thou give *me* a pledge, till thou send *it?*
18 And he said, What pledge shall I give thee? And she said, Thy signet, and thy bracelets, and thy staff that *is* in thine hand. And he gave *it* her, and came in unto her, and she conceived by him.
19 And she arose, and went away, and laid by her vail from her, and put on the garments of her widowhood.
20 And Judah sent the kid by the hand of his friend the Adullamite, to receive *his* pledge from the woman's hand: but he found her not.
21 Then he asked the men of that place, saying, Where *is* the harlot, that *was* openly by the way side? And they said, There was no harlot in this *place*.
22 And he returned to Judah, and said, I cannot find her; and also the men of the place said, *that* there was no harlot in this *place*.
23 And Judah said, Let her take *it* to her, lest we be shamed: behold, I sent this kid, and thou hast not found her.
24 And it came to pass about three months after, that it was told Judah, saying, Tamar thy daughter in law

תִּתֵּן עֵרָבוֹן עַד שָׁלְחֶךָ׃ וַיֹּאמֶר מָה 18
[is] What :said he And .sending thy until pledge a give wilt thou

הָעֵרָבוֹן אֲשֶׁר אֶתֶּן־לָּךְ וַתֹּאמֶר חֹתָמְךָ
ring signet Thy : said she And ? thee to give shall I which pledge the

וּפְתִילֶךָ וּמַטְּךָ אֲשֶׁר בְּיָדֶךָ וַיִּתֶּן־
gave he and ; hand thy in [is] which staff thy and ,cord thy and

לָהּ וַיָּבֹא אֵלֶיהָ וַתַּהַר לוֹ׃
.him by conceived she and ,her unto in came and ,her to

19 וַתָּקָם וַתֵּלֶךְ וַתָּסַר צְעִיפָהּ מֵעָלֶיהָ
,her upon from veil her removed and ,went and arose she And

20 וַתִּלְבַּשׁ בִּגְדֵי אַלְמְנוּתָהּ׃ וַיִּשְׁלַח יְהוּדָה
Judah sent And .widowhood her of garments the on put and

אֶת־גְּדִי הָעִזִּים בְּיַד רֵעֵהוּ הָעֲדֻלָּמִי
,Adullamite the friend his of hand the by goats the of kid the

לָקַחַת הָעֵרָבוֹן מִיַּד הָאִשָּׁה וְלֹא
[3]not and ; woman the of hand the from pledge the take to

21 מְצָאָהּ׃ וַיִּשְׁאַל אֶת־אַנְשֵׁי מְקֹמָהּ[a] לֵאמֹר[b]
: saying place her of men the asked he And .her find [2]did [1]he

אַיֵּה הַקְּדֵשָׁה הִוא[c] בָעֵינַיִם עַל־הַדָּרֶךְ[c]
? way the by Enaim at ,[1]that [2]harlot [is] Where

22 וַיֹּאמְרוּ לֹא־הָיְתָה בָזֶה קְדֵשָׁה׃ וַיָּשָׁב
returned he And .harlot a here been not Has :said they And

אֶל־יְהוּדָה וַיֹּאמֶר לֹא מְצָאתִיהָ וְגַם
also and ; her found [2]have [1]I [3]Not :said and ,Judah unto

אַנְשֵׁי הַמָּקוֹם אָמְרוּ לֹא־הָיְתָה בָזֶה קְדֵשָׁה׃
.harlot a here been not Has :said place the of men the

23 וַיֹּאמֶר יְהוּדָה תִּקַּח־לָהּ פֶּן נִהְיֶה
become we lest ,herself for take her Let :Judah said And

לָבוּז הִנֵּה שָׁלַחְתִּי הַגְּדִי הַזֶּה וְאַתָּה
thou and ,[1]this [2]kid sent I behold ; laughing-stock a (for)

24 לֹא מְצָאתָהּ׃ וַיְהִי כְּמִשְׁלֹשׁ
three about after pass to came it And .her find [1]didst [2]not

חֳדָשִׁים וַיֻּגַּד לִיהוּדָה לֵאמֹר זָנְתָה
whoredom committed Has : saying Judah to told was it (and) ,months

thou give me a pledge, till thou send it?
18 And he said, What pledge shall I give thee? And she said, Thy signet and thy cord, and thy staff that is in thine hand. And he gave them to her, and came in unto her, and she conceived by him.
19 And she arose, and went away, and put off her veil from her, and put on the garments of her widowhood.
20 And Judah sent the kid of the goats by the hand of his friend the Adullamite, to receive the pledge from the woman's hand: but he found her not.
21 Then he asked the men of her place, saying, Where is the harlot, that was at Enaim by the way side? And they said, There hath been no harlot here.
22 And he returned to Judah, and said, I have not found her; and also the men of the place said, There hath been no harlot here.
23 And Judah said, Let her take it to her, lest we be put to shame: behold, I sent this kid, and thou hast not found her.
24 And it came to pass about three months after, that it was told Judah, saying, Tamar thy daughter in law

---

a Sm., G., S. have, *the place*, המקם.
b G. omits.
c S., V. have, *who sat at the parting of the ways.*

hath played the harlot; and also, behold, she *is* with child by whoredom. And Judah said, Bring her forth, and let her be burnt. 25 When she *was* brought forth, she sent to her father in law, saying, By the man, whose these *are*, *am* I with child: and she said, Discern, I pray thee, whose *are* these, the signet, and bracelets, and staff. 26 And Judah acknowledged *them*, and said, She hath been more righteous than I; because that I gave her not to Shelah my son. And he knew her again no more.

27 And it came to pass in the time of her travail, that, behold, twins *were* in her womb. 28 And it came to pass, when she travailed, that *the one* put out *his* hand: and the midwife took and bound upon his hand a scarlet thread, saying, This came out first. 29 And it came to pass, as he drew back his hand, that, behold, his brother came out: and she said, How hast thou broken forth? *this* breach *be* upon thee: therefore his name was called Pharez. 30 And afterward came out his brother, that had the

תָּמָר כַּלָּתֶךָ וְגַם הִנֵּה הָרָה
pregnant [is she] behold also and ;daughter-in-law thy Tamar

לִזְנוּנִים וַיֹּאמֶר יְהוּדָה הוֹצִיאוּהָ וְתִשָּׂרֵף׃
.burned be her let and ,out her Bring :Judah said And .whoredom by

25 הִוא מוּצֵאת וְהִיא שָׁלְחָה אֶל־חָמִיהָ
,father-in-law her unto sent she and ,out brought being [was] She

לֵאמֹר[a] לְאִישׁ אֲשֶׁר־אֵלֶּה לּוֹ אָנֹכִי
I (him to) [are] these whom [to] man a By :saying

הָרָה וַתֹּאמֶר הַכֶּר־נָא לְמִי
whom to ,now ,Observe :said she and ;pregnant [am]

הַחֹתֶמֶת וְהַפְּתִילִים וְהַמַּטֶּה הָאֵלֶּה׃
.these ,staff the and cord the and ring signet the [are]

26 וַיַּכֵּר יְהוּדָה וַיֹּאמֶר צָדְקָה[b] מִמֶּנִּי
;I than righteous [more] is She :said and Judah observed And

כִּי־עַל־כֵּן לֹא־נְתַתִּיהָ לְשֵׁלָה בְנִי
.son my Shelah to her give not did I that because

27 וְלֹא־יָסַף עוֹד לְדַעְתָּהּ׃ וַיְהִי
pass to came it And .her know to again continue not did he And

בְּעֵת לִדְתָּהּ וְהִנֵּה[c] תְאוֹמִים בְּבִטְנָהּ׃
.womb her in twins behold that ,forth bringing her of time the in

28 וַיְהִי בְלִדְתָּהּ[d] וַיִּתֶּן־יָד[d]
;hand a gave [one] (and) forth bringing her in pass to came it And

וַתִּקַּח הַמְיַלֶּדֶת וַתִּקְשֹׁר עַל־יָדוֹ שָׁנִי[e]
,crimson hand his upon bound and midwife the took and

29 לֵאמֹר זֶה יָצָא רִאשֹׁנָה׃ וַיְהִי
pass to came it And .first out came one This :saying

כְּמֵשִׁיב יָדוֹ וְהִנֵּה יָצָא אָחִיו
,brother his out came behold (and) ,hand his back drawing [his] at

וַתֹּאמֶר מַה־פָּרַצְתָּ עָלֶיךָ פָּרֶץ וַיִּקְרָא[f]
called one and ?rent a thyself for torn thou hast How :said she and

30 שְׁמוֹ פָּרֶץ׃ וְאַחַר יָצָא אָחִיו אֲשֶׁר
(who) brother his out came afterwards And .Perez name his

hath played the harlot; and moreover, behold, she is with child by whoredom. And Judah said, Bring her forth, and let her be burnt. 25 When she was brought forth, she sent to her father in law, saying, By the man, whose these are, am I with child: and she said, Discern, I pray thee, whose are these, the signet, and the cords, and the staff. 26 And Judah acknowledged them, and said, She is more righteous than I; forasmuch as I gave her not to Shelah my son. And he knew her again no more.

27 And it came to pass in the time of her travail, that, behold, twins were in her womb. 28 And it came to pass, when she travailed, that one put out a hand: and the midwife took and bound upon his hand a scarlet thread, saying, This came out first. 29 And it came to pass, as he drew back his hand, that, behold, his brother came out: and she said, Wherefore hast thou made a breach for thyself? therefore his name was called Perez. 30 And afterward came out his brother, that

---

a S. omits.
b G. adds, *Tamar*.
c G. omits הנה, and adds, *to her*.
d S. has, *when the infant put forth his hand;* V. *one of the infants put forth a hand.*
e S. puts after המילדת.
f Sm., S. have, *and she called.*

scarlet thread
upon his hand:
and his name
was called Za-
rah.

עַל־יָדוֹ הַשָּׁנִי [a]וַיִּקְרָא שְׁמוֹ זָרַח׃
.Zerah name his called one and ;crimson the hand whose upon

had the scarlet
thread upon his
hand: and his
name was called
Zerah.

39

1 וְיוֹסֵף הוּרַד[b] מִצְרָיְמָה
,Egypt to down brought been having Joseph And

וַיִּקְנֵהוּ פּוֹטִיפַר סְרִיס פַּרְעֹה[c] שַׂר
of chief the ,Pharaoh of officer an ,Potiphar him bought (and)

הַטַּבָּחִים אִישׁ מִצְרִי מִיַּד הַיִּשְׁמְעֵאלִים[d]
Ishmaelites the of hand the from ,[1]Egyptian [2]man a ,executioners the

2 אֲשֶׁר הוֹרִדֻהוּ שָׁמָּה׃ וַיְהִי יְהוָֹה אֶת־
with Jehovah was And .thither down him brought had who

יוֹסֵף וַיְהִי אִישׁ מַצְלִיחַ וַיְהִי[e]
was he and ;[1]prosperous [2]man a was he and ,Joseph

3 בְּבֵית אֲדֹנָיו הַמִּצְרִי׃ וַיַּרְא אֲדֹנָיו
master his saw And .Egyptian the ,master his of house the in

כִּי יְהוָֹה אִתּוֹ וְכֹל אֲשֶׁר־הוּא עֹשֶׂה
doing [was] he which all and ; him with [was] Jehovah that

4 יְהוָֹה מַצְלִיחַ בְּיָדוֹ׃ וַיִּמְצָא יוֹסֵף
Joseph found And .hand his in prosperous making [was] Jehovah

חֵן בְּעֵינָיו[f] וַיְשָׁרֶת אֹתוֹ וַיַּפְקִדֵהוּ
him appointed he and ;him to ministered and ,eyes his in favor

עַל־בֵּיתוֹ וְכָל[g]־יֶשׁ־לוֹ נָתַן בְּיָדוֹ׃
.hand his into gave he him to was [which] all and ,house his over

5 וַיְהִי מֵאָז הִפְקִיד אֹתוֹ
him appointed he that time the from pass to came it And

בְּבֵיתוֹ וְעַל כָּל־אֲשֶׁר יֶשׁ־לוֹ וַיְבָרֶךְ
blessed (and) ; him to was which all over and house his over

יְהוָֹה אֶת־בֵּית הַמִּצְרִי בִּגְלַל יוֹסֵף
;Joseph of sake the for Egyptian the of house the Jehovah

וַיְהִי בִּרְכַּת יְהוָֹה בְּכָל־אֲשֶׁר יֶשׁ־לוֹ
,him to was which all on Jehovah of blessing the was and

AND Joseph
was brought
down to Egypt;
and Potiphar,
an officer of
Pharaoh, cap-
tain of the
guard, an Egyp-
tian, bought
him of the hands
of the Ishmee-
lites, which had
brought him
down thither. 2
And the LORD
was with Jo-
seph, and he
was a prosper-
ous man; and
he was in the
house of his
master the E-
gyptian. 3 And
his master saw
that the LORD
was with him,
and that the
LORD made all
that he did to
prosper in his
hand. 4 And Jo-
seph found
grace in his
sight, and he
served him: and
he made him
overseer over
his house, and
all *that* he had
he put into his
hand. 5 And it
came to pass
from the time
that he had
made him over-
seer in his
house, and over
all that he had,
that the LORD
blessed the E-
gyptian's house
for Joseph's
sake; and the
blessing of the
LORD was up-
on all that he

And Joseph
was brought
down to Egypt;
and Potiphar,
an officer of
Pharaoh's, the
captain of
the guard, an
Egyptian,
bought him of
the hand of the
Ishmaelites,
which had
brought him
down thither. 2
And the LORD
was with Jo-
seph, and he
was a prosper-
ous man; and
he was in the
house of his
master the E-
gyptian. 3 And
his master
saw that the
LORD was with
him, and that
the LORD made
all that he did
to prosper in his
hand. 4 And
Joseph found
grace in his
sight, and he
ministered unto
him: and he
made him over-
seer over his
house, and all
that he had he
put into his
hand. 5 And it
came to pass
from the time
that he made
him overseer in
his house, and
over all that he
had, that the
LORD blessed
the Egyptian's
house for Jo-
seph's sake; and
the blessing of
the LORD was
upon all that

---

a Sm., S. have, *and she called.*
b S. has, *the Midianites led.*
c S. puts after הטבחים.
d S., T. have, *the Arabs.*
e S. omits.
f G., Sm., V. have, *in the eyes of his master.*
g G., S., T. add, *which*, reading וכל אשר, cf. v. 5.

had in the
house, and in the
field. 6 And he
left all that he
had in Joseph's
hand; and he
knew not ought
he had, save the
bread which he
did eat. And
Joseph was *a*
goodly *person*,
and well favour-
ed.

7 And it came
to pass after
these things,
that his mas-
ter's wife cast
her eyes upon
Joseph; and
she said, Lie
with me. 8 But
he refused, and
said unto his
master's wife,
Behold, my
master wotteth
not what *is* with
me in the house,
and he hath
committed all
that he hath to
my hand; 9
There is none
greater in this
house than I;
neither hath he
kept back any
thing from
me but thee,
because thou *art*
his wife: how
then can I do
this great wick-
edness, and sin
against God? 10
And it came to
pass, as she
spake to Joseph
day by day, that
he hearkened
not unto her, to
lie by her, *or*
to be with her.
11 And it came
to pass about
this time, that
Joseph went into
the house to do
his business; and
there was none

6 בַּבַּ֫יִת וּבַשָּׂדֶה׃ וַיַּעֲזֹב כָּל־אֲשֶׁר־לוֹ
him to [was] which all left he And .field the in and house the in

בְּיַד־יוֹסֵף וְלֹא־יָדַע אִתּוֹ מְאוּמָה
,thing a him with know not did he and ; Joseph of hand the in

כִּי אִם־הַלֶּחֶם אֲשֶׁר־הוּא אוֹכֵל וַיְהִי
was and ; eating [was] he which bread the (if) but

יוֹסֵף יְפֵה־תֹאַר וִיפֵה מַרְאֶה׃ [a]
.appearance of beautiful and form of beautiful Joseph

7 וַיְהִי אַחַר הַדְּבָרִים הָאֵלֶּה וַתִּשָּׂא
raised (and) ,[1]these [2]things after pass to came it And

אֵשֶׁת־אֲדֹנָיו אֶת־עֵינֶיהָ אֶל־יוֹסֵף וַתֹּאמֶר [b]
:said and ,Joseph unto eyes her master his of wife the

8 שִׁכְבָה עִמִּי׃ וַיְמָאֵן ׀ וַיֹּאמֶר אֶל־אֵשֶׁת
of wife the unto said and refused he And .me with Lie

אֲדֹנָיו הֵן אֲדֹנִי לֹא־יָדַע אִתִּי
me with know not does master my ,Behold :master his

[c] מַה־בַּבָּיִת [d] וְכֹל אֲשֶׁר־יֶשׁ־לוֹ נָתַן
given has he him to is which all and ; house the in [is] what

9 בְּיָדִי׃ אֵינֶנּוּ גָדוֹל בַּבַּיִת [e] הַזֶּה [e] מִמֶּנִּי
; I than [1]this [2]house in greater not is He .hand my into

וְלֹא־חָשַׂךְ מִמֶּנִּי מְאוּמָה כִּי אִם־אוֹתָךְ בַּאֲשֶׁר
because ,thee (if) but ,thing a me from witheld not has he and

אַתְּ־אִשְׁתּוֹ וְאֵיךְ אֶעֱשֶׂה הָרָעָה [f] הַגְּדֹלָה
[2]great [3]evil do I should how and ; wife his [art] thou

10 הַזֹּאת וְחָטָאתִי לֵאלֹהִים׃ וַיְהִי [g] כְּדַבְּרָהּ
speaking her at ,pass to came it And ? God against sin and ,[1]this

אֶל־יוֹסֵף יוֹם ׀ יוֹם וְלֹא־שָׁמַע אֵלֶיהָ
,her unto hearken not did he and ,day [by] day Joseph unto

11 לִשְׁכַּב אֶצְלָהּ [h] לִהְיוֹת עִמָּהּ׃ וַיְהִי כְּהַיּוֹם [i]
[2]day about pass to came it (and) ; her with be to her by lie to

הַזֶּה וַיָּבֹא [j] הַבַּיְתָה לַעֲשׂוֹת מְלַאכְתּוֹ [k] וְאֵין
not was and ,work his do to house the to in came he (and) ,[1]this

he had, in
the house and
in the field. 6
And he left all
that he had in
Joseph's hand;
and he knew
not aught *that*
was with him,
save the bread
which he did
eat. And Joseph
was comely, and
well favoured.

7 And it came
to pass after
these things,
that his mas-
ter's wife cast
her eyes upon
Joseph; and she
said, Lie with
me. 8 But he re-
fused, and said
unto his mas-
ter's wife, Be-
hold, my master
knoweth not
what is with me
in the house,
and he hath put
all that he hath
into my hand;
9 there is none
greater in this
house than I;
neither hath he
kept back any
thing from me
but thee, be-
cause thou art
his wife: how
then can I do
this great wick-
edness, and sin
against God? 10
And it came to
pass, as she
spake to Joseph
day by day, that
he hearkened
not unto her, to
lie by her, *or* to
be with her. 11
And it came to
pass about this
time, that he
went into the
house to do his
work; and there
was none of the

---

a G. adds, *exceedingly*.
b S. adds, *to him*.
c For מה Sm., G. have, *a thing*, מאומה, cf. v. 6.
d Sm., G., S., V. have, *in his house*, בביתו.
e G. has, *in his house*, בביתו.
f G., V. have. *this evil thing*.
g G., S. omit יהי; V. omits ויהי.
h Sm., S. add, *and*, ו.
i G. omits כ.
j Sm., G., S., V. add, *Joseph*.
k Sm. adds, *in the house*, בבית.

of the men of the house there within. 12 And she caught him by his garment, saying, Lie with me: and he left his garment in her hand, and fled, and got him out.

13 And it came to pass, when she saw that he had left his garment in her hand, and was fled forth, 14 That she called unto the men of her house, and spake unto them, saying, See, he hath brought in an Hebrew unto us to mock us; he came in unto me to lie with me, and I cried with a loud voice: 15 And it came to pass, when he heard that I lifted up my voice and cried, that he left his garment with me, and fled, and got him out. 16 And she laid up his garment by her, until his lord came home. 17 And she spake unto him according to these words, saying, The Hebrew servant, which thou hast brought unto us, came in unto me to mock me: 18 And it came to pass, as I lifted up my voice and cried, that he left his gar-

אִ֫ישׁ מֵאַנְשֵׁ֣י[a] הַבַּ֔יִת שָׁ֖ם[a] בַּבָּֽיִת[b]׃
man a | of men the from | house the | there | ; house the in

12 וַתִּתְפְּשֵׂ֧הוּ בְּבִגְד֛וֹ לֵאמֹ֖ר[c] שִׁכְבָ֣ה עִמִּ֑י
him seized she and | garment his by | : saying | Lie | ; me with

וַיַּעֲזֹ֤ב בִּגְדוֹ֙ בְּיָדָ֔הּ[d] וַיָּ֖נָס וַיֵּצֵ֥א הַחֽוּצָה׃
left he and | garment his | hand her in | fled and | went and | .outside

13 וַֽיְהִי֙ כִּרְאוֹתָ֔הּ כִּֽי־עָזַ֥ב בִּגְד֖וֹ
,pass to came it And | seeing her at | left had he that | garment his

14 בְּיָדָ֑הּ וַיָּ֖נָס[e] הַחֽוּצָה׃ וַתִּקְרָ֞א לְאַנְשֵׁ֣י
,hand her in | fled had and | ; outside | called she (and) | of men the (to)

בֵיתָ֗הּ וַתֹּ֤אמֶר לָהֶם֙ לֵאמֹ֔ר[f] רְא֗וּ הֵ֥בִיא
house her | said and | them to | : saying | ,See | in brought has he

לָ֛נוּ אִ֥ישׁ[g] עִבְרִ֖י לְצַ֣חֶק בָּ֑נוּ בָּ֥א אֵלַי֙
us to | ²man a | ¹Hebrew | wanton to | ; us with | in came he | me unto

15 לִשְׁכַּ֣ב[h] עִמִּ֔י[h] וָאֶקְרָ֖א בְּק֥וֹל גָּדֽוֹל׃ וַיְהִ֣י[i]
lie to | ,me with | cried I and | ²voice a with | .¹loud | ,pass to came it And

כְשָׁמְע֔וֹ כִּֽי־הֲרִימֹ֥תִי קוֹלִ֖י וָאֶקְרָ֑א וַיַּעֲזֹ֤ב
hearing his at | raised I that | voice my | ,cried and | left he (and)

16 בִּגְדוֹ֙ אֶצְלִ֔י[j] וַיָּ֖נָס וַיֵּצֵ֥א הַחֽוּצָה׃ וַתַּנַּ֥ח
garment his | ,me by | fled and | went and | .outside | kept she And

בִּגְד֖וֹ אֶצְלָ֑הּ עַד־בּ֥וֹא אֲדֹנָ֖יו אֶל־
garment his | ,her by | of coming the until | master his | unto

17 בֵּיתֽוֹ׃ וַתְּדַבֵּ֣ר אֵלָ֔יו כַּדְּבָרִ֥ים הָאֵ֖לֶּה
.house his | spoke she And | him unto | ²words like | ,¹these

לֵאמֹ֑ר[k] בָּ֣א אֵלַ֞י הָעֶ֤בֶד הָֽעִבְרִי֙ אֲשֶׁר־
: saying | Came in | me unto | ²slave the | ¹Hebrew | whom

18 הֵבֵ֥אתָ לָּ֖נוּ לְצַ֥חֶק בִּֽי[l]׃ וַיְהִ֕י[m]
thou hast brought in | ,us to | wanton to | .me with | ,pass to came it And

כַּהֲרִימִ֥י קוֹלִ֖י וָאֶקְרָ֑א וַיַּעֲזֹ֤ב בִּגְדוֹ֙
at my raising | voice my | ,crying and | left he (and) | garment his

men of the house there within. 12 And she caught him by his garment, saying, Lie with me: and he left his garment in her hand, and fled, and got him out.

13 And it came to pass, when she saw that he had left his garment in her hand, and was fled forth, 14 that she called unto the men of her house, and spake unto them, saying, See, he hath brought in an Hebrew unto us to mock us; he came in unto me to lie with me, and I cried with a loud voice: 15 and it came to pass, when he heard that I lifted up my voice and cried, that he left his garment by me, and fled, and got him out. 16 And she laid up his garment by her, until his master came home. 17 And she spake unto him according to these words, saying, The Hebrew servant, which thou hast brought unto us, came in unto me to mock me: 18 and it came to pass, as I lifted up my voice and cried, that he left his garment

---

a G. omits.

b G. adds, *within.*

c S. adds, *to him.*

d G. omits.

e V. omits; Sm., G. add, *and he went*, ויצא; cf. vs. 12, 15.

f S., V. omit.

g G., S. have, *slave*, עבד; cf. v. 17.

h G. has, *saying, Lie with me.*

i G., S., V. omit יהי.

j Sm., S. have, *in my hand*, בידי; V. has, *which I held.*

k S., V. omit.

l G. adds, *and he said unto me, Lie with me.*

m G., S., V. omit יהי.

ment with me, and fled out. 19 And it came to pass, when his master heard the words of his wife, which she spake unto him, saying, After this manner did thy servant to me; that his wrath was kindled. 20 And Joseph's master took him, and put him into the prison, a place where the king's prisoners *were* bound: and he was there in the prison.

21 But the LORD was with Joseph, and shewed him mercy, and gave him favour in the sight of the keeper of the prison. 22 And the keeper of the prison committed to Joseph's hand all the prisoners that *were* in the prison; and whatsoever they did there, he was the doer *of it*. 23 The keeper of the prison looked not to any thing *that was* under his hand; because the LORD was with him, and *that* which he did, the LORD made *it* to prosper.

אֶצְלִי [a]וַיָּנָס הַחוּצָה׃ [b]וַיְהִי כִּשְׁמֹעַ 19
[3]hearing at ,pass to came it And .outside fled and me by

אֲדֹנָיו אֶת־דִּבְרֵי אִשְׁתּוֹ אֲשֶׁר דִּבְּרָה
spoke she which ,wife his of words the [2]master's [1]his

אֵלָיו [c]לֵאמֹר כַּדְּבָרִים הָאֵלֶּה עָשָׂה לִי
me to did [1]these [2]words Like :saying him unto

עַבְדֶּךָ וַיִּחַר אַפּוֹ׃ וַיִּקַּח אֲדֹנֵי 20
of master the took And .anger his glowed (and) ,slave thy

[d]יוֹסֵף [e]אֹתוֹ וַיִּתְּנֵהוּ אֶל־בֵּית הַסֹּהַר
;enclosure of house the into him put and ,him Joseph

מְקוֹם אֲשֶׁר־אֲסוּרֵי הַמֶּלֶךְ אֲסוּרִים
;imprisoned [were] king the of prisoners the where place the

[f]וַיְהִי־שָׁם בְּבֵית הַסֹּהַר׃ וַיְהִי יְהוָה 21
Jehovah was And .enclosure of house the in there was he and

אֶת־יוֹסֵף וַיֵּט אֵלָיו חָסֶד וַיִּתֵּן
gave he and ,kindness him unto extended and ,Joseph with

[g]חִנּוֹ בְּעֵינֵי שַׂר בֵּית־הַסֹּהַר׃
.enclosure of house the of governor the of eyes the in favor his

וַיִּתֵּן שַׂר בֵּית־הַסֹּהַר בְּיַד־ 22
of hand the into enclosure of house the of governor the gave And

יוֹסֵף אֵת כָּל־הָאֲסִירִם אֲשֶׁר בְּבֵית
of house the in [were] who prisoners the all Joseph

הַסֹּהַר וְאֵת כָּל־אֲשֶׁר עֹשִׂים שָׁם הוּא[h]
he ,there doing [were they] which all and ;enclosure

הָיָה עֹשֶׂה׃ [h]אֵין שַׂר בֵּית־הַסֹּהַר 23
enclosure of house the of governor the not Was .doing was

רֹאֶה אֶת־כָּל־מְאוּמָה [i]בְּיָדוֹ בַּאֲשֶׁר יְהוָה
Jehovah that in ;hand his in thing any seeing

אִתּוֹ [j]וַאֲשֶׁר־הוּא עֹשֶׂה יְהוָה
Jehovah doing [was] he what and ,him with [was]

[k]מַצְלִיחַ׃
.prosperous making [was]

by me, and fled out. 19 And it came to pass, when his master heard the words of his wife, which she spake unto him, saying, After this manner did thy servant to me; that his wrath was kindled. 20 And Joseph's master took him, and put him into the prison, the place where the king's prisoners were bound: and he was there in the prison.

21 But the LORD was with Joseph, and shewed kindness unto him, and gave him favour in the sight of the keeper of the prison. 22 And the keeper of the prison committed to Joseph's hand all the prisoners that were in the prison; and whatsoever they did there, he was the doer of it. 23 The keeper of the prison looked not to any thing that was under his hand, because the LORD was with him; and that which he did, the LORD made it to prosper.

---

a G., S. add, *and he went*, ויצא.
b S. omits יהי; V. omits ויהי.
c S. omits.
d S. has, *him*.
e G. omits.
f G. omits.
g G., S., T., V. have, *to him favor*.
h G. omits.
i G. adds, *for all was by the hand of Joseph*.
j For ואשר Sm., S., V. have, *and all which*, וכל אשר.
k G. adds, *in his hands*.

40

AND it came to pass after these things, *that* the butler of the king of Egypt and *his* baker had offended t h e i r lord the king of Egypt. 2 And Pharaoh w a s wroth against two *of* his officers, against the chief of the butlers, and against the chief of the bakers. 3 And he put them in ward in the house of the captain of the guard, into the prison, the place where Joseph *was* bound. 4 And the captain of the guard charged Joseph with them, and he served them: and they continued a season in ward.

5 And they d r e a m e d a dream both of them, each man his dream in one night, each man according to the interpretation of his dream, the butler and the baker of the king of Egypt, which *w e r e* bound in the prison. 6 And Joseph came in unto them in the morning, a n d looked u p o n them, and, behold, they *were* sad. 7 And he asked Pharaoh's officers that

1 וַיְהִי אַחַר הַדְּבָרִים הָאֵלֶּה חָטְאוּ
sinned ,¹these ²things after pass to came it And

מַשְׁקֵה*ᵃ* מֶלֶךְ־מִצְרַיִם וְהָאֹפֶה*ᵇ* לַאֲדֹנֵיהֶם
,lord their against baker the and Egypt of king the of cupbearer the

לְמֶלֶךְ מִצְרָיִם: וַיִּקְצֹף פַּרְעֹה עַל
against Pharaoh angry was And .Egypt of king the against

2 שְׁנֵי סָרִיסָיו עַל שַׂר הַמַּשְׁקִים וְעַל
against and cupbearers the of chief the against ,officers ¹his ²two

3 שַׂר הָאֹפִים: וַיִּתֵּן אֹתָם בְּמִשְׁמַר
,custody into them gave he And .bakers the of chief the

בֵּית שַׂר הַטַּבָּחִים אֶל־בֵּית
of house the into ,executioners the of chief the of house the in

הַסֹּהַר מְקוֹם אֲשֶׁר יוֹסֵף אָסוּר
imprisoned [was] Joseph where place the ; enclosure

4 שָׁם: וַיִּפְקֹד שַׂר הַטַּבָּחִים אֶת־יוֹסֵף
Joseph executioners the of chief the appointed And .(there)

אִתָּם וַיְשָׁרֶת אֹתָם וַיִּהְיוּ יָמִים
days were they and ; them to ministered he and ,them with

5 בְּמִשְׁמָר: וַיַּחַלְמוּ חֲלוֹם שְׁנֵיהֶם אִישׁ
each ,them of both dream a dreamed they And .custody in

חֲלֹמוֹ בְּלַיְלָה אֶחָד אִישׁ*ᶜ* כְּפִתְרוֹן
of interpretation the to according each ,¹one ²night in dream his

חֲלֹמוֹ*ᶜ* הַמַּשְׁקֶה וְהָאֹפֶה אֲשֶׁר לְמֶלֶךְ
of king the to [were] who baker the and cupbearer the ; dream his

מִצְרַיִם אֲשֶׁר אֲסוּרִים*ᵈ* בְּבֵית הַסֹּהַר:
.enclosure of house the in imprisoned [were] who ,Egypt

6 וַיָּבֹא אֲלֵיהֶם יוֹסֵף בַּבֹּקֶר וַיַּרְא
saw he and ; morning the in Joseph them unto in came And

7 אֹתָם וְהִנָּם זֹעֲפִים: וַיִּשְׁאַל אֶת־סָרִיסֵי
of officers the asked he And .despondent behold and ,them

And it came to pass after these things, that the butler of the king of Egypt and his baker offended their lord the king of Egypt. 2 And Pharaoh was wroth against his two officers, against the chief of the butlers, and against the chief of the bakers. 3 And he put them in ward in the house of the captain of the guard, into the prison, the place where Joseph was bound. 4 And the captain of the guard charged Joseph with them, and he ministered unto them: and they continued a season in ward.

5 And they d r e a m e d a dream both of them, each man his dream, in one night, each man according to the interpretation of his dream, the butler and the baker of the king of Egypt, which were bound in the prison. 6 A n d Joseph came in unto them in the morning, a n d saw them, and, behold, they were sad. 7 And he asked Pharaoh's officers

---

a G., S. have, *the chief cupbearer.*
b G., S. have, *and the chief baker.*

c G. has, *the vision of his dream.*
d G. omits.

were with him
in the ward of
his lord's house,
saying, Where-
fore look ye *so*
sadly to day ? 8
And they said
unto him, We
have dreamed a
dream, and
there is no in-
terpreter of it.
And Joseph said
unto them, *Do*
not interpreta-
tions *belong* to
God ? tell me
them, I pray
you.

9 And the
chief butler told
his dream to
Joseph, and said
to him, In my
dream, behold,
a vine *was* be-
fore me; 10 And
in the vine *were*
three branches :
and it *was* as
though it bud-
ded, *and* her
blossoms shot
forth ; and the
clusters thereof
brought forth
ripe grapes: 11
And Pharaoh's
cup *was* in my
hand; and I
took the grapes,
and pressed
them into Pha-
raoh's cup, and
I gave the cup
into Pharaoh's
hand. 12 And
Joseph said un-
to him, This *is*
the interpreta-
tion of it: The
three branches
are three days:
13 Yet within
three days shall
Pharaoh lift up
thine head, and
restore thee un-
to thy place :
and thou shalt
deliver Pha-
raoh's cup into
his hand, after

פַּרְעֹה אֲשֶׁר אִתּוֹ בְמִשְׁמַר בֵּית
of house the in ,custody in him with [were] who Pharaoh

אֲדֹנָיו לֵאמֹר[a] מַדּוּעַ פְּנֵיכֶם רָעִים הַיּוֹם׃
?today evil faces your [are] Why :saying ,lord his

8 וַיֹּאמְרוּ אֵלָיו חֲלוֹם חָלַמְנוּ וּפֹתֵר
interpreter an and ,dreamed have we dream A :him unto said they And

אֵין אֹתוֹ וַיֹּאמֶר אֲלֵהֶם יוֹסֵף הֲלוֹא
not [Are] :Joseph them unto said and ;it [of] not is

9 לֵאלֹהִים פִּתְרֹנִים סַפְּרוּ־נָא לִי[b]׃ וַיְסַפֵּר
related And .me to ,now ,relate ?interpretations God to

שַׂר־הַמַּשְׁקִים אֶת־חֲלֹמוֹ לְיוֹסֵף וַיֹּאמֶר
said and ,Joseph to dream his cupbearers the of chief the

[c]לוֹ בַּחֲלוֹמִי [d]וְהִנֵּה־גֶפֶן לְפָנָי׃
.me before vine a behold (and) ,dream my In :him to

10 וּבַגֶּפֶן שְׁלֹשָׁה שָׂרִיגִם וְהִוא [e]כְּפֹרַחַת
budding its at ,it and ;shoots three vine the in And

עָלְתָה נִצָּהּ הִבְשִׁילוּ אַשְׁכְּלֹתֶיהָ עֲנָבִים׃
.grapes [to] clusters its ripened ,blossom its up went

11 וְכוֹס פַּרְעֹה בְּיָדִי וָאֶקַּח
took I (and) ,hand my in [being] Pharaoh of cup the And

אֶת־הָעֲנָבִים וָאֶשְׂחַט אֹתָם אֶל־כּוֹס פַּרְעֹה[f]
;Pharaoh of cup the into them pressed and grapes the

12 וָאֶתֵּן אֶת־הַכּוֹס עַל־כַּף פַּרְעֹה׃ וַיֹּאמֶר
said And .Pharaoh of hand the into cup the gave I and

לוֹ יוֹסֵף זֶה פִּתְרֹנוֹ[g] שְׁלֹשֶׁת
three the ;interpretation its [is] This :Joseph him to

13 הַשָּׂרִגִים שְׁלֹשֶׁת יָמִים הֵם׃ בְּעוֹד שְׁלֹשֶׁת
three yet In .they [are] days three ,shoots

יָמִים יִשָּׂא[h] פַרְעֹה אֶת־רֹאשֶׁךָ[h] וַהֲשִׁיבְךָ
thee return will and ,head thy Pharaoh up lift will days

עַל־כַּנֶּךָ וְנָתַתָּ כוֹס־פַּרְעֹה בְּיָדוֹ
,hand his into Pharaoh of cup the give wilt thou and ;place thy unto

that were with
him in ward in
his master's
house, saying,
Wherefore look
ye so sadly to-
day? 8 And they
said unto him,
We have dream-
ed a dream, and
there is none
that can inter-
pret it. And Jo-
seph said unto
them, Do not in-
terpretations be-
long to God ?
tell it me, I pray
you.

9 And the
chief butler told
his dream to Jo-
seph, and said
to him, In my
dream, behold,
a vine was be-
fore me; 10 and
in the vine were
three branches :
and it was as
though it bud-
ded, *and* its
blossoms shot
forth ; *and* the
clusters thereof
brought forth
ripe grapes: 11
and Pharaoh's
cup was in my
hand; and I
took the grapes,
and pressed
them into Pha-
raoh's cup, and I
gave the cup in-
to Pharaoh's
hand. 12 And
Joseph said un-
to him, This is
the interpreta-
tion of it: the
three branches
are three days;
13 within yet
three days shall
Pharaoh lift up
thine head, and
restore thee un-
to thine office :
and thou shalt
give Pharaoh's
cup into his
hand, after the

***

a S. adds, *to them.*

b V. adds, *what you have seen.*

c G., V. omit.

d G. omits; S. omits, *and*, ו.

e G. has, *budding*, perhaps מפרחת.

f G. omits; V. omits and adds, *which I held.*

g S., V. have, *the interpretation of thy dream.*

h G. has, *and Pharaoh will remember thy office ;* S., T., V. are similar.

the former man-
ner when thou
wast his butler.
14 But think on
me when it shall
be well with
thee, and shew
kindness, I pray
thee, unto me,
and make men-
tion of me unto
Pharaoh, and
bring me out of
this house: 15
For indeed I
was stolen a-
way out of the
land of the He-
brews: and here
also have I done
nothing that
they should put
me into the
dungeon.

כְּמִשְׁפָּט הָרִאשׁוֹן אֲשֶׁר הָיִיתָ מַשְׁקֵהוּ׃
.cupbearer his wast thou when ,[1]former [2]custom the like

14 כִּי אִם־זְכַרְתַּנִי אִתְּךָ כַּאֲשֶׁר
when ,thyself with me remember thou mayest (if) But

יִיטַב לָךְ וְעָשִׂיתָ־נָּא עִמָּדִי [a]חָסֶד
,kindness me with ,pray I ,do and ; thee to well is it

וְהִזְכַּרְתַּנִי אֶל־פַּרְעֹה וְהוֹצֵאתַנִי מִן
from out me bring and ,Pharaoh unto me mention and

15 הַבַּיִת[b] הַזֶּה׃ כִּי־גֻנֹּב גֻּנַּבְתִּי מֵאֶרֶץ
of land the from stolen was I surely For .[1]this [2]house

הָעִבְרִים וְגַם־פֹּה לֹא־עָשִׂיתִי מְאוּמָה
,thing a done not have I here also and ; Hebrews the

16 כִּי־שָׂמוּ אֹתִי בַּבּוֹר׃ וַיַּרְא
saw And .dungeon the into me put have should they that

שַׂר־הָאֹפִים כִּי טוֹב פָּתָר וַיֹּאמֶר
said he and ,interpretation the [was] good that bakers the of chief the

אֶל־יוֹסֵף אַף־אֲנִי[c] בַּחֲלוֹמִי[d] וְהִנֵּה שְׁלֹשָׁה
three behold (and) ,dream my in I Also : Joseph unto

17 סַלֵּי חֹרִי עַל־רֹאשִׁי׃ וּבַסַּל
[2]basket the in and ; head my upon bread white of baskets

הָעֶלְיוֹן מִכֹּל מַאֲכַל פַּרְעֹה[e] מַעֲשֵׂה
of work the ,Pharaoh of food the all from [some] [1]upper

אֹפֶה וְהָעוֹף[f] אֹכֵל אֹתָם מִן־הַסַּל
basket the from them eating birds the and ; baker a

18 מֵעַל רֹאשִׁי׃ וַיַּעַן יוֹסֵף וַיֹּאמֶר[g] זֶה
This : said and Joseph answered And .head my upon from

פִּתְרֹנוֹ[h] שְׁלֹשֶׁת הַסַּלִּים שְׁלֹשֶׁת יָמִים
days three ,baskets three the ; interpretation its [is]

19 הֵם׃ בְּעוֹד שְׁלֹשֶׁת יָמִים יִשָּׂא פַרְעֹה
Pharaoh up lift will ,days three yet In .they [are]

אֶת־רֹאשְׁךָ מֵעָלֶיךָ וְתָלָה אוֹתְךָ עַל־עֵץ
,tree a upon thee hang and ,thee upon from head thy

וְאָכַל הָעוֹף[i] אֶת־בְּשָׂרְךָ מֵעָלֶיךָ׃
.thee upon from flesh thy birds the eat will and

16 When
the chief
baker saw that
the interpreta-
tion was good,
he said unto Jo-
seph, I also *was*
in my dream,
and, behold, *I*
had three white
baskets on my
head: 17 And in
the uppermost
basket *there was*
of all manner of
bakemeats for
Pharaoh; and
the birds did eat
them out of the
basket upon my
head. 18 And
Joseph answer-
ed and said,
This *is* the in-
terpretation
thereof: The
three baskets
are three days:
19 Yet within
three days
shall Pha-
raoh lift up thy
head from off
thee, and shall
hang thee on a
tree; and the
birds shall eat
thy flesh from
off thee.

former manner
when thou wast
his butler. 14
But have me in
thy remem-
brance when it
shall be well
with thee, and
shew kindness,
I pray thee, un-
to me, and
make mention
of me unto Pha-
raoh, and bring
me out of this
house: 15 for
indeed I was
stolen away out
of the land of
the Hebrews;
and here also
have I done
nothing that
they should put
me into the
dungeon.

16 When
the chief
baker saw that
the interpreta-
tion was good,
he said unto Jo-
seph, I also was
in my dream,
and, behold,
three baskets of
white bread
were on my
head: 17 and in
the uppermost
basket there was
of all manner
of bakemeats for
Pharaoh; and
the birds did eat
them out of the
basket upon my
head. 18 And
Joseph answer-
ed and said,
This is the in-
terpretation
thereof: the
three baskets are
three days; 19
within yet three
days shall Pha-
raoh lift up thy
head from off
thee, and shall
hang thee on a
tree; and the
birds shall eat
thy flesh from
off thee.

---

a S. has *kindness and justice.*
b G., S., T., V. apparently add, *of inclosure,* הסהר.
c S. adds, *and,* ו.
d G., V. have, *saw a dream.*
e G. has, *of which king Pharaoh eats.*
f G. adds, *of the heaven.*
g G., S. add, *to him.*
h S., V. have, *the interpretation of thy dream.*
i G. adds, *of the heaven.*

20 וַיְהִי ׀ בַּיּוֹם הַשְּׁלִישִׁי יוֹם הֻלֶּדֶת
of birth the   of day the   ,[1]third   [2]day the on   ,pass to came it And

אֶת־פַּרְעֹה וַיַּעַשׂ מִשְׁתֶּה לְכָל־עֲבָדָיו
; servants his all for   feast a   made he (and)   ,Pharaoh

וַיִּשָּׂא אֶת־רֹאשׁ ׀ שַׂר הַמַּשְׁקִים וְאֶת־
and   ,cupbearers the   of chief the   of head the   up lifted he and

רֹאשׁ שַׂר הָאֹפִים בְּתוֹךְ עֲבָדָיו׃
.servants his   of midst the in   ,bakers the   of chief the   of head the

21 וַיָּשֶׁב אֶת־שַׂר הַמַּשְׁקִים עַל־
unto   cupbearers the   of chief the   returned he And

מַשְׁקֵהוּ וַיִּתֵּן הַכּוֹס עַל־כַּף
of hand the into   cup the   gave he and   ;cupbearer [of office] his

22 פַּרְעֹה׃ וְאֵת שַׂר הָאֹפִים תָּלָה כַּאֲשֶׁר
as   ,hanged he   bakers the   of chief the   And   .Pharaoh

23 פָּתַר לָהֶם יוֹסֵף׃ וְלֹא־זָכַר שַׂר־
of chief the   remember not did And   .Joseph   them to   interpreted

הַמַּשְׁקִים אֶת־יוֹסֵף וַיִּשְׁכָּחֵהוּ׃
.him forgot but   ,Joseph   cupbearers the

41

1 וַיְהִי מִקֵּץ שְׁנָתַיִם יָמִים[a]
,days   ,years two   of end the from   pass to came it And

וּפַרְעֹה חֹלֵם[b] וְהִנֵּה עֹמֵד עַל־
by   standing [was he]   behold and   ,dreaming [was]   Pharaoh and

2 הַיְאֹר׃ וְהִנֵּה[c] מִן־הַיְאֹר עֹלֹת
up going [were]   river the from   behold And   .[Nile] river the

שֶׁבַע פָּרוֹת יְפוֹת מַרְאֶה וּבְרִיאֹת בָּשָׂר
; flesh   of fat and   appearance   of beautiful   ,cows   seven

3 וַתִּרְעֶינָה בָּאָחוּ׃ וְהִנֵּה שֶׁבַע פָּרוֹת
[2]cows   seven   behold And   .reeds the in   feeding were they and

אֲחֵרוֹת עֹלוֹת אַחֲרֵיהֶן מִן־הַיְאֹר רָעוֹת
of evil   ,river the from   them after   up going [were]   [1]other

20 And it came to pass the third day, *which was* Pharaoh's birthday, that he made a feast unto all his servants: and he lifted up the head of the chief butler and of the chief baker among his servants.

21 And he restored the chief butler unto his butlership again; and he gave the cup into Pharaoh's hand:
22 But he hanged the chief baker; as Joseph had interpreted to them.
23 Yet did not the chief butler remember Joseph, but forgat him.

AND it came to pass at the end of two full years, that Pharaoh dreamed: and, behold, he stood by the river.
2 And, behold, there came up out of the river seven well favoured kine and fatfleshed; and they fed in a meadow.
3 And, behold, seven other kine came up after them out of the river, ill favoured and

20 And it came to pass the third day, which was Pharaoh's birthday, that he made a feast unto all his servants: and he lifted up the head of the chief butler and the head of the chief baker among his servants.

21 And he restored the chief butler unto his butlership again; and he gave the cup into Pharaoh's hand:
22 but he hanged the chief baker: as Joseph had interpreted to them.
23 Yet did not the chief butler remember Joseph, but forgat him.

And it came to pass at the end of two full years, that Pharaoh dreamed: and behold, he stood by the river.
2 And, behold, there came up out of the river seven kine, well favoured and fatfleshed; and they fed in the reed-grass.
3 And, behold, seven other kine came up after them out of the river, ill favoured and lean-

a S., T., V. omit.
b S. adds, *a dream.*
c G. adds, *as if.*

leanfleshed; and
stood by the
other kine upon
the brink of the
river. 4 And the
ill favoured and
leanfleshed kine
did eat up the
seven well favoured and fat
kine. So Pharaoh awoke. 5
And he slept
and dreamed the
second time:
and, behold,
seven ears of
corn came up
upon one stalk,
rank and good.
6 And, behold,
seven thin ears
and blasted with
the east wind
sprung up after
them. 7 And the
seven thin ears
devoured the
seven rank and
full ears. And
Pharaoh awoke,
and, behold, *it*
was a dream. 8
And it came to
pass in the
morning that
his spirit was
troubled; and
he sent and called for all the
magicians of Egypt, and all the
wise men thereof: and Pharaoh told them
his dream; but
there was none
that could interpret them unto
Pharaoh.
9 Then spake
the chief butler
unto Pharaoh,

מַרְאֶה וְדַקּוֹת בָּשָׂר וַתַּעֲמֹדְנָה אֵצֶל[a]
by standing were they and ; flesh of lean and appearance

4 הַפָּרוֹת עַל־שְׂפַת הַיְאֹר[b]: וַתֹּאכַלְנָה
eating were And .river the of bank the upon ,cows the

הַפָּרוֹת[c] רָעוֹת הַמַּרְאֶה[d] וְדַקֹּת הַבָּשָׂר אֶת שֶׁבַע
seven the flesh of lean and appearance of evil cows the

הַפָּרוֹת יְפֹת הַמַּרְאֶה וְהַבְּרִיאֹת[e] וַיִּיקַץ
awoke and ; fat and appearance of beautiful cows

5 פַּרְעֹה: וַיִּישָׁן[f] וַיַּחֲלֹם שֵׁנִית וְהִנֵּה
behold and ; time second a dreamed and slept he And .Pharaoh

שֶׁבַע שִׁבֳּלִים עֹלוֹת בְּקָנֶה אֶחָד בְּרִיאוֹת
fat ,one stalk on up going grain of ears seven

6 וְטֹבוֹת: וְהִנֵּה[g] שֶׁבַע שִׁבֳּלִים דַּקּוֹת
lean grain of ears seven behold And .good and

וּשְׁדוּפֹת קָדִים צֹמְחוֹת אַחֲרֵיהֶן:
.them after forth sprouting [were] [wind] east the [by] (of) blasted and

7 וַתִּבְלַעְנָה הַשִּׁבֳּלִים[h] הַדַּקּוֹת[i] אֵת שֶׁבַע
seven the [1]lean [2]ears the swallowing were And

הַשִּׁבֳּלִים הַבְּרִיאוֹת וְהַמְּלֵאוֹת וַיִּיקַץ
awoke and ; full and fat ears

8 פַּרְעֹה וְהִנֵּה[j] חֲלוֹם: וַיְהִי בַבֹּקֶר
,morning the in pass to came it And .dream a behold and ,Pharaoh

וַתִּפָּעֶם רוּחוֹ[k] וַיִּשְׁלַח וַיִּקְרָא אֶת־כָּל־
all called and sent he and ; spirit his troubled was (and)

חַרְטֻמֵּי מִצְרַיִם[l] וְאֶת־כָּל־חֲכָמֶיהָ[m] וַיְסַפֵּר
related and ; men wise its all and ,Egypt of scribes the

פַּרְעֹה לָהֶם אֶת־חֲלֹמוֹ[n] וְאֵין־פּוֹתֵר
interpreting one not was [there] and ,dream his them to Pharaoh

9 אוֹתָם[o] לְפַרְעֹה: וַיְדַבֵּר שַׂר הַמַּשְׁקִים
cupbearers the of chief the spoke And .Pharaoh to them

fleshed; and
stood by the other kine upon the
brink of the
river. 4 And the
ill favoured and
leanfleshed kine
did eat up the
seven well favoured and fat
kine. So Pharaoh awoke. 5
And he slept
and dreamed a second
time: and, behold, seven ears
of corn came up
upon one stalk,
rank and good.
6 And, behold,
seven ears, thin
and blasted with
the east wind,
sprung up after
them. 7 And the
thin ears swallowed up the
seven rank and
full ears. And
Pharaoh awoke,
and, behold, it
was a dream. 8
And it came to
pass in the morning that his
spirit was
troubled; and he
sent and called
for all the magicians of Egypt, and all
the wise men
thereof: and
Pharaoh told
them his dream;
but there was
none that could
interpret them
unto Pharaoh.
9 Then spake
the chief butler
unto Pharaoh,

---

a G. omits.
b G. adds, *in the reeds,* באחו; cf. v. 2.
c G. adds, *seven.*
d G. omits.
e G. adds, *of flesh,* בשר.
f G. omits.
g G., V. omit הנה and add, *other.*
h G. adds, *seven.*
i G. adds, *and blasted by the east wind,* ושרופת קרים.
j G. omits.
k S. has, *the spirit of Pharaoh.*
l S. omits.
m For חכמיה S. has, *the wise men of Pharaoh.*
n Sm., S. have pl., *his dreams.*
o G., T. have sing., *it,* אותו.

saying, I do re-
member my
faults this day:
10 Pharaoh was
wroth with his
servants, and
put me in ward
in the captain of
the guard's
house, *both* me
and the chief
baker: 11 And
we dreamed a
dream in one
night, I and he;
we dreamed
each man ac-
cording to the
interpretation of
his dream. 12
And *there was*
there with us a
young man, an
Hebrew, servant
to the captain of
the guard; and
we told him, and
he interpreted
to us our
dreams; to each
man according
to his dream he
did interpret. 13
And it came to
pass, as he in-
terpreted to us,
so it was; me he
restored unto
mine office, and
him he hanged.

14 Then Pha-
raoh sent and
called Joseph,
and they
brought him
hastily out of
the dungeon:
and he shaved
himself, and
changed his rai-
ment, and came
in unto Pha-
raoh. 15 And
Pharaoh said
unto Joseph, I
have dreamed a
dream, and
there is none
that can inter-
pret it: and I
have heard say

אֶת־פַּרְעֹה[a] לֵאמֹר אֶת־חֲטָאַי אֲנִי מַזְכִּיר
mentioning [am] I sins My :saying ,Pharaoh with

10 הַיּוֹם׃ פַּרְעֹה קָצַף עַל־עֲבָדָיו וַיִּתֵּן
gave and ,servants his against angry was Pharaoh .today

אֹתִי[b] בְּמִשְׁמַר בֵּית שַׂר הַטַּבָּחִים
,executioners the of chief the of house the in ,custody into me

11 אֹתִי וְאֵת שַׂר הָאֹפִים׃ וַנַּחַלְמָה
dreamed we And .bakers the of chief the and me

חֲלוֹם בְּלַיְלָה אֶחָד אֲנִי וָהוּא אִישׁ
each ;he and I ,[1]one [2]night in dream a

12 כְּפִתְרוֹן[c] חֲלֹמוֹ[c] חָלָמְנוּ׃ וְשָׁם
there And .dreamed we dream his of interpretation the to according

אִתָּנוּ נַעַר עִבְרִי עֶבֶד לְשַׂר
of chief the to slave a ,[1]Hebrew [2]youth a [was] us with

הַטַּבָּחִים וַנְּסַפֶּר־לוֹ וַיִּפְתָּר־לָנוּ
us to interpreted he and ,him to related we and ;executioners the

אֶת־חֲלֹמֹתֵינוּ[d] אִישׁ כַּחֲלֹמוֹ פָּתָר[d]׃
.interpreted he dream his to according each ,dreams our

13 וַיְהִי[e] כַּאֲשֶׁר פָּתַר־לָנוּ כֵּן
so ,us to interpreted had he as ,pass to came it And

הָיָה[f] אֹתִי הֵשִׁיב עַל־כַּנִּי וְאֹתוֹ תָלָה׃
.hanged he him and ,place my unto returned he me ;was it

14 וַיִּשְׁלַח פַּרְעֹה וַיִּקְרָא אֶת־יוֹסֵף
,Joseph called and Pharaoh sent And

וַיְרִיצֻהוּ[g] מִן־הַבּוֹר וַיְגַלַּח
himself shaved he and ;dungeon the from run him made they and

וַיְחַלֵּף שִׂמְלֹתָיו וַיָּבֹא אֶל־פַּרְעֹה׃
.Pharaoh unto in came and ,clothing his changed and

15 וַיֹּאמֶר פַּרְעֹה אֶל־יוֹסֵף חֲלוֹם חָלַמְתִּי
,dreamed have I dream A :Joseph unto Pharaoh said And

וּפֹתֵר אֵין אֹתוֹ וַאֲנִי שָׁמַעְתִּי
heard have I and ;it [3]not [2]is [[1]there] [5]interpreting [4]one and

saying, I do re-
member my
faults this day:
10 Pharaoh was
wroth with his
servants, and
put me in ward
in the house of
the captain of
the guard, me
and the chief
baker: 11 and
we dreamed a
dream in one
night, I and he;
we dreamed
each man ac-
cording to the
interpretation of
his dream. 12
And there was
with us there a
young man, an
Hebrew, servant
to the captain of
the guard; and
we told him,
and he interpret-
ed to us our
dreams; to each
man according
to his dream he
did interpret. 13
And it came to
pass, as he in-
terpreted to us,
so it was; me he
restored unto
mine office, and
him he hanged.

14 Then Pha-
raoh sent and
called Joseph,
and they
brought him
hastily out of the
dungeon: and
he shaved him-
self, and chang-
ed his raiment,
and came in un-
to Pharaoh. 15
And Pharaoh
said unto Jo-
seph, I have
dreamed a
dream, and
there is none
that can inter-
pret it: and I
have heard say

---

a Sm., G. have, *unto*, אל.
b G., S. have, *us*, אתנו; Sm. *them*, אתם.
c G. has, *according to his dream.*
d G. omits.
e S. omits יהי.
f S. adds, *to us.*
g G. has, *and they brought him out*, ויציאהו.

of thee, *that*
thou canst un-
derstand a
dream to inter-
pret it. 16 And
Joseph answer-
ed Pharaoh, say-
ing, *It is* not in
me: God shall
give Pharaoh an
answer of peace.
17 And Phara-
oh said unto Jo-
seph, In my
dream, behold,
I stood upon
the bank of the
river: 18 And,
behold, there
came up out of
the river seven
kine, fatfleshed
and well favour-
ed; and they
fed in a mead-
ow: 19 And, be-
hold, seven oth-
er kine came up
after them, poor
and very ill fa-
voured and lean-
fleshed, such as I
never saw in all
the land of E-
gypt for bad-
ness: 20 And
the lean and the
ill favoured kine
did eat up the
first seven fat
kine: 21 And
when they had
eaten them up,
it could not be
known that they
had eaten them;
but they *were*
still ill favoured,
as at the begin-
ning. So I a-
woke. 22 And I
saw in my
dream, and, be-
hold, seven ears
came up in one

עָלֶיךָ לֵאמֹר[a] תִּשְׁמַע חֲלוֹם לִפְתֹּר
interpret to dream a hearest Thou :saying ,thee concerning

אֹתוֹ׃ וַיַּעַן יוֹסֵף אֶת־פַּרְעֹה לֵאמֹר[b] בִּלְעָדָי[c] 16
;I Not :saying ,Pharaoh Joseph answered And .it

אֱלֹהִים[d c] יַעֲנֶה[e] אֶת־שְׁלוֹם פַּרְעֹה׃ וַיְדַבֵּר 17
spoke And .Pharaoh of welfare the answer will God

פַּרְעֹה אֶל־יוֹסֵף[f] בַּחֲלֹמִי הִנְנִי עֹמֵד
standing [was] I behold ,dream my In :Joseph unto Pharaoh

עַל־שְׂפַת הַיְאֹר׃ וְהִנֵּה מִן־הַיְאֹר 18
river the from behold And .river the of bank the upon

עֹלֹת שֶׁבַע פָּרוֹת בְּרִיאוֹת[g] בָּשָׂר[g] וִיפֹת
of beautiful and flesh of fat ,cows seven up going [were]

תֹּאַר וַתִּרְעֶינָה בָּאָחוּ׃ וְהִנֵּה שֶׁבַע פָּרוֹת 19
[2]cows seven behold And .reeds the in feeding were and ,form

אֲחֵרוֹת עֹלוֹת אַחֲרֵיהֶן[h] דַּלּוֹת וְרָעוֹת תֹּאַר
form of evil and poor ,them after up going [were] [1]other

מְאֹד[i] וְרַקּוֹת בָּשָׂר[j] לֹא־רָאִיתִי כָהֵנָּה
them like seen not have I ;flesh of lean and ,exceedingly

בְּכָל־אֶרֶץ מִצְרַיִם לָרֹעַ׃ וַתֹּאכַלְנָה הַפָּרוֹת[k] 20
,cows the ate And .badness for Egypt of land the all in

הָרַקּוֹת וְהָרָעוֹת אֵת שֶׁבַע הַפָּרוֹת הָרִאשֹׁנוֹת[l]
[1]former [3]cows seven the ,evil the and lean the

הַבְּרִיאֹת׃ וַתָּבֹאנָה אֶל־קִרְבֶּנָה וְלֹא נוֹדַע 21
known be [2]could [1]it [3]not and ,them into went they And .[2]fat

כִּי־בָאוּ אֶל־קִרְבֶּנָה וּמַרְאֵיהֶן
appearance their and ;them into gone had they that

רַע כַּאֲשֶׁר בַּתְּחִלָּה וָאִיקָץ[m]׃ וָאֵרֶא[n] 22
saw I And .awoke I and ;beginning the at as evil [was]

בַּחֲלֹמִי וְהִנֵּה שֶׁבַע שִׁבֳּלִים עֹלֹת
up going [were] grain of ears seven behold and ,dream my in

of thee, that
when thou hear-
est a dream thou
canst interpret
it. 16 And Jo-
seph answered
Pharaoh, say-
ing, It is not in
me: God shall
give Pharaoh an
answer of peace.
17 And Phara-
oh spake unto
Joseph, In my
dream, behold,
I stood upon the
brink of the
river: 18 and, be-
hold, there came
up out of the
river seven kine,
fatfleshed and
well favoured;
and they fed in
the reed-grass:
19 and, behold,
seven other kine
came up after
them, poor and
very ill favoured
and leanfleshed,
such as I never
saw in all the
land of Egypt
for badness: 20
and the lean and
ill favoured kine
did eat up the
first seven fat
kine: 21 and
when they had
eaten them up,
it could not be
known that they
had eaten them;
but they were
still ill favoured,
as at the begin-
ning. So I a-
woke. 22 And I
saw in my
dream, and, be-
hold, seven ears
came up upon

---

a S. omits.
b S. adds, *dost thou think that ?*
c G., S. have, *without God.*
d Sm., G. add, *not*, לא.
e G., T. have, *will be answered*, יֵעָנֶה.
f G. adds, *saying.*
g G., V. put after תאר.
h G. adds, *from the river.*
i S. puts after בשר; G., V. omit.
j G. adds, *and fed in the reeds.*
k G. adds, *seven.*
l G. adds, *fair and.*
m G. adds, *I lay down.*
n G., S. add, *again.*

stalk, full and
good: 23 And,
behold, seven
ears, withered,
thin, *and* blasted
with the east
wind, sprung up
after them: 24
And the thin
ears devoured
the seven good
ears: and I told
this unto the
magicians; but
there was none
that could de-
clare *it* to me.

25 And Jo-
seph said unto
Pharaoh, The
dream of Pha-
raoh *is* one: God
hath shewed
Pharaoh what
he *is* about to
do. 26 The seven
good kine *are*
seven years; and
the seven good
ears *are* seven
years: the
dream *is* one. 27
And the seven
thin and ill fa-
voured kine that
came up after
them *are* seven
years; and the
seven empty ears
blasted with the
east wind shall
be seven years
of famine. 28
This *is* the thing
which I have
spoken unto
Pharaoh: What
God *is* about to
do he sheweth
unto Pharaoh.
29 Behold, there
come seven
years of great
plenty through-
out all the land
of Egypt: 30
And there shall
arise after them
seven years of

23 בְּקָנֶה אֶחָד מְלֵאֹת וְטֹבוֹת׃ וְהִנֵּה[a]
behold And .good and full ,[1]one [2]stalk on

שֶׁבַע שִׁבֳּלִים צְנֻמוֹת[b] דַּקּוֹת[c] שְׁדֻפוֹת קָדִים
[wind] east the [by] (of) blasted ,lean ,withered ,ears seven

24 צֹמְחוֹת אַחֲרֵיהֶם׃ וַתִּבְלַעְןָ[d]
swallowing were And .them after forth sprouting [were]

הַשִּׁבֳּלִים הַדַּקֹּת[e] אֵת שֶׁבַע הַשִּׁבֳּלִים הַטֹּבוֹת[f]
; [1]good [2]ears seven the [1]lean [2]ears the

וָאֹמַר אֶל־הַחַרְטֻמִּים וְאֵין מַגִּיד
known making one not is [there] but ,scribes the unto spoke I and

25 לִי׃ וַיֹּאמֶר יוֹסֵף אֶל־פַּרְעֹה חֲלוֹם
of dream The :Pharaoh unto Joseph said And .me to

פַּרְעֹה[g] אֶחָד הוּא אֵת אֲשֶׁר הָאֱלֹהִים עֹשֶׂה
,do to about [is] God what ; it [is] one ,Pharaoh

26 הִגִּיד לְפַרְעֹה׃ שֶׁבַע פָּרֹת הַטֹּבֹת שֶׁבַע
seven ,[1]good [2]cows seven The .Pharaoh to known made has he

שָׁנִים הֵנָּה וְשֶׁבַע הַשִּׁבֳּלִים הַטֹּבֹת שֶׁבַע שָׁנִים
years seven ,[1]good [2]ears seven the and ;they [are] years

27 הֵנָּה חֲלוֹם[h] אֶחָד הוּא׃ וְשֶׁבַע הַפָּרוֹת
cows seven the And .it [is] [1]one [2]dream ; they [are]

הָרַקּוֹת וְהָרָעֹת[i] הָעֹלֹת אַחֲרֵיהֶן שֶׁבַע שָׁנִים הֵנָּה
; they [are] years seven ,them after up going evil and lean

וְשֶׁבַע הַשִּׁבֳּלִים הָרֵקוֹת[j] שְׁדֻפוֹת הַקָּדִים יִהְיוּ
be will [wind] east the [by] (of) blasted lean ears seven the and

28 שֶׁבַע שְׁנֵי רָעָב׃ [k]הוּא הַדָּבָר אֲשֶׁר דִּבַּרְתִּי
spoke I which word the [is] That .famine of years seven

אֶל־פַּרְעֹה אֲשֶׁר הָאֱלֹהִים עֹשֶׂה הֶרְאָה
shown has he do to about [is] God What : Pharaoh unto

29 אֶת־פַּרְעֹה׃ הִנֵּה שֶׁבַע שָׁנִים בָּאוֹת שָׂבָע גָּדוֹל
[1]great [2]plenty ,coming [are] years seven Behold .Pharaoh

30 בְּכָל־אֶרֶץ מִצְרָיִם׃ וְקָמוּ שֶׁבַע שְׁנֵי
of years seven arise will And .Egypt of land the all in

one stalk, full
and good: 23
and, behold,
seven ears,
withered, thin,
and blasted
with the east
wind, sprung up
after them: 24
and the thin ears
swallowed up
the seven good
ears: and I told
it unto the ma-
gicians; but
there was none
that could de-
clare it to me.

25 And Jo-
seph said unto
Pharaoh, The
dream of Pha-
raoh is one:
what God is a-
bout to do he
hath declared
unto Pharaoh. 26
The seven good
kine are seven
years; and the
seven good ears
are seven years:
the dream is
one. 27 And the
seven lean and
ill favoured kine
that came up
after them are
seven years, and
also the seven
empty ears
blasted with the
east wind; they
shall be seven
years of famine.
28 That is the
thing which I
spake unto Pha-
raoh: what God
is about to do he
hath shewed un-
to Pharaoh. 29
Behold, there
come seven
years of great
plenty through-
out all the land
of Egypt: 30
and there shall
arise after them
seven years of

---

a G., V. omit הנה and add, *other*.
b G., S., V. omit; cf. v. 6.
c G., S., V. add, *and*, ו.
d G. adds, *seven*.
e G. adds, *and blasted by the east wind*, ושדפות קדים.
f G. adds, *and the full*, והמלאת.
g V. has, *the king*.
h G. adds, *of Pharaoh*.
i G. omits.
j Sm., G., V. add, *and*, ו.
k G. omits, and adds, *and*.

famine; and all
the plenty shall
be forgotten in
the land of E-
gypt; and the
famine shall
consume the
land; 31 And
the plenty shall
not be known in
the land by
reason of that
famine follow-
ing; for it *shall*
be very grievous.
32 And for that
the dream was
doubled unto
Pharaoh twice;
it is because the
thing *is* estab-
lished by God,
and God will
shortly bring it
to pass.

33 Now there-
fore let Pharaoh
look out a man
discreet and
wise, and set
him over
the land of E-
gypt. 34 Let
Pharaoh do *this*,
and let him ap-
point officers
over the land,
and take up the
fifth part of the
land of Egypt
in the seven
plenteous years.
35 And let them
gather all the
food of those
good years that
come, and lay
up corn under
the hand of
Pharaoh, and let
them keep food
in the cities. 36
And that food
shall be for
store to the land
against the sev-
en years of fa-
mine, which
shall be in the
land of Egypt;
that the land
perish not
through the
famine.

רָעָב אַחֲרֵיהֶן וְנִשְׁכַּח [a] כָּל־הַשָּׂבָע
plenty the all forgotten be will and ,them after famine

[b] בְּאֶרֶץ מִצְרָיִם וְכִלָּה הָרָעָב אֶת־
the famine the consume will and ; Egypt of land the in

31 הָאָרֶץ׃ וְלֹא־יִוָּדַע הַשָּׂבָע בָּאָרֶץ
,land the in plenty the known be not will And .land

מִפְּנֵי הָרָעָב הַהוּא אַחֲרֵי־כֵן כִּי־כָבֵד הוּא
it [is] heavy for ;afterwards 1that 2famine before from

32 מְאֹד׃ וְעַל הִשָּׁנוֹת הַחֲלוֹם אֶל־
unto 2dream's 1the 4repeated 3being concerning And .exceedingly

פַּרְעֹה פַּעֲמָיִם כִּי־נָכוֹן הַדָּבָר מֵעִם
with from thing the [is] settled because ,twice Pharaoh

33 הָאֱלֹהִים וּמְמַהֵר הָאֱלֹהִים לַעֲשֹׂתוֹ׃ וְעַתָּה
now And .it do to God hastening [is] and ,God

יֵרֶא פַרְעֹה [c] אִישׁ נָבוֹן וְחָכָם וִישִׁיתֵהוּ
him put and ,wise and intelligent man a 1Pharaoh 3for 2look let

34 עַל־אֶרֶץ מִצְרָיִם׃ [d] יַעֲשֶׂה פַרְעֹה וְיַפְקֵד
appoint him let and ,Pharaoh act Let .Egypt of land the over

פְּקִדִים עַל־הָאָרֶץ [e] וְחִמֵּשׁ [f] אֶת־אֶרֶץ [g]
of land the of part fifth a take and ,land the over overseers

35 מִצְרָיִם בְּשֶׁבַע שְׁנֵי הַשָּׂבָע׃ וְיִקְבְּצוּ
gather them let And .plenty of years seven the in Egypt

אֶת־כָּל־אֹכֶל הַשָּׁנִים הַטֹּבוֹת הַבָּאֹת הָאֵלֶּה
; 1these 2coming 3good 4years of food the all

וְיִצְבְּרוּ־בָר תַּחַת יַד־פַּרְעֹה אֹכֶל
food [as] Pharaoh of hand the under grain up heap them let and

36 בֶּעָרִים וְשָׁמָרוּ [h]׃ וְהָיָה הָאֹכֶל לְפִקָּדוֹן
store a for food the be let And .keep them let and ,cities the in

לָאָרֶץ לְשֶׁבַע שְׁנֵי הָרָעָב אֲשֶׁר תִּהְיֶיןָ
be will which famine of years seven the for ,land the for

בְּאֶרֶץ מִצְרָיִם וְלֹא־תִכָּרֵת הָאָרֶץ
land the off cut be not let and ,Egypt of land the in

famine; and all
the plenty shall
be forgotten in
the land of E-
gypt; and the
famine shall
consume the
land; 31 and the
plenty shall not
be known in the
land by reason
of that famine
which follow-
eth; for it shall
be very grievous.
32 And for that
the dream was
doubled unto
Pharaoh twice,
it is because the
thing is estab-
lished by God,
and God will
shortly bring it
to pass.

33 Now there-
fore let Pharaoh
look out a man
discreet and
wise, and set him
over the land of
Egypt. 34 Let
Pharaoh do *this*,
and let him ap-
point overseers
over the land,
and take up the
fifth part of the
land of Egypt
in the seven
plenteous years.
35 And let them
gather all the
food of these
good years that
come, and lay
up corn under
the hand of
Pharaoh for
food in the
cities, and let
them keep it. 36
And the food
shall be for a
store to the land
against the sev-
en years of fam-
ine, which shall
be in the land of
Egypt; that the
land perish not
through the
famine.

---

a G. omits.
b G., S. have, *in all the land.*
c G. omits; V. has, *the king.*
d Sm., G., S. add, *and,* ו.
e S. adds, *of Egypt.*
f G., S., T. have pl.
g G. has, *all the products of the land.*
h Sm., S. have, *let them keep,* יִשְׁמְרוּ; G. *let be kept,* יִשָּׁמֵר.

37 And the
thing was good
in the eyes of
Pharaoh, and in
the eyes of all
his servants. 38
And Pharaoh
said unto his
servants, Can
we find *such a*
one as this *is*, a
man in whom
the Spirit of
God *is*? 39 And
Pharaoh said
unto Joseph,
Forasmuch as
God hath shew-
ed thee all this,
there is none so
discreet and
wise as thou *art*:
40 Thou shalt
be over my
house, and ac-
cording unto thy
word shall all my
people be ruled:
only in the thro-
ne will I be grea-
ter than thou.

41 And Pha-
raoh said unto
Joseph, See,
I have set thee
over all the
land of Egypt.
42 And Pharaoh
took off his ring
from his hand,
and put it upon
Joseph's hand,
and arrayed him
in vestures of
fine linen, and
put a gold chain
about his neck;
43 And he made
him to ride in
the second char-
iot which he
had, and they
cried before
him, Bow the
knee: and he
made him *ruler*
over all the land
of Egypt. 44
And Pharaoh
said unto Jo-

37 בְּרָעָב׃ וַיִּיטַב הַדָּבָר בְּעֵינֵי פַרְעֹה
,Pharaoh of eyes the in word the good was And .famine the by

38 וּבְעֵינֵי [a]כָּל־עֲבָדָיו׃ וַיֹּאמֶר פַּרְעֹה
Pharaoh said And .servants his all of eyes the in and

[b]אֶל־עֲבָדָיו הֲנִמְצָא כָזֶה אִישׁ אֲשֶׁר
whom [in] man a ,this like find we Can :servants his unto

39 רוּחַ אֱלֹהִים בּוֹ׃ וַיֹּאמֶר פַּרְעֹה אֶל־
unto Pharaoh said And ?(him in) God of spirit the [is]

יוֹסֵף אַחֲרֵי הוֹדִיעַ אֱלֹהִים אוֹתְךָ אֶת־כָּל־זֹאת
,this all thee [1]God [3]taught [2]has Since :Joseph

40 [c]אֵין־נָבוֹן וְחָכָם כָּמוֹךָ[d]׃ אַתָּה תִּהְיֶה
be shalt Thou .thee like wise and intelligent one not is [there]

עַל־בֵּיתִי וְעַל־פִּיךָ [e]יִשַּׁק כָּל־עַמִּי
; people my all submit shall mouth thy upon and ,house my over

רַק הַכִּסֵּא אֶגְדַּל מִמֶּךָּ׃
.thou than greater be will I throne the to respect with only

41 וַיֹּאמֶר פַּרְעֹה אֶל־יוֹסֵף רְאֵה נָתַתִּי
placed have I See :Joseph unto Pharaoh said And

42 אֹתְךָ[f] עַל כָּל־אֶרֶץ מִצְרָיִם׃ וַיָּסַר פַּרְעֹה
Pharaoh removed And .Egypt of land the all over thee

אֶת־טַבַּעְתּוֹ מֵעַל יָדוֹ וַיִּתֵּן אֹתָהּ עַל־
upon it gave and ,hand his upon from ring signet his

יַד יוֹסֵף וַיַּלְבֵּשׁ אֹתוֹ בִּגְדֵי־
garments [with] him clothed he and ;Joseph of hand the

שֵׁשׁ וַיָּשֶׂם רְבִד הַזָּהָב עַל־צַוָּארוֹ׃
;neck his upon gold of chain the put and ,byssus of

43 וַיַּרְכֵּב אֹתוֹ בְּמִרְכֶּבֶת הַמִּשְׁנֶה אֲשֶׁר־
which second the ,chariot a in him ride to caused he and

לוֹ [g]וַיִּקְרְאוּ לְפָנָיו [h]אַבְרֵךְ וְנָתוֹן
put he and ;Avrek :him before called they and ;him to [was]

44 אֹתוֹ עַל כָּל־אֶרֶץ מִצְרָיִם׃ וַיֹּאמֶר פַּרְעֹה
Pharaoh said And .Egypt of land the all over him

37 And the
thing was good
in the eyes of
Pharaoh, and in
the eyes of all
his servants. 38
And Pharaoh
said unto his
servants, Can we
find such a one
as this, a man in
whom the spirit
of God is? 39
And Pharaoh
said unto Jo-
seph, Foras-
much as God
hath shewed
thee all this,
there is none so
discreet and
wise as thou: 40
thou shalt be
over my house,
and according
unto thy word
shall all my
people be ruled:
only in the
throne will I be
greater than
thou.

41 And Pha-
raoh said unto
Joseph, See, I
have set thee
over all the land
of Egypt. 42 And
Pharaoh took
off his signet
ring from his
hand, and put it
upon Joseph's
hand, and ar-
rayed him in
vestures of fine
linen, and put a
gold chain about
his neck; 43 and
he made him to
ride in the sec-
ond chariot
which he had;
and they cried
before him,
Bow the knee:
and he set him
over all the land
of Egypt. 44
And Pharaoh
said unto Jo-

a S. omits.
b For אל G. has, *unto all.*
c G. adds, *a man.*
d G., V. have, *more than thee,* ממך.
e G., V. have, *shall obey;* T. *shall be fed;* S. *shall receive judgment.*
f G. adds, *today.*
g Sm., G., S., Aq. have sing.
h G. has, *a herald;* S. *father and ruler;* T. *this is the father of the king;* Aq. *to kneel.*

seph, I *am*
Pharaoh, and
without thee
shall no man lift
up his hand or
foot in all the
land of Egypt.
45 And Pharaoh
called Joseph's
name Zaphnath-
paaneah; and
he gave him to
wife Asenath
the daughter of
Poti-pherah
priest of On.
And Joseph
went out over *all*
the land of E-
gypt.

אֶל־יוֹסֵף אֲנִי פַּרְעֹה[a] וּבִלְעָדֶיךָ[b]
thee without and ,Pharaoh [am] I :Joseph unto

לֹא־יָרִים אִישׁ אֶת־יָדוֹ וְאֶת־רַגְלוֹ[c] בְּכָל־
all in foot his and hand his man a up lift not shall

45 אֶרֶץ מִצְרָיִם׃ וַיִּקְרָא פַרְעֹה שֵׁם־יוֹסֵף
Joseph of name the Pharaoh called And .Egypt of land the

צָפְנַת פַּעְנֵחַ[d] וַיִּתֶּן־לוֹ אֶת־אָסְנַת
Asenath him to gave he and ;Paneah Zaphenath

בַּת־פּוֹטִי פֶרַע כֹּהֵן אֹן לְאִשָּׁה
;wife a for On of priest Phera Poti of daughter the

46 וַיֵּצֵא יוֹסֵף[e] עַל־אֶרֶץ[f] מִצְרָיִם׃ וְיוֹסֵף
Joseph And .Egypt of land the over Joseph out went and

בֶּן־שְׁלֹשִׁים שָׁנָה בְּעָמְדוֹ לִפְנֵי פַּרְעֹה
Pharaoh before standing his in ,[old] years thirty (of son a) [was]

46 And Jo-
seph *was* thirty
years old when
he stood before
Pharaoh king of
Egypt. And Jo-
seph went out
from the pres-
ence of Pha-
raoh, and went
throughout all
the land of E-
gypt. 47 And in
the seven plen-
teous years the
earth brought
forth by hand-
fuls. 48 And he
gathered up all
the food of the
seven years,
which were in
the land of E-
gypt, and laid
up the food in
the cities: the
food of the field,
which *was* round
about every city,
laid he up in the
same. 49 And
Joseph gathered
corn as the sand
of the sea, very
much, until he
left numbering;
for *it was* with-
out number. 50
And unto Jo-

מֶלֶךְ־מִצְרָיִם וַיֵּצֵא יוֹסֵף מִלִּפְנֵי
before (to) from Joseph out went and ;Egypt of king

פַּרְעֹה וַיַּעֲבֹר בְּכָל־אֶרֶץ מִצְרָיִם׃
.Egypt of land the all in over passed and ,Pharaoh

47 וַתַּעַשׂ[g] הָאָרֶץ בְּשֶׁבַע שְׁנֵי הַשָּׂבָע
plenty of years seven the in land the produced And

48 לִקְמָצִים[h]׃ וַיִּקְבֹּץ אֶת־כָּל־אֹכֶל שֶׁבַע
seven the of food the all gathered he And .handfuls by

שָׁנִים אֲשֶׁר[i] הָיוּ[i] בְּאֶרֶץ מִצְרַיִם וַיִּתֶּן־אֹכֶל
food put he and ,Egypt of land the in were which years

בֶּעָרִים אֹכֶל שְׂדֵה־הָעִיר אֲשֶׁר[j]
[was] which city the of field the of food the ;cities the in

49 סְבִיבֹתֶיהָ נָתַן בְּתוֹכָהּ׃ וַיִּצְבֹּר יוֹסֵף
Joseph up heaped And .it of midst the in put he ,it about round

בָּר כְּחוֹל הַיָּם הַרְבֵּה מְאֹד עַד כִּי־
that until ;exceedingly much ,sea the of sand the like grain

50 חָדַל לִסְפֹּר כִּי־אֵין מִסְפָּר׃ וּלְיוֹסֵף
Joseph to And .number not was because ,number to ceased he

seph, I am Pha-
raoh, and with-
out thee shall no
man lift up his
hand or his foot
in all the land of
Egypt. 45 And
Pharaoh called
Joseph's name
Zaphenath-pa-
neah; and he
gave him to
wife Asenath the
daughter of Po-
ti-phera priest of
On. And Jo-
seph went out
over the land of
Egypt.

46 And Jo-
seph was thirty
years old when
he stood before
Pharaoh king of
Egypt. And Jo-
seph went out
from the pres-
ence of Pha-
raoh, and went
throughout all
the land of E-
gypt. 47 And in
the seven plen-
teous years the
earth brought
forth by hand-
fuls. 48 And he
gathered up all
the food of the
seven years
which were in
the land of E-
gypt, and laid
up the food in
the cities: the
food of the field,
which was round
about every city,
laid he up in the
same. 49 And
Joseph laid up
corn as the sand
of the sea, very
much, until he
left numbering;
for it was with-
out number. 50
And unto Jo-

---

a S. adds, *have ordained.*

b G. omits, *and,* ו.

c G. omits.

d S. adds, *to whom secrets are revealed;* so T. omitting צפנת פענה.

e G. omits; T. adds, *a ruler.*

f S, adds, *all,* reading, על כל ארץ.

g S. has, *and was collected;* T. *and collected the inhabitants of.*

h S., T. have, *in granaries.*

i G. has, *in which was abundance;* so Sm.

j S. adds, *and,* ו.

seph were born
two sons before
the years of
famine came,
which Asenath
the daughter of
Poti-pherah
priest of On,
bare unto him.
51 And Joseph
called the name
of the firstborn
Manasseh: For
God, *said he*,
hath made me
forget all my
toil, and all my
father's house.
52 And the
name of the
second called
he Ephraim:
For God hath
caused me to be
fruitful in the
land of my
affliction.

53 And the
seven years of
plenteousness,
that was in the
land of Egypt,
were ended. 54
And the seven
years of dearth
began to come,
according as
Joseph had said:
and the dearth
was in all lands;
but in all the
land of Egypt
there was bread.
55 And when all
the land of E-
gypt was fam-
ished, the peo-
ple cried to
Pharaoh for
bread: and
Pharaoh said
unto all the
Egyptians, Go
unto Joseph;
what he saith to
you, do. 56 And
the famine was
over all the face
of the earth: and
Joseph opened
all the store-
houses, and sold
unto the Egyp-

יֻלַּד שְׁנֵי בָנִים בְּטֶרֶם תָּבוֹא שְׁנַת[a]
of year the in came before ,sons two born were

הָרָעָב אֲשֶׁר יָלְדָה־לּוֹ אָסְנַת בַּת־
of daughter the Asenath him to bore whom ;famine the

51 פּוֹטִי פֶרַע כֹּהֵן אוֹן׃ וַיִּקְרָא יוֹסֵף אֶת־
the Joseph called And .On of priest Phera Poti

שֵׁם[b] הַבְּכוֹר מְנַשֶּׁה[c] כִּי־נַשַּׁנִי אֱלֹהִים
God forget me made has For ;Manasseh firstborn the of name

52 אֶת־כָּל־עֲמָלִי וְאֵת כָּל־בֵּית אָבִי׃ וְאֵת
And .father my of house the all and ,toil my all

שֵׁם הַשֵּׁנִי קָרָא אֶפְרָיִם כִּי־הִפְרַנִי
fruitful me made has For ;Ephraim called he second the of name the

53 אֱלֹהִים בְּאֶרֶץ עָנְיִי׃ וַתִּכְלֶינָה שֶׁבַע[d]
seven the ended were And .affliction my of land the in God

שְׁנֵי הַשָּׂבָע אֲשֶׁר הָיָה בְּאֶרֶץ מִצְרָיִם׃
.Egypt of land the in were which ,plenty of years

54 וַתְּחִלֶּינָה שֶׁבַע שְׁנֵי הָרָעָב לָבוֹא כַּאֲשֶׁר
as ,in come to famine of years seven the began And

אָמַר יוֹסֵף וַיְהִי רָעָב בְּכָל־הָאֲרָצוֹת
,lands the all in famine was and ;Joseph said had

55 וּבְכָל־אֶרֶץ מִצְרַיִם הָיָה[e] לָחֶם׃ וַתִּרְעַב
hungered And .bread was Egypt of land the all in and

כָּל־אֶרֶץ מִצְרַיִם וַיִּצְעַק הָעָם[f] אֶל־פַּרְעֹה
Pharaoh unto people the cried and ,Egypt of land the all

לַלָּחֶם וַיֹּאמֶר פַּרְעֹה לְכָל־מִצְרַיִם לְכוּ אֶל־
unto Go :Egypt all to Pharaoh said and ;bread for

56 יוֹסֵף אֲשֶׁר־יֹאמַר[g] לָכֶם תַּעֲשׂוּ׃ וְהָרָעָב
famine the And .do ,you to says he what ;Joseph

הָיָה עַל כָּל־פְּנֵי[h] הָאָרֶץ וַיִּפְתַּח יוֹסֵף
Joseph opened and ;land the of face the all upon was

אֶת־כָּל־אֲשֶׁר[i] בָּהֶם[i] וַיִּשְׁבֹּר לְמִצְרַיִם[j]
;Egyptians the to sold and ,[was there] (them in) which [in] all

seph were born
two sons before
the year of fam-
ine came, which
Asenath the
daughter of
Poti-phera
priest of On bare
unto him. 51
And Joseph call-
ed the name of
the firstborn
Manasseh: For,
said he, God
hath made me
forget all my
toil, and all my
father's house.
52 And the
name of the
second called he
Ephraim: For
God hath made
me fruitful in
the land of my
affliction.

53 And the
seven years of
plenty, that was
in the land of
Egypt, came to
an end. 54 And
the seven years
of famine began
to come, ac-
cording as Jo-
seph had said:
and there was
famine in all
lands; but in all
the land of E-
gypt there
was bread. 55
And when all
the land of E-
gypt was fam-
ished, the peo-
ple cried to Pha-
raoh for bread:
and Pharaoh
said unto all the
Egyptians, Go
unto Joseph;
what he saith to
you, do. 56 And
the famine was
over all the face
of the earth: and
Joseph opened
all the store-
houses, and sold
unto the Egyp-

---

a G. has, *seven years.*
b S. adds, *his son.*
c G., V. add, *saying.*
d S. omits.
e G., S. have, *was not*, לא היה.
f G. adds, *all*, reading כל העם.
g Sm., G., S., V. add, *and*, ו.
h Sm., G., S. transpose, reading פני כל.
i For אשר בהם, G., S., V. have, *granaries;* Sm., *in which was corn;* T., *the granaries in which was corn.*
j G. has, *to all Egypt.*

tians; and the
famine waxed
sore in the land
of Egypt. 57
And all coun-
tries came into
Egypt to Joseph
for to buy *corn*;
because that the
famine was *so*
sore in all lands.

57 וַיֶּחֱזַק[a] הָרָעָב בְּאֶרֶץ מִצְרָיִם[a]׃ וְכָל־
all And .Egypt of land the in famine the strong was and

הָאָרֶץ בָּאוּ מִצְרַיְמָה לִשְׁבֹּר אֶל־יוֹסֵף כִּי־
for ;Joseph unto ,buy to Egypt to in came earth the

חָזַק הָרָעָב בְּכָל־הָאָרֶץ[b]׃
.earth the all in famine the strong was

tians; and the
famine was sore
in the land of
Egypt. 57 And
all countries
came into E-
gypt to Joseph
for to buy corn;
because the fam-
ine was sore in
all the earth.

42

Now when
Jacob saw that
there was corn
in Egypt, Jacob
said unto his
sons, Why do ye
look one upon
another? 2 And
he said, Behold,
I have heard
that there is corn
in Egypt: get
you down thith-
er, and buy for
us from thence;
that we may
live, and not die.
3 And Jo-
seph's ten breth-
ren went down
to buy corn in
Egypt. 4 But
Benjamin, Jo-
seph's brother,
Jacob sent not
with his breth-
ren; for he said,
Lest peradven-
ture mischief be-
fall him. 5 And
the sons of Is-
rael came to
buy *corn* a-
mong those that
came: for the
famine was in
the land of Ca-
naan. 6 And Jo-
seph *was* the
governor over
the land, *and* he
it was that sold
to all the peo-
ple of the land;
and Joseph's
brethren came,

1 וַיַּרְא יַעֲקֹב כִּי יֶשׁ־שֶׁבֶר בְּמִצְרָיִם
,Egypt in grain was [there] that Jacob saw And

וַיֹּאמֶר יַעֲקֹב[c] לְבָנָיו לָמָּה[d] תִּתְרָאוּ[d]׃
?other each at look you do Why :sons his to Jacob said and

2 וַיֹּאמֶר[e] הִנֵּה שָׁמַעְתִּי כִּי יֶשׁ־שֶׁבֶר
grain is [there] that heard have I Behold :said he And

בְּמִצְרָיִם רְדוּ־שָׁמָּה וְשִׁבְרוּ־לָנוּ מִשָּׁם[f]
,thence from us for buy and thither down go ;Egypt in

3 וְנִחְיֶה וְלֹא נָמוּת׃ וַיֵּרְדוּ אֲחֵי־
of brothers the down went And .die not and live may we that

4 יוֹסֵף עֲשָׂרָה לִשְׁבֹּר בָּר מִמִּצְרָיִם׃ וְאֶת־
And .Egypt from grain buy to ,ten ,Joseph

בִּנְיָמִין אֲחִי יוֹסֵף לֹא־שָׁלַח יַעֲקֹב[g]
Jacob send not did Joseph of brother the Benjamin

אֶת־אֶחָיו כִּי אָמַר פֶּן־יִקְרָאֶנּוּ אָסוֹן׃
.harm him to happen Lest :said he because ,brethren his with

5 וַיָּבֹאוּ בְּנֵי יִשְׂרָאֵל לִשְׁבֹּר בְּתוֹךְ
of midst the in buy to Israel of sons the in came And

הַבָּאִים כִּי־הָיָה[h] הָרָעָב בְּאֶרֶץ כְּנָעַן׃
.Canaan of land the in famine the was for ,in coming those

6 וְיוֹסֵף הוּא[i] הַשַּׁלִּיט עַל־הָאָרֶץ הוּא
[being] he ,land the over governor the [being] he ,Joseph And

הַמַּשְׁבִּיר לְכָל־עַם הָאָרֶץ וַיָּבֹאוּ
in came (and) ;earth the of people the all to selling one the

Now Jacob
saw that there
was corn in E-
gypt, and Ja-
cob said unto
his sons, Why
do ye look one
upon another?
2 And he said,
Behold, I have
heard that there
is corn in E-
gypt: get you
down thither,
and buy for us
from thence;
that we may
live, and not die.
3 And Jo-
seph's ten breth-
ren went down
to buy corn from
Egypt. 4 But
Benjamin, Jo-
seph's brother,
Jacob sent not
with his breth-
ren; for he said,
Lest peradven-
ture mischief be-
fall him. 5 And
the sons of Is-
rael came to buy
among those
that came: for
the famine was
in the land of
Canaan. 6 And
Joseph was the
governor over
the land; he it
was that sold to
all the people of
the land: and
Joseph's breth-

a G. omits.
b S. adds, *Egypt*.
c G. omits.
d S. has, *do not fear;* V., *why are ye neglectful?*
e G., S., V. omit.
f G. has, *a little food;* cf. 43: 2.
g G. omits.
h S. has, *was strong*, חזק.
i Sm., S., V. add, *and*, ו.

and bowed down themselves before him *with* their faces to the earth. 7 And Joseph saw his brethren, and he knew them, but made himself strange unto them, and spake roughly unto them; and he said unto them, Whence come ye? And they said, From the land of Canaan to buy food. 8 And Joseph knew his brethren, but they knew not him. 9 And Joseph remembered the dreams which he dreamed of them, and said unto them, Ye *are* spies; to see the nakedness of the land ye are come. 10 And they said unto him, Nay, my lord, but to buy food are thy servants come.

11 We *are* all one man's sons; we *are* true *men*; thy servants are no spies. 12 And he said unto them, Nay, but to see the nakedness of the land ye are come. 13 And they said, Thy servants *are* twelve brethren, the sons of one man in the land of Canaan; and, behold, the youngest *is* this day with our

אֲחֵי יוֹסֵף וַיִּשְׁתַּחֲווּ־לוֹ אַפַּיִם
face the ,him to themselves prostrated and Joseph of brethren the

7 אָרְצָה׃ וַיַּרְא יוֹסֵף אֶת־אֶחָיו וַיַּכִּרֵם
,them recognized and ,brethren his Joseph saw And .earth the to

[a]וַיִּתְנַכֵּר אֲלֵיהֶם[a] וַיְדַבֵּר אִתָּם קָשׁוֹת
,things harsh them with spoke and ,them towards dissembled and

וַיֹּאמֶר אֲלֵהֶם מֵאַיִן בָּאתֶם[b] וַיֹּאמְרוּ
: said they And ? come you have Whence :them unto said and

8 מֵאֶרֶץ כְּנַעַן[c] לִשְׁבָּר־אֹכֶל׃ וַיַּכֵּר
recognized And .food buy to Canaan of land the From

יוֹסֵף אֶת־אֶחָיו וְהֵם לֹא הִכִּרֻהוּ׃
.him [2]recognize [1]did [3]not they but ,brethren his Joseph

9 וַיִּזְכֹּר יוֹסֵף אֵת הַחֲלֹמוֹת אֲשֶׁר חָלַם
dreamed had he which dreams the Joseph remembered And

לָהֶם[d] וַיֹּאמֶר אֲלֵהֶם מְרַגְּלִים אַתֶּם
; you [are] Spies : them unto said he and ;them concerning

10 [e]לִרְאוֹת אֶת־עֶרְוַת הָאָרֶץ בָּאתֶם׃ וַיֹּאמְרוּ
said they And .come have you land the of bareness the see to

אֵלָיו[f] לֹא אֲדֹנִי [g]וַעֲבָדֶיךָ בָּאוּ לִשְׁבָּר־
buy to come have servants thy but ,lord my ,No : him unto

11 אֹכֶל׃ כֻּלָּנוּ בְּנֵי־אִישׁ אֶחָד נָחְנוּ [h]כֵּנִים
[are] honest ; we [are] [1]one [2]man of sons us of All .food

12 אֲנַחְנוּ [h]לֹא־הָיוּ עֲבָדֶיךָ מְרַגְּלִים׃ וַיֹּאמֶר
said he And .spies servants thy been not have ,we

אֲלֵהֶם[i] לֹא [j]כִּי־עֶרְוַת הָאָרֶץ בָּאתֶם
come have you land the of bareness the but ,No : them unto

13 לִרְאוֹת׃ [k]וַיֹּאמְרוּ שְׁנֵים עָשָׂר עֲבָדֶיךָ
,servants thy [are] ten [and] Two ; said they And .see to

אַחִים אֲנַחְנוּ בְּנֵי־אִישׁ[l] אֶחָד[l] בְּאֶרֶץ
of land the in [1]one [2]man of sons ,we [are] brethren

כְּנָעַן וְהִנֵּה הַקָּטֹן אֶת־אָבִינוּ הַיּוֹם
,today father our with [is] youngest the behold and ; Canaan

ren came, and bowed down themselves to him with their faces to the earth. 7 And Joseph saw his brethren, and he knew them, but made himself strange unto them, and spake roughly with them; and he said unto them, Whence come ye? And they said, From the land of Canaan to buy food. 8 And Joseph knew his brethren, but they knew not him. 9 And Joseph remembered the dreams which he dreamed of them, and said unto them, Ye are spies; to see the nakedness of the land ye are come. 10 And they said unto him, Nay, my lord, but to buy food are thy servants come.

11 We are all one man's sons; we are true men, thy servants are no spies. 12 And he said unto them, Nay, but to see the nakedness of the land ye are come. 13 And they said, We thy servants are twelve brethren, the sons of one man in the land of Canaan; and, behold, the youngest is this day with our

a T. has, *and he thought what he should say with them.*
b S. has, *you,* אתם.
c S. adds, *we come.*
d G., V. omit.
e S. adds, *and,* ו.
f G., S., V. omit.
g G., S. omit ו.
h S. adds, *and,* ו.
i S. adds, *Joseph.*
j S., V. omit.
k S. adds, *to him.*
l G. omits.

father, and one *is* not. 14 And Joseph said unto them, That *is it* that I spake unto you, saying, Ye *are* spies: 15 Hereby ye shall be proved: By the life of Pharaoh ye shall not go forth hence, except your youngest brother come hither. 16 Send one of you, and let him fetch your brother, and ye shall be kept in prison, that your words may be proved, whether *there be any* truth in you: or else by the life of Pharaoh surely ye *are* spies.

17 And he put them all together into ward three days. 18 And Joseph said unto them the third day, This do, and live; *for* I fear God: 19 If ye *be* true *men*, let one of your brethren be bound in the house of your prison: go ye, carry corn for the famine of your houses: 20 But bring your youngest brother unto me; so shall your words be verified, and ye shall not die. And they did so.

21 And they said one to an-

14 וְהָאֶחָד [a] אֵינֶנּוּ׃ [b] וַיֹּאמֶר אֲלֵהֶם יוֹסֵף הוּא
[is] That : Joseph them unto said And ,not is he ,one and

אֲשֶׁר דִּבַּרְתִּי אֲלֵכֶם לֵאמֹר [c] מְרַגְּלִים אַתֶּם׃
.you [are] Spies :saying you unto spoke I what

15 בְּזֹאת תִּבָּחֵנוּ חֵי פַרְעֹה אִם־
(if) Pharaoh lives [as] ; proved be shall you this By

תֵּצְאוּ מִזֶּה כִּי אִם־בְּבוֹא
of coming the in (if) except ,here from out go [not] shall you

16 אֲחִיכֶם הַקָּטֹן הֵנָּה׃ שִׁלְחוּ מִכֶּם אֶחָד
,one you of Send .hither [1]youngest [2]brother your

וְיִקַּח [d] אֶת־אֲחִיכֶם וְאַתֶּם הֵאָסְרוּ
,bound be [1]do [2]ye and ; brother your take him let and

וְיִבָּחֲנוּ דִּבְרֵיכֶם הַאֱמֶת אִתְּכֶם [e] וְאִם־
if and ; you with [is] truth whether ,words your proved be let and

לֹא חֵי פַרְעֹה כִּי מְרַגְּלִים אַתֶּם׃ [f]
.you [are] spies surely ,Pharaoh lives [as] ,not

17 וַיֶּאֱסֹף אֹתָם אֶל־מִשְׁמָר שְׁלֹשֶׁת יָמִים׃
.days three custody into them gathered he And

18 וַיֹּאמֶר אֲלֵהֶם יוֹסֵף [g] בַּיּוֹם הַשְּׁלִישִׁי זֹאת
This :[1]third [2]day the on Joseph them unto said And

19 עֲשׂוּ וִחְיוּ אֶת־הָאֱלֹהִים אֲנִי יָרֵא׃ אִם־
If .fear I God ; live and ye do

כֵּנִים אַתֶּם אֲחִיכֶם אֶחָד יֵאָסֵר בְּבֵית
of house the in bound be let ,one ,brother your ,you [are] honest

מִשְׁמַרְכֶם וְאַתֶּם לְכוּ הָבִיאוּ שֶׁבֶר רַעֲבוֹן
of famine the of grain bring ,go ye and ; custody your

20 בָּתֵּיכֶם׃ וְאֶת־אֲחִיכֶם הַקָּטֹן תָּבִיאוּ
ye bring [1]youngest [2]brother your and ; houses your

אֵלַי וְיֵאָמְנוּ דִבְרֵיכֶם וְלֹא [h] תָמוּתוּ
; die [2]shall [1]you [3]not and ,words your confirmed be let and ,me unto

21 וַיַּעֲשׂוּ־כֵן׃ וַיֹּאמְרוּ אִישׁ אֶל־אָחִיו
: brother his unto each ,said they And .so did they and

father, and one is not. 14 And Joseph said unto them, That is it that I spake unto you, saying, Ye are spies: 15 hereby ye shall be proved: by the life of Pharaoh ye shall not go forth hence, except your youngest brother come hither. 16 Send one of you, and let him fetch your brother, and ye shall be bound, that your words may be proved, whether there be truth in you; or else by the life of Pharaoh surely ye are spies.

17 And he put them all together into ward three days. 18 And Joseph said unto them the third day, This do, and live; for I fear God: 19 if ye be true men, let one of your brethren be bound in your prison house; but go ye, carry corn for the famine of your houses: 20 and bring your youngest brother unto me; so shall your words be verified, and ye shall not die. And they did so.

21 And they said one to an-

---

a G., V. have, *and the other*, והאחר.
b S., V. omit ו.
c S., V. omit.
d G. has, *and take ye*, וקחו.
e S., T. have, *you have spoken*.
f Sm. adds 44:22, except ונאמר אל-אדני.
g G., V. omit.
h G. has, *and if not*.

other, We *are*
verily guilty
concerning our
brother, in that
we saw the an-
guish of his soul,
when he be-
sought us, and
we would not
hear; therefore
is this distress
come upon us.

22 And Reuben
answered them,
saying, Spake I
not unto you,
saying, Do not
sin against the
child; and ye
would not hear?
therefore, be-
hold, also his
blood is requir-
ed. 23 And they
knew not that
Joseph under-
stood *them*; for
he spake unto
them by an in-
terpreter. 24
And he turned
himself about
from them, and
wept; and re-
turned to them
again, and com-
muned with
them, and took
from them Sim-
eon, and
bound him be-
fore their eyes.

25 Then Jo-
seph command-
ed to fill their
sacks with corn,
and to restore
every man's
money into his
sack, and to give
them provision
for the way: and
thus did he unto
them. 26 And
they laded their
asses with the
corn, and de-
parted thence.
27 And as one
of them opened
his sack to give
his ass proven-
der in the inn,

אֲבָל אֲשֵׁמִים ׀ אֲנַחְנוּ עַל־אָחִינוּ
,brother our of account on — we [are] — guilty — ,Truly

אֲשֶׁר רָאִינוּ צָרַת נַפְשׁוֹ בְּהִתְחַנְנוֹ
entreated he when — ,soul whose — of distress the — saw we — (who)

אֵלֵינוּ וְלֹא שָׁמָעְנוּ עַל־כֵּן בָּאָה
come has — therefore — ; hear [2]did [1]we — [3]not and — ,us (unto)

22 אֵלֵינוּ הַצָּרָה הַזֹּאת׃ וַיַּעַן רְאוּבֵן
Reuben — answered And — .[1]this — [2]distress — us unto

אֹתָם[a] לֵאמֹר[b] הֲלוֹא אָמַרְתִּי אֲלֵיכֶם ׀ לֵאמֹר
: saying — you unto — speak [2]I [1]did — [3]Not — ; saying — them

אַל־תֶּחֶטְאוּ בַיֶּלֶד וְלֹא שְׁמַעְתֶּם[c]
? hear [2]did [1]you — [3]not and — ,youth the against — sin not Do

23 וְגַם־דָּמוֹ הִנֵּה נִדְרָשׁ׃ וְהֵם לֹא
[2]not — they And — .required is — ,behold — ,blood his also and

יָדְעוּ כִּי שֹׁמֵעַ יוֹסֵף כִּי הַמֵּלִיץ
interpreter the — because — ,[1]Joseph — [3]hearing [[2]was] — that — know [1]did

24 בֵּינֹתָם׃ וַיִּסֹּב מֵעֲלֵיהֶם וַיֵּבְךְּ[d]
,wept and — them (upon) from — away turned he And — .them between [was]

וַיָּשָׁב אֲלֵהֶם וַיְדַבֵּר אֲלֵהֶם וַיִּקַּח
took he and — ; them unto — spoke and — ,them unto — returned and

מֵאִתָּם אֶת־שִׁמְעוֹן וַיֶּאֱסֹר אֹתוֹ
him — bound and — ,Simeon — them (with) from

25 לְעֵינֵיהֶם׃ וַיְצַו יוֹסֵף וַיְמַלְאוּ[e]
filled they and — ,Joseph — commandment gave And — .eyes their before

אֶת־כְּלֵיהֶם בָּר וּלְהָשִׁיב כַּסְפֵּיהֶם אִישׁ
each — ,money their — return to and — ,grain — [with] vessels their

אֶל־שַׂקּוֹ וְלָתֵת לָהֶם צֵדָה לַדָּרֶךְ
; way the for — provision — them to — give to and — ,sack his into

26 וַיַּעַשׂ[f] לָהֶם כֵּן׃ וַיִּשְׂאוּ אֶת־שִׁבְרָם
grain their — loaded they And — .so — them to — did one and

27 עַל־חֲמֹרֵיהֶם וַיֵּלְכוּ מִשָּׁם׃ וַיִּפְתַּח הָאֶחָד[g]
one — opened And — .thence — went and — ,asses their upon

אֶת־שַׂקּוֹ לָתֵת מִסְפּוֹא לַחֲמֹרוֹ בַּמָּלוֹן
; place lodging the in — ass his to — fodder — give to — sack his

other, We are
verily guilty
concerning our
brother, in that
we saw the dis-
tress of his soul,
when he be-
sought us, and
we would not
hear; therefore
is this distress
come upon us.

22 And Reuben
answered them,
saying, Spake I
not unto you,
saying, Do not
sin against the
child; and ye
would not hear?
therefore also,
behold, his
blood is requir-
ed. 23 And they
knew not that
Joseph under-
stood them; for
there was an in-
terpreter be-
tween them. 24
And he turned
himself about
from them, and
wept; and he re-
turned to them,
and spake to
them, and took
Simeon from a-
mong them,
and bound him
before their
eyes.

25 Then Jo-
seph command-
ed to fill their
vessels with
corn, and to re-
store every
man's money
into his sack,
and to give
them provision
for the way: and
thus was it done
unto them. 26
And they laded
their asses with
their corn, and
departed thence.
27 And as one
of them opened
his sack to give
his ass proven-
der in the lodg-

a G., S. omit.
b G., S. add, *to them.*
c G., V. add, *me.*
d G. adds, *Joseph.*
e G., V. have, *to fill*, למלאות.
f S., V. have pl.
g S. adds, *from them.*

he espied his money; for, behold, it *was* in his sack's mouth. 28 And he said unto his brethren, My money is restored; and, lo, *it is* even in my sack: and their heart failed *them*, and they were afraid, saying one to another, What *is* this *that* God hath done unto us?

29 And they came unto Jacob their father unto the land of Canaan, and told him all that befell unto them; saying, 30 The man, *who is* the lord of the land, spake roughly to us, and took us for spies of the country. 31 And we said unto him, We *are* true *men*; we are no spies: 32 We *be* twelve brethren, sons of our father; one *is* not, and the youngest *is* this day with our father in the land of Canaan. 33 And the man, the lord of the country, said unto us, Hereby shall I know that ye *are* true *men*; leave one of your brethren *here* with me, and take *food for* the famine of your households, and be gone; 34 And bring your youngest brother unto me: then shall I know that ye

וַיַּרְא אֶת־כַּסְפּוֹ וְהִנֵּה־הוּא[a] בְּפִי
of mouth the in [being] it behold (and) ,money his saw he and

28 אַמְתַּחְתּוֹ׃ וַיֹּאמֶר אֶל־אֶחָיו הוּשַׁב
returned been Has :brethren his unto said he And .sack his

כַּסְפִּי וְגַם הִנֵּה בְאַמְתַּחְתִּי וַיֵּצֵא[b]
forth went and ;sack my in behold also and ,money my

לִבָּם וַיֶּחֶרְדוּ אִישׁ אֶל־אָחִיו לֵאמֹר
:saying ,brother his unto each terrified were they and ,heart their

29 מַה־זֹּאת עָשָׂה אֱלֹהִים לָנוּ׃ וַיָּבֹאוּ
in came they And ?us to God done has [which] this is What

אֶל־יַעֲקֹב אֲבִיהֶם אַרְצָה כְּנָעַן וַיַּגִּידוּ
told and ,Canaan of land the to father their Jacob unto

30 לוֹ אֵת כָּל־הַקֹּרֹת אֹתָם לֵאמֹר[c]׃ דִּבֶּר
Spoke ;saying ,them to happening things the all him to

הָאִישׁ אֲדֹנֵי הָאָרֶץ אִתָּנוּ קָשׁוֹת
,things harsh us with ,land the of lord the ,man the

31 וַיִּתֵּן אֹתָנוּ[d] כִּמְרַגְּלִים אֶת־הָאָרֶץ׃ וַנֹּאמֶר
said we And .land the spying those as us considered and

אֵלָיו כֵּנִים אֲנַחְנוּ לֹא הָיִינוּ מְרַגְּלִים׃
.spies been [2]have [1]we [3]not ,we [are] Honest :him unto

32 שְׁנֵים־עָשָׂר אֲנַחְנוּ אַחִים בְּנֵי אָבִינוּ
;father our of sons ,brethren ,we [are] Twelve

[e]הָאֶחָד אֵינֶנּוּ וְהַקָּטֹן הַיּוֹם אֶת־אָבִינוּ
father our with [is] today youngest the and ,not is he ,one

33 בְּאֶרֶץ כְּנָעַן׃ וַיֹּאמֶר אֵלֵינוּ הָאִישׁ
,man the us unto said And .Canaan of land the in

אֲדֹנֵי הָאָרֶץ בְּזֹאת אֵדַע כִּי כֵנִים
honest that know shall I this By :land the of lord the

אַתֶּם אֲחִיכֶם הָאֶחָד הַנִּיחוּ אִתִּי וְאֶת־
[for] and ,me with leave ,one ,brother your ;you [are]

34 רַעֲבוֹן[f] בָּתֵּיכֶם קְחוּ וָלֵכוּ׃ וְהָבִיאוּ
in bring And .go and take houses your of famine the

אֶת־אֲחִיכֶם הַקָּטֹן אֵלַי וְאֵדְעָה כִּי
that know may I that ,me unto [1]youngest [2]brother your

ing place, he espied his money; and, behold, it was in the mouth of his sack. 28 And he said unto his brethren, My money is restored; and, lo, it is even in my sack: and their heart failed them, and they turned trembling one to another, saying, What is this that God hath done unto us?

29 And they came unto Jacob their father unto the land of Canaan, and told him all that had befallen them; saying, 30 The man, the lord of the land, spake roughly with us, and took us for spies of the country. 31 And we said unto him, We are true men; we are no spies: 32 we be twelve brethren, sons of our father; one is not, and the youngest is this day with our father in the land of Canaan. 33 And the man, the lord of the land, said unto us, Hereby shall I know that ye are true men; leave one of your brethren with me, and take corn *for* the famine of your houses, and go your way: 34 and bring your youngest brother unto me: then shall I know that ye

---

a S. has, *put*; V. omits.
b S. has, *and trembled.*
c S. adds, *to him.*
d G. adds, *into custody*, במשמר.
e Sm., S. add. *and*, ו
f G., S., T., V. add, *grain*, reading ואת שבר רעבון.

are no spies,
but *that* ye *are*
true *men:* so
will I deliver
you your broth-
er, and ye shall
traffic in the
land.

35 And it
came to pass as
they emptied
their sacks, that,
behold, every
man's bundle of
money *was* in
his sack: and
when *both* they
and their father
saw the bundles
of money, they
were afraid. 36
And Jacob their
father said unto
them, Me have
ye bereaved *of*
my children:
Joseph *is* not,
and Simeon *is*
not, and ye will
take Benjamin
away: all these
things are
against me. 37
And Reuben
spake unto his
father, saying,
Slay my two
sons, if I bring
him not to thee:
deliver him into
my hand, and I
will bring him to
thee again. 38
And he said,
My son shall not
go down with
you; for his
brother is dead,
and he is left
alone: if mis-
chief befall him
by the way in
the which ye go,
then shall ye
bring down my
gray hairs with
sorrow to the
grave.

לֹא מְרַגְּלִים אַתֶּם כִּי כֵנִים אַתֶּם
,you [are] honest but ,you [are] spies not

אֶת־אֲחִיכֶם[a] אֶתֵּן לָכֶם וְאֶת־הָאָרֶץ
land the and ,you to give will I brother your

35 תִּסְחָרוּ׃ וַיְהִי הֵם מְרִיקִים
emptying [were] they [as] ,pass to came it And .through go may you

שַׂקֵּיהֶם וְהִנֵּה־אִישׁ צְרוֹר־כַּסְפּוֹ
money his of bundle the ,one each behold (and) ,sacks their

בְּשַׂקּוֹ וַיִּרְאוּ אֶת־צְרֹרוֹת כַּסְפֵּיהֶם
,money their of bundles the saw they and ;sack his in [was]

36 הֵמָּה וַאֲבִיהֶם וַיִּירָאוּ׃ וַיֹּאמֶר אֲלֵהֶם
them unto said And .feared they and ,father their and they

יַעֲקֹב אֲבִיהֶם אֹתִי שִׁכַּלְתֶּם יוֹסֵף אֵינֶנּוּ
,not is he ,Joseph ;bereaved have you Me :father their Jacob

[b]וְשִׁמְעוֹן אֵינֶנּוּ וְאֶת־בִּנְיָמִן תִּקָּחוּ עָלַי
me upon ; take will you Benjamin and ,not is he ,Simeon and

37 [c]הָיוּ כֻלָּנָה[c]׃ וַיֹּאמֶר רְאוּבֵן אֶל־אָבִיו
,father his unto Reuben said And .them of all are

לֵאמֹר אֶת־שְׁנֵי בָנַי תָּמִית אִם־לֹא אֲבִיאֶנּוּ
him bring ²do ¹I ³not if ,slay mayest thou sons ¹my ²Two :saying

אֵלֶיךָ תְּנָה אֹתוֹ עַל־יָדִי וַאֲנִי אֲשִׁיבֶנּוּ
him return will I and ,hand my into him give ; thee unto

38 אֵלֶיךָ׃ וַיֹּאמֶר לֹא־יֵרֵד בְּנִי עִמָּכֶם
; you with son my down go not Shall :said he And .thee unto

כִּי־אָחִיו מֵת וְהוּא לְבַדּוֹ נִשְׁאָר[d] וּקְרָאָהוּ
him to happen [if] and ;left is only he and ,dead is brother his for

אָסוֹן בַּדֶּרֶךְ אֲשֶׁר תֵּלְכוּ־בָהּ וְהוֹרַדְתֶּם
down bring would you (and) ,(it in) go you which [in] ,way the in harm

אֶת־שֵׂיבָתִי בְּיָגוֹן שְׁאוֹלָה׃
.Sheol to sorrow in hair gray my

are no spies, but
that ye are
true men: so
will I deliver
you your broth-
er, and ye shall
traffick in the
land.

35 And it
came to pass as
they emptied
their sacks, that,
behold, every
man's bundle of
money was in
his sack: and
when they and
their father saw
their bundles of
money, they
were afraid. 36
And Jacob their
father said unto
them, Me have
ye bereaved of
my children:
Joseph is not,
and Simeon is
not, and ye will
take Benjamin
away; all these
things are a-
gainst me. 37
And Reuben
spake unto his
father, saying,
Slay my two
sons, if I bring
him not to thee:
deliver him into
my hand, and I
will bring him
to thee again.
38 And he said,
My son shall not
go down with
you; for his
brother is dead,
and he only is
left: if mischief
befall him by
the way in the
which ye go,
then shall ye
bring down my
gray hairs with
sorrow to the
grave.

43

AND the fam-
ine *was* sore in
the land. 2 And
it came to pass,

1 וְהָרָעָב כָּבֵד בָּאָרֶץ׃
2 וַיְהִי[e]
pass to came it And .land the in heavy was famine the And

And the fam-
ine was sore in
the land. 2 And
it came to pass,

---

a G., S., V. add, *and*, ו.
b G., V. omit ו.
c S. has, *all of them are completed.*
d S. adds, *to his mother.*
e S. omits ויהי.

when they had
eaten up the
corn which they
had brought out
of Egypt, their
father said unto
them, Go again,
buy us a little
food. 3 And Ju-
dah spake unto
him, saying,
The man did
solemnly protest
unto us, saying,
Ye shall not see
my face, except
your brother *be*
with you. 4 If
thou wilt send
our brother with
us, we will go
down and buy
thee food: 5 But
if thou wilt not
send *him*, we
will not go
down: for the
man said unto
us, Ye shall not
see my face, ex-
cept your broth-
er *be* with you.

6 And Israel
said, Wherefore
dealt ye *so* ill
with me, *as* to
tell the man
whether ye had
yet a brother? 7
And they said,
The man asked
us straitly of our
state, and of our
kindred, saying,
Is your father
yet alive? have
ye *another*
brother? and we
told him accord-
ing to the tenor
of these words:
could we cer-
tainly know
that he would
say, Bring your
brother down?
8 And Judah
said unto Israel

כַּאֲשֶׁר כִּלּוּ לֶאֱכֹל אֶת־הַשֶּׁבֶר אֲשֶׁר הֵבִיאוּ
brought had they which grain the eat to finished had they when

מִמִּצְרָיִם וַיֹּאמֶר אֲלֵיהֶם [a] אֲבִיהֶם [b] שֻׁבוּ
,Return :father their them unto said (and) ,Egypt from

3 שִׁבְרוּ־לָנוּ מְעַט־אֹכֶל׃ וַיֹּאמֶר אֵלָיו יְהוּדָה לֵאמֹר [c]
:saying ,Judah him unto said And .food little a us for buy

הָעֵד הֵעִד בָּנוּ הָאִישׁ לֵאמֹר לֹא־תִרְאוּ
see not shall You :saying ,man the us to protested Protesting

4 פָּנַי בִּלְתִּי אֲחִיכֶם אִתְּכֶם [d]׃ אִם־יֶשְׁךָ
art thou If .you with [be] brother your except ,face my

מְשַׁלֵּחַ אֶת־אָחִינוּ אִתָּנוּ נֵרְדָה וְנִשְׁבְּרָה
buy and down go will we ,us with brother our sending

5 לְךָ [e] אֹכֶל׃ וְאִם־אֵינְךָ מְשַׁלֵּחַ [f] לֹא נֵרֵד
;down go [2]will [1]we [3]not ,sending not art thou if And .food thee for

כִּי־הָאִישׁ אָמַר אֵלֵינוּ [g] לֹא־תִרְאוּ פָנַי בִּלְתִּי
except ,face my see not shall You :us unto said man the for

6 אֲחִיכֶם [h] אִתְּכֶם׃ וַיֹּאמֶר [i] יִשְׂרָאֵל [j] לָמָה הֲרֵעֹתֶם
evil do ye did Why :Israel said And .you with [be] brother your

לִי לְהַגִּיד לָאִישׁ הַעוֹד לָכֶם
you to [was there] still whether man the to tell to ,me to

7 אָח׃ וַיֹּאמְרוּ שָׁאוֹל שָׁאַל־הָאִישׁ לָנוּ
us after man the asked Asking :said they And ?brother a

וּלְמוֹלַדְתֵּנוּ לֵאמֹר הַעוֹד אֲבִיכֶם חַי הֲיֵשׁ
[there] Is ?alive father your still [Is] :saying ,kindred our after and

לָכֶם אָח וַנַּגֶּד־לוֹ עַל־פִּי [k] הַדְּבָרִים
[2]words of mouth the upon him to told we And ?brother a you to

הָאֵלֶּה [k] הֲיָדוֹעַ נֵדַע כִּי יֹאמַר [l]
:say would he that know we could knowing ;[1]these

8 הוֹרִידוּ אֶת־אֲחִיכֶם׃ וַיֹּאמֶר יְהוּדָה אֶל־
unto Judah said And ?brother your down Bring

when they had
eaten up the
corn which they
had brought
out of Egypt,
their father said
unto them, Go
again, buy us a
little food. 3
And Judah
spake unto him,
saying, The
man did sol-
emnly protest
unto us, saying,
Ye shall not see
my face, except
your brother be
with you. 4 If
thou wilt send
our brother with
us, we will go
down and buy
thee food: 5 but
if thou wilt not
send him, we
will not go
down: for the
man said unto
us, Ye shall not
see my face, ex-
cept your broth-
er be with you.

6 And Israel
said, Wherefore
dealt ye so ill
with me, as to
tell the man
whether ye had
yet a brother?
7 And they said,
The man asked
straitly concern-
ing ourselves,
and concerning
our kindred,
saying, Is your
father yet alive?
have ye *another*
brother? and
we told him ac-
cording to the
tenor of these
words: could we
in any wise
know that he
would say,
Bring your
brother down? 8
And Judah said
unto Israel his

---

a S. adds, *Jacob.*

b V. has, *Jacob.*

c S. omits.

d G. has, *the younger come down unto me;* V. *the younger you bring down with you.*

e S. has, *for us,* לנו.

f G. adds, *our brother with us,* cf. v. 4.

g G., V. add, *saying.*

h G., V. add, *the younger.*

i S., V. omit ו and add, *to them.*

j S. adds, *their father.*

k G. has, *according to his asking.*

l S. adds, *to us.*

his father, Send
the lad with me,
and we will a-
rise and go; that
we may live, and
not die, both
we, and thou,
and also our
little ones. 9 I
will be surety
for him; of my
hand shalt thou
require him: if
I bring him not
unto thee, and
set him before
thee, then let me
bear the blame
for ever: 10 For
except we had
lingered, surely
now we had re-
turned this sec-
ond time.

11 And their
father Israel
said unto them,
If *it must be* so
now, do this;
take of the best
fruits in the
land in your
vessels, and
carry down the
man a present,
a little balm,
and a little
honey, spices,
and myrrh, nuts,
and almonds: 12
And take double
money in your
hand; and the
money that was
brought again
in the mouth of
your sacks, carry
it again in your
hand; perad-
venture it *was*
an oversight:

13 Take also
your brother,
and arise, go
again unto the
man: 14 And
God Almighty
give you
mercy be-

יִשְׂרָאֵל אָבִיו שִׁלְחָה הַנַּעַר אִתִּי [a] וְנָקוּמָה
rise us let and ,me with youth the Send : father his Israel

וְנֵלֵכָה וְנִחְיֶה וְלֹא נָמוּת גַּם־אֲנַחְנוּ
,we both ,die not and live may we that ;go and

9 גַּם־אַתָּה גַּם־טַפֵּנוּ׃ [b] אָנֹכִי אֶעֶרְבֶנּוּ
; him for surety be will I .ones little our and ,thou and

מִיָּדִי תְּבַקְשֶׁנּוּ אִם־לֹא הֲבִיאֹתִיו
him bring [2]do [1]I [3]not if ; him require mayest thou hand my from

אֵלֶיךָ וְהִצַּגְתִּיו לְפָנֶיךָ וְחָטָאתִי
sinner a be shall I (and) ,thee before him set and ,thee unto

10 לְךָ [c] כָּל־הַיָּמִים׃ כִּי לוּלֵא הִתְמַהְמָהְנוּ
,delayed [2]had [1]we [3]not if For .days the all thee against

11 כִּי־עַתָּה שַׁבְנוּ זֶה פַעֲמָיִם׃ וַיֹּאמֶר
said And .twice here returned have should we now indeed

אֲלֵהֶם יִשְׂרָאֵל אֲבִיהֶם אִם־כֵּן ׀ אֵפוֹא
,then so If : father their Israel them unto

זֹאת עֲשׂוּ קְחוּ מִזִּמְרַת הָאָרֶץ
land the of produce the from take ; do this

בִּכְלֵיכֶם וְהוֹרִידוּ לָאִישׁ מִנְחָה מְעַט [d]
little a ; present a man the to down bring and ,vessels your in

צֳרִי וּמְעַט [e] דְּבַשׁ [f] נְכֹאת וָלֹט [g] בָּטְנִים
nuts pistachio ,ladanum and tragacanth ,honey little a and balsam

12 וּשְׁקֵדִים׃ וְכֶסֶף מִשְׁנֶה קְחוּ בְיֶדְכֶם
; hand your in take double money And .almonds and

[h] וְאֶת־הַכֶּסֶף הַמּוּשָׁב בְּפִי אַמְתְּחֹתֵיכֶם
,sacks your of mouth the in returned money the and

תָּשִׁיבוּ בְיֶדְכֶם אוּלַי מִשְׁגֶּה הוּא׃
.it [was] mistake a perhaps ,hand your in return

13 וְאֶת־אֲחִיכֶם קָחוּ וְקוּמוּ שׁוּבוּ אֶל־
unto return ,arise and ,take brother your And

14 הָאִישׁ׃ וְאֵל [i] שַׁדַּי יִתֵּן לָכֶם רַחֲמִים
mercy you to give [1]may [3]Almighty [2]God And .man the

father, Send the
lad with me,
and we will a-
rise and go; that
we may live,
and not die,
both we, and
thou, and also
our little ones.
9 I will be sure-
ty for him; of
my hand shalt
thou require
him: if I bring
him not unto
thee, and set
him before thee,
then let me bear
the blame for
ever: 10 for ex-
cept we had
lingered, surely
we had now re-
turned a second
time.

11 And their
father Israel
said unto them,
If it be so now,
do this; take of
the choice fruits
of the land in
your vessels, and
carry down the
man a present,
a little balm,
and a little
honey, spicery
and myrrh,
nuts, and al-
monds: 12 and
take double
money in your
hand; and the
money that was
returned in the
mouth of your
sacks carry a-
gain in your
hand; peradven-
ture it was an
oversight:

13 Take also
your brother,
and arise, go
again unto
the man: 14
and God Al-
mighty give you
mercy before the

---

a S. has, *us*, אתנו.
b G. adds, *and*, ו.
c S., T. have, *to my father*, לאבי, cf. 44: 32.
d G. omits.
e G. omits מעט.
f S., V. add *and*, ו.
g G., S., V. add, *and*, ו.
h G. omits ו.
i G. has, *my God;* V. *my God omnipotent*.

fore the man, that he may send away your other brother, and Benjamin. If I be bereaved *of my children*, I am bereaved.

15 And the men took that present, and they took double money in their hand, and Benjamin; and rose up, and went down to Egypt, and stood before Joseph. 16 And when Joseph saw Benjamin with them, he said to the ruler of his house, Bring *these* men home, and slay, and make ready; for *these* men shall dine with me at noon. 17 And the man did as Joseph bade; and the man brought the men into Joseph's house.

18 And the men were afraid, because they were brought into Joseph's house; and they said, Because of the money that was returned in our sacks at the first time are we brought in; that he may seek occasion against us, and fall upon us, and take

לִפְנֵי הָאִישׁ וְשִׁלַּח לָכֶם [a] אֶת־אֲחִיכֶם
[2]brother your you for send he may and ,man the before

אַחֵר [b] וְאֶת־בִּנְיָמִין וַאֲנִי כַּאֲשֶׁר שָׁכֹלְתִּי
,bereaved am I if ,I and ; Benjamin and [1]other

15 שָׁכָלְתִּי׃ וַיִּקְחוּ הָאֲנָשִׁים אֶת־הַמִּנְחָה
[2]present men the took And .bereaved am I

הַזֹּאת וּמִשְׁנֶה־כֶּסֶף לָקְחוּ בְיָדָם
,hand their in took they money double and ,[1]this

וְאֶת־בִּנְיָמִן [c] וַיָּקֻמוּ וַיֵּרְדוּ מִצְרַיִם
,Egypt to down went and arose they and ;Benjamin and

16 וַיַּעַמְדוּ לִפְנֵי יוֹסֵף׃ וַיַּרְא יוֹסֵף אִתָּם
them with Joseph saw And .Joseph before stood and

[d] אֶת־בִּנְיָמִין [e] וַיֹּאמֶר לַאֲשֶׁר עַל־בֵּיתוֹ
:house his over [was] who one the to said and ,Benjamin

הָבֵא אֶת־הָאֲנָשִׁים [f] הַבָּיְתָה וּטְבֹחַ
slaughter and ,house the to men the in Bring

טֶבַח וְהָכֵן כִּי אִתִּי יֹאכְלוּ
eat shall me with for ; prepare and ,slaughtering a

17 הָאֲנָשִׁים בַּצָּהֳרָיִם׃ וַיַּעַשׂ הָאִישׁ [g] כַּאֲשֶׁר
as man the did And .noon at men the

אָמַר יוֹסֵף וַיָּבֵא הָאִישׁ [h] אֶת־הָאֲנָשִׁים
men the man the in brought and ; Joseph said had

18 בֵּיתָה יוֹסֵף׃ וַיִּירְאוּ [i] הָאֲנָשִׁים [j] כִּי
because men the feared And .Joseph of house the to

הוּבְאוּ [k] בֵּית יוֹסֵף וַיֹּאמְרוּ
:said they and ,Joseph of house the into brought were they

עַל־דְּבַר הַכֶּסֶף הַשָּׁב בְּאַמְתְּחֹתֵינוּ
,sacks our in returned that ,money the of account On

בַּתְּחִלָּה אֲנַחְנוּ מוּבָאִים לְהִתְגֹּלֵל
himself roll to ,in brought are we ,time former the at

עָלֵינוּ וּלְהִתְנַפֵּל עָלֵינוּ וְלָקַחַת [l] אֹתָנוּ
us take to and ,us upon fall to and ,us upon

man, that he may release unto you your other brother and Benjamin. And if I be bereaved of my children, I am bereaved.

15 And the men took that present, and they took double money in their hand, and Benjamin; and rose up, and went down to Egypt, and stood before Joseph. 16 And when Joseph saw Benjamin with them, he said to the steward of his house, Bring the men into the house, and slay, and make ready; for the men shall dine with me at noon. 17 And the man did as Joseph bade; and the man brought the men into Joseph's house.

18 And the men were afraid, because they were brought into Joseph's house; and they said, Because of the money that was returned in our sacks at the first time are we brought in; that he may seek occasion against us, and fall upon us, and take

a G. omits.
b Sm., G. have, *one*, האחד.
c S., T. have, *and they took with them Benjamin.*
d G., V. add, *and*, ו.
e G. adds, *his brother of the same mother;* cf. v. 29.
f G. adds, *bread.*
g S. has, *the slave;* V. omits.
h G., S., V. omit.
i G. has, *and they saw*, ויראו.
j S. omits.
k S. has, *they brought them.*
l G., S. omit ו.

us for bondmen,
and our asses.

19 And they
came near to
the steward of
Joseph's house,
and they com-
muned with him
at the door of
the house, 20
And said, O sir,
we came indeed
down at the
first time to buy
food: 21 And it
came to pass,
when we came
to the inn, that
we opened our
sacks, and, be-
hold, *every*
man's money
was in the
mouth of his
sack, our money
in full weight:
and we have
brought it a-
gain in our
hand. 22 And
other money
have we brought
down in our
hands, to buy
food: we can-
not tell who
put our money
in our sacks.

23 And he said,
Peace *be* to you!
fear not: your
God, and the
God of your
father, hath giv-
en you treasure
in your sacks: I
had your money.
And he brought
Simeon out unto
them. 24 And
the man brought
the men into
Joseph's house,
and gave *them*
water, and they
washed their

19 לַעֲבָדִים וְאֶת־חֲמֹרֵינוּ׃ וַיִּגְּשׁוּ אֶל־הָאִישׁ
man the unto | near came they And | .asses our and | ,slaves for

אֲשֶׁר עַל־בֵּית יוֹסֵף וַיְדַבְּרוּ אֵלָיו
him unto | spoke and | ,Joseph | of house the over | [was] who

20 פֶּתַח הַבָּיִת׃ וַיֹּאמְרוּ[a] בִּי אֲדֹנִי
,lord my | O | :said they And | .house the | of door the at

יָרֹד יָרַדְנוּ בַּתְּחִלָּה לִשְׁבָּר־אֹכֶל׃
.food buy to | time former the at | down came we | surely

21 [b]וַיְהִי כִּי־בָאנוּ אֶל־הַמָּלוֹן
,place lodging the unto | came we when | ,pass to came it And

[c]וַנִּפְתְּחָה אֶת־אַמְתְּחֹתֵינוּ וְהִנֵּה כֶסֶף־
money the | behold (and) | ,sacks our | opened and

אִישׁ בְּפִי אַמְתַּחְתּוֹ כַּסְפֵּנוּ
money our | ,sack his | of mouth the in | one each of

בְּמִשְׁקָלוֹ [d]וַנָּשֶׁב אֹתוֹ בְּיָדֵנוּ[e]׃
.hand our in | it | returned have we and | ; weight its in

22 וְכֶסֶף אַחֵר הוֹרַדְנוּ בְיָדֵנוּ
hand our in | down brought have we | [1]other | [2]money And

לִשְׁבָּר־אֹכֶל לֹא יָדַעְנוּ מִי־שָׂם כַּסְפֵּנוּ
money our | put who | know [2]do [1]we | [3]not | ; food buy to

23 בְּאַמְתְּחֹתֵינוּ[f]׃ וַיֹּאמֶר[g] שָׁלוֹם לָכֶם אַל־תִּירָאוּ
; fear not do | ,you to | Peace | : said he And | .sacks our in

אֱלֹהֵיכֶם [h]וֵאלֹהֵי אֲבִיכֶם נָתַן לָכֶם
you to | given has | father your | of God the and | God your

מַטְמוֹן בְּאַמְתְּחֹתֵיכֶם כַּסְפְּכֶם בָּא
came | money your | ; sacks your in | treasure a

אֵלָי וַיּוֹצֵא אֲלֵהֶם אֶת־שִׁמְעוֹן׃
.Simeon | them unto | out brought he and | ; me unto

24 וַיָּבֵא[i] הָאִישׁ[j] אֶת־הָאֲנָשִׁים בֵּיתָה
of house the to | men the | man the | in brought And

יוֹסֵף[i] וַיִּתֶּן־מַיִם וַיִּרְחֲצוּ רַגְלֵיהֶם
; feet their | washed they and | ,water gave he and | ; Joseph

us for bondmen,
and our asses.

19 And they
came near to
the steward of
Joseph's house,
and they spake
unto him at the
door of the
house, 20 and
said, Oh my
lord, we came
indeed down at
the first time to
buy food: 21
and it came to
pass, when we
came to the
lodging place,
that we opened
our sacks, and,
behold, every
man's money
was in the
mouth of his
sack, our mon-
ey in full weight:
and we have
brought it a-
gain in our
hand. 22 And
other money
have we brought
down in our
hand to buy
food: we know
not who put
our money in
our sacks.

23 And he said,
Peace be to
you, fear not:
your God, and
the God of your
father, hath giv-
en you treasure
in your sacks: I
had your money.
And he brought
Simeon out unto
them. 24 And
the man brought
the men into Jo-
seph's house,
and gave them
water, and they
washed their

---

a S. adds, *to him.*
b S. omits יהי.
c S., V. omit *and,*
d G., S. omit, *and,* ו.
e G. has, *in our sacks.*
f S. has, *in the mouth of our sacks,*
g G. adds, *to them the man;* S. adds, *to them.*
h S. omits ו.
i G. omits; V. omits האיש, את-האנשים, and יוסף.
j S. has, *the slave,* העבד.

feet; and he
gave their asses
provender. 25
And they made
ready the pres-
ent against Jo-
seph came at
noon: for they
heard that they
should eat bread
there.

26 And when
Joseph came
home, they
brought him the
present which
was in their
hand into the
house, and bow-
ed themselves
to him to the
earth. 27 And
he asked them
of *their* welfare,
and said, *Is*
your father
well, the old
man of whom
ye spake? *Is*
he yet alive? 28
And they an-
swered, Thy
servant our fa-
ther *is* in good
health, he *is* yet
alive. And they
bowed down
their heads, and
made obeisance.

29 And he
lifted up his
eyes, and saw
his brother
Benjamin, his
mother's son,
and said, *Is*
this your young-
er brother, of
whom ye spake
unto me? And
he said, God be
gracious unto
thee, my son.
30 And Joseph
made haste; for
his bowels did
yearn upon his
brother: and he
sought *where* to
weep; and he
entered into *his*
chamber, and
wept there. 31

25 וַיִּתֵּן מִסְפּוֹא לַחֲמֹרֵיהֶם׃ וַיָּכִינוּ
prepared they And .asses their for fodder gave he and

אֶת־הַמִּנְחָה עַד־בּוֹא יוֹסֵף בַּצָּהֳרָיִם
;noon at Joseph of coming the for ,present the

כִּי שָׁמְעוּ כִּי־שָׁם יֹאכְלוּ[a] לָחֶם׃
.bread eat would they there that heard had they for

26 וַיָּבֹא יוֹסֵף הַבַּיְתָה וַיָּבִיאוּ לוֹ
him to in brought they and ,house the into Joseph came And

אֶת־הַמִּנְחָה אֲשֶׁר־בְּיָדָם הַבָּיְתָה
:house the into ,hand their in [was] which present the

27 וַיִּשְׁתַּחֲווּ־לוֹ[b] אָרְצָה׃ וַיִּשְׁאַל
asked he And .earth the to him to themselves prostrated they and

לָהֶם לְשָׁלוֹם וַיֹּאמֶר[c] הֲשָׁלוֹם
peace [Is] :said and ,welfare concerning them (to)

אֲבִיכֶם הַזָּקֵן אֲשֶׁר אֲמַרְתֶּם[d] הַעוֹדֶנּוּ
still he [is] ?spoke you whom [of] ,man old the ,father your [to]

28 חָי׃ וַיֹּאמְרוּ שָׁלוֹם לְעַבְדְּךָ לְאָבִינוּ
;father our to servant thy to Peace :said they And ?alive

עוֹדֶנּוּ[e] חָי[f] וַיִּקְּדוּ וַיִּשְׁתַּחֲוּ׃
.themselves prostrated and bowed they and ;alive [is] still he

29 וַיִּשָּׂא עֵינָיו וַיַּרְא[g] אֶת־בִּנְיָמִין אָחִיו בֶּן־
of son the brother his Benjamin saw and eyes his raised he And

אִמּוֹ וַיֹּאמֶר[h] הֲזֶה אֲחִיכֶם הַקָּטֹן
,[1]youngest [2]brother your this [Is] :said he and ,mother his

אֲשֶׁר אֲמַרְתֶּם אֵלָי[i] וַיֹּאמַר אֱלֹהִים
[2]God :said he And ?me unto spoke you whom [of]

30 יָחְנְךָ בְּנִי׃ וַיְמַהֵר יוֹסֵף כִּי־
because ,Joseph hastened And .son my ,thee to gracious be [1]may

נִכְמְרוּ רַחֲמָיו אֶל־אָחִיו וַיְבַקֵּשׁ
sought he and ;brother his towards feelings his agitated were

לִבְכּוֹת וַיָּבֹא הַחַדְרָה וַיֵּבְךְּ שָׁמָּה׃
.there wept and ,room inner the to in came he and ,weep to

feet; and he
gave their asses
provender. 25
And they made
ready the
present against
Joseph came at
noon: for they
heard that they
should eat bread
there.

26 And when
Joseph came
home, they
brought him
the present
which was in
their hand into
the house, and
bowed down
themselves to
him to the earth.
27 And he asked
them of their
welfare, and
said, Is your fa-
ther well, the
old man of
whom ye spake?
Is he yet alive?
28 And they
said, Thy serv-
ant our father is
well, he is yet a-
live. And they
bowed the head,
and made obei-
sance.

29 And he
lifted up his
eyes, and saw
Benjamin his
brother, his
mother's son,
and said, Is this
your youngest
brother, of
whom ye spake
unto me? And
he said, God be
gracious unto
thee, my son. 30
And Joseph
made haste; for
his bowels did
yearn upon his
brother: and he
sought where to
weep; and he
entered into his
chamber, and
wept there. 31

---

a G. has sing.
b G., V. add, *the face*, אפים.
c S., V. add, *to them.*
d S. adds, *to me.*
e S. adds, *and*, ו.
f Sm., G. add, *blessed be that man before God.*
g G. adds, *Joseph.*
h G., S. add, *to them.*
i G. adds, *to bring.*

And he washed
his face, and
went out, and
refrained him-
self, and said,
Set on bread.
32 And they set
on for him by
himself, and for
them by them-
selves, and for
the Egyptians,
which did eat
with him, by
themselves: be-
cause the Egyp-
tians might not
eat bread with
the Hebrews;
for that *is* an
abomination
unto the Egyp-
tians. 33 And
they sat before
him, the first-
born according
to his birthright,
and the young-
est according to
his youth: and
the men mar-
velled one at an-
other. 34 And
he took *and sent*
messes unto
them from be-
fore him: but
Benjamin's
mess was five
times so much
as any of theirs.
And they drank,
and were merry
with him.

31 וַיִּרְחַץ פָּנָיו וַיֵּצֵא וַיִּתְאַפַּק
himself controlled and ,out went and ,face his washed he And

32 וַיֹּאמֶר שִׂימוּ לָחֶם׃ וַיָּשִׂימוּ לוֹ לְבַדּוֹ
,himself by him for on put they And .bread on Put ,said and

וְלָהֶם לְבַדָּם וְלַמִּצְרִים הָאֹכְלִים
eating Egyptians the for and ,themselves by them for and

אִתּוֹ לְבַדָּם כִּי לֹא יוּכְלוּן הַמִּצְרִים
Egyptians the able [1]are [2]not for ;themselves by him with

לֶאֱכֹל אֶת־הָעִבְרִים לֶחֶם כִּי־תוֹעֵבָה
abomination an for ;bread Hebrews the with eat to

33 הִוא לְמִצְרָיִם׃ [a] וַיֵּשְׁבוּ לְפָנָיו הַבְּכֹר
firstborn the ,him before sat they And .Egypt to [is] it

כִּבְכֹרָתוֹ וְהַצָּעִיר כִּצְעִרָתוֹ
;youth his to according younger the and ,birthright his to according

וַיִּתְמְהוּ הָאֲנָשִׁים אִישׁ אֶל־רֵעֵהוּ׃
.neighbor his unto each ,men the astonished were and

34 וַיִּשָּׂא [b] מַשְׂאֹת מֵאֵת פָּנָיו אֲלֵהֶם
,them unto face his (with) from portions bore one And

וַתֵּרֶב מַשְׂאַת בִּנְיָמִן מִמַּשְׂאֹת
of portions the than Benjamin of portion the greater was and

כֻּלָּם חָמֵשׁ יָדוֹת וַיִּשְׁתּוּ וַיִּשְׁכְּרוּ
drunken were and drank they and ;times five ,them of all

עִמּוֹ׃
.him with

44

1 וַיְצַו [c] אֶת־אֲשֶׁר עַל־בֵּיתוֹ לֵאמֹר
:saying ,house his over [was] who one the commanded he And

מַלֵּא אֶת־אַמְתְּחֹת הָאֲנָשִׁים אֹכֶל כַּאֲשֶׁר
as ,food [with] men the of sacks the Fill

יוּכְלוּן שְׂאֵת וְשִׂים כֶּסֶף־אִישׁ בְּפִי
of mouth the in one each of money the put and ,carry to able are they

2 אַמְתַּחְתּוֹ׃ וְאֶת־גְּבִיעִי [d] גְּבִיעַ הַכֶּסֶף תָּשִׂים [e]
put ,silver of cup the ,cup my And .sack his

AND he com-
manded the
steward of his
house, saying,
Fill the men's
sacks *with* food,
as much as they
can carry, and
put every man's
money in his
sack's mouth. 2
And put my cup,
the silver cup,

And he washed
his face, and
came out; and
he refrained
himself, and
said, Set on
bread. 32 And
they set on for
him by himself,
and for them by
themselves, and
for the Egyp-
tians, which did
eat with him,
by themselves:
because the E-
gyptians might
not eat bread
with the He-
brews; for that
is an abomina-
tion unto the
Egyptians. 33
And they sat
before him, the
firstborn accord-
ing to his birth-
right, and the
youngest ac-
cording to his
youth: and the
men marvelled
one with anoth-
er. 34 And he
took *and sent*
messes unto
them from be-
fore him: but
Benjamin's
mess was five
times so much
as any of theirs.
And they drank,
and were merry
with him.

And he com-
manded the
steward of his
house, saying,
Fill the men's
sacks with food,
as much as they
can carry, and
put every man's
money in his
sack's mouth. 2
And put my
cup, the silver
cup, in the

a G. adds, *every shepherd of sheep.*
b G., S. have pl.
c G., V. add, *Joseph.*
d S. has, *and take my cup.*
e S. adds, *and,* ו

in the sack's mouth of the youngest, and his corn money. And he did according to the word that Joseph had spoken. 3 As soon as the morning was light, the men were sent away, they and their asses. 4 *And* when they were gone out of the city, *and* not *yet* far off, Joseph said unto his steward, Up, follow after the men; and when thou dost overtake them, say unto them, Wherefore have ye rewarded evil for good? 5 *Is* not this *it* in which my lord drinketh, and whereby indeed he divineth? ye have done evil in so doing.

בְּפִי אַמְתַּחַת הַקָּטֹן וְאֵת כֶּסֶף
of money the and ,youngest the of sack the of mouth the in

שִׁבְרוֹ וַיַּעַשׂ[a] כִּדְבַר יוֹסֵף אֲשֶׁר[b]
which Joseph of word the to according did he and ; grain his

3 דִּבֵּר[b]׃ הַבֹּקֶר אוֹר וְהָאֲנָשִׁים
men the (and) ,light [become having] morning The .spoke he

4 שֻׁלְּחוּ[c] הֵמָּה וַחֲמֹרֵיהֶם׃ הֵם יָצְאוּ
from out gone had They .asses their and they ,away sent were

אֶת־הָעִיר[d] לֹא הִרְחִיקוּ וְיוֹסֵף אָמַר לַאֲשֶׁר
who one the to said Joseph and ,far gone having not ,city the

עַל־בֵּיתוֹ[e] קוּם רְדֹף אַחֲרֵי הָאֲנָשִׁים
; men the after pursue ,Rise : house his over [was]

וְהִשַּׂגְתָּם וְאָמַרְתָּ אֲלֵהֶם לָמָּה שִׁלַּמְתֶּם[f]
repaid you have Why :them unto say and them overtake and

5 רָעָה תַּחַת טוֹבָה[g]׃ הֲלוֹא[h] זֶה[h] אֲשֶׁר
which [by] that this not [Is] ? good of instead evil

יִשְׁתֶּה אֲדֹנִי בּוֹ וְהוּא נַחֵשׁ
surely he [which by] and ,(it by) lord my drink to accustomed is

יְנַחֵשׁ בּוֹ הֲרֵעֹתֶם
evil done have You ? (it by) divination practice to accustomed is

6 אֲשֶׁר עֲשִׂיתֶם׃ וַיַּשִּׂגֵם וַיְדַבֵּר אֲלֵהֶם
them unto spoke and ,them overtook he And .done have you what

6 And he overtook them, and he spake unto them these same words. 7 And they said unto him, Wherefore saith my lord these words? God forbid that thy servants should do according to this thing: 8 Behold, the money, which we found in our sacks' mouths, we brought again unto thee out of the land of Canaan: how

7 אֶת־הַדְּבָרִים[i] הָאֵלֶּה׃ וַיֹּאמְרוּ אֵלָיו לָמָּה
Why : him unto said they And .[1]these [2]words

יְדַבֵּר אֲדֹנִי כַּדְּבָרִים[j] הָאֵלֶּה חָלִילָה
it be Far ? [1]these [2]words to according lord my speak should

8 לַעֲבָדֶיךָ מֵעֲשׂוֹת כַּדָּבָר[k] הַזֶּה׃ הֵן
,Behold .[1]this [2]word to according doing from servants thy from

כֶּסֶף אֲשֶׁר מָצָאנוּ בְּפִי אַמְתְּחֹתֵינוּ
,sacks our of mouth the in found we which money

הֱשִׁיבֹנוּ אֵלֶיךָ[l] מֵאֶרֶץ כְּנָעַן וְאֵיךְ[m]
how and ; Canaan of land the from thee unto returned we

sack's mouth of the youngest, and his corn money. And he did according to the word that Joseph had spoken. 3 As soon as the morning was light, the men were sent away, they and their asses. 4 *And* when they were gone out of the city, and were not yet far off, Joseph said unto his steward, Up, follow after the men; and when thou dost overtake them, say unto them, Wherefore have ye rewarded evil for good? 5 Is not this it in which my lord drinketh, and whereby he indeed divineth? ye have done evil in so doing.

6 And he overtook them, and he spake unto them these words. 7 And they said unto him, Wherefore speaketh my lord such words as these? God forbid that thy servants should do such a thing. 8 Behold, the money, which we found in our sacks' mouths, we brought again unto thee out of the land of Canaan: how

a S. adds, *the slave.*
b S., V. omit.
c S. adds, *to depart.*
d Sm., S., V. add, *and,* ו.
e G. adds, *saying.*
f G. adds, *to me.*
g G. adds, *why have you stolen my silver cup?*
h S. has, *this cup;* V. *the cup which you have stolen.*
i G., S. have, *like words.*
j S. omits כ.
k S. omits כ.
l S. omits.
m G., S. omit ו.

then should we
steal out of thy
lord's house sil-
ver or gold? 9
With whomso-
ever of thy serv-
ants it be found,
both let him die,
and we also will
be my lord's
bondmen. 10
And he said,
Now also *let* it
be according un-
to your words:
he with whom
it is found shall
be my servant;
and ye shall be
blameless. 11
Then they
speedily took
down every man
his sack to the
ground, and o-
pened every
man his sack. 12
And he search-
ed, *and* began
at the eldest,
and left at the
youngest: and
the cup was
found in Ben-
jamin's sack. 13
Then they rent
their clothes,
and laded every
man his ass, and
returned to the
city.

נִגְנֹב מִבֵּית אֲדֹנֶיךָ כֶּסֶף אוֹ זָהָב׃
?gold or silver lord thy of house the from steal we should

9 אֲשֶׁר יִמָּצֵא אִתּוֹ מֵעֲבָדֶיךָ
,servants thy of (him with) found be it whomsoever [With]

וָמֵת וְגַם־אֲנַחְנוּ נִהְיֶה לַאדֹנִי לַעֲבָדִים׃
.slaves (for) lord my to become will we also and ;die shall he (and)

10 וַיֹּאמֶר[a] גַּם־עַתָּה כְדִבְרֵיכֶם כֶּן־הוּא
; it so ,words your to according now Also : said he And

אֲשֶׁר[b] יִמָּצֵא אִתּוֹ[c] יִהְיֶה־לִּי
me for become shall he ,(him with) found be it whomsoever [with]

11 עָבֶד וְאַתֶּם תִּהְיוּ נְקִיִּם׃ וַיְמַהֲרוּ
,hastened they And .innocent be shall you and ,slave a

וַיּוֹרִדוּ אִישׁ אֶת־אַמְתַּחְתּוֹ אָרְצָה
;earth the to sack his one each down brought and

12 וַיִּפְתְּחוּ אִישׁ אַמְתַּחְתּוֹ׃ וַיְחַפֵּשׂ
,searched he And .sack his one each opened they and

בַּגָּדוֹל הֵחֵל וּבַקָּטֹן כִּלָּה
; finishing youngest the with and beginning eldest the with

13 וַיִּמָּצֵא[d] הַגָּבִיעַ בְּאַמְתַּחַת בִּנְיָמִן׃ וַיִּקְרְעוּ
rent they And .Benjamin of sack the in cup the found was and

שִׂמְלֹתָם וַיַּעֲמֹס אִישׁ[e] עַל־חֲמֹרוֹ
,ass his (upon) one each loaded they and ; clothes their

14 וַיָּשֻׁבוּ הָעִירָה׃ וַיָּבֹא יְהוּדָה וְאֶחָיו
brethren his and Judah in came And .city the to returned and

then should we
steal out of thy
lord's house sil-
ver or gold?
9 With whomso-
ever of thy serv-
ants it be found,
let him die, and
we also will be
my lord's bonds-
men. 10 And he
said, Now also
let it be accord-
ing unto your
words: he with
whom it is found
shall be my
bondman; and
ye shall be
blameless. 11
Then they hast-
ed, and took
down every man
his sack to the
ground, and o-
pened every
man his sack. 12
And he search-
ed, *and* began
at the eldest,
and left at the
youngest: and
the cup was
found in Ben-
jamin's sack. 13
Then they rent
their clothes,
and laded ev-
ery man his
ass, and re-
turned to the
city.

14 And Judah
and his brethren
came to Jo-
seph's house;
for he *was* yet
there: and they
fell before him
on the ground.
15 And Joseph
said unto them,
What deed *is*
this that ye
have done? wot
ye not that such
a man as I can
certainly divine?
16 And Judah
said, What shall
we say unto my
lord? what shall

בֵּיתָה[f] יוֹסֵף[f] וְהוּא עוֹדֶנּוּ שָׁם
; there (he) still [being] he (and) ,Joseph of house the to

15 וַיִּפְּלוּ לְפָנָיו אָרְצָה׃ וַיֹּאמֶר לָהֶם יוֹסֵף
: Joseph them to said And .earth the to him before fell they and

מָה הַמַּעֲשֶׂה הַזֶּה אֲשֶׁר עֲשִׂיתֶם הֲלוֹא יְדַעְתֶּם
know [2]you [1]did [3]Not ? done have you which [1]this [2]deed [is] What

כִּי־נַחֵשׁ יְנַחֵשׁ אִישׁ אֲשֶׁר כָּמֹנִי׃
?me like [is] who man a divination practise would surely that

16 וַיֹּאמֶר יְהוּדָה מַה־נֹּאמַר לַאדֹנִי מַה־[g]
what ?lord my to say we can What : Judah said And

14 And Judah
and his breth-
ren came to Jo-
seph's house;
and he was yet
there: and they
fell before him
on the ground.
15 And Joseph
said unto them,
What deed is
this that ye have
done? know ye
not that such a
man as I can
indeed divine?
16 And Judah
said, What shall
we say unto my
lord? what shall

---

a S., V. have, *he said to them*.
b G. has, *the man with whom*.
c G. adds, *the cup*.
d G., V. have, *and he found*, וַיִּמְצָא.
e G. adds, *his sack*.
f G., S., V. have, *to Joseph*.

we speak? or
how shall we
clear ourselves?
God hath found
out the iniquity
of thy servants:
behold, we *are*
my lord's serv-
ants, both we,
and *he* also with
whom the cup is
found. 17 And
he said, God
forbid that I
should do so:
but the man in
whose hand the
cup is found, he
shall be my serv-
ant; and as for
you, get you up
in peace unto
your father.

18 Then Ju-
dah came near
unto him, and
said, O my lord,
let thy servant,
I pray thee,
speak a word in
my lord's ears,
and let not
thine anger burn
against thy serv-
ant: for thou
art even as
Pharaoh. 19 My
lord asked his
servants, say-
ing, Have ye a
father, or a
brother? 20 And
we said unto my
lord, We have a
father, an old
man, and a
child of his old
age, a little one;
and his brother
is dead, and he
alone is left of
his mother, and
his father lov-
eth him. 21 And
thou saidst unto
thy servants,
Bring him down
unto me, that I
may set mine
eyes upon him.
22 And we said
unto my lord,
The lad cannot
leave his father:
for *if* he should
leave his father,
his father would

נְדַבֵּר וּמַה־נִּצְטַדָּק [a]הָאֱלֹהִים מָצָא
found has God ?ourselves justify we can what in and ,speak we can

אֶת־עֲוֺן עֲבָדֶיךָ הִנֶּנּוּ עֲבָדִים לַאדֹנִי
,lord my to slaves [are] we behold ;servants thy of iniquity the

גַּם־אֲנַחְנוּ גַּם אֲשֶׁר־נִמְצָא הַגָּבִיעַ בְּיָדוֹ׃
.³hand ²whose ¹in ⁷cup ⁶the ⁵found ⁴was (who) he and we both

17 [b]וַיֹּאמֶר חָלִילָה לִּי מֵעֲשׂוֹת זֹאת הָאִישׁ
man the ;this doing from me from it be Far :said he And

אֲשֶׁר נִמְצָא הַגָּבִיעַ בְּיָדוֹ הוּא יִהְיֶה־
become shall he ,³hand ²whose ¹in ⁷cup ⁶the ⁵found ⁴was (who)

לִּי עָבֶד וְאַתֶּם עֲלוּ לְשָׁלוֹם אֶל־אֲבִיכֶם׃
.father your unto peace in up go ,ye and ;slave a me to

18 וַיִּגַּשׁ אֵלָיו יְהוּדָה וַיֹּאמֶר בִּי אֲדֹנִי
,lord my O :said and Judah him unto near came And

יְדַבֶּר־נָא עַבְדְּךָ דָבָר [c]בְּאָזְנֵי [c]אֲדֹנִי
,lord my of ears the in word a servant thy ,pray I ,speak let

וְאַל־יִחַר אַפְּךָ בְּעַבְדֶּךָ כִּי כָמוֹךָ
,thee like for ;servant thy against anger thy glow not let and

19 כְּפַרְעֹה׃ אֲדֹנִי שָׁאַל אֶת־עֲבָדָיו לֵאמֹר הֲיֵשׁ־
[there] Is :saying servants his asked lord My .Pharaoh like

20 לָכֶם אָב אוֹ־אָח׃ וַנֹּאמֶר אֶל־אֲדֹנִי יֶשׁ־
is [There] :lord my unto said we And ?brother a or father a you to

לָנוּ אָב זָקֵן וְיֶלֶד זְקֻנִים קָטָן
;¹young ⁵age ⁴old ³of ²child a and ,¹aged ²father a us to

וְאָחִיו מֵת וַיִּוָּתֵר הוּא לְבַדּוֹ [d]לְאִמּוֹ
,mother his to alone he left is and ,dead is brother his and

21 וְאָבִיו אֲהֵבוֹ׃ וַתֹּאמֶר אֶל־עֲבָדֶיךָ
:servants thy unto saidst thou And .him loves father his and

הוֹרִדֻהוּ אֵלָי וְאָשִׂימָה עֵינִי עָלָיו׃
.him upon eye my put me let and ,me unto down him Bring

22 וַנֹּאמֶר אֶל־אֲדֹנִי לֹא־יוּכַל הַנַּעַר לַעֲזֹב
leave to youth the able not Is :lord my unto said we And

אֶת־אָבִיו וְעָזַב אֶת־אָבִיו וָמֵת׃
.die would he (and) ,father his leave should he [if] and ;father his

we speak? or
how shall we
clear ourselves?
God hath found
out the iniquity
of thy servants:
behold, we are
my lord's bond-
men, both we,
and he also in
whose hand the
cup is found. 17
And he said,
God forbid that
I should do so:
the man in
whose hand the
cup is found,
he shall be my
bondman; but
as for you, get
you up in peace
unto your fath-
er.

18 Then Ju-
dah came near
unto him, and
said, Oh my
lord, let thy
servant, I pray
thee, speak a
word in my
lord's ears, and
let not thine
anger burn a-
gainst thy serv-
ant: for thou art
even as Pha-
raoh. 19 My lord
asked his serv-
ants, saying,
Have ye a fath-
er, or a brother?
20 And we said
unto my lord,
We have a fath-
er, an old man,
and a child of his
old age, a little
one; and his
brother is dead,
and he alone is
left of his moth-
er, and his fath-
er loveth him.
21 And thou
saidst unto thy
servants, Bring
him down unto
me, that I may
set mine eyes
upon him. 22
And we said un-
to my lord, The
lad cannot leave
his father: for if
he should leave
his father, his
father would

---

a Sm., G. add, *and*, ו.
b G., V. add, *Joseph;* S. adds, *to them.*
c G., S. have, *before thee;* T. has, *before my lord;* V., *in thine ears.*
d G. has, *to his father.*

die. 23 And thou saidst unto thy servants, Except your youngest brother come down with you, ye shall see my face no more.

24 And it came to pass when we came up unto thy servant my father, we told him the words of my lord. 25 And our father said, Go again, *and* buy us a little food. 26 And we said, We cannot go down: if our youngest brother be with us, then will we go down: for we may not see the man's face, except our youngest brother *be* with us. 27 And thy servant my father said unto us, Ye know that my wife bare me two *sons:* 28 And the one went out from me, and I said, Surely he is torn in pieces; and I saw him not since: 29 And if ye take this also from me, and mischief befall him, ye shall bring down my gray hairs with sorrow to the grave. 30 Now therefore when I come to thy servant my father, and the lad *be* not with us; seeing that his life is bound up in the lad's life; 31 It shall come to pass,

23 וַתֹּאמֶר אֶל־עֲבָדֶיךָ אִם־לֹא יֵרֵד
down come 1does 2not If : servants thy unto saidst thou And

אֲחִיכֶם הַקָּטֹן אִתְּכֶם לֹא תֹסִפוּן לִרְאוֹת
see to continue 2shall 1ye 3not ,you with 1youngest 2brother your

24 פָּנָי׃ וַיְהִי[a] כִּי עָלִינוּ אֶל־עַבְדְּךָ
servant thy unto up gone had we when ,pass to came it And .face my

25 אָבִי[b] וַנַּגֶּד־לוֹ אֵת דִּבְרֵי אֲדֹנִי׃ וַיֹּאמֶר[c]
said And .lord my of words the him to told we (and) father my

26 אָבִינוּ שֻׁבוּ שִׁבְרוּ־לָנוּ מְעַט־אֹכֶל׃ וַנֹּאמֶר[d]
: said we And .food little a us for buy ,Return : father our

לֹא נוּכַל לָרֶדֶת אִם־יֵשׁ[e] אָחִינוּ הַקָּטֹן
1youngest 2brother our is if ; down go to able 2are 1we 3Not

אִתָּנוּ וְיָרַדְנוּ כִּי־לֹא נוּכַל לִרְאוֹת
see to able 2are 1we 3not for ; down go will we (and) ,us with

פְּנֵי הָאִישׁ וְאָחִינוּ הַקָּטֹן אֵינֶנּוּ
being not (he) 1youngest 2brother our (and) ,man the of face the

27 אִתָּנוּ׃ וַיֹּאמֶר[f] עַבְדְּךָ אָבִי[g] אֵלֵינוּ אַתֶּם
You : us unto father my servant thy said And .us with

28 יְדַעְתֶּם כִּי שְׁנַיִם יָלְדָה־לִּי אִשְׁתִּי׃ וַיֵּצֵא הָאֶחָד
one out went And .wife my me to bore two that know

מֵאִתִּי וָאֹמַר[h] אַךְ טָרֹף טֹרָף
; pieces in torn is he surely Indeed : said I and ,me (with) from

29 וְלֹא רְאִיתִיו עַד־הֵנָּה׃ וּלְקַחְתֶּם גַּם־אֶת־זֶה
one this also take ye [if] And .now until seen 2have 1I 3not and

מֵעִם פָּנַי וְקָרָהוּ אָסוֹן[i] וְהוֹרַדְתֶּם
down bring will ye (and) ; harm him to happen and ,face my (with) from

30 אֶת־שֵׂיבָתִי בְּרָעָה שְׁאֹלָה׃ וְעַתָּה כְּבֹאִי[j]
coming my at now And .Sheol to misfortune in hair gray my

אֶל־עַבְדְּךָ אָבִי[k] וְהַנַּעַר אֵינֶנּוּ אִתָּנוּ
,us with being not (he) youth the (and) ,father my servant thy unto

31 וְנַפְשׁוֹ קְשׁוּרָה בְנַפְשׁוֹ׃[l] וְהָיָה[m]
be shall it (and) ; soul his to bound [being] soul his and

die. 23 And thou saidst unto thy servants, Except your youngest brother come down with you, ye shall see my face no more.

24 And it came to pass when we came up unto thy servant my father, we told him the words of my lord. 25 And our father said, Go again, buy us a little food. 26 And we said, We cannot go down: if our youngest brother be with us, then will we go down: for we may not see the man's face, except our youngest brother be with us. 27 And thy servant my father said unto us, Ye know that my wife bare me two sons: 28 and the one went out from me, and I said, Surely he is torn in pieces; and I have not seen him since: 29 and if ye take this one also from me, and mischief befall him, ye shall bring down my gray hairs with sorrow to the grave. 30 Now therefore when I come to thy servant my father, and the lad be not with us; seeing that his life is bound up in the lad's life; 31 it shall come to pass when he

a S., V. omit יהי.
b Sm., S., V. have, *our father;* G., *and our father.*
c G. adds, *to us;* S. *to thy servant.*
d S. adds, *to our father.*
e G., S., V. have, *if goes down.*
f S. adds, *to us.*
g Sm., G., S. have, *our father.*
h G., V. have, *and you said.*
i G., V. add, *in the way.*
j S. has, *when we come in.*
k S., V. have, *our father;* G. has, *and our father.*
l S., T. have, *like his soul,* כנפשו
m S., V. omit יהי.

when he seeth
that the lad *is*
not *with us*,
that he will die:
and thy serv-
ants shall bring
down the gray
hairs of thy
servant our
father with sor-
row to the
grave. 32 For
thy servant be-
came surety for
the lad unto my
father, saying,
If I bring him
not unto thee,
then I shall bear
the blame to my
father for ever.
33 Now there-
fore, I pray
thee, let thy
servant abide in-
stead of the lad
a bondman to
my lord; and let
the lad go up
with his breth-
ren. 34 For how
shall I go up to
my father, and
the lad *be* not
with me? lest
peradventure I
see the evil that
shall come on
my father.

כִּרְאוֹתוֹ כִּי־אֵין הַנַּעַר[a] וָמֵת וְהוֹרִידוּ
down bring will and ; die will he (and) ,youth the not is that seeing his at

עֲבָדֶיךָ אֶת־שֵׂיבַת עַבְדְּךָ אָבִינוּ בְּיָגוֹן
sorrow in father our servant thy of hair gray the servants thy

32 שְׁאֹלָה׃ כִּי עַבְדְּךָ עָרַב אֶת־הַנַּעַר מֵעִם
(with) from youth the for surety was servant thy For .Sheol to

אָבִי לֵאמֹר אִם־לֹא אֲבִיאֶנּוּ אֵלֶיךָ[b]
,thee unto him bring 2do 1I 3not If : saying ,father my

33 וְחָטָאתִי לְאָבִי כָּל־הַיָּמִים׃ וְעַתָּה
,now And .days the all father my against sinner a be shall I (and)

יֵשֶׁב־נָא עַבְדְּךָ תַּחַת הַנַּעַר עֶבֶד לַאדֹנִי
;lord my to slave a ,youth the of instead servant thy ,pray I ,remain let

34 וְהַנַּעַר יַעַל עִם־אֶחָיו׃ כִּי־אֵיךְ אֶעֱלֶה
up go I can how For .brethren his with up go let ,youth the and

אֶל־אָבִי וְהַנַּעַר אֵינֶנּוּ אִתִּי[c] פֶּן
lest ?me with being not (he) youth the (and) ,father my unto

אֶרְאֶה בָרָע אֲשֶׁר יִמְצָא אֶת־אָבִי׃
.father my find will which evil the upon look I

seeth that the
lad is not *with
us*, that he will
die: and thy serv-
ants shall bring
down the gray
hairs of thy serv-
ant our father
with sorrow to
the grave. 32
For thy servant
became surety
for the lad unto
my father, say-
ing, If I bring
him not unto
thee, then shall I
bear the blame
to my father for
ever. 33 Now
therefore, let
thy servant, I
pray thee, a-
bide instead of
the lad a bond-
man to my lord;
and let the lad
go up with his
brethren. 34 For
how shall I go
up to my father,
and the lad be
not with me?
lest I see the
evil that shall
come on my
father.

45

THEN Joseph
could not re-
frain himself
before all them
that stood by
him; and he
cried, Cause ev-
ery man to go
out from me.
And there stood
no man with
him, while Jo-
seph made him-
self known unto
his brethren. 2
And he wept a-
loud: and the E-
gyptians and the
house of Pha-
raoh heard. 3
And Joseph said
unto his breth-

1 וְלֹא־יָכֹל יוֹסֵף לְהִתְאַפֵּק לְכֹל
all to regard with himself control to Joseph able not was And

הַנִּצָּבִים עָלָיו וַיִּקְרָא הוֹצִיאוּ כָל־אִישׁ
man every out go to Cause : called he and ,him by standing those

מֵעָלָי וְלֹא־עָמַד אִישׁ אִתּוֹ[d]
him with man a stand not did and ; me (upon) from

2 בְּהִתְוַדַּע יוֹסֵף אֶל־אֶחָיו׃ וַיִּתֵּן[e]
gave he And .brethren his unto 1Joseph's 4known 3himself 2making in

אֶת־קֹלוֹ בִּבְכִי וַיִּשְׁמְעוּ[f] מִצְרַיִם וַיִּשְׁמַע[g]
heard and ,Egyptians the heard and ; weeping in voice his

3 בֵּית פַּרְעֹה׃ וַיֹּאמֶר יוֹסֵף אֶל־אֶחָיו
: brethren his unto Joseph said And .Pharaoh of house the

Then Joseph
could not re-
frain himself
before all them
that stood by
him; and he
cried, Cause ev-
ery man to go
out from me.
And there stood
no man with
him, while Jo-
seph made him-
self known unto
his brethren. 2
And he wept a-
loud: and the E-
gyptians heard,
and the house of
Pharaoh heard.
3 And Joseph
said unto his
brethren, I am

---

a Sm., G., S., V. have, *with us*, אתנו.
b G. adds, *and put him before thee;* cf. 43: 9.
c G. has, *us*, אתנו.
d G. has, *with Joseph*.
e S., T., V. have, *and he raised*.
f G. adds, *all*.
g G., S. have, *and it was heard*, וַיִּשָּׁמַע.

ren, I *am* Joseph; doth my father yet live? And his brethren could not answer him; for they were troubled at his presence. 4 And Joseph said unto his brethren, Come near to me, I pray you. And they came near. And he said, I *am* Joseph your brother, whom ye sold into Egypt.

5 Now therefore be not grieved, nor angry with yourselves, that ye sold me hither: for God did send me before you to preserve life. 6 For these two years *hath* the famine *been* in the land: and yet *there are* five years, in the which *there shall* neither *be* earing nor harvest. 7 And God sent me before you to preserve you a posterity in the earth, and to save your lives by a great deliverance. 8 So now *it was* not you *that* sent me hither, but God: and he hath made me a father to Pharaoh, and lord of all his house, and a ruler throughout all the land of Egypt. 9 Haste ye, and go up to my father, and say unto him, Thus saith thy son Joseph, God hath made me lord of

אֲנִי יוֹסֵף[a] הַעוֹד אָבִי חָי וְלֹא־יָכְלוּ
able not were And ?alive father my still [is] ,Joseph [am] I

אֶחָיו לַעֲנוֹת אֹתוֹ[b] כִּי נִבְהֲלוּ
dismayed were they for ,him answer to brethren his

4 מִפָּנָיו׃[c] וַיֹּאמֶר יוֹסֵף אֶל־אֶחָיו גְּשׁוּ־
,near Come :brethren his unto Joseph said And .him before from

נָא אֵלַי וַיִּגָּשׁוּ[d] וַיֹּאמֶר[e] אֲנִי יוֹסֵף
Joseph [am] I :said he and ; near came they and ;me unto ,now

אֲחִיכֶם אֲשֶׁר־מְכַרְתֶּם אֹתִי מִצְרָיְמָה׃
.Egypt into (me) sold you whom ,brother your

5 וְעַתָּה אַל־תֵּעָצְבוּ וְאַל־יִחַר בְּעֵינֵיכֶם
,eyes your in be anger not let and ,grieved be not do ,now And

כִּי־מְכַרְתֶּם אֹתִי הֵנָּה כִּי לְמִחְיָה
life of preservation the for for ; hither me sold you because

6 שְׁלָחַנִי אֱלֹהִים לִפְנֵיכֶם׃ כִּי־זֶה שְׁנָתַיִם
years two now For .you before God me sent

הָרָעָב בְּקֶרֶב הָאָרֶץ וְעוֹד חָמֵשׁ
five [are] still and ; land the of midst the in [been has] famine the

7 שָׁנִים אֲשֶׁר אֵין־חָרִישׁ וְקָצִיר׃ וַיִּשְׁלָחֵנִי
me sent And .harvest and plowing not is which [in] ,years

אֱלֹהִים לִפְנֵיכֶם לָשׂוּם לָכֶם שְׁאֵרִית בָּאָרֶץ[f]
; land the in remnant a you for put to ,you before God

8 וּלְהַחֲיוֹת לָכֶם לִפְלֵיטָה[g] גְּדֹלָה׃ וְעַתָּה
now And .[1]great [2]deliverance a (for) you for alive preserve to and

לֹא־אַתֶּם שְׁלַחְתֶּם אֹתִי הֵנָּה כִּי הָאֱלֹהִים
; God but ,hither me sent you not

וַיְשִׂימֵנִי לְאָב לְפַרְעֹה וּלְאָדוֹן לְכָל־
all to lord a for and ,Pharaoh to father a for me put has he and

9 בֵּיתוֹ וּמֹשֵׁל בְּכָל־אֶרֶץ מִצְרָיִם׃ מַהֲרוּ
Hasten .Egypt of land the all in ruler a and ,house his

וַעֲלוּ אֶל־אָבִי וַאֲמַרְתֶּם אֵלָיו כֹּה אָמַר
says Thus :him unto say and ,father my unto up go and

בִּנְךָ יוֹסֵף שָׂמַנִי אֱלֹהִים לְאָדוֹן לְכָל־
all to lord a for God me put Has :Joseph son thy

Joseph; doth my father yet live? And his brethren could not answer him; for they were troubled at his presence. 4 And Joseph said unto his brethren, Come near to me, I pray you. And they came near. And he said, I am Joseph your brother, whom ye sold into Egypt.

5 And now be not grieved, nor angry with yourselves, that ye sold me hither: for God did send me before you to preserve life. 6 For these two years hath the famine been in the land: and there are yet five years, in the which there shall be neither plowing nor harvest. 7 And God sent me before you to preserve you a remnant in the earth, and to save you alive by a great deliverance. 8 So now it was not you that sent me hither, but God: and he hath made me a father to Pharaoh, and lord of all his house, and ruler over all the land of Egypt. 9 Haste ye, and go up to my father, and say unto him, Thus saith thy son Joseph, God hath made me lord of all

a G. adds, *your brother, whom ye sold into Egypt;* cf. v. 4; S. adds, *your brother.*
b S., T. add, *a word.*
c G., V. omit.
d S. adds, *to him;* G. omits from beginning of verse.
e S. adds, *to them.*
f S. transposes to end of verse.
g G., S. omit ל.

all Egypt: come
down unto me,
tarry not: 10
and thou shalt
dwell in the
land of Goshen,
And thou shalt
be near unto
me, thou, and
thy children,
and thy child-
ren's children,
and thy flocks,
and thy herds,
and all that thou
hast: 11 And
there will I
nourish thee;
for yet *there
are* five years
of famine; lest
thou, and thy
household, and
all that thou
hast, come to
poverty. 12 And,
behold, your
eyes see, and
the eyes of my
brother Benja-
min, that *it is*
my mouth that
speaketh unto
you. 13 And ye
shall tell my
father of all my
glory in Egypt,
and of all that
ye have seen;
and ye shall
haste and bring
down my father
hither. 14 And
he fell upon his
brother Benja-
min's neck, and
wept; and Ben-
jamin wept up-
on his neck. 15
Moreover he
kissed all his
brethren, and
wept upon
them: and after
that his brethren
talked with him.
16 And the
fame thereof
was heard in
Pharaoh's
house, saying,
Joseph's breth-
ren are come:
and it pleased
Pharaoh well,
and his serv-
ants. 17 And
Pharaoh said
unto Joseph,
Say unto thy
brethren, This

10 מִצְרַיִם רְדָה אֵלַי אַל־תַּעֲמוֹד׃ וְיָשַׁבְתָּ
dwell shalt thou And .delay not do ,me unto down come ;Egypt

בְאֶרֶץ־גֹּשֶׁן [a] וְהָיִיתָ קָרוֹב אֵלַי אַתָּה
,thou ;me unto near be shalt thou and ,Goshen of land the in

וּבָנֶיךָ וּבְנֵי [b] בָנֶיךָ [b] [c] וְצֹאנְךָ וּבְקָרְךָ
,herds thy and ,flocks thy and ,sons thy of sons the and ,sons thy and

11 וְכָל־אֲשֶׁר־לָךְ [d]׃ וְכִלְכַּלְתִּי אֹתְךָ [e] שָׁם כִּי־עוֹד
[are] still for ,there thee nourish will I And .thee to [is] which all and

חָמֵשׁ שָׁנִים רָעָב פֶּן־תִּוָּרֵשׁ אַתָּה
thou ,property of deprived be thou lest ;famine ,years five

12 וּבֵיתְךָ וְכָל־אֲשֶׁר־לָךְ׃ [f] וְהִנֵּה עֵינֵיכֶם
eyes your behold And .thee to [is] which all and house thy and

רֹאוֹת וְעֵינֵי אָחִי בִנְיָמִין כִּי־פִי [g]
mouth my that ,Benjamin brother my of eyes the and ,seeing [are]

13 הַמְדַבֵּר [g] אֲלֵיכֶם׃ וְהִגַּדְתֶּם לְאָבִי אֶת־
father my to tell ye do And .you unto speaking one the [is]

כָּל־כְּבוֹדִי בְּמִצְרַיִם וְאֵת כָּל־אֲשֶׁר רְאִיתֶם
;seen have you which all and ,Egypt in honor my all

14 וּמִהַרְתֶּם וְהוֹרַדְתֶּם אֶת־אָבִי הֵנָּה׃ וַיִּפֹּל
fell he And .hither father my down bring and ,hasten and

עַל־צַוְּארֵי בִנְיָמִן־אָחִיו וַיֵּבְךְּ וּבִנְיָמִן
Benjamin and ,wept and brother his Benjamin of neck the upon

15 בָּכָה עַל־צַוָּארָיו׃ וַיְנַשֵּׁק לְכָל־אֶחָיו וַיֵּבְךְּ
wept and ,brethren his all (to) kissed he And .neck his upon wept

עֲלֵהֶם וְאַחֲרֵי כֵן דִּבְּרוּ אֶחָיו אִתּוֹ׃
.him with brethren his spoke afterwards and ;them upon

16 וְהַקֹּל נִשְׁמַע בֵּית פַּרְעֹה לֵאמֹר
:saying ,Pharaoh of house the in heard was voice the And

בָּאוּ אֲחֵי יוֹסֵף [h] וַיִּיטַב בְּעֵינֵי
of eyes the in good was it And .Joseph of brethren the come Have

17 פַּרְעֹה וּבְעֵינֵי עֲבָדָיו׃ וַיֹּאמֶר פַּרְעֹה
Pharaoh said And .servants his of eyes the in and ,Pharaoh

אֶל־יוֹסֵף אֱמֹר אֶל־אַחֶיךָ זֹאת עֲשׂוּ טַעֲנוּ
Load :do This ,brethren thy unto Say :Joseph unto

Egypt: come
down unto me,
tarry not: 10
and thou shalt
dwell in the land
of Goshen, and
thou shalt be
near unto me,
thou, and thy
children, and
thy children's
children, and
thy flocks, and
thy herds, and
all that thou
hast: 11 and
there will I
nourish thee;
for there are
yet five years of
famine; lest
thou come to
poverty, thou,
and thy house-
hold, and all
that thou hast.
12 And, behold,
your eyes see,
and the eyes of
my brother Ben-
jamin, that it is
my mouth that
speaketh unto
you. 13 And ye
shall tell my fa-
ther of all my
glory in Egypt,
and of all that
ye have seen;
and ye shall
haste and bring
down my father
hither. 14 And
he fell upon his
brother Benja-
min's neck, and
wept; and Ben-
jamin wept up-
on his neck. 15
And he kissed
all his brethren,
and wept upon
them: and after
that his breth-
ren talked with
him.
16 And the
fame thereof
was heard in
Pharaoh's
house, saying,
Joseph's breth-
ren are come:
and it pleased
Pharaoh well,
and his servants.
17 And Pharaoh
said unto Jo-
seph, Say unto
thy brethren,
This do ye; lade

a G. adds, *of Arabia*.
b S. has, *and the sons of thy house*.
c G., V. omit ו.
d G. adds, *there*.
e S. has, *you*, אתכם.
f G. omits ו.
g T. has, *that in your tongue I am speaking*.
h S. adds, *the word*.

do ye; lade your
beasts, and go,
get you unto
the land of Ca-
naan; 18 And
take your fa-
ther and your
households, and
come unto me:
and I will give
you the good of
the land of E-
gypt, and ye
shall eat the fat
of the land. 19
Now thou art
commanded,
this do ye; take
you wagons out
of the land of
Egypt for your
little ones, and
for your wives,
and bring your
father, and
come. 20 Also
regard not your
stuff; for the
good of all the
land of Egypt *is*
yours.

21 And the
children of
Israel did so:
and Joseph
gave them wag-
ons, according
to the com-
mandment of
Pharaoh, and
gave them pro-
vision for the
way. 22 To
all of them
he gave each
man changes of
raiment; but to
Benjamin he
gave three hun-
dred *pieces* of
silver, and five
changes of rai-
ment. 23 And
to his father he
sent after this
manner; ten
asses laden with
the good things

אֶת־בְּעִירְכֶם[a] וּלְכוּ־בֹאוּ[b] אַרְצָה כְּנָעַן׃
.Canaan of land the unto go ,depart and ,beasts your

18 וּקְחוּ אֶת־אֲבִיכֶם וְאֶת־בָּתֵּיכֶם וּבֹאוּ[c]
come and ,houses your and ,father your take And

אֵלָי וְאֶתְּנָה לָכֶם אֶת־טוּב[d] אֶרֶץ
of land the of good the you to give will I and ;me unto

19 מִצְרַיִם וְאִכְלוּ אֶת־חֵלֶב הָאָרֶץ׃ וְאַתָּה[e]
,thou And .land the of fat the ye eat and ; Egypt

צֻוֵּיתָה[f] זֹאת עֲשׂוּ[g] קְחוּ־לָכֶם[h] מֵאֶרֶץ
of land the from yourselves for take ; ye do this ;commanded art thou

מִצְרַיִם עֲגָלוֹת לְטַפְּכֶם וְלִנְשֵׁיכֶם
; wives your for and ,ones little your for ,wagons Egypt

20 וּנְשָׂאתֶם אֶת־אֲבִיכֶם וּבָאתֶם׃ וְעֵינְכֶם
,eye your And .come and father your up take and

אַל־תָּחֹס עַל־כְּלֵיכֶם כִּי־טוּב כָּל־אֶרֶץ
of land the all of good the for ,vessels your (upon) spare not it let

21 מִצְרַיִם לָכֶם הוּא׃ וַיַּעֲשׂוּ־כֵן בְּנֵי יִשְׂרָאֵל
,Israel of sons the so did And .[is] it you to ,Egypt

וַיִּתֵּן לָהֶם יוֹסֵף עֲגָלוֹת עַל־פִּי
of mouth the upon wagons Joseph them to gave and

פַרְעֹה[i] וַיִּתֵּן לָהֶם צֵדָה לַדָּרֶךְ׃
.way the for provision them to gave he and ; Pharaoh

22 לְכֻלָּם[j] נָתַן לָאִישׁ[k] חֲלִפוֹת שְׂמָלֹת
,clothing of changes ,one each to ,gave he them of all To

וּלְבִנְיָמִן נָתַן שְׁלֹשׁ מֵאוֹת כֶּסֶף
silver [of shekels] hundred three gave he Benjamin to and

23 וְחָמֵשׁ חֲלִפֹת שְׂמָלֹת׃ וּלְאָבִיו שָׁלַח כְּזֹאת
:this like sent he father his to And .clothing of changes five and

[l]עֲשָׂרָה חֲמֹרִים נֹשְׂאִים מִטּוּב[m]
of things good the from bearing asses ten

your beasts, and
go, get you unto
the land of Ca-
naan; 18 and
take your fa-
ther and your
households, and
come unto me:
and I will give
you the good of
the land of E-
gypt, and ye
shall eat the fat
of the land. 19
Now thou art
commanded,
this do ye; take
you wagons out
of the land of
Egypt for your
little ones, and
for your wives,
and bring your
father, and
come. 20 Also
regard not your
stuff; for the
good of all the
land of Egypt is
yours.

21 And the
sons of Is-
rael did so: and
Joseph gave
them wagons,
according to the
commandment
of Pharaoh, and
gave them provi-
sion for the way.
22 To all of
them he gave
each man
changes of rai-
ment; but to
Benjamin he
gave three hun-
dred pieces of
silver, and five
changes of rai-
ment. 23 And
to his father he
sent after this
manner; ten ass-
es laden with
the good things

---

a S. adds, *with grain.*

b G. omits באו.

c S. has, *and bring.*

d G., V. have, *all the good.*

e S. has, *and thou, behold, hast power, say to thy brethren.*

f G. has, *command,* צַוֵּה; T. has, *commanding.*

g G. omits; V. omits זאת־עשו.

h G. has, *to take for them*; V. omits לכם.

i G. adds, *the king.*

j S. joins with v. 21; G. has ולכלם.

k G., V. omit.

l G. S., V. add, *and,* ו.

m G. adds, *all,* reading מכל טוב.

of Egypt, and
ten she asses
laden with corn
and bread and
meat for his
father by the
way. 24 So he
sent his breth-
ren away, and
they departed:
and he said un-
to them, See
that ye fall not
out by the way.

25 And they
went up out of
Egypt, and
came into the
land of Canaan
unto Jacob their
father, 26 And
told him, say-
ing, Joseph *is*
yet alive, and he
is governor over
all the land of
Egypt. And Ja-
cob's heart faint-
ed, for he be-
lieved them not.
27 And they
told him all the
words of Jo-
seph, which he
had said unto
them: and when
he saw the
wagons which
Joseph had sent
to carry him, the
spirit of Jacob
their father re-
vived: 28 And
Israel said, *It is*
enough; Joseph
my son *is* yet a-
live: I will go
and see him be-
fore I die.

מִצְרַיִם וְעֶשֶׂר אֲתֹנֹת נֹשְׂאֹת בָּר[a] וָלֶחֶם[a b]
,bread and ,grain bearing she-asses ten and ,Egypt

24 וּמָזוֹן לְאָבִיו לַדָּרֶךְ׃ וַיְשַׁלַּח
away sent he And .way the for father his for victuals and

אֶת־אֶחָיו[c] וַיֵּלֵכוּ וַיֹּאמֶר אֲלֵהֶם
:them unto said he and ;went they and ,brethren his

25 אַל־תִּרְגְּזוּ בַּדָּרֶךְ׃ וַיַּעֲלוּ מִמִּצְרָיִם
,Egypt from up went they And .way the in quarrel not Do

וַיָּבֹאוּ אֶרֶץ כְּנַעַן אֶל־יַעֲקֹב אֲבִיהֶם׃
.father their Jacob unto ,Canaan of land the to in came and

26 וַיַּגִּדוּ לוֹ לֵאמֹר עוֹד[d] יוֹסֵף[e] חַי
,alive [is] Joseph Still :saying him to told they And

וְכִי־הוּא מֹשֵׁל בְּכָל־אֶרֶץ מִצְרָיִם וַיָּפָג
cold grew and ;Egypt of land the all in ruler [is] he (that) and

27 לִבּוֹ[f] כִּי לֹא־הֶאֱמִין לָהֶם׃ וַיְדַבְּרוּ
spoke they And .them (to) believe not did he for ,heart his

אֵלָיו אֵת כָּל־דִּבְרֵי יוֹסֵף[g] אֲשֶׁר דִּבֶּר
spoken had he which Joseph of words the all him unto

אֲלֵהֶם וַיַּרְא אֶת־הָעֲגָלוֹת אֲשֶׁר־שָׁלַח
sent had which wagons the saw he and ;them unto

יוֹסֵף לָשֵׂאת אֹתוֹ וַתְּחִי רוּחַ יַעֲקֹב
Jacob of spirit the revived and ;him bear to Joseph

28 אֲבִיהֶם׃ וַיֹּאמֶר יִשְׂרָאֵל[h] רַב[i] עוֹד־יוֹסֵף בְּנִי
[is] son my Joseph still ,Enough ;Israel said And .father their

חָי אֵלְכָה וְאֶרְאֶנּוּ[j] בְּטֶרֶם אָמוּת׃
.die I before him see and go will I ;alive

of Egypt, and
ten she-asses
laden with corn
and bread and
victual for his
father by the
way. 24 So he
sent his breth-
ren away, and
they departed:
and he said un-
to them, See
that ye fall not
out by the way.

25 And they
went up out of
Egypt, and
came into the
land of Canaan
unto Jacob their
father. 26 And
they told him,
saying, Joseph
is yet alive, and
he is ruler over
all the land of
Egypt. And his
heart fainted,
for he believed
them not. 27
And they told
him all the
words of Jo-
seph, which he
had said un-
to them: and
when he saw the
wagons which
Joseph had sent
to carry him,
the spirit of Ja-
cob their father
revived: 28 and
Israel said, It is
enough; Joseph
my son is yet a-
live: I will go
and see him be-
fore I die.

46

AND Israel
took his jour-
ney with all
that he had, and
came to Beer-
she ba, and offer-
ed sacrifices un-
to the God of

1 וַיִּסַּע יִשְׂרָאֵל[k] וְכָל־אֲשֶׁר־לוֹ וַיָּבֹא
came he and ,him to [was] which all and Israel departed And

בְּאֵרָה שָׁבַע וַיִּזְבַּח[l] זְבָחִים לֵאלֹהֵי
of God the to sacrifices sacrificed he and ;Sheba Beer to

And Israel
took his jour-
ney with all that
he had, and
came to Beer-
sheba, and offer-
ed sacrifices un-
to the God of

a G. omits.
b S. has, *and wine.*
c S. has, *them.*
d G., V. omit; G. adds, *thy son.*
e V. adds, *thy son.*
f G. has, *the heart of Jacob.*
g S. puts after דבר.
h S., V. omit.
i G., S., V., T. add, *to me;* T. also adds, *joy.*
j S. omits ו.
k G., S. have, *he and all.*
l G., V. add, *there.*

his father I-
saac. 2 And
God spake un-
to Israel in
the visions
of the night,
and said, Ja-
cob, Jacob. And
he said, Here *am*
I. 3 And he
said, I *am* God,
the God of thy
father: fear not
to go down in-
to Egypt; for I
will there make
of thee a great
nation: 4 I will
go down with
thee into Egypt;
and I will also
surely bring thee
up *again*: and
Joseph shall put
his hand upon
thine eyes. 5
And Jacob rose
up from Beer-
sheba: and the
sons of Israel
carried Jacob
their father, and
their little ones,
and their wives,
in the wagons
which Pharaoh
had sent to
carry him. 6
And they took
their cattle, and
their goods,
which they had
gotten in the
land of Canaan,
and came into
Egypt, Jacob,
and all his seed
with him: 7
His sons, and
his sons' sons
with him, his
daughters, and
his sons' daugh-
ters, and all his
seed brought he
with him into
Egypt.

2 אָבִיו יִצְחָק׃ וַיֹּאמֶר אֱלֹהִים לְיִשְׂרָאֵל בְּמַרְאֹת
of visions in Israel to God said And .Isaac father his

הַלַּיְלָה וַיֹּאמֶר יַעֲקֹב יַעֲקֹב וַיֹּאמֶר הִנֵּנִי׃
.me Behold :said he and ,Jacob ,Jacob :said he and ,night the

3 וַיֹּאמֶר[a] אָנֹכִי הָאֵל[b] אֱלֹהֵי אָבִיךָ אַל־
not do ;father thy of God the ,El [am] I :said he And

תִּירָא מֵרְדָה מִצְרַיְמָה כִּי־לְגוֹי גָּדוֹל
[1]great [2]nation a (to) for ;Egypt to down going from fear

4 אֲשִׂימְךָ שָׁם׃ [c]אָנֹכִי אֵרֵד עִמְּךָ מִצְרַיְמָה[d]
,Egypt to thee with down go will I .there thee make will I

וְאָנֹכִי אַעַלְךָ גַם־עָלֹה[e] וְיוֹסֵף יָשִׁית
put shall Joseph and ;surely also up thee bring will I and

5 יָדוֹ עַל־עֵינֶיךָ׃ וַיָּקָם יַעֲקֹב מִבְּאֵר
Beer from Jacob arose And .eyes thine upon hand his

שָׁבַע וַיִּשְׂאוּ בְנֵי־יִשְׂרָאֵל אֶת־יַעֲקֹב אֲבִיהֶם
,father their Jacob Israel of sons the carried and ;Sheba

וְאֶת־טַפָּם וְאֶת־נְשֵׁיהֶם בָּעֲגָלוֹת אֲשֶׁר־
which wagons the in ,wives their and ,ones little their and

6 שָׁלַח פַּרְעֹה[f] לָשֵׂאת אֹתוֹ׃ וַיִּקְחוּ[g]
took they And .him carry to Pharaoh sent had

אֶת־מִקְנֵיהֶם[g] וְאֶת[h]־רְכוּשָׁם אֲשֶׁר רָכְשׁוּ
acquired had they which ,property movable their and ,cattle their

בְּאֶרֶץ כְּנַעַן וַיָּבֹאוּ מִצְרַיְמָה יַעֲקֹב
Jacob ,Egypt to in came they and ;Canaan of land the in

7 וְכָל־זַרְעוֹ אִתּוֹ׃ בָּנָיו וּבְנֵי בָנָיו
sons his of sons the and sons His .him with seed his all and

אִתּוֹ בְּנֹתָיו וּבְנוֹת בָּנָיו[i] וְכָל־
all and ,sons his of daughters the and daughters his ,him with

זַרְעוֹ הֵבִיא אִתּוֹ[j] מִצְרָיְמָה׃
.Egypt to him with brought he seed his

his father I-
saac. 2 And
God spake un-
to Israel in
the visions
of the night,
and said, Jacob,
Jacob. And he
said, Here am I.
3 And he said, I
am God, the
God of thy fa-
ther: fear not to
go down into
Egypt; for I
will there make
of thee a great
nation; 4 I will
go down with
thee into Egypt;
and I will also
surely bring thee
up again: and
Joseph shall
put his hand
upon thine eyes.
5 And Jacob
rose up from
Beer-sheba: and
the sons of Is-
rael carried Ja-
cob their father,
and their little
ones, and their
wives, in the
wagons which
Pharaoh had
sent to carry
him. 6 And they
took their cattle,
and their goods,
which they had
gotten in the
land of Canaan,
and came into
Egypt, Jacob,
and all his seed
with him: 7 his
sons, and his
sons' sons with
him, his daugh-
ters, and his
sons' daughters,
and all his seed
brought he with
him into Egypt.

8 And these
are the names
of the children
of Israel, which
came into E-

8 וְאֵלֶּה שְׁמוֹת בְּנֵי־יִשְׂרָאֵל הַבָּאִים
in coming those ,Israel of sons the of names the [were] these And

8 And these
are the names of
the children of
Israel, which
came into E-

---

a S., V. add, *to him.*
b G. omits.
c G. adds, *and*, ו.
d S. omits; V. has, *thither.*
e G. has, *at the end;* S. omits.
f G. has, *Joseph;* cf. 45: 27.
g V. omits.
h G., V. add, *all.*
i G. adds, *with him*, אתו.
j G. omits.

gypt, Jacob and
his sons: Reu-
ben, Jacob's
firstborn. 9 And
the sons of Reu-
ben; Hanoch,
and Phallu, and
Hezron, and
Carmi.
10 And the
sons of Simeon;
Jemuel, and
Jamin, and O-
had, and Ja-
chin, and Zo-
har, and Shaul
the son of a
Canaanitish
woman.
11 And the
sons of Levi;
Gershon, Ko-
hath, and Me-
rari.
12 And the
sons of Judah;
Er, and Onan,
and Shelah, and
Pharez, and
Zarah: but Er
and Onan died
in the land of
Canaan. And
the sons of Pha-
rez were Hez-
ron and Hamul.
13 And the
sons of Issachar;
Tola, and Phu-
vah, and Job,
and Shimron.
14 And the
sons of Zebulun;
Sered, and E-
lon, and Jahleel.
15 These *be*
the sons of
Leah, which she
bare unto Jacob
in Padan-aram,
with his daugh-
ter Dinah: all
the souls of his
sons and his
daughters *were*
thirty and three.
16 And the
sons of Gad;
Ziphion, and
Haggi, Shuni,
and Ezbon, Eri,
and Arodi, and
Areli.
17 And the
sons of Asher;
Jimnah, and
Ishuah, and I-
sui, and Beriah,
and Serah their
sister: and the
sons of Beriah;
Heber, and

מִצְרַיְמָה יַעֲקֹב וּבָנָיו בְּכֹר יַעֲקֹב
,Jacob of firstborn the ;sons his and Jacob ;Egypt to

9 רְאוּבֵן׃ [a]וּבְנֵי רְאוּבֵן חֲנוֹךְ וּפַלּוּא
,Pallu and ,Hanoch ;Reuben of sons the And .Reuben

10 וְחֶצְרֹן וְכַרְמִי׃ וּבְנֵי שִׁמְעוֹן יְמוּאֵל
,Jemuel ;Simeon of sons the And .Carmi and ,Hezron and

וְיָמִין וְאֹהַד וְיָכִין וְצֹחַר וְשָׁאוּל בֶּן־
of son the Shaul and ,Zohar and ,Jachin ,Ohad and ,Jamin and

11 הַכְּנַעֲנִית׃ וּבְנֵי לֵוִי גֵּרְשׁוֹן [b]קְהָת
,Kohath ,Gershon ;Levi of sons the And .Canaanitess a

12 וּמְרָרִי׃ וּבְנֵי יְהוּדָה עֵר וְאוֹנָן וְשֵׁלָה
,Shelah and ,Onan and ,Er ;Judah of sons the And .Merari and

וָפֶרֶץ וָזָרַח וַיָּמָת עֵר וְאוֹנָן בְּאֶרֶץ
of land the in Onan and Er died and ;Zerah and ,Perez and

כְּנַעַן וַיִּהְיוּ בְנֵי־פֶרֶץ חֶצְרֹן וְחָמוּל׃
.Hamul and ,Hezron ;Perez of sons the were and ;Canaan

13 וּבְנֵי יִשָּׂשכָר תּוֹלָע וּפֻוָּה וְיוֹב
,Iob and ,Puvah and ,Tola ;Issachar of sons the And

14 וְשִׁמְרֹן׃ וּבְנֵי זְבֻלוּן סֶרֶד וְאֵלוֹן
,Elon and ,Sered ;Zebulun of sons the And .Shimron and

15 וְיַחְלְאֵל׃ אֵלֶּה בְּנֵי לֵאָה אֲשֶׁר יָלְדָה
bore she whom ,Leah of sons the [were] These .Jahleel and

לְיַעֲקֹב בְּפַדַּן אֲרָם וְאֵת דִּינָה בִתּוֹ
;daughter his Dinah and ,Aram Paddan in Jacob to

כָּל־נֶפֶשׁ בָּנָיו וּבְנוֹתָיו שְׁלֹשִׁים וְשָׁלֹשׁ׃
.three and thirty [were] daughters his and sons his of souls the all

16 וּבְנֵי גָד צִפְיוֹן וְחַגִּי [c]שׁוּנִי וְאֶצְבֹּן
,Ezbon and ,Shuni ,Haggi and ,Ziphyon ;Gad of sons the And

17 [c]עֵרִי וַאֲרוֹדִי וְאַרְאֵלִי׃ וּבְנֵי אָשֵׁר
;Asher of sons the And .Areli and ,Arodi and ,Eri

יִמְנָה וְיִשְׁוָה וְיִשְׁוִי וּבְרִיעָה וְשֶׂרַח
Serah and ,Beriah and ,Jishvi and ,Jishvah and ,Jimnah

אֲחֹתָם וּבְנֵי בְרִיעָה חֶבֶר וּמַלְכִּיאֵל׃
.Malchiel and ,Heber ;Beriah of sons the and ;sister their

gypt, Jacob and
his sons: Reu-
ben, Jacob's
firstborn. 9 And
the sons of Reu-
ben; Hanoch,
and Pallu, and
Hezron, and
Carmi.
10 And the
sons of Simeon;
Jemuel, and Ja-
min, and Ohad,
and Jachin, and
Zohar, and
Shaul the son
of a Canaanitish
woman.
11 And the
sons of Levi;
Gershon, Ko-
hath, and Me-
rari.
12 And the
sons of Judah;
Er, and Onan,
and Shelah, and
Perez, and Ze-
rah: but Er and
Onan died in
the land of Ca-
naan. And the
sons of Perez
were Hezron
and Hamul.
13 And the
sons of Issachar;
Tola, and
Puvah, and Iob,
and Shimron.
14 And the
sons of Zebulun;
Sered, and E-
lon, and Jahleel.
15 These are the
sons of Leah,
which she bare
unto Jacob in
Paddan-aram,
with his daugh-
ter Dinah: all
the souls of his
sons and his
daughters were
thirty and three.
16 And the
sons of Gad;
Ziphion, and
Haggi, Shuni,
and Ezbon, Eri,
and Arodi, and
Areli.
17 And the
sons of Asher;
Imnah, and Ish-
vah, and Ishvi,
and Beriah, and
Serah their sis-
ter; and the sons
of Beriah; He-
ber, and Mal-

---

a S., V. omit ו.
b S., V. add, *and*, ו.
c G., S., V. add, *and*, ו.

Malchiel. 18
These *are* the
sons of Zilpah,
whom Laban
gave to Leah
his daughter;
and these she
bare unto Jacob,
even sixteen
souls. 19 The
sons of Rachel
Jacob's wife;
Joseph, and
Benjamin.
20 And unto
Joseph in the
land of Egypt
were born Manasseh and E-
phraim, which
Asenath the
daughter of Po-
tipherah priest
of On bare un-
to him.
21 And the
sons of Benja-
min *were* Be-
lah, and Be-
cher, and Ash-
bel, Gera, and
Naaman, Ehi,
and Rosh, Mup-
pim, and Hup-
pim, and Ard.
22 These *are* the
sons of Rachel,
which were born
to Jacob: all the
souls *were* four-
teen. 23 And the
sons of Dan;
Hushim.
24 And the
sons of Naph-
tali; Jahzeel,
and Guni, and
Jezer, and Shil-
lem. 25 These
are the sons of
Bilhah, which
Laban gave un-
to Rachel his
daughter, and
she bare these
unto Jacob: all
the souls *were*
seven. 26 All
the souls that
came with Jacob
into Egypt,
which came out
of his loins, be-
sides Jacob's

18 אֵלֶּה בְּנֵי זִלְפָּה אֲשֶׁר־נָתַן לָבָן לְלֵאָה
Leah to Laban gave whom ,Zilpah of sons the [were] These

בִתּוֹ וַתֵּלֶד אֶת־אֵלֶּה לְיַעֲקֹב שֵׁשׁ
[and] six ,Jacob to these bore she and ;daughter his

19 עֶשְׂרֵה נָפֶשׁ׃ [a]בְּנֵי רָחֵל אֵשֶׁת יַעֲקֹב יוֹסֵף
,Joseph ;Jacob of wife the Rachel of sons The .souls ten

20 וּבִנְיָמִן׃ [b]וַיִּוָּלֵד [b]לְיוֹסֵף בְּאֶרֶץ מִצְרַיִם
,Egypt of land the in Joseph to born were And .Benjamin and

אֲשֶׁר יָלְדָה־לּוֹ אָסְנַת בַּת־פּוֹטִי פֶרַע
Phera Poti of daughter the Asenath him to bore whom

21 כֹּהֵן אֹן אֶת־מְנַשֶּׁה וְאֶת־אֶפְרָיִם׃[c] וּבְנֵי
of sons the And .Ephraim and Manasseh ,On of priest

בִנְיָמִן בֶּלַע וָבֶכֶר וְאַשְׁבֵּל[d] [e]גֵּרָא וְנַעֲמָן
,Naaman and ,Gera ,Ashbel and ,Becher and ,Bela ;Benjamin

22 [f]אֵחִי וָרֹאשׁ [f]מֻפִּים וְחֻפִּים וָאָרְדְּ׃[g] אֵלֶּה
These .Ard and ,Huppim and ,Muppim ,Rosh and ,Ehi

בְּנֵי רָחֵל אֲשֶׁר יֻלַּד[h] לְיַעֲקֹב כָּל־נֶפֶשׁ
,souls the all ;Jacob to born were which ,Rachel of sons the [were]

23
24 אַרְבָּעָה[i] עָשָׂר[i]׃ וּבְנֵי־דָן חֻשִׁים׃ וּבְנֵי
of sons the And .Hushim ,Dan of sons the And .ten [and] four

25 נַפְתָּלִי יַחְצְאֵל וְגוּנִי וְיֵצֶר וְשִׁלֵּם׃ אֵלֶּה
These .Shillem and ,Jezer and ,Guni and ,Jahzeel ;Naphtali

בְּנֵי בִלְהָה אֲשֶׁר־נָתַן לָבָן לְרָחֵל
Rachel to Laban gave whom ,Bilhah of sons the [were]

בִּתּוֹ וַתֵּלֶד אֶת־אֵלֶּה לְיַעֲקֹב כָּל־נֶפֶשׁ
souls the all ,Jacob to these bore she and ;daughter his

26 שִׁבְעָה׃ כָּל־הַנֶּפֶשׁ הַבָּאָה לְיַעֲקֹב[j] מִצְרַיְמָה
,Egypt to Jacob to in coming souls the All .seven

יֹצְאֵי יְרֵכוֹ מִלְּבַד נְשֵׁי בְנֵי־יַעֲקֹב
,Jacob of sons the of wives the besides ,loins his of out going those

chiel. 18 These
are the sons of
Zilpah, which
Laban gave to
Leah his daugh-
ter, and these
she bare unto
Jacob, even six-
teen souls. 19
The sons of Ra-
chel Jacob's
wife; Joseph
and Benjamin,
20 And unto
Joseph in the
land of Egypt
were born Ma-
nasseh and E-
phraim, which
Asenath the
daughter of
Potiphera priest
of On bare unto
him.
21 And the
sons of Benja-
min; Bela, and
Becher, and
Ashbel, Gera,
and Naaman,
Ehi, and Rosh,
Muppim, and
Huppim, and
Ard. 22 These
are the sons of
Rachel, which
were born to
Jacob: all the
souls were four-
teen. 23 And the
sons of Dan;
Hushim.
24 And the
sons of Naph-
tali; Jahzeel,
and Guni, and
Jezer, and Shil-
lem. 25 These
are the sons of
Bilhah, which
Laban gave un-
to Rachel his
daughter, and
these she bare
unto Jacob: all
the souls were
seven. 26 All the
souls that came
with Jacob into
Egypt, which
came out of his
loins, besides
Jacob's sons'

---

a G., S. add, *and*, ו.

b V. adds, *sons;* G. has, *and were the sons of Joseph.*

c G. adds, *and were the sons of Manasseh, whom the Syrian concubine bore to him, Machir; and Machir begat Galaad. And the sons of Ephraim the brother of Manasseh, Sutalam, and Taam; and the sons of Sutalam, Edem.* Cf. Num. 26: 35, 36.

d G. adds, *and the sons of Bela were.*

e S., V. add, *and*, ו.

f G., S., V. add, *and*, ו.

g G. has, *and Gera begat Arad.*

h Sm., G., S., V. have, *she bore*, יָלְדָה; T. has pl. יְלִדוּ.

i G. has, *eighteen.*

j G., S., V. have, *with Jacob.*

sons' wives, all
the souls *were*
threescore and
six; 27 And the
sons of Joseph,
which were
born him in
Egypt, *were* two
souls: all the
souls of the
house of Jacob,
which came in-
to Egypt, *were*
threescore and
ten.

28 And he
sent Judah be-
fore him unto
Joseph, to direct
his face unto
Goshen; and
they came into
the land of Go-
shen. 29 And
Joseph made
ready his char-
iot, and went up
to meet Israel
his father, to
Goshen, and
presented him-
self unto him;
and he fell on
his neck, and
wept on his neck
a good while. 30
And Israel said
unto Joseph,
Now let me die,
since I have
seen thy face,
because thou
art yet alive.
31 And Joseph
said unto his
brethren, and
unto his father's
house, I will go
up, and shew
Pharaoh, and
say unto him,
My brethren,
and my father's
house, which
were in the land
of Canaan, are
come unto me;
32 And the men
are shepherds,
for their trade
hath been to
feed cattle; and
they have
brought their
flocks, and their
herds, and all

כָּל־נֶפֶשׁ שִׁשִּׁים וָשֵׁשׁ׃ וּבְנֵי יוֹסֵף 27
Joseph of sons the And .six and sixty [were] souls the all

אֲשֶׁר־יֻלַּד־לוֹ[a] בְמִצְרַיִם נֶפֶשׁ שְׁנָיִם[b] כָּל־הַנֶּפֶשׁ
souls the all ;¹two ²souls ,Egypt in him to born were which

לְבֵית־יַעֲקֹב הַבָּאָה מִצְרַיְמָה שִׁבְעִים׃[c]
.seventy [were] ,Egypt to in coming ,Jacob of house the to

וְאֶת־יְהוּדָה שָׁלַח לְפָנָיו אֶל־יוֹסֵף לְהוֹרֹת[d] 28
information give to ,Joseph unto him before sent he Judah And

לְפָנָיו[d] גֹּשְׁנָה[e] וַיָּבֹאוּ[f] אַרְצָה גֹּשֶׁן׃
.Goshen of land the to in came they and ;Goshen to him before

וַיֶּאְסֹר יוֹסֵף מֶרְכַּבְתּוֹ וַיַּעַל לִקְרַאת־ 29
meet to up went and ,chariot his Joseph prepared And

יִשְׂרָאֵל אָבִיו גֹּשְׁנָה וַיֵּרָא אֵלָיו
,him unto appeared he and ;Goshen to ,father his Israel

וַיִּפֹּל עַל־צַוָּארָיו וַיֵּבְךְּ[g] עַל־צַוָּארָיו עוֹד[g]׃
.repeatedly neck his upon wept and ,neck his upon fell and

וַיֹּאמֶר יִשְׂרָאֵל אֶל־יוֹסֵף אָמוּתָה הַפָּעַם 30
,time this die me Let ;Joseph unto Israel said And

אַחֲרֵי רְאוֹתִי אֶת־פָּנֶיךָ[h] כִּי עוֹדְךָ חָי׃
.alive [art] thou still because ,face thy seeing my after

וַיֹּאמֶר יוֹסֵף אֶל־אֶחָיו וְאֶל־בֵּית[i] 31
of house the unto and ,brethren his unto Joseph said And

אָבִיו[i] אֶעֱלֶה וְאַגִּידָה לְפַרְעֹה
,Pharaoh to known make and up go will I :father his

וְאֹמְרָה אֵלָיו אַחַי וּבֵית־אָבִי
,father my of house the and brethren My :him unto say will I and

אֲשֶׁר בְּאֶרֶץ־כְּנַעַן בָּאוּ אֵלָי׃
.me unto in come have Canaan of land the in [were] who

וְהָאֲנָשִׁים רֹעֵי צֹאן כִּי־אַנְשֵׁי מִקְנֶה 32
cattle of men for ,flocks of shepherds [are] men the And

הָיוּ וְצֹאנָם וּבְקָרָם וְכָל־אֲשֶׁר
[is] which all and ,herds their and ,flocks their and ;been have they

wives, all the
souls were
threescore and
six; 27 and the
sons of Joseph,
which were born
to him in Egypt,
were two souls:
all the souls of
the house of Ja-
cob, which came
into Egypt,
were threescore
and ten.

28 And he sent
Judah before
him unto Jo-
seph, to shew
the way before
him unto Go-
shen; and they
came into the
land of Goshen.
29 And Joseph
made ready his
chariot, and
went up to meet
Israel his father,
to Goshen; and
he presented
himself unto
him, and fell on
his neck, and
wept on his
neck a good
while. 30 And
Israel said unto
Joseph, Now let
me die, since I
have seen thy
face, that thou
art yet alive. 31
And Joseph said
unto his breth-
ren, and unto
his father's
house, I will go
up, and tell Pha-
raoh, and will
say unto him,
My brethren,
and my father's
house, which
were in the land
of Canaan, are
come unto me;
32 and the men
are shepherds,
for they have
been keepers of
cattle; and they
have brought
their flocks, and
their herds, and
all that they

---

a For ילד Sm., G., S., V., T. have pl. יָלְדוּ.

b G. has, *nine.*

c G. has, *seventy-five.*

d G. has, *to meet him;* V, *to announce to him and meet;* S. *to appear before him.*

e G. has, *to Hieropolis.*

f G. omits.

g G. has, *with a great weeping.*

h S. adds, *my son.*

i G. omits.

that they have.
33 And it shall
come to pass,
when Pharaoh
shall call you,
and shall say,
What *is* your oc-
cupation? 34
That ye shall
say, Thy serv-
ants' trade hath
been about cat-
tle from our
youth even un-
til now, both we,
and also our fa-
thers: that ye
may dwell in the
land of Goshen;
for every shep-
herd *is* an a-
bomination un-
to the Egyp-
tians.

לָהֶם הֵבִיאוּ׃ וְהָיָה[a] כִּי־יִקְרָא 33
them to .in brought have they ,pass to come shall it And when calls

לָכֶם פַּרְעֹה וְאָמַר[b] מַה־מַּעֲשֵׂיכֶם׃
you (to) Pharaoh : says and ?work your [is] What

וַאֲמַרְתֶּם[c] אַנְשֵׁי מִקְנֶה הָיוּ עֲבָדֶיךָ 34
: say shall ye (and) of Men cattle been have servants thy

מִנְּעוּרֵינוּ וְעַד־עַתָּה[d] גַּם־אֲנַחְנוּ גַּם־אֲבֹתֵינוּ
youth our from ,now until (and) we both ; fathers our and

בַּעֲבוּר תֵּשְׁבוּ בְּאֶרֶץ גֹּשֶׁן כִּי־
that order in dwell may ye of land the in ,Goshen for

תוֹעֲבַת מִצְרַיִם כָּל־רֹעֵה צֹאן׃
of abomination the Egypt of shepherd every [is] .flocks

have. 33 And it
shall come to
pass, when Pha-
raoh shall call
you, and shall
say, What is
your occupa-
tion? 34 that ye
shall say, Thy
servants have
been keepers of
cattle from our
youth even until
now, both we,
and our fathers:
that ye may
dwell in the
land of Goshen;
for every shep-
herd is an a-
bomination un-
to the Egyp-
tians.

47

THEN Joseph
came and told
Pharaoh, and
said, My father
and my breth-
ren, and their
flocks, and their
herds, and all
that they have,
are come out of
the land of Ca-
naan; and, be-
hold, they *are*
in the land of
Goshen. 2 And
he took some of
his brethren,
even five men,
and presented
them unto Pha-
raoh. 3 And
Pharaoh said un-
to his brethren,
What *is* your
occupation?
And they said
unto Pharaoh,
Thy servants
are shepherds,
both we, *and* al-
so our fathers. 4
They said more-
over unto Pha-
raoh, For to so-
journ in the land
are we come;
for thy servants

וַיָּבֹא יוֹסֵף וַיַּגֵּד לְפַרְעֹה וַיֹּאמֶר[e] 1
in came And ,Joseph known made and ,Pharaoh to :said and

אָבִי וְאַחַי וְצֹאנָם וּבְקָרָם וְכָל־
father My ,brethren my and flocks their and ,herds their and all and

אֲשֶׁר לָהֶם בָּאוּ מֵאֶרֶץ כְּנָעַן
[is] which ,them to in come have of land the from ,Canaan

וְהִנָּם בְּאֶרֶץ גֹּשֶׁן׃ וּמִקְצֵה[f] 2
[are] they behold and of land the in .Goshen of body the from And

אֶחָיו לָקַח[g] חֲמִשָּׁה אֲנָשִׁים וַיַּצִּגֵם לִפְנֵי
brethren his took he five ,men them set and before

פַרְעֹה׃ וַיֹּאמֶר פַּרְעֹה אֶל־אֶחָיו[h] מַה־ 3
.Pharaoh said And Pharaoh ; brethren his unto [is] What

מַּעֲשֵׂיכֶם וַיֹּאמְרוּ אֶל־פַּרְעֹה רֹעֵה[i] צֹאן
?work your said they And ; Pharaoh unto of Shepherds flocks

עֲבָדֶיךָ גַּם־אֲנַחְנוּ גַּם־אֲבוֹתֵינוּ[j]׃ וַיֹּאמְרוּ 4
,servants thy [are] we both .fathers our and said they And

אֶל־פַּרְעֹה לָגוּר בָּאָרֶץ בָּאנוּ כִּי־
; Pharaoh unto sojourn To land the in ; come have we because

Then Joseph
went in and told
Pharaoh, and
said, My father
and my breth-
ren, and their
flocks, and their
herds, and all
that they have,
are come out of
the land of Ca-
naan; and, be-
hold, they are in
the land of
Goshen. 2 And
from among his
brethren he took
five men, and
presented them
unto Pharaoh. 3
And Pharaoh
said unto his
brethren, What
is your occupa-
tion? And they
said unto Pha-
raoh, Thy serv-
ants are shep-
herds, both we,
and our fathers.
4 And they said
unto Pharaoh,
To sojourn in
the land are we
come; for there

---

a G., S., V. omit היה.
b G., S. add, *to you.*
c S. adds, *to him.*
d G., T., V. omit ו.
e S. adds, *to him.*
f G., S. have, *from.*
g Sm. adds, *with him.*
h Sm., G., S. have, *the brethren of Joseph.*
i Sm., G., S., T. have pl.
j S. adds, *from our youth.*

have no pasture
for their flocks;
for the famine *is*
sore in the land
of Canaan: now
therefore, we
pray thee, let
thy servants
dwell in the land
of Goshen. 5
And Pharaoh
spake unto Jo-
seph, saying,
Thy father and
thy brethren are
come unto thee:
6 The land of
Egypt *is* before
thee; in the
best of the land
make thy father
and brethren to
dwell; in the
land of Goshen
let them dwell:
and if thou
knowest *any*
men of activity
among them,
then make them
rulers over my
cattle. 7 And
Joseph brought
in Jacob his fa-
ther and set him
before Pharaoh:
and Jacob bless-
ed Pharaoh. 8
And Pharaoh
said unto Jacob,
How old *art*
thou?

אֵ֣ין מִרְעֶ֗ה לַצֹּאן֙ אֲשֶׁ֣ר לַעֲבָדֶ֔יךָ
; servants thy to [are] which flocks the for pasturage not is [there]

כִּֽי־כָבֵ֥ד הָרָעָ֖ב בְּאֶ֣רֶץ כְּנָ֑עַן וְעַתָּ֛ה
now and ; Canaan of land the in famine the heavy is for

5 [a]יֵֽשְׁבוּ־נָ֥א עֲבָדֶ֖יךָ[b] בְּאֶ֣רֶץ גֹּ֑שֶׁן׃ וַיֹּ֣אמֶר
said And .Goshen of land the in servants thy ,pray ,dwell let

פַּרְעֹ֔ה אֶל־יוֹסֵ֖ף לֵאמֹ֑ר[c d] אָבִ֥יךָ וְאַחֶ֖יךָ
brethren thy and father Thy : saying Joseph unto Pharaoh

6 בָּ֥אוּ אֵלֶֽיךָ׃ אֶ֤רֶץ מִצְרַ֙יִם֙ לְפָנֶ֣יךָ הִ֔וא
,it [is] thee before ,Egypt of land The .thee unto in come have

בְּמֵיטַ֣ב הָאָ֔רֶץ הוֹשֵׁ֥ב אֶת־אָבִ֖יךָ וְאֶת־
and father thy dwell to cause land the of best the in

אַחֶ֑יךָ יֵשְׁבוּ֙ בְּאֶ֣רֶץ גֹּ֔שֶׁן וְאִם־
if and ; Goshen of land the in dwell them let ; brethren thy

יָדַ֗עְתָּ וְיֶשׁ־בָּם֙[e] אַנְשֵׁי־חַ֔יִל
,ability of men them among are [there] and knowest thou

וְשַׂמְתָּ֛ם שָׂרֵ֥י מִקְנֶ֖ה עַל־אֲשֶׁר־לִֽי׃[f]
.me to [is] what over cattle of chiefs [as] them put (and)

7 וַיָּבֵ֤א יוֹסֵף֙ אֶת־יַעֲקֹ֣ב אָבִ֔יו וַיַּֽעֲמִדֵ֖הוּ
him placed and ,father his Jacob Joseph in brought And

8 לִפְנֵ֣י פַרְעֹ֑ה וַיְבָ֥רֶךְ יַעֲקֹ֖ב אֶת־פַּרְעֹֽה׃ וַיֹּ֥אמֶר
said And .Pharaoh [1]Jacob [2]blessed and ; Pharaoh before

פַּרְעֹ֖ה אֶֽל־יַעֲקֹ֑ב כַּמָּ֕ה יְמֵ֖י שְׁנֵ֥י
of years the of days the [are] what Like : Jacob unto Pharaoh

9 חַיֶּֽיךָ׃ וַיֹּ֤אמֶר יַעֲקֹב֙ אֶל־פַּרְעֹ֔ה יְמֵי֙
of days The : Pharaah unto Jacob said And ? life thy

שְׁנֵ֣י מְגוּרַ֔י שְׁלֹשִׁ֥ים וּמְאַ֖ת שָׁנָ֑ה
; years hundred a and thirty [are] sojourning my of years the

מְעַ֣ט[g] וְרָעִ֗ים הָיוּ֙ יְמֵי֙ שְׁנֵ֣י חַיַּ֔י
;life my of years the of days the been have evil and few

וְלֹ֣א הִשִּׂ֗יגוּ אֶת־יְמֵי֙[h] שְׁנֵ֣י חַיֵּ֔י
of life the of years the of days the unto attained [2]have [1]they [3]not and

is no pasture
for thy servants'
flocks; for the
famine is sore
in the land of
Canaan: now
therefore, we
pray thee, let thy
servants dwell in
the land of Go-
shen. 5 And
Pharaoh spake
unto Joseph,
saying, Thy
father and thy
brethren are
come unto thee:
6 the land of E-
gypt is before
thee; in the best
of the land
make thy father
and thy breth-
ren to dwell; in
the land of Go-
shen let them
dwell: and if
thou knowest
any able men a-
mong them,
then make them
rulers over my
cattle. 7 And
Joseph brought
in Jacob his fa-
ther, and set
him before
Pharaoh: and
Jacob blessed
Pharaoh. 8 And
Pharaoh said
unto Jacob,
How many are
the days of the
years of thy life?

9 And Ja-
cob said unto
Pharaoh, The
days of the
years of my pil-
grimage *are* an
hundred and
thirty years: few
and evil have
the days of the
years of my life
been, and have
not attained un-
to the days of
the years of the
life of my fa-

9 And Jacob
said unto Pha-
raoh, The days
of the years of
my pilgrimage
are an hundred
and thirty years:
few and evil
have been the
days of the
years of my life,
and they have
not attained un-
to the days of
the years of the
life of my fa-

a G. has, *let us dwell.*

b G. omits.

c G., S., V. omit.

d G. transfers here v. 6 b, from ישבו to the end, and then adds, *and Jacob and his sons came unto Egypt to Joseph; and Pharaoh king of Egypt heard. And Pharaoh spoke unto Joseph saying.*

e V. omits ו; Sm. has היש; S. *that there are.*

f For על S. has, *over all.*

g G., S., T., V. have pl.

h S. omits.

thers in the days of their pilgrimage. 10 And Jacob blessed Pharaoh, and went out from before Pharaoh.

11 And Joseph placed his father and his brethren, and gave them a possession in the land of Egypt, in the best of the land, in the land of Rameses, as Pharaoh had commanded. 12 And Joseph nourished his father, and his brethren, and all his father's household, with bread, according to *their* families.

13 And *there was* no bread in all the land; for the famine *was* very sore, so that the land of Egypt and *all* the land of Canaan fainted by reason of the famine. 14 And Joseph gathered up all the money that was found in the land of Egypt, and in the land of Canaan, for the corn which they bought: and Joseph brought the money into Pharaoh's house. 15 And when money failed in the land of Egypt, and in the land of Canaan, all the Egyptians came unto Joseph, and said, Give us bread: for why should we die in thy

10 אֲבֹתַי בִּימֵי מְגוּרֵיהֶם׃ וַיְבָרֶךְ יַעֲקֹב
[1]Jacob [2]blessed And .sojournings their of days the in ,fathers my

אֶת־פַּרְעֹה וַיֵּצֵא[a] מִלִּפְנֵי פַרְעֹה[b]׃
.Pharaoh before (to) from out went he and ,Pharaoh

11 וַיּוֹשֵׁב יוֹסֵף אֶת־אָבִיו וְאֶת־אֶחָיו
,brethren his and father his Joseph dwell to caused And

וַיִּתֵּן לָהֶם אֲחֻזָּה בְּאֶרֶץ מִצְרַיִם בְּמֵיטַב
of best the in ; Egypt of land the in possession a them to gave and

הָאָרֶץ בְּאֶרֶץ רַעְמְסֵס כַּאֲשֶׁר צִוָּה פַרְעֹה׃
.Pharaoh commanded as ,Ramses of land the in ,land the

12 וַיְכַלְכֵּל יוֹסֵף אֶת־אָבִיו וְאֶת־אֶחָיו וְאֵת
and ,brethren his and ,father his Joseph nourished And

כָּל־בֵּית אָבִיו לֶחֶם לְפִי הַטָּף׃
.ones little the of mouth the at ,bread [with] father his of house the all

13 וְלֶחֶם אֵין בְּכָל־הָאָרֶץ כִּי־כָבֵד
heavy was because ,land the all in being not bread And

הָרָעָב מְאֹד וַתֵּלַהּ[c] אֶרֶץ מִצְרַיִם
Egypt of land the exhausted were (and) ;exceedingly famine the

14 וְאֶרֶץ כְּנַעַן מִפְּנֵי הָרָעָב׃ וַיְלַקֵּט
up gathered And .famine the before from Canaan of land the and

יוֹסֵף אֶת־כָּל־הַכֶּסֶף הַנִּמְצָא בְאֶרֶץ־מִצְרַיִם
Egypt of land the in found money the all Joseph

וּבְאֶרֶץ כְּנַעַן בַּשֶּׁבֶר אֲשֶׁר־הֵם
they which grain the for ,Canaan of land the in and

שֹׁבְרִים[d] וַיָּבֵא יוֹסֵף[e] אֶת־הַכֶּסֶף בֵּיתָה
of house the to money the Joseph in brought and ;buying [were]

15 פַרְעֹה׃ וַיִּתֹּם[f] הַכֶּסֶף מֵאֶרֶץ מִצְרַיִם
,Egypt of land the from money the failed And .Pharaoh

וּמֵאֶרֶץ כְּנַעַן וַיָּבֹאוּ כָל־מִצְרַיִם אֶל־
unto Egypt all in came and ;Canaan of land the from and

יוֹסֵף לֵאמֹר[g] הָבָה־לָּנוּ לֶחֶם וְלָמָּה[h] נָמוּת
die we should why and ,bread us to Give :saying Joseph

thers in the days of their pilgrimage. 10 And Jacob blessed Pharaoh, and went out from the presence of Pharaoh.

11 And Joseph placed his father and his brethren, and gave them a possession in the land of Egypt, in the best of the land, in the land of Rameses, as Pharaoh had commanded. 12 And Joseph nourished his father, and his brethren, and all his father's household, with bread, according to their families.

13 And there was no bread in all the land; for the famine was very sore, so that the land of Egypt and the land of Canaan fainted by reason of the famine. 14 And Joseph gathered up all the money that was found in the land of Egypt, and in the land of Canaan, for the corn which they bought: and Joseph brought the money into Pharaoh's house. 15 And when the money was all spent in the land of Egypt, and in the land of Canaan, all the Egyptians came unto Joseph, and said, Give us bread: for why should we die in thy pres-

---

a S. adds, *Jacob.*
b G. has, *him.*
c S. adds, *all.*
d G. adds, *and he was dealing out grain to them.*
e G. adds, *all.*
f G. adds, *all.*
g S. adds, *to him.*
h S. has, *that we may live and not.*

presence? for
the money fail-
eth. 16 And Jo-
seph said, Give
your cattle; and
I will give you
for your cattle,
if money fail. 17
And they
brought their
cattle unto Jo-
seph: and Jo-
seph gave them
bread *in ex-
change* for hors-
es, and for the
flocks, and for
the cattle of the
herds, and for
the asses: and
he fed them
with bread for
all their cattle
for that year.
18 When that
year was
ended, they
came unto him
the second year,
and said unto
him, We will
not hide *it* from
my lord, how
that our money
is spent; my
lord also hath
our herds of
cattle; there is
not ought left
in the sight of
my lord, but
our bodies, and
our lands:

19 Wherefore
shall we die
before thine
eyes, both we
and our land?
buy us and our
land for bread,
and we and our
land will be
servants unto
Pharaoh: and
give *us* seed,
that we may
live, and not
die, that the
land be not des-
olate. 20 And
Joseph bought
all the land of

16 נֶגְדֶּךָ כִּי אָפֵס כָּסֶף׃ וַיֹּאמֶר [a] יוֹסֵף
: Joseph said And .money ceased has for ? presence thy in

הָבוּ[b] מִקְנֵיכֶם וְאֶתְּנָה לָכֶם[c] בְּמִקְנֵיכֶם אִם־
if ,cattle your for you to give will I and ,cattle your Give

17 אָפֵס כָּסֶף׃ וַיָּבִיאוּ אֶת־מִקְנֵיהֶם אֶל־
unto cattle their in brought they And .money ceased has

יוֹסֵף[d] וַיִּתֵּן לָהֶם יוֹסֵף לֶחֶם בַּסּוּסִים
,horses the for bread Joseph them to gave and ; Joseph

וּבְמִקְנֵה הַצֹּאן וּבְמִקְנֵה הַבָּקָר
,herds of possessions the for and ,flocks of possessions the for and

וּבַחֲמֹרִים וַיְנַהֲלֵם בַּלֶּחֶם בְּכָל־מִקְנֵהֶם
cattle their all for bread with them satisfied he and ; asses the for and

18 בַּשָּׁנָה הַהִוא׃ וַתִּתֹּם הַשָּׁנָה הַהִוא וַיָּבֹאוּ
in came they and ,[1]that [2]year ended And .[1]that [2]year in

אֵלָיו בַּשָּׁנָה הַשֵּׁנִית וַיֹּאמְרוּ לוֹ
: him to said and ,[1]second [2]year the in him unto

לֹא־נְכַחֵד מֵאֲדֹנִי כִּי אִם־תַּם[e] הַכֶּסֶף
,money the failed has if but ; lord my from conceal not can We

וּמִקְנֵה [f]הַבְּהֵמָה אֶל־אֲדֹנִי [g]לֹא נִשְׁאַר[h]
left [1]is [2]not ,lord my unto [be] cattle of possessions the and

לִפְנֵי אֲדֹנִי בִּלְתִּי אִם־גְּוִיָּתֵנוּ וְאַדְמָתֵנוּ׃
.ground our and bodies our (if) except ,lord my before

19 לָמָּה נָמוּת לְעֵינֶיךָ גַּם־אֲנַחְנוּ[i] גַּם־
and we both ,eyes thine before die we should Why

אַדְמָתֵנוּ[j] קְנֵה־אֹתָנוּ וְאֶת־אַדְמָתֵנוּ בַּלָּחֶם
; bread for ground our and us Buy ? ground our

וְנִהְיֶה אֲנַחְנוּ וְאַדְמָתֵנוּ עֲבָדִים לְפַרְעֹה
; Pharaoh to slaves ,ground our and we ,become us let and

וְתֶן־זֶרַע[k] וְנִחְיֶה וְלֹא נָמוּת וְהָאֲדָמָה
ground the and ,die not and live may we that ,seed give and

20 לֹא תֵשָׁם׃ וַיִּקֶן יוֹסֵף אֶת־כָּל־אַדְמַת
of ground the all Joseph bought And .desolate be not

ence? for *our*
money faileth.
16 And Joseph
said, Give your
cattle; and I
will give you for
your cattle, if
money fail. 17
And they
brought their
cattle unto Jo-
seph: and Jo-
seph gave them
bread in ex-
change for the
horses, and for
the flocks, and
for the herds,
and for the ass-
es: and he fed
them with bread
in exchange for
all their cattle
for that year. 18
And when that
year was ended,
they came unto
him the second
year, and said
unto him, We
will not hide
from my lord,
how that our
money is all
spent; and the
herds of cattle
are my lord's;
there is nought
left in the sight
of my lord, but
our bodies, and
our lands:

19 wherefore
should we die
before thine
eyes, both we
and our land?
buy us and our
land for bread,
and we and our
land will be
servants unto
Pharaoh: and
give us seed,
that we may
live, and not
die, and that
the land be not
desolate. 20 So
Joseph bought
all the land of

---

a G. adds, *to them;* S. has, *he said to them.*
b S. adds, *to me.*
c Sm., G., V. add, *bread.*
d V. omits: S. has, *unto him.*
e S. adds, *all.*
f G. adds, *and,* ו.
g G. adds, *and,* ו.
h G. adds, *to us.*
i G. omits.
j G. has, *and our land should be desolated.*
k G. adds, *that we may sow,* ונזרע.

Egypt for Pharaoh; for the Egyptians sold every man his field, because the famine prevailed over them: so the land became Pharaoh's.
21 And as for the people, he removed them to cities from *one* end of the borders of Egypt even to the *other* end thereof.
22 Only the land of the priests bought he not; for the priests had a portion *assigned them* of Pharaoh, and did eat their portion which Pharaoh gave them: wherefore they sold not their lands.

23 Then Joseph said unto the people, Behold, I have bought you this day and your land for Pharaoh: lo, *here is* seed for you, and ye shall sow the land.
24 And it shall come to pass in the increase, that ye shall give the fifth *part* unto Pharaoh, and four parts shall be your own, for seed of the field, and for your food, and for them of your households, and for food for your little ones.
25 And they said, Thou hast saved our lives: let us find grace in the sight of my lord,

מִצְרַיִם לְפַרְעֹה כִּי־מָכְרוּ מִצְרַיִם אִישׁ[a] שָׂדֵהוּ[a]
,field his one each Egypt sold because ; Pharaoh for Egypt

כִּי־חָזַק עֲלֵהֶם הָרָעָב וַתְּהִי הָאָרֶץ
land the became and ;famine the them upon strong was because

21 לְפַרְעֹה׃ וְאֶת־הָעָם הֶעֱבִיר[b] אֹתוֹ
them over pass to caused he ,people the And .Pharaoh to

לֶעָרִים[cb] מִקְצֵה גְבוּל־מִצְרַיִם וְעַד־קָצֵהוּ׃[d]
.end its unto and Egypt of border the of end the from ,cities the to

22 רַק אַדְמַת הַכֹּהֲנִים לֹא קָנָה[e] כִּי
,for ; buy [2]did [1]he [3]not priests the of ground the Only

חֹק לַכֹּהֲנִים מֵאֵת פַּרְעֹה
,Pharaoh (with) from priests the to [being] portion appointed an

וְאָכְלוּ אֶת־חֻקָּם אֲשֶׁר
which ,portion appointed their eat to accustomed were they (and)

נָתַן לָהֶם פַּרְעֹה עַל־כֵּן לֹא מָכְרוּ
sell [2]did [1]they [3]not therefore ; Pharaoh them to gave

23 אֶת־אַדְמָתָם׃ וַיֹּאמֶר יוֹסֵף אֶל־הָעָם[f]
: people the unto Joseph said And .ground their

הֵן קָנִיתִי אֶתְכֶם הַיּוֹם וְאֶת־אַדְמַתְכֶם
ground your and today you bought have I ,Behold

לְפַרְעֹה הֵא־לָכֶם[g] זֶרַע וּזְרַעְתֶּם אֶת־הָאֲדָמָה׃
.ground the ye sow and ,seed you to ,behold ;Pharaoh for

24 וְהָיָה בַּתְּבוּאֹת וּנְתַתֶּם
give shall ye (and) ,ingatherings the at ,pass to come shall it And

חֲמִישִׁית לְפַרְעֹה וְאַרְבַּע הַיָּדֹת יִהְיֶה לָכֶם
,you to be shall parts four and ; Pharaoh to part fifth a

לְזֶרַע הַשָּׂדֶה וּלְאָכְלְכֶם וְלַאֲשֶׁר[h]
[are] who those for and ,food your for and field the of seed for

25 בְּבָתֵּיכֶם[h] וְלֶאֱכֹל[i] לְטַפְּכֶם׃[i] וַיֹּאמְרוּ
: said they And .ones little your for eating for and ,houses your in

הֶחֱיִתָנוּ נִמְצָא־חֵן בְּעֵינֵי אֲדֹנִי
,lord my of eyes the in favor find us let ; lives our saved hast Thou

Egypt for Pharaoh; for the Egyptians sold every man his field, because the famine was sore upon them: and the land became Pharaoh's.
21 And as for the people, he removed them to the cities from one end of the border of Egypt even to the other end thereof.
22 Only the land of the priests bought he not; for the priests had a portion from Pharaoh, and did eat their portion which Pharaoh gave them; wherefore they sold not their land.

23 Then Joseph said unto the people, Behold, I have bought you this day and your land for Pharaoh: lo, here is seed for you, and ye shall sow the land.
24 And it shall come to pass at the ingatherings, that ye shall give a fifth unto Pharaoh, and four parts shall be your own, for seed of the field, and for your food, and for them of your households, and for food for your little ones.
25 And they said, Thou hast saved our lives: let us find grace in the sight of my lord, and we

a G. has, *their land to Pharaoh.*
b Sm., G. have, *he made them slaves,* העביר אתו לעבדים; so essentially V.
c S., T. have, *from city to city.*
d G., V. omit ו.
e G. adds, *this Joseph.*
f G. has, *all the Egyptians.*
g G., V. have, *take.*
h S. has, *and for food of your houses.*
i G. omits.

and we will be
Pharaoh's serv-
ants. 26 And Jo-
seph made it a
law over the
land of Egypt
unto this day,
that Pharaoh
should have the
fifth *part*; ex-
cept the land of
the priests only,
which became
not Pharaoh's.
27 And Israel
dwelt in the
land of Egypt,
in the country
of Goshen; and
they had posses-
ions therein, and
grew, and mul-
tiplied exceed-
ingly. 28 And
Jacob lived in
the land of E-
gypt seventeen
years: so the
whole age of Ja-
cob was an hun-
dred forty and
seven years. 29
And the time
drew nigh that
Israel must die:
and he called his
son Joseph, and
said unto him,
If now I have
found grace in
thy sight, put, I
pray thee, thy
hand under my
thigh, and deal
kindly and truly
with me; bury
me not, I pray
thee, in Egypt:
30 But I will lie
with my fathers,
and thou shalt
carry me out of
Egypt, and bury
me in their bury-
ingplace. And
he said, I will

וְהָיִינוּ עֲבָדִים לְפַרְעֹה׃ וַיָּשֶׂם אֹתָהּ 26
it put And .Pharaoh to slaves become will we and

יוֹסֵף לְחֹק עַד־הַיּוֹם הַזֶּה עַל־
upon ,[1]this [2]day until ordinance an for Joseph

אַדְמַת מִצְרַיִם לְפַרְעֹה לַחֹמֶשׁ רַק
only ; part fifth the (for) Pharaoh to ,Egypt of ground the

אַדְמַת הַכֹּהֲנִים לְבַדָּם[a] לֹא הָיְתָה
become [2]did [1]it [3]not ,alone priests the of ground the

לְפַרְעֹה׃ וַיֵּשֶׁב יִשְׂרָאֵל בְּאֶרֶץ מִצְרַיִם 27
,Egypt of land the in Israel dwelt And .Pharaoh to

[b]בְּאֶרֶץ גֹּשֶׁן וַיֵּאָחֲזוּ בָהּ
,it in fast themselves held they and ; Goshen of land the in

[c]וַיִּפְרוּ וַיִּרְבּוּ מְאֹד׃
.exceedingly multiplied and fruitful were and

וַיְחִי יַעֲקֹב בְּאֶרֶץ מִצְרַיִם שְׁבַע עֶשְׂרֵה 28
ten [and] seven Egypt of land the in Jacob lived And

שָׁנָה וַיְהִי יְמֵי־יַעֲקֹב שְׁנֵי חַיָּיו
,life his of years the ,Jacob of days the were and ; years

שֶׁבַע שָׁנִים וְאַרְבָּעִים וּמְאַת שָׁנָה׃
.years hundred a and forty and years seven

וַיִּקְרְבוּ יְמֵי־יִשְׂרָאֵל לָמוּת וַיִּקְרָא לִבְנוֹ 29
son his (to) called he and ,die to Israel of days the near drew And

לְיוֹסֵף וַיֹּאמֶר לוֹ אִם־נָא מָצָאתִי חֵן
favor found have I ,now ,If : him to said and ,Joseph (to)

בְּעֵינֶיךָ שִׂים־נָא יָדְךָ תַּחַת יְרֵכִי[d] וְעָשִׂיתָ
do and ; thigh my under hand thy ,pray ,put ,eyes thine in

עִמָּדִי חֶסֶד וֶאֱמֶת [e]אַל־נָא[f] תִקְבְּרֵנִי[f]
me bury ,pray ,not [do] ,truth and kindness me with

בְּמִצְרָיִם׃ וְשָׁכַבְתִּי עִם־אֲבֹתַי וּנְשָׂאתַנִי 30
me carry and ,fathers my with lie me let and ; Egypt in

מִמִּצְרַיִם וּקְבַרְתַּנִי בִּקְבֻרָתָם וַיֹּאמַר[g] אָנֹכִי
I : said he And .grave their in me bury and ,Egypt from

will be Pha-
raoh's servants.
26 And Joseph
made it a statute
concerning the
land of Egypt
unto this day,
that Pharaoh
should have the
fifth; only the
land of the
priests alone
became not Pha-
raoh's.
27 And Israel
dwelt in the
land of Egypt,
in the land of
Goshen; and
they gat them
possessions
therein, and
were fruitful,
and multiplied
exceedingly. 28
And Jacob liv-
ed in the land of
Egypt seventeen
years: so the
days of Jacob,
the years of his
life, were an
hundred forty
and seven years.
29 And the time
drew near that
Israel must die:
and he called his
son Joseph, and
said unto him,
If now I have
found grace in
thy sight, put, I
pray thee, thy
hand under my
thigh, and deal
kindly and truly
with me; bury
me not, I pray
thee, in Egypt:
30 but when I
sleep with my
fathers, thou
shalt carry me
out of Egypt,
and bury me in
their burying-
place. And he
said, I will do as

a S., V. omit; S. adds, *which.*

b S. adds, *and,* ו.

c G. omits.

d S. adds, *and I will cause thee to swear by the Lord.*

e S. adds *and,* ו.

f G., V. have, *to not bury me.*

g S., V. add, *Joseph.*

do as thou hast
said. 31 And he
said, Swear un-
to me. And he
sware unto him.
And Israel bow-
ed himself upon
the bed's head.

31 אֶעֱשֶׂה כִּדְבָרֶךָ׃ וַיֹּאמֶר הִשָּׁבְעָה לִי
;me to Swear :said he And .word thy to according do will

וַיִּשָּׁבַע לוֹ וַיִּשְׁתַּחוּ יִשְׂרָאֵל עַל־
upon Israel himself prostrated and ;him to swore he and

רֹאשׁ הַמִּטָּה[a]׃
.bed the of head the

thou hast said.
31 And he said,
Swear unto me:
and he sware
unto him. And
Israel bowed
himself upon
the bed's head.

48

AND it came
to pass after
these things,
that *one* told Jo-
seph, Behold,
thy father *is*
sick: and he
took with him
his two sons,
Manasseh and
Ephraim. 2 And
one told Jacob,
and said, Be-
hold, thy son
Joseph cometh
unto thee: and
Israel strength-
ened himself,
and sat upon the
bed. 3 And Ja-
cob said unto
Joseph, God Al-
mighty appear-
ed unto me at
Luz in the land
of Canaan, and
blessed me, 4
And said unto
me, Behold, I
will make thee
fruitful, and
multiply thee,
and I will make
of thee a multi-
tude of people;
and will give
this land to thy
seed after thee
for an everlast-
ing possession.
5 And now
thy two sons,
Ephraim and
Manasseh,
which were born
unto thee in the
land of Egypt,
before I came
unto thee into

1 וַיְהִי אַחֲרֵי הַדְּבָרִים הָאֵלֶּה וַיֹּאמֶר
said one (and) ,[1]these [2]things after pass to came it And

לְיוֹסֵף הִנֵּה אָבִיךָ חֹלֶה וַיִּקַּח אֶת־שְׁנֵי
[2]two took he and ;sick [is] father thy Behold :Joseph to

בָנָיו עִמּוֹ[b] אֶת־מְנַשֶּׁה וְאֶת־אֶפְרָיִם[c]׃
.Ephraim and Manasseh ,him with sons [1]his

2 וַיַּגֵּד לְיַעֲקֹב וַיֹּאמֶר[d] הִנֵּה בִּנְךָ יוֹסֵף בָּא
come has Joseph son thy Behold :said and Jacob to told one And

אֵלֶיךָ וַיִּתְחַזֵּק יִשְׂרָאֵל וַיֵּשֶׁב עַל־
upon sat and ,Israel himself strengthened and ;thee unto

3 הַמִּטָּה׃ וַיֹּאמֶר יַעֲקֹב אֶל־יוֹסֵף אֵל[e] שַׁדַּי[e]
Almighty God :Joseph unto Jacob said And .bed the

נִרְאָה־אֵלַי בְּלוּז בְּאֶרֶץ כְּנָעַן וַיְבָרֶךְ
blessed and ,Canaan of land the in Luz in me unto appeared

4 אֹתִי׃ וַיֹּאמֶר אֵלַי הִנְנִי מַפְרְךָ[f]
,fruitful thee make will I Behold :me unto said and ;me

וְהִרְבִּיתִךָ וּנְתַתִּיךָ לִקְהַל עַמִּים
;peoples of company a (for) thee make and ,thee multiply and

וְנָתַתִּי אֶת־הָאָרֶץ הַזֹּאת לְזַרְעֲךָ[g] אַחֲרֶיךָ
,thee after seed thy to [1]this [2]land give will I and

5 אֲחֻזַּת עוֹלָם׃ וְעַתָּה שְׁנֵי־בָנֶיךָ הַנּוֹלָדִים
born those ,sons two thy now And .eternity of possession a

לְךָ בְּאֶרֶץ מִצְרַיִם עַד־בֹּאִי אֵלֶיךָ
thee unto coming my to up Egypt of land the in thee to

And it came
to pass after
these things,
that one said to
Joseph, Behold,
thy father is
sick: and he
took with him
his two sons,
Manasseh and
Ephraim. 2 And
one told Jacob,
and said, Be-
hold, thy son
Joseph cometh
unto thee: and
Israel strength-
ened himself,
and sat upon
the bed. 3 And
Jacob said unto
Joseph, God Al-
mighty appear-
ed unto me at
Luz in the land
of Canaan, and
blessed me, 4
and said unto
me, Behold, I
will make thee
fruitful, and
multiply thee,
and I will make
of thee a com-
pany of peoples;
and will give
this land to thy
seed after thee
for an everlast-
ing possession.
5 And now
thy two sons,
which were born
unto thee in the
land of Egypt
before I came
unto thee into

---

a S., G. have, *his staff*, הַמַּטֶּה, cf. Heb. 11: 21.

b G. omits.

c G. adds, *he came to Jacob;* V. adds, *he proceeded to go.*

d S. adds, *to him.*

e G. has, *my God.*

f S. has, *will bless thee.*

g G., V. have, *to thee and to thy seed.*

Egypt, *are* mine; as Reuben and Simeon, they shall be mine. 6 And thy issue, which thou begettest after them, shall be thine, *and* shall be called after the name of their brethren in their inheritance. 7 And as for me, when I came from Padan, Rachel died by me in the land of Canaan in the way, when yet *there was* but a little way to come unto Ephrath: and I buried her there in the way of Ephrath; the same *is* Beth-lehem. 8 And Israel beheld Joseph's sons, and said, Who *are* these? 9 And Joseph said unto his father, They *are* my sons, whom God hath given me in this *place*. And he said, Bring them, I pray thee, unto me, and I will bless them. 10 Now the eyes of Israel were dim for age, *so that* he could not see. And he brought them near unto him; and he kissed them and embraced them.

11 And Israel said unto Joseph, I had not thought to see thy face: and, lo, God hath shewed me also thy seed. 12 And

מִצְרַיְמָה לִי־הֵם אֶפְרַיִם וּמְנַשֶּׁה[a] כִּרְאוּבֵן
Reuben like ,Manasseh and Ephraim ; they [are] me for , Egypt to

וְשִׁמְעוֹן יִהְיוּ־לִי׃ וּמוֹלַדְתְּךָ אֲשֶׁר־ 6
which offspring thy And .me for be shall they ,Simeon and

הוֹלַדְתָּ אַחֲרֵיהֶם לְךָ[b] יִהְיוּ עַל
to according ; be shall they thee for ,them after begettest thou

שֵׁם אֲחֵיהֶם יִקָּרְאוּ בְּנַחֲלָתָם׃
.inheritance their in called be shall they brethren their of name the

וַאֲנִי בְּבֹאִי מִפַּדָּן[c] מֵתָה עָלַי[d] רָחֵל[e] 7
Rachel me upon died ,Paddan from coming my in ,I And

בְּאֶרֶץ כְּנַעַן בַּדֶּרֶךְ[f] בְּעוֹד כִּבְרַת־אֶרֶץ
land of kibrah a still with ,way the in Canaan of land the in

לָבֹא אֶפְרָתָה וָאֶקְבְּרֶהָ שָּׁם[g] בְּדֶרֶךְ אֶפְרָת
,Ephrath of way the in there her buried I and ; Ephrath to come to

הִוא בֵּית לָחֶם׃ וַיַּרְא יִשְׂרָאֵל אֶת־בְּנֵי 8
of sons the Israel saw And .Lehem Beth [being] it

יוֹסֵף וַיֹּאמֶר[h] מִי־אֵלֶּה[i]׃ וַיֹּאמֶר יוֹסֵף 9
Joseph said And ? these [are] Who : said he and ,Joseph

אֶל־אָבִיו בָּנַי הֵם אֲשֶׁר־נָתַן־לִי אֱלֹהִים
God me to given has whom ,[are] they sons My : father his unto

בָּזֶה וַיֹּאמַר[j] קָחֶם־נָא אֵלַי וַאֲבָרְכֵם׃
.them bless will I and ,me unto ,now ,them take : said he And .here

וְעֵינֵי יִשְׂרָאֵל כָּבְדוּ מִזֹּקֶן[k] לֹא יוּכַל 10
able [2]was [1]he [3]not ,age from heavy being Israel of eyes the (And)

לִרְאוֹת[l] וַיַּגֵּשׁ אֹתָם אֵלָיו וַיִּשַּׁק
kissed he and ,him unto them near brought he and ;see to

לָהֶם וַיְחַבֵּק לָהֶם׃ וַיֹּאמֶר יִשְׂרָאֵל אֶל־ 11
unto Israel said And .them (to) embraced and ,them (to)

יוֹסֵף רְאֹה פָנֶיךָ לֹא פִלָּלְתִּי וְהִנֵּה
behold and ,think [2]did [1]I [3]not face thy see To : Joseph

הֶרְאָה אֹתִי אֱלֹהִים גַּם אֶת־זַרְעֶךָ׃
.seed thy also God [1]me [3]see [2]to caused has

Egypt, are mine; Ephraim and Manasseh, even as Reuben and Simeon, shall be mine. 6 And thy issue, which thou begettest after them, shall be thine; they shall be called after the name of their brethren in their inheritance. 7 And as for me, when I came from Paddan, Rachel died by me in the land of Canaan in the way, when there was still some way to come unto Ephrath: and I buried her there in the way to Ephrath (the same is Beth-lehem). 8 And Israel beheld Joseph's sons, and said, Who are these? 9 And Joseph said unto his father, They are my sons, whom God hath given me here. And he said, Bring them, I pray thee, unto me, and I will bless them. 10 Now the eyes of Israel were dim for age, so that he could not see. And he brought them near unto him; and he kissed them, and embraced them.

11 And Israel said unto Joseph, I had not thought to see thy face: and, lo, God hath let me see thy seed also. 12 And Jo-

---

a S. adds, *for me are they*, לי הם.
b G. omits.
c Sm., G., S. add, *Aram*, ארם.
d G. omits.
e Sm., G. add, *thy mother*.
f G. omits.
g G., V. omit.
h S., V. add, *to him*.
i Sm., G. add, *to thee*.
j G. adds, *Jacob*.
k G., S., V. add, *and*, ו.
l S., V. add, *clearly*.

Joseph brought them out from between his knees, and he bowed himself with his face to the earth. 13 And Joseph took them both, Ephraim in his right hand toward Israel's left hand, and Manasseh in his left hand toward Israel's right hand, and brought *them* near unto him. 14 And Israel stretched out his right hand, and laid *it* upon Ephraim's head, who *was* the younger, and his left hand upon Manasseh's head, guiding his hands wittingly; for Manasseh *was* the firstborn.

15 And he blessed Joseph, and said, God, before whom my fathers Abraham and Isaac did walk, the God which fed me all my life long unto this day, 16 The Angel which redeemed me from all evil, bless the lads; and let my name be named on them, and the name of my fathers Abraham and Isaac; and let them grow into a multitude in the midst of the earth. 17 And when Joseph saw that his father laid his right hand up-

12 וַיּוֹצֵא יוֹסֵף אֹתָם מֵעִם בִּרְכָּיו
; knees his (with) from them Joseph out brought And

13 וַיִּשְׁתַּחוּ לְאַפָּיו[a] אָרְצָה׃ וַיִּקַּח
took And .earth the to face his (to) ,himself prostrated he and

יוֹסֵף אֶת־שְׁנֵיהֶם[b] אֶת־אֶפְרַיִם בִּימִינוֹ
hand right his in Ephraim ,them of both Joseph

מִשְּׂמֹאל יִשְׂרָאֵל וְאֶת־מְנַשֶּׁה בִשְׂמֹאלוֹ
hand left his in Manasseh and ,Israel of left the from

מִימִין יִשְׂרָאֵל וַיַּגֵּשׁ[c] אֵלָיו׃
.him unto near brought he and ; Israel of right the from

14 וַיִּשְׁלַח יִשְׂרָאֵל אֶת־יְמִינוֹ וַיָּשֶׁת עַל־
upon put and ,hand right his Israel out stretched And

רֹאשׁ אֶפְרַיִם וְהוּא הַצָּעִיר וְאֶת־שְׂמֹאלוֹ
hand left his and ; younger the [being] he (and) ,Ephraim of head the

עַל־רֹאשׁ מְנַשֶּׁה שִׂכֵּל אֶת־יָדָיו כִּי[d]
for ; hands his crossing ,Manasseh of head the upon

15 מְנַשֶּׁה הַבְּכוֹר[d]׃ וַיְבָרֶךְ[e] אֶת־יוֹסֵף[f] וַיֹּאמַר
: said and Joseph blessed he And .firstborn the [was] Manasseh

הָאֱלֹהִים אֲשֶׁר הִתְהַלְּכוּ אֲבֹתַי לְפָנָיו
,(him before) fathers my walked whom [before] God The

אַבְרָהָם וְיִצְחָק הָאֱלֹהִים הָרֹעֶה אֹתִי
me for caring one the ,God the ; Isaac and Abraham

16 מֵעוֹדִי[g] [h]עַד־הַיּוֹם הַזֶּה׃ הַמַּלְאָךְ[i] הַגֹּאֵל
redeeming one the ,angel the ; [1]this [2]day until existence my since

אֹתִי מִכָּל־רָע יְבָרֵךְ אֶת־הַנְּעָרִים
; youths the bless he may ,evil every from me

וְיִקָּרֵא בָהֶם שְׁמִי וְשֵׁם אֲבֹתַי
fathers my of name the and name my them in called be may and

אַבְרָהָם וְיִצְחָק וְיִדְגּוּ לָרֹב[j] בְּקֶרֶב
of midst the in multitude a to increase they may and ;Isaac and Abraham

17 הָאָרֶץ׃ וַיַּרְא יוֹסֵף כִּי־יָשִׁית אָבִיו יַד־יְמִינוֹ
hand right his father his placing was that Joseph saw And .earth the

seph brought them out from between his knees; and he bowed himself with his face to the earth. 13 And Joseph took them both, Ephraim in his right hand toward Israel's left hand, and Manasseh in his left hand toward Israel's right hand, and brought them near unto him. 14 And Israel stretched out his right hand, and laid it upon Ephraim's head, who was the younger, and his left hand upon Manasseh's head, guiding his hands wittingly; for Manasseh was the firstborn.

15 And he blessed Joseph, and said, The God before whom my fathers Abraham and Isaac did walk, the God which hath fed me all my life long unto this day, 16 the angel which hath redeemed me from all evil, bless the lads; and let my name be named on them, and the name of my fathers Abraham and Isaac; and let them grow into a multitude in the midst of the earth. 17 And when Joseph saw that his father laid his right hand

a G. has, *to him, upon the face, unto the ground.*

b G., S. have, *his two sons.*

c G., S., V. add, *them.*

d G. omits.

e S., V. add, *Jacob.*

f G. has, *them;* V. *the sons of Joseph;* S. *Joseph his son.*

g G. has, *from youth;* S., V. have, *from my youth.*

h S. adds, *and,* ו.

i Sm. has, *the king,* המלך.

j G. has, *unto a great multitude;* S. adds, *multiply,* V. has *into a multitude.* For וידגו לרוב T. has, *like fish of the sea may they multiply.*

on the head of
Ephraim, it dis-
pleased him: and
he held up his
father's hand,
to remove it
from Ephraim's
head unto Ma-
nasseh's head.
18 And Joseph
said unto his fa-
ther, Not so, my
father: for this
is the firstborn;
put thy right
hand upon his
head. 19 And
his father re-
fused, and said,
I know *it*, my
son, I know *it*:
he also shall be-
come a people,
and he also
shall be great:
but truly his
younger brother
shall be greater
than he, and
his seed shall
become a multi-
tude of nations.
20 And he bless-
ed them that
day, saying, In
thee shall Israel
bless, saying,
God make thee
as Ephraim and
as Manasseh:
and he set Eph-
raim before Ma-
nasseh. 21 And
Israel said unto
Joseph, Behold,
I die; but God
shall be with
you, and bring
you again unto
the land of your
fathers.

22 Moreover I
have given to
thee one portion
above thy breth-
ren, which I
took out of the
hand of the Am-
orite with my
sword and with
my bow.

עַל־רֹאשׁ אֶפְרַיִם וַיֵּרַע בְּעֵינָיו
; eyes his in — evil was it and — ,Ephraim — of head the upon

וַיִּתְמֹךְ יַד־אָבִיו לְהָסִיר אֹתָהּ מֵעַל
upon from — it — remove to — ,father his of hand the — of hold took he and

18 רֹאשׁ־אֶפְרַיִם[a] עַל־רֹאשׁ מְנַשֶּׁה׃ וַיֹּאמֶר יוֹסֵף
Joseph — said And — .Manasseh — of head the unto — Ephraim of head the

אֶל־אָבִיו לֹא־כֵן אָבִי כִּי־זֶה הַבְּכֹר
; firstborn the [is] — one this for — ,father my — ,so Not — : father his unto

19 שִׂים יְמִינְךָ עַל־רֹאשׁוֹ׃ וַיְמָאֵן אָבִיו
father his — refused And — .head his upon — hand right thy — put

וַיֹּאמֶר יָדַעְתִּי בְנִי יָדַעְתִּי גַּם־הוּא יִהְיֶה־
become shall — also he — ; know I — ,son my — ,know I — : said and

לְּעָם וְגַם־הוּא יִגְדָּל וְאוּלָם אָחִיו הַקָּטֹן
[1]younger — [2]brother his — but — ; great become shall also he and — ,people a (for)

יִגְדַּל מִמֶּנּוּ וְזַרְעוֹ יִהְיֶה מְלֹא־
of fulness a — become shall — seed his and — ,he than — greater become shall

20 הַגּוֹיִם׃ וַיְבָרֲכֵם בַּיּוֹם הַהוּא לֵאמוֹר בְּךָ[b]
thee In — :saying — [1]that — [2]day in — them blessed he And — .nations

יְבָרֵךְ[c] יִשְׂרָאֵל לֵאמֹר יְשִׂמְךָ אֱלֹהִים כְּאֶפְרַיִם
,Ephraim like — God — thee put May — : saying — ,Israel — bless shall

וְכִמְנַשֶּׁה וַיָּשֶׂם אֶת־אֶפְרַיִם לִפְנֵי מְנַשֶּׁה׃
.Manasseh — before — Ephraim — put he and — ; Manasseh like and

21 וַיֹּאמֶר יִשְׂרָאֵל אֶל־יוֹסֵף הִנֵּה אָנֹכִי מֵת
; die — I — Behold — : Joseph unto — Israel — said And

וְהָיָה אֱלֹהִים עִמָּכֶם וְהֵשִׁיב אֶתְכֶם אֶל־
unto — you — return will and — ,you with — God — be will and

22 אֶרֶץ אֲבֹתֵיכֶם׃ וַאֲנִי נָתַתִּי לְךָ שְׁכֶם
[3]ridge [2]mountain — thee to — give — I And — .fathers your — of land the

אַחַד עַל־אַחֶיךָ אֲשֶׁר לָקַחְתִּי מִיַּד
of hand the from — took I — which — ,brethren thy beyond — [1]one

הָאֱמֹרִי בְּחַרְבִּי[d] וּבְקַשְׁתִּי׃[d]
.bow my with and — sword my with — Amorite the

upon the head
of Ephraim, it
displeased him:
and he held up
his father's
hand, to remove
it from Eph-
raim's head un-
to Manasseh's
head. 18 And
Joseph said un-
to his father,
Not so, my fa-
ther: for this is
the firstborn;
put thy right
hand upon his
head. 19 And
his father re-
fused, and said,
I know *it*, my
son, I know *it*:
he also shall be-
come a people,
and he also
shall be great:
howbeit his
younger brother
shall be greater
than he, and his
seed shall be-
come a multi-
tude of nations.
20 And he bless-
ed them that
day, saying, In
thee shall Israel
bless, saying,
God make thee
as Ephraim and
as Manasseh:
and he set Eph-
raim before Ma-
nasseh. 21 And
Israel said unto
Joseph, Behold,
I die: but God
shall be with
you, and bring
you again unto
the land of your
fathers.

22 Moreover I
have given to
thee one portion
above thy breth-
ren, which I
took out of the
hand of the Am-
orite with my
sword and with
my bow.

---

a S. adds, *and he might put it;* T. *to put it.*
b G. has, *in you,* בכם.
c G., S., V. have passive, יְבֹרַךְ.
d T. has, *by my prayer and my entreaty.*

49

AND Jacob
called unto his
sons, and said,
Gather your-
selves together,
that I may tell
you *that* which
shall befall you
in the last days.
2 Gather your-
selves together,
and hear, ye
sons of Jacob;
and hearken un-
to Israel your
father.

3 Reuben,
thou *art* my
firstborn, my
might, and the
beginning of my
strength, the
excellency of
dignity, and the
excellency of
power: 4 Un-
stable as water,
thou shalt not
excel; because
thou wentest up
to thy father's
bed; then de-
filedst thou *it*:
he went up to
my couch.

5 Simeon and
Levi *are* breth-
ren; instru-
ments of cruel-
ty. *are in* their
habitations. 6 O
my soul, come
not thou into
their secret; un-
to their as-
sembly, mine
honour, be not
thou united: for
in their anger
they slew a man,
and in their self-
will they digged
down a wall. 7
Cursed *be* their
anger, for *it*
was fierce; and
their wrath, for
it was cruel: I
will divide them
in Jacob, and
scatter them in
Israel.

1 וַיִּקְרָא יַעֲקֹב אֶל־בָּנָיו וַיֹּאמֶר[a] הֵאָסְפוּ
,yourselves Assemble :said and sons his (unto) Jacob called And

וְאַגִּידָה לָכֶם אֵת אֲשֶׁר־יִקְרָא אֶתְכֶם בְּאַחֲרִית
after in you to happen will what you to tell will I and

2 הַיָּמִים׃ הִקָּבְצוּ וְשִׁמְעוּ בְּנֵי יַעֲקֹב וְשִׁמְעוּ[b]
hearken and ;Jacob of sons ,hear and yourselves Gather .days

3 אֶל־יִשְׂרָאֵל[c] אֲבִיכֶם׃ רְאוּבֵן בְּכֹרִי אַתָּה
;thou [art] firstborn my ,Reuben .father your Israel unto

כֹּחִי וְרֵאשִׁית אוֹנִי יֶתֶר שְׂאֵת
,dignity of excellence ;vigor my of firstfruits the and strength my

4 וְיֶתֶר עָז׃ פַּחַז[d] כַּמַּיִם אַל־
not do ,water like over boiling A .might of excellence and

תּוֹתַר כִּי עָלִיתָ מִשְׁכְּבֵי אָבִיךָ
;father thy of bed the to up wentest thou for ;preeminence have thou

אָז חִלַּלְתָּ יְצוּעִי[e] עָלָה[e]׃
.up went he couch my [to] , defile didst thou then

5 שִׁמְעוֹן וְלֵוִי אַחִים כְּלֵי[f] חָמָס
[are] violence of instruments ;brethren ,Levi and Simeon

6 מְכֵרֹתֵיהֶם׃ בְּסֹדָם אַל־תָּבֹא נַפְשִׁי
; soul my come not let council their Into .weapons their

[g]בִּקְהָלָם אַל־תֵּחַד כְּבֹדִי[h] כִּי בְאַפָּם
anger their in for ;honor my united be not let assembly their with

הָרְגוּ אִישׁ וּבִרְצֹנָם עִקְּרוּ־שׁוֹר[i]׃
.oxen houghed they wrath wanton their in and ;men killed they

7 אָרוּר אַפָּם כִּי עָז וְעֶבְרָתָם כִּי
for ,wrath their and ;fierce was it for ,anger their [be] Cursed

קָשָׁתָה אֲחַלְּקֵם בְּיַעֲקֹב וַאֲפִיצֵם
them scatter will I and ,Jacob in them divide will I ;unrelenting was it

בְּיִשְׂרָאֵל׃
.Israel in

And Jacob
called unto his
sons, and said:
Gather your-
selves together,
that I may tell
you that which
shall befall you
in the latter
days. 2 As-
semble your-
selves, and hear,
ye sons of Ja-
cob; And heark-
en unto Israel
your father.

3 Reuben,
thou art my first-
born, my might,
and the begin-
ning of my
strength; The ex-
cellency of dig-
nity, and the ex-
cellency of pow-
er. 4 Unstable
as water, thou
shalt not have
the excellency;
Because thou
wentest up to
thy father's bed:
Then defiledst
thou it: he went
up to my couch.

5 Simeon and
Levi are breth-
ren; Weapons of
violence are
their swords. 6
O my soul, come
not thou into
their council;
Unto their as-
sembly, my glo-
ry, be not thou
united; For in
their anger they
slew a man,
And in their
selfwill they
houghed an ox.
7 Cursed be
their anger, for
it was fierce;
And their wrath,
for it was cruel:
I will divide
them in Jacob,
And scatter
them in Israel.

---

a G., S., V. add, *to them*.

b G., S., V. omit ו; T. has, *and receive instruction*.

c G. adds, *hear*.

d Sm., G., Sym., S., V. have verb, פָּחַזְתָּ.

e G. has, *the couch to which thou wentest up*; V. *his couch*; S. *my couch, and thou wentest up*.

f Sm., G., T. have, *they have ended*, כָּלוּ.

g G., S. add, *and*, ו.

h S., T. have *from my glory*.

i S. has, *wall*, שׁוּר; also V., Aq., Sym.; T. has, *the wall of enemies*.

8 Judah, thou
art he whom
thy brethren
shall praise : thy
hand *shall be* in
the neck of
thine enemies ;
thy father's chil-
dren shall bow
down before
thee. 9 Judah *is*
a lion's whelp :
from the prey,
my son, thou art
gone up : he
stooped down,
he couched as a
lion, and as an
old lion ; who
shall rouse him
up ? 10 The
sceptre shall not
depart from Ju-
dah, nor a law-
giver from be-
tween his feet,
until Shiloh
come ; and unto
him *shall* the
gathering of the
people *be.* 11
Binding his foal
unto the vine,
and his ass's
colt unto the
choice vine ; he
washed his gar-
ments in wine,
and his clothes
in the blood of
grapes : 12 His
eyes *shall be*
red with wine,
and his teeth
white with milk.

13 Zebulun
shall dwell at
the haven of the
sea; and he *shall*
be for an haven
of ships; and his
border *shall be*
unto Zidon.

14 Issachar *is*
a strong ass
couching down
between two
burdens: 15 And
he saw that rest
was good, and

8 יְהוּדָה אַתָּה יוֹדוּךָ אַחֶיךָ
;brethren thy thee praise may ,thou ,Judah

יָדְךָ בְּעֹרֶף אֹיְבֶיךָ יִשְׁתַּחֲווּ
themselves prostrate may ;enemies thy of neck the on [be] hand thy [may]

9 לְךָ בְּנֵי אָבִיךָ׃ גּוּר אַרְיֵה יְהוּדָה
; Judah [is] lion a of whelp A .father thine of sons the thee to

מִטֶּרֶף בְּנִי עָלִיתָ כָּרַע רָבַץ[a]
crouches he ,stoops he ; up gone hast thou ,son my ,prey from

כְּאַרְיֵה וּכְלָבִיא מִי יְקִימֶנּוּ׃
? him rouse would who ,lion strong a like and ; lion a like

10 לֹא־יָסוּר שֵׁבֶט[b] מִיהוּדָה וּמְחֹקֵק
staff leader's the and ,Judah from sceptre the depart not Shall

מִבֵּין רַגְלָיו[c] עַד כִּי־יָבֹא שִׁילֹה[d] וְלוֹ
him to and ,tranquility come that until ; feet his between from

11 יִקְּהַת[e] עַמִּים׃ אֹסְרִי לַגֶּפֶן עִירֹה
; foal his vine the for Binding .nations of obedience [be]

וְלַשֹּׂרֵקָה בְּנִי אֲתֹנוֹ כִּבֵּס
washes he ; [1]his [5]ass [4]an [3]of [2]son vine choice the for and

בַּיַּיִן לְבֻשׁוֹ וּבְדַם־עֲנָבִים סוּתֹה׃
.raiment his grapes of blood the in and ,clothing his wine in

12 חַכְלִילִי עֵינַיִם מִיָּיִן וּלְבֶן־שִׁנַּיִם מֵחָלָב׃
.milk from teeth of white and ,wine from eyes of Dark

13 זְבוּלֻן לְחוֹף יַמִּים יִשְׁכֹּן וְהוּא
he and ,dwell shall he seas of shore the at ,Zebulun

לְחוֹף אֳנִיֹּת וְיַרְכָתוֹ עַל־צִידֹן׃
.Zidon by border his (and) ,ships of shore a at

14 יִשָּׂשכָר חֲמֹר[f] גָּרֶם[f] רֹבֵץ בֵּין
between crouching ,bone of ass an ,Issachar

15 הַמִּשְׁפְּתָיִם׃ וַיַּרְא מְנֻחָה כִּי טוֹב
,good [was it] that resting-place a saw he And .sheep-folds the

8 Judah, thee
shall thy breth-
ren praise : Thy
hand shall be on
the neck of thine
enemies; Thy fa-
ther's sons shall
bow down be-
fore thee. 9 Ju-
dah is a lion's
whelp; From the
prey, my son,
thou art gone
up : He stooped
down, he couch-
ed as a lion, And
as a lioness ;
who shall rouse
him up ? 10 The
sceptre shall
not depart from
Judah, Nor the
ruler's staff from
between his
feet, Until Shi-
loh come ; And
unto him shall
the obedience of
the peoples be.
11 Binding his
foal unto the
vine, And his
ass's colt unto
the choice vine ;
He hath washed
his garments in
wine, And his
vesture in the
blood of grapes:
12 His eyes
shall be red with
wine, And his
teeth white with
milk.

13 Zebulun
shall dwell at
the haven of
the sea : And he
shall be for an
haven of ships ;
And his border
shall be upon
Zidon.

14 Issachar is
a strong ass,
Couching down
between the
sheepfolds:
15 And he saw a
resting place
that it was good,

---

a S. adds, *and*, ו.

b G., T. have, *ruler.*

c Sm. has, *his banners*, דגליו.

d G. has, *the things prepared for him ;* S. *he whose it is ;* Aq., Sym., *he for whom it is prepared ;* all reading probably שֶׁלֹּה; T. *the Messiah whose is the kingdom;* V. *he who is sent ;* I read שֶׁלֵו.

e G., V. have, *the expectation ;* S. *expect* (verb); T. *shall obey ;* Sm. *shall be assembled,* similar is Aq.

f G. has, *desired the noble thing ;* T. *rich in substance ;* S. *strong man.*

the land that *it was* pleasant; and bowed his shoulder to bear, and became a servant unto tribute.

16 Dan shall judge his people, as one of the tribes of Israel.
17 Dan shall be a serpent by the way, an adder in the path, that biteth the horse heels, so that his rider shall fall backward.
18 I have waited for thy salvation, O LORD.

19 Gad, a troop shall overcome him: but he shall overcome at the last.

20 Out of Asher his bread *shall be* fat, and he shall yield royal dainties.

21 Naphtali *is* a hind let loose: he giveth goodly words.

22 Joseph *is* a fruitful bough, *even* a fruitful bough by a well; *whose* branches run over the wall: 23 The archers have sorely grieved him, and shot *at him*, and hated him: 24 But his

וְאֶת־הָאָרֶץ כִּי נָעֵמָה וַיֵּט שִׁכְמוֹ
shoulder his bowed he and ; pleasant [was it] that land the and
לִסְבֹּל וַיְהִי לְמַס־עֹבֵד[a]׃
.serving one of service forced the for became and ,bear to

16 דָּן יָדִין עַמּוֹ כְּאַחַד שִׁבְטֵי
of tribes the of one as ,people his judge will Dan
17 יִשְׂרָאֵל׃ יְהִי־דָן נָחָשׁ עֲלֵי־דֶרֶךְ שְׁפִיפֹן[b]
snake horned a ,way the upon serpent a be Dan Let .Israel
עֲלֵי־אֹרַח הַנֹּשֵׁךְ עִקְּבֵי־סוּס וַיִּפֹּל[c] רֹכְבוֹ
rider its falls and ,horse a of heels the bites that ; path the upon
18 אָחוֹר׃ לִישׁוּעָתְךָ קִוִּיתִי יְהוָה׃
.Jehovah ,wait I blessing thy For .backward

19 גָּד גְּדוּד יְגוּדֶנּוּ וְהוּא
he and ,him upon press will throng warlike a ,Gad
יָגֻד[d] עָקֵב׃
.heel [their] upon press shall

20 מֵאָשֵׁר[e] שְׁמֵנָה לַחְמוֹ וְהוּא יִתֵּן
give shall he and ,bread his [is] fat ,Asher (From)
מַעֲדַנֵּי־מֶלֶךְ[f]׃
.king a of dainties

21 נַפְתָּלִי אַיָּלָה[g] שְׁלֻחָה[g] הַנֹּתֵן אִמְרֵי־
of sayings giving one ,loose let hind a ,Naphtali
שָׁפֶר[h]׃
.beauty

22 בֵּן פֹּרָת יוֹסֵף בֵּן[i] פֹּרָת
tree fruitful a of son a ,Joseph [is] tree fruitful a of son A
23 עֲלֵי־עָיִן[j] בָּנוֹת צָעֲדָה עֲלֵי־שׁוּר[ji]׃ וַיְמָרֲרֻהוּ
,him harass And .wall a upon run branches ; fountain a by
24 וָרֹבּוּ וַיִּשְׂטְמֻהוּ בַּעֲלֵי חִצִּים[k]׃ וַתֵּשֶׁב
remains but ; arrows of masters him for wait in lie and ,shoot and

And the land that it was pleasant; And he bowed his shoulder to bear, And became a servant under taskwork.

16 Dan shall judge his people, As one of the tribes of Israel.
17 Dan shall be a serpent in the way, An adder in the path, That biteth the horse's heels, So that his rider falleth backward.
18 I have waited for thy salvation, O LORD.

19 Gad, a troop shall press upon him: But he shall press upon their heel.

20 Out of Asher his bread shall be fat, And he shall yield royal dainties.

21 Naphtali is a hind let loose: He giveth goodly words.

22 Joseph is a fruitful bough, A fruitful bough by a fountain; His branches run over the wall.
23 The archers have sorely grieved him, And shot at him, and persecuted him:
24 But his bow a-

---

a G. has, *a man tilling the ground.*

b G. has, *lying in wait.*

c S. has, *and causes to fall,* וַיַּפֵּל.

d G. adds, *him.*

e G., S., V. omit מ.

f G., S., V. have, *to rulers.*

g G. has, *a tree trunk let loose*, reading perhaps אֵילָה for אַיָּלָה; S. *a swift messenger.*

h G. has, *in the fruit beauty.*

i G. has, *my son increased, happy, the son of my youth, unto me return,* perhaps reading for בנות צעדה, בני צעירי; so also Sm.

j S. has, *go up to the fountain, a fortified building which rises with a wall.*

k S. has, *troops.*

bow abode in strength, and the arms of his hands were made strong by the hands of the mighty *God* of Jacob; (from thence *is* the shepherd, the stone of Israel:) 25 *Even* by the God of thy father, who shall help thee; and by the Almighty, who shall bless thee with blessings of heaven above, blessings of the deep that lieth under, blessings of the breasts, and of the womb; 26 The blessings of thy father have prevailed above the blessings of my progenitors unto the utmost bound of the everlasting hills: they shall be on the head of Joseph, and on the crown of the head of him that was separate from his brethren.

27 Benjamin shall ravin *as* a wolf: in the morning he shall devour the prey, and at night he shall divide the spoil.

28 All these *are* the twelve tribes of Israel: and this *is it* that their father spake unto them, and blessed them; every one according to his blessing he

בְּאֵיתָן קַשְׁתּוֹ וַיָּפֹזּוּ זְרֹעֵי יָדָיו
;hands his of arms the active are and ,bow his firmness in

מִידֵי אֲבִיר יַעֲקֹב מִשָּׁם[a][b]
,thence from ,Jacob of one mighty the of hands the from

25 רֹעֶה אֶבֶן יִשְׂרָאֵל[b]׃ מֵאֵל[c]
of God the From .Israel of stone the ,shepherd the [from]

אָבִיךָ וְיַעְזְרֶךָּ[d] וְאֵת[e] שַׁדַּי[e]
,Almighty the with and ,thee help he may and ,father thy

וִיבָרְכֶךָּ בִּרְכֹת שָׁמַיִם מֵעָל
,above from heaven of blessings [with] ; thee bless he may and

בִּרְכֹת תְּהוֹם רֹבֶצֶת תָּחַת בִּרְכֹת
of blessings ,beneath crouching abyss the of blessings

26 שָׁדַיִם וָרָחַם׃ בִּרְכֹת אָבִיךָ[f] גָּבְרוּ עַל־
(upon) surpass father thy of blessings The .womb and breasts

בִּרְכֹת הוֹרַי[g] עַד־תַּאֲוַת[g] גִּבְעֹת
of hills the of desire the ,everlastingness of mountains the of blessings the

עוֹלָם תִּהְיֶיןָ לְרֹאשׁ יוֹסֵף
,Joseph of head the to be they may ,eternity

וּלְקָדְקֹד נְזִיר אֶחָיו׃
.brethren his of prince the of head the of crown the to and

27 בִּנְיָמִין זְאֵב יִטְרָף בַּבֹּקֶר יֹאכַל
devours he morning the in ; tears that wolf a ,Benjamin

28 עַד[h] וְלָעֶרֶב יְחַלֵּק שָׁלָל׃ כָּל־אֵלֶּה
these All .spoil divides he evening at and ,prey

שִׁבְטֵי[i] יִשְׂרָאֵל[i] שְׁנֵים עָשָׂר וְזֹאת
this and ; ten [and] two ,Israel of tribes the [were]

אֲשֶׁר־דִּבֶּר[j] לָהֶם[k] אֲבִיהֶם[l] וַיְבָרֶךְ אוֹתָם[m]
,them blessed he and ; father their them to spoke what [is]

אִישׁ אֲשֶׁר[n] כְּבִרְכָתוֹ בֵּרַךְ
blessed he blessing his to according [was] what [with] one each

bode in strength, And the arms of his hands were made strong, By the hands of the Mighty One of Jacob, (From thence is the shepherd, the stone of Israel,) 25 Even by the God of thy father, who shall help thee, And by the Almighty, who shall bless thee, With blessings of heaven above, Blessings of the deep that coucheth beneath, Blessings of the breasts, and of the womb. 26 The blessings of thy father Have prevailed above the blessings of my progenitors Unto the utmost bound of the everlasting hills: They shall be on the head of Joseph, And on the crown of the head of him that was separate from his brethren.

27 Benjamin is a wolf that ravineth: In the morning he shall devour the prey, And at even he shall divide the spoil.

28 All these are the twelve tribes of Israel: and this is it that their father spake unto them and blessed them; every one according to his blessing he

---

a Sm. has *from the name*, מִשֵּׁם; S. *and from the name*, וּמִשֵּׁם.

b G. has, *thence the one having overpowered Israel.*

c S., V. omit מ.

d S., V, omit ו.

e G. has, *my God;* Sm., S., V. *God Almighty*, ואל שדי.

f G. has, *thy father and thy mother.*

g G. has, *the enduring mountains and over the blessings;* Sm. is similar; I read הַרֲרֵי.

h G. has, *still*, עֹד.

i G. has, *sons of Jacob.*

j G., V. omit אשר.

k S. adds, *Jacob.*

l S. adds, *he said to them.*

m G. adds, *the father.*

n Sm., G., S. omit אשר.

blessed them. 29 And he charged them, and said unto them, I am to be gathered unto my people: bury me with my fathers in the cave that *is* in the field of Ephron the Hittite, 30 In the cave that *is* in the field of Machpelah, which *is* before Mamre, in the land of Canaan, which Abraham bought with the field of Ephron the Hittite for a possession of a buryingplace. 31 There they buried Abraham and Sarah his wife; there they buried Isaac and Rebekah his wife; and there I buried Leah. 32 The purchase of the field and of the cave that *is* therein *was* from the children of Heth. 33 And when Jacob had made an end of commanding his sons, he gathered up his feet into the bed, and yielded up the ghost, and was gathered unto his people.

29 אֹתָם׃ וַיְצַו[a] אוֹתָם[a] וַיֹּאמֶר אֲלֵהֶם[b]
: them unto said and them commanded he And .them

אֲנִי נֶאֱסָף אֶל־עַמִּי קִבְרוּ אֹתִי
me bury ; people my unto gathered be to about [am] I

אֶל־אֲבֹתָי אֶל־הַמְּעָרָה אֲשֶׁר בִּשְׂדֵה
of field the in [is] which cave the at ,fathers my by

30 עֶפְרוֹן הַחִתִּי׃ בַּמְּעָרָה[c] אֲשֶׁר[d] בִּשְׂדֵה[d]
of field the in [is] which cave the in ; Hittite the Ephron

הַמַּכְפֵּלָה[c] אֲשֶׁר־עַל־פְּנֵי מַמְרֵא בְּאֶרֶץ
of land the in ,Mamre before [is] which ,Machpelah

כְּנָעַן אֲשֶׁר קָנָה אַבְרָהָם אֶת־הַשָּׂדֶה[e] מֵאֵת
(with) from ,field the with Abraham bought which ;Canaan

31 עֶפְרֹן הַחִתִּי לַאֲחֻזַּת־קָבֶר׃ שָׁמָּה קָבְרוּ
buried they There .possession burial a for ,Hittite the Ephron

אֶת־אַבְרָהָם וְאֵת שָׂרָה אִשְׁתּוֹ שָׁמָּה[f] קָבְרוּ
buried they there ,wife his Sarah and Abraham

אֶת־יִצְחָק וְאֵת רִבְקָה אִשְׁתּוֹ וְשָׁמָּה[g] קָבַרְתִּי
buried I there and ; wife his Rebekah and Isaac

32 אֶת־לֵאָה׃ מִקְנֵה[h] הַשָּׂדֶה וְהַמְּעָרָה אֲשֶׁר־בּוֹ
it in [is] which cave the and field the of purchase the ; Leah

33 מֵאֵת בְּנֵי־חֵת[i]׃ וַיְכַל יַעֲקֹב לְצַוֹּת
command to Jacob finished And .Heth of sons the (with) from

אֶת־בָּנָיו וַיֶּאֱסֹף רַגְלָיו אֶל־הַמִּטָּה וַיִּגְוַע
,expired he and ; bed the into feet his gathered he and ,sons his

וַיֵּאָסֶף אֶל־עַמָּיו׃
.people his unto gathered was and

blessed them. 29 And he charged them, and said unto them, I am to be gathered unto my people: bury me with my fathers in the cave that is in the field of Ephron the Hittite, 30 in the cave that is in the field of Machpelah, which is before Mamre, in the land of Canaan, which Abraham bought with the field from Ephron the Hittite for a possession of a buryingplace: 31 there they buried Abraham and Sarah his wife; there they buried Isaac and Rebekah his wife; and there I buried Leah: 32 the field and the cave that is therein, which was purchased from the children of Heth. 33 And when Jacob made an end of charging his sons, he gathered up his feet into the bed, and yielded up the ghost, and was gathered unto his people.

50

And Joseph fell upon his father's face, and wept upon him, and kissed him. 2 And Joseph command-

1 וַיִּפֹּל יוֹסֵף עַל־פְּנֵי אָבִיו וַיֵּבְךְּ
wept and ,father his of face the upon Joseph fell And

2 עָלָיו וַיִּשַּׁק־לוֹ׃ וַיְצַו יוֹסֵף
Joseph commanded And .him (to) kissed and him upon

And Joseph fell upon his father's face, and wept upon him, and kissed him. 2 And Joseph command-

---

a G. omits.
b S. adds, *their father*.
c V. omits.
d G. omits.
e G. has, *the cave*, המערה
f Sm. has, *and there*, ושם ; so apparently S.
g G. omits ו.
h G. adds, *in*.
i V. omits the verse.

ed his servants
the physicians to
embalm his
father: and the
physicians em-
balmed Israel. 3
And forty days
were fulfilled for
him; for so are
fulfilled the days
of those which
are embalmed:
and the Egyp-
tians mourned
for him three-
score and ten
days. 4 And
when the days
of his mourn-
ing were past,
Joseph spake
unto the house
of Pharaoh, say-
ing, If now I
have found
grace in your
eyes, speak, I
pray you, in the
ears of Pharaoh,
saying, 5 My
father made me
swear, saying,
Lo, I die: in
my grave which
I have digged
for me in the
land of Canaan,
there shalt thou
bury me. Now
therefore let me
go up, I pray
thee, and bury
my father, and
I will come a-
gain. 6 And
Pharaoh said,
Go up, and
bury thy father,
according as he
made thee
swear.
7 And Joseph
went up to bury
his father: and
with him went
up all the serv-
ants of Pharaoh,
the elders of
his house, and
all the elders of
the land of E-
gypt, 8 And all
the house of Jo-
seph, and his
brethren, and
his father's
house: only
their little ones,

אֶת־עֲבָדָיו אֶת־הָרֹפְאִים לַחֲנֹט אֶת־אָבִיו

; father his   embalm to   physicians the   slaves his

3 וַיַּחַנְטוּ הָרֹפְאִים אֶת־יִשְׂרָאֵל׃ וַיִּמְלְאוּ־לוֹ

him for continued And   .Israel   physicians the   embalmed and

אַרְבָּעִים יוֹם כִּי כֵּן יִמְלְאוּ יְמֵי הַחֲנֻטִים

; embalmed those   of days the   continue   so   for   ,days   forty

4 וַיִּבְכּוּ אֹתוֹ מִצְרַיִם שִׁבְעִים יוֹם׃ וַיַּעַבְרוּ

by passed And   .days   seventy   Egypt   him   for wept and

יְמֵי בְכִיתוֹ וַיְדַבֵּר יוֹסֵף אֶל־בֵּית

of house the unto   Joseph   spoke and   ,weeping his   of days the

פַּרְעֹה לֵאמֹר אִם־נָא מָצָאתִי חֵן בְּעֵינֵיכֶם

,eyes your in   favor   found have I   ,now ,If   : saying   ,Pharaoh

5 דַּבְּרוּ־נָא[a] בְּאָזְנֵי פַרְעֹה לֵאמֹר[b]׃ אָבִי

father My   : saying   Pharaoh   of ears the in   ,pray ,ye speak

הִשְׁבִּיעַנִי לֵאמֹר[c] הִנֵּה[d] אָנֹכִי מֵת[d] בְּקִבְרִי

grave my in   ; die   I   Behold   : saying   ,swear me made

אֲשֶׁר כָּרִיתִי[e] לִי בְּאֶרֶץ כְּנַעַן שָׁמָּה

there   ,Canaan   of land the in   myself for   dug have I   which

תִּקְבְּרֵנִי [f]וְעַתָּה אֶעֱלֶה־נָּא [f]וְאֶקְבְּרָה

bury and   ,pray I ,up go me let   now and   ; me bury shalt thou

6 אֶת־אָבִי[g] וְאָשׁוּבָה׃ וַיֹּאמֶר פַּרְעֹה עֲלֵה [h]וּקְבֹר

bury and   ,up Go   : Pharaoh   said And   .return and   ,father my

7 אֶת־אָבִיךָ כַּאֲשֶׁר הִשְׁבִּיעֶךָ׃ וַיַּעַל יוֹסֵף

Joseph   up went And   .swear thee made he   as   ,father thy

לִקְבֹּר אֶת־אָבִיו וַיַּעֲלוּ אִתּוֹ כָּל־עַבְדֵי

of servants the all   him with   up went and   ; father his   bury to

פַרְעֹה [i]זִקְנֵי בֵיתוֹ וְכֹל זִקְנֵי אֶרֶץ־

of land the   of elders the   all and   ,house his   of elders the   ,Pharaoh

8 מִצְרָיִם׃ וְכֹל בֵּית יוֹסֵף וְאֶחָיו

brethren his and   ,Joseph   of house the   all And   .Egypt

וּבֵית[j] אָבִיו[k] רַק טַפָּם וְצֹאנָם

,flocks their and   ,ones little their   only   ; father his   of house the and

ed his servants
the physicians
to embalm his
father: and the
physicians em-
balmed Israel. 3
And forty days
were fulfilled for
him; for so are
fulfilled the days
of embalming:
and the Egyp-
tians wept for
him threescore
and ten days. 4
And when
the days of
weeping for him
were past, Jo-
seph spake unto
the house of
Pharaoh, saying,
If now I have
found grace in
your eyes,
speak, I pray
you, in the ears
of Pharaoh, say-
ing, 5 My father
made me swear,
saying, Lo, I die:
in my grave
which I have
digged for me
in the land of
Canaan, there
shalt thou bury
me. Now there-
fore let me go
up, I pray thee,
and bury my
father, and I
will come again.
6 And Pharaoh
said, Go up,
and bury thy
father, accord-
ing as he made
thee swear.
7 And Joseph
went up to bury
his father: and
with him went
up all the serv-
ants of Pharaoh,
the elders of his
house, and all
the elders of the
land of Egypt,
8 and all the
house of Joseph,
and his breth-
ren, and his
father's house:
only their little
ones, and their
flocks, and their

a G. adds, *concerning me.*

b S., V. omit.

c S. adds, *to me.*

d G. omits.

e S. has, *I have purchased;* T., *I have prepared for myself.*

f S. omits ו.

g Sm. adds, *as he made me swear.*

h G. omits ו.

i G., S. add, *and,* ו.

j G. adds, *all,* reading וכל בית.

k S. adds, *went up with him.*

and their flocks, and their herds, they left in the land of Goshen. 9 And there went up with him both chariots and horsemen: and it was a very great company. 10 And they came to the threshing floor of Atad, which *is* beyond Jordan, and there they mourned with a great and very sore lamentation: and he made a mourning for his father seven days. 11 And when the inhabitants of the land, the Canaanites, saw the mourning in the floor of Atad, they said, This *is* a grievous mourning to the Egyptians: wherefore the name of it was called Abel-mizraim, which *is* beyond Jordan. 12 And his sons did unto him according as he commanded them: 13 For his sons carried him into the land of Canaan, and buried him in the cave of the field of Machpelah, which Abraham bought with the field for a possession of a buryingplace of Ephron the Hittite, before Mamre.

וּבְקָרָם עָזְבוּ בְּאֶרֶץ גֹּשֶׁן׃ וַיַּעַל 9
,herds their and left they of land the in .Goshen up went And

עִמּוֹ גַּם־רֶכֶב גַּם־פָּרָשִׁים וַיְהִי הַמַּחֲנֶה
him with chariots both ; horsemen and was and camp the

כָּבֵד מְאֹד׃ וַיָּבֹאוּ עַד־גֹּרֶן 10
heavy .exceedingly came they And of threshing-floor the as far as

הָאָטָד אֲשֶׁר בְּעֵבֶר הַיַּרְדֵּן וַיִּסְפְּדוּ·
,thorns which of side other the on [is] ;Jordan mourned they and

שָׁם מִסְפֵּד גָּדוֹל וְכָבֵד מְאֹד[a] וַיַּעַשׂ
there mourning a with great heavy and ; exceedingly made he and

לְאָבִיו אֵבֶל שִׁבְעַת יָמִים׃ וַיַּרְא 11
father his for lamentation a seven .days saw And

יוֹשֵׁב הָאָרֶץ הַכְּנַעֲנִי אֶת־הָאֵבֶל
of inhabitants the ,land the ,Canaanites the lamentation the

בְּגֹרֶן הָאָטָד וַיֹּאמְרוּ אֵבֶל־כָּבֵד
of threshing-floor the in ; thorns : said they and lamentation heavy A

זֶה לְמִצְרָיִם עַל־כֵּן קָרָא שְׁמָהּ אָבֵל
this [is] ; Egypt to therefore called one ,name its Abel

מִצְרַיִם אֲשֶׁר בְּעֵבֶר הַיַּרְדֵּן׃ וַיַּעֲשׂוּ 12
; Mizraim [is] which of side other the on .Jordan did And

בָנָיו לוֹ כֵּן [b]כַּאֲשֶׁר צִוָּם[b]׃ וַיִּשְׂאוּ 13
sons his ,him to so as .them commanded had he carried And

אֹתוֹ בָנָיו[c] אַרְצָה כְּנַעַן וַיִּקְבְּרוּ אֹתוֹ
him sons his of land the to ,Canaan buried and him

בִּמְעָרַת שְׂדֵה[d] הַמַּכְפֵּלָה אֲשֶׁר קָנָה אַבְרָהָם
of cave the in of field the ;Machpelah which bought Abraham

אֶת־הַשָּׂדֶה[e] לַאֲחֻזַּת־קֶבֶר מֵאֵת עֶפְרֹן
field the with ,possession burial a for (with) from Ephron

הַחִתִּי עַל־פְּנֵי מַמְרֵא׃
Hittite the before .Mamre

herds, they left in the land of Goshen. 9 And there went up with him both chariots and horsemen: and it was a very great company. 10 And they came to the threshing-floor of Atad, which is beyond Jordan, and there they lamented with a very great and sore lamentation: and he made a mourning for his father seven days. 11 And when the inhabitants of the land, the Canaanites, saw the mourning in the floor of Atad, they said, This is a grievous mourning to the Egyptians: wherefore the name of it was called Abel-mizraim, which is beyond Jordan. 12 And his sons did unto him according as he commanded them: 13 for his sons carried him into the land of Canaan, and buried him in the cave of the field of Machpelah, which Abraham bought with the field, for a possession of a buryingplace, of Ephron the Hittite, before Mamre.

14 And Joseph returned into Egypt, he, and his brethren, and all that went up with him to bury his father, after he

וַיָּשָׁב יוֹסֵף מִצְרַיְמָה הוּא וְאֶחָיו 14
returned And Joseph ,Egypt to he brethren his and

[f]וְכָל־הָעֹלִים אִתּוֹ לִקְבֹּר אֶת־אָבִיו אַחֲרֵי[g]
up going those all and him with bury to ,father his after

14 And Joseph returned into Egypt, he, and his brethren, and all that went up with him to bury his father, after he

a S., V. omit.
b G. has, *and they buried him there.*
c S. omits, and adds, *and bore him.*
d G., V. omit.
e G. has, *the cave,* המערה.
f G. omits כל.
g G. omits; S. adds, *and,* reading, ואחרי

had buried his
father.

15 And when
Joseph's breth-
ren saw that
their father was
dead, they said,
Joseph will per-
adventure hate
us, and will
certainly requite
us all the evil
which we did
unto him. 16
And they sent a
messenger unto
Joseph, saying,
Thy father did
command be-
fore he died,
saying, 17 So
shall ye say un-
to Joseph, For-
give, I pray thee
now, the tres-
pass of thy
brethren, and
their sin; for
they did unto
thee evil: and
now, we pray
thee, forgive the
trespass of the
servants of the
God of thy fa-
ther. And Jo-
seph wept when
they spake unto
him. 18 And his
brethren also
went and fell
down before his
face; and they
said, Behold, we
be thy servants.
19 And Joseph
said unto them,
Fear not: for
am I in the
place of God?
20 But as for
you, ye thought
evil against me;
but God meant
it unto good, to
bring to pass,
as *it is* this day,
to save much
people alive. 21
Now therefore
fear ye not: I

קָבְרוֹ[a] אֶת־אָבִיו׃ וַיִּרְאוּ אֲחֵי־יוֹסֵף כִּי 15
that Joseph of brethren the saw And .father his burying his

מֵת אֲבִיהֶם[b] וַיֹּאמְרוּ לוּ יִשְׂטְמֵנוּ
us to hostile be should If :said they and ,father their dead was

יוֹסֵף וְהָשֵׁב יָשִׁיב לָנוּ אֵת כָּל־הָרָעָה
evil the all us to repay should repaying and ,Joseph

אֲשֶׁר גָּמַלְנוּ אֹתוֹ׃ וַיְצַוּוּ[dc] אֶל־יוֹסֵף 16
Joseph unto message a sent they And .—him to did we which

לֵאמֹר[d] אָבִיךָ צִוָּה[e] לִפְנֵי מוֹתוֹ לֵאמֹר׃
:saying death his before commanded father Thy :saying

כֹּה־תֹאמְרוּ לְיוֹסֵף אָנָּא שָׂא נָא 17
,now ,forgive ,pray We :Joseph to say shall ye Thus

פֶּשַׁע אַחֶיךָ[f] וְחַטָּאתָם כִּי־רָעָה
evil for ,sin their and brethren thy of transgression the

גְמָלוּךָ וְעַתָּה שָׂא נָא לְפֶשַׁע
of transgression the (to) ,pray ,forgive now and ;thee to did they

עַבְדֵי אֱלֹהֵי אָבִיךָ וַיֵּבְךְּ יוֹסֵף
Joseph wept and ;father thy of God the of servants the

בְּדַבְּרָם אֵלָיו׃ וַיֵּלְכוּ גַּם־אֶחָיו[g] וַיִּפְּלוּ 18
fell and ,brethren his also went And .him unto speaking their in

לְפָנָיו[g] וַיֹּאמְרוּ הִנֶּנּוּ לְךָ לַעֲבָדִים׃
.slaves (for) thee to [are] we Behold :said and ,him before

וַיֹּאמֶר אֲלֵהֶם יוֹסֵף אַל־תִּירָאוּ כִּי הֲתַחַת[h] 19
of instead for ,fear not Do :Joseph them unto said And

אֱלֹהִים[h] אָנִי׃ וְאַתֶּם[i] חֲשַׁבְתֶּם עָלַי רָעָה 20
,evil me against purposed you ,you And ?I [am] God

[j]אֱלֹהִים חֲשָׁבָהּ[k] לְטֹבָה לְמַעַן עֲשֹׂה כַּיּוֹם
[2]day like do to order in ;good for it purposed God

הַזֶּה [l]לְהַחֲיֹת עַם־רָב׃ וְעַתָּה[m] אַל־תִּירָאוּ 21
,fear not do ,now And .people numerous a alive keep to ,[1]this

had buried his
father.

15 And when
Joseph's breth-
ren saw that
their father was
dead, they said,
It may be that
Joseph will hate
us, and will
fully requite us
all the evil
which we did
unto him. 16
And they sent a
message unto
Joseph, saying,
Thy father did
command before
he died, say-
ing, 17 So shall
ye say unto Jo-
seph, Forgive, I
pray thee now,
the transgres-
sion of thy breth-
ren, and their
sin, for that they
did unto thee
evil: and now,
we pray thee,
forgive the
transgression of
the servants of
the God of thy
father. And Jo-
seph wept when
they spake un-
to him. 18 And
his brethren al-
so went and fell
down before his
face; and they
said, Behold,
we be thy serv-
ants. 19 And
Joseph said un-
to them, Fear
not: for am I
in the place of
God? 20 And as
for you, ye
meant evil a-
gainst me; but
God meant it
for good, to
bring to pass,
as it is this day,
to save much
people alive. 21
Now therefore
fear ye not: I

a G. omits.

b S. adds, *and they feared;* so essentially V.

c G. has, *and they drew near.*

d S. has, *and they drew near to Joseph and said to him.*

e G. has, *swore.*

f G. has, *to them.*

g G. omits, and adds, *to him.*

h G. has, *of God;* S., *under God,* omitting question; T. *I fear God;* V., *are we able to resist the will of God?*

i G., S., V. omit ו.

j G., S., V. add, *and,* ו.

k G. adds, *concerning me.*

l S., V. add, *and,* ו.

m G. has, *and he said to them;* V. omits.

will nourish
you, and your
little ones. And
he comforted
them, and spake
kindly unto
them.

22 And Jo-
seph dwelt in
Egypt, he, and
his father's
house: and Jo-
seph lived an
hundred and
ten years. 23
And Joseph saw
Ephraim's chil-
dren of the
third *genera-
tion:* the chil-
dren also of
Machir the son
of Manasseh
were brought
up upon Jo-
seph's knees.
24 And Joseph
said unto his
brethren, I die:
and God will
surely visit you,
and bring you
out of this land
unto the land
which he sware
to Abraham, to
Isaac, and to
Jacob. 25 And
Joseph took an
oath of the
children of Is-
rael, saying,
God will surely
visit you, and
ye shall carry up
my bones from
hence. 26 So
Joseph died,
being an hun-
dred and ten
years old: and
they embalmed
him, and he was
put in a coffin in
Egypt.

אָנֹכִי אֲכַלְכֵּל אֶתְכֶם וְאֶת־טַפְּכֶם וַיְנַחֵם
comforted he and ; ones little your and you nourish will I

אוֹתָם וַיְדַבֵּר עַל־לִבָּם׃ וַיֵּשֶׁב יוֹסֵף 22
Joseph dwelt And .heart their unto spoke and ,them

בְּמִצְרַיִם הוּא[a] וּבֵית[b] אָבִיו וַיְחִי יוֹסֵף
Joseph lived and ; father his of house the and he ,Egypt in

מֵאָה וָעֶשֶׂר שָׁנִים׃ וַיַּרְא יוֹסֵף לְאֶפְרַיִם בְּנֵי 23
of sons Ephraim to Joseph saw And .years ten and hundred a

שִׁלֵּשִׁים גַּם בְּנֵי מָכִיר בֶּן־מְנַשֶּׁה
Manasseh of son the Machir of sons the also ; generation third the

יֻלְּדוּ עַל־בִּרְכֵּי[c] יוֹסֵף׃ וַיֹּאמֶר יוֹסֵף אֶל־ 24
unto Joseph said And .Joseph of knees the upon born were

אֶחָיו[d] אָנֹכִי מֵת וֵאלֹהִים פָּקֹד יִפְקֹד אֶתְכֶם
,you visit will visiting God and ,die I :brethren his

וְהֶעֱלָה אֶתְכֶם מִן־הָאָרֶץ הַזֹּאת אֶל־הָאָרֶץ
land the unto ,[1]this [2]land from you up bring and

אֲשֶׁר נִשְׁבַּע[e] לְאַבְרָהָם לְיִצְחָק וּלְיַעֲקֹב׃
.Jacob to and Isaac to Abraham to swore he which

וַיַּשְׁבַּע יוֹסֵף אֶת־בְּנֵי יִשְׂרָאֵל לֵאמֹר פָּקֹד 25
Visiting :saying Israel of sons the Joseph swear made And

יִפְקֹד אֱלֹהִים אֶתְכֶם וְהַעֲלִתֶם אֶת־עַצְמֹתַי
bones my up bring shall ye and ,you God visit will

מִזֶּה[f]׃ וַיָּמָת יוֹסֵף בֶּן־מֵאָה וָעֶשֶׂר 26
ten and hundred a (of son a) ,Joseph died And .hence from

שָׁנִים וַיַּחַנְטוּ[g] אֹתוֹ וַיִּישֶׂם בָּאָרוֹן
coffin a in put and ,him embalmed they and ; [old] years

בְּמִצְרָיִם׃
.Egypt in

will nourish you,
and your little
ones. And he
comforted them,
and spake kind-
ly unto them.

22 And Jo-
seph dwelt in
Egypt, he, and
his father's
house: and Jo-
seph lived an
hundred and
ten years. 23
And Joseph saw
Ephraim's chil-
dren of the third
generation: the
children also of
Machir the son
of Manasseh
were born upon
Joseph's knees.
24 And Joseph
said unto his
brethren, I die:
but God will
surely visit you,
and bring you
up out of this
land unto the
land which he
sware to Abra-
ham, to Isaac,
and to Jacob. 25
And Joseph
took an oath of
the children of
Israel, saying,
God will surely
visit you, and ye
shall carry up
my bones from
hence. 26 So Jo-
seph died, being
an hundred and
ten years old:
and they em-
balmed him,
and he was put
in a coffin in
Egypt.

---

a G. adds, *and his brethren.*
b G., S., V. add, *all*, reading וכל בית.
c Sm. has, *in the days of*, בימי.
d G. adds, *saying.*
e G. adds, *God to your fathers.*
f G., S., V., add, *with you.*
g G. has, *and they buried.*

EXODUS—ואלה שמות

1

Now these
are the names
of the children
of Israel, which
came into E-
gypt; every man
and his house-
hold came with
Jacob. 2 Reu-
ben, Simeon,
Levi, and Ju-
dah, 3 Issachar,
Zebulun, and
Benjamin, 4
Dan, and Naph-
tali, Gad, and
Asher. 5 And
all the souls that
came out of the
loins of Jacob
were seventy
souls: for Jo-
seph was in E-
gypt *already*. 6
And Joseph
died, and all
his brethren,
and all that
generation.

7 And the chil-
dren of Israel
were fruitful,
and increased
abundantly, and
multiplied, and
waxed exceed-
ingly mighty;
and the land
was filled with
them. 8 Now
there arose up a
new king over
Egypt, which
knew not Jo-
seph. 9 And he
said unto his
people, Behold,

1 וְאֵלֶּה שְׁמוֹת בְּנֵי יִשְׂרָאֵל הַבָּאִים
in came who Israel of sons the of names the [were] these And

מִצְרָיְמָה אֵת יַעֲקֹב[a] אִישׁ וּבֵיתוֹ בָּאוּ׃
; in came they house his and one each ;Jacob with Egypt to

2 רְאוּבֵן [b]שִׁמְעוֹן [b]לֵוִי [c]וִיהוּדָה׃ [d]יִשָּׂשכָר [d]זְבוּלֻן
3 ,Zebulun ,Issachar ,Judah and ,Levi ,Simeon ,Reuben

4 וּבִנְיָמִן׃ [e]דָּן וְנַפְתָּלִי [e]גָּד וְאָשֵׁר׃ וַיְהִי
5 were And .Asher and ,Gad ,Naphtali and ,Dan ,Benjamin and

כָּל־נֶפֶשׁ יֹצְאֵי יֶרֶךְ־יַעֲקֹב שִׁבְעִים[f]
seventy Jacob of loins the from out came that souls the all

6 נָפֶשׁ וְיוֹסֵף[g] הָיָה בְמִצְרָיִם[g]׃ וַיָּמָת יוֹסֵף
Joseph died And .Egypt in being Joseph (and) ,souls

וְכָל־אֶחָיו וְכֹל הַדּוֹר הַהוּא׃
.[1]that [2]generation all and ,brethren his all and

7 וּבְנֵי יִשְׂרָאֵל פָּרוּ וַיִּשְׁרְצוּ
swarmed and fruitful were Israel of children the [since] And

וַיִּרְבּוּ וַיַּעַצְמוּ בִּמְאֹד מְאֹד
,exceedingly exceedingly (in) strong grew and multiplied and

וַתִּמָּלֵא הָאָרֶץ אֹתָם׃
.them [with] land the filled was (and)

8 וַיָּקָם מֶלֶךְ־חָדָשׁ[h] עַל־מִצְרָיִם אֲשֶׁר
who ,Egypt over king new a arose And

9 לֹא־יָדַע אֶת־יוֹסֵף׃ וַיֹּאמֶר אֶל־עַמּוֹ הִנֵּה
Behold :people his unto said he And .Joseph known not had

Now these are
the names of
the sons of Is-
rael, which
came into E-
gypt; every man
and his house-
hold came with
Jacob. 2 Reu-
ben, Simeon,
Levi, and Ju-
dah; 3 Issachar,
Zebulun, and
Benjamin; 4
Dan and Naph-
tali, Gad and
Asher. 5 And
all the souls that
came out of the
loins of Jacob
were seventy
souls: and Jo-
seph was in
Egypt already. 6
And Joseph
died, and all his
brethren, and all
that generation.

7 And the
children of Is-
rael were fruit-
ful, and in-
creased abun-
dantly, and
multiplied, and
waxed exceed-
ing mighty; and
the land was
filled with them.
8 Now there
arose a new
king over E-
gypt, which
knew not Jo-
seph. 9 And he
said unto his
people, Behold,

---

a G. adds, *their father*.
b S. adds, *and*, ו.
c G., V. omit ו.
d S. adds *and*, ו.
e S. adds, *and*, ו.
f G. has, *seventy-five*.
g G. transposes to beginning of verse.
h G. has, *another*.

the people of the children of Israel *are* more and mightier than we: 10 Come on, let us deal wisely with them; lest they multiply, and it come to pass, that, when there falleth out any war, they join also unto our enemies, and fight against us, and *so* get them up out of the land. 11 Therefore they did set over them taskmasters to afflict them with their burdens. And they built for Pharaoh treasure cities, Pithom and Raamses. 12 But the more they afflicted them, the more they multiplied and grew. And they were grieved because of the children of Israel. 13 And the Egyptians made the children of Israel to serve with rigour: 14 And they made their lives bitter with hard bondage, in morter, and in brick, and in all manner of service in the field: all their service, wherein they made them serve, *was* with rigour.

עַם בְּנֵי יִשְׂרָאֵל רַב [a] וְעָצוּם

strong and numerous [more] [are] Israel of children the of people the

10 מִמֶּנּוּ׃ הָבָה נִתְחַכְּמָה לוֹ פֶּן־יִרְבֶּה

,multiply they lest ;them towards craftily deal us let ,Come .we than

[b] וְהָיָה כִּי־תִקְרֶאנָה מִלְחָמָה וְנוֹסַף

joined be will (and) ,war us to happens when ,pass to come it and

גַּם־הוּא עַל־שֹׂנְאֵינוּ וְנִלְחַם־בָּנוּ וְעָלָה [c]

up go and ,us against fight will and ,enemies our with they also

11 מִן־הָאָרֶץ׃ [d] וַיָּשִׂימוּ עָלָיו שָׂרֵי [e]

of superintendents them over put they And .land the from

[e] מִסִּים לְמַעַן עַנֹּתוֹ בְּסִבְלֹתָם וַיִּבֶן

built they and ; burdens their with them afflict to order in ,labor forced

עָרֵי מִסְכְּנוֹת לְפַרְעֹה אֶת־פִּתֹם וְאֶת־רַעַמְסֵס׃ [f]

.Ramses and Pithom ,Pharaoh for [1]store [2]cities

12 וְכַאֲשֶׁר יְעַנּוּ אֹתוֹ כֵּן יִרְבֶּה וְכֵן יִפְרֹץ [g]

; spread they so and multiplied they so ,them afflicted they as And

[h] וַיָּקֻצוּ מִפְּנֵי בְּנֵי יִשְׂרָאֵל׃

.Israel of children the before from horror a had they and

13 וַיַּעֲבִדוּ מִצְרַיִם אֶת־בְּנֵי יִשְׂרָאֵל

Israel of children the [2]Egyptians [1]the [4]serve [3]made And

14 בְּפָרֶךְ׃ וַיְמָרְרוּ אֶת־חַיֵּיהֶם בַּעֲבֹדָה

[2]work through lives their bitter made they And .oppression with

קָשָׁה בְּחֹמֶר וּבִלְבֵנִים וּבְכָל־עֲבֹדָה בַּשָּׂדֶה

,field the in work all in and ,bricks in and clay in ,[1]hard

[i] אֵת [i] כָּל־עֲבֹדָתָם אֲשֶׁר־עָבְדוּ בָהֶם

them through wrought they which work their all

בְּפָרֶךְ׃

.oppression with

the people of the children of Israel are more and mightier than we: 10 come, let us deal wisely with them; lest they multiply, and it come to pass, that, when there falleth out any war, they also join themselves unto our enemies, and fight against us, and get them up out of the land. 11 Therefore they did set over them taskmasters to afflict them with their burdens. And they built for Pharaoh store cities, Pithom and Raamses. 12 But the more they afflicted them, the more they multiplied and the more they spread abroad. And they were grieved because of the children of Israel. 13 And the Egyptians made the children of Israel to serve with rigour: 14 and they made their lives bitter with hard service, in mortar and in brick, and in all manner of service in the field, all their service, wherein they made them serve with rigour.

15 And the king of Egypt spake to the Hebrew midwives, of which the name of the

15 וַיֹּאמֶר מֶלֶךְ מִצְרַיִם לַמְיַלְּדֹת הָעִבְרִיֹּת

,Hebrews the of midwives the to Egypt of king the said And

אֲשֶׁר שֵׁם הָאַחַת שִׁפְרָה וְשֵׁם

of name the and ,Shiphrah [being] one the of name the whom of

15 And the king of Egypt spake to the Hebrew midwives, of which the name of the

---

a G. has, *a great multitude.*

b G., S. omit היה.

c S. has, *and cast us out.*

d G. has sing.

e S., T. have, *evil rulers.*

f G. adds, *and On, which is the city of the sun.*

g G. adds, *exceedingly.*

h G., T., V. add, *the Egyptians.*

i For את כל G. has, *according to all*, ככל.

one *was* Shiphrah, and the name of the other Puah: 16 And he said, When ye do the office of a midwife to the Hebrew women, and see *them* upon the stools; if it *be* a son, then ye shall kill him; but if it *be* a daughter, then she shall live. 17 But the midwives feared God, and did not as the king of Egypt commanded them, but saved the men children alive. 18 And the king of Egypt called for the midwives, and said unto them, Why have ye done this thing, and have saved the men children alive? 19 And the midwives said unto Pharaoh, Because the Hebrew women *are* not as the Egyptian women; for they *are* lively, and are delivered ere the midwives come in unto them. 20 Therefore God dealt well with the midwives: and the people multiplied, and waxed very mighty. 21 And it came to pass, because the midwives feared God, that he made them houses. 22 And Pharaoh charged all his people, saying,

16 הַשֵּׁנִית פּוּעָה׃ וַיֹּאמֶר[a] בְּיַלֶּדְכֶן
to midwives as acting your In : said he and ; Puah ,second the

אֶת־הָעִבְרִיּוֹת וּרְאִיתֶן[b] עַל־הָאָבְנָיִם[b] אִם־בֵּן
son a if ; birthstools the on look (and) ,women Hebrew the

הוּא וַהֲמִתֶּן אֹתוֹ וְאִם־בַּת הִוא
,[is] it daughter a if and ,it kill shall ye (and) ,[is] it

17 וָחָיָה׃ וַתִּירֶאןָ הַמְיַלְּדֹת אֶת־הָאֱלֹהִים
,God midwives the feared And .live shall it (and)

וְלֹא עָשׂוּ כַּאֲשֶׁר דִּבֶּר[c] אֲלֵיהֶן מֶלֶךְ
of king the them unto spoken had as do 2did 1they 3not and

18 מִצְרָיִם וַתְּחַיֶּיןָ אֶת־הַיְלָדִים׃[d] וַיִּקְרָא
called And .children male the alive kept they and ; Egypt

מֶלֶךְ־מִצְרַיִם לַמְיַלְּדֹת וַיֹּאמֶר לָהֶן מַדּוּעַ
Why : them to said and ,midwives the to Egypt of king the

עֲשִׂיתֶן הַדָּבָר הַזֶּה וַתְּחַיֶּיןָ אֶת־הַיְלָדִים׃[e]
? children male the alive keep and ,1this 2thing do ye do

19 וַתֹּאמַרְןָ הַמְיַלְּדֹת אֶל־פַּרְעֹה כִּי[f] לֹא כַנָּשִׁים
2women the like not Because : Pharaoh unto midwives the said And

הַמִּצְרִיֹּת הָעִבְרִיֹּת כִּי־חָיוֹת[g] הֵנָּה
; they [are] vigorous for ,women Hebrew the [are] 1Egyptian

בְּטֶרֶם תָּבוֹא אֲלֵהֶן הַמְיַלֶּדֶת וְיָלָדוּ׃
.bear they (and) ,midwife the them unto comes before

20 וַיֵּיטֶב אֱלֹהִים לַמְיַלְּדֹת[h] וַיִּרֶב הָעָם
people the multiplied and ; midwives the to God well did And

21 וַיַּעַצְמוּ מְאֹד׃ וַיְהִי[i] כִּי־יָרְאוּ
feared because ,pass to came it And .exceedingly strong became and

הַמְיַלְּדֹת אֶת־הָאֱלֹהִים וַיַּעַשׂ לָהֶם בָּתִּים׃
.houses them for made he (and) ,God midwives the

22 וַיְצַו פַּרְעֹה לְכָל־עַמּוֹ לֵאמֹר כָּל־הַבֵּן
son Every : saying people his all (to) Pharaoh commanded And

one was Shiphrah, and the name of the other Puah: 16 and he said, When ye do the office of a midwife to the Hebrew women, and see them upon the birthstool; if it be a son, then ye shall kill him; but if it be a daughter, then she shall live. 17 But the midwives feared God, and did not as the king of Egypt commanded them, but saved the men children alive. 18 And the king of Egypt called for the midwives, and said unto them, Why have ye done this thing, and have saved the men children alive? 19 And the midwives said unto Pharaoh, Because the Hebrew women are not as the Egyptian women; for they are lively, and are delivered ere the midwife come unto them. 20 And God dealt well with the midwives: and the people multiplied, and waxed very mighty. 21 And it came to pass, because the midwives feared God, that he made them houses. 22 And Pharaoh charged all his people, saying, Every son that is

---

a S., V. add, *to them.*

b G. has, *and they are about to bear;* S., *see when they bow themselves;* T., *and thou seest in bearing;* V., *and the time of bearing has arrived.*

c G. has, *commanded;* so essentially V.

d Sm., G., V. have, *the males.*

e Sm., G. have, *the males;* V. *the boys.*

f G., S. omit.

g G. has, *they bore;* S. *midwives;* T., *wise;* V. *have knowledge of obstetrics.*

h S. adds, *because they had done this thing.*

i G., V. omit.

Every son that is born ye shall cast into the river, and every daughter ye shall save alive.

הַיִּלּוֹד[a] הַיְאֹרָה תַּשְׁלִיכֻהוּ וְכָל־הַבַּת

daughter every and ;him cast shall you river the into ,born is that

תְּחַיּוּן׃

.alive keep shall you

born ye shall cast into the river, and every daughter ye shall save alive.

2

AND there went a man of the house of Levi, and took *to wife* a daughter of Levi. 2 And the woman conceived, and bare a son; and when she saw him that he *was* a goodly *child*, she hid him three months. 3 And when she could not longer hide him, she took for him an ark of bulrushes, and daubed it with slime and with pitch, and put the child therein; and she laid *it* in the flags by the river's brink. 4 And his sister stood afar off, to wit what would be done to him.

5 And the daughter of Pharaoh came down to wash *herself* at the river; and her maidens walked along by the river's side; and when she saw the ark among the flags, she sent her maid to fetch it. 6 And when she had opened *it*, she

1 וַיֵּלֶךְ[b] אִישׁ מִבֵּית לֵוִי וַיִּקַּח

took and ,Levi of house the from man a went And

2 אֶת־בַּת־לֵוִי׃ וַתַּהַר הָאִשָּׁה[c] וַתֵּלֶד בֵּן

; son a bore and woman the conceived And .Levi of daughter a

וַתֵּרֶא[d] אֹתוֹ כִּי־טוֹב הוּא וַתִּצְפְּנֵהוּ[e]

him concealed she and ,he [was] beautiful that him saw she and

3 שְׁלֹשָׁה יְרָחִים׃ וְלֹא־יָכְלָה עוֹד הַצְּפִינוֹ

;him conceal to still able not was she And .months three

וַתִּקַּח־לוֹ[f] תֵּבַת גֹּמֶא[g] וַתַּחְמְרָה בַחֵמָר

bitumen with daubed and ,papyrus of basket a him for took she and

וּבַזָּפֶת[h] וַתָּשֶׂם בָּהּ אֶת־הַיֶּלֶד וַתָּשֶׂם בַּסּוּף

reeds the in put and ,child the it in put she and ,pitch with and

4 עַל־שְׂפַת[i] הַיְאֹר׃ וַתֵּתַצַּב[j] אֲחֹתוֹ

sister his stand her took And .river the of bank the upon

5 מֵרָחֹק לְדֵעָה מַה־יֵּעָשֶׂה לוֹ׃ וַתֵּרֶד

down went And .him to done be would what know to ,distance a from

בַּת־פַּרְעֹה לִרְחֹץ עַל־הַיְאֹר

,river the at bathe to Pharaoh of daughter the

וְנַעֲרֹתֶיהָ הֹלְכֹת עַל־יַד הַיְאֹר

; river the of side the upon walking [were] maidens her [while] (and)

וַתֵּרֶא אֶת־הַתֵּבָה בְּתוֹךְ הַסּוּף וַתִּשְׁלַח

sent and ,reeds the of midst the in basket the saw she and

6 אֶת־אֲמָתָהּ[k] וַתִּקָּחֶהָ׃ וַתִּפְתַּח וַתִּרְאֵהוּ

(him) saw and opened she And .it took and ,slave female her

And there went a man of the house of Levi, and took to wife a daughter of Levi. 2 And the woman conceived, and bare a son: and when she saw him that he was a goodly child, she hid him three months. 3 And when she could not longer hide him, she took for him an ark of bulrushes, and daubed it with slime and with pitch; and she put the child therein, and laid it in the flags by the river's brink. 4 And his sister stood afar off, to know what would be done to him.

5 And the daughter of Pharaoh came down to bathe at the river; and her maidens walked along by the river side; and she saw the ark among the flags, and sent her handmaid to fetch it. 6 And she opened it, and saw the

---

a G., T. add, *to the Hebrews.*
b G. has, ויהי.
c G. omits.
d G. has pl., *and they saw.*
e G. has pl., *and they concealed.*
f Sm.. G. add, *his mother*, אמו.
g G. omits.
h G. omits ו.
i G. has, *by the river.*
j G. has, *and observed closely.*
k S. has pl., *her female slaves;* V. *one of her female slaves.*

saw the child:
and, behold, the
babe wept. And
she had compas-
sion on him,
and said, This *is*
one of the He-
brews' children.
7 Then said his
sister to Pha-
raoh's daughter,
Shall I go and
call to thee a
nurse of the He-
brew women,
that she may
nurse the child
for thee? 8 And
Pharaoh's
daughter said to
her, Go. And
the maid went
and called the
child's mother. 9
And Pharaoh's
daughter said
unto her, Take
this child away,
and nurse it for
me, and I will
give *thee* thy
wages. And the
woman took the
child, and nurs-
ed it. 10 And the
child grew, and
she brought him
unto Pharaoh's
daughter, and
he became her
son. And she
called his name
Moses: and she
said, Because I
drew him out of
the water.

11 And it
came to pass in
those days,
when Moses was
grown, that he
went out unto
his brethren,
and looked on
their burdens:
and he spied an
Egyptian smit-
ing a Hebrew,
one of his breth-
ren. 12 And he
looked this way
and that way,

אֶת־הַיֶּלֶד וְהִנֵּה־נַעַר[a] בֹּכֶה[b] וַתַּחְמֹל
compassion had she and ; weeping boy a behold and ,child the

עָלָיו[c] וַתֹּאמֶר מִיַּלְדֵי הָעִבְרִים זֶה׃
.one this [is] Hebrews the of children the Of : said and ,him on

7 וַתֹּאמֶר אֲחֹתוֹ אֶל־בַּת־פַּרְעֹה הַאֵלֵךְ[d]
go I Shall : Pharaoh of daughter the unto sister his said And

וְקָרָאתִי לָךְ אִשָּׁה מֵינֶקֶת מִן הָעִבְרִיֹּת
,women Hebrew the of nurse a woman a thee for call and

8 וְתֵינִק לָךְ אֶת־הַיָּלֶד׃ וַתֹּאמֶר־לָהּ[e]
her to said And ? child the thee for nurse may she that

בַּת־פַּרְעֹה לֵכִי וַתֵּלֶךְ הָעַלְמָה וַתִּקְרָא
called and maid the went and ; Go ,Pharaoh of daughter the

9 אֶת־אֵם הַיָּלֶד׃ וַתֹּאמֶר לָהּ בַּת־פַּרְעֹה
: Pharaoh of daughter the her to said And .child the of mother the

הֵילִיכִי[f] אֶת־הַיֶּלֶד הַזֶּה וְהֵינִקִהוּ לִי וַאֲנִי
I and ,me for him nurse and [1]this [2]child away Carry

אֶתֵּן אֶת־שְׂכָרֵךְ וַתִּקַּח הָאִשָּׁה הַיֶּלֶד
child the woman the took and ; wages thy give will

10 וַתְּנִיקֵהוּ׃ וַיִּגְדַּל הַיֶּלֶד וַתְּבִאֵהוּ
him brought she and ,child the grew And .him nursed and

לְבַת־פַּרְעֹה וַיְהִי־לָהּ לְבֵן
.son a (for) her to became he and ,Pharaoh of daughter the to

וַתִּקְרָא שְׁמוֹ מֹשֶׁה וַתֹּאמֶר כִּי מִן־
from Because : said and ,Moses name his called she And

11 הַמַּיִם מְשִׁיתִהוּ׃ וַיְהִי בַּיָּמִים[g] הָהֵם
,[1]those [2]days in pass to came it And .him drew I water the

וַיִּגְדַּל מֹשֶׁה וַיֵּצֵא אֶל־אֶחָיו[h]
,brethren his unto out went he and Moses up grown was (and)

וַיַּרְא בְּסִבְלֹתָם וַיַּרְא אִישׁ מִצְרִי מַכֶּה
smiting [1]Egyptian [2]man a saw he and ; burdens their on looked and

12 אִישׁ־עִבְרִי מֵאֶחָיו[i]׃ וַיִּפֶן כֹּה וָכֹה
,there and here turned he And .brethren his of ,man Hebrew a

child: and, be-
hold, the babe
wept. And she
had compassion
on him, and
said, This is one
of the Hebrews'
children. 7 Then
said his sister to
Pharaoh's
daughter, Shall
I go and call
thee a nurse of
the Hebrew
women, that she
may nurse the
child for thee?
8 And Pha-
raoh's daughter
said to her, Go.
And the maid
went and called
the child's moth-
er. 9 And Pha-
raoh's daughter
said unto her,
Take this child
away, and nurse
it for me, and I
will give thee
thy wages. And
the woman took
the child, and
nursed it. 10
And the child
grew, and she
brought him un-
to Pharaoh's
daughter, and
he became her
son. And she
called his name
Moses, and said,
Because I drew
him out of the
water.

11 And it
came to pass in
those days,
when Moses was
grown up, that
he went out un-
to his brethren,
and looked on
their burdens:
and he saw an
Egyptian smit-
ing an Hebrew,
one of his breth-
ren. 12 And he
looked this way
and that way,

---

a G., V. omit.

b G. adds, *in the ark.*

c G. adds, *the daughter of Pharaoh.*

d G. has, *dost thou wish?* V. *dost thou wish that I should go?*

e G., V. omit לה.

f G. has, *watch for me;* S. *behold to thee.*

g G. adds, *many,* cf. vs. 23.

h G. adds, *the sons of Israel.*

i G., S. add, *the sons of Israel.*

and when he
saw that *there*
was no man, he
slew the Egyp-
tian, and hid
him in the sand.

13 And when he
went out the
second day, be-
hold, two men
of the Hebrews
strove together:
and he said to
him that did
the wrong,
Wherefore smit-
est thou thy fel-
low? 14 And he
said, Who made
thee a prince
and a judge over
us? intendest
thou to kill me,
as thou killedst
the Egyptian?
And Moses fear-
ed, and said,
Surely this
thing is known.
15 Now when
Pharaoh heard
this thing, he
sought to slay
Moses. But Mo-
ses fled from the
face of Pharaoh,
and dwelt in the
land of Midian:
and he sat down
by a well. 16
Now the priest
of Midian had
seven daugh-
ters: and they
came and drew
water, and filled
the troughs to
water their fa-
ther's flock. 17
And the shep-
herds came and
drove them a-
way: but Moses
stood up and
helped them,
and watered
their flock. 18
And when they
came to Reuel
their father, he
said, How *is it*
that ye are come

וַיַּרְא כִּי־אֵין אִישׁ וַיַּךְ אֶת־הַמִּצְרִי
,Egyptian the   smote he and   ; man a   not was [there] that   saw and

13 וַיִּטְמְנֵהוּ בַּחוֹל׃ וַיֵּצֵא בַּיּוֹם הַשֵּׁנִי
,[1]second   [2]day the on   out went he And   .sand the in   him hid and

וְהִנֵּה[a] שְׁנֵי־אֲנָשִׁים עִבְרִים נִצִּים וַיֹּאמֶר
said he and   ; fighting   Hebrews   men two   behold and

לָרָשָׁע לָמָּה תַכֶּה רֵעֶךָ׃
? neighbor thy   smite thou shouldst   Why   : one guilty the to

14 וַיֹּאמֶר מִי שָׂמְךָ לְאִישׁ שַׂר וְשֹׁפֵט
judge a and   prince a   man a for   thee put   Who   : said he and

עָלֵינוּ הַלְהָרְגֵנִי אַתָּה אֹמֵר כַּאֲשֶׁר הָרַגְתָּ[b]
killedst thou   as   ,saying   thou [art]   me kill To   ? us over

אֶת־הַמִּצְרִי וַיִּירָא מֹשֶׁה וַיֹּאמַר אָכֵן נוֹדַע
known is   Surely   : said and   Moses   feared And   ? Egyptian the

15 הַדָּבָר׃ וַיִּשְׁמַע פַּרְעֹה אֶת־הַדָּבָר הַזֶּה
,[1]this   [2]word   Pharaoh   heard And   .thing the

וַיְבַקֵּשׁ לַהֲרֹג אֶת־מֹשֶׁה וַיִּבְרַח מֹשֶׁה מִפְּנֵי
before from   Moses   fled and   ; Moses   kill to   sought he and

פַּרְעֹה וַיֵּשֶׁב[c] בְּאֶרֶץ־מִדְיָן וַיֵּשֶׁב[d] עַל־
by   sat and   ,Midian of land the in   dwelt and   ,Pharaoh

16 הַבְּאֵר׃ וּלְכֹהֵן מִדְיָן שֶׁבַע בָּנוֹת[e]
,daughters   seven [being]   Midian   of priest the to And   .well the

וַתָּבֹאנָה וַתִּדְלֶנָה וַתְּמַלֶּאנָה אֶת־הָרְהָטִים
troughs the   filled and   drew and   came they (and)

17 לְהַשְׁקוֹת צֹאן אֲבִיהֶן[f]׃ וַיָּבֹאוּ הָרֹעִים
shepherds the   came And   .father their   of flocks the   water to

וַיְגָרְשׁוּם וַיָּקָם מֹשֶׁה וַיּוֹשִׁעָן[g]
,them delivered and   Moses   arose and   ; away them drove and

18 וַיַּשְׁקְ אֶת־צֹאנָם׃ וַתָּבֹאנָה אֶל־רְעוּאֵל
Reuel unto   came they And   .flock their   watered and

אֲבִיהֶן וַיֹּאמֶר[h] מַדּוּעַ מִהַרְתֶּן בֹּא
come to   hastened ye have   Why   : said he and   ,father their

and when he
saw that there
was no man, he
smote the Egyp-
tian, and hid
him in the sand.

13 And he went
out the second
day, and, be-
hold, two men
of the Hebrews
strove together:
and he said to
him that did the
wrong, Where-
fore smitest
thou thy fellow?
14 And he said,
Who made thee
a prince and a
judge over us?
thinkest thou to
kill me, as thou
killedst the E-
gyptian? And
Moses feared,
and said, Surely
the thing is
known. 15 Now
when Pharaoh
heard this thing,
he sought to
slay Moses. But
Moses fled from
the face of
Pharaoh, and
dwelt in the
land of Midian:
and he sat down
by a well. 16
Now the priest
of Midian had
seven daughters:
and they came
and drew water,
and filled the
troughs to water
their father's
flock. 17 And
the shepherds
came and drove
them away: but
Moses stood up
and helped
them, and wa-
tered their flock.
18 And when
they came to
Reuel their fa-
ther, he said,
How is it that
ye are come so

---

a G., V. have, *he saw;* S., *and he saw and behold.*
b G., S., V. add, *yesterday.*
c S. has, *and he went.*
d G. has, *and coming to the land of Midian he sat.*
e G. adds, *feeding the sheep of their father Jethro.*
f G. adds, *Jethro.*
g G. adds, *and drew water for them.*
h G., S. add, *to them.*

so soon to day ?
19 And they
said, An Egyp-
tian delivered us
out of the hand
of the shep-
herds, and also
drew *water*
enough for us,
and watered the
flock. 20 And he
said unto his
daughters, And
where *is* he ?
why *is* it *that* ye
have left the
man ? call him,
that he may eat
bread. 21 And
Moses was con-
tent to dwell
with the man :
and he gave
Moses Zipporah
his daughter. 22
And she bare
him a son, and
he called his
name Gershom :
for he said, I
have been a
stranger in a
strange land.

19 הַיּוֹם׃ וַתֹּאמַרְןָ [a] אִישׁ מִצְרִי הִצִּילָנוּ
us rescued [1]Egyptian [2]man A : said they And ?today

מִיַּד הָרֹעִים וְגַם־דָּלֹה דָלָה לָנוּ
,us for drew he drawing also and ; shepherds the of hand the from

20 וַיַּשְׁקְ אֶת־הַצֹּאן׃ [b] וַיֹּאמֶר אֶל־בְּנֹתָיו
: daughters his unto said he And .flock the watered and

וְאַיּוֹ [c] לָמָּה זֶּה עֲזַבְתֶּן אֶת־הָאִישׁ [d]
?man the left ye have then why ? he [is] where And

21 קִרְאֶן לוֹ וְיֹאכַל לָחֶם׃ [e] וַיּוֹאֶל מֹשֶׁה
Moses consented And .bread eat him let and ,him (to) call

[e] לָשֶׁבֶת אֶת־הָאִישׁ וַיִּתֵּן אֶת־צִפֹּרָה בִתּוֹ
daughter his Zipporah gave he and ; man the with dwell to

22 לְמֹשֶׁה׃ [f] [g] וַתֵּלֶד בֵּן [h] וַיִּקְרָא אֶת־שְׁמוֹ
name his called he and ,son a bore she And .Moses to

גֵּרְשֹׁם כִּי אָמַר גֵּר הָיִיתִי בְּאֶרֶץ
[2]land a in become have I sojourner A :said he for ; Gershom

נָכְרִיָּה׃ [i]
.[1]strange

soon to-day ?
19 And they
said, An Egyp-
tian delivered us
out of the hand
of the shep-
herds, and
moreover he
drew water for
us, and watered
the flock. 20 And
he said unto his
daughters, And
where is he ?
why is it that
ye have left the
man ? call him,
that he may eat
bread. 21 And
Moses was con-
tent to dwell
with the man :
and he gave
Moses Zipporah
his daughter. 22
And she bare a
son, and he call-
ed his name
Gershom : for
he said, I have
been a sojourner
in a strange
land.

23 And it
came to pass in
process of time,
that the king of
Egypt died: and
the children of
Israel sighed by
reason of the
bondage, and
they cried, and
their cry came
up unto God by
reason of the
bondage. 24
And God heard
their groaning,
and God re-
membered his
covenant with
Abraham, with
Isaac, and with
Jacob. 25 And
God looked up-
on the children
of Israel, and
God had respect
unto *them*.

23 [j] וַיְהִי בַיָּמִים הָרַבִּים הָהֵם וַיָּמָת
died (and) ,[1]those [2]many [3]days in pass to came it And

מֶלֶךְ מִצְרַיִם וַיֵּאָנְחוּ בְנֵי־יִשְׂרָאֵל מִן־
from Israel of children the groaned and ,Egypt of king the

הָעֲבֹדָה וַיִּזְעָקוּ וַתַּעַל שַׁוְעָתָם אֶל־
unto cry their up went and ; cried they and ,service the

24 הָאֱלֹהִים מִן־הָעֲבֹדָה׃ וַיִּשְׁמַע אֱלֹהִים אֶת־נַאֲקָתָם
,lamentation their God heard And .service the from God

וַיִּזְכֹּר אֱלֹהִים אֶת־בְּרִיתוֹ אֶת־אַבְרָהָם [k] אֶת־
with ,Abraham with covenant his God remembered and

25 יִצְחָק וְאֶת־יַעֲקֹב׃ וַיַּרְא אֱלֹהִים אֶת־בְּנֵי
of children the God saw And .Jacob with and ,Isaac

יִשְׂרָאֵל [l] וַיֵּדַע אֱלֹהִים׃
.God [them] knew and ,Israel

23 And it
came to pass in
the course of
those many
days, that the
king of Egypt
died : and the
children of Is-
rael sighed by
reason of the
bondage, and
they cried, and
their cry came
up unto God by
reason of the
bondage. 24
And God heard
their groaning,
and God re-
membered his
covenant with
Abraham, with
Isaac, and with
Jacob. 25 And
God saw the
children of Is-
rael, and God
took knowledge
of *them*.

---

a S. adds, *to him.*
b G., S. have, *our flocks.*
c G. adds, *and,* ו.
d S. adds, *go.*
e G. has, *and Moses dwelt.*
f Sm., G. add, *for a wife ;* S. has, *to him for a wife.*
g G. adds, *and the woman conceived.*
h G. adds, *Moses.*
i S. adds, *and she bore again a second son to Moses, and he called his name Eliezer ; because the God of my fathers has helped me and has delivered me from the sword of Pharaoh ;* so essentially V.
j V. omits ; G. omits ויהי.
k G., S. add, *and,* ו.
l V. has, *and he knew them* ; G. *and he was known to them,* וַיִּוָּדַע אֲלֵיהֶם.

3

Now Moses
kept the flock of
Jethro his fa-
ther in law, the
priest of Midian:
and he led the
flock to the back-
side of the des-
ert, and came to
the mountain of
God, *even* to
Horeb.

2 And the
angel of the
LORD appeared
unto him in a
flame of fire
out of the
midst of a bush:
and he looked,
and, behold, the
bush burned
with fire, and
the bush *was*
not consum-
ed. 3 And
Moses said, I
will now turn a-
side, and see
this great sight,
why the bush is
not burnt. 4 And
when the LORD
saw that he
turned aside to
see, God called
unto him out of
the midst of the
bush, and said,
Moses, Moses.
And he said,
Here *am* I. 5
And he said,
Draw not nigh
hither: put off
thy shoes from
off thy feet, for
the place where-
on thou stand-
est *is* holy
ground. 6 More-
over he said, I
am the God of
thy father, the
God of Abra-
ham, the God of
Isaac, and the
God of Jacob.
And Moses hid
his face; for he
was afraid to

1 וּמֹשֶׁה הָיָה רֹעֶה אֶת־צֹאן יִתְרוֹ
Jethro of flock the tending was Moses [while] And

חֹתְנוֹ כֹּהֵן מִדְיָן וַיִּנְהַג אֶת־הַצֹּאן
flock the led he (and) ,Midian of priest the father-in-law his

אַחַר[a] הַמִּדְבָּר[a] וַיָּבֹא אֶל־הַר הָאֱלֹהִים[b]
,God of mountain the unto came and ,wilderness the behind

2 חֹרֵבָה׃ וַיֵּרָא מַלְאַךְ יְהוָה אֵלָיו בְּלַבַּת־
of flame a in him unto Jehovah of angel the appeared And .Horeb to

אֵשׁ מִתּוֹךְ הַסְּנֶה וַיַּרְא וְהִנֵּה[c]
behold and ,looked he and ;bush thorn a of midst the from fire

הַסְּנֶה בֹּעֵר בָּאֵשׁ וְהַסְּנֶה אֵינֶנּוּ
not was (it) bush thorn the and ,fire with burning [was] bush thorn the

3 אֻכָּל׃ וַיֹּאמֶר מֹשֶׁה אָסֻרָה־נָּא וְאֶרְאֶה
see and ,now ,aside turn will I :Moses said And .consumed

אֶת־הַמַּרְאֶה הַגָּדֹל הַזֶּה מַדּוּעַ[d] לֹא־יִבְעַר הַסְּנֶה׃
.bush thorn the burned not is why ,[1]this [2]great [3]sight

4 וַיַּרְא יְהוָה כִּי סָר לִרְאוֹת וַיִּקְרָא
called and ,see to aside turned he that Jehovah saw And

אֵלָיו אֱלֹהִים[e] מִתּוֹךְ הַסְּנֶה וַיֹּאמֶר
:said and ,bush thorn the of midst the from God him unto

5 מֹשֶׁה מֹשֶׁה וַיֹּאמֶר הִנֵּנִי׃ וַיֹּאמֶר[f]
:said he And .me Behold :said he and ;Moses ,Moses

אַל־תִּקְרַב הֲלֹם שַׁל־נְעָלֶיךָ מֵעַל
upon from sandals thy off pull ,hither near come not Do

רַגְלֶיךָ כִּי הַמָּקוֹם אֲשֶׁר אַתָּה עוֹמֵד
standing [art] thou which [upon] place the for ;feet thy

6 עָלָיו [g]אַדְמַת־קֹדֶשׁ הוּא׃ וַיֹּאמֶר אָנֹכִי
[am] I :said he And .it [is] holiness of ground ,(it upon)

אֱלֹהֵי אָבִיךָ אֱלֹהֵי אַבְרָהָם [h]אֱלֹהֵי יִצְחָק
,Isaac of God the ,Abraham of God the ,father thy of God the

[i]וֵאלֹהֵי יַעֲקֹב וַיַּסְתֵּר מֹשֶׁה פָּנָיו כִּי יָרֵא
feared he for ,face his Moses hid and ;Jacob of God the and

Now Moses
was keeping the
flock of Jethro
his father in
law, the priest
of Midian: and
he led the flock
to the back of
the wilderness,
and came to the
mountain of
God, unto Ho-
reb.

2 And the
angel of the
LORD appeared
unto him in a
flame of fire out
of the midst of
a bush: and he
looked, and, be-
hold, the bush
burned with fire,
and the bush
was not con-
sumed. 3 And
Moses said, I
will turn aside
now, and see
this great sight,
why the bush is
not burnt. 4 And
when the LORD
saw that he
turned aside to
see, God called
unto him out of
the midst of the
bush, and said,
Moses, Moses.
And he said,
Here am I. 5
And he said,
Draw not nigh
hither: put off
thy shoes from
off thy feet, for
the place where-
on thou stand-
est is holy
ground. 6 More-
over he said, I
am the God of
thy father, the
God of Abra-
ham, the God of
Isaac, and the
God of Jacob.
And Moses hid
his face; for he
was afraid to

a G., S. have, *to the wilderness.*
b G. omits.
c G., S., V. apparently omit.
d G. has, *that.*
e V. omits; G. has, *Lord*, יהוה.
f S. adds, *to him.*
g S., T. have, *place.*
h G. adds, *and*, ו.
i S. omits ו.

look upon God.
7 And the
LORD said, I
have surely seen
the affliction of
my people which
are in Egypt,
and have heard
their cry by
reason of their
taskmasters; for
I know their
sorrows; 8 And
I am come down
to deliver them
out of the hand
of the Egyp-
tians, and to
bring them up
out of that land
unto a good
land and a large,
unto a land
flowing with
milk and honey;
unto the place
of the Canaan-
ites, and the
Hittites, and
the Amorites,
and the Periz-
zites, and the
Hivites, and the
Jebusites. 9 Now
therefore, be-
hold, the cry of
the children of
Israel is come
unto me: and I
have also seen
the oppression
wherewith the
Egyptians op-
press them. 10
Come now
therefore, and I
will send thee
unto Pharaoh,
that thou mayest
bring forth my
people the chil-
dren of Israel
out of Egypt.
11 And Moses
said unto God,
Who *am* I, that
I should go un-
to Pharaoh, and
that I should
bring forth the
children of Is-
rael out of E-
gypt? 12 And he
said, Certainly I
will be with
thee; and this
shall be a token

מַבִּיט אֶל־הָאֱלֹהִים׃ וַיֹּאמֶר יְהוָה [a] רָאֹה 7
Seeing : Jehovah said And .God unto looking from

רָאִיתִי אֶת־עֳנִי עַמִּי אֲשֶׁר בְּמִצְרָיִם
,Egypt in [are] who people my of affliction the seen have I

וְאֶת־צַעֲקָתָם שָׁמַעְתִּי מִפְּנֵי נֹגְשָׂיו כִּי
for ;taskmasters their before from heard have I cry their and

יָדַעְתִּי אֶת־מַכְאֹבָיו׃ וָאֵרֵד לְהַצִּילוֹ 8
them deliver to down come have I And .sorrows their know I

מִיַּד מִצְרַיִם וּלְהַעֲלֹתוֹ מִן־הָאָרֶץ
[2]land from up them bring to and ,Egyptians the of hand the from

הַהִוא [b] אֶל־אֶרֶץ טוֹבָה וּרְחָבָה אֶל־אֶרֶץ
land a unto ,broad and good land a unto [1]that

זָבַת חָלָב וּדְבָשׁ אֶל־מְקוֹם הַכְּנַעֲנִי
,Canaanites the of place the unto ;honey and milk [with] (of) flowing

וְהַחִתִּי וְהָאֱמֹרִי וְהַפְּרִזִּי [c] וְהַחִוִּי
,Hivites the and ,Perizzites the and ,Amorites the and ,Hittites the and

וְהַיְבוּסִי׃ וְעַתָּה הִנֵּה צַעֲקַת בְּנֵי־יִשְׂרָאֵל 9
Israel of children the of cry the behold now And .Jebusites the and

בָּאָה אֵלָי וְגַם־רָאִיתִי אֶת־הַלַּחַץ אֲשֶׁר
which [with] ,oppression the seen have I also and ,me unto come has

מִצְרַיִם לֹחֲצִים אֹתָם׃ וְעַתָּה לְכָה 10
,come ,now And .them oppressing [are] Egyptians the

וְאֶשְׁלָחֲךָ אֶל־פַּרְעֹה [d] וְהוֹצֵא [e] אֶת־עַמִּי
people my out bring thou do and ,Pharaoh unto thee send will I and

בְנֵי־יִשְׂרָאֵל מִמִּצְרָיִם׃ וַיֹּאמֶר מֹשֶׁה אֶל־ 11
unto Moses said And .Egypt from Israel of children the

הָאֱלֹהִים מִי אָנֹכִי כִּי אֵלֵךְ אֶל־פַּרְעֹה [f]
,Pharaoh unto go should I that ,I [am] Who : God

וְכִי אוֹצִיא אֶת־בְּנֵי יִשְׂרָאֵל מִמִּצְרָיִם׃
? Egypt from Israel of children the out bring should I that and

וַיֹּאמֶר [g] כִּי־אֶהְיֶה עִמָּךְ וְזֶה־לְּךָ הָאוֹת 12
sign the [is] thee for this and ,thee with be will I(That) ,said he And

look upon God.
7 And the
LORD said, I
have surely seen
the affliction of
my people
which are in E-
gypt, and have
heard their cry
by reason of
their taskmas-
ters; for I know
their sorrows; 8
and I am come
down to deliver
them out of the
hand of the E-
gyptians, and to
bring them up
out of that land
unto a good
land and a large,
unto a land
flowing with
milk and honey;
unto the place
of the Canaan-
ite, and the Hit-
tite, and the Am-
orite, and the
Perizzite, and the
Hivite, and the
Jebusite. 9 And
now, behold,
the cry of the
children of Is-
rael is come un-
to me: moreover
I have seen the
oppression
wherewith the
Egyptians op-
press them. 10
Come now
therefore, and I
will send thee
unto Pharaoh,
that thou may-
est bring forth
my people the
children of Is-
rael out of E-
gypt.
11 And Moses
said unto
God, Who am
I, that I should
go unto Pha-
raoh, and that I
should bring
forth the chil-
dren of Israel
out of Egypt?
12 And he said,
Certainly I will
be with thee;
and this shall be

---

a G. adds, *unto Moses;* V. adds, *unto him.*

b G. adds, *and to bring them in.*

c Sm., G. add, *and Girgashites.*

d G. adds, *king of Egypt.*

e G. has, *and thou shalt bring out;* V., *that thou mayest bring out.*

f G. adds, *king of Egypt.*

g G. adds, *God to Moses saying;* S., V. add, *to him.*

unto thee, that
I have sent thee:
When thou hast
brought forth
the people out of
Egypt, ye shall
serve God upon
this mountain.
13 And Mo-
ses said unto
God, Behold,
when I come
unto the chil-
dren of Israel,
and shall say
unto them, The
God of your fa-
thers hath sent
me unto you;
and they shall
say to me, What
is his name?
what shall I
say unto them?
14 And God
said unto Moses,
I AM THAT I
AM: and he
said, Thus shalt
thou say unto
the children of
Israel, I AM
hath sent me
unto you. 15
And God said
moreover unto
Moses, Thus
shalt thou say
unto the chil-
dren of Israel,
The LORD God
of your fathers,
the God of A-
braham, the
God of Isaac,
and the God of
Jacob, hath sent
me unto you:
this *is* my name
for ever, and
this *is* my me-
morial unto all
generations. 16
Go, and gather
the elders of Is-
rael together,
and say unto
them, The
LORD God of
your fathers, the
God of Abra-
ham, of Isaac,
and of Jacob,
appeared unto
me, saying, I
have surely visit-
ed you, and *seen*

כִּי אָנֹכִי שְׁלַחְתִּיךָ בְּהוֹצִיאֲךָ אֶת־הָעָם [a]
people the out bringing thy in ; thee sent have I that

מִמִּצְרַיִם תַּעַבְדוּן אֶת־הָאֱלֹהִים עַל הָהָר הַזֶּה׃
.¹this ²mountain upon God serve shall you Egypt from

[b] וַיֹּאמֶר מֹשֶׁה אֶל־הָאֱלֹהִים הִנֵּה אָנֹכִי בָא אֶל־ 13
unto come [shall] I ,Behold : God unto Moses said And

בְּנֵי יִשְׂרָאֵל וְאָמַרְתִּי לָהֶם אֱלֹהֵי אֲבוֹתֵיכֶם
fathers your of God The :them to say and ,Israel of children the

שְׁלָחַנִי אֲלֵיכֶם וְאָמְרוּ־לִי מַה־שְּׁמוֹ
? name his [is] What : me to say will they and ; you unto me sent has

מָה אֹמַר אֲלֵהֶם׃ וַיֹּאמֶר אֱלֹהִים אֶל־מֹשֶׁה [c] 14
: Moses unto God said And ? them unto say I shall what

אֶהְיֶה אֲשֶׁר אֶהְיֶה וַיֹּאמֶר כֹּה תֹאמַר
say shalt thou Thus : said he and ; am I which that am I

לִבְנֵי יִשְׂרָאֵל אֶהְיֶה שְׁלָחַנִי אֲלֵיכֶם׃ וַיֹּאמֶר 15
said And .you unto me sent has Am I ,Israel of children the to

עוֹד אֱלֹהִים אֶל־מֹשֶׁה כֹּה תֹאמַר אֶל־
unto say shalt thou Thus : Moses unto God again

בְּנֵי יִשְׂרָאֵל יְהוָה אֱלֹהֵי אֲבֹתֵיכֶם
,fathers your of God the Jehovah : Israel of children the

אֱלֹהֵי אַבְרָהָם [d] אֱלֹהֵי יִצְחָק [e] וֵאלֹהֵי יַעֲקֹב
Jacob of God the and ,Isaac of God the ,Abraham of God the

שְׁלָחַנִי אֲלֵיכֶם זֶה־שְּׁמִי לְעֹלָם וְזֶה
[is] this and ,ever for name my [is] this ;you unto me sent has

זִכְרִי לְדֹר דֹּר׃ לֵךְ וְאָסַפְתָּ אֶת־ 16
the gather and ,Go .generation [and] generation for title my

זִקְנֵי יִשְׂרָאֵל [f] וְאָמַרְתָּ אֲלֵהֶם יְהוָה אֱלֹהֵי
of God the Jehovah :them unto say and ,Israel of elders

אֲבֹתֵיכֶם נִרְאָה אֵלַי אֱלֹהֵי אַבְרָהָם יִצְחָק [g]
Isaac Abraham of God the ,me unto appeared has fathers your

[g] וְיַעֲקֹב לֵאמֹר פָּקֹד [h] פָּקַדְתִּי [h] אֶתְכֶם וְאֶת־
and ,you visited have I Visiting : saying ,Jacob and

the token unto
thee, that I
have sent
thee: when thou
hast brought
forth the peo-
ple out of E-
gypt, ye shall
serve God upon
this mountain.
13 And Moses
said unto God,
Behold, when I
come unto the
children of Is-
rael, and shall
say unto them,
The God of
your fathers
hath sent me
unto you; and
they shall say to
me, What is his
name? what
shall I say un-
to them? 14
And God said
unto Moses, I
AM THAT I AM:
and he said,
Thus shalt thou
say unto the
children of Is-
rael, I AM hath
sent me unto
you. 15 And
God said more-
over unto Mo-
ses, Thus shalt
thou say unto
the children of
Israel, The
LORD, the God
of your fathers,
the God of A-
braham, the
God of Isaac,
and the God of
Jacob, hath sent
me unto you:
this is my name
for ever, and
this is my me-
morial unto all
generations. 16
Go, and gather
the elders of Is-
rael together,
and say unto
them, The
LORD, the God
of your fathers,
the God of A-
braham, of I-
saac, and of Ja-
cob, hath ap-
peared unto me,
saying, I have

---

a G., V. have, *my people.*

b G. omits ו.

c G. adds, *saying.*

d Sm., G. add, *and*, ו.

e S. omits ו.

f G., S. have, *sons of Israel.*

g G., V. have, *and the God of Isaac and the God of Jacob;* S. adds, *and*, reading ויצחק.

h S., T. have, *remembering I have remembered.*

that which is done to you in Egypt: 17 And I have said, I will bring you up out of the affliction of Egypt unto the land of the Canaanites, and the Hittites, and the Amorites, and the Perizzites, and the Hivites, and the Jebusites, unto a land flowing with milk and honey. 18 And they shall hearken to thy voice: and thou shalt come, thou, and the elders of Israel, unto the king of Egypt, and ye shall say unto him, The LORD God of the Hebrews hath met with us: and now let us go, we beseech thee, three days' journey into the wilderness, that we may sacrifice to the LORD our God.
19 And I am sure that the king of Egypt will not let you go, no, not by a mighty hand. 20 And I will stretch out my hand, and smite Egypt with all my wonders which I will do in the midst thereof: and after that he will let you go. 21 And I will give this people favour in the sight of the Egyptians: and it shall come to pass, that, when ye go, ye shall not go

17 הֶעָשׂוּי[a] לָכֶם בְּמִצְרָיִם׃ וָאֹמַר[b] אַעֲלֶה
up bring will I :said have I And .Egypt in you to done is [what]

אֶתְכֶם מֵעֳנִי מִצְרַיִם אֶל־אֶרֶץ הַכְּנַעֲנִי
,Canaanites the of land the unto ,Egypt of affliction the from you

וְהַחִתִּי וְהָאֱמֹרִי וְהַפְּרִזִּי[c] וְהַחִוִּי
,Hivites the and ,Perizzites the and ,Amorites the and ,Hittites the

וְהַיְבוּסִי אֶל־אֶרֶץ זָבַת חָלָב וּדְבָשׁ׃
.honey and milk [with] (of) flowing land a unto ,Jebusites the and

18 וְשָׁמְעוּ לְקֹלֶךָ וּבָאתָ אַתָּה
thou ,in come shalt thou and ;voice thy to hearken will they And

וְזִקְנֵי יִשְׂרָאֵל אֶל[d]־מֶלֶךְ מִצְרַיִם וַאֲמַרְתֶּם[e]
say shall you and ,Egypt of king the unto Israel of elders the and

אֵלָיו יְהוָה[f] אֱלֹהֵי הָעִבְרִיִּים נִקְרָה[g] עָלֵינוּ[g]
;us (upon) met has Hebrews the of God the Jehovah :him unto

וְעַתָּה נֵלֲכָה־נָּא דֶּרֶךְ שְׁלֹשֶׁת יָמִים
days three of journey a ,pray ,go us let ,now and

בַּמִּדְבָּר וְנִזְבְּחָה לַיהוָה[h] אֱלֹהֵינוּ׃
.God our Jehovah to sacrifice us let and ,wilderness the into

19 וַאֲנִי יָדַעְתִּי כִּי לֹא־יִתֵּן אֶתְכֶם[i] מֶלֶךְ מִצְרַיִם
Egypt of king the you give not will that know I And

20 לַהֲלֹךְ וְלֹא[j] בְּיָד חֲזָקָה׃ וְשָׁלַחְתִּי
out stretch will I And .[1]strong [2]hand a by not even ,go to

אֶת־יָדִי וְהִכֵּיתִי אֶת־מִצְרַיִם בְּכֹל נִפְלְאֹתַי אֲשֶׁר
which ,wonders my all with Egypt smite and hand my

אֶעֱשֶׂה בְּקִרְבּוֹ וְאַחֲרֵי־כֵן יְשַׁלַּח אֶתְכֶם׃
.you away send will he afterward and ,midst its in do will I

21 וְנָתַתִּי אֶת־חֵן הָעָם־הַזֶּה בְּעֵינֵי מִצְרָיִם
;Egypt of eyes the in people this [to] favor give will I And

וְהָיָה[k] כִּי תֵלֵכוּן לֹא תֵלְכוּ רֵיקָם׃
.empty go [2]will [1]you [3]not ,go you when ,pass to come will it and

surely visited you, and *seen* that which is done to you in Egypt: 17 and I have said, I will bring you up out of the affliction of Egypt unto the land of the Canaanite, and the Hittite, and the Amorite, and the Perizzite, and the Hivite, and the Jebusite, unto a land flowing with milk and honey. 18 And they shall hearken to thy voice: and thou shalt come, thou and the elders of Israel, unto the king of Egypt, and ye shall say unto him, The LORD, the God of the Hebrews, hath met with us: and now let us go, we pray thee, three days' journey into the wilderness, that we may sacrifice to the LORD our God.
19 And I know that the king of Egypt will not give you leave to go, no, not by a mighty hand. 20 And I will put forth my hand, and smite Egypt with all my wonders which I will do in the midst thereof: and after that he will let you go. 21 And I will give this people favour in the sight of the Egyptians: and it shall come to pass, that, when ye go, ye shall

---

a G. has, *and whatever has happened;* S. *and the thing which has been done;* T. *and what has been done;* V. *all which has happened.*

b G. has, *and he said,* ויאמר.

c Sm., G. add, *and the Girgashites.*

d G. adds, *Pharaoh.*

e G., V. have sing.

f G. omits.

g G. has, *has summoned us;* S. *has appeared to us.*

h G. omits יהוה.

i G. adds, *Pharaoh.*

j G., V. have, *unless,* אִם לֹא; Sm., *not?* הֲלֹא.

k G., S., V. omit היה.

empty: 22 But
every woman
shall borrow of
her neighbour,
and of her that
sojourneth in
her house, jew-
els of silver,
and jewels of
gold, and rai-
ment: and ye
shall put *them*
upon your sons,
and upon your
daughters; and
ye shall spoil the
Egyptians.

22 וּמִגָּרַת מִשְּׁכֶנְתָּהּ אִשָּׁה [a]וְשָׁאֲלָה
in sojourner the from and ,neighbor her from woman each ask shall And
וּשְׂמָלֹת זָהָב וּכְלֵי כְּלֵי־כֶסֶף בֵּיתָהּ
;garments and ,gold of articles and ,silver of articles ,house her
וְעַל־בְּנֹתֵיכֶם עַל־בְּנֵיכֶם וְשַׂמְתֶּם
,daughters your upon and sons your upon put shall ye and
אֶת־מִצְרָיִם׃ וְנִצַּלְתֶּם
.Egypt plunder shall ye and

not go empty: 22
but every wom-
an shall ask of
her neighbour,
and of her that
sojourneth in
her house, jew-
els of silver, and
jewels of gold,
and raiment:
and ye shall put
them upon your
sons, and upon
your daughters;
and ye shall
spoil the Egyp-
tians.

4

AND Moses
answered and
said, But, be-
hold, they will
not believe me,
nor hearken un-
to my voice:
for they will say,
The LORD hath
not appeared
unto thee. 2 And
the LORD said
unto him, What
is that in thine
hand? And he
said, A rod. 3
And he said,
Cast it on the
ground. And he
cast it on the
ground, and it
became a ser-
pent; and Moses
fled from before
it. 4 And
the LORD
said unto Mo-
ses, Put forth
thine hand, and
take it by the
tail. And he put
forth his hand,
and caught it,
and it became a
rod in his hand:
5 That they may
believe that the
LORD God of
their fathers, the
God of Abra-
ham, the God of
Isaac, and the
God of Jacob,
hath appeared
unto thee.

1 לֹא־יַאֲמִינוּ וְהֵן וַיֹּאמֶר מֹשֶׁה וַיַּעַן
believe not will they ,behold And :said and Moses answered And
יֹאמְרוּ כִּי בְּקֹלִי יִשְׁמְעוּ וְלֹא לִי
:say will they for ;voice my to hearken [1]will [2]not and ,me (to)
2 אֵלָיו וַיֹּאמֶר יְהוָה׃[b] אֵלֶיךָ לֹא־נִרְאָה
him unto said And .Jehovah thee unto appeared not Has
מַטֶּה׃ וַיֹּאמֶר בְיָדֶךָ מַזֶּה יְהוָה
.staff A ;said he and ?hand thy in this [is] What :Jehovah
3 אַרְצָה וַיַּשְׁלִכֵהוּ אַרְצָה הַשְׁלִיכֵהוּ וַיֹּאמֶר
,earth the to it cast he and ;earth the to it Cast :said he And
מִפָּנָיו׃ מֹשֶׁה וַיָּנָס לְנָחָשׁ וַיְהִי
.it before from Moses fled and ;serpent a (for) became it and
4 וֶאֱחֹז יָדְךָ שְׁלַח אֶל־מֹשֶׁה יְהוָה וַיֹּאמֶר
seize and ,hand thy out Stretch :Moses unto Jehovah said And
[c]בּוֹ וַיַּחֲזֶק יָדוֹ וַיִּשְׁלַח בִּזְנָבוֹ
,it (in) caught and hand his out stretched he and ;tail its by
5 [d]יַאֲמִינוּ לְמַעַן בְּכַפּוֹ׃ לְמַטֶּה וַיְהִי
believe may they that order in ;hand his in staff a (for) became it and
אֲבֹתָם אֱלֹהֵי [e]יְהוָה אֵלֶיךָ כִּי־נִרְאָה
,fathers their of God the Jehovah thee unto appeared has that
[g]וֵאלֹהֵי יִצְחָק [f]אֱלֹהֵי אַבְרָהָם אֱלֹהֵי
of God the and ,Isaac of God the ,Abraham of God the

And Moses
answered and
said, But, be-
hold, they will
not believe me,
nor hearken un-
to my voice:
for they will say,
The LORD hath
not appeared
unto thee. 2 And
the LORD said
unto him, What
is that in thine
hand? And he
said, A rod. 3
And he said,
Cast it on the
ground. And he
cast it on the
ground, and it
became a ser-
pent; and Mo-
ses fled from be-
fore it. 4 And
the LORD said
unto Moses,
Put forth thine
hand, and take
it by the tail:
(and he put
forth his hand,
and laid hold of
it, and it be-
came a rod in
his hand:). 5
that they may
believe that the
LORD, the God
of their fathers,
the God of A-
braham, the
God of Isaac,
and the God of
Jacob, hath ap-
peared unto
thee.

---

a G., S. omit ו.
b G. has, *God*, and adds, *what shall I say unto them?*
c G. has, *the tail;* V. omits.
d G. adds, *thee.*
e G. omits.
f Sm., G. add, *and*, ו
g S. omits ו.

6 And the
LORD said fur-
thermore unto
him, Put now
thine hand into
thy bosom. And
he put his hand
into his bosom:
and when he
took it out, be-
hold, his hand
was leprous as
snow. 7 And he
said, Put thine
hand into thy
bosom again.
And he put his
hand into his
bosom again;
and plucked it
outof his bosom,
and, behold, it
was turned a-
gain as his *other*
flesh. 8 And it
shall come to
pass, if they
will not believe
thee, neither
hearken to the
voice of the first
sign, that they
will believe the
voice of the lat-
ter sign. 9 And
it shall come to
pass, if they will
not believe also
these two signs,
neither hearken
unto thy voice,
that thou shalt
take of the wa-
ter of the river,
and pour *it* up-
on the dry *land:*
and the water
which thou tak-
est out of the
river shall be-
come blood up-
on the dry *land.*

6 יַעֲקֹב׃ וַיֹּאמֶר יְהוָה לוֹ עוֹד הָבֵא־נָא יָדְךָ
hand thy ,now ,Bring : again him to Jehovah said And .Jacob

בְּחֵיקֶךָ וַיָּבֵא יָדוֹ בְּחֵיקוֹ
,bosom his into hand his brought he and ; bosom thy into

וַיּוֹצִאָהּ[a] וְהִנֵּה[b] יָדוֹ מְצֹרַעַת[c]
leprous [was] hand his behold and ,out it brought he and

7 כַּשָּׁלֶג׃ וַיֹּאמֶר[d] הָשֵׁב יָדְךָ אֶל־חֵיקֶךָ
; bosom thy into hand thy Return : said he And .snow like

וַיָּשֶׁב יָדוֹ אֶל־חֵיקוֹ וַיּוֹצִאָהּ
out it brought he and ,bosom his into hand his returned he and

מֵחֵיקוֹ וְהִנֵּה־שָׁבָה[e] כִּבְשָׂרוֹ׃
.flesh his like turned had it behold and ,bosom his from

8 וְהָיָה[f] אִם־לֹא יַאֲמִינוּ לָךְ[g]
,thee (to) believe ²will ¹they ³not if ,pass to come will it And

וְלֹא יִשְׁמְעוּ לְקֹל הָאֹת הָרִאשׁוֹן
,¹first ²sign the of voice the to hearken ¹will ²not and

וְהֶאֱמִינוּ[h] לְקֹל הָאֹת הָאַחֲרוֹן׃
.¹later ²sign the of voice the (to) believe will they (and)

9 וְהָיָה[i] אִם־לֹא יַאֲמִינוּ[j] גַּם לִשְׁנֵי
²two (to) also believe ²will ¹they ³not if ,pass to come shall it And

הָאֹתוֹת הָאֵלֶּה וְלֹא יִשְׁמְעוּן לְקֹלֶךָ
,voice thy to hearken ¹will ²not and ,¹these ³signs

וְלָקַחְתָּ מִמֵּימֵי הַיְאֹר וְשָׁפַכְתָּ
pour and ,river the of water the of take shalt thou (and)

הַיַּבָּשָׁה וְהָיוּ[k] הַמַּיִם אֲשֶׁר תִּקַּח
takest thou which water the become shall and ; land dry the upon

מִן־הַיְאֹר וְהָיוּ[l] לְדָם בַּיַּבָּשֶׁת׃
.land dry the on blood (for) become shall it (and) ,river the from

10 וַיֹּאמֶר מֹשֶׁה אֶל־יְהוָה בִּי אֲדֹנָי לֹא אִישׁ[m]
of man a not ,Lord O : Jehovah unto Moses said And

דְּבָרִים[m] אָנֹכִי גַּם מִתְּמוֹל גַּם מִשִּׁלְשֹׁם גַּם
and ,day third the from and yesterday from both ,I [am] words

6 And the
LORD said fur-
thermore unto
him, Put now
thine hand into
thy bosom. And
he put his hand
into his bosom:
and when he
took it out, be-
hold, his hand
was leprous, as
white as snow.
7 And he said,
Put thine hand
into thy bosom
again. (And he
put his hand in-
to his bosom a-
gain; and when
he took it out
of his bosom,
behold, it was
turned again as
his *other* flesh.)
8 And it shall
come to pas, if
they will not be-
lieve thee, nei-
ther hearken to
the voice of the
first sign, that
they will believe
the voice of the
latter sign. 9
And it shall
come to pass, if
they will not be-
lieve even these
two signs, nei-
ther hearken un-
to thy voice,
that thou shalt
take of the wa-
ter of the river,
and pour it up-
on the dry land:
and the water
which thou tak-
est out of the
river shall be-
come blood up-
on the dry land.

10 And Moses
said unto the
LORD, O my
Lord, I *am* not
eloquent, nei-
ther heretofore,
nor since thou

10 And Mo-
ses said unto the
LORD, Oh Lord,
I am not elo-
quent, neither
heretofore, nor

a Sm., G. have, *and he brought out his hand from his bosom.*

b G. has, *and had become.*

c G. omits.

d S. adds, *to him the Lord.*

e S. has, *and it was to him.*

f V. omits; G., S. omit היה.

g S. omits.

h G. has, *they will believe for thee.*

i S. omits היה.

j G. adds, *thee.*

k S., V. omit.

l G. omits.

m G. has, *sufficient.*

hast spoken un-
to thy servants
but I *am* slow of
speech, and of a
slow tongue. 11
And the LORD
said unto him,
Who hath made
man's mouth?
or who maketh
the dumb, or
deaf, or the see-
ing, or the
blind? have not
I the LORD? 12
Now therefore
go, and I will be
with thy mouth,
and teach thee
what thou shalt
say. 13 And he
said, O my
Lord, send, I
pray thee, by
the hand *of him*
whom thou wilt
send.
14 And the
anger of the
LORD was kin-
dled against
Moses, and he
said, *Is* not
Aaron the Le-
vite thy brother?
I know that he
can speak well.
And also, be-
hold, he cometh
forth to meet
thee: and when
he seeth thee,
he will be glad
in his heart. 15
And thou shalt
speak unto him,
and put words
in his mouth:
and I will be
with thy mouth,
and with his
mouth, and will
teach you what
ye shall do. 16
And he shall be
thy spokesman
unto the peo-
ple: and he shall
be, *even* he shall
be to thee in-
stead of a
mouth, and thou
shalt be to him
instead of God.
17 And thou
shalt take this

מֵאָז דַּבֶּרְךָ אֶל־עַבְדֶּךָ כִּי כְבַד־פֶּה
mouth of heavy for ; servant thy unto speaking thy since

11 וּכְבַד לָשׁוֹן אָנֹכִי׃ וַיֹּאמֶר יְהוָה אֵלָיו[a]
: him unto Jehovah said And .I [am] tongue of heavy and

מִי שָׂם פֶּה לָאָדָם אוֹ מִי־יָשׂוּם אִלֵּם אוֹ
or dumb makes who or ?man to mouth made has Who

12 חֵרֵשׁ אוֹ[b] פִקֵּחַ אוֹ עִוֵּר הֲלֹא אָנֹכִי יְהוָה[c]׃ וְעַתָּה
now And ?Jehovah I not [do] ?blind or seeing or deaf

לֵךְ וְאָנֹכִי אֶהְיֶה[d] [d]עִם־פִּיךָ וְהוֹרֵיתִיךָ
thee teach will and ,mouth thy with be will I and ,go

13 אֲשֶׁר תְּדַבֵּר׃ וַיֹּאמֶר[e] בִּי אֲדֹנָי שְׁלַח־נָא
,pray I ,send ,Lord O : said he And .speak shalt thou what

14 בְּיַד־תִּשְׁלָח׃ וַיִּחַר־אַף
of anger the glowed And .send wilt thou [whom him of] hand the by

יְהוָה בְּמֹשֶׁה וַיֹּאמֶר[f] הֲלֹא[g] אַהֲרֹן אָחִיךָ
[7]brother [6]thy [5]Aaron [3]Not : said he and ,Moses against Jehovah

הַלֵּוִי יָדַעְתִּי כִּי־דַבֵּר יְדַבֵּר[h] הוּא וְגַם
also And ?he speak can speaking that ,[4]know [2]I [1]do [9]Levite [8]the

הִנֵּה־הוּא יֹצֵא לִקְרָאתֶךָ וְרָאֲךָ
,thee see will he and ,thee meet to out going [is] he behold

15 וְשָׂמַח בְּלִבּוֹ׃ וְדִבַּרְתָּ אֵלָיו
,him unto speak shalt thou And .heart his in rejoice and

וְשַׂמְתָּ אֶת־הַדְּבָרִים[i] בְּפִיו וְאָנֹכִי אֶהְיֶה
be will I and ;mouth his in words the put shalt thou and

עִם־פִּיךָ וְעִם־פִּיהוּ וְהוֹרֵיתִי אֶתְכֶם אֵת
you teach will I and ,mouth his with and ,mouth thy with

16 אֲשֶׁר תַּעֲשׂוּן׃ וְדִבֶּר־הוּא לְךָ אֶל־הָעָם
; people the unto thee for speak shall he And .do shall you what

וְהָיָה[j] הוּא יִהְיֶה־לְּךָ לְפֶה
,mouth a (for) thee for become shall he pass to come shall it and

17 וְאַתָּה תִּהְיֶה־לּוֹ לֵאלֹהִים׃ וְאֶת־הַמַּטֶּה הַזֶּה[k]
[1]this [2]staff And .God a (for) him for become shalt thou and

since thou hast
spoken unto thy
servant: for I
am slow of
speech, and of a
slow tongue. 11
And the LORD
said unto him,
Who hath made
man's mouth?
or who maketh
a man dumb, or
deaf, or seeing,
or blind? is it not
I the LORD? 12
Now therefore
go, and I will
be with thy
mouth, and
teach thee what
thou shalt
speak. 13 And
he said, Oh
Lord, send, I
pray thee, by
the hand of him
whom thou wilt
send.
14 And the
anger of the
LORD was kin-
dled against
Moses, and he
said, Is there
not Aaron thy
brother the Le-
vite? I know
that he can
speak well. And
also, behold, he
cometh forth to
meet thee: and
when he seeth
thee, he will be
glad in his heart.
15 And thou
shalt speak un-
to him, and put
the words in his
mouth: and I
will be with thy
mouth, and with
his mouth, and
will teach you
what ye shall do.
16 And he shall
be thy spokes-
man unto the
people: and it
shall come to
pass, that he
shall be to thee
a mouth, and
thou shalt be to
him as God. 17
And thou shalt

a G. has, *unto Moses.*
b G., V. omit.
c G. has, *God;* V. omits.
d G. has, *will open;* so in V. 15.
e G. adds, *Moses;* S., *to him Moses.*
f S. adds, *to him.*
g G. has, *Is not, behold?* S., *Behold;* V. omits.
h G. adds, *for thee.*
i G., S., V. have, *my words.*
j G., S., V. omit היה.
k G. adds, *the one which turned into a serpent*; cf. chap. 7:15.

rod in thine
hand, where-
with thou shalt
do signs.

18 And Mo-
ses went and re-
turned to Jethro
his father in law,
and said unto
him, Let me go,
I pray thee, and
return unto my
brethren which
are in Egypt,
and see whether
they be yet a-
live. And Jethro
said to Moses,
Go in peace. 19
And the LORD
said unto Mo-
ses in Midian,
Go, return into
Egypt: for all
the men are
dead which
sought thy life.
20 And Moses
took his wife
and his sons, and
set them upon
an ass, and he
returned to the
land of Egypt:
and Moses took
the rod of God
in his hand. 21
And the LORD
said unto Mo-
ses, When thou
goest to return
into Egypt, see
that thou do all
those wonders
before Pharaoh,
which I have put
in thine hand:
but I will hard-
en his heart, that
he shall not let
the people go.
22 And thou
shalt say
unto Pharaoh,
Thus saith the
LORD, Israel *is*
my son, *even*
my firstborn: 23
And I say unto
thee, Let my
son go, that he
may serve me:
and if thou re-
fuse to let him
go, behold, I

תִּקַּח בְּיָדֶךָ אֲשֶׁר תַּעֲשֶׂה־בּוֹ
take shalt thou | ,hand thy in | which [by] | (it by) doest thou

18 אֶת־הָאֹתֹת׃ וַיֵּלֶךְ מֹשֶׁה וַיָּשָׁב אֶל־יֶתֶר
.signs the | went And | Moses | returned and | Jethro unto

חֹתְנוֹ וַיֹּאמֶר לוֹ[a] אֵלְכָה נָּא וְאָשׁוּבָה
,father-in-law his | said and | : him to | ,go me Let | ,pray | return and

אֶל־אַחַי אֲשֶׁר־בְּמִצְרַיִם וְאֶרְאֶה הַעוֹדָם
brethren my unto | ,Egypt in [are] who | see and | [are] still they whether

19 חַיִּים וַיֹּאמֶר יִתְרוֹ לְמֹשֶׁה לֵךְ לְשָׁלוֹם׃ וַיֹּאמֶר
.alive | said And | Jethro | : Moses to | Go | .peace in | said And

יְהוָה אֶל־מֹשֶׁה בְּמִדְיָן לֵךְ שֻׁב מִצְרָיִם
Jehovah | Moses unto | : Midian in | ,Go | return | ; Egypt to

כִּי־מֵתוּ כָּל־הָאֲנָשִׁים הַמְבַקְשִׁים אֶת־נַפְשֶׁךָ׃
dead are for | ,men the all | seeking those | .life thy

20 וַיִּקַּח מֹשֶׁה אֶת־אִשְׁתּוֹ וְאֶת־בָּנָיו וַיַּרְכִּבֵם
took And | Moses | wife his | ,sons his and | ride them made and

עַל־הַחֲמֹר וַיָּשָׁב אַרְצָה[b] מִצְרָיִם וַיִּקַּח
,ass an upon | returned and | of land the to | ; Egypt | took and

21 מֹשֶׁה אֶת־מַטֵּה הָאֱלֹהִים בְּיָדוֹ׃ וַיֹּאמֶר יְהוָה
Moses | of staff the | God | .hand his in | said And | Jehovah

אֶל־מֹשֶׁה בְּלֶכְתְּךָ לָשׁוּב מִצְרַיְמָה רְאֵה כָּל־
: Moses unto | going thy In | return to | ,Egypt to | see | all

הַמֹּפְתִים אֲשֶׁר־שַׂמְתִּי בְיָדֶךָ [c]וַעֲשִׂיתָם לִפְנֵי
wonders the | put have I which | ,hand thy in | them do and | before

פַרְעֹה וַאֲנִי אֲחַזֵּק אֶת־לִבּוֹ וְלֹא
; Pharaoh | I and | harden will | ,heart his | [3]not and

22 יְשַׁלַּח אֶת־הָעָם׃ וְאָמַרְתָּ אֶל־
away send [2]will [1]he | .people the | speak shalt thou And | unto

פַּרְעֹה כֹּה אָמַר יְהוָה בְּנִי בְכֹרִי
: Pharaoh | Thus | says | : Jehovah | ,son My | [is] firstborn my

23 יִשְׂרָאֵל׃ וָאֹמַר אֵלֶיךָ שַׁלַּח אֶת־בְּנִי
.Israel | said I And | : thee unto | away Send | ,son my

וְיַעַבְדֵנִי וַתְּמָאֵן לְשַׁלְּחוֹ[d] הִנֵּה אָנֹכִי
,me serve him let and | refusedst thou and | ; him send to | behold | I

take in thine
hand this rod,
wherewith thou
shalt do the
signs.

18 And Moses
went and re-
turned to Jethro
his father in
law, and said
unto him, Let
me go, I pray
thee, and re-
turn unto my
brethren which
are in Egypt,
and see whether
they be yet a-
live. And Jeth-
ro said to Mo-
ses, Go in peace.
19 And the
LORD said un-
to Moses in
Midian, Go, re-
turn into Egypt:
for all the men
are dead which
sought thy life.
20 And Moses
took his wife
and his sons,
and set them up-
on an ass, and
he returned to
the land of E-
gypt: and Mo-
ses took the rod
of God in his
hand. 21 And
the LORD said
unto Moses,
When thou go-
est back into E-
gypt, see that
thou do before
Pharaoh all the
wonders which I
have put in thine
hand: but I will
harden his
heart, and he
will not let the
people go. 22
And thou shalt
say unto Pha-
raoh, Thus saith
the LORD, Is-
rael is my son,
my firstborn: 23
and I have said
unto thee, Let
my son go, that
he may serve
me; and thou
hast refused to
let him go: be-

---

a G. omits.
b S. omits, and adds, *to go;* G., V. omit.
c G., S., V. omit ו.
d S. has, *to send forth my son*.

will slay thy son,
even thy first-
born.
24 And it
came to pass by
the way in the
inn, that the
LORD met him,
and sought to
kill him. 25
Then Zipporah
took a sharp
stone, and cut
off the foreskin
of her son, and
cast *it* at his
feet, and said,
Surely a bloody
husband *art*
thou to me. 26
So he let him
go: then she
said, A bloody
husband *thou*
art, because of
the circum-
cision.
27 And the
LORD said to
Aaron, Go into
the wilderness
to meet Moses.
And he went,
and met him in
the mount of
God, and kissed
him. 28 And
Moses told
Aaron all the
words of the
LORD who had
sent him, and
all the signs
which he had
commanded
him.
29 And Mo-
ses and Aaron
went and gath-
ered together
all the elders of
the children of
Israel: 30 And
Aaron spake all
the words which
the LORD had
spoken unto
Moses, and did
the signs in the
sight of the
people. 31 And
the people be-
lieved: and
when they heard
that the LORD

24 הָרֹג אֶת־בִּנְךָ בְּכֹרֶךָ׃ וַיְהִי[a]
pass to came it And .firstborn thy son thy kill to about [am]
בַדֶּרֶךְ בַּמָּלוֹן וַיִּפְגְּשֵׁהוּ יְהוָה[b]
,Jehovah him met (and) ,place lodging the in ,way the on
25 וַיְבַקֵּשׁ הֲמִיתוֹ׃[c] וַתִּקַּח צִפֹּרָה צֹר וַתִּכְרֹת
off cut and ,stone a Zipporah took And .him slay to sought and
אֶת־עָרְלַת בְּנָהּ וַתַּגַּע לְרַגְלָיו וַתֹּאמֶר כִּי[d]
(That) :said she and ;feet his at put and ,son her of foreskin the
26 חֲתַן־דָּמִים אַתָּה לִי׃[d] וַיִּרֶף מִמֶּנּוּ
;him from desisted he And .me to thou [art] blood of bridegroom a
אָז אָמְרָה חֲתַן[e] דָּמִים לַמּוּלֹת׃[e]
.circumcision the for ,blood of bridegroom A :said she then
27 וַיֹּאמֶר יְהוָה אֶל־אַהֲרֹן לֵךְ לִקְרַאת מֹשֶׁה[f]
Moses meet to Go :Aaron unto Jehovah said And
הַמִּדְבָּרָה וַיֵּלֶךְ וַיִּפְגְּשֵׁהוּ בְּהַר
of mountain the in him met and went he And .wilderness the to
28 הָאֱלֹהִים[g] וַיִּשַּׁק־לוֹ׃[h] וַיַּגֵּד מֹשֶׁה לְאַהֲרֹן
Aaron to Moses told And .him (to) kissed he and ;God
אֵת כָּל־דִּבְרֵי יְהוָה אֲשֶׁר שְׁלָחוֹ וְאֵת
and ,him sent had he which [with] Jehovah of words the all
29 כָּל־הָאֹתֹת[i] אֲשֶׁר צִוָּהוּ׃[j] וַיֵּלֶךְ מֹשֶׁה
Moses went And .him commanded had he which signs the all
וְאַהֲרֹן וַיַּאַסְפוּ אֶת־כָּל־[k]זִקְנֵי בְּנֵי יִשְׂרָאֵל׃
.Israel of children the of elders the all gathered and Aaron and
30 וַיְדַבֵּר אַהֲרֹן אֵת כָּל־הַדְּבָרִים[l] אֲשֶׁר־דִּבֶּר
spoken had which words the all Aaron spoke And
יְהוָה[m] אֶל־מֹשֶׁה וַיַּעַשׂ הָאֹתֹת לְעֵינֵי
of eyes the before signs the did he and ;Moses unto Jehovah
31 הָעָם׃ וַיַּאֲמֵן הָעָם וַיִּשְׁמְעוּ[n] כִּי־פָקַד
visited had that heard they and ;people the believed And .people the

hold, I will slay
thy son, thy
firstborn.
24 And it
came to pass on
the way at the
lodging place,
that the LORD
met him, and
sought to kill
him. 25 Then
Zipporah took a
flint, and cut off
the foreskin of
her son, and
cast it at his
feet; and she
said, Surely a
bridegroom of
blood art thou to
me. 26 So he let
him alone. Then
she said, A
bridegroom of
blood *art thou*,
because of the
circumcision.
27 And the
LORD said to
Aaron, Go into
the wilderness
to meet Moses.
And he went,
and met him in
the mountain of
God, and kissed
him. 28 And
Moses told
Aaron all the
words of the
LORD where-
with he had
sent him, and
all the signs
wherewith he
had charged
him.
29 And Moses
and Aaron went
and gathered to-
gether all the
elders of the
children of Is-
rael: 30 and
Aaron spake all
the words which
the LORD had
spoken unto
Moses, and did
the signs in the
sight of the peo-
ple. 31 And the
people believed:
and when they
heard that the

a S. adds, *Moses.*

b G., T. have, *an angel of the Lord.*

c S. has, *to kill Moses.*

d T. has, *by the blood of this circumcision is given my husband to me.*

e G. has, [*there*] *lies the blood of the circumcision of my son;* T., *except for the blood of this circumcision would have been condemned to death my husband.*

f S. adds, *thy brother.*

g S. adds, *Horeb.*

h G. has, *and they kissed each other.*

i G. has, *the words.*

j S. adds, *to do.*

k G. omits.

l G. has, *these words.*

m G. has, *God.*

n G. has, *and rejoiced,* וישמחו.

had visited the children of Israel, and that he had looked upon their affliction, then they bowed their heads and worshipped.

[a]יְהוָה אֶת־בְּנֵי יִשְׂרָאֵל וְכִי רָאָה

seen had he that and ,Israel of children the Jehovah

אֶת־עָנְיָם [b]וַיִּקְּדוּ [c]וַיִּשְׁתַּחֲוּוּ׃

.themselves prostrated and ,down bowed they and ; affliction their

LORD had visited the children of Israel, and that he had seen their affliction, then they bowed their heads and worshipped.

5

AND afterward Moses and Aaron went in, and told Pharaoh, Thus saith the LORD God of Israel, Let my people go, that they may hold a feast unto me in the wilderness. 2 And Pharaoh said, Who *is* the Lord, that I should obey his voice to let Israel go? I know not the LORD, neither will I let Israel go. 3 And they said, The God of the Hebrews hath met with us: let us go, we pray thee, three days' journey into the desert, and sacrifice unto the LORD our God; lest he fall upon us with pestilence, or with the sword.

1 וְאַחַר בָּאוּ מֹשֶׁה וְאַהֲרֹן וַיֹּאמְרוּ[d] אֶל־

unto said and ,Aaron and Moses in came afterwards And

[d]פַּרְעֹה כֹּה־אָמַר יְהוָה אֱלֹהֵי יִשְׂרָאֵל

: Israel of God the Jehovah says Thus : Pharaoh

שַׁלַּח אֶת־עַמִּי וְיָחֹגּוּ לִי

me to feast a hold may they that ,people my away Send

2 בַּמִּדְבָּר׃ וַיֹּאמֶר פַּרְעֹה מִי [e]יְהוָה

,Jehovah [is] Who : Pharaoh said And .wilderness the in

אֲשֶׁר אֶשְׁמַע בְּקֹלוֹ לְשַׁלַּח

away send to [3]voice [2]whose [1]to [6]hearken [5]should [4]I (who)

אֶת־יִשְׂרָאֵל לֹא יָדַעְתִּי אֶת־יְהוָה וְגַם אֶת־יִשְׂרָאֵל

Israel also and ,Jehovah know [2]do [1]I [3]Not ? Israel

3 לֹא אֲשַׁלֵּחַ׃ וַיֹּאמְרוּ[f] אֱלֹהֵי הָעִבְרִים

Hebrews the of God The : said they And .away send [2]will [1]I [3]not

[g]נִקְרָא עָלֵינוּ[g] נֵלֲכָה נָּא דֶּרֶךְ שְׁלֹשֶׁת

three of journey a ,now ,go us let ; us (upon) met has

יָמִים בַּמִּדְבָּר וְנִזְבְּחָה לַיהוָה[h]

Jehovah to sacrifice us let and ,wilderness the into days

אֱלֹהֵינוּ פֶּן־יִפְגָּעֵנוּ [i]בַּדֶּבֶר אוֹ בֶחָרֶב[i]׃

.sword with or pestilence with us strike he lest ; God our

4 And the king of Egypt said unto them, Wherefore do ye, Moses and Aaron, let the people from their works? get you unto your

4 וַיֹּאמֶר אֲלֵהֶם מֶלֶךְ מִצְרַיִם לָמָּה מֹשֶׁה

Moses ,Why : Egypt of king the them unto said And

וְאַהֲרֹן תַּפְרִיעוּ אֶת־הָעָם מִמַּעֲשָׂיו לְכוּ

ye go ; work their from people the disturb ye do ,Aaron and

And afterward Moses and Aaron came, and said unto Pharaoh, Thus saith the LORD, the God of Israel, Let my people go, that they may hold a feast unto me in the wilderness. 2 And Pharaoh said, Who is the LORD, that I should hearken unto his voice to let Israel go? I know not the LORD, and moreover I will not let Israel go. 3 And they said, The God of the Hebrews hath met with us: let us go, we pray thee, three days' journey into the wilderness, and sacrifice unto the LORD our God; lest he fall upon us with pestilence, or with the sword.

4 And the king of Egypt said unto them, Wherefore do ye, Moses and Aaron, loose the people from their works? get you unto your

---

a G. has, *God.*

b S. adds, *the people.*

c S. adds, *before the Lord.*

d G. has, *unto Pharaoh and said to him.*

e G. omits.

f G. adds, *to him;* S., *the Lord,* יהוה

g G. has, *has summoned us;* S., T. have, *appeared to us.*

h G. omits יהוה.

i G. has, *death, or murder;* S. *with sword, or with death;* T., *with death, or with murder.*

burdens. 5 And
Pharaoh said,
Behold, the
people of the
land now *are*
many, and ye
make them rest
from their bur-
dens. 6 And
Pharaoh com-
manded the
same day the
taskmasters of
the people, and
their officers,
saying, 7 Ye
shall no more
give the peo-
ple straw to
make brick, as
heretofore: let
them go and
gather straw for
themselves. 8
And the tale of
the bricks, which
they did make
heretofore, ye
shall lay upon
them; ye shall
not diminish
ought thereof:
for they *be* idle;
therefore they
cry, saying, Let
us go *and* sac-
rifice to our
God. 9 Let there
more work be
laid upon the
men, that they
may labour
therein; and let
them not regard
vain words.

10 And the
taskmasters of
the people went
out, and their
officers, and
they spake to
the people, say-
ing, Thus saith
Pharaoh, I will
not give you
straw. 11 Go ye,
get you straw
where ye can
find it: yet not

5 לְסִבְלֹתֵיכֶם[a]׃ וַיֹּאמֶר[b] פַּרְעֹה הֵן־רַבִּים עַתָּה
,now ,many Behold :Pharaoh said And .burdens your to

עַם[c] הָאָרֶץ[d] וְהִשְׁבַּתֶּם אֹתָם
[1]them [2]cease make you (and) ,land the of people the [being]

6 מִסִּבְלֹתָם׃ וַיְצַו פַּרְעֹה בַּיּוֹם[e] הַהוּא[e]
[1]that [2]day in Pharaoh commanded And .burdens their from

אֶת־הַנֹּגְשִׂים בָּעָם וְאֶת־שֹׁטְרָיו לֵאמֹר[f]׃
: saying ,overseers their and people the [of] (in) taskmasters the

7 לֹא תֹאסִפוּן לָתֵת תֶּבֶן לָעָם לִלְבֹּן
make to people the to straw give to continue [2]shall [1]you [3]Not

הַלְּבֵנִים כִּתְמוֹל שִׁלְשֹׁם הֵם יֵלְכוּ
go shall they ; day third the [and] yesterday like ,bricks

8 וְקֹשְׁשׁוּ לָהֶם תֶּבֶן׃ וְאֶת־מַתְכֹּנֶת
of quantity fixed the And .straw themselves for up pick and

הַלְּבֵנִים אֲשֶׁר הֵם עֹשִׂים תְּמוֹל שִׁלְשֹׁם
,day third the [and] yesterday making [were] they which bricks the

תָּשִׂימוּ עֲלֵיהֶם לֹא תִגְרְעוּ מִמֶּנּוּ[g]
;it from diminish [2]shall [1]you [3]not ,them upon put shall you

כִּי־נִרְפִּים הֵם עַל־כֵּן הֵם צֹעֲקִים לֵאמֹר
: saying ,crying [are] they therefore ,they [are] lazy for

9 נֵלְכָה נִזְבְּחָה[h] לֵאלֹהֵינוּ׃ תִּכְבַּד הָעֲבֹדָה
service the heavy be Let .God our to sacrifice us let ,go us Let

עַל־הָאֲנָשִׁים[i] וְיַעֲשׂוּ־בָהּ[j] וְאַל־יִשְׁעוּ
trust not may and ,it in work may they that ,men the upon

10 בְּדִבְרֵי־שָׁקֶר׃ וַיֵּצְאוּ[k] נֹגְשֵׂי הָעָם
people the of taskmasters the out went And .falsehood of words to

וְשֹׁטְרָיו וַיֹּאמְרוּ אֶל־הָעָם לֵאמֹר כֹּה
Thus : saying people the unto spoke and ,overseers their and

11 אָמַר פַּרְעֹה אֵינֶנִּי נֹתֵן לָכֶם תֶּבֶן׃ אַתֶּם לְכוּ
,go ,Ye .straw you to give not will I :Pharaoh said has

קְחוּ לָכֶם תֶּבֶן מֵאֲשֶׁר תִּמְצָאוּ כִּי
for ;find may you whence from straw yourselves for take

burdens. 5 And
Pharaoh said,
Behold, the peo-
ple of the land
are now many,
and ye make
them rest from
their burdens. 6
And the same
day Pharaoh
commanded the
taskmasters of
the people, and
their officers,
saying, 7 Ye
shall no more
give the people
straw to make
brick, as here-
tofore: let them
go and gather
straw for them-
selves. 8 And
the tale of the
bricks, which
they did make
heretofore, ye
shall lay upon
them; ye shall
not diminish
aught thereof:
for they be idle;
therefore they
cry, saying, Let
us go and sac-
rifice to our
God. 9 Let
heavier work be
laid upon the
men, that they
may labour
therein; and
let them not re-
gard lying
words.

10 And the
taskmasters of
the people went
out, and their
officers, and
they spake to
the people, say-
ing, Thus saith
Pharaoh, I will
not give you
straw. 11 Go
yourselves, get
you straw where
ye can find it:

---

a G. has, *each of you to his work.*
b S. adds, *to them.*
c Sm. has, *than the people,* מעם.
d G. omits.
e G. omits.
f S. adds, *to them.*
g G., V. have, *anything.*
h G. adds, *and,* ו.
i Sm., G. add, *these.*
j Sm., G., S., T. have, *and let them be concerned,* וישעו.
k G. has, *and urged them,* וַיָּאצוּם.

ought of your
work shall be
diminished. 12
So the people
were scattered
abroad through-
out all the land
of Egypt to
gather stubble
instead of straw.
13 And the
taskmasters
hasted *them*,
saying, Fulfil
your works,
your daily tasks,
as when there
was straw. 14
And the officers
of the children
of Israel, which
Pharaoh's task-
masters had set
over them, were
beaten, *and*
demanded,
Wherefore have
ye not fulfilled
your task in
making brick
both yesterday
and to day, as
heretofore?

15 Then the
officers of the
children of Is-
rael came and
cried unto Pha-
raoh, saying,
Wherefore deal-
est thou thus
with thy serv-
ants? 16 There
is no straw given
unto thy serv-
ants, and they
say to us, Make
brick: and, be-
hold, thy serv-
ants *are* beaten;
but the fault *is*
in thine own
people. 17 But
he said, Ye *are*
idle, *ye are* idle:
therefore ye say,
Let us go *and*
do sacrifice to
the LORD. 18
Go therefore
now, *and* work;
for there shall
no straw be
given you, yet
shall ye deliver
the tale of

12 אֵין נִגְרַע מֵעֲבֹדַתְכֶם דָּבָר׃ וַיָּפֶץ
scattered And .thing a work your from diminished be not shall

הָעָם בְּכָל־אֶרֶץ מִצְרָיִם לְקֹשֵׁשׁ קַשׁ לַתֶּבֶן׃
.straw for stubble up pick to ,Egypt of land the all in people the

13 וְהַנֹּגְשִׂים אָצִים[a] לֵאמֹר כַּלּוּ מַעֲשֵׂיכֶם
,work your Complete :saying ,urging [were] taskmasters the And

דְּבַר־יוֹם בְּיוֹמוֹ כַּאֲשֶׁר בִּהְיוֹת[b] הַתֶּבֶן׃
.straw being [there] in as ,day its in day a of matter the

14 וַיֻּכּוּ שֹׁטְרֵי בְּנֵי יִשְׂרָאֵל אֲשֶׁר־
whom Israel of children the of overseers the beaten were And

שָׂמוּ עֲלֵהֶם נֹגְשֵׂי פַרְעֹה לֵאמֹר
: saying ,Pharaoh of taskmasters the them over put had

מַדּוּעַ לֹא כִלִּיתֶם חָקְכֶם לִלְבֹּן
,bricks make to task fixed your completed [2]you [1]have [3]not Why

כִּתְמוֹל שִׁלְשֹׁם גַּם־תְּמוֹל[c] גַּם־הַיּוֹם׃
? today and yesterday both ,day third the [and] yesterday like

15 וַיָּבֹאוּ שֹׁטְרֵי בְּנֵי יִשְׂרָאֵל וַיִּצְעֲקוּ
cried and ,Israel of children the of overseers the in came And

אֶל־פַּרְעֹה לֵאמֹר לָמָּה תַעֲשֶׂה כֹה
thus do thou dost Why : saying Pharaoh unto

16 לַעֲבָדֶיךָ׃ תֶּבֶן אֵין נִתָּן לַעֲבָדֶיךָ וּלְבֵנִים
,bricks and ,servants thy to given not is Straw ?servants thy to

אֹמְרִים לָנוּ עֲשׂוּ וְהִנֵּה עֲבָדֶיךָ
servants thy behold and ; ye make ,us to saying [are] they

17 מֻכִּים וְחָטָאת[d] עַמֶּךָ[d]׃ וַיֹּאמֶר[e] נִרְפִּים אַתֶּם
,ye [are] Lazy : said he And .people thy sins but ,beaten are

נִרְפִּים עַל־כֵּן אַתֶּם אֹמְרִים נֵלְכָה
,go us Let : saying [are] you therefore ; lazy

18 נִזְבְּחָה לַיהוָה[f]׃ וְעַתָּה לְכוּ עִבְדוּ וְתֶבֶן
straw and ,work ,go ,now And .Jehovah to sacrifice us let

לֹא־יִנָּתֵן לָכֶם וְתֹכֶן לְבֵנִים
bricks of quantity fixed a and ;you to given be not shall

for nought of
your work shall
be diminished.
12 So the peo-
ple were scatter-
ed abroad
throughout all
the land of E-
gypt to gather
stubble for
straw. 13 And
the taskmasters
were urgent,
saying, Fulfil
your works,
your daily tasks,
as when there
was straw. 14
And the officers
of the children
of Israel, which
Pharaoh's task-
masters had set
over them, were
beaten, and
demanded,
Wherefore have
ye not fulfilled
your task both
yesterday and
to-day, in mak-
ing brick as
heretofore?

15 Then the
officers of the
children of Is-
rael came and
cried unto Pha-
raoh, saying,
Wherefore deal-
est thou thus
with thy serv-
ants? 16 There
is no straw giv-
en unto thy
servants, and
they say to us,
Make brick:
and, behold, thy
servants are
beaten; but the
fault is in thine
own people. 17
But he said, Ye
are idle, ye are
idle: therefore
ye say, Let us
go and sacrifice
to the LORD. 18
Go therefore
now, and work;
for there shall
no straw be giv-
en you, yet shall
ye deliver the

---

a G. has, *urged them.*
b Sm., G., S., T. have, *when was given.*
c G. omits.
d G., S. have, *thou wilt treat unjustly thy people*, reading וְחָטָאתָ לְעַמֶּךָ; V. has, *unjustly it is done toward thy people.*
e G. adds, *to them;* S. adds, *to them Pharaoh.*
f G. has, *to our God.* cf. v. 8

bricks. 19 And
the officers of
the children of
Israel did see
that they *were*
in evil *case*, af-
ter it was said,
Ye shall not
minish *ought*
from your bricks
of your daily
task.

20 And they
met Moses and
Aaron, who
stood in the way,
as they came
forth from Pha-
raoh: 21 And
they said unto
them, The
LORD look up-
on you, and
judge; because
ye have made
our savour to be
abhorred in the
eyes of Pha-
raoh, and in the
eyes of his
servants, to put
a sword in their
hand to slay us.
22 And Moses
returned unto
the LORD, and
said, Lord,
wherefore hast
thou *so* evil en-
treated this peo-
ple? why *is* it
that thou hast
sent me? 23
For since I
came to Pha-
raoh to speak in
thy name, he
hath done evil
to this people;
neither hast
thou delivered
thy people at all.

19 תִּתֵּנוּ׃ וַיִּרְאוּ שֹׁטְרֵי בְנֵי־יִשְׂרָאֵל
Israel of children the of overseers the saw And .give shall you
אֹתָם בְּרָע לֵאמֹר[a] לֹא־תִגְרְעוּ
diminish not shall You : saying ,extremity an in themselves
20 מִלִּבְנֵיכֶם דְּבַר־יוֹם בְּיוֹמוֹ׃ וַיִּפְגְּעוּ
met they And .day its in day a of matter the ,bricks your from
אֶת־מֹשֶׁה וְאֶת־אַהֲרֹן נִצָּבִים[b] לִקְרָאתָם בְּצֵאתָם
out going their at ,them meet to standing Aaron and Moses
21 מֵאֵת פַּרְעֹה׃ וַיֹּאמְרוּ אֲלֵהֶם יֵרֶא
[2]look May ; them unto said they And .Pharaoh with from
יְהוָה[c] עֲלֵיכֶם וְיִשְׁפֹּט אֲשֶׁר הִבְאַשְׁתֶּם אֶת־רֵיחֵנוּ
savour our evil made have who ; judge and you upon [1]Jehovah
בְּעֵינֵי פַרְעֹה וּבְעֵינֵי עֲבָדָיו לָתֶת־
give to ,servants his of eyes the in and ,Pharaoh of eyes the in
22 חֶרֶב בְּיָדָם[d] לְהָרְגֵנוּ׃ וַיָּשָׁב מֹשֶׁה אֶל־
unto Moses returned And .us kill to hands their into sword a
יְהוָה וַיֹּאמַר אֲדֹנָי לָמָה הֲרֵעֹתָה לָעָם
[2]people to evil done thou hast why ,Lord : said and Jehovah
23 הַזֶּה[e] לָמָּה זֶּה שְׁלַחְתָּנִי׃ וּמֵאָז בָּאתִי אֶל־
unto in came I since And ? me sent thou hast then why ? [1]this
פַּרְעֹה לְדַבֵּר בִּשְׁמֶךָ הֵרַע לָעָם הַזֶּה
;[1]this [2]people to evil done has he ,name thy in speak to Pharaoh
וְהַצֵּל לֹא־הִצַּלְתָּ אֶת־עַמֶּךָ׃
.people thy delivered not hast thou delivering and

tale of bricks. 19
And the officers
of the children
of Israel did see
that they were
in evil case,
when it was
said, Ye shall
not minish
aught from your
bricks, *your*
daily tasks.

20 And they
met Moses and
Aaron, who
stood in the
way, as they
came forth from
Pharaoh: 21 and
they said unto
them, The
LORD look up-
on you, and
judge; because
ye have made
our savour
to be abhorred
in the eyes of
Pharaoh, and in
the eyes of his
servants, to put
a sword in their
hand to slay us.
22 And Moses
returned unto
the LORD, and
said, Lord,
wherefore hast
thou evil en-
treated this peo-
ple? why is it
that thou hast
sent me? 23 For
since I came to
Pharaoh to
speak in thy
name, he hath
evil entreated
this people; nei-
ther hast thou
delivered thy
people at all.

6

THEN the
LORD said unto
Moses, Now
shalt thou see
what I will do to
Pharaoh: for
with a strong

1 וַיֹּאמֶר יְהוָה אֶל־מֹשֶׁה עַתָּה תִרְאֶה אֲשֶׁר
what see wilt thou Now : Moses unto Jehovah said And
אֶעֱשֶׂה לְפַרְעֹה כִּי בְיָד חֲזָקָה
[1]strong [2]hand a with for ; Pharaoh to do will I

And the LORD
said unto Mo-
ses, Now shalt
thou see what I
will do to Pha-
raoh: for by a
strong hand

---

a S. has, *and they said to them;* V., *because it was said to them.*

b G. has, *coming.*

c G. has, *God.*

d Sm., G. have, *in his hand*, בידו; so essentially V.

e G., S., T. add, *and*, ו.

hand shall he let
them go, and
with a strong
hand shall he
drive them out
of his land.

2 And God
spake unto Mo-
ses, and said
unto him, I *am*
the LORD: 3
And I appeared
unto Abraham,
unto Isaac, and
unto Jacob, by
the name of God
Almighty; but
by my name JE-
HOVAH was I
not known to
them. 4 And I
have also estab-
lished my cove-
nant with them,
to give them the
land of Canaan,
the land of their
pilgrimage,
wherein they
were strangers.
5 And I have al-
so heard the
groaning of the
children of Is-
rael, whom the
Egyptians keep
in bondage; and
I have remem-
bered my cove-
nant. 6 Where-
fore say unto
the children of
Israel, I *am* the
LORD, and I
will bring you
out from under
the burdens of
the Egyptians,
and I will rid
you out of their
bondage, and I
will redeem you
with a stretched
out arm, and
with great judg-
ments: 7 And I
will take you to
me for a people,
and I will be to
you a God: and

יְשַׁלְּחֵם וּבְיָד [a] חֲזָקָה [a] יְגָרְשֵׁם׃
out them drive will he ¹strong ²hand a with and ,away them send will he

מֵאַרְצוֹ׃
.land his from

2 וַיְדַבֵּר אֱלֹהִים [b] אֶל־מֹשֶׁה וַיֹּאמֶר אֵלָיו
: him unto said and ,Moses unto God spoke And

3 אֲנִי יְהוָה׃ וָאֵרָא אֶל־אַבְרָהָם [c] אֶל־יִצְחָק
,Isaac unto ,Abraham unto appeared I and ;Jehovah [am] I

וְאֶל־יַעֲקֹב בְּאֵל [d] שַׁדָּי [d] וּשְׁמִי יְהוָה
Jehovah name my [by] and ,Almighty God as ,Jacob unto and

4 לֹא נוֹדַעְתִּי [e] לָהֶם׃ וְגַם הֲקִמֹתִי
established I also And .them to known myself make ¹did ²I ³not

אֶת־בְּרִיתִי אִתָּם לָתֵת לָהֶם אֶת־אֶרֶץ כְּנָעַן
; Canaan of land the them to give to ,them with covenant my

אֵת אֶרֶץ מְגֻרֵיהֶם אֲשֶׁר־גָּרוּ בָהּ׃
.(it in) sojourned they which [in] ,sojournings their of land the

5 וְגַם ׀ אֲנִי שָׁמַעְתִּי אֶת־נַאֲקַת בְּנֵי
of children the of lamentation the heard have I also And

יִשְׂרָאֵל אֲשֶׁר מִצְרַיִם מַעֲבִדִים אֹתָם
; (them) serve to making [are] Egyptians the whom ,Israel

6 וָאֶזְכֹּר אֶת־בְּרִיתִי [f]׃ לָכֵן [g] אֱמֹר
say Therefore .covenant my remembered have I and

לִבְנֵי־יִשְׂרָאֵל [h] אֲנִי יְהוָה [i] וְהוֹצֵאתִי
out bring will I and ,Jehovah [am] I : Israel of children the to

אֶתְכֶם מִתַּחַת סִבְלֹת מִצְרַיִם וְהִצַּלְתִּי
deliver will and ,Egypt of burdens the under from you

אֶתְכֶם מֵעֲבֹדָתָם וְגָאַלְתִּי אֶתְכֶם [j] בִּזְרוֹעַ
arm an with you redeem will I and ; service their from you

7 נְטוּיָה וּבִשְׁפָטִים גְּדֹלִים׃ וְלָקַחְתִּי אֶתְכֶם
you take will I And .¹great ²judgments with and ,out stretched

לִי לְעָם וְהָיִיתִי לָכֶם לֵאלֹהִים
; God a for you for be will I and ,people a for myself for

shall he let them
go, and by a
strong hand
shall he drive
them out of his
land.

2 And God
spake unto Mo-
ses, and said
unto him, I am
JEHOVAH: 3 and
I appeared un-
to Abraham, un-
to Isaac, and un-
to Jacob, as God
Almighty, but
by my name JE-
HOVAH I was
not known to
them. 4 And I
have also estab-
lished my cove-
nant with them,
to give them the
land of Canaan,
the land of their
sojournings,
wherein they so-
journed. 5 And
moreover I have
heard the groan-
ing of the chil-
dren of Israel,
whom the Egyp-
tians keep in
bondage; and I
have remember-
ed my covenant.
6 Wherefore say
unto the chil-
dren of Israel, I
am Jehovah,
and I will bring
you out from un-
der the burdens
of the Egyp-
tians, and I will
rid you out of
their bondage,
and I will re-
deem you with a
stretched out
arm, and with
great judg-
ments: 7 and I
will take you to
me for a people,
and I will be to
you a God: and

---

a G., S. have, *and with a stretched out arm.*
b Sm., S., V. have, *the Lord*, יהוה.
c G., S. add *and*, ו.
d G. has, *being their God;* S. adds, *God.*
e Sm., G., S., T. have, *I made known.*
f G. has, *our covenant.*
g G. has, *go*, הָבָה.
h G. adds, *saying.*
i S. adds, *your God.*
j S. adds, *with a strong hand and.*

ye shall know that I *am* the LORD your God, which bringeth you out from under the burdens of the Egyptians. 8 And I will bring you in unto the land, concerning the which I did swear to give it to Abraham, to Isaac, and to Jacob; and I will give it you for an heritage: I *am* the LORD.

9 And Moses spake so unto the children of Israel: but they hearkened not unto Moses for anguish of spirit, and for cruel bondage. 10 And the LORD spake unto Moses saying, 11 Go in, speak unto Pharaoh king of Egypt, that he let the children of Israel go out of his land. 12 And Moses spake before the LORD, saying, Behold, the children of Israel have not hearkened unto me; how then shall Pharaoh hear me, who *am* of uncircumcised lips?

13 And the LORD spake unto Moses and unto Aaron, and gave them a charge unto the children of Israel,

וִֽידַעְתֶּם כִּֽי־אֲנִי יְהוָה אֱלֹהֵיכֶם
,God your Jehovah [am] I that know shall you and

הַמּוֹצִיא אֶתְכֶם מִתַּחַת סִבְלוֹת מִצְרָיִם׃
.Egypt of burdens the under from you out bringing one the

8 וְהֵבֵאתִי אֶתְכֶם אֶל־הָאָרֶץ אֲשֶׁר נָשָׂאתִי
raised I which land the into you bring will I And

אֶת־יָדִי לָתֵת אֹתָהּ לְאַבְרָהָם [a] לְיִצְחָק וְלְיַעֲקֹב
;Jacob to and ,Isaac to ,Abraham to (it) give to hand my

וְנָתַתִּי אֹתָהּ לָכֶם מוֹרָשָׁה אֲנִי יְהוָה׃
.Jehovah [am] I ; possession a [as] you to it give will I and

9 וַיְדַבֵּר מֹשֶׁה כֵּן אֶל־בְּנֵי יִשְׂרָאֵל וְלֹא
[3]not and ;Israel of children the unto so Moses spoke And

שָׁמְעוּ אֶל־מֹשֶׁה מִקֹּצֶר רוּחַ
spirit of shortness from ,Moses unto hearken [2]did [1]they

וּמֵעֲבֹדָה קָשָׁה[b]׃
.[1]hard [2]bondage from and

10 11 וַיְדַבֵּר יְהוָה אֶל־מֹשֶׁה לֵּאמֹר׃ בֹּא דַבֵּר
speak ,Go :saying Moses unto Jehovah spoke And

אֶל־פַּרְעֹה מֶלֶךְ מִצְרָיִם וִישַׁלַּח אֶת־בְּנֵי־
of children the away send may he that ;Egypt of king Pharaoh unto

12 יִשְׂרָאֵל מֵאַרְצוֹ׃ וַיְדַבֵּר מֹשֶׁה לִפְנֵי יְהוָה
Jehovah before Moses spoke And .land his from Israel

לֵאמֹר[c] הֵן בְּנֵי־יִשְׂרָאֵל לֹא־שָׁמְעוּ אֵלַי
;me unto hearkened not have Israel of children the Behold :saying

[d]וְאֵיךְ יִשְׁמָעֵנִי פַּרְעֹה וַאֲנִי עֲרַל[e]
of uncircumcised [being] I (and) ,Pharaoh me hear should how and

שְׂפָתָיִם[e]׃
?lips

13 וַיְדַבֵּר יְהוָה אֶל־מֹשֶׁה וְאֶל־אַהֲרֹן
,Aaron unto and Moses unto Jehovah spoke And

וַיְצַוֵּם אֶל־בְּנֵי[f] יִשְׂרָאֵל[f]
Israel of children the concerning them commanded he and

ye shall know that I am Jehovah your God, which bringeth you out from under the burdens of the Egyptians. 8 And I will bring you in unto the land, concerning which I lifted up my hand to give it to Abraham, to Isaac, and to Jacob; and I will give it you for an heritage: I am Jehovah.

9 And Moses spake so unto the children of Israel: but they hearkened not unto Moses for anguish of spirit, and for cruel bondage. 10 And the LORD spake unto Moses, saying, 11 Go in, speak unto Pharaoh king of Egypt, that he let the children of Israel go out of his land. 12 And Moses spake before the LORD, saying, Behold, the children of Israel have not hearkened unto me; how then shall Pharaoh hear me, who am of uncircumcised lips?

13 And the LORD spake unto Moses and unto Aaron, and gave them a charge unto the children of Israel,

---

a G., S. add, *and*, ו.

b Sm. adds, *And they said to Moses, Cease from us that we may serve the Egyptians; for it is better for us to serve the Egyptians than to die in the wilderness;* cf. 14; 12.

c S., V. omit.

d S. omits, ו.

e Most of the versions paraphrase, giving the same meaning.

f G. omits.

and unto Pha-
raoh king of E-
gypt, to bring
the children of
Israel out of the
land of Egypt.

14 These *be*
the heads of
their fathers'
houses: The
sons of Reuben
the firstborn of
Israel; Hanoch,
and Pallu, Hez-
ron, and Car-
mi: these *be* the
families of Reu-
ben. 15 And the
sons of Simeon;
Jemuel, and Ja-
min, and Ohad,
and Jachin, and
Zohar, and
Shaul the son of
a Canaanitish
woman: these
are the families
of Simeon.

16 And these
are the names
of the sons of
Levi according
to their genera-
tions; Gershon,
and Kohath,
and Merari: and
the years of the
life of Levi *were*
an hundred thir-
ty and seven
years. 17 The
sons of Ger-
shon; Libni,
and Shimi, ac-
cording to their
families. 18 And
the sons of Ko-
hath; Amram,
and Izhar, and
Hebron, and
Uzziel: and the
years of the life
of Kohath *were*
an hundred thir-
ty and three
years. 19 And
the sons of
Merari; Ma-
hali and Mushi:
these *are* the
families of Levi
according to
their genera-
tions. 20 And
Amram took

[a]וְאֶל־פַּרְעֹה מֶלֶךְ מִצְרָיִם לְהוֹצִיא אֶת־בְּנֵי־
of children the out bring to ; Egypt of king Pharaoh concerning and

יִשְׂרָאֵל מֵאֶרֶץ מִצְרָיִם׃
.Egypt of land the from Israel

14 [b]אֵלֶּה רָאשֵׁי בֵית־אֲבֹתָם בְּנֵי
of sons the ; fathers their of houses the of heads the [were] These

רְאוּבֵן בְּכֹר יִשְׂרָאֵל חֲנוֹךְ וּפַלּוּא [c]חֶצְרֹן
,Hezron ,Pallu and ,Hanoch : Israel of firstborn the Reuben

15 וְכַרְמִי אֵלֶּה מִשְׁפְּחֹת רְאוּבֵן׃ וּבְנֵי
of sons the And .Reuben of families the [were] these ; Carmi and

שִׁמְעוֹן יְמוּאֵל וְיָמִין וְאֹהַד וְיָכִין וְצֹחַר
,Zohar and ,Jachin and ,Ohad and ,Jamin and ,Jemuel : Simeon

וְשָׁאוּל [d]בֶּן־הַכְּנַעֲנִית אֵלֶּה מִשְׁפְּחֹת
of families the [were] these ; Canaanitess the of son the Shaul and

16 שִׁמְעוֹן׃ וְאֵלֶּה שְׁמוֹת בְּנֵי־לֵוִי
Levi of sons the of names the [were] these And .Simeon

לְתֹלְדֹתָם גֵּרְשׁוֹן וּקְהָת וּמְרָרִי וּשְׁנֵי
of years the and ; Merari and ,Kohath and ,Gershon :generations their by

חַיֵּי לֵוִי שֶׁבַע וּשְׁלֹשִׁים וּמְאַת שָׁנָה׃
.years hundred a and thirty and seven [were] Levi of life the

17 [e]בְּנֵי גֵרְשׁוֹן לִבְנִי וְשִׁמְעִי לְמִשְׁפְּחֹתָם׃
.families their by ,Shimei and ,Libni : Gershon of sons The

18 וּבְנֵי קְהָת עַמְרָם וְיִצְהָר וְחֶבְרוֹן
,Hebron and ,Izhar and ,Amram : Kohath of sons the And

וְעֻזִּיאֵל וּשְׁנֵי חַיֵּי קְהָת [f]שָׁלֹשׁ
three [were] Kohath of life the of years the and ; Uzziel and

19 וּשְׁלֹשִׁים [f]וּמְאַת שָׁנָה׃ וּבְנֵי מְרָרִי מַחְלִי
,Mahli : Merari of sons the And .years hundred a and thirty and

וּמוּשִׁי אֵלֶּה מִשְׁפְּחֹת הַלֵּוִי לְתֹלְדֹתָם׃
.generations their by Levites the of families the [were] these ; Mushi and

20 וַיִּקַּח עַמְרָם אֶת־יוֹכֶבֶד [g]דֹּדָתוֹ לוֹ לְאִשָּׁה
,wife a for him to aunt his Jochebed Amram took And

and unto Pha-
raoh king of E-
gypt, to bring
the children of
Israel out of the
land of Egypt.

14 These are
the heads of
their fathers'
houses: the sons
of Reuben the
firstborn of Is-
rael; Hanoch,
and Pallu, Hez-
ron, and Carmi:
these are the
families of Reu-
ben. 15 And the
sons of Simeon;
Jemuel, and Ja-
min, and Ohad,
and Jachin, and
Zohar, and
Shaul the son of
a Canaanitish
woman: these
are the families
of Simeon.

16 And these
are the names
of the sons of
Levi according
to their genera-
tions; Gershon,
and Kohath,
and Merari: and
the years of the
life of Levi
were an hun-
dred thirty and
seven years. 17
The sons of
Gershon; Libni
and Shimei,
according to
their families.
18 And the sons
of Kohath; Am-
ram, and Izhar,
and Hebron,
and Uzziel: and
the years of the
life of Kohath
were an hun-
dred thirty and
three years. 19
And the sons
of Merari; Mah-
li and Mushi.
These are the
families of the
Levites accord-
ing to their gen-
erations. 20 And
Amram took

---

a G. omits ו.

b G., S. add, *and*, ו.

c S. adds, *and*, ו.

d G. has, *the Phenician woman.*

e G. adds, *and these*; S. *and* ו.

f G. has, *a hundred and thirty.*

g G. has, *the daughter of the brother of his father*; S. has, *the daughter of his uncle*; V., *his paternal cousin.*

him Jochebed his father's sister to wife; and she bare him Aaron and Moses: and the years of the life of Amram *were* an hundred and thirty and seven years.

21 And the sons of Izhar; Korah, and Nepheg, and Zichri. 22 And the sons of Uzziel; Mishael, and Elzaphan, and Zithri. 23 And Aaron took him Elisheba, daughter of Amminadab, sister of Naashon, to wife; and she bare him Nadab, and Abihu, Eleazar, and Ithamar. 24 And the sons of Korah; Assir, and Elkanah, and Abiasaph: these *are* the families of the Korhites. 25 And Eleazar Aaron's son took him *one* of the daughters of Putiel to wife; and she bare him Phinehas: these *are* the heads of the fathers of the Levites according to their families. 26 These *are* that Aaron and Moses, to whom the LORD said, Bring out the children of Israel from the land of Egypt according to their armies. 27 These *are* they which spake to Pharaoh king of

וַתֵּלֶד לוֹ אֶת־אַהֲרֹן וְאֶת־מֹשֶׁה [a] וּשְׁנֵי
of years the and ; Moses and Aaron him to bore she and

חַיֵּי עַמְרָם שֶׁבַע [b] וּשְׁלֹשִׁים וּמְאַת [b] שָׁנָה׃
.years hundred a and thirty and seven [were] Amram of life the

21 וּבְנֵי יִצְהָר קֹרַח וָנֶפֶג וְזִכְרִי׃
.Zikri and ,Nepheg and ,Korah : Izhar of sons the And

22 וּבְנֵי עֻזִּיאֵל מִישָׁאֵל [c] וְאֶלְצָפָן [d] וְסִתְרִי׃
.Sithri and ,Elzaphan and ,Mishael : Uzziel of sons the And

23 וַיִּקַּח אַהֲרֹן אֶת־אֱלִישֶׁבַע בַּת־עַמִּינָדָב
,Amminadab of daughter the Elisheba Aaron took And

אֲחוֹת נַחְשׁוֹן לוֹ לְאִשָּׁה וַתֵּלֶד לוֹ
him to bore she and ; wife a for him to Nahshon of sister the

אֶת־נָדָב וְאֶת־אֲבִיהוּא [e] אֶת־אֶלְעָזָר וְאֶת־אִיתָמָר׃
.Ithamar and ,Eleazar ,Abihu and ,Nadab

24 וּבְנֵי קֹרַח אַסִּיר וְאֶלְקָנָה וַאֲבִיאָסָף אֵלֶּה
these ; Abiasaph and ,Elkanah and ,Assir : Korah of sons the And

25 מִשְׁפְּחֹת הַקָּרְחִי׃ וְאֶלְעָזָר בֶּן־אַהֲרֹן
Aaron of son the Eleazar And .Korahites the of families the [were]

לָקַח־לוֹ מִבְּנוֹת פּוּטִיאֵל לוֹ לְאִשָּׁה
; wife a for him to Putiel of daughters the of [one] him to took

וַתֵּלֶד לוֹ אֶת־פִּינְחָס אֵלֶּה רָאשֵׁי
of heads the [were] these ; Phinehas him to bore she and

26 אֲבוֹת הַלְוִיִּם לְמִשְׁפְּחֹתָם׃ הוּא אַהֲרֹן
Aaron [is] That .families their by Levites the of fathers the

וּמֹשֶׁה אֲשֶׁר אָמַר יְהוָֹה [f] לָהֶם הוֹצִיאוּ
out Bring :(them to) Jehovah said whom [to] Moses and

אֶת־בְּנֵי יִשְׂרָאֵל מֵאֶרֶץ מִצְרַיִם [g] עַל־
to according Egypt of land the from Israel of children the

27 צִבְאֹתָם׃ הֵם הַמְדַבְּרִים אֶל־פַּרְעֹה
Pharaoh unto speaking ones the [were] Those .hosts their

him Jochebed his father's sister to wife; and she bare him Aaron and Moses: and the years of the life of Amram were an hundred and thirty and seven years.

21 And the sons of Izhar; Korah, and Nepheg, and Zichri. 22 And the sons of Uzziel; Mishael, and Elzaphan, and Sithri. 23 And Aaron took him Elisheba, the daughter of Amminadab, the sister of Nahshon to wife; and she bare him Nadab and Abihu, Eleazar and Ithamar. 24 And the sons of Korah; Assir, and Elkanah, and Abiasaph; these are the families of the Korahites. 25 And Eleazar Aaron's son took him one of the daughters of Putiel to wife; and she bare him Phinehas. These are the heads of the fathers' *houses* of the Levites according to their families. 26 These are that Aaron and Moses, to whom the LORD said, Bring out the children of Israel from the land of Egypt according to their hosts. 27 These are they which spake to Pharaoh king of

a Sm., G. add, *and Miriam their sister;* S. adds, *and Miriam;* cf. Num. 26 : 59.

b G. has, *one hundred and thirty-two.*

c G. omits.

d G. omits ו.

e G., S., V. add, *and,* ו.

f G. adds, *God.*

g For על S. has, *all* כל.

Egypt, to bring
out the chil-
dren of Israel
from Egypt:
these *are* that
Moses and Aa-
ron.

מֶלֶךְ־מִצְרַיִם לְהוֹצִיא אֶת־בְּנֵי־יִשְׂרָאֵל מִמִּצְרָיִם[a]
,Egypt of king | out bring to | Israel of children the | ,Egypt from

הוּא מֹשֶׁה[b] וְאַהֲרֹן[b]׃
[was] that | Moses | .Aaron and

Egypt, to bring
out the children
of Israel from
Egypt: these
are that Moses
and Aaron.

28 And it
came to pass
on the day *when*
the LORD spake
unto Moses in
the land of E-
gypt, 29 That
the LORD spake
unto Moses, say-
ing, I *am* the
LORD: speak
thou unto Pha-
raoh king of E-
gypt all that I
say unto thee. 30
And Moses said
before the
LORD, Behold,
I *am* of uncir-
cumcised lips,
and how shall
Pharaoh heark-
en unto me?

28 וַיְהִי[c] בְּיוֹם דִּבֶּר יְהוָה אֶל־
,pass to came it And | day the on | spoke [that] | Jehovah | unto

29 מֹשֶׁה בְּאֶרֶץ מִצְרָיִם׃ וַיְדַבֵּר יְהוָה אֶל־
Moses | of land the in | ; Egypt | spoke (and) | Jehovah | unto

מֹשֶׁה לֵּאמֹר[d] אֲנִי יְהוָה דַּבֵּר אֶל־פַּרְעֹה
Moses | :saying | I | ; Jehovah [am] | speak | Pharaoh unto

מֶלֶךְ מִצְרַיִם אֵת[e] [e]כָּל־אֲשֶׁר אֲנִי דֹּבֵר אֵלֶיךָ׃
of king | Egypt | which all | I | speak to about [am] | .thee unto

30 וַיֹּאמֶר מֹשֶׁה לִפְנֵי יְהוָה הֵן אֲנִי
said And | Moses | before | : Jehovah | Behold | I

עֲרַל[f] שְׂפָתַיִם[f] וְאֵיךְ[g] יִשְׁמַע אֵלַי
of uncircumcised [being] | ,lips | how (and) | hearken could | me unto

פַּרְעֹה׃
?Pharaoh

28 And it
came to pass on
the day when
the LORD spake
unto Moses in
the land of E-
gypt, 29 that the
LORD spake un-
to Moses, say-
ing, I am the
LORD: speak
thou unto Pha-
raoh king of E-
gypt all that I
speak unto thee.
30 And Moses
said before the
LORD, Behold,
I am of uncir-
cumcised lips,
and how shall
Pharaoh heark-
en unto me?

7

AND the
LORD said unto
Moses, See, I
have made thee
a god to Pha-
raoh; and Aa-
ron thy broth-
er shall be thy
prophet. 2 Thou
shalt speak all
that I command
thee: and Aaron
thy brother shall
speak unto Pha-
raoh, that he
send the chil-
dren of Israel
out of his land.
3 And I will
harden Pha-
raoh's heart,
and multiply
my signs and

1 וַיֹּאמֶר יְהוָה אֶל־מֹשֶׁה[h] רְאֵה נְתַתִּיךָ
said And | Jehovah | : Moses unto | ,See | thee make I

אֱלֹהִים לְפַרְעֹה וְאַהֲרֹן אָחִיךָ יִהְיֶה נְבִיאֶךָ׃
God a | ; Pharaoh to | Aaron and | brother thy | is | .prophet thy

2 [i]אַתָּה תְדַבֵּר[j] אֵת כָּל־אֲשֶׁר אֲצַוֶּךָּ וְאַהֲרֹן
Thou | speak shalt | which all | ,thee command I | Aaron and

אָחִיךָ יְדַבֵּר אֶל־פַּרְעֹה וְשִׁלַּח
brother thy | speak shall | ; Pharaoh unto | away send shall he and

3 אֶת־בְּנֵי־יִשְׂרָאֵל מֵאַרְצוֹ׃ וַאֲנִי אַקְשֶׁה
Israel of children the | .land his from | I And | harden will

אֶת־לֵב פַּרְעֹה וְהִרְבֵּיתִי אֶת־אֹתֹתַי
of heart the | ; Pharaoh | multiply will I and | signs my

And the
LORD said unto
Moses, See, I
have made thee
a god to Pha-
raoh: and Aa-
ron thy broth-
er shall be thy
prophet. 2 Thou
shalt speak all
that I command
thee: and Aa-
ron thy brother
shall speak un-
to Pharaoh,
that he let the
children of Is-
rael go out of
his land. 3 And I
will harden
Pharaoh's heart,
and multiply my
signs and my

a Sm., G., S. have, *from the land of Egypt.*
b G. has, *Aaron and Moses.*
c G., V. omit.
d S. adds, *to him.*
e G. omits, and adds, *and*, ו.
f Most of the versions paraphrase, giving the same meaning.
g S., V. omit, ו.
h G. adds, *saying.*
i G. adds, *and*, ו.
j G., V. add, *to him.*

my wonders in
the land of E-
gypt. 4 But
Pharaoh shall
not hearken un-
to you, that I
may lay my
hand upon E-
gypt, and bring
forth mine ar-
mies, *and* my
people the chil-
dren of Israel,
out of the land
of Egypt by
great judg-
ments. 5 And
the Egyptians
shall know that
I *am* the LORD,
when I stretch
forth mine hand
upon Egypt,
and bring out
the children of
Israel from a-
mong them. 6
And Moses and
Aaron did as
the LORD com-
manded them,
so did they. 7
And Moses *was*
fourscore years
old, and Aaron
fourscore and
three years old,
when they spake
unto Pharaoh.

8 And the
LORD spake un-
to Moses and
unto Aaron,
saying, 9 When
Pharaoh shall
speak unto you,
saying, Shew a
miracle for you:
then thou shalt
say unto Aaron,
Take thy rod,
and cast *it* be-
fore Pharaoh,
and it shall be-
come a serpent.

10 And Moses
and Aaron went
in unto Pha-
raoh, and
they did so
as the LORD
had command-
ed: and Aaron
cast down his

וְאֶת־מוֹפְתַי בְּאֶרֶץ מִצְרָיִם׃ וְלֹא־יִשְׁמַע 4
wonders my and of land the in .Egypt hearken not will And

אֲלֵכֶם פַּרְעֹה וְנָתַתִּי אֶת־יָדִי בְּמִצְרָיִם
you unto ; Pharaoh lay will I and hand my ,Egypt on

וְהוֹצֵאתִי אֶת־צִבְאֹתַי[a] אֶת־עַמִּי בְנֵי־יִשְׂרָאֵל
out bring will and ,hosts my ,people my Israel of children the

מֵאֶרֶץ מִצְרַיִם בִּשְׁפָטִים גְּדֹלִים׃ [b]וְיָדְעוּ 5
of land the from Egypt [2]judgments with .[1]great know shall And

מִצְרַיִם כִּי־אֲנִי יְהוָה בִּנְטֹתִי אֶת־יָדִי
Egyptians the I that ,Jehovah [am] out stretch I when hand my

עַל־מִצְרָיִם וְהוֹצֵאתִי אֶת־בְּנֵי־יִשְׂרָאֵל מִתּוֹכָם׃
,Egypt upon out bring and Israel of children the .midst their from

וַיַּעַשׂ מֹשֶׁה וְאַהֲרֹן כַּאֲשֶׁר צִוָּה יְהוָה 6
did And Moses ,Aaron and as commanded Jehovah

אֹתָם כֵּן עָשׂוּ׃ וּמֹשֶׁה בֶּן־שְׁמֹנִים שָׁנָה 7
,them so .did they Moses And [was] (of son a) eighty [old] years,

וְאַהֲרֹן[c] בֶּן־שָׁלֹשׁ וּשְׁמֹנִים שָׁנָה בְּדַבְּרָם
Aaron and three (of son a) eighty and [old] years speaking their in

אֶל־פַּרְעֹה׃
.Pharaoh unto

וַיֹּאמֶר יְהוָה אֶל־מֹשֶׁה וְאֶל־אַהֲרֹן לֵאמֹר[d]׃ 8
spoke And Jehovah Moses unto Aaron unto and :saying

[e]כִּי יְדַבֵּר אֲלֵכֶם פַּרְעֹה לֵאמֹר[f] תְּנוּ לָכֶם[g] 9
When speaks you unto Pharaoh :saying Give yourselves for

מוֹפֵת[h] וְאָמַרְתָּ אֶל־אַהֲרֹן[i] קַח אֶת־מַטְּךָ
; wonder a say shalt thou (and) : Aaron unto Take staff thy

וְהַשְׁלֵךְ[j] לִפְנֵי־פַרְעֹה[k] [l]יְהִי לְתַנִּין׃ וַיָּבֹא 10
cast and ,Pharaoh before become it let .serpent a (for) came And

מֹשֶׁה וְאַהֲרֹן אֶל־פַּרְעֹה וַיַּעֲשׂוּ כֵן כַּאֲשֶׁר
Moses Aaron and ,Pharaoh unto did they and ,so as

צִוָּה[m] יְהוָה וַיַּשְׁלֵךְ אַהֲרֹן אֶת־מַטֵּהוּ לִפְנֵי
commanded had ; Jehovah cast and Aaron staff his before

wonders in the
land of Egypt. 4
But Pharaoh
will not heark-
en unto you,
and I will lay
my hand upon
Egypt, and
bring forth my
hosts, my peo-
ple the chil-
dren of Israel,
out of the land
of Egypt by
great judg-
ments. 5 And
the Egyptians
shall know that
I am the LORD,
when I stretch
forth mine hand
upon Egypt,
and bring out
the children of
Israel from a-
mong them. 6
And Moses and
Aaron did so; as
the LORD com-
manded them,
so did they. 7
And Moses was
fourscore years
old, and Aaron
fourscore and
three years old,
when they spake
unto Pharaoh.

8 And the
LORD spake un-
to Moses and
unto Aaron,
saying, 9 When
Pharaoh shall
speak unto you,
saying, Shew a
wonder for you:
then thou shalt
say unto Aaron,
Take thy rod,
and cast it down
before Pharaoh,
that it become a
serpent.

10 And Moses
and Aaron went
in unto Pha-
raoh, and they
did so, as the
LORD had com-
manded: and
Aaron cast down
his rod before

a G. has, *with my power.*
b Sm., G. add, *all.*
c G. adds, *his brother.*
d S. omits.
e G. adds, *and,* ו.
f S., V. omit.
g G. has, *to us;* S., *to me.*
h G. has, *a sign or a wonder;* V., *signs;* S., T. have, *sign.*
i G. adds, *thy brother.*
j G adds, *upon the earth,* cf. 4:3.
k G. adds, *and before his servants,* so v. 10 a.
l Sm., G., S. add, *and,* ו.
m G., S. add, *them.*

rod before Pha-
raoh, and be-
fore his serv-
ants, and it be-
came a serpent.
11 Then Pha-
raoh also called
the wise men
and the sorcer-
ers: now the
magicians of E-
gypt, they also
did in like man-
ner with their
enchantments.
12 For they cast
down every man
his rod, and
they became
serpents: but
Aaron's rod
swallowed up
their rods. 13
And he harden-
ed Pharaoh's
heart, that he
hearkened not
unto them; as
the LORD had
said.
14 And the
LORD said unto
Moses, Pha-
raoh's heart *is*
hardened, he re-
fuseth to let the
people go. 15
Get thee unto
Pharaoh in the
morning; lo,
he goeth out un-
to the water;
and thou shalt
stand by the
river's brink a-
gainst he come;
and the rod
which was turn-
ed to a serpent
shalt thou take
in thine hand.
16 And thou
shalt say unto
him, The LORD
God of the He-
brews hath sent
me unto thee,
saying, Let my
people go, that
they may serve
me in the wil-
derness: and,
behold, hitherto
thou wouldest
not hear. 17
Thus saith the
LORD, In this
thou shalt know

פַּרְעֹה וְלִפְנֵי עֲבָדָיו וַיְהִי לְתַנִּין׃
.serpent a (for) became it and ; servants his before and Pharaoh

11 וַיִּקְרָא גַּם־פַּרְעֹה לַחֲכָמִים[a] וְלַמְכַשְּׁפִים וַיַּעֲשׂוּ
did and ; magicians (to) and men wise (to) Pharaoh also called And

גַם־הֵם חַרְטֻמֵּי מִצְרַיִם בְּלַהֲטֵיהֶם כֵּן׃
.so ,arts secret their by ,Egypt of scribes the ,they also

12 וַיַּשְׁלִיכוּ אִישׁ מַטֵּהוּ[b] וַיִּהְיוּ לְתַנִּינִם
; serpents (for) became they and ,staff his one each ,down cast they And

13 וַיִּבְלַע מַטֵּה־אַהֲרֹן אֶת־מַטֹּתָם׃ וַיֶּחֱזַק
hard was And .staffs their Aaron of staff the swallowed but

לֵב פַּרְעֹה וְלֹא שָׁמַע[c] אֲלֵהֶם
,them unto hearken ²did ¹he ³not and ,Pharaoh of heart the

כַּאֲשֶׁר דִּבֶּר[d] יְהוָה׃
.Jehovah spoken had as

14 וַיֹּאמֶר יְהוָה אֶל־מֹשֶׁה כָּבֵד לֵב
of heart the heavy [Is] :Moses unto Jehovah said And

15 פַּרְעֹה מֵאֵן לְשַׁלַּח הָעָם׃ לֵךְ אֶל־
unto thou Go .people the away send to refuses he ,Pharaoh

פַּרְעֹה בַּבֹּקֶר הִנֵּה יֹצֵא הַמַּיְמָה
,water the to out go to about [is he] behold ,morning the in Pharaoh

וְנִצַּבְתָּ[e] לִקְרָאתוֹ[e] עַל־שְׂפַת הַיְאֹר וְהַמַּטֶּה
staff the and ; river the of bank the upon him meet to thou stand and

אֲשֶׁר־נֶהְפַּךְ לְנָחָשׁ תִּקַּח בְּיָדֶךָ׃
.hand thy in take shalt thou serpent a into turned was which

16 וְאָמַרְתָּ אֵלָיו יְהוָה אֱלֹהֵי הָעִבְרִים
Hebrews the of God the Jehovah :him unto say shalt thou And

שְׁלָחַנִי אֵלֶיךָ לֵאמֹר שַׁלַּח אֶת־עַמִּי
,people my away Send : saying ,thee unto me sent has

וְיַעַבְדֻנִי בַּמִּדְבָּר וְהִנֵּה לֹא־שָׁמַעְתָּ
heard not hast thou behold and ;wilderness the in me serve may they that

17 עַד־כֹּה׃ כֹּה אָמַר יְהוָה בְּזֹאת תֵּדַע
know shalt thou this By : Jehovah says Thus .now until

Pharaoh and
before his serv-
ants, and it be-
came a serpent.
11 Then Pha-
raoh also called
for the wise men
and the sorcer-
ers: and they
also, the ma-
gicians of E-
gypt, did in like
manner with
their enchant-
ments. 12 For
they cast down
every man his
rod, and they
became ser-
pents: but Aa-
ron's rod swal-
lowed up their
rods. 13 And
Pharaoh's heart
was hardened,
and he hearken-
ed not unto
them; as the
LORD had spok-
en.
14 And the
LORD said un-
to Moses, Pha-
raoh's heart is
stubborn, he re-
fuseth to let the
people go. 15
Get thee unto
Pharaoh in the
morning; lo, he
goeth out unto
the water; and
thou shalt stand
by the river's
brink to meet
him; and the
rod which was
turned to a ser-
pent shalt thou
take in thine
hand. 16 And
thou shalt say
unto him, The
LORD, the God
of the Hebrews,
hath sent me un-
to thee, saying,
Let my people
go, that they
may serve me in
the wilderness:
and, behold,
hitherto thou
hast not heark-
ened. 17 Thus
saith the LORD,
In this thou
shalt know that

a G. adds, *of Egypt.*
b S. adds, *before Pharaoh.*
c S. has, *did send away.*
d G. has, *had commanded them.*
e G. has, *and thou shalt be meeting him;* S. omits ו.

that I *am* the
LORD: behold,
I will smite with
the rod that *is* in
mine hand upon
the waters which
are in the river,
and they shall
be turned to
blood. 18 And
the fish that *is*
in the river
shall die, and
the river shall
stink; and the
Egyptians shall
lothe to drink
of the water of
the river.

19 And the
LORD spake un-
to Moses, Say
unto Aaron,
Take thy rod,
and stretch out
thine hand up-
on the waters of
Egypt, upon
their streams,
upon their riv-
ers, and upon
their ponds, and
upon all their
pools of water,
that they may
become blood;
and *that* there
may be blood
throughout all
the land of E-
gypt, both in
vessels of wood,
and in *vessels of*
stone. 20 And
Moses and
Aaron did so, as
the LORD com-
manded; and he
lifted up the
rod, and smote
the waters that
were in the riv-
er, in the sight
of Pharaoh, and
in the sight of
his servants;
and all the wa-
ters that *were*
in the river were
turned to blood.
21 And the fish
that *was* in the

כִּי אֲנִי יְהוָה הִנֵּה אָנֹכִי מַכֶּה׀
smite to about [am] I behold ; Jehovah [am] I that

בַּמַּטֶּה אֲשֶׁר־בְּיָדִי עַל־הַמַּיִם אֲשֶׁר
[is] which water the upon hand my in [is] which staff the with

בַּיְאֹר וְנֶהֶפְכוּ[b] לְדָם׃ וְהַדָּגָה אֲשֶׁר 18
which fish the And .blood to turned be shall it and ,river the in

בַּיְאֹר תָּמוּת וּבָאַשׁ הַיְאֹר וְנִלְאוּ[b]
weary become will and ,river the stink will and ,die will river the in [are]

מִצְרַיִם לִשְׁתּוֹת מַיִם [c]מִן־הַיְאֹר׃
.river the from water drinking [of] (to) Egyptians the

וַיֹּאמֶר יְהוָה אֶל־מֹשֶׁה אֱמֹר אֶל־אַהֲרֹן[d] 19
: Aaron unto Say :Moses unto Jehovah said And

קַח מַטְּךָ[e] וּנְטֵה־יָדְךָ עַל־מֵימֵי
of waters the over hand thy out stretch and ,staff thy Take

מִצְרַיִם [f]עַל־נַהֲרֹתָם׀ [g]עַל־יְאֹרֵיהֶם וְעַל־אַגְמֵיהֶם
,pools their over and ,canals their over ,rivers their over ,Egypt

וְעַל [h]כָּל־מִקְוֵה מֵימֵיהֶם וְיִהְיוּ־דָם
; blood become may they that ,waters their of collection every over and

וְהָיָה דָם בְּכָל־אֶרֶץ מִצְרַיִם וּבָעֵצִים
[vessels] wood in both ,Egypt of land the all in blood be shall and

וּבָאֲבָנִים׃ וַיַּעֲשׂוּ־כֵן מֹשֶׁה וְאַהֲרֹן כַּאֲשֶׁר׀ 20
as ,Aaron and Moses so did And .[vessels] stone in and

צִוָּה[i] יְהוָה וַיָּרֶם[j] בַּמַּטֶּה[k] וַיַּךְ
smote and ,staff the (with) up lifted he and ; Jehovah commanded had

אֶת־הַמַּיִם אֲשֶׁר בַּיְאֹר לְעֵינֵי פַרְעֹה
,Pharaoh of eyes the before river the in [was] which water the

וּלְעֵינֵי עֲבָדָיו וַיֵּהָפְכוּ כָּל־הַמַּיִם
water the all turned was and ; servants his of eyes the before and

אֲשֶׁר־בַּיְאֹר לְדָם׃ וְהַדָּגָה אֲשֶׁר־ 21
[were] which fish the And .blood to river the in [was] which

I am the LORD:
behold, I will
smite with the
rod that is in
mine hand
upon the waters
which are in the
river, and they
shall be turned
to blood. 18 And
the fish that is
in the river shall
die, and the riv-
er shall stink;
and the Egyp-
tians shall loathe
to drink water
from the river.

19 And the
LORD said unto
Moses, Say un-
to Aaron, Take
thy rod, and
stretch out thine
hand over the
waters of E-
gypt, over their
rivers, over their
streams, and
over their pools,
and over all
their ponds of
water, that they
may become
blood; and there
shall be blood
throughout all
the land of E-
gypt, both in
vessels of wood
and in vessels of
stone. 20 And
Moses and
Aaron did so,
as the LORD
commanded;
and he lifted up
the rod, and
smote the wa-
ters that were
in the river, in
the sight of Pha-
raoh, and in
the sight of his
servants; and
all the waters
that were in the
river were turn-
ed to blood. 21
And the fish that
was in the river

---

a S. adds, *and shall become.*

b G. has, *and shall not be able*; cf. v. 21.

c Sm. adds, *and came Moses and Aaron to Pharaoh and said to him, Jehovah God of the Hebrews has sent us to thee*, etc., repeating vs. 16--18.

d G. adds, *thy brother.*

e G. adds, *in thy hand.*

f Sm., G., V. add, *and*, ו.

g Sm., G., S., V. add, *and*, ו.

h S. omits כל.

i G., S. have, *had commanded them*, צום.

j S. adds, *Aaron.*

k S. adds, *in his hand.*

river died; and
the river stank,
and the Egyp-
tians could not
drink of the wa-
ter of the river;
and there was
blood through-
out all the land
of Egypt. 22
And the ma-
gicians of E-
gypt did so with
their enchant-
ments: and Pha-
raoh's heart was
hardened, nei-
ther did he
hearken unto
them; as the
LORD had said.
23 And Pharaoh
turned and went
into his house,
neither did he
set his heart to
this also. 24 And
all the Egyp-
tians digged
round about the
river for water
to drink; for
they could not
drink of the
water of the
river. 25 And
seven days were
fulfilled, after
that the LORD
had smitten the
river.

AND the
LORD spake un-
to Moses, Go
unto Pharaoh,
and say unto
him, Thus saith
the LORD, Let
my people go,
that they may
serve me. 2
And if thou re-
fuse to let *them*
go, behold, I
will smite all
thy borders with
frogs: 3 And
the river shall
bring forth frogs
abundantly,
which shall go
up and come
into thine house,
and into thy
bedchamber,
and upon thy
bed, and into
the house of thy
servants, and

בַּיְאֹר מֵתָה וַיִּבְאַשׁ הַיְאֹר וְלֹא־יָכְלוּ
able not were and ; river the stank and ,died river the in

מִצְרַיִם לִשְׁתּוֹת מַיִם מִן־הַיְאֹר וַיְהִי הַדָּם
blood the was and ; river the from water drink to Egyptians the

22 בְּכָל־אֶרֶץ מִצְרָיִם׃ וַיַּעֲשׂוּ־כֵן חַרְטֻמֵּי מִצְרַיִם
Egypt of scribes the so did And .Egypt of land the all in

בְּלָטֵיהֶם וַיֶּחֱזַק לֵב־פַּרְעֹה
,Pharaoh of heart the hard was and ; arts secret their by

וְלֹא־שָׁמַע אֲלֵהֶם כַּאֲשֶׁר דִּבֶּר יְהוָה׃
.Jehovah spoken had as ,them unto hearken not did he and

23 וַיִּפֶן פַּרְעֹה וַיָּבֹא אֶל־בֵּיתוֹ וְלֹא־שָׁת
direct not did he and ;house his into went and Pharaoh turned And

24 לִבּוֹ גַּם־לָזֹאת׃ וַיַּחְפְּרוּ כָל־מִצְרַיִם סְבִיבֹת
about round Egyptians the all dug And .this to even heart his

הַיְאֹר מַיִם [a] לִשְׁתּוֹת [a] כִּי לֹא יָכְלוּ לִשְׁתֹּת
drink to able [2]were [1]they [3]not for ; drink to water river the

25 מִמֵּימֵי הַיְאֹר׃ וַיִּמָּלֵא שִׁבְעַת יָמִים
,days seven completed were And .river the of water the from

אַחֲרֵי הַכּוֹת־יְהוָה אֶת־הַיְאֹר׃
.river the smiting Jehovah's after

26 וַיֹּאמֶר יְהוָה אֶל־מֹשֶׁה בֹּא אֶל־פַּרְעֹה
,Pharaoh unto Go : Moses unto Jehovah said And

וְאָמַרְתָּ אֵלָיו כֹּה אָמַר יְהוָה שַׁלַּח
away Send : Jehovah says Thus : him unto say and

27 אֶת־עַמִּי וְיַעַבְדֻנִי׃ וְאִם־מָאֵן אַתָּה
[[2]art] [1]thou [3]refusing if And .me serve may they that people my

לְשַׁלֵּחַ הִנֵּה אָנֹכִי נֹגֵף אֶת־כָּל־גְּבוּלְךָ
territory thy all smite to about [am] I behold ,away send to

28 בִּצְפַרְדְּעִים׃ וְשָׁרַץ הַיְאֹר צְפַרְדְּעִים
; frogs [with] river the swarm shall And .frogs with

וְעָלוּ וּבָאוּ בְּבֵיתֶךָ וּבַחֲדַר
of chamber the into and ,house thy into enter and up go shall they and

מִשְׁכָּבְךָ וְעַל־מִטָּתֶךָ וּבְבֵית עֲבָדֶיךָ
,servants thy of house the into and ,couch thy upon and ,bed thy

died; and the riv-
er stank, and the
Egyptians could
not drink water
from the river;
and the blood
was throughout
all the land of
Egypt. 22 And
the magicians of
Egypt did in
like manner
with their en-
chantments: and
Pharaoh's heart
was hardened,
and he heark-
ened not unto
them; as the
LORD had spok-
en. 23 And Pha-
raoh turned and
went into his
house, neither
did he lay even
this to heart. 24
And all the E-
gyptians digged
round about the
river for water
to drink; for
they could not
drink of the
water of the
river. 25 And
seven days were
fulfilled, after
that the LORD
had smitten the
river.

And the
LORD spake
unto Moses, Go
in unto Pha-
raoh, and say
unto him,
Thus saith the
LORD, Let my
people go, that
they may serve
me. 2 And if
thou refuse to
let them go,
behold, I will
smite all thy
borders with
frogs: 3 and
the river shall
swarm with
frogs, which
shall go up and
come into thine
house, and into
thy bedcham-
ber, and upon
thy bed, and in-
to the house of
thy servants,

---

a G. has, *so as to drink water from the river.*

upon thy people, and into thine ovens, and into thy kneadingtroughs: 4 And the frogs shall come up both on thee, and upon thy people, and upon all thy servants.

וּבְעַמֶּ֫ךָ[a] וּבְתַנּוּרֶ֫יךָ וּבְמִשְׁאֲרוֹתֶ֫יךָ׃
; kneading-vessels thy into and ,ovens thine into and ,people thy on and

29 וּבְכָה וּֽבְעַמְּךָ[b] וּבְכָל־עֲבָדֶ֫יךָ[c] יַעֲלוּ
up come shall ,servants thy all on and ,people thy on and ,thee on and

הַֽצְפַרְדְּעִים[d]׃
.frogs the

and upon thy people, and into thine ovens, and into thy kneadingtroughs: 4 and the frogs shall come up both upon thee, and upon thy people, and upon all thy servants.

8

5 And the LORD spake unto Moses, Say unto Aaron, Stretch forth thine hand with thy rod over the streams, over the rivers, and over the ponds, and cause frogs to come up upon the land of Egypt. 6 And Aaron stretched out his hand over the waters of Egypt; and the frogs came up, and covered the land of Egypt. 7 And the magicians did so with their enchantments, and brought up frogs upon the land of Egypt.

8 Then Pharaoh called for Moses and Aaron, and said, Intreat the LORD, that he may take away the frogs from me, and from my people; and I will let the people go, that they may do sacrifice unto the LORD.

1 וַיֹּאמֶר יְהוָה אֶל־מֹשֶׁה אֱמֹר אֶל־אַהֲרֹן[e]
: Aaron unto Say : Moses unto Jehovah said And

נְטֵה אֶת־יָדְךָ בְּמַטֶּךָ עַל־הַנְּהָרֹת[f] עַל־
over ,rivers the over staff thy with hand thy out Stretch

הַיְאֹרִים וְעַל־הָאֲגַמִּים וְהַעַל אֶת־הַצְפַרְדְּעִים
frogs the up bring and ; pools the over and ,canals the

2 עַל־אֶרֶץ[g] מִצְרָיִם[g]׃ וַיֵּט אַהֲרֹן אֶת־יָדוֹ
hand his Aaron out stretched And .Egypt of land the upon

עַל מֵימֵי מִצְרָיִם וַתַּעַל הַצְפַרְדֵּעַ
,frogs the up went and ; Egypt of waters the over

3 וַתְּכַס אֶת־אֶרֶץ מִצְרָיִם׃ וַיַּעֲשׂוּ־כֵן הַחַרְטֻמִּים
scribes the so did And .Egypt of land the covered and

בְּלָטֵיהֶם וַיַּעֲלוּ אֶת־הַצְפַרְדְּעִים
frogs the up brought they and ,arts secret their with

4 עַל־אֶרֶץ מִצְרָיִם׃ וַיִּקְרָא פַרְעֹה לְמֹשֶׁה
Moses (to) Pharaoh called And .Egypt of land the upon

וּֽלְאַהֲרֹן וַיֹּאמֶר[h] הַעְתִּירוּ[i] אֶל־יְהוָה
,Jehovah unto Entreat : said and ,Aaron (to) and

וְיָסֵר הַצְפַרְדְּעִים מִמֶּנִּי וּמֵעַמִּי
; people my from and me from frogs the remove may he that

וַאֲשַׁלְּחָה אֶת־הָעָם[j] וְיִזְבְּחוּ לַיהוָה׃
.Jehovah to sacrifice may they that ,people the away send will I and

5 And the LORD said unto Moses, Say unto Aaron, Stretch forth thine hand with thy rod over the rivers, over the streams and over the pools, and cause frogs to come up upon the land of Egypt. 6 And Aaron stretched out his hand over the waters of Egypt; and the frogs came up, and covered the land of Egypt. 7 And the magicians did in like manner with their enchantments, and brought up frogs upon the land of Egypt.

8 Then Pharaoh called for Moses and Aaron, and said, Intreat the LORD, that he take away the frogs from me, and from my people; and I will let the people go, that they may sacrifice un-

---

a G. has, *and thy people*, omitting ב.

b G. puts after the next word; S. adds, *all*, reading, ובכל עמך.

c S. omits; G. omits כל.

d. Sm. adds, *and came Moses and Aaron unto Pharaoh and said to him*, etc., repeating vs. 26-29.

e G., S. add, *thy brother*.

f G., S., V. add, *and*, ו.

g G. omits; Sm. adds, *and said Moses to Aaron*, etc., repeating v. 1b.

h S., V. add, *to them.*

i G. adds, *for me.*

j G. has, *with them.*

9 And Moses said unto Pharaoh, Glory over me: when shall I intreat for thee, and for thy servants, and for thy people, to destroy the frogs from thee and thy houses, *that* they may remain in the river only? 10 And he said, To morrow. And he said, *Be it* according to thy word: that thou mayest know that *there is* none like unto the LORD our God. 11 And the frogs shall depart from thee, and from thy houses, and from thy servants, and from thy people; they shall remain in the river only. 12 And Moses and Aaron went out from Pharaoh: and Moses cried unto the LORD because of the frogs which he had brought against Pharaoh. 13 And the LORD did according to the word of Moses; and the frogs died out of the houses, out of the villages, and out of the fields. 14 And they gathered them together upon heaps: and the land stank. 15 But when Pharaoh saw that there was respite, he hardened his heart,

5 וַיֹּאמֶר מֹשֶׁה לְפַרְעֹה הִתְפָּאֵר[a] עָלַי[a] לְמָתַי
when for ; me over Glory : Pharaoh to Moses said And

אַעְתִּיר לְךָ וְלַעֲבָדֶיךָ וּלְעַמְּךָ
,people thy for and servants thy for and thee for entreat I shall

לְהַכְרִית הַצְפַרְדְּעִים מִמְּךָ[b] וּמִבָּתֶּיךָ[c] רַק[d]
only ,house thy from and ,thee from frogs the off cut to

6 בַּיְאֹר תִּשָּׁאַרְנָה[d]: וַיֹּאמֶר[e] לְמָחָר
.tomorrow For ,said he And ? left be shall they river the in

וַיֹּאמֶר[f] כִּדְבָרְךָ לְמַעַן תֵּדַע
know mayest thou that order in ; word thy to According :said he And

7 כִּי־אֵין כַּיהוָה אֱלֹהֵינוּ[g]: וְסָרוּ
depart shall And .God our Jehovah like not is [there] that

הַצְפַרְדְּעִים מִמְּךָ וּמִבָּתֶּיךָ[h] וּמֵעֲבָדֶיךָ
,servants thy from and ,houses thy from and ,thee from frogs the

וּמֵעַמֶּךָ רַק בַּיְאֹר תִּשָּׁאַרְנָה:
.left be shall they river the in only ,people thy from and

8 וַיֵּצֵא מֹשֶׁה וְאַהֲרֹן מֵעִם פַּרְעֹה
; Pharaoh (with) from Aaron and Moses out went And

וַיִּצְעַק מֹשֶׁה אֶל־יְהוָה עַל־דְּבַר הַצְפַרְדְּעִים
,frogs the of matter the upon Jehovah unto Moses cried and

9 אֲשֶׁר־שָׂם[i] לְפַרְעֹה[i]: וַיַּעַשׂ יְהוָה
Jehovah did And .Pharaoh to appointed had he [as] (which)

כִּדְבַר מֹשֶׁה וַיָּמֻתוּ הַצְפַרְדְּעִים מִן־
from frogs the died and ; Moses of word the to according

10 הַבָּתִּים מִן־הַחֲצֵרֹת וּמִן־הַשָּׂדֹת: וַיִּצְבְּרוּ
collected they And .fields the from and ,courts the from ,houses the

11 אֹתָם חֳמָרִם חֳמָרִם וַתִּבְאַשׁ הָאָרֶץ: וַיַּרְא
saw And .land the stank and ; heaps ,heaps [in] them

פַרְעֹה כִּי הָיְתָה הָרְוָחָה וְהַכְבֵּד אֶת־לִבּוֹ
,heart his heavy made he and ;relief the was [there] that Pharaoh

to the LORD. 9 And Moses said unto Pharaoh, Have thou this glory over me: against what time shall I intreat for thee, and for thy servants, and for thy people, that the frogs be destroyed from thee and thy houses, and remain in the river only? 10 And he said, Against to-morrow. And he said, Be it according to thy word: that thou mayest know that there is none like unto the LORD our God. 11 And the frogs shall depart from thee and from thy houses, and from thy servants, and from thy people; they shall remain in the river only. 12 And Moses and Aaron went out from Pharaoh: and Moses cried unto the LORD concerning the frogs which he had brought upon Pharaoh. 13 And the LORD did according to the word of Moses; and the frogs died out of the houses, out of the courts, and out of the fields. 14 And they gathered them together in heaps: and the land stank. 15 But when Pharaoh saw that there was respite, he hardened his heart,

---

a G., V. have, *appoint thou unto me;* S. has, *ask for thyself a time;* T., *ask for thyself an omen and give for thyself a time.*

b G., Sm. add, *and from thy people.*

c G. has suffix plural; V. adds, *and from thy servants and from thy people.*

d S. omits.

e S. adds, *to him.*

f S. adds, *to him.*

g G. omits.

h G. has suffix plural, and adds, *and from thy courts;* cf. v. 9.

i G., V. have, *as he had appointed to Pharaoh.*

and hearkened not unto them; as the LORD had said.
16 And the LORD said unto Moses, Say unto Aaron, Stretch out thy rod, and smite the dust of the land, that it may become lice throughout all the land of Egypt. 17 And they did so; for Aaron stretched out his hand with his rod, and smote the dust of the earth, and it became lice in man, and in beast; all the dust of the land became lice throughout all the land of Egypt. 18 And the magicians did so with their enchantments to bring forth lice, but they could not: so there were lice upon man, and upon beast. 19 Then the magicians said unto Pharaoh, This *is* the finger of God: and Pharaoh's heart was hardened, and he hearkened not unto them; as the LORD had said.
20 And the LORD said unto Moses, Rise up early in the morning, and stand before Pharaoh; lo, he cometh forth to the water; and say unto him, Thus saith the LORD, Let my people go, that they may serve me. 21 Else, if thou wilt not let

וְלֹא שָׁמַע אֲלֵהֶם כַּאֲשֶׁר דִּבֶּר יְהוָה׃[a]
.Jehovah spoken had as ,them unto hearken [2]did [1]he [3]not and

12 וַיֹּאמֶר יְהוָה אֶל־מֹשֶׁה אֱמֹר אֶל־אַהֲרֹן
:Aaron unto Say : Moses unto Jehovah said And

נְטֵה[b] אֶת־מַטְּךָ וְהַךְ אֶת־עֲפַר הָאָרֶץ
,earth the of dust the smite and staff thy out Stretch

13 וְהָיָה לְכִנִּם[c] בְּכָל־אֶרֶץ מִצְרָיִם׃ וַיַּעֲשׂוּ
did they And .Egypt of land the all in gnats (for) become it let and

כֵן[d] וַיֵּט אַהֲרֹן אֶת־יָדוֹ בְמַטֵּהוּ וַיַּךְ
smote and ,staff his with hand his Aaron out stretched and ,so

אֶת־עֲפַר הָאָרֶץ וַתְּהִי הַכִּנָּם בָּאָדָם וּבַבְּהֵמָה
; beast on and man on gnats the were and ,earth the of dust the

[e]כָּל־עֲפַר הָאָרֶץ הָיָה כִנִּים בְּכָל־אֶרֶץ מִצְרָיִם׃
.Egypt of land the all in gnats became earth the of dust the all

14 וַיַּעֲשׂוּ־כֵן הַחַרְטֻמִּים בְּלָטֵיהֶם לְהוֹצִיא[f]
forth bring to ,arts secret their with scribes the so did And

אֶת־הַכִּנִּים[f] וְלֹא יָכֹלוּ וַתְּהִי הַכִּנָּם בָּאָדָם
man on gnats the were and ; able [2]were [1]they [3]not and ,gnats the

15 וּבַבְּהֵמָה׃ וַיֹּאמְרוּ הַחַרְטֻמִּם אֶל־פַּרְעֹה אֶצְבַּע
of finger The :Pharaoh unto scribes the said And .beast on and

אֱלֹהִים הִוא וַיֶּחֱזַק לֵב־פַּרְעֹה
Pharaoh of heart the hard was and ; it [is] God

וְלֹא־שָׁמַע אֲלֵהֶם כַּאֲשֶׁר דִּבֶּר יְהוָה׃
.Jehovah spoken had as ,them unto hearken not did he and

16 וַיֹּאמֶר יְהוָה אֶל־מֹשֶׁה הַשְׁכֵּם בַּבֹּקֶר
,morning the in early Rise : Moses unto Jehovah said And

וְהִתְיַצֵּב לִפְנֵי פַרְעֹה הִנֵּה יוֹצֵא הַמָּיְמָה
,water the to out go to about [is] he behold ,Pharaoh before stand and

וְאָמַרְתָּ אֵלָיו כֹּה אָמַר יְהוָה שַׁלַּח
away Send :Jehovah says Thus :him unto say thou do and

17 עַמִּי וְיַעַבְדֻנִי׃[g] כִּי אִם־אֵינְךָ מְשַׁלֵּחַ
away sending not art thou if For .me serve may they that people my

and hearkened not unto them; as the LORD had spoken.
16 And the LORD said unto Moses, Say unto Aaron, Stretch out thy rod, and smite the dust of the earth, that it may become lice throughout all the land of Egypt. 17 And they did so; and Aaron stretched out his hand with his rod, and smote the dust of the earth, and there were lice upon man, and upon beast; all the dust of the earth became lice throughout all the land of Egypt. 18 And the magicians did so with their enchantments to bring forth lice, but they could not: and there were lice upon man, and upon beast. 19 Then the magicians said unto Pharaoh, This is the finger of God: and Pharaoh's heart was hardened, and he hearkened not unto them; as the LORD had spoken.
20 And the LORD said unto Moses, Rise up early in the morning, and stand before Pharaoh; lo, he cometh forth to the water; and say unto him, Thus saith the LORD, Let my people go, that they may serve me. 21 Else, if thou wilt not let

---

a S. adds, *to Moses.*
b G. adds, *with the hand;* Sm. essentially the same.
c G. adds, *upon men and upon beasts and;* cf. v. 13.
d G. omits; S. has singular.
e S. adds, *and,* ו; G. adds, *and in.*
f S. puts after יכלו.
g G. adds, *in the wilderness.*

my people go, behold, I will send swarms *of flies* upon thee, and upon thy servants, and upon thy people, and into thy houses: and the houses of the Egyptians shall be full of swarms *of flies*, and also the ground whereon they *are*. 22 And I will sever in that day the land of Goshen, in which my people dwell, that no swarms *of flies* shall be there; to the end thou mayest know that I *am* the LORD in the midst of the earth. 23 And I will put a division between my people and thy people: to morrow shall this sign be. 24 And the LORD did so; and there came a grievous swarm *of flies* into the house of Pharaoh, and *into* his servants' houses, and into all the land of Egypt: the land was corrupted by reason of the swarm *of flies*.

25 And Pharaoh called for Moses and for Aaron, and said, Go ye, sacrifice to your God in the land. 26 And Moses said, It is not meet so to do; for we shall sacrifice the a-

אֶת־עַמִּי הִנְנִי מַשְׁלִיחַ בְּךָ וּבַעֲבָדֶיךָ[a]
servants thy on and ,thee on send to about [am] I behold ,people my

וּבְעַמְּךָ וּבְבָתֶּיךָ[b] אֶת־הֶעָרֹב וּמָלְאוּ
full be will and ; flies ,house thy on and ,people thy on and

בָּתֵּי מִצְרַיִם אֶת־הֶעָרֹב וְגַם הָאֲדָמָה
ground the also and ,flies [of] Egyptians the of houses the

18 אֲשֶׁר־הֵם עָלֶיהָ׃ וְהִפְלֵיתִי בַיּוֹם הַהוּא
[1]that [2]day in separate will I And .(it upon) [are] they which [upon]

אֶת־אֶרֶץ גֹּשֶׁן אֲשֶׁר עַמִּי עֹמֵד
abiding [are] people my which [upon] ,Goshen of land the

עָלֶיהָ לְבִלְתִּי הֱיוֹת־שָׁם עָרֹב לְמַעַן תֵּדַע
know mayest thou that order in ;flies there be not to ,(it upon)

19 כִּי אֲנִי יְהוָה בְּקֶרֶב[c] הָאָרֶץ[c]׃ וְשַׂמְתִּי
put will I And .land the of midst the in Jehovah [am] I that

פְדֻת[d] בֵּין עַמִּי וּבֵין עַמֶּךָ
; people thy (between) and people my between deliverance

20 לְמָחָר יִהְיֶה הָאֹת[e] הַזֶּה[f e]׃ וַיַּעַשׂ יְהוָה
Jehovah did And .[1]this [2]sign be shall tomorrow for

כֵּן וַיָּבֹא[g] עָרֹב כָּבֵד בֵּיתָה פַרְעֹה
,Pharaoh of house the into numerous flies came and ,so

וּבֵית עֲבָדָיו וּבְכָל־אֶרֶץ מִצְרָיִם
; Egypt of land the all into and ,servants his of house the and

21 [h]תִּשָּׁחֵת הָאָרֶץ מִפְּנֵי הֶעָרֹב׃ וַיִּקְרָא[i] פַרְעֹה
Pharaoh called And .flies the before from land the destroyed was

אֶל־מֹשֶׁה וּלְאַהֲרֹן וַיֹּאמֶר לְכוּ זִבְחוּ
sacrifice ,ye Go : said and ,Aaron (to) and Moses (unto)

22 לֵאלֹהֵיכֶם[j] בָּאָרֶץ׃ וַיֹּאמֶר מֹשֶׁה לֹא נָכוֹן
admissible [2]is [1]it [3]Not :Moses said And .land the in God your to

לַעֲשׂוֹת כֵּן[k] כִּי תּוֹעֲבַת[l] מִצְרַיִם נִזְבַּח
sacrifice we Egyptians the of abomination the for ,so do to

my people go, behold, I will send swarms of flies upon thee, and upon thy servants, and upon thy people, and into thy houses: and the houses of the Egyptians shall be full of swarms of flies, and also the ground whereon they are. 22 And I will sever in that day the land of Goshen, in which my people dwell, that no swarms of flies shall be there; to the end thou mayest know that I am the LORD in the midst of the earth. 23 And I will put a division between my people and thy people: by to-morrow shall this sign be. 24 And the LORD did so; and there came grievous swarms of flies into the house of Pharaoh, and into his servants' houses: and in all the land of Egypt the land was corrupted by reason of the swarms of flies.

25 And Pharaoh called for Moses and for Aaron, and said, Go ye, sacrifice to your God in the land. 26 And Moses said, It is not meet so to do; for we shall sacrifice

a S. omits.
b G. has suffix plural.
c G. has, *the Lord of all the earth;* T., *the ruler in the midst of the earth.*
d G., S., V. have, *distinction.*
e G. has, *this upon the earth.*
f Sm. adds, *and came Moses and Aaron to Pharaoh and said to him*, etc., adding vs. 16b-19.
g S. has, *and he brought*, וַיָּבֵא.
h Sm., G., S., V. add, *and*, ו.
i S., V. add, *to them.*
j S. has, *before the Lord your God.*
k G. adds, *this word.*
l T. has, *the animals which the Egyptians worship.*

bomination of
the Egyptians to
the LORD our
God: lo, shall
we sacrifice the
abomination of
the Egyptians
before their
eyes, and will
they not stone
us? 27 We will
go three days'
journey into the
wilderness, and
sacrifice to the
LORD our God,
as he shall com-
mand us. 28 And
Pharaoh said, I
will let you go,
that ye may
sacrifice to the
LORD your God
in the wilder-
ness; only ye
shall not go very
far away: in-
treat for me. 29
And Moses said,
Behold, I go
out from thee,
and I will in-
treat the LORD
that the swarms
of flies may de-
part from Pha-
raoh, from his
servants, and
from his peo-
ple, to morrow:
but let not Pha-
raoh deal deceit-
fully any more
in not letting
the people go to
sacrifice to the
LORD. 30 And
Moses went out
from Pharaoh,
and intreated
the LORD. 31
And the LORD
did according
to the word of
Moses; and he
removed the
swarms *of flies*
from Pharaoh,
from his serv-
ants, and from
his people; there
remained not

לַיהוָה אֱלֹהֵינוּ הֵן [a] נִזְבַּח אֶת־תּוֹעֲבַת [b]
of abomination the sacrifice we [if] ,behold ; God our Jehovah to

מִצְרַיִם לְעֵינֵיהֶם וְלֹא יִסְקְלֻנוּ [c]:
? us stone [2]they [1]will [3]not (and) ,eyes their before Egyptians the

23 דֶּרֶךְ שְׁלֹשֶׁת יָמִים נֵלֵךְ בַּמִּדְבָּר
,wilderness the into go us let days three of journey A

וְזָבַחְנוּ לַיהוָה [d] אֱלֹהֵינוּ כַּאֲשֶׁר יֹאמַר [e] אֵלֵינוּ:
.us unto say may he as ,God our Jehovah to sacrifice and

24 וַיֹּאמֶר פַּרְעֹה אָנֹכִי אֲשַׁלַּח אֶתְכֶם וּזְבַחְתֶּם
sacrifice may ye and ,you away send will I : Pharaoh said And

לַיהוָה [f] אֱלֹהֵיכֶם בַּמִּדְבָּר רַק הַרְחֵק
distant making only ; wilderness the in God your Jehovah to

25 לֹא־תַרְחִיקוּ לָלֶכֶת הַעְתִּירוּ [g] בַּעֲדִי [h]: וַיֹּאמֶר
said And .behalf my on entreat ; go to distant make not shall you

מֹשֶׁה [i] הִנֵּה אָנֹכִי יוֹצֵא מֵעִמָּךְ
,thee with from out go to about [am] I Behold : Moses

וְהַעְתַּרְתִּי אֶל־יְהוָה [j] וְסָר הֶעָרֹב
flies the depart will and ; Jehovah (unto) entreat to and

מִפַּרְעֹה [k] מֵעֲבָדָיו [l] וּמֵעַמּוֹ מָחָר
; tomorrow ,people his from and ,servants his from ,Pharaoh from

רַק אַל־יֹסֵף פַּרְעֹה הָתֵל לְבִלְתִּי שַׁלַּח
away send not to ,deceive to Pharaoh continue not let only

26 אֶת־הָעָם לִזְבֹּחַ לַיהוָה: וַיֵּצֵא מֹשֶׁה
Moses out went And .Jehovah to sacrifice to people the

27 מֵעִם פַּרְעֹה וַיֶּעְתַּר אֶל־יְהוָה: וַיַּעַשׂ
did And .Jehovah (unto) entreated he and ; Pharaoh (with) from

יְהוָה כִּדְבַר מֹשֶׁה וַיָּסַר הֶעָרֹב
flies the departed and ,Moses of word the to according Jehovah

מִפַּרְעֹה מֵעֲבָדָיו [m] וּמֵעַמּוֹ [n] לֹא נִשְׁאַר
left was not ; people his from and ,servants his from ,Pharaoh from

the abomina-
tion of the E-
gyptians to the
LORD our God;
lo, shall we sac-
rifice the abom-
ination of the
Egyptians be-
fore their eyes,
and will they
not stone us? 27
We will go three
days' journey in-
to the wilder-
ness, and sac-
rifice to the
LORD our God,
as he shall com-
mand us. 28
And Pharaoh
said, I will let
you go, that ye
may sacrifice to
the LORD your
God in the
wilderness; only
ye shall not go
very far away:
intreat for me.
29 And Moses
said, Behold, I
go out from
thee, and I will
intreat the
LORD that the
swarms of flies
may depart
from Pharaoh,
from his serv-
ants, and from
his people, to-
morrow: only
let not Pharaoh
deal deceitfully
any more in not
letting the peo-
ple go to sac-
rifice to the
LORD. 30 And
Moses went out
from Pharaoh,
and intreated
the LORD. 31
And the LORD
did according
to the word of
Moses; and he
removed the
swarms of flies
from Pharaoh,
from his serv-
ants, and from

---

a G. has, *for if*; S., *and if*.

b S. has, *gods of*; T. *the animals, which the Egyptians worship*; so essentially V.

c G. has, *we shall be stoned*.

d G. omits יהוה.

e G., V. translate by past, *said*; G. adds, *the Lord*, יהוה.

f G. omits יהוה.

g S., V. add, *also*; G. adds, *therefore*; S. adds preceding, *and*, ו.

h G. adds, *unto the Lord*.

i S. adds, *to Pharaoh*.

j G. has, *God*.

k G. has, *from thee*, the following suffixes and יסף being in the second person.

l G., S., V., T. add, *and*, ו.

m G., S., V. add, *and*, ו.

n G., S. add, *and*, ו.

one. 32 And
Pharaoh hard-
ened his heart
at this time also,
neither would
he let the peo-
ple go.

28 אֶחָד׃ וַיַּכְבֵּד פַּרְעֹה אֶת־לִבּוֹ גַּם בַּפַּעַם הַזֹּאת
,[1]this [2]time also ,heart his Pharaoh heavy made And .one

וְלֹא שִׁלַּח אֶת־הָעָם׃
.people the away send [2]did [1]he [3]not and

his people; there remained not one. 32 And Pharaoh hardened his heart this time also, and he did not let the people go.

9

THEN the
LORD said unto
Moses, Go in
unto Pharaoh,
and tell him,
Thus saith the
LORD God of
the Hebrews,
Let my people
go, that they
may serve me.
2 For if thou re-
fuse to let *them*
go, and wilt
hold them still,
3 Behold, the
hand of the
LORD is upon
thy cattle which
is in the field,
upon the horses,
upon the asses,
upon the camels,
upon the oxen,
and upon the
sheep: *there*
shall be a very
grievous mur-
rain. 4 And the
LORD shall sev-
er between the
cattle of Israel
and the cattle of
Egypt: and
there shall noth-
ing die of all
that is the chil-
dren's of Israel.

1 וַיֹּאמֶר יְהוָה אֶל־מֹשֶׁה בֹּא אֶל־פַּרְעֹה
,Pharaoh unto in Go : Moses unto Jehovah said And

וְדִבַּרְתָּ אֵלָיו כֹּה־אָמַר יְהוָה אֱלֹהֵי
of God the Jehovah says Thus : him unto speak and

2 הָעִבְרִים שַׁלַּח אֶת־עַמִּי וְיַעַבְדֻנִי׃ כִּי
For .me serve may they that ,people my away Send ,Hebrews the

אִם־מָאֵן אַתָּה לְשַׁלֵּחַ[a] וְעוֹדְךָ מַחֲזִיק
grasping [art] thou still and ,away send to thou [art] refusing if

3 בָּם׃ הִנֵּה יַד־יְהוָה הוֹיָה בְּמִקְנְךָ
cattle thy on be to about [is] Jehovah of hand the behold ; them (on)

אֲשֶׁר בַּשָּׂדֶה [b]בַּסּוּסִים [c]בַּחֲמֹרִים [c]בַּגְּמַלִּים
,camels the on ,asses the on ,horses the on ,field the in [are] which

[c]בַּבָּקָר וּבַצֹּאן דֶּבֶר כָּבֵד מְאֹד׃
.exceedingly heavy pestilence a ,flocks the on and ,herds the on

4 וְהִפְלָה[d] יְהוָה[e] בֵּין מִקְנֵה יִשְׂרָאֵל
Israel of cattle the between Jehovah separate will And

וּבֵין מִקְנֵה מִצְרָיִם וְלֹא יָמוּת מִכָּל־
all from die [1]will [2]not and ; Egypt of cattle the (between) and

5 לִבְנֵי יִשְׂרָאֵל דָּבָר׃ וַיָּשֶׂם יְהוָה
Jehovah set And .thing a Israel of sons the to [belonging]

מוֹעֵד לֵאמֹר[f] מָחָר יַעֲשֶׂה יְהוָה
Jehovah do will Tomorrow : saying time appointed an

6 הַדָּבָר הַזֶּה בָּאָרֶץ[g]׃ וַיַּעַשׂ יְהוָה אֶת־הַדָּבָר
[2]thing Jehovah did And .land the in [1]this [2]thing

הַזֶּה מִמָּחֳרָת וַיָּמָת כֹּל מִקְנֵה מִצְרָיִם
; Egypt of cattle the all died and ; morrow the from [1]this

Then the LORD said unto Moses, Go in unto Pharaoh, and tell him, Thus saith the LORD, the God of the Hebrews, Let my people go, that they may serve me. 2 For if thou refuse to let them go, and wilt hold them still, 3 behold, the hand of the LORD is upon thy cattle which is in the field, upon the horses, upon the asses, upon the camels, upon the herds, and upon the flocks: *there shall be* a very grievous murrain. 4 And the LORD shall sever between the cattle of Israel and the cattle of Egypt: and there shall nothing die of all that belongeth to the children of Israel.

5 And the
LORD appoint-
ed a set time,
saying, To
morrow the
LORD shall do
this thing in the
land. 6 And the
LORD did that
thing on the
morrow, and all
the cattle of E-

5 And the LORD appointed a set time, saying, To-morrow the LORD shall do this thing in the land. 6 And the LORD did that thing on the morrow, and all the cattle

a G. adds, *my people*, עַמִּי; V. omits.
b G., V. add, *and*, וּ.
c G., S., V. add, *and*, וּ.
d G. has first person.
e G. omits, and adds, *at that season.*
f S. omits.
g Sm. adds, *and came Moses and Aaron to Pharaoh and said to him etc.*, repeating essentially 1b—5.

gypt died: but
of the cattle of
the children of
Israel died not
one. 7 And Pha-
raoh sent, and,
behold, there
was not one of
the cattle of the
Israelites dead.
And the heart
of Pharaoh was
hardened, and
he did not let
the people go.

8 And the
LORD said unto
Moses and unto
Aaron, Take to
you handfuls of
ashes of the
furnace, and let
Moses sprinkle
it toward the
heaven in the
sight of Pha-
raoh. 9 And it
shall become
small dust in all
the land of E-
gypt, and shall
be a boil break-
ing forth *with*
blains upon
man, and upon
beast, through-
out all the land
of Egypt. 10
And they took
ashes of the
furnace, and
stood before
Pharaoh; and
Moses sprinkled
it up toward
heaven; and it
became a boil
breaking forth
with blains up-
on man, and
upon beast. 11
And the magi-
cians could not
stand before
Moses because
of the boils; for
the boil was up-
on the magi-
cians, and upon
all the Egyp-
tians. 12 And
the LORD hard-
ened the heart

וּמִמִּקְנֵה בְּנֵי־יִשְׂרָאֵל לֹא־מֵת אֶחָד׃
.one die not did Israel of children the of cattle the from and

7 וַיִּשְׁלַח[a] פַּרְעֹה וְהִנֵּה[b] לֹא־מֵת מִמִּקְנֵה[c]
of cattle the from dead not was ,behold and ,Pharaoh sent And

יִשְׂרָאֵל[d] עַד־אֶחָד וַיִּכְבַּד לֵב פַּרְעֹה וְלֹא
3not and ,Pharaoh of heart the heavy was and ;one even Israel

שִׁלַּח אֶת־הָעָם׃
.people the away send 2did 1he

8 וַיֹּאמֶר יְהוָה אֶל־מֹשֶׁה וְאֶל־אַהֲרֹן[e] קְחוּ
Take : Aaron unto and Moses unto Jehovah said And

לָכֶם מְלֹא חָפְנֵיכֶם פִּיחַ כִּבְשָׁן
,smelting-oven the of soot hands your of fulness the you for

וּזְרָקוֹ מֹשֶׁה הַשָּׁמַיְמָה לְעֵינֵי
of eyes the before heavens the towards Moses it sprinkle let and

9 פַרְעֹה[f]׃ וְהָיָה לְאָבָק עַל כָּל־אֶרֶץ
of land the all upon dust (for) become it let And .Pharaoh

מִצְרָיִם וְהָיָה עַל־הָאָדָם וְעַל־הַבְּהֵמָה
cattle upon and man upon become it let and ,Egypt

לִשְׁחִין פֹּרֵחַ אֲבַעְבֻּעֹת[g] בְּכָל־אֶרֶץ מִצְרָיִם׃
.Egypt of land the all in boils [in] out breaking ulcer an (for)

10 וַיִּקְחוּ[h] אֶת־פִּיחַ הַכִּבְשָׁן וַיַּעַמְדוּ[i] לִפְנֵי
before stood and ,smelting-oven the of soot took they And

פַרְעֹה וַיִּזְרֹק אֹתוֹ מֹשֶׁה הַשָּׁמָיְמָה[j]
;heavens the towards Moses it sprinkled and ;Pharaoh

וַיְהִי שְׁחִין אֲבַעְבֻּעֹת פֹּרֵחַ בָּאָדָם
man on out breaking ,boils of ulcer an became it and

11 וּבַבְּהֵמָה׃ וְלֹא־יָכְלוּ הַחַרְטֻמִּים לַעֲמֹד לִפְנֵי
before stand to scribes the able not were And .cattle on and

מֹשֶׁה מִפְּנֵי הַשְּׁחִין כִּי־הָיָה הַשְּׁחִין[k] בַּחַרְטֻמִּם
scribes the on ulcer the was for ;ulcer the before from ,Moses

12 וּבְכָל־מִצְרָיִם׃ וַיְחַזֵּק יְהוָה אֶת־לֵב
of heart the Jehovah hardened And .Egyptians the all on and

of Egypt died:
but of the cattle
of the children
of Israel died
not one. 7 And
Pharaoh sent,
and, behold,
there was not
so much as one
of the cattle of
the Israelites
dead. But the
heart of Pha-
raoh was stub-
born, and he
did not let the
people go.

8 And the
LORD said unto
Moses and unto
Aaron, Take to
you handfuls of
ashes of the
furnace, and let
Moses sprinkle
it toward the
heaven in the
sight of Pha-
raoh. 9 And it
shall become
small dust over
all the land of
Egypt, and shall
be a boil break-
ing forth with
blains upon
man and upon
beast, through-
out all the land
of Egypt. 10
And they took
ashes of the
furnace, and
stood before
Pharaoh; and
Moses sprinkled
it up toward
heaven; and it
became a boil
breaking forth
with blains up-
on man and up-
on beast. 11
And the magi-
cians could not
stand before
Moses because
of the boils; for
the boils were
upon the ma-
gicians, and up-
on all the Egyp-
tians. 12 And
the LORD hard-
ened the heart

a G. has, *and seeing;* V., *and sent to see.*
b G. has, *that;* S. *and saw that.*
c G. adds, *all*, reading מכל מקנה.
d G. omits עד.
e G. adds, *saying.*
f G. adds, *and before his servants.*
g G. adds, *on men and on beasts and.*
h G. has singular.
i G. omits.
j S. adds, *before the eyes of Pharaoh.*
k S. omits; so apparently V.

of Pharaoh, and he hearkened not unto them; as the LORD had spoken unto Moses.

13 And the LORD said unto Moses, Rise up early in the morning, and stand before Pharaoh, and say unto him, Thus saith the LORD God of the Hebrews, Let my people go, that they may serve me. 14 For I will at this time send all my plagues upon thine heart, and upon thy servants, and upon thy people; that thou mayest know that *there is* none like me in all the earth. 15 For now I will stretch out my hand, that I may smite thee and thy people with pestilence; and thou shalt be cut off from the earth. 16 And in very deed for this *cause* have I raised thee up, for to shew *in* thee my power; and that my name may be declared throughout all the earth. 17 As yet exaltest thou thyself against my people, that thou wilt not let them go? 18 Behold, to morrow about this time I will cause it to rain a very grievous hail, such as hath not been in Egypt since the foundation thereof even until now. 19 Send therefore now, *and* gather thy cattle, and all that

פַּרְעֹה וְלֹא שָׁמַע אֲלֵהֶם כַּאֲשֶׁר דִּבֶּר
spoken had as ;them unto hearken [2]did [1]he [3]not and ,Pharaoh

יְהוָה אֶל־מֹשֶׁה[a] : וַיֹּאמֶר יְהוָה אֶל־מֹשֶׁה 13
: Moses unto Jehovah said And .Moses unto Jehovah

הַשְׁכֵּם בַּבֹּקֶר וְהִתְיַצֵּב לִפְנֵי פַרְעֹה וְאָמַרְתָּ
say and ,Pharaoh before stand and ,morning the in early Rise

אֵלָיו כֹּה־אָמַר יְהוָה אֱלֹהֵי הָעִבְרִים
, Hebrews the of God the Jehovah says Thus :him unto

שַׁלַּח אֶת־עַמִּי וְיַעַבְדֻנִי : כִּי בַּפַּעַם 14
[2]time at For .me serve may they that people my away Send

הַזֹּאת אֲנִי שֹׁלֵחַ אֶת־כָּל־מַגֵּפֹתַי[b] אֶל־לִבְּךָ
,heart thy unto plagues my all send to about [am] I [1]this

וּבַעֲבָדֶיךָ וּבְעַמֶּךָ בַּעֲבוּר תֵּדַע
know mayest thou that order in ;people thy on and ,servants thy on and

כִּי אֵין כָּמֹנִי[c] בְּכָל־הָאָרֶץ : כִּי עַתָּה 15
now For .land the all in me like not is [there] that

שָׁלַחְתִּי אֶת־יָדִי וָאַךְ אוֹתְךָ וְאֶת־עַמְּךָ
people thy and thee smitten and hand my out stretched had I [if]

בַּדָּבֶר[d] וַתִּכָּחֵד מִן־הָאָרֶץ : וְאוּלָם 16
but — earth the from destroyed been hast thou and ,pestilence with

בַּעֲבוּר זֹאת הֶעֱמַדְתִּיךָ בַּעֲבוּר הַרְאֹתְךָ
see to thee cause to order in ,thee preserved have I this of account on

אֶת־כֹּחִי וּלְמַעַן סַפֵּר שְׁמִי בְּכָל־הָאָרֶץ :
.land the all in name my declare to order in and ,power my

עוֹדְךָ מִסְתּוֹלֵל בְּעַמִּי לְבִלְתִּי 17
not to ,people my against thyself exalting [art] thou Still

שַׁלְּחָם : הִנְנִי מַמְטִיר כָּעֵת מָחָר 18
,tomorrow time [this] about rain will I Behold .away them send

בָּרָד כָּבֵד מְאֹד אֲשֶׁר לֹא־הָיָה כָמֹהוּ
(it like) been not has it which [like] ; exceedingly heavy hail

בְּמִצְרַיִם לְמִן־הַיּוֹם הִוָּסְדָה וְעַד־עָתָּה :
.now until and founded being [its] of day the from (to) ,Egypt in

וְעַתָּה שְׁלַח הָעֵז אֶת־מִקְנְךָ וְאֵת כָּל־אֲשֶׁר 19
[is] which all and ,cattle thy security into bring ,send now And

of Pharaoh, and he hearkened not unto them; as the LORD had spoken unto Moses.

13 And the LORD said unto Moses, Rise up early in the morning, and stand before Pharaoh, and say unto him, Thus saith the LORD, the God of the Hebrews, Let my people go, that they may serve me. 14 For I will this time send all my plagues upon thine heart, and upon thy servants, and upon thy people; that thou mayest know that there is none like me in all the earth. 15 For now I had put forth my hand, and smitten thee and thy people with pestilence, and thou hadst been cut off from the earth: 16 but in very deed for this cause have I made thee to stand, for to shew thee my power, and that my name may be declared throughout all the earth. 17 As yet exaltest thou thyself against my people, that thou wilt not let them go? 18 Behold, to-morrow about this time I will cause it to rain a very grievous hail, such as hath not been in Egypt since the day it was founded even until now. 19 Now therefore send, hasten in thy cattle and all

a G. omits.
b S. has, *my plague.*
c G. adds, *another;* T. *a ruler.*
d G. has, *I will put to death.*

thou hast in the field; *for upon* every man and beast which shall be found in the field, and shall not be brought home, the hail shall come down upon them, and they shall die. 20 He that feared the word of the LORD among the servants of Pharaoh made his servants and his cattle flee into the houses: 21 And he that regarded not the word of the LORD left his servants and his cattle in the field.

22 And the LORD said unto Moses, Stretch forth thine hand toward heaven, that there may be hail in all the land of Egypt, upon man, and upon beast, and upon every herb of the field, throughout the land of Egypt. 23 And Moses stretched forth his rod toward heaven: and the LORD sent thunder and hail, and the fire ran along upon the ground; and the LORD rained hail upon the land of Egypt. 24 So there was hail, and fire mingled with the hail, very grievous, such as there was none like it in all the land of Egypt since it became a na-

לְךָ֖ בַּשָּׂדֶ֑ה[a] כָּל־הָ֨אָדָ֜ם וְהַבְּהֵמָ֗ה אֲשֶׁר־יִמָּצֵ֤א
found are which cattle and men all ;field the in thee to

בַשָּׂדֶה֙ וְלֹ֣א יֵאָסֵף֙ הַבַּ֔יְתָה וְיָרַ֧ד
down come will (and) ,house the to gathered ¹are ²not and field the in

עֲלֵהֶ֛ם הַבָּרָ֖ד וָמֵֽתוּ׃[b] הַיָּרֵא֙ אֶת־דְּבַ֣ר 20
of word the fearing one The .die will they and ,hail the them upon

יְהוָ֔ה מֵעַבְדֵ֖י פַּרְעֹ֑ה הֵנִ֛יס אֶת־עֲבָדָ֥יו[c]
slaves his flee to made Pharaoh of servants the of Jehovah

וְאֶת־מִקְנֵ֖הוּ אֶל־הַבָּתִּֽים׃ וַאֲשֶׁ֥ר לֹא־שָׂ֛ם לִבּ֖וֹ 21
heart his direct not did who he And .houses the unto cattle his and

אֶל־דְּבַ֣ר יְהוָ֑ה וַֽיַּעֲזֹ֛ב אֶת־עֲבָדָ֥יו[d] וְאֶת־מִקְנֵ֖הוּ
cattle his and slaves his left (and) ,Jehovah of word the unto

בַּשָּׂדֶֽה׃
.field the in

וַיֹּ֨אמֶר יְהוָ֜ה אֶל־מֹשֶׁ֗ה נְטֵ֤ה אֶת־יָֽדְךָ֙ 22
hand thy out Stretch :Moses unto Jehovah said And

עַל־הַשָּׁמַ֔יִם וִיהִ֥י בָרָ֖ד בְּכָל־אֶ֣רֶץ מִצְרָ֑יִם
;Egypt of land the all in hail be may that ,heavens the unto

עַל־הָאָדָ֤ם וְעַל־הַבְּהֵמָה֙ וְעַ֨ל כָּל־עֵ֣שֶׂב הַשָּׂדֶ֔ה
field the of herb every upon and ,cattle upon and ,man upon

בְּאֶ֖רֶץ מִצְרָֽיִם׃[e] וַיֵּ֨ט מֹשֶׁ֣ה אֶת־מַטֵּהוּ֮[f] 23
staff his Moses out stretched And .Egypt of land the in

עַל־הַשָּׁמַיִם֒ וַֽיהוָ֗ה נָתַ֤ן קֹלֹת֙ וּבָרָ֔ד וַתִּֽהֲלַךְ־
came and ;hail and thunder gave Jehovah and ,heavens the unto

אֵ֖שׁ אָ֑רְצָה וַיַּמְטֵ֧ר יְהוָ֛ה בָּרָ֖ד עַל־אֶ֥רֶץ
of land the upon hail Jehovah rained and ;earth the unto fire

מִצְרָֽיִם׃ וַיְהִ֣י בָרָ֔ד וְאֵ֕שׁ מִתְלַקַּ֖חַת בְּת֣וֹךְ 24
of midst the in incessant fire and ,hail was [there] And .Egypt

הַבָּרָ֑ד[g] כָּבֵ֣ד מְאֹ֔ד אֲשֶׁ֨ר לֹא־הָיָ֤ה כָמֹ֨הוּ֙
(it like) not was it which [like] ,exceedingly heavy ,hail the

בְּכָל־אֶ֣רֶץ[h] מִצְרַ֔יִם[h] מֵאָ֖ז הָיְתָ֥ה לְגֽוֹי׃[i]
.nation a (for) became it since ,Egypt of land the all in

that thou hast in the field; *for* every man and beast which shall be found in the field, and shall not be brought home, the hail shall come down upon them, and they shall die. 20 He that feared the word of the LORD among the servants of Pharaoh made his servants and his cattle flee into the houses: 21 and he that regarded not the word of the LORD left his servants and his cattle in the field.

22 And the LORD said unto Moses, Stretch forth thine hand toward heaven, that there may be hail in all the land of Egypt, upon man, and upon beast, and upon every herb of the field, throughout the land of Egypt. 23 And Moses stretched forth his rod toward heaven: and the LORD sent thunder and hail, and fire ran down unto the earth; and the LORD rained hail upon the land of Egypt. 24 So there was hail, and fire mingled with the hail, very grievous, such as had not been in all the land of Egypt since it became a na-

---

a G. adds, *for*.

b Sm. adds, *and came Moses and Aaron to Pharaoh and said unto him* etc., repeating 13b—19.

c G. omits.

d G. omits.

e G. omits.

f G. has, *his hand*.

g G. adds, *and the hail*.

h Sm., G. have, *in Egypt*.

i G. has, *upon it a nation*.

tion. 25 And the
hail smote
throughout all
the land of E-
gypt all that *was*
in the field, both
man and beast;
and the hail
smote every
herb of the field,
and brake every
tree of the field.
26 Only in the
land of Goshen,
where the chil-
dren of Israel
were, was there
no hail.

27 And Pha-
raoh sent, and
called for Moses
and Aaron, and
said unto them,
I have sinned
this time: the
LORD *is* right-
eous, and I and
my people *are*
wicked. 28 In-
treat the LORD
(for *it* *is*
enough) that
there be no
more mighty
thunderings and
hail; and I will
let you go, and
ye shall stay no
longer. 29 And
Moses said unto
him, As soon as
I am gone out
of the city, I
will spread a-
broad my hands
unto the LORD;
and the thunder
shall cease, nei-
ther shall there
be any more
hail; that thou
mayest know
how that the
earth *is* the
LORD'S. 30 But
as for thee and
thy servants, I
know that ye
will not yet fear
the LORD God.
31 And the flax
and the barley
was smitten: for

25 וַיַּךְ הַבָּרָד בְּכָל־אֶרֶץ מִצְרַיִם אֵת כָּל־אֲשֶׁר
[was] which all Egypt of land the all in hail the smote And

בַּשָּׂדֶה [a] מֵאָדָם וְעַד־בְּהֵמָה וְאֵת כָּל־עֵשֶׂב הַשָּׂדֶה
field the of herb every and ;cattle unto and man from ,field the in

הִכָּה הַבָּרָד וְאֶת־כָּל־עֵץ הַשָּׂדֶה שִׁבֵּר [b]׃
.pieces in broke it field the of tree every and ,hail the smote

26 רַק בְּאֶרֶץ גֹּשֶׁן אֲשֶׁר־שָׁם [c] בְּנֵי
of children the [were] where ,Goshen of land the in Only

27 יִשְׂרָאֵל לֹא הָיָה בָּרָד׃ וַיִּשְׁלַח פַּרְעֹה
Pharaoh sent And .hail [2]was [1][there] [3]not ,Israel

וַיִּקְרָא לְמֹשֶׁה וּלְאַהֲרֹן וַיֹּאמֶר אֲלֵהֶם
:them unto said and ,Aaron (to) and Moses (to) called and

חָטָאתִי הַפָּעַם יְהוָה הַצַּדִּיק
,one righteous the [being] Jehovah ,time [this] sinned have I

28 וַאֲנִי וְעַמִּי הָרְשָׁעִים׃ הַעְתִּירוּ [d] אֶל־יְהוָה
,Jehovah unto ye Entreat .ones wicked the people my and I and

וְרַב [e] מִהְיֹת קֹלֹת אֱלֹהִים וּבָרָד [f]
;hail and God of thunder the being of enough [being it] (and)

וַאֲשַׁלְּחָה אֶתְכֶם וְלֹא תֹסִפוּן לַעֲמֹד׃
.remain to continue [2]shall [1]you [3]not and ,you away send will I and

29 וַיֹּאמֶר אֵלָיו [g] מֹשֶׁה כְּצֵאתִי אֶת־הָעִיר
,city the of out going my At :Moses him unto said And

אֶפְרֹשׂ אֶת־כַּפַּי אֶל־יְהוָה [h] הַקֹּלוֹת
thunder the ;Jehovah unto hands my out spread will I

יֶחְדָּלוּן וְהַבָּרָד [i] לֹא יִהְיֶה־עוֹד לְמַעַן
that order in ;still ,be [1]shall [2]not hail the and ,cease shall

30 תֵּדַע כִּי לַיהוָה הָאָרֶץ׃ וְאַתָּה
thou And .land the [is] Jehovah to that know mayest thou

וַעֲבָדֶיךָ יָדַעְתִּי כִּי טֶרֶם תִּירְאוּן מִפְּנֵי [j]
before from fear you do yet not that know I ,servants thy and

31 יְהוָה אֱלֹהִים׃ וְהַפִּשְׁתָּה וְהַשְּׂעֹרָה נֻכָּתָה כִּי
for ;smitten were barley the and flax the And .God Jehovah

tion. 25 And the
hail smote
throughout all
the land of E-
gypt all that
was in the field,
both man and
beast; and the
hail smote every
herb of the field,
and brake every
tree of the field.
26 Only in the
land of Goshen,
where the chil-
dren of Israel
were, was there
no hail.

27 And Pha-
raoh sent, and
called for Mo-
ses and Aaron,
and said unto
them, I have
sinned this time:
the LORD is
righteous, and I
and my people
are wicked. 28
Intreat the
LORD; for there
hath been e-
nough of *these*
mighty thunder-
ings and hail;
and I will let
you go, and ye
shall stay no
longer. 29 And
Moses said unto
him, As soon as
I am gone out
of the city, I will
spread abroad
my hands unto
the LORD; the
thunders shall
cease, neither
shall there be
any more hail:
that thou may-
est know that
the earth is the
LORD'S. 30 But
as for thee and
thy servants, I
know that ye
will not yet fear
the LORD God.
31 And the flax
and the barley
were smitten:

---

a G. omits.

b G. adds, *the hail.*

c S. adds, *were dwelling.*

d G. adds, *therefore for me.*

e G. has, *and let it cease;* S., *and there is much delay with him;* so essentially T.; V. has, *that may cease.*

f G. adds, *and fire.*

g S. has, *unto Pharaoh;* V. omits.

h G. omits.

i G. adds, *and the rain;* cf. v. 34.

j G. omits.

the barley *was*
in the ear, and
the flax *was*
bolled. 32 But
the wheat and
the rie were not
smitten: for
they *were* not
grown up. 33
And Moses went
out of the city
from Pharaoh,
and spread a-
broad his hands
unto the LORD:
and the thun-
ders and hail
ceased, and the
rain was not
poured upon the
earth. 34 And
when Pharaoh
saw that the
rain and the
hail and the
thunders were
ceased, he sin-
ned yet more,
and hardened
his heart, he and
his servants. 35
And the heart of
Pharaoh was
hardened, nei-
ther would he
let the children
of Israel go; as
the LORD had
spoken by Mo-
ses.

הַשְּׂעֹרָה אָבִיב וְהַפִּשְׁתָּה גִּבְעֹל׃
.blossom [in was] flax the and ,ear [in was] barley the

וְהַחִטָּה וְהַכֻּסֶּמֶת לֹא נֻכּוּ כִּי אֲפִילֹת 32
[are] late for ; smitten [1]were [2]not spelt the and wheat the And

הֵנָּה׃ וַיֵּצֵא מֹשֶׁה מֵעִם פַּרְעֹה אֶת־הָעִיר 33
,city the [from] Pharaoh with from Moses out went And .they

וַיִּפְרֹשׂ כַּפָּיו[a] אֶל־יְהוָה וַיַּחְדְּלוּ הַקֹּלוֹת
thunder the ceased and ; Jehovah unto hands his out spread and

וְהַבָּרָד וּמָטָר לֹא־נִתַּךְ אָרְצָה׃ וַיַּרְא 34
saw And .earth the unto out poured not was rain and ,hail the and

פַּרְעֹה כִּי־חָדַל הַמָּטָר וְהַבָּרָד וְהַקֹּלֹת
,thunder the and hail the and rain the ceased had that Pharaoh

וַיֹּסֶף לַחֲטֹא וַיַּכְבֵּד לִבּוֹ[b] הוּא
he ,heart his heavy made he and ; sin to continued he and

וַעֲבָדָיו׃ וַיֶּחֱזַק לֵב פַּרְעֹה וְלֹא 35
[3]not and ,Pharaoh of heart the hard was And .servants his and

שִׁלַּח אֶת־בְּנֵי יִשְׂרָאֵל כַּאֲשֶׁר דִּבֶּר
spoken had as ; Israel of children the away send [2]did [1]he

יְהוָה בְּיַד־מֹשֶׁה[c]׃
.Moses of hand the by Jehovah

for the barley
was in the ear,
and the flax was
bolled. 32 But
the wheat and
the spelt were
not smitten: for
they were not
grown up. 33
And Moses went
out of the city
from Pharaoh,
and spread a-
broad his hands
unto the LORD:
and the thun-
ders and hail
ceased, and the
rain was not
poured upon
the earth. 34
And when Pha-
raoh saw that
the rain and the
hail and the
thunders were
ceased, he sin-
ned yet more,
and hardened
his heart, he and
his servants. 35
And the heart of
Pharaoh was
hardened, and
he did not let
the children of
Israel go; as
the LORD had
spoken by Mo-
ses.

10

AND the
LORD said unto
Moses, Go in
unto Pharaoh:
for I have hard-
ened his heart,
and the heart of
his servants,
that I might
shew these my
signs before
him: 2 And that
thou mayest tell
in the ears of
thy son, and of
thy son's son,
what things I
have wrought in
Egypt, and my

וַיֹּאמֶר יְהוָה אֶל־מֹשֶׁה[d] בֹּא אֶל־פַּרְעֹה כִּי־ 1
for ,Pharaoh unto in Go : Moses unto Jehovah said And

אֲנִי הִכְבַּדְתִּי אֶת־לִבּוֹ וְאֶת־לֵב עֲבָדָיו
,servants his of heart the and heart his heavy made have I

לְמַעַן שִׁתִי[e] אֹתֹתַי אֵלֶּה בְּקִרְבּוֹ[f]׃
; midst their in [1]these [3]signs [2]my putting my to order in

וּלְמַעַן תְּסַפֵּר[g] בְּאָזְנֵי בִנְךָ וּבֶן־ 2
of son the and son thy of ears the in relate mayest thou that order in and

בִּנְךָ אֵת אֲשֶׁר הִתְעַלַּלְתִּי בְּמִצְרַיִם וְאֶת־אֹתֹתַי
signs my and ,Egypt in wrought have I what son thy

And the LORD
said unto Moses,
Go in unto
Pharaoh: for I
have hardened
his heart, and
the heart of his
servants, that I
might shew
these my signs
in the midst of
them: 2 And
that thou may-
est tell in the
ears of thy son,
and of thy son's
son, what things
I have wrought
upon Egypt,
and my signs

---

a S. adds, *towards heaven.*
b S. has, *the heart of Pharaoh.*
c G. has, *to Moses.*
d G. adds, *saying.*
e G. has, *might come successively.*
f G., S., T. have, *in the midst of them*, בקרבם.
g G. has pl.

signs which I
have done a-
mong them;
that ye may
know how that
I *am* the LORD.
3 And Moses
and Aaron came
in unto Pha-
raoh, and said
unto him, Thus
saith the LORD
God of the He-
brews, How
long wilt thou
refuse to hum-
ble thyself be-
fore me? let my
people go, that
they may serve
me. 4 Else, if
thou refuse to
let my people
go, behold, to-
morrow will I
bring the locusts
into thy coast:
5 And they shall
cover the face of
the earth, that
one cannot be
able to see the
earth: and they
shall eat the
residue of that
which is escap-
ed, which re-
maineth unto
you from the
hail, and shall
eat every tree
which groweth
for you out of
the field: 6 And
they shall fill thy
houses, and the
houses of all
thy servants,
and the houses
of all the Egyp-
tians; which
neither thy fa-
thers, nor thy
father's fathers
have seen, since
the day that
they were upon
the earth unto
this day. And
he turned him-
self, and went
out from Pha-

אֲשֶׁר־שַׂמְתִּי בָּם וִידַעְתֶּם כִּי־אֲנִי
[am] I that know may you and ,them among put have I which

3 יְהוָה׃ וַיָּבֹא[a] משֶׁה וְאַהֲרֹן אֶל־פַּרְעֹה וַיֹּאמְרוּ
said and ,Pharaoh unto Aaron and Moses in went And .Jehovah

[b]אֵלָיו כֹּה־אָמַר יְהוָה אֱלֹהֵי הָעִבְרִים
: Hebrews the of God the Jehovah says Thus :him unto

עַד־מָתַי מֵאַנְתָּ לֵעָנֹת מִפָּנָי
? me before from thyself humble to refuse thou dost when Until

4 שַׁלַּח עַמִּי וְיַעַבְדֻנִי׃ כִּי אִם־מָאֵן
[art] refusing if For .me serve may they that ,people my away Send

אַתָּה לְשַׁלֵּחַ אֶת־עַמִּי הִנְנִי מֵבִיא
bring to about [am] I behold ,people my away send to thou

5 [b]מָחָר אַרְבֶּה בִּגְבֻלֶךָ[c b]׃ וְכִסָּה אֶת־עֵין
of eye the cover will they And .territory thy into locusts tomorrow

הָאָרֶץ וְלֹא יוּכַל לִרְאֹת אֶת־הָאָרֶץ
;land the see to able be [2]will [1]one [3]not and ,land the

וְאָכַל אֶת־יֶתֶר[d] הַפְּלֵטָה הַנִּשְׁאֶרֶת[e]
left is that ,escaped which that of remnant the eat will they and

לָכֶם[e] מִן־הַבָּרָד וְאָכַל אֶת־כָּל־הָעֵץ
tree every eat will they and ;hail the from you to

6 הַצֹּמֵחַ לָכֶם מִן־הַשָּׂדֶה[f]׃ וּמָלְאוּ בָתֶּיךָ
,houses thy full be will And .field the from you to sprouts that

וּבָתֵּי[g] כָל־עֲבָדֶיךָ וּבָתֵּי[h] כָל־מִצְרַיִם
; Egyptians the all of houses the and ,servants thy all of houses the and

אֲשֶׁר לֹא־רָאוּ אֲבֹתֶיךָ וַאֲבוֹת אֲבֹתֶיךָ
,fathers thy of fathers the and ,fathers thy seen not have which

מִיּוֹם הֱיוֹתָם עַל־הָאֲדָמָה עַד הַיּוֹם הַזֶּה[i]
.[1]this [2]day until ground the upon being their of day the from

7 וַיִּפֶן[j] וַיֵּצֵא[k] מֵעִם פַּרְעֹה׃ וַיֹּאמְרוּ
said And .Pharaoh with from out went and turned he And

which I have
done among
them; that ye
may know that I
am the LORD. 3
And Moses and
Aaron went in
unto Pharaoh,
and said unto
him, Thus saith
the LORD, the
God of the He-
brews, How
long wilt thou
refuse to hum-
ble thyself be-
fore me? let my
people go, that
they may serve
me. 4 Else, if
thou refuse to
let my people
go, behold, to-
morrow will I
bring locusts in-
to thy border: 5
and they shall
cover the face
of the earth,
that one shall
not be able to
see the earth:
and they shall
eat the residue
of that which is
escaped, which
remaineth unto
you from the
hail, and shall
eat every tree
which groweth
for you out of
the field: 6 and
thy houses shall
be filled, and
the houses of
all thy servants,
and the houses
of all the Egyp-
tians; as nei-
ther thy fathers
nor thy fathers'
fathers have
seen, since the
day that they
were upon the
earth unto this
day. And he
turned, and
went out from

---

a Sm. omits, and adds, *and thou shalt say unto Pharaoh.*

b G. has, *at this hour tomorrow many locusts upon all thy borders.*

c S. has, *upon all thy borders.*

d G. has, *all the residue of the land.*

e G., S. have, *which the hail left to you.*

f G. has, *upon the earth.*

g G. omits.

h G. has, *and all the houses.*

i Sm. adds, *and came in Moses and Aaron unto Pharaoh and said unto him*, etc., repeating from v. 3b to this point in v. 6.

j G. adds, *Moses;* S. has plural.

k S. has pl.

raoh. 7 And
Pharaoh's serv-
ants said unto
him, How long
shall this man be
a snare unto us?
let the men go,
that they may
serve the LORD
their God:
knowest thou
not yet that E-
gypt is destroy-
ed? 8 And Mo-
ses and Aaron
were brought a-
gain unto Pha-
raoh: and he
said unto them,
Go, serve the
LORD your God:
but who *are*
they that shall
go? 9 And Mo-
ses said, We
will go with our
young and with
our old, with
our sons and
with our daugh-
ters, with our
flocks and with
our herds will
we go; for we
must hold a
feast unto the
LORD. 10 And
he said unto
them, Let the
LORD be so with
you, as I will let
you go, and
your little ones:
look *to it;* for
evil *is* before
you. 11 Not so:
go now ye *that*
are men, and
serve the LORD;
for that ye did
desire. And they
were driven out
from Pharaoh's
presence.

עַבְדֵי פַרְעֹה אֵלָיו עַד־מָתַי יִהְיֶה זֶה[a]
one this be shall when Until :him unto Pharaoh of servants the

לָנוּ לְמוֹקֵשׁ[a] שַׁלַּח אֶת־הָאֲנָשִׁים וְיַעַבְדוּ
serve may they that ,men the away Send ? snare a (for) us to

אֶת־יְהוָה[b] אֱלֹהֵיהֶם הֲטֶרֶם[c] תֵּדַע[c] כִּי אָבְדָה
perishes that know [2]thou [1]dost [4]yet [3]not ; God their Jehovah

מִצְרָיִם׃ וַיּוּשַׁב[d] אֶת־מֹשֶׁה וְאֶת־אַהֲרֹן אֶל־ 8
unto Aaron and Moses back brought were And ? Egypt

פַּרְעֹה וַיֹּאמֶר אֲלֵהֶם לְכוּ[e] עִבְדוּ אֶת־יְהוָה[f]
Jehovah serve ,Go : them unto said he and ,Pharaoh

אֱלֹהֵיכֶם מִי[g] וָמִי הַהֹלְכִים׃ וַיֹּאמֶר[h] מֹשֶׁה 9
; Moses said And ? going ones the [are] who and who ; God your

בִּנְעָרֵינוּ וּבִזְקֵנֵינוּ נֵלֵךְ בְּבָנֵינוּ
sons our with ; go will we old our with and young our With

וּבִבְנוֹתֵנוּ בְּצֹאנֵנוּ[i] וּבִבְקָרֵנוּ נֵלֵךְ[j]
; go will we herds our with and flocks our with ,daughters our with and

כִּי חַג־יְהוָה לָנוּ[k]׃ וַיֹּאמֶר אֲלֵהֶם יְהִי 10
be May : them unto said he And .us to [is] Jehovah of feast a for

כֵן יְהוָה עִמָּכֶם כַּאֲשֶׁר אֲשַׁלַּח אֶתְכֶם וְאֶת־
and you away send I as ,you with Jehovah so

טַפְּכֶם רְאוּ כִּי רָעָה נֶגֶד פְּנֵיכֶם׃ לֹא כֵן 11
; so Not .face your before [is] evil for ,see ; ones little your

לְכוּ נָא הַגְּבָרִים וְעִבְדוּ אֶת־יְהוָה[l] כִּי אֹתָהּ[m] אַתֶּם
you it for ; Jehovah serve and ,men [1]now [2]ye go

מְבַקְשִׁים וַיְגָרֶשׁ[n] אֹתָם מֵאֵת פְּנֵי
of face the (with) from them out drove he and ; seeking [were]

פַרְעֹה׃
.Pharaoh

Pharaoh. 7 And
Pharaoh's serv-
ants said unto
him, How long
shall this man be
a snare unto us?
let the men go,
that they may
serve the LORD
their God:
knowest thou
not yet that E-
gypt is destroy-
ed? 8 And Mo-
ses and Aaron
were brought a-
gain unto Pha-
raoh: and he
said unto them,
Go, serve the
LORD your God:
but who are
they that shall
go? 9 And Mo-
ses said, We
will go with
our young and
with our old,
with our sons
and with our
daughters, with
our flocks and
with our herds
will we go; for
we must hold a
feast unto the
LORD. 10 And
he said unto
them, So be the
LORD with you,
as I will let you
go, and your
little ones: look
to it; for evil is
before you. 11
Not so: go now
ye that are men,
and serve the
LORD; for that
is what ye de-
sire. And they
were driven out
from Pharaoh's
presence.

12 And the
LORD said unto
Moses, Stretch
out thine hand

12 וַיֹּאמֶר יְהוָה אֶל־מֹשֶׁה נְטֵה יָדְךָ
hand thy out Stretch : Moses unto Jehovah said And

12 And the
LORD said unto
Moses, Stretch
out thine hand

---

a S. has, *to us this snare.*
b G. omits.
c G. has, *dost thou wish to know?*
d Sm., G., S., V. have, *and they brought back.*
e G. adds, *and,* ו.
f G. omits.
g G., S. have, *but who.*
h S. adds, *to him.*
i G. adds, *and,* ו.
j G., V. omit.
k G., V. have, *it is.*
l G. has, *God.*
m S. has, *rest.*
n Sm., G., S. have pl.

over the land of
Egypt for the
locusts, that
they may come
up upon the
land of Egypt,
and eat every
herb of the land,
even all that the
hail hath left. 13
And Moses
stretched forth
his rod over the
land of Egypt,
and the LORD
brought an east
wind upon the
land all that
day, and all *that*
night; *and* when
it was morning,
the east wind
brought the lo-
custs. 14 And
the locusts went
up over all the
land of Egypt,
and rested in all
the coasts of E-
gypt: very griev-
ous *were they;*
before them
there were no
such locusts as
they, neither
after them shall
be such. 15 For
they covered
the face of the
whole earth, so
that the land
was darkened;
and they did
eat every herb
of the land, and
all the fruit of
the trees which
the hail had left:
and there re-
mained not any
green thing in
the trees, or in
the herbs of the
field, through
all the land of
Egypt.

16 Then Pha-
raoh called for
Moses and Aa-
ron in haste;
and he said, I
have sinned a-

עַל-אֶרֶץ מִצְרַיִם בָּאַרְבֶּה[a] וְיַעַל עַל-
upon up go may they that ; locusts the for Egypt of land the over

אֶרֶץ מִצְרָיִם[b] וְיֹאכַל אֶת-כָּל-עֵשֶׂב[c] הָאָרֶץ אֵת
,land the of herb every eat may and ,Egypt of land the

13 כָּל-אֲשֶׁר[d] הִשְׁאִיר הַבָּרָד׃ וַיֵּט מֹשֶׁה
Moses out stretched And .hail the left which all

אֶת-מַטֵּהוּ עַל-אֶרֶץ[e] מִצְרַיִם[e] וַיהוָה[f] נִהַג
brought Jehovah and ,Egypt of land the over staff his

רוּחַ-קָדִים בָּאָרֶץ כָּל-הַיּוֹם הַהוּא וְכָל-הַלָּיְלָה
; night the all and ¹that ²day all land the on wind east an

הַבֹּקֶר הָיָה וְרוּחַ הַקָּדִים נָשָׂא
bore ¹east (the) (of) ²wind the (and) ,was morning [when]

14 אֶת-הָאַרְבֶּה׃ וַיַּעַל הָאַרְבֶּה[g] עַל כָּל-אֶרֶץ
of land the all over locusts the up went And .locusts the

מִצְרַיִם וַיָּנַח בְּכֹל גְּבוּל מִצְרָיִם כָּבֵד
numerous ,Egypt of territory the all on rested and ,Egypt

מְאֹד[h] לְפָנָיו לֹא-הָיָה כֵן אַרְבֶּה כָּמֹהוּ
,them like locusts so not were them before ; exceedingly

15 וְאַחֲרָיו לֹא יִהְיֶה-כֵּן׃ וַיְכַס אֶת-עֵין[i] כָּל-
all of eye the covered they And .so be ¹will ²not them after and

הָאָרֶץ וַתֶּחְשַׁךְ הָאָרֶץ וַיֹּאכַל אֶת-כָּל-עֵשֶׂב
of herb every ate they and ; land the dark became and ,earth the

הָאָרֶץ וְאֵת כָּל-פְּרִי הָעֵץ אֲשֶׁר הוֹתִיר הַבָּרָד
; hail the left had which ,trees the of fruit all and ,land the

[j]וְלֹא-נוֹתַר כָּל-יֶרֶק בָּעֵץ וּבְעֵשֶׂב[k]
of herbs the in and trees the in greenness any left not was and

16 הַשָּׂדֶה בְּכָל-אֶרֶץ[l] מִצְרָיִם׃ וַיְמַהֵר פַּרְעֹה
Pharaoh hastened And .Egypt of land the all in ,field the

לִקְרֹא לְמֹשֶׁה וּלְאַהֲרֹן וַיֹּאמֶר[m] חָטָאתִי
sinned have I :said he and ,Aaron (to) and Moses (to) call to

over the land of
Egypt for the
locusts, that
they may come
up upon the
land of Egypt,
and eat every
herb of the land,
even all that the
hail hath left.
13 And Moses
stretched forth
his rod over the
land of Egypt,
and the LORD
brought an east
wind upon the
land all that
day, and all the
night; and when
it was morning,
the east wind
brought the lo-
custs. 14 And
the locusts went
up over all the
land of Egypt,
and rested in
all the borders
of Egypt; very
grievous were
they; before
them there were
no such locusts
as they, neither
after them shall
be such. 15 For
they covered the
face of the
whole earth, so
that the land
was darkened;
and they did eat
every herb of
the land, and all
the fruit of the
trees which the
hail had left:
and there re-
mained not any
green thing, ei-
ther tree or herb
of the field,
through all the
land of Egypt.

16 Then Pha-
raoh called for
Moses and Aa-
ron in haste;
and he said, I
have sinned a-

---

a G. puts after ויעל, omitting ב; T. has, *that locusts may come.*

b G. omits.

c S. omits כל.

d Sm., G. have, *and all the fruit of the trees which;* S. adds, *and,* ו; cf. v. 15.

e G. has, *unto the heaven.*

f G. omits יהוה.

g G. has, *it.*

h S. adds, *and,* ו.

i G. omits.

j G. omits ו.

k G. adds, *all,* reading ובכל עשב; S. has, *and herb in the field.*

l G. omits כל.

m S., V. add, *to them.*

gainst the LORD
your God, and
against you. 17
Now therefore
forgive, I pray
thee, my sin
only this once,
and intreat the
LORD your God,
that he may
take away from
me this death
only. 18 And he
went out from
Pharaoh, and
intreated the
LORD. 19 And
the LORD turn-
ed a mighty
strong west
wind, which
took away the
locusts, and cast
them into the
Red sea; there
remained not
one locust in all
the coasts of
Egypt. 20 But
the LORD hard-
ened Pharaoh's
heart, so that he
would not let
the children of
Israel go.

21 And the
LORD said unto
Moses, Stretch
out thine hand
toward heaven,
that there may
be darkness over
the land of E-
gypt, even dark-
ness *which* may
be felt. 22 And
Moses stretched
forth his hand
toward heaven;
and there was a
thick darkness
in all the land of
Egypt three
days: 23 They
saw not one an-
other, neither
rose any from
his place for
three days: but
all the children
of Israel had
light in their
dwellings.

לַיהוָה אֱלֹהֵיכֶם וְלָכֶם׃ וְעַתָּה שָׂא[a] 17
,forgive now And .you against and God your Jehovah against

נָא חַטָּאתִי אַךְ הַפַּעַם וְהַעְתִּירוּ לַיהוָה
Jehovah (to) entreat and ,time [this] only sin my ,pray

אֱלֹהֵיכֶם וְיָסֵר מֵעָלַי רַק[b] אֶת־הַמָּוֶת
[2]death only me upon from remove may he that ,God your

הַזֶּה׃ וַיֵּצֵא[c] מֵעִם פַּרְעֹה וַיֶּעְתַּר 18
entreated he and ,Pharaoh (with) from out went he And .[1]this

אֶל־יְהוָה[d]׃ וַיַּהֲפֹךְ[e] יְהוָה רוּחַ־יָם חָזָק 19
strong ,wind west a [to] Jehovah [it] changed And .Jehovah (unto)

מְאֹד[f] וַיִּשָּׂא אֶת־הָאַרְבֶּה וַיִּתְקָעֵהוּ יָמָּה
of sea the into them threw and ,locusts the bore it and ,exceedingly

סוּף לֹא[g] נִשְׁאַר אַרְבֶּה אֶחָד בְּכֹל גְּבוּל[h]
of territory the all in ,[1]one [2]locust left [1]was [2]not ;reeds

מִצְרָיִם׃ וַיְחַזֵּק יְהוָה אֶת־לֵב פַּרְעֹה וְלֹא 20
[3]not and Pharaoh of heart the Jehovah hardened And .Egypt

שִׁלַּח אֶת־בְּנֵי יִשְׂרָאֵל׃
.Israel of children the away send [2]did [1]he

וַיֹּאמֶר יְהוָה אֶל־מֹשֶׁה נְטֵה יָדְךָ עַל־ 21
unto hand thy out Stretch :Moses unto Jehovah said And

הַשָּׁמַיִם וִיהִי חֹשֶׁךְ עַל־אֶרֶץ מִצְרָיִם
,Egypt of land the upon darkness be may that ,heavens the

וְיָמֵשׁ חֹשֶׁךְ׃ וַיֵּט מֹשֶׁה אֶת־יָדוֹ 22
hand his Moses out stretched And .darkness feel may one and

עַל־הַשָּׁמָיִם וַיְהִי חֹשֶׁךְ־אֲפֵלָה בְּכָל־אֶרֶץ
of land the all in gloom of darkness was and ,heavens the unto

מִצְרַיִם שְׁלֹשֶׁת יָמִים׃ לֹא־רָאוּ אִישׁ אֶת־אָחִיו[i] 23
,brother his one each see not did they ;days three Egypt

וְלֹא־קָמוּ אִישׁ מִתַּחְתָּיו שְׁלֹשֶׁת יָמִים
;days three ,place his from one each ,arise not did they and

וּלְכָל־בְּנֵי יִשְׂרָאֵל הָיָה אוֹר בְּמוֹשְׁבֹתָם[j]׃
.dwellings their in light was Israel of children the all to and

gainst the LORD
your God, and
against you. 17
Now therefore
forgive, I pray
thee, my sin
only this once,
and intreat the
LORD your
God, that he
may take away
from me this
death only. 18
And he went
out from Pha-
raoh, and in-
treated the
LORD. 19 And
the LORD turn-
ed an exceeding
strong west
wind, which
took up the
locusts, and
drove them into
the Red Sea;
there remained
not one locust
in all the border
of Egypt. 20
But the LORD
hardened Pha-
raoh's heart,
and he did not
let the children
of Israel go.

21 And the
LORD said unto
Moses, Stretch
out thine hand
toward heaven,
that there may
be darkness over
the land of E-
gypt, even dark-
ness which may
be felt. 22 And
Moses stretched
forth his hand
toward heaven;
and there was a
thick darkness
in all the land of
Egypt three
days; 23 they saw
not one another,
neither rose any
from his place
for three days;
but all the chil-
dren of Israel
had light in
their dwellings.

---

a Sm., G., S., V. have pl., שאו.
b G., S., V. omit.
c G., S., V. add, *Moses*.
d G. has, *God*.
e S. has, *and turned*, *brought*.
f G. apparently omits.
g G., S. add, *and*, ו.
h G. has, *land*.
i G. adds, *three days*.
j G. adds, *all*.

24 And Pha-
raoh called unto
Moses, and said,
Go ye, serve
the LORD; only
let your flocks
and your herds
be stayed: let
your little ones
also go with
you. 25 And
Moses said,
Thou must give
us also sacrifices
and burnt offer-
ings, that we
may sacrifice un-
to the LORD our
God. 26 Our
cattle also shall
go with us;
there shall not
an hoof be left
behind; for
thereof must we
take to serve the
LORD our God;
and we know
not with what
we must serve
the LORD, until
we come thither.
27 But the
LORD hardened
Pharaoh's
heart, and he
would not let
them go. 28
And Pharaoh
said unto him,
Get thee from
me, take heed to
thyself, see my
face no more;
for in *that* day
thou seest my
face thou shalt
die. 29 And Mo-
ses said, Thou
hast spoken
well, I will see
thy face again
no more.

24 וַיִּקְרָא פַרְעֹה אֶל־מֹשֶׁה[a] וַיֹּאמֶר[b] לְכוּ עִבְדוּ
serve ,ye Go ; said and Moses unto Pharaoh called And

אֶת־יְהוָה[c] רַק צֹאנְכֶם וּבְקַרְכֶם יֻצָּג
;behind left be let herds your and flocks your only ; Jehovah

25 גַּם־טַפְּכֶם יֵלֵךְ עִמָּכֶם׃ וַיֹּאמֶר[d] מֹשֶׁה[e] גַּם־אַתָּה
thou Also : Moses said And .you with go may ones little your

תִּתֵּן בְּיָדֵנוּ זְבָחִים וְעֹלֹת וְעָשִׂינוּ
prepare may we that ,offerings burnt and sacrifices hand our into give must

26 לַיהוָה אֱלֹהֵינוּ׃ וְגַם־מִקְנֵנוּ יֵלֵךְ עִמָּנוּ[f] לֹא
not ,us with go shall cattle our also And .God our Jehovah for

תִשָּׁאֵר[g] פַּרְסָה כִּי מִמֶּנּוּ נִקַּח לַעֲבֹד
serve to take shall we them from for ; hoof a left be shall

אֶת־יְהוָה אֱלֹהֵינוּ וַאֲנַחְנוּ לֹא־נֵדַע מַה־נַּעֲבֹד
serve shall we what [with] know not do we and ; God our Jehovah

27 אֶת־יְהוָה[h] עַד־בֹּאֵנוּ שָׁמָּה׃ וַיְחַזֵּק יְהוָה
Jehovah hardened And .thither come we until ,Jehovah

אֶת־לֵב פַּרְעֹה וְלֹא אָבָה לְשַׁלְּחָם׃
.away them send to willing [2]was [1]he [3]not and ,Pharaoh of heart the

28 וַיֹּאמֶר־לוֹ[i] פַרְעֹה לֵךְ מֵעָלָי הִשָּׁמֶר
careful be ; me (upon) from Go : Pharaoh him to said And

לְךָ אַל־תֹּסֶף רְאוֹת פָּנַי כִּי בְּיוֹם
of day the in for ,face my see to continue not do ,thyself for

29 רְאֹתְךָ פָנַי תָּמוּת׃ וַיֹּאמֶר[j] מֹשֶׁה כֵּן[k]
Rightly : Moses said And .die shalt thou face my seeing thy

דִּבַּרְתָּ לֹא־אֹסִף עוֹד רְאוֹת פָּנֶיךָ׃
.face thy see to again continue not will I ;spoken hast thou

24 And Pha-
raoh called unto
Moses and said,
Go ye, serve the
LORD; only let
your flocks and
your herds be
stayed: let your
little ones also
go with you. 25
And Moses said,
Thou must also
give into our
hand sacrifices
and burnt offer-
ings, that we
may sacrifice
unto the LORD
our God. 26
Our cattle also
shall go with us;
there shall not
an hoof be left
behind; for
thereof must we
take to serve the
LORD our God;
and we know
not with what
we must serve
the LORD, until
we come thither.
27 But the
LORD hardened
Pharaoh's
heart, and he
would not let
them go. 28
And Pharaoh
said unto him,
Get thee from
me, take heed to
thyself, see my
face no more;
for in the day
thou seest my
face thou shalt
die. 29 And
Moses said,
Thou hast spok-
en well; I will
see thy face a-
gain no more.

11

AND the
LORD said unto
Moses, Yet will
I bring one

1 וַיֹּאמֶר יְהוָה אֶל־מֹשֶׁה עוֹד נֶגַע אֶחָד
[1]one [2]plague [1]Still : Moses unto Jehovah said And

And the LORD
said unto Moses,
Yet one plague

---

a Sm., G., V. add, *and Aaron.*
b S. adds, *to him;* V., *to them.*
c G., S. add, *your God.*
d S. adds, *to Pharaoh.*
e G. adds, *but.*
f G., S. add, *and,* ו.
g S. has, *from us here.*
h G. adds, *our God.*
i G. omits לו; S., V. have, *to Moses.*
j S. adds, *to him,*
k G. omits; S., T. have, *well.*

plague *more* up-
on Pharaoh,
and upon E-
gypt; after-
wards he will
let you go
hence: when he
shall let *you*
go, he shall
surely thrust
you out hence
altogether. 2
Speak now in
the ears of the
people, and let
every man bor-
row of his
neighbour, and
every woman of
her neighbour,
jewels of silver,
and jewels of
gold. 3 And the
LORD gave the
people favour
in the sight of
the Egyptians.
Moreover the
man Moses *was*
very great in the
land of Egypt,
in the sight of
Pharaoh's serv-
ants, and in the
sight of the peo-
ple. 4 And Mo-
ses said, Thus
saith the
LORD, About
midnight will I
go out into the
midst of Egypt:
5 And all the
firstborn in the
land of Egypt
shall die, from
the firstborn of
Pharaoh that
sitteth upon his
throne, even un-
to the firstborn
of the maid-
servant that *is*
behind the mill;
and all the first-
born of beasts. 6
And there shall
be a great cry
throughout all
the land of E-

אָבִיא עַל־פַּרְעֹה וְעַל־מִצְרַיִם [a] אַחֲרֵי־כֵן
afterwards ; Egypt upon and Pharaoh upon bring will I

יְשַׁלַּח [b] אֶתְכֶם מִזֶּה כְּשַׁלְּחוֹ [c] כָּלָה [d]
,entirely away sending his at ; hence you away send will he

גָּרֵשׁ יְגָרֵשׁ אֶתְכֶם מִזֶּה׃ [e] דַּבֶּר־נָא [f] בְּאָזְנֵי 2
of ears the in ,now ,Speak .hence you out drive will he surely

הָעָם וְיִשְׁאֲלוּ אִישׁ מֵאֵת רֵעֵהוּ
,neighbor his (with) from man each ,ask them let and ,people the

וְאִשָּׁה [g] מֵאֵת [g] רְעוּתָהּ [g] כְּלֵי־כֶסֶף
silver of articles ,neighbor her (with) from woman each and

וּכְלֵי זָהָב׃ [h] וַיִּתֵּן [i] יְהוָה אֶת־חֵן הָעָם 3
people the [to] favor Jehovah gave And .gold of articles and

בְּעֵינֵי מִצְרָיִם [j] גַּם [k] הָאִישׁ מֹשֶׁה גָּדוֹל
great [being] Moses man the also ; Egyptians the of eyes the in

מְאֹד בְּאֶרֶץ [l] מִצְרַיִם בְּעֵינֵי עַבְדֵי־
of servants the of eyes the in ,Egypt of land the in exceedingly

פַרְעֹה וּבְעֵינֵי הָעָם׃ [l]
.people the of eyes the in and ,Pharaoh

וַיֹּאמֶר [m] מֹשֶׁה כֹּה אָמַר יְהוָה [m] כַּחֲצֹת 4
of middle the About : Jehovah says Thus :Moses said And

הַלַּיְלָה אֲנִי יוֹצֵא בְּתוֹךְ מִצְרָיִם׃ וּמֵת 5
die shall And .Egypt of midst the in out go will I night the

כָּל־בְּכוֹר בְּאֶרֶץ מִצְרַיִם מִבְּכוֹר פַּרְעֹה
Pharaoh of firstborn the from ;Egypt of land the in firstborn every

הַיֹּשֵׁב עַל־כִּסְאוֹ [n] עַד בְּכוֹר הַשִּׁפְחָה
slave female the of firstborn the unto ,throne his upon sitting one the

אֲשֶׁר אַחַר הָרֵחָיִם וְכֹל [o] בְּכוֹר בְּהֵמָה׃
.cattle of firstborn every and ; hand-mill the behind [is] who

וְהָיְתָה צְעָקָה גְדֹלָה בְּכָל־אֶרֶץ [p] מִצְרָיִם 6
; Egypt of land the all in [1]great [2]cry a be shall And

more will I bring
upon Pharaoh,
and upon E-
gypt; after-
wards he will let
you go hence:
when he shall
let you go, he
shall surely
thrust you out
hence altogeth-
er. 2 Speak now
in the ears of
the people, and
let them ask ev-
ery man of his
neighbour, and
every woman of
her neighbour,
jewels of silver,
and jewels of
gold. 3 And the
LORD gave the
people favour in
the sight of the
Egyptians.
Moreover the
man Moses was
very great in the
land of Egypt,
in the sight of
Pharaoh's serv-
ants, and in the
sight of the peo-
ple. 4 And Mo-
ses said, Thus
saith the LORD,
About midnight
will I go out in-
to the midst of
Egypt: 5 and all
the firstborn in
the land of E-
gypt shall die,
from the first-
born of Pha-
raoh that sitteth
upon his throne,
even unto the
firstborn of the
maidservant
that is behind
the mill; and all
the firstborn of
cattle. 6 And
there shall be a
great cry
throughout all
the land of E-

a G., S., V. add, *and*, ו.

b S. has, *I will send away.*

c S. has, *and when I send you away all of you, depart for yourselves hence.*

d G. has, *with all;* V. *and compel to go forth.*

e G. omits.

f G. adds, *secretly.*

g G. omits.

h Sm., G. add, *and clothing;* cf. 12: 35.

i Sm., V. have, *and will give.*

j G. adds, *and they lent to them;* Sm. *and they will lend to them.*

k Sm. omits to the end of the verse.

l G. has, *before the Egyptians, and before Pharaoh and before all his servants.*

m Sm. omits.

n G., S. add, *and*, ו.

o Sm., G. have, *and unto the firstborn of all cattle.*

p Sm., S. omit כל.

gypt, such as there was none like it, nor shall be like it any more. 7 But against any of the children of Israel shall not a dog move his tongue, against man or beast: that ye may know how that the LORD doth put a difference between the Egyptians and Israel. 8 And all these thy servants shall come down unto me, and bow down themselves unto me, saying, Get thee out, and all the people that follow thee: and after that I will go out. And he went out from Pharaoh in a great anger. 9 And the LORD said unto Moses, Pharaoh shall not hearken unto you; that my wonders may be multiplied in the land of Egypt. 10 And Moses and Aaron did all these wonders before Pharaoh: and the LORD hardened Pharaoh's heart, so that he would not let the children of Israel go out of his land.

אֲשֶׁר כָּמֹהוּ לֹא נִהְיָתָה וְכָמֹהוּ לֹא
³not which like and ,been ²has ¹[there] ³not (it) ¹like ²which

7 תֹּסִף׃ וּלְכֹל בְּנֵי יִשְׂרָאֵל
,Israel of children the all towards And .again be ²shall [¹there]

לֹא יֶחֱרַץ־כֶּלֶב לְשֹׁנוֹ לְמֵאִישׁ וְעַד־בְּהֵמָה
; cattle unto and man from (to) ,tongue his dog a sharpen ¹shall ²not

לְמַעַן תֵּדְעוּן[a] אֲשֶׁר יַפְלֶה יְהוָה בֵּין
between Jehovah separates that know may you that order in

8 מִצְרַיִם וּבֵין יִשְׂרָאֵל׃[b] וְיָרְדוּ כָל־
all down come will And .Israel (between) and Egypt

עֲבָדֶיךָ אֵלֶּה אֵלַי וְהִשְׁתַּחֲווּ־לִי
me to themselves prostrate and ,me unto ¹these ³servants ²thy

לֵאמֹר[c] צֵא אַתָּה וְכָל־הָעָם אֲשֶׁר־בְּרַגְלֶיךָ
; feet thy at [are] who people the all and thou ,out Go :saying

וְאַחֲרֵי־כֵן אֵצֵא וַיֵּצֵא מֵעִם־פַּרְעֹה
Pharaoh (with) from out went he And .out go will I afterwards and

בָּחֳרִי־אָף׃
.anger of heat in

9 וַיֹּאמֶר יְהוָה אֶל־מֹשֶׁה לֹא־יִשְׁמַע
hearken not Will : Moses unto Jehovah said had And

אֲלֵיכֶם פַּרְעֹה לְמַעַן רְבוֹת[d] מוֹפְתַי בְּאֶרֶץ
of land the in wonders my multiply to order in ; Pharaoh you unto

10 מִצְרָיִם׃ וּמֹשֶׁה וְאַהֲרֹן עָשׂוּ אֶת־כָּל־הַמֹּפְתִים[e]
²wonders all did Aaron and Moses And .Egypt

הָאֵלֶּה[f] לִפְנֵי פַרְעֹה וַיְחַזֵּק יְהוָה אֶת־לֵב
of heart the Jehovah hardened and ; Pharaoh before ¹these

פַּרְעֹה וְלֹא־שִׁלַּח[g] אֶת־בְּנֵי־יִשְׂרָאֵל מֵאַרְצוֹ[h]׃
.land his from Israel of children the away send not did he and ,Pharaoh

gypt, such as there hath been none like it, nor shall be like it any more. 7 But against any of the children of Israel shall not a dog move his tongue, against man or beast: that ye may know how that the LORD doth put a difference between the Egyptians and Israel. 8 And all these thy servants shall come down unto me, and bow down themselves unto me, saying, Get thee out, and all the people that follow thee: and after that I will go out. And he went out from Pharaoh in hot anger. 9 And the LORD said unto Moses, Pharaoh will not hearken unto you: that my wonders may be multiplied in the land of Egypt. 10 And Moses and Aaron did all these wonders before Pharaoh: and the LORD hardened Pharaoh's heart, and he did not let the children of Israel go out of his land.

12

AND the LORD spake unto Moses and Aaron in the land of E-

1 וַיֹּאמֶר יְהוָה אֶל־מֹשֶׁה וְאֶל־אַהֲרֹן בְּאֶרֶץ
of land the in ,Aaron unto and Moses unto Jehovah spoke And

And the LORD spake unto Moses and Aaron in the land of Egypt,

---

a Sm., G. have sing.

b Sm. adds, 11: 3b and says, *and Moses said unto Pharaoh*, and adds essentially 4: 22b, 23 and 11: 4b—7.

c S. adds, *to me.*

d G. has, *I may increase my signs and.*

e S. omits כל; G. has, *signs and wonders.*

f G. adds, *in the land of Egypt.*

g G. has, *he hearkened to send away.*

h G. has, *from the land of Egypt.*

gypt, saying. 2
This month
shall be unto
you the begin-
ning of months:
it *shall be* the
first month of
the year to you.
3 Speak ye
unto all the
congregation of
Israel, saying,
In the tenth *day*
of this month
they shall take
to them every
man a lamb,
according to
the house of
their fathers, a
lamb for an
house: 4 And if
the household
be too little for
the lamb, let
him and his
neighbour next
unto his house
take *it* accord-
ing to the num-
ber of the souls;
every man ac-
cording to his
eating shall
make your
count for the
lamb. 5 Your
lamb shall be
without blem-
ish a male of
the first year: ye
shall take *it* out
from the sheep,
or from the
goats: 6 And ye
shall keep it up
until the four-
teenth day of the
same month:
and the whole
assembly of the
congregation of
Israel shall kill
it in the eve-
ning. 7 And they
shall take of the
blood, and
strike *it* on the
two side posts
and on the up-
per door post of
the houses,
wherein they
shall eat it. 8
And they shall
eat the flesh in
that night, roast

2 מִצְרַיִם לֵאמֹר[a]׃ הַחֹדֶשׁ הַזֶּה לָכֶם רֹאשׁ
of head [be let] you for [1]this [2]Month : saying ,Egypt

חֳדָשִׁים רִאשׁוֹן הוּא לָכֶם לְחָדְשֵׁי[b] הַשָּׁנָה׃
.year the of months the to you for [be] it [let] first ,months

3 דַּבְּרוּ[c] אֶל־כָּל־עֲדַת יִשְׂרָאֵל לֵאמֹר[d]
: saying Israel of congregation the all unto ye Speak

בֶּעָשֹׂר לַחֹדֶשׁ הַזֶּה וְיִקְחוּ לָהֶם
,themselves for take shall they (and) ,[1]this [2]month to [day] tenth the On

4 אִישׁ שֶׂה לְבֵית־אָבֹת[e] שֶׂה[f] לַבָּיִת׃ וְאִם־
if And .house a for lamb a ,house fathers' a for lamb a one each

יִמְעַט[g] הַבַּיִת מִהְיוֹת מִשֶּׂה וְלָקַח הוּא
he take shall (and) ,lamb a for being from house the small be

וּשְׁכֵנוֹ הַקָּרֹב אֶל־בֵּיתוֹ בְּמִכְסַת
of number the by ,house his unto next neighbor his and

נְפָשֹׁת אִישׁ לְפִי אָכְלוֹ תָּכֹסּוּ
count shall you ,eating his of mouth the to according one each ,souls

5 עַל־הַשֶּׂה׃ שֶׂה תָמִים זָכָר בֶּן־שָׁנָה
[old] year a (of son) male perfect lamb A .lamb the concerning

יִהְיֶה לָכֶם מִן־הַכְּבָשִׂים וּמִן־הָעִזִּים תִּקָּחוּ׃
.take shall ye goats the from or sheep the from ; you to be shall

6 וְהָיָה לָכֶם לְמִשְׁמֶרֶת עַד אַרְבָּעָה עָשָׂר
tenth [and] four the until keep to you for be shall it And

יוֹם לַחֹדֶשׁ הַזֶּה וְשָׁחֲטוּ אֹתוֹ כֹּל קְהַל
of assembly the all it kill shall and ; [1]this [2]month to day

7 עֲדַת־יִשְׂרָאֵל בֵּין[h] הָעַרְבָּיִם[h]׃ וְלָקְחוּ
take shall they And .evenings the between Israel of congregation the

מִן־הַדָּם וְנָתְנוּ עַל־שְׁתֵּי הַמְּזוּזֹת וְעַל־
upon and posts door side two the upon put and blood the from

הַמַּשְׁקוֹף עַל[i] הַבָּתִּים אֲשֶׁר־יֹאכְלוּ אֹתוֹ
it eat they which [in] houses the upon ; post door upper the

8 בָּהֶם׃ וְאָכְלוּ אֶת־הַבָּשָׂר בַּלַּיְלָה הַזֶּה
; [1]this [2]night in flesh the eat shall they And .(them in)

saying, 2 This
month shall be
unto you the
beginning of
months: it shall
be the first
month of the
year to you.

3 Speak ye
unto all the
congregation of
Israel, saying,
In the tenth *day*
of this month
they shall take
to them every
man a lamb, ac-
cording to their
fathers' houses,
a lamb for an
household: 4
and if the house-
hold be too lit-
tle for a lamb,
then shall he
and his neigh-
bour next unto
his house take
one according to
the number of
the souls; ac-
cording to every
man's eating ye
shall make your
count for the
lamb. 5 Your
lamb shall be
without blem-
ish, a male of
the first year:
ye shall take it
from the sheep,
or from the
goats: 6 and ye
shall keep it up
until the four-
teenth day of
the same month:
and the whole
assembly of the
congregation of
Israel shall kill
it at even. 7
And they shall
take of the
blood, and put it
on the two side
posts and on the
lintel, upon the
houses wherein
they shall eat it.
8 And they shall
eat the flesh in
that night, roast

a S., V. omit.

b S. adds, *all*, reading לכל חרשי.

c G. has sing.

d S. omits.

e G. adds, *each;* S. transfers אבת to the end of the verse.

f S. adds, *and*, ו.

g G., S., T., V. paraphrase the verse but apparently have the same text.

h G., V. have, *at evening;* S. has, *at the setting of the sun.*

i S. adds, *and*, ו.

with fire, and
unleavened
bread; *and* with
bitter *herbs* they
shall eat it. 9
Eat not of it
raw, nor sodden
at all with wa-
ter, but roast
with fire; his
head with his
legs, and with
the purtenance
thereof. 10 And
ye shall let noth-
ing of it remain
until the morn-
ing; and that
which remaineth
of it until the
morning ye shall
burn with fire.

11 And thus
shall ye eat it;
with your loins
girded, your
shoes on your
feet, and your
staff in your
hand; and ye
shall eat it in
haste: it *is* the
LORD'S pass-
over. 12 For I
will pass
through the land
of Egypt this
night, and will
smite all the
firstborn in the
land of Egypt,
both man and
beast; and a-
gainst all the
gods of Egypt I
will execute
judgment: I *am*
the LORD. 13
And the blood
shall be to you
for a token up-
on the houses
where ye *are*:
and when I see
the blood, I will
pass over you,
and the plague
shall not be up-
on you to de-
stroy *you*, when
I smite the land
of Egypt. 14
And this day
shall be unto

צְלִי־אֵשׁ וּמַצּוֹת עַל־מְרֹרִים
,[herbs] bitter with ,bread unleavened and ,fire of roasted

יֹאכְלֻהוּ׃ אַל־תֹּאכְלוּ מִמֶּנּוּ נָא וּבָשֵׁל[a] מְבֻשָּׁל 9
cooked ,cooked or raw it from eat not Do .it eat shall they

בַּמָּיִם כִּי אִם־צְלִי־אֵשׁ [b]רֹאשׁוֹ עַל־כְּרָעָיו וְעַל־
and legs its with head its ; fire of roasted (if) but ,water in

קִרְבּוֹ׃ [c]וְלֹא־תוֹתִירוּ[d] מִמֶּנּוּ עַד־בֹּקֶר[e] 10
; morning until it from leave not shall you And .entrails its with

וְהַנֹּתָר מִמֶּנּוּ עַד־בֹּקֶר[f] בָּאֵשׁ תִּשְׂרֹפוּ׃
.burn shall you fire with ,morning until it from left that and

וְכָכָה תֹּאכְלוּ אֹתוֹ מָתְנֵיכֶם חֲגֻרִים [g]נַעֲלֵיכֶם 11
sandals your ,girded loins your ; it eat shall you thus And

בְּרַגְלֵיכֶם וּמַקֶּלְכֶם בְּיֶדְכֶם וַאֲכַלְתֶּם אֹתוֹ
it eat shall you and ;hand your in staff your and ,feet your on

בְּחִפָּזוֹן פֶּסַח הוּא לַיהוָה׃
.Jehovah to [is] it passover a ,haste anxious in

וְעָבַרְתִּי בְאֶרֶץ־מִצְרַיִם בַּלַּיְלָה הַזֶּה 12
,[1]this [2]night in Egypt of land the in through pass will I And

וְהִכֵּיתִי[h] כָל־בְּכוֹר בְּאֶרֶץ מִצְרַיִם מֵאָדָם
man from Egypt of land the in firstborn every smite will I and

[i]וְעַד־בְּהֵמָה וּבְכָל־אֱלֹהֵי מִצְרַיִם אֶעֱשֶׂה
do will I Egypt of gods the all on and ; cattle unto and

שְׁפָטִים אֲנִי יְהוָה׃ וְהָיָה הַדָּם 13
blood the be shall And .Jehovah [am] I ,judgments

לָכֶם לְאֹת עַל הַבָּתִּים אֲשֶׁר אַתֶּם שָׁם
; (there) [are] you where houses the upon ,sign a (for) you for

וְרָאִיתִי אֶת־הַדָּם וּפָסַחְתִּי עֲלֵיכֶם
; you (upon) over pass will I and ,blood the see will I and

וְלֹא־יִהְיֶה בָכֶם נֶגֶף לְמַשְׁחִית בְּהַכֹּתִי
smiting my at ,destroy to plague a you on be not shall and

בְּאֶרֶץ מִצְרָיִם׃ וְהָיָה הַיּוֹם הַזֶּה לָכֶם 14
you to [1]this [2]day be shall And .Egypt of land the (in)

with fire, and
unleavened
bread; with
bitter herbs they
shall eat it. 9
Eat not of it
raw, nor sodden
at all with wa-
ter, but roast
with fire; its
head with its
legs and with
the inwards
thereof. 10 And
ye shall let noth-
ing of it remain
until the morn-
ing; but that
which remain-
eth of it until
the morning ye
shall burn with
fire.

11 And thus
shall ye eat it;
with your loins
girded, your
shoes on your
feet, and your
staff in your
hand: and ye
shall eat it in
haste: it is the
LORD'S pass-
over. 12 For I
will go through
the land of E-
gypt in that
night, and will
smite all the
firstborn in the
land of Egypt,
both man and
beast; and a-
gainst all the
gods of Egypt I
will execute
judgments: I
am the LORD.
13 And the
blood shall be to
you for a token
upon the houses
where ye are:
and when I see
the blood, I will
pass over you,
and there shall
no plague be
upon you to de-
stroy you, when
I smite the land
of Egypt. 14
And this day
shall be unto

a G. apparently omits בשל.
b S. adds, *and*, ו.
c G., S. omit ו.
d G. has, *shall be left*.
e G. adds, *and a bone shall not be broken from it*; cf. v. 46.
f V. omits.
g G., S., V. add, *and*, ו.
h S. has, *and shall die*.
i G., V. omit ו.

you for a me-
morial; and ye
shall keep it a
feast to the
LORD through-
out your gener-
ations; ye shall
keep it a feast
by an ordinance
for ever. 15
Seven days shall
ye eat unleaven-
ed bread; even
the first day ye
shall put away
leaven out of
your houses;
for whosoever
eateth leavened
bread from the
first day until
the seventh day,
that soul shall
be cut off from
Israel. 16 And
in the first day
there shall be an
holy convoca-
tion, and in the
seventh day
there shall be an
holy convoca-
tion to you; no
manner of work
shall be done in
them, save that
which every man
must eat, that
only may be
done of you. 17
And ye shall ob-
serve *the feast*
of unleavened
bread; for in
this selfsame
day have I
brought your
armies out of the
land of Egypt:
therefore shall
ye observe this
day in your gen-
erations by an
ordinance for
ever.

18 In the first
month, on the
fourteenth day
of the month at
even, ye shall
eat unleavened
bread, until the
one and twenti-
eth day of the
month at even.

לְזִכָּרוֹן וְחַגֹּתֶם אֹתוֹ חַג לַיהוָה
;Jehovah to feast a [as] it celebrate shall you and ,remembrance for

לְדֹרֹתֵיכֶם[a] חֻקַּת עוֹלָם תְּחָגֻּהוּ[b]:
.it celebrate shall you eternity of ordinance an [as] ,generations your for

שִׁבְעַת יָמִים מַצּוֹת תֹּאכֵלוּ אַךְ בַּיּוֹם 15
²day the on indeed ;eat shall you bread unleavened days Seven

הָרִאשׁוֹן תַּשְׁבִּיתוּ שְּׂאֹר מִבָּתֵּיכֶם כִּי
for ;houses your from leaven cease to cause shall you ¹first

כָּל־אֹכֵל חָמֵץ[c] וְנִכְרְתָה הַנֶּפֶשׁ
²soul off cut be shall (and) ,leavened anything eating one any

הַהִוא מִיִּשְׂרָאֵל מִיּוֹם הָרִאשֹׁן עַד־יוֹם
²day the until ¹first ²day the from ,Israel from ¹that

הַשְּׁבִעִי: וּבַיּוֹם[d] הָרִאשׁוֹן מִקְרָא־קֹדֶשׁ 16
,holiness of convocation a ¹first ²day the on And .¹seventh

וּבַיּוֹם[e] הַשְּׁבִיעִי מִקְרָא־קֹדֶשׁ יִהְיֶה לָכֶם
;you to be shall holiness of convocation a ¹seventh ²day the on and

כָּל־מְלָאכָה לֹא־יֵעָשֶׂה[f] בָהֶם אַךְ אֲשֶׁר
what only ;them on done be not may work any

יֵאָכֵל[g] לְכָל־נֶפֶשׁ הוּא לְבַדּוֹ יֵעָשֶׂה לָכֶם:
.you by done be may alone that ,soul any by eaten be must

וּשְׁמַרְתֶּם אֶת־הַמַּצּוֹת[h] כִּי בְּעֶצֶם 17
(of bone the) in for ,bread unleavened the observe shall you And

הַיּוֹם הַזֶּה הוֹצֵאתִי אֶת־צִבְאוֹתֵיכֶם מֵאֶרֶץ
of land the from hosts your out brought I ¹this ²day

מִצְרָיִם וּשְׁמַרְתֶּם אֶת־הַיּוֹם הַזֶּה לְדֹרֹתֵיכֶם
,generations your for ¹this ²day observe shall you and ;Egypt

חֻקַּת עוֹלָם: בָּרִאשֹׁן[i] בְּאַרְבָּעָה 18
[and] four the on ,[month] first the In .eternity of ordinance an

עָשָׂר יוֹם לַחֹדֶשׁ[j] בָּעֶרֶב תֹּאכְלוּ מַצֹּת
;bread unleavened eat shall you ,evening at ,month the to day tenth

עַד יוֹם הָאֶחָד וְעֶשְׂרִים לַחֹדֶשׁ בָּעָרֶב:
.evening at ,month the to [day] twentieth and one the of day the until

you for a me-
morial, and ye
shall keep it a
feast to the
LORD: through-
out your genera-
tions ye shall
keep it a feast
by an ordinance
for ever. 15
Seven days shall
ye eat unleaven-
ed bread; even
the first day ye
shall put away
leaven out of
your houses: for
whosoever eat-
eth leavened
bread from the
first day until
the seventh day,
that soul shall
be cut off from
Israel. 16 And
in the first day
there shall be to
you an holy
convocation,
and in the sev-
enth day an
holy convoca-
tion; no manner
of work shall be
done in them,
save that which
every man must
eat, that only
may be done of
you. 17 And ye
shall observe
the *feast of* un-
leavened bread;
for in this self-
same day have I
brought your
hosts out of the
land of Egypt:
therefore shall
ye observe this
day throughout
your genera-
tions by an or-
dinance for ev-
er.

18 In the first
month, on the
fourteenth day
of the month at
even, ye shall
eat unleavened
bread, until the
one and twen-
tieth day of the
month at even.

---

a G. has, *to all your generations.*
b S. has, *you shall make it;* V. omits.
c S. adds, *from your houses.*
d G. has, **and the day;** S., *the day.*
e G., S. have, *and the day.*
f G., V. have, *ye shall do.*
g G. has, *must be done,* יֵעָשֶׂה.
h Sm., G. have, *this command;* cf. v. 24.
i T. has, *Nisan.*
j G. adds, *first.*

19 Seven days
shall there be no
leaven found in
your houses:
for whosoever
eateth that
which is leaven-
ed, even that
soul shall be cut
off from the
congregation of
Israel, whether
he be a stranger,
or born in the
land. 20 Ye
shall eat noth-
ing leavened;
in all your hab-
itations shall ye
eat unleavened
bread.

21 Then Mo-
ses called for
all the elders of
Israel, and said
unto them,
Draw out and
take you a lamb
according to
your families,
and kill the pass-
over. 22 And ye
shall take a
bunch of hyssop,
and dip *it* in
the blood that *is*
in the bason,
and strike the
lintel and the
two side posts
with the blood
that *is* in the
bason; and none
of you shall go
out at the door
of his house un-
til the morning.
23 For the LORD
will pass
through to smite
the Egyptians;
and when he
seeth the blood
upon the lintel,
and on the two
side posts, the
LORD will pass
over the door,
and will not
suffer the de-
stroyer to come
in unto your
houses to smite
you. 24 And ye
shall observe
this thing for an
ordinance to
thee and to thy

19 שִׁבְעַת יָמִים שְׂאֹר לֹא יִמָּצֵא בְּבָתֵּיכֶם כִּי
for ; houses your in found be ¹shall ²not leaven days seven

כָּל־אֹכֵל מַחְמֶצֶת וְנִכְרְתָה הַנֶּפֶשׁ
²soul off cut be shall (and) ,leavened anything eating one any

הַהִוא מֵעֲדַת יִשְׂרָאֵל בַּגֵּר
strangers the among ,Israel of congregation the from ¹that

20 וּבְאֶזְרַח הָאָרֶץ׃ כָּל־מַחְמֶצֶת לֹא
³not leavened Anything .land the of natives the among and

תֹאכֵלוּ [a]בְּכֹל מוֹשְׁבֹתֵיכֶם תֹּאכְלוּ מַצּוֹת׃
.bread unleavened eat shall you habitations your all in ; eat ²shall ¹you

21 וַיִּקְרָא מֹשֶׁה לְכָל־זִקְנֵי יִשְׂרָאֵל וַיֹּאמֶר
said and ,Israel of elders the all (to) Moses called And

אֲלֵהֶם מִשְׁכוּ וּקְחוּ לָכֶם צֹאן לְמִשְׁפְּחֹתֵיכֶם
,families your for lambs yourselves for take and forth Go ;them unto

22 וְשַׁחֲטוּ הַפָּסַח׃ וּלְקַחְתֶּם אֲגֻדַּת אֵזוֹב וּטְבַלְתֶּם
dip and ,hyssop of bunch a ye take And .passover the kill and

בַּדָּם אֲשֶׁר־בַּסַּף[b] וְהִגַּעְתֶּם אֶל־
(unto) touch to cause and ; basin the in [is] which blood the in

הַמַּשְׁקוֹף וְאֶל־שְׁתֵּי הַמְּזוּזֹת מִן־הַדָּם[c]
blood the of [some] posts door side two the (unto) and post door upper the

אֲשֶׁר בַּסָּף[dc] וְאַתֶּם לֹא תֵצְאוּ אִישׁ
one any ,out go ¹shall ²not you and ; basin the in [is] which

23 מִפֶּתַח־בֵּיתוֹ עַד־בֹּקֶר׃ וְעָבַר
through pass will And .morning until ,house his of door the from

יְהוָה לִנְגֹּף אֶת־מִצְרַיִם וְרָאָה אֶת־הַדָּם עַל־
upon blood the see will he and ; Egypt smite to Jehovah

הַמַּשְׁקוֹף וְעַל שְׁתֵּי הַמְּזוּזֹת וּפָסַח
over pass will and ;posts door side two the upon and post door upper the

יְהוָה עַל־הַפֶּתַח וְלֹא יִתֵּן הַמַּשְׁחִית
destroyer the allow ²will ¹he ³not and ,door the upon Jehovah

24 לָבֹא אֶל־בָּתֵּיכֶם לִנְגֹּף׃ וּשְׁמַרְתֶּם
observe shall you And .smite to houses your into come to

אֶת־הַדָּבָר הַזֶּה [e]לְחָק־לְךָ וּלְבָנֶיךָ עַד־
for sons thy for and thee for ordinance an for ¹this ²word

19 Seven days
shall there be no
leaven found in
your houses:
for whosoever
eateth that
which is leaven-
ed, that soul
shall be cut off
from the con-
gregation of Is-
rael, whether he
be a sojourner,
or one that is
born in the land.
20 Ye shall eat
nothing leaven-
ed; in all your
habitations shall
ye eat unleaven-
ed bread.

21 Then Mo-
ses called for all
the elders of Is-
rael, and said
unto them,
Draw out, and
take you lambs
according to
your families,
and kill the
passover. 22
And ye shall
take a bunch of
hyssop, and dip
it in the blood
that is in the
bason, and
strike the lintel
and the two side
posts with the
blood that is in
the bason; and
none of you
shall go out of
the door of his
house until the
morning. 23 For
the LORD will
pass through to
smite the Egyp-
tians; and when
he seeth the
blood upon the
lintel, and on
the two side
posts, the LORD
will pass over
the door, and
will not suffer
the destroyer to
come in unto
your houses to
smite you. 24
And ye shall ob-
serve this thing
for an ordinance
to thee and to

---

a G. adds, *but*, ו.

b G. has, *which is by the door;* V., *which is on the threshold;* S., *of the lamb.*

c V. omits.

d G. has, *by the door.*

e S. has, *and this law.*

sons for ever. 25
And it shall
come to pass,
when ye be
come to the
land which the
LORD will give
you, according
as he hath
promised, that
ye shall keep
this service. 26
And it shall
come to pass,
when your chil-
dren shall say
unto you, What
mean ye by this
service? 27 That
ye shall say, It *is*
the sacrifice of
the LORD's pass-
over, who pass-
ed over the
houses of the
children of Is-
rael in Egypt,
when he smote
the Egyptians,
and delivered
our houses. And
the people bow-
ed the head and
worshipped. 28
And the chil-
dren of Israel
went away, and
did as the LORD
had command-
ed Moses and
Aaron, so did
they.

29 And it
came to pass,
that at midnight
the LORD smote
all the firstborn
in the land of
Egypt, from the
firstborn of Pha-
raoh that sat on
his throne unto
the firstborn of
the captive that
was in the dun-
geon; and all
the firstborn of
cattle. 30 And
Pharaoh rose up
in the night, he,
and all his serv-
ants, and all the
Egyptians; and
there was a
great cry in E-

25 עוֹלָם׃ וְהָיָה[a] כִּי־תָבֹאוּ אֶל־הָאָרֶץ אֲשֶׁר
which land the into come you when ,be shall it And .ever

יִתֵּן יְהוָה לָכֶם כַּאֲשֶׁר דִּבֵּר וּשְׁמַרְתֶּם
observe shall you (and) ,spoken has he as ,you to Jehovah give will

26 אֶת־הָעֲבֹדָה הַזֹּאת׃ וְהָיָה כִּי־יֹאמְרוּ אֲלֵיכֶם
you unto say when ,be shall it And .[1]this [2]service

27 בְּנֵיכֶם מָה הָעֲבֹדָה הַזֹּאת לָכֶם[b]׃ וַאֲמַרְתֶּם[c]
:say shall you (and) ?you to [1]this [2]service [is] What ; sons your

זֶבַח־פֶּסַח הוּא לַיהוָה אֲשֶׁר פָּסַח עַל־
upon over passed who ,Jehovah to [is] it passover a of sacrifice A

בָּתֵּי בְנֵי־יִשְׂרָאֵל בְּמִצְרַיִם בְּנָגְפּוֹ
smiting his at ,Egypt in Israel of children the of houses the

אֶת־מִצְרַיִם וְאֶת־בָּתֵּינוּ הִצִּיל וַיִּקֹּד הָעָם
people the bowed and ; delivered he houses our and ,Egypt

28 וַיִּשְׁתַּחֲווּ[d]׃ וַיֵּלְכוּ וַיַּעֲשׂוּ בְּנֵי
of children the did and went And .themselves prostrated and

יִשְׂרָאֵל כַּאֲשֶׁר צִוָּה יְהוָה אֶת־מֹשֶׁה
Moses Jehovah commanded had as ; Israel

וְאַהֲרֹן[e] כֵּן עָשׂוּ׃
.did they so ,Aaron and

29 וַיְהִי בַּחֲצִי הַלַּיְלָה וַיהוָה
Jehovah (and) ,night the of middle the at ,pass to came it And

הִכָּה כָל־בְּכוֹר בְּאֶרֶץ מִצְרַיִם מִבְּכֹר
of firstborn the from ; Egypt of land the in firstborn every smote

פַּרְעֹה הַיֹּשֵׁב עַל־כִּסְאוֹ עַד בְּכוֹר
of firstborn the unto ,throne his upon sitting one the ,Pharaoh

הַשְּׁבִי אֲשֶׁר בְּבֵית הַבּוֹר וְכֹל[f] בְּכוֹר
of firstborn every and ,pit the of house the in [was] who captive the

30 בְּהֵמָה[f]׃ וַיָּקָם פַּרְעֹה לַיְלָה[g] הוּא[g] וְכָל־עֲבָדָיו[h]
,servants his all and ,he ,night by Pharaoh arose And .cattle

וְכָל־מִצְרַיִם וַתְּהִי צְעָקָה גְדֹלָה בְּמִצְרָיִם[i]
,Egypt in [1]great [2]cry a was and ; Egyptians the all and

thy sons for ev-
er. 25 And it
shall come to
pass, when ye
be come to the
land which the
LORD will give
you, according
as he hath prom-
ised, that ye
shall keep this
service. 26 And
it shall come to
pass, when your
children shall
say unto you,
What mean ye
by this service?
27 that ye shall
say, It is the
sacrifice of the
LORD's pass-
over, who pass-
ed over the
houses of the
children of Is-
rael in Egypt,
when he smote
the Egyptians,
and delivered
our houses. And
the people bow-
ed the head and
worshipped. 28
And the chil-
dren of Israel
went and did
so; as the LORD
had command-
ed Moses and
Aaron, so did
they.

29 And it
came to pass at
midnight, that
the LORD smote
all the firstborn
in the land of
Egypt, from the
firstborn of Pha-
raoh that sat on
his throne unto
the firstborn of
the captive that
was in the dun-
geon; and all
the firstborn of
cattle. 30 And
Pharaoh rose up
in the night,
he, and all his
servants, and all
the Egyptians;
and there was a
great cry in E-

a G., S., V. omit היה.
b G., S., V. apparently omit.
c G., S., V. add, *to them.*
d S. adds, *before the Lord.*
e G. omits.
f G. has, *and unto the firstborn of all cattle.*
g G., V. omit הוא; S. has, *in that night.*
h G. omits כל.
i G. has, *in all the land of Egypt;* S., *in the land of Egypt.*

gypt; for *there*
was not a house
where *there was*
not one dead.
31 And he
called for Moses
and Aaron by
night, and said,
Rise up, *and*
get you forth
from among my
people, both ye
and the children
of Israel; and
go, serve the
LORD, as ye
have said. 32
Also take your
flocks and your
herds, as ye
have said, and
be gone; and
bless me also. 33
And the Egyp-
tians were ur-
gent upon the
people, that
they might send
them out of the
land in haste; for
they said, We
be all dead *men*.
34 And the peo-
ple took their
dough before it
was leavened,
their kneading-
troughs being
bound up in
their clothes up-
on their shoul-
ders. 35 And the
children of Is-
rael did accord-
ing to the word
of Moses; and
they borrowed
of the Egyp-
tians jewels of
silver, and jew-
els of gold, and
raiment: 36 And
the LORD gave
the people fa-
vour in the
sight of the E-
gyptians, so that
they lent unto
them *such*
things as they
required. And
they spoiled the
Egyptians.
37 And the
children of Is-
rael journeyed
from Rameses

כִּי־אֵין בַּיִת אֲשֶׁר אֵין־שָׁם [a] מֵת׃
.one dead a (there) not was where ,house a not was for

31 וַיִּקְרָא [b] לְמֹשֶׁה וּלְאַהֲרֹן לַיְלָה [c] וַיֹּאמֶר [d]
:said and ,night by Aaron (to) and Moses (to) called he And

קוּמוּ צְּאוּ [e] מִתּוֹךְ עַמִּי גַּם־אַתֶּם גַּם־
and you both ,people my of midst the from out go ,Arise

בְּנֵי יִשְׂרָאֵל וּלְכוּ [f] עִבְדוּ [f] אֶת־יְהוָה [g]
Jehovah serve ,go and ; Israel of children the

32 כְּדַבֶּרְכֶם׃ גַּם־צֹאנְכֶם גַּם־בְּקַרְכֶם
herds your and flocks your Both .speaking your to according

קְחוּ כַּאֲשֶׁר [h] דִּבַּרְתֶּם [h] וָלֵכוּ וּבֵרַכְתֶּם גַּם־אֹתִי׃
.me also bless and ; go and ,spoke you as ,take

33 וַתֶּחֱזַק מִצְרַיִם עַל־הָעָם לְמַהֵר לְשַׁלְּחָם
away them send to hasten to ,people the upon Egyptians the pressed And

מִן־הָאָרֶץ כִּי אָמְרוּ כֻּלָּנוּ מֵתִים׃
.die to about [are] us of All : said they for ; land the from

34 וַיִּשָּׂא הָעָם אֶת־בְּצֵקוֹ טֶרֶם יֶחְמָץ
,leavened was it before ,dough their people the up took And

מִשְׁאֲרֹתָם [i] צְרֻרֹת בְּשִׂמְלֹתָם [j] עַל־
upon clothing their in up bound being kneading-vessels their

35 שִׁכְמָם׃ [i] וּבְנֵי־יִשְׂרָאֵל עָשׂוּ כִּדְבַר [k]
of word the to according did Israel of children the And .shoulders their

מֹשֶׁה וַיִּשְׁאֲלוּ מִמִּצְרַיִם כְּלֵי־כֶסֶף
silver of vessels Egyptians the from asked they and ; Moses

36 וּכְלֵי זָהָב וּשְׂמָלֹת׃ וַיהוָה נָתַן אֶת־חֵן
favor gave Jehovah And .clothing and ,gold of vessels and

הָעָם בְּעֵינֵי מִצְרָיִם
,Egyptians the of eyes the in people the [to]

וַיַּשְׁאִלוּם וַיְנַצְּלוּ אֶת־מִצְרָיִם׃
.Egypt plundered they And ; ask to them encouraged they and

37 וַיִּסְעוּ בְנֵי־יִשְׂרָאֵל מֵרַעְמְסֵס סֻכֹּתָה
,Succoth to Ramses from Israel of children the journeyed And

gypt; for there
was not a house
where there was
not one dead.
31 And he
called for Mo-
ses and Aaron
by night, and
said, Rise up,
get you forth
from among my
people, both ye
and the children
of Israel; and
go, serve the
LORD, as ye
have said. 32
Take both your
flocks and your
herds, as ye
have said, and
be gone; and
bless me also.
33 And the E-
gyptians were
urgent upon the
people, to send
them out of the
land in haste;
for they said,
We be all dead
men. 34 And
the people took
their dough be-
fore it was
leavened, their
kneading-
troughs being
bound up in
their clothes up-
on their shoul-
ders. 35 And the
children of Is-
rael did accord-
ing to the word
of Moses; and
they asked of
the Egyptians
jewels of silver,
and jewels of
gold, and rai-
ment: 36 and
the LORD gave
the people fa-
vour in the
sight of the E-
gyptians, so that
they let them
have what they
asked. And they
spoiled the E-
gyptians.
37 And the
children of Is-
rael journeyed
from Rameses
to Succoth, a-

a G., S. have, *in it*.
b G., S. add, *Pharaoh*.
c S. has, *in that night*.
d G., S. add, *to them*.
e G. adds, *and*, ו.
f G. has, *go and serve*, לכו ועבדו; V., *go sacrifice*.
g G. adds, *your God*.
h G. omits.
i V. has, *and binding in the garments put upon their shoulders*.
j S. adds, *and put*.
k G. has, *as commanded them*; V., *as commanded*.

to Succoth, a-
bout six hun-
dred thousand
on foot *that*
were men, be-
side children.
38 And a mixed
multitude went
up also with
them; and
flocks, and
herds, *even* very
much cattle. 39
And they baked
unleavened
cakes of the
dough which
they brought
forth out of E-
gypt, for it was
not leavened;
because they
were thrust out
of Egypt, and
could not tarry,
neither had they
prepared for
themselves any
victual.

40 Now the
sojourning of
the children of
Israel, who
dwelt in Egypt,
was four hun-
dred and thirty
years. 41 And it
came to pass at
the end of the
four hundred
and thirty years,
even the self-
same day it
came to pass,
that all the
hosts of the
LORD went out
from the land of
Egypt. 42 It *is*
a night to be
much observed
unto the LORD
for bringing
them out from
the land of E-
gypt: this *is*
that night of the
LORD to be ob-
served of all the
children of Is-
rael in their
generations.
43 And the
LORD said unto
Moses and Aa-
ron, This *is* the

כְּשֵׁשׁ־מֵאוֹת אֶלֶף רַגְלִי הַגְּבָרִים לְבַד מִטָּף׃
.ones little from aside ,men the ,foot on thousand hundred six about

38 וְגַם־עֵרֶב רַב עָלָה אִתָּם
,them with up went [1]numerous [3]throng [2]mingled a also And

39 וְצֹאן וּבָקָר [a]מִקְנֶה כָּבֵד מְאֹד׃ וַיֹּאפוּ
baked they And .exceedingly heavy cattle ,herds and flocks and

אֶת־הַבָּצֵק אֲשֶׁר הוֹצִיאוּ מִמִּצְרַיִם עֻגֹת
[2]cakes [into] Egypt from out brought they which dough the

מַצּוֹת כִּי לֹא חָמֵץ כִּי־גֹרְשׁוּ[b]
out driven were they because ; leavened [2]was [1]it [3]not for ,[1]unleavened

מִמִּצְרַיִם[b] וְלֹא יָכְלוּ לְהִתְמַהְמֵהַּ וְגַם־
also and ; delay to able [2]were [1]they [3]not and ,Egypt from

צֵדָה לֹא־עָשׂוּ לָהֶם׃[c]
.themselves for made not had they journey a for food

40 וּמוֹשַׁב בְּנֵי יִשְׂרָאֵל[d] אֲשֶׁר
which ,Israel of children the of dwelling of time the And

יָשְׁבוּ בְּמִצְרָיִם[e] שְׁלֹשִׁים שָׁנָה וְאַרְבַּע מֵאוֹת[f]
hundred four and years thirty [was] ,Egypt in dwelt they

41 שָׁנָה׃ וַיְהִי מִקֵּץ שְׁלֹשִׁים שָׁנָה
years thirty of end the from ,pass to came it And .years

וְאַרְבַּע מֵאוֹת[g] שָׁנָה וַיְהִי[h] בְּעֶצֶם
(of bone the) on ,pass to came it (and) ,years hundred four and

הַיּוֹם הַזֶּה[h] יָצְאוּ כָּל־צִבְאוֹת יְהוָֹה מֵאֶרֶץ
of land the from Jehovah of hosts the all out went ,[1]this [2]day

42 מִצְרָיִם׃[i] לֵיל שִׁמֻּרִים הוּא לַיהוָֹה לְהוֹצִיאָם
out them bringing for ,Jehovah to it [is] celebration of night A .Egypt

מֵאֶרֶץ מִצְרָיִם הוּא־הַלַּיְלָה הַזֶּה לַיהוָֹה
,Jehovah to [1]this [2]night [is] it ; Egypt of land the from

שִׁמֻּרִים לְכָל־בְּנֵי יִשְׂרָאֵל לְדֹרֹתָם׃
.generations their to Israel of children the all for celebration a

43 וַיֹּאמֶר יְהוָֹה אֶל־מֹשֶׁה וְאַהֲרֹן[j] זֹאת
This : Aaron and Moses unto Jehovah said And

bout six hun-
dred thousand
on foot that
were men, be-
side chil-
dren. 38 And a
mixed multitude
went up also
with them; and
flocks, and
herds, even very
much cattle. 39
And they baked
unleavened
cakes of the
dough which
they brought
forth out of
Egypt, for it
was not leaven-
ed; because
they were thrust
out of Egypt,
and could not
tarry, neither
had they pre-
pared for them-
selves any vic-
tual.
40 Now the
sojourning of
the children of
Israel, which
they sojourned
in Egypt, was
four hundred
and thirty years.
41 And it came
to pass at the
end of four hun-
dred and thirty
years, even the
selfsame day it
came to pass,
that all the
hosts of the
LORD went out
from the land of
Egypt. 42 It is a
night to be
much observed
unto the LORD
for bringing
them out from
the land of E-
gypt: this is
that night of the
LORD, to be
much observed
of all the chil-
dren of Israel
throughout
their genera-
tions.
43 And the
LORD said unto
Moses and Aa-
ron, This is the

---

a G., S., V. add, *and*, ו.
b Sm., G., S. have, *for the Egyptians drove them out*, כִּי־גֵרְשׁוּם מצרים.
c G. adds, *for the way.*
d Sm. adds, *and their fathers.*
e G. has, *in the land of Egypt and in the land of Canaan;* so Sm. in reverse order.
f G. has, *four hundred and thirty-five.*
g G. has, *four hundred and thirty-five.*
h G. omits; S. omits ויהי.
i G. adds, *by night*, transferring from following verse.
j G. adds, *saying.*

ordinance of the
passover: There
shall no strang-
er eat thereof:
44 But every
man's servant
that is bought
for money, when
thou hast cir-
cumcised him,
then shall he
eat thereof. 45
A foreigner and
an hired serv-
ant shall not eat
thereof. 46 In
one house shall
it be eaten; thou
shalt not carry
forth ought of
the flesh abroad
out of the house:
neither shall ye
break a bone
thereof. 47 All
the congrega-
tion of Israel
shall keep it. 48
And when a
stranger shall
sojourn with
thee, and will
keep the pass-
over to the
LORD, let all
his males be cir-
cumcised, and
then let him
come near and
keep it; and he
shall be as one
that is born in
the land; for no
uncircumcised
person shall eat
thereof. 49 One
law shall be to
him that is
homeborn, and
unto the strang-
er that sojourn-
eth among you.
50 Thus did all
the children of
Israel; as the
LORD com-
manded Moses
and Aaron, so
did they. 51 And
it came to pass
the selfsame
day, *that* the
LORD did bring
the children of
Israel out of the
land of Egypt
by their armies.

חֻקַּת הַפָּסַח כָּל־בֶּן־נֵכָר לֹא־יֹאכַל
eat not may strangeness of son any ; passover the of ordinance the

44 בּוֹ׃ וְכָל־עֶבֶד אִישׁ[a] מִקְנַת־כָּסֶף
,money of purchase a ,man a of slave every And .it of

45 וּמַלְתָּה אֹתוֹ אָז יֹאכַל בּוֹ׃ תּוֹשָׁב
foreigner A .it of eat may he then ,him circumcise shalt thou (and)

46 וְשָׂכִיר לֹא־יֹאכַל בּוֹ׃ בְּבַיִת אֶחָד יֵאָכֵל
,eaten be shall it ¹one ²house In .it of eat not may servant hired a and

[b] לֹא־תוֹצִיא מִן־הַבַּיִת מִן־הַבָּשָׂר חוּצָה
; outside flesh the of [any] house the from forth carry not shalt thou

47 וְעֶצֶם לֹא תִשְׁבְּרוּ־בוֹ׃ כָּל־עֲדַת יִשְׂרָאֵל
Israel of congregation the All .it in break not shall you bone a and

48 יַעֲשׂוּ אֹתוֹ׃ וְכִי־יָגוּר[c] אִתְּךָ גֵּר
,sojourner a thee with sojourns when And .it prepare shall

וְעָשָׂה[d] פֶסַח לַיהוָֹה הִמּוֹל לוֹ
him to circumcised be let ; Jehovah to passover the prepares and

כָל־זָכָר וְאָז יִקְרַב לַעֲשֹׂתוֹ וְהָיָה
be shall he and ; it prepare to near come may he then and ,male every

כְּאֶזְרַח הָאָרֶץ וְכָל־עָרֵל[e] לֹא־יֹאכַל בּוֹ׃
.it of eat not may uncircumcised one any and ; land the of native a like

49 תּוֹרָה אַחַת יִהְיֶה לָאֶזְרָח וְלַגֵּר
,sojourner the to and ,native the to be shall ¹one ²Law

50 הַגָּר בְּתוֹכְכֶם׃ וַיַּעֲשׂוּ כָּל־בְּנֵי
of children the all did And .you of midst the in sojourning one the

יִשְׂרָאֵל כַּאֲשֶׁר צִוָּה יְהוָֹה אֶת־מֹשֶׁה וְאֶת־אַהֲרֹן[f]
,Aaron and Moses Jehovah commanded as ; Israel

51 כֵּן עָשׂוּ׃ וַיְהִי בְּעֶצֶם הַיּוֹם הַזֶּה
,¹this ²day (of bone the) on ,pass to came it And .did they so

הוֹצִיא יְהוָֹה אֶת־בְּנֵי יִשְׂרָאֵל מֵאֶרֶץ
of land the from Israel of children the Jehovah out brought

מִצְרַיִם עַל־צִבְאֹתָם[g]׃
.hosts their by Egypt

ordinance of the
passover: there
shall no alien
eat thereof: 44
but every man's
servant that is
bought for mon-
ey, when thou
hast circumcised
him, then shall
he eat thereof.
45 A sojourner
and an hired
servant shall not
eat thereof. 46 In
one house shall
it be eaten; thou
shalt not carry
forth aught of
the flesh abroad
out of the house;
neither shall ye
break a bone
thereof. 47 All
the congrega-
tion of Israel
shall keep it. 48
And when a
stranger shall
sojourn with
thee, and will
keep the pass-
over to the
LORD, let all his
males be cir-
cumcised, and
then let him
come near and
keep it; and he
shall be as one
that is born in
the land: but no
uncircumcised
person shall eat
thereof. 49 One
law shall be to
him that is
homeborn, and
unto the strang-
er that sojourn-
eth among you.
50 Thus did all
the children of
Israel; as the
LORD com-
manded Moses
and Aaron, so
did they. 51
And it came to
pass the self-
same day, that
the LORD did
bring the chil-
dren of Israel
out of the land
of Egypt by
their hosts.

---

a G. has apparently, *or*, או.
b G., S. add, *and*, ו; Sm., G., S., T., V., have pl.
c G. has, *approaches*.
d G. has, *to do*.
e G. omits ו.
f G. adds, *unto them*.
g S. has, *all*, כל.

AND the
LORD spake un-
to Moses, say-
ing, 2 Sanctify
unto me all the
firstborn, what-
soever openeth
the womb a-
mong the chil-
dren of Israel,
both of man and
of beast: it *is*
mine.
3 And Moses
said unto the
people, Re-
member this
day, in which ye
came out from
Egypt, out of
the house of
bondage; for by
strength of hand
the LORD
brought you out
from this *place:*
there shall no
leavened bread
be eaten. 4 This
day came ye out
in the month
Abib.
5 And it shall
be when the
LORD shall
bring thee into
the land of the
Canaanites, and
the Hittites, and
the Amorites,
and the Hivites,
and the Jebu-
sites, which he
sware unto thy
fathers to give
thee, a land
flowing with
milk and honey,
that thou shalt
keep this service
in this month. 6
Seven days thou
shalt eat un-
leavened bread,
and in the sev-
enth day *shall*
be a feast to the
LORD. 7 Unleav-
ened bread shall
be eaten seven
days; and there
shall no leaven-
ed bread be
seen with thee,
neither shall
there be leaven
seen with thee
in all thy quar-
ters.

13

1 2 וַיְדַבֵּר יְהוָה אֶל־מֹשֶׁה לֵּאמֹר[a]׃ קַדֶּשׁ־לִי
me to Sanctify :saying Moses unto Jehovah spoke And
כָל־בְּכוֹר פֶּטֶר כָּל־רֶחֶם בִּבְנֵי יִשְׂרָאֵל
,Israel of children the among ,womb every of opener the ,firstborn every
3 בָּאָדָם וּבַבְּהֵמָה לִי הוּא׃ וַיֹּאמֶר מֹשֶׁה
Moses said And .it [is] me to ;cattle among and men among
אֶל־הָעָם זָכוֹר אֶת־הַיּוֹם הַזֶּה אֲשֶׁר יְצָאתֶם
out went you which [in] ,¹this ²day Remember :people the unto
מִמִּצְרַיִם מִבֵּית עֲבָדִים כִּי בְּחֹזֶק יָד
hand of strength by For .slaves of house the from Egypt from
הוֹצִיא יְהוָה אֶתְכֶם מִזֶּה וְלֹא יֵאָכֵל
eaten be shall not and ;hence from you Jehovah out brought
4 חָמֵץ׃ הַיּוֹם[b] אַתֶּם יֹצְאִים בְּחֹדֶשׁ הָאָבִיב׃
.Abib of month the in ,out going [are] you Today .bread leavened
5 וְהָיָה כִי־יְבִיאֲךָ יְהוָה[c] אֶל־אֶרֶץ
of land the into Jehovah thee brings when ,be shall it And
הַכְּנַעֲנִי וְהַחִתִּי וְהָאֱמֹרִי[d] וְהַחִוִּי
,Hivites the and ,Amorites the and ,Hittites the and ,Canaanites the
וְהַיְבוּסִי אֲשֶׁר נִשְׁבַּע לַאֲבֹתֶיךָ לָתֶת לָךְ אֶרֶץ
land a ,thee to give to ,fathers thy to swore he which ,Jebusites the and
זָבַת חָלָב וּדְבָשׁ וְעָבַדְתָּ אֶת־הָעֲבֹדָה
²service keep shalt thou (and) ;honey and milk [with] (of) flowing
6 הַזֹּאת בַּחֹדֶשׁ הַזֶּה׃ שִׁבְעַת[e] יָמִים תֹּאכַל מַצֹּת
;bread unleavened eat shalt thou days Seven .¹this ²month in ¹this
7 וּבַיּוֹם הַשְּׁבִיעִי חַג לַיהוָה׃ מַצּוֹת
bread Unleavened .Jehovah to feast a ,¹seventh ²day the on and
יֵאָכֵל[f] אֵת שִׁבְעַת הַיָּמִים וְלֹא־יֵרָאֶה לְךָ
thee for seen be not shall and ;days seven the eaten be shall
חָמֵץ וְלֹא־יֵרָאֶה[g] לְךָ שְׂאֹר[g] בְּכָל־גְּבֻלֶךָ׃
.territory thy all in leaven thee for seen be not shall and ,bread leavened

And the LORD
spake unto Mo-
ses, saying, 2
Sanctify unto
me all the first-
born, whatso-
ever openeth the
womb among
the children of
Israel, both of
man and of
beast: it is
mine.
3 And Moses
said unto the
people, Re-
member this
day, in which ye
came out from
Egypt, out of
the house of
bondage; for by
strength of hand
the LORD
brought you out
from this place:
there shall no
leavened bread
be eaten. 4 This
day ye go forth
in the month
Abib.
5 And it shall
be when the
LORD shall
bring thee into
the land of the
Canaanite, and
the Hittite, and
the Amorite,
and the Hivite,
and the Jebu-
site, which he
sware unto thy
fathers to give
thee, a land
flowing with
milk and honey,
and thou shalt
keep this service
in this month. 6
Seven days thou
shalt eat un-
leavened bread,
and in the sev-
enth day shall
be a feast to the
LORD. 7 Un-
leavened bread
shall be eaten
throughout the
seven days; and
there shall no
leavened bread
be seen with
thee, neither
shall there be
leaven seen with
thee, in all thy
borders.

---

a S. omits.
b G. adds, *for*.
c G. adds, *thy God*.
d Sm. adds, *the Perizzites and the Girgashites;* so G. with changes in order; S. adds, *the Perizzites*.
e Sm., G. have, *six*, ששת.
f G., S. have, *ye shall eat*.
g S. omits; so essentially V.

8 And thou
shalt shew thy
son in that day,
saying, *This is*
done because of
that *which* the
LORD did unto
me when I came
forth out of E-
gypt. 9 And it
shall be for a
sign unto thee
upon thine
hand, and for a
memorial be-
tween thine
eyes, that the
LORD's law may
be in thy mouth:
for with a strong
hand hath the
LORD brought
thee out of E-
gypt. 10 Thou
shalt therefore
keep this or-
dinance in his
season from
year to year.

11 And it shall
be when the
LORD shall
bring thee into
the land of the
Canaanites, as
he sware unto
thee and to thy
fathers, and
shall give it
thee, 12 That
thou shalt set a-
part unto the
LORD all that
openeth the ma-
trix, and every
firstling that
cometh of a
beast which
thou hast; the
males *shall be*
the LORD's. 13
And every first-
ling of an ass
thou shalt re-
deem with a
lamb; and if
thou wilt not
redeem it, then
thou shalt break
his neck: and
all the firstborn

8 וְהִגַּדְתָּ לְבִנְךָ בַּיּוֹם הַהוּא לֵאמֹר[a] בַּעֲבוּר
of account On : saying ,[1]that [2]day on son thy to tell shalt thou And

זֶה עָשָׂה יְהוָֹה[b] לִי בְּצֵאתִי מִמִּצְרָיִם׃
.Egypt from out going my at ,me to Jehovah did [which] this

9 וְהָיָה לְךָ לְאוֹת עַל־יָדְךָ
,hand thy upon sign a (for) thee to be shall it And

וּלְזִכָּרוֹן בֵּין עֵינֶיךָ לְמַעַן תִּהְיֶה
be may that order in ; eyes thine between memorial a (for) and

תּוֹרַת יְהוָֹה בְּפִיךָ כִּי בְּיָד חֲזָקָה
[1]strong [2]hand a with for ; mouth thy in Jehovah of law the

10 הוֹצִאֲךָ יְהוָֹה[c] מִמִּצְרָיִם׃ וְשָׁמַרְתָּ
keep shalt thou And .Egypt from Jehovah out thee brought

אֶת־הַחֻקָּה[d] הַזֹּאת[d] לְמוֹעֲדָהּ[e] מִיָּמִים
(days) [year] from ,time appointed its at [1]this [2]ordinance

יָמִימָה׃
.(days) [year] to

11 וְהָיָה כִּי־יְבִאֲךָ יְהוָֹה[f] אֶל־אֶרֶץ
of land the into Jehovah thee brings when ,be shall it And

הַכְּנַעֲנִי כַּאֲשֶׁר נִשְׁבַּע לְךָ[g] וְלַאֲבֹתֶיךָ[h]
,fathers thy to and thee to swore he as ,Canaanites the

12 וּנְתָנָהּ לָךְ׃ וְהַעֲבַרְתָּ כָל־פֶּטֶר[i]
of opener every over pass to make shalt thou (and) ;thee to it gives and

רֶחֶם[j] לַיהוָֹה וְכָל־פֶּטֶר שֶׁגֶר בְּהֵמָה[k]
cattle of young the ,firstling every and ,Jehovah to womb a

13 אֲשֶׁר יִהְיֶה לְךָ הַזְּכָרִים[l] לַיהוָֹה׃ וְכָל־[m]
every And .Jehovah to [are] males the ;thee to is which

פֶּטֶר[n] חֲמֹר[n] תִּפְדֶּה[o] בְשֶׂה וְאִם־לֹא
[3]not if and ; lamb a with redeem shalt thou ass an of firstling

תִפְדֶּה[p] וַעֲרַפְתּוֹ[q] וְכֹל בְּכוֹר
of firstborn every and ;neck its break shalt thou (and) ,redeem [2]dost [1]thou

8 And thou
shalt tell thy
son in that day,
saying, It is be-
cause of that
which the LORD
did for me
when I came
forth out of E-
gypt. 9 And it
shall be for a
sign unto thee
upon thine
hand, and for a
memorial be-
tween thine
eyes, that the
law of the LORD
may be in thy
mouth: for with
a strong hand
hath the LORD
brought thee
out of Egypt. 10
Thou shalt
therefore keep
this ordinance
in its season
from year to
year.

11 And it shall
be when the
LORD shall
bring thee into
the land of the
Canaanite, as he
sware unto thee
and to thy fa-
thers, and shall
give it thee, 12
that thou shalt
set apart unto
the LORD all
that openeth the
womb, and ev-
ery firstling
which thou hast
that cometh of a
beast; the males
shall be the
LORD's. 13 And
every firstling of
an ass thou
shalt redeem
with a lamb;
and if thou wilt
not redeem it,
then thou shalt
break its neck:
and all the first-
born of man a-

---

a S. omits.
b G. adds, *God;* S., *my God.*
c G. adds, *God.*
d S. has, *this commandment and this law.*
e G. omits.
f Sm., G. add, *thy God.*
g G. omits.
h G. omits ו.
i S. adds, *firstborn.*
j G. adds, *the males.*
k G. has, *from the herds or in thy flocks.*
l G., V., T. add, *thou shalt sanctify.*
m G. omits ו.
n S. has, *and every firstborn male opening the womb of cattle.*
o G., V. have, *exchange.*
p G. has, *exchange.*
q G. has, *thou shalt redeem it.*

of man among
thy children
shalt thou re-
deem.
14 And it
shall be when
thy son asketh
thee in time to
come, saying,
What *is* this?
that thou shalt
say unto him,
By strength of
hand the LORD
brought us out
from Egypt,
from the house
of bondage: 15
And it came to
pass, when Pha-
raoh would
hardly let us go,
that the LORD
slew all the
firstborn in the
land of Egypt,
both the first-
born of man,
and the first-
born of beast:
therefore I sac-
rifice to the
LORD all that
openeth the ma-
trix, being
males; but all
the firstborn of
my children I
redeem. 16 And
it shall be for a
token upon
thine hand, and
for frontlets be-
tween thine
eyes: for by
strength of hand
the LORD
brought us forth
out of Egypt.
17 And it
came to pass,
when Pharaoh
had let the peo-
ple go, that God
led them not
through the way
of the land of
the Philistines,
although that
was near; for
God said, Lest
peradventure
the people re-
pent when they
see war, and
they return to
Egypt: 18 But
God led the peo-
ple about,
through the way

אָדָם בְּבָנֶיךָ תִּפְדֶּה׃ וְהָיָה[a] כִּי־ 14
when ,be shall it And .redeem shalt thou sons thy among men

יִשְׁאָלְךָ בִנְךָ מָחָר לֵאמֹר[b] מַה־זֹּאת
? this [is] What :saying tomorrow son thy thee asks

וְאָמַרְתָּ אֵלָיו בְּחֹזֶק יָד הוֹצִיאָנוּ
out us brought hand of strength By :him unto say shalt thou (and)

יְהוָה מִמִּצְרַיִם מִבֵּית עֲבָדִים׃ וַיְהִי[c] 15
,pass to came it And .slaves of house the from ,Egypt from Jehovah

כִּי־הִקְשָׁה פַרְעֹה לְשַׁלְּחֵנוּ וַיַּהֲרֹג
slew (and) ,away us sending against Pharaoh himself hardened when

יְהוָה[d] כָּל־בְּכוֹר בְּאֶרֶץ מִצְרַיִם מִבְּכֹר
of firstborn the from ;Egypt of land the in firstborn every Jehovah

אָדָם [e]וְעַד־בְּכוֹר בְּהֵמָה עַל־כֵּן אֲנִי
I therefore ;cattle of firstborn the unto and ,men

זֹבֵחַ[f] לַיהוָה כָּל־פֶּטֶר רֶחֶם הַזְּכָרִים
,males the ,womb a of opener every Jehovah to sacrificing [am]

וְכָל־בְּכוֹר בָּנַי אֶפְדֶּה׃ וְהָיָה לְאוֹת 16
sign a (for) be shall it And .redeem I sons my of firstborn every and

עַל־יָדְכָה וּלְטוֹטָפֹת בֵּין עֵינֶיךָ כִּי
for ;eyes thine between frontlets (for) and hand thy upon

בְּחֹזֶק יָד הוֹצִיאָנוּ[g] יְהוָה מִמִּצְרָיִם׃
.Egypt from Jehovah out us brought hand of strength by

וַיְהִי[h] בְּשַׁלַּח פַּרְעֹה אֶת־הָעָם 17
,people the [1]Pharaoh's [3]away [2]sending in ,pass to came it And

וְלֹא־נָחָם אֱלֹהִים דֶּרֶךְ אֶרֶץ
of land the of way the [by] God them lead not did (and)

פְּלִשְׁתִּים כִּי קָרוֹב הוּא כִּי אָמַר אֱלֹהִים
:God said for ;it [was] near because ,Philistines the

פֶּן־יִנָּחֵם הָעָם בִּרְאֹתָם מִלְחָמָה וְשָׁבוּ
return and ,war seeing their at people the repent Lest

מִצְרָיְמָה׃ וַיַּסֵּב אֱלֹהִים אֶת־הָעָם דֶּרֶךְ 18
of way the towards people the God turn made But .Egypt to

mong thy sons
shalt thou re-
deem.
14 And it shall
be when thy son
asketh thee in
time to come,
saying, What is
this? that thou
shalt say unto
him, By strength
of hand the
LORD brought
us out from E-
gypt, from the
house of bond-
age: 15 and it
came to pass,
when Pharaoh
would hardly let
us go, that the
LORD slew all
the firstborn in
the land of E-
gypt, both the
firstborn of man,
and the firstborn
of beast: there-
fore I sacrifice to
the LORD all
that openeth the
womb, being
males; but all
the firstborn of
my sons I re-
deem. 16 And it
shall be for a
sign upon thine
hand, and for
frontlets be-
tween thine
eyes: for by
strength of hand
the LORD
brought us forth
out of Egypt.
17 And it
came to pass,
when Pharaoh
had let the peo-
ple go, that God
led them not by
the way of the
land of the Phi-
listines, al-
though that was
near; for God
said, Lest per-
adventure the
people repent
when they see
war, and they
return to Egypt:
18 but God led
the people a-
bout, by the way

a G., S., V. omit היה.
b S. adds, *to thee.*
c G., S. omit יהי.
d G. omits.
e G., V. omit ו.
f G. adds, *every firstborn.*
g Sm., G., S. have suffix, *thee.*
h G., S., V. omit יהי.

of the wilder-
ness of the Red
sea: and the chil-
dren of Israel
went up har-
nessed out
of the land of
Egypt. 19
And Moses
took the bones
of Joseph with
him: for he had
straitly sworn
the children of
Israel, saying,
God will surely
visit you; and
ye shall carry up
my bones away
hence with you.
20 And they
took their jour-
ney from Suc-
coth, and en-
camped in E-
tham, in the
edge of the
wilderness. 21
And the LORD
went before
them by day
in a pillar
of a cloud, to
lead them the
way; and by
night in a pillar
of fire, to give
them light; to
go by day and
night: 22 He
took not away
the pillar of the
cloud by day,
nor the pillar of
fire by night,
from before the
people.

הַמִּדְבָּר יַם־סוּף וַחֲמֻשִׁים [a] עָלוּ בְנֵי־יִשְׂרָאֵל
Israel of children the up went armed and ;reeds of sea the ,wilderness the

19 מֵאֶרֶץ מִצְרָיִם׃ וַיִּקַּח מֹשֶׁה אֶת־עַצְמוֹת יוֹסֵף
Joseph of bones the Moses took And .Egypt of land the from

עִמּוֹ כִּי הַשְׁבֵּעַ הִשְׁבִּיעַ אֶת־בְּנֵי
of children the swear to made had he surely for ;him with

יִשְׂרָאֵל לֵאמֹר פָּקֹד יִפְקֹד אֱלֹהִים [b] אֶתְכֶם
,you God visit will Visiting :saying Israel

וְהַעֲלִיתֶם אֶת־עַצְמֹתַי מִזֶּה אִתְּכֶם׃
.you with hence from bones my up carry shall you and

20 וַיִּסְעוּ [c] מִסֻּכֹּת וַיַּחֲנוּ בְאֵתָם
,Etham at encamped they and ,Succoth from journeyed they And

21 בִּקְצֵה הַמִּדְבָּר׃ וַיהוָה הֹלֵךְ לִפְנֵיהֶם
them before going [was] Jehovah And .wilderness the of edge the in

יוֹמָם בְּעַמּוּד עָנָן לַנְחֹתָם הַדֶּרֶךְ וְלַיְלָה
night by and ;way the [in] them lead to ,cloud of pillar a in day by

בְּעַמּוּד אֵשׁ לְהָאִיר [d] לָהֶם לָלֶכֶת יוֹמָם וָלָיְלָה [a]׃
.night by and day by go to ,them to light give to ,fire of pillar a in

22 [e] לֹא־יָמִישׁ עַמּוּד הֶעָנָן יוֹמָם וְעַמּוּד הָאֵשׁ
fire of pillar the and ,day by cloud of pillar the cease not Did

לָיְלָה לִפְנֵי הָעָם [f]׃
.people the before ,night by

of the wilder-
ness by the Red
Sea: and the
children of Is-
rael went up
armed out of
the land of E-
gypt. 19 And
Moses took the
bones of Joseph
with him: for he
had straitly
sworn the chil-
dren of Israel,
saying, God will
surely visit you;
and ye shall
carry up my
bones away
hence with you.
20 And they
took their jour-
ney from Suc-
coth, and en-
camped in E-
tham, in the
edge of the
wilderness.
21 And the
LORD went be-
fore them by
day in a pillar of
cloud, to lead
them the way;
and by night in
a pillar of fire,
to give them
light; that they
might go by
day and by
night: 22 the
pillar of cloud
by day, and the
pillar of fire by
night, departed
not from before
the people.

14

AND the
LORD spake un-
to Moses, say-
ing, 2 Speak un-
to the children
of Israel, that
they turn and
encamp before
Pi-hahiroth, be-
tween Migdol
and the sea,
over against
Baal-zephon:
before it shall ye
encamp by the
sea. 3 For Pha-

1 2 וַיְדַבֵּר יְהוָה אֶל־מֹשֶׁה לֵּאמֹר [g]׃ דַּבֵּר אֶל־
unto Speak :saying Moses unto Jehovah spoke And

בְּנֵי יִשְׂרָאֵל וְיָשֻׁבוּ וְיַחֲנוּ לִפְנֵי
before encamp and return them let and Israel of children the

פִּי [h] הַחִירֹת [h] בֵּין מִגְדֹּל וּבֵין הַיָּם לִפְנֵי
before ;sea the (between) and Migdol between ,Hahiroth Pi

3 בַּעַל צְפֹן נִכְחוֹ תַחֲנוּ עַל־הַיָּם׃ וְאָמַר
say will And .sea the by encamp shall you it opposite ,Zephon Baal

And the LORD
spake unto Mo-
ses, saying, 2
Speak unto the
children of Is-
rael, that they
turn back and
encamp before
Pi-hahiroth, be-
tween Migdol
and the sea, be-
fore Baal-ze-
phon: over a-
gainst it shall ye
encamp by the
sea. 3 And Pha-

a Sm., G. have, *in the fifth generation.*
b G. has, *Lord,* יהוה.
c G. adds, *the sons of Israel.*
d G. omits.
e G. adds, *but,* ו.
f G. has, *all the people.*
g S. adds, *to him.*
h G. has, *farm buildings;* S., *at the mouth of the canal;* so in v. 9.

raoh will say of the children of Israel, They *are* entangled in the land, the wilderness hath shut them in. 4 And I will harden Pharaoh's heart, that he shall follow after them; and I will be honoured upon Pharaoh, and upon all his host; that the Egyptians may know that I *am* the LORD. And they did so.

5 And it was told the king of Egypt that the people fled: and the heart of Pharaoh and of his servants was turned against the people, and they said, Why have we done this, that we have let Israel go from serving us? 6 And he made ready his chariot, and took his people with him: 7 And he took six hundred chosen chariots, and all the chariots of Egypt, and captains over every one of them. 8 And the LORD hardened the heart of Pharaoh king of Egypt, and he pursued after the children of Israel: and the children of Israel went out with an high hand. 9 But the Egyptians pursued after them, all the horses

פַּרְעֹה[a] לִבְנֵי[b] יִשְׂרָאֵל נְבֻכִים
aimlessly Wandering :Israel of children the concerning Pharaoh

הֵם בָּאָרֶץ סָגַר עֲלֵיהֶם הַמִּדְבָּר׃
.wilderness the them upon shut has ,land the in they [are]

4 וְחִזַּקְתִּי[c] אֶת־לֵב־פַּרְעֹה וְרָדַף אַחֲרֵיהֶם
; you after pursue will he and ,Pharaoh of heart the harden will I And

וְאִכָּבְדָה בְּפַרְעֹה וּבְכָל־חֵילוֹ
; army his all through and ,Pharaoh through honored be will I And

וְיָדְעוּ מִצְרַיִם[d] כִּי־אֲנִי יְהוָה וַיַּעֲשׂוּ־כֵן׃
.so did they and ;Jehovah [am] I that Egyptians the know shall and

5 וַיֻּגַּד לְמֶלֶךְ מִצְרַיִם כִּי בָרַח הָעָם
; people the fled had that Egypt of king the to told was it And

וַיֵּהָפֵךְ לְבַב פַּרְעֹה וַעֲבָדָיו[e] אֶל־
servants his and Pharaoh of heart the turned was and

הָעָם וַיֹּאמְרוּ מַה־זֹּאת עָשִׂינוּ
?done have we this [is] What :said they and ; people the concerning

6 כִּי־שִׁלַּחְנוּ אֶת־יִשְׂרָאֵל מֵעָבְדֵנוּ׃ וַיֶּאְסֹר[f]
prepared he And .us serving from Israel away sent have we for

7 אֶת־רִכְבּוֹ וְאֶת־עַמּוֹ[g] לָקַח עִמּוֹ׃ וַיִּקַּח
took he And .him with took he people his and ,chariots his

שֵׁשׁ־מֵאוֹת רֶכֶב בָּחוּר וְכֹל[h] רֶכֶב[i h] מִצְרָיִם
,Egypt of chariots the all and ,chosen chariots hundred six

8 וְשָׁלִשִׁם[j] עַל־כֻּלּוֹ׃ וַיְחַזֵּק יְהוָה אֶת־לֵב
of heart the Jehovah hardened And .them of all over warriors and

פַּרְעֹה מֶלֶךְ מִצְרַיִם[k] וַיִּרְדֹּף אַחֲרֵי בְּנֵי
of children the after pursued he and ,Egypt of king Pharaoh

יִשְׂרָאֵל וּבְנֵי יִשְׂרָאֵל יֹצְאִים
out going [were] Israel of children the [while] (and) ; Israel

9 בְּיָד רָמָה׃ וַיִּרְדְּפוּ מִצְרַיִם אַחֲרֵיהֶם
,them after Egyptians the pursued And .exalted hand a with

וַיַּשִּׂיגוּ אוֹתָם חֹנִים עַל־הַיָּם[l] כָּל־סוּס
of horses the all ,sea the by encamping them overtook they and

raoh will say of the children of Israel, they are entangled in the land, the wilderness hath shut them in. 4 And I will harden Pharaoh's heart, and he shall follow after them; and I will get me honour upon Pharaoh, and upon all his host; and the Egyptians shall know that I am the LORD. And they did so.

5 And it was told the king of Egypt that the people were fled: and the heart of Pharaoh and of his servants was changed towards the people, and they said, What is this we have done, that we have let Israel go from serving us? 6 And he made ready his chariot, and took his people with him: 7 and he took six hundred chosen chariots, and all the chariots of Egypt, and captains over all of them. 8 And the LORD hardened the heart of Pharaoh king of Egypt, and he pursued after the children of Israel: for the children of Israel went out with an high hand. 9 And the Egyptians pursued after them, all the horses

---

a G. adds, *to his people.*
b G. omits ל.
c S. adds, *and said the Lord to Moses.*
d G. has, *all the Egyptians.*
e G. has, *and the heart of his servants.*
f G. adds, *Pharaoh.*
g G. has, *all his people.*
h S. has, *and all of them.*
i G. has, *horse,* סוס.
j S., T. have, *strong men.*
k G. adds, *and of his servants.*
l G. adds, *and,* ו.

and chariots of Pharaoh, and his horsemen, and his army, and overtook them encamping by the sea, beside Pi-hahiroth, before Baal-zephon.

10 And when Pharaoh drew nigh, the children of Israel lifted up their eyes, and, behold, the Egyptians marched after them; and they were sore afraid: and the children of Israel cried out unto the LORD.
11 And they said unto Moses, Because *there were* no graves in Egypt, hast thou taken us away to die in the wilderness? wherefore hast thou dealt thus with us, to carry us forth out of Egypt? 12 *Is* not this the word that we did tell thee in Egypt, saying, Let us alone, that we may serve the Egyptians? For *it had been* better for us to serve the Egyptians, than that we should die in the wilderness.

13 And Moses said unto the people, Fear ye not, stand still, and see the salvation of the LORD, which he will shew to you to day: for the Egyptians whom ye have seen to day, ye shall see them again no more for ever. 14 The

רֶכֶב[a] פַּרְעֹה וּפָרָשָׁיו וְחֵילוֹ[b] עַל־פִּי
Pi by ;army his and horsemen his and ,Pharaoh of chariots the

10 הַחִירֹת לִפְנֵי בַּעַל צְפֹן׃ וּפַרְעֹה הִקְרִיב
;near came Pharaoh And .Zephon Baal before ,Hahiroth

וַיִּשְׂאוּ בְנֵי־יִשְׂרָאֵל אֶת־עֵינֵיהֶם[c] וְהִנֵּה[d] מִצְרַיִם
Egyptians the behold and ,eyes their Israel of children the raised and

נֹסֵעַ[e] אַחֲרֵיהֶם וַיִּירְאוּ מְאֹד וַיִּצְעֲקוּ
cried and ,exceedingly feared they and ;them after marching

11 בְנֵי־יִשְׂרָאֵל אֶל־יְהוָֹה׃ וַיֹּאמְרוּ אֶל־מֹשֶׁה
:Moses unto said they And .Jehovah unto Israel of children the

הֲמִבְּלִי אֵין־קְבָרִים בְּמִצְרַיִם לְקַחְתָּנוּ
away us taken thou hast ,Egypt in graves (no) being not From

לָמוּת בַּמִּדְבָּר מַה־זֹּאת עָשִׂיתָ לָּנוּ
,us to done hast thou this [is] What ?wilderness the in die to

12 לְהוֹצִיאָנוּ מִמִּצְרָיִם׃ הֲלֹא־זֶה הַדָּבָר אֲשֶׁר
which word the this not [Is] ?Egypt from out us bring to

דִּבַּרְנוּ אֵלֶיךָ בְמִצְרַיִם לֵאמֹר[f] חֲדַל מִמֶּנּוּ
,us from Cease :saying Egypt in thee unto spoke we

וְנַעַבְדָה אֶת־מִצְרָיִם כִּי טוֹב לָנוּ עֲבֹד
serve to us for good [is it] For ?Egyptians the serve us let and

אֶת־מִצְרַיִם מִמֻּתֵנוּ בַּמִּדְבָּר[g]׃
.wilderness the in dying our than [rather] ,Egyptians the

13 וַיֹּאמֶר מֹשֶׁה אֶל־הָעָם אַל־תִּירָאוּ הִתְיַצְּבוּ
,stand your take ;fear not Do :people the unto Moses said And

וּרְאוּ אֶת־יְשׁוּעַת יְהוָֹה[h] אֲשֶׁר־יַעֲשֶׂה לָכֶם הַיּוֹם
;today you for make will he which ,Jehovah of salvation the see and

כִּי אֲשֶׁר[i] רְאִיתֶם אֶת־מִצְרַיִם הַיּוֹם לֹא תֹסִפוּ
continue [2]shall [1]you [3]not ,today Egyptians the see you as for

14 לִרְאֹתָם עוֹד עַד־עוֹלָם׃ יְהוָֹה יִלָּחֵם לָכֶם
,you for fight will Jehovah .forever again them see to

וְאַתֶּם תַּחֲרִשׁוּן[j]׃
.silent keep you [while] (and)

and chariots of Pharaoh, and his horsemen, and his army, and overtook them encamping by the sea, beside Pi-hahiroth, before Baal-zephon.

10 And when Pharaoh drew nigh, the children of Israel lifted up their eyes, and, behold, the Egyptians marched after them; and they were sore afraid: and the children of Israel cried out unto the LORD.
11 And they said unto Moses, Because there were no graves in Egypt, hast thou taken us away to die in the wilderness? wherefore hast thou dealt thus with us, to bring us forth out of Egypt? 12 Is not this the word that we spake unto thee in Egypt, saying, Let us alone, that we may serve the Egyptians? For it were better for us to serve the Egyptians, than that we should die in the wilderness.

13 And Moses said unto the people, Fear ye not, stand still, and see the salvation of the LORD, which he will work for you to-day: for the Egyptians whom ye have seen to-day, ye shall see them again no more for ever. 14 The

---

a G., V. add, *and*, ו; so essentially S.
b S. adds, *encamping*.
c Sm., G., S., V. add, *they see*.
d S., V. omit; G. omits הנה.
e Sm., G., S., T. have pl; V. omits.
f S. omits.
g G., S. add, *this*.
h G. has, *God*.
i G., S., T. apparently have כאשר.
j S. adds, *and cried Moses before the Lord*.

LORD shall fight
for you, and ye
shall hold your
peace.
15 And the
LORD said unto
Moses, Where-
fore criest thou
unto me? speak
unto the chil-
dren of Israel,
that they go for-
ward: 16 But
lift thou up thy
rod, and stretch
out thine hand
over the sea, and
divide it: and
the children of
Israel shall go
on dry *ground*
through the
midst of the
sea. 17 And I,
behold, I will
harden the
hearts of the E-
gyptians, and
they shall follow
them: and I
will get me
honour upon
Pharaoh, and
upon all his
host, upon his
chariots, and
upon his horse-
men. 18 And the
Egyptians shall
know that I *am*
the LORD, when
I have gotten
me honour up-
on Pharaoh, up-
on his chariots,
and upon his
horsemen.
19 And the
angel of God,
which went be-
fore the camp of
Israel, removed
and went be-
hind them; and
the pillar of the
cloud went from
before their
face, and stood
behind them:
20 And it came
between the
camp of the E-
gyptians and
the camp of Is-
rael; and it was
a cloud and
darkness *to*
them, but it gave

15 וַיֹּאמֶר יְהוָה אֶל־מֹשֶׁה מַה־תִּצְעַק אֵלָי

?me unto cry thou dost Why :Moses unto Jehovah said And

דַּבֵּר אֶל־בְּנֵי־יִשְׂרָאֵל וְיִסָּעוּ׃

.forward move them let and ,Israel of children the unto Speak

16 וְאַתָּה הָרֵם אֶת־מַטְּךָ וּנְטֵה אֶת־יָדְךָ עַל־

over hand thy out stretch and ,staff thy raise ,thou And

הַיָּם וּבְקָעֵהוּ וְיָבֹאוּ בְנֵי־יִשְׂרָאֵל בְּתוֹךְ

of midst the in Israel of children the go may that :it divide and ,sea the

17 הַיָּם בַּיַּבָּשָׁה׃ וַאֲנִי הִנְנִי מְחַזֵּק

harden to about [am] I behold ,I and .ground dry on sea the

אֶת־לֵב מִצְרַיִם[a] וְיָבֹאוּ אַחֲרֵיהֶם

;them after go will they and ,Egyptians the of heart the

וְאִכָּבְדָה בְּפַרְעֹה וּבְכָל־חֵילוֹ

,army his all through and ,Pharaoh through honored be will I and

18 [b]בְּרִכְבּוֹ וּבְפָרָשָׁיו׃ וְיָדְעוּ

know shall And .horsemen his through and ,chariots his through

מִצְרַיִם[c] כִּי־אֲנִי יְהוָה בְּהִכָּבְדִי

honored being my at ,Jehovah [am] I that Egyptians the

[d]בְּפַרְעֹה [e]בְּרִכְבּוֹ וּבְפָרָשָׁיו׃

.horsemen his through and ,chariots his through ,Pharaoh through

19 וַיִּסַּע מַלְאַךְ הָאֱלֹהִים הַהֹלֵךְ לִפְנֵי מַחֲנֵה

of camp the before going one the ,God of angel the withdrew And

יִשְׂרָאֵל וַיֵּלֶךְ מֵאַחֲרֵיהֶם וַיִּסַּע עַמּוּד

of pillar the withdrew and ;them behind (from) went he and ,Israel

20 הֶעָנָן מִפְּנֵיהֶם וַיַּעֲמֹד מֵאַחֲרֵיהֶם׃ וַיָּבֹא

came it And .them behind (from) stood it and ,them before from cloud

בֵּין מַחֲנֵה מִצְרַיִם וּבֵין מַחֲנֵה יִשְׂרָאֵל[f]

;Israel of camp the (between) and Egypt of camp the between

וַיְהִי הֶעָנָן[g] וְהַחֹשֶׁךְ[h] וַיָּאֶר[i] אֶת־הַלָּיְלָה[i]

.night the to light gave it and ,darkness and cloud was it and

וְלֹא־קָרַב זֶה אֶל־זֶה כָּל־הַלָּיְלָה׃

.night all one this unto one this near come not did And

LORD shall fight
for you, and ye
shall hold your
peace.
15 And the
LORD said unto
Moses, Where-
fore criest thou
unto me? speak
unto the chil-
dren of Israel,
that they go for-
ward. 16 And
lift thou up thy
rod, and stretch
out thine hand
over the sea, and
divide it: and
the children of
Israel shall go
into the midst
of the sea on
dry ground. 17
And I, behold, I
will harden the
hearts of the E-
gyptians, and
they shall go in
after them:
and I will get
me honour up-
on Pharaoh,
and upon all his
host, upon his
chariots, and
upon his horse-
men. 18 And
the Egyptians
shall know that
I am the LORD,
when I have
gotten me hon-
our upon Pha-
raoh, upon his
chariots, and
upon his horse-
men.
19 And the
angel of God,
which went be-
fore the camp of
Israel, removed
and went behind
them; and the
pillar of cloud
removed from
before them,
and stood be-
hind them: 20
and it came be-
tween the camp
of Egypt and
the camp of Is-
rael; and there
was the cloud
and the dark-
ness, yet gave it
light by night:

a G. has, *of Pharaoh and of all the Egyptians.*
b G., S., V. add, *and*, ו.
c Sm., G. have, *all the Egyptians.*
d S. adds, *and in all his host.*
e G., S., V. add, *and*, ו.
f G. adds, *and stood.*
g G. has, *darkness;* S. has, *and it gave light all night to the children of Israel;* so essentially T.
h Sm. omits ו; S. adds, *all the night;* T. adds, *to the Egyptians.*
i G. has, *and passed the night.*

light by night
to these: so that
the one came
not near the oth-
er all the night.
21 And Moses
stretched out
his hand over
the sea; and the
LORD caused the
sea to go *back*
by a strong east
wind all that
night, and made
the sea dry *land*,
and the waters
were divided. 22
And the chil-
dren of Israel
went into the
midst of the sea
upon the dry
ground: and
the waters *were*
a wall unto
them on their
right hand, and
on their left.
23 And the
Egyptians pur-
sued, and went
in after them to
the midst of the
sea, *even* all
Pharaoh's hors-
es, his chariots,
and his horse-
men. 24 And it
came to pass,
that in the
morning watch
the LORD look-
ed unto the host
of the Egyptians
through the
pillar of fire and
of the cloud,
and troubled the
host of the E-
gyptians, 25
And took off
their chariot
wheels, that
they drave them
heavily; so that
the Egyptians
said, Let us flee
from the face of
Israel; for the
LORD fighteth
for them against
the Egyptians.
26 And the
LORD said unto
Moses, Stretch
out thine hand
over the sea,
that the waters
may come again

21 וַיֵּט מֹשֶׁה אֶת־יָדוֹ עַל־הַיָּם וַיּוֹלֶךְ
go to caused and ,sea the over hand his Moses out stretched And
יְהוָה אֶת־הַיָּם בְּרוּחַ קָדִים עַזָּה כָּל־הַלַּיְלָה
; night all ,strong ,east the of wind a by sea the Jehovah
וַיָּשֶׂם אֶת־הַיָּם לֶחָרָבָה וַיִּבָּקְעוּ הַמָּיִם׃
.waters the divided were and ,land dry (for) sea the made he and
22 וַיָּבֹאוּ בְנֵי־יִשְׂרָאֵל בְּתוֹךְ הַיָּם בַּיַּבָּשָׁה
; ground dry on sea the of midst the into Israel of children the came And
וְהַמַּיִם לָהֶם חוֹמָה מִימִינָם
hand right their from wall a them to [being] waters the (and)
23 וּמִשְּׂמֹאלָם׃ [a] וַיִּרְדְּפוּ מִצְרַיִם וַיָּבֹאוּ
came and ,Egyptians the pursued And .hand left their from and
אַחֲרֵיהֶם [b] כֹּל סוּס פַּרְעֹה [c] רִכְבּוֹ וּפָרָשָׁיו
,horsemen his and ,chariots his ,Pharaoh of horses the all them after
24 אֶל־תּוֹךְ הַיָּם׃ וַיְהִי בְּאַשְׁמֹרֶת
of watch the in ,pass to came it And .sea the of midst the into
הַבֹּקֶר וַיַּשְׁקֵף יְהוָה אֶל־מַחֲנֵה מִצְרַיִם
Egyptians the of camp the upon Jehovah looked (and) ,morning the
בְּעַמּוּד אֵשׁ וְעָנָן וַיָּהָם אֵת מַחֲנֵה
of camp the confused he and ; cloud and fire of pillar the in
25 מִצְרָיִם׃ וַיָּסַר [d] אֵת אֹפַן מַרְכְּבֹתָיו
,chariots their of wheels the bound he And .Egyptians the
וַיְנַהֲגֵהוּ [e] בִּכְבֵדֻת וַיֹּאמֶר [f] מִצְרַיִם
:Egyptians the said and ; difficulty with drive them made and
אָנוּסָה [g] מִפְּנֵי יִשְׂרָאֵל כִּי יְהוָה נִלְחָם
fighting [is] Jehovah for ; Israel of face the from flee will I
לָהֶם בְּמִצְרָיִם׃
.Egyptians the against them for

26 וַיֹּאמֶר יְהוָה אֶל־מֹשֶׁה נְטֵה אֶת־יָדְךָ
hand thine out Stretch : Moses unto Jehovah said And
עַל־הַיָּם וְיָשֻׁבוּ הַמַּיִם [h] עַל־מִצְרַיִם עַל־
upon ,Egyptians the upon waters the return let and ; sea the over

and the one
came not near
the other all the
night. 21 And
Moses stretched
out his hand o-
ver the sea; and
the LORD caus-
ed the sea to go
back by a strong
east wind all the
night, and made
the sea dry land,
and the waters
were divided. 22
And the chil-
dren of Israel
went into the
midst of the sea
upon the dry
ground: and
the waters were
a wall unto them
on their right
hand, and on
their left.
23 And the
Egyptians pur-
sued, and went
in after them
into the midst
of the sea, all
Pharaoh's hors-
es, his chariots,
and his horse-
men. 24 And it
came to pass in
the morning
watch, that the
LORD looked
forth upon the
host of the
Egyptians
through the pil-
lar of fire and of
cloud, and dis-
comfited the
host of the E-
gyptians. 25
And he took off
their chariot
wheels, that they
drave them
heavily: so that
the Egyptians
said, Let us flee
from the face of
Israel; for the
LORD fighteth
for them against
the Egyptians.
26 And the
LORD said unto
Moses, Stretch
out thine hand
over the sea,
that the waters
may come a-
gain upon the

---

a G. has, *and a wall from the left;* so v. 29.
b G., V. add, *and,* ו.
c G., S. add, *and,* ו.
d Sm., G. have, *and he bound,* ויאסר; S. has, *and they bound.*
e S., T. have pl.
f Sm., G., S., T., V., have pl.
g Sm., G., S., T., V. have pl.
h G. adds, *and cover.*

upon the Egyp-
tians, upon their
chariots, and
upon their
horsemen. 27
And Moses
stretched forth
his hand over
the sea, and the
sea returned to
his strength
when the morn-
ing appeared;
and the Egyp-
tians fled a-
gainst it; and
the LORD over-
threw the Egyp-
tians in the
midst of the sea.
28 And the wa-
ters returned,
and covered the
chariots, and
the horsemen,
and all the host
of Pharaoh that
came into the
sea after them;
there remained
not so much as
one of them. 29
But the children
of Israel walked
upon dry *land*
in the midst of
the sea; and the
waters *were* a
wall unto them
on their right
hand, and on
their left.

30 Thus the
LORD saved Is-
rael that day
out of the hand
of the Egyp-
tians; and Is-
rael saw the
Egyptians dead
upon the sea
shore. 31 And
Israel saw that
great work
which the LORD
did upon the
Egyptians: and
the people fear-
ed the LORD,
and believed the
LORD, and his
servant Moses.

רִכְבּוֹ וְעַל־פָּרָשָׁיו׃ וַיֵּט מֹשֶׁה 27
Moses out stretched And .horsemen their upon and ,chariots their

אֶת־יָדוֹ עַל־הַיָּם וַיָּשָׁב הַיָּם[a] לִפְנוֹת
of turning the at ,sea the returned and ,sea the over hand his

בֹּקֶר לְאֵיתָנוֹ[b] וּמִצְרַיִם נָסִים
fleeing [were] Egyptians the [while] (and) ,flow usual its to ,morning

לִקְרָאתוֹ[c] וַיְנַעֵר יְהוָה אֶת־מִצְרַיִם בְּתוֹךְ
of midst the into Egyptians the Jehovah off shook and ; it meet to

הַיָּם׃ וַיָּשֻׁבוּ הַמַּיִם וַיְכַסּוּ אֶת־הָרֶכֶב 28
chariots the covered and ,waters the returned And .sea the

וְאֶת־הַפָּרָשִׁים לְכֹל[d] חֵיל פַּרְעֹה
,Pharaoh of army the all with together ,horsemen the and

הַבָּאִים אַחֲרֵיהֶם בַּיָּם לֹא־נִשְׁאַר[e] בָּהֶם
them among left not was ; sea the into them after going those

עַד־אֶחָד׃ וּבְנֵי יִשְׂרָאֵל הָלְכוּ בַיַּבָּשָׁה[f] 29
ground dry on walked had Israel of children the And .one even

בְּתוֹךְ הַיָּם וְהַמַּיִם לָהֶם חֹמָה[g]
,wall a them to [being] waters the (and) ,sea the of midst the in

מִימִינָם וּמִשְּׂמֹאלָם׃ וַיּוֹשַׁע יְהוָה 30
Jehovah saved And .hand left their from and hand right their from

בַּיּוֹם הַהוּא אֶת־יִשְׂרָאֵל מִיַּד מִצְרָיִם וַיַּרְא
saw and ; Egypt of hand the from Israel [1]that [2]day in

יִשְׂרָאֵל אֶת־מִצְרַיִם מֵת עַל־שְׂפַת הַיָּם׃
.sea the of shore the upon dead Egyptians the Israel

וַיַּרְא יִשְׂרָאֵל אֶת־הַיָּד הַגְּדֹלָה אֲשֶׁר עָשָׂה יְהוָה 31
Jehovah done had which ,[1]great [2]hand the Israel saw And

בְּמִצְרַיִם וַיִּירְאוּ הָעָם אֶת־יְהוָה וַיַּאֲמִינוּ
believed they and ; Jehovah people the feared and ,Egypt against

בַּיהוָה[h] וּבְמֹשֶׁה עַבְדּוֹ׃
.servant his Moses in and Jehovah in

Egyptians, up-
on their chari-
ots, and upon
their horsemen.
27 And Moses
stretched forth
his hand over
the sea, and the
sea returned
to its strength
when the morn-
ing appeared:
and the Egyp-
tians fled a-
gainst it; and
the LORD over-
threw the Egyp-
tians in the
midst of the sea.
28 And the wa-
ters returned,
and covered the
chariots, and
the horsemen,
even all the host
of Pharaoh that
went in after
them into the
sea; there re-
mained not so
much as one of
them. 29 But the
children of Is-
rael walked up-
on dry land in
the midst of the
sea; and the
waters were a
wall unto them
on their right
hand, and on
their left.

30 Thus the
LORD saved Is-
rael that day
out of the
hand of the
Egyptians; and
Israel saw the
Egyptians dead
upon the sea
shore. 31 And
Israel saw the
great work
which the LORD
did upon the
Egyptians, and
the people fear-
ed the LORD;
and they believ-
ed in the LORD,
and in his serv-
ant Moses.

---

a G. has, *the water*, המים.
b G. has, *upon* [*its*] *place;* V., *to its former place;* S. *to its place.*
c G. has, *under the water.*
d G., S. have, *and all*, וכל.
e G., S. add, *and*, ו.
f S. has, *as on dry land.*
g S. V. have, *like a wall.*
h G. has, *in God.*

15

THEN sang Moses and the children of Israel this song unto the LORD, and spake, saying, I will sing unto the LORD, for he hath triumphed gloriously: the horse and his rider hath he thrown into the sea. 2 The LORD *is* my strength and my song, and he is become my salvation: he *is* my God, and I will prepare him an habitation: my father's God, and I will exalt him. 3 The LORD *is* a man of war: the LORD *is* his name. 4 Pharaoh's chariots and his host hath he cast into the sea: his chosen captains also are drowned in the Red sea. 5 The depths have covered them: they sank into the bottom as a stone. 6 Thy right hand, O LORD, is become glorious in power: thy right hand, O LORD, hath dashed in pieces the enemy. 7 And in the greatness of thine excellency thou hast overthrown them that rose up against thee: thou sentest forth thy wrath,

1 אז ישיר־משה ובני ישראל את־השירה
[2]song Israel of children the and Moses sung Then

הזאת ליהוה[a] ויאמרו לאמר[b] אשירה[c] ליהוה
,Jehovah to sing will I :saying spoke and ,Jehovah to [1]this

כי־גאה[d] גאה סוס[d] ורכבו רמה בים:
.sea the into thrown has he rider its and horse ;exalted is he surely for

2 עזי[e] וזמרת יה[fe] ויהי־לי[g] לישועה
; salvation (for) me to become has he and ,Jah [is] song and praise My

זה אלי ואנוהו[h] אלהי אבי
father my of God the ,him glorify will I and ,God my [is] this

3 וארממנהו[h]: יהוה איש[i] מלחמה[i] יהוה
Jehovah ; war of man a [is] Jehovah .him exalt will I and

4 שמו: מרכבת פרעה וחילו ירה
cast has he army his and Pharaoh of chariots The .name his [is]

בים ומבחר[j] שלשיו טבעו[k] בים־
of sea the in drowned are warriors his of choice the and ; sea the into

5 סוף: תהמת[l] יכסימו[l] ירדו במצולת[m]
depths the into down gone have they ,them cover Floods .reeds

6 כמו־אבן: ימינך יהוה נאדרי בכח
; power in glorified [is] ,Jehovah O ,hand right Thy .stone a like

ימינך יהוה תרעץ אויב:
.enemy the pieces to dashes ,Jehovah O ,hand right thy

7 וברב[n] גאונך תהרס
down pullest thou majesty thy of greatness the in And

קמיך תשלח חרנך יאכלמו[o]
them consumes it ,wrath thy forth sendest thou ;thee against up rising those

8 כקש: וברוח[p] אפיך נערמו־מים
;waters up heaped were nostrils thy of breath the with And .stubble like

Then sang Moses and the children of Israel this song unto the LORD, and spake, saying, I will sing unto the LORD, for he hath triumphed gloriously: The horse and his rider hath he thrown into the sea. 2 The LORD is my strength and song, And he is become my salvation: This is my God, and I will praise him; My father's God, and I will exalt him. 3 The LORD is a man of war: The LORD is his name. 4 Pharaoh's chariots and his host hath he cast into the sea: And his chosen captains are sunk in the Red Sea. 5 The deeps cover them: They went down into the depths like a stone. 6 Thy right hand, O LORD, is glorious in power, Thy right hand, O LORD, dasheth in pieces the enemy. 7 And in the greatness of thine excellency thou overthrowest them that rise up against thee: Thou sendest forth thy wrath, it consumeth them as stubble. 8 And with the

a G. has, *to God.*
b S. omits.
c Sm., S., T., V. have pl.
d S. has, *glorious, who has been glorified upon the horses;* so in v. 21.
e G. has, *strength and covering.*
f S. adds, *the Lord*, יהוה.
g G. omits ו.
h S. omits ו.
i G. has, *destroying enemies;* S., *a hero and a warrior.*
j G., V. omit ו; G. adds, *horsemen.*
k S. has, *he has sunk*, טבע.
l G. has, *in the sea he covered them.*
m S. adds, *and have sunk.*
n S. omits ו.
o G., S. add, *and*, ו.
p S. omits ו.

which consum-
ed them as
stubble. 8 And
with the blast of
thy nostrils the
waters were
gathered to-
gether, the
floods stood up-
right as an heap,
and the depths
were congealed
in the heart of
the sea. 9 The
enemy said, I
will pursue, I
will overtake, I
will divide the
spoil; my lust
shall be satis-
fied upon them;
I will draw my
sword, my hand
shall destroy
them. 10 Thou
didst blow with
thy wind, the
sea covered
them: they sank
as lead in the
mighty waters.
11 Who *is* like
unto thee, O
LORD, among
the gods? who
is like thee,
glorious in holi-
ness, fearful *in*
praises, doing
wonders? 12
Thou stretch-
edst out thy
right hand, the
earth swallow-
ed them. 13
Thou in thy
mercy hast led
forth the people
which thou hast
redeemed: thou
hast guided
them in thy
strength unto
thy holy habita-
tion. 14 The
people shall
hear, *and* be a-
fraid: sorrow
shall take hold
on the inhabi-
tants of Pales-
tina. 15 Then
the dukes of
Edom shall be
amazed; the
mighty men of
Moab, trem-
bling shall take
hold upon
them: all the in-

נִצְּבוּ כְמוֹ־נֵד נֹזְלִים קָפְאוּ תְהֹמֹת
floods curdled ;[waters] running the wall a like stood

9 בְּלֶב־יָם׃ אָמַר אוֹיֵב אֶרְדֹּף
,pursue will I : enemy the Said .sea the of heart the in

[a]אַשִּׂיג [a]אֲחַלֵּק שָׁלָל [a]תִּמְלָאֵמוֹ נַפְשִׁי
,soul my them [with] filled be shall ; plunder divide will ,overtake will

10 אָרִיק חַרְבִּי תּוֹרִישֵׁמוֹ יָדִי׃ נָשַׁפְתָּ
blow didst Thou .hand my them destroy shall ,sword my draw will I

בְרוּחֲךָ [b]כִּסָּמוֹ יָם צָלֲלוּ כַּעוֹפֶרֶת
lead like sank they ;sea the them covered ,wind thy with

11 בְּמַיִם אַדִּירִים׃ מִי־כָמֹכָה [c]בָּאֵלִם יְהוָה
?Jehovah O ,gods the among thee like [is] Who .[1]mighty [2]waters in

מִי כָּמֹכָה נֶאְדָּר בַּקֹּדֶשׁ נוֹרָא [d]תְהִלֹּת
,praises [in] fearful ,holiness in glorified ,thee like [is] Who

12 [e]עֹשֵׂה־פֶלֶא׃ נָטִיתָ יְמִינְךָ [f]תִּבְלָעֵמוֹ
them swallows ,hand right thy out stretchedst Thou ? wonders of doer

13 אָרֶץ׃ נָחִיתָ בְחַסְדְּךָ עַם־זוּ
whom people the mercy thy in leddest Thou .earth the

גָּאָלְתָּ נֵהַלְתָּ בְעָזְּךָ אֶל־נְוֵה
of habitation the unto strength thy in guidedst thou ; redeemed hadst thou

14 קָדְשֶׁךָ׃ שָׁמְעוּ עַמִּים [g]יִרְגָּזוּן [h]חִיל אָחַז
seized trembling ; tremble they ,peoples Heard .holiness thy

15 יֹשְׁבֵי פְּלָשֶׁת׃ אָז נִבְהֲלוּ אַלּוּפֵי
of princes the confounded were Then .Philistia of inhabitants the

אֱדוֹם אֵילֵי מוֹאָב יֹאחֲזֵמוֹ רָעַד נָמֹגוּ
melted were ;shaking them seizes ,Moab of leaders the ; Edom

16 כֹּל יֹשְׁבֵי כְּנָעַן׃ תִּפֹּל עֲלֵיהֶם אֵימָתָה
terror them upon Fall .Canaan of inhabitants the all

וָפַחַד בִּגְדֹל זְרוֹעֲךָ יִדְּמוּ כָּאָבֶן
; stone a as silent are they arm thine of greatness the by ,anguish and

עַד־יַעֲבֹר עַמְּךָ יְהוָה עַד־יַעֲבֹר
through pass until ,Jehovah O ,people thy through pass until

blast of thy
nostrils the wa-
ters were piled
up, The floods
stood upright as
an heap; The
deeps were con-
gealed in the
heart of the sea.
9 The enemy
said, I will pur-
sue, I will over-
take, I will
divide the spoil:
My lust shall be
satisfied upon
them; I will
draw my sword,
my hand shall
destroy them.
10 Thou didst
blow with thy
wind, the sea
covered them:
They sank as
lead in the
mighty waters.
11 Who is like
unto thee, O
LORD, among
the gods? Who
is like thee, glo-
rious in holi-
ness, Fearful in
praises, doing
wonders? 12
Thou stretch-
edst out thy
right hand, The
earth swallowed
them. 13 Thou
in thy mercy
hast led the
people which
thou hast re-
deemed: Thou
hast guided
them in thy
strength to thy
holy habitation.
14 The peoples
have heard, they
tremble: Pangs
have taken hold
on the inhabi-
tants of Philis-
tia. 15 Then
were the dukes
of Edom a-
mazed; The
mighty men of
Moab, trem-
bling taketh
hold upon them:
All the inhabi-
tants of Canaan
are melted a-
way. 16 Terror
and dread fall-
eth upon them;

a S., V. add, *and*, ו.
b S., V. add, *and*, ו.
c S. omits.
d S., V. have, *and praiseworthy*.
e S. adds, *and*, ו.
f S., V. add, *and*, ו.
g G., S., V. add, *and*, ו.
h S. adds, *and*, ו

habitants of
Canaan shall
melt away. 16
Fear and dread
shall fall upon
them; by the
greatness of
thine arm they
shall be *as* still
as a stone; till
thy people pass
over, O LORD,
till the people
pass over,
which thou
hast purchased.
17 Thou shalt
bring them in,
and plant them
in the mountain
of thine inher-
itance, *in* the
place, O LORD,
which thou hast
made for thee to
dwell in, *in* the
Sanctuary, O
LORD, *which*
thy hands have
established. 18
The LORD shall
reign for ever
and ever. 19
For the horse of
Pharaoh went
in with his char-
iots and with his
horsemen into
the sea, and the
LORD brought
again the wa-
ters of the sea
upon them; but
the children of
Israel went on
dry *land* in the
midst of the sea.
20 And Mir-
iam the proph-
etess, the sister
of Aaron, took
a timbrel in her
hand; and all
the women went
out after her
with timbrels
and with dan-
ces. 21 And
Miriam answer-
ed them, Sing
ye to the LORD,
for he hath
triumphed glo-
riously; the
horse and his
rider hath he
thrown into the
sea. 22 So Mo-
ses brought Is-
rael from the

17 עַם־זוּ קָנִיתָ׃ תְּבִאֵמוֹ
,in them bringest Thou .acquired hast thou whom people the

וְתִטָּעֵמוֹ בְּהַר נַחֲלָתְךָ מָכוֹן
place the ; inheritance thine of mountain the in them plantest and

לְשִׁבְתְּךָ פָּעַלְתָּ יְהוָה מִקְּדָשׁ
,sanctuary the ; Jehovah O ,made hast thou dwelling thy for [which]

18 אֲדֹנָי כּוֹנְנוּ יָדֶיךָ׃ יְהוָה ׀ יִמְלֹךְ
reigns Jehovah .hands thy prepared have [which] ,Lord O

19 לְעֹלָם וָעֶד[a]׃ כִּי בָא סוּס פַּרְעֹה
Pharaoh of horses the in went For .ever and ever for

בְּרִכְבּוֹ וּבְפָרָשָׁיו בַּיָּם וַיָּשֶׁב
back brought and ,sea the into horsemen his and chariots his with

יְהוָה עֲלֵהֶם אֶת־מֵי הַיָּם וּבְנֵי
of children the and ; sea the of waters the them upon Jehovah

יִשְׂרָאֵל הָלְכוּ בַיַּבָּשָׁה בְּתוֹךְ הַיָּם׃
.sea the of midst the in ground dry on went Israel

20 וַתִּקַּח מִרְיָם הַנְּבִיאָה אֲחוֹת אַהֲרֹן
,Aaron of sister the ,prophetess the Miriam took And

אֶת־הַתֹּף בְּיָדָהּ וַתֵּצֶאןָ כָל־הַנָּשִׁים אַחֲרֶיהָ
her after women the all out went and ; hand her in timbrel the

21 בְּתֻפִּים וּבִמְחֹלֹת׃ וַתַּעַן לָהֶם מִרְיָם[b]
: Miriam them to answered And .dances with and timbrels with

שִׁירוּ לַיהוָה כִּי־גָאֹה גָּאָה סוּס וְרֹכְבוֹ
rider its and horse ,exalted is he surely for ,Jehovah to Sing

רָמָה בַיָּם׃
.sea the into thrown has he

22 וַיַּסַּע מֹשֶׁה אֶת־יִשְׂרָאֵל מִיַּם־סוּף
,reeds of sea the from Israel Moses journey to caused And

וַיֵּצְאוּ[c] אֶל־מִדְבַּר־שׁוּר וַיֵּלְכוּ[d]
went they and ; Shur of wilderness the into out went they and

23 שְׁלֹשֶׁת־יָמִים בַּמִּדְבָּר וְלֹא־מָצְאוּ מָיִם[e]׃ וַיָּבֹאוּ
came they And .water find not did and ,wilderness the in days three

By the greatness
of thine arm
they are as still
as a stone; Till
thy people pass
over, O LORD,
Till the people
pass over which
thou hast pur-
chased. 17 Thou
shalt bring them
in, and plant
them in the
mountain of
thine inher-
itance, The
place, O LORD,
which thou hast
made for thee to
dwell in, The
sanctuary, O
LORD, which
thy hands have
established. 18
The LORD shall
reign for ever
and ever. 19 For
the horses of
Pharaoh went
in with his char-
iots and with
his horsemen
into the sea,
and the LORD
brought again
the waters of
the sea upon
them; but the
children of Is-
rael walked on
dry land in the
midst of the
sea.
20 And Mir-
iam the proph-
etess, the sister
of Aaron, took
a timbrel in her
hand; and all
the women went
out after her
with timbrels
and with dances.
21 And Miriam
answered them,
Sing ye to the
LORD, for he
hath triumphed
gloriously; The
horse and his
rider hath he
thrown into the
sea. 22 And Mo-
ses led Israel on-
ward from the
Red Sea, and
they went out in-
to the wilder-
ness of Shur;
and they went

a G. has, *and still*, וְעֹד.

b G., V. add, *saying*.

c Sm., G. have, *and he led them*, וַיּוֹצִאֵהוּ.

d Sm. adds, *a journey of*, דרך; so S. essentially; cf. Num. 33: 8.

e G. adds, *so as to drink*.

Red sea, and
they went out
into the wilder-
ness of Shur;
and they went
three days in the
wilderness, and
found no water.
23 And when
they came to
Marah, they
could not drink
of the waters of
Marah, for they
were bitter:
therefore the
name of it was
called Marah.
24 And the peo-
ple murmured
against Moses,
saying, What
shall we drink?
25 And he cried
unto the LORD;
and the LORD
shewed him a
tree, *which*
when he had
cast into the
waters, the wa-
ters were made
sweet: there he
made for them
a statute and an
ordinance, and
there he proved
them, 26 And
said, If thou
wilt diligently
hearken to the
voice of the
LORD thy God,
and wilt do that
which is right
in his sight, and
wilt give ear to
his command-
ments, and keep
all his statutes,
I will put none
of these diseases
upon thee,
which I have
brought upon
the Egyptians:
for I *am* the
LORD that heal-
eth thee.
27 And they
came to Elim,
where *were*
twelve wells of
water, and
threescore and
ten palm trees:
and they en-
camped there
by the waters.
AND they

מָרָ֫תָה וְלֹא יָֽכְלוּ לִשְׁתֹּת מַ֫יִם [a] מִמָּרָה
,Marah from water drink to able ²were ¹they ³not and ,Marah to

כִּי מָרִים הֵם עַל־כֵּן קָרָא־שְׁמָהּ [b] מָרָה׃
.Marah name its called one therefore ; it [was] bitter for

וַיִּלֹּנוּ הָעָם עַל־מֹשֶׁה לֵּאמֹר [c] מַה־נִּשְׁתֶּה׃ 24
? drink we shall What : saying Moses against people the murmured And

וַיִּצְעַק [d] אֶל־יְהוָה וַיּוֹרֵהוּ יְהוָה עֵץ 25
,tree a Jehovah him showed and ,Jehovah unto cried he And

וַיַּשְׁלֵךְ אֶל־הַמַּיִם וַיִּמְתְּקוּ הַמָּיִם שָׁם שָׂם
put he There .water the sweet became and ,water the into cast he and

לוֹ חֹק וּמִשְׁפָּט וְשָׁם נִסָּהוּ׃
; them tried he there and ,ordinance an and statute a them for

וַיֹּאמֶר [e] אִם־שָׁמוֹעַ תִּשְׁמַע לְקוֹל יְהוָה 26
Jehovah of voice the to hearkenest thou hearkening If : said he and

אֱלֹהֶיךָ וְהַיָּשָׁר בְּעֵינָיו תַּעֲשֶׂה וְהַאֲזַנְתָּ
ear givest thou and ,doest thou eyes his in right the and ,God thy

לְמִצְוֹתָיו וְשָׁמַרְתָּ כָּל־חֻקָּיו כָּל־הַמַּחֲלָה
diseases the all ; statutes his all keepest and ,commandments his to

אֲשֶׁר־שַׂמְתִּי בְמִצְרַיִם לֹא־אָשִׂים עָלֶיךָ כִּי אֲנִי
I for ;thee upon put not will I Egypt on put I which

יְהוָה [f] רֹפְאֶךָ׃
.healer thy Jehovah [am]

וַיָּבֹאוּ אֵילִמָה וְשָׁם שְׁתֵּים עֶשְׂרֵה 27
ten [and] two [being] there (and) ,Elim to came they And

עֵינֹת מַיִם וְשִׁבְעִים תְּמָרִים וַיַּחֲנוּ־שָׁם
there encamped they and ;trees palm seventy and ,water of springs

עַל־הַמָּיִם׃
.waters the by

16

וַיִּסְעוּ מֵאֵילִם וַיָּבֹאוּ כָּל־עֲדַת 1
of congregation the all came and ,Elim from journeyed they And

three days in the
wilderness, and
found no water.
23 And when
they came to
Marah, they
could not drink
of the waters of
Marah, for they
were bitter:
therefore the
name of it was
called Marah. 24
And the people
murmured a-
gainst Moses,
saying, What
shall we drink?
25 And he cried
unto the LORD;
and the LORD
shewed him a
tree, and he cast
it into the wa-
ters, and the
waters were
made sweet.
There he made
for them a
statute and an
ordinance, and
there he proved
them; 26 and he
said, If thou
wilt diligently
hearken to the
voice of the
LORD thy God,
and wilt do that
which is right in
his eyes, and
wilt give ear to
his command-
ments, and keep
all his statutes,
I will put none
of the diseases
upon thee,
which I have
put upon the
Egyptians: for
I am the LORD
that healeth
thee.
27 And they
came to Elim,
where were
twelve springs
of water, and
threescore and
ten palm trees:
and they en-
camped there by
the waters.

And they took
their journey
from Elim, and
all the congre-

---

a G. omits.
b G., S. have, *the name of that place*.
c S. adds, *to him*.
d Sm., G., S. add, *Moses*.
e S. adds, *to him*.
f G. adds, *thy God*.

took their jour-
ney from Elim,
and all the con-
gregation of the
children of Is-
rael came unto
the wilderness
of Sin, which *is*
between Elim
and Sinai, on
the fifteenth
day of the
second month
after their de-
parting out of
the land of E-
gypt. 2 And the
whole congre-
gation of the
children of Is-
rael murmured
against Moses
and Aaron in
the wilderness:
3 And the chil-
dren of Israel
said unto them,
Would to God
we had died by
the hand of the
LORD in the
land of Egypt,
when we sat by
the flesh pots,
and when we
did eat bread to
the full; for ye
have brought us
forth into this
wilderness, to
kill this whole
assembly with
hunger.
4 Then said
the LORD unto
Moses, Behold,
I will rain bread
from heaven for
you; and the
people shall go
out and gather
a certain rate
every day, that
I may prove
them, whether
they will walk
in my law, or
no. 5 And it
shall come to
pass, that on
the sixth day
they shall pre-
pare *that* which
they bring in;
and it shall be
twice as much
as they gather
daily. 6 And Mo-

בְּנֵי־יִשְׂרָאֵל אֶל־מִדְבַּר־סִין אֲשֶׁר בֵּין־
between [is] which ,Sin of wilderness the unto ; Israel of children the
אֵילִם וּבֵין סִינָי [a]בַּחֲמִשָּׁה עָשָׂר יוֹם
day tenth [and] five the on ; Sinai (between) and Elim
לַחֹדֶשׁ הַשֵּׁנִי [b]לְצֵאתָם מֵאֶרֶץ מִצְרָיִם׃
.Egypt of land the from out going their to [1]second [2]month the to
2 [c]וַיִּלִּינוּ כָּל־עֲדַת בְּנֵי־יִשְׂרָאֵל עַל־
against Israel of children the of congregation the all murmured And
3 מֹשֶׁה וְעַל־אַהֲרֹן בַּמִּדְבָּר׃[d] וַיֹּאמְרוּ אֲלֵהֶם
them unto said And .wilderness the in Aaron against and Moses
בְּנֵי יִשְׂרָאֵל מִי־יִתֵּן מוּתֵנוּ בְיַד־
of hand the by died had we that Would :Israel of children the
יְהוָה בְּאֶרֶץ מִצְרַיִם בְּשִׁבְתֵּנוּ עַל־סִיר
of pots the by sitting our in ,Egypt of land the in Jehovah
הַבָּשָׂר [e]בְּאָכְלֵנוּ לֶחֶם לָשֹׂבַע כִּי־הוֹצֵאתֶם
out brought have you for ; satisfaction to bread eating our in ,flesh
אֹתָנוּ אֶל־הַמִּדְבָּר הַזֶּה לְהָמִית אֶת־כָּל־הַקָּהָל הַזֶּה[f]
[1]this [2]assembly all slay to ,[1]this [2]wilderness into us
בָּרָעָב׃
.famine with

4 וַיֹּאמֶר יְהוָה אֶל־מֹשֶׁה הִנְנִי מַמְטִיר
rain to about [am] I Behold : Moses unto Jehovah said And
לָכֶם לֶחֶם מִן־הַשָּׁמַיִם וְיָצָא הָעָם
people the out go shall and ; heavens the from bread you for
וְלָקְטוּ [g]דְּבַר־יוֹם בְּיוֹמוֹ לְמַעַן אֲנַסֶּנּוּ
,them try may I that order in ;day its in day a of matter the ,up pick and
5 הֲיֵלֵךְ בְּתוֹרָתִי אִם־לֹא׃ וְהָיָה
,pass to come shall it and .not or law my in walk will they whether
בַּיּוֹם הַשִּׁשִּׁי וְהֵכִינוּ אֵת אֲשֶׁר־יָבִיאוּ
;in bring they what prepare shall they (and) ,[1]sixth [2]day the on
וְהָיָה מִשְׁנֶה עַל אֲשֶׁר־יִלְקְטוּ יוֹם יוֹם׃
.day [by] day up pick they what upon double be shall it and

gation of the
children of Is-
rael came unto
the wilderness
of Sin, which is
between Elim
and Sinai, on
the fifteenth day
of the second
month after
their departing
out of the land
of Egypt. 2 And
the whole con-
gregation of the
children of Is-
rael murmured
against Moses
and against Aa-
ron in the wil-
derness: 3 and
the children of
Israel said unto
them, Would
that we had
died by the
hand of the
LORD in the
land of Egypt,
when we sat by
the flesh pots,
when we did eat
bread to the
full; for ye have
brought us forth
into this wilder-
ness, to kill this
whole assembly
with hunger.
4 Then said
the LORD unto
Moses, Behold,
I will rain bread
from heaven for
you; and the
people shall go
out and gather
a day's portion
every day, that
I may prove
them, whether
they will walk
in my law, or
no. 5 And it
shall come to
pass on the
sixth day, that
they shall pre-
pare that which
they bring in,
and it shall be
twice as much
as they gather
daily. 6 And

a G. adds, *but*, ו.
b S. has, *in the time in which went forth the children of Israel.*
c G. omits ו.
d G. omits.
e G., S., T., V. add, *and*, ו.
f S. has, *of the children of Israel;* V. omits.
g S. has, *food.*

ses and Aaron said unto all the children of Israel, At even, then ye shall know that the LORD hath brought you out from the land of Egypt: 7 And in the morning, then ye shall see the glory of the LORD; for that he heareth your murmurings against the LORD: and what *are* we, that ye murmur against us? 8 And Moses said, *This shall be*, when the LORD shall give you in the evening flesh to eat, and in the morning bread to the full; for that the LORD heareth your murmurings which ye murmur against him: and what *are* we? your murmurings *are* not against us, but against the LORD.

9 And Moses spake unto Aaron, Say unto all the congregation of the children of Israel, Come near before the LORD: for he hath heard your murmurings. 10 And it came to pass, as Aaron spake unto the whole congregation of the children of Israel, that they looked toward the wilderness, and, behold, the glory of the LORD appeared in the cloud.

11 And the LORD spake unto Moses, saying, 12 I have

6 וַיֹּאמֶר מֹשֶׁה וְאַהֲרֹן אֶל־כָּל־בְּנֵי[a] יִשְׂרָאֵל
; Israel of children the all unto Aaron and Moses said And

עֶרֶב וִידַעְתֶּם[b] כִּי יְהוָה הוֹצִיא
out brought has Jehovah that know shall you (and) ,evening At

7 אֶתְכֶם מֵאֶרֶץ מִצְרָיִם׃ וּבֹקֶר
,morning the in and ; Egypt of land the from you

וּרְאִיתֶם[c] אֶת־כְּבוֹד יְהוָה בְּשָׁמְעוֹ
hearing his in ,Jehovah of glory the see shall you (and)

אֶת־תְּלֻנֹּתֵיכֶם עַל־יְהוָה[d] וְנַחְנוּ מָה כִּי תַלּוֹנוּ
murmur you that ,what ,we and ; Jehovah against murmurings your

8 עָלֵינוּ׃ וַיֹּאמֶר[e] מֹשֶׁה בְּתֵת יְהוָה לָכֶם
you to ¹Jehovah's ²giving In : Moses said And ? us against

בָּעֶרֶב בָּשָׂר לֶאֱכֹל וְלֶחֶם בַּבֹּקֶר
morning the in bread and ,eat to flesh evening the in

לִשְׂבֹּעַ בִּשְׁמֹעַ יְהוָה אֶת־תְּלֻנֹּתֵיכֶם אֲשֶׁר־
which murmurings your ¹Jehovah's ²hearing in ; satisfaction to

אַתֶּם מַלִּינִם עָלָיו[f] וְנַחְנוּ מָה[g] לֹא־עָלֵינוּ
us against not ? what ,we and ; him against murmuring [are] you

9 תְלֻנֹּתֵיכֶם כִּי עַל־יְהוָה[h]׃ וַיֹּאמֶר מֹשֶׁה אֶל־
unto Moses said And .Jehovah against but ,murmurings your

אַהֲרֹן אֱמֹר אֶל־כָּל־עֲדַת בְּנֵי יִשְׂרָאֵל
; Israel of children the of congregation the all unto Say : Aaron

קִרְבוּ לִפְנֵי יְהוָה כִּי שָׁמַע[i] אֵת תְּלֻנֹּתֵיכֶם׃
.murmurings your heard has he for ;Jehovah before near Come

10 וַיְהִי[j] כְּדַבֵּר אַהֲרֹן אֶל־כָּל־עֲדַת
of congregation the all unto ¹Aaron's ²speaking at ,pass to came it And

בְּנֵי־יִשְׂרָאֵל וַיִּפְנוּ אֶל־הַמִּדְבָּר
; wilderness the towards turned they (and) ,Israel of children the

וְהִנֵּה[k] כְּבוֹד יְהוָה נִרְאָה בֶּעָנָן׃
.cloud the in appeared Jehovah of glory the behold and

11 12 וַיְדַבֵּר יְהוָה אֶל־מֹשֶׁה לֵּאמֹר[l]׃ שָׁמַעְתִּי
heard have I :saying ,Moses unto Jehovah spoke And

Moses and Aaron said unto all the children of Israel, At even, then ye shall know that the LORD hath brought you out from the land of Egypt: 7 and in the morning, then ye shall see the glory of the LORD; for that he heareth your murmurings against the LORD: and what are we, that ye murmur against us? 8 And Moses said, *This shall be*, when the LORD shall give you in the evening flesh to eat, and in the morning bread to the full; for that the LORD heareth your murmurings which ye murmur against him: and what are we? your murmurings are not against us, but against the LORD.

9 And Moses said unto Aaron, Say unto all the congregation of the children of Israel, Come near before the LORD: for he hath heard your murmurings. 10 And it came to pass, as Aaron spake to the whole congregation of the children of Israel, that they looked toward the wilderness, and, behold, the glory of the LORD appeared in the cloud.

11 And the LORD spake unto Moses, saying, 12 I have

a G. has, *unto all the congregation*.
b Sm., G., V., S. omit ו.
c Sm., G., S., V. omit ו.
d G. has, *God*.
e S. adds, *to them*.
f G. has, *against us*.
g G. adds, *for*.
h G. adds, *God*.
i S. adds, *the Lord*, יהוה; so essentially T.
j G., V. omit יהי.
k G. omits הנה.
l S. omits.

heard the mur-
murings of the
children of Is-
rael: speak un-
to them, saying,
At even ye shall
eat flesh, and in
the morning ye
shall be filled
with bread; and
ye shall know
that I *am* the
LORD your God.
13 And it came
to pass, that at
even the quails
came up, and
covered the
camp: and in
the morning the
dew lay round
about the host.
14 And when
the dew that
lay was gone up,
behold, upon
the face of the
wilderness *there*
lay a small
round thing, *as*
small as the
hoar frost on
the ground. 15
And when the
children of Is-
rael saw *it*, they
said one to an-
other, It *is* man-
na: for they
wist not what it
was. And Mo-
ses said unto
them, This *is*
the bread which
the LORD hath
given you to
eat.

16 This *is* the
thing which the
LORD hath com-
manded, Gather
of it every man
according to his
eating, an omer
for every man,
according to the
number of your
persons: take ye
every man for
them which *are*
in his tents. 17
And the chil-
dren of Israel
did so, and gath-

אֶת־תְּלוּנֹּת בְּנֵי יִשְׂרָאֵל דַּבֵּר אֲלֵהֶם
them unto speak ; Israel of children the of murmurings the

לֵאמֹר[a] בֵּין הָעַרְבַּיִם תֹּאכְלוּ בָשָׂר
,flesh eat shall you evenings the Between : saying

וּבַבֹּקֶר תִּשְׂבְּעוּ־לָחֶם וִידַעְתֶּם
know shall you and ; bread [with] satisfied be shall you morning the in and

כִּי אֲנִי יְהוָה אֱלֹהֵיכֶם׃ וַיְהִי 13
,pass to came it And .God your Jehovah [am] I that

[b]בָּעֶרֶב וַתַּעַל הַשְּׂלָו וַתְּכַס אֶת־הַמַּחֲנֶה
; camp the covered and quail the up came (and) ,evening the in

[c]וּבַבֹּקֶר הָיְתָה שִׁכְבַת הַטַּל סָבִיב לַמַּחֲנֶה׃
.camp the (to) around dew of layer a was morning the in and

[d]וַתַּעַל שִׁכְבַת הַטָּל[d] וְהִנֵּה עַל־פְּנֵי 14
of face the upon behold and ,dew of layer the up went And

הַמִּדְבָּר דַּק[e] מְחֻסְפָּס[f] דַּק כַּכְּפֹר
hoar-frost the like small ,scale-like ,small [something] wilderness the

עַל־הָאָרֶץ׃ וַיִּרְאוּ בְנֵי־יִשְׂרָאֵל וַיֹּאמְרוּ 15
,said they and ,Israel of children the saw And .earth the upon

אִישׁ אֶל־אָחִיו מָן הוּא כִּי לֹא יָדְעוּ
know [2]did [1]they [3]not for ? that [is] What : brother his unto one each

מַה־הוּא וַיֹּאמֶר מֹשֶׁה אֲלֵהֶם הוּא הַלֶּחֶם
bread the [is] That : them unto Moses said And .[was] it what

אֲשֶׁר נָתַן יְהוָה לָכֶם לְאָכְלָה׃ [g]זֶה הַדָּבָר 16
thing the [is] This .food for you to Jehovah given has which

אֲשֶׁר צִוָּה יְהוָה לִקְטוּ מִמֶּנּוּ אִישׁ
one each ,it from up Pick : Jehovah commanded has which

לְפִי אָכְלוֹ עֹמֶר לַגֻּלְגֹּלֶת
,head a for omer an ; eating his of mouth the to according

מִסְפַּר נַפְשֹׁתֵיכֶם אִישׁ לַאֲשֶׁר[h] בְּאָהֳלוֹ[h]
tent his in [are] who those for one each ,souls your of number the [by]

תִּקָּחוּ׃ וַיַּעֲשׂוּ־כֵן בְּנֵי יִשְׂרָאֵל וַיִּלְקְטוּ 17
,up picked they and ; Israel of children the so did And .take shall you

heard the
murmurings of
the children of
Israel: speak un-
to them, say-
ing, At even ye
shall eat flesh,
and in the morn-
ing ye shall be
filled with
bread; and ye
shall know that
I am the LORD
your God. 13
And it came to
pass at even,
that the quails
came up, and
covered the
camp: and in
the morning the
dew lay round
about the camp.
14 And when the
dew that lay
was gone up,
behold, upon
the face of the
wilderness a
small round
thing, small as
the hoar frost
on the ground.
15 And when
the children of
Israel saw it,
they said one to
another, What
is it? for they
wist not what it
was. And Moses
said unto them,
It is the bread
which the LORD
hath given you
to eat.

16 This is the
thing which the
LORD hath com-
manded, Gather
ye of it every
man according
to his eating; an
omer a head,
according to the
number of your
persons, shall
ye take it, every
man for them
which are in his
tent. 17 And the
children of Is-
rael did so, and
gathered some

---

a S., V. omit.
b G. omits ב.
c G. omits וב.
d G. omits; so apparently V.
e S., V. add, *and*, ו; G., has, *like coriander;* cf. v. 31.
f G. has, *white;* S., *and formed;* V. apparently omits.
g S. adds, *and*, ו.
h G. has, *with those in his tent.*

ered, some
more, some less.
18 And when
they did mete *it*
with an omer,
he that gathered
much had noth-
ing over, and he
that gathered
little had no
lack; they gath-
ered every
man according
to his eating. 19
And Moses said,
Let no man
leave of it till
the morning. 20
Notwithstand-
ing they heark-
ened not unto
Moses; but
some of them
left of it until the
morning, and it
bred worms,
and stank: and
Moses was
wroth with
them. 21 And
they gathered it
every morning,
every man ac-
cording to his
eating: and
when the sun
waxed hot, it
melted.
22 And it
came to pass,
that on the
sixth day they
gathered twice
as much bread,
two omers for
one *man*: and
all the rulers of
the congrega-
tion came and
told Moses. 23
And he said un-
to them, This
is that which
the LORD hath
said, To mor-
row *is* the rest
of the holy sab-
bath unto the
LORD: bake *that*
which ye will
bake *to day*, and
seethe that
ye will
seethe; and
that which
remaineth over
lay up for you
to be kept until
the morning. 24
And they laid it
up till the morn-
ing, as Moses

הַמַּרְבֶּה וְהַמַּמְעִיט׃ וַיָּמֹדּוּ 18
measured they And .few making one the and much making one the

בָעֹמֶר וְלֹא הֶעְדִּיף הַמַּרְבֶּה
,much making one the excess an have [1]did [2]not and ,omer an with

וְהַמַּמְעִיט לֹא הֶחְסִיר אִישׁ
one each ; need have [1]did [2]not little making one the and

לְפִי־אָכְלוֹ לָקָטוּ׃ וַיֹּאמֶר מֹשֶׁה 19
Moses said And .up picked they eating his of mouth the to according

אֲלֵהֶם אִישׁ אַל־יוֹתֵר מִמֶּנּוּ עַד־בֹּקֶר׃
.morning until it from leave not let one Any :them unto

וְלֹא־שָׁמְעוּ אֶל־מֹשֶׁה וַיּוֹתִרוּ אֲנָשִׁים מִמֶּנּוּ 20
it from [1]some [2]left and ,Moses unto hearken not did they And

עַד־בֹּקֶר וַיָּרֻם תּוֹלָעִים וַיִּבְאַשׁ
; stank and ,worms [with] putrid became it and ; morning until

וַיִּקְצֹף עֲלֵהֶם מֹשֶׁה׃ וַיִּלְקְטוּ אֹתוֹ 21
it up picked they And .Moses them against angry was and

בַּבֹּקֶר בַּבֹּקֶר[a] אִישׁ[b] כְּפִי
of mouth the to according one each ,morning the in ,morning the in

אָכְלוֹ[b] וְחַם הַשֶּׁמֶשׁ וְנָמָס׃ וַיְהִי 22
,pass to came it And .melted it and ,sun the hot became and ;eating his

בַּיּוֹם הַשִּׁשִּׁי לָקְטוּ לֶחֶם מִשְׁנֶה שְׁנֵי הָעֹמֶר
omers two ,double bread up picked they ,[1]sixth [2]day the on

לָאֶחָד וַיָּבֹאוּ כָּל־נְשִׂיאֵי הָעֵדָה וַיַּגִּידוּ
told and ,congregation the of chiefs the all came and ; one for

לְמֹשֶׁה׃ וַיֹּאמֶר[c] אֲלֵהֶם הוּא אֲשֶׁר דִּבֶּר יְהוָֹה 23
: Jehovah spoke what [is] That : them unto said he And .Moses to

שַׁבָּתוֹן שַׁבַּת־קֹדֶשׁ לַיהוָֹה מָחָר אֵת
; tomorrow [is] Jehovah to holiness of rest a ,rest of festival A

אֲשֶׁר־תֹּאפוּ אֵפוּ וְאֵת אֲשֶׁר־תְּבַשְּׁלוּ בַּשֵּׁלוּ וְאֵת כָּל־
all and ; boil ,boil you what and ,bake ,bake you what

הָעֹדֵף הַנִּיחוּ לָכֶם[d] לְמִשְׁמֶרֶת עַד־הַבֹּקֶר׃
.morning the until keep to ,yourselves for by lay excess the

וַיַּנִּיחוּ אֹתוֹ עַד־הַבֹּקֶר כַּאֲשֶׁר צִוָּה[e] מֹשֶׁה 24
;Moses commanded as ,morning the until it by laid they And

more, some less.
18 And when
they did mete it
with an omer,
he that gather-
ed much had
nothing over,
and he that
gathered little
had no lack;
they gathered
every man ac-
cording to his
eating. 19 And
Moses said unto
them, Let no
man leave of it
till the morning.
20 Notwith-
standing they
hearkened not
unto Moses; but
some of them
left of it until
the morning,
and it bred
worms, and
stank: and Mo-
ses was wroth
with them. 21
And they gath-
ered it morn-
ing by morn-
ing, every man
according to his
eating: and
when the sun
waxed hot, it
melted.
22 And it
came to pass,
that on the
sixth day they
gathered twice
as much bread,
two omers for
each one: and
all the rulers of
the congrega-
tion came and
told Moses. 23
And he said un-
to them, This is
that which the
LORD hath
spoken, To-
morrow is a
solemn rest, a
holy sabbath un-
to the LORD:
bake that which
ye will bake,
and seethe that
which ye will
seethe; and all
that remaineth
over lay up for
you to be kept
until the morn-
ing. 24 And they
laid it up till

a G. omits.
b G. omits.
c G. adds, *Lord*, יהוה; Sm., S. add, *Moses*.
d G., V. apparently omit.
e G., S. add, *them*.

bade: and it did
not stink, neith-
er was there any
worm therein.25
And Moses said,
Eat that to day;
for to day *is* a
sabbath unto
the LORD:
to day ye shall
not find it in the
field. 26 Six
days ye shall
gather it; but on
the seventh day,
which is the sab-
bath, in it there
shall be none.
27 And it
came to pass,
that there went
out *some* of the
people on the
seventh day for
to gather, and
they found
none. 28 And
the LORD said
unto Moses,
How long re-
fuse ye to keep
my command-
ments and my
laws? 29 See,
for that the
LORD hath giv-
en you the sab-
bath, therefore
he giveth you on
the sixth day
the bread of
two days: abide
ye every man in
his place, let no
man go out of
his place on the
seventh day. 30
So the people
rested on the
seventh day. 31
And the house
of Israel called
the name there-
of Manna: and
it *was* like
coriander seed,
white; and the
taste of it *was*
like wafers *made*
with honey.
32 And Mo-
ses said, This *is*
the thing which
the LORD
commandeth,
Fill an omer
of it to be

25 וְלֹא הִבְאִישׁ וְרִמָּה לֹא־הָיְתָה־בּוֹ׃ וַיֹּאמֶר
said And .it in not was worm a and ,stink [2]did [1]it [3]not and

מֹשֶׁה אִכְלֻהוּ[a] הַיּוֹם כִּי־שַׁבָּת הַיּוֹם לַיהוָֹה
; Jehovah to today [is] sabbath a for ,today it Eat : Moses

26 הַיּוֹם[b] לֹא תִמְצָאֻהוּ בַּשָּׂדֶה׃ שֵׁשֶׁת יָמִים
days Six .field the in it find [2]will [1]you [3]not today

תִּלְקְטֻהוּ וּבַיּוֹם[c] הַשְּׁבִיעִי שַׁבָּת[d] לֹא
not ,sabbath a [is] [1]seventh [2]day the on and ; up it pick shall you

27 יִהְיֶה־בּוֹ׃ . וַיְהִי בַּיּוֹם הַשְּׁבִיעִי
,[1]seventh [2]day the on ,pass to came it And .it in [any] be shall

יָצְאוּ מִן־הָעָם לִלְקֹט וְלֹא מָצָאוּ׃
.find [2]did [1]they [3]not and ; up pick to people the of [some] out went

28 וַיֹּאמֶר יְהוָֹה אֶל־מֹשֶׁה עַד־אָנָה מֵאַנְתֶּם
refuse you do long how Until : Moses unto Jehovah said And

29 לִשְׁמֹר מִצְוֹתַי וְתוֹרֹתָי׃ רְאוּ כִּי־יְהוָֹה
Jehovah because ,See ? laws my and commandments my keep to

נָתַן לָכֶם הַשַּׁבָּת עַל־כֵּן הוּא[e] נֹתֵן לָכֶם
you to giving [is] he therefore ,sabbath the you to given has

בַּיּוֹם הַשִּׁשִּׁי לֶחֶם יוֹמָיִם שְׁבוּ אִישׁ
one each ye remain ; days two of bread [1]sixth [2]day the on

תַּחְתָּיו[f] אַל־יֵצֵא אִישׁ מִמְּקֹמוֹ[g] בַּיּוֹם
[2]day the on place his from one any out go not let ,place his in

30 הַשְּׁבִיעִי׃ וַיִּשְׁבְּתוּ הָעָם בַּיּוֹם הַשְּׁבִעִי׃
.[1]seventh [2]day the on people the rested And .[1]seventh

31 וַיִּקְרְאוּ בֵית־יִשְׂרָאֵל[h] אֶת־שְׁמוֹ מָן וְהוּא
[being] it (and) ,Manna name its Israel of house the called And

כְּזֶרַע גַּד לָבָן וְטַעְמוֹ כְּצַפִּיחִת בִּדְבָשׁ׃
.honey with cakes like taste its and ,white ,coriander of seed the like

32 וַיֹּאמֶר מֹשֶׁה זֶה הַדָּבָר אֲשֶׁר צִוָּה
commanded has which thing the [is] This : Moses said And

יְהוָֹה מְלֹא[i] הָעֹמֶר מִמֶּנּוּ[j] לְמִשְׁמֶרֶת לְדֹרֹתֵיכֶם
; generations your for keep to ,it from omer an Fill : Jehovah

the morning, as
Moses bade: and
it did not stink,
neither was
there any worm
therein. 25 And
Moses said, Eat
that to-day; for
to-day is a sab-
bath unto the
LORD: to-day
ye shall not
find it in the
field. 26 Six
days ye shall
gather it; but
on the seventh
day is the sab-
bath, in it there
shall be none.
27 And it
came to pass on
the seventh day,
that there went
out some of the
people for to
gather, and they
found none. 28
And the LORD
said unto Mo-
ses, How long
refuse ye to keep
my command-
ments and my
laws? 29 See,
for that the
LORD hath giv-
en you the sab-
bath, therefore
he giveth you
on the sixth day
the bread of two
days; abide ye
every man in
his place, let no
man go out of
his place on the
seventh day. 30
So the people
rested on the
seventh day. 31
And the house
of Israel called
the name there-
of Manna: and
it was like
coriander seed,
white; and the
taste of it
was like wafers
made with
honey.
32 And Mo-
ses said, This is
the thing which
the LORD hath
commanded,

a G. omits suffix.
b G. omits.
c S. has, *and the day*, והיום.
d G. adds, *that*.
e S. has, *Lord*, יהוה.
f G. has, *in your houses*.
g S. has, *from the door of his house*.
h G., S. have, *sons of Israel;* so 22: 18.
i Sm., G. have, *fill ye*, מִלְאוּ.
j G. has, *of manna*.

kept for your
generations;
that they may
see the bread
wherewith I
have fed you in
the wilderness,
when I brought
you forth from
the land of E-
gypt. 33 And
Moses said unto
Aaron, Take a
pot, and put an
omer full of
manna therein,
and lay it up be-
fore the LORD,
to be kept for
your genera-
tions. 34 As the
LORD com-
manded Moses,
so Aaron laid it
up before the
Testimony, to
be kept. 35 And
the children of
Israel did eat
manna forty
years, until they
came to a land
inhabited; they
did eat manna,
until they came
unto the borders
of the land of
Canaan. 36 Now
an omer *is* the
tenth *part* of an
ephah.

לְמַעַן יִרְאוּ אֶת־הַלֶּחֶם אֲשֶׁר הֶאֱכַלְתִּי[a]
eat to caused I | which | bread the | see may they | that order in

אֶתְכֶם[a] בַּמִּדְבָּר בְּהוֹצִיאִי[b] אֶתְכֶם מֵאֶרֶץ
of land the from | you | out bringing my at | ,wilderness the in | you

מִצְרָיִם׃ וַיֹּאמֶר מֹשֶׁה אֶל־אַהֲרֹן קַח צִנְצֶנֶת[c] 33
[2]pitcher | Take | :Aaron unto | Moses | said And | .Egypt

אַחַת וְתֶן־שָׁמָּה מְלֹא־הָעֹמֶר מָן וְהַנַּח
deposit and | ;manna | ,omer an of fulness the | there put and | ,[1]one

אֹתוֹ לִפְנֵי יְהוָה[d] לְמִשְׁמֶרֶת לְדֹרֹתֵיכֶם׃ כַּאֲשֶׁר 34
As | .generations your for | keep to | ,Jehovah | before | it

צִוָּה יְהוָה אֶל־מֹשֶׁה וַיַּנִּיחֵהוּ אַהֲרֹן
Aaron | it deposited (and) | ,Moses (unto) | Jehovah | commanded

לִפְנֵי הָעֵדֻת[e] לְמִשְׁמָרֶת׃ וּבְנֵי יִשְׂרָאֵל 35
Israel | of children the And | .keep to | testimony the | before

אָכְלוּ אֶת־הַמָּן אַרְבָּעִים שָׁנָה עַד־בֹּאָם אֶל־
unto | coming their until | ,years | forty | manna the | ate

אֶרֶץ נוֹשָׁבֶת אֶת־הַמָּן אָכְלוּ עַד־בֹּאָם
coming their until | ,ate they | manna the | ;inhabited | land a

אֶל־קְצֵה אֶרֶץ[f] כְּנָעַן׃ וְהָעֹמֶר 36
omer the (and) | ;Canaan | of land the | of end the unto

עֲשִׂרִית הָאֵפָה[g] הוּא׃
.(it) | ephah the | of tenth the [being]

Let an omerful
of it be kept for
your genera-
tions; that they
may see the
bread where-
with I fed you
in the wilder-
ness, when I
brought you
forth from the
land of Egypt.
33 And Moses
said unto Aa-
ron, Take a pot,
and put an
omerful of man-
na therein, and
lay it up before
the LORD, to be
kept for your
generations. 34
As the LORD
commanded
Moses, so Aa-
ron laid it up
before the Tes-
timony, to be
kept. 35 And
the children of
Israel did eat
the manna forty
years, until they
came to a land
inhabited; they
did eat the
manna, until
they came unto
the borders of
the land of
Canaan. 36 Now
an omer is the
tenth part of an
ephah.

17

AND all the
congregation of
the children of
Israel journeyed
from the wilder-
ness of Sin, af-
ter their jour-
neys, according
to the com-
mandment of
the LORD, and
pitched in Re-
phidim: and
there was no
water for the
people to drink.
2 Wherefore the
people did chide

וַיִּסְעוּ כָּל־עֲדַת בְּנֵי־יִשְׂרָאֵל 1
Israel of children the | of congregation the all | journeyed And

מִמִּדְבַּר־סִין לְמַסְעֵיהֶם עַל־פִּי
of mouth the upon | ,journeys their to according | ,Sin of wilderness the from

יְהוָה וַיַּחֲנוּ בִּרְפִידִים וְאֵין מַיִם
water | not was and | ,Rephidim in | encamped they and | ;Jehovah

לִשְׁתֹּת הָעָם׃ וַיָּרֶב הָעָם עִם־ 2
with | people the | quarrelled And | .people the | of drinking the for

And all the
congregation of
the children of
Israel journeyed
from the wilder-
ness of Sin, by
their journeys,
according to the
commmand-
ment of the
LORD, and
pitched in Reph-
idim: and
there was no
water for the
people to drink.
2 Wherefore the
people strove

---

a G. has, *ye ate.*
b G. omits suffix and adds, *Lord.*
c G. adds, *gold.*
d G. has, *God.*
e G. has, *God;* V., *in the tabernacle.*
f G. has, *Phoenicia.*
g S. has, *the seah;* T., *three seahs;* G., *three measures.*

with Moses, and
said, Give us
water that we
may drink. And
Moses said unto
them, Why
chide ye with
me? wherefore
do ye tempt the
LORD? 3 And
the people
thirsted there
for water;
and the people
murmured a-
gainst Moses,
and said,
Wherefore *is*
this *that* thou
hast brought us
up out of E-
gypt, to kill us
and our chil-
dren and our
cattle with
thirst? 4 And
Moses cried un-
to the LORD,
saying, What
shall I do unto
this people?
they be almost
ready to stone
me. 5 And the
LORD said unto
Moses, Go on
before the peo-
ple, and take
with thee of the
elders of Israel;
and thy rod,
wherewith thou
smotest the riv-
er, take in thine
hand, and go. 6
Behold, I will
stand before
thee there upon
the rock in
Horeb; and thou
shalt smite the
rock, and there
shall come wa-
ter out of it,
that the people
may drink. And
Moses did so in
the sight of the
elders of Israel.
7 And he called
the name of the
place Massah,
and Meribah,
because of the
chiding of the
children of Is-
rael, and be-

מֹשֶׁה וַיֹּאמְרוּ[a] [b]תְּנוּ־לָנוּ מַיִם וְנִשְׁתֶּה וַיֹּאמֶר
said And .drink may we that ,water us to Give : said and ,Moses

לָהֶם מֹשֶׁה מַה־תְּרִיבוּן עִמָּדִי [c]מַה־תְּנַסּוּן
try you do why ?me with quarrel you do Why : Moses them to

3 אֶת־יְהוָה׃ וַיִּצְמָא שָׁם הָעָם לַמַּיִם [d]וַיָּלֶן
murmured and ,water for people the there thirsted And ? Jehovah

הָעָם עַל־מֹשֶׁה [e]וַיֹּאמֶר לָמָּה זֶּה
,then ,Why :said and ,Moses against people the

הֶעֱלִיתָנוּ מִמִּצְרַיִם לְהָמִית אֹתִי[f] וְאֶת־בָּנַי
children my and me kill to ,Egypt from up us brought thou hast

4 וְאֶת־מִקְנַי בַּצָּמָא׃ וַיִּצְעַק מֹשֶׁה אֶל־יְהוָה
,Jehovah unto Moses cried And ?thirst with cattle my and

לֵאמֹר מָה אֶעֱשֶׂה לָעָם הַזֶּה עוֹד מְעַט
,little a yet ?[1]this [2]people to do I shall What : saying

5 וּסְקָלֻנִי׃ וַיֹּאמֶר יְהוָה אֶל־מֹשֶׁה עֲבֹר
by Pass : Moses unto Jehovah said And .me stone will they and

לִפְנֵי הָעָם וְקַח אִתְּךָ מִזִּקְנֵי
of elders the of [some] thee with take and ,people the before

יִשְׂרָאֵל וּמַטְּךָ אֲשֶׁר הִכִּיתָ בּוֹ
(it with) smotest thou which [with] ,staff thy and ; Israel

6 אֶת־הַיְאֹר קַח בְּיָדְךָ וְהָלָכְתָּ׃ [g]הִנְנִי עֹמֵד
stand will I Behold .go and ,hand thy in take ,river the

לְפָנֶיךָ שָּׁם עַל־הַצּוּר בְּחֹרֵב וְהִכִּיתָ
smite shalt thou and .Horeb in rock the upon there thee before

בַצּוּר וְיָצְאוּ מִמֶּנּוּ מַיִם וְשָׁתָה
drink will and ,water it from out come will and ,rock the (on)

הָעָם וַיַּעַשׂ כֵּן מֹשֶׁה [h]לְעֵינֵי זִקְנֵי
of elders the of eyes the before Moses so did and ; people the

7 יִשְׂרָאֵל׃[h] וַיִּקְרָא שֵׁם הַמָּקוֹם מַסָּה וּמְרִיבָה
;Meribah and Massah place the of name the called one And .Israel

עַל־רִיב ׀ בְּנֵי יִשְׂרָאֵל וְעַל
of account on and ,Israel of children the of quarrelling the of account on

with Moses, and
said, Give us
water that we
may drink. And
Moses said unto
them, Why
strive ye with
me? wherefore
do ye tempt the
LORD? 3 And
the people
thirsted there
for water; and
the people mur-
mured against
Moses, and said,
Wherefore hast
thou brought us
up out of E-
gypt, to kill us
and our chil-
dren and our
cattle with
thirst? 4 And
Moses cried unto
the LORD, say-
ing, What shall
I do unto this
people? they be
almost ready to
stone me. 5 And
the LORD said
unto Moses,
Pass on before
the people, and
take with thee
of the elders of
Israel; and thy
rod, wherewith
thou smotest
the river, take
in thine hand,
and go. 6 Be-
hold, I will
stand before
thee there
upon the
rock in Horeb;
and thou shalt
smite the rock,
and there shall
come water out
of it, that the
people may
drink. And Mo-
ses did so in
the sight of the
elders of Israel.
7 And he called
the name of the
place Massah,
and Meribah,
because of the
striving of the
children of Is-
rael, and be-
cause they

---

a S. adds, *to him.*
b Sm., G., S. have sing.
c G., S. add, *and*, ו.
d G. adds, *there.*
e S. adds, *to him.*
f G., S., V. have pl; so the following suffixes.
g S. adds, *and*, ו.
h G. has, *before the sons of Israel.*

cause they
tempted the
LORD, saying,
Is the LORD a-
mong us, or
not?

8 Then came
Amalek, and
fought with Is-
rael in Rephi-
dim. 9 And
Moses said unto
Joshua, Choose
us out men, and
go out, fight
with Amalek:
to morrow I will
stand on the top
of the hill with
the rod of God
in mine hand.

10 So Joshua
did as Moses
had said to him,
and fought with
Amalek: and
Moses, Aaron,
and Hur went
up to the top of
the hill. 11 And
it came to pass,
when Moses
held up his
hand, that Is-
rael prevailed:
and when he let
down his hand,
Amalek pre-
vailed. 12 But
Moses' hands
were heavy; and
they took a
stone, and put
it under him,
and he sat
thereon; and
Aaron and Hur
stayed up his
hands, the one
on the one side,
and the other on
the other side;
and his hands
were steady un-
til the going
down of the
sun. 13 And
Joshua discom-
fited Amalek
and his people
with the edge of

נִסִּתָם אֶת־יְהוָה לֵאמֹר הֲיֵשׁ יְהוָה בְּקִרְבֵּנוּ
,midst our in Jehovah Is :saying ,Jehovah trying their

אִם־אָיִן׃
?not or

8 וַיָּבֹא עֲמָלֵק וַיִּלָּחֶם[a] עִם־יִשְׂרָאֵל בִּרְפִידִם׃
.Rephidim in Israel against fought and Amalek came And

9 וַיֹּאמֶר מֹשֶׁה אֶל־יְהוֹשֻׁעַ בְּחַר־לָנוּ[b] אֲנָשִׁים
,men us for Choose :Joshua unto Moses said And

וְצֵא הִלָּחֵם בַּעֲמָלֵק מָחָר[c] אָנֹכִי נִצָּב
upon stand will I tomorrow ;Amalek against fight ,go and

עַל־רֹאשׁ הַגִּבְעָה וּמַטֵּה הָאֱלֹהִים בְּיָדִי׃
.hand my in [being] God of staff the (and) ,hill the of summit the

10 וַיַּעַשׂ יְהוֹשֻׁעַ כַּאֲשֶׁר אָמַר־לוֹ מֹשֶׁה
,Moses him to said had as Joshua did And

לְהִלָּחֵם[d] בַּעֲמָלֵק וּמֹשֶׁה[e] אַהֲרֹן וְחוּר עָלוּ
up went Hur and ,Aaron ,Moses and ;Amalek against fight to

11 רֹאשׁ הַגִּבְעָה׃ וְהָיָה כַּאֲשֶׁר יָרִים
up lifted when ,was it And .hill the of summit the [to]

מֹשֶׁה יָדוֹ[f] וְגָבַר יִשְׂרָאֵל וְכַאֲשֶׁר יָנִיחַ
rested he when and ;Israel conquered (and) ,hand his Moses

12 יָדוֹ[f] וְגָבַר עֲמָלֵק׃ וִידֵי מֹשֶׁה
Moses of hands the And .Amalek conquered (and) ,hand his

כְּבֵדִים וַיִּקְחוּ־אֶבֶן וַיָּשִׂימוּ תַחְתָּיו
,him under put and ,stone a took they (and) ,heavy [being]

וַיֵּשֶׁב עָלֶיהָ וְאַהֲרֹן וְחוּר תָּמְכוּ בְיָדָיו
,hands his (on) supported Hur and Aaron and ;it upon sat he and

מִזֶּה אֶחָד וּמִזֶּה אֶחָד וַיְהִי
were and ;one [side] this from and ,one [side] this from

יָדָיו אֱמוּנָה עַד־בֹּא הַשָּׁמֶשׁ׃
.sun the of down going the until steadiness [in] hands his

13 וַיַּחֲלֹשׁ יְהוֹשֻׁעַ אֶת־עֲמָלֵק וְאֶת־עַמּוֹ[g] לְפִי־
of mouth the at people his and Amalek Joshua defeated And

tempted the
LORD, saying,
Is the LORD a-
mong us, or not?

8 Then came
Amalek, and
fought with Is-
rael in Rephi-
dim. 9 And Mo-
ses said unto
Joshua, Choose
us out men, and
go out, fight
with Amalek:
to-morrow I will
stand on the top
of the hill with
the rod of God
in mine hand.

10 So Joshua
did as Moses
had said to him,
and fought with
Amalek: and
Moses, Aaron,
and Hur went
up to the top of
the hill. 11 And
it came to pass,
when Moses
held up his
hand, that Is-
rael prevailed:
and when he let
down his hand,
Amalek pre-
vailed. 12 But
Moses' hands
were heavy; and
they took a
stone, and put it
under him, and
he sat thereon;
and Aaron and
Hur stayed up
his hands, the
one on the one
side, and the
other on the
other side; and
his hands were
steady until the
going down of
the sun. 13 And
Joshua discom-
fited Amalek
and his people
with the edge of

---

a S. has, *to fight.*
b G., S. have, *for thyself;* V. omits.
c G., S. add, *and behold.*
d G. has, *and going forth he fought;* S. *and he went forth to fight;* V., *and fought.*
e G., S., V. add, *and,* ו.
f Sm., G., S., T., V. have pl. like v. 12.
g G. has, *all his people.*

the sword. 14
And the LORD
said unto Moses, Write this
for a memorial
in a book, and
rehearse *it* in the
ears of Joshua:
for I will utterly
put out the
remembrance
of Amalek from
under heaven.
15 And Moses
built an altar,
and called the
name of it Jehovah-nissi:
16 For he said,
Because the
LORD hath
sworn *that* the
LORD *will have*
war with Amalek from generation to generation.

חָרֶב׃ וַיֹּאמֶר יְהוָה אֶל־מֹשֶׁה כְּתֹב זֹאת 14
this Write :Moses unto Jehovah said And .sword the

זִכָּרוֹן בַּסֵּפֶר וְשִׂים בְּאָזְנֵי יְהוֹשֻׁעַ[a] כִּי
for ;Joshua of ears the in put and ,book a in record a [as]

מָחֹה אֶמְחֶה אֶת־זֵכֶר עֲמָלֵק מִתַּחַת
under from Amalek of remembrance the off wipe will I off wiping

הַשָּׁמָיִם׃ וַיִּבֶן מֹשֶׁה מִזְבֵּחַ[b] וַיִּקְרָא שְׁמוֹ 15
,name its called he and ;altar an Moses built And .heavens the

יְהוָה נִסִּי׃ וַיֹּאמֶר[c] כִּי־יָד[d] עַל־כֵּס 16
of throne the upon hand a (That) :said he and ;Nissi Jehovah

יָהּ[d] מִלְחָמָה לַיהוָה בַּעֲמָלֵק מִדֹּר
[to] generation from Amalek against Jehovah to war ,Jah

דֹּר׃
.generation

the sword. 14
And the LORD
said unto Moses, Write this
for a memorial
in a book, and
rehearse it in
the ears of Joshua: that I
will utterly blot
out the remembrance of Amalek from under heaven. 15
And Moses
built an altar,
and called the
name of it Jehovah-nissi: 16
and he said,
The LORD hath
sworn: the
LORD will have
war with Amalek from generation to generation.

18

WHEN Jethro, the priest of
Midian, Moses'
father in law,
heard of all that
God had done
for Moses, and
for Israel his
people, *and*
that the LORD
had brought Israel out of Egypt; 2 Then
Jethro, Moses'
father in law,
took Zipporah,
Moses' wife, after he had sent
her back, 3 And
her two sons;
of which the
name of the one
was Gershom;
for he said, I
have been an
alien in a
strange land: 4
And the name
of the other *was*
Eliezer; for the
God of my father, *said he,*
was mine help,

וַיִּשְׁמַע יִתְרוֹ כֹהֵן מִדְיָן חֹתֵן 1
of father-in-law the ,Midian of priest the ,Jethro heard And

מֹשֶׁה אֵת כָּל־אֲשֶׁר עָשָׂה אֱלֹהִים[e] לְמֹשֶׁה[f] [g]וּלְיִשְׂרָאֵל
Israel for and ,Moses for God done had which all ,Moses

עַמּוֹ [h]כִּי־הוֹצִיא יְהוָה אֶת־יִשְׂרָאֵל מִמִּצְרָיִם׃
.Egypt from Israel Jehovah out brought had that ,people his

וַיִּקַּח יִתְרוֹ חֹתֵן מֹשֶׁה אֶת־צִפֹּרָה[i] 2
Zipporah ,Moses of father-in-law the ,Jethro took And

אֵשֶׁת מֹשֶׁה אַחַר שִׁלּוּחֶיהָ׃ וְאֵת שְׁנֵי בָנֶיהָ 3
;sons [1]her [2]two and ;away sending her after ,Moses of wife the

אֲשֶׁר שֵׁם הָאֶחָד גֵּרְשֹׁם כִּי אָמַר
:said he for ,Gershom [was] one of name the whom [of]

גֵּר הָיִיתִי בְּאֶרֶץ נָכְרִיָּה׃ וְשֵׁם 4
of name the and ;[1]strange [2]land a in become have I sojourner A

הָאֶחָד[j] אֱלִיעֶזֶר[k] כִּי־אֱלֹהֵי אָבִי בְּעֶזְרִי
,help my (in) [was] father my of God the for ,Eliezer [was] one

Now Jethro,
the priest of
Midian, Moses'
father in law,
heard of all that
God had done
for Moses, and
for Israel his
people, how
that the LORD
had brought Israel out of Egypt. 2 And
Jethro, Moses'
father in law,
took Zipporah,
Moses' wife,
after he had sent
her away, and
her two sons; 3
of which the
name of the one
was Gershom;
for he said, I
have been a sojourner in a
strange land: 4
and the name of
the other was Eliezer; for *he*
said, The God
of my father
was my help,

---

a S. has, *son of Nun.*

b G. adds, *to the Lord.*

c G. omits.

d G. has, *with a concealed hand;* Sm., S. have, *upon the throne.*

e G. has, *the Lord,* יהוה.

f G. omits.

g G. omits ו.

h S., V. add, *and,* ו.

i S. adds, *his daughter.*

j G. has, *the second;* S. V. have, *the other.*

k G. adds, *saying;* so essentially V.

and delivered me from the sword of Pharaoh:
5 And Jethro, Moses' father in law, came with his sons and his wife unto Moses into the wilderness, where he encamped at the mount of God:
6 And he said unto Moses, I thy father in law Jethro am come unto thee, and thy wife, and her two sons with her.

7 And Moses went out to meet his father in law, and did obeisance, and kissed him; and they asked each other of *their* welfare; and they came into the tent.
8 And Moses told his father in law all that the LORD had done unto Pharaoh and to the Egyptians for Israel's sake, *and* all the travail that had come upon them by the way, and *how* the LORD delivered them.
9 And Jethro rejoiced for all the goodness which the LORD had done to Israel, whom he had delivered out of the hand of the Egyptians.
10 And Jethro said, Blessed *be* the LORD, who hath delivered you out of the hand of the Egyptians, and out of the hand of Pharaoh, who hath

5 וַיַּצִּלֵנִי מֵחֶרֶב [a] פַּרְעֹה׃ וַיָּבֹא יִתְרוֹ
,Jethro came And .Pharaoh of sword the from me delivered and

חֹתֵן מֹשֶׁה וּבָנָיו וְאִשְׁתּוֹ אֶל־מֹשֶׁה
,Moses unto ,wife his and ,sons his and ,Moses of father-in-law the

אֶל־הַמִּדְבָּר אֲשֶׁר־הוּא חֹנֶה שָׁם
,(there) encamping [was] he where wilderness the unto

6 הַר הָאֱלֹהִים׃ וַיֹּאמֶר אֶל־מֹשֶׁה אֲנִי [b]
I :Moses unto said he And .God of mount the [at]

חֹתֶנְךָ יִתְרוֹ בָּא אֵלֶיךָ וְאִשְׁתְּךָ
,wife thy and ,thee unto come have Jethro father-in-law thy

7 וּשְׁנֵי בָנֶיהָ עִמָּהּ׃ וַיֵּצֵא מֹשֶׁה לִקְרַאת
meet to Moses out went And .her with sons [1]thy [2]two and

חֹתְנוֹ וַיִּשְׁתַּחוּ וַיִּשַּׁק־לוֹ
,him (to) kissed and ,himself prostrated and ,father-in-law his

וַיִּשְׁאֲלוּ אִישׁ־לְרֵעֵהוּ לְשָׁלוֹם
;welfare [their] about ,neighbor his to each ,asked they and

8 וַיָּבֹאוּ [c] הָאֹהֱלָה׃ וַיְסַפֵּר מֹשֶׁה לְחֹתְנוֹ
father-in-law his to Moses related And .tent the to in came they and

אֵת כָּל־אֲשֶׁר עָשָׂה יְהוָֹה לְפַרְעֹה וּלְמִצְרַיִם עַל
on ,Egypt to and Pharaoh to Jehovah done had which all

אוֹדֹת יִשְׂרָאֵל [d] אֵת כָּל־הַתְּלָאָה אֲשֶׁר מְצָאָתַם
them found had which trouble the all ,Israel of account

9 בַּדֶּרֶךְ וַיַּצִּלֵם יְהוָֹה׃ [e] וַיִּחַדְּ יִתְרוֹ
Jethro rejoiced And .Jehovah them delivered had and ,way the in

עַל כָּל־הַטּוֹבָה אֲשֶׁר־עָשָׂה יְהוָֹה לְיִשְׂרָאֵל [f]
,Israel to Jehovah done had which good the all concerning

10 אֲשֶׁר הִצִּילוֹ מִיַּד מִצְרָיִם [g]׃ וַיֹּאמֶר
said And .Egypt of hand the from (him) delivered had he whom

יִתְרוֹ בָּרוּךְ יְהוָֹה אֲשֶׁר הִצִּיל אֶתְכֶם [h]
you delivered has who Jehovah [be] Blessed :Jethro

מִיַּד מִצְרַיִם וּמִיַּד פַּרְעֹה אֲשֶׁר [i]
who ;Pharaoh of hand the from and ,Egypt of hand the from

and delivered me from the sword of Pharaoh;
5 and Jethro, Moses' father in law, came with his sons and his wife unto Moses into the wilderness where he was encamped, at the mount of God:
6 and he said unto Moses, I thy father in law Jethro am come unto thee, and thy wife, and her two sons with her.

7 And Moses went out to meet his father in law, and did obeisance, and kissed him; and they asked each other of their welfare; and they came into the tent.
8 And Moses told his father in law all that the LORD had done unto Pharaoh and to the Egyptians for Israel's sake, all the travail that had come upon them by the way, and how the LORD delivered them.
9 And Jethro rejoiced for all the goodness which the LORD had done to Israel, in that he had delivered them out of the hand of the Egyptians.
10 And Jethro said, Blessed be the LORD, who hath delivered you out of the hand of the Egyptians, and out of the hand of Pharaoh; who

---

a G. has, *from the hand.*
b G., S. have, *behold.*
c G. has, *and he brought him*, וַיְבִאֵהוּ.
d G., S., V. add, *and* ו.
e G. adds, *from the hand of Pharaoh and from the hand of the Egyptians.*
f G. adds, *to them.*
g G., S. add, *and from the hand of Pharaoh.*
h G. has, *them.*
i G. omits.

delivered the
people from un-
der the hand of
the Egyptians.
11 Now I know
that the LORD *is*
greater than all
gods: for in the
thing wherein
they dealt
proudly *he was*
above them. 12
And Jethro,
Moses' father in
law, took a
burnt offering
and sacrifices
for God: and
Aaron came,
and all the
elders of Israel,
to eat bread
with Moses' fa-
ther in law be-
fore God.

13 And it
came to pass on
the morrow,
that Moses sat
to judge the
people: and the
people stood by
Moses from the
morning unto
the evening. 14
And when Mo-
ses' father in
law saw all that
he did to the
people, he said,
What *is* this
thing that thou
doest to the
people? Why
sittest thou thy-
self alone, and
all the people
stand by thee
from morning
unto even? 15
And Moses said
unto his father
in law, Because
the people come
unto me to in-
quire of God:
16 When they
have a matter,
they come unto
me; and I judge
between one and
another, and I
do make *them*
know the stat-
utes of God,
and his laws. 17
And Moses' fa-
ther in law said

הִצִּיל אֶת־הָעָם מִתַּחַת יַד־מִצְרָיִם׃ עַתָּה 11
Now .Egypt of hand the under from people the delivered has

יָדַעְתִּי כִּי־גָדוֹל יְהוָה מִכָּל־הָאֱלֹהִים כִּי
,indeed ;gods the all than Jehovah [is] greater that know I

בַדָּבָר אֲשֶׁר זָדוּ עֲלֵיהֶם׃ וַיִּקַּח 12
took And .them against insolent were they that matter the in

יִתְרוֹ חֹתֵן מֹשֶׁה עֹלָה וּזְבָחִים
sacrifices and offering burnt a Moses of father-in-law the Jethro

לֵאלֹהִים וַיָּבֹא אַהֲרֹן וְכֹל זִקְנֵי יִשְׂרָאֵל לֶאֱכָל־
eat to Israel of elders the all and Aaron came and ;God to

לֶחֶם עִם־חֹתֵן מֹשֶׁה לִפְנֵי הָאֱלֹהִים׃
.God before ,Moses of father-in-law the with bread

וַיְהִי מִמָּחֳרָת וַיֵּשֶׁב מֹשֶׁה לִשְׁפֹּט 13
judge to Moses sat (and) ,morrow the on ,pass to came it And

אֶת־הָעָם וַיַּעֲמֹד הָעָם[a] עַל־מֹשֶׁה מִן־הַבֹּקֶר
morning the from Moses by people the stood and ;people the

עַד־הָעָרֶב׃ וַיַּרְא חֹתֵן[b] מֹשֶׁה[b] אֵת כָּל־ 14
all Moses of father-in-law the saw And .evening the until

אֲשֶׁר־הוּא עֹשֶׂה לָעָם וַיֹּאמֶר[c] מָה־הַדָּבָר
[2]thing [is] What :said he and ,people the to doing [was] he which

הַזֶּה אֲשֶׁר אַתָּה עֹשֶׂה לָעָם מַדּוּעַ אַתָּה
thou [art] Why ?people the to doing [art] thou which [1]this

יוֹשֵׁב לְבַדֶּךָ וְכָל־הָעָם נִצָּב עָלֶיךָ מִן
from thee by standing [are] people the all and ,thyself by sitting

בֹּקֶר עַד־עָרֶב׃ וַיֹּאמֶר מֹשֶׁה לְחֹתְנוֹ 15
: father-in-law his to Moses said And ?evening until morning

כִּי־יָבֹא אֵלַי הָעָם לִדְרֹשׁ אֱלֹהִים[d]׃ כִּי־יִהְיֶה 16
is When .God seek to people the me unto come (That)

לָהֶם דָּבָר בָּא[e] אֵלַי וְשָׁפַטְתִּי בֵּין אִישׁ
man between judge I and ,me unto come they ,matter a them to

וּבֵין רֵעֵהוּ וְהוֹדַעְתִּי[f] אֶת־חֻקֵּי
of statutes the know to [them] make I and ;neighbor his (between) and

הָאֱלֹהִים וְאֶת־תּוֹרֹתָיו׃ וַיֹּאמֶר חֹתֵן מֹשֶׁה 17
Moses of father-in-law the said And .laws his and God

hath delivered
the people from
under the hand
of the Egyp-
tians. 11 Now I
know that the
LORD is greater
than all gods:
yea, in the
thing wherein
they dealt
proudly against
them. 12 And
Jethro, Moses'
father in law,
took a burnt
offering and
sacrifices for
God: and Aa-
ron came, and
all the elders of
Israel, to eat
bread with Mo-
ses' father in
law before God.

13 And it
came to pass on
the morrow,
that Moses sat
to judge the
people: and the
people stood a-
bout Moses
from the morn-
ing unto the
evening. 14 And
when Moses' fa-
ther in law saw
all that he did
to the people,
he said, What is
this thing that
thou doest to
the people? why
sittest thou thy-
self alone, and
all the people
stand about
thee from morn-
ing unto even?
15 And Moses
said unto his fa-
ther in law,
Because the
people come un-
to me to inquire
of God: 16 when
they have a mat-
ter, they come
unto me; and
I judge between
a man and his
neighbour, and
I make them
know the stat-
utes of God,
and his laws. 17
And Moses' fa-
ther in law said

a G. adds, *all*, כל.
b G. has. *Jethro.*
c S. adds, *to him.*
d G. has, *judgment from God;* so essentially V.; S. has, *word from God*; T. *instruction from before God.*
e G. adds, *and*, ו; Sm., G., T., S., V. have pl.
f Sm., G., T., S. add, *them.*

unto him, The thing that thou doest *is* not good. 18 Thou wilt surely wear away, both thou, and this people that *is* with thee: for this thing *is* too heavy for thee; thou art not able to perform it thyself alone. 19 Hearken now unto my voice, I will give thee counsel, and God shall be with thee: Be thou for the people to God-ward, that thou mayest bring the causes unto God: 20 And thou shalt teach them ordinances and laws, and shalt shew them the way wherein they must walk, and the work that they must do. 21 Moreover thou shalt provide out of all the people able men, such as fear God, men of truth, hating covetousness; and place *such* over them, *to be* rulers of thousands, *and* rulers of hundreds, rulers of fifties, and rulers of tens: 22 And let them judge the people at all seasons: and it shall be, *that* every great matter they shall bring unto thee, but every small matter they shall judge: so

אֵלָיו לֹא־טוֹב הַדָּבָר[a] אֲשֶׁר[a] אַתָּה עֹשֶׂה׃
.doing [art] thou which thing the [is] good Not :him unto

נָבֹל תִּבֹּל גַּם־אַתָּה גַּם־הָעָם[b] הַזֶּה 18
[1]this [2]people and thou both ,out wear wilt thou Surely

אֲשֶׁר עִמָּךְ כִּי־כָבֵד מִמְּךָ הַדָּבָר
,thing the [is] thee for heavy [too] for ;thee with [is] which

לֹא־תוּכַל עֲשֹׂהוּ לְבַדֶּךָ׃ עַתָּה שְׁמַע בְּקֹלִי 19
,voice my to hearken ,Now .thyself by it do to able not art thou

[c]אִיעָצְךָ וִיהִי אֱלֹהִים עִמָּךְ הֱיֵה אַתָּה
thou be ;thee with God be may and ,thee counsel will I

לָעָם[d] מוּל[d] הָאֱלֹהִים וְהֵבֵאתָ אַתָּה אֶת־הַדְּבָרִים
matters the thou bring and ,God before people the for

אֶל־הָאֱלֹהִים׃ וְהִזְהַרְתָּה אֶתְהֶם[e] אֶת־הַחֻקִּים[f] 20
statutes the [concerning] them admonish thou do And .God unto

[g]וְאֶת־הַתּוֹרֹת וְהוֹדַעְתָּ לָהֶם אֶת־הַדֶּרֶךְ
way the them to known make and ;laws the and

יֵלְכוּ בָהּ וְאֶת־הַמַּעֲשֶׂה אֲשֶׁר יַעֲשׂוּן׃
.do should they which work the and ,[2]which [1]in [5]walk [4]should [3]they

וְאַתָּה תֶחֱזֶה[h] מִכָּל־הָעָם אַנְשֵׁי־חַיִל 21
,ability of men people the all from out look thou do ,thou And

יִרְאֵי אֱלֹהִים אַנְשֵׁי אֱמֶת [i]שֹׂנְאֵי בָצַע
;gain unjust of haters ,truth of men ,God of fearers

וְשַׂמְתָּ עֲלֵהֶם שָׂרֵי אֲלָפִים [j]שָׂרֵי
of rulers ,thousands of rulers [as] ,them over put thou do and

מֵאוֹת [k]שָׂרֵי חֲמִשִּׁים וְשָׂרֵי עֲשָׂרֹת׃ וְשָׁפְטוּ 22
judge them let And .tens of rulers and ,fifties of rulers ,hundreds

אֶת־הָעָם בְּכָל־עֵת וְהָיָה[l] כָּל־הַדָּבָר הַגָּדֹל
[1]great [2]matter every ,be shall it and ;times all at people the

יָבִיאוּ אֵלֶיךָ וְכָל־הַדָּבָר הַקָּטֹן יִשְׁפְּטוּ־הֵם
;judge shall they [1]small [2]matter every and ,thee unto bring shall they

unto him, The thing that thou doest is not good. 18 Thou wilt surely wear away, both thou, and this people that is with thee: for the thing is too heavy for thee; thou art not able to perform it thyself alone. 19 Hearken now unto my voice, I will give thee counsel, and God be with thee: be thou for the people to God-ward, and bring thou the causes unto God: 20 and thou shalt teach them the statutes and the laws, and shalt shew them the way wherein they must walk, and the work that they must do. 21 Moreover thou shalt provide out of all the people able men, such as fear God, men of truth, hating unjust gain; and place such over them, to be rulers of thousands, rulers of hundreds, rulers of fifties, and rulers of tens: 22 and let them judge the people at all seasons: and it shall be, that every great matter they shall bring unto thee, but every small matter they shall judge themselves: so

---

a S. apparently omits.

b G., S. add, *all*, reading גם כל העם.

c G., S., T. add, *and*, ו.

d S. has, *teaching the people from God;* T., *to the people seeking instruction from before God.*

e S. adds, *that they should observe.*

f G. adds, *of God.*

g G. adds, *his.*

h Sm., G. add, *for thee.*

i S., V. add, *and*, ו.

j G., S., T., V. add, *and*, ו.

k G., S., V. add, *and*, ו.

l Sm., G., T. omit היה; S. has, *and when shall be to them.*

shall it be easier
for thyself, and
they shall bear
the burden with
thee. 23 If thou
shalt do this
thing, and God
command thee
so, then thou
shalt be able to
endure, and all
this people shall
also go to their
place in peace.
24 So Moses
hearkened to the
voice of his fa-
ther in law, and
did all that he
had said. 25 And
Moses chose
able men out of
all Israel, and
made them
heads over the
people, rulers
of thousands,
rulers of hun-
dreds, rulers of
fifties, and rul-
ers of tens. 26
And they judg-
ed the people at
all seasons: the
hard causes
they brought
unto Moses, but
every small mat-
ter they judged
themselves.
27 And Mo-
ses let his father
in law depart;
and he went his
way into his
own land.

וְהָקֵל מֵעָלֶיךָ וְנָשְׂאוּ אִתָּךְ׃
.thee with bear them let and ,thee upon from easy [it] thou make and

23 אִם אֶת־הַדָּבָר הַזֶּה תַּעֲשֶׂה [a]וְצִוְּךָ אֱלֹהִים
,God thee commands and ,doest thou ¹this ²thing If

וְיָכָלְתָּ עֲמֹד וְגַם כָּל־הָעָם הַזֶּה
¹this ²people all also and ; stand to able be wilt thou (and)

24 [b]עַל־מְקֹמוֹ יָבֹא בְשָׁלוֹם׃ וַיִּשְׁמַע מֹשֶׁה
Moses hearkened And .peace in go will place their unto

לְקוֹל חֹתְנוֹ וַיַּעַשׂ כֹּל אֲשֶׁר אָמָר׃[c]
.said had he which all did he and ,father-in-law his of voice the to

25 וַיִּבְחַר מֹשֶׁה אַנְשֵׁי־חַיִל מִכָּל־יִשְׂרָאֵל וַיִּתֵּן
made and ,Israel all from ability of men Moses chose And

אֹתָם רָאשִׁים[d] עַל־הָעָם[e] שָׂרֵי אֲלָפִים [f]שָׂרֵי
of rulers ,thousands of rulers ; people the over heads them

מֵאוֹת [f]שָׂרֵי חֲמִשִּׁים וְשָׂרֵי עֲשָׂרֹת׃
.tens of rulers and ,fifties of rulers ,hundreds

26 וְשָׁפְטוּ אֶת־הָעָם בְּכָל־עֵת [g]אֶת־הַדָּבָר
²matter the ; times all at people the judged they And

הַקָּשֶׁה יְבִיאוּן אֶל־מֹשֶׁה [h]וְכָל־הַדָּבָר הַקָּטֹן
¹small ²matter every and ,Moses unto brought they ¹hard

27 יִשְׁפּוּטוּ הֵם׃ וַיְשַׁלַּח מֹשֶׁה אֶת־חֹתְנוֹ
,father-in-law his Moses away sent And .they ,judged they

וַיֵּלֶךְ לוֹ אֶל־אַרְצוֹ׃
.land his unto himself for went he and

shall it be easier
for thyself, and
they shall bear
the burden with
thee. 23 If thou
shalt do this
thing, and God
command thee
so, then thou
shalt be able to
endure, and all
this people also
shall go to their
place in peace.
24 So Moses
hearkened to
the voice of his
father in law,
and did all that
he had said. 25
And Moses
chose able men
out of all Is-
rael, and made
them heads over
the people,
rulers of thou-
sands, rulers of
hundreds, rulers
of fifties, and
rulers of tens. 26
And they judg-
ed the people
at all seasons:
the hard causes
they brought
unto Moses,
but every small
matter they
judged them-
selves.
27 And Moses
let his father in
law depart; and
he went his way
into his own
land.

19

IN the third
month, when
the children of
Israel were gone
forth out of the
land of Egypt,
the same day
came they *into*
the wilderness of
Sinai. 2 For
they were de-
parted from
Rephidim, and
were come *to* the

1 בַּחֹדֶשׁ הַשְּׁלִישִׁי לְצֵאת בְּנֵי־יִשְׂרָאֵל
Israel of children the of out going the to ¹third ²month the In

מֵאֶרֶץ מִצְרָיִם בַּיּוֹם הַזֶּה בָּאוּ מִדְבַּר
of wilderness the [to] came they ¹this ²day on ,Egypt of land the from

2 סִינָי׃ וַיִּסְעוּ מֵרְפִידִים וַיָּבֹאוּ
came and ,Rephidim from journeyed they And .Sinai

In the third
month after the
children of Is-
rael were gone
forth out of the
land of Egypt,
the same day
came they into
the wilderness
of Sinai. 2 And
when they were
departed from
Rephidim, and
were come to

---

a G. has, *shall strengthen thee;* so essentially S.
b S. has, *his house.*
c G., S. add, *to him.*
d G. omits.
e G. has, *over them,* עליהם.
f G., S. add, *and,* ו. Instead of v. 25, Sm. has, *and Moses said to the people* etc., adding essentially Deut. 1: 9—18.
g G. adds, *all.*
h S. omits כל.

desert of Sinai,
and had pitched
in the wilder-
ness; and there
Israel camped
before the
mount. 3 And
Moses went up
unto God, and
the LORD called
unto him out of
the mountain,
saying, Thus
shalt thou say
to the house of
Jacob, and tell
the children of
Israel; 4 Ye have
seen what I did
unto the Egyp-
tians, and *how*
I bare you on
eagles' wings,
and brought you
unto myself. 5
Now therefore,
if ye will obey
my voice indeed,
and keep my
covenant, then
ye shall be a
peculiar treas-
ure unto me a-
bove all people:
for all the earth
is mine: 6 And
ye shall be unto
me a kingdom of
priests, and an
holy nation.
These *are* the
words which
thou shalt speak
unto the chil-
dren of Israel.

7 And Moses
came and called
for the elders of
the people, and
laid before their
faces all these
words which the
LORD com-
manded him. 8
And all the peo-
ple answered to-
gether, and said,
All that the
LORD hath
spoken we will
do. And Moses
returned the

מִדְבַּר סִינַי וַֽיַּחֲנוּ[a] בַּמִּדְבָּר
;wilderness the in encamped they and ,Sinai of wilderness the [to]

וַיִּֽחַן־שָׁם יִשְׂרָאֵל נֶגֶד הָהָר׃ וּמֹשֶׁה עָלָה 3
up went Moses And .mountain the before Israel there encamped and

אֶל[b]־הָאֱלֹהִים וַיִּקְרָא אֵלָיו יְהוָה[c] מִן־הָהָר[d]
mountain the from Jehovah him unto called and ; God unto

לֵאמֹר כֹּה תֹאמַר לְבֵית יַעֲקֹב וְתַגֵּיד
tell and ,Jacob of house the to say shalt thou Thus :saying

לִבְנֵי יִשְׂרָאֵל׃ אַתֶּם רְאִיתֶם אֲשֶׁר עָשִׂיתִי 4
did I what seen have You .Israel of children the to

לְמִצְרָיִם וָאֶשָּׂא אֶתְכֶם עַל[e]־כַּנְפֵי נְשָׁרִים
,eagles of wings upon you bore I and ,Egypt to

וָאָבִא אֶתְכֶם אֵלָי׃ וְעַתָּה אִם־שָׁמוֹעַ תִּשְׁמְעוּ 5
hearken will you hearkening if now And .me unto you brought and

בְּקֹלִי וּשְׁמַרְתֶּם אֶת־בְּרִיתִי וִהְיִיתֶם
become shall you (and) ,covenant my keep will and ,voice my to

לִי[f] סְגֻלָּה מִכָּל־הָעַמִּים[g] כִּי־לִי
me to for ,nations the all above possession personal a me for

כָּל־הָאָרֶץ[h]׃ וְאַתֶּם תִּהְיוּ־לִי מַמְלֶכֶת 6
of kingdom a me for become shall you And .earth the all [is]

כֹּהֲנִים[i] וְגוֹי קָדוֹשׁ אֵלֶּה[j] הַדְּבָרִים אֲשֶׁר[j]
which words the [are] these ; [1]holy [2]nation a and ,priests

תְּדַבֵּר אֶל־בְּנֵי יִשְׂרָאֵל׃ וַיָּבֹא מֹשֶׁה 7
Moses came And .Israel of children the unto speak shalt thou

וַיִּקְרָא לְזִקְנֵי הָעָם וַיָּשֶׂם לִפְנֵיהֶם אֵת
them before put he and ; people the of elders the (to) called and

כָּל־הַדְּבָרִים הָאֵלֶּה אֲשֶׁר צִוָּהוּ יְהוָה[k]׃
.Jehovah him commanded had which [1]these [2]words all

וַיַּעֲנוּ כָל־הָעָם יַחְדָּו וַיֹּאמְרוּ כֹּל אֲשֶׁר־ 8
which All : said and ,together people the all answered And

דִּבֶּר יְהוָה[l] נַעֲשֶׂה[m] וַיָּשֶׁב מֹשֶׁה
Moses back brought and ; do will we Jehovah spoken has

the wilderness
of Sinai, they
pitched in the
wilderness; and
there Israel
camped before
the mount. 3
And Moses went
up unto God,
and the LORD
called unto him
out of the
mountain, say-
ing, Thus shalt
thou say to the
house of Jacob,
and tell the
children of Is-
rael; 4 Ye have
seen what I did
unto the Egyp-
tians, and how
I bare you on
eagles' wings,
and brought
you unto my-
self. 5 Now
therefore, if ye
will obey my
voice indeed,
and keep my
covenant, then
ye shall be a
peculiar treas-
ure unto me
from among all
peoples: for all
the earth is
mine: 6 and ye
shall be unto
me a kingdom
of priests, and
an holy nation.
These are the
words which
thou shalt speak
unto the chil-
dren of Israel.

7 And Moses
came and called
for the elders of
the people, and
set before them
all these words
which the LORD
commanded
him. 8 And all
the people
answered to-
gether, and said,
All that the
LORD hath
spoken we will
do. And Moses
reported the

a G. omits.
b G. adds, *mount of*.
c G., S. have, *God*.
d G. has, *the heaven*.
e G., S., T. have כעל.
f G. adds, *people;* cf. Deut. 7:6.
g S. adds, *of the earth*.
h S. omits כל.
i S. adds, *and*, ו.
j G., S. have, *these words*.
k G. has, *God*.
l G. has, *God*.
m G. adds, *and will hear*.

words of the people unto the LORD. 9 And the LORD said unto Moses, Lo, I come unto thee in a thick cloud, that the people may hear when I speak with thee, and believe thee for ever. And Moses told the words of the people unto the LORD.

10 And the LORD said unto Moses, Go unto the people, and sanctify them to day and to morrow, and let them wash their clothes, 11 And be ready against the third day: for the third day the LORD will come down in the sight of all the people upon mount Sinai. 12 And thou shalt set bounds unto the people round about, saying, Take heed to yourselves, *that ye* go *not* up into the mount, or touch the border of it: whosoever toucheth the mount shall be surely put to death: 13 There shall not an hand touch it, but he shall surely be stoned, or shot through; whether *it be* beast or man, it shall not live: when the trumpet soundeth long, they shall come up to the mount.

14 And Moses went down

9 אֶת־דִּבְרֵי[a] הָעָם[a] אֶל־יְהוָה[b]׃ וַיֹּאמֶר יְהוָה אֶל־

unto Jehovah said And .Jehovah unto people the of words the

מֹשֶׁה הִנֵּה אָנֹכִי בָּא אֵלֶיךָ בְּעַב הֶעָנָן

,clouds of darkness in thee unto come I Behold : Moses

בַּעֲבוּר יִשְׁמַע הָעָם בְּדַבְּרִי עִמָּךְ וְגַם־

and ,thee with speaking my at people the hear may that order in

בְּךָ יַאֲמִינוּ לְעוֹלָם וַיַּגֵּד מֹשֶׁה

Moses told and ; ever for believe may they thee in

10 אֶת־דִּבְרֵי הָעָם אֶל־יְהוָה׃ וַיֹּאמֶר יְהוָה אֶל־

unto Jehovah said And .Jehovah unto people the of words the

מֹשֶׁה לֵךְ[c] אֶל־הָעָם וְקִדַּשְׁתָּם הַיּוֹם וּמָחָר

,tomorrow and today them sanctify and people the unto Go : Moses

11 וְכִבְּסוּ שִׂמְלֹתָם׃ וְהָיוּ נְכֹנִים

prepared be them let and ; garments their wash them let and

לַיּוֹם הַשְּׁלִישִׁי כִּי בַּיּוֹם הַשְּׁלִשִׁי יֵרֵד

down go will [1]third [2]day the on for ; [1]third [2]day the for

יְהוָה לְעֵינֵי כָל־הָעָם עַל־הַר[d] סִינָי[d]׃

.Sinai of mountain the upon people the all of eyes the before Jehovah

12 וְהִגְבַּלְתָּ אֶת־הָעָם[e] סָבִיב לֵאמֹר[f]

: saying ,about round people the to limits set shalt thou And

הִשָּׁמְרוּ לָכֶם עֲלוֹת בָּהָר

,mountain the into up going [from] yourselves for careful Be

וּנְגֹעַ בְּקָצֵהוּ כָּל־הַנֹּגֵעַ בָּהָר

mountain the (on) touching one every ; end its (on) touching and

13 מוֹת יוּמָת[g]׃ לֹא־תִגַּע בּוֹ יָד כִּי־

but ,hand a him (on) touch not Shall .death to put be shall surely

סָקוֹל יִסָּקֵל אוֹ־יָרֹה יִיָּרֶה

; through shot be shall he surely or ,stoned be shall he surely

אִם־בְּהֵמָה אִם־אִישׁ לֹא יִחְיֶה בִּמְשֹׁךְ[h]

of sounding the At .live [2]shall [1]he [3]not ,man or beast if

14 הַיֹּבֵל[h] הֵמָּה[i] יַעֲלוּ בָהָר׃ וַיֵּרֶד

down went And .mountain the into up go shall they ,horn ram's the

words of the people unto the LORD. 9 And the LORD said unto Moses, Lo, I come unto thee in a thick cloud, that the people may hear when I speak with thee, and may also believe thee for ever. And Moses told the words of the people unto the LORD.

10 And the LORD said unto Moses, Go unto the people, and sanctify them to-day and to-morrow, and let them wash their garments, 11 and be ready against the third day: for the third day the LORD will come down in the sight of all the people upon mount Sinai. 12 And thou shalt set bounds unto the people round about, saying, Take heed to yourselves, that ye go not up into the mount, or touch the border of it: whosoever toucheth the mount shall be surely put to death: 13 no hand shall touch him, but he shall surely be stoned, or shot through; whether it be beast or man, it shall not live: when the trumpet soundeth long, they shall come up to the mount.

14 And Moses went down

---

a G. has, *these words.*

b G. has, *God.*

c G. adds, *witness;* cf. v. 21.

d G. puts before לעיני.

e Sm. has, *the mountain;* cf. v. 23.

f S., V. add, *to them;* Sm. adds, *to the people.*

g Sm., G. have, *shall die,* יָמוּת.

h G. has, *whenever the voices and the trumpet-calls* [*come*] *and cloud departs from the mount.*

i S. has, *you.*

from the mount
unto the peo-
ple, and sanc-
tified the peo-
ple; and they
washed their
clothes. 15 And
he said unto the
people, Be ready
against the third
day: come not
at *your* wives.

16 And it
came to pass on
the third day in
the morning,
that there were
thunders and
lightnings, and
a thick cloud
upon the
mount, and the
voice of the
trumpet exceed-
ing loud; so
that all the peo-
ple that *was* in
the camp trem-
bled. 17 And
Moses brought
forth the peo-
ple out of the
camp to meet
with God; and
they stood at
the nether part
of the mount. 18
And mount
Sinai was alto-
gether on a
smoke, because
the LORD de-
scended upon it
in fire: and the
smoke thereof
ascended as the
smoke of a fur-
nace, and the
whole mount
quaked greatly.
19 And when
the voice of the
trumpet sound-
ed long, and
waxed louder
and louder, Mo-
ses spake, and
God answered
him by a voice.
20 And the
LORD came
down upon
mount Sinai, on
the top of the
mount: and the
LORD called

מֹשֶׁה מִן־הָהָר אֶל־הָעָם וַיְקַדֵּשׁ
sanctified he and ; people the unto mountain the from Moses

15 אֶת־הָעָם וַיְכַבְּסוּ שִׂמְלֹתָם׃ וַיֹּאמֶר אֶל־
unto said he And .garments their washed they and ,people the

הָעָם הֱיוּ נְכֹנִים לִשְׁלֹשֶׁת יָמִים אַל־תִּגְּשׁוּ
approach not do ,day third the for prepared Be : people the

16 אֶל־אִשָּׁה׃ וַיְהִי בַיּוֹם הַשְּׁלִישִׁי
,[1]third [2]day the on ,pass to came it And .woman a (unto)

בִּהְיֹת הַבֹּקֶר וַיְהִי קֹלֹת וּבְרָקִים
,lightnings and thunders were (and) ,morning being [its] in

וְעָנָן כָּבֵד עַל־הָהָר[a] וְקֹל שֹׁפָר
trumpet a of voice a and ,mountain the upon [1]heavy [2]cloud a and

חָזָק מְאֹד וַיֶּחֱרַד כָּל־הָעָם אֲשֶׁר
who people the all trembled and ;exceedingly strong

17 בַּמַּחֲנֶה׃ וַיּוֹצֵא מֹשֶׁה אֶת־הָעָם
people the Moses out brought And .camp the in [were]

לִקְרַאת הָאֱלֹהִים מִן־הַמַּחֲנֶה וַיִּתְיַצְּבוּ
stand their took they and ; camp the from ,God meet to

18 בְּתַחְתִּית הָהָר[b]׃ וְהַר סִינַי
Sinai of mountain the And .mountain the of part lower the at

עָשַׁן כֻּלּוֹ מִפְּנֵי אֲשֶׁר יָרַד עָלָיו
it upon down came that before from ,it of all ,smoking was

יְהוָה[c] בָּאֵשׁ וַיַּעַל עֲשָׁנוֹ כְּעֶשֶׁן
of smoke the like smoke its up went and ; fire in Jehovah

הַכִּבְשָׁן וַיֶּחֱרַד כָּל־הָהָר[d] מְאֹד׃
.exceedingly mountain the all trembled and smelting-oven a

19 וַיְהִי קוֹל הַשֹּׁפָר הוֹלֵךְ
going [was] trumpet the of voice the [while] ,pass to came it And

וְחָזֵק מְאֹד מֹשֶׁה[e] יְדַבֵּר וְהָאֱלֹהִים
God and ,speaks Moses ,exceedingly strong becoming and

20 יַעֲנֶנּוּ בְקוֹל׃ וַיֵּרֶד יְהוָה עַל־
upon Jehovah down came And .voice a by him answers

הַר סִינַי אֶל־רֹאשׁ הָהָר וַיִּקְרָא
called and ; mountain the of summit the unto ,Sinai of mountain the

from the mount
unto the peo-
ple, and sancti-
fied the people;
and they
washed their
garments. 15
And he said un-
to the people,
Be ready against
the third day:
come not near
a woman.

16 And it
came to pass on
the third day,
when it was
morning, that
there were thun-
ders and light-
nings, and a
thick cloud up-
on the mount,
and the voice of
a trumpet ex-
ceeding loud;
and all the peo-
ple that were in
the camp trem-
bled. 17 And
Moses brought
forth the peo-
ple out of the
camp to meet
God; and they
stood at the
nether part of
the mount. 18
And Mount
Sinai was alto-
gether on smoke,
because the
LORD descend-
ed upon it in
fire: and the
smoke thereof
ascended as the
smoke of a fur-
nace, and the
whole mount
quaked greatly.
19 And when
the voice of the
trumpet waxed
louder and loud-
er, Moses spake,
and God an-
swered him by
a voice. 20 And
the LORD came
down upon
mount Sinai, to
the top of the
mount: and the
LORD called

---

a G. adds, *Sinai.*
b G. adds, *Sinai.*
c G. has, *God.*
d G. has, *the people.*
e S. adds, *and,* ו.

Moses *up* to the
top of the
mount; and Mo-
ses went up. 21
And the LORD
said unto Mo-
ses, Go down,
charge the peo-
ple, lest they
break through
unto the LORD
to gaze, and
many of them
perish. 22
And let the
priests also,
which come near
to the LORD,
sanctify them-
selves, lest the
LORD break
forth upon
them. 23 And
Moses said unto
the LORD, the
people cannot
come up to
mount Sinai: for
thou chargedst
us, saying, Set
bounds about
the mount, and
sanctify it. 24
And the LORD
said unto him,
Away, get thee
down, and thou
shalt come up,
thou, and Aa-
ron with thee:
but let not the
priests and the
people break
through to come
up unto the
LORD, lest he
break forth up-
on them. 25 So
Moses went
down unto the
people, and
spake unto
them.

יְהוָה׃ לְמֹשֶׁה אֶל־רֹאשׁ הָהָר וַיַּעַל
up went and ,mountain the of summit the unto Moses (to) Jehovah

21 מֹשֶׁה׃ וַיֹּאמֶר יְהוָה[a] אֶל־מֹשֶׁה[b] רֵד הָעֵד
warn ,down Go :Moses unto Jehovah said And .Moses

בָּעָם פֶּן־יֶהֶרְסוּ אֶל־יְהוָה[c] לִרְאוֹת
,see to Jehovah unto through break they lest ; people the (in)

22 וְנָפַל מִמֶּנּוּ רָב׃ וְגַם הַכֹּהֲנִים הַנִּגָּשִׁים
approaching those ,priests the also And .many them from fall and

אֶל־יְהוָה[d] יִתְקַדָּשׁוּ פֶּן־יִפְרֹץ בָּהֶם
them among forth burst lest ,themselves sanctify them let ,Jehovah (unto)

23 יְהוָה׃ וַיֹּאמֶר מֹשֶׁה אֶל־יְהוָה[e] לֹא־יוּכַל הָעָם
people the able are Not :Jehovah unto Moses said And .Jehovah

לַעֲלֹת אֶל־הַר סִינָי כִּי־אַתָּה הַעֵדֹתָה
warnedst thou for ; Sinai of mountain the unto up come to

בָּנוּ לֵאמֹר[f] הַגְבֵּל אֶת־הָהָר וְקִדַּשְׁתּוֹ׃
.it sanctify and mountain the to limits Set :saying ,us (in)

24 וַיֹּאמֶר אֵלָיו יְהוָה לֶךְ־רֵד וְעָלִיתָ אַתָּה
thou ,up come and ;down go ,Come :Jehovah him unto said And

וְאַהֲרֹן[g] עִמָּךְ וְהַכֹּהֲנִים וְהָעָם
,people the and priests the and ; thee with Aaron and

אַל־יֶהֶרְסוּ לַעֲלֹת אֶל־יְהוָה[h] פֶּן־יִפְרָץ־
forth burst he lest ,Jehovah unto up come to through break not them let

25 בָּם׃[i] וַיֵּרֶד מֹשֶׁה אֶל־הָעָם וַיֹּאמֶר
said and ,people the unto Moses down went And .them among

אֲלֵהֶם׃
.them unto

Moses to the
top of the
mount; and Mo-
ses went up. 21
And the LORD
said unto Mo-
ses, Go down,
charge the peo-
ple, lest they
break through
unto the LORD
to gaze, and
many of them
perish. 22 And
let the priests
also, which
come near to
the LORD, sanc-
tify themselves,
lest the LORD
break forth up-
on them. 23
And Moses said
unto the LORD,
The people can-
not come up to
mount Sinai:
for thou didst
charge us, say-
ing, Set bounds
about the
mount, and
sanctify it. 24
And the LORD
said unto him,
Go, get thee
down; and thou
shalt come up,
thou, and Aa-
ron with thee:
but let not the
priests and the
people break
through to come
up unto the
LORD, lest he
break forth up-
on them. 25
So Moses went
down unto the
people, and told
them.

20

AND God
spake all these
words, saying,
2 I *am* the LORD
thy God, which
have brought
thee out of the

1 וַיְדַבֵּר אֱלֹהִים[j] אֵת כָּל־הַדְּבָרִים הָאֵלֶּה לֵאמֹר׃[k]
:saying ,[1]these [2]words all God spoke And

2 אָנֹכִי יְהוָה אֱלֹהֶיךָ אֲשֶׁר הוֹצֵאתִיךָ
out thee brought have who ,God thy Jehovah [am] I

And God
spake all these
words, saying,
2 I am the LORD
thy God, which
brought thee
out of the land

---

a G. has, *God.*
b G. adds, *saying.*
c G. has, *God.*
d G. adds, *God.*
e G. has, *God.*
f S. adds, *to me.*
g S. adds, *thy brother.*
h G. has, *God.*
i G. adds, *the Lord*, יהוה.
j Sm., G. have יהוה.
k S., V. omit.

land of Egypt,
out of the house
of bondage. 3
Thou shalt
have no other
gods before me.
4 Thou shalt
not make unto
thee any graven
image, or any
likeness *of any
thing* that *is* in
heaven above,
or that *is* in the
earth beneath,
or that *is* in the
water under the
earth: 5 Thou
shalt not bow
down thyself to
them, nor serve
them: for I the
LORD thy God
am a jealous
God, visiting
the iniquity of
the fathers up-
on the children
unto the third
and fourth *gen-
eration* of them
that hate me;

6 And shewing
mercy unto
thousands of
them that love
me, and keep
my command-
ments. 7 Thou
shalt not take
the name of the
LORD thy God
in vain; for the
LORD will not
hold him guilt-
less that taketh
his name in
vain. 8 Remem-
ber the sabbath
day, to keep it
holy. 9 Six days
shalt thou la-
bour, and do all
thy work: 10
But the seventh
day *is* the sab-
bath of the
LORD thy God:
in it thou shalt
not do any
work, thou, nor
thy son, nor
thy daughter,

3 מֵאֶרֶץ מִצְרַיִם מִבֵּית עֲבָדִים׃ לֹא־יִהְיֶה
be not Shall .slaves of house the from ,Egypt of land the from

4 לְךָ אֱלֹהִים אֲחֵרִים עַל־פָּנָי׃ לֹא־תַעֲשֶׂה־
make not shalt Thou .me besides [1]another [2]god thee to

לְךָ [a] פֶסֶל וְכָל־תְּמוּנָה אֲשֶׁר בַּשָּׁמַיִם
heavens the in [is] which form any and ; image graven a thyself for

מִמַּעַל וַאֲשֶׁר בָּאָרֶץ מִתַּחַת וַאֲשֶׁר
which and ,beneath (from) earth the in [is] which and ,above (from)

5 בַּמַּיִם מִתַּחַת לָאָרֶץ׃ לֹא־תִשְׁתַּחֲוֶה
thyself prostrate not shalt thou—earth the (to) under (from) water the in [is]

לָהֶם וְלֹא תָעָבְדֵם כִּי אָנֹכִי יְהוָה
Jehovah [am] I for ; them serve [2]shalt [1]thou [3]not and ,them to

אֱלֹהֶיךָ אֵל קַנָּא פֹּקֵד עֲוֺן אָבֹת עַל־
upon fathers of iniquity the visiting ,[1]jealous [2]God a ,God thy

בָּנִים עַל־שִׁלֵּשִׁים וְעַל־רִבֵּעִים
,generation fourth the upon and ,generation third the upon ,children

6 לְשֹׂנְאָי׃ וְעֹשֶׂה חֶסֶד לַאֲלָפִים [b]
,thousands to kindness doing and ; me hating those to

7 לְאֹהֲבַי וּלְשֹׁמְרֵי מִצְוֺתָי׃ לֹא
[3]Not .commandments my keeping those to and ,me loving those to

תִשָּׂא [c] אֶת־שֵׁם־יְהוָה אֱלֹהֶיךָ לַשָּׁוְא כִּי
for ; vanity for God thy Jehovah of name the utter [2]shalt [1]thou

לֹא יְנַקֶּה יְהוָה [d] אֵת אֲשֶׁר־יִשָּׂא [e] אֶת־שְׁמוֹ
name his utters who him Jehovah unpunished leave will not

8 לַשָּׁוְא׃ זָכוֹר אֶת־יוֹם הַשַּׁבָּת לְקַדְּשׁוֹ׃
.it sanctify to ,sabbath the of day the Remember .vanity for

9 שֵׁשֶׁת יָמִים תַּעֲבֹד וְעָשִׂיתָ כָּל־מְלַאכְתֶּךָ׃
; work thy all do and ,labor mayest thou days Six

10 וְיוֹם הַשְּׁבִיעִי שַׁבָּת לַיהוָה אֱלֹהֶיךָ
,God thy Jehovah to sabbath a [is] [1]seventh [2]day the (and)

לֹא־תַעֲשֶׂה [f] כָל־מְלָאכָה אַתָּה וּבִנְךָ־וּבִתֶּךָ
,daughter thy and ,son thy and ,thou ,work any do not shalt thou

of Egypt, out of
the house of
bondage. 3
Thou shalt have
none other gods
before me. 4
Thou shalt not
make unto thee
a graven image,
nor *the likeness*
of any form that
is in heaven a-
bove, or that is
in the earth be-
neath, or that is
in the water un-
der the earth:
5 thou shalt
not bow down
thyself unto
them, nor serve
them; for I the
LORD thy God
am a jealous
God, visiting
the iniquity of
the fathers up-
on the children,
upon the third
and upon the
fourth genera-
tion of them
that hate me;

6 and shewing
mercy unto
thousands, of
them that love
me and keep
my command-
ments. 7 Thou
shalt not take
the name of the
LORD thy God
in vain; for the
LORD will not
hold him guilt-
less that taketh
his name in
vain. 8 Remem-
ber the sabbath
day, to keep it
holy. 9 Six days
shalt thou la-
bour, and do all
thy work: 10 but
the seventh day
is a sabbath un-
to the LORD thy
God: *in it* thou
shalt not do any
work, thou, nor
thy son, nor thy
daughter, thy

---

a S. adds, *any*, כל.

b S., T. have, *to a thousand generations*, לְאֶלֶף דּוֹר; cf. Deut. 7:9.

c S., T. have, *swear*.

d G. adds, *thy God*.

e S., T. have, *swear*.

f G., S. add, *in it*.

thy manservant,
nor thy maid-
servant, nor thy
cattle, nor thy
stranger that *is*
within thy gates:
11 For *in* six
days the LORD
made heaven
and earth, the
sea, and all that
in them *is*, and
rested the sev-
enth day:
wherefore the
LORD blessed
the sabbath
day, and hal-
lowed it.

12 Honour thy
father and thy
mother: that
thy days may be
long upon the
land which the
LORD thy God
giveth thee. 13
Thou shalt not
kill. 14 Thou
shalt not com-
mit adultery. 15
Thou shalt not
steal. 16 Thou
shalt not bear
false witness a-
gainst thy
neighbour. 17
Thou shalt not
covet thy neigh-
bour's house,
thou shalt not
covet thy neigh-
bour's wife, nor
his manservant,
nor his maid-
servant, nor his
ox, nor his ass,
nor any thing
that *is* thy
neighbour's.

18 And all the
people saw the
thunderings,
and the light-
nings, and the
noise of the
trumpet, and
the mountain
smoking: and
when the peo-
ple saw *it*, they
removed, and
stood afar off.

עַבְדְּךָ וַאֲמָתְךָ וּבְהֶמְתֶּךָ[a] וְגֵרְךָ
sojourner thy and ,cattle thy and ,slave female thy and ,slave male thy

11 אֲשֶׁר[b] בִּשְׁעָרֶיךָ[b]׃ כִּי שֵׁשֶׁת־יָמִים עָשָׂה יְהוָה
Jehovah made days six [in] For .gates thy in [is] who

אֶת־הַשָּׁמַיִם וְאֶת־הָאָרֶץ[c] אֶת־הַיָּם וְאֶת־כָּל־אֲשֶׁר־בָּם
,them in [is] which all and ,sea the ,earth the and ,heavens the

וַיָּנַח בַּיּוֹם הַשְּׁבִיעִי עַל־כֵּן בֵּרַךְ
blessed therefore ;[1]seventh [2]day the on rested he and

12 יְהוָה אֶת־יוֹם הַשַּׁבָּת וַיְקַדְּשֵׁהוּ׃ כַּבֵּד
Honor .it sanctified and ,sabbath the of day the Jehovah

אֶת־אָבִיךָ וְאֶת־אִמֶּךָ לְמַעַן[d] יַאֲרִכוּן יָמֶיךָ
days thy long be may that order in ;mother thy and father thy

עַל הָאֲדָמָה[e] אֲשֶׁר־יְהוָה אֱלֹהֶיךָ נֹתֵן לָךְ׃
.thee to giving [is] God thy Jehovah which ,ground the upon

13 14 לֹא תִּרְצָח׃ לֹא תִּנְאָף׃
.adultery commit [2]shalt [1]thou [3]Not .kill [2]shalt [1]thou [3]Not

15 16 לֹא תִּגְנֹב׃ לֹא־תַעֲנֶה בְרֵעֲךָ
neighbor thy against witness not shalt Thou .steal [2]shalt [1]thou [3]Not

17 עֵד שָׁקֶר׃ לֹא תַחְמֹד בֵּית[f]
of house the covet [2]shalt [1]thou [3]Not .falsehood of witness a [as]

רֵעֶךָ לֹא־תַחְמֹד אֵשֶׁת[g] רֵעֶךָ[h]
,neighbor thy of wife the covet not shalt thou ,neighbor thy

וְעַבְדּוֹ וַאֲמָתוֹ וְשׁוֹרוֹ וַחֲמֹרוֹ[i] וְכֹל
anything or ,ass his or ,ox his or ,slave female his or ,slave male his or

אֲשֶׁר לְרֵעֶךָ[j]׃
.neighbor thy to [is] which

18 וְכָל־הָעָם רֹאִים אֶת־הַקּוֹלֹת וְאֶת־הַלַּפִּידִם
,lightnings the and ,thunders the seeing [were] people the all And

וְאֵת קוֹל הַשֹּׁפָר וְאֶת־הָהָר עָשֵׁן וַיַּרְא[k]
saw and ;smoking mountain the and ,trumpet the of voice the and

הָעָם וַיָּנֻעוּ וַיַּעַמְדוּ מֵרָחֹק׃
.distance a from stood they and ,shook they and ,people the

manservant, nor
thy maidserv-
ant, nor thy
cattle, nor thy
stranger that is
within thy gates:
11 for in six
days the LORD
made heaven
and earth, the
sea, and all that
in them is, and
rested the sev-
enth day:
wherefore the
LORD blessed
the sabbath
day, and hal-
lowed it.

12 Honour
thy father and
thy mother:
that thy days
may be long up-
on the land
which the LORD
thy God giveth
thee. 13 Thou
shalt do no
murder. 14
Thou shalt not
commit adul-
tery. 15 Thou
shalt not steal.
16 Thou shalt
not bear false
witness against
thy neighbour.
17 Thou shalt
not covet thy
neighbour's
house, thou
shalt not covet
thy neighbour's
wife, nor his
manservant, nor
his maidserv-
ant, nor his
ox, nor his ass,
nor any thing
that is thy
neighbour's.

18 And all the
people saw the
thunderings,
and the light-
nings, and the
voice of the
trumpet, and
the mountain
smoking: and
when the peo-
ple saw it, they
trembled, and
stood afar off.

---

a G. has, *thine ox and thine ass and all thy cattle.*

b S. has, *who is in thy cities;* T., *who is in thy city;* G., *who dwells with thee.*

c S., V. add, *and,* ו; G. omits.

d G. adds, *it may be well for thee and.*

e G. adds, *the good.*

f G. has, *wife,* אשת.

g G. has, *house,* בית.

h Sm., G. add, *nor his field.*

i G. adds, *nor any property of his.*

j Sm. makes a long addition, giving the substance of Deut. 37 : 2-7, with the substitution of *Gerizim* for *Ebal*, and many other changes.

k V. has, *they feared;* Sm., G. omit, and add, *all,* כל.

19 And they
said unto Mo-
ses, Speak thou
with us, and we
will hear: but
let not God
speak with us,
lest we die. 20
And Moses said
unto the peo-
ple, Fear not:
for God is come
to prove you,
and that his
fear may be be-
fore your faces,
that ye sin not.
21 And the peo-
ple stood afar
off, and Moses
drew near unto
the thick dark-
ness where God
was.

22 And the
LORD said unto
Moses, Thus
thou shalt say
unto the chil-
dren of Israel,
Ye have seen
that I have
talked with you
from heaven. 23
Ye shall not
make with me
gods of silver,
neither shall ye
make unto you
gods of gold.

24 An altar of
earth thou shalt
make unto me,
and shalt sac-
rifice thereon
thy burnt offer-
ings, and thy
peace offerings,
thy sheep, and
thine oxen: in
all places where
I record my
name I will
come unto thee,
and I will bless
thee. 25 And if
thou wilt make
me an altar of
stone, thou shalt
not build it of

19 וַיֹּאמְרוּ אֶל־מֹשֶׁה [a] דַּבֵּר־אַתָּה עִמָּנוּ וְנִשְׁמָעָה [b]
; hear will we and ,us with thou Speak : Moses unto said they And

20 וְאַל־יְדַבֵּר עִמָּנוּ אֱלֹהִים פֶּן־נָמוּת׃ וַיֹּאמֶר מֹשֶׁה
Moses said And .die we lest ,God us with speak not let and

אֶל־הָעָם [c] אַל־תִּירָאוּ כִּי לְבַעֲבוּר נַסּוֹת אֶתְכֶם בָּא
come has you try to order in for ,fear not Do : people the unto

הָאֱלֹהִים [d] וּבַעֲבוּר תִּהְיֶה יִרְאָתוֹ עַל־פְּנֵיכֶם
,faces your upon fear his be may that order in and ; God

21 לְבִלְתִּי תֶחֱטָאוּ׃ וַיַּעֲמֹד הָעָם מֵרָחֹק
,distance a from people the stood And .sin [2]may [1]you [3]not that

וּמֹשֶׁה נִגַּשׁ אֶל־הָעֲרָפֶל אֲשֶׁר־שָׁם
[was] where darkness thick the (unto) approached Moses and

הָאֱלֹהִים׃
.God

22 וַיֹּאמֶר יְהוָה אֶל־מֹשֶׁה [e] כֹּה תֹאמַר [f]
say shalt thou Thus : Moses unto Jehovah said And

אֶל־בְּנֵי יִשְׂרָאֵל אַתֶּם רְאִיתֶם כִּי מִן־הַשָּׁמַיִם
heavens the from that seen have You : Israel of children the unto

23 דִּבַּרְתִּי עִמָּכֶם׃ לֹא תַעֲשׂוּן אִתִּי [g] אֱלֹהֵי
of gods ; me with make [2]shall [1]you [3]Not .you with spoken have I

כֶּסֶף וֵאלֹהֵי זָהָב לֹא תַעֲשׂוּ לָכֶם׃
.yourselves for make [2]shall [1]you [3]not gold of gods and ,silver

24 מִזְבַּח אֲדָמָה תַּעֲשֶׂה־לִּי וְזָבַחְתָּ
sacrifice shalt thou and ,me for make shalt thou earth of altar An

עָלָיו אֶת־עֹלֹתֶיךָ וְאֶת־שְׁלָמֶיךָ [h] אֶת־צֹאנְךָ
sheep thy ,offerings peace thy and offerings burnt thy it upon

וְאֶת־בְּקָרֶךָ בְּכָל־הַמָּקוֹם אֲשֶׁר אַזְכִּיר [i]
remembered be to cause I which [in] place every in ; cattle thy and

25 אֶת־שְׁמִי [j] אָבוֹא אֵלֶיךָ וּבֵרַכְתִּיךָ׃ וְאִם־
if And .thee bless will and ,thee unto come will I ,name my

מִזְבַּח אֲבָנִים תַּעֲשֶׂה־לִּי לֹא־תִבְנֶה אֶתְהֶן
them build not shalt thou ,me for makest thou stones of altar an

19 And they
said unto Mo-
ses, Speak thou
with us, and we
will hear: but
let not God
speak with us,
lest we die. 20
And Moses said
unto the peo-
ple, Fear not:
for God is come
to prove you,
and that his
fear may be be-
fore you, that
ye sin not. 21
And the peo-
ple stood afar
off, and Moses
drew near unto
the thick dark-
ness where God
was.

22 And the
LORD said unto
Moses, Thus
thou shalt say
unto the chil-
dren of Israel,
Ye yourselves
have seen that I
have talked
with you from
heaven. 23 Ye
shall not make
other gods
with me; gods
of silver, or gods
of gold, ye
shall not make
unto you.

24 An altar of
earth thou shalt
make unto me,
and shalt sacri-
fice thereon thy
burnt offerings,
and thy peace
offerings, thy
sheep, and thine
oxen: in every
place where I
record my name
I will come un-
to thee and I
will bless thee.
25 And if thou
make me an
altar of stone,
thou shalt not

a Sm. has a long addition, from Deut. 5: 21-24.

b G. omits.

c G. has, *God.*

d G., T. add, *to you.*

e Sm. makes a long addition, containing Deut. 5: 25, 26 and 18: 15-22, with slight changes.

f G. adds, *to the house of Jacob and announce.*

g G. has, *for yourselves;* V. omits; S. has, *for yourselves with me.*

h G., S. add, *and,* ו.

i S. has, *thou rememberest.*

j G., T. add, *there.*

hewn stone: for
if thou lift up
thy tool upon it,
thou hast polluted it. 26
Neither shall
thou go up by
steps unto mine
altar, that thy
nakedness be
not discovered
thereon.

גָּזִית כִּי חַרְבְּךָ[a] הֵנַפְתָּ עָלֶיהָ
;stone hewn [as] when tool thy swingest thou ,it upon

26 וַתְּחַלְלֶהָ[b]: וְלֹא־תַעֲלֶה[c] בְמַעֲלֹת עַל־
.it profanest thou (and) And thou shalt not go up by steps upon

מִזְבְּחִי אֲשֶׁר לֹא־תִגָּלֶה[d] עֶרְוָתְךָ עָלָיו:
,altar mine that may not be uncovered nakedness thy .it upon

build it of hewn
stones: for if
thou lift up thy
tool upon it,
thou hast polluted it. 26
Neither shall
thou go up by
steps unto mine
altar, that thy
nakedness be
not discovered
thereon.

21

Now these
are the judgments which
thou shalt set
before them. 2 If
thou buy an Hebrew servant, six
years he shall
serve: and in
the seventh he
shall go out free
for nothing. 3 If
he came in by
himself, he shall
go out by himself: if he were
married, then
his wife shall go
out with him. 4
If his master
have given him
a wife, and she
have born him
sons or daughters; the wife
and her children shall be her
master's, and he
shall go out by
himself. 5 And
if the servant
shall plainly say,
I love my master, my wife,
and my children; I will not
go out free: 6
Then his master
shall bring him
unto the judges;
he shall also
bring him to the
door, or unto
the door post;

1 וְאֵלֶּה הַמִּשְׁפָּטִים אֲשֶׁר תָּשִׂים לִפְנֵיהֶם:
.them before put shalt thou which judgments the [are] these And

2 כִּי תִקְנֶה עֶבֶד עִבְרִי שֵׁשׁ שָׁנִים יַעֲבֹד[e]
;serve shall he years six ,[1]Hebrew [2]slave a buyest thou When

3 וּבַשְּׁבִעִת יֵצֵא לַחָפְשִׁי חִנָּם: אִם־
If .nothing for ,free (for) out go shall he seventh the in and

בְּגַפּוֹ יָבֹא בְּגַפּוֹ[f] יֵצֵא[g] אִם־
if ;out go shall he body his with ,in comes he body his with

בַּעַל[h] אִשָּׁה הוּא[h] וְיָצְאָה אִשְׁתּוֹ עִמּוֹ:
.him with wife his out go shall (and) ,he [was] wife a of husband the

4 אִם־אֲדֹנָיו[i] יִתֶּן־לוֹ אִשָּׁה וְיָלְדָה־לוֹ בָנִים
sons him to bears she and ,wife a him to gives master his If

אוֹ בָנוֹת הָאִשָּׁה וִילָדֶיהָ תִּהְיֶה לַאדֹנֶיהָ[j]
,master her to be shall children her and wife the ;daughters or

5 וְהוּא יֵצֵא בְגַפּוֹ: וְאִם־אָמֹר[k] יֹאמַר[k]
says saying if And .body his with out go shall he and

הָעֶבֶד אָהַבְתִּי אֶת־אֲדֹנִי[l] אֶת־אִשְׁתִּי וְאֶת־בָּנָי
;children my and ,wife my ,master my love I :slave the

6 לֹא אֵצֵא חָפְשִׁי: וְהִגִּשׁוֹ אֲדֹנָיו אֶל־
unto master his him bring shall (and) ;free out go [2]will [1]I [3]not

הָאֱלֹהִים[m] וְהִגִּישׁוֹ אֶל־הַדֶּלֶת אוֹ[n] אֶל־הַמְּזוּזָה
;post door the unto or door the unto him bring shall one and ,God

Now these are
the judgments
which thou shalt
set before them.
2 If thou buy an
Hebrew servant,
six years he
shall serve: and
in the seventh
he shall go out
free for nothing.
3 If he come in
by himself, he
shall go out by
himself: if he
be married, then
his wife shall go
out with him. 4
If his master
give him a wife,
and she bear
him sons or
daughters; the
wife and her
children shall be
her master's,
and he shall go
out by himself.
5 But if the
servant shall
plainly say, I
love my master,
my wife, and
my children; I
will not go out
free; 6 then his
master shall
bring him unto
God, and shall
bring him to the
door, or unto
the door post;

---

a S. has, *iron.*

b G. has passive, *and they are defiled;* V., *it is defiled.*

c G. omits ו.

d G. has active, *thou mayest reveal,* תְּגַלֶּה.

e Sm., G., S., V. add, *thee.*

f G. adds, *and,* ו.

g S. adds, *and,* ו.

h G. has, *and if a wife came in with him.*

i G., S. add, *and,* ו.

j G., S., T. have, *to his master,* לאדניו.

k G. has, *answering says.*

l G., S., V. add, *and,* ו.

m G. has, *the judgment place of God;* Sm., S., T. have, *the judges.*

n G. omits; so apparently T.; V. has, *and.*

and his master shall bore his ear through with an aul; and he shall serve him for ever.

7 And if a man sell his daughter to be a maidservant, she shall not go out as the menservants do. 8 If she please not her master, who hath betrothed her to himself, then shall he let her be redeemed: to sell her unto a strange nation he shall have no power, seeing he hath dealt deceitfully with her. 9 And if he have betrothed her unto his son, he shall deal with her after the manner of daughters. 10 If he take him another *wife;* her food, her raiment, and her duty of marriage, shall he not diminish. 11 And if he do not these three unto her, then shall she go out free without money.

12 He that smiteth a man, so that he die, shall be surely put to death. 13 And if a man lie not in wait, but God deliver *him* into his hand; then I will appoint thee a place whither he shall flee. 14 But if a man come presumptuously upon his neighbour, to slay him

וְרָצַע אֲדֹנָיו אֶת־אָזְנוֹ בַּמַּרְצֵעַ וַעֲבָדוֹ
him serve shall he and ,awl an with ear his master his pierce shall and

לְעֹלָם׃
.ever for

7 וְכִי־יִמְכֹּר אִישׁ אֶת־בִּתּוֹ לְאָמָה לֹא
[3]not ;slave female a for daughter his man a sells when And

8 תֵצֵא כְּצֵאת הָעֲבָדִים[a]׃ אִם־
If .slaves male the of out going the like ,out go [2]shall [1]she

רָעָה בְּעֵינֵי אֲדֹנֶיהָ אֲשֶׁר־לֹא[b]
himself for who ,master her of eyes the in displeasing is she

יְעָדָהּ וְהֶפְדָּהּ לְעַם[c]
[2]people a to ;redemption her allow shall he (and) ,her appointed has

נָכְרִי לֹא־יִמְשֹׁל לְמָכְרָהּ בְּבִגְדוֹ־בָהּ׃
.her (in) deceiving his in ,her sell to power have not shall he [1]strange

9 וְאִם־לִבְנוֹ יִיעָדֶנָּה כְּמִשְׁפַּט הַבָּנוֹת
daughters of custom the like ,her appoints he son his for if And

10 יַעֲשֶׂה־לָּהּ׃ [d]אִם־אַחֶרֶת יִקַּח־לוֹ שְׁאֵרָהּ
,flesh her ,himself for takes he [wife] another If .her to do shall he

11 [e]כְּסוּתָהּ וְעֹנָתָהּ לֹא יִגְרָע׃ וְאִם־
if And .diminish [2]shall [1]he [3]not right conjugal her and ,clothing her

שְׁלָשׁ־אֵלֶּה לֹא יַעֲשֶׂה לָהּ וְיָצְאָה
out go shall she (and) ,her for do [2]does [1]he [3]not three these

חִנָּם אֵין כָּסֶף׃
.money without ,nothing for

12 מַכֵּה[f] אִישׁ[f] וָמֵת מוֹת יוּמָת׃
.death to put be shall surely ,dies he that so ,man a of smiter The

13 וַאֲשֶׁר לֹא צָדָה[g] וְהָאֱלֹהִים אִנָּה לְיָדוֹ
,hand his into fall lets God and ,wait in lie [1]does [2]not who he And

וְשַׂמְתִּי[h] לְךָ מָקוֹם אֲשֶׁר יָנוּס שָׁמָּה[i]׃
.(there) flee may he whither place a thee for appoint will I (and)

14 וְכִי־יָזִד אִישׁ עַל־רֵעֵהוּ לְהָרְגוֹ
him kill to neighbor his against man a insolently acts when And

and his master shall bore his ear through with an awl; and he shall serve him for ever.

7 And if a man sell his daughter to be a maidservant, she shall not go out as the menservants do. 8 If she please not her master, who hath espoused her to himself, then shall he let her be redeemed: to sell her unto a strange people he shall have no power, seeing he hath dealt deceitfully with her. 9 And if he espouse her unto his son, he shall deal with her after the manner of daughters. 10 If he take him another *wife;* her food, her raiment, and her duty of marriage, shall he not diminish. 11 And if he do not these three unto her, then shall she go out for nothing, without money.

12 He that smiteth a man, so that he die, shall surely be put to death. 13 And if a man lie not in wait, but God deliver *him* into his hand; then I will appoint thee a place whither he shall flee. 14 And if a man come presumptuously upon his neighbour, to slay

---

a G., V. have feminine.
b G., T., V. have, *to him*, לוֹ.
c G. adds, *and*, וְ.
d G., S. add, *and*, וְ.
e G., S., V. add, *and*, וְ.
f G. has, *and if one smite another*.
g S., T. add, *for him*.
h S. has imperative, *make thou*.
i G. adds, *the murderer*.

with guile; thou
shalt take him
from mine altar,
that he may die.
15 And he
that smiteth his
father, or his
mother, shall be
surely put to
death.
16 And he
that stealeth a
man, and selleth
him, or if he be
found in his
hand, he shall
surely be put to
death.
17 And he that
curseth his fa-
ther, or his
mother, shall
surely be put to
death.
18 And if men
strive together,
and one smite
another with a
stone, or with
his fist, and he
die not, but
keepeth *his* bed:
19 If he rise a-
gain, and walk
abroad upon
his staff, then
shall he that
smote *him* be
quit: only he
shall pay *for*
the loss of his
time, and shall
cause *him* to be
thoroughly
healed.
20 And if a
man smite his
servant, or his
maid, with a
rod, and he die
under his hand;
he shall be sure-
ly punished. 21
Notwithstanding,
ing, if he con-
tinue a day or
two, he shall
not be punished:
for he *is* his
money.
22 If men
strive, and hurt
a woman with
child, so that
her fruit depart
from her, and
yet no mischief
follow: he shall

בְּעָרְמָה[a] מֵעִם מִזְבְּחִי תִּקָּחֶנּוּ לָמוּת׃[b]
.die to ,him take shalt thou altar my (with) from ;stratagem by

15 וּמַכֵּה אָבִיו וְאִמּוֹ מוֹת יוּמָת׃
.death to put be shall surely ,mother his or father his of smiter the And

16 וְגֹנֵב[c] אִישׁ[d] וּמְכָרוֹ וְנִמְצָא בְיָדוֹ
,hand his in found is he or ,him sells and ,man a steals who he And

17 מוֹת יוּמָת׃ וּמְקַלֵּל אָבִיו
father his of curser the And .death to put be shall he surely

18 וְאִמּוֹ מוֹת יוּמָת׃ וְכִי־יְרִיבֻן
quarrel when And .death to put be shall surely ,mother his or

אֲנָשִׁים[e] וְהִכָּה־אִישׁ אֶת־רֵעֵהוּ בְּאֶבֶן אוֹ
or stone a with neighbor his smites one and ,men

19 בְאֶגְרֹף וְלֹא יָמוּת וְנָפַל לְמִשְׁכָּב׃ אִם־
if ;bed [his] upon falls but ,die ²does ¹he ³not and ;fist a with

יָקוּם[f] וְהִתְהַלֵּךְ בַּחוּץ עַל־מִשְׁעַנְתּוֹ
,staff his upon street the in about walks and rises he

וְנִקָּה הַמַּכֶּה רַק שִׁבְתּוֹ יִתֵּן
,give shall he sitting his only ;smiter the innocent be shall (and)

20 וְרַפֹּא יְרַפֵּא׃ וְכִי־יַכֶּה אִישׁ
man a smites when And .healed be to him cause shall surely and

אֶת־עַבְדּוֹ אוֹ אֶת־אֲמָתוֹ בַּשֵּׁבֶט וּמֵת תַּחַת
under dies he and ,rod a with slave female his or slave male his

21 יָדוֹ נָקֹם יִנָּקֵם׃ אַךְ אִם־יוֹם אוֹ יוֹמַיִם
days two or day a if But .avenged be shall he surely ;hand his

יַעֲמֹד לֹא יֻקָּם כִּי כַסְפּוֹ הוּא׃
.he [is] money his for ,avenged be ²shall ¹he ³not ,continues he

22 וְכִי־יִנָּצוּ אֲנָשִׁים[g] וְנָגְפוּ אִשָּׁה הָרָה
,¹pregnant ²woman a strike they and ,men contend when And

וְיָצְאוּ[h] יְלָדֶיהָ[i] וְלֹא יִהְיֶה אָסוֹן עָנוֹשׁ יֵעָנֵשׁ
,fined be shall he surely ;injury is not and ,child her forth goes and

כַּאֲשֶׁר יָשִׁית עָלָיו בַּעַל הָאִשָּׁה וְנָתַן[j]
give shall he and ,woman the of husband the him upon put may as

him with guile;
thou shalt take
him from mine
altar, that he
may die.
15 And he
that smiteth his
father, or his
mother, shall be
surely put to
death.
16 And he
that stealeth a
man, and selleth
him, or if he be
found in his
hand, he shall
surely be put to
death.
17 And he
that curseth his
father, or his
mother, shall
surely be put to
death.
18 And if men
contend, and
one smiteth the
other with a
stone, or with
his fist, and he
die not, but keep
his bed: 19 if he
rise again, and
walk abroad
upon his staff,
then shall he
that smote him
be quit: only
he shall pay for
the loss of his
time, and shall
cause him to be
thoroughly
healed.
20 And if a
man smite his
servant, or his
maid, with a
rod, and he die
under his hand;
he shall surely
be punished.
21 Notwith-
standing, if he
continue a day
or two, he shall
not be punished:
for he is his
money.
22 And if men
strive together,
and hurt a
woman with
child, so that
her fruit de-
part, and yet no
mischief follow:

a G. adds, *and flees.*

b G., T. have, *to put to death;* S. has, *to put him to death.*

c G. transposes vs. 16, 17.

d G., T. add, *one of the sons of Israel.*

e G., S. have, *two men.*

f G. adds, *the man.*

g G., S. have, *two men.*

h S. has, *and they cause to go forth.*

i Sm., G., S. have sing.

j G. omits ו.

be surely punished, according as the woman's husband will lay upon him; and he shall pay as the judges *determine*. 23 And if *any* mischief follow, then thou shalt give life for life, 24 Eye for eye, tooth for tooth, hand for hand, foot for foot, 25 Burning for burning, wound for wound, stripe for stripe.

26 And if a man smite the eye of his servant, or the eye of his maid, that it perish; he shall let him go free for his eye's sake. 27 And if he smite out his manservant's tooth, or his maidservant's tooth; he shall let him go free for his tooth's sake.

28 If an ox gore a man or a woman, that they die: then the ox shall be surely stoned, and his flesh shall not be eaten; but the owner of the ox *shall be* quit. 29 But if the ox were wont to push with his horn in time past, and it hath been testified to his owner, and he hath not kept him in, but that he hath killed a man or a woman; the ox shall be stoned, and his owner also shall be put to death. 30 If there be laid on him a sum of money, then he shall give for

23 בִּפְלִלִים׃ וְאִם־אָסוֹן יִהְיֶה [a]וְנָתַתָּה נֶפֶשׁ
soul give shalt thou (and) ,is injury if And .judges the with
24 תַּחַת נָפֶשׁ׃ עַיִן תַּחַת עַיִן שֵׁן תַּחַת שֵׁן יָד
hand ,tooth for tooth ,eye for eye ,soul for
25 תַּחַת יָד רֶגֶל תַּחַת רָגֶל׃ כְּוִיָּה תַּחַת כְּוִיָּה
,branding for branding ,foot for foot ,hand for
26 פֶּצַע תַּחַת פָּצַע חַבּוּרָה תַּחַת חַבּוּרָה׃ וְכִי־יַכֶּה
smites when And .stripe for stripe ,wound for wound
אִישׁ אֶת־עֵין עַבְדּוֹ אוֹ־אֶת־עֵין אֲמָתוֹ
,slave female his of eye the or ,slave male his of eye the man a
וְשִׁחֲתָהּ לַחָפְשִׁי יְשַׁלְּחֶנּוּ תַּחַת עֵינוֹ׃
.eye his for away him send shall he free (for) ; it destroys and
27 וְאִם־שֵׁן עַבְדּוֹ אוֹ־שֵׁן אֲמָתוֹ
slave female his of tooth the or ,slave male his of tooth the if And
יַפִּיל לַחָפְשִׁי יְשַׁלְּחֶנּוּ תַּחַת שִׁנּוֹ׃
.tooth his for away him send shall he free (for) ; fall to makes he

28 וְכִי־יִגַּח שׁוֹר[b] אֶת־אִישׁ אוֹ אֶת־אִשָּׁה
,woman a or man a ox an gores when And
וָמֵת סָקוֹל יִסָּקֵל הַשּׁוֹר וְלֹא יֵאָכֵל
eaten be [1]shall [2]not and ox the stoned be shall surely ; dies he that so
29 אֶת־בְּשָׂרוֹ וּבַעַל הַשּׁוֹר נָקִי׃ וְאִם שׁוֹר
ox an if And .innocent [is] ox the of owner the and ,flesh its
נַגָּח הוּא מִתְּמֹל שִׁלְשֹׁם
,day third the [and] yesterday from he [was] gore to apt
וְהוּעַד בִּבְעָלָיו וְלֹא יִשְׁמְרֶנּוּ
,him watch [2]does [1]he [3]not and ,owner its to given is warning and
וְהֵמִית אִישׁ אוֹ אִשָּׁה הַשּׁוֹר יִסָּקֵל
,stoned be shall ox the ; woman a or man a kills he and
30 וְגַם־בְּעָלָיו יוּמָת׃ [c]אִם־כֹּפֶר יוּשַׁת[d]
put is ransom a If .death to put be shall owner its also and
עָלָיו וְנָתַן[e] פִּדְיֹן נַפְשׁוֹ כְּכֹל
all to according ,soul his of redemption the give shall he (and) ,him upon

he shall be surely fined, according as the woman's husband shall lay upon him; and he shall pay as the judges determine. 23 But if any mischief follow, then thou shalt give life for life, 24 eye for eye, tooth for tooth, hand for hand, foot for foot, 25 burning for burning, wound for wound, stripe for stripe.

26 And if a man smite the eye of his servant, or the eye of his maid, and destroy it; he shall let him go free for his eye's sake. 27 And if he smite out his manservant's tooth, or his maidservant's tooth; he shall let him go free for his tooth's sake.

28 And if an ox gore a man or a woman, that they die, the ox shall be surely stoned, and his flesh shall not be eaten; but the owner of the ox shall be quit. 29 But if the ox were wont to gore in time past, and it hath been testified to his owner, and he hath not kept him in, but that he hath killed a man or a woman; the ox shall be stoned, and his owner also shall be put to death. 30 If there be laid on him a ransom, then he shall give for the redemption of his

a S., G., V. omit ו.
b Sm. adds, *or any beast;* similar in vs. 29-31.
c G., S. add, *and,* ו.
d S., T. have, *they put.*
e G., S., V. omit ו.

the ransom of his life whatsoever is laid upon him. 31 Whether he have gored a son, or have gored a daughter, according to this judgment shall it be done unto him. 32 If the ox shall push a manservant or a maidservant; he shall give unto their master thirty shekels of silver, and the ox shall be stoned.

33 And if a man shall open a pit, or if a man shall dig a pit, and not cover it, and an ox or an ass fall therein; 34 The owner of the pit shall make *it* good, *and* give money unto the owner of them; and the dead *beast* shall be his.

35 And if one man's ox hurt another's, that he die; then they shall sell the live ox, and divide the money of it; and the dead *ox* also they shall divide. 36 Or if it be known that the ox hath used to push in time past, and his owner hath not kept him in; he shall surely pay ox for ox; and the dead shall be his own.

IF a man shall steal an ox, or a sheep, and kill it, or sell it;

אֲשֶׁר־יוּשַׁת[a] עָלָיו׃ [b]אוֹ־בֵן יִגָּח[c] אוֹ־בַת 31
daughter a or gores he son a Whether .him upon put is which

יִגָּח[d] כַּמִּשְׁפָּט הַזֶּה יֵעָשֶׂה לּוֹ׃
.him to done be shall it [1]this [2]judgment to according ,gores he

אִם־עֶבֶד[e] יִגַּח הַשּׁוֹר אוֹ אָמָה כֶּסֶף 32
,silver ; slave female a or ,ox the gores slave male a If

שְׁלֹשִׁים שְׁקָלִים יִתֵּן לַאדֹנָיו וְהַשּׁוֹר
ox the and ,master his to give shall he ,shekels thirty

יִסָּקֵל׃
.stoned be shall

וְכִי־יִפְתַּח אִישׁ בּוֹר אוֹ כִּי־יִכְרֶה אִישׁ בֹּר 33
,pit a man a digs when or ,pit a man a opens when And

וְלֹא יְכַסֶּנּוּ וְנָפַל־שָׁמָּה שּׁוֹר אוֹ חֲמוֹר׃[f]
; ass an or ox an thither falls and ,it [2]cover [1]does [3]not and

בַּעַל הַבּוֹר יְשַׁלֵּם כֶּסֶף יָשִׁיב[g] 34
return shall he money ,pay shall pit the of owner the

לִבְעָלָיו וְהַמֵּת יִהְיֶה־לּוֹ׃ וְכִי־יִגֹּף 35
strikes when And .him to be shall dead the and ,owner its to

שׁוֹר־אִישׁ אֶת־שׁוֹר רֵעֵהוּ וָמֵת וּמָכְרוּ
sell shall they (and) ;dies he and ,neighbor his of ox the man a of ox the

אֶת־הַשּׁוֹר הַחַי וְחָצוּ אֶת־כַּסְפּוֹ וְגַם
also and ,money its halve shall they and ,[1]living [2]ox the

אֶת־הַמֵּת יֶחֱצוּן׃ [h]אוֹ נוֹדַע כִּי שׁוֹר 36
ox an that known was it Or .halve shall they dead the

נַגָּח הוּא מִתְּמוֹל שִׁלְשֹׁם[i] וְלֹא
[2]not and ,day third the [and] yesterday from he [was] gore to apt

יִשְׁמְרֶנּוּ בְּעָלָיו[j] שַׁלֵּם יְשַׁלֵּם שׁוֹר תַּחַת הַשּׁוֹר
,ox for ox pay shall he surely ; owner his him watch [1]does

וְהַמֵּת יִהְיֶה־לּוֹ׃
.him to be shall dead the and

כִּי[k] יִגְנֹב־אִישׁ שׁוֹר אוֹ־שֶׂה וּטְבָחוֹ 37
,it slaughters and ,sheep a or ox an man a steals When

life whatsoever is laid upon him. 31 Whether he have gored a son, or have gored a daughter, according to this judgment shall it be done unto him. 32 If the ox gore a manservant or maidservant; he shall give unto their master thirty shekels of silver, and the ox shall be stoned.

33 And if a man shall open a pit, or if a man shall dig a pit and not cover it, and an ox or an ass fall therein, 34 the owner of the pit shall make it good; he shall give money unto the owner of them, and the dead *beast* shall be his.

35 And if one man's ox hurt another's, that he die; then they shall sell the live ox, and divide the price of it; and the dead also they shall divide. 36 Or if it be known that the ox was wont to gore in time past, and his owner hath not kept him in; he shall surely pay ox for ox, and the dead *beast* shall be his own.

If a man shall steal an ox, or a sheep, and kill it, or sell it; he

---

a G., T. have, *they put;* S. has, *they ask.*
b G., S. add, *and,* ו.
c G., S., V. omit.
d S. adds, *the ox.*
e G., S. add, *and,* ו.
f Sm. adds, *or any beast.*
g S., V. omit.
h G., S. add, *and,* ו.
i G. adds, *and they testified to the master;* cf. v. 29.
j G. omits.
k G., S. add, *and,* ו.

he shall restore
five oxen for an
ox, and four
sheep for a
sheep.

2 If a thief be
found breaking
up, and be
smitten that he
die, *there shall*
no blood *be*
shed for him. 3
If the sun be
risen upon him,
there shall be
blood *shed* for
him; *for* he
should make
full restitution:
if he have noth-
ing, then he
shall be sold for
his theft. 4 If
the theft be
certainly found
in his hand a-
live, whether it
be ox, or ass, or
sheep; he shall
restore double.
5 If a man
shall cause a
field or vine-
yard to be eaten,
and shall put in
his beast, and
shall feed in
another man's
field; of the
best of his own
field, and of the
best of his own
vineyard, shall
he make resti-
tution.
6 If fire break
out, and catch in
thorns, so that
the stacks of
corn, or the
standing corn,
or the field, be
consumed
therewith; he
that kindled the
fire shall surely
make restitu-
tion.
7 If a man
shall deliver un-
to his neighbour
money or stuff

אוֹ מְכָרוֹ חֲמִשָּׁה בָקָר יְשַׁלֵּם תַּחַת הַשּׁוֹר
,ox the for pay shall he cattle five ; it sells or

וְאַרְבַּע־צֹאן[a] תַּחַת הַשֶּׂה׃
.sheep the for sheep four and

22

1 [b]אִם־בַּמַּחְתֶּרֶת יִמָּצֵא הַגַּנָּב וְהֻכָּה וָמֵת
;dies and smitten is and ,thief the found is in breaking in If

2 אֵין לוֹ דָּמִים׃ [c]אִם־זָרְחָה הַשֶּׁמֶשׁ עָלָיו
,him upon sun the risen has If .blood him for not is

דָּמִים לוֹ שַׁלֵּם[d] יְשַׁלֵּם[d] [e]אִם־אֵין לוֹ
,[anything] him to not is if ,pay shall he surely ; him for [is] blood

3 וְנִמְכַּר בִּגְנֵבָתוֹ׃ [f]אִם־הִמָּצֵא[g] תִמָּצֵא[g]
found is indeed If .stolen thing the for sold be shall he (and)

בְיָדוֹ הַגְּנֵבָה מִשּׁוֹר[h] עַד־חֲמוֹר עַד־שֶׂה[h i]
,sheep unto ,ass unto ,ox from ,stolen thing the hand his in

חַיִּים שְׁנַיִם יְשַׁלֵּם׃
.pay shall he double ; living

4 [j]כִּי יַבְעֶר־אִישׁ שָׂדֶה אוֹ־כֶרֶם וְשִׁלַּח
loose lets he and ,vineyard a or field a man a pastures When

אֶת־בְּעִירֹה וּבִעֵר בִּשְׂדֵה אַחֵר[k] מֵיטַב שָׂדֵהוּ
,field his of best the ; another of field the in feeds it and beast his

5 וּמֵיטַב כַּרְמוֹ יְשַׁלֵּם׃ [l]כִּי־תֵצֵא אֵשׁ
,fire out goes When .pay shall he vineyard his of best the and

וּמָצְאָה קֹצִים וְנֶאֱכַל[m] גָּדִישׁ אוֹ הַקָּמָה
,standing or ,grain shocked consumed is and ,thorns finds and

אוֹ הַשָּׂדֶה שַׁלֵּם יְשַׁלֵּם הַמַּבְעִר אֶת־הַבְּעֵרָה׃
.fire the kindling one the repay shall surely ;field the or

6 [n]כִּי־יִתֵּן אִישׁ אֶל־רֵעֵהוּ כֶּסֶף אוֹ־כֵלִים
vessels or money neighbor his unto man a gives When

shall pay five
oxen for an ox,
and four sheep
for a sheep.

2 If the thief
be found break-
ing in, and be
smitten that he
die, there shall
be no blood-
guiltiness for
him. 3 If the
sun be risen up-
on him, there
shall be blood-
guiltiness for
him: he should
make restitu-
tion; if he have
nothing, then
he shall be sold
for his theft. 4
If the theft be
found in his
hand alive,
whether it be
ox, or ass, or
sheep; he shall
pay double.
5 If a man
shall cause a
field or vine-
yard to be eat-
en, and shall let
his beast loose,
and it feed in
another man's
field; of the
best of his own
field, and of the
best of his own
vineyard, shall
he make restitu-
tion.
6 If fire break
out, and catch
in thorns, so
that the shocks
of corn, or the
standing corn,
or the field, be
consumed; he
that kindled the
fire shall surely
make restitu-
tion.
7 If a man
shall deliver un-
to his neigh-
bour money or

a S. adds, *he shall repay.*
b G., S. add, *and,* ו.
c G., S. add, *and,* ו.
d G. has, *he shall die;* V., *and he shall die.*
e G., S. add, *and,* ו.
f G., S. add, *and,* ו.
g G. has, *if he is seized and is found.*
h G. has, *from ass unto sheep.*
i Sm. adds, *unto all cattle.*
j G., S. add, *and,* ו.
k Sm., G. add, *he shall repay from his field according to its fruit; and if it consumes all the field.*
l G., S. add, *and,* ו.
m G. has, *and burns besides;* S., *and consumes;* V., *and shall seize,* all being active.
n G., S. add, *and,* ו.

to keep, and it be stolen out of the man's house; if the thief be found, let him pay double. 8 If the thief be not found, then the master of the house shall be brought unto the judges, *to see* whether he have put his hand unto his neighbour's goods. 9 For all manner of trespass, *whether it be* for ox, for ass, for sheep, for raiment, *or* for any manner of lost thing, which *another* challengeth to be his, the cause of both parties shall come before the judges; *and* whom the judges shall condemn, he shall pay double unto his neighbour. 10 If a man deliver unto his neighbour an ass, or an ox, or a sheep, or any beast, to keep; and it die, or be hurt, or driven away, no man seeing *it*: 11 *Then* shall an oath of the LORD be between them both, that he hath not put his hand unto his neighbour's goods; and the owner of it shall accept *thereof*, and he shall not make *it* good. 12 And if it be stolen from him, he shall make restitution unto the owner thereof. 13 If it be torn in pieces, *then*

לִשְׁמֹר וְגֻנַּב מִבֵּית הָאִישׁ אִם־יִמָּצֵא
found is if ; man the of house the from stolen is it and ,keep to

הַגַּנָּב יְשַׁלֵּם שְׁנָיִם׃ [a]אִם־לֹא יִמָּצֵא הַגַּנָּב 7
,thief the found [1]is [2]not If .double repay shall he ,thief the

וְנִקְרַב[b] בַּעַל־הַבַּיִת אֶל־הָאֱלֹהִים[c]
; God unto house the of master the near brought be shall (and)

אִם־לֹא שָׁלַח יָדוֹ בִּמְלֶאכֶת[d]
of affair the to hand his out stretched [2]has [1]he [3]not whether

רֵעֵהוּ׃ עַל־כָּל־דְּבַר־פֶּשַׁע [e]עַל־שׁוֹר 8
,ox concerning ,trespass of case every For .neighbor his

[f]עַל־חֲמוֹר [f]עַל־שֶׂה [f]עַל־שַׂלְמָה [f]עַל־
concerning ,clothing concerning ,sheep concerning ,ass concerning

כָּל־אֲבֵדָה אֲשֶׁר יֹאמַר כִּי־הוּא זֶה עַד
unto ,this [is] it (That) ,says one which [of] ,lost anything

הָאֱלֹהִים יָבֹא דְּבַר־שְׁנֵיהֶם [g]אֲשֶׁר יַרְשִׁיעֻן
guilty declares whom ; them of both of case the come shall God

אֱלֹהִים יְשַׁלֵּם שְׁנַיִם לְרֵעֵהוּ׃ [h]כִּי־יִתֵּן אִישׁ 9
man a gives When .neighbor his to double repay shall he ,God

אֶל־רֵעֵהוּ חֲמוֹר אוֹ־שׁוֹר אוֹ־שֶׂה וְכָל־בְּהֵמָה
cattle any or ,sheep a or ,ox an or ass an neighbor his unto

לִשְׁמֹר וּמֵת אוֹ־נִשְׁבַּר אוֹ־נִשְׁבָּה אֵין רֹאֶה׃
; seeing one any without ,captured is or injured is or dies and ; keep to

שְׁבֻעַת יְהוָה תִּהְיֶה בֵּין שְׁנֵיהֶם אִם־לֹא 10
[3]not whether ,them of both between be shall Jehovah of oath the

שָׁלַח יָדוֹ[i] בִּמְלֶאכֶת רֵעֵהוּ
; neighbor his of affair the to hand his out stretched [2]has [1]he

וְלָקַח בְּעָלָיו[j] וְלֹא יְשַׁלֵּם׃ וְאִם־גָּנֹב 11
indeed if And .repay [2]shall [1]he [3]not and ,owner its accept shall and

יִגָּנֵב מֵעִמּוֹ יְשַׁלֵּם לִבְעָלָיו׃ [k]אִם־טָרֹף 12
indeed If .master its to repay shall he ,him (with) from stolen is it

יִטָּרֵף יְבִאֵהוּ עֵד[l] הַטְּרֵפָה[l]
torn the ; witness a [as] it bring shall he ,pieces in torn is it

stuff to keep, and it be stolen out of the man's house; if the thief be found, he shall pay double. 8 If the thief be not found, then the master of the house shall come near unto God, *to see* whether he have not put his hand unto his neighbour's goods. 9 For every matter of trespass, whether it be for ox, for ass, for sheep, for raiment, *or* for any manner of lost thing, whereof one saith, This is it, the cause of both parties shall come before God; he whom God shall condemn shall pay double unto his neighbour. 10 If a man deliver unto his neighbour an ass, or an ox, or a sheep, or any beast, to keep; and it die, or be hurt, or driven away, no man seeing it: 11 the oath of the LORD shall be between them both, whether he hath not put his hand unto his neighbour's goods; and the owner thereof shall accept it, and he shall not make restitution. 12 But if it be stolen from him, he shall make restitution unto the owner thereof. 13 If it be torn in pieces, let him bring it

a G., S. add, *and*, ו.
b G., S. have, *shall come near*.
c G., V. add, *and shall swear*.
d G. has, *in all* etc.
e G., V. add, *and*, ו.
f G., V., S. add, *and*, ו.
g G., S., V. add, *and*, ו.
h G., S. add, *and*, ו.
i G. adds, *at all*.
j S., V. add, *the oath;* T. adds, *from him the oath*.
k G., S. add, *and*, ו.
l G. has, *unto the game;* V. is similar.

let him bring it *for* witness, *and* he shall not make good that which was torn.
14 And if a man borrow *ought* of his neighbour, and it be hurt, or die, the owner thereof *being* not with it, he shall surely make *it* good.
15 *But* if the owner thereof *be* with it, he shall not make *it* good: if it *be* an hired *thing*, it came for his hire.
16 And if a man entice a maid that is not betrothed, and lie with her, he shall surely endow her to be his wife. 17 If her father utterly refuse to give her unto him, he shall pay money according to the dowry of virgins.
18 Thou shalt not suffer a witch to live.
19 Whosoever lieth with a beast shall surely be put to death.
20 He that sacrificeth unto *any* god, save unto the LORD only, he shall be utterly destroyed.
21 Thou shalt neither vex a stranger, nor oppress him: for ye were strangers in the land of Egypt.
22 Ye shall

13 [a]לֹא יְשַׁלֵּם׃ וְכִי־יִשְׁאַל אִישׁ מֵעִם
(with) from man a asks when And .repay [2]shall [1]he [3]not

[b]רֵעֵהוּ וְנִשְׁבַּר אוֹ־מֵת[c] בְּעָלָיו אֵין־עִמּוֹ
,it with being not owner its ,dies or ,injured is it and ,neighbor his

14 שַׁלֵּם יְשַׁלֵּם׃ [d]אִם־בְּעָלָיו עִמּוֹ לֹא יְשַׁלֵּם
; repay [2]shall [1]he [3]not ,it with [is] master its If .repay shall he surely

15 [e]אִם־שָׂכִיר הוּא בָּא[f] בִּשְׂכָרוֹ[f]׃ וְכִי־יְפַתֶּה אִישׁ
man a seduces when And .hire its for comes it ,it [is] hired if

בְּתוּלָה אֲשֶׁר לֹא־אֹרָשָׂה וְשָׁכַב עִמָּהּ מָהֹר
surely ,her with lies and ,betrothed not is who virgin a

16 יִמְהָרֶנָּה לּוֹ לְאִשָּׁה׃ [g]אִם־מָאֵן יְמָאֵן[h]
refuses refusing If .wife a for himself to her purchase shall he

אָבִיהָ לְתִתָּהּ לוֹ[i] כֶּסֶף יִשְׁקֹל[j]
weigh shall he money ,him to her give to father her

17 כְּמֹהַר הַבְּתוּלֹת׃ מְכַשֵּׁפָה לֹא
[3]not sorceress A .virgins of dowry the to according

18 תְחַיֶּה׃ [k]כָּל־שֹׁכֵב עִם־בְּהֵמָה מוֹת
surely ,beast a with lying one Any .live to allow [2]shalt [1]thou

יוּמָת[l]׃
.death to put be shall

19 זֹבֵחַ לָאֱלֹהִים[m] יָחֳרָם בִּלְתִּי[n]
except ,destruction to devoted be shall god a to sacrificing One

20 לַיהוָה לְבַדּוֹ[n]׃ וְגֵר לֹא־תוֹנֶה וְלֹא
[3]not and vex not shalt thou sojourner a And .alone Jehovah to

תִלְחָצֶנּוּ כִּי־גֵרִים הֱיִיתֶם בְּאֶרֶץ מִצְרָיִם׃
.Egypt of land the in were you sojourners for ; oppress [2]shalt [1]thou

21 [o]כָּל־אַלְמָנָה וְיָתוֹם לֹא תְעַנּוּן׃ [p]אִם־עַנֵּה
22 afflicting If .afflict [2]shall [1]you [3]not orphan or widow Any

for witness; he shall not make good that which was torn.
14 And if a man borrow aught of his neighbour, and it be hurt, or die, the owner thereof not being with it, he shall surely make restitution. 15 If the owner thereof be with it, he shall not make it good: if it be an hired thing, it came for its hire.
16 And if a man entice a virgin that is not betrothed, and lie with her, he shall surely pay a dowry for her to be his wife. 17 If her father utterly refuse to give her unto him, he shall pay money according to the dowry of virgins.
18 Thou shalt not suffer a sorceress to live.
19 Whosoever lieth with a beast shall surely be put to death.
20 He that sacrificeth unto any god, save unto the LORD only, shall be utterly destroyed.
21 And a stranger shalt thou not wrong, neither shalt thou oppress him: for ye were strangers

---

a G., V. add, *and*, ו.
b S. adds, *cattle;* V. *anything of theirs in common.*
c G. adds, *or be taken captive.*
d G., S. add, *and*, ו.
e G., S. add, *and*, ו.
f G. has, *it shall be to him instead of his wages;* S., *it shall be taken from his wages.*
g G., S. add, *and*, ו.
h G. adds, *and is not willing.*
i G. adds, *for wife.*
j G. adds, *to the father.*
k S. adds, *and*, ו.
l G. has, *you shall kill them.*
m Sm. adds, *other;* T. has, *the idols of the nations.*
n Sm. omits.
o S. adds, *and*, ו.
p G., S. add, *and*, ו.

not afflict any
widow, or fa-
therless child. 23
If thou afflict
them in any
wise, and they
cry at all unto
me, I will surely
hear their cry; 24
And my wrath
shall wax hot,
and I will kill
you with the
sword; and your
wives shall be
widows, and
your children
fatherless.
25 If thou
lend money to
any of my peo-
ple *that is* poor
by thee, thou
shalt not be
to him as an
usurer, neither
shalt thou lay
upon him usury.
26 If thou at
all take thy
neighbour's
raiment to
pledge, thou
shalt deliver it
unto him by
that the sun
goeth down: 27
For that *is* his
covering only, it
is his raiment for
his skin: where-
in shall he sleep?
and it shall
come to pass,
when he crieth
unto me, that I
will hear; for I
am gracious.
28 Thou shalt
not revile the
gods, nor curse
the ruler of thy
people. 29 Thou
shalt not delay
to offer the
first of thy
ripe fruits, and
of thy liq-
uors: the first-
born of thy sons
shalt thou give
unto me. 30
Likewise shalt
thou do with
thine oxen, *and*
with thy sheep:
seven days it
shall be with his

תְּעַנֶּה אֹתוֹ כִּי[a] אִם־צָעֹק[a] יִצְעַק אֵלַי
,me unto cries he crying if truly ,him afflict dost thou

23 שָׁמֹעַ אֶשְׁמַע צַעֲקָתוֹ׃ וְחָרָה אַפִּי וְהָרַגְתִּי
kill will I and ,anger my glow shall and ; cry his hear will I hearing

אֶתְכֶם בֶּחָרֶב וְהָיוּ נְשֵׁיכֶם אַלְמָנוֹת
,widows wives your become shall and ;sword the with you

וּבְנֵיכֶם יְתֹמִים׃
.orphans sons your and

24 [b]אִם־כֶּסֶף׀ תַּלְוֶה אֶת־עַמִּי[c] אֶת־הֶעָנִי עִמָּךְ
,thee with poor the ,people my [to] lendest thou money If

לֹא־תִהְיֶה לוֹ כְּנֹשֶׁה לֹא־תְשִׂימוּן עָלָיו
him upon put not shall you ; creditor a as him to be not shalt thou

25 נֶשֶׁךְ׃ [d]אִם־חָבֹל תַּחְבֹּל שַׂלְמַת
of garment outer the pledge as takest thou indeed If .interest

רֵעֶךָ עַד־בֹּא הַשֶּׁמֶשׁ תְּשִׁיבֶנּוּ
it return shalt thou sun the of down going the by ,neighbor thy

26 לוֹ׃ כִּי הִוא כְסוּתֹה לְבַדָּהּ הִוא שִׂמְלָתוֹ
garment his [is] that ,alone covering his [is] that for ;him to

לְעֹרוֹ בַּמֶּה יִשְׁכָּב וְהָיָה[e] כִּי־יִצְעַק
cries he when ,be shall it and ?down lie he shall what in ;skin his for

27 אֵלַי וְשָׁמַעְתִּי כִּי־חַנּוּן אָנִי׃ אֱלֹהִים
God .I [am] compassionate for ,hear will I (and) ,me unto

לֹא תְקַלֵּל וְנָשִׂיא בְעַמְּךָ לֹא
[3]not people thy among ruler a and ,revile [2]shalt [1]thou [3]not

28 תָאֹר׃ מְלֵאָתְךָ[f] וְדִמְעֲךָ[f] לֹא תְאַחֵר
;delay [2]shalt [1]thou [3]not sap thy and fulness Thy .curse [2]shalt [1]thou

29 בְּכוֹר בָּנֶיךָ תִּתֶּן־לִּי׃ כֵּן־תַּעֲשֶׂה
do shalt thou So .me to give shalt thou sons thy of firstborn the

לְשֹׁרְךָ [g]לְצֹאנֶךָ שִׁבְעַת יָמִים יִהְיֶה עִם־
with be shall it days seven ;sheep thy to ,oxen thine to

אִמּוֹ [h]בַּיּוֹם הַשְּׁמִינִי תִּתְּנוֹ־לִי׃
.me to it give shalt thou [1]eighth [2]day the on ,mother its

in the land of
Egypt.
22 Ye shall
not afflict any
widow, or fa-
therless child. 23
If thou afflict
them in any
wise, and they
cry at all unto
me, I will sure-
ly hear their
cry; 24 and my
wrath shall wax
hot, and I will
kill you with the
sword; and your
wives shall be
widows, and
your children
fatherless.
25 If thou
lend money to
any of my peo-
ple with thee
that is poor,
thou shalt not
be to him as a
creditor; nei-
ther shall ye
lay upon him
usury.
26 If thou at
all take thy
neighbour's gar-
ment to pledge,
thou shalt re-
store it unto
him by that the
sun goeth down:
27 for that is
his only cover-
ing, it is his gar-
ment for his
skin: wherein
shall he sleep?
and it shall
come to pass,
when he crieth
unto me, that I
will hear; for I
am gracious.
28 Thou shalt
not revile God,
nor curse a rul-
er of thy people.
29 Thou shalt
not delay to
offer of the a-
bundance of thy
fruits, and of
thy liquors. The
firstborn of thy
sons shalt thou
give unto me. 30
Likewise shalt
thou do with
thine oxen, *and*

---

a G., S. have, *and;* V. omits.
b G., S. add, *and,* ו.
c G. has, *the brother.*
d G., S. add, *and,* ו.
e V. omits; G., S. omit היה.
f G. has, *the first fruits of threshing-floor and wine-press;* so essentially S.; V. has, *thy tithes and thy first fruits.*
g G., S., V. add, *and,* ו; G. also adds, *and thine ass.*
h G., S. add, *and,* ו.

dam; on the
eighth day thou
shalt give it me.
31 And ye
shall be holy
men unto me:
neither shall ye
eat *any* flesh
that is torn of
beasts in the
field; ye shall
cast it to the
dogs.

30 וְאַנְשֵׁי־קֹדֶשׁ תִּהְיוּן לִי וּבָשָׂר בַּשָּׂדֶה[a]
field the in flesh and ; me to be shall you holiness of men And

טְרֵפָה[a] לֹא תֹאכֵלוּ לַכֶּלֶב תַּשְׁלִכוּן אֹתוֹ׃
.it cast shall you dogs the to ,eat 2shall 1you 3not pieces in torn

with thy sheep:
seven days it
shall be with its
dam; on the
eighth day thou
shalt give it me.
31 And ye
shall be holy
men unto me:
therefore ye
shall not eat
any flesh that is
torn of beasts in
the field; ye
shall cast it to
the dogs.

23

THOU shalt
not raise a false
report: put not
thine hand with
the wicked to
be an unright-
eous witness.
2 Thou shalt
not follow a
multitude to *do*
evil; neither
shalt thou speak
in a cause to de-
cline after many
to wrest *judg-*
ment: 3 Neither
shalt thou coun-
tenance a poor
man in his
cause.
4 If thou
meet thine en-
emy's ox or his
ass going astray,
thou shalt sure-
ly bring it back
to him again. 5
If thou see the
ass of him that
hateth thee ly-
ing under his
burden, and
wouldest for-
bear to help
him, thou shalt
surely help with
him.
6 Thou shalt
not wrest
the judgment of
thy poor in his
cause. 7 Keep
thee far from a
false matter;
and the in-
nocent and
righteous slay
thou not: for I
will not justify
the wicked.

1 לֹא תִשָּׂא שֵׁמַע שָׁוְא אַל־תָּשֶׁת
put not do ,vanity of report a utter 2shalt 1thou 3Not

יָדְךָ עִם־רָשָׁע לִהְיֹת עֵד חָמָס׃
.violence of witness a become to ,wicked the with hand thy

2 לֹא־תִהְיֶה אַחֲרֵי־רַבִּים לְרָעֹת וְלֹא־תַעֲנֶה
witness not shalt thou and ;things evil to many after be not shalt Thou

עַל־רִב[b] לִנְטֹת אַחֲרֵי רַבִּים לְהַטֹּת׃
.[justice] pervert to many after aside turn to ,law-suit a concerning

3 וְדָל לֹא תֶהְדַּר בְּרִיבוֹ׃ [c]כִּי
4 When .law-suit his in favor 2shalt 1thou 3not lowly the And

תִפְגַּע שׁוֹר אֹיִבְךָ אוֹ חֲמֹרוֹ תֹּעֶה
,wandering ass his or ,enemy thy of ox the upon happenest thou

5 הָשֵׁב תְּשִׁיבֶנּוּ לוֹ׃ [d]כִּי־תִרְאֶה חֲמוֹר
of ass the seest thou When .him to it return shalt thou returning

שֹׂנַאֲךָ רֹבֵץ תַּחַת מַשָּׂאוֹ וְחָדַלְתָּ[e]
refrain shalt thou (and) ,burden its under crouching thee hating one

6 מֵעֲזֹב לוֹ עָזֹב תַּעֲזֹב עִמּוֹ׃[e] לֹא
3Not .him with release shalt thou surely ,him to [it] leaving from

תַטֶּה מִשְׁפַּט אֶבְיֹנְךָ בְּרִיבוֹ׃
.law-suit his in needy thy of judgment the pervert 2shalt 1thou

7 [f]מִדְּבַר־שֶׁקֶר תִּרְחָק וְנָקִי
innocent the and ; away keep shalt thou falsehood of matter a From

וְצַדִּיק אַל־תַּהֲרֹג [g]כִּי לֹא־אַצְדִּיק [g]רָשָׁע׃
.wicked the justify not do I for ; kill not do righteous the and

Thou shalt
not take up a
false report:
put not thine
hand with the
wicked to be an
unrighteous wit-
ness.
2 Thou shalt
not follow a
multitude to do
evil; neither
shalt thou speak
in a cause to
turn aside after
a multitude to
wrest *judg-*
ment: 3 neither
shalt thou fa-
vour a poor man
in his cause.
4 If thou meet
thine enemy's
ox or his ass
going astray,
thou shalt sure-
ly bring it back
to him again. 5
If thou see the
ass of him that
hateth thee ly-
ing under his
burden, and
wouldest for-
bear to help
him, thou shalt
surely help with
him.
6 Thou shalt
not wrest
the judgment of
thy poor in his
cause. 7 Keep
thee far from a
false matter;
and the inno-
cent and right-
eous slay thou
not: for I will
not justify the
wicked.

---

a S., T. have, *torn from a living animal;* V. has, *which from beasts has been torn beforehand.*

b G. has, *multitude*, רֹב.

c G. S. add, *and*, ו.

d G., S. add, *and*, ו.

e G., V. have, *thou shalt not pass him by, but shalt aid him in lifting it.*

f S. adds, *and*, ו; G. adds, *every.*

g G. has, *and thou shalt not justify the wicked for a reward.*

8 And thou
shalt take no
gift: for the
gift blindeth the
wise, and per-
verteth the
words of the
righteous. 9
Also thou shalt
not oppress a
stranger: for ye
know the heart
of a stranger,
seeing ye were
strangers in the
land of Egypt.
10 And six
years thou
shalt sow thy
land, and
shalt gather in
the fruits there-
of: 11 But the
seventh *year*
thou shalt let it
rest and lie still;
that the poor of
thy people may
eat: and what
they leave the
beasts of the
field shall eat. In
like manner
thou shalt deal
with thy vine-
yard, *and* with
thy oliveyard. 12
Six days thou
shalt do thy
work, and on
the seventh day
thou shalt rest:
that thine ox
and thine ass
may rest, and
the son of thy
handmaid, and
the stranger,
may be refresh-
ed. 13 And in
all *things* that I
have said unto
you be circum-
spect: and make
no mention of
the name of
other gods, nei-
ther let it be
heard out of thy
mouth.
14 Three
times thou shalt
keep a feast un-
to me in the
year. 15 Thou
shalt keep the
feast of un-
leavened bread:
(thou shalt eat

8 וְשֹׁחַד לֹא תִקָּח כִּי הַשֹּׁחַד [a]יְעַוֵּר פִּקְחִים[b]
,seeing the blinds bribe the for ,take ²shalt ¹thou ³not bribe a And

9 וִיסַלֵּף דִּבְרֵי צַדִּיקִים׃ וְגֵר לֹא
³not sojourner a And .righteous the of words the perverts and

תִלְחָץ וְאַתֶּם יְדַעְתֶּם אֶת־נֶפֶשׁ הַגֵּר
,sojourner the of soul the know you and ;oppress ²shalt ¹thou

כִּי־גֵרִים הֱיִיתֶם בְּאֶרֶץ מִצְרָיִם׃
.Egypt of land the in were you sojourners for

10 [c]וְשֵׁשׁ שָׁנִים תִּזְרַע אֶת־אַרְצֶךָ וְאָסַפְתָּ
gather shalt thou and ,land thy sow shalt thou years six And

11 אֶת־תְּבוּאָתָהּ׃ וְהַשְּׁבִיעִת תִּשְׁמְטֶנָּה וּנְטַשְׁתָּהּ
;it leave and ,it release shalt thou ,seventh the and ;produce its

וְאָכְלוּ אֶבְיֹנֵי עַמֶּךָ וְיִתְרָם תֹּאכַל
eat shall leaving their and ,people thy of needy the eat shall and

חַיַּת הַשָּׂדֶה כֵּן־תַּעֲשֶׂה לְכַרְמְךָ [d]לְזֵיתֶךָ׃
.oliveyard thy to ,vineyard thy to do shall thou so ;field the of beasts the

12 שֵׁשֶׁת יָמִים תַּעֲשֶׂה מַעֲשֶׂיךָ וּבַיּוֹם הַשְּׁבִיעִי
¹seventh ²day the on and ,work thy do shalt thou days Six

תִּשְׁבֹּת לְמַעַן יָנוּחַ שׁוֹרְךָ וַחֲמֹרֶךָ
,ass thy and ox thy rest have may that order in ;rest shalt thou

וְיִנָּפֵשׁ בֶּן־אֲמָתְךָ וְהַגֵּר[e]׃
.sojourner the and ,slave female thy of son the breath take may and

13 וּבְכֹל אֲשֶׁר־אָמַרְתִּי אֲלֵיכֶם תִּשָּׁמֵרוּ וְשֵׁם
of name the and ;careful be you unto said have I which all in And

אֱלֹהִים אֲחֵרִים לֹא תַזְכִּירוּ [f]לֹא יִשָּׁמַע
heard be ²shall ¹it ³not ,mention ²shall ¹you ³not ¹another ²god

עַל־פִּיךָ[f]׃
.mouth thy upon

14 שָׁלֹשׁ רְגָלִים תָּחֹג לִי בַּשָּׁנָה׃
.year the in me to feast a make shalt thou times Three

15 אֶת־חַג הַמַּצּוֹת [g]תִּשְׁמֹר שִׁבְעַת יָמִים
days seven ;keep shalt thou bread unleavened of feast The

8 And thou
shalt take no
gift: for a gift
blindeth them
that have sight,
and perverteth
the words of
the righteous. 9
And a stranger
shalt thou not
oppress: for ye
know the heart
of a stranger,
seeing ye were
strangers in the
land of Egypt.
10 And six
years thou
shalt sow
thy land, and
shalt gather in
the increase
thereof: 11 but
the seventh year
thou shalt let it
rest and lie fal-
low; that the
poor of thy peo-
ple may eat:
and what they
leave the beast
of the field shall
eat. In like
manner thou
shalt deal with
thy vineyard,
and with thy
oliveyard. 12 Six
days thou shalt
do thy work,
and on the
seventh day
thou shalt rest:
that thine ox
and thine ass
may have rest,
and the son of
thy handmaid,
and the stran-
ger, may be re-
freshed. 13 And
in all things
that I have said
unto you take
ye heed: and
make no men-
tion of the name
of other gods,
neither let it be
heard out of
thy mouth.
14 Three
times thou shalt
keep a feast un-
to me in the
year. 15 The
feast of unleav-
ened bread shalt
thou keep: sev-

a Sm., G., S. add, *the eyes,* עיני.

b S. adds, *in judgment.*

c G., S. omit ו.

d G., S., V. add, *and,* ו.

e S. adds, *who is in thy cities.*

f S. has, *and they shall not go up on thy heart.*

g G. has, *you shall observe to do.*

unleavened
bread seven
days, as I com-
manded thee, in
the time ap-
pointed of the
month Abib;
for in it thou
camest out
from Egypt:
and none shall
appear before
me empty:) 16
And the feast of
harvest, the
firstfruits of thy
labours, which
thou hast sown
in the field:
and the feast of
ingathering,
which is in the
end of the year,
when thou hast
gathered in thy
labours out of
the field. 17
Three times in
the year all thy
males shall ap-
pear before the
Lord GOD. 18
Thou shalt not
offer the blood
of my sacrifice
with leavened
bread; neither
shall the fat of
my sacrifice re-
main until the
morning. 19 The
first of the first-
fruits of thy
land thou shalt
bring into the
house of the
LORD thy God.
Thou shalt not
seethe a kid in
his mother's
milk.

20 Behold I
send an Angel
before thee, to
keep thee in the
way, and to
bring thee into
the place which
I have prepared.

21 Beware of
him, and obey
his voice, pro-

תֹּאכַל מַצּוֹת כַּאֲשֶׁר צִוִּיתִךָ
,thee commanded have I as ,bread unleavened eat shalt thou

לְמוֹעֵד[a] חֹדֶשׁ הָאָבִיב כִּי־בוֹ יָצָאתָ
out camest thou it in for ,Abib of month the of time appointed the at

מִמִּצְרָיִם וְלֹא־יֵרָאוּ[b] פָנַי רֵיקָם׃
.empty me before appear not shall they and ;Egypt from

16 וְחַג הַקָּצִיר בִּכּוּרֵי מַעֲשֶׂיךָ[c] אֲשֶׁר
what [of] ,work thy of firstfruits the ,harvest of feast the And

תִּזְרַע בַּשָּׂדֶה וְחַג הָאָסִף בְּצֵאת
of out going the at ,gathering of feast the and ;field the in sowest thou

הַשָּׁנָה בְּאָסְפְּךָ אֶת־מַעֲשֶׂיךָ מִן־הַשָּׂדֶה׃
.field the from work thy gathering thy at ,year the

17 שָׁלֹשׁ פְּעָמִים בַּשָּׁנָה יֵרָאֶה כָּל־זְכוּרְךָ
thine of male every appear shall year the in times Three

18 אֶל־פְּנֵי הָאָדֹן[d] יְהוָה׃[d] לֹא־תִזְבַּח[e] עַל־חָמֵץ
bread leavened with offer not shalt Thou .Jehovah Lord the before unto

דַּם־זִבְחִי וְלֹא־יָלִין חֵלֶב־חַגִּי
,feast my of fat the night the pass not shall and ;sacrifice my of blood the

19 עַד־בֹּקֶר׃ רֵאשִׁית בִּכּוּרֵי[f] אַדְמָתְךָ[f]
,ground thy of firstfruits the ,first The .morning until

תָּבִיא בֵּית יְהוָה אֱלֹהֶיךָ
;God thy Jehovah of house the [to] bring shalt thou

לֹא־תְבַשֵּׁל גְּדִי בַּחֲלֵב אִמּוֹ׃[g]
.mother its of milk the in kid a boil not shalt thou

20 הִנֵּה[h] אָנֹכִי שֹׁלֵחַ מַלְאָךְ[i] לְפָנֶיךָ
,thee before angel an send to about [am] I Behold

לִשְׁמָרְךָ בַּדָּרֶךְ וְלַהֲבִיאֲךָ אֶל־הַמָּקוֹם[j] אֲשֶׁר
which place the unto thee bring to and ,way the in thee guard to

21 הֲכִנֹתִי׃ הִשָּׁמֶר מִפָּנָיו[k] וּשְׁמַע בְּקֹלוֹ
,voice his to hearken and ,him before from careful Be .prepared have I

en days thou
shalt eat unleav-
ened bread, as
I commanded
thee, at the time
appointed in the
month Abib (for
in it thou camest
out from E-
gypt); and none
shall appear be-
fore me empty:
16 and the feast
of harvest, the
firstfruits of thy
labours, which
thou sowest in
the field: and
the feast of in-
gathering, at
the end of the
year, when thou
gatherest in thy
labours out of
the field. 17
Three times in
the year all thy
males shall ap-
pear before the
Lord GOD. 18
Thou shalt not
offer the blood
of my sacrifice
with leavened
bread; neither
shall the fat of
my feast re-
main all night
until the morn-
ing. 19 The
first of the
firstfruits of
thy ground thou
shalt bring into
the house of the
LORD thy God.
Thou shalt not
seethe a kid in
its mother's
milk.

20 Behold, I
send an angel
before thee, to
keep thee by the
way, and to
bring thee into
the place which
I have prepared.

21 Take ye
heed of him,
and hearken un-
to his voice;

---

a S. omits.

b G., V. have, *thou shalt appear*; S., T., *you shall appear*; Sm. has, *they shall see.*

c G. adds, *thou shalt make*; cf. 34:22.

d G., S., V. have, *the Lord thy God.*

e G. adds, *for when I cast out nations from thy presence and make broad thy borders.*

f G. has, *thy firstfruits.*

g Sm. adds, *for he who does this has forgotten what he sacrifices, and this is indignation to the God of Jacob*; cf. Deut. 14:21.

h G. adds, *and*, ו.

i Sm., G., V. have, *my angel.*

j G., S. have, *the land.*

k G. has, *for thyself.*

voke him not ;
for he will not
pardon your
transgressions :
for my name *is*
in him. 22 But if
thou shalt in-
deed obey his
voice, and do all
that I speak ;
then I will be
an enemy unto
thine enemies,
and an adver-
sary unto thine
adversaries. 23
For mine Angel
shall go before
thee, and bring
thee in unto the
Amorites, and
the Hittites, and
the Perizzites,
and the Cana-
anites, the Hi-
vites, and the
Jebusites : and I
will cut them
off. 24 Thou
shalt not bow
down to their
gods, nor serve
them, nor do af-
ter their works :
but thou shalt
utterly over-
throw them, and
quite break
down their im-
ages. 25 And ye
shall serve the
LORD your God,
and he shall
bless thy bread,
and thy water ;
and I will take
sickness away
from the midst
of thee.

26 There shall
nothing cast
their young, nor
be barren, in
thy land : the
number of thy
days I will ful-
fil. 27 I will
send my fear be-
fore thee, and
will destroy all
the people to
whom thou
shalt come; and
I will make all

אַל־תַּמֵּר בּוֹ כִּי לֹא יִשָּׂא
forgive ²will ¹he ³not for ; him against rebellious be not do

22 לְפִשְׁעֲכֶם כִּי שְׁמִי בְּקִרְבּוֹ׃ [a]כִּי אִם־שָׁמוֹעַ
hearkening if For .him in [is] name my for ,transgression your (to)

תִּשְׁמַע בְּקֹלוֹ[b] וְעָשִׂיתָ כֹּל אֲשֶׁר אֲדַבֵּר
; speak I which all doest and ,voice his to hearken dost thou

וְאָיַבְתִּי אֶת־אֹיְבֶיךָ וְצַרְתִּי
to adversary an be will and ,enemies thine to enemy an be will I (and)

23 אֶת־צֹרְרֶיךָ׃ כִּי־יֵלֵךְ מַלְאָכִי לְפָנֶיךָ וֶהֱבִיאֲךָ
thee bring and ,thee before angel mine go shall For .adversaries thy

אֶל־הָאֱמֹרִי וְהַחִתִּי[c] וְהַפְּרִזִּי וְהַכְּנַעֲנִי[d]
,Canaanites the and ,Perizzites the and ,Hittites the and ,Amorites the unto

[e]הַחִוִּי וְהַיְבוּסִי וְהִכְחַדְתִּיו׃
.them destroy will I and ; Jebusites the and ,Hivites the

24 לֹא־תִשְׁתַּחֲוֶה לֵאלֹהֵיהֶם וְלֹא תָעָבְדֵם
,them serve ²shalt ¹thou ³not and ,gods their to thyself prostrate not shalt Thou

וְלֹא תַעֲשֶׂה כְּמַעֲשֵׂיהֶם כִּי הָרֵס
surely but ; works their like do ²shalt ¹thou ³not and

תְּהָרְסֵם וְשַׁבֵּר תְּשַׁבֵּר
pieces in break shalt thou surely and ,down them tear shalt thou

25 מַצֵּבֹתֵיהֶם׃ וַעֲבַדְתֶּם אֵת יְהוָה אֱלֹהֵיכֶם
,God your Jehovah serve shall you And .pillars memorial their

וּבֵרַךְ אֶת־לַחְמְךָ[f] וְאֶת־מֵימֶיךָ וַהֲסִרֹתִי
remove will I and ; water thy and bread thy bless will he and

26 מַחֲלָה מִקִּרְבֶּךָ[g]׃ לֹא־תִהְיֶה מְשַׁכֵּלָה וַעֲקָרָה
,barren a or ,aborting one be not Shall .midst thy from sickness

27 בְּאַרְצֶךָ אֶת־מִסְפַּר יָמֶיךָ אֲמַלֵּא׃ [h]אֶת־אֵימָתִי
terror My .fill will I days thy of number the ; land thy in

אֲשַׁלַּח לְפָנֶיךָ וְהַמֹּתִי אֶת־כָּל־הָעָם
[among] people the all confound will I and ,thee before send will I

אֲשֶׁר תָּבֹא בָּהֶם וְנָתַתִּי אֶת־
make will I and ; (them among) comest thou whom

provoke him
not : for he will
not pardon
your transgres-
sion ; for my
name is in him.
22 But if thou
shalt indeed
hearken unto
his voice, and
do all that I
speak ; then I
will be an enemy
unto thine en-
emies, and an
adversary unto
thine adversa-
ries. 23 For
mine angel
shall go before
thee, and bring
thee in unto the
Amorite, and
the Hittite, and
the Perizzite,
and the Canaan-
ite, the Hivite,
and the Jebu-
site : and I will
cut them off.
24 Thou shalt
not bow down
to their gods,
nor serve them,
nor do after
their works: but
thou shalt utter-
ly overthrow
them, and break
in pieces their
pillars. 25 And
ye shall serve
the LORD your
God, and he
shall bless thy
bread, and thy
water ; and I
will take sick-
ness away from
the midst of
thee.

26 There shall
none cast her
young, nor be
barren, in thy
land : the num-
ber of thy days
I will fulfil. 27
I will send my
terror before
thee, and will
discomfit all the
people to whom
thou shalt come,
and I will make

a G. adds, 19 : 5,6.
b Sm., G. have, *unto my voice.*
c Sm. adds, *and Girgashites.*
d G. adds, *and Girgashites.*
e G., S., V. add, *and*, ו.
f G. adds, *and thy wine.*
g S. has, *from your houses.*
h G., S. add, *and*, ו.

thine enemies
turn their backs
unto thee. 28
And I will send
hornets before
thee, which shall
drive out the
Hivite, the Ca-
naanite, and the
Hittite, from be-
fore thee. 29 I
will not drive
them out from
before thee in
one year; lest
the land become
desolate, and
the beast of the
field multiply a-
gainst thee. 30
By little and
little I will
drive them out
from before
thee, until thou
be increased,
and inherit the
land. 31 And I
will set thy
bounds from the
Red sea even
unto the sea of
the Philistines,
and from the
desert unto the
river: for I will
deliver the in-
habitants of the
land into your
hand; and thou
shalt drive them
out before thee.
32 Thou shalt
make no cove-
nant with them,
nor with their
gods. 33 They
shall not dwell
in thy land, lest
they make thee
sin against me:
for if thou serve
their gods, it
will surely be a
snare unto thee.

כָּל־אֹיְבֶיךָ[a] אֵלֶיךָ עֹרֶף׃ וְשָׁלַחְתִּי אֶת־הַצִּרְעָה 28
hornets send will I And .necks thee towards enemies thine all

לְפָנֶיךָ וְגֵרְשָׁה[b] [c]אֶת־הַחִוִּי אֶת־הַכְּנַעֲנִי
,Canaanites the ,Hivites the out drive shall they and ,thee before

וְאֶת־הַחִתִּי מִלְּפָנֶיךָ׃ לֹא אֲגָרְשֶׁנּוּ 29
out them drive ²will ¹I ³Not .thee before from Hittites the and

מִפָּנֶיךָ[d] בְּשָׁנָה אֶחָת פֶּן־תִּהְיֶה הָאָרֶץ שְׁמָמָה
,desolation a land the become lest ;¹one ²year in thee before from

וְרַבָּה עָלֶיךָ חַיַּת הַשָּׂדֶה׃ מְעַט מְעַט 30
little [by] Little .field the of beasts the thee upon multiply and

אֲגָרְשֶׁנּוּ מִפָּנֶיךָ עַד אֲשֶׁר תִּפְרֶה
,fruitful art thou that until ;thee before from out them drive will I

וְנָחַלְתָּ אֶת־הָאָרֶץ׃ וְשַׁתִּי אֶת־גְּבֻלְךָ 31
,border thy put will I And .land the possessest and

מִיַּם־סוּף וְעַד־יָם פְּלִשְׁתִּים
,Philistines the of sea the as far as (and) reeds of sea the from

וּמִמִּדְבָּר עַד־הַנָּהָר[e] כִּי ׀ אֶתֵּן
give will I for ;river the as far as wilderness the from and

בְּיֶדְכֶם אֵת יֹשְׁבֵי הָאָרֶץ וְגֵרַשְׁתָּמוֹ[f]
out them drive shalt thou and ;land the of inhabitants the hand your into

מִפָּנֶיךָ[g]׃ לֹא־תִכְרֹת לָהֶם וְלֵאלֹהֵיהֶם 32
gods their for and them for cut not shalt Thou .thee before from

בְּרִית׃ [h]לֹא יֵשְׁבוּ בְּאַרְצְךָ פֶּן־יַחֲטִיאוּ 33
sin to cause they lest ,land thy in dwell ²shall ¹they ³Not .covenant a

אֹתְךָ לִי כִּי תַעֲבֹד אֶת־אֱלֹהֵיהֶם כִּי־
,indeed gods their servest thou when ;me towards thee

יִהְיֶה[i] לְךָ לְמוֹקֵשׁ׃
.snare a (for) thee to be will it

all thine en-
emies turn their
backs unto thee.
28 And I will
send the hor-
net before thee,
which shall
drive out the
Hivite, the Ca-
naanite, and
the Hittite,
from before
thee. 29 I will
not drive them
out from before
thee in one
year; lest the
land become
desolate, and
the beast of the
field multiply a-
gainst thee. 30
By little and
little I will
drive them out
from before
thee, until thou
be increased,
and inherit the
land. 31 And I
will set thy bor-
der from the
Red Sea even
unto the sea of
the Philistines,
and from the
wilderness unto
the River: for I
will deliver the
inhabitants of
the land into
your hand; and
thou shalt drive
them out be-
fore thee. 32
Thou shalt
make no cove-
nant with them,
nor with their
gods. 33 They
shall not dwell
in thy land, lest
they make thee
sin against me:
for if thou serve
their gods, it
will surely be a
snare unto thee.

24

AND he said
unto Moses,
Come up unto
the LORD, thou,

וְאֶל־מֹשֶׁה אָמַר עֲלֵה אֶל־יְהוָה אַתָּה 1
,thou ,Jehovah unto up Come :said he Moses unto And

And he said
unto Moses,
Come up unto
the LORD, thou,

---

a S. omits כל.

b G. has, *and thou shalt drive out*, and adds, *the Amorites;* S. has, *and I will drive out;* Sm. adds all the nations mentioned in v. 23.

c G., V. add, *and*, ו; S. omits.

d G. omits.

e G. has, *the great river Euphrates.*

f G., V. have, *and I will drive them out.*

g S. omits.

h G., S. add, *and*, ו.

i Sm. G., S., T. have pl.

and Aaron,
Nadab, and A-
bihu, and sev-
enty of the eld-
ers of Israel;
and worship ye
afar off. 2 And
Moses alone
shall come near
the LORD: but
they shall not
come nigh; nei-
ther shall the
people go up
with him.

3 And Moses
came and told
the people all
the words of the
LORD, and all
the judgments:
and all the peo-
ple answered
with one voice,
and said, All
the words which
the LORD hath
said will we do.
4 And Moses
wrote all the
words of the
LORD, and rose
up early in the
morning, and
builded an altar
under the hill,
and twelve pil-
lars, according
to the twelve
tribes of Israel.
5 And he sent
young men of
the children of
Israel, which
offered burnt
offerings and
sacrificed peace
offerings of ox-
en unto the
LORD. 6 And
Moses took half
of the blood,
and put *it* in
basons; and half
of the blood he
sprinkled on the
altar. 7 And he
took the book of
the covenant,
and read in the
audience of the
people: and they
said, All that
the LORD hath
said will we do,

וְאַהֲרֹן [a] נָדָב וַאֲבִיהוּא [b] וְשִׁבְעִים מִזִּקְנֵי
of elders the from seventy and ,Abihu and ,Nadab ,Aaron and

2 יִשְׂרָאֵל וְהִשְׁתַּחֲוִיתֶם מֵרָחֹק [c]׃ וְנִגַּשׁ
approach let And .distance a from yourselves prostrate and ;Israel

מֹשֶׁה לְבַדּוֹ אֶל־יְהוָֹה וְהֵם לֹא יִגָּשׁוּ
;approach [1]shall [2]not they and ,Jehovah unto himself by Moses

3 וְהָעָם לֹא יַעֲלוּ עִמּוֹ [d]׃ וַיָּבֹא מֹשֶׁה
Moses came And .him with up go [1]shall [2]not people the and

וַיְסַפֵּר לָעָם אֵת כָּל־דִּבְרֵי יְהוָֹה וְאֵת [e] כָּל־
all and ,Jehovah of words the all people the to related and

הַמִּשְׁפָּטִים וַיַּעַן כָּל־הָעָם קוֹל אֶחָד
,[1]one [2]voice [with] people the all answered and ;judgments the

וַיֹּאמְרוּ כָּל־הַדְּבָרִים אֲשֶׁר־דִּבֶּר יְהוָֹה נַעֲשֶׂה [f]׃
.do will we Jehovah spoken has which words the All :said and

4 וַיִּכְתֹּב מֹשֶׁה אֵת כָּל־דִּבְרֵי יְהוָֹה וַיַּשְׁכֵּם
early rose he and ;Jehovah of words the all Moses wrote And

בַּבֹּקֶר וַיִּבֶן מִזְבֵּחַ תַּחַת הָהָר וּשְׁתֵּים
[and] two and ,mountain the below altar an built and ,morning the in

עֶשְׂרֵה מַצֵּבָה [g] לִשְׁנֵים עָשָׂר שִׁבְטֵי
of tribes ten [and] two the for pillars memorial ten

5 יִשְׂרָאֵל׃ וַיִּשְׁלַח אֶת־נַעֲרֵי בְּנֵי יִשְׂרָאֵל
,Israel of children the of youths sent he And .Israel

וַיַּעֲלוּ עֹלֹת וַיִּזְבְּחוּ זְבָחִים
,sacrifices sacrificed and offerings burnt up offered they and

6 שְׁלָמִים לַיהוָֹה פָּרִים׃ וַיִּקַּח מֹשֶׁה חֲצִי
of half Moses took And .oxen ,Jehovah to ,offerings peace

הַדָּם וַיָּשֶׂם בָּאַגָּנֹת וַחֲצִי הַדָּם זָרַק
sprinkled he blood the of half and ;basins in put he and ,blood the

7 עַל־הַמִּזְבֵּחַ׃ וַיִּקַּח סֵפֶר הַבְּרִית וַיִּקְרָא
read he and ,covenant the of book the took he And .altar the upon

בְּאָזְנֵי הָעָם וַיֹּאמְרוּ כֹּל אֲשֶׁר־דִּבֶּר
spoken has which All :said they and ;people the of ears the in

and Aaron, Na-
dab, and Abihu,
and seventy of
the elders of Is-
rael; and wor-
ship ye afar off:
2 and Moses
alone shall come
near unto the
LORD; but they
shall not come
near; neither
shall the peo-
ple go up with
him.

3 And Moses
came and told
the people all
the words of the
LORD, and all
the judgments:
and all the peo-
ple answered
with one voice,
and said, All
the words which
the LORD hath
spoken will we
do. 4 And Mo-
ses wrote all the
words of the
LORD, and rose
up early in the
morning, and
builded an altar
under the
mount, and
twelve pillars,
according to the
twelve tribes of
Israel. 5 And he
sent young men
of the children
of Israel, which
offered burnt
offerings, and
sacrificed peace
offerings of ox-
en unto the
LORD. 6 And
Moses took half
of the blood,
and put it in
basons; and
half of the blood
he sprinkled on
the altar. 7 And
he took the
book of the cov-
enant, and read
in the audience
of the people:
and they said,
All that the
LORD hath
spoken will we

a G., S. add, *and*, ו.
b Sm. adds, *Eleazar and Ithamar*.
c G. adds, *before the Lord*.
d G. has, *with them*.
e G., V. omit כל.
f G. adds, *and will hear*.
g Sm., G. have, *stones*.

and be obedient.
8 And Moses
took the blood,
and sprinkled *it*
on the people,
and said, Be-
hold the blood
of the covenant,
which the LORD
hath made with
you concerning
all these words.

9 Then went
up Moses, and
Aaron, Nadab,
and Abihu, and
seventy of the
elders of Israel:
10 And they saw
the God of Is-
rael: and *there*
was under his
feet as it were a
paved work of a
sapphire stone,
and as it were
the body of
heaven in *his*
clearness. 11
And upon the
nobles of the
children of Is-
rael he laid not
his hand: also
they saw God,
and did eat and
drink.

12 And the
LORD said unto
Moses, Come up
to me into the
mount, and be
there: and I
will give thee
tables of stone,
and a law, and
commandments
which I have
written; that
thou mayest
teach them. 13
And Moses rose
up, and his min-
ister Joshua: and
Moses went up
into the mount
of God. 14 And
he said unto the
elders, Tarry ye
here for us, un-

8 יְהוָה נַעֲשֶׂה וְנִשְׁמָע׃ וַיִּקַּח מֹשֶׁה
Moses took And .hear will and ,do will we Jehovah

אֶת־הַדָּם וַיִּזְרֹק עַל־הָעָם וַיֹּאמֶר הִנֵּה
Behold :said and ,people the upon sprinkled and ,blood the

דַם־הַבְּרִית אֲשֶׁר כָּרַת יְהוָה עִמָּכֶם
you with Jehovah cut has which ,covenant the of blood the

9 עַל כָּל־הַדְּבָרִים הָאֵלֶּה׃ וַיַּעַל מֹשֶׁה
,Moses up went And .¹these ²words all concerning

וְאַהֲרֹן [a] נָדָב [b] וַאֲבִיהוּא וְשִׁבְעִים מִזִּקְנֵי
of elders the from seventy and ,Abihu and ,Nadab ,Aaron and

10 יִשְׂרָאֵל׃ וַיִּרְאוּ [c] אֵת אֱלֹהֵי יִשְׂרָאֵל וְתַחַת
under and ;Israel of God the saw they And .Israel

רַגְלָיו כְּמַעֲשֵׂה לִבְנַת הַסַּפִּיר וּכְעֶצֶם [d]
(of bone the) like and ,sapphire of plate a of work the like feet his

11 הַשָּׁמַיִם לָטֹהַר׃ וְאֶל־אֲצִילֵי בְּנֵי
of children the of nobles the upon And .clearness for heavens the

יִשְׂרָאֵל לֹא [e] שָׁלַח יָדוֹ [e] וַיֶּחֱזוּ [f]
saw they and ;hand his out stretch ²did ¹he ³not Israel

אֶת־הָאֱלֹהִים [f] וַיֹּאכְלוּ וַיִּשְׁתּוּ׃
.drank and ate they and ,God

12 וַיֹּאמֶר יְהוָה אֶל־מֹשֶׁה עֲלֵה אֵלַי
me unto up Come :Moses unto Jehovah said And

הָהָרָה וֶהְיֵה־שָׁם וְאֶתְּנָה לְךָ
thee to give will I and ;there be and ,mountain the to

אֶת־לֻחֹת הָאֶבֶן [g] וְהַתּוֹרָה וְהַמִּצְוָה אֲשֶׁר
which ,commandment the and ,law the and ,stone of tablets the

13 כָּתַבְתִּי לְהוֹרֹתָם׃ וַיָּקָם מֹשֶׁה וִיהוֹשֻׁעַ
Joshua and ,Moses arose And .them teach to ,written have I

מְשָׁרְתוֹ וַיַּעַל [h] מֹשֶׁה [i] אֶל־הַר הָאֱלֹהִים׃
.God of mountain the unto Moses up went and ;attendant his

14 וְאֶל־הַזְּקֵנִים אָמַר [j] שְׁבוּ־לָנוּ בָזֶה עַד
until ,[place] this in us for Sit :said had he elders the unto And

do, and be obe-
dient. 8 And
Moses took the
blood, and
sprinkled it on
the people, and
said, Behold the
blood of the
covenant, which
the LORD hath
made with you
concerning all
these words.

9 Then went
up Moses, and
Aaron, Nadab,
and Abihu, and
seventy of the
elders of Israel:
10 and they saw
the God of Is-
rael; and there
was under his
feet as it were a
paved work of
sapphire stone,
and as it were
the very heaven
for clearness. 11
And upon the
nobles of the
children of Is-
rael he laid not
his hand: and
they beheld
God, and did
eat and drink.

12 And the
LORD said unto
Moses, Come
up to me into
the mount, and
be there: and I
will give thee
the tables of
stone, and the
law and the
commandment,
which I have
written, that
thou mayest
teach them. 13
And Moses rose
up, and Joshua
his minister:
and Moses went
up into the
mount of God.
14 And he said
unto the elders,
Tarry ye here
for us, until we

---

a G., S. add, *and*, ו.

b Sm. adds, *Eleazar and Ithamar*.

c G. adds, *the place where stood*; T. adds, *the glory of*.

d G. has, *and as the form of the firmament of*.

e G. has, *did not perish even one*.

f G. has, *and they appeared in the place of God*; T., *and they saw the glory of God*.

g Sm., G. omit ו.

h G. has pl.

i G. omits.

j G. has pl.

til we come a-
gain unto you :
and, behold,
Aaron and Hur
are with you : if
any man have
any matters to
do, let him come
unto them. 15
And Moses went
up into the
mount, and a
cloud covered
the mount. 16
And the glory
of the LORD a-
bode upon
mount Sinai,
and the cloud
covered it six
days : and the
seventh day he
called unto Mo-
ses out of the
midst of the
cloud. 17 And
the sight of the
glory of the
LORD *was* like
devouring fire
on the top of
the mount in
the eyes of the
children of Is-
rael. 18 And
Moses went into
the midst of the
cloud, and gat
him up into the
mount: and Mo-
ses was in the
mount forty
days and forty
nights.

אֲשֶׁר־נָשׁוּב אֲלֵיכֶם וְהִנֵּה אַהֲרֹן וְחוּר
Hur and | Aaron | ,behold and | ; you unto | return we that

עִמָּכֶם מִי־בַעַל דְּבָרִים יִגַּשׁ
approach him let | ,matters | of master [is] whoever | ,you with [being]

15 אֲלֵהֶם׃ וַיַּעַל מֹשֶׁה [a] אֶל־הָהָר וַיְכַס
covered and | ; mountain the into | Moses | up went And | .them unto

16 הֶעָנָן אֶת־הָהָר׃ [b] וַיִּשְׁכֹּן [c] כְּבוֹד־יְהוָה [d] עַל־
upon | Jehovah of glory the | dwelt And | .mountain the | cloud a

הַר סִינַי וַיְכַסֵּהוּ הֶעָנָן שֵׁשֶׁת יָמִים
; days | six | cloud the | it covered and | ,Sinai | of mountain the

[e] וַיִּקְרָא אֶל־מֹשֶׁה בַּיּוֹם הַשְּׁבִיעִי מִתּוֹךְ
of midst the from | [1]seventh | [2]day the on | Moses unto | called he and

17 הֶעָנָן׃ וּמַרְאֵה [f] כְּבוֹד יְהוָה כְּאֵשׁ
fire like [was] | Jehovah | of glory the | of appearance the And | .cloud the

אֹכֶלֶת בְּרֹאשׁ הָהָר לְעֵינֵי
of eyes the before | ,mountain the | of summit the on | consuming

18 [g] בְּנֵי יִשְׂרָאֵל׃ וַיָּבֹא מֹשֶׁה בְּתוֹךְ
of midst the into | Moses | came And | .Israel | of children the

הֶעָנָן וַיַּעַל אֶל־הָהָר וַיְהִי מֹשֶׁה [h]
Moses | was and | ; mountain the into | up went he and | ,cloud the

בָּהָר אַרְבָּעִים יוֹם וְאַרְבָּעִים לָיְלָה׃
.nights | forty and | days | forty | mountain the in

come again un-
to you : and,
behold, Aaron
and Hur are
with you : who-
soever hath a
cause, let him
come near unto
them. 15 And
Moses went up
into the mount,
and the cloud
covered the
mount. 16 And
the glory of the
LORD abode up-
on mount Sinai,
and the cloud
covered it six
days : and the
seventh day he
called unto Mo-
ses out of the
midst of the
cloud. 17 And
the appearance
of the glory of
the LORD was
like devouring
fire on the top
of the mount in
the eyes of the
children of Is-
rael. 18 And Mo-
ses entered into
the midst of the
cloud, and went
up into the
mount: and Mo-
ses was in the
mount forty
days and forty
nights.

25

AND the
LORD spake un-
to Moses, say-
ing, 2 Speak un-
to the children
of Israel, that
they bring me
an offering : of
every man that
giveth it willing-
ly with his heart
ye shall take my
offering. 3 And
this *is* the offer-
ing which ye
shall take of

1 וַיְדַבֵּר יְהוָה אֶל־מֹשֶׁה לֵּאמֹר׃ [i] דַּבֵּר אֶל־
2 unto | Speak | :saying | Moses unto | Jehovah | spoke And

בְּנֵי יִשְׂרָאֵל וְיִקְחוּ־לִי תְּרוּמָה
; contribution a | me for take them let and | ,Israel | of children the

מֵאֵת כָּל־אִישׁ אֲשֶׁר יִדְּבֶנּוּ לִבּוֹ תִּקְחוּ
take them let | [1]heart (his) | [3]him [2]impels | whose | man every | (with) from

3 אֶת־תְּרוּמָתִי׃ וְזֹאת הַתְּרוּמָה אֲשֶׁר תִּקְחוּ
take shall you | which | contribution the | [is] this And | .contribution my

And the
LORD spake un-
to Moses, say-
ing, 2 Speak un-
to the children
of Israel, that
they take for
me an offering :
of every man
whose heart
maketh him
willing ye shall
take my offer-
ing. 3 And this
is the offering
which ye shall
take of them ;

---

a G. adds, *and Joshua.*
b S. has, *him.*
c G. has, *and descended.*
d G. has, *God.*
e G., S. add, *the Lord*, יהוה.
f S. has, *and he saw.*
g S. adds, *all*, כל.
h G., V. have, *there*, שם.
i S. adds, *to him.*

them; gold, and silver, and brass, 4 And blue, and purple, and scarlet, and fine linen, and goats' *hair*, 5 And rams' skins dyed red, and badgers' skins, and shittim wood, 6 Oil for the light, spices for anointing oil, and for sweet incense, 7 Onyx stones, and stones to be set in the ephod, and in the breastplate. 8 And let them make me a sanctuary; that I may dwell among them. 9 According to all that I shew thee, *after* the pattern of the tabernacle, and the pattern of all the instruments thereof, even so shall ye make *it*.

10 And they shall make an ark *of* shittim wood: two cubits and a half *shall be* the length thereof, and a cubit and a half the breadth thereof, and a cubit and a half the height thereof. 11 And thou shalt overlay it with pure gold, within and without shalt thou overlay it, and shalt make upon it a crown of gold round about. 12 And thou shalt cast four rings of gold for it, and put *them* in the four corners thereof; and two rings *shall be* in the one

4 מֵאִתָּם זָהָב וָכֶסֶף וּנְחֹשֶׁת׃ וּתְכֵלֶת
,blue and ; bronze and ,silver and ,gold ; them (with) from

וְאַרְגָּמָן וְתוֹלַעַת שָׁנִי וְשֵׁשׁ וְעִזִּים׃
; [hair] goats and ,byssus and ,crimson (of worm) and ,purple and

5 וְעֹרֹת אֵילִם מְאָדָּמִים וְעֹרֹת תְּחָשִׁים וַעֲצֵי
of wood of pieces and ,dolphins of skins and ,red dyed rams of skins and

6 שִׁטִּים׃ [a] שֶׁמֶן לַמָּאֹר בְּשָׂמִים לְשֶׁמֶן הַמִּשְׁחָה
,anointing of oil the for spices ,light the for oil ; acacia

7 וְלִקְטֹרֶת הַסַּמִּים׃ [b] אַבְנֵי־שֹׁהַם וְאַבְנֵי
(of) stones and ,onyx of stones ; perfumes of incense the for and

8 מִלֻּאִים לָאֵפֹד וְלַחֹשֶׁן׃ וְעָשׂוּ
make them let And .breastplate the for and ,ephod the for ,setting [for]

9 לִי מִקְדָּשׁ וְשָׁכַנְתִּי בְּתוֹכָם׃ [c] כְּכֹל
all to According .midst their in dwell may I that ,sanctuary a me for

אֲשֶׁר אֲנִי מַרְאֶה אוֹתְךָ [d] אֵת תַּבְנִית
of plan the ,thee see to cause to about [am] I which

הַמִּשְׁכָּן וְאֵת תַּבְנִית [e] כָּל־כֵּלָיו וְכֵן [f] תַּעֲשׂוּ׃ [f]
.do shall you so and ; vessels its all of plan the and habitation the

10 וְעָשׂוּ [g] אֲרוֹן [h] עֲצֵי שִׁטִּים אַמָּתַיִם
cubits two ;acacia of wood of pieces of ark an make shall they And

וָחֵצִי אָרְכּוֹ וְאַמָּה וָחֵצִי רָחְבּוֹ וְאַמָּה
cubit a and ,width its half a and cubit a and ,length its half a and

11 וָחֵצִי קֹמָתוֹ׃ וְצִפִּיתָ אֹתוֹ זָהָב
[2]gold [with] it overlay shalt thou And .height its half a and

טָהוֹר מִבַּיִת וּמִחוּץ תְּצַפֶּנּוּ
; it overlay shalt thou outside (from) and inside (from) ,[1]pure

וְעָשִׂיתָ עָלָיו זֵר זָהָב סָבִיב׃
.about round gold of wreath a it upon make shalt thou and

12 וְיָצַקְתָּ לּוֹ אַרְבַּע טַבְּעֹת זָהָב וְנָתַתָּה
put shalt and ,gold of rings four it for cast shalt thou And

עַל אַרְבַּע פַּעֲמֹתָיו [i] וּשְׁתֵּי טַבָּעֹת עַל־צַלְעוֹ
side its upon rings two (and) ; feet [1]its [2]four upon

gold, and silver, and brass; 4 and blue, and purple, and scarlet, and fine linen, and goats' *hair;* 5 and rams' skins dyed red, and sealskins, and acacia wood; 6 oil for the light, spices for the anointing oil, and for the sweet incense; 7 onyx stones, and stones to be set, for the ephod, and for the breastplate. 8 And let them make me a sanctuary; that I may dwell among them. 9 According to all that I shew thee, the pattern of the tabernacle, and the pattern of all the furniture thereof, even so shall ye make it.

10 And they shall make an ark of acacia wood: two cubits and a half shall be the length thereof, and a cubit and a half the breadth thereof, and a cubit and a half the height thereof. 11 And thou shalt overlay it with pure gold, within and without shalt thou overlay it, and shalt make upon it a crown of gold round about. 12 And thou shalt cast four rings of gold for it, and put them in the four feet thereof; and two rings shall be on the one side

---

a G. omits verse.
b G., S. add, *and*, ו.
c G. adds, *and thou shalt make for me.*
d Sm., G. add, *in the mount.*
e S., V. omit.
f Sm., G. have, *so thou shalt do;* S. omits ו.
g Sm., G. have, *and thou shalt make;* V. omits.
h G. adds, *of witness.*
i G., S., V. omit ו.

side of it, and
two rings in the
other side of it.
13 And thou
shalt make
staves *of* shit-
tim wood, and
overlay them
with gold. 14
And thou shalt
put the staves
into the rings by
the sides of the
ark, that the ark
may be borne
with them. 15
The staves shall
be in the rings
of the ark: they
shall not be
taken from it. 16
And thou shalt
put into the ark
the testimony
which I shall
give thee. 17
And thou shalt
make a mercy
seat *of* pure
gold: two cubits
and a half *shall*
be the length
thereof, and a
cubit and a half
the breadth
thereof. 18 And
thou shalt make
two cherubim *of*
gold, *of* beaten
work shalt thou
make them, in
the two ends of
the mercy seat.
19 And make
one cherub on
the one end, and
the other cherub
on the other
end: *even* of the
mercy seat shall
ye make the
cherubim on the
two ends there-
of. 20 And the
cherubim shall
stretch forth
their wings on
high, covering
the mercy seat
with their
wings, and their
faces *shall look*
one to another;
toward the mer-
cy seat shall the
faces of the
cherubim be. 21

13 הָאֶחָת וּשְׁתֵּי טַבָּעֹת עַל־צַלְעוֹ הַשֵּׁנִית׃ וְעָשִׂיתָ
make shalt thou And .second side its upon rings two and ,one

בַדֵּי עֲצֵי שִׁטִּים וְצִפִּיתָ אֹתָם
them overlay shalt thou and ;acacia of wood of pieces of poles

14 זָהָב׃ וְהֵבֵאתָ אֶת־הַבַּדִּים בַּטַּבָּעֹת
,rings the into poles the bring shalt thou And .gold [with]

עַל צַלְעֹת הָאָרֹן לָשֵׂאת אֶת־הָאָרֹן בָּהֶם׃
.them by ark the carry to ,ark the of sides the upon

15 בְּטַבְּעֹת הָאָרֹן יִהְיוּ הַבַּדִּים לֹא[a] יָסֻרוּ
depart ²shall ¹they ³not ,poles the be shall ark the of rings the In

16 מִמֶּנּוּ׃[a] וְנָתַתָּ אֶל־הָאָרֹן אֵת הָעֵדֻת
testimony the ark the into put shalt thou And .it from

17 אֲשֶׁר אֶתֵּן אֵלֶיךָ׃ וְעָשִׂיתָ כַפֹּרֶת
of lid expiating an make shalt thou And .thee unto give shall I which

זָהָב טָהוֹר אַמָּתַיִם וָחֵצִי אָרְכָּהּ וְאַמָּה
cubit a and ,length its half a and cubits two ;¹pure ²gold

18 וָחֵצִי רָחְבָּהּ׃ וְעָשִׂיתָ שְׁנַיִם כְּרֻבִים
of cherubs two make shalt thou And .width its half a and

זָהָב מִקְשָׁה תַּעֲשֶׂה[b] אֹתָם מִשְּׁנֵי קְצוֹת
of ends two the from ,them make shalt thou work chased [of] ;gold

19 הַכַּפֹּרֶת׃ וַעֲשֵׂה[c] כְּרוּב אֶחָד מִקָּצָה מִזֶּה
,here end the from ¹one ²cherub make And .lid expiating the

וּכְרוּב־אֶחָד מִקָּצָה מִזֶּה מִן־הַכַּפֹּרֶת[d] תַּעֲשׂוּ[e]
make shall you lid expiating the from ;there end the from cherub one and

20 אֶת־הַכְּרֻבִים[f] עַל־שְׁנֵי קְצוֹתָיו׃[d] וְהָיוּ הַכְּרֻבִים
cherubs the be shall And .ends ¹its ²two upon cherubs the

פֹּרְשֵׂי כְנָפַיִם לְמַעְלָה סֹכְכִים בְּכַנְפֵיהֶם עַל־
upon wings their with covering ,above (to) wings out spreading

הַכַּפֹּרֶת וּפְנֵיהֶם אִישׁ אֶל־אָחִיו
;brother its towards each [being] faces their and ,lid expiating the

אֶל־הַכַּפֹּרֶת יִהְיוּ פְּנֵי הַכְּרֻבִים׃
.cherubs the of faces the be shall lid expiating the towards

of it, and two
rings on the
other side of it.
13 And thou
shalt make
staves of acacia
wood, and over-
lay them with
gold. 14 And
thou shalt put
the staves into
the rings on the
sides of the ark,
to bear the ark
withal. 15 The
staves shall be
in the rings of
the ark: they
shall not be
taken from it. 16
And thou shalt
put into the ark
the testimony
which I shall
give thee. 17
And thou shalt
make a mercy-
seat of pure
gold: two cubits
and a half *shall*
be the length
thereof, and a
cubit and a half
the breadth
thereof. 18 And
thou shalt make
two cherubim of
gold; of beaten
work shalt thou
make them, at
the two ends of
the mercy-seat.
19 And make
one cherub at
the one end,
and one cherub
at the other end:
of one piece
with the mercy-
seat shall ye
make the cheru-
bim on the two
ends thereof. 20
And the cheru-
bim shall spread
out their wings
on high, cover-
ing the mercy-
seat with their
wings, with
their faces one
to another; to-
ward the mercy-
seat shall the
faces of the cher-
ubim be. 21 And

---

a G. has, *immovable.*
b G. has, *and thou shalt put.*
c Sm., V. have, *and shall be made.*
d V. omits.
e G., S. have, *and thou shalt make;* Sm. has, *thou shalt make.*
f G., S. add, *two.*

And thou shalt
put the mercy
seat above upon
the ark; and in
the ark thou
shalt put the
testimony that I
shall give thee.
22 And there I
will meet with
thee, and I will
commune with
thee from above
the mercy seat,
from between
the two cheru-
bims which *are*
upon the ark of
the testimony,
of all *things*
which I will give
thee in com-
mandment unto
the children of
Israel.
23 Thou shalt
also make a
table *of* shittim
wood: two cu-
bits *shall be* the
length there-
of, and a cubit
the breadth
thereof, and a
cubit and a half
the height there-
of. 24 And thou
shalt overlay it
with pure gold,
and make there-
to a crown of
gold round a-
bout. 25 And
thou shalt make
unto it a border
of an hand-
breadth round
about, and thou
shalt make a
golden crown to
the border there-
of round about.
26 And thou
shalt make for
it four rings of
gold, and put
the rings in the
four corners
that *are* on the
four feet there-
of. 27 Over a-
gainst the bor-
der shall the

21 וְנָתַתָּ אֶת־הַכַּפֹּרֶת עַל־הָאָרֹן מִלְמָעְלָה
And thou shalt put the expiating lid upon the ark from (to) above;

וְאֶל־הָאָרֹן תִּתֵּן אֶת־הָעֵדֻת אֲשֶׁר אֶתֵּן
and into the ark thou shalt put the testimony, which I shall give

22 אֵלֶיךָ׃ וְנוֹעַדְתִּי[a] לְךָ שָׁם וְדִבַּרְתִּי אִתְּךָ
unto thee. And I will meet (to) thee there, and will speak with thee,

מֵעַל הַכַּפֹּרֶת מִבֵּין שְׁנֵי הַכְּרֻבִים
from upon the expiating lid, from between the two cherubs,

אֲשֶׁר עַל־אֲרוֹן הָעֵדֻת אֵת כָּל־אֲשֶׁר אֲצַוֶּה
which [are] upon the ark of testimony, all which I shall command

אוֹתְךָ אֶל־בְּנֵי יִשְׂרָאֵל׃
thee concerning the children of Israel.

23 וְעָשִׂיתָ שֻׁלְחָן עֲצֵי[b] שִׁטִּים[b]
And thou shalt make a table, [of] pieces of wood of acacia;

אַמָּתַיִם אָרְכּוֹ וְאַמָּה רָחְבּוֹ וְאַמָּה וָחֵצִי
two cubits its length, and a cubit its width, and a cubit and a half

24 קֹמָתוֹ׃ וְצִפִּיתָ[c] אֹתוֹ זָהָב טָהוֹר[c]
its height. And thou shalt overlay it [with] [2]gold [1]pure;

וְעָשִׂיתָ לּוֹ זֵר זָהָב[d] סָבִיב׃
and thou shalt make for it a wreath of gold round about.

25 וְעָשִׂיתָ[e] לּוֹ מִסְגֶּרֶת טֹפַח סָבִיב
And thou shalt make for it a border of a handbreadth round about;

וְעָשִׂיתָ[f] זֵר־זָהָב לְמִסְגַּרְתּוֹ סָבִיב׃
and thou shalt make a wreath of gold to its border round about.

26 וְעָשִׂיתָ לּוֹ[g] אַרְבַּע טַבְּעֹת זָהָב
And thou shalt make for it four rings of gold;

וְנָתַתָּ[h] אֶת־הַטַּבָּעֹת[h] עַל אַרְבַּע הַפֵּאֹת
and thou shalt put the rings upon the four corners,

27 אֲשֶׁר[i] לְאַרְבַּע רַגְלָיו׃ לְעֻמַּת[j] הַמִּסְגֶּרֶת תִּהְיֶיןָ[k]
which [are] to [2]four [1]its feet. Near the border shall be

thou shalt put
the mercy-seat
above upon the
ark; and in the
ark thou shalt
put the testi-
mony that I
shall give thee.
22 And there I
will meet with
thee, and I will
commune with
thee from above
the mercy-seat,
from between
the two cher-
ubim which are
upon the ark of
the testimony,
of all things
which I will
give thee in
commandment
unto the chil-
dren of Israel.
23 And thou
shalt make a
table of acacia
wood: two cu-
bits *shall be* the
length thereof,
and a cubit the
breadth there-
of, and a cubit
and a half the
height thereof.
24 And thou
shalt overlay it
with pure gold,
and make there-
to a crown of
gold round a-
bout. 25 And
thou shalt make
unto it a border
of an hand-
breadth round
about, and thou
shalt make a
golden crown to
the border there-
of round about.
26 And thou
shalt make for
it four rings of
gold, and put
the rings in the
four corners
that are on the
four feet there-
of. 27 Close by
the border shall

---

a G. has, *and I will be known*, ונדעתי.

b G. has, *golden*, *of pure gold*.

c G. has, *and thou shalt make for it waving mouldings of gold round about*.

d G. has, *of a skilful man*.

e For the verse G. has, *and thou shalt make a waving moulding for the crown round about*.

f S. adds, *for it*.

g G., V. omit.

h S. has, *and thou shalt make four rings of gold*.

i G. has, *of its feet*.

j G., V. have, *under the crown*, G. joining with v. 26.

k G. adds, *and*, ו.

rings be for
places of the
staves to bear
the table. 28
And thou shalt
make the staves
of shittim wood,
and overlay
them with gold,
that the table
may be borne
with them. 29
And thou shalt
make the dishes
thereof, and
spoons thereof,
and covers
thereof, and
bowls thereof,
to cover withal:
of pure gold
shalt thou make
them. 30 And
thou shalt set
upon the table
shewbread be-
fore me alway.

31 And thou
shalt make a
candlestick *of*
pure gold: *of*
beaten work
shall the candle-
stick be made:
his shaft, and
his branches,
his bowls, his
knops, and his
flowers, shall be
of the same. 32
And six branch-
es shall come out
of the sides of it;
three branches
of the candle-
stick out of the
one side, and
three branches
of the candle-
stick out of the
other side: 33
Three bowls
made like unto
almonds, *with* a
knop and flower
in one branch;
and three bowls
made like al-
monds in the
other branch,
with a knop and
a flower: so in
the six branch-

הַטַּבָּעֹת לְבָתִּים לְבַדִּים לָשֵׂאת אֶת־הַשֻּׁלְחָן׃ [a]
.table the carry to ,poles the for houses for ,rings the

28 וְעָשִׂיתָ אֶת־הַבַּדִּים עֲצֵי שִׁטִּים
,acacia of wood of pieces [of] poles the make shalt thou And

וְצִפִּיתָ אֹתָם זָהָב[b] וְנִשָּׂא־בָם
them by carried be shall and ;gold [with] them overlay shalt thou and

29 אֶת־הַשֻּׁלְחָן׃ וְעָשִׂיתָ קְעָרֹתָיו וְכַפֹּתָיו
,bowls its and ,platters its make shalt thou And .table the

וּקְשׂוֹתָיו וּמְנַקִּיֹּתָיו אֲשֶׁר יֻסַּךְ
made is libation a which [with] cups sacrificial its and ,pitchers its and

בָּהֵן זָהָב טָהוֹר תַּעֲשֶׂה אֹתָם׃
.them make shalt thou ¹pure ²gold [of] ;(them with)

30 וְנָתַתָּ עַל־הַשֻּׁלְחָן לֶחֶם פָּנִים לְפָנַי
me before face the of bread table the upon put shalt thou And

תָּמִיד׃
.continually

31 וְעָשִׂיתָ מְנֹרַת זָהָב טָהוֹר מִקְשָׁה
work chased [of] ;¹pure ²gold of lampstand a make shalt thou And

תֵּיעָשֶׂה[c] הַמְּנוֹרָה יְרֵכָהּ וְקָנָהּ [d]גְּבִיעֶיהָ
,calixes its ;stalk its and thigh its ,lampstand the made be shall

32 [e]כַּפְתֹּרֶיהָ וּפְרָחֶיהָ מִמֶּנָּה יִהְיוּ׃ וְשִׁשָּׁה קָנִים
stalks six And .be shall it from ,blossoms its and ,knobs its

יֹצְאִים מִצִּדֶּיהָ שְׁלֹשָׁה ׀ קְנֵי מְנֹרָה[f]
lamp the of stalks three ;sides its from out going

מִצִּדָּהּ הָאֶחָד וּשְׁלֹשָׁה קְנֵי מְנֹרָה[g] מִצִּדָּהּ
,side its from lamp the of stalks three and ,one the ,side its from

33 הַשֵּׁנִי׃ שְׁלֹשָׁה גְבִעִים מְשֻׁקָּדִים בַּקָּנֶה הָאֶחָד
,¹one ²stalk the on almond-like calixes three ;second the

כַּפְתֹּר וָפֶרַח וּשְׁלֹשָׁה[h] גְבִעִים מְשֻׁקָּדִים
almond-like calixes three and ;blossom and knob [with]

בַּקָּנֶה הָאֶחָד כַּפְתֹּר וָפֶרַח[h] כֵּן לְשֵׁשֶׁת
six the for so ;blossom and knob [with] ,¹one ²stalk the on

the rings be, for
places for the
staves to bear
the table. 28
And thou shalt
make the staves
of acacia wood,
and overlay
them with gold,
that the table
may be borne
with them. 29
And thou shalt
make the dishes
thereof, and the
spoons thereof,
and the flagons
thereof, and the
bowls thereof,
to pour out
withal: of pure
gold shalt thou
make them. 30
And thou shalt
set upon the
table shewbread
before me al-
ways.
31 And thou
shalt make a
candlestick of
pure gold: of
beaten work
shall the candle-
stick be made,
even its base,
and its shaft;
its cups, its
knops, and its
flowers, shall be
of one piece
with it: 32 and
there shall be
six branches
going out of the
sides thereof;
three branches
of the candle-
stick out of the
one side thereof,
and three
branches of the
candlestick out
of the other side
thereof: 33 three
cups made like
almond-blos-
soms in one
branch, a knop
and a flower; and
three cups made
like almond-
blossoms in the
other branch, a
knop and a
flower: so for
the six branches

---

a G. adds, *by them.*
b G. adds, *pure.*
c Sm., G., S. have, *thou shalt make.*
d G., S. add, *and*, ו.
e G., S., V. add, *and*, ו.
f S. puts after האחד; V. omits.
g S., V. omit.
h G. omits.

es that come out
of the candle-
stick. 34 And in
the candlestick
shall be four
bowls made like
unto almonds,
with their knops
and their flow-
ers. 35 And
there shall be a
knop under two
branches of the
same, and a
knop under two
branches of the
same, and a
knop under two
branches of the
same, accord-
ing to the six
branches that
proceed out of
the candlestick.
36 Their knops
and their
branches shall
be of the same:
all it *shall be*
one beaten
work *of* pure
gold. 37 And
thou shalt make
the seven lamps
thereof: and
they shall light
the lamps there-
of, that they
may give light
over against it.
38 And the
tongs thereof,
and the snuff-
dishes thereof,
shall be of pure
gold. 39 *Of* a
talent of pure
gold shall he
make it, with
all these vessels.
40 And look
that thou make
them after their
pattern, which
was shewed thee
in the mount.

הַקָּנִים הַיֹּצְאִים מִן־הַמְּנֹרָה׃ וּבַמְּנֹרָה 34
lampstand the on And .lampstand the from out going those ,stalks

אַרְבָּעָה גְבִעִים מְשֻׁקָּדִים[a] כַּפְתֹּרֶיהָ וּפְרָחֶיהָ׃
.blossoms its and knobs its [with] ,almond-like calixes four

וְכַפְתֹּר[b] תַּחַת שְׁנֵי הַקָּנִים מִמֶּנָּה וְכַפְתֹּר תַּחַת 35
under knob a and ;it of stalks two under knob a And

שְׁנֵי[c] הַקָּנִים מִמֶּנָּה וְכַפְתֹּר[d] תַּחַת־שְׁנֵי הַקָּנִים
stalks two under knob a and ;it of stalks two

מִמֶּנָּה[e] לְשֵׁשֶׁת הַקָּנִים הַיֹּצְאִים מִן־הַמְּנֹרָה׃[f]
.lampstand the from out going those ,stalks six the to ;it of

כַּפְתֹּרֵיהֶם וּקְנֹתָם מִמֶּנָּה יִהְיוּ כֻּלָּהּ 36
it of all ,be shall it of stalks their and knobs Their

מִקְשָׁה אַחַת זָהָב טָהוֹר׃ וְעָשִׂיתָ 37
make shalt thou And .[1]pure [2]gold ,one ,work chased

אֶת־נֵרֹתֶיהָ שִׁבְעָה וְהֶעֱלָה[g] אֶת־נֵרֹתֶיהָ
,lamps its up set shall one and ;seven lamps its

וְהֵאִיר[h] עַל־עֵבֶר פָּנֶיהָ׃[h] וּמַלְקָחֶיהָ[i] 38
,snuffers its And .face its against over (upon) light give shall they and

וּמַחְתֹּתֶיהָ[j] זָהָב טָהוֹר׃ כִּכַּר זָהָב טָהוֹר 39
[1]pure [2]gold of talent a [Of] .[1]pure [2]gold ,pans its and

יַעֲשֶׂה[lk] אֹתָהּ[k] [m]אֵת כָּל־הַכֵּלִים הָאֵלֶּה׃ וּרְאֵה 40
see And .[1]these [2]vessels all with ,it make shall one

וַעֲשֵׂה בְּתַבְנִיתָם אֲשֶׁר־אַתָּה[n] מָרְאֶה[n]
see to caused [wert] thou which plans their by make and

בָּהָר׃
.mountain the in

going out of
the candlestick:
34 and in the
candlestick four
cups made like
almond-blos-
soms, the knops
thereof, and the
flowers thereof:
35 and a knop
under two
branches of one
piece with it,
and a knop un-
der two branch-
es of one piece
with it, and a
knop under two
branches of one
piece with it,
for the six
branches going
out of the
candlestick. 36
Their knops and
their branches
shall be of one
piece with it:
the whole of it
one beaten work
of pure gold. 37
And thou shalt
make the lamps
thereof, seven:
and they shall
light the lamps
thereof, to give
light over a-
gainst it. 38 And
the tongs there-
of, and the
snuffdishes
thereof, shall be
of pure gold. 39
Of a talent of
pure gold shall
it be made,
with all these
vessels. 40 And
see that thou
make them af-
ter their pattern,
which hath been
shewed thee in
the mount.

26

MOREOVER
thou shalt make
the tabernacle
with ten cur-

וְאֶת־הַמִּשְׁכָּן תַּעֲשֶׂה עֶשֶׂר יְרִיעֹת שֵׁשׁ 1
byssus ;curtains ten ,make shalt thou habitation the And

Moreover
thou shalt make
the tabernacle
with ten cur-
tains; of fine

---

a G. adds, *in the one stalk*; S. omits.
b G., S., V. omit ו.
c G. has, *four*.
d Some manuscripts of G. omit.
e G., S. add, *thus*.
f G. adds, v. 34 a.
g Sm., G., T., V. have second person.
h Sm., S., T., V. have pl; G. has, *and they shall appear from the one face*.
i S. adds, *thou shalt make;* G. similar.
j V. adds, *shall be made*.
k G. omits.
l S. has second person.
m Sm., S. add, *and*, ו.
n S. has, *which I showed to thee*.

מָשְׁזָר וּתְכֵלֶת וְאַרְגָּמָן וְתֹלַעַת שָׁנִי
,crimson (of worm) and ,purple and ,blue and ,twisted

כְּרֻבִים מַעֲשֵׂה חֹשֵׁב תַּעֲשֶׂה אֹתָם׃
.them make shalt thou ,workman skilled a of work a cherubs

2 אֹרֶךְ הַיְרִיעָה הָאַחַת שְׁמֹנֶה וְעֶשְׂרִים
twenty and eight [1]one [2]curtain the of length The

בָּאַמָּה וְרֹחַב אַרְבַּע בָּאַמָּה הַיְרִיעָה
[2]curtain the ,cubit the by four ,width the and ; cubit the by

3 הָאֶחָת מִדָּה אַחַת לְכָל־הַיְרִיעֹת׃ חֲמֵשׁ הַיְרִיעֹת
curtains Five .curtains the all to [1]one [2]measure ; [1]one

תִּהְיֶיןָ חֹבְרֹת אִשָּׁה אֶל־אֲחֹתָהּ וְחָמֵשׁ יְרִיעֹת
curtains five and ; sister her unto each ,joined be shall

4 חֹבְרֹת אִשָּׁה אֶל־אֲחֹתָהּ׃ וְעָשִׂיתָ[a] לֻלְאֹת
of loops make shalt thou And .sister her unto each ,joined

תְּכֵלֶת עַל שְׂפַת הַיְרִיעָה הָאֶחָת מִקָּצָה
end the from ,[1]one [2]curtain the of lip the upon ,blue

בַּחֹבָרֶת וְכֵן תַּעֲשֶׂה בִּשְׂפַת הַיְרִיעָה
[2]curtain the of lip the at do shalt thou so and ; joining the at

5 הַקִּיצוֹנָה בַּמַּחְבֶּרֶת הַשֵּׁנִית׃ חֲמִשִּׁים לֻלָאֹת תַּעֲשֶׂה
make shalt thou loops Fifty .[1]second [2]joining the at [1]last

בַּיְרִיעָה[b] הָאֶחָת וַחֲמִשִּׁים לֻלָאֹת תַּעֲשֶׂה
make shalt thou loops fifty and ; [1]one [2]curtain the on

בִּקְצֵה הַיְרִיעָה[c] אֲשֶׁר בַּמַּחְבֶּרֶת הַשֵּׁנִית
; [1]second [2]joining the at [is] which curtain the of end the in

מַקְבִּילֹת הַלֻּלָאֹת אִשָּׁה אֶל־אֲחֹתָהּ׃
.sister her unto each loops the [be shall] corresponding

6 וְעָשִׂיתָ חֲמִשִּׁים קַרְסֵי זָהָב וְחִבַּרְתָּ
join shalt thou and ; gold of hooks fifty make shalt thou And

אֶת־הַיְרִיעֹת אִשָּׁה אֶל־אֲחֹתָהּ בַּקְּרָסִים וְהָיָה
become shall and ,hooks the by ,sister her unto each ,curtains the

7 הַמִּשְׁכָּן אֶחָד׃ וְעָשִׂיתָ יְרִיעֹת עִזִּים
,goats [of hair] of curtains make shalt thou And .one habitation the

לְאֹהֶל עַל־הַמִּשְׁכָּן עַשְׁתֵּי־עֶשְׂרֵה יְרִיעֹת תַּעֲשֶׂה
make shalt thou curtains eleven ; habitation the over tent a for

tains *of* fine twined linen, and blue, and purple, and scarlet: *with* cherubim of cunning work shalt thou make them.
2 The length of one curtain *shall be* eight and twenty cubits, and the breadth of one curtain four cubits: and every one of the curtains shall have one measure.
3 The five curtains shall be coupled together one to another; and *other* five curtains *shall be* coupled one to another.
4 And thou shalt make loops of blue upon the edge of the one curtain from the selvedge in the coupling; and likewise shalt thou make in the uttermost edge of *another* curtain, in the coupling of the second.
5 Fifty loops shalt thou make in the one curtain, and fifty loops shalt thou make in the edge of the curtain that *is* in the coupling of the second; that the loops may take hold one of another.
6 And thou shalt make fifty taches of gold, and couple the curtains together with the taches: and it shall be one tabernacle.

7 And thou shalt make curtains *of* goats' *hair* to be a covering upon the tabernacle: eleven curtains

twined linen, and blue, and purple, and scarlet, with cherubim the work of the cunning workman shalt thou make them.
2 The length of each curtain shall be eight and twenty cubits, and the breadth of each curtain four cubits: all the curtains shall have one measure.
3 Five curtains shall be coupled together one to another; and *the other* five curtains shall be coupled one to another.
4 And thou shalt make loops of blue upon the edge of the one curtain from the selvedge in the coupling; and likewise shalt thou make in the edge of the curtain that is outmost in the second coupling.
5 Fifty loops shalt thou make in the one curtain, and fifty loops shalt thou make in the edge of the curtain that is in the second coupling; the loops shall be opposite one to another.
6 And thou shalt make fifty clasps of gold, and couple the curtains one to another with the clasps: and the tabernacle shall be one.

7 And thou shalt make curtains of goats' *hair* for a tent over the tabernacle: eleven curtains shalt

a G. adds, *for them.*
b S. has, בקצה היריעה.
c S. adds, *the other.*

shalt thou make.
8 The length of
one curtain
shall be thirty
cubits, and the
breadth of one
curtain four cu-
bits: and the
eleven curtains
shall be all of
one measure. 9
And thou shalt
couple five cur-
tains by them-
selves, and six
curtains by
themselves, and
shalt double the
sixth curtain in
the forefront of
the tabernacle.
10 And thou
shalt make fifty
loops on the
edge of the one
curtain *that is*
outmost in the
coupling, and
fifty loops in
the edge of the
curtain which
coupleth the
second. 11 And
thou shalt make
fifty taches of
brass, and put
the taches into
the loops, and
couple the tent
together, that it
may be one. 12
And the rem-
nant that re-
maineth of the
curtains of the
tent, the half
curtain that re-
maineth, shall
hang over the
backside of the
tabernacle. 13
And a cubit on
the one side,
and a cubit on
the other side of
that which re-
maineth in the
length of the
curtains of the
tent, it shall
hang over the
sides of the

8 אֹתָם׃ אֹרֶךְ הַיְרִיעָה הָאַחַת[a] שְׁלֹשִׁים בָּאַמָּה
,cubit the by thirty ,[1]one [2]curtain the of length The .them

וְרֹחַב אַרְבַּע בָּאַמָּה הַיְרִיעָה הָאֶחָת
;[2]one [2]curtain the ,cubit the by four width the and

מִדָּה אַחַת לְעַשְׁתֵּי[b] עֶשְׂרֵה יְרִיעֹת׃
.curtains ten [and] one the to [1]one [2]measure

9 וְחִבַּרְתָּ אֶת־חֲמֵשׁ הַיְרִיעֹת לְבָד וְאֶת־שֵׁשׁ
six the and ,separately curtains five the join shalt thou And

הַיְרִיעֹת לְבָד וְכָפַלְתָּ אֶת־הַיְרִיעָה
[2]curtain the double take shalt thou and ;separately curtains

10 הַשִּׁשִּׁית אֶל־מוּל פְּנֵי הָאֹהֶל׃ וְעָשִׂיתָ
make shalt thou And .tent the of face the before unto [1]sixth

חֲמִשִּׁים לֻלָאֹת[c] עַל שְׂפַת הַיְרִיעָה הָאֶחָת הַקִּיצֹנָה
last the ,[1]one [2]curtain the of lip the upon loops fifty

בַּחֹבָרֶת וַחֲמִשִּׁים לֻלָאֹת עַל שְׂפַת הַיְרִיעָה[d]
curtain the of lip the upon loops fifty and ; joining the at

11 הַחֹבֶרֶת הַשֵּׁנִית׃ וְעָשִׂיתָ קַרְסֵי נְחֹשֶׁת
,bronze of hooks make shalt thou And .second the ,joins that

חֲמִשִּׁים וְהֵבֵאתָ אֶת־הַקְּרָסִים בַּלֻּלָאֹת וְחִבַּרְתָּ
join and ,loops the in hooks the put shalt thou and ; fifty

12 אֶת־הָאֹהֶל[e] וְהָיָה אֶחָד׃ וְסֶרַח[f]
of part overhanging the And .one become shall it and ,tent the

הָעֹדֵף בִּירִיעֹת הָאֹהֶל חֲצִי[g h] הַיְרִיעָה
,curtain a of half the ,tent the of curtains the in ,excess the

הָעֹדֶפֶת[g] תִּסְרַח עַל אֲחֹרֵי
of part back the upon over hang shall ,over remaining one the

13 הַמִּשְׁכָּן׃ וְהָאַמָּה מִזֶּה וְהָאַמָּה
cubit the and ,[side] this from cubit the And .habitation the

מִזֶּה בָּעֹדֵף[i] בְּאֹרֶךְ יְרִיעֹת הָאֹהֶל
,tent the of curtains the of length the in ,excess in ,[side] this from

יִהְיֶה סָרוּחַ עַל־צִדֵּי הַמִּשְׁכָּן מִזֶּה
,[side] this from habitation the of sides the upon over hung be shall

thou make
them. 8 The
length of
each curtain
shall be thirty
cubits, and the
breadth of each
curtain four cu-
bits: the eleven
curtains shall
have one meas-
ure. 9 And thou
shalt couple five
curtains by
themselves, and
six curtains by
themselves, and
shalt double o-
ver the sixth
curtain in the
forefront of the
tent. 10 And
thou shalt make
fifty loops on
the edge of the
one curtain that
is outmost in
the coupling,
and fifty loops
upon the edge
of the curtain
which is *outmost*
in the second
coupling. 11
And thou shalt
make fifty clasps
of brass, and
put the clasps
into the loops,
and couple the
tent together,
that it may be
one. 12 And
the overhang-
ing part that
remaineth of the
curtains of the
tent, the half
curtain that re-
maineth, shall
hang over the
back of the
tabernacle. 13
And the cubit
on the one side,
and the cubit on
the other side,
of that which
remaineth in the
length of the
curtains of the
tent, shall hang
over the sides
of the taber-
nacle on this

---

a S. has, *of them.*

b S. adds, *all*, reading לכל עשתי; so V. adds, *all*, omitting *eleven.*

c G. adds, *thou shalt make.*

d S., V. add, *the other.*

e G. has, *the screens.*

f G. has, *and thou shalt place under.*

g G. omits.

h V. has, *one.*

i G. adds, יריעת.

tabernacle on
this side and on
that side, to
cover it. 14 And
thou shalt make
a covering for
the tent *of*
rams' skins dyed
red, and a
covering above
of badgers'
skins.

15 And thou
shalt make
boards for the
tabernacle *of*
shittim wood
standing up. 16
Ten cubits *shall*
be the length of
a board, and a
cubit and a half
shall be the
breadth of one
board. 17 Two
tenons *shall*
there be in one
board, set in
order one a-
gainst another:
thus shalt thou
make for all the
boards of the
tabernacle. 18
And thou shalt
make the boards
for the taber-
nacle, twenty
boards on the
south side south-
ward. 19 And
thou shalt
make forty
sockets of silver
under the
twenty boards;
two sockets un-
der one board
for his two ten-
ons, and two
sockets under
another board
for his two ten-
ons. 20 And for
the second side
of the taber-
nacle on the
north side *there*
shall be twenty
boards: 21 And
their forty sock-
ets *of* silver;
two sockets un-

וּמִזֶּה לְכַסֹּתוֹ׃ וְעָשִׂיתָ מִכְסֶה 14
cover a make shalt thou And .it cover to ,[side] this from and

לָאֹהֶל עֹרֹת אֵילִם מְאָדָּמִים וּמִכְסֵה עֹרֹת
of skins of cover a and ; red dyed rams of skins ,tent the for

תְּחָשִׁים מִלְמָעְלָה׃
.above (to) from dolphins

15 וְעָשִׂיתָ אֶת־הַקְּרָשִׁים לַמִּשְׁכָּן
,habitation the for boards the make shalt thou And

16 עֲצֵי שִׁטִּים עֹמְדִים[a]׃ עֶשֶׂר אַמּוֹת [b]אֹרֶךְ
of length the cubits Ten .standing ,acacia of wood of pieces

הַקֶּרֶשׁ[c] וְאַמָּה וַחֲצִי הָאַמָּה רֹחַב
of width the cubit a of half a and cubit a and ; board the

17 הַקֶּרֶשׁ הָאֶחָד׃ שְׁתֵּי יָדוֹת לַקֶּרֶשׁ הָאֶחָד
,¹one ²board the to [pins] (hands) Two .¹one ²board the

מְשֻׁלָּבֹת אִשָּׁה אֶל־אֲחֹתָהּ כֵּן תַּעֲשֶׂה לְכֹל
all to do shalt thou so ; sister her unto each ,connected

18 קַרְשֵׁי הַמִּשְׁכָּן׃ וְעָשִׂיתָ אֶת־הַקְּרָשִׁים
boards the make shalt thou And .habitation the of boards the

לַמִּשְׁכָּן עֶשְׂרִים קֶרֶשׁ לִפְאַת נֶגְבָּה
,south the of direction the for boards twenty ; habitation the for

19 תֵּימָנָה׃ וְאַרְבָּעִים אַדְנֵי־כֶסֶף תַּעֲשֶׂה תַּחַת
under make shalt thou silver of sockets forty And .southward

עֶשְׂרִים הַקָּרֶשׁ שְׁנֵי אֲדָנִים תַּחַת־הַקֶּרֶשׁ הָאֶחָד
,¹one ²board the under sockets two ; boards twenty the

לִשְׁתֵּי יְדֹתָיו וּשְׁנֵי[d] אֲדָנִים תַּחַת־הַקֶּרֶשׁ
²board the under sockets two and ,[pins] (hands) ¹its ²two for

20 הָאֶחָד לִשְׁתֵּי יְדֹתָיו[d]׃ וּלְצֶלַע הַמִּשְׁכָּן[e]
,habitation the of side the for And .[pins] (hands) ¹its ²two for ¹one

הַשֵּׁנִית לִפְאַת צָפוֹן עֶשְׂרִים קָרֶשׁ׃
.boards twenty ,north the of direction the for ,second the

21 וְאַרְבָּעִים אַדְנֵיהֶם כָּסֶף שְׁנֵי אֲדָנִים תַּחַת
under sockets two ; silver of sockets their forty And

הַקֶּרֶשׁ הָאֶחָד וּשְׁנֵי[f] אֲדָנִים תַּחַת הַקֶּרֶשׁ
²board the under sockets two and ,¹one ²board the

side and on that
side, to cover it.
14 And thou
shalt make a
covering for the
tent of rams'
skins dyed red,
and a covering
of sealskins a-
bove.

15 And thou
shalt make the
boards for the
tabernacle of
acacia wood,
standing up. 16
Ten cubits shall
be the length of
a board, and a
cubit and a half
the breadth of
each board. 17
Two tenons
shall there be
in each board,
joined one to
another: thus
shalt thou make
for all the
boards of the
tabernacle. 18
And thou shalt
make the boards
for the taber-
nacle, twenty
boards for the
south side south-
ward. 19 And
thou shalt make
forty sockets of
silver under the
twenty boards;
two sockets un-
der one board
for its two ten-
ons, and two
sockets under
another board
for its two ten-
ons: 20 and for
the second side
of the taber-
nacle, on the
north side,
twenty boards:
21 and their
forty sockets of
silver; two sock-
ets under one
board, and two

a G. apparently omits.
b G. has, *thou shalt make*.
c Sm., G., S. add, *one*, האחד.
d V. omits, also some manuscripts of G.
e G. omits.
f V. omits, and some manuscripts of G.; some manuscripts of G. add, לשתי ידתיו.

der one board, and two sockets under another board. 22 And for the sides of the tabernacle westward thou shalt make six boards. 23 And two boards shalt thou make for the corners of the tabernacle in the two sides. 24 And they shall be coupled together beneath, and they shall be coupled together above the head of it unto one ring: thus shall it be for them both; they shall be for the two corners. 25 And they shall be eight boards, and their sockets *of* silver, sixteen sockets; two sockets under one board, and two sockets under another board. 26 And thou shalt make bars *of* shittim wood; five for the boards of the one side of the tabernacle, 27 And five bars for the boards of the other side of the tabernacle, and five bars for the boards of the side of the tabernacle, for the two sides westward. 28 And the middle bar in the midst of the boards shall reach from end to end. 29 And thou shalt overlay the boards with gold, and make their rings *of* gold *for* places for the

22 הָאֶחָד[a]׃ וּלְיַרְכְּתֵי הַמִּשְׁכָּן יָמָּה תַּעֲשֶׂה
make shalt thou ,westward habitation the of thighs the for And .[1]one

23 שִׁשָּׁה קְרָשִׁים׃ וּשְׁנֵי קְרָשִׁים תַּעֲשֶׂה
make shalt thou boards two And .boards six

24 לִמְקֻצְעֹת הַמִּשְׁכָּן בַּיַּרְכָתָיִם׃ וְיִהְיוּ
be shall they And .thighs the in ,habitation the of corners the for

תֹאֲמִם מִלְּמַטָּה וְיַחְדָּו יִהְיוּ תַמִּים
complete be shall they manner like in and ; below (to) from double

עַל־רֹאשׁוֹ אֶל־הַטַּבַּעַת הָאֶחָת כֵּן יִהְיֶה לִשְׁנֵיהֶם[b]
;them of both to be shall it so ; [1]one [2]ring the unto ,top its upon

25 לִשְׁנֵי הַמִּקְצֹעֹת יִהְיוּ׃ וְהָיוּ שְׁמֹנָה
eight be shall And .be shall they corners two the for

קְרָשִׁים וְאַדְנֵיהֶם כֶּסֶף שִׁשָּׁה עָשָׂר אֲדָנִים[c]
; sockets ten [and] six ,silver sockets their and ,boards

שְׁנֵי אֲדָנִים תַּחַת הַקֶּרֶשׁ הָאֶחָד[d] וּשְׁנֵי
two and ,[1]one [2]board the under sockets two

26 אֲדָנִים תַּחַת הַקֶּרֶשׁ הָאֶחָד׃ וְעָשִׂיתָ
make shalt thou And .[1]one [2]board the under sockets

בְרִיחִם עֲצֵי שִׁטִּים חֲמִשָּׁה לְקַרְשֵׁי[e]
of boards the to five ;acacia of wood of pieces ,bars

27 צֶלַע־הַמִּשְׁכָּן הָאֶחָד׃ וַחֲמִשָּׁה בְרִיחִם לְקַרְשֵׁי[f]
of boards the to bars five And .one the ,habitation the of side the

צֶלַע־הַמִּשְׁכָּן הַשֵּׁנִית וַחֲמִשָּׁה בְרִיחִם לְקַרְשֵׁי[g]
of boards the to bars five and ;second the ,habitation the of side the

28 צֶלַע הַמִּשְׁכָּן לַיַּרְכָתַיִם יָמָּה׃ וְהַבְּרִיחַ
[2]bar the And .westward ,thighs the to ,habitation the of side the

הַתִּיכֹן בְּתוֹךְ הַקְּרָשִׁים מַבְרִחַ מִן־הַקָּצֶה
end from through going ,boards the of midst the in [1]middle

29 אֶל־הַקָּצֶה׃ וְאֶת־הַקְּרָשִׁים תְּצַפֶּה זָהָב
,gold [with] overlay shalt thou boards the And .end unto

וְאֶת־טַבְּעֹתֵיהֶם תַּעֲשֶׂה זָהָב בָּתִּים לַבְּרִיחִם
,bars the for houses ,gold make shalt thou rings their and

sockets under another board. 22 And for the hinder part of the tabernacle westward thou shalt make six boards. 23 And two boards shalt thou make for the corners of the tabernacle in the hinder part. 24 And they shall be double beneath, and in like manner they shall be entire unto the top thereof unto one ring: thus shall it be for them both; they shall be for the two corners. 25 And there shall be eight boards, and their sockets of silver, sixteen sockets; two sockets under one board, and two sockets under another board.
26 And thou shalt make bars of acacia wood; five for the boards of the one side of the tabernacle, 27 and five bars for the boards of the other side of the tabernacle, and five bars for the boards of the side of the tabernacle, for the hinder part westward. 28 And the middle bar in the midst of the boards shall pass through from end to end. 29 And thou shalt overlay the boards with gold, and make their rings of gold for places for the bars:

---

a S. has, *thou shalt make,* תעשה ; S. omits.
b S. has, לשני אדנים; V. has, לשני קרשים.
c G., S., V. omit.
d G. adds, לשתי ידתיו.
e G. has, *to the one pillar.*
f G. has, *to the one pillar.*
g G. has, *to the hinder pillar.*

bars: and thou
shalt overlay
the bars with
gold. 30 And
thou shalt rear
up the taber-
nacle according
to the fashion
thereof which
was shewed
thee in the
mount.

31 And thou
shalt make a
vail *of* blue, and
purple, and
scarlet, and fine
twined linen of
cunning work:
with cherubim
shall it be made.
32 And thou
shalt hang it
upon four pil-
lars of shittim
wood overlaid
with gold: their
hooks *shall be*
of gold, upon
the four sockets
of silver.

33 And thou
shalt hang up
the vail under
the taches, that
thou mayest
bring in thither
within the vail
the ark of the
testimony: and
the vail shall
divide unto you
between the
holy *place* and
the most holy.
34 And thou
shalt put the
mercy seat up-
on the ark of
the testimony
in the most
holy *place*. 35
And thou shalt
set the table
without the vail,
and the candle-
stick over a-
gainst the table
on the side of
the tabernacle
toward the
south: and thou
shalt put the
table on the
north side. 36
And thou shalt

30 וְצִפִּיתָ אֶת־הַבְּרִיחִם זָהָב׃ וַהֲקֵמֹתָ
up set shalt thou And .gold [with] bars the overlay shalt thou and

אֶת־הַמִּשְׁכָּן כְּמִשְׁפָּטוֹ אֲשֶׁר הָרְאֵיתָ
see to caused wast thou which ordinance its to according habitation the

בָּהָר׃
.mountain the in

31 וְעָשִׂיתָ פָרֹכֶת תְּכֵלֶת וְאַרְגָּמָן
,purple and ,blue ,veil a make shalt thou And

וְתוֹלַעַת שָׁנִי וְשֵׁשׁ מָשְׁזָר מַעֲשֵׂה
of work a ;twisted byssus and ,crimson (of worm) and

חֹשֵׁב יַעֲשֶׂה[a] אֹתָהּ כְּרֻבִים׃
.cherubs [and] ,it make shall one workman skilful a

32 וְנָתַתָּה אֹתָהּ עַל־אַרְבָּעָה עַמּוּדֵי שִׁטִּים
,acacia of pillars four upon it put shalt thou And

מְצֻפִּים זָהָב וָוֵיהֶם זָהָב [b]עַל־
upon ; gold [being] nails their ,gold [with] overlaid

33 אַרְבָּעָה אַדְנֵי־כָסֶף׃ וְנָתַתָּה אֶת־הַפָּרֹכֶת
veil the put shalt thou And .silver of sockets four

תַּחַת הַקְּרָסִים[c] וְהֵבֵאתָ שָׁמָּה מִבֵּית
within from thither bring shalt thou and ;hooks the under

לַפָּרֹכֶת אֵת אֲרוֹן הָעֵדוּת וְהִבְדִּילָה הַפָּרֹכֶת
veil the divide shall and ;testimony of ark the veil the to

לָכֶם בֵּין הַקֹּדֶשׁ וּבֵין קֹדֶשׁ הַקֳּדָשִׁים׃
.holies of holy the (between) and ,place holy the between you for

34 [d]וְנָתַתָּ אֶת־הַכַּפֹּרֶת עַל [d]אֲרוֹן הָעֵדֻת
,testimony of ark the upon lid expiating the put shalt thou And

35 בְּקֹדֶשׁ הַקֳּדָשִׁים׃ וְשַׂמְתָּ אֶת־הַשֻּׁלְחָן
table the set shalt thou And .holies of holy the in

מִחוּץ לַפָּרֹכֶת וְאֶת־הַמְּנֹרָה נֹכַח הַשֻּׁלְחָן
,table the against over lamp the and ,veil the to without from

עַל צֶלַע הַמִּשְׁכָּן תֵּימָנָה וְהַשֻּׁלְחָן
table the and ;southward habitation the of side the upon

36 תִּתֵּן [e]עַל־צֶלַע [f]צָפוֹן׃ וְעָשִׂיתָ
make shalt thou And .north the of side the upon put shalt thou

and thou shalt
overlay the bars
with gold. 30
And thou shalt
rear up the tab-
ernacle accord-
ing to the
fashion thereof
which hath been
shewed thee in
the mount.

31 And thou
shalt make a
veil of blue, and
purple, and
scarlet, and fine
twined linen:
with cherubim
the work of the
cunning work-
man shall it be
made: 32 and
thou shalt hang
it upon four
pillars of acacia
overlaid with
gold, their hooks
shall be of gold,
upon four sock-
ets of silver.

33 And thou
shalt hang up
the veil under
the clasps, and
shalt bring in
thither within
the veil the ark
of the testi-
mony: and the
veil shall di-
vide unto you
between the
holy place and
the most holy.
34 And thou
shalt put the
mercy-seat up-
on the ark of
the testimony
in the most
holy place. 35
And thou shalt
set the table
without the veil,
and the candle-
stick over a-
gainst the table
on the side of
the tabernacle
toward the
south: and thou
shalt put the
table on the
north side. 36
And thou shalt

---

a G., S. have, *thou shalt make;* V. omits.
b G. has, *and,* ו; V. has, *but,* ו.
c G., S. have, *the pillars,* הקרשים.
d G. has, *and thou shalt cover with the veil the ark.*
e G. adds, *the dwelling,* המשכן.
f Sm. adds ch. 30: 1-10.

make an hang-
ing for the door
of the tent, *of*
blue, and pur-
ple, and scarlet,
and fine twined
linen, wrought
with needle-
work. 37 And
thou shalt make
for the hanging
five pillars *of*
shittim *wood*,
and overlay
them with gold,
and their hooks
shall be of gold:
and thou shalt
cast five sock-
ets of brass for
them.

מָסָךְ לְפֶתַח[a] הָאֹהֶל[a] תְּכֵלֶת וְאַרְגָּמָן
,purple and ,blue ;tent the of door the for screen a

וְתוֹלַעַת שָׁנִי וְשֵׁשׁ מָשְׁזָר מַעֲשֵׂה רֹקֵם׃
.embroiderer an of work the ,twisted byssus and ,crimson (of worm) and

37 וְעָשִׂיתָ לַמָּסָךְ חֲמִשָּׁה עַמּוּדֵי [b]שִׁטִּים
,acacia of pillars five screen the for make shalt thou And

וְצִפִּיתָ אֹתָם זָהָב וָוֵיהֶם
nails their ,gold [with] them overlay shalt thou and

זָהָב וְיָצַקְתָּ לָהֶם חֲמִשָּׁה אַדְנֵי נְחֹשֶׁת׃
.bronze of sockets five them for cast shalt thou and ;gold [being]

make a screen
for the door of
the Tent, of
blue, and pur-
ple, and scar-
let, and fine
twined linen,
the work of the
embroiderer. 37
And thou shalt
make for the
screen five pil-
lars of acacia,
and overlay
them with gold;
their hooks shall
be of gold: and
thou shalt cast
five sockets of
brass for them.

27

AND thou
shalt make an
altar *of* shittim
wood, five cu-
bits long, and
five cubits
broad; the altar
shall be four-
square: and the
height thereof
shall be three
cubits. 2 And
thou shalt make
the horns of it
upon the four
corners there-
of: his horns
shall be of the
same: and thou
shalt overlay it
with brass. 3
And thou shalt
make his pans
to receive his
ashes, and his
shovels, and his
basons, and his
fleshhooks, and
his firepans: all
the vessels
thereof thou
shalt make *of*
brass. 4 And
thou thalt make
for it a grate of
network *of*
brass; and up-

1 וְעָשִׂיתָ אֶת־הַמִּזְבֵּחַ עֲצֵי שִׁטִּים חָמֵשׁ
five ;acacia of timbers ,altar the make shalt thou And

אַמּוֹת אֹרֶךְ וְחָמֵשׁ אַמּוֹת רֹחַב רָבוּעַ
four-sided ; width [in] cubits five and ,length [in] cubits

יִהְיֶה הַמִּזְבֵּחַ וְשָׁלֹשׁ אַמּוֹת קֹמָתוֹ׃
.height its cubits three and ; altar the be shall

2 וְעָשִׂיתָ קַרְנֹתָיו עַל אַרְבַּע פִּנֹּתָיו
,corners [1]its [2]four upon horns its make shalt thou And

מִמֶּנּוּ תִּהְיֶיןָ קַרְנֹתָיו וְצִפִּיתָ אֹתוֹ[c]
[with] it overlay shalt thou and ;corners its be shall it of

3 נְחֹשֶׁת׃ וְעָשִׂיתָ סִּירֹתָיו[d] לְדַשְּׁנוֹ[d]
,ashes its remove to pots its make shalt thou And .bronze

וְיָעָיו וּמִזְרְקֹתָיו וּמִזְלְגֹתָיו וּמַחְתֹּתָיו
;pans its and ,flesh-forks its and ,bowls sacrificial its and ,shovels its and

4 [e]לְכָל־כֵּלָיו תַּעֲשֶׂה נְחֹשֶׁת׃ וְעָשִׂיתָ
make shalt thou And .bronze make shalt thou vessels its all to

לוֹ[f] מִכְבָּר מַעֲשֵׂה רֶשֶׁת נְחֹשֶׁת וְעָשִׂיתָ
make shalt thou and ;bronze of [1]net [2]work a ,grating a it for

And thou
shalt make the
altar of acacia
wood, five cu-
bits long, and
five cubits
broad; the al-
tar shall be
foursquare: and
the height there-
of shall be three
cubits. 2 And
thou shalt make
the horns of it
upon the four
corners thereof:
the horns there-
of shall be of
one piece with
it: and thou
shalt overlay it
with brass. 3
And thou shalt
make its pots
to take away its
ashes, and its
shovels, and its
basons, and its
fleshhooks, and
its firepans: all
the vessels
thereof thou
shalt make of
brass. 4 And
thou shalt make
for it a grating
of network of

---

a G. omits.
b G. omits.
c G. has, *them*, אתם.
d G. has, *a crown for the altar*.
e G., S. have, *and all*, וכל; V. has, *all*, כל.
f S., V. omit.

on the net shalt thou make four brazen rings in the four corners thereof. 5 And thou shalt put it under the compass of the altar beneath, that the net may be even to the midst of the altar. 6 And thou shalt make staves for the altar, staves *of* shittim wood, and overlay them with brass. 7 And the staves shall be put into the rings, and the staves shall be upon the two sides of the altar, to bear it. 8 Hollow with boards shalt thou make it: as it was shewed thee in the mount, so shall they make *it*.

9 And thou shalt make the court of the tabernacle: for the south side southward *there shall be* hangings for the court *of* fine twined linen of an hundred cubits long for one side: 10 And the twenty pillars thereof and their twenty sockets *shall be of* brass; the hooks of the pillars and their fillets *shall be of* silver. 11 And likewise for the north side in length *there shall be* hangings of an hundred *cubits* long, and his twenty pillars and their twenty sockets *of* brass;

עַל־הָרֶשֶׁת אַרְבַּע טַבְּעֹת נְחֹשֶׁת עַל אַרְבַּע
²four upon bronze of rings four net the upon

5 קְצוֹתָיו׃ וְנָתַתָּה אֹתָהּ[a] תַּחַת כַּרְכֹּב
of ledge the under it put shalt thou And .ends ¹its

הַמִּזְבֵּחַ מִלְּמָטָּה וְהָיְתָה הָרֶשֶׁת עַד חֲצִי
of half as far as net the be shall and ; below (to) from altar the

6 הַמִּזְבֵּחַ׃ וְעָשִׂיתָ בַדִּים לַמִּזְבֵּחַ בַּדֵּי
of poles ,altar the for poles make shalt thou And .altar the

עֲצֵי שִׁטִּים וְצִפִּיתָ אֹתָם נְחֹשֶׁת׃
.bronze [with] them overlay shalt thou and ; acacia of timbers

7 וְהוּבָא[b] אֶת־בַּדָּיו בַּטַּבָּעֹת וְהָיוּ
be shall and ; rings the into poles its brought be shall And

הַבַּדִּים[c] עַל־שְׁתֵּי[d] צַלְעֹת הַמִּזְבֵּחַ בִּשְׂאֵת אֹתוֹ׃
.it carrying in ,altar the of sides two the upon poles the

8 נְבוּב לֻחֹת תַּעֲשֶׂה אֹתוֹ כַּאֲשֶׁר
as ,it make shalt thou tablets [with] (of) Hollow

הֶרְאָה אֹתְךָ בָּהָר כֵּן יַעֲשׂוּ[e]׃
.make shall they so ,mountain the in thee see to caused he

9 וְעָשִׂיתָ אֵת חֲצַר הַמִּשְׁכָּן
; habitation the of court the make shalt thou And

לִפְאַת נֶגֶב־תֵּימָנָה קְלָעִים לֶחָצֵר
,court the for hangings southward south the of direction the for

שֵׁשׁ מָשְׁזָר מֵאָה בָאַמָּה אֹרֶךְ לַפֵּאָה
²direction the for ,length [in] cubit the by hundred a ,twisted byssus

10 הָאֶחָת׃ וְעַמֻּדָיו עֶשְׂרִים וְאַדְנֵיהֶם עֶשְׂרִים
,twenty sockets their and ,twenty pillars its And .¹one

נְחֹשֶׁת וָוֵי הָעַמֻּדִים וַחֲשֻׁקֵיהֶם כָּסֶף׃
.silver ,bands their and pillars the of nails the ; bronze

11 וְכֵן לִפְאַת צָפוֹן[f] בָּאֹרֶךְ קְלָעִים
hangings ,length in north the of direction the for so And

מֵאָה אֹרֶךְ[g] וְעַמֻּדָו עֶשְׂרִים וְאַדְנֵיהֶם
sockets their and twenty pillars its and ; length [in] hundred a

brass; and upon the net shalt thou make four brasen rings in the four corners thereof. 5 And thou shalt put it under the ledge round the altar beneath, that the net may reach halfway up the altar. 6 And thou shalt make staves for the altar, staves of acacia wood, and overlay them with brass. 7 And the staves thereof shall be put into the rings, and the staves shall be upon the two sides of the altar, in bearing it. 8 Hollow with planks shalt thou make it: as it hath been shewed thee in the mount, so shall they make it.

9 And thou shalt make the court of the tabernacle: for the south side southward there shall be hangings for the court of fine twined linen an hundred cubits long for one side: 10 and the pillars thereof shall be twenty, and their sockets twenty, of brass; the hooks of the pillars and their fillets *shall be* of silver. 11 And likewise for the north side in length there shall be hangings an hundred cubits long, and the pillars thereof twenty, and their sockets

a G., V. have, *them.*
b Sm., G., S., V. have, *and thou shalt bring in.*
c S. omits.
d G. omits.
e G. has, *thou shalt make it.*
f G. has, *east.*
g Sm., G., S., V. have, *cubits.*

the hooks of the
pillars and their
fillets *of* silver.
12 And *for* the
breadth of the
court on the
west side *shall*
be hangings of
fifty cubits: their
pillars ten, and
their sockets
ten. 13 And the
breadth of the
court on the
east side east-
ward *shall be*
fifty cubits. 14
The hangings of
one side *of the*
gate shall be
fifteen cubits:
their pillars
three, and their
sockets three. 15
And on the
other side *shall*
be hangings fif-
teen *cubits:*
their pillars
three, and their
sockets three.
16 And for
the gate of the
court *shall be* an
hanging of
twenty cubits,
of blue, and
purple, and
scarlet, and fine
twined linen,
wrought with
needlework:
and their pillars
shall be four,
and their sock-
ets four. 17 All
the pillars round
about the court
shall be filleted
with silver;
their hooks
shall be of sil-
ver, and their
sockets *of* brass.
18 The length
of the court
shall be an hun-
dred cubits, and
the breadth fifty
every where,
and the height
five cubits *of*
fine twined lin-
en, and their
sockets *of* brass.
19 All the ves-
sels of the tab-

עֶשְׂרִים נְחֹשֶׁת וָוֵי הָעַמֻּדִים וַחֲשֻׁקֵיהֶם[a]
,bands their and pillars the of nails the ; bronze ,twenty

12 כָּסֶף׃ וְרֹחַב הֶחָצֵר לִפְאַת־יָם
,west the of direction the for court the of width the And .silver

קְלָעִים חֲמִשִּׁים אַמָּה עַמֻּדֵיהֶם עֲשָׂרָה וְאַדְנֵיהֶם
sockets their and ten pillars their ; cubits fifty hangings

13 עֲשָׂרָה׃ וְרֹחַב הֶחָצֵר לִפְאַת קֵדְמָה[b]
east the of direction the for court the of width the And .ten

14 מִזְרָחָה[cb] חֲמִשִּׁים אַמָּה׃ וַחֲמֵשׁ עֶשְׂרֵה אַמָּה
cubits ten [and] five And .cubits fifty ,eastward

קְלָעִים[d] לַכָּתֵף[d] עַמֻּדֵיהֶם שְׁלֹשָׁה וְאַדְנֵיהֶם
sockets their and ,three. pillars their ; side the to hangings the

15 שְׁלֹשָׁה׃ וְלַכָּתֵף הַשֵּׁנִית חֲמֵשׁ עֶשְׂרֵה
,ten [and] five ,¹second ²side the to And .three

קְלָעִים[e] עַמֻּדֵיהֶם שְׁלֹשָׁה וְאַדְנֵיהֶם שְׁלֹשָׁה׃
.three sockets their and ,three pillars their ; hangings

16 וּלְשַׁעַר הֶחָצֵר מָסָךְ עֶשְׂרִים אַמָּה[f]
,cubits ten ,screen a ,court the of gate the for And

תְּכֵלֶת וְאַרְגָּמָן וְתוֹלַעַת שָׁנִי וְשֵׁשׁ מָשְׁזָר
,twisted byssus and ,crimson (of worm) and ,purple and ,blue

מַעֲשֵׂה רֹקֵם עַמֻּדֵיהֶם אַרְבָּעָה וְאַדְנֵיהֶם
sockets their and ,four pillars their ; embroiderer an of work the

17 אַרְבָּעָה׃ כָּל־עַמּוּדֵי הֶחָצֵר סָבִיב מְחֻשָּׁקִים
united [be shall] about round court the of pillars the All .four

כֶּסֶף וָוֵיהֶם כָּסֶף וְאַדְנֵיהֶם נְחֹשֶׁת׃
.bronze sockets their and ; silver nails their ,silver [with]

18 אֹרֶךְ הֶחָצֵר מֵאָה בָּאַמָּה[g] וְרֹחַב
width the and ,cubit the by hundred a court the of length The

חֲמִשִּׁים בַּחֲמִשִּׁים[h] וְקֹמָה חָמֵשׁ אַמּוֹת שֵׁשׁ
byssus ,cubits five height the and ,fifty by fifty

19 מָשְׁזָר וְאַדְנֵיהֶם נְחֹשֶׁת׃ לְכֹל[i] כְּלֵי
of vessels the all Concerning .bronze sockets their and ; twisted

twenty, of brass;
the hooks of the
pillars and their
fillets of silver.
12 And for the
breadth of the
court on the
west side shall
be hangings of
fifty cubits;
their pillars ten,
and their sock-
ets ten. 13 And
the breadth of
the court on
the east side
eastward shall
be fifty cubits.
14 The hang-
ings for the one
side *of the gate*
shall be fifteen
cubits: their pil-
lars three, and
their sockets
three. 15 And
for the other
side shall be
hangings of fif-
teen cubits:
their pillars
three, and their
sockets three.
16 And for the
gate of the
court shall be a
screen of twenty
cubits, of blue,
and purple, and
scarlet, and fine
twined linen,
the work of the
embroiderer:
their pillars
four, and their
sockets four. 17
All the pillars
of the court
round about
shall be filleted
with silver; their
hooks of silver,
and their sock-
ets of brass.
18 The length
of the court
shall be an hun-
dred cubits,
and the breadth
fifty every
where, and the
height five cu-
bits, of fine
twined linen,
and their sock-
ets of brass. 19
All the instru-

---

a G. adds, ואדניהם.
b G. has, *south.*
c G. adds, *curtains,* קלעים.
d G. has, *the height of the curtains in one direction.*
e G. has, *cubits, the height of the curtains.*
f G. adds, *the height.*
g G. has, *by a hundred,* במאה.
h Sm. has, *by the cubit,* באמה; V. omits.
i G. has, *and all,* וכל; S., V. have, *all,* כל; Sm. has *and thou shalt make,* ועשית.

ernacle in all the service thereof, and all the pins thereof, and all the pins of the court, *shall be of* brass.

20 And thou shalt command the children of Israel, that they bring thee pure oil olive beaten for the light, to cause the lamp to burn always. 21 In the tabernacle of the congregation without the vail, which *is* before the testimony, Aaron and his sons shall order it from evening to morning before the LORD: *it shall be* a statute for ever unto their generations on the behalf of the children of Israel.

הַמִּשְׁכָּן [a] בְּכֹל [b] עֲבֹדָתוֹ וְכָל־יְתֵדֹתָיו [c] וְכָל־יִתְדֹת
of pins the all and ,pins its all and ,service its all in ,habitation the

הֶחָצֵר נְחֹשֶׁת׃
.bronze ,court the

20 וְאַתָּה תְּצַוֶּה ׀ אֶת־בְּנֵי יִשְׂרָאֵל
,Israel of children the command shalt thou And

וְיִקְחוּ אֵלֶיךָ שֶׁמֶן זַיִת זָךְ כָּתִית לַמָּאוֹר
;light the for beaten pure olive of oil thee unto take them let and

21 לְהַעֲלֹת נֵר תָּמִיד׃ בְּאֹהֶל מוֹעֵד
,meeting of tent the In .continually lamps up set to

מִחוּץ לַפָּרֹכֶת אֲשֶׁר עַל־הָעֵדֻת יַעֲרֹךְ
arrange shall ,testimony the by [is] which veil the (to) outside (from)

אֹתוֹ אַהֲרֹן וּבָנָיו מֵעֶרֶב עַד־בֹּקֶר
morning until evening from sons his and Aaron them

לִפְנֵי יְהוָה חֻקַּת עוֹלָם לְדֹרֹתָם [d]
,generations their for eternity of statute a ;Jehovah before

מֵאֵת בְּנֵי יִשְׂרָאֵל׃
.Israel of children the (with) from

ments of the tabernacle in all the service thereof, and all the pins thereof, and all the pins of the court, shall be of brass.

20 And thou shalt command the children of Israel, that they bring unto thee pure olive oil beaten for the light, to cause a lamp to burn continually. 21 In the tent of meeting, without the veil which is before the testimony, Aaron and his sons shall order it from evening to morning before the LORD: it shall be a statute for ever throughout their generations on the behalf of the children of Israel.

28

AND take thou unto thee Aaron thy brother, and his sons with him, from among the children of Israel, that he may minister unto me in the priest's office, *even* Aaron, Nadab and Abihu, Eleazar and Ithamar, Aaron's sons. 2 And thou shalt make holy garments for Aaron thy brother, for glory and for beauty. 3 And thou shalt speak unto all *that are* wise hearted, whom I have filled with the spirit of wisdom, that they may make Aa-

1 וְאַתָּה הַקְרֵב אֵלֶיךָ אֶת־אַהֲרֹן אָחִיךָ
,brother thy Aaron thyself unto near bring ,thou And

וְאֶת־בָּנָיו אִתּוֹ [e] מִתּוֹךְ בְּנֵי יִשְׂרָאֵל
,Israel of children the of midst the from ,him with sons his and

לְכַהֲנוֹ־לִי אַהֲרֹן נָדָב וַאֲבִיהוּא אֶלְעָזָר
,Eleazar ,Abihu and ,Nadab ,Aaron ;me to priest as officiating his for

2 וְאִיתָמָר בְּנֵי אַהֲרֹן׃ וְעָשִׂיתָ בִגְדֵי־
of garments make shalt thou And .Aaron of sons the ,Ithamar and

3 קֹדֶשׁ לְאַהֲרֹן אָחִיךָ לְכָבוֹד וּלְתִפְאָרֶת׃ וְאַתָּה
thou And .beauty for and honor for ,brother thy Aaron for holiness

תְּדַבֵּר אֶל־כָּל־חַכְמֵי־לֵב אֲשֶׁר מִלֵּאתִיו
with filled have I whom ,heart of wise the all unto speak shalt

רוּחַ חָכְמָה וְעָשׂוּ אֶת־בִּגְדֵי [f] אַהֲרֹן
Aaron of garments the make shall they and ;wisdom of spirit a

And bring thou near unto thee Aaron thy brother, and his sons with him, from among the children of Israel, that he may minister unto me in the priest's office, even Aaron, Nadab and Abihu, Eleazar and Ithamar, Aaron's sons. 2 And thou shalt make holy garments for Aaron thy brother, for glory and for beauty. 3 And thou shalt speak unto all that are wise hearted, whom I have filled with the spirit of wisdom, that

---

a G. omits.
b S. omits ב.
c G. omits כל.
d Sm., G., S. have, *to your generations*, לדרתכם.
e G. omits.
f G., S. add, *holy*, קדש.

ron's garments
to consecrate
him, that he
may minister
unto me in the
priest's office. 4
And these *are*
the garments
which they shall
make; a breast-
plate, and an
ephod, and a
robe, and a
broidered coat,
a mitre, and a
girdle: and they
shall make holy
garments for Aa-
ron thy broth-
er, and his
sons, that he
may minister
unto me in the
priest's office. 5
And they shall
take gold, and
blue, and pur-
ple, and scarlet,
and fine linen.

6 And they
shall make the
ephod *of* gold,
of blue, and *of*
purple, *of* scar-
let, and fine
twined linen,
with cunning
work. 7 It shall
have the two
shoulderpieces
thereof joined
at the two edges
thereof; and *so*
it shall be joined
together. 8 And
the curious
girdle of the
ephod, which *is*
upon it, shall be
of the same, ac-
cording to the
work thereof;
even of gold, *of*
blue, and pur-
ple, and scarlet,
and fine twined
linen. 9 And
thou shalt take
two onyx stones,
and grave on
them the names
of the children
of Israel: 10 Six
of their names
on one stone,

4 לְקַדְּשׁוֹ לְכַהֲנוֹ־לִי׃ וְאֵלֶּה
[are] these And .me to priest as officiating his for ,him sanctify to

הַבְּגָדִים אֲשֶׁר יַעֲשׂוּ[a] חֹשֶׁן וְאֵפוֹד
,ephod an and ,breastplate a ; make shall they which garments the

וּמְעִיל וּכְתֹנֶת תַּשְׁבֵּץ מִצְנֶפֶת וְאַבְנֵט
; girdle a and ,mitre a ,stuff woven of tunic a and ,robe a and

וְעָשׂוּ בִגְדֵי־קֹדֶשׁ לְאַהֲרֹן אָחִיךָ
,brother thy Aaron for holiness of garments make shall they and

5 וּלְבָנָיו לְכַהֲנוֹ־לִי׃ וְהֵם
they And .me to priest as officiating his for ,sons his for and

יִקְחוּ אֶת־הַזָּהָב וְאֶת־הַתְּכֵלֶת וְאֶת־הָאַרְגָּמָן
,purple the and ,blue the and ,gold the take shall

וְאֶת־תּוֹלַעַת הַשָּׁנִי וְאֶת־הַשֵּׁשׁ׃
.byssus the and ,crimson (of worm) the and

6 וְעָשׂוּ אֶת־הָאֵפֹד זָהָב[b] תְּכֵלֶת
,blue ,gold [of] ; ephod the make shall they And

וְאַרְגָּמָן תּוֹלַעַת שָׁנִי[b] וְשֵׁשׁ[c] מָשְׁזָר מַעֲשֵׂה
of work the ,twisted byssus and ,crimson (of worm) ,purple and

7 חֹשֵׁב׃ שְׁתֵּי כְתֵפֹת חֹבְרֹת יִהְיֶה־לּוֹ[d]
,it to be shall joining shoulderpieces two .workman skilful a

8 אֶל־שְׁנֵי קְצוֹתָיו וְחֻבָּר[e]׃ וְחֵשֶׁב
of band the And .joined be shall it and ; ends [1]its [2]two at

אֲפֻדָּתוֹ[f] אֲשֶׁר עָלָיו כְּמַעֲשֵׂהוּ מִמֶּנּוּ יִהְיֶה
; be shall it it of ,work its like ,it upon [is] which fastening its

זָהָב תְּכֵלֶת וְאַרְגָּמָן וְתוֹלַעַת שָׁנִי וְשֵׁשׁ
byssus and ,crimson (of worm) and ,purple and ,blue ,gold

9 מָשְׁזָר׃ וְלָקַחְתָּ אֶת־שְׁתֵּי אַבְנֵי־שֹׁהַם
; onyx of stones two take shalt thou And .twisted

וּפִתַּחְתָּ עֲלֵיהֶם שְׁמוֹת בְּנֵי
of children the of names the them upon engrave shalt thou and

10 יִשְׂרָאֵל׃ שִׁשָּׁה מִשְּׁמֹתָם[g] עַל הָאֶבֶן הָאֶחָת
; [1]one [2]stone the upon names their of Six .Israel

they make Aa-
ron's garments
to sanctify him,
that he may
minister unto
me in the
priest's office. 4
And these are
the garments
which they shall
make; a breast-
plate, and an
ephod, and a
robe, and a coat
of chequer
work, a mitre,
and a girdle:
and they shall
make holy gar-
ments for Aa-
ron thy brother,
and his sons,
that he may
minister unto
me in the
priest's office. 5
And they shall
take the gold,
and the blue,
and the purple,
and the scarlet,
and the fine lin-
en.
6 And they
shall make the
ephod of gold,
of blue, and
purple, scarlet,
and fine twined
linen, the work
of the cunning
workman. 7 It
shall have two
shoulderpieces
joined to the
two ends there-
of; that it may
be joined to-
gether. 8 And
the cunningly
woven band,
which is upon it,
to gird it on
withal, shall be
like the work
thereof, *and* of
the same piece;
of gold, of blue,
and purple, and
scarlet, and fine
twined linen. 9
And thou shalt
take two onyx
stones, and
grave on them
the names of
the children of
Israel: 10 six of

---

a S. adds, *for them.*
b G. omits.
c G. has, *from byssus*, משש.
d G. adds, *each to each.*
e Sm., G. have, *joined*, יְחֻבַּר, cf. 39: 4.
f G. has, *the ephods;* S., *the ephod.*
g S. adds, *engrave.*

and *the other* six
names of the rest
on the other
stone, according
to their birth. 11
With the work
of an engraver
in stone, *like* the
engravings of a
signet, shalt
thou engrave
the two stones
with the names
of the children
of Israel: thou
shalt make them
to be set in
ouches of gold.
12 And thou
shalt put the
two stones up-
on the shoul-
ders of the eph-
od *for* stones
of memorial un-
to the children
of Israel: and
Aaron shall
bear their names
before the LORD
upon his two
shoulders for a
memorial.

13 And thou
shalt make
ouches *of* gold;
14 And two
chains *of* pure
gold at the ends;
of wreathen
work shalt thou
make them, and
fasten the
wreathen chains
to the ouches.

15 And thou
shalt make the
breastplate of
judgment with
cunning work;
after the work
of the ephod
thou shalt make
it; *of* gold, *of*
blue, and *of*
purple, and *of*
scarlet, and *of*
fine twined lin-
en, shalt thou
make it. 16
Foursquare it
shall be *being*
doubled; a span
shall be the

וְאֵת־שְׁמוֹת הַשִּׁשָּׁה הַנּוֹתָרִים [a] עַל־הָאֶבֶן הַשֵּׁנִית
,¹second ²stone the upon remaining six the of names the and

11 כְּתוֹלְדֹתָם׃ מַעֲשֵׂה חָרַשׁ אֶבֶן
,stone of engraver an of work The .birth their to according

פִּתּוּחֵי חֹתָם תְּפַתַּח אֶת־שְׁתֵּי
two the engrave shalt thou ,signet a of engravings the[like]

הָאֲבָנִים עַל־שְׁמֹת [b] בְּנֵי יִשְׂרָאֵל [b]
;Israel of children the of names the to according ,stones

[c] מֻסַבֹּת מִשְׁבְּצוֹת זָהָב תַּעֲשֶׂה אֹתָם׃
.them make shalt thou gold of work plaited [in] set

12 [d] וְשַׂמְתָּ אֶת־שְׁתֵּי הָאֲבָנִים [d] עַל כִּתְפֹת
of shoulderpieces the upon stones two the put shalt thou And

הָאֵפֹד אַבְנֵי זִכָּרֹן לִבְנֵי יִשְׂרָאֵל
;Israel of children the for remembrance of stones ,ephod the

וְנָשָׂא אַהֲרֹן אֶת־שְׁמוֹתָם [e] לִפְנֵי יְהוָה
Jehovah before names their Aaron bear shall and

13 עַל־שְׁתֵּי כְתֵפָיו לְזִכָּרֹן [f]׃ וְעָשִׂיתָ
make shalt thou And .remembrance for shoulders ¹his ²two upon

14 מִשְׁבְּצֹת זָהָב [g]׃ וּשְׁתֵּי שַׁרְשְׁרֹת זָהָב טָהוֹר
,¹pure ²gold of chains two and ;gold of work plaited

מִגְבָּלֹת תַּעֲשֶׂה אֹתָם [h] מַעֲשֵׂה עֲבֹת
; cords of work a ,them make shalt thou ropes

וְנָתַתָּה [i] אֶת־שַׁרְשְׁרֹת הָעֲבֹתֹת עַל־הַמִּשְׁבְּצֹת [j]׃
.work plaited the upon cords of chains the put shalt thou and

15 וְעָשִׂיתָ חֹשֶׁן מִשְׁפָּט מַעֲשֵׂה
of work a ,judgment of breastplate a make shalt thou And

חֹשֵׁב כְּמַעֲשֵׂה אֵפֹד תַּעֲשֶׂנּוּ
; it make shalt thou ephod the of work the like ,workman skilful a

זָהָב תְּכֵלֶת וְאַרְגָּמָן וְתוֹלַעַת שָׁנִי וְשֵׁשׁ
byssus and ,crimson (of worm) and ,purple and ,blue ,gold

16 מָשְׁזָר תַּעֲשֶׂה אֹתוֹ׃ רָבוּעַ יִהְיֶה כָּפוּל
;double taken ,be shall it Foursided .it make shalt thou ,twisted

their names on
the one stone,
and the names
of the six that
remain on the
other stone, ac-
cording to their
birth. 11 With
the work of an
engraver in
stone, like the
engravings of a
signet, shalt
thou engrave
the two stones,
according to the
names of the
children of Is-
rael: thou shalt
make them to
be inclosed in
ouches of gold.
12 And thou
shalt put the two
stones upon the
shoulderpieces
of the ephod, to
be stones of
memorial for the
children of Is-
rael: and Aar-
on shall bear
their names be-
fore the LORD
upon his two
shoulders for a
memorial.
13 And thou
shalt make
ouches of gold:
14 and two
chains of pure
gold; like cords
shalt thou make
them, of wreath-
en work: and
thou shalt put
the wreathen
chains on the
ouches.
15 And thou
shalt make a
breastplate of
judgment, the
work of the
cunning work-
man; like the
work of the
ephod thou
shalt make it;
of gold, of blue,
and purple, and
scarlet, and fine
twined linen,
shalt thou make
it. 16 Four-
square it shall

---

a S. adds, *engrave.*
b G. omits in some manuscripts.
c G. omits.
d G. omits in some manuscripts.
e G. has, *the names of the sons of Israel.*
f G. adds, *concerning them.*
g G. adds, *pure.*
h G. omits.
i S. adds, *two.*
j G. adds, *over the shoulder clothing from the front.*

length thereof,
and a span *shall*
be the breadth
thereof. 17 And
thou shalt set
in it settings of
stones, *even* four
rows of stones:
the first row
shall be a sar-
dius, a topaz,
and a carbuncle:
this shall be the
first row. 18 And
the second row
shall be an
emerald, a sap-
phire, and a
diamond. 19
And the third
row a ligure, an
agate, and an
amethyst. 20
And the fourth
row a beryl, and
an onyx, and a
jasper: they
shall be set in
gold in their in-
closings. 21 And
the stones shall
be with the
names of the
children of Is-
rael, twelve, ac-
cording to their
names, *like* the
engravings of a
signet; every
one with his
name shall they
be according to
the twelve
tribes.
22 And thou
shalt make up-
on the breast-
plate chains at
the ends *of*
wreathen work
of pure gold. 23
And thou shalt
make upon the
breastplate two
rings of gold,
and shalt put
the two rings on
the two ends of
the breastplate.
24 And thou
shalt put
the two wreath-
en *chains* of
gold in the two
rings *which are*
on the ends of
the breastplate.
25 And *the other*

17 זֶרֶת אָרְכּוֹ וְזֶרֶת רָחְבּוֹ׃ וּמִלֵּאתָ בוֹ
it in fill shalt thou And .width its span a and ,length its span a

מִלֻּאַת אֶבֶן [a]אַרְבָּעָה טוּרִים אֶבֶן [b a]טוּר אֹדֶם
,cornelian of row a ;stones ,rows four ,stones of settings

18 פִּטְדָה וּבָרֶקֶת הַטּוּר הָאֶחָד׃ וְהַטּוּר הַשֵּׁנִי
,[1]second [2]row the And .[1]one [2]row the ,smaragd and ,topaz

19 נֹפֶךְ סַפִּיר וְיָהֲלֹם׃ וְהַטּוּר הַשְּׁלִישִׁי
,[1]third [2]row the And .jasper and ,sapphire ,carbuncle

20 לֶשֶׁם שְׁבוֹ וְאַחְלָמָה׃ וְהַטּוּר הָרְבִיעִי
,[1]fourth [2]row the And .amethyst and ,agate ,amber

תַּרְשִׁישׁ וְשֹׁהַם וְיָשְׁפֵה [c]מְשֻׁבָּצִים [d]זָהָב יִהְיוּ
be shall they gold [with] plaited ;beryl and ,onyx and ,chrysolite

21 [e]בְּמִלּוּאֹתָם׃ וְהָאֲבָנִים תִּהְיֶיןָ עַל־שְׁמֹת
of names the to according be shall stones the And .settings their in

בְּנֵי־יִשְׂרָאֵל שְׁתֵּים עֶשְׂרֵה עַל־שְׁמֹתָם
;names their to according ten [and] two ,Israel of children the

פִּתּוּחֵי חוֹתָם אִישׁ עַל־שְׁמוֹ תִּהְיֶיןָ
,be shall they ,name his to according each ,signet a of engravings the

22 לִשְׁנֵי עָשָׂר שָׁבֶט׃ וְעָשִׂיתָ עַל־
upon make shalt thou And .tribes ten [and] two the for

הַחֹשֶׁן שַׁרְשֹׁת גַּבְלֻת מַעֲשֵׂה עֲבֹת זָהָב
[2]gold ,cords of work a ,ropes of chains breastplate the

23 [f]טָהוֹר׃ [g]וְעָשִׂיתָ [h]עַל־הַחֹשֶׁן שְׁתֵּי טַבְּעוֹת
of rings two breastplate the upon make shalt thou And .[1]pure

[i]זָהָב וְנָתַתָּ אֶת־שְׁתֵּי הַטַּבָּעוֹת עַל־שְׁנֵי
two the upon rings two the put shalt thou and ;gold

24 קְצוֹת [h]הַחֹשֶׁן׃ וְנָתַתָּה אֶת־שְׁתֵּי עֲבֹתֹת
of cords two the put shalt thou And .breastplate the of ends

הַזָּהָב עַל־שְׁתֵּי הַטַּבָּעֹת אֶל־קְצוֹת [j]הַחֹשֶׁן׃
.breastplate the of ends the at ,rings two the upon gold

25 וְאֵת [k]שְׁתֵּי [k]קְצוֹת שְׁתֵּי הָעֲבֹתֹת תִּתֵּן עַל־
upon put shalt thou cords two the of ends two the And

be *and* double;
a span shall be
the length there-
of, and a span
the breadth
thereof. 17 And
thou shalt set in
it settings of
stones, four
rows of stones:
a row of sar-
dius, topaz, and
carbuncle shall
be the first row;
18 and the sec-
ond row an
emerald, a sap-
phire, and a
diamond; 19
and the third
row a jacinth,
an agate, and
an amethyst; 20
and the fourth
row a beryl,
and an onyx,
and a jasper:
they shall be in-
closed in gold
in their settings.
21 And the
stones shall be
according to the
names of the
children of Is-
rael, twelve, ac-
cording to their
names; like the
engravings of a
signet, every
one according to
his name, they
shall be for the
twelve tribes.
22 And thou
shalt make upon
the breastplate
chains like
cords, of
wreathen work
of pure gold. 23
And thou shalt
make upon the
breastplate two
rings of gold,
and shalt put
the two rings on
the two ends of
the breastplate.
24 And thou
shalt put the
wreathen chains
of gold on the
two rings at the
ends of the
breastplate. 25
And the *other*
two ends of the

a G. has, *four-rowed, a row of stones shall be.*

b S., T., V. add, *the first.*

c S. has, *set and made firm.*

d G. adds, *bound together with silver;* S. adds, *make them.*

e G., V. have, *according to their rows.*

f G. transfers to this place v. 29.

g Vs. 23—28 are very much abbreviated in G.

h For החשן S. has, הכפרת.

i S. adds, *pure.*

j S. has, הכפרת.

k S. omits.

two ends of the two wreathen *chains* thou shalt fasten in the two ouches, and put *them* on the shoulderpieces of the ephod before it.

26 And thou shalt make two rings of gold, and thou shalt put them upon the two ends of the breastplate in the border thereof, which *is* in the side of the ephod inward. 27 And two *other* rings of gold thou shalt make, and shalt put them on the two sides of the ephod underneath, toward the forepart thereof, over against the *other* coupling thereof, above the curious girdle of the ephod. 28 And they shall bind the breastplate by the rings thereof unto the rings of the ephod with a lace of blue, that *it* may be above the curious girdle of the ephod, and that the breastplate be not loosed from the ephod. 29 And Aaron shall bear the names of the children of Israel in the breastplate of judgment upon his heart, when he goeth in unto the holy *place*, for a memorial before the LORD continually.

30 And thou shalt put in the breastplate of judgment the

שְׁתֵּי הַמִּשְׁבְּצוֹת וְנָתַתָּה עַל־כִּתְפוֹת
of sholderpieces the upon put shalt thou and ; plaitings two the

26 הָאֵפֹד אֶל־מוּל פָּנָיו׃ וְעָשִׂיתָ שְׁתֵּי
two make shalt thou And .face its before unto ,ephod the

טַבְּעוֹת זָהָב וְשַׂמְתָּ אֹתָם עַל־שְׁנֵי
two the upon them put shalt thou and ,gold of rings

קְצוֹת הַחֹשֶׁן[a] עַל־שְׂפָתוֹ אֲשֶׁר אֶל־עֵבֶר
against over (unto) [is] which ,lip its upon ;breastplate the of ends

27 הָאֵפֹד בָּיְתָה׃ וְעָשִׂיתָ שְׁתֵּי טַבְּעוֹת זָהָב
,gold of rings two make shalt thou And .inward ephod the

וְנָתַתָּה אֹתָם עַל־שְׁתֵּי כִתְפוֹת הָאֵפוֹד
ephod the of shoulderpieces two the upon them put shalt thou and

מִלְּמַטָּה מִמּוּל פָּנָיו לְעֻמַּת מַחְבַּרְתּוֹ מִמַּעַל
above (from) ,joining its near face its before from, ,below (to) from

28 לְחֵשֶׁב הָאֵפוֹד׃ וְיִרְכְּסוּ אֶת־הַחֹשֶׁן
breastplate the fasten shall they And .ephod the of band the (to)

מִטַּבְּעֹתָו אֶל־טַבְּעֹת הָאֵפוֹד בִּפְתִיל תְּכֵלֶת
,blue of ribbon a with ephod the of rings the unto rings its from

לִהְיוֹת עַל־חֵשֶׁב הָאֵפוֹד וְלֹא־יִזַּח[b]
itself move not may and ; ephod the of band the above be to

29 הַחֹשֶׁן[b] מֵעַל הָאֵפוֹד׃ וְנָשָׂא אַהֲרֹן
Aaron bear shall And .ephod the upon from breastplate the

אֶת־שְׁמוֹת בְּנֵי־יִשְׂרָאֵל בְּחֹשֶׁן הַמִּשְׁפָּט
judgment of breastplate the on Israel of children the of names the

עַל־לִבּוֹ בְּבֹאוֹ אֶל־הַקֹּדֶשׁ לְזִכָּרֹן
remembrance for ,place holy the into going his in ,heart his upon

30 לִפְנֵי־יְהוָה תָּמִיד[c]׃ וְנָתַתָּ אֶל־חֹשֶׁן
of breastplate the into put shalt thou And .continually Jehovah before

הַמִּשְׁפָּט אֶת־הָאוּרִים וְאֶת־הַתֻּמִּים וְהָיוּ
be shall they and ,Thummim the and Urim the judgment

עַל־לֵב[d] אַהֲרֹן[d] בְּבֹאוֹ[e] לִפְנֵי יְהוָה׃
:Jehovah before in going his in Aaron of heart the upon

two wreathen chains thou shalt put on the two ouches, and put them on the shoulderpieces of the ephod, in the forepart thereof.

26 And thou shalt make two rings of gold, and thou shalt put them upon the two ends of the breastplate, upon the edge thereof, which is toward the side of the ephod inward. 27 And thou shalt make two rings of gold, and shalt put them on the two shoulderpieces of the ephod underneath, in the forepart thereof, close by the coupling thereof, above the cunningly woven band of the ephod. 28 And they shall bind the breastplate by the rings thereof unto the rings of the ephod with a lace of blue, that it may be upon the cunningly woven band of the ephod, and that the breastplate be not loosed from the ephod. 29 And Aaron shall bear the names of the children of Israel in the breastplate of judgment upon his heart, when he goeth in unto the holy place, for a memorial before the LORD continually.

30 And thou shalt put in the breastplate of

a S. has, הכפרת.
b S. has, *may pass over upon the breastplate.*
c G. omits.
d S. has, *upon his heart.*
e G. adds, *into the holy place.*

Urim and the
Thummim; and
they shall be
upon Aaron's
heart, when he
goeth in before
the LORD: and
Aaron shall bear
the judgment
of the children
of Israel upon
his heart before
the LORD continually.
31 And thou
shalt make the
robe of the
ephod all *of*
blue. 32 And
there shall be an
hole in the top
of it, in the
midst thereof:
it shall have a
binding of woven work round
about the hole
of it, as it were
the hole of an
habergeon, that
it be not rent.
33 And *beneath* upon the
hem of it thou
shalt make
pomegranates *of*
blue, and *of*
purple, and *of*
scarlet, round
about the hem
thereof; and
bells of gold between them
round about; 34
A golden bell
and a pomegranate, a golden
bell and a pomegranate, upon
the hem of the
robe round about. 35 And it
shall be upon
Aaron to minister: and his
sound shall be
heard when he
goeth in unto
the holy *place*
before the
LORD, and
when he cometh
out, that he die
not.
36 And thou
shalt make a
plate *of* pure
gold, and grave

וְנָשָׂא אַהֲרֹן אֶת־מִשְׁפַּט בְּנֵי־יִשְׂרָאֵל
Israel of children the of judgment the Aaron bear shall and

עַל־לִבּוֹ לִפְנֵי יְהוָה תָּמִיד׃
.continually Jehovah before heart his upon

31 וְעָשִׂיתָ אֶת־מְעִיל הָאֵפוֹד[a] כְּלִיל תְּכֵלֶת׃
.blue entirely ephod the of robe the make shalt thou And

32 וְהָיָה פִי־רֹאשׁוֹ בְּתוֹכוֹ שָׂפָה יִהְיֶה
be shall lip a ; midst its in head its of mouth the be shall And

לְפִיו סָבִיב מַעֲשֵׂה אֹרֵג כְּפִי[b]
of mouth the like ; weaver a of work a ,about round mouth its to

תַחְרָא יִהְיֶה־לּוֹ[b] לֹא יִקָּרֵעַ׃
.rent be [2]may [1]it [3]not [that] ,it to be shall it mail of coat a

33 וְעָשִׂיתָ עַל־שׁוּלָיו[c] רִמֹּנֵי תְּכֵלֶת
,blue of pomegranates hem its upon make shalt thou And

וְאַרְגָּמָן וְתוֹלַעַת שָׁנִי[d] עַל־שׁוּלָיו[e] סָבִיב
; about round hem its upon ,crimson (of worm) and ,purple and

34 וּפַעֲמֹנֵי[f] זָהָב[f] בְּתוֹכָם סָבִיב׃ פַּעֲמֹן[g]
of bell a ; about round them of midst the in gold of bells and

זָהָב וְרִמּוֹן פַּעֲמֹן[h] זָהָב וְרִמּוֹן[g h]
; pomegranate a and gold of bell a ,pomegranate a and gold

35 עַל־שׁוּלֵי הַמְּעִיל סָבִיב׃ וְהָיָה עַל־
upon be shall it And .about round robe the of hem the upon

אַהֲרֹן לְשָׁרֵת וְנִשְׁמַע קוֹלוֹ בְּבֹאוֹ
going his in voice its heard be shall and ; ministering for Aaron

אֶל־הַקֹּדֶשׁ לִפְנֵי יְהוָה וּבְצֵאתוֹ וְלֹא
[3]not and ,out coming his in and Jehovah before place holy the into

יָמוּת׃
.die [2]shall [1]he

36 וְעָשִׂיתָ צִּיץ זָהָב טָהוֹר
; [1]pure [2]gold of plate a make shalt thou And

וּפִתַּחְתָּ עָלָיו פִּתּוּחֵי חֹתָם קֹדֶשׁ
Holiness ,signet a of engravings the it upon engrave shalt thou and

judgment the
Urim and the
Thummim; and
they shall be
upon Aaron's
heart, when he
goeth in before
the LORD: and
Aaron shall
bear the judgment of the
children of Israel upon his
heart before the
LORD continually.
31 And thou
shalt make the
robe of the
ephod all of
blue. 32 And it
shall have a
hole for the
head in the
midst thereof:
it shall have a
binding of woven work round
about the hole
of it, as it were
the hole of a
coat of mail,
that it be not
rent.
33 And upon
the skirts of it
thou shalt make
pomegranates
of blue, and of
purple, and of
scarlet, round about the skirts
thereof; and
bells of gold
between them
round about: 34
a golden bell and
a pomegranate, a golden
bell and a pomegranate, upon
the skirts of the
robe round about. 35 And it
shall be upon
Aaron to minister: and the
sound thereof
shall be heard
when he goeth
in unto the holy
place before the
LORD, and
when he cometh
out, that he die
not.
36 And thou
shalt make a

a G. has, *reaching to the feet.*

b G. has, *the edge woven together from it, in order that.*

c G. has, *upon the border of the undergarment beneath, like a blossoming pomegranate.*

d Sm., G. add, *and twisted byssus.*

e G. has, *upon the border of the undergarment.*

f G. has, *the same form of golden pomegranate and of bell.*

g G. has, *by the golden pomegranate, a bell, and bright colored.*

h S. omits.

upon it, like
the engravings
of a signet,
HOLINESS
TO THE
LORD. 37 And
thou shalt put it
on a blue lace,
that it may be
upon the mitre;
upon the fore-
front of the
mitre it shall be.
38 And it shall
be upon Aa-
ron's forehead,
that Aaron may
bear the iniquity
of the holy
things, which
the children
of Israel shall
hallow in all
their holy gifts;
and it shall be
always upon his
forehead, that
they may be ac-
cepted before
the LORD. 39
And thou shalt
embroider the
coat of fine lin-
en, and thou
shalt make the
mitre *of* fine
linen, and thou
shalt make the
girdle *of* needle-
work. 40 And
for Aaron's sons
thou shalt make
coats, and thou
shalt make for
them girdles,
and bonnets
shalt thou make
for them, for
glory and for
beauty. 41 And
thou shalt put
them upon Aar-
on thy brother,
and his sons
with him; and
shalt anoint
them, and con-
secrate them,
and sanctify
them, that they
may minister
unto me in the
priest's office.
42 And thou
shalt make them
linen breeches to
cover their
nakedness; from
the loins even
unto the thighs
they shall reach:

37 לַיהוָה׃ וְשַׂמְתָּ אֹתוֹ עַל־פְּתִיל תְּכֵלֶת
,blue of ribbon a upon it put shalt thou And .Jehovah to

וְהָיָה עַל־הַמִּצְנָפֶת אֶל־מוּל פְּנֵי־הַמִּצְנֶפֶת
mitre the of face the before unto ; mitre the upon be shall it and

38 יִהְיֶה׃ וְהָיָה עַל־מֵצַח אַהֲרֹן וְנָשָׂא
bear shall and ,Aaron of forehead the upon be shall it And .be shall it

אַהֲרֹן אֶת־עֲוֹן הַקֳּדָשִׁים אֲשֶׁר יַקְדִּישׁוּ
sanctify will which things holy the of iniquity the Aaron

בְּנֵי יִשְׂרָאֵל לְכָל־מַתְּנֹת קָדְשֵׁיהֶם
; holiness [1]their [3]of [2]gifts all to ,Israel of children the

וְהָיָה עַל־מִצְחוֹ [a] תָּמִיד לְרָצוֹן לָהֶם
them for acceptance for ,continually forehead his upon be shall it and

39 לִפְנֵי יְהוָה׃ וְשִׁבַּצְתָּ [b] הַכְּתֹנֶת שֵׁשׁ
; byssus ,tunic the weave shalt thou And .Jehovah before

וְעָשִׂיתָ מִצְנֶפֶת שֵׁשׁ וְאַבְנֵט תַּעֲשֶׂה
,make shalt thou girdle a and ,byssus of mitre a make shalt thou and

40 מַעֲשֵׂה רֹקֵם׃ וְלִבְנֵי אַהֲרֹן
Aaron of sons the for And .embroiderer an of work a

תַּעֲשֶׂה כֻתֳּנֹת וְעָשִׂיתָ [c] לָהֶם [c] אַבְנֵטִים
; girdles them for make shalt thou and ,tunics make shalt thou

וּמִגְבָּעוֹת תַּעֲשֶׂה לָהֶם לְכָבוֹד וּלְתִפְאָרֶת׃
.beauty for and honor for ,them for make shalt thou turbans and

41 וְהִלְבַּשְׁתָּ אֹתָם אֶת־אַהֲרֹן אָחִיךָ וְאֶת־
and brother thy Aaron them [with] clothe shalt thou And

בָּנָיו אִתּוֹ וּמָשַׁחְתָּ אֹתָם וּמִלֵּאתָ
fill shalt thou and ,them anoint shalt thou and ; him with sons his

אֶת־יָדָם וְקִדַּשְׁתָּ אֹתָם וְכִהֲנוּ
priests as officiate shall they and ,them sanctify shalt thou and ,hand their

42 לִי׃ וַעֲשֵׂה לָהֶם מִכְנְסֵי־בָד לְכַסּוֹת בְּשַׂר
of flesh the cover to ,linen of breeches them for make And .me to

עֶרְוָה מִמָּתְנַיִם וְעַד־יְרֵכַיִם יִהְיוּ׃
.be shall they thighs the as far as and loins the from ,nakedness

43 וְהָיוּ עַל־אַהֲרֹן וְעַל־בָּנָיו בְּבֹאָם
going their in ,sons his upon and Aaron upon be shall they And

plate of pure
gold, and grave
upon it, like the
engravings of a
signet, HOLY TO
THE LORD. 37
And thou shalt
put it on a lace
of blue, and it
shall be upon
the mitre; upon
the forefront of
the mitre it shall
be. 38 And it
shall be upon
Aaron's fore-
head, and Aar-
on shall bear
the iniquity of
the holy things,
which the chil-
dren of Israel
shall hallow
in all their holy
gifts; and it
shall be always
upon his fore-
head, that they
may be accept-
ed before the
LORD. 39 And
thou shalt weave
the coat in cheq-
uer work of fine
linen, and thou
shalt make a
mitre of fine lin-
en, and thou
shalt make a
girdle, the work
of the embroid-
erer. 40 And for
Aaron's sons
thou shalt make
coats, and thou
shalt make for
them girdles,
and headtires
shalt thou make
for them, for
glory and for
beauty. 41 And
thou shalt put
them upon Aar-
on thy brother,
and upon his
sons with him;
and shalt anoint
them, and con-
secrate them,
and sanctify
them, that they
may minister
unto me in the
priest's office. 42
And thou shalt
make them linen
breeches to cov-
er the flesh of
their nakedness;
from the loins

a G. has, *upon the forehead of Aaron.*
b G. has, *and the fringes*; S. has, *and make.*
c G. omits, reading simply, *and*, ו.

43 And they
shall be upon
Aaron, and up-
on his sons,
when they come
in unto the tab-
ernacle of the
congregation, or
when they come
near unto the
altar to minister
in the holy
place; that they
bear not iniq-
uity, and die:
it shall be a
statute for ever
unto him and
his seed after
him.

אל־אהל מועד [a]או בגשתם [b]אל־המזבח
altar the unto approaching their in or ,meeting of tent the into

לשרת [c]בקדש [d]ולא־ישאו עון
iniquity bear not shall they so and ;sanctuary the in minister to

ומתו חקת עולם לו ולזרעו אחריו׃
.him after seed his for and him for ,eternity of statute a ; die and

29

AND this *is*
the thing that
thou shalt do
unto them to
hallow them, to
minister unto
me in the priest's
office: Take one
young bullock,
and two rams
without blem-
ish, 2 And un-
leavened bread,
and cakes un-
leavened tem-
pered with oil,
and wafers un-
leavened anoint-
ed with oil: *of*
wheaten flour
shalt thou make
them. 3 And
thou shalt put
them into one
basket, and
bring them in
the basket, with
the bullock and
the two rams. 4
And Aaron and
his sons thou
shalt bring unto
the door of the
tabernacle of
the congrega-
tion, and shalt
wash them with
water. 5 And
thou shalt take
the garments,
and put upon
Aaron the coat,
and the robe of
the ephod, and

1 וזה הדבר [e]אשר־תעשה להם לקדש
sanctify to ,them to do shalt thou which thing the [is] this And

אתם לכהן לי לקח פר אחד בן
of son a ,[1]one [2]bullock take ; me to priests as officiate to them

2 בקר ואילם שנים תמימם׃ ולחם מצות
,unleavened (of) bread and ;perfect ,[1]two [2]rams and ,herd the

[f]וחלת [f]מצת בלולת בשמן ורקיקי
(of) wafers and ,oil with over poured unleavened (of) cakes and

מצות משחים בשמן סלת חטים
wheat of flour fine [of] ; oil with anointed unleavened

3 תעשה אתם׃ ונתת אותם על־סל
basket into them put shalt thou And .them make shalt thou

אחד והקרבת אתם בסל ואת־הפר
bullock the and ,basket the in them near bring shalt and ,one

4 ואת שני האילם׃ ואת־אהרן ואת־בניו תקריב
near bring shalt thou sons his and Aaron And .rams two the and

אל־פתח אהל מועד ורחצת אתם
them wash shalt thou and ; meeting of tent the of door the unto

5 במים׃ ולקחת את־הבגדים והלבשת
clothe shalt thou and ,garments the take shalt thou And .water in

[g]את־אהרן [h i]את־הכתנת ואת [j]מעיל [k i]האפד ואת־
and ,ephod the of robe the and ,tunic the [with] Aaron

even unto the
thighs they shall
reach: 43 and
they shall be up-
on Aaron, and
upon his sons,
when they go in
unto the tent of
meeting, or
when they come
near unto the
altar to minister
in the holy
place; that they
bear not in-
iquity, and die:
it shall be a
statute for ever
unto him and
unto his seed af-
ter him.

And this is the
thing that thou
shalt do unto
them to hallow
them, to minis-
ter unto me in
the priest's
office: take one
young bullock
and two rams
without blem-
ish, 2 and un-
leavened bread,
and cakes un-
leavened min-
gled with oil,
and wafers un-
leavened anoint-
ed with oil: of
fine wheaten
flour shalt thou
make them. 3
And thou shalt
put them into
one basket, and
bring them in
the basket, with
the bullock and
the two rams. 4
And Aaron and
his sons thou
shalt bring unto
the door of the
tent of meeting,
and shalt wash
them with wa-
ter. 5 And thou
shalt take the
garments, and
put upon Aar-
on the coat,
and the robe of
the ephod, and

---

a G. apparently omits; S. has, *and*.
b G. puts after לשרת.
c G. omits ב.
d G. adds, *unto themselves*.
e S., V. omit.
f G. omits; S. omits ו.
g G. adds, *thy brother*.
h Sm. adds, *and thou shalt gird him with the girdle*.
i G. has, *and the tunic reaching to the feet*, apparently omitting ואת מעיל.
j S. has, מצנפת.
k S. has, מעיל.

the ephod, and
the breastplate,
and gird him
with the cu-
rious girdle of
the ephod: 6
And thou shalt
put the mitre
upon his head,
and put the
holy crown up-
on the mitre. 7
Then shalt thou
take the anoint-
ing oil, and
pour *it* upon his
head, and a-
noint him. 8 And
thou shalt bring
his sons, and
put coats upon
them. 9 And
thou shalt gird
them with gir-
dles, Aaron and
his sons, and
put the bonnets
on them: and
the priest's office
shall be their's
for a perpetual
statute: and
thou shalt con-
secrate Aaron
and his sons.
10 And thou
shalt cause a
bullock to be
brought before
the tabernacle
of the con-
gregation:
and Aaron and
his sons shall
put their hands
upon the head of
the bullock. 11
And thou shalt
kill the bullock
before the
LORD, *by* the
door of the tab-
ernacle of the
congregation.
12 And thou
shalt take of the
blood of the
bullock, and put
it upon the
horns of the al-
tar with thy
finger, and pour
all the blood be-
side the bottom
of the altar. 13
And thou shalt
take all the fat

הָאֵפֹד וְאֶת־הַחֹשֶׁן[a] וְאָפַדְתָּ[b] לוֹ
him to | bind shalt thou and | ; breastplate the and | ,ephod the

6 בְּחֵשֶׁב הָאֵפֹד׃ וְשַׂמְתָּ הַמִּצְנֶפֶת עַל־
upon | mitre the | put shalt thou And | .ephod the | of band the with

רֹאשׁוֹ וְנָתַתָּ אֶת־נֵזֶר הַקֹּדֶשׁ עַל־הַמִּצְנָפֶת׃
.mitre the upon | holiness | of diadem the | put shalt thou and | ; head his

7 וְלָקַחְתָּ אֶת־שֶׁמֶן הַמִּשְׁחָה וְיָצַקְתָּ עַל־
upon | pour shalt and | ,anointing | of oil the | take shalt thou And

8 רֹאשׁוֹ וּמָשַׁחְתָּ אֹתוֹ׃ וְאֶת־בָּנָיו תַּקְרִיב
,near bring shalt thou | sons his And | .him | anoint shalt and | ,head his

9 וְהִלְבַּשְׁתָּם כֻּתֳּנֹת׃ וְחָגַרְתָּ אֹתָם
them | gird shalt thou And | .tunics [with] | them clothe shalt and

אַבְנֵט אַהֲרֹן[c] וּבָנָיו וְחָבַשְׁתָּ לָהֶם
them for | bind shalt thou and | ,sons his and | Aaron | ,girdles with

מִגְבָּעֹת וְהָיְתָה לָהֶם כְּהֻנָּה לְחֻקַּת[d]
of statute a for | office priest's the | them for | be shall and | ;turbans

עוֹלָם[d] וּמִלֵּאתָ יַד־אַהֲרֹן וְיַד־בָּנָיו׃
.sons his of hand the and | Aaron of hand the | fill shalt thou and | ,eternity

10 וְהִקְרַבְתָּ אֶת־הַפָּר לִפְנֵי[e] אֹהֶל
of tent the | before | bullock the | near bring shalt thou And

מוֹעֵד וְסָמַךְ אַהֲרֹן וּבָנָיו אֶת־יְדֵיהֶם עַל־
upon | hands their | sons his and | Aaron | lay shall and | ; meeting

11 רֹאשׁ הַפָּר[f]׃ וְשָׁחַטְתָּ אֶת־הַפָּר
bullock the | slaughter shalt thou And | .bullock the | of head the

לִפְנֵי יְהוָה פֶּתַח אֹהֶל מוֹעֵד׃
.meeting | of tent the | of door the [at] | ,Jehovah | before

12 וְלָקַחְתָּ מִדַּם הַפָּר וְנָתַתָּה
put shalt and | ,bullock the | of blood the of [some] | take shalt thou And

עַל־קַרְנֹת הַמִּזְבֵּחַ בְּאֶצְבָּעֶךָ וְאֶת־כָּל־הַדָּם[g]
blood the all and | ;finger thy with | altar the | of horns the upon

13 תִּשְׁפֹּךְ אֶל־יְסוֹד הַמִּזְבֵּחַ׃ וְלָקַחְתָּ
take shalt thou And | .altar the | of foundation the at | out pour shalt thou

the ephod, and
the breastplate,
and gird him
with the cun-
ningly woven
band of the eph-
od: 6 and
thou shalt set
the mitre upon
his head, and
put the holy
crown upon the
mitre. 7 Then
shalt thou take
the anointing
oil, and pour it
upon his head,
and anoint him.
8 And thou shalt
bring his sons,
and put coats
upon them. 9
And thou shalt
gird them with
girdles, Aaron
and his sons,
and bind head-
tires on them:
and they shall
have the priest-
hood by a per-
petual statute:
and thou shalt
consecrate Aar-
on and his
sons.
10 And thou
shalt bring
the bullock be-
fore the tent of
meeting: and
Aaron and his
sons shall lay
their hands up-
on the head of
the bullock. 11
And thou shalt
kill the bullock
before the
LORD, at the
door of the tent
of meeting. 12
And thou shalt
take of the
blood of the
bullock, and put
it upon the
horns of the al-
tar with thy
finger; and thou
shalt pour out
all the blood at
the base of the
altar. 13 And
thou shalt take
all the fat that

---

a S. puts after הכתנת.

b G. has, *unto the ephod.*

c G. omits.

d G. has, *to me for ever.*

e G. has, *at the door of;* Sm. adds, *Jehovah, at the door of.*

f G. adds, *before the Lord at the door of the tent of witness.*

g G. has, *and the rest, all the blood;* V., *and the rest of the blood.*

that covereth
the inwards, and
the caul *that is*
above the liver,
and the two
kidneys, and the
fat that *is* upon
them, and burn
them upon the
altar. 14 But the
flesh of the
bullock, and his
skin, and his
dung, shalt thou
burn with fire
without the
camp: it *is* a
sin offering.

15 Thou shalt
also take one
ram; and Aar-
on and his
sons shall put
their hands up-
on the head of
the ram. 16 And
thou shalt slay
the ram, and
thou shalt take
his blood, and
sprinkle *it*
round about up-
on the altar. 17
And thou shalt
cut the ram in
pieces, and wash
the inwards of
him, and his
legs, and put
them unto his
pieces, and unto
his head. 18 And
thou shalt burn
the whole ram
upon the altar:
it *is* a burnt
offering unto the
LORD: it *is* a
sweet savour,
an offering
made by fire
unto the LORD.
19 And thou
shalt take the
other ram; and
Aaron and his
sons shall put
their hands up-
on the head of
the ram. 20
Then shalt thou
kill the ram, and
take of his

אֶת־כָּל־הַחֵלֶב הַמְכַסֶּה אֶת־הַקֶּרֶב וְאֵת הַיֹּתֶרֶת
lobe the and ,inwards the covering that ,fat the all

עַל־הַכָּבֵד וְאֵת שְׁתֵּי הַכְּלָיֹת וְאֶת־הַחֵלֶב אֲשֶׁר
[is] which fat the and ,kidneys two the and ,liver the upon

14 עֲלֵיהֶן וְהִקְטַרְתָּ הַמִּזְבֵּחָה׃ וְאֶת־בְּשַׂר
of flesh the And .altar the on burn shalt thou and ;them upon

הַפָּר וְאֶת־עֹרוֹ וְאֶת־פִּרְשׁוֹ תִּשְׂרֹף בָּאֵשׁ
,fire with burn shalt thou ,dung its and ,skin its and ,bullock the

15 מִחוּץ לַמַּחֲנֶה חַטָּאת הוּא׃ וְאֶת־הָאַיִל
[2]ram the And .it [is] sin-offering a ;camp the (to) outside (from)

הָאֶחָד תִּקָּח וְסָמְכוּ אַהֲרֹן וּבָנָיו
sons his and Aaron lay shall and ;take shalt thou [1]one

16 אֶת־יְדֵיהֶם עַל־רֹאשׁ הָאָיִל׃ וְשָׁחַטְתָּ
slaughter shalt thou And .ram the of head the upon hands their

אֶת־הָאָיִל[a] וְלָקַחְתָּ אֶת־דָּמוֹ[b] וְזָרַקְתָּ עַל־
upon sprinkle shalt and ,blood its take shalt thou and ;ram the

17 הַמִּזְבֵּחַ סָבִיב׃ וְאֶת־הָאַיִל תְּנַתֵּחַ לִנְתָחָיו
;pieces its into cut shalt thou ram the And .about round altar the

וְרָחַצְתָּ קִרְבּוֹ וּכְרָעָיו[c] וְנָתַתָּ עַל־
upon put shalt and ,legs its and inwards its wash shalt thou and

18 נְתָחָיו[d] וְעַל־רֹאשׁוֹ׃ וְהִקְטַרְתָּ אֶת־כָּל־
all burn shalt thou And .head its upon and ,pieces its

הָאַיִל הַמִּזְבֵּחָה עֹלָה הוּא לַיהוָה
;Jehovah to it [is] burnt-offering a ,altar the on ram the

רֵיחַ נִיחוֹחַ אִשֶּׁה[e] לַיהוָה הוּא׃
.it [is] Jehovah to offering fire a ,acceptance of odor an

19 וְלָקַחְתָּ אֵת הָאַיִל הַשֵּׁנִי וְסָמַךְ אַהֲרֹן
Aaron lay shall and ;[1]second [2]ram the take shalt thou And

וּבָנָיו אֶת־יְדֵיהֶם עַל־רֹאשׁ הָאָיִל׃
.ram the of head the upon hands their sons his and

20 וְשָׁחַטְתָּ אֶת־הָאַיִל[f] וְלָקַחְתָּ
take shalt thou and ;ram the slaughter shalt thou And

covereth the in-
wards, and the
caul upon the
liver, and the
two kidneys,
and the fat that
is upon them,
and burn them
upon the altar.
14 But the flesh
of the bullock,
and its skin, and
its dung, shalt
thou burn with
fire without the
camp: it is a sin
offering.

15 Thou shalt
also take the
one ram; and
Aaron and his
sons shall lay
their hands up-
on the head of
the ram. 16 And
thou shalt slay
the ram, and
thou shalt take
its blood, and
sprinkle it round
about upon the
altar. 17 And
thou shalt cut
the ram into its
pieces, and
wash its in-
wards, and its
legs, and put
them with its
pieces, and with
its head. 18 And
thou shalt burn
the whole ram
upon the altar:
it is a burnt of-
fering unto the
LORD: it is a
sweet savour, an
offering made
by fire unto the
LORD. 19 And
thou shalt take
the other ram;
and Aaron and
his sons shall
lay their hands
upon the head
of the ram. 20
Then shalt thou
kill the ram, and
take of its

---

a G. has, *him.*

b S., V. have, *from his blood.*

c G. adds, *with water.*

d G. has, *the pieces with the head.*

e S., T., V. have, *a gift*, קרבן; they give the same translation in many other places.

f G. has, *him.*

blood, and put
it upon the tip
of the right ear
of Aaron, and
upon the tip of
the right ear of
his sons, and
upon the thumb
of their right
hand, and upon
the great toe of
their right foot,
and sprinkle the
blood upon the
altar round a-
bout. 21 And
thou shalt take
of the blood
that *is* upon the
altar, and of the
anointing oil,
and sprinkle *it*
upon Aaron,
and upon his
garments, and
upon his sons,
and upon the
garments of his
sons with him:
and he shall be
hallowed, and
his garments,
and his sons,
and his sons'
garments with
him.

22 Also thou
shalt take
of the ram the
fat and the
rump, and the
fat that cover-
eth the inwards,
and the caul
above the liver,
and the two
kidneys, and the
fat that *is* upon
them, and the
right shoulder;
for it *is* a ram
of consecration:
23 And one loaf
of bread, and
one cake of oil-
ed bread, and
one wafer out of
the basket of the
unleavened
bread that *is* be-
fore the LORD:
24 And thou
shalt put all in

מִדָּמוֹ וְנָתַתָּה עַל־תְּנוּךְ אֹזֶן אַהֲרֹן [a]
,Aaron of ear the of tip the upon put shalt and ,blood its of [some]

וְעַל־תְּנוּךְ [b] אֹזֶן בָּנָיו [b] הַיְמָנִית וְעַל־
upon and ,right the ,sons his of ear the of tip the upon and

בֹּהֶן יָדָם [c] הַיְמָנִית וְעַל־בֹּהֶן
of toe great the upon and ,right the ,hand their of thumb the

רַגְלָם [c] הַיְמָנִית [d] וְזָרַקְתָּ [e] אֶת־הַדָּם עַל־
upon blood the sprinkle shalt thou and ;right the ,foot their

הַמִּזְבֵּחַ סָבִיב [e]: וְלָקַחְתָּ [f] מִן־הַדָּם 21
blood the of [some] take shalt thou And .about round altar the

אֲשֶׁר עַל־הַמִּזְבֵּחַ וּמִשֶּׁמֶן הַמִּשְׁחָה
,anointing of oil the of and ,altar the upon [is] which

וְהִזֵּיתָ עַל־אַהֲרֹן וְעַל־בְּגָדָיו
,garments his upon and Aaron upon sprinkle shalt thou and

וְעַל־בָּנָיו וְעַל־בִּגְדֵי בָנָיו אִתּוֹ
;him with sons his of garments the upon and sons his upon and

וְקָדַשׁ הוּא וּבְגָדָיו וּבָנָיו
,sons his and ,garments his and he ,holy be shall he and

וּבִגְדֵי בָנָיו אִתּוֹ: וְלָקַחְתָּ מִן־ 22
from take shalt thou And .him with sons his of garments the and

הָאַיִל הַחֵלֶב וְהָאַלְיָה [g] וְאֶת־הַחֵלֶב ׀ הַמְכַסֶּה
covering that ,fat the and ,tail fat the and ,fat the ram the

אֶת־הַקֶּרֶב וְאֵת יֹתֶרֶת הַכָּבֵד וְאֵת ׀ שְׁתֵּי הַכְּלָיֹת
,kidneys two the and ,liver the of lobe the and ,inwards the

וְאֶת־הַחֵלֶב אֲשֶׁר עֲלֵיהֶן וְאֵת שׁוֹק הַיָּמִין
;[1]right [2]shoulder the and ,them upon [is] which fat the and

כִּי אֵיל מִלֻּאִים הוּא: וְכִכַּר לֶחֶם אַחַת 23
,[1]one [4]bread [3]of [2]loaf and ;it [is] consecration of ram a for

וְחַלַּת [h] לֶחֶם [h] שֶׁמֶן אַחַת וְרָקִיק אֶחָד מִסַּל
of basket the from ,[1]one [2]wafer and ,[1]one [6]oil [5]of [4]bread [3]of [2]cake and

הַמַּצּוֹת אֲשֶׁר לִפְנֵי יְהוָה: וְשַׂמְתָּ 24
put shalt thou And .Jehovah before [is] which bread unleavened

blood, and put
it upon the tip
of the right ear
of Aaron, and
upon the tip of
the right ear of
his sons, and
upon the thumb
of their right
hand, and upon
the great toe of
their right foot,
and sprinkle the
blood upon the
altar round a-
bout. 21 And
thou shalt take
of the blood that
is upon the al-
tar, and of the
anointing oil,
and sprinkle it
upon Aaron,
and upon his
garments, and
upon his sons,
and upon the
garments of his
sons with him:
and he shall be
hallowed, and
his garments,
and his sons,
and his sons'
garments with
him.

22 Also thou
shalt take of
the ram the
fat, and the fat
tail, and the fat
that covereth
the inwards,
and the caul of
the liver, and
the two kidneys,
and the fat that
is upon them,
and the right
thigh; for it is a
ram of conse-
cration: 23 and
one loaf of
bread, and one
cake of oiled
bread, and one
wafer, out of the
basket of un-
leavened bread
that is before
the LORD: 24
and thou shalt
put the whole

---

a S. adds, *the right.*

b G. omits.

c G. omits suffix.

d G. adds, *and upon the lobes of the right ears of his sons, and upon the thumbs of their right hands, and upon the great toes of their right feet.*

e G. transfers to end of v. 21, adding *goat* after הדם.

f Sm. puts v. 21 after v. 28.

g G. omits.

h G. omits.

the hands of
Aaron, and in
the hands of
his sons; and
shalt wave them
for a wave offer-
ing before the
LORD. 25 And
thou shalt re-
ceive them of
their hands, and
burn *them* upon
the altar for a
burnt offering,
for a sweet sa-
vour before the
LORD: it *is* an
offering made
by fire unto the
LORD. 26 And
thou shalt take
the breast of the
ram of Aaron's
consecration,
and wave it *for*
a wave offering
before the
LORD: and it
shall be thy
part. 27 And
thou shalt sanc-
tify the breast of
the wave offer-
ing, and the
shoulder of the
heave offering,
which is waved,
and which is
heaved up, of
the ram of the
consecration, *e-
ven* of *that*
which *is* for Aar-
on, and of *that*
which is for his
sons: 28 And it
shall be Aaron's
and his sons' by
a statute for ev-
er from the chil-
dren of Israel:
for it *is* an heave
offering: and it
shall be an heave
offering from
the children of
Israel of the sac-
rifice of their
peace offerings,
even their heave
offering unto
the LORD.

29 And the
holy garments
of Aaron shall
be his sons' af-
ter him, to be

הַכֹּל עַל כַּפֵּי אַהֲרֹן וְעַל כַּפֵּי
of palms the upon and ,Aaron of palms the upon whole the

בָּנָיו וְהֵנַפְתָּ אֹתָם תְּנוּפָה לִפְנֵי יְהוָה׃
.Jehovah before offering wave a them wave shalt thou and ; sons his

25 וְלָקַחְתָּ אֹתָם מִיָּדָם וְהִקְטַרְתָּ[a]
burn shalt thou and ,hand their from them take shalt thou And

הַמִּזְבֵּחָה[b] עַל־הָעֹלָה[b] לְרֵיחַ נִיחוֹחַ
acceptance of odor an for ,offering burnt the upon altar the on

לִפְנֵי יְהוָה אִשֶּׁה הוּא לַיהוָה׃
.Jehovah to it [is] offering fire a ,Jehovah before

26 וְלָקַחְתָּ אֶת־הֶחָזֶה מֵאֵיל הַמִּלֻּאִים
,consecration of ram the from breast the take shalt thou And

אֲשֶׁר לְאַהֲרֹן וְהֵנַפְתָּ אֹתוֹ תְּנוּפָה
offering wave a ,it wave shalt thou and ; Aaron to [is] which

לִפְנֵי יְהוָה וְהָיָה לְךָ לְמָנָה׃
.share a for thee to be shall it and ; Jehovah before

27 וְקִדַּשְׁתָּ אֵת חֲזֵה הַתְּנוּפָה וְאֵת
and ,offering wave the of breast the sanctify shalt thou And

שׁוֹק הַתְּרוּמָה אֲשֶׁר הוּנַף וַאֲשֶׁר
which and waved is which ,contribution the of shoulder the

הוּרָם מֵאֵיל הַמִּלֻּאִים מֵאֲשֶׁר[c] לְאַהֲרֹן
,Aaron to [is] what from ,consecration of ram the from ,away taken is

28 וּמֵאֲשֶׁר לְבָנָיו׃[c] וְהָיָה לְאַהֲרֹן
Aaron for be shall it And .sons his to [is] what from and

וּלְבָנָיו לְחָק־עוֹלָם מֵאֵת בְּנֵי
of children the (with) from ,eternity of statute a for sons his for and

יִשְׂרָאֵל כִּי תְרוּמָה הוּא וּתְרוּמָה
contribution a and ; it [is] contribution a because ,Israel

יִהְיֶה מֵאֵת בְּנֵי־יִשְׂרָאֵל מִזִּבְחֵי
of sacrifices the from ,Israel of children the (with) from be shall it

29 שַׁלְמֵיהֶם[d] תְּרוּמָתָם לַיהוָה׃ וּבִגְדֵי
of garments the And .Jehovah to contribution their ,offerings peace your

הַקֹּדֶשׁ אֲשֶׁר לְאַהֲרֹן יִהְיוּ לְבָנָיו אַחֲרָיו[e]
,him after sons his to be shall Aaron to [are] which holiness

upon the hands
of Aaron, and
upon the hands
of his sons: and
shalt wave them
for a wave offer-
ing before the
LORD. 25 And
thou shalt take
them from their
hands, and burn
them on the al-
tar upon the
burnt offering,
for a sweet
savour before
the LORD: it is
an offering
made by fire
unto the LORD.
26 And thou
shalt take the
breast of Aar-
on's ram of
consecration,
and wave it for
a wave offering
before the
LORD: and it
shall be thy por-
tion. 27 And
thou shalt sanc-
tify the breast of
the wave offer-
ing, and the
thigh of the
heave offering,
which is waved,
and which is
heaved up, of
the ram of con-
secration, even
of that which is
for Aaron, and
of that which is
for his sons: 28
and it shall be
for Aaron and
his sons as a due
for ever from
the children of
Israel: for it is
an heave offer-
ing: and it shall
be an heave of-
fering from the
children of Is-
rael of the sac-
rifices of their
peace offerings,
even their heave
offering unto
the LORD.

29 And the
holy garments
of Aaron shall
be for his sons
after him, to be

a S. adds, *the breast of the ram.*
b G. has, *upon the altar of burnt-offering.*
c G. has, *from Aaron and from his sons.*
d G. has, *the peace offerings of the sons of Israel.*
e G. has, *with him.*

anointed therein, and to be consecrated in them.
30 *And* that son that is priest in his stead shall put them on seven days, when he cometh into the tabernacle of the congregation to minister in the holy *place.*
31 And thou shalt take the ram of the consecration, and seethe his flesh in the holy place.
32 And Aaron and his sons shall eat the flesh of the ram, and the bread that *is* in the basket, *by* the door of the tabernacle of the congregation.
33 And they shall eat those things wherewith the atonement was made, to consecrate *and* to sanctify them: but a stranger shall not eat *thereof*, because they *are* holy.
34 And if ought of the flesh of the consecrations, or of the bread, remain unto the morning, then thou shalt burn the remainder with fire: it shall not be eaten, because it *is* holy.
35 And thus shalt thou do unto Aaron, and to his sons, according to all *things* which I have commanded thee: seven days shalt thou consecrate them.
36 And thou shalt offer every day a bullock *for* a sin offering for atonement; and thou shalt

לְמָשְׁחָה בָהֶם וּלְמַלֵּא־בָם אֶת־יָדָם׃
.hand their them in filling for and them in anointing for

30 שִׁבְעַת יָמִים יִלְבָּשָׁם הַכֹּהֵן תַּחְתָּיו
him of place in priest the on them put shall days Seven

מִבָּנָיו אֲשֶׁר יָבֹא אֶל־אֹהֶל מוֹעֵד
,meeting of tent the into comes who ,sons his from

31 לְשָׁרֵת בַּקֹּדֶשׁ׃ וְאֵת אֵיל הַמִּלֻּאִים
consecration of ram the And .sanctuary the in minister to

תִּקָּח וּבִשַּׁלְתָּ אֶת־בְּשָׂרוֹ בְּמָקֹם קָדֹשׁ׃
.[1]holy [2]place a in flesh its boil shalt thou and ,take shalt thou

32 וְאָכַל אַהֲרֹן וּבָנָיו אֶת־בְּשַׂר הָאַיִל
,ram the of flesh the sons his and Aaron eat shall And

וְאֶת־הַלֶּחֶם אֲשֶׁר בַּסָּל פֶּתַח אֹהֶל
of tent the of door the [at] ,basket the in [is] which bread the and

33 מוֹעֵד׃ וְאָכְלוּ אֹתָם אֲשֶׁר
which [by] [things] those eat shall they And .meeting

כֻּפַּר בָּהֶם לְמַלֵּא אֶת־יָדָם לְקַדֵּשׁ
sanctify to ,hand their fill to ,(them by) made is atonement

34 אֹתָם וְזָר לֹא־יֹאכַל[a] כִּי־קֹדֶשׁ הֵם׃ וְאִם־
if And .they [are] holy for ,eat not shall stranger a and ;them

יִוָּתֵר מִבְּשַׂר הַמִּלֻּאִים[b] וּמִן־הַלֶּחֶם עַד־
until bread the of and consecration of flesh the of [any] left is

הַבֹּקֶר וְשָׂרַפְתָּ אֶת־הַנּוֹתָר בָּאֵשׁ לֹא
[3]not ,fire with remainder the burn shalt thou (and) ,morning the

35 יֵאָכֵל כִּי־קֹדֶשׁ הוּא׃ וְעָשִׂיתָ לְאַהֲרֹן
Aaron to do shalt thou And .it [is] holy for ,eaten be [2]shall [1]it

וּלְבָנָיו כָּכָה[c] כְּכֹל[c] אֲשֶׁר־צִוִּיתִי[c]
commanded have I which all to according ,so sons his to and

36 אֹתָכָה שִׁבְעַת יָמִים תְּמַלֵּא יָדָם׃ וּפַר
of bullock a And .hand their fill shalt thou days seven ;thee

חַטָּאת תַּעֲשֶׂה לַיּוֹם עַל־הַכִּפֻּרִים[d]
,atonement for daily offer shalt thou sin-offering a

וְחִטֵּאתָ עַל־הַמִּזְבֵּחַ בְּכַפֶּרְךָ עָלָיו
;it for atonement making thy in altar the (upon) purify shalt thou and

anointed in them, and to be consecrated in them.
30 Seven days shall the son that is priest in his stead put them on, when he cometh into the tent of meeting to minister in the holy place.
31 And thou shalt take the ram of consecration, and seethe its flesh in a holy place.
32 And Aaron and his sons shall eat the flesh of the ram, and the bread that is in the basket, at the door of the tent of meeting.
33 And they shall eat those things wherewith atonement was made, to consecrate *and* to sanctify them: but a stranger shall not eat thereof, because they are holy.
34 And if aught of the flesh of the consecration, or of the bread, remain unto the morning, then thou shalt burn the remainder with fire: it shall not be eaten, because it is holy.
35 And thus shalt thou do unto Aaron, and to his sons, according to all that I have commanded thee: seven days shalt thou consecrate them.
36 And every day shalt thou offer the bullock of sin offering for atonement: and thou shalt cleanse the altar, when thou makest atonement for it;

---

a G. adds, *from it;* V., *from them.*
b G. has, *sacrifice of completeness.*
c S. has, *as.*
d G. omits עַל.

cleanse the al-
tar, when thou
hast made an a-
tonement for it,
and thou shalt
anoint it, to
sanctify it. 37
Seven days thou
shalt make an
atonement for
the altar, and
sanctify it ; and
it shall be an al-
tar most holy:
whatsoever
toucheth the al-
tar shall be holy.
38 Now this
is that which
thou shalt offer
upon the altar;
two lambs of the
first year day by
day continually.
39 The one
lamb thou shalt
offer in the
morning; and
the other lamb
thou shalt offer
at even: 40 And
with the one
lamb a tenth
deal of flour
mingled with
the fourth part
of an hin of beat-
en oil; and the
fourth part of an
hin of wine *for*
a drink offering.
41 And the
other lamb thou
shalt offer at
even, and
shalt do thereto
according to the
meat offering of
the morning,
and according
to the drink of-
fering thereof,
for a sweet
savour, an offer-
ing made by
fire unto the
LORD. 42 *This*
shall be a con-
tinual burnt of-
fering through-
out your gen-
erations *at* the
door of the tab-
ernacle of the
congregation be-
fore the LORD;
where I will
meet you, to
speak there un-

37 וּמָשַׁחְתָּ אֹתוֹ לְקַדְּשׁוֹ׃ שִׁבְעַת יָמִים
days Seven .it sanctify to it anoint shalt thou and
תְּכַפֵּר עַל־הַמִּזְבֵּחַ וְקִדַּשְׁתָּ אֹתוֹ
;it sanctify shalt and ,altar the for atonement make shalt thou
וְהָיָה הַמִּזְבֵּחַ קֹדֶשׁ קָדָשִׁים כָּל־הַנֹּגֵעַ
touching thing every ,holies of holy altar the become shall and
בַּמִּזְבֵּחַ יִקְדָּשׁ׃
.holy becomes altar the (on)

38 וְזֶה אֲשֶׁר תַּעֲשֶׂה עַל־הַמִּזְבֵּחַ כְּבָשִׂים
,lambs ; altar the upon offer shalt thou what [is] this And
39 בְּנֵי־שָׁנָה[a] שְׁנַיִם לַיּוֹם[b] תָּמִיד[c]׃ אֶת־הַכֶּבֶשׂ
[2]lamb The .continually daily two ,[old] year a (of sons)
הָאֶחָד תַּעֲשֶׂה בַבֹּקֶר וְאֵת הַכֶּבֶשׂ הַשֵּׁנִי
[1]second [2]lamb the and ; morning the in offer shalt thou [1]one
40 תַּעֲשֶׂה בֵּין הָעַרְבָּיִם׃ וְעִשָּׂרֹן
[of ephah an] of tenth a And .evenings the between offer shalt thou
סֹלֶת בָּלוּל בְּשֶׁמֶן כָּתִית רֶבַע הַהִין
,hin a of fourth a ,beaten oil with upon poured ,flour fine
וְנֵסֶךְ רְבִיעִת הַהִין יָיִן לַכֶּבֶשׂ הָאֶחָד׃
.[1]one [2]lamb the for ,wine ,hin a of fourth a ,libation a and
41 וְאֵת הַכֶּבֶשׂ הַשֵּׁנִי תַּעֲשֶׂה בֵּין הָעַרְבָּיִם
; evenings the between offer shalt thou [1]second [2]lamb the And
כְּמִנְחַת הַבֹּקֶר וּכְנִסְכָּהּ
libation its like and morning the of offering vegetable the like
תַּעֲשֶׂה־לָּהּ[d] לְרֵיחַ נִיחֹחַ אִשֶּׁה
offering fire a ,acceptance of odor an for ,it to do shalt thou
42 לַיהוָה׃ עֹלַת תָּמִיד לְדֹרֹתֵיכֶם
,generations your to continuance of offering burnt A .Jehovah to
פֶּתַח אֹהֶל־מוֹעֵד לִפְנֵי יְהוָה אֲשֶׁר
where ; Jehovah before ,meeting of tent the of door the [at]
אִוָּעֵד[e] לָכֶם[f] שָׁמָּה לְדַבֵּר אֵלֶיךָ[g] שָׁם[h]׃
.there thee unto speak to ,(there) you (to) meet I

and thou shalt
anoint it, to
sanctify it. 37
Seven days thou
shalt make a-
tonement for
the altar, and
sanctify it: and
the altar shall
be most holy;
whatsoever
toucheth the al-
tar shall be
holy.

38 Now this is
that which thou
shalt offer upon
the altar; two
lambs of the
first year day by
day continually.
39 The one
lamb thou shalt
offer in the
morning; and
the other lamb
thou shalt offer
at even: 40 and
with the one
lamb a tenth
part *of an ephah*
of fine flour
mingled with
the fourth part
of an hin of
beaten oil; and
the fourth part
of an hin of
wine for a drink
offering. 41 And
the other lamb
thou shalt offer
at even, and
shalt do thereto
according to the
meal offering of
the morning,
and according
to the drink of-
fering thereof,
for a sweet sa-
vour, an offer-
ing made by fire
unto the LORD.
42 It shall be
a continual
burnt offering
throughout
your genera-
tions at the
door of the tent
of meeting be-
fore the LORD:
where I will
meet with you,
to speak there
unto thee. 43

a G. adds, *without blemish;* cf. Num. 28:3.
b G. adds, *upon the altar*, על המזבח.
c G. adds, *a continual offering.*
d G. omits לה.
e G. has, *I shall be known.*
f Sm., G. have, *to thee*, לך.
g S. has, *unto you*, אליכם.
h G., S. omit.

to thee. 43 And
there I will meet
with the children
of Israel, and *the*
tabernacle shall
be sanctified by
my glory. 44
And I will sanc-
tify the taber-
nacle of the
congregation,
and the altar: I
will sanctify al-
so both Aaron
and his sons, to
minister to me
in the priest's
office.
45 And I will
dwell among
the children of
Israel, and will
be their God. 46
And they shall
know that I *am*
the LORD their
God, that
brought them
forth out of the
land of Egypt,
that I may dwell
among them: I
am the LORD
their God.

43 וְנֹעַדְתִּי שָׁמָּה לִבְנֵי יִשְׂרָאֵל
; Israel of children the (to) there meet will I And

44 וְנִקְדַּשׁ בִּכְבֹדִי׃ וְקִדַּשְׁתִּי אֶת־אֹהֶל
of tent the sanctify will I And .glory my by sanctified be shall it and

מוֹעֵד וְאֶת־הַמִּזְבֵּחַ וְאֶת־אַהֲרֹן וְאֶת־בָּנָיו אֲקַדֵּשׁ
sanctify will I sons his and Aaron and ,altar the and meeting

45 לְכַהֵן לִי׃ וְשָׁכַנְתִּי[a] בְּתוֹךְ
of midst the in dwell will I And .me to priests as officiate to

בְּנֵי יִשְׂרָאֵל וְהָיִיתִי לָהֶם לֵאלֹהִים׃
.God a (for) them to be will I and ;Israel of children the

46 וְיָדְעוּ כִּי אֲנִי יְהוָה אֱלֹהֵיהֶם אֲשֶׁר
who ,God their Jehovah [am] I that know shall they And

הוֹצֵאתִי אֹתָם מֵאֶרֶץ מִצְרַיִם לְשָׁכְנִי[b]
dwelling my for ,Egypt of land the from them out brought

בְתוֹכָם אֲנִי[c] יְהוָה[c] אֱלֹהֵיהֶם׃
.God their Jehovah [am] I ;midst their in

And there I will
meet with the
children of Is-
rael; and *the*
Tent shall be
sanctified by my
glory. 44 And I
will sanctify the
tent of meeting,
and the altar:
Aaron also and
his sons will I
sanctify, to min-
ister to me in
the priest's of-
fice.
45 And I will
dwell among
the children of
Israel, and will
be their God. 46
And they shall
know that I am
the LORD their
God, that
brought them
forth out of the
land of Egypt,
that I may dwell
among them: I
am the LORD
their God.

30

AND thou
shalt make an
altar to burn in-
cense upon: *of*
shittim wood
shalt thou make
it. 2 A cubit
shall be the
length thereof,
and a cubit the
breadth there-
of; foursquare
shall it be: and
two cubits *shall*
be the height
thereof: the
horns thereof
shall be of the
same. 3 And
thou shalt over-
lay it with pure
gold, the top
thereof, and the
sides thereof
round about,
and the horns
thereof; and
thou shalt make
unto it a crown
of gold round

1 וְעָשִׂיתָ[d] מִזְבֵּחַ מִקְטַר קְטֹרֶת
; incense burning of place a ,altar an make shalt thou And

2 עֲצֵי שִׁטִּים תַּעֲשֶׂה[e] אֹתוֹ׃ אַמָּה
cubit A .it make shalt thou acacia of wood of pieces [of]

אָרְכּוֹ וְאַמָּה רָחְבּוֹ רָבוּעַ יִהְיֶה וְאַמָּתַיִם
cubits two and ;be shall it foursided ,width its cubit a and ,length its

3 קֹמָתוֹ מִמֶּנּוּ קַרְנֹתָיו׃ וְצִפִּיתָ אֹתוֹ
[with] it overlay shalt thou And .horns its it from ;height its

זָהָב טָהוֹר אֶת־גַּגּוֹ וְאֶת־קִירֹתָיו סָבִיב וְאֶת־קַרְנֹתָיו
; horns its and ,about round walls its and ,roof its ,[1]pure [2]gold

4 וְעָשִׂיתָ לּוֹ זֵר זָהָב סָבִיב׃ וּשְׁתֵּי
two And .about round gold of wreath a it for make shalt thou and

And thou
shalt make an
altar to burn
incense upon:
of acacia wood
shalt thou make
it. 2 A cubit
shall be the
length thereof,
and a cubit the
breadth there-
of; foursquare
shall it be: and
two cubits shall
be the height
thereof: the
horns thereof
shall be of one
piece with it. 3
And thou shalt
overlay it with
pure gold, the
top thereof, and
the sides thereof
round about,
and the horns
thereof; and
thou shalt make
unto it a crown
of gold round a-

---

a G. has, *and I will be called upon.*
b G. has, *to be called upon;* S., *and I will dwell.*
c G. has, *and to be.*
d Sm. transfers to ch. 26, vs. 1—10, as noted.
e G. adds, *and* ו, connecting with following verse.

about. 4 And
two golden
rings shalt thou
make to it un-
der the crown of
it, by the two
corners thereof,
upon the two
sides of it shalt
thou make *it*;
and they shall
be for places
for the staves to
bear it withal. 5
And thou shalt
make the staves
of shittim wood,
and overlay
them with gold.
6 And thou
shalt put it be-
fore the vail
that *is* by the
ark of the testi-
mony, before
the mercy seat
that *is* over the
testimony,
where I will
meet with thee.

7 And Aaron
shall burn there-
on sweet in-
cense every
morning: when
he dresseth the
lamps, he shall
burn incense up-
on it. 8 And
when Aaron
lighteth the
lamps at even,
he shall burn in-
cense upon it, a
perpetual in-
cense before the
LORD through-
out your gen-
erations. 9 Ye
shall offer no
strange incense
thereon, nor
burnt sacrifice,
nor meat offer-
ing; neither
shall ye pour
drink offering
thereon. 10 And
Aaron shall
make an atone-
ment upon the
horns of it once
in a year with
the blood of
the sin offering
of atonements:

טַבְּעֹת זָהָב[a] תַּעֲשֶׂה־לּוֹ[b] מִתַּחַת לְזֵרוֹ
,wreath its (to) under (from) ,it for make shalt thou gold of rings

עַל שְׁתֵּי צַלְעֹתָיו תַּעֲשֶׂה עַל־שְׁנֵי צִדָּיו
;sides [1]its [2]two upon ,make shalt thou corners [1]its [2]two upon

וְהָיָה לְבָתִּים לְבַדִּים לָשֵׂאת אֹתוֹ בָּהֵמָּה׃
.them by it carry to ,poles for houses for be shall they and

5 וְעָשִׂיתָ אֶת־הַבַּדִּים עֲצֵי שִׁטִּים
; acacia of wood of pieces ,poles the make shalt thou And

6 וְצִפִּיתָ אֹתָם זָהָב׃ וְנָתַתָּה
put shalt thou And .gold [with] them overlay shalt thou and

אֹתוֹ לִפְנֵי הַפָּרֹכֶת אֲשֶׁר עַל־אֲרֹן הָעֵדֻת
; testimony the of ark the by [is] which ,veil the before it

לִפְנֵי[c] הַכַּפֹּרֶת אֲשֶׁר עַל־הָעֵדֻת[c] אֲשֶׁר
where ,testimony the over [is] which lid expiating the before

7 אִוָּעֵד לְךָ שָׁמָּה׃ וְהִקְטִיר עָלָיו אַהֲרֹן
Aaron it upon burn shall And .(there) thee (to) meet I

קְטֹרֶת סַמִּים[d] בַּבֹּקֶר בַּבֹּקֶר בְּהֵיטִיבוֹ
dressing his at ,morning the in ,morning the in ; perfumes of incense

8 אֶת־הַנֵּרֹת יַקְטִירֶנָּה׃ וּבְהַעֲלֹת אַהֲרֹן
[1]Aaron's [3]up [2]setting at And .it burn shall he lamps the

אֶת־הַנֵּרֹת בֵּין הָעַרְבַּיִם יַקְטִירֶנָּה קְטֹרֶת
of incense ; it burn shall he ,evenings the between lamps the

תָּמִיד לִפְנֵי יְהוָה לְדֹרֹתֵיכֶם׃
.generations your to Jehovah before continuance

9 לֹא־תַעֲלוּ עָלָיו קְטֹרֶת זָרָה וְעֹלָה
,offering burnt and ,[1]strange [2]incense it upon up offer not shall You

וּמִנְחָה וְנֵסֶךְ לֹא תִסְּכוּ
out pour [2]shall [1]you [3]not libation a and ; offering vegetable and

10 עָלָיו׃ וְכִפֶּר[e] אַהֲרֹן עַל־קַרְנֹתָיו[f] אַחַת
once horns its upon Aaron atonement make shall And . .it upon

בַּשָּׁנָה מִדַּם חַטַּאת הַכִּפֻּרִים
atonement of offering sin the of blood the from ; year the in

bout. 4 And two
golden rings
shalt thou make
for it under the
crown thereof,
upon the two
ribs thereof, up-
on the two sides
of it shalt thou
make them;
and they shall
be for places
for staves to
bear it withal. 5
And thou shalt
make the staves
of acacia wood,
and overlay
them with gold.
6 And thou shalt
put it before the
veil that is by
the ark of the
testimony, be-
fore the mercy-
seat that is over
the testimony,
where I will
meet with thee.

7 And Aaron
shall burn there-
on incense of
sweet spices:
every morning,
when he dress-
eth the lamps,
he shall burn it.
8 And when Aar-
on lighteth the
lamps at even,
he shall burn it,
a perpetual in-
cense before the
LORD through-
out your gen-
erations. 9 Ye
shall offer no
strange incense
thereon, nor
burnt offering,
nor meal offer-
ing; and ye
shall pour no
drink offering
thereon. 10 And
Aaron shall
make atone-
ment upon
the horns of it
once in the year:
with the blood
of the sin offer-
ing of atone-
ment once in

a G. adds, *pure.*
b G. omits לוֹ.
c Sm., G. omit.
d G. has, *compounded, delicate.*
e G. adds, *concerning it.*
f S. has, *the horns of the altar.*

once in the year
shall he make
atonement up-
on it through-
out your gen-
erations: it *is*
most holy unto
the LORD.
11 And the
LORD spake un-
to Moses, say-
ing, 12 When
thou takest the
sum of the chil-
dren of Israel aft-
er their number,
then shall
they give every
man a ransom
for his soul unto
the LORD, when
thou numberest
them; that there
be no plague a-
mong them,
when *thou* num-
berest them. 13
This they shall
give, every one
that passeth a-
mong them
that are num-
bered, half a
shekel after the
shekel of the
sanctuary: (a
shekel *is* twenty
gerahs:) an half
shekel *shall be*
the offering of
the LORD. 14
Every one that
passeth among
them that are
numbered, from
twenty years
old and above,
shall give an of-
fering unto the
LORD. 15 The
rich shall not
give more, and
the poor shall
not give less
than half a she-
kel, when *they*
give an offer-
ing unto the
LORD, to make
an atonement
for your souls.
16 And thou
shalt take the a-
tonement mon-
ey of the chil-
dren of Israel,
and shalt ap-
point it for the
service of the
tabernacle of
the congrega-
tion; that it may

אַחַת בַּשָּׁנָה יְכַפֵּר עָלָיו לְדֹרֹתֵיכֶם[a]
; generations your to it upon atonement make shall he year the in once
קֹדֶשׁ־קָדָשִׁים הוּא לַיהוָה׃
.Jehovah to it [is] holies of holy
11 וַיְדַבֵּר יְהוָה אֶל־מֹשֶׁה לֵּאמֹר[b]׃ כִּי
12 When : saying Moses unto Jehovah spoke And
תִשָּׂא אֶת־רֹאשׁ בְּנֵי־יִשְׂרָאֵל לִפְקֻדֵיהֶם
,mustered those to ,Israel of children the of sum the up liftest thou
וְנָתְנוּ אִישׁ כֹּפֶר נַפְשׁוֹ לַיהוָה
Jehovah to soul his of ransom the one each give shall they (and)
בִּפְקֹד[c] אֹתָם[c] וְלֹא־יִהְיֶה בָהֶם נֶגֶף
plague a them among be not shall and ; them mustering in
13 בִּפְקֹד אֹתָם׃ זֶה יִתְּנוּ כָּל־הָעֹבֵר
over passing one every ,give shall they This .them mustering in
עַל־הַפְּקֻדִים מַחֲצִית הַשֶּׁקֶל בְּשֶׁקֶל הַקֹּדֶשׁ
,sanctuary the of shekel the by ,shekel a of half ,mustered the unto
עֶשְׂרִים גֵּרָה הַשֶּׁקֶל מַחֲצִית הַשֶּׁקֶל תְּרוּמָה
contribution a ,shekel a of half ; shekel the [being] gerahs twenty
14 לַיהוָה׃ כֹּל הָעֹבֵר עַל־הַפְּקֻדִים
,mustered the unto over passing one Every .Jehovah to
מִבֶּן עֶשְׂרִים שָׁנָה וָמָעְלָה יִתֵּן
give shall ,upwards and [old] years twenty (of son a) from
15 תְּרוּמַת יְהוָה׃ הֶעָשִׁיר לֹא־יַרְבֶּה
,increase not shall rich The .Jehovah of contribution the
וְהַדַּל לֹא יַמְעִיט מִמַּחֲצִית הַשָּׁקֶל לָתֵת
give to ,shekel a of half from diminish [1]shall [2]not poor the and
אֶת־תְּרוּמַת יְהוָה לְכַפֵּר עַל־נַפְשֹׁתֵיכֶם׃
.souls your for atonement make to ,Jehovah of contribution the
16 וְלָקַחְתָּ אֶת־כֶּסֶף הַכִּפֻּרִים[d] מֵאֵת
(with) from atonement the of money the take shalt thou And
בְּנֵי יִשְׂרָאֵל וְנָתַתָּ אֹתוֹ עַל־עֲבֹדַת
of service the unto it give shalt thou and ,Israel of children the
אֹהֶל מוֹעֵד וְהָיָה לִבְנֵי יִשְׂרָאֵל
Israel of children the for be shall it and ; meeting of tent the

the year shall
he make aton-
ement for it
throughout
your genera-
tions: it is most
holy unto the
LORD.
11 And the
LORD spake un-
to Moses, say-
ing, 12 When
thou takest the
sum of the chil-
dren of Israel, ac-
cording to those
that are num-
bered of them,
then shall they
give every man
a ransom for his
soul unto the
LORD, when
thou numberest
them; that there
be no plague a-
mong them,
when thou num-
berest them. 13
This they shall
give, every one
that passeth o-
ver unto them
that are num-
bered, half a
shekel after the
shekel of the
sanctuary: (the
shekel is twenty
gerahs:) half a
shekel for an
offering to the
LORD. 14 Every
one that passeth
over unto them
that are num-
bered, from
twenty years old
and upward,
shall give the
offering of the
LORD. 15 The
rich shall not
give more, and
the poor shall
not give less,
than the half
shekel, when
they give the of-
fering of the
LORD, to make
atonement for
your souls. 16
And thou shalt
take the atone-
ment money
from the chil-
dren of Israel,
and shalt ap-
point it for the
service of the
tent of meeting;

a G. has, *to their generations.*
b S. adds, *to him.*
c G., V. omit.
d G. apparently has התרומה.

be a memorial unto the children of Israel before the LORD, to make an atonement for your souls.

17 And the LORD spake unto Moses, saying, 18 Thou shalt also make a laver *of* brass, and his foot *also of* brass, to wash *withal:* and thou shalt put it between the tabernacle of the congregation and the altar, and thou shalt put water therein. 19 For Aaron and his sons shall wash their hands and their feet thereat: 20 When they go into the tabernacle of the congregation, they shall wash with water, that they die not; or when they come near to the altar to minister, to burn offering made by fire unto the LORD: 21 So they shall wash their hands and their feet, that they die not: and it shall be a statute for ever to them, *even* to him and to his seed throughout their generations.

22 Moreover the LORD spake unto Moses, saying, 23 Take thou also unto thee principal spices, of pure myrrh five hundred *shekels*, and of sweet cinnamon half so much, *even*

לְזִכָּרוֹן לִפְנֵי יְהוָה לְכַפֵּר עַל־
for atonement make to ,Jehovah before remembrance for

17 נַפְשֹׁתֵיכֶם[a]: וַיְדַבֵּר יְהוָה אֶל־מֹשֶׁה לֵּאמֹר[b]:
:saying ,Moses unto Jehovah spoke And .souls your

18 וְעָשִׂיתָ כִּיּוֹר נְחֹשֶׁת וְכַנּוֹ[c] נְחֹשֶׁת
,bronze base its and ,bronze of laver a make shalt thou And

לְרָחְצָה וְנָתַתָּ אֹתוֹ בֵּין־אֹהֶל מוֹעֵד
meeting of tent the between it put shalt thou and ;washing for

וּבֵין הַמִּזְבֵּחַ וְנָתַתָּ שָׁמָּה מָיִם:
.water there put shalt thou and ,altar the (between) and

19 וְרָחֲצוּ אַהֲרֹן וּבָנָיו מִמֶּנּוּ אֶת־יְדֵיהֶם
hands their ,it from sons his and Aaron wash shall And

20 וְאֶת־רַגְלֵיהֶם[d]: בְּבֹאָם אֶל־אֹהֶל מוֹעֵד
meeting of tent the into going their at ;feet their and

יִרְחֲצוּ־מַיִם וְלֹא יָמֻתוּ אוֹ
or ;die [1]shall [2]not and ,water [with] wash shall they

בְגִשְׁתָּם אֶל־הַמִּזְבֵּחַ לְשָׁרֵת לְהַקְטִיר אִשֶּׁה
offering fire a burn to ,minister to altar the unto approaching their at

21 לַיהוָה: וְרָחֲצוּ[e] יְדֵיהֶם וְרַגְלֵיהֶם[f] וְלֹא
[2]not and ,feet their and hands their wash shall they and ;Jehovah to

יָמֻתוּ וְהָיְתָה לָהֶם חָק־עוֹלָם לוֹ
him to ,eternity of statute a them to be shall it and ;die [1]shall

וּלְזַרְעוֹ[g] לְדֹרֹתָם[g]:
.generations their to seed his to and

22 וַיְדַבֵּר יְהוָה אֶל־מֹשֶׁה לֵּאמֹר[h]: וְאַתָּה
23 ,thou And :saying Moses unto Jehovah spoke And

קַח־לְךָ בְּשָׂמִים רֹאשׁ מָר־דְּרוֹר חֲמֵשׁ
five myrrh flowing ,best the ,spices thyself for take

מֵאוֹת וְקִנְּמָן־בֶּשֶׂם מַחֲצִיתוֹ חֲמִשִּׁים
fifty ,half its cinnamon spicy and ,[shekels] hundred

that it may be a memorial for the children of Israel before the LORD, to make atonement for your souls.

17 And the LORD spake unto Moses, saying, 18 Thou shalt also make a laver of brass, and the base thereof of brass, to wash withal: and thou shalt put it between the tent of meeting and the altar, and thou shalt put water therein. 19 And Aaron and his sons shall wash their hands and their feet thereat: 20 when they go into the tent of meeting, they shall wash with water, that they die not; or when they come near to the altar to minister, to burn an offering made by fire unto the LORD: 21 so they shall wash their hands and their feet, that they die not: and it shall be a statute for ever to them, even to him and to his seed throughout their generations.

22 Moreover the LORD spake unto Moses, saying, 23 Take thou also unto thee the chief spices, of flowing myrrh five hundred *shekels*, and of sweet cinnamon half so much,

---

a S., V. have, *for their souls.*
b S. adds, *to him.*
c G. adds, *to it.*
d G. adds, *with water.*
e G., S. omit ו.
f G. adds, *with water; whenever they come in into the tent of witness, they shall wash with water.*
g G. has, *and to his generations with him.*
h S. adds, *to him.*

וּמָאתָיִם וּקְנֵה־בֹשֶׂם חֲמִשִּׁים וּמָאתָיִם׃
; hundred two and fifty calamus aromatic and ,hundred two and

24 וְקִדָּה חֲמֵשׁ מֵאוֹת בְּשֶׁקֶל הַקֹּדֶשׁ
; sanctuary the of shekel the by hundred five cassia and

25 וְשֶׁמֶן זַיִת הִין׃ וְעָשִׂיתָ אֹתוֹ שֶׁמֶן
of oil an it make shalt thou And .hin a ,olive the of oil and

מִשְׁחַת־קֹדֶשׁ רֹקַח מִרְקַחַת מַעֲשֵׂה [a]
of work a ,ointment preparing of ointment an ,holiness of anointing

רֹקֵחַ שֶׁמֶן מִשְׁחַת־קֹדֶשׁ יִהְיֶה׃
.be shall it holiness of anointing of oil an ; ointment of preparer a

26 וּמָשַׁחְתָּ בוֹ אֶת־אֹהֶל מוֹעֵד וְאֵת אֲרוֹן
of ark the and ,meeting of tent the it with anoint shalt thou And

27 הָעֵדֻת׃ וְאֶת־הַשֻּׁלְחָן [b] וְאֶת־כָּל־כֵּלָיו [b] וְאֶת־
and ,vessels its all and table the and ; testimony the

הַמְּנֹרָה וְאֶת־כֵּלֶיהָ [c] וְאֵת מִזְבַּח הַקְּטֹרֶת׃
; incense of altar the and ,vessels its and lamp-stand the

28 וְאֶת־מִזְבַּח הָעֹלָה וְאֶת־כָּל־כֵּלָיו [d] וְאֶת־הַכִּיֹּר
laver the and ; vessels its all and ,offering burnt of altar the and

29 וְאֶת־כַּנּוֹ׃ [e] וְקִדַּשְׁתָּ אֹתָם וְהָיוּ
become shall they and them sanctify shalt thou And .base its and

קֹדֶשׁ קָדָשִׁים כָּל־הַנֹּגֵעַ בָּהֶם יִקְדָּשׁ׃
.holy becomes them (on) touching one every ; holies of holy

30 וְאֶת־אַהֲרֹן וְאֶת־בָּנָיו תִּמְשָׁח וְקִדַּשְׁתָּ
consecrate shalt thou and ,anoint shalt thou sons his and Aaron And

31 אֹתָם לְכַהֵן לִי׃ וְאֶל־בְּנֵי
of children the unto And .me to priests as officiate to them

יִשְׂרָאֵל תְּדַבֵּר לֵאמֹר שֶׁמֶן מִשְׁחַת־קֹדֶשׁ
holiness of anointing of Oil : saying speak shalt thou Israel

32 יִהְיֶה זֶה לִי [f] לְדֹרֹתֵיכֶם׃ עַל־בְּשַׂר
of flesh the Upon .generations your to me for this be shall

אָדָם לֹא יִיסָךְ וּבְמַתְכֻּנְתּוֹ לֹא
[3]not proportion its in and ,poured be [2]shall [1]it [3]not man

תַעֲשׂוּ [g] כָּמֹהוּ קֹדֶשׁ הוּא [h] קֹדֶשׁ יִהְיֶה
be shall it holy ,it [is] holy ; it like make [2]shall [1]you

two hundred
and fifty *shek-
els*, and of
sweet calamus
two hundred
and fifty *shekels*,
24 And of cassia
five hundred
shekels, after
the shekel of the
sanctuary, and
of oil olive an
hin: 25 And
thou shalt make
it an oil of holy
ointment, an
ointment com-
pound after the
art of the apoth-
ecary: it shall be
an holy anoint-
ing oil. 26 And
thou shalt a-
noint the tab-
ernacle of the
congregation
therewith, and
the ark of the
testimony, 27
And the table
and all his ves-
sels, and the
candlestick and
his vessels, and
the altar of in-
cense, 28 And
the altar of
burnt offering
with all his ves-
sels, and the
laver and his
foot. 29 And
thou shalt sanc-
tify them, that
they may be
most holy:
whatsoever
toucheth them
shall be holy. 30
And thou shalt
anoint Aaron
and his sons,
and consecrate
them, that *they*
may minister
unto me in the
priest's office. 31
And thou shalt
speak unto the
children of Is-
rael, saying,
This shall be an
holy anointing
oil unto me
throughout your
generations. 32
Upon man's
flesh shall it not
be poured, nei-
ther shall ye
make *any other*

even two hun-
dred and fifty,
and of sweet
calamus two
hundred and
fifty, 24 and of
cassia five hun-
dred, after the
shekel of the
sanctuary, and
of olive oil an
hin: 25 and
thou shalt make
it an holy a-
nointing oil, a
perfume com-
pounded after
the art of the
perfumer: it
shall be an holy
anointing oil. 26
And thou shalt
anoint there-
with the tent of
meeting, and
the ark of the
testimony, 27
and the table
and all the ves-
sels thereof, and
the candlestick
and the vessels
thereof, 28 and
the altar of in-
cense, and the
altar of burnt
offering with all
the vessels there-
of, and the laver
and the base
thereof. 29 And
thou shalt sanc-
tify them,
that they may
be most holy:
whatsoever
toucheth them
shall be holy. 30
And thou shalt
anoint Aaron
and his sons,
and sanctify
them, that they
may minister
unto me in the
priest's office.
31 And thou
shalt speak unto
the children of
Israel, saying,
This shall be an
holy anointing
oil unto me
throughout your
generations. 32
Upon the flesh
of man shall it
not be poured,
neither shall ye
make any like it,
according to the

a S. has, *make*.
b G. omits.
c Sm., G. add, *all*, reading ואת כל כליה.
d G. adds, *and the table and all its vessels*.
e G. omits.
f G. has, *to you*; S. puts before זה.
g G. adds, *for you*, לכם.
h G., S., V. add, *and*, ו.

like it, after the
composition of
it: it *is* holy,
and it shall be
holy unto you.
33 Whosoever
compoundeth
any like it, or
whosoever putteth
any of it
upon a stranger,
shall even be
cut off from his
people.
34 And the
LORD said unto
Moses, Take unto
thee sweet
spices, stacte,
and onycha, and
galbanum; *these*
sweet spices
with pure frankincense:
of each
shall there be a
like *weight*: 35
And thou shalt
make it a perfume,
a confection
after the
art of the apothecary,
tempered
together, pure
and holy: 36
And thou shalt
beat *some* of it
very small, and
put of it before
the testimony in
the tabernacle
of the congregation,
where I
will meet with
thee: it shall be
unto you most
holy. 37 And *as
for* the perfume
which thou shalt
make, ye shall
not make to
yourselves according
to the
composition
thereof: it shall
be unto thee holy
for the LORD.
38 Whosoever
shall make like
unto that, to
smell thereto,
shall even be
cut off from his
people.
AND the
LORD spake unto
Moses, saying,
2 See, I
have called by
name Bezaleel
the son of Uri,
the son of Hur,

33 לָכֶם׃ אִישׁ אֲשֶׁר יִרְקַח כָּמֹהוּ וַאֲשֶׁר יִתֵּן

gives who or ,it like prepares who man A .you to

מִמֶּנּוּ עַל־זָר וְנִכְרַת מֵעַמָּיו׃

.people his from off cut be shall he (and) ,stranger a upon it from

34 וַיֹּאמֶר יְהוָה אֶל־מֹשֶׁה קַח־לְךָ סַמִּים

; perfumes thyself for Take : Moses unto Jehovah said And

נָטָף ׀ וּשְׁחֵלֶת וְחֶלְבְּנָה סַמִּים וּלְבֹנָה

frankincense and ,perfumes ,galbanum and ,onycha and ,storax

35 זַכָּה בַּד בְּבַד יִהְיֶה׃ וְעָשִׂיתָ[a] אֹתָהּ

it make shalt thou And .be shall part a for part a ;pure

קְטֹרֶת רֹקַח מַעֲשֵׂה רוֹקֵחַ מְמֻלָּח

,salted ,ointment of preparer a of work a ,ointment an ,incense

36 טָהוֹר קֹדֶשׁ׃ וְשָׁחַקְתָּ מִמֶּנָּה הָדֵק[b] וְנָתַתָּה

put and ,fine it of [some] grind shalt thou And .holy ,pure

מִמֶּנָּה[c] לִפְנֵי הָעֵדֻת בְּאֹהֶל מוֹעֵד אֲשֶׁר

where ,meeting of tent the in testimony the before it of [some]

אִוָּעֵד[d] לְךָ שָׁמָּה קֹדֶשׁ קָדָשִׁים תִּהְיֶה

be shall it holies of holy ;(there) thee (to) meet I

37 לָכֶם׃ וְהַקְּטֹרֶת אֲשֶׁר[e] תַּעֲשֶׂה[e] בְּמַתְכֻּנְתָּהּ

proportion its in ,makest thou which incense the And .you to

לֹא תַעֲשׂוּ לָכֶם קֹדֶשׁ תִּהְיֶה לְךָ

thee to be shall it holy ;yourselves for make [2]shall [1]you [3]not

38 לַיהוָה׃ אִישׁ אֲשֶׁר־יַעֲשֶׂה כָמוֹהָ לְהָרִיחַ בָּהּ

,it by smell to it like makes who man A .Jehovah for

וְנִכְרַת מֵעַמָּיו׃

.people his from off cut be shall he (and)

31

1
2 וַיְדַבֵּר יְהוָה אֶל־מֹשֶׁה לֵּאמֹר[f]׃ רְאֵה

,See :saying Moses unto Jehovah spoke And

קָרָאתִי בְשֵׁם בְּצַלְאֵל בֶּן־אוּרִי בֶן־חוּר

,Hur of son the Uri of son the Bezalel name by called have I

composition
thereof: it is
holy, *and* it shall
be holy unto
you. 33 Whosoever
compounded
eth any like it,
or whosoever
putteth any of it
upon a stranger,
he shall be cut
off from his people.
34 And the
LORD said unto
Moses, Take unto
thee sweet
spices, stacte,
and onycha, and
galbanum;
sweet spices
with pure frankincense:
of each
shall there be a
like weight; 35
and thou shalt
make of it incense,
a perfume
after the
art of the perfumer,
seasoned
with salt, pure
and holy: 36 and
thou shalt beat
some of it very
small, and put
of it before the
testimony in the
tent of meeting,
where I will
meet with thee:
it shall be unto
you most holy.
37 And the incense
which
thou shalt make,
according to the
composition
thereof ye shall
not make for
yourselves: it
shall be unto
thee holy for the
LORD. 38 Whosoever
shall
make like unto
that, to smell
thereto, he shall
be cut off from
his people.

And the LORD
spake unto Moses,
saying, 2
See, I have
called by name
Bezalel the son
of Uri, the son
of Hur, of the

a G. has, *and they shall make.*
b S., T. have, *and pulverize.*
c G. omits.
d G. has, *I will be known.*
e G., V. omit; S. has pl.
f S. adds, *to him.*

of the tribe of Judah: 3 And I have filled him with the spirit of God, in wisdom, and in understanding, and in knowledge, and in all manner of workmanship, 4 To devise cunning works, to work in gold, and in silver, and in brass, 5 And in cutting of stones, to set *them*, and in carving of timber, to work in all manner of workmanship. 6 And I, behold, I have given with him Aholiab, the son of Ahisamach, of the tribe of Dan: and in the hearts of all that are wise hearted I have put wisdom, that they may make all that I have commanded thee; 7 The tabernacle of the congregation, and the ark of the testimony, and the mercy seat that *is* thereupon, and all the furniture of the tabernacle, 8 And the table and his furniture, and the pure candlestick with all his furniture, and the altar of incense, 9 And the altar of burnt offering with all his furniture, and the laver and his foot, 10 And the cloths of service, and the holy garments

3 לְמַטֵּה יְהוּדָה׃ וָאֲמַלֵּא אֹתוֹ רוּחַ
of spirit the [with] him filled have I And .Judah of tribe the to

אֱלֹהִים בְּחָכְמָה וּבִתְבוּנָה וּבְדַעַת וּבְכָל־
all in and ,knowledge in and ,intelligence in and ,wisdom in ,God

4 מְלָאכָה׃ לַחְשֹׁב [a] מַחֲשָׁבֹת [a] לַעֲשׂוֹת בַּזָּהָב וּבַכֶּסֶף
,silver in and ,gold in work to ,designs plan to ; workmanship

5 וּבַנְּחֹשֶׁת [b]׃ וּבַחֲרֹשֶׁת אֶבֶן לְמַלֹּאת [c] וּבַחֲרֹשֶׁת
of hewing in and ,setting for stones of cutting in and ; bronze in and

6 עֵץ לַעֲשׂוֹת [d] בְּכָל־מְלָאכָה׃ וַאֲנִי הִנֵּה נָתַתִּי
given have I behold ,I And .workmanship all in work to ,wood

אִתּוֹ אֵת אָהֳלִיאָב בֶּן־אֲחִיסָמָךְ לְמַטֵּה־דָן
; Dan of tribe the to ,Ahisamach of son the Oholiab him with

וּבְלֵב [e] כָּל־חֲכַם־לֵב נָתַתִּי חָכְמָה
,wisdom given have I heart of wise one every of heart the in and

וְעָשׂוּ אֵת כָּל־אֲשֶׁר צִוִּיתִךָ׃
; them commanded have I which all make shall they and

7 אֵת אֹהֶל מוֹעֵד וְאֶת־הָאָרֹן לָעֵדֻת וְאֶת־
and ,testimony the for ark the and ,meeting of tent the

הַכַּפֹּרֶת אֲשֶׁר עָלָיו וְאֵת כָּל־כְּלֵי [f] הָאֹהֶל׃
;tent the of vessels the all and ,it upon [is] which lid expiating the

8 וְאֶת־הַשֻּׁלְחָן [g] וְאֶת־כֵּלָיו [h] וְאֶת־הַמְּנֹרָה הַטְּהֹרָה
,[1]pure [2]lamp-stand the and ,vessels its and ,table the and

9 וְאֶת־כָּל־כֵּלֶיהָ וְאֵת [i] מִזְבַּח הַקְּטֹרֶת׃ וְאֵת מִזְבַּח [j]
of altar the and ; incense of altar the and ,vessels its all and

הָעֹלָה וְאֶת־כָּל־כֵּלָיו [j] וְאֶת־הַכִּיֹּר וְאֶת־כַּנּוֹ׃
; base its and laver the and ,vessels its all and ,offering burnt

10 וְאֵת בִּגְדֵי הַשְּׂרָד [k] וְאֶת־בִּגְדֵי [l] הַקֹּדֶשׁ
holiness of garments the and ,weaving of garments the and

לְאַהֲרֹן הַכֹּהֵן [l] וְאֶת־בִּגְדֵי בָנָיו לְכַהֵן [m]׃
; priests as officiate to sons his of garments the and ,priest the Aaron for

tribe of Judah: 3 and I have filled him with the spirit of God, in wisdom, and in understanding, and in knowledge, and in all manner of workmanship, 4 to devise cunning works, to work in gold, and in silver, and in brass, 5 and in cutting of stones for setting, and in carving of wood, to work in all manner of workmanship. 6 And I, behold, I have appointed with him Oholiab, the son of Ahisamach, of the tribe of Dan; and in the hearts of all that are wise hearted I have put wisdom, that they may make all that I have commanded thee: 7 the tent of meeting, and the ark of the testimony, and the mercy-seat that is thereupon, and all the furniture of the Tent; 8 and the table and its vessels, and the pure candlestick with all its vessels, and the altar of incense; 9 and the altar of burnt offering with all its vessels, and the laver and its base; 10 and the finely wrought garments, and the holy garments for Aaron the priest, and the gar-

---

a G. has, *to plan and to construct.*

b G. adds, *and blue and purple and crimson.*

c G. apparently omits.

d S. omits ב.

e G. has, *and to every wise heart.*

f G. omits כל.

g G. adds, *and the altar.*

h G. adds, *all*, reading ואת כל כליו; Sm., S. have the same.

i G. omits.

j G. omits.

k G. adds, *of Aaron.*

l G. omits.

m G., S. add, *to me.*

for Aaron the
priest, and the
garments of his
sons, to minis-
ter in the priest's
office, 11 And
the anointing
oil, and sweet
incense for the
holy *place:* ac-
cording to all
that I have
commanded
thee shall they
do.
12 And the
LORD spake un-
to Moses, say-
ing, 13 Speak
thou also unto
the children of
Israel, saying,
Verily my sab-
baths ye shall
keep: for it *is* a
sign between me
and you
throughout your
generations;
that *ye* may
know that I *am*
the LORD that
doth sanctify
you. 14 Ye
shall keep the
sabbath there-
fore; for it *is*
holy unto you.
Every one that
defileth it shall
surely be put to
death: for who-
soever doeth
any work there-
in, that soul
shall be cut off
from among his
people. 15 Six
days may work
be done; but in
the seventh *is*
the sabbath of
rest, holy to the
LORD: whoso-
ever doeth *any*
work in the
sabbath day, he
shall surely be
put to death. 16
Wherefore the
children of Is-
rael shall keep
the sabbath, to
observe the sab-
bath through-
out their gen-
erations, *for* a

11 וְאֵת שֶׁמֶן הַמִּשְׁחָה וְאֶת־קְטֹרֶת הַסַּמִּים
perfumes of incense the and ,anointing of oil the and
לַקֹּדֶשׁ [a]כְּכֹל אֲשֶׁר־צִוִּיתִךָ
,thee commanded have I which all to according ;sanctuary the for
יַעֲשׂוּ׃
.do shall they

12 וַיֹּאמֶר יְהוָה אֶל־מֹשֶׁה לֵּאמֹר[b]׃ וְאַתָּה דַּבֵּר
13 speak ,thou And :saying Moses unto Jehovah said And
אֶל־בְּנֵי יִשְׂרָאֵל לֵאמֹר[c] אַךְ[d] אֶת־שַׁבְּתֹתַי
sabbaths my Indeed :saying Israel of children the unto
תִּשְׁמֹרוּ כִּי אוֹת הִוא בֵּינִי וּבֵינֵיכֶם
you (between) and me between ,it [is] sign a for ;keep shall you
לְדֹרֹתֵיכֶם לָדַעַת כִּי אֲנִי [e]יְהוָה מְקַדִּשְׁכֶם׃
.sanctifier your Jehovah [am] I that know to ;generations your to
14 וּשְׁמַרְתֶּם אֶת־הַשַּׁבָּת כִּי קֹדֶשׁ[f] הִוא לָכֶם[g]
,you for it [is] holy for ,sabbath the keep shall you And
מְחַלְלֶיהָ מוֹת יוּמָת כִּי[h] כָּל־הָעֹשֶׂה
doing one every for ;death to put be shall surely it of profaners the
בָהּ מְלָאכָה וְנִכְרְתָה הַנֶּפֶשׁ הַהִוא מִקֶּרֶב
of midst the from [1]that [2]soul off cut be shall (and) ,work it in
15 עַמֶּיהָ׃ שֵׁשֶׁת יָמִים יֵעָשֶׂה[i] מְלָאכָה וּבַיּוֹם
[2]day the on and ;work done be may days Six .people his
הַשְּׁבִיעִי שַׁבַּת שַׁבָּתוֹן קֹדֶשׁ לַיהוָה
;Jehovah to holy ,rest of festival a of sabbath a [is] [1]seventh
כָּל־הָעֹשֶׂה מְלָאכָה בְּיוֹם הַשַּׁבָּת מוֹת
surely ,sabbath the of day the on work doing one every
16 יוּמָת׃ וְשָׁמְרוּ בְנֵי־יִשְׂרָאֵל
Israel of children the keep shall And .death to put be shall
אֶת־הַשַּׁבָּת[j] לַעֲשׂוֹת אֶת־הַשַּׁבָּת[k] לְדֹרֹתָם[l]
,generations their for sabbath the observe to ,sabbath the

ments of his
sons, to minis-
ter in the priest's
office; 11 and
the anointing
oil, and the in-
cense of sweet
spices for the
holy place: ac-
cording to all
that I have
commanded
thee shall they
do.
12 And the
LORD spake un-
to Moses, say-
ing, 13 Speak
thou also unto
the children of
Israel, saying,
Verily ye shall
keep my sab-
baths: for it is a
sign between
me and you
throughout your
generations;
that ye may
know that I am
the LORD which
sanctify you. 14
Ye shall keep
the sabbath
therefore; for it
is holy unto you:
every one that
profaneth it
shall surely be
put to death:
for whosoever
doeth any work
therein, that
soul shall be cut
off from among
his people. 15
Six days shall
work be done;
but on the sev-
enth day is a
sabbath of
solemn rest, ho-
ly to the LORD:
whosoever do-
eth any work in
the sabbath day,
he shall surely
be put to death.
16 Wherefore
the children of
Israel shall keep
the sabbath, to
observe the sab-
bath through-
out their gen-
erations, for a

---

a S., V. omit כ.
b S. omits.
c S. omits.
d G. has, *see and;* V., *see that;* S. omits.
e S. adds, *your God.*
f G. adds, *of the Lord.*
g G., S. add, *all.*
h G., V. omit; S. has, *and.*
i Sm., G. have, *thou shalt do;* S., V., *you shall do.*
j S. adds, *to the Lord,* ליהוה.
k G. has, *them;* V., *it.*
l S. has, *to your generations.*

perpetual covenant. 17 It *is* a sign between me and the children of Israel for ever: for *in* six days the LORD made heaven and earth, and on the seventh day he rested, and was refreshed.

17 בְּרִית עוֹלָם׃ בֵּינִי וּבֵין בְּנֵי
of children the between and me Between .eternity of covenant a
יִשְׂרָאֵל אוֹת הִוא[a] לְעֹלָם כִּי־שֵׁשֶׁת יָמִים עָשָׂה
made days six [in] for ;ever for it is sign a ,Israel
יְהוָה אֶת־הַשָּׁמַיִם וְאֶת־הָאָרֶץ[b] וּבַיּוֹם
[2]day the on and ,earth the and heavens the Jehovah
הַשְּׁבִיעִי שָׁבַת וַיִּנָּפַשׁ׃
.breath took and ,rested he [1]seventh

perpetual covenant. 17 It is a sign between me and the children of Israel for ever: for in six days the LORD made heaven and earth, and on the seventh day he rested, and was refreshed.

18 And he gave unto Moses, when he had made an end of communing with him upon mount Sinai, two tables of testimony, tables of stone, written with the finger of God.

18 וַיִּתֵּן אֶל־מֹשֶׁה כְּכַלֹּתוֹ לְדַבֵּר אִתּוֹ
him with speak to finishing his at ,Moses unto gave he And
בְּהַר סִינַי שְׁנֵי לֻחֹת הָעֵדֻת לֻחֹת
of tablets ,testimony of tablets two the ,Sinai of mountain the on
אֶבֶן כְּתֻבִים בְּאֶצְבַּע אֱלֹהִים׃
.God of finger the with written ,stone

18 And he gave unto Moses, when he had made an end of communing with him upon mount Sinai, two tables of the testimony, tables of stone, written with the finger of God.

32

AND when the people saw that Moses delayed to come down out of the mount, the people gathered themselves together unto Aaron, and said unto him, Up, make us gods, which shall go before us; for *as for* this Moses, the man that brought us up out of the land of Egypt, we wot not what is become of him. 2 And Aaron said unto them, Break off the golden earrings, which *are* in the ears of your wives, of your sons, and of your daughters, and bring *them* unto me. 3 And all the people brake off the golden

1 וַיַּרְא הָעָם כִּי־בֹשֵׁשׁ מֹשֶׁה לָרֶדֶת
down come to Moses neglected that people the saw And
מִן־הָהָר וַיִּקָּהֵל הָעָם עַל־אַהֲרֹן
,Aaron unto people the themselves gathered (and) ,mountain the from
וַיֹּאמְרוּ אֵלָיו קוּם עֲשֵׂה־לָנוּ אֱלֹהִים אֲשֶׁר יֵלְכוּ
go may who god a us for make Arise :him unto said they and
לְפָנֵינוּ כִּי־זֶה[c] מֹשֶׁה הָאִישׁ[c] אֲשֶׁר הֶעֱלָנוּ
up us brought who man the ,Moses ,now ,for ;us before
מֵאֶרֶץ מִצְרַיִם לֹא יָדַעְנוּ מֶה־הָיָה
become has what know [2]do [1]we [3]not ,Egypt of land the from
2 לוֹ׃ וַיֹּאמֶר אֲלֵהֶם אַהֲרֹן פָּרְקוּ נִזְמֵי
of rings the off Tear :Aaron them unto said And .him to
הַזָּהָב אֲשֶׁר בְּאָזְנֵי נְשֵׁיכֶם בְּנֵיכֶם[d]
,sons your ,wives your of ears the in [are] which gold
3 וּבְנֹתֵיכֶם וְהָבִיאוּ אֵלָי׃ וַיִּתְפָּרְקוּ כָּל־
all off tore And .me unto bring and ;daughters your and

And when the people saw that Moses delayed to come down from the mount, the people gathered themselves together unto Aaron, and said unto him, Up, make us gods, which shall go before us; for as for this Moses, the man that brought us up out of the land of Egypt, we know not what is become of him. 2 And Aaron said unto them, Break off the golden rings, which are in the ears of your wives, of your sons, and of your daughters, and bring them unto me. 3 And all the people brake off

a G. adds, *with me.*
b S. adds, *and the sea and all which is in them.*
c G., V. have, *for Moses, this man;* S. has, *because this man Moses.*
d G. omits.

earrings which
were in their
ears, and
brought *them*
unto Aaron. 4
And he received
them at their
hand, and fash-
ioned it with a
graving tool,
after he had
made it a molten
calf: and they
said, These *be*
thy gods, O Is-
rael, which
brought thee up
out of the land
of Egypt. 5
And when Aar-
on saw *it*, he
built an altar be-
fore it; and Aar-
aron made proc-
lamation, and
said, To mor-
row *is* a feast to
the LORD. 6
And they rose
up early on the
morrow, and
offered burnt
offerings, and
brought peace
offerings; and
the people sat
down to eat and
to drink, and
rose up to play.
7 And the
LORD said un-
to Moses, Go,
get thee down;
for thy people,
which thou
broughtest out
of the land of
Egypt, have cor-
rupted *them-*
selves: 8 They
have turned a-
side quickly out
of the way which
I commanded
them: they have
made them a
molten calf, and
have worship-
ped it, and have
sacrificed there-
unto and
said, These *be*
thy gods, O
Israel, which
have brought
thee up out of
the land of E-

הָעָם אֶת־נִזְמֵי הַזָּהָב[a] אֲשֶׁר בְּאָזְנֵיהֶם
,ears their in [were] which gold of rings the people the

4 וַיָּבִיאוּ אֶל־אַהֲרֹן׃ וַיִּקַּח מִיָּדָם
,hand their from took he And .Aaron unto brought they and

וַיָּצַר אֹתוֹ בַּחֶרֶט וַיַּעֲשֵׂהוּ עֵגֶל
of calf a it made he and ,chisel a with it formed he and

מַסֵּכָה וַיֹּאמְרוּ[b] אֵלֶּה אֱלֹהֶיךָ יִשְׂרָאֵל אֲשֶׁר
who ,Israel O ,god thy [is] This :said they and ;casting

5 הֶעֱלוּךָ מֵאֶרֶץ מִצְרָיִם׃ וַיַּרְא[c] אַהֲרֹן
,Aaron saw And .Egypt of land the from up thee brought

וַיִּבֶן מִזְבֵּחַ לְפָנָיו וַיִּקְרָא אַהֲרֹן וַיֹּאמַר
:said and Aaron called and ;it before altar an built he and

6 חַג לַיהוָה מָחָר׃ וַיַּשְׁכִּימוּ[d] מִמָּחֳרָת
,morrow the from early rose they And .tomorrow Jehovah to feast A

וַיַּעֲלוּ עֹלֹת וַיַּגִּשׁוּ שְׁלָמִים[e d]
;offerings peace brought and ,offerings burnt up offered they and

וַיֵּשֶׁב הָעָם לֶאֱכֹל וְשָׁתוֹ וַיָּקֻמוּ לְצַחֵק[f]׃
.wanton to arose they and ;drink and eat to people the sat and

7 וַיְדַבֵּר יְהוָה אֶל־מֹשֶׁה[g] לֶךְ־רֵד[h]
,down go ,Come :Moses unto Jehovah spoke And

כִּי שִׁחֵת עַמְּךָ אֲשֶׁר הֶעֱלֵיתָ
up broughtest thou whom people thy corruptly done have for

8 מֵאֶרֶץ מִצְרָיִם׃ סָרוּ מַהֵר
quickly swerved have they ;Egypt of land the from

מִן־הַדֶּרֶךְ אֲשֶׁר צִוִּיתִם[i] עָשׂוּ
made have they ;them commanded I which way the from

לָהֶם עֵגֶל מַסֵּכָה[j] וַיִּשְׁתַּחֲווּ־לוֹ
,it to themselves prostrated have and ,casting of calf a themselves for

וַיִּזְבְּחוּ־לוֹ[k] וַיֹּאמְרוּ אֵלֶּה אֱלֹהֶיךָ יִשְׂרָאֵל
,Israel O ,god thy [is] This :said have and ,it to sacrificed have and

9 אֲשֶׁר הֶעֱלוּךָ מֵאֶרֶץ מִצְרָיִם׃ וַיֹּאמֶר[l]
said And .Egypt of land the from up thee brought who

the golden rings
which were in
their ears, and
brought them
unto Aaron. 4
And he received
it at their hand,
and fashioned
it with a graving
tool, and made
it a molten calf:
and they said,
These be thy
gods, O Israel,
which brought
thee up out of
the land of E-
gypt. 5 And
when Aaron saw
this, he built an
altar before it;
and Aaron made
proclamation,
and said, To-
morrow shall be
a feast to the
LORD. 6 And
they rose up ear-
ly on the mor-
row, and offered
burnt offerings,
and brought
peace offerings;
and the people
sat down to eat
and to drink,
and rose up to
play.
7 And the
LORD spake un-
to Moses, Go,
get thee down;
for thy people,
which thou
broughtest up
out of the land
of Egypt, have
corrupted them-
selves: 8 they
have turned a-
side quickly out
of the way which
I commanded
them: they have
made them a
molten calf, and
have worship-
ped it, and have
sacrificed unto
it, and said,
These be thy
gods, O Israel,
which brought
thee up out of
the land of E-
gypt. 9 And the

a S., V. omit.
b G. has sing., *he said.*
c S. has, *and feared*, וַיִּרָא.
d G. has sing. in all the verbs.
e S. adds, *and brought gifts.*
f S. has, *to laugh and play.*
g Sm., G., V. add, *saying.*
h G. has, *go quickly hence, go down*; S. *come, go hence for thyself.*
i G., V. have, *thou commandedst them*, צִוִּיתָם.
j G. omits.
k G. omits.
l G. omits the verse.

gypt. 9 And
the LORD said
unto Moses, I
have seen this
people, and, be-
hold, it is a stiff-
necked people:

10 Now there-
fore let me alone,
that my wrath
may wax hot a-
gainst them,
and that I may
consume them:
and I will make
of thee a great
nation. 11 And
Moses besought
the LORD his
God, and said,
LORD, why doth
thy wrath wax
hot against thy
people, which
thou hast
brought forth
out of the land
of Egypt with
great power, and
with a mighty
hand? 12
Wherefore
should the E-
gyptians speak,
and say, For
mischief did he
bring them out,
to slay them in
the mountains,
and to consume
them from the
face of the
earth? Turn
from thy fierce
wrath, and re-
pent of this evil
against thy peo-
ple. 13 Remem-
ber Abraham,
Isaac, and Israel,
thy servants, to
whom thou
swarest by
thine own self,
and saidst unto
them, I will
multiply your
seed as the stars
of heaven, and
all this land that
I have spoken of
will I give unto
your seed, and
they shall inherit

יְהוָה׃ אֶל־מֹשֶׁה רָאִיתִי אֶת־הָעָם הַזֶּה וְהִנֵּה
,behold and ,[1]this [2]people seen have I : Moses unto Jehovah

10 עַם־קְשֵׁה־עֹרֶף הוּא׃ וְעַתָּה הַנִּיחָה לִּי
,me (to) alone leave now And .it [is] neck of hard people a

וְיִחַר־אַפִּי בָהֶם וַאֲכַלֵּם
;them consume may I and ,them against anger my glow may that

11 וְאֶעֱשֶׂה אוֹתְךָ לְגוֹי גָּדוֹל׃ וַיְחַל מֹשֶׁה
Moses appeased And .[1]great [2]nation a (for) thee make will I and

אֶת־פְּנֵי יְהוָה אֱלֹהָיו וַיֹּאמֶר לָמָה יְהוָה
,Jehovah O ,Why :said he and ,God his Jehovah of face the

יֶחֱרֶה אַפְּךָ בְּעַמֶּךָ אֲשֶׁר הוֹצֵאתָ
out brought hast thou whom people thy against anger thine glows

מֵאֶרֶץ מִצְרַיִם בְּכֹחַ גָּדוֹל וּבְיָד[a] חֲזָקָה׃
?strong hand a with and ,great power with Egypt of land the from

12 לָמָּה יֹאמְרוּ מִצְרַיִם לֵאמֹר[b] בְּרָעָה
misfortune With :saying ,Egyptians the say should Why

הוֹצִיאָם לַהֲרֹג אֹתָם בֶּהָרִים
,mountains the in them kill to out them brought has he

וּלְכַלֹּתָם מֵעַל פְּנֵי הָאֲדָמָה שׁוּב
Turn ?ground the of face the upon from them consume to and

מֵחֲרוֹן אַפֶּךָ וְהִנָּחֵם
purpose thy change and ,anger thine of fierceness the from

13 עַל־הָרָעָה לְעַמֶּךָ׃ זְכֹר לְאַבְרָהָם
,Abraham (to) Remember .people thy to evil the concerning

לְיִצְחָק וּלְיִשְׂרָאֵל[c] עֲבָדֶיךָ אֲשֶׁר נִשְׁבַּעְתָּ
swarest thou whom [to] ,servants thy ,Israel (to) and ,Isaac (to)

לָהֶם בָּךְ וַתְּדַבֵּר אֲלֵהֶם[d] אַרְבֶּה
multiply will I :them unto spokest thou and ,thyself by (them to)

אֶת־זַרְעֲכֶם כְּכוֹכְבֵי הַשָּׁמָיִם וְכָל־הָאָרֶץ הַזֹּאת
[1]this [2]land all and ;heavens the of stars the like seed your

אֲשֶׁר אָמַרְתִּי[e] אֶתֵּן לְזַרְעֲכֶם[f] וְנָחֲלוּ
possess shall they and ,seed your to give will I of spoken have I which

LORD said unto
Moses, I have
seen this people,
and, behold, it
is a stiffnecked
people:

10 now there-
fore let me
alone, that my
wrath may wax
hot against
them, and that
I may consume
them: and I will
make of thee a
great nation. 11
And Moses be-
sought the
LORD his
God, and said,
LORD, why doth
thy wrath wax
hot against thy
people, which
thou hast
brought forth
out of the land
of Egypt with
great power and
with a mighty
hand? 12
Wherefore
should the E-
gyptians speak,
saying, For evil
did he bring
them forth, to
slay them in the
mountains, and
to consume
them from the
face of the
earth? Turn
from thy fierce
wrath, and re-
pent of this evil
against thy peo-
ple. 13 Re-
member A-
braham, Isaac,
and Israel, thy
servants, to
whom thou
swarest by thine
own self, and
saidst unto them,
I will multiply
your seed as the
stars of heaven,
and all this land
that I have spok-
en of will I give
unto your seed,
and they shall
inherit it for

---

a Sm., G., S. have, *and with thy arm exalted.*
b S., V. omit.
c Sm., G. have, *Jacob.*
d G. adds, *saying.*
e G. has, *thou saidst.*
f G. has, *to them.*

it for ever. 14
And the LORD
repented of the
evil which he
thought to do
unto his people.
15 And Moses
turned, and
went down from
the mount, and
the two tables
of the testimony
were in his hand:
the tables *were*
written on both
their sides; on
the one side and
on the other
were they written.
16 And the
tables *were* the
work of God,
and the writing
was the writing
of God, graven
upon the tables.
17 And when
Joshua heard
the noise of the
people as they
shouted, he said
unto Moses,
There is a noise
of war in the
camp. 18 And
he said, *It is* not
the voice of
them that shout
for mastery,
neither *is it* the
voice of *them*
that cry for being
overcome:
but the noise of
them that sing
do I hear. 19
And it came to
pass, as soon as
he came nigh
unto the camp,
that he saw the
calf, and the
dancing: and
Moses' anger
waxed hot, and
he cast the tables
out of his hands,
and brake them
beneath the
mount. 20 And
he took the calf
which they had
made, and burnt
it in the fire, and
ground *it* to
powder, and
strawed *it* upon
the water, and

14 לְעֹלָם׃ וַיִּנָּחֶם יְהוָה עַל־הָרָעָה [a] אֲשֶׁר
which evil the concerning Jehovah purpose his changed And .ever for

דִּבֶּר לַעֲשׂוֹת לְעַמּוֹ׃ [a]
.people his to do to spoken had he

15 וַיִּפֶן וַיֵּרֶד מֹשֶׁה מִן־הָהָר וּשְׁנֵי
two the (and) ,mountain the from Moses down went and turned And

לֻחֹת הָעֵדֻת בְּיָדוֹ לֻחֹת [b] כְּתֻבִים מִשְּׁנֵי
²two from written tablets ;hand his in [being] testimony of tablets

עֶבְרֵיהֶם מִזֶּה וּמִזֶּה הֵם כְּתֻבִים׃
.written [were] they this from and this from ,sides ¹their

16 וְהַלֻּחֹת מַעֲשֵׂה אֱלֹהִים הֵמָּה וְהַמִּכְתָּב
,writing the and ;they [were] God of work the ,tablets the And

17 מִכְתַּב אֱלֹהִים הוּא חָרוּת עַל־הַלֻּחֹת׃ וַיִּשְׁמַע
heard And .tablets the upon engraved ,it [was] God of writing the

יְהוֹשֻׁעַ אֶת־קוֹל הָעָם בְּרֵעֹה וַיֹּאמֶר
said he and ,shouting their in people the of voice the Joshua

18 אֶל־מֹשֶׁה קוֹל מִלְחָמָה בַּמַּחֲנֶה׃ וַיֹּאמֶר אֵין
not is It :said he And .camp the in war of voice A :Moses unto

קוֹל עֲנוֹת גְּבוּרָה וְאֵין קוֹל עֲנוֹת [c] חֲלוּשָׁה
;defeat of cry a of voice a not and ,victory of cry a of voice a

19 [d] קוֹל עַנּוֹת [e] אָנֹכִי שֹׁמֵעַ׃ וַיְהִי כַּאֲשֶׁר
as ,pass to came it And .hearing [am] I singing of voice a

קָרַב אֶל־הַמַּחֲנֶה וַיַּרְא אֶת־הָעֵגֶל וּמְחֹלֹת
,dances and calf the saw and ,camp the unto near came he

וַיִּחַר־אַף מֹשֶׁה וַיַּשְׁלֵךְ מִיָּדָו
hands his from cast he and ,Moses of anger the glowed (and)

20 אֶת־הַלֻּחֹת [f] וַיְשַׁבֵּר אֹתָם תַּחַת הָהָר׃ וַיִּקַּח
took he And .mountain the below them broke he and ,tablets the

אֶת־הָעֵגֶל אֲשֶׁר עָשׂוּ וַיִּשְׂרֹף בָּאֵשׁ וַיִּטְחַן [g]
ground and ,fire with burned and ,made had they which calf the

עַד [h] אֲשֶׁר־דָּק [h] וַיִּזֶר [i] עַל־פְּנֵי הַמָּיִם
,water of face the upon scattered he and ;fine was it that until

ever. 14 And
the LORD repented
of the
evil which he
said he would
do unto his
people.
15 And Moses
turned, and
went down from
the mount, with
the two tables of
the testimony in
his hand; tables
that were written
on both
their sides; on
the one side and
on the other
were they written.
16 And the
tables were the
work of God,
and the writing
was the writing
of God, graven
upon the tables.
17 And when
Joshua heard
the noise of the
people as they
shouted, he said
unto Moses,
There is a noise
of war in the
camp. 18 And
he said, It is not
the voice of
them that shout
for mastery,
neither is it the
voice of them
that cry for being
overcome:
but the noise of
them that sing
do I hear. 19
And it came to
pass, as soon as
he came nigh
unto the camp,
that he saw the
calf and the
dancing: and
Moses' anger
waxed hot, and
he cast the tables
out of his hands,
and brake them
beneath the
mount. 20 And
he took the calf
which they had
made, and burnt
it with fire,
and ground it to
powder, and
strewed it upon

a G. has, *to preserve his people.*
b G. adds, *stone.*
c S. omits.
d G. adds, *but*; S., *for.*
e G. adds, *of wine*; Sm., S. have, *sins*, עֲוֹנוֹת; Sym. has, *humiliation*, עֱנוּת.
f G. adds, *two.*
g S. adds, *with a file.*
h G. has, *fine*; S. *until it was pulverized like dust.*
i S. adds, *its powder.*

made the chil-
dren of Israel
drink *of it.* 21
And Moses said
unto Aaron,
What did this
people unto
thee, that thou
hast brought so
great a sin upon
them. 22 And
Aaron said, Let
not the anger of
my lord wax hot:
thou knowest
the people, that
they *are set* on
mischief. 23
For they said
unto me, Make
us gods, which
shall go before
us: for *as for*
this Moses, the
man that
brought us up
out of the land
of Egypt, we
wot not what is
become of him.
24 And I said
unto them,
Whosoever hath
any gold, let
them break *it*
off. So they gave
it me: then I
cast it into the
fire, and there
came out this
calf.
25 And when
Moses saw that
the people *were*
naked; (for Aar-
on had made
them naked un-
to *their* shame
among their en-
emies:) 26 Then
Moses stood in
the gate of the
camp, and said,
Who *is* on the
LORD'S side?
let him come un-
to me. And all
the sons of Levi
gathered them-
selves together
unto him. 27
And he said un-
to them, Thus
saith the LORD
God of Israel,

וַיַּשְׁקְ אֶת־בְּנֵי יִשְׂרָאֵל׃ וַיֹּאמֶר מֹשֶׁה 21
Moses said And .Israel of children the drink to caused he and

אֶל־אַהֲרֹן מֶה־עָשָׂה לְךָ הָעָם הַזֶּה
,¹this ²people thee to done has What : Aaron unto

כִּי־הֵבֵאתָ עָלָיו חֲטָאָה גְדֹלָה׃ וַיֹּאמֶר 22
said And ? ¹great ²sin a them upon brought hast thou that

אַהֲרֹן[a] אַל־יִחַר אַף אֲדֹנִי[b] אַתָּה יָדַעְתָּ
knowest thou ; lord my of anger the glow not Let : Aaron

אֶת־הָעָם[c] כִּי בְרָע[d] הוּא[c]׃ וַיֹּאמְרוּ לִי 23
: me to said they And .it [is] [disposition] evil in that ,people the

עֲשֵׂה־לָנוּ אֱלֹהִים אֲשֶׁר יֵלְכוּ לְפָנֵינוּ כִּי־זֶה[e] מֹשֶׁה
,Moses ,now ,for ; us before go may who ,god a us for Make

הָאִישׁ[e] אֲשֶׁר הֶעֱלָנוּ מֵאֶרֶץ מִצְרַיִם לֹא
³not ,Egypt of land the from up us brought who man the

יָדַעְנוּ מֶה־הָיָה לוֹ׃ וָאֹמַר לָהֶם לְמִי 24
whom To : them to said I And .him to become has what know ²do ¹we

זָהָב הִתְפָּרָקוּ[f] וַיִּתְּנוּ־לִי וָאַשְׁלִכֵהוּ
it cast I and ,me to gave they and ; off tear them let ,gold [is]

בָאֵשׁ וַיֵּצֵא[g] הָעֵגֶל הַזֶּה׃ וַיַּרְא מֹשֶׁה 25
Moses saw And .¹this ²calf out came and ,fire the into

אֶת־הָעָם כִּי פָרֻעַ הוּא כִּי־פְרָעֹה אַהֲרֹן
,Aaron unbridled it made had for ; it [was] unbridled that ,people the

לְשִׁמְצָה[h] בְּקָמֵיהֶם[h]׃ וַיַּעֲמֹד מֹשֶׁה 26
Moses stood And .opponents their among whispering a for

בְּשַׁעַר הַמַּחֲנֶה וַיֹּאמֶר מִי לַיהוָה אֵלָי[i]
! me unto ,Jehovah for Who : said and ,camp the of gate the in

וַיֵּאָסְפוּ אֵלָיו[j] כָּל־בְּנֵי לֵוִי׃ וַיֹּאמֶר 27
said he And .Levi of sons the all him unto themselves gathered And

לָהֶם[k] כֹּה־אָמַר יְהוָה אֱלֹהֵי יִשְׂרָאֵל שִׂימוּ
ye Put : Israel of God ,Jehovah says Thus ; them to

the water, and
made the chil-
dren of Israel
drink of it. 21
And Moses said
unto Aaron,
What did this
people unto
thee, that thou
hast brought a
great sin upon
them? 22 And
Aaron said, Let
not the anger of
my lord wax hot:
thou knowest
the people, that
they are *set* on
evil. 23 For
they said unto
me, Make us
gods, which
shall go before
us: for as for
this Moses, the
man that
brought us up
out of the land
of Egypt, we
know not what
is become of
him. 24 And I
said unto them,
Whosoever hath
any gold, let
them break it
off; so they
gave it me:
and I cast it into
the fire, and
there came out
this calf.
25 And when
Moses saw that
the people were
broken loose; for
Aaron had let
them loose for a
derision among
their enemies:
26 then Moses
stood in the gate
of the camp,
and said, Whoso
is on the LORD'S
side, *let him*
come unto me.
And all the sons
of Levi gathered
themselves to-
gether unto him.
27 And he said
unto them, Thus
saith the LORD,
the God of Isra-

---

a G. adds, *to Moses.*

b G., V. add, *for.*

c G. has, *the violence of this people.*

d Sm. has, בְּרָע.

e G. has, *for Moses this man;* S., V. have, *because this Moses.*

f S. has, *let them give to me.*

g S. has, *and it became.*

h S. has, *that they might be an offensive name among their descendants;* T., *to defile themselves with an evil name in their generations.*

i G. adds, *let him come*; so ess. S., T., V.

j G. omits.

k S. adds, *Moses.*

Put every man
his sword by his
side, *and* go in
and out from
gate to gate
throughout the
camp, and slay
every man his
brother, and
every man his
companion, and
every man his
neighbour. 28
And the children
of Levi did ac-
cording to the
word of Moses:
and there fell of
the people that
day about three
thousand men.
29 For Moses
had said, Conse-
crate yourselves
to day to the
LORD, even
every man upon
his son, and
upon his broth-
er; that he may
bestow upon you
a blessing this
day.
30 And it
came to pass on
the morrow,
that Moses said
unto the people,
Ye have sinned
a great sin: and
now I will go up
unto the LORD;
peradventure I
shall make an
atonement for
your sin. 31
And Moses re-
turned unto the
LORD, and said,
Oh, this people
have sinned a
great sin, and
have made them
gods of gold. 32
Yet now, if
thou wilt for-
give their sin—;
and if not, blot
me, I pray thee,
out of thy book
which thou hast
written. 33 And
the LORD said
unto Moses,
Whosoever

אִישׁ־חַרְבּוֹ עַל־יְרֵכוֹ עִבְרוּ וָשׁוּבוּ מִשַּׁעַר
gate from return and over pass ;thigh his upon sword his one each

לָשַׁעַר בַּמַּחֲנֶה וְהִרְגוּ אִישׁ־אֶת־אָחִיו וְאִישׁ
one each and ,brother his one each kill and ;camp the in gate to

28 אֶת־רֵעֵהוּ וְאִישׁ אֶת־קְרֹבוֹ׃ וַיַּעֲשׂוּ בְנֵי־לֵוִי
Levi of sons the did And .relative his one each and ,neighbor his

כִּדְבַר מֹשֶׁה וַיִּפֹּל מִן־הָעָם בַּיּוֹם
[2]day on people the of fell and ;Moses of word the to according

29 הַהוּא כִּשְׁלֹשֶׁת אַלְפֵי אִישׁ׃ וַיֹּאמֶר[a] מֹשֶׁה מִלְאוּ
Fill :Moses said And .men thousand three about [1]that

יֶדְכֶם הַיּוֹם לַיהוָה כִּי[b] אִישׁ בִּבְנוֹ
son his against [was] one each since ,Jehovah for today hands your

וּבְאָחִיו וְלָתֵת[c] עֲלֵיכֶם הַיּוֹם[d] בְּרָכָה׃
.blessing a today you unto give to order in and ;brother his against and

30 וַיְהִי מִמָּחֳרָת וַיֹּאמֶר מֹשֶׁה
Moses said (and) ,morrow the from ,pass to came it And

אֶל־הָעָם אַתֶּם חֲטָאתֶם חֲטָאָה גְדֹלָה[e] וְעַתָּה
,now and ;[1]great [2]sin a sinned have You :people the unto

אֶעֱלֶה אֶל־יְהוָה[f] אוּלַי אֲכַפְּרָה[g] בְּעַד
for atonement make can I perhaps ,Jehovah unto up go will I

31 חַטַּאתְכֶם׃ וַיָּשָׁב מֹשֶׁה אֶל־יְהוָה וַיֹּאמַר אָנָּא[h]
,Ah :said and Jehovah unto Moses returned And .sin your

חָטָא הָעָם הַזֶּה חֲטָאָה גְדֹלָה וַיַּעֲשׂוּ
made have they and ,[1]great [2]sin a [1]this [2]people sinned has

32 לָהֶם אֱלֹהֵי זָהָב׃ וְעַתָּה אִם־תִּשָּׂא
forgive wilt thou if ,now And .gold of god a themselves for

חַטָּאתָם[i] וְאִם־אַיִן מְחֵנִי נָא מִסִּפְרְךָ אֲשֶׁר
which book thy from ,pray I ,off me wipe ,not if and !sin their

33 כָּתָבְתָּ׃ וַיֹּאמֶר יְהוָה אֶל־מֹשֶׁה מִי אֲשֶׁר
(who) Whoever :Moses unto Jehovah said And .written hast thou

el, Put ye every
man his sword
upon his thigh,
and go to and
fro from gate to
gate throughout
the camp, and
slay every man
his brother, and
every man his
companion, and
every man his
neighbour. 28
And the sons of
Levi did accord-
ing to the word
of Moses: and
there fell of the
people that day
about three
thousand men.
29 And Moses
said, Consecrate
yourselves to-
day to the
LORD, yea every
man against his
son, and against
his brother; that
he may bestow
upon you a
blessing this
day.
30 And it
came to pass on
the morrow,
that Moses said
unto the people,
Ye have sinned
a great sin: and
now I will go up
unto the LORD;
peradventure I
shall make a-
tonement for
your sin. 31
And Moses re-
turned unto the
LORD, and said,
Oh, this people
have sinned a
great sin, and
have made them
gods of gold. 32
Yet now, if thou
wilt forgive their
sin—; and if not,
blot me, I pray
thee, out of thy
book which thou
hast written. 33
And the LORD
said unto Moses,
Whosoever

---

a G., S. add, *to them.*
b G., S., V. omit.
c G., S., V. omit ו.
d G., V. omit.
e S. adds, *this.*
f G. has, *God.*
g S. has, *he will forgive.*
h G. adds, *Lord;* S. adds, *Lord God.*
i Sm., G. add, *forgive,* שָׂא.

34 חָטָא־לִי[a] אֶמְחֶנּוּ מִסִּפְרִי׃ וְעַתָּה[b]
now And .book my from off him wipe will I ,me against sinned has

לֵךְ[c] נְחֵה אֶת־הָעָם אֶל[d] אֲשֶׁר־דִּבַּרְתִּי לָךְ הִנֵּה
behold ;thee to of spoken have I what unto people the lead ,go

מַלְאָכִי יֵלֵךְ לְפָנֶיךָ וּבְיוֹם פָּקְדִי
,visiting my of day the in and ;thee before go shall angel my

35 וּפָקַדְתִּי עֲלֵהֶם חַטָּאתָם׃ וַיִּגֹּף יְהוָה
Jehovah plagues sent And .sin their them upon visit will I (and)

אֶת־הָעָם עַל[e] אֲשֶׁר עָשׂוּ[f] אֶת־הָעֵגֶל אֲשֶׁר עָשָׂה
made which ,calf the made they that because ,people the [upon]

אַהֲרֹן׃
.Aaron

hath sinned against me, him will I blot out of my book. 34 And now go, lead the people unto *the place* of which I have spoken unto thee: behold, mine angel shall go before thee: nevertheless in the day when I visit, I will visit their sin upon them. 35 And the LORD smote the people, because they made the calf, which Aaron made.

ıath sinned a-
;ainst me, him
vill I blot out of
ny book. 34
Therefore now
;o, lead the peo-
ɔle unto *the*
place of which
have spoken
ınto thee: be-
ıold, mine An-
;el shall go be-
ore thee: nev-
rtheless, in the
ay when I visit
will visit their
in upon them.
5 And the
ORD plagued
he people, be-
ause they made
he calf, which
Aaron made.

33

1 וַיְדַבֵּר יְהוָה אֶל־מֹשֶׁה לֵךְ עֲלֵה מִזֶּה אַתָּה
thou ,hence up go ,Come : Moses unto Jehovah spoke And

וְהָעָם אֲשֶׁר הֶעֱלִיתָ מֵאֶרֶץ מִצְרָיִם
,Egypt of land the from up brought hast thou whom people the and

אֶל־הָאָרֶץ אֲשֶׁר נִשְׁבַּעְתִּי לְאַבְרָהָם לְיִצְחָק וּלְיַעֲקֹב
,Jacob to and ,Isaac to ,Abraham to swore I which land the unto

2 לֵאמֹר[g] לְזַרְעֲךָ אֶתְּנֶנָּה׃ וְשָׁלַחְתִּי לְפָנֶיךָ
thee before send will I And .it give will I seed thy To ,saying

מַלְאָךְ[h] וְגֵרַשְׁתִּי[i] אֶת־הַכְּנַעֲנִי הָאֱמֹרִי
,Amorites the ,Canaanites the out drive will I and ,angel an

וְהַחִתִּי[j] וְהַפְּרִזִּי[k] הַחִוִּי[l] וְהַיְבוּסִי׃
;Jebusites the and ,Hivites the ,Perizzites the and ,Hittites the and

3 אֶל־אֶרֶץ[m] זָבַת חָלָב וּדְבָשׁ כִּי לֹא
[3]not for ;honey and milk [with] (of) flowing land a unto

אֶעֱלֶה בְּקִרְבְּךָ כִּי עַם־קְשֵׁה־עֹרֶף
neck of hard people a because ,thee of midst the in up go [2]will [1]I

And the LORD spake unto Moses, Depart, go up hence, thou and the people which thou hast brought up out of the land of Egypt, unto the land of which I sware unto Abraham, to Isaac, and to Jacob, saying, Unto thy seed will I give it: 2 and I will send an angel before thee; and I will drive out the Canaanite, the Amorite, and the Hittite, and the Perizzite, the Hivite, and the Jebusite: 3 unto a land flowing with milk and honey: for I will not go up in the midst of thee; for thou art a stiffnecked peo-

AND the LORD
aid unto Moses,
Depart, *and* go
p hence, thou
nd the people
vhich thou hast
rought up out
f the land of E-
ypt, unto the
and which I
ware unto A-
raham, to Isaac,
nd to Jacob,
aying, Unto
hy seed will I
ive it: 2 And
will send an
ngel before
hee; and I will
rive out the
Canaanite, the
Amorite, and
he Hittite, and
he Perizzite, the
Hivite, and the
ebusite: 3
Unto a land
owing with
nilk and honey:
or I will not go
p in the midst
f thee; for thou
rt a stiffnecked

---

a G. omits.

b G., V. have, *and thou*, ואתה.

c G. adds, *go down and.*

d G., T. add, *the place*, המקום.

e G. has, *on account of the making.*

f Sm., S., T. have, *they had worshipped.*

g S. adds, *to them.*

h G. has, *my angel*, מלאכי.

i G. has, *and thou shalt drive out*, וְגֵרַשְׁתָּ; S. *and he will destroy*, וגרש.

j S. adds, *and the Girgashite.*

k G. adds, *and the Girgashite.*

l G., S., V. add, *and*, ו.

m G. adds, *and I will bring thee;* V., *and thou shalt enter.*

people: lest I consume thee in the way.

4 And when the people heard these evil tidings, they mourned: and no man did put on him his ornaments. 5 For the LORD had said unto Moses, Say unto the children of Israel, Ye *are* a stiffnecked people: I will come up into the midst of thee in a moment, and consume thee: therefore now put off thy ornaments from thee, that I may know what to do unto thee. 6 And the children of Israel stripped themselves of their ornaments by the mount Horeb.

7 And Moses took the tabernacle, and pitched it without the camp, afar off from the camp, and called it the Tabernacle of the congregation. And it came to pass, *that* every one which sought the LORD went out unto the tabernacle of the congregation, which *was* without the camp. 8 And it came to pass, when Moses went out unto the tabernacle, *that* all the people rose up, and stood every man *at* his tent door, and looked after Mo-

אַתָּה פֶּן־אֲכֶלְךָ בַּדָּרֶךְ׃ וַיִּשְׁמַע הָעָם 4
people the heard And .way the in thee consume I lest ,thou [art]

אֶת־הַדָּבָר הָרָע הַזֶּה וַיִּתְאַבָּלוּ [a]וְלֹא־שָׁתוּ
put not did they and ;mourned they and ,[1]this [2]evil [3]word

אִישׁ עֶדְיוֹ עָלָיו[a]׃ וַיֹּאמֶר יְהוָה אֶל־ 5
unto Jehovah said And .himself upon ornaments his one any

מֹשֶׁה[b] אֱמֹר[b] אֶל־בְּנֵי־יִשְׂרָאֵל אַתֶּם עַם־קְשֵׁה־
of hard people a [are] You :Israel of children the unto Say :Moses

עֹרֶף [c]רֶגַע אֶחָד אֶעֱלֶה בְקִרְבְּךָ
,thee of midst the in up go I [1]one [2]instant [if] ;neck

וְכִלִּיתִיךָ וְעַתָּה הוֹרֵד[d] עֶדְיְךָ
ornaments thine off lay now and ;thee consume should I (and)

מֵעָלֶיךָ[e] וְאֵדְעָה[f] מָה אֶעֱשֶׂה־לָּךְ׃
.thee to do shall I what know may I that ,thee upon from

וַיִּתְנַצְּלוּ בְנֵי־יִשְׂרָאֵל אֶת־עֶדְיָם[g] מֵהַר 6
of mountain the from ,ornaments their Israel of children the off pulled And

חוֹרֵב׃
.Horeb

וּמֹשֶׁה יִקַּח אֶת־הָאֹהֶל[h] וְנָטָה־לוֹ 7
him for pitch to and ,tent the take to accustomed was Moses And

מִחוּץ לַמַּחֲנֶה הַרְחֵק מִן־הַמַּחֲנֶה וְקָרָא
call to and ,camp the from distant making ,camp the (to) outside (from)

לוֹ אֹהֶל מוֹעֵד וְהָיָה כָּל־מְבַקֵּשׁ
seeking one every ,pass to came it And .meeting of Tent ,it (to)

יְהוָה יֵצֵא אֶל־אֹהֶל מוֹעֵד[i] אֲשֶׁר
[was] which ,meeting of tent the unto out go to accustomed was Jehovah

מִחוּץ לַמַּחֲנֶה׃ וְהָיָה כְּצֵאת 8
[3]out [2]going at ,pass to came it And .camp the (to) outside (from)

מֹשֶׁה אֶל־הָאֹהֶל[j] יָקוּמוּ[k] כָּל־הָעָם
,people the all rise to accustomed were ,tent the unto [1]Moses'

וְנִצְּבוּ[k] אִישׁ פֶּתַח אָהֳלוֹ וְהִבִּיטוּ אַחֲרֵי
after look to and ,tent his of door the [at] one each stand to and

ple: lest I con sume thee in th way.

4 And whe the people hear these evil tid ings, the mourned: an no man di put on him hi ornaments. And the LORI said unto Moses Say unto th children of Isra el, Ye are a stiff necked people if I go up int the midst of the for one moment I shall consum thee: therefor now put off th ornaments fron thee, that I ma know what to d unto thee. And the chil dren of Israe stripped them selves of thei ornaments fron mount Horel onward.

7 Now Mose used to take th tent and to pitc it without th camp, afar o from the camp and he called i The tent c meeting. And came to pass that every on which sough the LORD wen out unto the ten of meeting which was wit out the camp. And it came t pass, when Mc ses went out ur to the Tent, tha all the peopl rose up, an stood, ever man at his ten door, and looke after Moses, ur

a G. has, *with grief.*
b G. omits.
c G. adds, *see lest.*
d G. adds, *the garments of.*
e G. has, *and the ornament.*
f G. has, *and I will show thee,* וְאֹרְאֶךָ; so essentially Sm.
g G. adds, *and the dress.*
h G., S. have, *his tent.*
i G. omits.
j G. adds, *without the camp.*
k G. has, *all the people stood looking.*

ses, until he was
gone into the
tabernacle. 9
And it came to
pass, as Moses
entered into the
tabernacle, the
cloudy pillar
descended, and
stood *at* the door
of the taber-
nacle, and *the*
Lord talked
with Moses. 10
And all the peo-
ple saw the
cloudy pillar
stand *at* the tab-
ernacle door:
and all the peo-
ple rose up and
worshipped, ev-
ery man *in* his
tent door. 11
And the LORD
spake unto Mo-
ses face to face,
as a man speak-
eth unto his
friend. And he
turned again
into the camp:
but his servant
Joshua, the son
of Nun, a young
man, departed
not out of the
tabernacle.

מֹשֶׁה [a] עַד־בֹּאוֹ הָאֹהֱלָה׃ וְהָיָה כְּבֹא 9
²going at ,pass to came it And .tent the into going his until Moses

מֹשֶׁה הָאֹהֱלָה יֵרֵד עַמּוּד הֶעָנָן
,cloud of pillar the descend to accustomed was, tent the into ¹Moses'

וְעָמַד פֶּתַח הָאֹהֶל וְדִבֶּר
speak to accustomed was He and ;tent the of door the [at] stand to and

עִם־מֹשֶׁה׃ וְרָאָה כָל־הָעָם אֶת־עַמּוּד 10
of pillar the people the all see to accustomed were And .Moses with

הֶעָנָן עֹמֵד פֶּתַח הָאֹהֶל וְקָם
rise to accustomed were and ;tent the of door the [at] standing cloud

כָּל־הָעָם וְהִשְׁתַּחֲווּ אִישׁ פֶּתַח
of door the [at] one each ,themselves prostrate to and ,people the all

אָהֳלוֹ׃ וְדִבֶּר יְהוָה אֶל־מֹשֶׁה פָּנִים 11
face ,Moses unto Jehovah speak to accustomed was And .tent his

אֶל־פָּנִים כַּאֲשֶׁר יְדַבֵּר אִישׁ אֶל־רֵעֵהוּ
.friend his unto man a speaks as ,face unto

וְשָׁב אֶל־הַמַּחֲנֶה וּמְשָׁרְתוֹ
,attendant his and ; camp the unto return to accustomed was he And

יְהוֹשֻׁעַ בִּן־נוּן נַעַר לֹא יָמִישׁ מִתּוֹךְ
of midst the from depart ¹did ²not ,youth a ,Nun of son the Joshua

הָאֹהֶל׃
.tent the

til he was gone
into the Tent. 9
And it came to
pass, when Mo-
ses entered into
the Tent, the
pillar of cloud
descended, and
stood at the
door of the
Tent: and *the*
Lord spake with
Moses. 10 And
all the people
saw the pillar of
cloud stand at
the door of the
Tent: and all
the people rose
up and wor-
shipped, every
man at his tent
door. 11 And
the LORD spake
unto Moses face
to face, as a man
speaketh unto
his friend. And
he turned again
into the camp:
but his minister
Joshua, the son
of Nun, a young
man, departed
not out of the
Tent.

12 And Moses
said unto the
LORD, See, thou
sayest unto me,
Bring up this
people: and
thou hast not let
me know whom
thou wilt send
with me. Yet
thou hast said,
I know thee by
name, and thou
hast also found
grace in my
sight. 13 Now
therefore, I pray
thee, if I have
found grace in
thy sight, shew
me now thy way,
that I may know
thee, that I may
find grace in thy

וַיֹּאמֶר מֹשֶׁה אֶל־יְהוָה רְאֵה אַתָּה אֹמֵר אֵלַי 12
,me unto saying [art] thou ,See :Jehovah unto Moses said And

הַעַל אֶת־הָעָם הַזֶּה וְאַתָּה לֹא הוֹדַעְתַּנִי אֵת
me told ²hast ¹thou ³not ,thou and ; ¹this ²people up Bring

אֲשֶׁר־תִּשְׁלַח עִמִּי וְאַתָּה אָמַרְתָּ [b] יְדַעְתִּיךָ
thee know I ,said hast thou yet and ;me with send wilt thou whom

בְשֵׁם [c] וְגַם־מָצָאתָ חֵן בְּעֵינָי׃ וְעַתָּה 13
,now And .eyes mine in favor found hast thou also and ,name by

אִם־נָא מָצָאתִי חֵן בְּעֵינֶיךָ הוֹדִעֵנִי נָא
,pray ,me show ,eyes thine in favor found have I ,pray I ,if

אֶת־דְּרָכֶךָ [d] וְאֵדָעֲךָ לְמַעַן אֶמְצָא־חֵן
favor find may I that order in ; thee know me let and ,ways thy

12 And Moses
said unto the
LORD, See, thou
sayest unto me,
Bring up this
people: and
thou hast not let
me know whom
thou wilt send
with me. Yet
thou hast said, I
know thee by
name, and thou
hast also found
grace in my
sight. 13 Now
therefore, I pray
thee, if I have
found grace
in thy sight,
shew me now
thy ways, that
I may know
thee, to the end
that I may find
grace in thy

a G. adds, *departing*.
b G. adds, *to me*.
c G. has, *beyond all*.
d G., V. have, *thy face*, פָּנֶיךָ.

sight: and consider that this nation *is* thy people. 14 And he said, My presence shall go *with thee*, and I will give thee rest. 15 And he said unto him, If thy presence go not *with me*, carry us not up hence. 16 For wherein shall it be known here that I and thy people have found grace in thy sight? *is it* not in that thou goest with us? so shall we be separated, I and thy people, from all the people that *are* upon the face of the earth.

17 And the LORD said unto Moses, I will do this thing also that thou hast spoken: for thou hast found grace in my sight, and I know thee by name. 18 And he said, I beseech thee, shew me thy glory. 19 And he said, I will make all my goodness pass before thee, and I will proclaim the name of the LORD before thee; and will be gracious to whom I will be gracious, and will shew mercy on whom I will shew mercy. 20 And he said, Thou canst not see my face: for there shall no man see me, and live. 21 And the

בְּעֵינֶ֑יךָ וּרְאֵ֕ה[a] כִּ֥י עַמְּךָ֖ הַגּ֥וֹי[b] הַזֶּֽה׃
.¹this ²nation [is] people thy that ,thou see and ;eyes thine in

14 וַיֹּאמַ֑ר פָּנַ֥י[c] יֵלֵ֖כוּ[c] וַהֲנִחֹ֥תִי לָֽךְ׃
?thee to rest give I and ,go ¹shall ³person ²My : said he And

15 וַיֹּ֖אמֶר אֵלָ֑יו אִם־אֵ֤ין פָּנֶ֙יךָ֙ הֹלְכִ֔ים[d]
,go to about person thy not is If :him unto said he And

16 אַל־תַּעֲלֵ֖נוּ מִזֶּֽה׃ וּבַמֶּ֣ה יִוָּדַ֣ע אֵפ֗וֹא[e]
,now ,known be it can what by And .hence up us bring not do

כִּֽי־מָצָ֨אתִי חֵ֤ן בְּעֵינֶ֙יךָ֙ אֲנִ֣י וְעַמֶּ֔ךָ הֲל֖וֹא
not [it is] ?people thy and I ,eyes thine in favor found have I that

בְּלֶכְתְּךָ֣ עִמָּ֑נוּ וְנִפְלֵ֙ינוּ֙ אֲנִ֣י וְעַמְּךָ֔
,people thy and I ,distinguished are we so and ,us with going thy in

17 מִכָּ֨ל־הָעָ֔ם אֲשֶׁ֖ר עַל־פְּנֵ֥י הָאֲדָמָֽה׃ וַיֹּ֤אמֶר
said And ?ground the of face the upon [are] which nations the all from

יְהוָה֙ אֶל־מֹשֶׁ֔ה גַּ֚ם אֶת־הַדָּבָ֥ר[f] הַזֶּ֛ה אֲשֶׁ֥ר דִּבַּ֖רְתָּ
spoken hast thou which ¹this ²thing Also :Moses unto Jehovah

אֶֽעֱשֶׂ֑ה כִּֽי־מָצָ֥אתָ חֵ֙ן֙ בְּעֵינַ֔י וָאֵדָעֲךָ֖
thee know I and ,eyes mine in favor found hast thou for ;do will I

18 19 בְּשֵֽׁם׃[g] וַיֹּאמַ֑ר הַרְאֵ֥נִי נָ֖א אֶת־כְּבֹדֶֽךָ׃[h] וַיֹּ֗אמֶר
:said he And .glory thy ,pray I ,see me Let ,said he And .name by

אֲנִ֨י אַעֲבִ֤יר כָּל־טוּבִי֙[i] עַל־פָּנֶ֔יךָ וְקָרָ֧אתִֽי
proclaim will I and ,face thy upon majesty my all by pass to cause will I

בְשֵׁ֛ם[j] יְהוָ֖ה לְפָנֶ֑יךָ וְחַנֹּתִי֙ אֶת־אֲשֶׁ֣ר
whom to favor show will I and ;thee before Jehovah of name the by

אָחֹ֔ן וְרִחַמְתִּ֖י אֶת־אֲשֶׁ֥ר
whom on compassion have will and ,favor show will I

20 אֲרַחֵֽם׃ וַיֹּ֕אמֶר לֹ֥א תוּכַ֖ל לִרְאֹ֣ת
see to able ²art ¹thou ³Not : said he And .compassion have will I

21 אֶת־פָּנָ֑י כִּ֛י לֹֽא־יִרְאַ֥נִי[k] הָאָדָ֖ם וָחָֽי׃ וַיֹּ֣אמֶר יְהוָ֔ה[l]
:Jehovah said And .live and man me see not can for ;face my

sight: and consider that this nation is thy people. 14 And he said, My presence shall go *with thee*, and I will give thee rest. 15 And he said unto him, If thy presence go not *with me*, carry us not up hence. 16 For wherein now shall it be known that I have found grace in thy sight, I and thy people? is it not in that thou goest with us, so that we be separated, I and thy people, from all the people that are upon the face of the earth?

17 And the LORD said unto Moses, I will do this thing also that thou hast spoken: for thou hast found grace in my sight, and I know thee by name. 18 And he said, Shew me, I pray thee, thy glory. 19 And he said, I will make all my goodness pass before thee, and will proclaim the name of the LORD before thee; and will be gracious to whom I will be gracious, and will shew mercy on whom I will shew mercy. 20 And he said, Thou canst not see my face: for man shall not see me and live. 21 And the LORD said, Be

---

a G. has, *and I may know*, וארע.

b G., S. add, *great*.

c G. has, *I myself will go before thee;* S., *go thou before me*.

d V., G. have, *if thou thyself dost not go;* so S. adding, *with us*.

e G. has, *truly*.

f S. has, *according to thy word*, כדברך

g G. has, *beyond all*.

h G. has apparently פניך.

i G. has, *my glory*.

j G. has, *by my name*, בשמי.

k G. has, *sees my face*.

l S. adds, *to Moses*.

Lord said, Be-
hold, *there is* a
place by me, and
thou shalt stand
upon a rock: 22
And it shall
come to pass,
while my glory
passeth by, that
I will put thee
in a clift of the
rock, and will
cover thee with
my hand while
I pass by: 23
And I will take
away mine
hand, and thou
shalt see my
back parts: but
my face shall not
be seen.

הִנֵּה מָקוֹם אִתִּי[a] וְנִצַּבְתָּ[b] עַל־הַצּוּר׃
.rock a upon stand shalt thou and ; me with place a ,Behold

22 וְהָיָה בַּעֲבֹר כְּבֹדִי וְשַׂמְתִּיךָ
thee put will I (and) ,[2]glory's [1]my [4]by [3]passing at ,be shall it And

בְּנִקְרַת הַצּוּר וְשַׂכֹּתִי כַפִּי עָלֶיךָ
thee over palm my cover will I and ; rock the of hole a in

23 עַד־עָבְרִי׃ וַהֲסִרֹתִי אֶת־כַּפִּי וְרָאִיתָ
see shalt thou and ,palm my remove will I And .by passing my during

אֶת־אֲחֹרָי וּפָנַי לֹא יֵרָאוּ[c]׃
.seen be [1]can [2]not face my but ; back my

hold, there is a
place by me,
and thou shalt
stand upon the
rock: 22 and it
shall come to
pass, while my
glory passeth
by, that I will
put thee in a
cleft of the rock,
and will cover
thee with my
hand until I
have passed by:
23 and I will
take away mine
hand, and thou
shalt see my
back: but my
face shall not
be seen.

34

And the
Lord said unto
Moses, Hew
thee two tables
of stone like un-
to the first: and
I will write up-
on *these* tables
the words that
were in the first
tables, which
thou brakest. 2
And be ready in
the morning,
and come up in
the morning un-
to mount Sinai,
and present thy-
self there to me
in the top of the
mount. 3 And
no man shall
come up with
thee, neither let
any man be seen
throughout all
the mount; nei-
ther let the flocks
nor herds feed
before that
mount. 4 And
he hewed two
tables of stone
like unto the
first; and Moses
rose up early in
the morning, and
went up unto
mount Sinai, as

1 וַיֹּאמֶר יְהוָה אֶל־מֹשֶׁה פְּסָל־לְךָ שְׁנֵי־לֻחֹת
of tablets two thyself for out Hew :Moses unto Jehovah said And

אֲבָנִים כָּרִאשֹׁנִים[d] וְכָתַבְתִּי עַל־הַלֻּחֹת
tablets the upon write will I and ; former the like ,stone

אֶת־הַדְּבָרִים אֲשֶׁר הָיוּ עַל־הַלֻּחֹת הָרִאשֹׁנִים אֲשֶׁר
which ,[1]former [2]tablets the upon were which words the

2 שִׁבַּרְתָּ׃ וֶהְיֵה נָכוֹן לַבֹּקֶר וְעָלִיתָ
up go and ,morning the in prepared be And .brokedst thou

בַבֹּקֶר[e] אֶל־הַר[f] סִינַי וְנִצַּבְתָּ לִי[g]
me by thyself place and ,Sinai of mountain the unto morning the in

3 שָׁם עַל־רֹאשׁ הָהָר׃ וְאִישׁ לֹא־יַעֲלֶה
up go not shall man a And .mountain the of summit the upon there

עִמָּךְ וְגַם־אִישׁ אַל־יֵרָא בְּכָל־הָהָר
;mountain the all on seen be not let man a also and ,thee with

גַּם־הַצֹּאן וְהַבָּקָר אַל־יִרְעוּ אֶל־מוּל הָהָר
[2]mountain before (unto) feed not let herds the and flocks the also

4 הַהוּא׃ וַיִּפְסֹל[h] שְׁנֵי־לֻחֹת אֲבָנִים כָּרִאשֹׁנִים
; former the like stone of tablets two out hewed he And .[1]that

וַיַּשְׁכֵּם מֹשֶׁה[i] בַבֹּקֶר וַיַּעַל אֶל־הַר
of mountain the unto up went and ,morning the in Moses early rose and

And the
Lord said unto
Moses, Hew
thee two tables
of stone like un-
to the first: and
I will write upon
the tables the
words that were
on the first ta-
bles, which thou
brakest. 2 And
be ready by the
morning, and
come up in the
morning unto
mount Sinai,
and present thy-
self there to me
on the top of the
mount. 3 And
no man shall
come up with
thee, neither let
any man be seen
throughout all
the mount; nei-
ther let the flocks
nor herds feed
before that
mount. 4 And
he hewed two
tables of stone
like unto the
first; and Moses
rose up early in
the morning,
and went up un-
to mount Sinai,

a S., T. have, *before me.*
b S. has, *stand thou;* G. omits ו.
c G. adds, *by thee.*
d G. adds, *and come up to me into the mountain.*
e G. omits.
f G. adds, *Sinai.*
g S. omits.
h Sm. adds, *Moses.*
i Sm., V. omit.

the LORD had
commanded
him, and took in
his hand the two
tables of stone.
5 And the LORD
descended in the
cloud, and stood
with him there,
and proclaimed
the name of the
LORD. 6 And
the LORD passed
by before him,
and proclaimed,
The LORD, The
LORD God, mer-
ciful and gra-
cious, long-
suffering, and
abundant in
goodness and
truth, 7 Keep-
ing mercy for
thousands, for-
giving iniquity
and transgres-
sion and sin, and
that will by no
means clear *the
guilty;* visiting
the iniquity of
the fathers upon
the children,
and upon the
children's chil-
dren, unto the
third and to the
fourth *genera-
tion.* 8 And Mo-
ses made haste,
and bowed his
head toward the
earth, and wor-
shipped 9 And
he said, If now
I have found
grace in thy
sight, O Lord,
let my Lord, I
pray thee, go a-
mong us; for
it *is* a stiffnecked
people; and par-
don our iniquity
and our sin, and
take us for thine
inheritance.
10 And he
said, Behold, I
make a cove-
nant: before all
thy people I will
do marvels, such
as have not been
done in all the
earth, nor in any

סִינַי כַּאֲשֶׁר צִוָּה יְהוָה אֹתוֹ וַיִּקַּח בְּיָדוֹ [a]
hand his in took he and ;him Jehovah commanded had as ,Sinai

5 שְׁנֵי לֻחֹת אֲבָנִים׃ וַיֵּרֶד יְהוָה בֶּעָנָן
;cloud the in Jehovah descended And .stone of tablets two

וַיִּתְיַצֵּב[b] עִמּוֹ שָׁם וַיִּקְרָא בְשֵׁם
of name the on called and ,there him with himself placed he and

6 יְהוָה׃ וַיַּעֲבֹר יְהוָה עַל־פָּנָיו וַיִּקְרָא
:proclaimed and ,face his upon Jehovah by passed And .Jehovah

יְהוָה יְהוָה אֵל רַחוּם וְחַנּוּן אֶרֶךְ אַפַּיִם
,anger of slow ,kind and compassionate God a ,Jehovah ,Jehovah

7 וְרַב־חֶסֶד וֶאֱמֶת׃ נֹצֵר חֶסֶד[c] לָאֲלָפִים
,thousands for mercy preserving ;truth and mercy of great and

נֹשֵׂא עָוֹן וָפֶשַׁע וְחַטָּאָה וְנַקֵּה לֹא
[1]not [3]entirely and ,sin and ,transgression and ,iniquity forgiving

יְנַקֶּה[d] פֹּקֵד עֲוֹן אָבוֹת עַל־בָּנִים
,children upon fathers of iniquity visiting ;unpunished [2]leaving

וְעַל־בְּנֵי בָנִים עַל־שִׁלֵּשִׁים וְעַל־רִבֵּעִים׃
.fourth unto and [generation] third unto ,children of children upon and

8 וַיְמַהֵר מֹשֶׁה וַיִּקֹּד אַרְצָה וַיִּשְׁתָּחוּ׃
.himself prostrated and ,earth the to bowed and ,Moses hastened And

9 וַיֹּאמֶר אִם־נָא מָצָאתִי חֵן בְּעֵינֶיךָ אֲדֹנָי
,Lord O ,eyes thine in favor found have I ,now ,If :said he And

יֵלֶךְ־נָא אֲדֹנָי בְּקִרְבֵּנוּ כִּי עַם־קְשֵׁה־עֹרֶף
[is] neck of hard people a for ;midst our in Lord the ,pray I ,go let

הוּא וְסָלַחְתָּ לַעֲוֹנֵנוּ וּלְחַטָּאתֵנוּ
,sin our (to) and iniquity our (to) forgive thou do and ;it

10 וּנְחַלְתָּנוּ׃[e] וַיֹּאמֶר[f] הִנֵּה אָנֹכִי כֹּרֵת[g]
cutting am I Behold :said he And .possession a as us take and

בְּרִית נֶגֶד כָּל־עַמְּךָ אֶעֱשֶׂה נִפְלָאֹת אֲשֶׁר
which ,things wonderful do will I people thy all before ,covenant a

לֹא־נִבְרְאוּ בְכָל־הָאָרֶץ וּבְכָל־הַגּוֹיִם
;nations all among and earth the all in created been not have

as the LORD
had commanded
him, and took in
his hand two ta-
bles of stone. 5
And the LORD
descended in the
cloud, and stood
with him there,
and proclaimed
the name of the
LORD. 6 And
the LORD passed
by before him,
and proclaimed,
The LORD, the
LORD, a God
full of compas-
sion and
gracious, slow
to anger, and
plenteous in
mercy and truth;
7 keeping mercy
for thousands,
forgiving iniq-
uity and trans-
gression and sin:
and that will by
no means clear
the guilty; visit-
ing the iniquity
of the fathers
upon the chil-
dren, and upon
the children's
children, upon
the third and up-
on the fourth ge-
neration. 8 And
Moses made
haste, and
bowed his head
toward the earth
and worship-
ped. 9 And he
said, If now I
have found grace
in thy sight, O
Lord, let the
Lord, I pray
thee, go in the
midst of us; for
it is a stiffnecked
people; and
pardon our iniq-
uity and our
sin, and take us
for thine inherit-
ance.
10 And he said,
Behold, I make
a covenant:
before all thy
people I will do
marvels, such
as have not been

a G. has, *Moses.*
b V. adds, *Moses.*
c G. has, *justice and mercy.*
d G. adds, *the guilty.*
e G. has, *and we shall be thine.*
f G. adds, *the Lord unto Moses;* V., *the Lord.*
g G. adds, *for thee.*

nation: and all the people among which thou *art* shall see the work of the LORD: for it *is* a terible thing that I will do with thee. 11 Observe thou that which I command thee this day: behold, I drive out before thee the Amorite, and the Canaanite, and the Hittite, and the Perizzite, and the Hivite, and the Jebusite. 12 Take heed to thyself, lest thou make a covenant with the inhabitants of the land whither thou goest, lest it be for a snare in the midst of thee: 13 But ye shall destroy their altars, break their images, and cut down their groves: 14 For thou shalt worship no other god: for the LORD, whose name *is* Jealous, *is* a jealous God. 15 Lest thou make a covenant with the inhabitants of the land, and they go a whoring after their gods, and do sacrifice unto their gods, and *one* call thee, and thou eat of his sacrifice; 16 And thou take of their daughters unto thy sons, and their daughters go a whoring after

וְרָאָה כָל־הָעָם אֲשֶׁר־אַתָּה בְקִרְבּוֹ
[3]midst [2]whose [1]in [[5]art] [4]thou (whom) people the all see shall and

אֶת־מַעֲשֵׂה יְהוָה כִּי־נוֹרָא הוּא אֲשֶׁר אֲנִי עֹשֶׂה
do to about [am] I which it [is] terrible for ,Jehovah of work the

11 עִמָּךְ׃ שְׁמָר־לְךָ [a]אֵת אֲשֶׁר אָנֹכִי מְצַוְּךָ
thee commanding [am] I what thyself for Observe .thee with

[b]הַיּוֹם הִנְנִי גֹרֵשׁ מִפָּנֶיךָ אֶת־הָאֱמֹרִי
,Amorites the thee before from out drive to about [am] I behold ;today

וְהַכְּנַעֲנִי וְהַחִתִּי[c] וְהַפְּרִזִּי וְהַחִוִּי[d]
,Hivites the and ,Perizzites the and ,Hittites the and ,Canaanites the and

12 וְהַיְבוּסִי׃ הִשָּׁמֶר לְךָ פֶּן־תִּכְרֹת בְּרִית
covenant a cut thou lest thyself for careful Be .Jebusites the and

לְיוֹשֵׁב הָאָרֶץ אֲשֶׁר אַתָּה בָּא
in going [art] thou which [unto] land the of inhabitants the for

13 עָלֶיהָ פֶּן־יִהְיֶה[e] לְמוֹקֵשׁ בְּקִרְבֶּךָ[f]׃ [g]כִּי אֶת־מִזְבְּחֹתָם
altars their But .midst thy in snare a (for) be it lest ;(it unto)

תִּתֹּצוּן וְאֶת־מַצֵּבֹתָם תְּשַׁבֵּרוּן
,break shall you pillars memorial their and ,down cut shall you

14 וְאֶת־אֲשֵׁרָיו תִּכְרֹתוּן[h]׃ כִּי לֹא תִשְׁתַּחֲוֶה
thyself prostrate [2]shalt [1]thou [3]not For .off cut shall you asheras their and

לְאֵל אַחֵר כִּי יְהוָה[i] קַנָּא שְׁמוֹ אֵל
[2]God a ,name his [is] jealous ,Jehovah for ;[1]another [2]god to

15 קַנָּא הוּא פֶּן־תִּכְרֹת בְּרִית לְיוֹשֵׁב[j]
of inhabitants the for covenant a cut thou lest ;he [is] [1]jealous

הָאָרֶץ וְזָנוּ אַחֲרֵי אֱלֹהֵיהֶם וְזָבְחוּ
sacrifice they and ,gods their after whoredom commit they and ,land the

לֵאלֹהֵיהֶם וְקָרָא לְךָ וְאָכַלְתָּ מִזִּבְחוֹ׃
;sacrifice their from eat thou and ,thee (to) call one and ,gods their to

16 וְלָקַחְתָּ מִבְּנֹתָיו לְבָנֶיךָ[k] וְזָנוּ
whoredom commit and ,sons thy for daughters their from take thou and

wrought in all the earth, nor in any nation: and all the people among which thou art shall see the work of the LORD, for it is a terrible thing that I do with thee. 11 Observe thou that which I command thee this day: behold, I drive out before thee the Amorite, and the Canaanite, and the Hittite, and the Perizzite, and the Hivite, and the Jebusite. 12 Take heed to thyself, lest thou make a covenant with the inhabitants of the land whither thou goest, lest it be for a snare in the midst of thee: 13 but ye shall break down their altars, and dash in pieces their pillars, and ye shall cut down their Asherim: 14 for thou shalt worship no other god: for the LORD, whose name is Jealous, is a jealous God: 15 lest thou make a covenant with the inhabitants of the land, and they go a whoring after their gods, and do sacrifice unto their gods, and one call thee and thou eat of his sacrifice; 16 and thou take of their daughters unto thy sons, and their daughters go a whor-

---

a G., V. add, *all.*

b G. omits.

c Sm. adds, *and the Girgashite.*

d G. adds, *and the Girgashite.*

e G., S., V. add, *to thee.*

f S., V. omit.

g G., S. omit.

h G. adds, *and the carvings of their gods you shall burn with fire.*

i G. adds, *the God.*

j G. adds, *to the foreigners upon.*

k G. adds, *and of thy daughters thou givest to their sons;* so essentially S.

their gods, and make thy sons go a whoring after their gods. 17 Thou shalt make thee no molten gods.

18 The feast of unleavened bread shalt thou keep. Seven days thou shalt eat unleavened bread, as I commanded thee, in the time of the month Abib: for in the month Abib thou camest out from Egypt. 19 All that openeth the matrix *is* mine; and every firstling among thy cattle, *whether* ox or sheep, *that is male*. 20 But the firstling of an ass thou shalt redeem with a lamb: and if thou redeem *him* not, then shalt thou break his neck. All the firstborn of thy sons thou shalt redeem. And none shall appear before me empty. 21 Six days thou shalt work, but on the seventh day thou shalt rest: in earing time and in harvest thou shalt rest. 22 And thou shalt observe the feast of weeks, of the firstfruits of wheat harvest, and the feast of ingathering at the year's end. 23 Thrice in the year shall all your menchildren appear be-

בְּנֹתָיו[a] אַחֲרֵי אֱלֹהֵיהֶן וְהִזְנוּ[b] אֶת־בָּנֶיךָ
sons thy whoredom to lead they and ,gods their after daughters their

17 אַחֲרֵי אֱלֹהֵיהֶן׃ אֱלֹהֵי מַסֵּכָה לֹא־תַעֲשֶׂה־לָּךְ׃
.thyself for make not shalt thou casting of Gods .gods their after

18 אֶת־חַג הַמַּצּוֹת תִּשְׁמֹר שִׁבְעַת יָמִים
days seven ,keep shalt thou bread unleavened of feast The

תֹּאכַל מַצּוֹת אֲשֶׁר צִוִּיתִךָ לְמוֹעֵד
,time fixed the at ,thee commanded I which ,bread unleavened eat shalt thou

חֹדֶשׁ הָאָבִיב כִּי בְּחֹדֶשׁ הָאָבִיב יָצָאתָ
out wentest thou Abib of month the in for ;Abib of month the

19 מִמִּצְרָיִם׃ כָּל־פֶּטֶר רֶחֶם לִי[c] וְכָל[d]־מִקְנְךָ[e]
cattle thy all and ; me for [is] womb a of opener Every .Egypt from

20 תִּזָּכָר[e][f][g] פֶּטֶר שׁוֹר וָשֶׂה[g]׃ וּפֶטֶר חֲמוֹר
ass an of firstling a And .sheep or ox of firstling a ,male are [that]

תִּפְדֶּה בְשֶׂה וְאִם־לֹא תִפְדֶּה
,redeem [2]dost [1]thou [3]not if and ,lamb a with redeem shalt thou

וַעֲרַפְתּוֹ[h] כֹּל בְּכוֹר בָּנֶיךָ
sons thy of firstborn every ; neck its break shalt thou (and)

21 תִּפְדֶּה וְלֹא־יֵרָאוּ[i] פָנַי רֵיקָם׃ שֵׁשֶׁת
Six .empty me before appear not shall they and ,redeem shalt thou

יָמִים תַּעֲבֹד וּבַיּוֹם הַשְּׁבִיעִי תִּשְׁבֹּת[j]
;rest shalt thou [1]seventh [2]day the on and ,work mayest thou days

22 בֶּחָרִישׁ וּבַקָּצִיר תִּשְׁבֹּת[j]׃ וְחַג שָׁבֻעֹת
weeks of feast a And .rest shalt thou harvest in and plowing in

תַּעֲשֶׂה לְךָ[k] בִּכּוּרֵי קְצִיר חִטִּים
; wheat of harvest the of firstfruits the ,thyself for make shalt thou

23 וְחַג הָאָסִיף תְּקוּפַת[l] הַשָּׁנָה׃ שָׁלֹשׁ
Three .year the of circuit the [at] gathering of feast the and

פְּעָמִים בַּשָּׁנָה יֵרָאֶה כָּל־זְכוּרְךָ אֶת־פְּנֵי הָאָדֹן[m]
Lord the before thine of male every appear shall year the in times

ing after their gods, and make thy sons go a whoring after their gods. 17 Thou shalt make thee no molten gods.

18 The feast of unleavened bread shalt thou keep. Seven days thou shalt eat unleavened bread, as I commanded thee, at the time appointed in the month Abib: for in the month Abib thou camest out from Egypt. 19 All that openeth the womb is mine; and all thy cattle that is male, the firstlings of ox and sheep. 20 And the firstling of an ass thou shalt redeem with a lamb: and if thou wilt not redeem it, then thou shalt break its neck. All the firstborn of thy sons thou shalt redeem. And none shall appear before me empty. 21 Six days thou shalt work, but on the seventh day thou shalt rest: in plowing time and in harvest thou shalt rest. 22 And thou shalt observe the feast of weeks, *even* of the firstfruits of wheat harvest, and the feast of ingathering at the year's end. 23 Three times in the year shall all thy males appear before

---

a G. has, *thy daughters*, בנתיך; S. has, *your daughters*.

b G. has וזנו.

c G. adds, *the males*.

d G. omits ו.

e G. omits.

f V. omits; T. has, *the males thou shalt sanctify*.

g S. has, *and firstborn of thy cattle, of the oxen and the sheep*.

h G. has, *thou shalt give the price*.

i Sm. has, *they shall see;* S. *you shall appear;* G., V. have, *thou shalt appear*.

j G. has, *a rest*.

k G. has, *for me*, לי.

l G. has, *middle*.

m Sm., G., S., V., T. have, *the Lord*.

fore the Lord
God, the God
of Israel. 24
For I will cast
out the nations
before thee, and
enlarge thy bor-
ders: neither
shall any man
desire thy land,
when thou shalt
go up to appear
before the Lord
thy God thrice
in the year. 25
Thou shalt not
offer the blood
of my sacrifice
with leaven;
neither shall the
sacrifice of the
feast of the pass-
over be left unto
the morning. 26
The first of the
firstfruits of thy
land thou shalt
bring unto the
house of the
Lord thy God.
Thou shalt not
seethe a kid in
his mother's
milk. 27 And the
Lord said unto
Moses, Write
thou these
words: for after
the tenor of
these words I
have made a
covenant with
thee and with
Israel. 28 And
he was there
with the Lord
forty days and
forty nights; he
did neither eat
bread, nor drink
water. And he
wrote upon the
tables the words
of the covenant,
the ten com-
mandments.

29 And it
came to pass,
when Moses
came down from
mount Sinai
with the two
tables of testi-
mony in Moses'
hand, when he
came down from
the mount, that
Moses wist not
that the skin of

24 יהוה [m] אלהי ישראל׃ כי־אוריש גוים
nations dispossess will I For .Israel of God the Jehovah

מפניך והרחבתי את־גבלך ולא־יחמד
covet not shall and ; territory thy broad make will and ,thee before from

איש את־ארצך בעלתך לראות את־פני יהוה
Jehovah before appear to up going thy at ,land thy one any

25 אלהיך שלש פעמים בשנה׃ לא־תשחט
slaughter not shalt Thou .year the in times three God thy

על־חמץ דם־זבחי ולא־ילין
night the pass not shall and ,sacrifice my of blood the bread leavened upon

26 לבקר זבח חג הפסח׃ ראשית
,first The .passover the of feast the of sacrifice the morning till

בכורי אדמתך תביא בית יהוה
Jehovah of house the [to] bring shalt thou ground thy of firstfruits the

אלהיך לא־תבשל גדי בחלב אמו׃
.mother its of milk the in kid a boil not shalt thou ; God thy

27 ויאמר יהוה אל־משה כתב־לך את־הדברים
[2]words thyself for Write : Moses unto Jehovah said And

האלה כי על־פי הדברים האלה כרתי אתך
thee with cut I [1]these [2]words of mouth the upon for ;[1]these

28 ברית ואת־ישראל[a]׃ ויהי־שם[b] עם־יהוה
Jehovah with there was he And .Israel with and ,covenant a

ארבעים יום וארבעים לילה לחם לא אכל
,eat [2]did [1]he [3]not bread ; nights forty and days forty

ומים לא שתה ויכתב על־הלחת[c] את[d]
tablets the upon wrote he and ; drink [2]did [1]he [3]not water and

דברי[d] הברית עשרת הדברים׃
.words ten ,covenant the of words the

29 ויהי ברדת משה מהר
of mountain the from [1]Moses' [3]down [2]going at ,pass to came it And

סיני ושני לחת העדת ביד־משה
,Moses of hand the in [being] testimony the of tablets two the (and) ,Sinai

ברדתו מן־ההר ומשה[e] לא־ידע
known having not Moses (and) ,mountain the from down going his at

the Lord God,
the God of Isra-
el. 24 For I will
cast out nations
before thee, and
enlarge thy
borders: neither
shall any man
desire thy land,
when thou goest
up to appear be-
fore the Lord
thy God three
times in the
year. 25 Thou
shalt not offer
the blood of my
sacrifice with
leavened bread;
neither shall the
sacrifice of the
feast of the pass-
over be left
unto the morn-
ing. 26 The first
of the firstfruits
of thy ground
thou shalt bring
unto the house
of the Lord thy
God. Thou shalt
not seethe a kid
in its mother's
milk. 27 And
the Lord said
unto Moses,
Write thou these
words: for after
the tenor of
these words I
have made a
covenant with
thee and with
Israel. 28 And
he was there
with the Lord
forty days and
forty nights; he
did neither eat
bread, nor drink
water. And he
wrote upon the
tables the words
of the covenant,
the ten com-
mandments.

29 And it
came to pass,
when Moses
came down from
mount Sinai
with the two
tables of the tes-
timony in Mo-
ses' hand, when
he came down
from the mount,
that Moses wist
not that the skin

a S. adds, *all*, reading ואת כל ישראל.
b G. adds, *Moses*.
c S. adds, *of stone*.
d G. puts before על and adds, *these*.
e Sm., G. omit ו.

his face shone while he talked with him. 30 And when Aaron and all the children of Israel saw Moses, behold, the skin of his face shone; and they were afraid to come nigh him. 31 And Moses called unto them; and Aaron and all the rulers of the congregation returned unto him: and Moses talked with them. 32 And afterward all the children of Israel came nigh: and he gave them in commandment all that the LORD had spoken with him in mount Sinai.

33 And *till* Moses had done speaking with them, he put a vail on his face. 34 But when Moses went in before the LORD to speak with him, he took the vail off, until he came out. And he came out, and spake unto the children of Israel *that* which he was commanded. 35 And the children of Israel saw the face of Moses, that the skin of Moses' face shone: and Moses put the vail upon his face again, until he went in to speak with him.

כִּי קָרַן[a] עוֹר פָּנָיו בְּדַבְּרוֹ
speaking his through face his of skin the shining become had that

30 אִתּוֹ׃ וַיַּרְא אַהֲרֹן וְכָל־בְּנֵי[b] יִשְׂרָאֵל אֶת־מֹשֶׁה[c]
,Moses Israel of children the all and Aaron saw that ; him with

וְהִנֵּה קָרַן[d] עוֹר פָּנָיו[e] וַיִּירְאוּ
feared they and ,face his of skin the shining become had behold and

31 מִגֶּשֶׁת אֵלָיו׃ וַיִּקְרָא אֲלֵהֶם מֹשֶׁה
; Moses them unto called And .him unto approaching from

וַיָּשֻׁבוּ אֵלָיו אַהֲרֹן וְכָל־הַנְּשִׂאִים בָּעֵדָה
,congregation the among chiefs the all and Aaron him unto returned and

32 וַיְדַבֵּר מֹשֶׁה אֲלֵהֶם׃ וְאַחֲרֵי־כֵן נִגְּשׁוּ[f] כָּל־
all approached afterwards And .them unto Moses spoke and

בְּנֵי יִשְׂרָאֵל וַיְצַוֵּם אֵת כָּל־אֲשֶׁר דִּבֶּר
spoken had which all them commanded he and ;Israel of children the

33 יְהוָה אִתּוֹ בְּהַר סִינָי׃ וַיְכַל מֹשֶׁה
Moses finished And .Sinai of mountain the in him with Jehovah

מִדַּבֵּר אִתָּם וַיִּתֵּן עַל־פָּנָיו מַסְוֶה׃
.veil a face his upon put he and ,them with speaking (from)

34 וּבְבֹא מֹשֶׁה לִפְנֵי יְהוָה לְדַבֵּר אִתּוֹ
,him with speak to Jehovah before [1]Moses' [3]in [2]coming at And

יָסִיר אֶת־הַמַּסְוֶה עַד־צֵאתוֹ
; out going his until veil the remove to accustomed was he

וְיָצָא וְדִבֶּר אֶל־בְּנֵי[g]
of children the unto speak to and out go to accustomed was he and

35 יִשְׂרָאֵל אֵת אֲשֶׁר יְצֻוֶּה׃ וְרָאוּ
see to accustomed were And .commanded was he what Israel

בְנֵי־יִשְׂרָאֵל אֶת־פְּנֵי מֹשֶׁה כִּי קָרַן
shining become had that ,Moses of face the Israel of children the

עוֹר פְּנֵי מֹשֶׁה וְהֵשִׁיב מֹשֶׁה
Moses return to accustomed was and ;Moses of face the of skin the

אֶת־הַמַּסְוֶה עַל־פָּנָיו עַד־בֹּאוֹ לְדַבֵּר אִתּוֹ׃
.him with speak to in going his until ,face his upon veil the

of his face shone by reason of his speaking with him. 30 And when Aaron and all the children of Israel saw Moses, behold, the skin of his face shone; and they were afraid to come nigh him. 31 And Moses called unto them; and Aaron and all the rulers of the congregation returned unto him: and Moses spake to them. 32 And afterward all the children of Israel came nigh: and he gave them in commandment all that the LORD had spoken with him in mount Sinai.

33 And when Moses had done speaking with them, he put a veil on his face. 34 But when Moses went in before the LORD to speak with him, he took the veil off, until he came out; and he came out, and spake unto the children of Israel that which he was commanded; 35 and the children of Israel saw the face of Moses, that the skin of Moses' face shone: and Moses put the veil upon his face again, until he went in to speak with him.

---

a G. adds, *the appearance.*
b In some manuscripts G. has, *elders,* זקני; S. omits.
c S. adds, *face,* reading את פני משה.
d G. adds, *the appearance.*
e S. has, *the face of Moses.*
f Sm., G., S., V. add, *to him.*
g G. adds, *all,* reading אל כל בני.

35

AND Moses
gathered all the
congregation of
the children of
Israel together,
and said unto
them, These *are*
the words which
the LORD hath
commanded,
that *ye* should do
them. 2 Six days
shall work be
done, but on the
seventh day
there shall be to
you an holy day,
a sabbath of rest
to the LORD:
whosoever do-
eth work therein
shall be put to
death. 3 Ye shall
kindle no fire
throughout your
habitations up-
on the sabbath
day.

4 And Moses
spake unto all
the congrega-
tion of the chil-
dren of Israel,
saying, This *is*
the thing which
the LORD com-
manded, say-
ing, 5 Take
ye from among
you an offering
unto the LORD:
whosoever *is* of
a willing heart,
let him bring it,
an offering of
the LORD; gold,
and silver, and
brass, 6 And
blue, and pur-
ple, and scarlet,
and fine linen,
and goats' *hair*,
7 And rams'
skins dyed red,
and badgers'
skins, and shit-
tim wood, 8
And oil for the
light, and spices
for anointing
oil, and for the

1 וַיַּקְהֵל מֹשֶׁה אֶת־כָּל־עֲדַת בְּנֵי
of children the of congregation the all Moses assembled And
יִשְׂרָאֵל וַיֹּאמֶר אֲלֵהֶם אֵלֶּה הַדְּבָרִים
words the [are] These : them unto said and ,Israel
2 אֲשֶׁר־צִוָּה יְהוָה לַעֲשֹׂת אֹתָם׃ שֵׁשֶׁת יָמִים
days Six .them do to ,Jehovah commanded has which
תֵּעָשֶׂה[a] מְלָאכָה וּבַיּוֹם הַשְּׁבִיעִי יִהְיֶה לָכֶם[b]
you to be shall it ,[1]seventh [2]day the on and ,work done be may
קֹדֶשׁ שַׁבַּת שַׁבָּתוֹן[c] לַיהוָה כָּל־הָעֹשֶׂה בוֹ
it in doing one every ;Jehovah to rest of festival a of sabbath a ,holy
3 מְלָאכָה יוּמָת[d]׃ לֹא־תְבַעֲרוּ אֵשׁ בְּכֹל
all in fire a kindle not shall You .death to put be shall work
מֹשְׁבֹתֵיכֶם בְּיוֹם הַשַּׁבָּת[e]׃
.sabbath the of day the on ,dwellings your

4 וַיֹּאמֶר מֹשֶׁה אֶל־כָּל־עֲדַת בְּנֵי־יִשְׂרָאֵל
Israel of children the of congregation the all unto Moses said And
לֵאמֹר[f] זֶה הַדָּבָר אֲשֶׁר־צִוָּה יְהוָה לֵאמֹר[g]׃
:saying Jehovah commanded which thing the [is] This :saying
5 קְחוּ מֵאִתְּכֶם תְּרוּמָה לַיהוָה כֹּל נְדִיב
of willing one every ,Jehovah to contribution a you with from Take
לִבּוֹ יְבִיאֶהָ אֵת תְּרוּמַת יְהוָה זָהָב וָכֶסֶף
silver and gold ;Jehovah of contribution the ,it bring shall heart his
6 וּנְחֹשֶׁת׃ וּתְכֵלֶת וְאַרְגָּמָן וְתוֹלַעַת שָׁנִי
,crimson (of worm) and ,purple and ,blue and ,bronze and
7 וְשֵׁשׁ[h] וְעִזִּים׃ וְעֹרֹת אֵילִם מְאָדָּמִים
,red dyed rams of skins and ,goats [of hair] and ,byssus and
8 וְעֹרֹת תְּחָשִׁים וַעֲצֵי שִׁטִּים׃ וְשֶׁמֶן[i]
oil and ,acacia of wood of pieces and ,dolphins of skins and
לַמָּאוֹר וּבְשָׂמִים לְשֶׁמֶן הַמִּשְׁחָה וְלִקְטֹרֶת
of incense the for and ,anointing of oil the for spices and ,light the for

And Moses
assembled all
the congrega-
tion of the chil-
dren of Israel,
and said unto
them, These are
the words which
the LORD hath
commanded,
that ye should
do them. 2 Six
days shall work
be done, but on
the seventh day
there shall be to
you an holy day,
a sabbath of
solemn rest to
the LORD: who-
soever doeth any
work therein
shall be put to
death. 3 Ye shall
kindle no fire
throughout your
habitations
upon the sab-
bath day.

4 And Moses
spake unto all
the congrega-
tion of the
children of
Israel, saying,
This is the thing
which the LORD
commanded,
saying, 5 Take
ye from among
you an offering
unto the LORD;
whosoever is of a
willing heart, let
him bring it,
the LORD's of-
fering; gold, and
silver, and brass;
6 and blue, and
purple, and
scarlet, and fine
linen, and goats'
hair; 7 and
rams' skins dyed
red, and seal-
skins, and acacia
wood; 8 and oil
for the light,
and spices for
the anointing
oil, and for the

a G., S. have, *thou shalt do*, תַּעֲשֶׂה; V. has, *you shall do*: Sm. has, יעשה.

b G. has, *a rest;* S. omits.

c S. adds, *holy*.

d G. has, *let him die*.

e G. adds, *I am the Lord*, אני יהוה.

f S., V. omit.

g S. has, *to do*.

h G., S. add, *twisted*.

i G. omits the verse.

sweet incense, 9
And onyx
stones, and
stones to be set
for the ephod,
and for the
breastplate. 10
And every wise
hearted among
you shall come,
and make all
that the LORD
hath command-
ed; 11 The
tabernacle, his
tent, and his
covering, his
taches, and his
boards, his bars,
his pillars, and
his sockets, 12
The ark, and the
staves thereof,
with the mercy
seat, and the vail
of the covering,
13 The table,
and his staves,
and all his ves-
sels, and the
shewbread, 14
The candlestick
also for the
light, and his fur-
niture, and his
lamps, with the
oil for the light,
15 And the in-
cense altar, and
his staves, and
the anointing
oil, and the
sweet incense,
and the hanging
for the door at
the entering in
of the taberna-
cle, 16 The al-
tar of burnt
offering, with
his brasen grate,
his staves, and
all his vessels,
the laver and his
foot, 17 The
hangings of the
court, his pillars,
and their sock-
ets, and the
hanging for the
door of the
court, 18 The

9 הַסַּמִּים׃ וְאַבְנֵי־שֹׁהַם וְאַבְנֵי מִלֻּאִים לָאֵפוֹד
ephod the for ,settings of stones and ,onyx of stones and ,perfumes

10 וְלַחֹשֶׁן׃ וְכָל־חֲכַם־לֵב בָּכֶם
,you among heart of wise one every And .breastplate the for and

יָבֹאוּ וְיַעֲשׂוּ אֵת כָּל־אֲשֶׁר צִוָּה יְהוָה׃
; Jehovah commanded has which all make and come them let

11 אֶת־הַמִּשְׁכָּן אֶת־אָהֳלוֹ וְאֶת־מִכְסֵהוּ אֶת־קְרָסָיו[a] וְאֶת־
and ,hooks its ,cover its and ,tent its ,habitation the

12 קְרָשָׁיו[a] אֶת־בְּרִיחָו אֶת־עַמֻּדָיו וְאֶת־אֲדָנָיו[a]׃ אֶת־
; sockets its and ,pillars its ,bars its ,boards its

הָאָרֹן[b] וְאֶת־בַּדָּיו אֶת־הַכַּפֹּרֶת וְאֵת פָּרֹכֶת הַמָּסָךְ[c]׃
; screen the of veil the and lid expiating the ,poles its and ,ark the

13 אֶת־הַשֻּׁלְחָן וְאֶת־בַּדָּיו[d] וְאֶת־כָּל־כֵּלָיו וְאֵת[e] לֶחֶם
of bread the and ,vessels its all and ,poles its and ,table the

14 הַפָּנִים[e]׃ וְאֶת־מְנֹרַת הַמָּאוֹר וְאֶת־כֵּלֶיהָ[f] [g]וְאֶת־
and ,vessels its and ,light the of lampstand the and ; face the

15 נֵרֹתֶיהָ[h] וְאֵת שֶׁמֶן הַמָּאוֹר׃ וְאֶת־מִזְבַּח[i] הַקְּטֹרֶת
incense of altar the and ; light the of oil the and ,lamps its

וְאֶת־בַּדָּיו[i] וְאֵת שֶׁמֶן הַמִּשְׁחָה וְאֵת קְטֹרֶת הַסַּמִּים
,perfumes of incense the and ,anointing of oil the and ,poles its and

16 וְאֶת־מָסַךְ[j] הַפֶּתַח[k] לְפֶתַח הַמִּשְׁכָּן׃ אֵת[l]
; habitation the of door the at ,door the of screen the and

מִזְבַּח הָעֹלָה וְאֶת־מִכְבַּר הַנְּחֹשֶׁת אֲשֶׁר־לוֹ
,it to [is] which bronze of grating the and ,offering burnt of altar the

17 אֶת־בַּדָּיו וְאֶת־כָּל־כֵּלָיו אֶת־הַכִּיֹּר וְאֶת־כַּנּוֹ׃ אֵת
; base its and ,laver the ,vessels its all and ,poles its

קַלְעֵי הֶחָצֵר אֶת־עַמֻּדָיו וְאֶת־אֲדָנֶיהָ[m] וְאֵת
and ,sockets its and ,pillars its ,court the of hangings the

18 מָסַךְ שַׁעַר הֶחָצֵר׃ אֶת־יִתְדֹת[n] הַמִּשְׁכָּן
,habitation the of pins the ; court the of gate the of screen the

sweet incense; 9
and onyx stones,
and stones to be
set, for the
ephod, and for
the breastplate.
10 And let every
wise hearted
man among you
come, and make
all that the
LORD hath com-
manded; 11 the
tabernacle, its
tent, and its
covering, its
clasps, and its
boards, its bars,
its pillars, and
its sockets; 12
the ark, and the
staves thereof,
the mercy-seat,
and the veil of
the screen; 13
the table, and
its staves, and
all its vessels,
and the shew-
bread; 14 the
candlestick also
for the light,
and its vessels,
and its lamps,
and the oil for
the light; 15 and
the altar of in-
cense, and its
staves, and the
anointing oil,
and the sweet
incense, and the
screen for the
door, at the door
of the taber-
nacle; 16 the al-
tar of burnt
offer'ng, with its
grating of brass,
its staves, and
all its vessels,
the laver and its
base; 17 the
hangings of the
court, the pillars
thereof, and
their sockets,
and the screen
for the gate of
the court; 18 the
pins of the tab-

---

a G. apparently omits.

b G. adds, *of witness*.

c The order of verses in G. is, 12, 17, 13, 14, 16, 19, 15, 20.

d G. omits.

e G. omits.

f Sm. has, *and all its vessels*.

g G. omits.

h Sm. omits.

i G. omits.

j G. omits.

k S., V. omit.

l For the verse G. has, *and the altar and all its vessels*.

m G. omits.

n G. omits the verse.

pins of the tab-
ernacle, and the
pins of the
court, and their
cords, 19 The
cloths of serv-
ice, to do serv-
ice in the holy
place, the holy
garments for
Aaron the priest,
and the gar-
ments of his
sons, to minis-
ter in the priest's
office.
20 And all the
congregation of
the children of
Israel departed
from the pres-
ence of Moses.
21 And they
came, every one
whose heart
stirred him up,
and every one
whom his spirit
made willing,
and they
brought the
LORD's offering
to the work of
the tabernacle
of the congrega-
tion, and for all
his service, and
for the holy gar-
ments. 22 And
they came, both
men and wom-
en, as many
as were willing
hearted, *and*
brought brace-
lets, and ear-
rings, and rings,
and tablets, all
jewels of gold:
and every man
that offered
offered an offer-
ing of gold unto
the LORD. 23
And every man,
with whom was
found blue, and
purple, and scar-
let, and fine
linen, and goats'
hair, and red
skins of rams,
and badgers'
skins, brought
them. 24 Every
one that did
offer an offer-
ing of silver and

19 וְאֶת־יִתְדֹת הֶחָצֵר וְאֶת־מֵיתְרֵיהֶם׃ אֶת־בִּגְדֵי [a] הַשְּׂרָד
,weaving of garments the ; cords their and ,court the of pins the and
לְשָׁרֵת בַּקֹּדֶשׁ [a] אֶת־בִּגְדֵי [b] הַקֹּדֶשׁ לְאַהֲרֹן
Aaron for holiness of garments the ,sanctuary the in minister to
הַכֹּהֵן וְאֶת־בִּגְדֵי בָנָיו לְכַהֵן [b]׃
.priests as officiate to ,sons his of garments the and ,priest the
20 וַיֵּצְאוּ כָּל־עֲדַת בְּנֵי־יִשְׂרָאֵל
Israel of children the of congregation the all out went And
21 מִלִּפְנֵי מֹשֶׁה׃ וַיָּבֹאוּ [c] כָּל־אִישׁ אֲשֶׁר־נְשָׂאוֹ
up lifted whom one every ,came they And .Moses before from
לִבּוֹ וְכֹל אֲשֶׁר נָדְבָה רוּחוֹ אֹתוֹ [d] הֵבִיאוּ
brought they ; (him) spirit his impelled whom one every and ,heart his
אֶת־תְּרוּמַת יְהוָה לִמְלֶאכֶת [e] אֹהֶל מוֹעֵד
,meeting of tent the of work the for Jehovah of contribution the
22 וּלְכָל־עֲבֹדָתוֹ וּלְבִגְדֵי [f] הַקֹּדֶשׁ׃ וַיָּבֹאוּ [g]
in came And .holiness of garments the for and ,service its all for and
הָאֲנָשִׁים עַל־הַנָּשִׁים כֹּל נְדִיב לֵב
; heart of willing one every ,women the with together men the
הֵבִיאוּ חָח וָנֶזֶם וְטַבַּעַת [h] וְכוּמָז
,brooches and ,rings and ,nose-rings and ,bangles in brought they
כָּל־כְּלִי זָהָב וְכָל־אִישׁ אֲשֶׁר הֵנִיף תְּנוּפַת
of wave-offering a waved who one every and ; gold of article every
23 זָהָב לַיהוָה׃ וְכָל־אִישׁ אֲשֶׁר־נִמְצָא אִתּוֹ
(him with) found was whom [with] one every And .Jehovah to gold
תְּכֵלֶת [i] וְאַרְגָּמָן וְתוֹלַעַת שָׁנִי [i] וְשֵׁשׁ
,byssus and ,crimson (of worm) and ,purple and ,blue
וְעִזִּים [j] וְעֹרֹת אֵילִם מְאָדָּמִים וְעֹרֹת
of skins and ,red dyed rams of skins and ,goats [of hair] and
24 תְּחָשִׁים הֵבִיאוּ׃ כָּל־מֵרִים תְּרוּמַת
of contribution a away taking one Every .brought they ,dolphins
כֶּסֶף וּנְחֹשֶׁת הֵבִיאוּ אֵת תְּרוּמַת יְהוָה
; Jehovah of contribution the brought they ,bronze and silver

ernacle, and the
pins of the court,
and their cords;
19 the finely
wrought gar-
ments, for min-
istering in the
holy place, the
holy garments
for Aaron the
priest, and the
garments of his
sons, to minister
in the priest's
office.
20 And all the
congregation of
the children of
Israel departed
from the pres-
ence of Moses.
21 And they
came, every one
whose heart
stirred him up,
and every one
whom his spirit
made willing,
and brought the
LORD's offer-
ing, for the
work of the tent
of meeting, and
for all the serv-
ice thereof, and
for the holy gar-
ments. 22 And
they came, both
men and wom-
en, as many as
were willing
hearted, *and*
brought brooch-
es, and earrings,
and signet-
rings, and arm-
lets, all jewels
of gold; even
every man that
offered an offer-
ing of gold un-
to the LORD. 23
And every man,
with whom was
found blue, and
purple, and
scarlet, and fine
linen, and goats'
hair, and rams'
skins dyed red,
and sealskins,
brought them.
24 Every one
that did offer an
offering of silver
and brass
brought the
LORD's offering:

---

a G. omits.
b G. has, *with which they minister*.
c Sm., S., G. have, *and they brought*, וַיָּבִיאוּ.
d G. adds, תרומה.
e G. adds, *all*, reading לכל מלאכת.
f G. adds, *all*, reading ולכל בגדי.
g Sm., G., S., T. have, *and they brought*, וַיָּבִיאוּ.
h Sm., G. add, *and woven things*, ועגיל.
i G. omits.
j G. omits.

brass brought the LORD'S offering: and every man, with whom was found shittim wood for any work of the service, brought *it.*
25 And all the women that were wise hearted did spin with their hands, and brought that which they had spun, *both* of blue, and of purple, *and* of scarlet, and of fine linen. 26
And all the women whose heart stirred them up in wisdom spun goats' *hair.* 27 And the rulers brought onyx stones, and stones to be set, for the ephod, and for the breastplate; 28
And spice, and oil for the light, and for the anointing oil, and for the sweet incense.
29 The children of Israel brought a willing offering unto the LORD, every man and woman, whose heart made them willing to bring for all manner of work, which the LORD had commanded to be made by the hand of Moses.
30 And Moses said unto the children of Israel, See, the LORD hath called by name Bezaleel the son of Uri, the son of Hur, of the tribe of Judah;
31 And he hath filled him with

וְכֹל אֲשֶׁר נִמְצָא אִתּוֹ עֲצֵי
of wood of pieces (him with) found were whom [with] one every and

שִׁטִּים לְכָל־מְלֶאכֶת הָעֲבֹדָה הֵבִיאוּ׃ 25 וְכָל־אִשָּׁה
woman every And .brought they ,service the of work any for acacia

חַכְמַת־לֵב בְּיָדֶיהָ טָווּ[a] וַיָּבִיאוּ
brought they and ; spun they hands their with ,heart of wise

מַטְוֶה אֶת־הַתְּכֵלֶת וְאֶת־הָאַרְגָּמָן אֶת־תּוֹלַעַת הַשָּׁנִי
,crimson (of worm) ,purple and ,blue ,yarn spun

וְאֶת־הַשֵּׁשׁ[b]׃ 26 וְכָל־הַנָּשִׁים אֲשֶׁר נָשָׂא לִבָּן אֹתָנָה
(them) hearts their up lifted whom women the all And .byssus and

בְּחָכְמָה טָווּ אֶת־הָעִזִּים׃ 27 וְהַנְּשִׂאִם הֵבִיאוּ אֵת
brought chiefs the And .goats [of hair] the spun wisdom in

אַבְנֵי הַשֹּׁהַם וְאֵת אַבְנֵי הַמִּלֻּאִים לָאֵפוֹד
ephod the for ,settings of stones the and onyx of stones the

וְלַחֹשֶׁן׃ 28 וְאֶת־הַבֹּשֶׂם וְאֶת־הַשָּׁמֶן לְמָאוֹר[c]
,light the for ,oil the and ,spice the and ; breastplate the for and

וּלְשֶׁמֶן[c] הַמִּשְׁחָה וְלִקְטֹרֶת[d] הַסַּמִּים׃
.perfumes of incense the for and ,anointing of oil the for and

29 כָּל־אִישׁ וְאִשָּׁה אֲשֶׁר נָדַב לִבָּם אֹתָם
(them) hearts their impelled whom woman and man Every

לְהָבִיא[e] [f]לְכָל־הַמְּלָאכָה אֲשֶׁר צִוָּה יְהוָה לַעֲשׂוֹת
do to Jehovah commanded which work the all for bring to

בְּיַד־מֹשֶׁה הֵבִיאוּ בְנֵי־יִשְׂרָאֵל נְדָבָה[g]
offering voluntary a Israel of children the brought ; Moses of hand the by

לַיהוָה׃
.Jehovah to

30 וַיֹּאמֶר מֹשֶׁה אֶל־בְּנֵי יִשְׂרָאֵל רְאוּ קָרָא
called has ,See : Israel of children the unto Moses said And

יְהוָה בְּשֵׁם בְּצַלְאֵל בֶּן־אוּרִי בֶן־חוּר
,Hur of son the Uri of son the Bezalel name by Jehovah

31 לְמַטֵּה יְהוּדָה׃ וַיְמַלֵּא אֹתוֹ רוּחַ
of spirit the [with] him filled has he and ; Judah of tribe the to

and every man, with whom was found acacia wood for any work of the service, brought it.
25 And all the women that were wise hearted did spin with their hands, and brought that which they had spun, the blue, and the purple, the scarlet, and the fine linen.
26 And all the women whose heart stirred them up in wisdom spun the goats' *hair.*
27 And the rulers brought the onyx stones, and the stones to be set, for the ephod, and for the breastplate; 28
and the spice, and the oil; for the light, and for the anointing oil, and for the sweet incense.
29 The children of Israel brought a freewill offering unto the LORD; every man and woman, whose heart made them willing to bring for all the work, which the LORD had commanded to be made by the hand of Moses.

30 And Moses said unto the children of Israel, See, the LORD hath called by name Bezalel the son of Uri, the son of Hur, of the tribe of Judah;
31 and he hath

a G. has, *to spin.*
b S. adds, *twisted.*
c G. omits.
d G. omits ל.
e G. has, *coming in to do.*
f G. omits ל.
g G., S. apparently have תרומה.

the spirit of God, in wisdom, in understanding, and in knowledge, and in all manner of workmanship;
32 And to devise curious works, to work in gold, and in silver, and in brass,
33 And in the cutting of stones, to set *them*, and in carving of wood, to make any manner of cunning work.
34 And he hath put in his heart that he may teach, *both* he, and Aholiab, the son of Ahisamach, of the tribe of Dan.
35 Them hath he filled with wisdom of heart, to work all manner of work, of the engraver, and of the cunning workman, and of the embroiderer, in blue, and in purple, in scarlet, and in fine linen, and of the weaver, *even* of them that do any work, and of those that devise cunning work.

אֱלֹהִים[a] בְּחָכְמָה[b] בִּתְבוּנָה וּבְדַעַת

,knowledge in and ,intelligence in ,wisdom in ,God

32 וּבְכָל־מְלָאכָה׃[c] וְלַחְשֹׁב[d] מַחֲשָׁבֹת[e] לַעֲשֹׂת בַּזָּהָב

,gold in work to ,designs plan to and ; workmanship all in and

33 וּבַכֶּסֶף וּבַנְּחֹשֶׁת׃ וּבַחֲרֹשֶׁת אֶבֶן לְמַלֹּאת[f]

,settings for stones of cutting in and ; bronze in and ,silver in and

וּבַחֲרֹשֶׁת עֵץ לַעֲשׂוֹת בְּכָל־מְלֶאכֶת מַחֲשָׁבֶת׃

.design of workmanship all in work to ,wood of hewing in and

34 וּלְהוֹרֹת נָתַן בְּלִבּוֹ הוּא וְאָהֳלִיאָב

Oholiab and he ,heart his in given has he teach to And

35 בֶּן־אֲחִיסָמָךְ לְמַטֵּה־דָן׃ מִלֵּא אֹתָם

them filled has He .Dan of tribe the to ,Ahisamach of son the

חָכְמַת־לֵב[g] לַעֲשׂוֹת[h] כָּל־מְלֶאכֶת חָרָשׁ[i]

,smith a of work every do to ,heart of wisdom [with]

וְחֹשֵׁב[j] וְרֹקֵם[k] בַּתְּכֵלֶת וּבָאַרְגָּמָן[k]

,purple in and ,blue in embroiderer an and ,workman skilful a and

בְּתוֹלַעַת הַשָּׁנִי וּבַשֵּׁשׁ[l] וְאֹרֵג עֹשֵׂי[m]

of doers ; weaver a and ,byssus in and ,crimson (of worm) in

כָּל־מְלָאכָה וְחֹשְׁבֵי[n] מַחֲשָׁבֹת׃

.designs of planners and ,work every

filled him with the spirit of God, in wisdom, in understanding, and in knowledge, and in all manner of workmanship; 32 and to devise cunning works, to work in gold, and in silver, and in brass, 33 and in cutting of stones for setting, and in carving of wood, to work in all manner of cunning workmanship. 34
And he hath put in his heart that he may teach, both he, and Oholiab, the son of Ahisamach, of the tribe of Dan. 35
Them hath he filled with wisdom of heart, to work all manner of workmanship, of the engraver, and of the cunning workman, and of the embroiderer, in blue, and in purple, in scarlet, and in fine linen, and of the weaver, even of them that do any workmanship, and of those that devise cunning works.

36

1 THEN wrought Bezaleel and Aholiab, and every wise hearted man, in whom the LORD put wisdom and understanding to know how to work all manner of work for the service of the

1 וְעָשָׂה בְצַלְאֵל וְאָהֳלִיאָב וְכֹל אִישׁ

one every and Oholiab and Bezalel make shall And

חֲכַם־לֵב אֲשֶׁר נָתַן[o] יְהוָה[p] חָכְמָה וּתְבוּנָה

intelligence and wisdom Jehovah given has whom [to] ,heart of wise

בָּהֵמָּה לָדַעַת לַעֲשֹׂת אֶת־כָּל־מְלֶאכֶת עֲבֹדַת

of service the of work every do to how know to ,(them to)

And Bezalel and Oholiab shall work, and every wise hearted man, in whom the LORD hath put wisdom and understanding to know how to work all the work for the

---

a G. omits.
b G. omits ב, also in the following words in this verse.
c G. omits ו.
d G., S. omit ו.
e G. has, *according to all the works of architecture.*
f G., V. apparently omit.
g G. has, *wisdom and understanding.*
h G. adds, *to understand how.*
i G. has, *holy,* קדש.
j G. apparently has, *and the woven things.*
k G. has, *and to weave embroideries.*
l G. omits.
m S. adds, *and,* ו; G. has, *to do.*
n G. has, *of architecture, of embroidery.*
o G. has, *had been given.*
p G. omits.

הַקֹּדֶשׁ לְכֹל [a] אֲשֶׁר־צִוָּה יְהוָה׃
.Jehovah commanded has which all to according ,sanctuary the

2 וַיִּקְרָא מֹשֶׁה אֶל־בְּצַלְאֵל וְאֶל־אָהֳלִיאָב וְאֶל
unto and ,Oholiab unto and ,Bezalel unto Moses called And

כָּל־אִישׁ חֲכַם־לֵב אֲשֶׁר נָתַן יְהוָה [b] חָכְמָה
[7]wisdom [4]Jehovah [6]given [5]had (whom) heart of wise one every

בְּלִבּוֹ כֹּל אֲשֶׁר נְשָׂאוֹ לִבּוֹ
[2]heart [1]whose [6]up [5]him [4]lifted [3]had (who) one every ,[3]heart [2]whose [1]in

3 לְקָרְבָה אֶל־הַמְּלָאכָה לַעֲשֹׂת אֹתָהּ׃ וַיִּקְחוּ מִלִּפְנֵי
before from took they And .it do to ,work the unto near come to

מֹשֶׁה אֵת כָּל־הַתְּרוּמָה אֲשֶׁר הֵבִיאוּ בְּנֵי יִשְׂרָאֵל
Israel of children the brought had which ,contribution every Moses

לִמְלֶאכֶת [c] [d] עֲבֹדַת הַקֹּדֶשׁ [d] לַעֲשֹׂת אֹתָהּ וְהֵם
they and ;it make to ,sanctuary the of service the of work the for

הֵבִיאוּ אֵלָיו [e] עוֹד נְדָבָה [f] בַּבֹּקֶר
,morning the in offerings voluntary still him unto brought

4 בַּבֹּקֶר [g]׃ וַיָּבֹאוּ [h] כָּל־הַחֲכָמִים הָעֹשִׂים אֵת כָּל־
every doing those ,men wise the all came And .morning the in

מְלֶאכֶת [i] הַקֹּדֶשׁ אִישׁ־אִישׁ מִמְּלַאכְתּוֹ אֲשֶׁר־הֵמָּה
[were] they which work his from ,each ,each ,sanctuary the of work

5 עֹשִׂים׃ וַיֹּאמְרוּ אֶל־מֹשֶׁה לֵּאמֹר [j] מַרְבִּים הָעָם
people the increasing [Are] :saying ,Moses unto said they And .doing

לְהָבִיא מִדֵּי הָעֲבֹדָה לַמְּלָאכָה
work the for service the [for] (of) sufficiency a than more ,bring to

6 אֲשֶׁר־צִוָּה יְהוָה לַעֲשֹׂת אֹתָהּ׃ וַיְצַו מֹשֶׁה
,Moses commanded And .it make to Jehovah commanded which

וַיַּעֲבִירוּ קוֹל בַּמַּחֲנֶה לֵאמֹר אִישׁ
Man :saying ,camp the in voice a over pass to caused they and

וְאִשָּׁה אַל־יַעֲשׂוּ־עוֹד מְלָאכָה לִתְרוּמַת
of contribution the for work a still make not them let ,woman and

הַקֹּדֶשׁ וַיִּכָּלֵא הָעָם מֵהָבִיא׃
.bringing from people the restrained were and ;sanctuary the

sanctuary, ac-
cording to all
that the LORD
had command-
ed.

2 And Moses
called Bezaleel
and Aholiab,
and every wise
hearted man, in
whose heart the
LORD had put
wisdom, *even*
every one whose
heart stirred him
up to come unto
the work to do
it: 3 And they
received of Mo-
ses all the offer-
ing, which the
children of Is-
rael had brought
for the work of
the service of
the sanctuary,
to make it *with-
al.* And they
brought yet unto
him free offer-
ings every morn-
ing. 4 And all
the wise men,
that wrought all
the work of the
sanctuary, came
every man from
his work which
they made; 5
And they spake
unto Moses, say-
ing, The people
bring much
more than
enough for the
service of the
work, which the
LORD command-
ed to make. 6
And Moses gave
commandment;
and they caused
it to be pro-
claimed
throughout the
camp, saying,
Let neither man
nor woman
make any more
work for the
offering of the
sanctuary. So
the people were
restrained from

service of the
sanctuary, ac-
cording to all
that the LORD
hath command-
ed.

2 And Moses
called Bezaleel
and Oholiab,
and every wise
hearted man, in
whose heart the
LORD had put
wisdom, even
every one whose
heart stirred him
up to come un-
to the work to
do it: 3 and they
received of Mo-
ses all the offer-
ing, which the
children of Is-
rael had brought
for the work of
the service of
the sanctuary, to
make it withal.
And they
brought yet unto
him freewill
offerings every
morning. 4 And
all the wise men,
that wrought all
the work of the
sanctuary, came
every man from
his work which
they wrought; 5
and they spake
unto Moses, say-
ing, The people
bring much
more than
enough for the
service of the
work, which the
LORD command-
ed to make. 6
And Moses gave
commandment,
and they caused
it to be pro-
claimed
throughout the
camp, saying,
Let neither man
nor woman
make any more
work for the
offering of the
sanctuary. So
the people were
restrained from

---

a S., V. apparently omit כל.
b G. has, *God.*
c G. has, *for all,* לכל.
d S. has, *for the work of the tent of meeting.*
e G., V. omit.
f G. adds, *from those bringing.*
g G. omits.
h S. has, *and brought,* וַיָּבִאוּ.
i G., S. omit כל.
j G., S., V. omit.

bringing. 7 For the stuff they had was sufficient for all the work to make it, and too much.

8 And every wise hearted man among them that wrought the work of the tabernacle made ten curtains *of* fine twined linen, and blue, and purple, and scarlet: *with* cherubims of cunning work made he them. 9 The length of one curtain *was* twenty and eight cubits, and the breadth of one curtain four cubits: the curtains *were* all of one size. 10 And he coupled the five curtains one unto another; and *the other* five curtains he coupled one unto another. 11 And he made loops of blue on the edge of one curtain from the selvedge in the coupling: likewise he made in the uttermost side of *another* curtain, in the coupling of the second. 12 Fifty loops made he in one curtain, and fifty loops made he in the edge of the curtain which *was* in the coupling of the second: the loops held one *curtain* to anoth-

וְהַמְּלָאכָה הָיְתָה[a] דַיָּם לְכָל־הַמְּלָאכָה לַעֲשׂוֹת 7
make to work the all for sufficiency their was matter the And

אֹתָהּ וְהוֹתֵר[b]׃
.superfluous was it and ,it

וַיַּעֲשׂוּ כָל־חֲכַם־לֵב בְּעֹשֵׂי[c] הַמְּלָאכָה[d] 8
work the of doers the among heart of wise one every made And

אֶת־הַמִּשְׁכָּן עֶשֶׂר יְרִיעֹת שֵׁשׁ[e] מָשְׁזָר וּתְכֵלֶת
,blue and ,twisted byssus ;curtains ten ,habitation the

וְאַרְגָּמָן וְתוֹלַעַת שָׁנִי כְּרֻבִים מַעֲשֵׂה
of work a cherubs ,crimson (of worm) and ,purple and

חֹשֵׁב עָשָׂה אֹתָם[e]׃ אֹרֶךְ הַיְרִיעָה 9
[2]curtain the of length The .them made he ,workman skilful a

הָאַחַת שְׁמֹנֶה וְעֶשְׂרִים בָּאַמָּה וְרֹחַב אַרְבַּע
four ,width the and ;cubit the by twenty and eight [1]one

בָּאַמָּה הַיְרִיעָה הָאֶחָת מִדָּה אַחַת לְכָל־הַיְרִיעֹת׃
.curtains the all to [1]one [2]measure ;[1]one [2]curtain the ,cubit the by

וַיְחַבֵּר[f] אֶת־חֲמֵשׁ הַיְרִיעֹת אַחַת[g] אֶל־אֶחָת[g] וְחָמֵשׁ 10
five and ;one unto one ,curtains five joined he And

יְרִיעֹת חִבַּר אַחַת אֶל־אֶחָת׃ וַיַּעַשׂ לֻלְאֹת תְּכֵלֶת 11
blue of loops made he And .one unto one ,joined he curtains

עַל שְׂפַת הַיְרִיעָה הָאֶחָת מִקָּצָה בַּמַּחְבָּרֶת
:joining the at end the from ,[1]one [2]curtain the of lip the upon

כֵּן עָשָׂה בִּשְׂפַת הַיְרִיעָה הַקִּיצוֹנָה בַּמַּחְבֶּרֶת
[2]joining the at [1]last [2]curtain the of lip the at did he so

הַשֵּׁנִית׃ חֲמִשִּׁים לֻלָאֹת עָשָׂה בַּיְרִיעָה הָאֶחָת 12
;[1]one [2]curtain the on made he loops Fifty .[1]second

וַחֲמִשִּׁים לֻלָאֹת עָשָׂה בִּקְצֵה הַיְרִיעָה[h] אֲשֶׁר
[was] which curtain the of end the on made he loops fifty and

בַּמַּחְבֶּרֶת הַשֵּׁנִית מַקְבִּילֹת הַלֻּלָאֹת אַחַת
one ,loops the [were] corresponding ;[1]second [2]joining the at

bringing. 7 For the stuff they had was sufficient for all the work to make it, and too much.
8 And every wise hearted man among them that wrought the work made the tabernacle with ten curtains; of fine twined linen, and blue, and purple, and scarlet, with cherubim the work of the cunning workman made he them. 9 The length of each curtain was eight and twenty cubits, and the breadth of each curtain four cubits: all the curtains had one measure. 10 And he coupled five curtains one to another: and *the other* five curtains he coupled one to another. 11 And he made loops of blue upon the edge of the one curtain from the selvedge in the coupling: likewise he made in the edge of the curtain that was outmost in the second coupling. 12 Fifty loops made he in the one curtain, and fifty loops made he in the edge of the curtain that was in the second coupling: the loops were opposite one to

a Sm., G. add, *for them.*

b Sm., G. have, *and they had left,* והותירו.

c S. has, *and the doers,* ועשי.

d From this point the order of G. varies much from H., being as follows: 39: 1b-31, 36: 8a-9, 34-38, 38: 9-23, 37: 1-23, 36: 34, 36, 38: 20, 1-7, 37: 29, 38: 8, 40: 30-32, 38: 24-31, 39: 32b, 1a, 33-43, 40: 1-6, 8-29,33-38, with omission of remainder, and some other slight omissions and transfers. G. also has in many cases a much briefer form of statement and in other places varies very greatly from H., making it unnecessary and unprofitable to record all its variations. The order of H. has many indications of being the original.

e G. omits.

f G. omits vss. 10-33.

g S. has, *like one.*

h S. adds, *one.*

er. 13 And he made fifty taches of gold, and coupled the curtains one unto another with the taches: so it became one tabernacle.

14 And he made curtains *of* goats' *hair* for the tent over the tabernacle: eleven curtains he made them. 15 The length of one curtain *was* thirty cubits, and four cubits *was* the breadth of one curtain: the eleven curtains *were* of one size. 16 And he coupled five curtains by themselves, and six curtains by themselves. 17 And he made fifty loops upon the uttermost edge of the curtain in the coupling, and fifty loops made he upon the edge of the curtain which coupleth the second. 18 And he made fifty taches *of* brass to couple the tent together, that it might be one. 19 And he made a covering for the tent *of* rams' skins dyed red, and a covering *of* badgers' skins above *that*.

20 And he made boards for the tabernacle *of* shittim wood, standing up. 21 The length of a board *was* ten cubits, and the breadth of a board one cubit and a half. 22 One board had two tenons, equally distant one from an-

13 אֶל־אֶחָת׃ וַיַּעַשׂ חֲמִשִּׁים קַרְסֵי זָהָב וַיְחַבֵּר
joined he and ;gold of hooks fifty made he And .one unto

אֶת־הַיְרִיעֹת אַחַת אֶל־אַחַת בַּקְּרָסִים וַיְהִי
became and ,hooks the by ,one unto one ,curtains the

14 הַמִּשְׁכָּן אֶחָד׃ וַיַּעַשׂ יְרִיעֹת עִזִּים
,goats [of hair] of curtains made he And .one habitation the

לְאֹהֶל עַל־הַמִּשְׁכָּן עַשְׁתֵּי־עֶשְׂרֵה יְרִיעֹת עָשָׂה אֹתָם׃
.them made he curtains eleven ;habitation the over tent a for

15 אֹרֶךְ הַיְרִיעָה הָאַחַת שְׁלֹשִׁים בָּאַמָּה וְאַרְבַּע
four and ,cubit the by thirty ,[1]one [2]curtain the of length The

אַמּוֹת רֹחַב הַיְרִיעָה הָאֶחָת מִדָּה אַחַת
[1]one [2]measure ;[1]one [2]curtain the of width the cubits

16 לְעַשְׁתֵּי עֶשְׂרֵה יְרִיעֹת׃ וַיְחַבֵּר אֶת־חֲמֵשׁ
five the joined he And .curtains ten [and] one the to

17 הַיְרִיעֹת לְבָד וְאֶת־שֵׁשׁ הַיְרִיעֹת לְבָד׃ וַיַּעַשׂ
made he And .separately curtains six the and ,separately curtains

לֻלָאֹת חֲמִשִּׁים [a] עַל שְׂפַת הַיְרִיעָה הַקִּיצֹנָה
[1]last [2]curtain the of lip the upon [1]fifty [2]loops

בַּמַּחְבָּרֶת וַחֲמִשִּׁים לֻלָאֹת עָשָׂה עַל־שְׂפַת הַיְרִיעָה
curtain the of lip the upon made he loops fifty and ;joining the at

18 הַחֹבֶרֶת הַשֵּׁנִית׃ וַיַּעַשׂ קַרְסֵי נְחֹשֶׁת חֲמִשִּׁים
,fifty ,bronze of hooks made he And .second the ,joined that

19 לְחַבֵּר אֶת־הָאֹהֶל לִהְיֹת אֶחָד׃ וַיַּעַשׂ מִכְסֶה
cover a made he And .one become to ,tent the join to

לָאֹהֶל עֹרֹת אֵילִם מְאָדָּמִים וּמִכְסֵה עֹרֹת
of skins of cover a and ;red dyed rams of skins ,tent the for

20 תְּחָשִׁים מִלְמָעְלָה׃ וַיַּעַשׂ אֶת־הַקְּרָשִׁים
boards the made he And .above (to) from dolphins

21 לַמִּשְׁכָּן עֲצֵי שִׁטִּים עֹמְדִים׃ עֶשֶׂר אַמֹּת
cubits Ten .standing ,acacia of timbers ,habitation the for

אֹרֶךְ הַקָּרֶשׁ [b] וְאַמָּה וַחֲצִי הָאַמָּה רֹחַב
of width the cubit a of half a and cubit a and ;board the of length the

22 הַקֶּרֶשׁ הָאֶחָד׃ שְׁתֵּי יָדֹת לַקֶּרֶשׁ הָאֶחָד [c]
,[1]one [2]board the to [pins] (hands) Two .[1]one [2]board the

another. 13 And he made fifty clasps of gold, and coupled the curtains one to another with the clasps: so the tabernacle was one.

14 And he made curtains of goats' *hair* for a tent over the tabernacle: eleven curtains he made them. 15 The length of each curtain was thirty cubits, and four cubits the breadth of each curtain: the eleven curtains had one measure. 16 And he coupled five curtains by themselves, and six curtains by themselves. 17 And he made fifty loops on the edge of the curtain that was outmost in the coupling, and fifty loops made he upon the edge of the curtain which was *outmost in* the second coupling. 18 And he made fifty clasps of brass to couple the tent together, that it might be one. 19 And he made a covering for the tent of rams' skins dyed red, and a covering of sealskins above.

20 And he made the boards for the tabernacle of acacia wood, standing up. 21 Ten cubits was the length of a board, and a cubit and a half the breadth of each board. 22 Each board had two tenons, joined one to

---

a S. adds, ללאת.
b Sm., S., V. add, *one*.
c S. adds, *and two tenons to the other beam*.

other: thus did
he make for all
the boards of the
tabernacle. 23
And he made
boards for the
tabernacle;
twenty boards
for the south
side southward:
24 And forty
sockets of silver
he made under
the twenty
boards; two
sockets under
one board for
his two tenons,
and two sockets
under another
board for his two
tenons. 25 And
for the other side
of the taber-
nacle, *which is*
toward the
north corner, he
made twenty
boards, 26 And
their forty sock-
ets of silver;
two sockets un-
der one board,
and two sockets
under another
board. 27 And
for the sides of
the tabernacle
westward he
made six boards.
28 And two
boards made he
for the corners
of the tabernacle
in the two sides.
29 And they
were coupled be-
neath, and coup-
led together at
the head there-
of, to one ring:
thus he did to
both of them in
both the corners.
30 And there
were eight
boards; and
their sockets
were sixteen
sockets of silver,
under every
board two sock-
ets.
31 And he
made bars of

מְשֻׁלָּבֹת אַחַת אֶל־אֶחָת כֵּן עָשָׂה לְכֹל קַרְשֵׁי
of boards the all to did he so ;one unto one ,connected

23 הַמִּשְׁכָּן׃ וַיַּעַשׂ אֶת־הַקְּרָשִׁים לַמִּשְׁכָּן עֶשְׂרִים
twenty ; habitation the for boards the made he And .habitation the

24 קְרָשִׁים לִפְאַת נֶגֶב תֵּימָנָה׃ וְאַרְבָּעִים
forty And .southward south the of direction the for boards

אַדְנֵי־כֶסֶף עָשָׂה תַּחַת עֶשְׂרִים הַקְּרָשִׁים שְׁנֵי
two ; boards twenty the under made he silver of sockets

אֲדָנִים תַּחַת־הַקֶּרֶשׁ הָאֶחָד לִשְׁתֵּי יְדֹתָיו וּשְׁנֵי
two and ,[pins] (hands) [1]its [2]two for [1]one [2]board the under sockets

אֲדָנִים תַּחַת־הַקֶּרֶשׁ הָאֶחָד לִשְׁתֵּי יְדֹתָיו[a]׃
.[pins] (hands) [1]its [2]two for [1]one [2]board the under sockets

25 וּלְצֶלַע הַמִּשְׁכָּן הַשֵּׁנִית לִפְאַת
of direction the to ,second the ,habitation the of side the for And

26 צָפוֹן עָשָׂה עֶשְׂרִים קְרָשִׁים׃ וְאַרְבָּעִים אַדְנֵיהֶם
,sockets their forty And .boards twenty made he ,north the

כֶּסֶף שְׁנֵי אֲדָנִים תַּחַת הַקֶּרֶשׁ הָאֶחָד וּשְׁנֵי
two and ,[1]one [2]board the under sockets two ; silver

27 אֲדָנִים תַּחַת הַקֶּרֶשׁ הָאֶחָד׃ וּלְיַרְכְּתֵי
of thighs the for And .[1]one [2]board the under sockets

28 הַמִּשְׁכָּן יָמָּה עָשָׂה שִׁשָּׁה קְרָשִׁים׃ וּשְׁנֵי
two And .boards six made he ,westward habitation the

קְרָשִׁים עָשָׂה לִמְקֻצְעֹת הַמִּשְׁכָּן בַּיַּרְכָתָיִם׃
.thighs the in ,habitation the of corners the for made he boards

29 וְהָיוּ תוֹאֲמִם מִלְּמַטָּה וְיַחְדָּו יִהְיוּ
were they manner like in and ,below (to) from double were they And

תַמִּים אֶל־רֹאשׁוֹ אֶל־הַטַּבַּעַת הָאֶחָת כֵּן עָשָׂה
did he so ;[1]one [2]ring the unto top its upon complete

30 לִשְׁנֵיהֶם לִשְׁנֵי הַמִּקְצֹעֹת׃ וְהָיוּ שְׁמֹנָה קְרָשִׁים
,boards eight were And .corners two the for ,them of both to

וְאַדְנֵיהֶם כֶּסֶף שִׁשָּׁה עָשָׂר אֲדָנִים[b] שְׁנֵי אֲדָנִים[c]
,sockets two ; sockets ten [and] six ,silver sockets their and

31 שְׁנֵי אֲדָנִים תַּחַת הַקֶּרֶשׁ הָאֶחָד׃ וַיַּעַשׂ בְרִיחֵי
of bars made he And .[1]one [2]board the under ,sockets two

another: thus
did he make for
all the boards of
the tabernacle.
23 And he made
the boards for
the tabernacle;
twenty boards
for the south
side southward:
24 and he made
forty sockets of
silver under the
twenty boards;
two sockets un-
der one board
for its two ten-
ons, and two
sockets under
another board
for its two ten-
ons. 25 And for
the second side
of the tabernacle
on the north
side, he made
twenty boards,
26 and their
forty sockets of
silver; two sock-
ets under one
board, and two
sockets under
another board.
27 And for the
hinder part of
the tabernacle
westward he
made six boards.
28 And two
boards made he
for the corners
of the tabernacle
in the hinder
part. 29 And
they were doub-
le beneath, and
in like manner
they were entire
unto the top
thereof unto one
ring: thus he
did to both of
them in the two
corners. 30 And
there were eight
boards, and
their sockets of
silver, sixteen
sockets; under
every board two
sockets.
31 And he
made bars of

---

a S. adds, *they made.*
b S., V. omit.
c S. adds, *under one beam;* cf. 26:25.

shittim wood; five for the boards of the one side of the tabernacle,
32 And five bars for the boards of the other side of the tabernacle, and five bars for the boards of the tabernacle for the sides westward.
33 And he made the middle bar to shoot through the boards from the one end to the other.
34 And he overlaid the boards with gold, and made their rings *of* gold *to be* places for the bars, and overlaid the bars with gold.

35 And he made a vail *of* blue, and purple, and scarlet, and fine twined linen: *with* cherubims made he it of cunning work.
36 And he made thereunto four pillars *of* shittim *wood*, and overlaid them with gold: their hooks *were* *of* gold; and he cast for them four sockets of silver.
37 And he made an hanging for the tabernacle door *of* blue, and purple, and scarlet, and fine twined linen, of needlework;
38 And the five pillars of it with their hooks: and he overlaid their

עצי שטים חמשה לקרשי צלע־
of side the of boards the to five ;acacia of wood of pieces

32 המשכן האחת: וחמשה בריחם לקרשי
of boards the to bars five and ;one the ,habitation the

צלע־המשכן השנית וחמשה בריחם לקרשי
of boards the to bars five and ;second the ,habitation the of side the

33 המשכן לירכתים ימה: ויעש את־הבריח
[2]bar the made he And .westward ,thighs the to ,habitation the

התיכן לברח בתוך הקרשים מן־הקצה
end from ,boards the of midst the in through go to ,[1]middle

34 אל־הקצה: ואת־הקרשים צפה זהב[a] ואת־
and ,gold [with] overlaid he boards the And .end unto

טבעתם עשה[b] זהב בתים[c] לבריחם[c] ויצף
overlaid he and ;poles the for houses ,gold made he rings the

35 את־הבריחם זהב: ויעש את־הפרכת תכלת
,blue ,veil the made he And .gold [with] bars the

וארגמן ותולעת שני ושש משזר מעשה
of work a ,twisted byssus and ,crimson (of worm) and ,purple and

36 חשב עשה[d] אתה[d] כרבים: ויעש[e]
made he And .cherubs [and] ,it made he workman skilful a

לה[e] ארבעה עמודי שטים ויצפם[f] זהב
,gold [with] them overlaid he and ,acacia of pillars four it for

וויהם זהב ויצק[hg] להם[h] ארבעה אדני־
of sockets four them for cast he and ;gold [being] nails their

37 כסף: ויעש מסך לפתח האהל[i] תכלת
,blue ,tent the of door the for screen a made he And .silver

וארגמן ותולעת שני ושש משזר מעשה
of work a ,twisted byssus and ,crimson (of worm) and ,purple and

38 רקם[j]: ואת־עמודיו חמשה ואת־וויהם[k] וצפה[l]
overlaid he and ;nails their and ,five pillars its and ;embroiderer an

acacia wood; five for the boards of the one side of the tabernacle,
32 and five bars for the boards of the other side of the tabernacle, and five bars for the boards of the tabernacle for the hinder part westward.
33 And he made the middle bar to pass through in the midst of the boards from the one end to the other.
34 And he overlaid the boards with gold, and made their rings of gold for places for the bars, and overlaid the bars with gold.

35 And he made the veil of blue, and purple, and scarlet, and fine twined linen: with cherubim the work of the cunning workman made he it.
36 And he made thereunto four pillars of acacia, and overlaid them with gold: their hooks were of gold; and he cast for them four sockets of silver.
37 And he made a screen for the door of the Tent, of blue, and purple, and scarlet, and fine twined linen, the work of the embroiderer;
38 and the five pillars of it with their hooks: and

---

a G. has, *silver*.
b G. adds, *for the pillar*.
c G. omits.
d G., V. omit.
e G. has, *and they put it upon*.
f G. has, *covered with*.
g S. has, *and they made*.
h G. has, *and*.
i G. adds, *of witness*.
j G. adds, *of cherubim*.
k S. apparently omits.
l S. has, *and the coverings of*.

chapiters and
their fillets with
gold: but their
five sockets *were*
of brass.

רָאשֵׁיהֶם וַחֲשֻׁקֵיהֶם זָהָב וְאַדְנֵיהֶם חֲמִשָּׁה
,five ,sockets their and ; gold [with] bands their and tops their

נְחֹשֶׁת׃
.bronze

he overlaid their
chapiters and
their fillets with
gold: and their
five sockets were
of brass.

37

AND Bezalel
made the ark *of*
shittim wood:
two cubits and a
half *was* the
length of it, and
a cubit and a
half the breadth
of it, and a cubit
and a half the
height of it: 2
And he overlaid
it with pure gold
within and with-
out, and made
a crown of gold
to it round a-
bout. 3 And he
cast for it four
rings of gold, *to*
be set by the
four corners of
it; even two
rings upon the
one side of it,
and two rings
upon the other
side of it. 4 And
he made staves
of shittim wood,
and overlaid
them with gold.
5 And he put
the staves into
the rings by the
sides of the ark,
to bear the ark.
6 And he made
the mercy seat
of pure gold:
two cubits and a
half *was* the
length thereof,
and one cubit
and a half the
breadth thereof.
7 And he made
two cherubims *of*
gold, beaten out
of one piece
made he them,
on the two ends
of the mercy
seat; 8 One
cherub on the
end on this side,
and another
cherub on the

1 וַיַּעַשׂ[a] בְּצַלְאֵל אֶת־הָאָרֹן עֲצֵי[b] שִׁטִּים[b]
;acacia of wood of pieces ,ark the Bezalel made And

אַמָּתַיִם וָחֵצִי אָרְכּוֹ וְאַמָּה וָחֵצִי רָחְבּוֹ
,width its half a and cubit a and ,length its half a and cubits two

2 וְאַמָּה וָחֵצִי קֹמָתוֹ׃ וַיְצַפֵּהוּ זָהָב
²gold (with) it overlaid he And .height its half a and cubit a and

טָהוֹר מִבַּיִת וּמִחוּץ וַיַּעַשׂ לוֹ
it for made he and ; outside (from) and inside (from) ,¹pure

3 זֵר זָהָב סָבִיב׃ וַיִּצֹק לוֹ אַרְבַּע
four it for cast he And .about round gold of wreath a

טַבְּעֹת זָהָב עַל אַרְבַּע פַּעֲמֹתָיו וּשְׁתֵּי[c] טַבָּעֹת[d]
rings two (and) ; feet ¹its ²four upon ,gold of rings

עַל־צַלְעוֹ הָאֶחָת וּשְׁתֵּי טַבָּעֹת[d] עַל־צַלְעוֹ הַשֵּׁנִית׃
.second side its upon rings two and ,one side its upon

4 וַיַּעַשׂ בַּדֵּי עֲצֵי שִׁטִּים וַיְצַף
overlaid he and ; acacia of wood of pieces of poles made he And

5 אֹתָם זָהָב׃ וַיָּבֵא אֶת־הַבַּדִּים בַּטַּבָּעֹת
,rings the into poles the brought he And .gold [with] them

6 עַל צַלְעֹת הָאָרֹן לָשֵׂאת אֶת־הָאָרֹן׃ וַיַּעַשׂ
made he And .ark the carry to ,ark the of sides the upon

כַּפֹּרֶת זָהָב טָהוֹר אַמָּתַיִם וָחֵצִי אָרְכָּהּ
,length its half a and cubits two ; ¹pure ²gold of lid expiating an

7 וְאַמָּה וָחֵצִי רָחְבָּהּ׃ וַיַּעַשׂ שְׁנֵי כְרֻבִים
,cherubs two made he And .width its half a and cubit a and

זָהָב מִקְשָׁה עָשָׂה אֹתָם מִשְּׁנֵי קְצוֹת
of ends two the from ,them made he work chased of : gold

8 הַכַּפֹּרֶת׃ כְּרוּב אֶחָד מִקָּצָה מִזֶּה וּכְרוּב־אֶחָד
cherub one and ,here end the from ¹one ²Cherub .lid expiating the

And Bezalel
made the ark of
acacia wood:
two cubits and a
half was the
length of it, and
a cubit and a half
the breadth of it,
and a cubit and
a half the height
of it: 2 and he
overlaid it with
pure gold with-
in and without,
and made a
crown of gold
to it round a-
bout. 3 And he
cast for it four
rings of gold, in
the four feet
thereof; even
two rings on the
one side of
it, and two
rings on the
other side of it.
4 And he made
staves of acacia
wood, and over-
laid them with
gold. 5 And he
put the staves
into the rings on
the sides of the
ark, to bear the
ark. 6 And he
made a mercy-
seat of pure
gold: two cubits
and a half *was*
the length there-
of, and a cubit
and a half the
breadth thereof.
7 And he made
two cherubim of
gold; of beaten
work made he
them, at the two
ends of the
mercy seat: 8
one cherub at
the one end, and
one cherub at

---

a Nearly every verse in this chapter is much abbreviated in G.

b G. omits.

c G., S., V. omit ו.

d G. omits.

other end on
that side : out of
the mercy seat
made he the
cherubims on the
two ends there-
of. 9 And the
cherubim spread
out *their* wings
on high, *and*
covered with
their wings over
the mercy seat,
with their faces
one to another ;
even to the
mercy seatward
were the faces of
the cherubims.

10 And he
made the table
of shittim wood:
two cubits *was*
the length there-
of, and a cubit
the breadth
thereof, and a
cubit and a half
the height there-
of: 11 And he
overlaid it with
pure gold, and
made thereunto
a crown of gold
round about. 12
Also he made
thereunto a bor-
der of an hand-
breadth round
about ; and
made a crown of
gold for the bor-
der thereof
round about. 13
And he cast for
it four rings of
gold, and put
the rings upon
the four corners
that *were* in the
four feet there-
of. 14 Over a-
gainst the bor-
der were the
rings, the places
for the staves to
bear the table.
15 And he made
the staves *of*
shittim wood,
and overlaid
them with gold,
to bear the table.
16 And he made
the vessels
which *were* up-
on the table, his
dishes, and his
spoons, and his
bowls, and his

מִקָּצָה מִזֶּה מִן־הַכַּפֹּרֶת[a] עָשָׂה אֶת־הַכְּרֻבִים
,cherubs the made he lid expiating the from ; there end the from

9 מִשְּׁנֵי קְצוֹתָו׃ וַיִּהְיוּ הַכְּרֻבִים פֹּרְשֵׂי
out spreading cherubs the were And .ends [1]its [2]two from

כְנָפַיִם לְמַעְלָה סֹכְכִים בְּכַנְפֵיהֶם עַל־הַכַּפֹּרֶת
lid expiating the upon wings their with covering ,above (to) wings

וּפְנֵיהֶם אִישׁ אֶל־אָחִיו אֶל־הַכַּפֹּרֶת
,lid expiating the toward; brother its toward each [being] faces their (and)

10 הָיוּ פְּנֵי הַכְּרֻבִים׃ וַיַּעַשׂ אֶת־הַשֻּׁלְחָן
,table the made he And .cherubs the of faces the were

עֲצֵי[b] שִׁטִּים[b] אַמָּתַיִם אָרְכּוֹ וְאַמָּה
cubit a and ,length its cubits two ; acacia of timbers [of]

11 רָחְבּוֹ וְאַמָּה וָחֵצִי קֹמָתוֹ׃ וַיְצַף[c] אֹתוֹ
it overlaid he And .height its half a and cubit a and ,width its

זָהָב טָהוֹר וַיַּעַשׂ לוֹ זֵר זָהָב[d]
gold of wreath a it for made he and ; [1]pure [2]gold [with]

12 סָבִיב׃ וַיַּעַשׂ לוֹ מִסְגֶּרֶת טֹפַח
handbreadth a of border a it for made he And .about round

סָבִיב וַיַּעַשׂ[e] זֵר־זָהָב לְמִסְגַּרְתּוֹ סָבִיב׃
.about round border its to gold of wreath a made he and ; about round

13 וַיִּצֹק לוֹ אַרְבַּע טַבְּעֹת זָהָב וַיִּתֵּן
put he and ; gold of rings four it for cast he And

אֶת־הַטַּבָּעֹת עַל אַרְבַּע הַפֵּאֹת אֲשֶׁר לְאַרְבַּע
[2]four to [were] which ,corners four the upon rings the

14 רַגְלָיו׃ לְעֻמַּת הַמִּסְגֶּרֶת הָיוּ הַטַּבָּעֹת בָּתִּים
houses ,rings the were border the Near .feet [1]its

15 לְבַדִּים לָשֵׂאת אֶת־הַשֻּׁלְחָן׃ וַיַּעַשׂ
made he And .table the carry to ,poles the for

אֶת־הַבַּדִּים עֲצֵי שִׁטִּים וַיְצַף אֹתָם
them overlaid he and ,acacia of wood of pieces [of] ,poles the

16 זָהָב לָשֵׂאת[f] אֶת־הַשֻּׁלְחָן׃ וַיַּעַשׂ אֶת־הַכֵּלִים
vessels the made he And .table the carry to ,gold [with]

אֲשֶׁר עַל־הַשֻּׁלְחָן אֶת־קְעָרֹתָיו וְאֶת־כַּפֹּתָיו וְאֵת
and ,bowls its and ,platters its ,table the upon [were] which

the other end :
of one piece
with the mercy-
seat made he
the cherubim at
the two ends
thereof. 9 And
the cherubim
spread out their
wings on high,
covering the
mercy-seat with
their wings,
with their faces
one to another;
toward the
mercy-seat were
the faces of the
cherubim.

10 And he
made the table
of acacia wood:
two cubits *was*
the length there-
of, and a cubit
the breadth
thereof, and a
cubit and a half
the height there-
of: 11 and he
overlaid it with
pure gold, and
made thereto a
crown of gold
round about. 12
And he made
unto it a border
of an hand-
breadth round
about, and made
a golden crown
to the border
thereof round
about. 13 And
he cast for it
four rings of
gold, and put
the rings in the
four corners that
were on the four
feet thereof. 14
Close by the
border were the
rings, the places
for the staves to
bear the table.
15 And he made
the staves of
acacia wood,
and overlaid
them with gold,
to bear the table.
16 And he made
the vessels
which were up-
on the table, the
dishes thereof,
and the spoons
thereof, and the
bowls thereof,

a S. has for מן *upon.*
b G. has, *of pure gold.*
c G. omits vss. 11, 12.
d S. adds, *upon its border*, למסגרתו.
e S. adds, *for it.*
f S. adds, *by them;* cf. 25: 29.

covers to cover withal, *of* pure gold.
17 And he made the candlestick *of* pure gold: *of* beaten work made he the candlestick; his shaft, and his branch, his bowls, his knops, and his flowers, were of the same: 18 And six branches going out of the sides thereof; three branches of the candlestick out of the one side thereof, and three branches of the candlestick out of the other side thereof: 19 Three bowls made after the fashion of almonds in one branch, a knop and a flower; and three bowls made like almonds in another branch, a knop and a flower: so throughout the six branches going out of the candlestick. 20 And in the candlestick *were* four bowls made like almonds, his knops, and his flowers: 21 And a knop under two branches of the same, and a knop under two branches of the same, and a knop under two branches of the same, according to the six branches going out of it. 22 Their knops and their branches were of the same: all of it *was* one beaten work *of* pure gold. 23 And he made his seven lamps, and his snuffers, and his

מְנַקִּיֹּתָיו וְאֶת־הַקְּשָׂוֹת אֲשֶׁר יֻסַּךְ
made is libation a which (with) ,pitchers its and ,cups sacrificial its

17 בָּהֵן זָהָב טָהוֹר׃ [a] וַיַּעַשׂ אֶת־הַמְּנֹרָה זָהָב
[2]gold ,lampstand the made he And .[1]pure [2]gold [of] ,(them with)

טָהוֹר מִקְשָׁה עָשָׂה אֶת־הַמְּנֹרָה יְרֵכָהּ
,thigh its ,lampstand the made he work chased [of] ;[1]pure

וְקָנָהּ גְּבִיעֶיהָ כַּפְתֹּרֶיהָ וּפְרָחֶיהָ מִמֶּנָּה הָיוּ׃
.were it from blossoms its and ,knobs its ,calixes its ; stalk its and

18 וְשִׁשָּׁה קָנִים יֹצְאִים מִצִּדֶּיהָ שְׁלֹשָׁה ׀ קְנֵי
of stalks three ; sides its from out going stalks six And

מְנֹרָה מִצִּדָּהּ הָאֶחָד וּשְׁלֹשָׁה קְנֵי מְנֹרָה
lampstand the of stalks three and ,one the ,side its from lampstand the

19 מִצִּדָּהּ הַשֵּׁנִי׃ שְׁלֹשָׁה גְבִעִים מְשֻׁקָּדִים
almond-like calixes Three .second the ,side its from

בַּקָּנֶה הָאֶחָד כַּפְתֹּר וָפֶרַח וּשְׁלֹשָׁה
three and ; blossom and knob [with] ,[1]one [2]stalk the on

גְבִעִים מְשֻׁקָּדִים בַּקָּנֶה אֶחָד כַּפְתֹּר וָפָרַח
; blossom and knob [with] ,[1]one [2]stalk the on almond-like calixes

כֵּן לְשֵׁשֶׁת הַקָּנִים הַיֹּצְאִים מִן־הַמְּנֹרָה׃
.lampstand the from out going those ,stalks six the for so

20 וּבַמְּנֹרָה אַרְבָּעָה גְבִעִים מְשֻׁקָּדִים
,almond-like calixes four lampstand the on And

21 כַּפְתֹּרֶיהָ וּפְרָחֶיהָ׃ וְכַפְתֹּר תַּחַת שְׁנֵי
two under knob a And .blossoms its and knobs its [with]

הַקָּנִים מִמֶּנָּה וְכַפְתֹּר תַּחַת שְׁנֵי הַקָּנִים מִמֶּנָּה
;it of ,stalks two under knob a and ; it of ,stalks

וְכַפְתֹּר תַּחַת־שְׁנֵי הַקָּנִים מִמֶּנָּה [b] לְשֵׁשֶׁת הַקָּנִים
,stalks six the to ; it of ,stalks two under knob a and

22 הַיֹּצְאִים מִמֶּנָּה׃ [c] כַּפְתֹּרֵיהֶם וּקְנֹתָם מִמֶּנָּה
it of stalks their and knobs Their .it from out going those

הָיוּ כֻּלָּהּ מִקְשָׁה אַחַת זָהָב טָהוֹר׃
.[1]pure [2]gold ,one ,work chased it of all ,were

23 וַיַּעַשׂ אֶת־נֵרֹתֶיהָ שִׁבְעָה וּמַלְקָחֶיהָ וּמַחְתֹּתֶיהָ
,pans its and ,snuffers its and ; seven lamps its made he And

and the flagons thereof, to pour out withal, of pure gold.
17 And he made the candlestick of pure gold: of beaten work made he the candlestick, even its base, and its shaft; its cups, its knops, and its flowers, were of one piece with it: 18 and there were six branches going out of the sides thereof; three branches of the candlestick out of the one side thereof, and three branches of the candlestick out of the other side thereof: 19 three cups made like almond-blossoms in one branch, a knop and a flower; and three cups made like almond-blossoms in the other branch, a knop and a flower: so for the six branches going out of the candlestick. 20 And in the candlestick were four cups made like almond-blossoms, the knops thereof, and the flowers thereof: 21 and a knop under two branches of one piece with it, and a knop under two branches of one piece with it, and a knop under two branches of one piece with it, for the six branches going out of it. 22 Their knops and their branches were of one piece with it: the whole of it was

---

a G. omits.
b S. adds, *thus.*
c Sm., S. have, *from the lamp-stand,* מן המנרה; cf. 25: 35.

snuffdishes, *of*
pure gold. 24 *Of*
a talent of pure
gold made he it,
and all the ves-
sels thereof.

25 And he
made the in-
cense altar *of*
shittim wood:
the length of it
was a cubit,
and the breadth
of it a cubit; *it*
was foursquare;
and two cubits
was the height
of it; the horns
thereof were of
the same. 26
And he overlaid
it with pure
gold, *both* the
top of it, and
the sides thereof
round about,
and the horns
of it: also he
made unto it a
crown of gold
round about. 27
And he made
two rings of
gold for it un-
der the crown
thereof, by the
two corners of
it, upon the two
sides thereof, to
be places for the
staves to bear it
withal. 28 And
he made the
staves *of* shittim
wood, and over-
laid them with
gold. 29 And he
made the holy
anointing oil,
and the pure in-
cense of sweet
spices, accord-
ing to the work
of the apoth-
ecary.

24 זָהָב טָהוֹר׃ כִּכַּר[a] זָהָב טָהוֹר עָשָׂה אֹתָהּ
,it made he [1]pure [2]gold of talent a [Of] .[1]pure [2]gold

וְאֵת כָּל־כֵּלֶיהָ׃
.vessels its all and

25 וַיַּעַשׂ אֶת־מִזְבַּח הַקְּטֹרֶת עֲצֵי
of wood of pieces [of] ,incense of altar the made he And

שִׁטִּים אַמָּה אָרְכּוֹ וְאַמָּה רָחְבּוֹ רָבוּעַ
,four-sided ,width its cubit a and ,length its cubit a ;acacia

26 וְאַמָּתַיִם קֹמָתוֹ מִמֶּנּוּ הָיוּ קַרְנֹתָיו׃ וַיְצַף
overlaid he And .horns its were it of ;height its cubits two and

אֹתוֹ זָהָב טָהוֹר אֶת־גַּגּוֹ וְאֶת־קִירֹתָיו סָבִיב
,about round walls its and roof its ,[1]pure [2]gold [with] it

וְאֶת־קַרְנֹתָיו וַיַּעַשׂ לוֹ זֵר זָהָב סָבִיב׃
.about round gold of wreath a it for made he and ;horns its and

27 וּשְׁתֵּי טַבְּעֹת זָהָב עָשָׂה־לּוֹ מִתַּחַת
under from ,it for made he gold of rings two And

לְזֵרוֹ עַל שְׁתֵּי צַלְעֹתָיו עַל שְׁנֵי צִדָּיו
;sides [1]its [2]two upon ,corners [1]its [2]two upon ,wreath its (to)

28 לְבָתִּים לְבַדִּים לָשֵׂאת אֹתוֹ בָּהֶם׃ וַיַּעַשׂ
made he And .them by it carry to ,poles for houses for

אֶת־הַבַּדִּים עֲצֵי שִׁטִּים וַיְצַף אֹתָם זָהָב׃
.gold [with] them overlaid he and ;acacia of wood of pieces ,poles the

29 וַיַּעַשׂ אֶת־שֶׁמֶן הַמִּשְׁחָה קֹדֶשׁ וְאֶת־קְטֹרֶת
[3]of [2]incense the and ,[1]holy [4]anointing [3]of [2]oil the made he And

הַסַּמִּים טָהוֹר מַעֲשֵׂה רֹקֵחַ׃
.ointment of preparer a of work a ,[1]pure [4]fragrance

one beaten work
of pure gold. 23
And he made
the lamps there-
of, seven, and
the tongs there-
of, and the snuff-
dishes thereof,
of pure gold. 24
Of a talent of
pure gold made
he it, and all the
vessels thereof.

25 And he
made the altar
of incense of
acacia wood:
a cubit was the
length thereof,
and a cubit the
breadth thereof,
foursquare; and
two cubits was
the height there-
of; the horns
thereof were of
one piece with
it. 26 And he
overlaid it with
pure gold, the
top thereof, and
the sides thereof
round about,
and the horns of
it: and he made
unto it a crown
of gold round a-
bout. 27 And he
made for it two
golden rings un-
der the crown
thereof, upon
the two ribs
thereof, upon
the two sides of
it, for places for
staves to bear it
withal. 28 And
he made the
staves of acacia
wood, and over-
laid them with
gold. 29 And he
made the holy
anointing oil,
and the pure in-
cense of sweet
spices, after the
art of the per-
fumer.

38

AND he made
the altar of
burnt offering *of*
shittim wood:
five cubits *was*
the length there-
of, and five cu-
bits the breadth

1 וַיַּעַשׂ[b] אֶת־מִזְבַּח הָעֹלָה עֲצֵי
of wood of pieces ,offering burnt of altar the made he And

שִׁטִּים חָמֵשׁ אַמּוֹת אָרְכּוֹ וַחֲמֵשׁ־אַמּוֹת רָחְבּוֹ
,width its cubits five and ,length its cubits five ;acacia

And he made
the altar of burnt
offering of
acacia wood:
five cubits was
the length there-
of, and five cu-
bits the breadth

---

a G. omits vss. 24—28.

b Most of the verses in this chapter are abbreviated in G.

thereof; *it was* foursquare; and three cubits the height thereof. 2 And he made the horns thereof on the four corners of it; the horns thereof were of the same: and he overlaid it with brass. 3 And he made all the vessels of the altar, the pots, and the shovels, and the basons, *and* the fleshhooks, and the firepans: all the vessels thereof made he *of* brass. 4 And he made for the altar a brasen grate of network under the compass thereof beneath unto the midst of it. 5 And he cast four rings for the four ends of the grate of brass, *to be* places for the staves. 6 And he made the staves *of* shittim wood, and overlaid them with brass. 7 And he put the staves into the rings on the sides of the altar, to bear it withal; he made the altar hollow with boards.

8 And he made the laver *of* brass, and the foot of it *of* brass, of the lookingglasses of *the women* assembling, which assembled *at* the door of the tabernacle of the congregation.

9 And he made the court: on the south side southward the hangings of the court *were of*

רָבוּעַ וְשָׁלֹשׁ אַמּוֹת קֹמָתוֹ׃ וַיַּעַשׂ 2
,four-sided three and cubits .height its And he made
קַרְנֹתָיו עַל אַרְבַּע פִּנֹּתָיו מִמֶּנּוּ הָיוּ קַרְנֹתָיו
horns its upon [2]four ,corners [1]its of it were horns its;
וַיְצַף אֹתוֹ נְחֹשֶׁת׃ וַיַּעַשׂ אֶת־כָּל־כְּלֵי 3
and he overlaid it [with] bronze. And he made the all vessels of
הַמִּזְבֵּחַ אֶת־הַסִּירֹת וְאֶת־הַיָּעִים וְאֶת־הַמִּזְרָקֹת[a] אֶת־
the altar; the pots, and the shovels, and the sacrificial bowls,
הַמִּזְלָגֹת וְאֶת־הַמַּחְתֹּת כָּל־כֵּלָיו עָשָׂה נְחֹשֶׁת׃
the flesh-forks, and the pans; all its vessels he made bronze.
וַיַּעַשׂ לַמִּזְבֵּחַ מִכְבָּר מַעֲשֵׂה רֶשֶׁת נְחֹשֶׁת 4
And he made for the altar a grating, a [2]work [1]net of bronze;
תַּחַת כַּרְכֻּבּוֹ מִלְּמַטָּה עַד־חֶצְיוֹ׃ וַיִּצֹק[b] אַרְבַּע 5
under its ledge from (to) below, as far as its half. And he cast four
טַבָּעֹת בְּאַרְבַּע הַקְּצָוֹת לְמִכְבַּר הַנְּחֹשֶׁת בָּתִּים
rings in the four ends to the grating of bronze, houses
לַבַּדִּים׃ וַיַּעַשׂ אֶת־הַבַּדִּים עֲצֵי שִׁטִּים 6
for the poles. And he made the poles, pieces of wood of acacia;
וַיְצַף אֹתָם נְחֹשֶׁת׃ וַיָּבֵא אֶת־הַבַּדִּים 7
and he overlaid them [with] bronze. And he brought the poles
בַּטַּבָּעֹת עַל צַלְעֹת הַמִּזְבֵּחַ לָשֵׂאת אֹתוֹ בָּהֶם
into the rings, upon the sides of the altar, to carry it with them;
נְבוּב לֻחֹת עָשָׂה אֹתוֹ׃ וַיַּעַשׂ אֵת 8
hollow [of] [with] tablets he made it. And he made
הַכִּיּוֹר נְחֹשֶׁת וְאֵת כַּנּוֹ נְחֹשֶׁת בְּמַרְאֹת[c]
the laver, bronze, and its base, bronze, of the mirrors of
הַצֹּבְאֹת אֲשֶׁר צָבְאוּ פֶּתַח אֹהֶל
the serving women who did service [at] the door of the tent of
מוֹעֵד׃
meeting.
וַיַּעַשׂ אֶת־הֶחָצֵר לִפְאַת נֶגֶב 9
And he made the court; for the direction of the south
תֵּימָנָה קַלְעֵי הֶחָצֵר שֵׁשׁ מָשְׁזָר
southward, the hangings of the court [were] byssus twisted,

thereof, foursquare; and three cubits the height thereof. 2 And he made the horns thereof upon the four corners of it; the horns thereof were of one piece with it: and he overlaid it with brass. 3 And he made all the vessels of the altar, the pots, and the shovels, and the basons, the fleshhooks, and the firepans: all the vessels thereof made he of brass. 4 And he made for the altar a grating of network of brass, under the ledge round it beneath, reaching halfway up. 5 And he cast four rings for the four ends of the grating of brass, to be places for the staves. 6 And he made the staves of acacia wood, and overlaid them with brass. 7 And he put the staves into the rings on the sides of the altar, to bear it withal; he made it hollow with planks.

8 And he made the laver of brass, and the base thereof of brass, of the mirrors of the serving women which served at the door of the tent of meeting.

9 And he made the court: for the south side southward the hangings of the court were of fine twined

---

a S. adds, *and the strainers.*
b S. adds, *for it.*
c For ב, S. has, *among.*

fine twined linen, an hundred cubits: 10 Their pillars *were* twenty, and their brazen sockets twenty; the hooks of the pillars and their fillets *were of* silver. 11 And for the north side *the hangings were* an hundred cubits, their pillars *were* twenty, and their sockets of brass twenty; the hooks of the pillars and their fillets *of* silver. 12 And for the west side *were* hangings of fifty cubits, their pillars ten, and their sockets ten; the hooks of the pillars and their fillets *of* silver. 13 And for the east side eastward fifty cubits. 14 The hangings of the one side *of the gate were* fifteen cubits; their pillars three, and their sockets three. 15 And for the other side of the court gate, on this hand and that hand, *were* hangings of fifteen cubits; their pillars three, and their sockets three. 16 All the hangings of the court round about *were* of fine twined linen. 17 And the sockets for the pillars *were of* brass; the hooks of the pillars and their fillets *of* silver; and the overlaying of their chapiters *of* silver; and all the pillars of

10 מֵאָה בָּאַמָּה׃ עַמּוּדֵיהֶם עֶשְׂרִים וְאַדְנֵיהֶם
sockets their and ,twenty pillars Their .cubit the by hundred a

עֶשְׂרִים נְחֹשֶׁת[a] וָוֵי הָעַמּוּדִים וַחֲשֻׁקֵיהֶם
,bands their and pillars the of nails the ;bronze ,twenty

11 כָּסֶף׃[a] וְלִפְאַת צָפוֹן מֵאָה בָאַמָּה[b]
;cubit the by hundred a ,north the of direction the for And .silver

עַמּוּדֵיהֶם עֶשְׂרִים וְאַדְנֵיהֶם עֶשְׂרִים נְחֹשֶׁת
;bronze ,twenty sockets their and twenty pillars their

וָוֵי הָעַמּוּדִים וַחֲשׁוּקֵיהֶם כָּסֶף׃
.silver ,bands their and pillars the of nails the

12 וְלִפְאַת־יָם קְלָעִים חֲמִשִּׁים בָּאַמָּה
;cubit the by fifty hangings ,west the of direction the for And

עַמּוּדֵיהֶם עֲשָׂרָה וְאַדְנֵיהֶם עֲשָׂרָה וָוֵי[c]
of nails the ;ten sockets their and ,ten pillars their

13 הָעַמֻּדִים וַחֲשׁוּקֵיהֶם כָּסֶף׃[c] וְלִפְאַת קֵדְמָה
east the of direction the for And .silver ,bands their and pillars the

14 מִזְרָחָה חֲמִשִּׁים אַמָּה׃ קְלָעִים חֲמֵשׁ־עֶשְׂרֵה אַמָּה
cubits fifteen ,Hangings .cubits fifty ,eastward

אֶל־הַכָּתֵף עַמּוּדֵיהֶם[d] שְׁלֹשָׁה וְאַדְנֵיהֶם שְׁלֹשָׁה[d]׃
.three sockets their and ,three pillars their ;side the unto

15 וְלַכָּתֵף הַשֵּׁנִית מִזֶּה וּמִזֶּה לְשַׁעַר הֶחָצֵר
,court the of gate the to there and here ,[1]second [2]side the for And

קְלָעִים חֲמֵשׁ עֶשְׂרֵה אַמָּה[e] עַמֻּדֵיהֶם שְׁלֹשָׁה
,three pillars their ;cubits ten [and] five hangings

16 וְאַדְנֵיהֶם שְׁלֹשָׁה׃ כָּל־קַלְעֵי הֶחָצֵר סָבִיב
about round court the of hangings the All .three sockets their and

17 שֵׁשׁ מָשְׁזָר׃ וְהָאֲדָנִים לָעַמֻּדִים נְחֹשֶׁת
,bronze pillars the to sockets the And .twisted byssus [were]

וָוֵי הָעַמּוּדִים[f] וַחֲשׁוּקֵיהֶם[f] כֶּסֶף
,silver ,bands their and ,pillars the of nails the

וְצִפּוּי רָאשֵׁיהֶם כָּסֶף וְהֵם מְחֻשָּׁקִים
united being they (and) ;silver ,tops their of overlaying the and

linen, an hundred cubits: 10 their pillars were twenty, and their sockets twenty, of brass; the hooks of the pillars and their fillets were of silver. 11 And for the north side an hundred cubits, their pillars twenty, and their sockets twenty, of brass; the hooks of the pillars and their fillets of silver. 12 And for the west side were hangings of fifty cubits, their pillars ten, and their sockets ten; the hooks of the pillars and their fillets of silver. 13 And for the east side eastward fifty cubits. 14 The hangings for the one side *of the gate* were fifteen cubits; their pillars three, and their sockets three; 15 and so for the other side: on this hand and that hand by the gate of the court were hangings of fifteen cubits; their pillars three, and their sockets three. 16 All the hangings of the court round about were of fine twined linen. 17 And the sockets for the pillars were of brass; the hooks of the pillars and their fillets of silver; and the overlaying of their chapiters of silver; and all the pillars of the

---

a G. omits.
b G. has, *by a hundred*, במאה.
c G. omits.
d G. omits.
e S. adds, *to the side.*
f Sm., G. omit.

the court *were*
filleted with
silver. 18 And
the hanging for
the gate of the
court *was*
needlework, *of*
blue, and pur-
ple, and scarlet,
and fine twined
linen: and
twenty cubits
was the length,
and the height
in the breadth
was five cubits,
answerable to
the hangings of
the court. 19
And their pillars
were four, and
their sockets *of*
brass four; their
hooks *of* silver,
and the overlay-
ing of their
chapiters and
their fillets *of*
silver. 20 And
all the pins of
the tabernacle,
and of the court
round about,
were of brass.

18 כֶּסֶף כֹּל עַמֻּדֵי הֶחָצֵר׃ וּמָסַךְ שַׁעַר
of gate the of screen the And .court the of pillars the all ,silver [with]

הֶחָצֵר מַעֲשֵׂה רֹקֵם תְּכֵלֶת וְאַרְגָּמָן
,purple and ,blue ,embroiderer an of work a [was] court the

וְתוֹלַעַת שָׁנִי וְשֵׁשׁ מָשְׁזָר וְעֶשְׂרִים אַמָּה
cubits twenty and ; twisted byssus and ,crimson (of worm) and

אֹרֶךְ וְקוֹמָה בְרֹחַב חָמֵשׁ אַמּוֹת לְעֻמַּת
near ,cubits five width the with height the and ,length [in]

19 קַלְעֵי הֶחָצֵר׃ וְעַמֻּדֵיהֶם אַרְבָּעָה וְאַדְנֵיהֶם
sockets their and ,four pillars their And .court the of hangings the

אַרְבָּעָה נְחֹשֶׁת וָוֵיהֶם כֶּסֶף וְצִפּוּי
of overlaying the and ,silver nails their ; bronze ,four

20 רָאשֵׁיהֶם וַחֲשֻׁקֵיהֶם כָּסֶף׃ וְכָל־הַיְתֵדֹת לַמִּשְׁכָּן[a]
habitation the for pins the all And .silver ,bands their and tops their

וְלֶחָצֵר[b] סָבִיב נְחֹשֶׁת׃
.bronze ,about round court the for and

court were
filleted with
silver. 18 And
the screen for
the gate of the
court was the
work of the
embroiderer, of
blue, and pur-
ple, and scarlet,
and fine twined
linen: and
twenty cubits
was the length,
and the height
in the breadth
was five cubits,
answerable to
the hangings of
the court. 19
And their pillars
were four, and
their sockets
four, of brass;
their hooks of
silver, and the
overlaying of
their chapiters
and their fillets
of silver. 20 And
all the pins of
the tabernacle,
and of the court
round about,
were of brass.

21 This is the
sum of the taber-
nacle, *even* of
the tabernacle of
testimony, as it
was counted, ac-
cording to the
commandment
of Moses, *for*
the service of
the Levites, by
the hand of
Ithamar, son to
Aaron the
priest. 22 And
Bezaleel the son
of Uri, the son
of Hur, of the
tribe of Judah,
made all that
the LORD com-
manded Moses.
23 And with him
was Aholiab,
son of Ahis-
amach, of the
tribe of Dan, an
engraver, and a
cunning work-
man, and an
embroiderer in

21 אֵלֶּה פְקוּדֵי הַמִּשְׁכָּן[c] מִשְׁכַּן
of habitation the ,habitation the of things mustered the [are] These

הָעֵדֻת אֲשֶׁר פֻּקַּד עַל־פִּי מֹשֶׁה
; Moses of mouth the upon mustered was which ,testimony

[d]עֲבֹדַת הַלְוִיִּם בְּיַד אִיתָמָר בֶּן־אַהֲרֹן
Aaron of son the Ithamar of hand the by Levites the of service the

22 הַכֹּהֵן׃ וּבְצַלְאֵל בֶּן־אוּרִי בֶן־חוּר[e] לְמַטֵּה
of tribe the to ,Hur of son the Uri of son the Bezalel And .priest the

יְהוּדָה עָשָׂה אֵת כָּל־אֲשֶׁר־צִוָּה יְהוָה אֶת־מֹשֶׁה׃
.Moses Jehovah commanded which all made ,Judah

23 וְאִתּוֹ אָהֳלִיאָב בֶּן־אֲחִיסָמָךְ לְמַטֵּה־דָן
,Dan of tribe the to ,Ahisamach of son the Oholiab him with And

חָרָשׁ וְחֹשֵׁב וְרֹקֵם בַּתְּכֵלֶת
,blue in embroiderer an and ,workman skilful a and ,smith a

21 This is the
sum of *the
things for* the
tabernacle, even
the tabernacle
of the testi-
mony, as they
were counted,
according to the
commandment
of Moses, for
the service of the
Levites, by the
hand of Itha-
mar, the son
of Aaron the
priest. 22 And
Bezalel the son
of Uri, the son
of Hur, of the
tribe of Judah,
made all that
the LORD com-
manded Moses.
23 And with him
was Oholiab,
the son of Ahis-
amach, of the
tribe of Dan, an
engraver, and a
cunning work-
man, and an em-
broiderer in

---

a G. omits.
b G. omits ו.
c G., V. omit.
d S. adds, *and*, ו.
e G. omits.

blue, and in pur-
ple, and in scar-
let, and fine
linen.
24 All the
gold that was
occupied for the
work in all the
work of the holy
place, even the
gold of the
offering, was
twenty and nine
talents, and
seven hundred
and thirty shek-
els, after the
shekel of the
sanctuary. 25
And the silver
of them that
were numbered
of the congrega-
tion *was* an hun-
dred talents, and
a thousand sev-
en hundred and
threescore and
fifteen shekels,
after the shekel
of the sanctuary:
26 A bekah for
every man, *that
is*, half a shekel,
after the shekel
of the sanctuary,
for every one
that went to be
numbered, from
twenty years old
and upward, for
six hundred
thousand and
three thousand
and five hundred
and fifty *men*.
27 And of the
hundred talents
of silver were
cast the sockets
of the sanctuary,
and the sockets
of the vail; an
hundred sockets
of the hundred
talents, a talent
for a socket. 28
And of the thou-
sand seven hun-
dred seventy
and five *shekels*
he made hooks
for the pillars,
and overlaid
their chapiters,
and filleted
them. 29 And
the brass of the

וּבָאַרְגָּמָן וּבְתוֹלַעַת הַשָּׁנִי וּבַשֵּׁשׁ׃
,purple in and (of worm) in and ,crimson .byssus in and

24 כָּל־הַזָּהָב הֶעָשׂוּי לַמְּלָאכָה בְּכֹל מְלֶאכֶת
gold the All used ,work the for all in of work the

הַקֹּדֶשׁ וַיְהִי זְהַב הַתְּנוּפָה תֵּשַׁע
; sanctuary the was (and) of gold the offering wave the nine

וְעֶשְׂרִים כִּכָּר וּשְׁבַע מֵאוֹת וּשְׁלֹשִׁים שֶׁקֶל
twenty and ,talents seven and hundred thirty and ,shekels

25 בְּשֶׁקֶל הַקֹּדֶשׁ׃ וְכֶסֶף פְּקוּדֵי
of shekel the by .sanctuary the And the silver of of mustered the

הָעֵדָה מְאַת כִּכָּר וְאֶלֶף וּשְׁבַע מֵאוֹת
congregation the ,hundred a ,talents thousand a and seven and hundred

26 וַחֲמִשָּׁה[a] וְשִׁבְעִים שֶׁקֶל בְּשֶׁקֶל[b] הַקֹּדֶשׁ[b]׃ בֶּקַע
five and seventy and ,shekels of shekel the by ;sanctuary the beka a

לַגֻּלְגֹּלֶת מַחֲצִית הַשֶּׁקֶל בְּשֶׁקֶל הַקֹּדֶשׁ
,head a for of half ,shekel a of shekel the by ,sanctuary the

לְכֹל[c] הָעֹבֵר עַל־הַפְּקֻדִים מִבֶּן עֶשְׂרִים
one every for over passing ,mustered the unto of son a from twenty

שָׁנָה וָמַעְלָה [d]לְשֵׁשׁ־מֵאוֹת אֶלֶף וּשְׁלֹשֶׁת
years ,upward and hundred six for ,thousand three and

27 אֲלָפִים וַחֲמֵשׁ מֵאוֹת וַחֲמִשִּׁים׃ וַיְהִי מְאַת
,thousand five and hundred .fifty and were And hundred the

כִּכַּר הַכֶּסֶף לָצֶקֶת אֵת אַדְנֵי הַקֹּדֶשׁ וְאֵת
of talents silver casting for of sockets the ,sanctuary the and

אַדְנֵי הַפָּרֹכֶת מְאַת אֲדָנִים לִמְאַת[e]
of sockets the ; veil the hundred a sockets hundred the for

28 הַכִּכָּר כִּכָּר לָאָדֶן׃ וְאֶת־הָאֶלֶף וּשְׁבַע הַמֵּאוֹת
,talents talent a for socket a. thousand the And seven and hundred

וַחֲמִשָּׁה וְשִׁבְעִים עָשָׂה וָוִים לָעַמּוּדִים
five and ,[shekels] seventy and made he nails ;pillars the for

29 וְצִפָּה רָאשֵׁיהֶם וְחִשַּׁק אֹתָם׃[f] וּנְחֹשֶׁת[g]
overlaid he and ,tops their united and .them of bronze the And

blue, and in
purple, and in
scarlet, and fine
linen.
24 All the
gold that was
used for the
work in all the
work of the
sanctuary, even
the gold of the
offering, was
twenty and nine
talents, and sev-
en hundred and
thirty shekels,
after the shekel
of the sanctuary.
25 And the
silver of them
that were num-
bered of the con-
gregation was
an hundred tal-
ents, and a
thousand seven
hundred and
threescore and
fifteen shekels,
after the shekel
of the sanctuary:
26 a beka a head,
that is, half a
shekel, after the
shekel of the
sanctuary, for
every one that
passed over to
them that were
numbered, from
twenty years old
and upward, for
six hundred
thousand and
three thousand
and five hun-
dred and fifty
men. 27 And
the hundred tal-
ents of silver
were for casting
the sockets of
the sanctuary,
and the sockets of
the veil; an hun-
dred sockets for
the hundred tal-
ents, a talent
for a socket. 28
And of the thou-
sand seven hun-
dred seventy
and five *shekels*
he made hooks
for the pillars,
and overlaid
their chapiters,
and made fillets

---

a S. omits.
b Sm., G., V. omit.
c G., S. omit ל.
d S. omits ל.
e For ל, S. has, *from*.
f S., V. add, *silver;* so essentially G.
g S. has, *all the bronze*.

offering *was*
seventy talents,
and two thou-
sand and four
hundred shek-
els. 30 and there-
with he made
the sockets to the
door of the tab-
ernacle of the
congregation,
and the brasen
altar, and the
brasen grate for
it, and all the
vessels of the
altar, 31 And the
sockets of the
court round
about, and the
sockets of the
court gate, and
all the pins of
the tabernacle,
and all the pins
of the court
round about.

הַתְּנוּפָה שִׁבְעִים כִּכָּר וְאַלְפַּיִם
thousand two and ,talents seventy [was] offering wave the

30 וְאַרְבַּע־מֵאוֹת שָׁקֶל׃ וַיַּעַשׂ בָּהּ אֶת־אַדְנֵי
of sockets the it with made he And .shekels hundred four and

פֶּתַח אֹהֶל מוֹעֵד וְאֵת מִזְבַּח הַנְּחֹשֶׁת
,bronze of altar the and ,meeting of tent the of door the

וְאֶת־מִכְבַּר הַנְּחֹשֶׁת אֲשֶׁר־לוֹ וְאֵת כָּל־כְּלֵי
of vessels the all and ; it to [was] which bronze of grating the and

31 הַמִּזְבֵּחַ׃ וְאֶת־אַדְנֵי הֶחָצֵר סָבִיב וְאֶת־אַדְנֵי
of sockets the and ,about round court the of sockets the and ; altar the

שַׁעַר הֶחָצֵר וְאֵת כָּל־יִתְדֹת הַמִּשְׁכָּן
,habitation the of pins the all and ; court the of gate the

וְאֶת־כָּל־יִתְדֹת הֶחָצֵר סָבִיב׃
.about round court the of pins the all and

for them. 29
And the brass of
the offering was
seventy talents,
and two thou-
sand and four
hundred shekels.
30 And therewith
he made the
sockets to the
door of the tent
of meeting, and
the brasen altar,
and the brasen
grating for it,
and all the ves-
sels of the altar,
31 and the sock-
ets of the court
round about,
and the sockets
of the gate of the
court, and all
the pins of the
tabernacle, and
all the pins of
the court round
about.

39

AND of the
blue, and pur-
ple, and scarlet,
they made
cloths of serv-
ice, to do serv-
ice in the holy
place, and made
the holy gar-
ments for Aar-
on; as the LORD
commanded Mo-
ses.

1 וּמִן־הַתְּכֵלֶת וְהָאַרְגָּמָן וְתוֹלַעַת הַשָּׁנִי
,crimson (of worm) the and ,purple the and ,blue the from And

עָשׂוּ בִגְדֵי־שְׂרָד לְשָׁרֵת בַּקֹּדֶשׁ
; place holy the in ministering for ,weaving of garments made they

וַיַּעֲשׂוּ אֶת־בִּגְדֵי הַקֹּדֶשׁ אֲשֶׁר לְאַהֲרֹן[a]
,Aaron to [were] which holiness of garments the made they and

2 כַּאֲשֶׁר צִוָּה יְהוָה אֶת־מֹשֶׁה׃ וַיַּעַשׂ אֶת־הָאֵפֹד
; ephod the made he And .Moses Jehovah commanded as

זָהָב תְּכֵלֶת וְאַרְגָּמָן וְתוֹלַעַת שָׁנִי וְשֵׁשׁ
byssus and ,crimson (of worm) and ,purple and ,blue ,gold [of]

3 מָשְׁזָר׃ וַיְרַקְּעוּ אֶת־פַּחֵי הַזָּהָב וְקִצֵּץ פְּתִילִם
,threads cut and ,gold of plates beat they And .twisted

לַעֲשׂוֹת בְּתוֹךְ הַתְּכֵלֶת וּבְתוֹךְ הָאַרְגָּמָן
,purple the of midst the in and ,blue the of midst the in work to

וּבְתוֹךְ תּוֹלַעַת הַשָּׁנִי[b] וּבְתוֹךְ
of midst the in and ,crimson (of worm) the of midst the in and

And of the
blue, and pur-
ple, and scarlet,
they made finely
wrought gar-
ments, for min-
istering in the
holy place, and
made the holy
garments for
Aaron; as the
LORD com-
manded Moses.

2 And he
made the ephod
of gold, blue,
and purple, and
scarlet, and fine
twined linen. 3
And they did
beat the gold in-
to thin plates,
and cut *it into*
wires, to work *it*
in the blue, and
in the purple,
and in the scar-
let, and in the

2 And he
made the ephod
of gold, blue,
and purple, and
scarlet, and fine
twined linen. 3
And they did
beat the gold in-
to thin plates,
and cut it into
wires, to work it
in the blue, and
in the purple,
and in the scar-
let, and in the

a G. adds, *the priest.*

b G. adds, *spun.*

fine linen, *with* cunning work. 4 They made shoulderpieces for it, to couple *it* together: by the two edges was it coupled together. 5 And the curious girdle of his ephod, that *was* upon it, *was* of the same, according to the work thereof; *of* gold, blue, and purple, and scarlet, and fine twined linen; as the LORD commanded Moses.

6 And they wrought onyx stones inclosed in ouches of gold, graven, as signets are graven, with the names of the children of Israel. 7 And he put them on the shoulders of the ephod, *that they should be* stones for a memorial to the children of Israel; as the LORD commanded Moses.

8 And he made the breastplate *of* cunning work, like the work of the ephod; *of* gold, blue, and purple, and scarlet, and fine twined linen. 9 It was foursquare; they made the breastplate double: a span *was* the length thereof, and a span the breadth thereof, *being* doubled. 10 And they set in it four rows of stones: *the first* row *was* a sardius, a topaz, and a carbuncle: this *was* the first row. 11 And the

4 הַשֵּׁשׁ[a] מַעֲשֵׂה חֹשֵׁב[b]׃ כְּתֵפֹת עָשׂוּ־לוֹ
,it to made they Shoulderpieces .workman skilful a of work a ,byssus the

5 חֹבְרֹת עַל־שְׁנֵי קְצוֹוֹתָו חֻבָּר׃ וְחֵשֶׁב
of band the And .joined was it ends ¹its ²two upon ;joining

אֲפֻדָּתוֹ[c] אֲשֶׁר עָלָיו מִמֶּנּוּ הוּא כְּמַעֲשֵׂהוּ
,work its like ,[was] it it of ,it upon [was] which fastening its

זָהָב תְּכֵלֶת וְאַרְגָּמָן וְתוֹלַעַת שָׁנִי[d] וְשֵׁשׁ
byssus and ,crimson (of worm) and ,purple and ,blue ,gold

6 מָשְׁזָר כַּאֲשֶׁר צִוָּה יְהוָה אֶת־מֹשֶׁה׃ וַיַּעֲשׂוּ[e]
made they And .Moses Jehovah commanded as ,twisted

אֶת־אַבְנֵי הַשֹּׁהַם מֻסַבֹּת מִשְׁבְּצֹת זָהָב מְפֻתָּחֹת
engraved ,gold of work plaited [in] set ,onyx of stones the

פִּתּוּחֵי חוֹתָם עַל־שְׁמוֹת בְּנֵי
of children the of names the to according ,signet a of engravings the [with]

7 יִשְׂרָאֵל׃ וַיָּשֶׂם אֹתָם עַל כִּתְפֹת
of shoulderpieces the upon them put he And .Israel

הָאֵפֹד אַבְנֵי זִכָּרוֹן לִבְנֵי יִשְׂרָאֵל
; Israel of children the for remembrance of stones ,ephod the

כַּאֲשֶׁר צִוָּה יְהוָה אֶת־מֹשֶׁה׃
.Moses Jehovah commanded as

8 וַיַּעַשׂ אֶת־הַחֹשֶׁן מַעֲשֵׂה חֹשֵׁב
,workman skilful a of work a ,breastplate the made he And

כְּמַעֲשֵׂה אֵפֹד זָהָב תְּכֵלֶת וְאַרְגָּמָן וְתוֹלַעַת
(of worm) and ,purple and ,blue ,gold ;ephod the of work the like

9 שְׁנִי[f] וְשֵׁשׁ מָשְׁזָר׃ רָבוּעַ הָיָה כָּפוּל
double taken ;was it Four-sided .twisted byssus and ,crimson

עָשׂוּ אֶת־הַחֹשֶׁן[g] זֶרֶת אָרְכּוֹ וְזֶרֶת רָחְבּוֹ
,width its span a and ,length its span a ;breastplate the made they

10 כָּפוּל[h]׃ וַיְמַלְאוּ־בוֹ אַרְבָּעָה טוּרֵי אָבֶן
; stones of rows four it in filled they And .double taken

טוּר[i] אֹדֶם פִּטְדָה וּבָרֶקֶת הַטּוּר הָאֶחָד׃
.¹one ²row the ,smaragd and ,topaz ,cornelian of row a

fine linen, the work of the cunning workman. 4 They made shoulderpieces for it, joined together: at the two ends was it joined together. 5 And the cunningly woven band, that was upon it, to gird it on withal, was of the same piece *and* like the work thereof; of gold, of blue, and purple, and scarlet, and fine twined linen; as the LORD commanded Moses.

6 And they wrought the onyx stones, inclosed in ouches of gold, graven with the engravings of a signet, according to the names of the children of Israel. 7 And he put them on the shoulderpieces of the ephod, to be stones of memorial for the children of Israel; as the LORD commanded Moses.

8 And he made the breastplate, the work of the cunning workman, like the work of the ephod; of gold, of blue, and purple, and scarlet, and fine twined linen. 9 It was foursquare; they made the breastplate double: a span was the length thereof, and a span the breadth thereof, being double. 10 And they set in it four rows of stones: a row of sardius, topaz, and car-

---

a G. adds, *twisted.*
b G. adds, *they made it.*
c S. has, *the ephod.*
d G. adds, *spun.*
e G., V. add, *two.*
f G. adds, *spun.*
g S. has הכפרת; so in vss. 15, 16, 17, 19, 21.
h Sm., V. omit.
i S., T., V. add, *first;* G. adds, *of stones.*

second row, an
emerald, a sap-
phire, and a dia-
mond. 12 And
the third row,
a ligure, an
agate, and an
amethyst. 13
And the fourth
row, a beryl, an
onyx, and a jas-
per: *they were*
inclosed in
ouches of gold
in their inclos-
ings. 14 And the
stones *were* ac-
cording to the
names of the
children of Isra-
el, twelve, ac-
cording to their
names, *like* the
engravings of a
signet, every
one with his
name, according
to the twelve
tribes. 15 And
they made upon
the breastplate
chains at the
ends, *of* wreath-
en work *of* pure
gold. 16 And
they made two
ouches *of* gold,
and two gold
rings, and put
the two rings in
the two ends of
the breastplate.
17 And they put
the two wreath-
en chains of
gold in the two
rings on the
ends of the
breastplate. 18
And the two
ends of the two
wreathen chains
they fastened in
the two ouches,
and put them on
the shoulder-
pieces of the
ephod, before
it. 19 And they
made two rings
of gold, and put
them on the two
ends of the
breastplate, up-
on the border of
it, which *was* on
the side of the
ephod inward.
20 And they
made two *other*

11 וְהַטּוּר הַשֵּׁנִי נֹפֶךְ סַפִּיר וְיָהֲלֹם׃
.jasper and ,sapphire ,carbuncle ,[1]second [2]row the And

12 וְהַטּוּר הַשְּׁלִישִׁי לֶשֶׁם שְׁבוֹ וְאַחְלָמָה׃
.amethyst and ,agate ,amber ,[1]third [2]row the And

13 וְהַטּוּר הָרְבִיעִי תַּרְשִׁישׁ שֹׁהַם וְיָשְׁפֵה מֽוּסַבֹּת
[in] set ; beryl and ,onyx ,chrysolite ,[1]fourth [2]row the And

14 מִשְׁבְּצֹת זָהָב בְּמִלֻּאֹתָם[a]׃ וְהָאֲבָנִים
,stones the And .settings their in gold of work plaited

עַל־שְׁמֹת בְּנֵי־יִשְׂרָאֵל הֵנָּה שְׁתֵּים
two ,they [were] Israel of children the of names the to according

עֶשְׂרֵה עַל־שְׁמֹתָם פִּתּוּחֵי חֹתָם אִישׁ
each ,signet a of engravings the ; names their to according ten [and]

15 עַל־שְׁמוֹ לִשְׁנֵים עָשָׂר שָׁבֶט׃ וַיַּעֲשׂוּ
made they And .tribes ten [and] two the for ,name his to according

עַל־הַחֹשֶׁן שַׁרְשְׁרֹת גַּבְלֻת מַעֲשֵׂה עֲבֹת זָהָב
[2]gold ,cords of work a ,ropes of chains breastplate the upon

16 טָהוֹר׃ וַיַּעֲשׂוּ שְׁתֵּי מִשְׁבְּצֹת זָהָב וּשְׁתֵּי
two and ,gold of plaitings two made they And .[1]pure

טַבְּעֹת זָהָב וַיִּתְּנוּ אֶת־שְׁתֵּי הַטַּבָּעֹת[b] עַל־שְׁנֵי
two the upon rings two the put they and ;gold of rings

17 קְצוֹת הַחֹשֶׁן׃ וַיִּתְּנוּ שְׁתֵּי הָעֲבֹתֹת הַזָּהָב
gold of cords two the put they And .breastplate the of ends

18 עַל־שְׁתֵּי הַטַּבָּעֹת עַל־קְצוֹת הַחֹשֶׁן׃ וְאֵת שְׁתֵּי
two the And .breastplate the of ends the upon ,rings two the upon

קְצוֹת שְׁתֵּי הָעֲבֹתֹת נָתְנוּ עַל־שְׁתֵּי הַמִּשְׁבְּצֹת
; settings two the upon put they cords two the of ends

וַיִּתְּנֻם עַל־כִּתְפֹת[c] הָאֵפֹד אֶל־מוּל
before (unto) ,ephod the of shoulderpieces the upon them put they and

19 פָּנָיו׃ וַיַּעֲשׂוּ שְׁתֵּי טַבְּעֹת זָהָב וַיָּשִׂימוּ
put they and ,gold of rings two made they and .face its

עַל־שְׁנֵי קְצוֹת[d] הַחֹשֶׁן עַל־שְׂפָתוֹ אֲשֶׁר
which ,lip its upon ; breastplate the of ends two the upon

20 אֶל־עֵבֶר הָאֵפֹד בָּיְתָה׃ וַיַּעֲשׂוּ שְׁתֵּי
two made they And .inward ephod the against over (unto) [was]

buncle was the
first row. 11
And the second
row, an emer-
ald, a sapphire,
and a diamond.
12 And the third
row, a jacinth,
an agate, and
an amethyst. 13
And the fourth
row, a beryl, an
onyx, and a jas-
per: they were
inclosed in
ouches of gold
in their settings.
14 And the
stones were ac-
cording to the
names of the
children of Isra-
el, twelve, ac-
cording to their
names; like the
engravings of a
signet, every one
according to his
name, for the
twelve tribes. 15
And they made
upon the breast-
plate chains like
cords, of wreath-
en work of
pure gold. 16
And they made
two ouches of
gold, and two
gold rings; and
put the two
rings on the two
ends of the
breastplate. 17
And they put
the two wreath-
en chains of
gold on the two
rings at the ends
of the breast-
plate. 18 And
the *other* two
ends of the two
wreathen chains
they put on the
two ouches, and
put them on the
shoulderpieces
of the ephod, in
the forepart
thereof. 19 And
they made two
rings of gold,
and put them
upon the two
ends of the
breastplate, up-
on the edge
thereof, which
was toward the
side of the eph-

a G. has, *and bound together with silver.*
b G. adds, *of gold.*
c S. has, *upon the two shoulder-pieces.*
d G. has, *the projections upon the edge of.*

golden rings,
and put them on
the two sides of
the ephod underneath,
toward the forepart
of it, over
against the *other*
coupling thereof,
above the
curious girdle
of the ephod. 21
And they did
bind the breastplate
by his
rings unto the
rings of the ephod
with a lace
of blue, that it
might be above
the curious
girdle of the ephod,
and that
the breastplate
might not be
loosed from the
ephod; as the
LORD commanded
Moses.

22 And he
made the robe
of the ephod *of*
woven work, all
of blue. 23 And
there was an hole
in the midst of
the robe, as the
hole of an habergeon,
with a
band round about
the hole,
that it should
not rend. 24
And they made
upon the hems
of the robe
pomegranates *of*
blue, and purple,
and scarlet,
and twined
linen. 25 And
they made bells
of pure gold, and
put the bells between
the pomegranates
upon
the hem of the
robe, round about
between
the pomegranates;
26 A bell
and a pomegranate,
a bell and
a pomegranate,
round about

טַבְּעֹת זָהָב וַיִּתְּנֻם עַל־שְׁתֵּי כִתְפֹת
of shoulderpieces two the upon them put they and ,gold of rings

הָאֵפֹד מִלְּמַטָּה מִמּוּל פָּנָיו לְעֻמַּת מַחְבַּרְתּוֹ
; joining its near face its before from ,below (to) from ephod the

21 מִמַּעַל לְחֵשֶׁב הָאֵפֹד׃ וַיִּרְכְּסוּ
fastened they And .ephod the of band the to above from

אֶת־הַחֹשֶׁן מִטַּבְּעֹתוֹ אֶל־טַבְּעֹת הָאֵפֹד
ephod the of rings the unto rings its from breastplate the

בִּפְתִיל תְּכֵלֶת לִהְיֹת עַל־חֵשֶׁב הָאֵפֹד
; ephod the of band the above be to ,blue of ribbon a with

וְלֹא־יִזַּח הַחֹשֶׁן מֵעַל הָאֵפֹד
; ephod the upon from breastplate the itself move not might and

כַּאֲשֶׁר צִוָּה יְהוָה אֶת־מֹשֶׁה׃
.Moses Jehovah commanded as

22 וַיַּעַשׂ אֶת־מְעִיל הָאֵפֹד מַעֲשֵׂה אֹרֵג
,weaver a of work a ,ephod the of robe the made he And

23 כְּלִיל תְּכֵלֶת׃ וּפִי־הַמְּעִיל בְּתוֹכוֹ
,midst its in [was] robe the of mouth the And .blue entirely

כְּפִי[a] תַחְרָא שָׂפָה לְפִיו סָבִיב
,about round mouth its to lip a ; mail of coat a of mouth the like

24 לֹא יִקָּרֵעַ׃ וַיַּעֲשׂוּ עַל־שׁוּלֵי
of hem the upon made they And .rent be [2]might [1]it [3]not [that]

הַמְּעִיל[b] רִמּוֹנֵי תְּכֵלֶת וְאַרְגָּמָן וְתוֹלַעַת שָׁנִי[c]
,crimson (of worm) and ,purple and ,blue of pomegranates robe the

25 מָשְׁזָר׃ וַיַּעֲשׂוּ פַעֲמֹנֵי זָהָב טָהוֹר[d]
; [1]pure [2]gold of bells made they And .twisted [byssus and]

וַיִּתְּנוּ אֶת־הַפַּעֲמֹנִים בְּתוֹךְ הָרִמֹּנִים
,pomegranates the of midst the in bells the put they and

עַל־שׁוּלֵי הַמְּעִיל סָבִיב בְּתוֹךְ[e]
of midst the in ,about round robe the of hem the upon

26 הָרִמֹּנִים[e]׃ פַּעֲמֹן[f] וְרִמֹּן פַּעֲמֹן[g]
bell a ,pomegranate a and bell a ; pomegranates the

od inward. 20
And they made
two rings of
gold, and put
them on the two
shoulderpieces
of the ephod underneath,
in the
forepart thereof,
close by the
coupling thereof,
above the
cunningly woven
band of the
ephod. 21 And
they did bind
the breastplate
by the rings
thereof unto the
rings of the ephod
with a lace
of blue, that it
might be upon
the cunningly
woven band of
the ephod, and
that the breastplate
might not
be loosed from
the ephod; as
the LORD commanded
Moses.

22 And he
made the robe
of the ephod of
woven work, all
of blue; 23 and
the hole of the
robe in the midst
thereof, as the
hole of a coat of
mail, with a
binding round
about the hole
of it, that it
should not be
rent. 24 And
they made upon
the skirts of the
robe pomegranates
of blue, and
purple, and scarlet,
and twined
linen. 25 And
they made bells
of pure gold,
and put the bells
between the
pomegranates
upon the skirts
of the robe
round about, between
the pomegranates;
26 a
bell and a pomegranate,
a bell
and a pomegran-

a G. has, *interwoven, twined together.*
b G. adds, *underneath as a blossoming pomegranate.*
c Sm., G., S., V. add, *and byssus,* וששׁ.
d G. omits.
e G. omits,
f Sm., G., S., V. add, *of gold.*
g Sm., G., S., V. omit.

the hem of the robe to minister *in;* as the LORD commanded Moses.

27 And they made coats *of* fine linen of woven work for Aaron, and for his sons,
28 And a mitre *of* fine linen, and goodly bonnets *of* fine linen, and linen breeches *of* fine twined linen,
29 And a girdle *of* fine twined linen, and blue, and purple, and scarlet, *of* needlework; as the LORD commanded Moses.

30 And they made the plate of the holy crown *of* pure gold, and wrote upon it a writing, *like to* the engravings of a signet, HOLINESS TO THE LORD.
31 And they tied unto it a lace of blue, to fasten *it* on high upon the mitre; as the LORD commanded Moses.

32 Thus was all the work of the tabernacle of the tent of the congregation finished: and the children of Israel did according to all that the LORD commanded Moses, so did they.

33 And they brought the tab-

וְרִמֹּן[a] עַל־שׁוּלֵי הַמְּעִיל סָבִיב
,about round robe the of hem the upon ,pomegranate a and

לְשָׁרֵת כַּאֲשֶׁר צִוָּה יְהוָה אֶת־מֹשֶׁה׃
.Moses Jehovah commanded as ,ministering for

27 וַיַּעֲשׂוּ אֶת־הַכָּתְנֹת שֵׁשׁ מַעֲשֵׂה אֹרֵג
; weaver a of work a ,byssus ,tunics the made they And

28 לְאַהֲרֹן וּלְבָנָיו׃ וְאֵת הַמִּצְנֶפֶת שֵׁשׁ
,byssus ,mitre the and ; sons his for and Aaron for

וְאֶת־פַּאֲרֵי הַמִּגְבָּעֹת שֵׁשׁ וְאֶת־מִכְנְסֵי[b] הַבָּד[b]
,linen of breeches the and ,byssus ,turbans the of beauty the and

29 שֵׁשׁ מָשְׁזָר[c]׃ וְאֶת־הָאַבְנֵט שֵׁשׁ מָשְׁזָר[d]
,twisted byssus ,girdle the and ; twisted byssus [of]

וּתְכֵלֶת וְאַרְגָּמָן וְתוֹלַעַת שָׁנִי מַעֲשֵׂה
of work a ,crimson (of worm) and ,purple and ,blue and

רֹקֵם כַּאֲשֶׁר צִוָּה יְהוָה אֶת־מֹשֶׁה׃
.Moses Jehovah commanded as ,embroiderer an

30 וַיַּעֲשׂוּ אֶת־צִיץ[e] נֵזֶר־הַקֹּדֶשׁ זָהָב טָהוֹר
; [1]pure [2]gold ,holiness of diadem the of plate the made they And

וַיִּכְתְּבוּ עָלָיו מִכְתַּב פִּתּוּחֵי חוֹתָם
,signet a of engravings the of writing the it upon wrote they and

31 קֹדֶשׁ לַיהוָה׃ וַיִּתְּנוּ עָלָיו[f] פְּתִיל[f] תְּכֵלֶת
,blue of ribbon a it upon put they And .Jehovah to Holiness

לָתֵת[g] עַל־הַמִּצְנֶפֶת מִלְמָעְלָה כַּאֲשֶׁר צִוָּה יְהוָה
Jehovah commanded as ; above (to) from mitre the upon put to

אֶת־מֹשֶׁה׃
.Moses

32 וַתֵּכֶל[h] כָּל־עֲבֹדַת מִשְׁכַּן אֹהֶל
of tent the of habitation the of work the all finished was And

מוֹעֵד[h] וַיַּעֲשׂוּ בְּנֵי יִשְׂרָאֵל כְּכֹל[i] אֲשֶׁר
which all to according Israel of children the did and ; meeting

33 צִוָּה יְהוָה אֶת־מֹשֶׁה כֵּן עָשׂוּ׃ וַיָּבִיאוּ
brought they And .did they so ,Moses Jehovah commanded had

ate, upon the skirts of the robe round about, to minister in; as the LORD commanded Moses.

27 And they made the coats of fine linen of woven work for Aaron, and for his sons,
28 and the mitre of fine linen, and the goodly headtires of fine linen, and the linen breeches of fine twined linen,
29 and the girdle of fine twined linen, and blue, and purple, and scarlet, the work of the embroiderer: as the LORD commanded Moses.

30 And they made the plate of the holy crown of pure gold, and wrote upon it a writing, like the engravings of a signet, HOLY TO THE LORD.
31 And they tied unto it a lace of blue, to fasten it upon the mitre above; as the LORD commanded Moses.

32 Thus was finished all the work of the tabernacle of the tent of meeting: and the children of Israel did according to all that the LORD commanded Moses, so did they.

33 And they brought the tab-

---

a Sm., G., S., V. omit.
b S. has, *and the band.*
c S., V. omit.
d G. omits,
e G. adds, *of gold.*
f G. has, *upon the hem.*
g S. has, *to be.*
h G. omits.
i Sm., G. omit כל; S., V. omit כ.

ernacle unto
Moses, the tent,
and all his furniture,
his taches, his boards, his bars,
and his pillars, and his sockets,
34 And the covering of rams' skins dyed red,
and the covering of badgers' skins, and the vail of the covering,
35 The ark of the testimony, and the staves thereof, and the mercy seat,
36 The table, *and* all the vessels thereof, and the shewbread,
37 The pure candlestick, *with* the lamps thereof, *even with* the lamps to be set in order, and all the vessels thereof, and the oil for light,
38 And the golden altar, and the anointing oil, and the sweet incense, and the hanging for the tabernacle door,
39 The brasen altar, and his grate of brass, his staves, and all his vessels, the laver and his foot,
40 The hangings of the court, his pillars, and his sockets, and the hanging for the court gate, his cords, and his pins, and all the vessels of the service of the tabernacle, for the tent of the congregation,
41 The cloths of service to do service in the holy *place*, and the holy garments for Aaron

אֶת־הַמִּשְׁכָּן אֶל־מֹשֶׁה אֶת־הָאֹהֶל וְאֶת־כָּל־כֵּלָיו
,vessels its all and ,tent the ,Moses unto habitation the

קְרָסָיו[b][a] קְרָשָׁיו[a] בְּרִיחָו[c] וְעַמֻּדָיו וַאֲדָנָיו׃[d]
; sockets its and ,pillars its and ,bars its ,boards its ,hooks its

34 וְאֶת־מִכְסֵה עוֹרֹת הָאֵילִם הַמְאָדָּמִים וְאֶת־מִכְסֵה
of cover the and ,red dyed rams of skins of cover the and

35 עֹרֹת הַתְּחָשִׁים וְאֵת[e] פָּרֹכֶת הַמָּסָךְ׃[e] אֶת־אֲרוֹן
of ark the ; screen the of veil the and ,dolphins of skins

36 הָעֵדֻת וְאֶת־בַּדָּיו וְאֵת[f] הַכַּפֹּרֶת׃[f] אֶת־הַשֻּׁלְחָן[g]
,table the ; lid expiating the and ,poles its and ,testimony

37 אֶת־כָּל־כֵּלָיו וְאֵת לֶחֶם הַפָּנִים׃ אֶת־הַמְּנֹרָה
[2]lampstand the ; face the of bread the and ,vessels its all

הַטְּהֹרָה אֶת־נֵרֹתֶיהָ נֵרֹת הַמַּעֲרָכָה וְאֶת־כָּל־כֵּלֶיהָ[h]
,vessels its all and ,arrangement of lamps the ,lamps its ,[1]pure

38 וְאֵת שֶׁמֶן הַמָּאוֹר׃ וְאֵת מִזְבַּח הַזָּהָב[i] וְאֵת
and ,gold of altar the and ; light the of oil the and

שֶׁמֶן הַמִּשְׁחָה וְאֵת קְטֹרֶת הַסַּמִּים וְאֵת[j] מָסַךְ
of screen the and ,perfumes of incense the and ,anointing of oil the

39 פֶּתַח הָאֹהֶל׃[j] אֵת[k] מִזְבַּח הַנְּחֹשֶׁת וְאֶת־מִכְבַּר
of grating the and ,bronze of altar the ; tent the of door the

הַנְּחֹשֶׁת אֲשֶׁר־לוֹ אֶת־בַּדָּיו וְאֶת־כָּל־כֵּלָיו אֶת־הַכִּיֹּר
,laver the ,vessels its all and ,poles its ,it to [was] which bronze

40 וְאֶת־כַּנּוֹ׃ אֵת קַלְעֵי הֶחָצֵר אֶת־עַמֻּדֶיהָ
,pillars its ,court the of hangings the ; base its and

וְאֶת־אֲדָנֶיהָ וְאֶת־הַמָּסָךְ לְשַׁעַר הֶחָצֵר אֶת־מֵיתָרָיו
,cords its ,court the of gate the for screen the and ,sockets its and

וִיתֵדֹתֶיהָ וְאֵת כָּל־כְּלֵי עֲבֹדַת הַמִּשְׁכָּן
,habitation the of service the of vessels the all and ,pins its and

41 לְאֹהֶל מוֹעֵד׃ אֶת־בִּגְדֵי[l] הַשְּׂרָד לְשָׁרֵת
ministering for ,weaving of garments the ; meeting of tent the for

בַּקֹּדֶשׁ[l] אֶת־בִּגְדֵי הַקֹּדֶשׁ לְאַהֲרֹן הַכֹּהֵן
,priest the Aaron for holiness of garments the ,sanctuary the in

ernacle unto Moses, the Tent, and all its furniture, its clasps, its boards, its bars, and its pillars, and its sockets;
34 and the covering of rams' skins dyed red, and the covering of sealskins, and the veil of the screen;
35 the ark of the testimony, and the staves thereof, and the mercy-seat;
36 the table, all the vessels thereof, and the shewbread;
37 the pure candlestick, the lamps thereof, even the lamps to be set in order, and all the vessels thereof, and the oil for the light;
38 and the golden altar, and the anointing oil, and the sweet incense, and the screen for the door of the Tent;
39 the brasen altar, and its grating of brass, its staves, and all its vessels, the laver and its base;
40 the hangings of the court, its pillars, and its sockets, and the screen for the gate of the court, the cords thereof, and the pins thereof, and all the instruments of the service of the tabernacle, for the tent of meeting;
41 the finely wrought garments for ministering in the holy place, and the holy garments for Aaron the priest,

---

a G. apparently omits.
b S. adds, *and the dishes.*
c S. adds, *and the nails.*
d The order in G. is 33, 35, 38, 37, 36, 41, 40, 34, 40b, 42, 43.
e G. has, *and the veils of the rest.*
f G. omits.
g G. adds פנים.
h G. omits.
i G. omits, and adds, *and all its vessels.*
j G. omits.
k G. omits the verse.
l G. omits.

the priest, and
his sons' gar-
ments, to min-
ister in the
priest's office. 42
According to all
that the LORD
commanded Mo-
ses, so the chil-
dren of Israel
made all the
work. 43 And
Moses did look
upon all the
work, and, be-
hold, they had
done it as the
LORD had com-
manded, even
so had they done
it: and Moses
blessed them.

42 וְאֵת־בִּגְדֵי בָנָיו לְכַהֵן׃ כְּכֹל[a]
all to According .priests as officiating for sons his of garments the and

אֲשֶׁר־צִוָּה יְהוָה אֶת־מֹשֶׁה כֵּן עָשׂוּ בְּנֵי
of children the did so ,Moses Jehovah commanded which

43 יִשְׂרָאֵל אֵת כָּל־הָעֲבֹדָה׃ וַיַּרְא מֹשֶׁה אֶת־כָּל־
all Moses saw And .work the all Israel

הַמְּלָאכָה וְהִנֵּה עָשׂוּ אֹתָהּ כַּאֲשֶׁר צִוָּה
commanded had as ,it done had they behold and ,work the

יְהוָה[b] כֵּן עָשׂוּ וַיְבָרֶךְ אֹתָם מֹשֶׁה׃
.Moses them blessed and ;done had they so ,Jehovah

and the gar-
ments of his
sons, to minister
in the priest's of-
fice. 42 Accord-
ing to all that
the LORD com-
manded Moses,
so the children
of Israel did all
the work. 43
And Moses saw
all the work,
and, behold,
they had done
it: as the LORD
had command-
ed, even so had
they done it:
and Moses
blessed them.

40

AND the
LORD spake un-
to Moses, say-
ing, 2 On the
first day of the
first month shalt
thou set up the
tabernacle of the
tent of the con-
gregation. 3
And thou shalt
put therein the
ark of the testi-
mony, and cover
the ark with the
vail. 4 And thou
shalt bring in
the table, and
set in order the
things that are
to be set in or-
der upon it; and
thou shalt bring
in the candle-
stick, and light
the lamps there-
of. 5 And thou
shalt set the
altar of gold for
the incense be-
fore the ark of
the testimony,
and put the hang-
ing of the door
to the tabernacle.
6 And thou shalt
set the altar of
the burnt offer-
ing before the
door of the tab-

1 וַיְדַבֵּר יְהוָה אֶל־מֹשֶׁה לֵּאמֹר[c]׃ בְּיוֹם־
2 of day the On :saying Moses unto Jehovah spoke And

הַחֹדֶשׁ הָרִאשׁוֹן בְּאֶחָד לַחֹדֶשׁ תָּקִים
up raise shalt thou ,month the to [day] first the on ,[1]first [2]month the

3 אֶת־מִשְׁכַּן אֹהֶל מוֹעֵד׃ וְשַׂמְתָּ[d] שָׁם אֵת
there put shalt thou And .meeting of tent the of habitation the

אֲרוֹן הָעֵדוּת[d] וְסַכֹּתָ עַל־הָאָרֹן[e] אֶת־
ark the upon cover shalt thou and ,testimony of ark the

4 הַפָּרֹכֶת[f]׃ וְהֵבֵאתָ אֶת־הַשֻּׁלְחָן וְעָרַכְתָּ אֶת־עֶרְכּוֹ
;arrangement its arrange and ,table the in bring shalt thou And .veil the

וְהֵבֵאתָ אֶת־הַמְּנֹרָה וְהַעֲלֵיתָ אֶת־נֵרֹתֶיהָ׃
.lamps its up set and ,lampstand the in bring shalt thou and

5 וְנָתַתָּה אֶת־מִזְבַּח הַזָּהָב לִקְטֹרֶת לִפְנֵי אֲרוֹן
of ark the before incense for gold of altar the put shalt thou And

הָעֵדֻת וְשַׂמְתָּ אֶת־מָסַךְ הַפֶּתַח לַמִּשְׁכָּן[g]׃
.habitation the to door the of screen the put shalt thou and ;testimony

6 וְנָתַתָּה אֵת מִזְבַּח הָעֹלָה לִפְנֵי פֶּתַח
of door the before offering burnt of altar the place shalt thou And

And the
LORD spake un-
to Moses, say-
ing, 2 On the
first day of the
first month shalt
thou rear up the
tabernacle of
the tent of meet-
ing. 3 And thou
shalt put therein
the ark of the
testimony, and
thou shalt screen
the ark with the
veil. 4 And thou
shalt bring in
the table, and
set in order the
things that are
upon it; and
thou shalt bring
in the candle-
stick, and light
the lamps there-
of. 5 And thou
shalt set the
golden altar for
incense before
the ark of the
testimony, and
put the screen
of the door to
the tabernacle.
6 And thou shalt
set the altar of
burnt offering
before the door

---

a G. omits; S., V. omit כל.
b G., S. add, *Moses.*
c S. omits.
d G. omits.
e G. adds, *of the testimony.*
f Sm. has, הכפרת.
g G. has, *the tent of witness.*

ernacle of the
tent of the con-
gregation. 7
And thou shalt
set the laver be-
tween the tent
of the congrega-
tion and the
altar, and shalt
put water there-
in. 8 And thou
shalt set up the
court round a-
bout, and hang
up the hanging
at the court
gate. 9 And
thou shalt take
the anointing
oil, and anoint
the tabernacle,
and all that *is*
therein, and
shalt hallow it,
and all the ves-
sels thereof:
and it shall be
holy. 10 And
thou shalt
anoint the altar
of the burnt of-
fering, and all
his vessels, and
sanctify the al-
tar: and it shall
be an altar most
holy. 11 And
thou shalt anoint
the laver and his
foot, and sanc-
tify it. 12 And
thou shalt bring
Aaron and his
sons unto the
door of the tab-
ernacle of the
congregation,
and wash them
with water. 13
And thou shalt
put upon Aaron
the holy gar-
ments, and
anoint him,
and sanctify
him; that he
may minister
unto me in the
priest's office.
14 And thou
shalt bring his
sons, and clothe
them with coats:
15 And thou
shalt anoint
them, as thou
didst anoint
their father, that
they may min-
ister unto me
in the priest's

מִשְׁכַּן אֹהֶל־מוֹעֵד׃ וְנָתַתָּ[a] אֶת־הַכִּיֹּר 7
laver the put shalt thou And .meeting of tent the of habitation the

בֵּין־אֹהֶל מוֹעֵד וּבֵין הַמִּזְבֵּחַ וְנָתַתָּ
place shalt thou and ; altar the between and meeting of tent the between

שָׁם מָיִם׃ וְשַׂמְתָּ אֶת־הֶחָצֵר סָבִיב 8
; about round court the put shalt thou And .water there

וְנָתַתָּ[b] אֶת־מָסַךְ שַׁעַר הֶחָצֵר[b]׃
.court the of gate the of screen the place shalt thou and

וְלָקַחְתָּ אֶת־שֶׁמֶן הַמִּשְׁחָה וּמָשַׁחְתָּ 9
anoint shalt thou and ,anointing of oil the take shalt thou And

אֶת־הַמִּשְׁכָּן וְאֶת־כָּל־אֲשֶׁר־בּוֹ וְקִדַּשְׁתָּ אֹתוֹ
it sanctify shalt thou and ; it in [is] which all and ,habitation the

וְאֶת־כָּל־כֵּלָיו וְהָיָה קֹדֶשׁ׃ וּמָשַׁחְתָּ 10
anoint shalt thou And .holy become shall it and ,vessels its all and

אֶת־מִזְבַּח הָעֹלָה וְאֶת־כָּל־כֵּלָיו וְקִדַּשְׁתָּ
sanctify shalt thou and ; vessels its all and offering burnt of altar the

אֶת־הַמִּזְבֵּחַ וְהָיָה הַמִּזְבֵּחַ קֹדֶשׁ קָדָשִׁים׃
.holies of holy altar the become shall and ,altar the

וּמָשַׁחְתָּ[c] אֶת־הַכִּיֹּר וְאֶת־כַּנּוֹ וְקִדַּשְׁתָּ 11
sanctify shalt thou and ,base its and laver the anoint shalt thou And

אֹתוֹ׃ וְהִקְרַבְתָּ אֶת־אַהֲרֹן וְאֶת־בָּנָיו אֶל־פֶּתַח 12
of door the unto sons his and Aaron near bring shalt thou And .it

אֹהֶל מוֹעֵד וְרָחַצְתָּ אֹתָם בַּמָּיִם׃
.water with them wash shalt thou and ; meeting of tent the

וְהִלְבַּשְׁתָּ אֶת־אַהֲרֹן אֵת בִּגְדֵי הַקֹּדֶשׁ 13
; holiness of garments the [with] Aaron clothe shalt thou And

וּמָשַׁחְתָּ אֹתוֹ וְקִדַּשְׁתָּ אֹתוֹ וְכִהֵן[d]
priest as officiate shall he and ,him sanctify and ,him anoint shalt thou and

לִי׃ וְאֶת־בָּנָיו תַּקְרִיב וְהִלְבַּשְׁתָּ 14
clothe shalt thou and ; near bring shalt thou sons his And .me for

אֹתָם כֻּתֳּנֹת׃ וּמָשַׁחְתָּ אֹתָם כַּאֲשֶׁר מָשַׁחְתָּ 15
anointedst thou as ,them anoint shalt thou And .tunics [with] them

אֶת־אֲבִיהֶם[e] וְכִהֲנוּ לִי וְהָיְתָה
be shall and ; me to priests as officiate shall they and ,father their

of the tabernacle
of the tent of
meeting. 7 And
thou shalt set
the laver be-
tween the tent
of meeting and
the altar, and
shalt put water
therein. 8 And
thou shalt set up
the court round
about, and hang
up the screen of
the gate of the
court. 9 And
thou shalt take
the anointing
oil, and anoint
the tabernacle,
and all that is
therein, and
shalt hallow it,
and all the fur-
niture thereof:
and it shall be
holy. 10 And
thou shalt a-
noint the altar
of burnt offer-
ing, and all its
vessels, and
sanctify the
altar: and the
altar shall be
most holy. 11
And thou shalt
anoint the laver
and its base, and
sanctify it. 12
And thou shalt
bring Aaron and
his sons unto
the door of the
tent of meeting,
and shalt wash
them with wa-
ter. 13 And thou
shalt put upon
Aaron the holy
garments; and
thou shalt a-
noint him, and
sanctify him,
that he may
minister unto
me in the priest's
office. 14 And
thou shalt bring
his sons, and
put coats upon
them: 15 and
thou shalt a-
noint them, as
thou didst a-
noint their fa-
ther, that they
may minister un-
to me in the
priest's office:
and their a-

---

a G. omits the verse.

b G. has, *and all belonging to it thou shalt sanctify round about.*

c G. omits the verse.

d G. has לְכֹהֵן.

e S. has, *Aaron thy brother.*

office: for their anointing shall surely be an everlasting priesthood throughout their generations. 16 Thus did Moses: according to all that the LORD commanded him, so did he.

17 And it came to pass in the first month in the second year, on the first *day* of the month, *that* the tabernacle was reared up. 18 And Moses reared up the tabernacle, and fastened his sockets, and set up the boards thereof, and put in the bars thereof, and reared up his pillars. 19 And he spread abroad the tent over the tabernacle, and put the covering of the tent above upon it; as the LORD commanded Moses. 20 And he took and put the testimony into the ark, and set the staves on the ark, and put the mercy seat above upon the ark; 21 And he brought the ark into the tabernacle, and set up the vail of the covering, and covered the ark of the testimony; as the LORD commanded Moses. 22 And he put the table in the tent of the congregation, upon the side of the tabernacle northward, without the vail. 23 And he set the bread

לִהְיֹת לָהֶם מָשְׁחָתָם לִכְהֻנַּת עוֹלָם
eternity of priesthood a for anointing their them for be to

16 לְדֹרֹתָם׃ וַיַּעַשׂ מֹשֶׁה [a]כְּכֹל אֲשֶׁר
which all to according ; Moses did And .generations their to

צִוָּה יְהוָה אֹתוֹ כֵּן עָשָׂה׃
.did he so ,him Jehovah commanded had

17 וַיְהִי בַּחֹדֶשׁ[b] הָרִאשׁוֹן[b] בַּשָּׁנָה
[2]year the in ,[1]first [2]month the in ,pass to came it And

הַשֵּׁנִית בְּאֶחָד[c] לַחֹדֶשׁ[c] הוּקַם הַמִּשְׁכָּן׃
.habitation the up raised was ,month the to [day] first the on ,[1]second

18 וַיָּקֶם מֹשֶׁה אֶת־הַמִּשְׁכָּן וַיִּתֵּן אֶת־אֲדָנָיו
,sockets its placed he and ; habitation the Moses up raised And

וַיָּשֶׂם[d] אֶת־קְרָשָׁיו[d] וַיִּתֵּן אֶת־בְּרִיחָיו וַיָּקֶם
up raised he and ,bars its placed he and ,boards its put he and

19 אֶת־עַמּוּדָיו׃ וַיִּפְרֹשׂ אֶת־הָאֹהֶל עַל־הַמִּשְׁכָּן
,habitation the over tent the out spread he And .pillars its

וַיָּשֶׂם אֶת־מִכְסֵה הָאֹהֶל עָלָיו מִלְמָעְלָה כַּאֲשֶׁר
as ,above (to) from it upon tent the of cover the put he and

20 צִוָּה יְהוָה אֶת־מֹשֶׁה׃ וַיִּקַּח[e] וַיִּתֵּן
placed and took he And .Moses Jehovah commanded had

אֶת־הָעֵדֻת אֶל־הָאָרֹן וַיָּשֶׂם אֶת־הַבַּדִּים עַל־הָאָרֹן[e]
; ark the upon poles the put he and ,ark the into testimony the

וַיִּתֵּן אֶת־הַכַּפֹּרֶת עַל־הָאָרֹן מִלְמָעְלָה׃
.above (to) from ark the upon lid expiating the placed he and

21 וַיָּבֵא אֶת־הָאָרֹן אֶל־הַמִּשְׁכָּן וַיָּשֶׂם אֵת
put he and ,habitation the into ark the brought he And

פָּרֹכֶת הַמָּסָךְ וַיָּסֶךְ עַל אֲרוֹן הָעֵדוּת
,testimony of ark the upon covered he and ,screen the of veil the

22 כַּאֲשֶׁר צִוָּה יְהוָה אֶת־מֹשֶׁה׃ וַיִּתֵּן
placed he And .Moses Jehovah commanded had as

אֶת־הַשֻּׁלְחָן בְּאֹהֶל מוֹעֵד עַל יֶרֶךְ הַמִּשְׁכָּן
habitation the of side the upon ,meeting of tent the in table the

23 צָפֹנָה מִחוּץ לַפָּרֹכֶת[f]׃ וַיַּעֲרֹךְ עָלָיו
it upon arranged he And .veil the (to) outside (from) ,northward

nointing shall be to them for an overlasting priesthood throughout their generations. 16 Thus did Moses: according to all that the LORD commanded him, so did he.

17 And it came to pass in the first month in the second year, on the first day of the month, that the tabernacle was reared up. 18 And Moses reared up the tabernacle, and laid its sockets, and set up the boards thereof, and put in the bars thereof, and reared up its pillars. 19 And he spread the tent over the tabernacle, and put the covering of the tent above upon it; as the LORD commanded Moses. 20 And he took and put the testimony into the ark, and set the staves on the ark, and put the mercy-seat above upon the ark: 21 and he brought the ark into the tabernacle, and set up the veil of the screen, and screened the ark of the testimony; as the LORD commanded Moses. 22 And he put the table in the tent of meeting, upon the side of the tabernacle northward, without the veil. 23 And he set the bread in or-

a G., S. omit כ.
b S. has, *on the first of the first month.*
c S. has, *on the first day of the week;* G. omits.
d G. apparently omits.
e G. omits.
f G. adds, *of the tent.*

in order upon it before the LORD; as the LORD had commanded Moses. 24 And he put the candlestick in the tent of the congregation, over against the table, on the side of the tabernacle southward. 25 And he lighted the lamps before the LORD; as the LORD commanded Moses. 26 And he put the golden altar in the tent of the congregation before the vail: 27 And he burnt sweet incense thereon; as the LORD commanded Moses. 28 And he set up the hanging *at* the door of the tabernacle.

29 And he put the altar of burnt offering *by* the door of the tabernacle of the tent of the congregation, and offered upon it the burnt offering and the meat offering; as the LORD commanded Moses. 30 And he set the laver between the tent of the congregation and the altar, and put water there, to wash *withal.* 31 And Moses and Aaron and his sons washed their hands and their feet thereat: 32 When they went into the tent of the congregation, and when they came near unto the altar, they washed; as the LORD com-

עֵרֶךְ[a] לֶחֶם[a] לִפְנֵי יְהֹוָה כַּאֲשֶׁר צִוָּה
commanded had as ,Jehovah before bread of arrangement an

24 יְהֹוָה אֶת־מֹשֶׁה׃ וַיָּשֶׂם אֶת־הַמְּנֹרָה בְּאֹהֶל
of tent the in lampstand the put he And .Moses Jehovah

מוֹעֵד נֹכַח הַשֻּׁלְחָן[b] עַל יֶרֶךְ הַמִּשְׁכָּן
habitation the of side the upon ;table the opposite ,meeting

25 נֶגְבָּה׃ וַיַּעַל הַנֵּרֹת לִפְנֵי יְהֹוָה כַּאֲשֶׁר
as ,Jehovah before lamps the up set he And .southward

26 צִוָּה יְהֹוָה אֶת־מֹשֶׁה׃ וַיָּשֶׂם אֶת־מִזְבַּח
of altar the put he And .Moses Jehovah commanded had

27 הַזָּהָב בְּאֹהֶל מוֹעֵד לִפְנֵי הַפָּרֹכֶת׃ וַיַּקְטֵר
burned he And .veil the before ,meeting of tent the in gold

עָלָיו קְטֹרֶת סַמִּים כַּאֲשֶׁר צִוָּה יְהֹוָה
Jehovah commanded had as ,perfumes of incense it upon

28 אֶת־מֹשֶׁה׃ וַיָּשֶׂם אֶת־מָסַךְ הַפֶּתַח לַמִּשְׁכָּן׃
.habitation the to door the of screen the put he And .Moses

29 וְאֵת מִזְבַּח הָעֹלָה שָׂם פֶּתַח
of door the [at] put he offering burnt of altar the And

מִשְׁכַּן אֹהֶל־מוֹעֵד[c] וַיַּעַל עָלָיו
it upon up offered he and ;meeting of tent the of habitation the

אֶת־הָעֹלָה וְאֶת־הַמִּנְחָה כַּאֲשֶׁר צִוָּה
commanded had as ,offering vegetable the and offering burnt the

30 יְהֹוָה אֶת־מֹשֶׁה[c]׃ וַיָּשֶׂם אֶת־הַכִּיֹּר בֵּין־אֹהֶל
of tent the between laver the put he And .Moses Jehovah

מוֹעֵד וּבֵין הַמִּזְבֵּחַ וַיִּתֵּן שָׁמָּה מַיִם
water there placed he and ;altar the between and meeting

31 לְרָחְצָה[d]׃ וְרָחֲצוּ מִמֶּנּוּ מֹשֶׁה וְאַהֲרֹן
Aaron and Moses it from wash to accustomed were And .washing for

32 וּבָנָיו אֶת־יְדֵיהֶם וְאֶת־רַגְלֵיהֶם׃ בְּבֹאָם
in coming their At .feet their and hands their sons his and

אֶל־אֹהֶל מוֹעֵד וּבְקָרְבָתָם אֶל־הַמִּזְבֵּחַ[e]
altar the unto near coming their at and ,meeting of tent the unto

יִרְחָצוּ[f] כַּאֲשֶׁר צִוָּה יְהֹוָה אֶת־
Jehovah commanded had as ,wash to accustomed were they

der upon it before the LORD; as the LORD commanded Moses. 24 And he put the candlestick in the tent of meeting, over against the table, on the side of the tabernacle southward. 25 And he lighted the lamps before the LORD; as the LORD commanded Moses. 26 And he put the golden altar in the tent of meeting before the veil: 27 and he burnt thereon incense of sweet spices; as the LORD commanded Moses. 28 And he put the screen of the door to the tabernacle.

29 And he set the altar of burnt offering at the door of the tabernacle of the tent of meeting, and offered upon it the burnt offering and the meal offering; as the LORD commanded Moses. 30 And he set the laver between the tent of meeting and the altar, and put water therein, to wash withal. 31 And Moses and Aaron and his sons washed their hands and their feet thereat; 32 when they went into the tent of meeting, and when they came near unto the altar, they washed: as the LORD com-

a G. apparently has לחם פנים.

b G. omits.

c G. omits.

d Sm., S. have, *and washed,* וירחצו.

e G. adds, *to minister.*

f G. adds, *from it.*

manded Moses.
33 And he
reared up the
court round a-
bout the taber-
nacle and the
altar, and set up
the hanging of
the court gate.
So Moses finish-
ed the work.

34 Then a
cloud covered
the tent of the
congregation,
and the glory of
the LORD filled
the tabernacle.
35 And Moses
was not able to
enter into the
tent of the con-
gregation, be-
cause the cloud
abode thereon,
and the glory of
the LORD filled
the tabernacle.
36 And when
the cloud was
taken up from
over the taber-
nacle, the chil-
dren of Israel
went onward in
all their jour-
neys: 37 But if
the cloud were
not taken up,
then they jour-
neyed not till
the day that it
was taken up.
38 For the cloud
of the LORD *was*
upon the taber-
nacle by day,
and fire was on
it by night, in
the sight of all
the house of Is-
rael, through-
out all their
journeys.

33 מֹשֶׁה׃ וַיָּקֶם אֶת־הֶחָצֵר סָבִיב לַמִּשְׁכָּן
habitation the to about round court the up raised he And .Moses

וְלַמִּזְבֵּחַ וַיִּתֵּן[a] אֶת־מָסַךְ שַׁעַר הֶחָצֵר[a]
;court the of gate the of screen the placed he and ;altar the to and

וַיְכַל מֹשֶׁה אֶת־הַמְּלָאכָה[b]׃
.work the Moses finished and

34 וַיְכַס הֶעָנָן אֶת־אֹהֶל מוֹעֵד וּכְבוֹד
of glory the and ;meeting of tent the cloud the covered And

35 יְהוָה מָלֵא אֶת־הַמִּשְׁכָּן׃ וְלֹא־יָכֹל מֹשֶׁה לָבוֹא
come to Moses able not was And .habitation the filled Jehovah

אֶל־אֹהֶל מוֹעֵד כִּי־שָׁכַן עָלָיו הֶעָנָן
,cloud the it upon dwelt because ,meeting of tent the into

36 וּכְבוֹד יְהוָה מָלֵא אֶת־הַמִּשְׁכָּן׃ וּבְהֵעָלוֹת
[3]arising at And .habitation the filled Jehovah of glory the and

הֶעָנָן מֵעַל הַמִּשְׁכָּן יִסְעוּ בְּנֵי
of children the journeyed ,habitation the upon from [2]cloud's [1]the

37 יִשְׂרָאֵל בְּכֹל[c] מַסְעֵיהֶם[c]׃ וְאִם־לֹא יֵעָלֶה
arise [1]did [2]not if And .journeyings their all in ,Israel

הֶעָנָן וְלֹא יִסְעוּ עַד־יוֹם הֵעָלֹתוֹ[d]׃
.arising its of day the until ,journey [2]did [1]they [3]not (and) ,cloud the

38 כִּי עֲנַן יְהוָה[e] עַל־הַמִּשְׁכָּן יוֹמָם
,day by habitation the upon [was] Jehovah of cloud the For

וְאֵשׁ תִּהְיֶה לַיְלָה בּוֹ לְעֵינֵי
of eyes the before ,it on night by be to accustomed was fire and

כָל־בֵּית־יִשְׂרָאֵל בְּכָל־מַסְעֵיהֶם׃
.journeyings their all in Israel of house the all

manded Moses.
33 And he rear-
ed up the court
round about the
tabernacle and
the altar, and
set up the screen
of the gate of
the court. So
Moses finished
the work.

34 Then the
cloud covered
the tent of meet-
ing, and the
glory of the
LORD filled the
tabernacle. 35
And Moses was
not able to enter
into the tent of
meeting, be-
cause the cloud
abode thereon,
and the glory of
the LORD filled
the tabernacle.
36 And when the
cloud was taken
up from over the
tabernacle, the
children of Isra-
el went onward,
throughout all
their journeys:
37 but if the
cloud were not
taken up, then
they journeyed
not till the day
that it was taken
up. 38 For the
cloud of the
LORD was upon
the tabernacle by
day, and there
was fire therein
by night, in the
sight of all the
house of Israel,
throughout all
their journeys.

---

a G. omits.
b Sm., G. add, *all*, reading את כל המלאכה.
c G. has, *with their movables;* V., *by their troops.*
d G. has, *went up the cloud.*
e G. omits.

The Value of HEBREW and GREEK to Clergymen.

1. Without *some* knowledge of Hebrew and Greek, you cannot understand the critical commentaries on the Scriptures, and a commentary that is *not* critical is of doubtful value.

2. Without *some* knowledge of Hebrew and Greek, you cannot satisfy yourself or those who look to you for help as to the changes which you will find in the Revised Old and New Testaments.

3. Without *some* knowledge of Hebrew and Greek, you cannot appreciate the critical discussions, now so frequent, relating to the books of the Old and New Testaments.

4. Without *some* knowledge of Hebrew and Greek, you cannot be certain, in a single instance, that in your sermon based on a Scripture text, you are presenting the correct teaching of that text.

5. Without *some* knowledge of Hebrew and Greek, you cannot be an independent student, or a reliable interpreter of the word of God.

6. As much knowledge of Hebrew can be secured, with the same method, under the same circumstances, by the same pupil, in *one* year, as can be gained of Latin in three years. Greek, though somewhat more difficult, may be readily acquired within a brief period with the aid of the Interlinear New Testament (which contains a lexicon) and an elementary Greek grammar.

7. The Hebrew language has, in all, about 7,000 words, and of these 1,000 occur in the Old Testament over 25 times each.

8. The Hebrew grammar has but *one* form for the Relative pronoun in all cases, numbers and genders; but *three* forms for the Demonstrative pronoun. The possible verbal forms are about 300 as compared with the 1,200 found in Greek. It has practically no declension.

9. Within ten years the average man wastes more time in fruitless reading and indifferent talk, than would be used in acquiring a good working knowledge of Hebrew and Greek that in turn would impart to his teaching that quality of independence and of reliability which so greatly enhances one's power as a teacher.

10. There is not *one* minister in *ten* who might not if he but *would*, find time and opportunity for such study of Hebrew and Greek as would enable him to make a thoroughly practical use of it in his work as a Bible-preacher and Bible-teacher.